WHAT WILL YOU FIND IN THE AN...

FISHING LOCATIONS IN ALL 50 UNITED STATES AND CANADA:
- 1,400 inland lakes and reservoirs
- 750 rivers and streams
- Atlantic and Pacific oceans
- Gulf of Mexico
- Great Lakes

INFORMATION AND SERVICE PROVIDERS:
- 640 bait and tackle stores
- 480 charter and party boats
- 460 professional fishing guides
- 155 marinas
- 350 fishing lodges, resorts, ranches and camps
- 32 International Destination travel agents
- 45 fish camps

COMPLETE BUSINESS PROFILES:
- Contact names and telephone numbers
- Rates, species and seasons
- Supplies and services
- Handicapped equipped guides, charters and facilities

AREA MAPS OF FISHING LOCATIONS:
- All 50 United States
- Canada

SPECIAL FEATURES:
- Hiring fishing guides and charter boats
- Planning and preparing for a fishing trip
- Questions to ask service providers

EASY TO USE FORMAT:
- Visual tables of contents
- Alphabetically arranged state-by-state
- Headings for each type of business
- Headings for every major fishable body of water
- Easy to read listings
- Index sections to ease searching:
    - Major and secondary fishing locations
    - Services by species of fish

Who are the angler's on the cover?

The *Angler's Yellow Pages* appeals to all types of fishermen and we have captured representative photos of some of them for the cover of the book. They are not famous - they are everyday folks like you and me. They are not trophy hunters - they catch the same size and variety of fish we all do. The thing they all have in common is a love of fishing. The same love we all share for the outdoors and this great sport of ours.

Following are brief profiles of each angler on the cover, beginning from the top left corner, moving left to right across and down the page.

Top left:
Alex was fishing in Raleigh, North Carolina on Falls Lake when she caught her first largemouth bass on a crankbait. Her expression shows that's she's thrilled about catching the fish, but still considers handling them a little "yucky" (notice the rag she's using to hold the fish?).

Center Top:
Bob is an accomplished veteran salmon fisherman and retired bomber pilot. He looks pretty happy about landing this 18 pounder on a guided canoe trip on the Matapedia River in Quebec, Canada.

Top Right:
This is a classic shot of a fly fisherman angling for striped bass at sunset off Martha's Vineyard in Massachusetts. He eventually landed over 20 stripers ranging in size from 2 to 20 pounds.

Second Row, Left:
Do you think Howard is happy about catching this 3 pound bonefish? He's obviously having the time of his life fly fishing on a guided trip to the Andros Islands in the Bahamas.

Second Row, Right:
This young lady landed several yellow perch while fishing on Lake Wallenpaupack in Pennsylvania. Sylvia's from near Towanda, Pennsylvania (does the T-shirt give it away?)

Third Row, Left:
Joey is an avid ocean fisherman and mate on a charter boat out of North Carolina. He hooked-up with this nice dolphin while fishing with his dad.

Bottom Row, Left:
Bass fishermen still flock to Florida for big fish and this guy's no exception. He looks pretty satisfied with the 9 pounder he caught while on a guided trip to the St. John's River.

Bottom Row, Right:
The Ashokan Reservoir in upstate New York is known for it's smallmouth bass, and Ron appears glad that he knows where to find them. Ron is a graphic artist when he's not fishing.

We strongly support catch and release. Most of the fish shown were released alive.

The Angler's Yellow Pages
Your silent fishing partner

1996-1997 edition

Outdoor Directory Group
Dallas, PA

Graphic Design & Creative Direction:

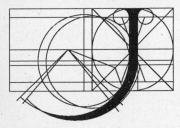

Jennings Design
1202 Applewood Acres
Clarks Summit, PA 18411

Voice: 717 586-4996
Transmission: 717 586-4997

Bruce Arthur Jennings
Principal • Creative Director

The Outdoor Directory Group does not endorse the businesses or service providers listed in the Angler's Yellow Pages and assumes no liability for their performance. Every effort has been made to ensure the accuracy and currency of information contained in this publication. The data Is based on information supplied by the businesses and service providers listed and is subject to change.

Copyright 1995 by the Outdoor Directory Group

All rights reserved. No part of this book may be reproduced or transmitted in any form or by any means, electronic or mechanical, including photocopying, recording, or by any information storage and retrieval system, without permission in writing from the publisher.

Printed in the United States
ISBN 0-9648467-7-2, $19.95

Published by

The Outdoor Directory Group, 15 Elm Drive, PO Box 488, Dallas, PA 18612-0488

TABLE OF CONTENTS

INTRODUCTION	7
COUPONS	17
ALABAMA	19
ALASKA	27
ARIZONA	37
ARKANSAS	43
CALIFORNIA	53
COLORADO	71
CONNECTICUT	77
DELAWARE	83
FLORIDA	87
GEORGIA	123
HAWAII	129
IDAHO	133
ILLINOIS	139
INDIANA	149
IOWA	155
KANSAS	161
KENTUCKY	165
LOUISIANA	171
MAINE	175
MARYLAND	179
MASSACHUSETTS	187
MICHIGAN	201
MINNESOTA	215
MISSISSIPPI	249
MISSOURI	255
MONTANA	267
NEBRASKA	285
NEVADA	291
NEW HAMPSHIRE	295
NEW JERSEY	299
NEW MEXICO	309
NEW YORK	313
NORTH CAROLINA	347
NORTH DAKOTA	355
OHIO	359
OKLAHOMA	369
OREGON	373
PENNSYLVANIA	391
RHODE ISLAND	399
SOUTH CAROLINA	403
SOUTH DAKOTA	411
TENNESSEE	415
TEXAS	421
UTAH	439
VERMONT	443
VIRGINIA	447
WASHINGTON	453
WEST VIRGINIA	461
WISCONSIN	465
WYOMING	483
CANADA	487
INTERNATIONAL DESTINATIONS	495
PRODUCTS	499
INDEXES	503

This book is dedicated to
the many people who have contributed
to making it possible
most of all Augustine

Acknowledgments

We would like to thank all of the businesses and service providers who supplied information about their operations. In all of our experience, we have never worked with a greater group of people.

INTRODUCTION

Welcome To The Angler's Yellow Pages

The Angler's Yellow Pages gives you the power of information and the convenience of choice. It was created by and for fishermen. No matter what kind of fisherman you are: fly fisherman, bass or walleye fisherman, muskie hunter or "big game" sportfisherman, the Angler's Yellow Pages offers you an abundant source of angling opportunities and information.

The Angler's Yellow Pages lets you examine all of your angling options, regardless of where you intend to fish, what species you are after, what technique you prefer, or how much you can afford to spend. Our goal is to put you in touch with the resource that meets your needs.

You will find the Angler's Yellow Pages an indispensable reference source when searching for adventures away from home, new opportunities close to home, planning a family vacation, or traveling on business and looking to mix in a little fishing pleasure. The Angler's Yellow Pages offers a geographically wide coverage area - virtually all of North America. In addition, there are lists of agencies that specialize in fishing excursions all over the world. Practically anywhere you want to fish, you will find it in the Angler's Yellow Pages.

Read the "How To Use This Book" section for a quick overview of the contents and how to make the most effective use of the Angler's Yellow Pages. If you plan to hire a professional fishing guide or charter boat captain, or plan to stay at a fishing lodge, ranch or camp, also read the "Getting The Most Out Of Your Trip" section for valuable guidelines and suggestions.

The Angler's Yellow Pages is published every twelve to eighteen months. Information is expanded and updated to keep pace with your angling interests and a rapidly changing industry. If you have a favorite service provider or other business you would like to see listed in the Angler's Yellow Pages, let us know and we will feature them in the next edition. And, if you, or someone you know would like additional copies of the Angler's Yellow Pages, call us toll fee at 1-800-242-9722 or use one of the postage paid order cards at the back of the book.

Thousands of hours of research have gone into creating the Angler's Yellow Pages. That's time you won't have to spend trying to find the same information - and a lot of it is hard to find. We hope you enjoy the Angler's Yellow Pages - it is our pleasure bringing it to you.

Mike Rittelmeyer
Outdoor Directory Group

INTRODUCTION

The Angler's Yellow Pages Format

The format of the Angler's Yellow Pages is designed for ease of use. There are 53 separate sections containing logically related groups of information - one for each USA state, Canada, International Destinations and Products. In addition, there are two Index sections to help you locate information quickly and easily.

USA State Sections

State sections begin with an area map, followed by alphabetized regional headings and business/service provider listings. The area maps provide a visual table of contents for each state; they show all of the major regions within each state and list all of the regional headings. To give you a better idea of where things are located, area maps also identify landmarks such as cities, towns, rivers and roadways.

Business and service provider listings begin with headings that identify major regions. Regions can be large bodies of water such as Lake Mead in Arizona, cities such as Dallas, TX, counties with large clusters of fishable waters such as Vilas County in Wisconsin, or wider geographic areas such as Eastern Montana. The idea is to make identifying and locating fishing spots as easy as possible.

Please note that every body of water will not have a regional heading - only the major ones - other bodies of water can be found in the Location Index. So, if you don't find what you are looking for under a regional heading, look in the Location Index.

Each regional heading contains one or more alphabetized category headings for each type of business such as Bait and Tackle, Guides, Marinas, Charter Boats, and Lodges. Business and service provider listings are alphabetized by company name under each business heading.

Canada

Canadian listings are formatted the same as USA State listings. The Canadian section begins with an area map, followed by alphabetized regional and business category headings. Canadian regions span the entire country - they are not separated by individual Province.

International Destinations

The International Destinations section lists a wide range of exciting "overseas" angling opportunities. This section is divided into country, continent or region. Examples include regional headings such as Mexico, Russia, South America and Latin America. Business and service provider listings are alphabetized by company name within each region.

Products

The Products section lists a number of industry manufacturers, the products they provide, and contact information. Manufacturers are listed alphabetically by company name.

INTRODUCTION

How To Use This Book

The way you locate information in the Angler's Yellow Pages depends on whether you are simply "exploring" (scanning the various sections to see what's available), looking for a specific location, or looking for a particular species of fish. Whatever your objective, the Angler's Yellow Pages makes it as easy as 1-2-3 to find information.

1 Exploring

If you are browsing through the Angler's Yellow Pages to see which locations are covered, the number and types of businesses and service providers, or the species of fish available, the best place to start is with each section's area map. The map provides a visual table of contents for the section. When you find a region you're interested in, turn to the regional heading with the same name for all of the detail information.

2 Location Search

If you are looking for a specific location - lake, river, stream - the best place to start is the Location Index. The Location index gives you the names and page numbers of *all* the fishing locations listed in the book. If you don't see the fishing location you're looking for when "exploring" or searching the USA state or Canadian sections, look in the Location Index.

3 Species Search

If you are looking for a business or service provider that offers a specific species of fish, the best place to start is with the Species Index. The Species index gives you the names and page numbers of all of the businesses and service providers listed in the book that can give you information about a specific species of fish.

Abbreviations

For ease of use, abbreviations have been kept to a minimum. However, you will find a few. They are explained below.

Telephone numbers:	(S) = Summer contact number, (W) = Winter contact number
Rates:	PP = charge per person, (1) = charge for 1 person, (1-2) = charge for 1 to 2 people and so on. All rates listed are 1995 rates and may be subject to change.
Species:	For consistency and ease of reference, the "official" names of the various species of fish are used instead of the wide variety of "nicknames".
Business Headings:	Business headings are self explanatory. The "Lodges..." heading includes all Lodges, Ranches, Resorts and Camps.

INTRODUCTION

How To Get The Most Out Of Your Fishing Trip

Introduction

Fishing trips, especially those involving professional services, represent a sizable financial investment. "How To Get The Most Out Of Your Fishing Trip" provides guidelines that assist you in making informed decisions, maximizing your investment, and selecting the service provider that meets your expectations.

Before you embark on a professionally guided fishing trip or charter boat excursion there are several things to consider - how to plan your trip, how to prepare for your trip, etiquette during the trip, and what to do at the conclusion of your trip. Increase your chances for a productive and enjoyable experience by reading those sections.

The section on fishing lodges, resorts, ranches and camps provides an overview of some appealing and unique opportunities. The combination of lodging and guided fishing services provides an ideal option for families and serious fishermen alike.

Finally, there are lists of questions to ask each category of service provider. These help you formulate specific questions which ensure that you get the most out of your trip.

Planning Your Trip

Make sure that you are able to enjoy the fishing experience you want, where you want, and when you want with advanced planning. Many service providers are booked well into the future. Furthermore, the availability of many species of fish is seasonal. If you don't plan early, you might miss the height of a season, or worse yet, miss it altogether.

Half the fun of any fishing trip is in the planning. Where to go? What species of fish to pursue? The Angler's Yellow Pages offers you a wealth of options. To help you sort it all out, and prioritize those things that are important, you must determine your objectives for the trip. Ask yourself the following questions:

- Are you going for quality (size) or quantity (numbers)?
- Do you expect to enhance your fishing expertise?
- Do you want to become more familiar with a body of water?
- Are you looking for a family, or group experience?
- What type of equipment do you prefer to use?
- What is your budget?
- What is important to you in the personality of the service provider?

These are some of the points you need to consider while planning your trip, others depend on your individual needs. The important thing is taking the time to think about what is important to you and finding a service provider that is compatible with your interests. Defining and prioritizing your objectives creates the basis for an intelligent selection of a service provider and forms the criteria against which you can judge the success of your trip.

Once you have determined your objectives, you are ready to locate a service provider. Using the Angler's Yellow Pages, select a list of names that most closely match your goals. Call the people on your list and spend some time talking to them. Establish a rapport with the service provider.

INTRODUCTION

Get a "feel" for their personality - confirm that there is a match. Most of them are more than willing to devote whatever time is necessary answering your questions (also see "Questions To Ask ..."). Tell the service provider your objectives and make certain they can satisfy them.

Preparing For Your Trip

After you have located and booked a service, you will need to prepare for your trip. The degree of preparation depends upon your personal preferences and range of options offered by the service provider. If the service provides everything from bait and beverages to tackle and rain gear, all you need to do is show up. Usually, there are usually several things you will want to do.

- Pack appropriate clothing including sunglasses, sun tan lotion and hat
- Ensure that your equipment is in excellent working order and strung with new line if you plan to bring your own
- Make sure your camera has new batteries and plenty of film
- Plan your travel to arrive on time

Types Of Trips

Professional Fishing Guides

Professional fishing guides specialize in fishing inland rivers, streams, lakes and reservoirs for bass, walleye, trout, salmon and a variety of other species. They use fly rods, spinning or bait casting gear from powered fishing boats, shore, canoes or drift boats. They may also provide shallow coastal water fishing using similar equipment and techniques in search of bonefish, permit and tarpon among others.

Fishing guides help you catch quality fish, quantities of fish, and can provide instruction on a variety of fishing techniques. Perhaps the biggest advantage of using a guide is that it increases your angling knowledge; they show you when, where, why and how to fish a body of water.

Guided Fishing Trip Etiquette

OK, you have done everything right up to this point - planned everything "to a T", located the perfect guide and spruced up your favorite equipment. The first order of business is meeting the guide on the prearranged date and time, and at the right location. Above all else, be on time!

When you arrive, discuss the day's game plan with the guide. Find out the strategy, locations and types of fishing techniques they intend to use. Review your list of objectives and expectations to ensure that you and the guide are working toward the same purpose. If you have any special needs or requests, make the guide aware of them before you launch.

When dealing with your guide, follow the golden rule; treat them as you would like to be treated. Guides love fishing, people and the outdoors - that's why they do what they do. Be honest with the guide about your fishing expertise. Guides are most helpful when they know your strengths and weaknesses.

Since one of the biggest benefits of guided fishing trips is the amount you can learn, ask questions. Ask about fishing techniques, seasonal fish locations and patterns, lure selection and

INTRODUCTION

other subjects of interest to you. You will find that most guides are willing to share a wealth of information, suggestions and recommendations.

Invite your guide to fish along with you. The result is a more enjoyable experience for everyone. This gesture also allows the guide to determine the location and "mood" of the fish and is a good way to observe and learn new fishing techniques.

As the day progresses, if you are not achieving the success you anticipated, talk to the guide. Ask them if there are other techniques or locations that might be worth trying. Also ask if there are opportunities for other species of fish. Often times, changing tactics turns the day in your favor, but you must let the guide know you are open to a change of plan.

Charter Boats

Charter boats are large vessels, usually in the 25 foot plus range, that ply the open waters of the ocean, bays, gulfs and great lakes for salmon, trout, blues, tuna, dolphin, marlin, sails, wahoo, and many other species of fish. They use trolling rigs, outriggers, downriggers, even fly rods. Charters boats charge by the day for exclusive use of the boat. Another class of charter boats, known as party boats, charge a reasonable per-person fee for non-exclusive use of a boat - you share the boat with other fishermen seeking the same species of fish.

Charter Boat Etiquette

When you meet the boat at the dock, discuss the game plan for the day with the captain or mate. Find out the strategy, locations and types of fishing techniques that will be used. Review your list of objectives to ensure you and the crew are working toward the same goals. If you have any special needs or requests, make the captain or mate aware of them before you leave the dock.

Once you are on the water, follow the safety directions from the captain and mate. One of the crew's many responsibilities is your personal safety, and many of the game fish sought by charter boats are large and/or potentially dangerous. Be careful and pay close attention to the instructions provided by the captain and mate. If you are not familiar with the equipment or species of fish, ask the mate how to operate the equipment and handle the fish.

Be aware that on many charter boats, the mate rigs the tackle, baits the hook, sets out the lines, and often times sets the hook on the fish. Discuss these procedures with the mate so that you know what to expect, especially if you prefer to do these things yourself.

Some charters have a policy of keeping a portion of the catch for themselves. Typically, this takes the form of a 50/50 split with customers. Settle this in advance if you plan on taking the fish home, or if catch and release is important to you.

On party boats you are often fishing shoulder-to-shoulder with other anglers. This can pose problems handling hooked fish unless you follow standard procedures. When another fisherman hooks-up they should indicate that they have a fish with an audible "fish on!" This is your cue to stand out of their way and pull your line from the water if necessary. By the same token, when you hook a fish, announce it with a loud "fish on!" This puts other fishermen on notice to yield to you and signals the mate to provide assistance if required.

INTRODUCTION

At The Conclusion Of Your Trip

If all goes well, at the end of the trip, you will have met all of the objectives you set out to achieve. However, in fishing, as in life, there are few guarantees. Although using a professional service greatly increases your chances for catching fish, it is no guarantee. Some service providers offer "special deals" for fishless days: future free trips, refunds, or partial rebates. However, this is generally not the case. If you expect something in return for a less than successful day, establish it with the service before booking the trip.

It is common practice to pay at the end of the trip unless other arrangements have been made. Payment includes the cost of services plus lunch, tackle usage, broken or lost equipment and gas. Understand all of the costs beforehand to avoid surprises at the end. Also make sure you know ahead of time what form of payment is acceptable: cash, personal check, or credit card.

Service providers work hard for you and it is customary to tip them. The amount is, of course, your decision and should be based on the quality of the entire experience. For a particularly good day, a 20 percent tip is a generous expression of your gratitude.

Fishing Lodges, Resorts, Ranches and Camps

Lodges, resorts, ranches and camps bring an added dimension to the fishing experience. Most of the facilities listed in the Angler's Yellow Pages also offer guide services. They deserve special mention because they offer some unique opportunities and introduce additional questions you will need to ask.

Lodges and Resorts range from luxury hideaways that can accommodate large groups to wilderness outposts suitable only for small groups. When contacting lodge owners, ask the right questions to ensure you get what you expect, and can afford.

Ranches, sometimes called dude ranches, offer a wide range of activities. These facilities are ideal for family trips. There is something for everyone: fishing for you, horseback riding, hiking, swimming, tennis, golf and more for the rest of the family. Many ranches specialize in fly fishing, and some offer lessons from certified guides.

Camps take many forms. They may be campgrounds, RV parks, remote fly-in cabins or small fishing camps. Generally, camps cater to the serious fisherman. If you want to live, eat and breath fishing, camps can be a good choice.

When calling and asking questions of lodge, resort, ranch or camp operators regarding accommodations, make sure you also speak to the fishing guide, or the person in charge of guides. Operators know the facility, but may not be familiar with current fishing conditions.

INTRODUCTION

List Of Questions To Ask Professional Fishing Guides

1. Rates: half day, full day; number of people? Include: gas, tackle, bait, beverages, lunch? Other charges? Volume discounts available (two or more days)? Any "special deals" on fishless days? Deposit required? How much? Cancellation refund policy? Forms of acceptable payment?
2. Tackle provided? If so, what type?
3. OK to bring own tackle? What kind of equipment? Maximum allowable equipment?
4. Lunch provided? Beverages?
5. OK to bring your own beverages? Cooler? Make sure you specify the type of beverage.
6. Rain gear provided?
7. Type of clothing to bring?
8. Length, in hours, of the trip?
9. Maximum number of people per trip?
10. Minimum age if bringing children?
11. Fishing techniques: live bait, artificial lures?
12. Years of experience fishing for the species in the area?
13. Any "unique" specialties, perhaps a technique or lure developed by them?
14. Best time of year for selected species and location?
15. Recent average catch for species and location?
16. Catch and release only?
17. Type of fishing: wading, drift boat, canoe, powered boat?
18. Will they, or an associate, be doing the guiding?
19. References?
20. Recommend local lodging if required?
21. When and where to purchase license if required?
22. Does the guide have a list of absolute "do's and don'ts"?
23. Where and when to meet?

List Of Questions To Ask Charter Boat Captains

1. Rates: half day, full day; number of people? Include: gas, tackle, bait, beverages, lunch? Other charges? Volume discounts available (two or more days)? Any "special deals" on fishless days? Deposit required? How much? Cancellation refund policy? Forms of acceptable payment?
2. Exclusive charter or party boat?
3. Tackle provided? If so, what type?
4. OK to bring own tackle? What kind of equipment? Maximum allowable equipment?
5. Lunch provided? Beverages?
6. OK to bring your own beverages? Cooler? Make sure you specify the type of beverage.
7. Rain gear provided?
8. Type of clothing to bring?
9. Length, in hours, of the trip?
10. Maximum number of people per trip?
11. Minimum age if bringing children?
12. Fishing techniques: live bait, artificial lures?
13. Years of experience fishing for the species in the area?
14. Any "unique" specialties, perhaps a technique or lure developed by them?
15. Best time of year for selected species and location?
16. Recent average catch for species and location?
17. Catch and release only?
18. Policy on sharing of the catch?
19. References?
20. Recommend local lodging if required?
21. License required? If so, when and where to purchase?
22. Does the boat have a list of absolute "do's and don'ts"?
23. Where and when to meet?

INTRODUCTION

List Of Questions To Ask Lodge, Ranch and Camp Operators

1. Rates: Day, week. Include: guides, tackle, bait, beverages, lunch? Other charges? Deposit required? How much? Cancellation refund policy? Forms of acceptable payment?
2. Pick up service provided from airport, train or bus stations?
3. Rental car recommended?
4. Pets allowed?
5. RV hook ups available?
6. Minimum length of stay?
7. Age of the facility?
8. Facility currently under renovation?
9. Lodging conditions (upscale, average, primitive)?
10. Shared or private bathrooms?
11. Range of non-fishing activities available?
12. Tackle provided? If so, what type?
13. OK to bring own tackle? What kind of equipment?
14. Lunch provided? Beverages?
15. OK to bring your own beverages? Cooler? Make sure you specify the type of beverage.
16. Type of clothing to bring?
17. Length, in hours, of guided trips?
18. Maximum number of people per trip?
19. Minimum age if bringing children?
20. Fishing techniques: live bait, artificial lures?
21. Guides years of experience fishing for the species in the area?
22. Need to book guide in advance?
23. Policy on tipping? Standard amount?
24. Best time of year for selected species and location?
25. Recent average catch for species and location?
26. Catch and release only?
27. References?
28. License required? If so, when and where to purchase?
29. Bait and tackle available?
30. How much fishing pressure in the area?
31. Problems with insects?
32. Does the facility have a list of absolute "do's and don'ts"?

Happy Angling!

Geographic Coverage

The Big Picture

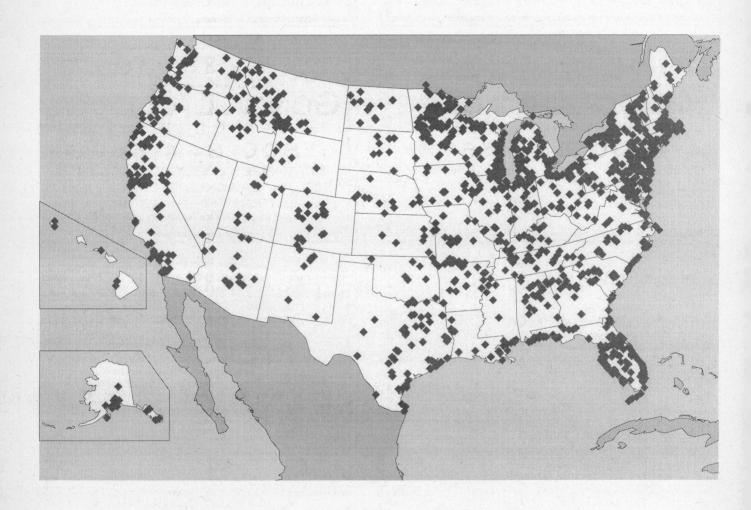

The map above illustrates the number and location of USA fishing spots listed in the Angler's Yellow Pages.

ANGLER'S COUPON

GUNGA-LA LODGE
RIVER OUTFITTERS
1 800 844-5606
FREE FLIES & LEADER OR BAIT & TERMINAL TACKLE ON ANY GUIDED TROUT FISHING TRIP.
SEE OUR AD IN "ARKANSAS STATE" SECTION

ANGLER'S COUPON

GUNGA-LA LODGE
RIVER OUTFITTERS
1 800 844-5606
FREE FLIES & LEADER OR BAIT & TERMINAL TACKLE ON ANY GUIDED TROUT FISHING TRIP.
SEE OUR AD IN "ARKANSAS STATE" SECTION

ANGLER'S COUPON

GUNGA-LA LODGE
RIVER OUTFITTERS
1 800 844-5606
FREE FLIES & LEADER OR BAIT & TERMINAL TACKLE ON ANY GUIDED TROUT FISHING TRIP.
SEE OUR AD IN "ARKANSAS STATE" SECTION

ANGLER'S COUPON

GUNGA-LA LODGE
RIVER OUTFITTERS
1 800 844-5606
FREE FLIES & LEADER OR BAIT & TERMINAL TACKLE ON ANY GUIDED TROUT FISHING TRIP.
SEE OUR AD IN "ARKANSAS STATE" SECTION

ANGLER'S COUPON

COFFEE CREEK RANCH
NORTHERN CALIFORNIA'S FINEST GUEST RANCH

- Private Cabins • Full American Plan • Heated Pool • HorsebackRiding
- X-C Skiing • Horse Drawn Hayrides & Sleighrides • Health Spa
- Trout/Fly Fishing • Youth Program (3-17 years) • Square Dancing
- Hunting (Deer and Bear) • Rifle Range • Fall Foliage • Trapshooting
- Holiday Parties & MORE!

10% OFF 2 OR MORE NIGHTS!

MEMBER NORTH AMERICAN FISHING CLUB

Call or write for brochure...
HC 2 Box 4940, Dept. AYP, Trinity Center, CA 96091
TOLL FREE 1-800-624-4480

OPEN ALL YEAR

ANGLER'S COUPON

COFFEE CREEK RANCH
NORTHERN CALIFORNIA'S FINEST GUEST RANCH

- Private Cabins • Full American Plan • Heated Pool • HorsebackRiding
- X-C Skiing • Horse Drawn Hayrides & Sleighrides • Health Spa
- Trout/Fly Fishing • Youth Program (3-17 years) • Square Dancing
- Hunting (Deer and Bear) • Rifle Range • Fall Foliage • Trapshooting
- Holiday Parties & MORE!

10% OFF 2 OR MORE NIGHTS!

MEMBER NORTH AMERICAN FISHING CLUB

Call or write for brochure...
HC 2 Box 4940, Dept. AYP, Trinity Center, CA 96091
TOLL FREE 1-800-624-4480

OPEN ALL YEAR

ANGLER'S COUPON

COFFEE CREEK RANCH
NORTHERN CALIFORNIA'S FINEST GUEST RANCH

- Private Cabins • Full American Plan • Heated Pool • HorsebackRiding
- X-C Skiing • Horse Drawn Hayrides & Sleighrides • Health Spa
- Trout/Fly Fishing • Youth Program (3-17 years) • Square Dancing
- Hunting (Deer and Bear) • Rifle Range • Fall Foliage • Trapshooting
- Holiday Parties & MORE!

10% OFF 2 OR MORE NIGHTS!

MEMBER NORTH AMERICAN FISHING CLUB

Call or write for brochure...
HC 2 Box 4940, Dept. AYP, Trinity Center, CA 96091
TOLL FREE 1-800-624-4480

OPEN ALL YEAR

ANGLER'S COUPON

COFFEE CREEK RANCH
NORTHERN CALIFORNIA'S FINEST GUEST RANCH

- Private Cabins • Full American Plan • Heated Pool • HorsebackRiding
- X-C Skiing • Horse Drawn Hayrides & Sleighrides • Health Spa
- Trout/Fly Fishing • Youth Program (3-17 years) • Square Dancing
- Hunting (Deer and Bear) • Rifle Range • Fall Foliage • Trapshooting
- Holiday Parties & MORE!

10% OFF 2 OR MORE NIGHTS!

MEMBER NORTH AMERICAN FISHING CLUB

Call or write for brochure...
HC 2 Box 4940, Dept. AYP, Trinity Center, CA 96091
TOLL FREE 1-800-624-4480

OPEN ALL YEAR

ANGLER'S COUPON

GUNGA-LA LODGE
RIVER OUTFITTERS
1 800 844-5606
FREE FLIES & LEADER OR BAIT & TERMINAL TACKLE ON ANY GUIDED TROUT FISHING TRIP.
SEE OUR AD IN "ARKANSAS STATE" SECTION

ANGLER'S COUPON

GUNGA-LA LODGE
RIVER OUTFITTERS
1 800 844-5606
FREE FLIES & LEADER OR BAIT & TERMINAL TACKLE ON ANY GUIDED TROUT FISHING TRIP.
SEE OUR AD IN "ARKANSAS STATE" SECTION

ANGLER'S COUPON

GUNGA-LA LODGE
RIVER OUTFITTERS
1 800 844-5606
FREE FLIES & LEADER OR BAIT & TERMINAL TACKLE ON ANY GUIDED TROUT FISHING TRIP.
SEE OUR AD IN "ARKANSAS STATE" SECTION

ANGLER'S COUPON

GUNGA-LA LODGE
RIVER OUTFITTERS
1 800 844-5606
FREE FLIES & LEADER OR BAIT & TERMINAL TACKLE ON ANY GUIDED TROUT FISHING TRIP.
SEE OUR AD IN "ARKANSAS STATE" SECTION

ANGLER'S COUPON

COFFEE CREEK RANCH
NORTHERN CALIFORNIA'S FINEST GUEST RANCH

- Private Cabins • Full American Plan • Heated Pool • HorsebackRiding
- X-C Skiing • Horse Drawn Hayrides & Sleighrides • Health Spa
- Trout/Fly Fishing • Youth Program (3-17 years) • Square Dancing
- Hunting (Deer and Bear) • Rifle Range • Fall Foliage • Trapshooting
- Holiday Parties & MORE!

10% OFF 2 OR MORE NIGHTS!

MEMBER NORTH AMERICAN FISHING CLUB
Call or write for brochure...
HC 2 Box 4940, Dept. AYP, Trinity Center, CA 96091
TOLL FREE 1-800-624-4480
OPEN ALL YEAR

ANGLER'S COUPON

COFFEE CREEK RANCH
NORTHERN CALIFORNIA'S FINEST GUEST RANCH

- Private Cabins • Full American Plan • Heated Pool • HorsebackRiding
- X-C Skiing • Horse Drawn Hayrides & Sleighrides • Health Spa
- Trout/Fly Fishing • Youth Program (3-17 years) • Square Dancing
- Hunting (Deer and Bear) • Rifle Range • Fall Foliage • Trapshooting
- Holiday Parties & MORE!

10% OFF 2 OR MORE NIGHTS!

MEMBER NORTH AMERICAN FISHING CLUB
Call or write for brochure...
HC 2 Box 4940, Dept. AYP, Trinity Center, CA 96091
TOLL FREE 1-800-624-4480
 OPEN ALL YEAR

ANGLER'S COUPON

COFFEE CREEK RANCH
NORTHERN CALIFORNIA'S FINEST GUEST RANCH

- Private Cabins • Full American Plan • Heated Pool • HorsebackRiding
- X-C Skiing • Horse Drawn Hayrides & Sleighrides • Health Spa
- Trout/Fly Fishing • Youth Program (3-17 years) • Square Dancing
- Hunting (Deer and Bear) • Rifle Range • Fall Foliage • Trapshooting
- Holiday Parties & MORE!

10% OFF 2 OR MORE NIGHTS!

MEMBER NORTH AMERICAN FISHING CLUB
Call or write for brochure...
HC 2 Box 4940, Dept. AYP, Trinity Center, CA 96091
TOLL FREE 1-800-624-4480
OPEN ALL YEAR

ANGLER'S COUPON

COFFEE CREEK RANCH
NORTHERN CALIFORNIA'S FINEST GUEST RANCH

- Private Cabins • Full American Plan • Heated Pool • HorsebackRiding
- X-C Skiing • Horse Drawn Hayrides & Sleighrides • Health Spa
- Trout/Fly Fishing • Youth Program (3-17 years) • Square Dancing
- Hunting (Deer and Bear) • Rifle Range • Fall Foliage • Trapshooting
- Holiday Parties & MORE!

10% OFF 2 OR MORE NIGHTS!

MEMBER NORTH AMERICAN FISHING CLUB
Call or write for brochure...
HC 2 Box 4940, Dept. AYP, Trinity Center, CA 96091
TOLL FREE 1-800-624-4480
  OPEN ALL YEAR

ALABAMA

1. Alabama River
2. Black Warrior River
3. Cahaba River
4. Dannelly Reservoir
5. Gulf of Mexico
6. Guntersville Lake
7. Harris Reservoir
8. Lake Eufaula
9. Lake Jordan
10. Lake Martin
11. Lay Lake
12. Lewis Smith Lake
13. Logan Martin Lake
14. Mitchell Lake
15. Mobile River Delta
16. Neely Henry Lake
17. Pickwick Lake
18. Tallapoosa River
19. Tennessee River
20. Weiss Lake
21. Wheeler Lake
22. Wilson Lake

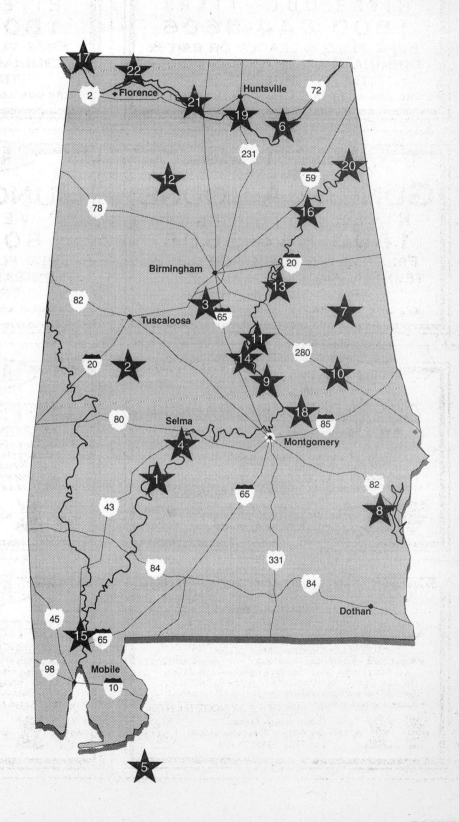

ALABAMA

ALABAMA RIVER - GULF OF MEXICO

ALABAMA RIVER

BAIT & TACKLE...

Kent Bait & Tackle
Tallassee 334-283-4414
Hours: 6am-7pm, 1-5pm Sun.
Carries: Live bait, lures, flies, maps, rods, reels, licenses
Bodies of water: Lake Martin, Tallapoosa River, Lake Jordan, Alabama River
Services & Products: Food, beverages, gas/oil
Guides: Yes
OK to call for current conditions: Yes

Maurice Sporting Goods
Marion 334-683-9100
Hours: 5am-7pm
Carries: Live bait, lures, flies, maps, rods, reels, licenses
Bodies of water: Black Warrior River, Alabama River, Cahaba River, Lake Land Farms
Services & Products: Food, beverages, gas/oil, fishing instruction
Guides: Yes
OK to call for current conditions: Yes
Contact: Maurice Nichols, Jr

Statesville Grocery
Selma 334-872-1385
Hours: 5am-8pm
Carries: Live bait, lures, flies, maps, rod, reels, licenses
Bodies of water: Alabama River, Jones Bluff Dam
Services & Products: Food, beverages, gas/oil
Guides: Yes
OK to call for current conditions: Yes
Contact: Leo Brewer

BLACK WARRIOR RIVER

BAIT & TACKLE...

Corner Bait & Tackle
Tuscaloosa 205-752-1379
Hours: 5:30am-6pm
Carries: Live bait, lures, flies, rods, reels, licenses
Bodies of water: Black Warrior River
Services & Products: Guide service, food, beverages, gas/oil, repair services
Guides: Yes
OK to call for current conditions: Yes

Maurice Sporting Goods
Marion 334-683-9100
Hours: 5am-7pm
Carries: Live bait, lures, flies, maps, rods, reels, licenses
Bodies of water: Black Warrior River, Alabama River, Cahaba River, Lake Land Farms
Services & Products: Food, beverages, gas/oil, fishing instruction
Guides: Yes
OK to call for current conditions: Yes
Contact: Maurice Nichols, Jr.

Reed's Grocery & Bait
Tuscaloosa 205-752-0520
Hours: 5:30am-8pm, 8am-8pm Sun.
Carries: Live bait, lures, licenses
Bodies of water: Lake Tuscaloosa, Lake Nichol, Lake Harris, Black Warrior River
Services & Products: Food, beverages, gas/oil
Guides: No
OK to call for current conditions: No

GUIDES...

Reed's Guide Service
Ensley 205-787-5133
Species & Seasons: Spotted Bass, SM Bass, LM Bass all year
Bodies of water: Coosa River, Weiss Lake, Neely Henry Lake, Logan Martin Lake, Tallapoosa River, Lake Martin, Harris Res., Warrior River, Tennessee River, Guntersville Lake, Wilson Lake, Wheeler Lake, Chatahoochee River, Lake Eufaula
Rates: Full day: $150(1), $200(2)
Call between: 7pm-10pm
Provides: Heavy tackle, lures
Handicapped equipped: No

CAHABA RIVER

BAIT & TACKLE...

Let's Go Fishing - Lake Purdy
3780 Boat Launch Road
Birmingham 35242
Carries: Live bait, lures, flies, maps, rods, reels, licenses
Bodies of water: Lake Purdy, Cahaba River
Guides: Yes
OK to call for current conditions: Yes
Contact: Ken Delap

Maurice Sporting Goods
Marion 334-683-9100
Hours: 5am-7pm
Carries: Live bait, lures, flies, maps, rods, reels, licenses
Bodies of water: Black Warrior River, Alabama River, Cahaba River, Lake Land Farms
Services & Products: Food, beverages, gas/oil, fishing instruction
Guides: Yes
OK to call for current conditions: Yes
Contact: Maurice Nichols, Jr

DANNELLY RESERVOIR

BAIT & TACKLE...

Shell Creek Minnow Bucket
Catherine 334-225-4458
Hours: 6am-6pm Mon.-Sat., 8am-4pm Sun.
Carries: Live bait, lures, flies, maps, rods, reels, licenses
Bodies of water: Dannelly Res. (one of the top 4 lakes in AL)
Services & Products: Food, beverages, gas/oil, repair services
Guides: Yes
OK to call for current conditions: Yes
Contact: Tenna Wilkerson

GULF OF MEXICO

CHARTERS...

Great Gulf Fishing Charters
Orange Beach 334-981-6507
Species & Seasons: Redfish, Speckled Trout, Flounder, Red Snapper all year, Sheepshead Mar-May, Spanish Mackerel, King Mackerel May-Oct, Pompano Mar-May
Bodies of water: Gulf of Mexico
Rates: Half day: $200(1-4), Full day: $350(1-4)
Call between: 6pm-10pm
Provides: Light tackle, lures, bait
Handicapped equipped: Yes
Certifications: USCG

Joe Nash
Orange Beach 334-981-2343
Species & Seasons: Speckled Trout, Redfish, Bluefish, Flounder, Mackerel, Red Snapper, Triggerfish, Amberjack all year
Bodies of water: Gulf of Mexico

GULF OF MEXICO - LAKE JORDAN

ALABAMA

Rates: 22' skiff (Inland, for Speckled Trout, Redfish, Bluefish, Flounder, Mackerel):
4 hrs: $200(1-4), 6 hrs: $300(1-4),
8 hrs: $350, all bait, tackle, licenses included 52', 22 passenger vessel available
Call between: Anytime
Provides: Light tackle, heavy tackle, bait
Handicapped equipped: No
Certifications: USCG

Outcast Charter Boat
Orange Beach.................. 334-981-5553
Species & Seasons: Red Snapper, Triggerfish, Vermillion Snapper all year, King Mackerel May-Aug, Cobia Mar-May, Amberjack Spring-Fall
Bodies of water: Gulf of Mexico
Rates: Varies
Call between: 8am-5pm
Provides: Heavy tackle, lures, bait
Handicapped equipped: Yes
Certifications: USCG

Underwriter Charters
Orange Beach.................. 334-981-3252
Species & Seasons: Red Snapper, Vermillion Snapper, Triggerfish all year, Blue Marlin, Sailfish May-Sept, Amberjack April-Sept, Cobia Mar-May, King Mackerel May-Aug
Bodies of water: Gulf of Mexico
Rates: Varies
Call between: 8am-9pm
Provides: Heavy tackle, lures, bait
Handicapped equipped: Yes
Certifications: USCG

MARINAS...

Fort Morgan Marina
Fort Morgan 334-540-2336
Hours: 6am-7pm, closed Mon.
Carries: Live bait, lures, maps, rods, reels, licenses
Bodies of water: Gulf of Mexico, Mobile Bay, Bon Secour Bay
Services & Products: Guide services, charter boat, boat ramp, food, beverages, gas/oil, repair services, boat storage
Guides: Yes
OK to call for current conditions: Yes
Contact: Jerry Bullard

Outcast Charter Docks, Inc.
Orange Beach.................. 334-981-5553
Hours: 8am-5pm
Bodies of water: Gulf of Mexico
Services & Products: Charter boat service, snacks, beverages
Guides: Yes
OK to call for current conditions: Yes

GUNTERSVILLE LAKE

GUIDES...

Reed's Guide Service
Ensley 205-787-5133
Species & Seasons: Spotted Bass, SM Bass, LM Bass all year
Bodies of water: Coosa River, Weiss Lake, Neely Henry Lake, Logan Martin Lake, Tallapoosa River, Lake Martin, Harris Res., Warrior River, Tennessee River, Guntersville Lake, Wilson Lake, Wheeler Lake, Chatahoochee River, Lake Eufaula
Rates: Full day: $150(1), $200(2)
Call between: 7pm-10pm
Provides: Heavy tackle, lure
Handicapped equipped: No

Top Guide Service
Guntersville 800-645-1585
.... 205-582-5463
Species & Seasons: LM Bass all year
Bodies of water: Guntersville Lake
Rates: Half day: $90(1-2),
Full day: $150(1-2)
Call between: 8am-9pm
Provides: Light tackle, heavy tackle, lures
Handicapped equipped: Yes

MARINAS...

Scott's Marina
Cullman 205-287-1635
Hours: 7am-6pm
Carries: Live bait, lures, flies, maps, rods, reels, licenses
Bodies of water: Lewis Smith Lake, Guntersville Lake, Lake Martin, Weiss Lake, Wheeler Lake, Logan Martin Lake
Services & Products: Boat ramp, food, beverages, gas/oil, fishing instruction, repair services
Guides: No
OK to call for current conditions: Yes

HARRIS RESERVOIR

GUIDES...

Reed's Guide Service
Ensley 205-787-5133
Species & Seasons: Spotted Bass, SM Bass, LM Bass all year
Bodies of water: Coosa River, Weiss Lake, Neely Henry Lake, Logan Martin Lake, Tallapoosa River, Lake Martin, Harris Res., Warrior River, Tennessee River, Guntersville Lake, Wilson Lake, Wheeler Lake, Chatahoochee River, Lake Eufaula
Rates: Full day: $150(1), $200(2)
Call between: 7pm-10pm
Provides: Heavy tackle, lures
Handicapped equipped: No

LAKE EUFAULA

BAIT & TACKLE...

White Oak Village
Abbeville 334-687-5088
Hours: 6am-8pm
Carries: Live bait, lures, flies, maps, rods, reels, licenses
Bodies of water: Lake Eufaula, Walter F. George Res.
Guides: Yes
OK to call for current conditions: Yes
Contact: Bob Knowles

LAKE JORDAN

BAIT & TACKLE...

Kent Bait & Tackle
Tallassee 334-283-4414
Hours: 6am-7pm, 1-5pm Sun.
Carries: Live bait, lures, flies, maps, rods, reels, licenses
Bodies of water: Lake Martin, Tallapoosa River, Lake Jordan, Alabama River
Services & Products: Food, beverages, gas/oil
Guides: Yes
OK to call for current conditions: Yes

YOUR SILENT FISHING PARTNER

ALABAMA
LAKE JORDAN - LOGAN MARTIN LAKE

GUIDES...

Reed's Guide Service
Ensley 205-787-5133
Species & Seasons: Spotted Bass, SM Bass, LM Bass all year
Bodies of water: Coosa River, Weiss Lake, Neely Henry Lake, Logan Martin Lake, Tallapoosa River, Lake Martin, Harris Res., Warrior River, Tennessee River, Guntersville Lake, Wilson Lake, Wheeler Lake, Chatahoochee River, Lake Eufaula
Rates: Full day: $150(1), $200(2)
Call between: 7pm-10pm
Provides: Heavy tackle, lures
Handicapped equipped: No

LAKE MARTIN

BAIT & TACKLE...

Hawthorne's Country Bait
Sylacauga 205-245-1486
Hours: 6am-7pm
Carries: Live bait, lures, flies, maps, rods, reels, licenses
Bodies of water: Lake Martin, Mitchell Lake, Lay Lake, Logan Martin Lake
Services & Products: Beverages
Guides: Yes
OK to call for current conditions: Yes
Contact: Robert Hawthorne

Kent Bait & Tackle
Tallassee 334-283-4414
Hours: 6am-7pm, 1-5pm Sun.
Carries: Live bait, lures, flies, maps, rods, reels, licenses
Bodies of water: Lake Martin, Tallapoosa River, Lake Jordan, Alabama River
Services & Products: Food, beverages, gas/oil
Guides: Yes
OK to call for current conditions: Yes

GUIDES...

Reed's Guide Service
Ensley 205-787-5133
Species & Seasons: Spotted Bass, SM Bass, LM Bass all year
Bodies of water: Coosa River, Weiss Lake, Neely Henry Lake, Logan Martin Lake, Tallapoosa River, Lake Martin, Harris Res., Warrior River, Tennessee River, Guntersville Lake, Wilson Lake, Wheeler Lake, Chatahoochee River, Lake Eufaula
Rates: Full day: $150(1), $200(2)
Call between: 7pm-10pm
Provides: Heavy tackle, lures
Handicapped equipped: No

MARINAS...

Scott's Marina
Cullman 205-287-1635
Hours: 7am-6pm
Carries: Live bait, lures, flies, maps, rods, reels, licenses
Bodies of water: Lewis Smith Lake, Guntersville Lake, Lake Martin, Weiss Lake, Wheeler Lake, Logan Martin Lake
Services & Products: Boat ramp, food, beverages, gas/oil, fishing instruction, repair services
Guides: No
OK to call for current conditions: Yes

LAY LAKE

BAIT & TACKLE...

Hawthorne's Country Bait
Sylacauga 205-245-1486
Hours: 6am-7pm
Carries: Live bait, lures, flies, maps, rods, reels, licenses
Bodies of water: Lake Martin, Mitchell Lake, Lay Lake, Logan Martin Lake
Services & Products: Beverages
Guides: Yes
OK to call for current conditions: Yes
Contact: Robert Hawthorne

LEWIS SMITH LAKE

GUIDES...

Welch Guide Service
Crane Hill 205-737-0541
Species & Seasons: Striped Bass, Spotted Bass all year, Crappie Jan-May
Bodies of water: Lewis Smith Lake, Joe Wheeler Dam tailrace
Rates: Full day: $150(1), $200(2)
Call between: 6pm-10pm
Provides: Heavy tackle, lures, bait
Handicapped equipped: Yes

MARINAS...

Hames Marina
Cullman 205-287-9785
Hours: 9am-6pm, closed in winter
Carries: Live bait, lures, maps, rods, licenses
Bodies of water: Lewis Smith Lake
Services & Products: Boat rentals, boat ramp, food, beverages, gas/oil, camping, trailer/rv lots, ice, boat slips
Guides: Yes
OK to call for current conditions: Yes
Contact: Carolyn Hames

Scott's Marina
Cullman 205-287-1635
Hours: 7am-6pm
Carries: Live bait, lures, flies, maps, rods, reels, licenses
Bodies of water: Lewis Smith Lake, Guntersville Lake, Lake Martin, Weiss Lake, Wheeler Lake, Logan Martin Lake
Services & Products: Boat ramp, food, beverages, gas/oil, fishing instruction, repair services
Guides: No
OK to call for current conditions: Yes

LOGAN MARTIN LAKE

BAIT & TACKLE...

Hawthorne's Country Bait
Sylacauga 205-245-1486
Hours: 6am-7pm
Carries: Live bait, lures, flies, maps, rods, reels, licenses
Bodies of water: Lake Martin, Mitchell Lake, Lay Lake, Logan Martin Lake
Services & Products: Beverages
Guides: Yes
OK to call for current conditions: Yes
Contact: Robert Hawthorne

GUIDES...

Don Massey
44214 Highway 78, Lot 110
Lincoln 35906
Species & Seasons: Bass Mar-Dec, Striped Bass July-Sept
Bodies of water: Logan Martin Lake
Rates: Half day: $75-$90(1-2), Full day: $150-$175(1-2)
Call between: 6am-10pm
Provides: Light tackle, lures, lunch
Handicapped equipped: No

LOGAN MARTIN LAKE - TALLAPOOSA RIVER / ALABAMA

Reed's Guide Service
Ensley 205-787-5133
Species & Seasons: Spotted Bass, SM Bass, LM Bass all year
Bodies of water: Coosa River, Weiss Lake, Neely Henry Lake, Logan Martin Lake, Tallapoosa River, Lake Martin, Harris Res., Warrior River, Tennessee River, Guntersville Lake, Wilson Lake, Wheeler Lake, Chatahoochee River, Lake Eufaula
Rates: Full day: $150(1), $200(2)
Call between: 7pm-10pm
Provides: Heavy tackle, lures
Handicapped equipped: No

MARINAS...

Aqualand Marina
Pell City 205-338-7726
Hours: 10am-5pm, closed Mon.
Carries: Maps
Bodies of water: Logan Martin Lake
Services & Products: Boat ramp, food, beverages, gas/oil, repair services
Guides: Yes
OK to call for current conditions: No

Scott's Marina
Cullman 205-287-1635
Hours: 7am-6pm
Carries: Live bait, lures, flies, maps, rods, reels, licenses
Bodies of water: Lewis Smith Lake, Guntersville Lake, Lake Martin, Weiss Lake, Wheeler Lake, Logan Martin Lake
Services & Products: Boat ramp, food, beverages, gas/oil, fishing instruction, repair services
Guides: No
OK to call for current conditions: Yes

MITCHELL LAKE

BAIT & TACKLE...

Hawthorne's Country Bait
Sylacauga 205-245-1486
Hours: 6am-7pm
Carries: Live bait, lures, flies, maps, rods, reels, licenses
Bodies of water: Lake Martin, Mitchell Lake, Lay Lake, Logan Martin Lake
Services & Products: Beverages
Guides: Yes
OK to call for current conditions: Yes
Contact: Robert Hawthorne

MOBILE RIVER DELTA

LODGING...

Dead Lake Fishing Lodge
Creola 334-675-0320
Guest Capacity: 4 cabins (4 people each), 40 RV spaces
Handicapped equipped: Yes
Seasons: All year
Rates: $19/day, $114/week
Contact: Fran Turner
Guides: Yes
Species & Seasons: LM Bass, Bream, Crappie, Catfish all year
Bodies of Water: Mobile River Delta
Types of fishing: Fly fishing, light tackle
Available: Fishing instruction, licenses, bait, tackle, boat rentals, family activities

NEELY HENRY LAKE

GUIDES...

Reed's Guide Service
Ensley 205-787-5133
Species & Seasons: Spotted Bass, SM Bass, LM Bass all year
Bodies of water: Coosa River, Weiss Lake, Neely Henry Lake, Logan Martin Lake, Tallapoosa River, Lake Martin, Harris Res., Warrior River, Tennessee River, Guntersville Lake, Wilson Lake, Wheeler Lake, Chatahoochee River, Lake Eufaula
Rates: Full day: $150(1), $200(2)
Call between: 7pm-10pm
Provides: Heavy tackle, lures
Handicapped equipped: No

MARINAS...

Coosa Willow Point Campground and Marina
Ohatchee 205-892-2717
Hours: 5am-8pm
Carries: Live bait, lures, flies, maps, rods, reels, licenses
Bodies of water: Neely Henry Lake
Services & Products: Boat rentals, guide services, boat ramp, food, beverages, gas/oil
OK to call for current conditions: Yes
Contact: Rick

PICKWICK LAKE

BAIT & TACKLE...

The Tackle Box
Florence 205-764-2446
Hours: 5:30am-6pm
Carries: Live bait, lures, flies, maps, rods, reels, licenses
Bodies of water: Tennessee River, Wheeler Lake, Wilson Lake, Pickwick Lake
Services & Products: Guide services, food, beverages, fishing instruction, repair services
OK to call for current conditions: Yes
Contact: Betty Munger

GUIDES...

Pickwick Smallmouth Guide Service
Tuscumbia 205-383-1058
Species & Seasons: SM Bass, LM Bass March-Dec
Bodies of water: Pickwick Lake, Wilson Lake, Wheeler Lake
Rates: Half day: $125(1), $150(2), Full day $200(1), $250(2), Discounts on multiple day trips
Call between: 8am-8pm
Provides: Light tackle, bait, beverages, lunch
Handicapped equipped: No

TALLAPOOSA RIVER

BAIT & TACKLE...

Kent Bait & Tackle
Tallassee 334-283-4414
Hours: 6am-7pm, 1-5pm Sun.
Carries: Live bait, lures, flies, maps, rods, reels, licenses
Bodies of water: Lake Martin, Tallapoosa River, Lake Jordan, Alabama River
Services & Products: Food, beverages, gas/oil
Guides: Yes
OK to call for current conditions: Yes

ALABAMA

TALLAPOOSA RIVER - WEISS LAKE

GUIDES...

Reed's Guide Service
Ensley 205-787-5133
Species & Seasons: Spotted Bass, SM Bass, LM Bass all year
Bodies of water: Coosa River, Weiss Lake, Neely Henry Lake, Logan Martin Lake, Tallapoosa River, Lake Martin, Harris Res., Warrior River, Tennessee River, Guntersville Lake, Wilson Lake, Wheeler Lake, Chatahoochee River, Lake Eufaula
Rates: Full day: $150(1), $200(2)
Call between: 7pm-10pm
Provides: Heavy tackle, lures
Handicapped equipped: No

TENNESSEE RIVER

BAIT & TACKLE...

The Tackle Box
Florence 205-764-2446
Hours: 5:30am-6pm
Carries: Live bait, lures, flies, maps, rods, reels, licenses
Bodies of water: Tennessee River, Wheeler Lake, Wilson Lake, Pickwick Lake
Services & Products: Guide services, food, beverages, fishing instruction, repair services
OK to call for current conditions: Yes
Contact: Betty Munger

GUIDES...

Reed's Guide Service
Ensley 205-787-5133
Species & Seasons: Spotted Bass, SM Bass, LM Bass all year
Bodies of water: Coosa River, Weiss Lake, Neely Henry Lake, Logan Martin Lake, Tallapoosa River, Lake Martin, Harris Res., Warrior River, Tennessee River, Guntersville Lake, Wilson Lake, Wheeler Lake, Chatahoochee River, Lake Eufaula
Rates: Full day: $150(1), $200(2)
Call between: 7pm-10pm
Provides: Heavy tackle, lures
Handicapped equipped: No

WEISS LAKE

GUIDES...

Reed's Guide Service
Ensley 205-787-5133
Species & Seasons: Spotted Bass, SM Bass, LM Bass all year
Bodies of water: Coosa River, Weiss Lake, Neely Henry Lake, Logan Martin Lake, Tallapoosa River, Lake Martin, Harris Res., Warrior River, Tennessee River, Guntersville Lake, Wilson Lake, Wheeler Lake, Chatahoochee River, Lake Eufaula
Rates: Full day: $150(1), $200(2)
Call between: 7pm-10pm
Provides: Heavy tackle, lures
Handicapped equipped: No

LODGING...

Bay Springs Motel and Campground
Centre 205-927-3618
Guest Capacity: 22 rooms
Handicapped equipped: Yes
Seasons: All year
Rates: $38/day double occupancy
Contact: Bill O'Brien
Guides: Yes
Species & Seasons: Crappie Feb-May, LM Bass Mar-June
Bodies of Water: Weiss Lake
Types of fishing: Light tackle
Available: Licenses, boat rentals

Big Oak Fish Camp
Cedar Bluff 205-526-8723
Guest Capacity: 175
Handicapped equipped: No
Seasons: All year
Rates: $10/day
Contact: Cotton Crow
Guides: Yes
Species & Seasons: Crappie Feb-May/Oct-Nov, Bream May-June, LM Bass Feb-Sept, Striped Bass May-Aug
Bodies of Water: Weiss Lake
Types of fishing: Fly fishing, light tackle, heavy tackle
Available: Licenses, bait, tackle, groceries, gas, ice

Lockridge Waterfront Cabins
Centre 205-927-5338
Guest Capacity: 8
Handicapped equipped: No
Seasons: All year
Rates: $125/day
Contact: Jerry G. Lockridge
Guides: Yes
Species & Seasons: LM Bass, Crappie Mar-Nov, Striped Bass, Saltwater Striped Bass Dec-Dec, Bream April-Oct
Bodies of Water: Weiss Lake
Types of fishing: Light tackle, wading, float trips

Pruett's Fish Camp & Cabins
Centre 205-475-3950
Guest Capacity: 80+
Handicapped equipped: Yes
Seasons: All year
Rates: $35-$150/day
Contact: Johnny or Betty Fann
Guides: Yes
Species & Seasons: Crappie Feb-May/Sept-Nov, LM Bass, Bream May-Sept, Catfish all year
Bodies of Water: Weiss Lake
Types of fishing: Fly fishing, light tackle, wading, float trips
Available: Fishing instruction, bait, tackle, boat rentals

Tysons Camp Ground
Centre 205-475-3015
Guest Capacity: 30 units
Handicapped equipped: No
Seasons: Mar 1 to Sept 30
Rates: Varies
Guides: Yes
Species & Seasons: LM Bass, Crappie, Catfish, Striped Bass all year, Bream, Bluegill May-Sept
Bodies of Water: Weiss Lake
Types of fishing: Fly fishing, light tackle, heavy tackle, wading
Available: Fishing instruction, bait, tackle, boat rentals, family activities

MARINAS...

Scott's Marina
Cullman 205-287-1635
Hours: 7am-6pm
Carries: Live bait, lures, flies, maps, rods, reels, licenses
Bodies of water: Lewis Smith Lake, Guntersville Lake, Lake Martin, Weiss Lake, Wheeler Lake, Logan Martin Lake

WEISS LAKE - WILSON LAKE — ALABAMA

Services & Products: Boat ramp, food, beverages, gas/oil, fishing instruction, repair services
Guides: No
OK to call for current conditions: Yes

WHEELER LAKE

BAIT & TACKLE...

The Tackle Box
Florence 205-764-2446
Hours: 5:30am-6pm
Carries: Live bait, lures, flies, maps, rods, reels, licenses
Bodies of water: Tennessee River, Wheeler Lake, Wilson Lake, Pickwick Lake
Services & Products: Guide services, food, beverages, fishing instruction, repair services
OK to call for current conditions: Yes
Contact: Betty Munger

GUIDES...

Pickwick Smallmouth Guide Service
Tuscumbia 205-383-1058
Species & Seasons: SM Bass, LM Bass March-Dec
Bodies of water: Pickwick Lake, Wilson Lake, Wheeler Lake
Rates: Half day: $125(1), $150(2), Full day $200(1),$250(2), Other: Discounts on multiple day trips
Call between: 8am-8pm
Provides: Light tackle, bait, beverages, lunch
Handicapped equipped: No

Reed's Guide Service
Ensley 205-787-5133
Species & Seasons: Spotted Bass, SM Bass, LM Bass all year
Bodies of water: Coosa River, Weiss Lake, Neely Henry Lake, Logan Martin Lake, Tallapoosa River, Lake Martin, Harris Res., Warrior River, Tennessee River, Guntersville Lake, Wilson Lake, Wheeler Lake, Chatahoochee River, Lake Eufaula
Rates: Full day: $150(1), $200(2)
Call between: 7pm-10pm
Provides: Heavy tackle, lures
Handicapped equipped: No

MARINAS...

Ditto Landing
Huntsville 205-883-9420
Hours: 8am-10pm
Carries: Maps
Bodies of water: Wheeler Lake
Services & Products: Boat ramp, beverages, gas/oil, campgrounds, transient slips
Guides: Yes
OK to call for current conditions: No

Scott's Marina
Cullman 205-287-1635
Hours: 7am-6pm
Carries: Live bait, lures, flies, maps, rods, reels, licenses
Bodies of water: Lewis Smith Lake, Guntersville Lake, Lake Martin, Weiss Lake, Wheeler Lake, Logan Martin Lake
Services & Products: Boat ramp, food, beverages, gas/oil, fishing instruction, repair services
Guides: No
OK to call for current conditions: Yes

WILSON LAKE

BAIT & TACKLE...

The Tackle Box
Florence 205-764-2446
Hours: 5:30am-6pm
Carries: Live bait, lures, flies, maps, rods, reels, licenses
Bodies of water: Tennessee River, Wheeler Lake, Wilson Lake, Pickwick Lake
Services & Products: Guide services, food, beverages, fishing instruction, repair services
OK to call for current conditions: Yes
Contact: Betty Munger

GUIDES...

Pickwick Smallmouth Guide Service
Tuscumbia 205-383-1058
Species & Seasons: SM Bass, LM Bass March-Dec
Bodies of water: Pickwick Lake, Wilson Lake, Wheeler Lake
Rates: Half day: $125(1), $150(2), Full day $200(1),$250(2), Discounts on multiple day trips
Call between: 8am-8pm
Provides: Light tackle, bait, beverages, lunch
Handicapped equipped: No

Reed's Guide Service
Ensley 205-787-5133
Species & Seasons: Spotted Bass, SM Bass, LM Bass all year
Bodies of water: Coosa River, Weiss Lake, Neely Henry Lake, Logan Martin Lake, Tallapoosa River, Lake Martin, Harris Res., Warrior River, Tennessee River, Guntersville Lake, Wilson Lake, Wheeler Lake, Chatahoochee River, Lake Eufaula
Rates: Full day: $150(1), $200(2)
Call between: 7pm-10pm
Provides: Heavy tackle, lures
Handicapped equipped: No

YOUR SILENT FISHING PARTNER

Thank you for using the Angler's Yellow Pages

ALASKA

1. Aleutian Range
2. Anchorage Area
3. Bristol Bay
4. Cook Inlet
5. Fairbanks Area
6. Gulf of Alaska
7. Kachemak Bay
8. Kenai Area
9. Ketchikan Area
10. Kodiak Area
11. Kvichak River
12. Lake Clark
13. Mulchatna River
14. Nushagak River
15. Pacific Ocean
16. Sitka Area

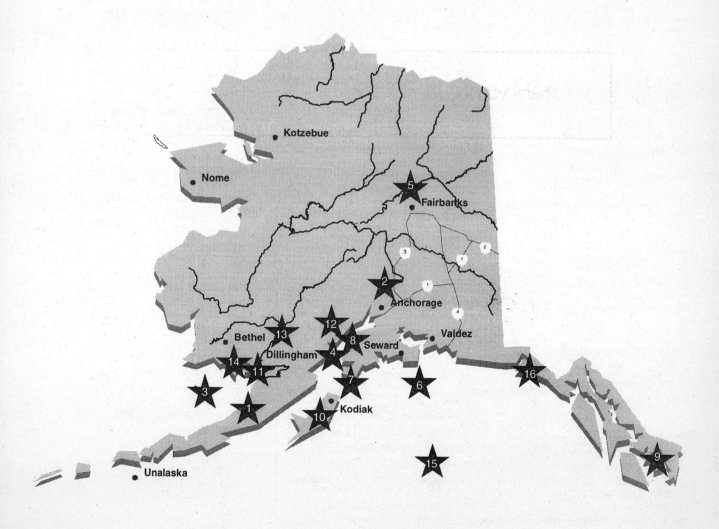

ALASKA
ALEUTIAN RANGE - ANCHORAGE AREA

ALEUTIAN RANGE

LODGING...

Ugashik Lake Lodge
Anchorage 907-248-3230
Guest Capacity: 8
Handicapped equipped: No
Seasons: June 1 to Sept 30
Rates: $2100/week
Contact: Gus Lamoureux
Guides: Yes
Species & Seasons: Chinook Salmon June-July, Sockeye Salmon July-Aug, Coho Salmon Aug-Sept, Arctic Char July-Oct, Arctic Grayling May-Oct, Northern Pike, Lake Trout all year
Bodies of Water: Becharof NWR, upper and lower Ugashik Lakes, Bristol Bay
Types of fishing: Fly fishing, light tackle, wading, fly-out trips
Available: Licenses, bait, tackle, animal viewing and photography

ANCHORAGE AREA

GUIDES...

Midnight Sun Outfitters
Gold Beach, OR 503-247-6284
Species & Seasons: King Salmon June-July, Rainbow Trout, Arctic Grayling June-Sept
Bodies of water: Talachulitna River
Rates: 7day float trip: $1900

Call between: 9am-9pm
Provides: Fly rod/reel, flies
Handicapped equipped: No

CHARTERS...

Susitna Riverover Charters
Wasilla 907-376-2630
Species & Seasons: Chinook Salmon May-July, Coho Salmon, Chum Salmon July-Aug, Rainbow Trout, Northern Pike May-Sept, Arctic Grayling Sept-Oct
Bodies of water: Susitna River, many others
Rates: Full day: $145(1-2)
Special rates for 5 or more, and for multiple day bookings
Call between: 8am-8pm
Provides: Light tackle, heavy tackle, lures, bait
Handicapped equipped: Yes
Certifications: USCG, NAFC

Trophy Catch Charters
Palmer 907-745-4101
Species & Seasons: Chinook Salmon May-July, Coho Salmon, Chum Salmon, Pink Salmon July-Aug, Sockeye Salmon July
Bodies of water: Little Susitna River
Rates: Half day: $90(1), $180(2), Full day: $150(1), $300(2)
Drop-off bank fishing
Call between: 7am-10pm

Provides: Light tackle, heavy tackle, lures, bait
Handicapped equipped: Yes, some restrictions
Certifications: Licensed and registered AK Guides

GUIDES...

Mahay's Riverboat Service
Talkeetna 907-733-2223
Species & Seasons: Rainbow Trout, Dolly Varden, Arctic Grayling May/June/Sept/Oct, Chinook Salmon June-July, Sockeye Salmon July-Aug, Coho Salmon Aug-Sept, Chum Salmon July-Sept, Pink Salmon July-Sept
Bodies of water: Talkeetna River, Upper Susitna River
Rates: Half day: $125(1), $250(2), Full day: $175(1), $350(2), Drop-off unguided: $50
Call between: 8am-10pm
Provides: Light tackle, lures, rain gear
Handicapped equipped: Yes
Certifications: USCG

LODGING...

Northwoods Lodge
Skwentna 800-999-6539
.... 907-733-3742
Guest Capacity: 12
Handicapped equipped: No
Seasons: All year
Rates: Winter: $120/day, Summer: $200/day
Contact: Eric or Shan Johnson
Guides: Yes
Species & Seasons: Chinook Salmon May-July, Coho Salmon July-Aug, Rainbow Trout, Arctic Grayling May-June/July-Sept, Northern Pike May-Sept, Pink Salmon July-Aug, Chum Salmon July-Sept
Bodies of Water: Lake Creek, 8 Mile Creek, Fish Creek, Donkey Creek, Indian Creek, Hewitt Creek, Malone Creek
Types of fishing: Fly fishing, light tackle, heavy tackle, wading, fly-out trips, float trips
Available: Fishing instruction, licenses, bait, tackle

ALASKA
Remote wilderness fishing & comfortable facilities in Bristol Bay. Five species of Salmon, Grayling, Pike, Lake Trout, Dolly Varden, & Arctic Char.

For Information contact:
907 248-3230 or
907 248-3012

Ugashik Lake Lodge
Master Guide: Gus Lamoureux
PO Box 90444-YP
Anchorage, Alaska 99509

BRISTOL BAY - COOK INLET — ALASKA

BRISTOL BAY

LODGING...

Ugashik Lake Lodge
Anchorage 907-248-3230
Guest Capacity: 8
Handicapped equipped: No
Seasons: June 1 to Sept 30
Rates: $2100/week
Contact: Gus Lamoureux
Guides: Yes
Species & Seasons: Chinook Salmon June-July, Sockeye Salmon July-Aug, Coho Salmon Aug-Sept, Arctic Char July-Oct, Arctic Grayling May-Oct, Northern Pike, Lake Trout all year
Bodies of Water: Becharof NWR, upper and lower Ugashik Lakes, Bristol Bay
Types of fishing: Fly fishing, light tackle, wading, fly-out trips
Available: Licenses, bait, tackle, animal viewing and photography

COOK INLET

CHARTERS...

Alaska Native Charters
Ninilchik 907-567-3972
Species & Seasons: Halibut May-Sept, Chinook Salmon June-July, Coho Salmon July-Sept
Bodies of water: Cook Inlet
Rates: Full day: $120(1), $240(2)
Call between: 8am-5pm
Provides: Light tackle, heavy tackle, lures, bait, rain gear, beverages
Certifications: USCG

Alaskan Game Fisher
Soldotna 800-320-2980
.... 907-262-2980
Species & Seasons: Halibut May-Sept, Chinook Salmon May-July, Coho Salmon Aug-Sept
Bodies of water: Kenai River, Cook Inlet
Rates: Half day: $125(1), Full day: $150-$195(1)
Call between: Anytime
Provides: Light tackle, heavy tackle, lures, bait
Handicapped equipped: Yes
Certifications: USCG

Ardison Charters
Ninilchik 907-567-3600
Species & Seasons: Halibut May-Sept, Chinook Salmon May-June/July, Coho Salmon Aug
Bodies of water: Cook Inlet
Rates: 6-8 hrs: $125(1), $110(3 or more)
Call between: 9am-4pm
Provides: Light tackle, heavy tackle, lures, bait, rain gear
Handicapped equipped: Yes
Certifications: USCG, CPR, First aid

Clearwater Adventures
Homer 907-235-8030
Species & Seasons: Halibut, Chinook Salmon May-Sept, Coho Salmon Aug-Sept
Bodies of water: Kachemak Bay, Cook Inlet
Rates: Full day: $120(1), $240(2), Other packages available
Call between: 8am-9pm
Provides: Light tackle, heavy tackle, lures, bait
Handicapped equipped: Yes
Certifications: USCG, State of AK Fish & Game, Pacific Halibut Comm.

Halibut King Charters
Homer 907-235-7303
Species & Seasons: Chinook Salmon Jan-Oct, Halibut Feb-Oct
Bodies of water: Kachemak Bay, Cook Inlet, Kenai River, Kasilof River
Rates: Varies ($125-$175)
Call between: Anytime
Provides: Light tackle, heavy tackle, fly rod/reel, lures, bait, beverages, lunch, licenses
Handicapped equipped: Yes
Certifications: USCG, FCC

Joyce Marie Charters
Ninilchik 907-567-3663
Species & Seasons: Chinook Salmon April-June/July, Coho Salmon Aug, Halibut May-Sept
Bodies of water: Cook Inlet, Kachemak Bay, Kodiac Island
Rates: Full day: $140-$165(1)
Call between: 8am-11pm
Provides: Light tackle, heavy tackle, lures, bait
Handicapped equipped: No
Certifications: USCG

7/25/95 King 86.1 lbs.

King of the River

- World famous largest king salmon at the Kenai River, Alaska.
- May to September
- King / Silver / Red Salmon / Halibut / Trout - Charters
- Unlimited tackle
- Accessible to disabled
- Lodging referrals
- RV - Campground
- 1/2 day to week long - Charters

1-800-478-9901
P.O. Box 107
Soldotna, AK 99669

ALASKA — COOK INLET

King of the River
Soldotna 800-478-9901
.... 907-279-3474
Species & Seasons: Chinook Salmon May-July, Coho Salmon Aug-Oct, Halibut April-Oct, Steelhead April-Oct, Sockeye Salmon July
Bodies of water: Kenai River, Cook Inlet, Kasilof River
Rates: Half day: $120-$140(1), Full day: $175-$205, 1/2 for 2nd person, other packages available
Call between: 8am-8pm
Provides: Light tackle, heavy tackle, fly rod/reel, lures, bait, rain gear, beverages
Handicapped equipped: Yes
Certifications: USCG, 100 tons Master

Ninilchik Saltwater Charters
Ninilchik 907-567-3611
Species & Seasons: Halibut April-Sept, Chinook Salmon May-July, Coho Salmon Aug-Sept, Sockeye Salmon June-July, Rainbow Trout, Dolly Varden July-Sept
Bodies of water: Cook Inlet, Kenai River, Kasilof River, Kachemak Bay
Call between: 7am-10pm
Provides: Light tackle, heavy tackle, lures, bait, rain gear, beverages
Handicapped equipped: Yes

Sea Flight Charters
Homer 907-235-7572
Species & Seasons: Halibut, Rockfish Mar-Oct, Chinook Salmon all year, Coho Salmon July-Aug
Bodies of water: Kachemak Bay, Cook Inlet
Rates: Full day: $165(1) more than one species, $125(1) pre/post season, $140(1) June, July, Aug. Special rate for whole boat(6)
Call between: Anytime
Provides: Light tackle, heavy tackle, lures, bait, By special arrangement: Beverages, lunch transportation, B&B
Handicapped equipped: Yes
Certifications: USCG, 100 ton Master

Tim Hiner's Alaska Fishing
Soldotna 907-262-9729
Species & Seasons: Chinook Salmon May-Aug, Coho Salmon Aug-Oct, Pink Salmon Aug-Sept, Sockeye Salmon Aug-Oct, Rainbow Trout, Dolly Varden Aug-Oct, Halibut May-Sept
Bodies of water: Kenai River, Cook Inlet
Rates: Half day: $120(1), $240(2), Full day: $240(1), $480(2), Full day: Halibut: $145(1)
Call between: 7am-8pm
Provides: Light tackle, heavy tackle, lures, bait
Certifications: USCG, CPR, First aid

GUIDES...

Johnson Brothers Fishing Guide
Soldotna 800-918-7233
Species & Seasons: Chinook Salmon May-July, Coho Salmon Aug-Sept, Halibut May-Sept
Bodies of water: Kenai River, Cook Inlet, Kasilof River
Provides: Light tackle, heavy tackle, rain gear
Handicapped equipped: Yes
Certifications: USCG

R W's Fishing Guide Service
Soldotna 907-262-7888
Species & Seasons: Chinook Salmon May-July, Halibut May-Sept, Coho Salmon July-Oct, Sockeye Salmon June-Aug, Rainbow Trout June-Oct
Bodies of water: Cook Inlet, Kenai River
Rates: Half day: $140(1), $280(2)
Call between: 8am-5pm
Provides: Heavy tackle, lures, bait
Handicapped equipped: Yes
Certifications: USCG

Smokin Joe's World Famous Guide Service
Soldotna 907-262-1575
Species & Seasons: Chinook Salmon May-July, Coho Salmon July-Sept, Sockeye Salmon June-Aug, Halibut May-Sept, Rainbow Trout, Dolly Varden June-Oct
Bodies of water: Kenai River, Kasilof River, Cook Inlet
Rates: Varies
Call between: 6am-8pm
Provides: Light tackle, heavy tackle, fly rod/reel, lures, bait
Handicapped equipped: Yes

Wes' Guide Service
Soldotna 907-262-9264
Species & Seasons: Chinook Salmon May-July, Coho Salmon, Pink Salmon Aug-Sept, Sockeye Salmon June-Aug, Halibut, Dolly Varden May-Sept, Rainbow Trout June-Sept
Bodies of water: Kenai River, Kasilof River, Cook Inlet
Rates: Half day: $110(1), Full day: $200(1)
Call between: 9am-9pm
Provides: Light tackle, heavy tackle, fly rod/reel, lures, bait, rain gear, beverages, lunch
Handicapped equipped: Yes
Certifications: USCG, CIPSA, TU, NAFC, IGFA

LODGING...

Orca Lodge
Soldotna 907-262-5649
Guest Capacity: 24
Handicapped equipped: No
Seasons: May to Oct
Rates: $120-$125/day
Guides: Yes
Species & Seasons: Chinook Salmon May-July, Sockeye Salmon June-Aug, Coho Salmon Aug-Sept, Rainbow Trout June-Sept, Halibut May-Sept
Bodies of Water: Kenai River, Kasilof River, Kachemak Bay, Cook Inlet
Types of fishing: Fly fishing, heavy tackle, wading, fly-out trips, float trips
Available: Fishing instruction, licenses, family activities

Orca Lodge
Deluxe Kenai Riverfront Log Cabins
• Lodging •
• Guided/Unguided Fishing •
• Hunting/Fishing Packages •

PO Box 4653, Soldota, AK 99669
907 262-5649

COOK INLET - KACHEMAK BAY
ALASKA

Riddles Lodge & Guide Service
Kenai 907-283-5853
Guest Capacity: 12
Handicapped equipped: No
Seasons: May to Oct
Rates: $60/day pp
Contact: Donna Ridde
Guides: Yes
Species & Seasons: Chinook Salmon May-July, Coho Salmon Aug-Sept, Sockeye Salmon June-Aug, Halibut May-Oct, Rainbow Trout, Steelhead June-Oct
Bodies of Water: Cook Inlet, Kenai River, Kasilof River
Types of fishing: Fly fishing, light tackle, heavy tackle, fly-out trips, float trips
Available: Wild Life viewing

FAIRBANKS AREA
CHARTERS...

Lake Clark Air
Port Alsworth 907-781-2211
Species & Seasons: Rainbow Trout June-Oct, Lake Trout May-Sept, Arctic Grayling May-Oct Arctic Char May-Sept, Chinook Salmon June-July, Sockeye Salmon July, Coho Salmon Aug-Sept, Chum Salmon, Pink Salmon July-Aug, Northern Pike June-Aug
Bodies of water: Lake Clark, Kvichak River, Nusagak River, Mulchatna River
Rates: Half day: $75(1), $50(pp2), Full day: $125(1), $75(pp2), Fly Out: $500 day
Call between: 7am-8am
Provides: Beverages, lunch
Handicapped equipped: Yes
Certifications: USCG

GUIDES...

Alaska Private Guide Service
Fairbanks 907-457-8318
Species & Seasons: Northern Pike, Sheafish, Arctic Grayling, Dolly Varden June-Oct, Chinook Salmon June-July, Coho Salmon Aug-Sept, Sockeye Salmon July-Aug, Rainbow Trout, Arctic Char May-Oct
Bodies of water: Yukon River, Tanana River, Nowitna River, Innoko River, Chena River, Salcha River, Nushagak River, many others
Rates: Half day: $175(1), $250(2), Full day: $250(1), $350(2), 5-10 day trips: $1000-$2500(pp) with group discounts

Call between: 12pm-12am est
Provides: Bait, beverages, lunch, camps
Handicapped equipped: Maybe
Certifications: USCG, AK registered

Elliott's Wilderness Fishing
Fairbanks 907-479-6323
Species & Seasons: Rainbow Trout, Arctic Grayling, Silver Salmon, Northern Pike, Lake Trout, Arctic Char May-Sept
Bodies of water: Fly-in wilderness lakes (complete packages)
Rates: Full day(24 hrs.): $155(1), $310(2)
Call between: 8am-8provides: Light tackle, fly rod/reel, lures, bait, rain gear, beverages, lunch
Handicapped equipped: No
Certifications: FAA, AK Dept. of Sport Fishing

GULF OF ALASKA
CHARTERS...

Sablefish Charters
Seward 907-224-3283
Species & Seasons: Halibut, Rockfish May-Aug, Coho Salmon July-Sept, Ling Cod July-Aug, Chinook Salmon May-June
Bodies of water: Resurrection Bay, Kenai Fjords, Gulf of Alaska
Rates: Full day: $130(1), Group rate: $700(6)
Call between: Anytime
Provides: Light tackle, heavy tackle, lures, bait
Handicapped equipped: Yes
Certifications: USCG, Master 100 ton

LODGING...

Lisianski Lodge & Charters
Pelican 907-735-2266
Guest Capacity: 8
Handicapped equipped: No
Seasons: May 1 to Sept 30
Rates: $350/pp day
Contact: Denny Corbin
Guides: Yes
Species & Seasons: Chinook Salmon, Halibut, Trout May-Sept
Bodies of Water: Cross Sound, Lisianski Inlet, Icy Straits, Gulf of Alaska
Types of fishing: Fly fishing, light tackle, heavy tackle, fly-out trips
Available: Fishing instruction, licenses, bait, tackle, boat rentals, family activities

KACHEMAK BAY
CHARTERS...

Clearwater Adventures
Homer 907-235-8030
Species & Seasons: Halibut, Chinook Salmon May-Sept, Coho Salmon Aug-Sept
Bodies of water: Kachemak Bay, Cook Inlet
Rates: Full day: $120(1), $240(2), other packages available
Call between: 8am-9pm
Provides: Light tackle, heavy tackle, lures, bait
Handicapped equipped: Yes
Certifications: USCG, State of AK Fish & Game, Pacific Halibut Comm.

Halibut King Charters
Homer 907-235-7303
Species & Seasons: Chinook Salmon Jan-Oct, Halibut Feb-Oct
Bodies of water: Kachemak Bay, Cook Inlet, Kenai River, Kasilof River
Rates: Varies ($125-$175)
Call between: Anytime
Provides: Light tackle, heavy tackle, fly rod/reel, lures, bait, beverages, lunch, licenses
Handicapped equipped: Yes
Certifications: USCG, FCC

Joyce Marie Charters
Ninilchik 907-567-3663
Species & Seasons: Chinook Salmon April-June/July, Coho Salmon Aug, Halibut May-Sept
Bodies of water: Cook Inlet, Kachemak Bay, Kodiac Island
Rates: Full day: $140-$165(1)
Call between: 8am-11pm
Provides: Light tackle, heavy tackle, lures, bait
Handicapped equipped: No
Certifications: USCG

Ninilchik Saltwater Charters
Ninilchik 907-567-3611
Species & Seasons: Halibut April-Sept, Chinook Salmon May-July, Coho Salmon Aug-Sept, Sockeye Salmon June-July, Rainbow Trout, Dolly Varden July-Sept
Bodies of water: Cook Inlet, Kenai River, Kasilof River, Kachemak Bay
Call between: 7am-10pm
Provides: Light tackle, heavy tackle, lures, bait, rain gear, beverages
Handicapped equipped: Yes

ALASKA
KACHEMAK BAY - KENAI AREA

Sea Flight Charters
Homer 907-235-7572
Species & Seasons: Halibut, Rockfish Mar-Oct, Chinook Salmon all year, Coho Salmon July-Aug
Bodies of water: Kachemak Bay, Cook Inlet
Rates: Full day: $165(1) more than one species, $125(1) pre/post season, $140(1) June, July, Aug, special rate for whole boat(6)
Call between: Anytime
Provides: Light tackle, heavy tackle, lures, bait, By special arrangement: Beverages, lunch transportation, B&B
Handicapped equipped: Yes
Certifications: USCG, 100 ton Master

LODGING...

Orca Lodge
Soldotna 907-262-5649
Guest Capacity: 24
Handicapped equipped: No
Seasons: May to Oct
Rates: $120-$125/day
Guides: Yes
Species & Seasons: Chinook Salmon May-July, Sockeye Salmon June-Aug, Coho Salmon Aug-Sept, Rainbow Trout June-Sept, Halibut May-Sept
Bodies of Water: Kenai River, Kasilof River, Kachemak Bay, Cook Inlet
Types of fishing: Fly fishing, heavy tackle, wading, fly-out trips, float trips
Available: Fishing instruction, licenses, family activities

KENAI AREA
CHARTERS...

Alaska Sunrise Fishing Adventures
Sterling 907-262-1250
Species & Seasons: Chinook Salmon, May-July, Silver Salmon Aug-Oct, Trout June-Oct
Bodies of water: Kenai River, Kasilof River
Rates: Half day: $125(1), Full day: $210(1)
Call between: 8am-10pm
Provides: Light tackle, heavy tackle, lures, bait
Handicapped equipped: Yes, moderately handicapped
Certifications: USCG

Alaskan Game Fisher
Soldotna 800-320-2980
.... 907-262-2980
Species & Seasons: Halibut May-Sept, Chinook Salmon May-July, Coho Salmon Aug-Sept
Bodies of water: Kenai River, Cook Inlet
Rates: Half day: $125(1), Full day: $150-$195(1)
Call between: Anytime
Provides: Light tackle, heavy tackle, lures, bait
Handicapped equipped: Yes
Certifications: USCG

HALIBUT ✳ SALMON
Ling Cod ✳ Rockfish
May thru September
licensed & insured
Gear & Bait provided
Call or Write
for Free Brochure
SABLEFISH CHARTERS
PO Box 1588
Seward, Alaska 99664
1 800 357-2253
907 224-3283

Halibut King Charters
Homer 907-235-7303
Species & Seasons: Chinook Salmon Jan-Oct, Halibut Feb-Oct
Bodies of water: Kachemak Bay, Cook Inlet, Kenai River, Kasilof River
Rates: Varies ($125-$175)
Call between: Anytime
Provides: Light tackle, heavy tackle, fly rod/reel, lures, bait, beverages, lunch, licenses
Handicapped equipped: Yes
Certifications: USCG, FCC

King of the River
Soldotna 800-478-9901
.... 907-279-3474
Species & Seasons: Chinook Salmon May-July, Coho Salmon Aug-Oct, Halibut April-Oct, Steelhead April-Oct, Sockeye Salmon July
Bodies of water: Kenai River, Cook Inlet, Kasilof River
Rates: Half day: $120-$140(1), Full day: $175-$205, 1/2 for 2nd person, other packages available

Call between: 8am-8pm
Provides: Light tackle, heavy tackle, fly rod/reel, lures, bait, rain gear, beverages
Handicapped equipped: Yes
Certifications: USCG, 100 tons Master

Ninilchik Saltwater Charters
Ninilchik 907-567-3611
Species & Seasons: Halibut April-Sept, Chinook Salmon May-July, Coho Salmon Aug-Sept, Sockeye Salmon June-July, Rainbow Trout, Dolly Varden July-Sept
Bodies of water: Cook Inlet, Kenai River, Kasilof River, Kachemak Bay
Call between: 7am-10pm
Provides: Light tackle, heavy tackle, lures, bait, rain gear, beverages
Handicapped equipped: Yes

Sablefish Charters
Seward 907-224-3283
Species & Seasons: Halibut, Rockfish May-Aug, Coho Salmon July-Sept, Ling Cod July-Aug, Chinook Salmon May-June
Bodies of water: Resurrection Bay, Kenai Fjords, Gulf of Alaska
Rates: Full day: $130(1), Group rate: $700(6)
Call between: Anytime
Provides: Light tackle, heavy tackle, lures, bait
Handicapped equipped: Yes
Certifications: USCG, Master 100 ton

Tim Hiner's Alaska Fishing
Soldotna 907-262-9729
Species & Seasons: Chinook Salmon May-Aug, Coho Salmon Aug-Oct, Pink Salmon Aug-Sept, Sockeye Salmon Aug-Oct, Rainbow Trout, Dolly Varden Aug-Oct, Halibut May-Sept
Bodies of water: Kenai River, Cook Inlet
Rates: Half day: $120(1), $240(2), Full day: $240(1), $480(2), Halibut: $145(1) Full day
Call between: 7am-8pm
Provides: Light tackle, heavy tackle, lures, bait
Certifications: USCG, CPR, First aid

GUIDES...

Gary and Val Early
Brookings, OR 503-469-0525
.... 907-262-6132
Species & Seasons: Chinook Salmon Aug-Dec, Steelhead Sept-Mar, Salmon April-Aug

KENAI AREA — ALASKA

Bodies of water: Kenai River
Rates: Full day: $125(1), $250(2), half days available in Alaska
Call between: 5pm-9pm
Provides: Light tackle, heavy tackle, fly rod/reel, lures, bait
Handicapped equipped: Yes
Certifications: USCG, Orvis, Red Cross

Fun Fishing with Tex
Soldotna 800-234-7406
.... 907-262-9655
Species & Seasons: Chinook Salmon May-July, Sockeye Salmon June-July, Coho Salmon July-Sept, Halibut May-Sept, Trout June-Oct, Steelhead April-May, Sheafish Aug-Sept
Bodies of water: Kasilof River, Kenai River, many others
Rates: Full day: $100(1), $200(2)
Call between: 9am-9pm
Provides: Light tackle, heavy tackle, lures, bait, beverages
Handicapped equipped: Yes

Johnson Brothers Fishing Guide
Soldotna 800-918-7233
Species & Seasons: Chinook Salmon May-July, Coho Salmon Aug-Sept, Halibut May-Sept
Bodies of water: Kenai River, Cook Inlet, Kasilof River
Provides: Light tackle, heavy tackle, rain gear
Handicapped equipped: Yes
Certifications: USCG

HALIBUT - AND - SALMON
- Kenai River Kings & Silvers
- Cook Inlet Salmon & Halibut

410 lb. Halibut - Caught 6/30/92
CAPT. MEL ERICKSON Local Resident & Guide
ALASKAN GAME FISHER
P.O. Box 1127-AK, Soldotna, AK 99669
1 800 320-2980

Kenai King Drifters-Drift Boat Guide Service & Outfitters
Kasilof 907-262-6654
.... 653-7648 off season
Species & Seasons: Chinook Salmon May-July, Silver Salmon Aug-Sept
Bodies of water: Kenai River, Kasilof River, Gulkana River
Rates: Full day: $125-$175(1), overnight packages available
Call between: 8am-9pm
Provides: Light tackle, heavy tackle, lures, bait
Handicapped equipped: Yes
Certifications: Licensed AK resident guide

R W's Fishing Guide Service
Soldotna 907-262-7888
Species & Seasons: Chinook Salmon May-July, Halibut May-Sept, Coho Salmon July-Oct, Sockeye Salmon June-Aug, Rainbow Trout June-Oct
Bodies of water: Cook Inlet, Kenai River
Rates: Half day: $140(1), $280(2)
Call between: 8am-5pm
Provides: Heavy tackle, lures, bait
Handicapped equipped: Yes
Certifications: USCG

Sehl Guide Service
Tidewater, OR 503-528-3382
Species & Seasons: Chinook Salmon May-July/Sept-Nov, Steelhead May-July/Dec-Feb, Sturgeon April-May
Bodies of water: Kenai River, American River, Susitna drainage
Rates: Full day: $100(1) Senior discount
Call between: 7:30-8am/6pm-8pm
Provides: Light tackle, heavy tackle, lures, bait, beverages, lunch
Handicapped equipped: Yes
Certifications: USCG

Smokin Joe's World Famous Guide Service
Soldotna 907-262-1575
Species & Seasons: Chinook Salmon May-July, Coho Salmon July-Sept, Sockeye Salmon June-Aug, Halibut May-Sept, Rainbow Trout, Dolly Varden June-Oct
Bodies of water: Kenai River, Kasilof River, Cook Inlet
Rates: Varies
Call between: 6am-8pm
Provides: Light tackle, heavy tackle, fly rod/reel, lures, bait
Handicapped equipped: Yes

Wes' Guide Service
Soldotna 907-262-9264
Species & Seasons: Chinook Salmon May-July, Coho Salmon, Pink Salmon Aug-Sept, Sockeye Salmon June-Aug, Halibut, Dolly Varden May-Sept, Rainbow Trout June-Sept
Bodies of water: Kenai River, Kasilof River, Cook Inlet
Rates: Half day: $110(1), Full day: $200(1)
Call between: 9am-9pm
Provides: Light tackle, heavy tackle, fly rod/reel, lures, bait, rain gear, beverages, lunch
Handicapped equipped: Yes
Certifications: USCG, CIPSA, TU, NAFC, IGFA

LODGING...

Orca Lodge
Soldotna 907-262-5649
Guest Capacity: 24
Handicapped equipped: No
Seasons: May to Oct
Rates: $120-$125/day
Guides: Yes
Species & Seasons: Chinook Salmon May-July, Sockeye Salmon June-Aug, Coho Salmon Aug-Sept, Rainbow Trout June-Sept, Halibut May-Sept
Bodies of Water: Kenai River, Kasilof River, Kachemak Bay, Cook Inlet
Types of fishing: Fly fishing, heavy tackle, wading, fly-out trips, float trips
Available: Fishing instruction, licenses, family activities

Riddles Lodge & Guide Service
Kenai 907-283-5853
Guest Capacity: 12
Handicapped equipped: No
Seasons: May to Oct
Rates: $60/day pp
Contact: Donna Ridde
Guides: Yes
Species & Seasons: Chinook Salmon May-July, Coho Salmon Aug-Sept, Sockeye Salmon June-Aug, Halibut May-Oct, Rainbow Trout, Steelhead June-Oct
Bodies of Water: Cook Inlet, Kenai River, Kasilof River
Types of fishing: Fly fishing, light tackle, heavy tackle, fly-out trips, float trips
Available: Wild Life viewing

ALASKA

KETCHIKAN AREA

CHARTERS...

Eagle Charters
Ketchikan.................. 907-247-3474
Species & Seasons: Chinook Salmon May-Aug, Coho Salmon July-Sept, Pink Salmon June-Aug, Halibut, Rockfish April-Oct
Bodies of water: Ketchikan area (inside waters)
Rates: Half day: $130(1), Full day: $185(1)
Call between: Anytime
Provides: Light tackle, heavy tackle, lures, bait, rain gear
Handicapped equipped: No
Certifications: USCG, 25 ton Masters

Ken's Charters
Ketchikan.................. 907-225-7290
Species & Seasons: Steelhead, April-May, Chinook Salmon May-June, Pink Salmon June-Aug, Halibut May-Sept, Coho Salmon, Aug-Oct, Cutthroat Trout, Rainbow Trout Spring-Fall
Bodies of water: Ketchikan area
Rates: Half day: $400(1), $480(4), $175(pp for 3-4), Multi-day trips available
Call between: 8am-10pm
Provides: Light tackle, heavy tackle, lures, bait, rain gear, beverages, lunch
Handicapped equipped: Yes, depending on handicap
Certifications: USCG

Northern Lights Charters
Ward Cove................. 907-247-8488
Species & Seasons: Chinook Salmon May-July, Pink Salmon, Chum Salmon June-Aug, Coho Salmon June-Sept, Halibut May-Sept, Shark June-Aug
Bodies of water: Ketchikan Area
Rates: Half day: $95(1), Full day: $150(1)
Call between: Anytime
Provides: Light tackle, heavy tackle, fly rod/reel, lures, bait, rain gear, beverages, lunch
Handicapped equipped: Yes
Certifications: USCG, Masters 50 ton

KODIAK AREA

CHARTERS...

Joyce Marie Charters
Ninilchik 907-567-3663
Species & Seasons: Chinook Salmon April-June/July, Coho Salmon Aug, Halibut May-Sept
Bodies of water: Cook Inlet, Kachemak Bay, Kodiac Island
Rates: Full day: $140-$165(1)
Call between: 8am-11pm
Provides: Light tackle, heavy tackle, lures, bait
Handicapped equipped: No
Certifications: USCG

LODGING...

Olga Bay Lodge, Inc.
Kodiak 907-486-5373
Guest Capacity:
Handicapped equipped: No
Seasons: June to Oct
Rates: $3000/week
Contact: James David Jones
Guides: Yes
Species & Seasons: Salmon, Trout June-Oct, Steelhead Sept-Oct
Bodies of Water: Southwest Kodiak Island
Types of fishing: Fly fishing, wading, fly-out trips
Available: Fishing instruction, licenses, bait, tackle

KVICHAK RIVER

CHARTERS...

Lake Clark Air
Port Alsworth 907-781-2211
Species & Seasons: Rainbow Trout June-Oct, Lake Trout May-Sept, Arctic Grayling May-Oct Arctic Char May-Sept, Chinook Salmon June-July, Sockeye Salmon July, Coho Salmon Aug-Sept, Chum Salmon, Pink Salmon July-Aug, Northern Pike June-Aug
Bodies of water: Lake Clark, Kvichak River, Nusagak River, Mulchatna River
Rates: Half day: $75(1), $50(pp2), Full day: $125(1), $75(pp2), Fly Out: $500 day
Call between: 7am-8am
Provides: Beverages, lunch
Handicapped equipped: Yes
Certifications: USCG

LAKE CLARK

CHARTERS...

Lake Clark Air
Port Alsworth 907-781-2211
Species & Seasons: Rainbow Trout June-Oct, Lake Trout May-Sept, Arctic Grayling May-Oct Arctic Char May-Sept, Chinook Salmon June-July, Sockeye Salmon July, Coho Salmon Aug-Sept, Chum Salmon, Pink Salmon July-Aug, Northern Pike June-Aug
Bodies of water: Lake Clark, Kvichak River, Nushagak River, Mulchatna River
Rates: Half day: $75(1), $50(pp2), Full day: $125(1), $75(pp2),
Fly Out: $500 day
Call between: 7am-8am
Provides: Beverages, lunch
Handicapped equipped: Yes
Certifications: USCG

MULCHATNA RIVER

CHARTERS...

Lake Clark Air
Port Alsworth 907-781-2211
Species & Seasons: Rainbow Trout June-Oct, Lake Trout May-Sept, Arctic Grayling May-Oct Arctic Char May-Sept, Chinook Salmon June-July, Sockeye Salmon July, Coho Salmon Aug-Sept, Chum Salmon, Pink Salmon July-Aug, Northern Pike June-Aug
Bodies of water: Lake Clark, Kvichak River, Nushagak River, Mulchatna River
Rates: Half day: $75(1), $50(pp2), Full day: $125(1), $75(pp2), Fly Out: $500 day
Call between: 7am-8am
Provides: Beverages, lunch
Handicapped equipped: Yes
Certifications: USCG

NUSHAGAK RIVER

CHARTERS...

Lake Clark Air
Port Alsworth 907-781-2211
Species & Seasons: Rainbow Trout June-Oct, Lake Trout May-Sept, Arctic Grayling May-Oct Arctic Char May-Sept, Chinook Salmon June-July, Sockeye Salmon July, Coho Salmon Aug-Sept, Chum Salmon, Pink Salmon July-Aug, Northern Pike June-Aug

NUSHAGAK RIVER - SITKA AREA — ALASKA

Bodies of water: Lake Clark, Kvichak River, Nushagak River, Mulchatna River
Rates: Half day: $75(1), $50(pp2), Full day: $125(1), $75(pp2), Fly Out: $500 day
Call between: 7am-8am
Provides: Beverages, lunch
Handicapped equipped: Yes
Certifications: USCG

GUIDES...

Alaska Private Guide Service
Fairbanks 907-457-8318
Species & Seasons: Northern Pike, Sheafish, Arctic Grayling, Dolly Varden June-Oct, Chinook Salmon June-July, Coho Salmon Aug-Sept, Sockeye Salmon July-Aug, Rainbow Trout, Arctic Char May-Oct
Bodies of water: Yukon River, Tanana River, Nowitna River, Innoko River, Chena River, Salcha River, Nushagak River, many others
Rates: Half day: $175(1), $250(2), Full day: $250(1), $350(2), 5-10 day trips: $1000-$2500(pp) with group discounts
Call between: 12pm-12am est
Provides: Bait, beverages, lunch, camps
Handicapped equipped: Maybe
Certifications: USCG, AK registered

PACIFIC OCEAN

CHARTERS...

Alaska Salmon Guaranteed Charters
Juneau 907-364-3474
Species & Seasons: Chinook Salmon May-Oct, Coho Salmon, Halibut July-Oct
Bodies of water: Pacific Ocean
Rates: Half day: $110 (1), $220(2), Full day: $175 (1), $350(2)
Call between: Anytime
Provides: Light tackle, heavy tackle, lures, bait, rain gear, beverages, lunch
Handicapped equipped: Yes
Certifications: USCG

Duke's Charter Fishing
Craig 907-826-3809
Species & Seasons: Chinook Salmon, Halibut June-Aug, Coho Salmon, Humpback Salmon July-Aug
Bodies of water: Pacific Ocean, inside waters

Rates: Half day: $200(1), $400(2), Full day: $400(1), $650(2), 3 or 4: $333 pp
Call between: 9am-1pm
Provides: Light tackle, heavy tackle, lures, bait, rain gear, beverages, lunch
Handicapped equipped: Yes
Certifications: USCG

LODGING...

Tanaku Lodge
Elfin Cove 907-239-2205
Guest Capacity: 12
Handicapped equipped: No
Seasons: May to Sept
Rates: $2395/6 days, 5 nights
Contact: Dennis Meier
Guides: Yes
Species & Seasons: Chinook Salmon, Halibut May-Sept, Coho Salmon July-Sept, Red Snapper, Ling Cod May-Sept
Bodies of Water: Pacific Ocean, sheltered coves, streams
Types of fishing: Fly fishing, light tackle
Available: Fishing instruction, licenses, bait, tackle, family activities

SITKA AREA

LODGING...

Lisianski Lodge & Charters
Pelican 907-735-2266
Guest Capacity: 8
Handicapped equipped: No
Seasons: May 1 to Sept 30
Rates: $350/pp day
Contact: Denny Corbin
Guides: Yes
Species & Seasons: Chinook Salmon, Halibut, Trout May-Sept
Bodies of Water: Cross Sound, Lisianski Inlet, Icy Straits, Gulf of Alaska
Types of fishing: Fly fishing, light tackle, heavy tackle, fly-out trips
Available: Fishing instruction, licenses, bait, tackle, boat rentals, family activities

The Angler's Yellow Pages lets you
tap the fishing information grapevine

ARIZONA

1. Alamo Lake
2. Apache Lake
3. Bartlett Reservoir
4. Colorado River
5. Eastern Region
6. Lake Havasu
7. Lake Mary
8. Lake Mead
9. Lake Mohave
10. Lake Pleasant
11. Lake Powell
12. Theodore Roosevelt Lake
13. Verde River
14. Western Region

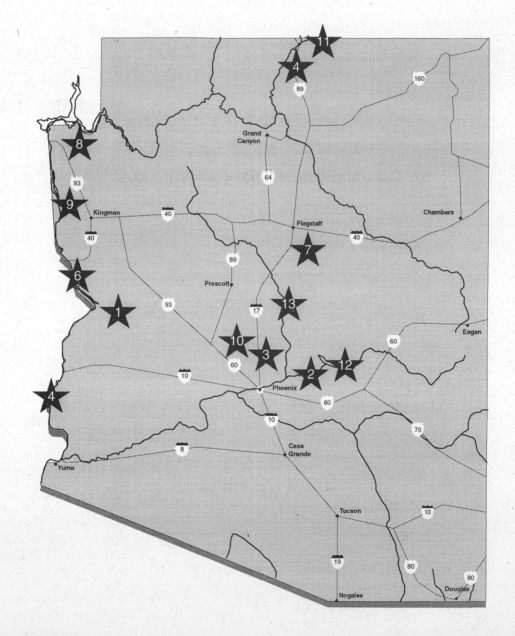

YOUR SILENT FISHING PARTNER

ARIZONA

ALAMO LAKE - COLORADO RIVER

ALAMO LAKE

BAIT & TACKLE...

Waterdog Willy's West
Glendale 602-435-1533
Hours: 6am-9pm
Carries: Live bait, lures, flies, maps, rods, reels, licenses
Bodies of water: Lake Pleasant, Bartlett Res., Theodore Roosevelt Lake, Alamo Lake
Services & Products: Guide services, food, beverages, fishing instruction, repair services
OK to call for current conditions: Yes
Contact: Craig Schultz

GUIDES...

Arizona Wildlife Outfitters
Kingman 520-753-4867
Species & Seasons: LM Bass, Striped Bass, Trout, Catfish Feb-Oct, Crappie Jan-Mar
Bodies of water: Alamo Lake, Lake Mead, Lake Mohave, Lake Havasu, Colorado River (Willow Beach)
Rates: Half day: $150(1), $175(2), Full day: $200(1), $225(2)
Call between: 5pm-10pm
Provides: Bait, beverages, lunch
Handicapped equipped: Yes
Certifications: AZ Game & Fish Dept.

APACHE LAKE

BAIT & TACKLE...

Punkin Center Bait Tackle
Tonto Basin 520-479-2221
Hours: 5:30am-7pm
Carries: Live bait, lures, maps, rods, reels, licenses
Bodies of water: Theodore Roosevelt Lake, Apache Lake
Services & Products: Food, beverages, repair services, camping supplies, marine parts and access.
Guides: Yes
OK to call for current conditions: Yes
Contact: Barb or Gary

GUIDES...

C&C Guide Service
Roosevelt 520-467-2770
Species & Seasons: LM Bass, Jan-Dec, SM Bass Dec-Mar, Crappie Sept-May, LM Bass (night) May-Sept
Bodies of water: Theodore Roosevelt Lake, Apache Lake
Rates: Half day: $125(1), $150(2), Full day: $200(1), $250(2)
Call between: 6pm-9pm
Provides: Light tackle, heavy tackle, lures, bait, rain gear
Handicapped equipped: No
Certifications: AZ Game & Fish, U.S. Forest Service

Thomas Holmquist
Gilbert 602-497-6038
Species & Seasons: LM Bass, SM Bass, Crappie, Walleye, Catfish, White Bass
Bodies of water: Apache Lake, Bartlett Res., Theodore Roosevelt Lake, Lake Pleasant, Canyon Lake, Saguaro Lake
Rates: Full day: $150(1), $250(2), $100pp per day over 2 people
Call between: 7-10am/5-9pm
Provides: Light tackle, lures, bait, beverages, lunch
Handicapped equipped: Yes

Billy W. Palmer
Globe 520-425-2270
Species & Seasons: LM Bass, SM Bass all year, Crappie Feb,-May
Bodies of water: Theodore Roosevelt Lake, Apache Lake, Statewide Arizona
Rates: Half day: $100(1), $150(2), Full day: $150(1), $200(2), children under 14 free with paid adult (one max)
Call between: 7pm-9pm
Provides: Light tackle, lures, bait, beverages
Handicapped equipped: No
Certifications: Liicensed and insured Pro. Bass Fisherman

BARTLETT RESERVOIR

BAIT & TACKLE...

Waterdog Willy's West
Glendale 602-435-1533
Hours: 6am-9pm
Carries: Live bait, lures, flies, maps, rods, reels, licenses
Bodies of water: Lake Pleasant, Bartlett Res., Theodore Roosevelt Lake, Alamo Lake
Services & Products: Guide services, food, beverages, fishing instruction, repair services
OK to call for current conditions: Yes
Contact: Craig Schultz

GUIDES...

Thomas Holmquist
Gilbert 602-497-6038
Species & Seasons: LM Bass, SM Bass, Crappie, Walleye, Catfish, White Bass
Bodies of water: Apache Lake, Bartlett Res., Theodore Roosevelt Lake, Lake Pleasant, Canyon Lake, Saguaro Lake
Rates: Full day: $150(1), $250(2), $100pp per day over 2 people
Call between: 7-10am/5-9pm
Provides: Light tackle, lures, bait, beverages, lunch
Handicapped equipped: Yes

COLORADO RIVER

BAIT & TACKLE...

Smitty's Bait & Tackle
Bullhead City 520-754-7111
Hours: 6am-7pm
Carries: Live bait, lures, maps, rods, reels, licenses
Bodies of water: Lake Mohave, lower part of Colorado River, Topock Marsh
Services & Products: Guide services, charter boat service, beverages, fishing instruction, repair services
Guides: Yes
OK to call for current conditions: Yes
Contact: Jong or Sam

GUIDES...

Arizona Wildlife Outfitters
Kingman 520-753-4867
Species & Seasons: LM Bass, Striped Bass, Trout, Catfish Feb-Oct, Crappie Jan-Mar
Bodies of water: Alamo Lake, Lake Mead, Lake Mohave, Lake Havasu, Colorado River (Willow Beach)
Rates: Half day: $150(1), $175(2), Full day: $200(1), $225(2)
Call between: 5pm-10pm
Provides: Bait, beverages, lunch
Handicapped equipped: Yes
Certifications: AZ Game & Fish Dept.

COLORADO RIVER - LAKE MOHAVE | ARIZONA

Jeffrey S. English
Marble Canyon 520-355-2261
Species & Seasons: Rainbow Trout Sept-June
Bodies of water: Colorado River at Lee's Ferry
Rates: Full day: $225(1), $275(2)
Call between: 7am-7pm
Provides: Fly rod/reel, lunch
Handicapped equipped: No
Certifications: USCG

Marble Canyon Guide Service
Marble Canyon 520-355-2245
Species & Seasons: Rainbow Trout all year
Bodies of water: Colorado River at Lee's Ferry
Rates: Full day: $200(1), $250(2), $300(3)
Provides: Fly rod/reel, lures, lunch
Handicapped equipped: Yes
Certifications: National Park Service, USCG, AZ Dept. Game & Fish

William Schultz
Flagstaff 520-355-2261
Species & Seasons: Rainbow Trout Sept-June
Bodies of water: Colorado River at Lee's Ferry
Rates: Full day: $225(1), $275(2)
Call between: 7am-6pm
Provides: Fly rod/reel, lunch
Handicapped equipped: No
Certifications: USCG

EASTERN REGION

GUIDES...

Chaparral Guides & Outfitters
Payson 520-474-9693
Rates: Full day: $300(1)
Call between: 6pm-9pm
Handicapped equipped: Yes

Harold Stephens
Lakeside 520-367-0516
Species & Seasons: Trout April-Oct
Bodies of water: N.W. New Mexico, Eastern & N. Eastern AZ, over 100 lakes
Rates: Full day: $150(1), $255(2)
Call between: 5pm-9pm
Provides: Light tackle, fly rod/reel, lures, beverages, lunch
Handicapped equipped: No

LAKE HAVASU

BAIT & TACKLE...

Fishermen's Bait & Tackle
Lake Havasu City 520-855-3474
Hours: 6am-6pm
Carries: Live bait, lures, maps, rods, reels, licenses
Bodies of water: Lake Havasu
Services & Products: Boat rentals, guide services, food, beverages, oil, fishing instruction, repair services
Guides: Yes
OK to call for current conditions: Yes
Contact: Sam or Pat

GUIDES...

Arizona Wildlife Outfitters
Kingman 520-753-4867
Species & Seasons: LM Bass, Striped Bass, Trout, Catfish Feb-Oct, Crappie Jan-Mar
Bodies of water: Alamo Lake, Lake Mead, Lake Mohave, Lake Havasu, Colorado River (Willow Beach)
Rates: Half day: $150(1), $175(2), Full day: $200(1), $225(2)
Call between: 5pm-10pm
Provides: Bait, beverages, lunch
Handicapped equipped: Yes
Certifications: AZ Game & Fish Dept.

Sam's Fishing Guide Service
Lake Havasu City 520-855-FISH
Species & Seasons: Striped Bass all year
Bodies of water: Lake Havasu
Rates: Half day: $100(1), $150(2)
Call between: 6am
Provides: Light tackle, heavy tackle, lures, bait, beverages
Handicapped equipped: Yes

LAKE MARY

BAIT & TACKLE...

Ralston's Outdoor Sports
Camp Verde 520-567-3550
Hours: 8am-5:30pm, closed Sun, Sept-April
Carries: Live bait, lures, flies, maps, rods, reels, licenses
Bodies of water: Verde River, Clear Creek, Beaver Creek, Oak Creek, Lake Mary
Services & Products: Beverages, repair services
Guides: Yes
OK to call for current conditions: Yes
Contact: Rick Ralston

LAKE MEAD

GUIDES...

Arizona Wildlife Outfitters
Kingman 520-753-4867
Species & Seasons: LM Bass, Striped Bass, Trout, Catfish Feb-Oct, Crappie Jan-Mar
Bodies of water: Alamo Lake, Lake Mead, Lake Mohave, Lake Havasu, Colorado River (Willow Beach)
Rates: Half day: $150(1), $175(2), Full day: $200(1), $225(2)
Call between: 5pm-10pm
Provides: Bait, beverages, lunch
Handicapped equipped: Yes
Certifications: AZ Game & Fish Dept.

LAKE MOHAVE

BAIT & TACKLE...

Smitty's Bait & Tackle
Bullhead City 520-754-7111
Hours: 6am-7pm
Carries: Live bait, lures, maps, rods, reels, licenses
Bodies of water: Lake Mohave, lower part of Colorado River, Topock Marsh
Services & Products: Guide services, charter boat service, beverages, fishing instruction, repair services
Guides: Yes
OK to call for current conditions: Yes
Contact: Jong or Sam

GUIDES...

Arizona Wildlife Outfitters
Kingman 520-753-4867
Species & Seasons: LM Bass, Striped Bass, Trout, Catfish Feb-Oct, Crappie Jan-Mar
Bodies of water: Alamo Lake, Lake Mead, Lake Mohave, Lake Havasu, Colorado River (Willow Beach)
Rates: Half day: $150(1), $175(2), Full day: $200(1), $225(2)
Call between: 5pm-10pm
Provides: Bait, beverages, lunch
Handicapped equipped: Yes
Certifications: AZ Game & Fish Dept.

ARIZONA

LAKE PLEASANT - VERDE RIVER

LAKE PLEASANT

BAIT & TACKLE...

Waterdog Willy's West
Glendale 602-435-1533
Hours: 6am-9pm
Carries: Live bait, lures, flies, maps, rods, reels, licenses
Bodies of water: Lake Pleasant, Bartlett Res., Theodore Roosevelt Lake, Alamo Lake
Services & Products: Guide services, food, beverages, fishing instruction, repair services
OK to call for current conditions: Yes
Contact: Craig Schultz

GUIDES...

Thomas Holmquist
Gilbert 602-497-6038
Species & Seasons: LM Bass, SM Bass, Crappie, Walleye, Catfish, White Bass
Bodies of water: Apache Lake, Bartlett Res., Theodore Roosevelt Lake, Lake Pleasant, Canyon Lake, Saguaro Lake
Rates: Full day: $150(1), $250(2), $100pp per day over 2 people
Call between: 7-10am/5-9pm
Provides: Light tackle, lures, bait, beverages, lunch
Handicapped equipped: Yes

LAKE POWELL

CHARTERS...

Capt. Dan's Charters
Page 520-353-4011
Species & Seasons: Striped Bass Mar-June/Sept-Oct, Catfish, Crappie June-Oct
Bodies of water: Lake Powell
Rates: Half day: $200 +tax, Full day: $280 +tax (4 people and under)
Call between: Anytime
Provides: Light tackle, fly rod/reel, bait, beverages
Handicapped equipped: Yes
Certifications: US Park service AZ Game & Fish

GUIDES...

Ray Young
Page 520-645-5505
Species & Seasons: Striped Bass all year, SM Bass, LM Bass April-Dec
Bodies of water: Lake Powell-AZ & UT
Rates: Half day: $250(1-2), Full day: $350(1-2)
Provides: Light tackle, lures, bait, beverages, lunch
Handicapped equipped: Yes
Certifications: USCG

THEODORE ROOSEVELT LAKE

BAIT & TACKLE...

Punkin Center Bait Tackle
Tonto Basin 520-479-2221
Hours: 5:30am-7pm
Carries: Live bait, lures, maps, rods, reels, licenses
Bodies of water: Theodore Roosevelt Lake, Apache Lake
Services & Products: Food, beverages, repair services, camping supplies, marine parts and access.
Guides: Yes
OK to call for current conditions: Yes
Contact: Barb or Gary

Waterdog Willy's West
Glendale 602-435-1533
Hours: 6am-9pm
Carries: Live bait, lures, flies, maps, rods, reels, licenses
Bodies of water: Lake Pleasant, Bartlett Res., Theodore Roosevelt Lake, Alamo Lake
Services & Products: Guide services, food, beverages, fishing instruction, repair services
OK to call for current conditions: Yes
Contact: Craig Schultz

GUIDES...

C&C Guide Service
Roosevelt 520-467-2770
Species & Seasons: LM Bass, Jan-Dec, SM Bass Dec-Mar, Crappie Sept-May, LM Bass (night) May-Sept
Bodies of water: Theodore Roosevelt Lake, Apache Lake
Rates: Half day: $125(1), $150(2), Full day: $200(1), $250(2)
Call between: 6pm-9pm
Provides: Light tackle, heavy tackle, lures, bait, rain gear
Handicapped equipped: No
Certifications: AZ Game & Fish, U.S. Forest Service

Thomas Holmquist
Gilbert 602-497-6038
Species & Seasons: LM Bass, SM Bass, Crappie, Walleye, Catfish, White Bass
Bodies of water: Apache Lake, Bartlett Res., Theodore Roosevelt Lake, Lake Pleasant, Canyon Lake, Saguaro Lake
Rates: Full day: $150(1), $250(2), $100pp per day over 2 people
Call between: 7-10am/5-9pm
Provides: Light tackle, lures, bait, beverages, lunch
Handicapped equipped: Yes

Billy W. Palmer
Globe 520-425-2270
Species & Seasons: LM Bass, SM Bass all year, Crappie Feb.-May
Bodies of water: Theodore Roosevelt Lake, Apache Lake, Statewide Arizona
Rates: Half day: $100(1), $150(2), Full day: $150(1), $200(2), children under 14 free with paid adult (one max)
Call between: 7pm-9pm
Provides: Light tackle, lures, bait, beverages
Handicapped equipped: No
Certifications: Liicensed and insured Pro. Bass Fisherman

VERDE RIVER

BAIT & TACKLE...

Ralston's Outdoor Sports
Camp Verde 520-567-3550
Hours: 8am-5:30pm, closed Sun, Sept-April
Carries: Live bait, lures, flies, maps, rods, reels, licenses
Bodies of water: Verde River, Clear Creek, Beaver Creek, Oak Creek, Lake Mary
Services & Products: Beverages, repair services
Guides: Yes
OK to call for current conditions: Yes
Contact: Rick Ralston

WESTERN REGION

GUIDES...

Chaparral Guides & Outfitters
Payson 520-474-9693
Rates: Full day: $300(1)
Call between: 6pm-9pm
Handicapped equipped: Yes

Troutback® Fly Fishing Guide Service
Springerville 520-333-2371
Species & Seasons: Rainbow Trout, Brown Trout, Apache Trout April-Nov, Arctic Grayling May-Oct
Bodies of water: Black River, Little Colorado River, Lee Valley Res., Nelson Res., Big Lake, Crescent Lake and more
Rates: Half day: $90(1), $125(2), Full day: $125(1), $200(2), Llama pack trips: $150 pp/day
Call between: 8am-8pm
Provides: Fly rod/reel, beverages, lunch
Handicapped equipped: Yes

Introduce a friend to "Your silent fishing partner..."
Use the postage paid order cards at the back of the book

ARKANSAS

1. Arkansas River
2. Beaver Lake
3. Buffalo River
4. Bull Shoals Lake
5. Crystal Lake
6. DeGray Lake
7. Greers Ferry Lake
8. Lake Charles
9. Lake Dardanelle
10. Lake Hamilton
11. Lake Ouachita
12. Lake Poinsett
13. Little Red River
14. Millwood Lake
15. Mississippi River
16. Nimrod Lake
17. Norfork Lake
18. Ouachita River
19. Red River
20. St. Francis River
21. White River

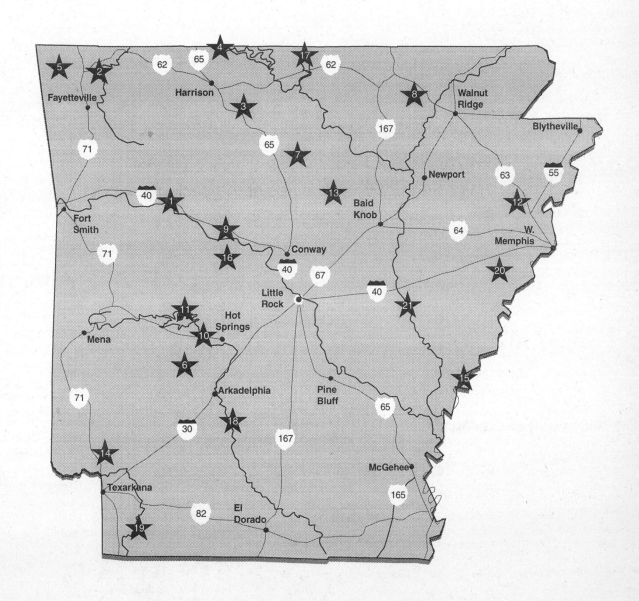

ARKANSAS

ARKANSAS RIVER — BUFFALO RIVER

ARKANSAS RIVER

BAIT & TACKLE...

Early Bird Outfitters
Russellville 501-967-1387
Hours: 5am-7pm
Carries: Live bait, lures, flies, maps, rods, reels, licenses
Bodies of water: Lake Dardanelle, Arkansas River, Piney River, Buffalo River, Illinois Bayou
Services & Products: Boat rentals, guide services, lodging, food, beverages, gas/oil
Guides: Yes
OK to call for current conditions: Yes
Contact: Doug Olson

Murphy's Sporting Goods
Dardanelle 501-229-3200
Hours: 7am-6pm
Carries: Live bait, lures, flies, maps, rods, reels
Bodies of water: Lake Dardanelle, Arkansas River, Nimrod Lake
Services & Products: Beverages, gas/oil, repair services
Guides: Yes
OK to call for current conditions: Yes
Contact: Joe Murphy

Webster's Chuck-Wagon
Marvell 501-829-2474
Hours: 5:30am-8 or 9pm
Carries: Live bait, lures, maps, rods, reels, licenses
Bodies of water: White River, Mississippi River, Arkansas River, Big Creek, White River National Wildlife Refuge Lakes
Services & Products: Guide services, food, beverages, fishing instruction
Guides: Yes
OK to call for current conditions: Yes

Wild Goose Corner One Stop
Tichnor 501-548-2778
Hours: 6am-8pm
Carries: Live bait, lures, flies, maps, rods, reels, licenses
Bodies of water: Lake Merrisack, White River, Arkansas River, Mississippi River, White River Refuge Lakes
Services & Products: Guide services, lodging, food, beverages, gas/oil, repair services
Guides: Yes
OK to call for current conditions: Yes
Contact: Mike or Carolyn Bell

BEAVER LAKE

BAIT & TACKLE...

Barnett's Pawn and Bait Shop
Gateway 501-656-3730
Hours: 8am-6pm
Carries: Live bait, lures, flies, rods, reels, licenses
Bodies of water: Beaver Lake, White River, Table Rock Lake
Guides: Yes
OK to call for current conditions: Yes
Contact: Sharon Barnett

BUFFALO RIVER

BAIT & TACKLE...

Early Bird Outfitters
Russellville 501-967-1387
Hours: 5am-7pm
Carries: Live bait, lures, flies, maps, rods, reels, licenses
Bodies of water: Lake Dardanelle, Arkansas River, Piney River, Buffalo River, Illinois Bayou
Services & Products: Boat rentals, guide services, lodging, food, beverages, gas/oil
Guides: Yes
OK to call for current conditions: Yes
Contact: Doug Olson

LODGING...

Cedar Hollow RV Park
Flippin 501-453-8643
Guest Capacity: 100
Handicapped equipped: Yes
Seasons: All year
Rates: $13/day and up
Contact: Don or Donna Wilkes
Guides: Yes
Species & Seasons: LM Bass, SM Bass, Crappie Mar-June, Trout, Catfish all year
Bodies of Water: Bull Shoals Lake, White River, Buffalo River
Types of fishing: Fly fishing, light tackle, wading, float trips

Gunga-La Lodge River Outfitters
Lakeview 501-431-5606
.... 800-844-5606
Guest Capacity: 10
Handicapped equipped: No
Seasons: All year
Rates: $70
Guides: Yes
Species & Seasons: Rainbow Trout, Brown Trout, Cutthroat Trout all year, SM Bass, Rock Bass May-Oct
Bodies of Water: White River, Bull Shoals Lake, Crooked Creek, Buffalo River
Types of fishing: Fly fishing, light tackle, wading, float trips
Available: Fishing instruction, licenses bait, tackle, boat rentals, canoes, rubber rafts

---

GUNGA-LA LODGE
RIVER OUTFITTERS
• HOME OF 3 WORLD RECORDS
• GUIDED TROUT FISHING TRIPS
• LOG CABINS ON RIVER
• BOAT, CANOE, RAFT RENTALS
FREE BRO. 1-800 844-5606
RT.1, BOX 147, LAKEVIEW, AR 72642

Sportsmen's Resort
Flippin 800-626-3474
Guest Capacity: 68
Handicapped equipped: No
Seasons: All year
Rates: $52-$58
Contact: Dick Bump
Guides: Yes
Species & Seasons: Trout all year, LM Bass, SM Bass, Mar-July

BUFFALO RIVER - BULL SHOALS LAKE — ARKANSAS

Bodies of Water: White River, Crooked Creek, Buffalo River, Norfork Lake, Bull Shoals Lake
Types of fishing: Fly fishing, light tackle, wading, float trips
Available: Licenses, bait, tackle, boat rentals, family activities

BULL SHOALS LAKE

BAIT & TACKLE...

Crawdad Hole
Flippin 501-453-8744
Hours: 6:30am-7pm
Carries: Live bait, lures, flies, maps, rods, reels, licenses
Bodies of water: White River, Bull Shoals Lake, Norfork Lake
Services & Products: Guide services, beverages, fishing instruction
Guides: Yes
OK to call for current conditions: Yes
Contact: Robert Whites

GUIDES...

Billy Bob's Fishing Service
Flippin 501-453-8744
Species & Seasons: Rainbow Trout, Brown Trout, LM Bass, Crappie, Catfish, SM Bass Feb-Nov
Bodies of water: White River, Bull Shoals Lake, Norfork Lake
Rates: Half day: $90(1), $115(2), Full day: $120(1), $150(2)
Call between: Anytime
Provides: Bait, beverages, lunch
Handicapped equipped: No

River Valley Guide Service
Russellville 501-967-6080
Species & Seasons: Crappie Dec-April, Bass, Trout all year
Bodies of water: Lake Dardanelle, Lake Ouachita, Bull Shoals Lake, Red River, White River (trout)
Rates: Half day: $75(1-2), Full day: $150(1-2), Other: $15 hr.(2)
Call between: 5:30 Pm 10:00 Pm
Provides: Light tackle, heavy tackle, fly rod/reel, lures, bait, Full day only: Beverages, lunch
Handicapped equipped: Yes

LODGING...

Black Oak Resort
Oakland 501-431-8363
Guest Capacity: 66
Handicapped equipped: No
Seasons: All year
Rates: $52/day
Contact: Mike Scrima
Guides: Yes
Species & Seasons: LM Bass, SM Bass, Walleye, Spotted Bass, Trout all open
Bodies of Water: Bull Shoals Lake, White River
Types of fishing: Light tackle, float trips, downrigger
Available: Fishing instruction, licenses, bait, tackle, boat rentals, baby sitting, pets welcome

Cedar Hollow RV Park
Flippin 501-453-8643
Guest Capacity: 100
Handicapped equipped: Yes
Seasons: All year
Rates: $13/day and up
Contact: Don or Donna Wilkes
Guides: Yes
Species & Seasons: LM Bass, SM Bass, Crappie Mar-June, Trout, Catfish all year
Bodies of Water: Bull Shoals Lake, White River, Buffalo River
Types of fishing: Fly fishing, light tackle, wading, float trips

Coon Creek Fishing Resort
Peel 501-436-5405
Guest Capacity: 12 kitchenettes
Handicapped equipped: No
Seasons: All year
Rates: $35-$40/day
Contact: Patricia Dell
Guides: Yes
Species & Seasons: LM Bass, SM Bass April-Dec, Crappie, Trout May-Dec, Catfish, Northern Pike, Walleye May-Jan
Bodies of Water: Bull Shoals Lake
Types of fishing: Light tackle, heavy tackle
Available: Licenses, bait, tackle, boat rentals

GUIDE FISHING — SHORE LUNCH

BILLY BOB'S FISHING SERVICE
CRAWDAD HOLE BAIT SHOP
FLIPPIN, ARKANSAS 72634
"Trout Capital of the World"

LAKE FISHING — 1 800 876-8567 — (501) 453-8744

Gunga-La Lodge River Outfitters
Lakeview 501-431-5606
.... 800-844-5606
Guest Capacity: 10
Handicapped equipped: No
Seasons: All year
Rates: $70
Guides: Yes
Species & Seasons: Rainbow Trout, Brown Trout, Cutthroat Trout all year, SM Bass, Rock Bass May-Oct
Bodies of Water: White River, Bull Shoals Lake, Crooked Creek, Buffalo River
Types of fishing: Fly fishing, light tackle, wading, float trips
Available: Fishing instruction, licenses, bait, tackle, boat rentals, canoe's, rubber rafts

ARKANSAS

BULL SHOALS LAKE - GREERS FERRY LAKE

Mar Mar Resort & Tackle Shop
Bull Shoals 800-332-BULL
.... 501-445-4444
Guest Capacity: 13 units, 29 beds
Handicapped equipped: No
Seasons: All year
Rates: $36-$48/day
Guides: Yes
Species & Seasons: Brown Trout, Rainbow Trout, LM Bass, SM Bass, Walleye, Catfish, Crappie, Bream, many others, call for fishing report
Bodies of Water: Bull Shoals Lake, White River
Types of fishing: Fly fishing, light tackle, heavy tackle, wading, float trips, overnight fish/camp trips
Available: Fishing instruction, licenses, bait, tackle, boat rentals, family activities

Sportsmen's Resort
Flippin 800-626-3474
Guest Capacity: 68
Handicapped equipped: No
Seasons: All year
Rates: $52-$58
Contact: Dick Bump
Guides: Yes
Species & Seasons: Trout all year, LM Bass, SM Bass, Mar-July
Bodies of Water: White River, Crooked Creek, Buffalo River, Norfork Lake, Bull Shoals Lake
Types of fishing: Fly fishing, light tackle, wading, float trips
Available: Licenses, bait, tackle, boat rentals, family activities

Sunset Point Resort
Midway 501-431-5372
Guest Capacity: 46
Handicapped equipped: No
Seasons: All year
Rates: $45-$270
Guides: Yes
Species & Seasons: Trout, Catfish all year, LM Bass, SM Bass, Walleye Jan-June
Bodies of Water: Bull Shoals Lake, White River
Types of fishing: Fly fishing, light tackle, wading, float trips
Available: Licenses, bait, tackle, boat rentals

CRYSTAL LAKE

BAIT & TACKLE...

Tree Leaf Archery & Bait Shop
Decatur 501-752-8496
Hours: 8am-5pm, closed Sunday
Carries: Live bait, lures, flies, rods, reels, licenses
Bodies of water: Crystal Lake, Swepco
Services & Products: Food, beverages, archery supplies
Guides: No
OK to call for current conditions: Yes
Contact: Nickie Smith

DEGRAY LAKE

BAIT & TACKLE...

Rob's Quick Sak
Ashdown.......................... 501-898-3520
Hours: 4:30am-10pm
Carries: Live bait, lures, maps, rods, reels, licenses
Bodies of water: Millwood Lake, Lake Wright Patmen, Deirks Lake, DeQueen Lake, Red River, Little River, Cossatot River, DeGray Lake
Services & Products: Food, beverages, gas/oil
Guides: No
OK to call for current conditions: Yes
Contact: Robert Jones

LODGING...

Arrowhead Cabin & Canoe Rentals
Caddo Gap 501-356-2944
Guest Capacity: 85
Handicapped equipped: No
Seasons: Feb 15 to Nov 1
Rates: Cabins: $50/day, Canoes: $30/day
Contact: John or Maxine
Guides: Yes
Species & Seasons: LM Bass, SM Bass, Catfish, Spotted Bass all year
Bodies of Water: Caddo River, Ouachita River, DeGray Lake, Lake Ouachita
Types of fishing: Fly fishing, light tackle, wading, float trips
Available: Licenses, boat rentals

Days Inn
Arkadelphia 501-246-3031
Guest Capacity: 53 rooms
Handicapped equipped: Yes
Seasons: All year
Rates: $43.80/day
Species & Seasons: Catfish, LM Bass, SM Bass, Bream, Crappie, Hybrids all year
Bodies of Water: DeGray Lake, Caddo River, Ouachita River
Types of fishing: Float trips
Available: Licenses, bait, tackle, boat rentals, family activities

GREERS FERRY LAKE

FLY SHOPS...

The Ozark Angler
Heber Springs 501-362-3597
Hours: 7am-6pm
Carries: Flies, maps, rods, reels
Bodies of water: Little Red River, White River, North Fork River, Greers Ferry Lake
Services & Products: Boat rentals, guide services, fishing instruction
OK to call for current conditions: Yes
Contact: Anyone

LODGING...

Lobo Landing Resort
Heber Springs 501-362-5802
Guest Capacity: 100
Handicapped equipped: No
Seasons: All year
Rates: $45-$80/night
Contact: Abe or Lesa Vogel
Guides: Yes
Species & Seasons: Brown Trout, Rainbow Trout, Cutthroat Trout all year
Bodies of Water: Little Red River, Greers Ferry Lake
Types of fishing: Fly fishing, light tackle, wading, float trips
Available: Fishing instruction, licenses, bait, tackle, boat rentals, guided fishing on pontoons

River Ranch Resort
Heber Springs 800-366-9003
Guest Capacity: 104
Handicapped equipped: Yes
Seasons: All year
Rates: Motel: $45, Single Unit: $65, Cabins: $76-$85, Bunk House: $100
Contact: Mickey

GREERS FERRY LAKE - LAKE OUACHITA — ARKANSAS

Guides: Yes
Species & Seasons: Brown Trout, Rainbow Trout, Cutthroat Trout
Bodies of Water: Little Red River, Greers Ferry Lake
Types of fishing: Fly fishing, light tackle
Available: Licenses, bait, tackle, boat rentals, family activities, baby sitting

LAKE CHARLES

BAIT & TACKLE...

Powhatan Landing Bait Shop
Powhatan 501-878-6030
Hours: 6am-8pm
Carries: Live bait, lures, flies, rods, reels, licenses
Bodies of water: Lake Charles, Black River, Spring River, Eleven Point River, Portia Bay, Hill Slough
Services & Products: Boat ramp, food, beverages, gas/oil, fishing instruction
OK to call for current conditions: Yes
Contact: Zim

LAKE DARDANELLE

BAIT & TACKLE...

Early Bird Outfitters
Russellville 501-967-1387
Hours: 5am-7pm
Carries: Live bait, lures, flies, maps, rods, reels, licenses
Bodies of water: Lake Dardanelle, Arkansas River, Piney River, Buffalo River, Illinois Bayou
Services & Products: Boat rentals, guide services, lodging, food, beverages, gas/oil
Guides: Yes
OK to call for current conditions: Yes
Contact: Doug Olson

Murphy's Sporting Goods
Dardanelle 501-229-3200
Hours: 7am-6pm
Carries: Live bait, lures, flies, maps, rods, reels
Bodies of water: Lake Dardanelle, Arkansas River, Nimrod Lake
Services & Products: Beverages, gas/oil, repair services
Guides: Yes
OK to call for current conditions: Yes
Contact: Joe Murphy

GUIDES...

River Valley Guide Service
Russellville 501-967-6080
Species & Seasons: Crappie Dec-April, Bass, Trout all year
Bodies of water: Lake Dardanelle, Lake Ouachita, Bull Shoals Lake, Red River, White River (trout)
Rates: Half day: $75(1-2), Full day: $150(1-2)
Call between: 5:30pm-10:00pm
Provides: Light tackle, heavy tackle, fly rod/reel, lures, bait, Full day only: Beverages, lunch
Handicapped equipped: Yes

LAKE HAMILTON

BAIT & TACKLE...

Dozhier's Bait Shop
Hot Springs 501-262-5608
Hours: 6:30am-7:30pm
Carries: Live bait, lures, flies, maps, rods, reels, licenses
Bodies of water: Lake Catherine, Lake Hamilton
Services & Products: Boat rentals, guide services, lodging, food, beverages, gas/oil
OK to call for current conditions: Yes

GUIDES...

Jim's Guide Service
Hot Springs 501-767-3711
Species & Seasons: Striped Bass all year
Bodies of water: Lake Ouachita, Lake Hamilton
Rates: Half day: $140(1-2)
Call between: 8am-10pm
Provides: Heavy tackle, bait
Handicapped equipped: Depends on handicap

John T. Hall's Professional Guide Service
Hot Springs 501-767-1468
Species & Seasons: Striped Bass, LM Bass all year
Bodies of water: Lake Ouachita, Lake Hamilton
Rates: Half day: $140(1-2), Full day: $250(1-2), $70 additional pp
Call between: 6pm-9pm
Provides: Light tackle, heavy tackle, lures, bait, rain gear, beverages
Handicapped equipped: Yes

LODGING...

Paradise Point Resort
Hot Springs 501-767-9251
Guest Capacity: 65
Handicapped equipped: No
Seasons: All year
Rates: $59/day
Contact: Sandy Baker
Guides: Yes
Species & Seasons: LM Bass, SM Bass, Crappie, Striped Bass, Spring-Fall
Bodies of Water: Lake Hamilton, Lake Ouachita
Types of fishing: Light tackle, float trips
Available: Boat rentals

LAKE OUACHITA

GUIDES...

Jim's Guide Service
Hot Springs 501-767-3711
Species & Seasons: Striped Bass all year
Bodies of water: Lake Ouachita, Lake Hamilton
Rates: Half day: $140(1-2)
Call between: 8am-10pm
Provides: Heavy tackle, bait
Handicapped equipped: Depends on handicap

John T. Hall's Professional Guide Service
Hot Springs 501-767-1468
Species & Seasons: Striped Bass, LM Bass all year
Bodies of water: Lake Ouachita, Lake Hamilton
Rates: Half day: $140(1-2), Full day: $250(1-2), $70 additional pp
Call between: 6pm-9pm
Provides: Light tackle, heavy tackle, lures, bait, rain gear, beverages
Handicapped equipped: Yes

ARKANSAS

LAKE OUACHITA - LITTLE RED RIVER

River Valley Guide Service
Russellville 501-967-6080
Species & Seasons: Crappie Dec-April, Bass, Trout all year
Bodies of water: Lake Dardanelle, Lake Ouachita, Bull Shoals Lake, Red River, White River (trout)
Rates: Half day: $75(1-2), Full day: $150(1-2), Other: $15 hr.(2)
Call between: 5:30pm 10:00pm
Provides: Light tackle, heavy tackle, fly rod/reel, lures, bait,
Full day only: Beverages, lunch
Handicapped equipped: Yes

LODGING...

Arrowhead Cabin & Canoe Rentals
Caddo Gap 501-356-2944
Guest Capacity: 85
Handicapped equipped: No
Seasons: Feb 15 to Nov 1
Rates: Cabins: $50/day, Canoes: $30/day
Contact: John or Maxine
Guides: Yes
Species & Seasons: LM Bass, SM Bass, Catfish, Spotted Bass all year
Bodies of Water: Caddo River, Ouachita River, DeGray Lake, Lake Ouachita
Types of fishing: Fly fishing, light tackle, wading, float trips
Available: Licenses, boat rentals

Crystal Inn & Restaurant, Inc.
Mt. Ida 501-867-2643
Guest Capacity: 40
Handicapped equipped: Yes
Seasons: All year
Rates: $32
Guides: Yes
Species & Seasons: LM Bass, SM Bass
Bodies of Water: Lake Ouachita

Mount Ida Motel
Mt. Ida 501-867-3456
Seasons: All year
Rates: $24-$45/day
Guides: Yes
Species & Seasons: LM Bass, SM Bass, Crappie, Striped Bass, Catfish
Bodies of Water: Lake Ouachita
Types of fishing: Light tackle, float trips

Mountain Harbor Resort
PO Box 807
Mt. Ida 71957
Guest Capacity: 250+
Handicapped equipped: Yes
Seasons: All year
Rates: In season: $62-$285, Off season: $43-$250
Contact: Pati Brown or Julie Rurys
Guides: Yes
Species & Seasons: LM Bass Jan-Nov, Striped Bass Jan-June, Crappie Jan-April
Bodies of Water: Lake Ouachita
Types of fishing: Light tackle
Available: Licenses, bait, tackle, boat rentals, family activities, baby sitting, horseback riding, restaurant

Paradise Point Resort
Hot Springs 501-767-9251
Guest Capacity: 65
Handicapped equipped: No
Seasons: All year
Rates: $59/day
Contact: Sandy Baker
Guides: Yes
Species & Seasons: LM Bass, SM Bass, Crappie, Striped Bass, Spring-Fall
Bodies of Water: Lake Hamilton, Lake Ouachita
Types of fishing: Light tackle, float trips
Available: Boat rentals

LAKE POINSETT

BAIT & TACKLE...

Vic's Bait & Tackle
Harrisburg 501-578-2765
Hours: 6am-7pm, closed Wed.
Carries: Live bait, lures, flies, maps, rods, reels,
Bodies of water: Lake Poinsett
Services & Products: Food, beverages
Guides: Yes
OK to call for current conditions: Yes

LITTLE RED RIVER

GUIDES...

Bob Brown Guide Service
Little Rock 800-880-8808
.... 501-791-2111
Species & Seasons: Brown Trout, Rainbow Trout, Cutthroat Trout all year
Bodies of water: Little Red River/Heber Springs
Rates: Half day: $100(1-2), Full day: $150(1-2)
Call between: Anytime
Provides: Light tackle, lures
Handicapped equipped: No

FLY SHOPS...

The Ozark Angler
Heber Springs 501-362-3597
Hours: 7am-6pm
Carries: Flies, maps, rods, reels
Bodies of water: Little Red River, White River, North Fork River, Greers Ferry Lake
Services & Products: Boat rentals, guide services, fishing instruction
OK to call for current conditions: Yes
Contact: Anyone

LODGING...

Lobo Landing Resort
Heber Springs 501-362-5802
Guest Capacity: 100
Handicapped equipped: No
Seasons: All year
Rates: $45-$80/night
Contact: Abe or Lesa Vogel
Guides: Yes
Species & Seasons: Brown Trout, Rainbow Trout, Cutthroat Trout all year
Bodies of Water: Little Red River, Greers Ferry Lake
Types of fishing: Fly fishing, light tackle, wading, float trips
Available: Fishing instruction, licenses, bait, tackle, boat rentals, guided fishing on pontoons

River Ranch Resort
Heber Springs 800-366-9003
Guest Capacity: 104
Handicapped equipped: Yes
Seasons: All year
Rates: Motel: $45, Single Unit: $65, Cabins: $76-$85, Bunk House: $100
Contact: Mickey
Guides: Yes
Species & Seasons: Brown Trout, Rainbow Trout, Cutthroat Trout
Bodies of Water: Little Red River, Greers Ferry Lake
Types of fishing: Fly fishing, light tackle
Available: Licenses, bait, tackle, boat rentals, family activities, baby sitting

LITTLE RED RIVER - NORFORK LAKE — ARKANSAS

Swinging Bridge Resort
Heber Springs 501-362-3327
Guest Capacity: 35
Handicapped equipped: No
Seasons: All year
Rates: $40-$80/day
Contact: George Heine
Guides: Yes
Species & Seasons: Rainbow Trout, Brown Trout, Cuthroat Trout all year
Bodies of Water: Little Red River
Types of fishing: Fly fishing, light tackle, wading, float trips
Available: Fishing instruction, licenses, bait, tackle, boat rentals

MILLWOOD LAKE

BAIT & TACKLE...

Rob's Quick Sak
Ashdown 501-898-3520
Hours: 4:30am-10pm
Carries: Live bait, lures, maps, rods, reels, licenses
Bodies of water: Millwood Lake, Lake Wright Patmen, Deirks Lake, DeQueen Lake, Red River, Little River, Cossatot River, DeGray Lake
Services & Products: Food, beverages, gas/oil
Guides: No
OK to call for current conditions: Yes
Contact: Robert Jones

MISSISSIPPI RIVER

BAIT & TACKLE...

Red Barn Sports Center
West Memphis 501-732-1484
Hours: 4am-8pm
Carries: Live bait, lures, maps, rods, reels, licenses
Bodies of water: Mississippi River, Horshoe Lake, Dacus Lake, Mid-Way, 96-Shoot, Blue Lake, Sardis
Services & Products: Food, beverages, gas/oil, fishing instruction, repair services
Guides: Yes
OK to call for current conditions: Yes
Contact: Kenneth or Jimmy Black

Webster's Chuck-Wagon
Marvell 501-829-2474
Hours: 5:30am-8 or 9pm
Carries: Live bait, lures, maps, rods, reels, licenses
Bodies of water: White River, Mississippi River, Arkansas River, Big Creek, White River National Wildlife Refuge Lakes
Services & Products: Guide services, food, beverages, fishing instruction
Guides: Yes
OK to call for current conditions: Yes

Wild Goose Corner One Stop
Tichnor 501-548-2778
Hours: 6am-8pm
Carries: Live bait, lures, flies, maps, rods, reels, licenses
Bodies of water: Lake Merrisack, White River, Arkansas River, Mississippi River, White River Refuge Lakes
Services & Products: Guide services, lodging, food, beverages, gas/oil, repair services
Guides: Yes
OK to call for current conditions: Yes
Contact: Mike or Carolyn Bell

NIMROD LAKE

BAIT & TACKLE...

Murphy's Sporting Goods
Dardanelle 501-229-3200
Hours: 7am-6pm
Carries: Live bait, lures, flies, maps, rods, reels
Bodies of water: Lake Dardanelle, Arkansas River, Nimrod Lake
Services & Products: Beverages, gas/oil, repair services
Guides: Yes
OK to call for current conditions: Yes
Contact: Joe Murphy

NORFORK LAKE

BAIT & TACKLE...

Crawdad Hole
Flippin 501-453-8744
Hours: 6:30am-7pm
Carries: Live bait, lures, flies, maps, rods, reels, licenses
Bodies of water: White River, Bull Shoals Lake, Norfork Lake
Services & Products: Guide services, beverages, fishing instruction
Guides: Yes
OK to call for current conditions: Yes
Contact: Robert Whites

GUIDES...

Billy Bob's Fishing Service
Flippin 501-453-8744
Species & Seasons: Rainbow Trout, Brown Trout, LM Bass, Crappie, Catfish, SM Bass Feb-Nov
Bodies of water: White River, Bull Shoals Lake, Norfork Lake
Rates: Half day: $90(1), $115(2), Full day: $120(1), $150(2)
Call between: Anytime
Provides: Bait, beverages, lunch
Handicapped equipped: No

Garry Sperry Professional Guide Service
Gamaliel 501-467-5448
Species & Seasons: Striped Bass Nov-Aug, LM Bass all year, Spotted Bass June-Oct, Crappie March-Nov
Bodies of water: Norfork Lake
Rates: Half day: $150(2), Full day: $225(2)
Call between: 7pm-10pm
Provides: Heavy tackle, lures, bait, beverages
Handicapped equipped: Yes
Certifications: USCG

LODGING...

Gene's Trout Fishing Resort & Lodge
Mountain Home 501-499-5381
.... 800-526-3625
Hours: 7am-8pm
Carries: Live bait, lures, flies, maps, rods, reels, licenses
Bodies of water: North Fork River (we are on river), White River, Norfork Lake
Services & Products: Boat rentals, guide services, charter boat service, lodging, gas/oil, fishing instruction, canoe rentals
Guides: Yes
OK to call for current conditions: Yes
Contact: Scott

ARKANSAS

NORFORK LAKE - WHITE RIVER

Oak Ridge Resort
Mountain Home 501-431-5575
Guest Capacity: 45
Handicapped equipped: No
Seasons: All year
Rates: $40-$105/day
Contact: David or Colleen Pearson
Guides: Yes
Species & Seasons: LM Bass, SM Bass all year, Lake Trout April-Aug, Catfish Mar-Aug, Crappie April-June/Nov-Dec
Bodies of Water: Bull Shoals Lake, Norfork Lake, White River
Types of fishing: Fly fishing, light tackle, float trips
Available: Fishing instruction, licenses, bait, tackle, boat rentals, family activities

Sportsmen's Resort
Flippin 800-626-3474
Guest Capacity: 68
Handicapped equipped: No
Seasons: All year
Rates: $52-$58
Contact: Dick Bump
Guides: Yes
Species & Seasons: Trout all year, LM Bass, SM Bass, Mar-July
Bodies of Water: White River, Crooked Creek, Buffalo River, Norfork Lake, Bull Shoals Lake
Types of fishing: Fly fishing, light tackle, wading, float trips
Available: Licenses, bait, tackle, boat rentals, family activities

OUACHITA RIVER

LODGING...

Arrowhead Cabin & Canoe Rentals
Caddo Gap 501-356-2944
Guest Capacity: 85
Handicapped equipped: No
Seasons: Feb 15 to Nov 1
Rates: Cabins: $50/day, Canoes: $30/day
Contact: John or Maxine
Guides: Yes
Species & Seasons: LM Bass, SM Bass, Catfish, Spotted Bass all year
Bodies of Water: Caddo River, Ouachita River, DeGray Lake, Lake Ouachita
Types of fishing: Fly fishing, light tackle, wading, float trips
Available: Licenses, boat rentals

Days Inn
Arkadelphia 501-246-3031
Guest Capacity: 53 rooms
Handicapped equipped: Yes
Seasons: All year
Rates: $43.80/day
Species & Seasons: Catfish, LM Bass, SM Bass, Bream, Crappie, Hybrids all year
Bodies of Water: DeGray Lake, Caddo River, Ouachita River
Types of fishing: Float trips
Available: Licenses, bait, tackle, boat rentals, family activities

RED RIVER

BAIT & TACKLE...

Rob's Quick Sak
Ashdown.......................... 501-898-3520
Hours: 4:30am-10pm
Carries: Live bait, lures, maps, rods, reels, licenses
Bodies of water: Millwood Lake, Lake Wright Patmen, Deirks Lake, DeQueen Lake, Red River, Little River, Cossatot River, Lake Degray
Services & Products: Food, beverages, gas/oil
Guides: No
OK to call for current conditions: Yes
Contact: Robert Jones

GUIDES...

River Valley Guide Service
Russellville 501-967-6080
Species & Seasons: Crappie Dec-April, Bass, Trout all year
Bodies of water: Lake Dardanelle, Lake Ouachita, Bull Shoals Lake, Red River, White River (trout)
Rates: Half day: $75(1-2), Full day: $150(1-2),
Call between: 5:30 Pm 10:00 Pm
Provides: Light tackle, heavy tackle, fly rod/reel, lures, bait,
Full day only: Beverages, lunch
Handicapped equipped: Yes

ST. FRANCIS RIVER

BAIT & TACKLE...

Davis & Son's Bait Shop
Colt 501-630-0725
Hours: 7am-7:30pm, closed Sun.
Carries: Live bait, lures, flies,
Bodies of water: Bear Creek Lake, St. Francis River, Lake Dunn Village Creek, Lake Aptell Village Creek, L'Anguille River
Services & Products: Food, beverages, fishing instruction
Guides: Yes
OK to call for current conditions: Yes

Flookie's Bait Shop
Trumann 501-483-5431
Hours: 6am-8pm
Carries: Live bait, lures, flies, maps, rods, reels, licenses
Bodies of water: St Francis River, Lake Poinsett
Services & Products: Beverages, fishing instruction, repair services
Guides: Yes
OK to call for current conditions: Yes
Contact: Floyd Walton

WHITE RIVER

BAIT & TACKLE...

Barnett's Pawn and Bait Shop
Gateway 501-656-3730
Hours: 8am-6pm
Carries: Live bait, lures, flies, rods, reels, licenses
Bodies of water: Beaver Lake, White River, Table Rock Lake
Guides: Yes
OK to call for current conditions: Yes
Contact: Sharon Barnett

Crawdad Hole
Flippin 501-453-8744
Hours: 6:30am-7pm
Carries: Live bait, lures, flies, maps, rods, reels, licenses
Bodies of water: White River, Bull Shoals Lake, Norfork Lake
Services & Products: Guide services, beverages, fishing instruction
Guides: Yes
OK to call for current conditions: Yes
Contact: Robert Whites

WHITE RIVER — ARKANSAS

Webster's Chuck-Wagon
Marvell 501-829-2474
Hours: 5:30am-8 or 9pm
Carries: Live bait, lures, maps, rods, reels, licenses
Bodies of water: White River, Mississippi River, Arkansas River, Big Creek, White River National Wildlife Refuge Lakes
Services & Products: Guide services, food, beverages, fishing instruction
Guides: Yes
OK to call for current conditions: Yes

Wild Goose Corner One Stop
Tichnor 501-548-2778
Hours: 6am-8pm
Carries: Live bait, lures, flies, maps, rods, reels, licenses
Bodies of water: Lake Merrisack, White River, Arkansas River, Mississippi River, White River Refuge Lakes
Services & Products: Guide services, lodging, food, beverages, gas/oil, repair services
Guides: Yes
OK to call for current conditions: Yes
Contact: Mike or Carolyn Bell

FLY SHOPS...

The Ozark Angler
Heber Springs 501-362-3597
Hours: 7am-6pm
Carries: Flies, maps, rods, reels
Bodies of water: Little Red River, White River, North Fork River, Greers Ferry Lake
Services & Products: Boat rentals, guide services, fishing instruction
OK to call for current conditions: Yes
Contact: Anyone

GUIDES...

Billy Bob's Fishing Service
Flippin 501-453-8744
Species & Seasons: Rainbow Trout, Brown Trout, LM Bass, Crappie, Catfish, SM Bass Feb-Nov
Bodies of water: White River, Bull Shoals Lake, Norfork Lake
Rates: Half day: $90(1), $115(2), Full day: $120(1), $150(2)
Call between: Anytime
Provides: Bait, beverages, lunch
Handicapped equipped: No

River Valley Guide Service
Russellville 501-967-6080
Species & Seasons: Crappie Dec-April, Bass, Trout all year
Bodies of water: Lake Dardanelle, Lake Ouachita, Bull Shoals Lake, Red River, White River (trout)
Rates: Half day: $75(1-2), Full day: $150(1-2)
Call between: 5:30 Pm 10:00 Pm
Provides: Light tackle, heavy tackle, fly rod/reel, lures, bait, Full day only: Beverages, lunch
Handicapped equipped: Yes

LODGING...

Black Oak Resort
Oakland 501-431-8363
Guest Capacity: 66
Handicapped equipped: No
Seasons: All year
Rates: $52/day
Contact: Mike Scrima
Guides: Yes
Species & Seasons: LM Bass, SM Bass, Walleye, Spotted Bass, Trout all open
Bodies of Water: Bull Shoals Lake, White River
Types of fishing: Light tackle, float trips, downrigger
Available: Fishing instruction, licenses, bait, tackle, boat rentals, baby sitting, pets welcome

Cedar Hollow RV Park
Flippin 501-453-8643
Guest Capacity: 100
Handicapped equipped: Yes
Seasons: All year
Rates: $13/day and up
Contact: Don or Donna Wilkes
Guides: Yes
Species & Seasons: LM Bass, SM Bass, Crappie Mar-June, Trout, Catfish all year
Bodies of Water: Bull Shoals Lake, White River, Buffalo River
Types of fishing: Fly fishing, light tackle, wading, float trips

Gene's Trout Fishing Resort & Lodge
Mountain Home 501-499-5381
 800-526-3625
Hours: 7am-8pm
Carries: Live bait, lures, flies, maps, rods, reels, licenses
Bodies of water: North Fork River (we are on river), White River, Norfork Lake

Services & Products: Boat rentals, guide services, charter boat service, lodging, gas/oil, fishing instruction, canoe rentals
Guides: Yes
OK to call for current conditions: Yes
Contact: Scott

Gunga-La Lodge River Outfitters
Lakeview 501-431-5606
 800-844-5606
Guest Capacity: 10
Handicapped equipped: No
Seasons: All year
Rates: $70
Guides: Yes
Species & Seasons: Rainbow Trout, Brown Trout, Cutthroat Trout all year, SM Bass, Rock Bass May-Oct
Bodies of Water: White River, Bull Shoals Lake, Crooked Creek, Buffalo River
Types of fishing: Fly fishing, light tackle, wading, float trips
Available: Fishing instruction, licenses, bait, tackle, boat rentals, canoes, rubber rafts
(see ad on page 44)

Mar Mar Resort & Tackle Shop
Bull Shoals 800-332-BULL
 501-445-4444
Guest Capacity: 13 units, 29 beds
Handicapped equipped: No
Seasons: All year
Rates: $36-$48/day
Guides: Yes
Species & Seasons: Brown Trout, Rainbow Trout, LM Bass, SM Bass, Walleye, Catfish, Crappie, Bream, many others, call for fishing report
Bodies of Water: Bull Shoals Lake, White River
Types of fishing: Fly fishing, light tackle, heavy tackle, wading, float trips, overnight fish/camp trips
Available: Fishing instruction, licenses, bait, tackle, boat rentals, family activities

ARKANSAS
WHITE RIVER

Oak Ridge Resort
Mountain Home 501-431-5575
Guest Capacity: 45
Handicapped equipped: No
Seasons: All year
Rates: $40-$105/day
Contact: David or Colleen Pearson
Guides: Yes
Species & Seasons: LM Bass, SM Bass all year, Lake Trout April-Aug, Catfish Mar-Aug, Crappie April-June/Nov-Dec
Bodies of Water: Bull Shoals Lake, Norfork Lake, White River
Types of fishing: Fly fishing, light tackle, float trips
Available: Fishing instruction, licenses, bait, tackle, boat rentals, family activities

Rainbow Drive Resort
Cotter 501-430-5217
Guest Capacity: 50
Handicapped equipped: No
Seasons: Feb to Nov
Rates: $72/day and up
Guides: Yes
Species & Seasons: Brown Trout, Cutthroat Trout, Rainbow Trout all year
Bodies of Water: White River, Bull Shoals tailwater
Types of fishing: Fly fishing, light tackle, wading, float trips
Available: Fishing instruction, licenses, bait, tackle, boat rentals

Red Bud Dock
Gassville 501-435-6303
Hours: 7am-6pm
Carries:
Bodies of water: White River
Services & Products: Boat rentals, guide services, lodging, boat ramp, gas/oil, motors
Guides: Yes
OK to call for current conditions: Yes
Contact: Jeff Evans

Sportsmen's Resort
Flippin 800-626-3474
Guest Capacity: 68
Handicapped equipped: No
Seasons: All year
Rates: $52-$58
Contact: Dick Bump
Guides: Yes
Species & Seasons: Trout all year, LM Bass, SM Bass, Mar-July
Bodies of Water: White River, Crooked Creek, Buffalo River, Norfork Lake, Bull Shoals Lake

Types of fishing: Fly fishing, light tackle, wading, float trips
Available: Licenses, bait, tackle, boat rentals, family activities

Sunset Point Resort
Midway 501-431-5372
Guest Capacity: 46
Handicapped equipped: No
Seasons: All year
Rates: $45-$270
Guides: Yes
Species & Seasons: Trout, Catfish all year, LM Bass, SM Bass Walleye Jan-June
Bodies of Water: Bull Shoals Lake, White River
Types of fishing: Fly fishing, light tackle, wading, float trips
Available: Licenses, bait, tackle, boat rentals

CALIFORNIA

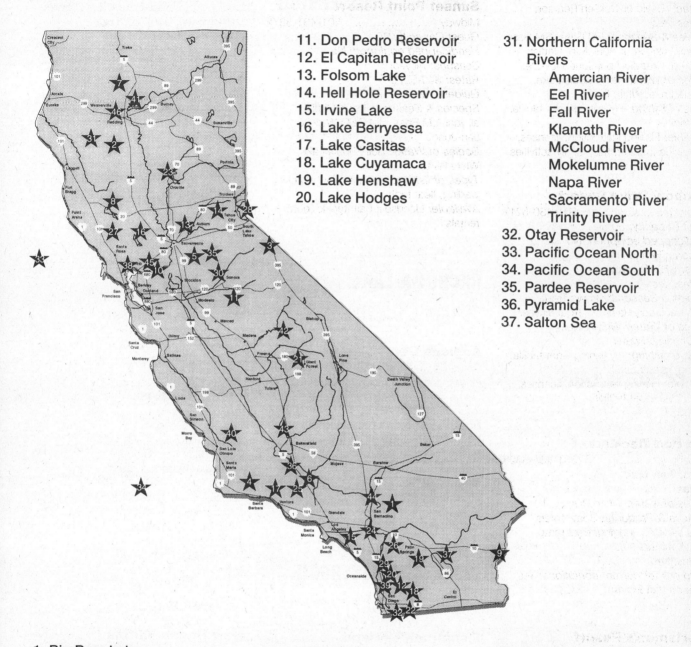

11. Don Pedro Reservoir
12. El Capitan Reservoir
13. Folsom Lake
14. Hell Hole Reservoir
15. Irvine Lake
16. Lake Berryessa
17. Lake Casitas
18. Lake Cuyamaca
19. Lake Henshaw
20. Lake Hodges
31. Northern California Rivers
    Amercian River
    Eel River
    Fall River
    Klamath River
    McCloud River
    Mokelumne River
    Napa River
    Sacramento River
    Trinity River
32. Otay Reservoir
33. Pacific Ocean North
34. Pacific Ocean South
35. Pardee Reservoir
36. Pyramid Lake
37. Salton Sea

1. Big Bear Lake
2. Black Butte Lake
3. Bridgeport Reservoir
4. Cachuma Lake
5. Camanche Reservoir
6. Castaic Lake
7. Clair Engle Lake
8. Clear Lake
9. Colorado River
10. Delta
21. Lake Kaweah
22. Lake Morena
23. Lake Oroville
24. Lake Perris
25. Lake Piru
26. Lake Skinner
27. Lake Sonoma
28. Lake Tahoe
29. Lake Wohlford
30. New Melones Lake
38. San Pablo Bay
39. San Vicente Lake
40. Santa Margarita Reservoir
41. Shasta Lake
42. Sierra National Forest Area
43. Siltcoos Lake
44. Silverwood Lake
45. Suison Bay
46. Whiskeytown Lake

YOUR SILENT FISHING PARTNER

CALIFORNIA
BIG BEAR LAKE - CAMANCHE RESERVOIR

BIG BEAR LAKE

BAIT & TACKLE...

Pratt's Sporting Goods
Redlands 909-793-3278
Hours: 10am-7pm Mon.-Fri.,
9am-6pm Sat.,10am-5pm Sun.
Carries: Live bait, lures, flies, maps, rods, reels, licenses
Bodies of water: Pacific Ocean, Lake Perris, Big Bear Lake, Silverwood Lake, Salton Sea
Guides: No
OK to call for current conditions: No

MARINAS...

Pleasure Point Landing
Big Bear Lake 909-866-2455
Hours: 6am-6pm (closed Dec.-Feb.)
Carries: Live bait, lures, licenses
Bodies of water: Big Bear Lake
Services & Products: Boat rentals, boat ramp, beverages, fishing instruction, repair services
OK to call for current conditions: Yes

BLACK BUTTE LAKE

BAIT & TACKLE...

Sportsman's Market
Orland 916-865-9273
Hours: 6am-10pm
Carries: Live bait, lures, maps, rods, reels, licenses
Bodies of water: Black Butte Lake, Stony Gorge Res, East Park Res.
Services & Products: Food, beverages, gas/oil, fishing instruction
Guides: No
OK to call for current conditions: Yes
Contact: Hennie or Barbara

MARINAS...

Black Butte Marina
Orland 916-865-2665
Hours: 7am-6pm, closed Mon. (open Mar.-Oct.)
Carries: Live bait, lures, maps, rods, reels, licenses
Bodies of water: Black Butte Lake
Services & Products: Boat rentals, boat ramp,food, beverages, gas/oil, over night dockage

Guides: No
OK to call for current conditions: Yes
Contact: Scott or Sharon

BRIDGEPORT RESERVOIR

BAIT & TACKLE...

Ken's Alpine Shops & Sporting
Bridgeport..................... 619-932-7707
Hours: 7am-8pm Mon.-Thurs., 7am-9pm Fri., Sat., 7am-6pm Sun.
Carries: Live bait, lures, flies, maps, rods, reels, licenses
Bodies of water: Bridgeport
Guides: Yes
OK to call for current conditions: Yes
Contact: Rick or Tracy

CACHUMA LAKE

BAIT & TACKLE...

Angler's Den
Camarillo..................... 805-388-1566
Hours: 10am-6pm, closed Sun., Mon.
Carries: Live bait, artificial, lures, maps, rods, reels, licenses
Bodies of water: Pacific Ocean, Cachuma Lake, Lake Casitas, Sespe River, Castaic Lake, Ventura River, Pyramid Lake, Lake Piru
Guides: Yes
OK to call for current conditions: Yes
Contact: Rick Graham

CAMANCHE RESERVOIR

BAIT & TACKLE...

Fisherman's Friend
Lodi 209-369-0204
Hours: 5am-5:30pm
Carries: Live bait, lures, flies, maps, rods, reels, licenses
Bodies of water: Camanche Res., Pardee Res., Lake Amador, New Melones Lake, San Joaquin River, Sacramento River, Delta
Services & Products: Guide services
Guides: Yes
OK to call for current conditions: Yes
Contact: Russ or Rick

Hook Line & Sinker
Oakley 510-625-2441
Hours: 6am-7pm
Carries: Live bait, lures, maps, rods, reels, licenses
Bodies of water: California Delta, Clear Lake, Shasta Lake, Lake Oroville, Folsom Lake, Don Pedro Res., Camanche Res.
Services & Products: Guide services, boat ramp, food, beverages, repair services
Guides: Yes
OK to call for current conditions: Yes
Contact: Gene Buchholz

GUIDES...

Don Payne Guide Service
Modesto 209-537-4486
Species & Seasons: Striped Bass Oct-Feb, LM Bass Dec-Jan
Bodies of water: Delta, Don Pedro Res., Lake McClure, New Melones Lake, Camanche Res., and most central California lakes
Rates: Full day: $200(1-2)
Call between: 7pm-9pm
Provides: Light tackle, lures, beverages
Handicapped equipped: No

Bob Lockhart
Ione 209-274-4739
Species & Seasons: LM Bass, Rainbow Trout fall-late spring, Bluegill May-Sept, Catfish May-Nov, Crappie Mar-June
Bodies of water: Camanche Res.
Rates: Half day: $65(1), $100(2), Full day: $150(1), $180(2), includes lunch
Call between: 7am-8am
Provides: Light tackle, heavy tackle, lures, bait, beverages, lunch
Handicapped equipped: Yes

MARINAS...

New Hogan Marina
Valley Springs 209-772-1462
Hours: 7am-Dark
Carries: Live bait, lures, flies, maps, rods, reels, licenses
Bodies of water: Lake Amador, Camanche Res., Pardee Res., New Melones Lake
Services & Products: Boat rentals, boat ramp, food, beverages, gas/oil, repair services
Guides: Yes
OK to call for current conditions: Yes

CASTAIC LAKE - DELTA / CALIFORNIA

CASTAIC LAKE

BAIT & TACKLE...

Angler's Den
Camarillo.......................... 805-388-1566
Hours: 10am-6pm, closed Sun., Mon.
Carries: Live bait, artificial lures, maps, rods, reels, licenses
Bodies of water: Pacific Ocean, Cachuma Lake, Lake Casitas, Sespe River, Castaic Lake, Ventura River, Pyramid Lake, Lake Piru
Guides: Yes
OK to call for current conditions: Yes

CLAIR ENGLE LAKE

MARINAS...

Pine Cove Marina
Lewiston 916-778-3770
Hours: 7am-7pm
Carries: Live bait, lures, flies, maps, reels
Bodies of water: Shasta Lake, Clair Engle Lake, Sacramento River, Trinity River, Lewiston Lake
Services & Products: Boat rentals, beverages, gas/oil, fishing instruction, repair services
Guides: Yes
OK to call for current conditions: Yes
Contact: Bret

CLEAR LAKE

BAIT & TACKLE...

Hook Line & Sinker
Oakley 510-625-2441
Hours: 6am-7pm
Carries: Live bait, lures, maps, rods, reels, licenses
Bodies of water: California Delta, Clear Lake, Shasta Lake, Lake Oroville, Folsom Lake, Don Pedro Res., Camanche Res.
Services & Products: Guide services, boat ramp, food, beverages, repair services
Guides: Yes
OK to call for current conditions: Yes
Contact: Gene Buchholz

Sweeney's Sports
Napa 707-255-5544
Hours: 9am-6pm
Carries: Live bait, lures, flies, maps, rods, reels, licenses
Bodies of water: San Pablo Bay, Napa River, Lake Berryessa, Clear Lake, Putah Creek, Pacific Ocean
Services & Products: Fishing instruction, repair services
Guides: Yes
OK to call for current conditions: Yes
Contact: Mike

LODGING...

Jim's Soda Bay Resort
Kelseyville 707-279-4837
Handicapped equipped: No
Seasons: All year
Rates: $49-$59/day
Guides: Yes
Species & Seasons: Catfish, LM Bass all year
Bodies of Water: Clear Lake
Types of fishing: Fly fishing, light tackle, heavy tackle
Available: Boat rentals, swimming, small beach

MARINAS...

Austin's Campground & Marina
Clearlake.......................... 707-994-7623
Hours: 8am-6pm
Carries: Live bait, lures, maps
Bodies of water: Clear Lake
Services & Products: Boat ramp, food, beverages, gas/oil, repair services
Guides: Yes
OK to call for current conditions: Yes
Contact: Howard McKenizie

Ferndale Resort & Marina
Kelseyville 707-279-4866
Hours: 7am-10pm
Carries: Live bait, lures, maps, rods, reels, licenses
Bodies of water: Clear Lake
Services & Products: Boat rentals, guide services, lodging, boat ramp, food, beverages, gas/oil, fishing instruction, repair services
Guides: Yes
OK to call for current conditions: Yes
Contact: Richard or Deb Todd

COLORADO RIVER

BAIT & TACKLE...

Brewer's Bait & Tackle
Palo Verde 619-854-3370
Hours: 6:30am-7pm
Carries: Live bait, lures, flies, maps
Bodies of water: Colorado River Oxboe Lake, Harvey's Fishing Hole, Cibola Lake
Services & Products: Food, beverages, gas/oil, repair services, beer, wine
Guides: No
OK to call for current conditions: Yes
Contact: Toni

DELTA

BAIT & TACKLE...

Fisherman's Friend
Lodi 209-369-0204
Hours: 5am-5:30pm
Carries: Live bait, lures, flies, maps, rods, reels, licenses
Bodies of water: Camanche Res., Pardee Res., Lake Amador, New Melones Lake, San Joaquin River, Sacramento River, Delta
Services & Products: Guide services
Guides: Yes
OK to call for current conditions: Yes
Contact: Russ or Rick

Grand Street Bait & Tackle
Alameda 510-521-2460
Hours: 7am-6pm
Carries: Live bait, lures, maps, rods, reels
Bodies of water: Pacific Ocean, San Francisco Bay, Sacramento River, Delta, Lake Chabot, Lake Merced
Services & Products: Guide services, charter boat service, boat ramp, food, beverages, fishing instruction, repair services
Guides: Yes
OK to call for current conditions: Yes
Contact: Anyone

CALIFORNIA

DELTA - DON PEDRO RESERVOIR

Hook Line & Sinker
Oakley 510-625-2441
Hours: 6am-7pm
Carries: Live bait, lures, maps, rods, reels, licenses
Bodies of water: California Delta, Clear Lake, Shasta Lake, Lake Oroville, Folsom Lake, Don Pedro Res., Camanche Res.
Services & Products: Guide services, boat ramp, food, beverages, repair services
Guides: Yes
OK to call for current conditions: Yes
Contact: Gene Buchholz

Jolly Joe Too Bait & Tackle
Stockton 209-948-6344
Hours: 5am-9pm
Carries: Live bait, maps, rods, reels, licenses
Bodies of water: Delta
Services & Products: Food, beverages, repair services
Guides: Yes
OK to call for current conditions: Yes
Contact: Kenney Beish

Martini's Bait Shop
Stockton 209-951-1692
Hours: 6am-7pm
Carries: Live bait, lures, maps, rods, reels, licenses
Bodies of water: Delta, Northern California lakes and rivers
Services & Products: Food, beverages, fishing instruction
Guides: Yes
OK to call for current conditions: Yes
Contact: Neal Hayden

Penny Bait Shop
West Sacramento 916-372-8813
Hours: 5am-11pm
Carries: Live bait, lures, flies, maps, rods, reels, licenses
Bodies of water: Sacramento River, American River, Folsom Lake, Delta
Services & Products: Beverages, repair services
Guides: Yes
OK to call for current conditions: Yes
Contact: Iho Chen

Romeo's Bait Shop No. 1
Sacramento 916-665-1788
Hours: 5am-8pm
Carries: Live bait, lures, maps, rods, reels, licenses
Bodies of water: Sacramento River, Delta

Services & Products: Beverages, repair services
Guides: Yes
OK to call for current conditions: Yes
Contact: Del

The Trap
Rio Vista 707-374-5554
Hours: 5am-8pm Mon.-Fri., 10pm Sat.-Sun.
Carries: Live bait, lures, maps, rods, reels, licenses
Bodies of water: Sacramento River, San Joaquin River, Delta
Services & Products: Guide services, boat ramp, food, beverages, fishing instruction
Guides: Yes
OK to call for current conditions: Yes
Contact: Sally Whitesides or Sylvia Vieira

GUIDES...

Don Payne Guide Service
Modesto 209-537-4486
Species & Seasons: Striped Bass Oct-Feb, LM Bass Dec-Jan
Bodies of water: Delta, Don Pedro Res., Lake McClure, New Melones Lake, Camanche Res., and most central California lakes
Rates: Full day: $200(1-2)
Call between: 7pm-9pm
Provides: Light tackle, lures, beverages
Handicapped equipped: No

LODGING...

Delta Bay Club
Isleton 916-777-5588
Guest Capacity: 500
Handicapped equipped: No
Seasons: All year
Rates: $24.95/night
Guides: Yes
Species & Seasons: Striped Bass all year
Bodies of Water: Sacramento River, San Joaquin River, Delta
Types of fishing: Light tackle, heavy tackle, float trips
Available: Bait, tackle, boat rentals, family activities

MARINAS...

Delta Marina-Yacht Harbor
Rio Vista 707-374-2315
Hours: 8am-5pm
Carries: Lures, maps, rods, reels
Bodies of water: Sacramento River, Delta
Services & Products: Boat ramp, food, beverages, gas/oil, repair services, RV sites
Guides: Yes
OK to call for current conditions: Yes
Contact: Roy Phillips

New Bridge Marina Inc.
Antioch 510-757-1500
Hours: 8am-5pm
Bodies of water: San Joaquin River, Sacramento River, Delta
Services & Products: Gas/oil, repair services
Guides: No
OK to call for current conditions: Yes
Contact: Jim Sutton

New Hope Landing
Thornton 209-794-2627
Hours: 8am-6pm
Carries: Lures, maps, rods, reels
Bodies of water: Mokelumne River, Delta
Services & Products: Boat ramp, beverages, camping
Guides: No
OK to call for current conditions: Yes

DON PEDRO RESERVOIR

BAIT & TACKLE...

Hook Line & Sinker
Oakley 510-625-2441
Hours: 6am-7pm
Carries: Live bait, lures, maps, rods, reels, licenses
Bodies of water: California Delta, Clear Lake, Shasta Lake, Lake Oroville, Folsom Lake, Don Pedro Res., Camanche Res.
Services & Products: Guide services, boat ramp, food, beverages, repair services
Guides: Yes
OK to call for current conditions: Yes
Contact: Gene Buchholz

DON PEDRO RESERVOIR - HELL HOLE RESERVOIR — CALIFORNIA

GUIDES...

Don Payne Guide Service
Modesto 209-537-4486
Species & Seasons: Striped Bass Oct-Feb, LM Bass Dec-Jan
Bodies of water: Delta, Don Pedro Res., Lake McClure, New Melones Lake, Camanche Res., and most central California lakes
Rates: Full day: $200(1-2)
Call between: 7pm-9pm
Provides: Light tackle, lures, beverages
Handicapped equipped: No

EL CAPITAN RESERVOIR

BAIT & TACKLE...

Angler's Arsenal
La Mesa 800-428-8730
Hours: 7am-4pm, closed Sat., Sun.
Carries: Lures, maps, rods, reels, mail order
Bodies of water: Pacific Ocean, San Vicente Lake, El Capitan Res., Lake Hodges
Guides: Yes
OK to call for current conditions: Yes
Contact: John Cassidy

Bobs Bait & Tackle
Chula Vista 619-420-1999
Encinitas 619-632-7051
Escondido 619-741-1570
Hemet 909-658-0208
San Diego 619-222-1261
                                    619-278-8055
San Marcos 619-736-4077
Santee 619-562-6984
Spring Valley 619-697-2160
Vista 619-774-4317
Hours: 7am-7pm
Carries: Live bait, lures, flies, maps, rods, reels, licenses
Bodies of water: Lake Hodges, San Vicente Lake, Otay Res., El Capitan Res., Lake Morena, Lake Dixon, Lake Wohlford, Sutherland, Pacific Ocean
Services & Products: Repair services
Guides: Yes
OK to call for current conditions: Yes

Fishing Adventures Bait & Tackle
San Diego 619-487-1691
Hours: 5:30am-7:00pm
Carries: Live bait, lures, flies, maps, rods, reels, licenses
Bodies of water: Pacific Ocean, San Vicente Lake, El Capitan Res., Lake Hodges, Lake Miramar, Lake Wohlford, Lake Poway
Services & Products: Guide services, repair services
Guides: Yes
OK to call for current conditions: Yes
Contact: Eric or Chris

Lakeside Sporting Goods
Lakeside 619-443-3859
Hours: 9am-6pm, closed Sun.
Carries: Live bait, lures, flies, maps, rods, reels, licenses
Bodies of water: Pacific Ocean, San Vicente Lake, El Capitan Res., Otay Res., Lake Hodges, Barrett Lake
Services & Products: Beverages, fishing instruction, repair services, rod building
Guides: Yes
OK to call for current conditions: Yes
Contact: Richard, Jimbo or Manny

GUIDES...

Dave Zimmerlee
San Diego 619-271-8726
Species & Seasons: LM Bass Jan-Dec
Bodies of water: Lower Otay Res., El Capitan Res., all San Diego lakes
Rates: Half day: $75(1), $100(2), Full day: $125(1), $150(2)
Call between: Anytime
Provides: Light tackle, lures, bait, rain gear, beverages, lunch
Handicapped equipped: Yes

FOLSOM LAKE

BAIT & TACKLE...

The Fishin' Hole
Roseville 916-791-2248
Hours: 5:30am-6pm
Carries: Live bait, lures, flies, maps, rods, reels, licenses
Bodies of water: Folsom Lake, Natomas Lake, Clementime Lake
Services & Products: Boat rentals, guide services, food, beverages, fishing instruction
Guides: Yes
OK to call for current conditions: Yes

Fruitridge Bait & Tackle Shop
Sacramento 916-456-7506
Hours: 8am-5pm, closed Sun. afternoon
Carries: Live bait, lures, flies, maps, licenses
Bodies of water: Sacramento River, American River, Folsom Lake
Services & Products: Beverages, fishing instruction
OK to call for current conditions: Yes

Hook Line & Sinker
Oakley 510-625-2441
Hours: 6am-7pm
Carries: Live bait, lures, maps, rods, reels, licenses
Bodies of water: California Delta, Clear Lake, Shasta Lake, Lake Oroville, Folsom Lake, Don Pedro Res., Camanche Res.
Services & Products: Guide services, boat ramp, food, beverages, repair services
Guides: Yes
OK to call for current conditions: Yes
Contact: Gene Buchholz

Penny Bait Shop
West Sacramento 916-372-8813
Hours: 5am-11pm
Carries: Live bait, lures, flies, maps, rods, reels, licenses
Bodies of water: Sacramento River, American River, Folsom Lake, Delta
Services & Products: Beverages, repair services
Guides: Yes
OK to call for current conditions: Yes
Contact: Iho Chen

HELL HOLE RESERVOIR

GUIDES...

Alpine Fly Fishing Service
S. Lake Tahoe 916-542-0759
Species & Seasons: Rainbow Trout, Cutthroat Trout, Brown Trout, Brook Trout April-Nov
Bodies of water: East Fork Carson River, West Fork Carson River, Silver Creek, Pleasant Valley Creek, Lost Lakes, Summit Lake, Tamarock, Hellhole Res., Indian Creek Res.
Rates: Half day: $95(1), $125(2), Full day: $175(1), $225(2)
Call between: 7am-6pm
Provides: Fly rod/reel, beverages, lunch
Handicapped equipped: No
Certifications: Endorsed by Fisher Rod Co., BLM & US forest Service Permittee

CALIFORNIA

IRVINE LAKE — LAKE HODGES

IRVINE LAKE

BAIT & TACKLE...

The Grant Boys
Costa Mesa 714-645-3400
Hours: 10-7 Mon.-Fri., 10-6 Sat., 10-5 Sun.
Carries: Live bait, lures, flies, maps, rods, reels, licenses
Bodies of water: Pacific Ocean, Irvine Lake, Santa Ana River Lakes, Laguna Niguel Lake
Services & Products: Camping equipment rentals
Guides: Yes
OK to call for current conditions: Yes
Contact: Fishing Department

LAKE BERRYESSA

BAIT & TACKLE...

A & M Market
Napa 707-255-0400
Hours: 6am-9pm
Carries: Live bait, lures, rods, reels, licenses
Bodies of water: Napa River, Lake Berryessa, Lake Hennessy
Services & Products: Food, beverages
Guides: Yes
OK to call for current conditions: Yes
Contact: Bob or Paulette

Sweeney's Sports
Napa 707-255-5544
Hours: 9am-6pm
Carries: Live bait, lures, flies, maps, rods, reels, licenses
Bodies of water: San Pablo Bay, Napa River, Lake Berryessa, Clear Lake, Putah Creek, Pacific Ocean
Services & Products: Fishing instruction, repair services
Guides: Yes
OK to call for current conditions: Yes
Contact: Mike

LODGING...

Spanish Flat Resort
Napa 707-966-7700
Guest Capacity: 120 campsites
Handicapped equipped: Yes
Seasons: All year
Rates: $16/night
Guides: No
Species & Seasons: Trout, LM Bass, Crappie, Bluegill Sept-June, Catfish all year
Bodies of Water: Lake Berryessa
Types of fishing: Fly fishing, light tackle, trolling
Available: Licenses, bait, tackle, boat rentals, camping

LAKE CASITAS

BAIT & TACKLE...

Angler's Den
Camarillo 805-388-1566
Hours: 10am-6pm, closed Sun., Mon.
Carries: Live bait, artificial, lures, maps, rods, reels, licenses
Bodies of water: Pacific Ocean, Cachuma Lake, Lake Casitas, Sespe River, Castaic Lake, Ventura River, Pyramid Lake, Lake Piru
Guides: Yes
OK to call for current conditions: Yes
Contact: Rick Graham

LAKE CUYAMACA

FLY SHOPS...

Stroud Tackle
San Diego 619-276-4822
Hours: 11am-6pm, closed Sun.
Carries: Flies, maps, rods, reels
Bodies of water: Pacific Ocean, Lake Morena, Lake Cuyamaca
Services & Products: Fishing instruction, repair services, fly fishing products
Guides: Yes
OK to call for current conditions: Yes
Contact: Bill or Eileen Stroud

LAKE HENSHAW

LODGING...

Lake Henshaw Resort
Santa Ysabel 619-782-3501
Handicapped equipped: No
Seasons: All year
Contact: Al Socin
Guides: No
Species & Seasons: Crappie Feb-Sept, LM Bass April-Oct, Channel Catfish Feb-Dec
Bodies of Water: Lake Henshaw
Types of fishing: Fly fishing, light tackle
Available: Bait, tackle, boat rentals, campground, cabins, RV/mobile home park

LAKE HODGES

BAIT & TACKLE...

Angler's Arsenal
La Mesa 800-428-8730
Hours: 7am-4pm, closed Sat., Sun.
Carries: Lures, maps, rods, reels, mail order
Bodies of water: Pacific Ocean, San Vicente Lake, El Capitan Res., Lake Hodges
Guides: Yes
OK to call for current conditions: Yes
Contact: John Cassidy

Bobs Bait & Tackle
Chula Vista 619-420-1999
Encinitas 619-632-7051
Escondido 619-741-1570
Hemet 909-658-0208
San Diego 619-222-1261
                                 619-278-8055
Santee 619-562-6984
Spring Valley 619-697-2160
Hours: 7am-7pm
Carries: Live bait, lures, flies, maps, rods, reels, licenses
Bodies of water: Lake Hodges, San Vicente Lake, Otay Res., El Capitan Res., Lake Morena, Lake Dixon, Lake Wohlford, Sutherland, Pacific Ocean
Services & Products: Repair Services
Guides: Yes
OK to call for current conditions: Yes

Fishing Adventures Bait & Tackle
San Diego 619-487-1691
Hours: 5:30am-7:00pm
Carries: Live bait, lures, flies, maps, rods, reels, licenses
Bodies of water: Pacific Ocean, San Vicente Lake, El Capitan Res., Lake Hodges, Lake Miramar, Lake Wohlford, Lake Poway
Services & Products: Guide services, repair services
Guides: Yes
OK to call for current conditions: Yes
Contact: Eric or Chris

LAKE HODGES - LAKE PIRU   CALIFORNIA

Lakeside Sporting Goods
Lakeside 619-443-3859
Hours: 9am-6pm, closed Sun.
Carries: Live bait, lures, flies, maps, rods, reels, licenses
Bodies of water: Pacific Ocean, San Vicente Lake, El Capitan Res., Otay Res., Lake Hodges, Barrett Lake
Services & Products: Beverages, fishing instruction, repair services, rod building
Guides: Yes
OK to call for current conditions: Yes
Contact: Richard, Jimbo or Manny

LAKE KAWEAH

BAIT & TACKLE...

Clouds Bait & Tackle
Lemon Cove 209-597-2427
Hours: 7:30am-7pm
Carries: Live bait, lures, flies, maps, rods, reels, licenses
Bodies of water: Lake Kaweah, Kaweah River
Services & Products: Food, beverages, fishing instruction, picnic supplies
Guides: No
OK to call for current conditions: Yes
Contact: Mary or Orville Cloud

MARINAS...

Kaweah Marina
Lemon Cove 209-597-2526
Hours: 8am-5pm (7am-7pm in summer)
Carries: Live bait, lures, maps, rods, reels
Bodies of water: Lake Kaweah
Services & Products: Boat rentals, food, beverages, gas/oil, repair services
Guides: No
OK to call for current conditions: Yes
Contact: Dale or Davindee

LAKE MORENA

BAIT, TACKLE & FLY SHOPS...

Bobs Bait & Tackle
Chula Vista 619-420-1999
Encinitas 619-632-7051
Escondido 619-741-1570
Hemet 909-658-0208
San Diego 619-222-1261
.... 619-278-8055
San Marcos 619-736-4077
Santee 619-562-6984
Spring Valley 619-697-2160
Vista 619-774-4317
Hours: 7am-7pm
Carries: Live bait, lures, flies, maps, rods, reels, licenses
Bodies of water: Lake Hodges, San Vicente Lake, Otay Res., El Capitan Res., Lake Morena, Lake Dixon, Lake Wohlford, Sutherland, Pacific Ocean
Services & Products: Repair Services
Guides: Yes
OK to call for current conditions: Yes

Stroud Tackle
San Diego 619-276-4822
Hours: 11am-6pm, closed Sun.
Carries: Flies, maps, rods, reels
Bodies of water: Pacific Ocean, Lake Morena, Lake Cuyamaca
Services & Products: Fishing instruction, repair services, fly fishing products
Guides: Yes
OK to call for current conditions: Yes
Contact: Bill or Eileen Stroud

LAKE OROVILLE

BAIT & TACKLE...

Hook Line & Sinker
Oakley 510-625-2441
Hours: 6am-7pm
Carries: Live bait, lures, maps, rods, reels, licenses
Bodies of water: California Delta, Clear Lake, Shasta Lake, Lake Oroville, Folsom Lake, Don Pedro Res., Camanche Res.
Services & Products: Guide services, boat ramp, food, beverages, repair services
Guides: Yes
OK to call for current conditions: Yes
Contact: Gene Buchholz

GUIDES...

Pro-Guide Fishing & Recreation
Oroville 916-533-1510
Species & Seasons: Spotted Bass, LM Bass, SM Bass Feb-Oct
Bodies of water: Lake Oroville
Rates: Half day: $130(1), $160(2), $190(3), Full day: $200(1), $250(2), $300(3)
Call between: Anytime
Provides: Light tackle, lures, rain gear, beverages, lunch
Handicapped equipped: No

LAKE PERRIS

BAIT & TACKLE...

Pratt's Sporting Goods
Redlands 909-793-3278
Hours: 10am-7pm Mon.-Fri., 9am-6pm Sat., 10am-5pm Sun.
Carries: Live bait, lures, flies, maps, rods, reels, licenses
Bodies of water: Pacific Ocean, Lake Perris, Big Bear Lake, Silverwood Lake, Salton Sea
Guides: No
OK to call for current conditions: No

LAKE PIRU

BAIT & TACKLE...

Angler's Den
Camarillo 805-388-1566
Hours: 10am-6pm, closed Sun., Mon.
Carries: Live bait, artificial, lures, maps, rods, reels, licenses
Bodies of water: Pacific Ocean, Cachuma Lake, Lake Casitas, Sespe River, Castaic Lake, Ventura River, Pyramid Lake, Lake Piru
Guides: Yes
OK to call for current conditions: Yes
Contact: Rick Graham

MARINAS...

Lake Piru
Piru 805-521-1500
.... 521-1231
Hours: Sunup-Sunset
Carries: Live bait, lures, maps, rods, reels, licenses
Bodies of water: Lake Piru
Services & Products: Boat rentals, boat ramp, food, beverages, gas/oil, fishing instruction, repair services, camping
Guides: Yes
OK to call for current conditions: Yes
Contact: Art Caldara

CALIFORNIA
LAKE SKINNER - NEW MELONES LAKE

LAKE SKINNER

MARINAS...

Lake Skinner Marina
Winchester 909-926-1505
Hours: 6am-10pm
Carries: Live bait, lures, maps, rods, reels, licenses
Bodies of water: Lake Skinner
Services & Products: Boat rentals, guide services, lodging, boat ramp, food, beverages, gas/oil, cafe, campgrounds
Guides: Yes
OK to call for current conditions: Yes

LAKE SONOMA

FLY SHOPS...

Fly Fishing Etc.
Petaluma 707-762-3073
Hours: 10am-5:30pm
Carries: Flies, maps, rods, reels
Bodies of water: Russian River, Gualala River, Sacramento River, Trinity River, Fall River, Hat Creek, Eel River, Lake Sonoma
Services & Products: Guide services, fishing instruction, repair services, fly tying lessons
Guides: Yes
OK to call for current conditions: Yes
Contact: Fernando Tabor or Liz

LAKE TAHOE

CHARTERS...

Mickey's Big Mack Charters
Tahoe City 800-877-1462
.... 916-546-4444
Species & Seasons: Mackinaw, Lake Trout, Rainbow Trout all year, Brown Trout Oct-June
Bodies of water: Lake Tahoe (North Shore)
Rates: Half day: $65(1), Week days 3 hour trip: $45
Call between: 6pm-11pm
Provides: Light tackle, lures, bait
Handicapped equipped: Yes
Certifications: USCG (Lic CA & NV Fish & Game)

Tahoe Sports Fishing
S. Lake Tahoe 916-541-5448
Species & Seasons: Mackinaw, Rainbow Trout, Brown Trout Jan-Jan
Bodies of water: Lake Tahoe
Rates: Half day: $65(2)
Call between: 9am-4pm
Provides: Light tackle, heavy tackle, lures, bait, beverages
Certifications: USCG

LAKE WOHLFORD

BAIT & TACKLE...

Bobs Bait & Tackle
Chula Vista 619-420-1999
Encinitas 619-632-7051
Escondido 619-741-1570
Hemet 909-658-0208
San Diego 619-222-1261
                                        619-278-8055
San Marcos 619-736-4077
Santee 619-562-6984
Spring Valley 619-697-2160
Vista 619-774-4317
Hours: 7am-7pm
Carries: Live bait, lures, flies, maps, rods, reels, licenses
Bodies of water: Lake Hodges, San Vicente Lake, Otay Res., El Capitan Res., Lake Morena, Lake Dixon, Lake Wohlford, Sutherland, Pacific Ocean
Services & Products: Repair Services
Guides: Yes
OK to call for current conditions: Yes

Fishing Adventures Bait & Tackle
San Diego 619-487-1691
Hours: 5:30am-7:00pm
Carries: Live bait, lures, flies, maps, rods, reels, licenses
Bodies of water: Pacific Ocean, San Vicente Lake, El Capitan Res., Lake Hodges, Lake Miramar, Lake Wohlford, Lake Poway
Services & Products: Guide services, repair services
Guides: Yes
OK to call for current conditions: Yes
Contact: Eric or Chris

NEW MELONES LAKE

BAIT & TACKLE...

Fisherman's Friend
Lodi 209-369-0204
Hours: 5am-5:30pm
Carries: Live bait, lures, flies, maps, rods, reels, licenses
Bodies of water: Camanche Res., Pardee Res., Lake Amador, New Melones Lake, San Joaquin River, Sacramento River, Delta
Services & Products: Guide services
Guides: Yes
OK to call for current conditions: Yes
Contact: Russ or Rick

GUIDES...

Don Payne Guide Service
Modesto 209-537-4486
Species & Seasons: Striped Bass Oct-Feb, LM Bass Dec-Jan
Bodies of water: Delta, Don Pedro Res., Lake McClure, New Melones Lake, Camanche Res., and most central California lakes
Rates: Full day: $200(1-2)
Call between: 7pm-9pm
Provides: Light tackle, lures, beverages
Handicapped equipped: No

MARINAS...

New Hogan Marina
Valley Springs 209-772-1462
Hours: 7am-Dark
Carries: Live bait, lures, flies, maps, rods, reels, licenses
Bodies of water: Lake Amador, Camanche Res., Pardee Res., New Melones Lake
Services & Products: Boat rentals, boat ramp, food, beverages, gas/oil, repair services
Guides: Yes
OK to call for current conditions: Yes

NORTHERN CALIFORNIA RIVERS

BAIT & TACKLE ...

A & M Market
Napa 707-255-0400
Hours: 6am-9pm
Carries: Live bait, lures, rods, reels, licenses
Bodies of water: Napa River, Lake Berryessa, Lake Hennessy
Services & Products: Food, beverages
Guides: Yes
OK to call for current conditions: Yes
Contact: Bob or Paulette

Fisherman's Friend
Lodi 209-369-0204
Hours: 5am-5:30pm
Carries: Live bait, lures, flies, maps, rods, reels, licenses
Bodies of water: Camanche Res., Pardee Res., Lake Amador, New Melones Lake, San Joaquin River, Sacramento River, Delta
Services & Products: Guide services
Guides: Yes
OK to call for current conditions: Yes
Contact: Russ or Rick

Fruitridge Bait & Tackle Shop
Sacramento 916-456-7506
Hours: 8am-5pm, closed Sun. afternoon
Carries: Live bait, lures, flies, maps, licenses
Bodies of water: Sacramento River, American River, Folsom Lake
Services & Products: Beverages, fishing instruction
OK to call for current conditions: Yes

Grand Street Bait & Tackle
Alameda 510-521-2460
Hours: 7am-6pm
Carries: Live bait, lures, maps, rods, reels,
Bodies of water: Pacific Ocean, San Francisco Bay, Sacramento River, Delta, Lake Chabot, Lake Merced
Services & Products: Guide services, charter boat service, boat ramp, food, beverages, fishing instruction, repair services
Guides: Yes
OK to call for current conditions: Yes
Contact: Anyone

Penny Bait Shop
West Sacramento 916-372-8813
Hours: 5am-11pm
Carries: Live bait, lures, flies, maps, rods, reels, licenses
Bodies of water: Sacramento River, American River, Folsom Lake, Delta
Services & Products: Beverages, repair services
Guides: Yes
OK to call for current conditions: Yes
Contact: Iho Chen

Romeo's Bait Shop No. 1
Sacramento 916-665-1788
Hours: 5am-8pm
Carries: Live bait, lures, maps, rods, reels, licenses
Bodies of water: Sacramento River, Delta
Services & Products: Beverages, repair services
Guides: Yes
OK to call for current conditions: Yes
Contact: Del

Shasta Angler
Fall River Mills 916-336-6600
Hours: 9am-5pm
Carries: Lures, flies, maps, rods, reels, licenses
Bodies of water: Fall River, Hat Creek, Pit River, Shasta Lake, McCloud River
Services & Products: Guide services, gas/oil, fishing instruction, repair services
Guides: Yes
OK to call for current conditions: Yes
Contact: Matt Nicholls

Sweeney's Sports
Napa 707-255-5544
Hours: 9am-6pm
Carries: Live bait, lures, flies, maps, rods, reels, licenses
Bodies of water: San Pablo Bay, Napa River, Lake Berryessa, Clear Lake, Putah Creek, Pacific Ocean
Services & Products: Fishing instruction, repair services
Guides: Yes
OK to call for current conditions: Yes
Contact: Mike

The Trap
Rio Vista 707-374-5554
Hours: 5am-8pm Mon.-Fri., 10pm Sat.-Sun.
Carries: Live bait, lures, maps, rods, reels, licenses
Bodies of water: Sacramento River, San Joaquin River, Delta
Services & Products: Guide services, boat ramp, food, beverages, fishing instruction
Guides: Yes
OK to call for current conditions: Yes
Contact: Sally Whitesides or Sylvia Vieira

FLY SHOPS...

Fly Fishing Etc.
Petaluma 707-762-3073
Hours: 10am-5:30pm
Carries: Flies, maps, rods, reels
Bodies of water: Russian River, Gualala River, Sacramento River, Trinity River, Fall River, Hat Creek, Eel River, Lake Sonoma
Services & Products: Guide services, fishing instruction, repair services, fly tying lessons
Guides: Yes
OK to call for current conditions: Yes
Contact: Fernando Tabor or Liz

CHARTERS...

Sacramento Sport Fishing
Sacramento 800-344-4871
.... 916-987-3392
Species & Seasons: Striped Bass Mar-May/Oct-Jan, Sturgeon Feb-May, Shad May-July, Salmon July-Jan, Steelhead Sept-Oct, Rainbow Trout April-July
Bodies of water: Sacramento River, American River, Feather River, San Joaquin River
Rates: Salmon, Steelhead, Rainbow Trout: $250(1-2), $100 each additional person Striped Bass, Sturgeon, Shad: $170(1-2) full day, $85 pp additional
Call between: 7am-7pm
Provides: Light tackle, heavy tackle, fly rod/reel, lures, bait
Handicapped equipped: Yes
Certifications: USCG

CALIFORNIA
NORTHERN CALIFORNIA RIVERS

GUIDES...

Fish Tales Guide Service
Hayfork 916-628-5176
Species & Seasons: Chinook Salmon July-Dec, Steelhead Oct-April, Trout April-Nov, American Shad June-Aug, SM Bass, LM Bass Mar-July
Bodies of water: Sacramento River, Klamath River, Trinity River, Eel River, Smith River, Shasta Lake, Oregon waters: Chetco River, Rogue River
Rates: Full day: $175(1), $250(2), $300(3), $400(4)
Call between: 6am-11pm
Provides: Light tackle, lures, bait
Certifications: USCG, CPR, First aid

Hart's Guide Service
Mt. Shasta 916-926-2431
Species & Seasons: Rainbow Trout Mar-Dec, Brown Trout July-Nov
Bodies of water: McCloud River, Upper Sacramento River
Rates: Half day:: $100(1), $125(2), Full day: $175(1), $225(2)
Call between: 8am-8pm
Provides: Beverages, lunch
Handicapped equipped: No

Klamath's Camper Corral
Klamath 707-482-5741
Species & Seasons: Chinook Salmon, Steelhead Aug-Oct, Coho Salmon Sept-Oct
Bodies of water: Klamath River
Rates: Half day: $90(1), $180(2), Full day: $125(1), $250(2), custom trips available
Call between: 9am-5pm
Provides: Light tackle, fly rod/reel, lures, bait
Handicapped equipped: Yes
Certifications: USCG, CPR, CA Guide

North Rivers Guide Service
Orleans 916-469-3492
Species & Seasons: Steelhead Aug-May, Salmon Aug-Nov, Trout Jan-Dec
Bodies of water: Klamath River, Trinity River, Sacramento River, Eel River, Mad River, Van Duzen River, Smith River, area lakes
Rates: Half day: $100(1), $200(2), Full day: $200(1), $300(2), varies with type of boat and number of people
Call between: 8am-9pm
Provides: Light tackle, fly rod/reel, lures, bait
Handicapped equipped: Yes
Certifications: USCG, FFF

Pipe Creek Guide Service
Garberville 707-923-9236
Species & Seasons: Steelhead Dec-Mar, Salmon April-June/Aug-Dec
Bodies of water: Eel River, Smith River, Klamath River, Chetco River, Rogue River, Elk River
Rates: Half day: $100(1), $200(2), Full day: $125(1), $250(2)
Call between: 6pm-10pm
Provides: Light tackle, heavy tackle, lures, bait
Handicapped equipped: No
Certifications: USCG, NACO, NCARG

Ted Fay Fly Shop & Guide Service
Dunsmuir 916-235-2969
Species & Seasons: Rainbow Trout, Brown Trout May-Nov
Bodies of water: Upper Sacramento River, McCloud River
Rates: Half day: $50(1), $50(2), only half day evening trips
Call between: 8am-4pm
Provides: Fly rod/reel
Handicapped equipped: No

LODGING...

Coffee Creek Ranch
Trinity Center 800-624-4480
Guest Capacity: 50
Handicapped equipped: Yes
Seasons: All year
Rates: Summer: $250-$695/week pp, call for other rates
Contact: Ruth G. Hartman
Guides: Yes
Species & Seasons: Rainbow Trout, Brook Trout, Brown Trout April-Nov, LM Bass, SM Bass, Kokanee, Catfish all year
Bodies of Water: Trinity Lake, Trinity River, Coffee Creek
Types of fishing: Fly fishing, light tackle, heavy tackle, horse/back pack, wading, float trips
Available: Fishing instruction, bait, tackle, family activities, children's program, baby sitting

Deer Lodge
Trinidad 707-677-3554
Guest Capacity: 250
Handicapped equipped: Yes
Seasons: All year
Rates: Cabins: $40-$105/day
Contact: Beverly Rolen
Guides: Yes
Species & Seasons: Salmon, Bottom Fish, Smelt May-Sept, Shellfish Dec-Aug, Steelhead Sept-Feb
Bodies of Water: Pacific Ocean, Klamath River, Trinity River, Eel River, VanDuzen River, Redwood Creek
Types of fishing: Light tackle, heavy tackle, ocean party boats
Available: Family activities

MARK & RUTH HARTMAN
Managing Owners

HC2, BOX 4940
TRINITY CENTER, CA 96091-9502
PHONE (916) 266-3343
FAX (916) 266-3597

RESERVATIONS TOLL FREE 1-800-624-4480

Delta Bay Club
Isleton 916-777-5588
Guest Capacity: 500
Handicapped equipped: No
Seasons: All year
Rates: $24.95/night
Guides: Yes
Species & Seasons: Striped Bass all year
Bodies of Water: Sacramento River, San Joaquin River, Delta
Types of fishing: Light tackle, heavy tackle, float trips
Available: Bait, tackle, boat rentals, family activities

NORTHERN CALIFORNIA RIVERS - OTAY RESERVOIR — CALIFORNIA

Rick's Lodge
Fall River Mills 916-336-5300
Guest Capacity: 30
Handicapped equipped: Yes
Seasons: April 1 to Dec 31
Rates: $75/day
Contact: Rick
Guides: Yes
Species & Seasons: Rainbow Trout, Brown Trout April-Nov
Bodies of Water: Fall River
Types of fishing: Fly fishing, horse/back pack, wading, float trips
Available: Fishing instruction, bait, tackle, boat rentals, family activities

MARINAS...

Delta Marina-Yacht Harbor
Rio Vista 707-374-2315
Hours: 8am-5pm
Carries: Lures, maps, rods, reels
Bodies of water: Sacramento River, Delta
Services & Products: Boat ramp, food, beverages, gas/oil, repair services, RV sites
Guides: Yes
OK to call for current conditions: Yes
Contact: Roy Phillips

Grimes Boat Landing
Grimes 916-437-2333
Carries: Lures, maps
Bodies of water: Sacramento River
Services & Products: Food, beverages, gas/oil, RV hook-ups, dockage, sling launch
Guides: Yes
OK to call for current conditions: Yes

New Bridge Marina Inc.
Antioch 510-757-1500
Hours: 8am-5pm
Bodies of water: San Joaquin River, Sacramento River, Delta
Services & Products: Gas/oil, repair services
Guides: No
OK to call for current conditions: Yes
Contact: Jim Sutton

New Hope Landing
Thornton 209-794-2627
Hours: 8am-6pm
Carries: Lures, maps, rods, reels
Bodies of water: Mokelumne River, Delta
Services & Products: Boat ramp, beverages, camping
Guides: No
OK to call for current conditions: Yes

Pine Cove Marina
Lewiston 916-778-3770
Hours: 7am-7pm
Carries: Live bait, lures, flies, maps, reels
Bodies of water: Shasta Lake, Clair Engle Lake, Sacramento River, Trinity River, Lewiston Lake
Services & Products: Boat rentals, beverages, gas/oil, fishing instruction, repair services
Guides: Yes
OK to call for current conditions: Yes
Contact: Bret

Tower Park Marina
Lodi 209-369-1041
Hours: 7am-10pm
Carries: Lures, flies, maps, rods, reels, licenses
Bodies of water: Little Potato Slough, Mokelumne River
Services & Products: Boat rentals, guide services, lodging, boat ramp, food, beverages, gas/oil, repair services
Guides: Yes
OK to call for current conditions: Yes

Walnut Grove Marina Inc.
Walnut Grove 916-776-1181
Hours: 8am-5pm
Carries: Lures, flies, maps
Bodies of water: Sacramento River, Snograss Slough, Mokelumne River
Services & Products: Boat ramp, food, beverages, gas/oil, fishing instruction, repair services
Guides: Yes
OK to call for current conditions: Yes
Contact: Stu Pratt

Windmill Cove Marina
Stockton 209-948-6995
Hours: 10am-12pm
Bodies of water: San Juaquin River, Sacramento River
Services & Products: Food, beverages, gas/oil, RV hook ups, camping
Guides: No
OK to call for current conditions: No

OTAY RESERVOIR

BAIT & TACKLE...

Bobs Bait & Tackle
Chula Vista 619-420-1999
Encinitas 619-632-7051
Escondido 619-741-1570
Hemet 909-658-0208
San Diego 619-222-1261
                                  619-278-8055
San Marcos 619-736-4077
Santee 619-562-6984
Spring Valley 619-697-2160
Vista 619-774-4317
Hours: 7am-7pm
Carries: Live bait, lures, flies, maps, rods, reels, licenses
Bodies of water: Lake Hodges, San Vicente Lake, Otay Res., El Capitan Res., Lake Morena, Lake Dixon, Lake Wohlford, Sutherland, Pacific Ocean
Services & Products: Repair Services
Guides: Yes
OK to call for current conditions: Yes

Lakeside Sporting Goods
Lakeside 619-443-3859
Hours: 9am-6pm, closed Sun.
Carries: Live bait, lures, flies, maps, rods, reels, licenses
Bodies of water: Pacific Ocean, San Vicente Lake, El Capitan Res., Otay Res., Lake Hodges, Barrett Lake
Services & Products: Beverages, fishing instruction, repair services, rod building
Guides: Yes
OK to call for current conditions: Yes
Contact: Richard, Jimbo or Manny

GUIDES...

Dave Zimmerlee
San Diego 619-271-8726
Species & Seasons: LM Bass Jan-Dec
Bodies of water: Lower Otay Res., El Capitan Res., all San Diego lakes
Rates: Half day: $75(1), $100(2), Full day: $125(1), $150(2)
Call between: Anytime
Provides: Light tackle, lures, bait, rain gear, beverages, lunch
Handicapped equipped: Yes

CALIFORNIA

PACIFIC OCEAN (NORTH)

PACIFIC OCEAN (NORTH)

BAIT & TACKLE...

Coastside #2 Bait & Tackle
Pacifica 415-359-9790
Hours: 6am-5pm
Carries: Live bait, lures, rods, reels, licenses
Bodies of water: Pacific Ocean
Services & Products: Beverages, repair services
Guides: Yes
OK to call for current conditions: Yes
Contact: Vasco Fernandez

Grand Street Bait & Tackle
Alameda 510-521-2460
Hours: 7am-6pm
Carries: Live bait, lures, maps, rods, reels,
Bodies of water: Pacific Ocean, San Francisco Bay, Sacramento River, Delta, Lake Chabot, Lake Merced
Services & Products: Guide services, charter boat service, boat ramp, food, beverages, fishing instruction, repair services
Guides: Yes
OK to call for current conditions: Yes
Contact: Anyone

Lucky Bait Shop
Berkeley 510-704-8990
Hours: 7am-6pm
Carries: Live bait, lures, flies, maps, rods, reels, licenses
Bodies of water: Pacific Ocean, San Francisco Bay
Services & Products: Charter boat service, beverages, fishing instruction
Guides: Yes
OK to call for current conditions: Yes
Contact: Daniel Owyang

Sweeney's Sports
Napa 707-255-5544
Hours: 9am-6pm
Carries: Live bait, lures, flies, maps, rods, reels, licenses
Bodies of water: San Pablo Bay, Napa River, Lake Berryessa, Clear Lake, Putah Creek, Pacific Ocean
Services & Products: Fishing instruction, repair services
Guides: Yes
OK to call for current conditions: Yes
Contact: Mike

Western Boat & Tackle
San Rafael 415-454-4177
Hours: 7am-6:30pm Mon.-Fri., 6am-5:30 Sat., 6am-5:00 Sun.
Carries: Live bait, lures, flies, maps, rods, reels, licenses
Bodies of water: San Pablo Bay, Pacific Ocean, San Francisco Bay
Services & Products: Food, beverages, gas/oil, repair services
Guides: Yes
OK to call for current conditions: Yes

Wong's Bait & Tackle Shop
San Francisco 415-563-9819
Hours: 7am-5pm, closed Mon.
Carries: Live bait, lures, flies, maps, rods, reels, licenses
Bodies of water: San Francisco Bay, Pacific Ocean, San Pablo Dam Resevoir, Lake Merced
Services & Products: Food, beverages, fishing instruction, repair services
Guides: Yes
OK to call for current conditions: Yes
Contact: James

CHARTERS...

Boat House Bodega Bay New Sea Angler & Jaws
Bodega Bay 707-875-3495
.... 875-3344
Species & Seasons: Salmon March-Oct, Rock Cod, Ling Cod all year, Halibut April-Sept, Dungeness Crab, Rockfish Nov-June
Bodies of water: Pacific Ocean (Sonoma Coast)
Rates: Rock Cod: $40, Salmon: $45, Live bait Halibut: $45, Comb. Crab and Rock Cod: $50, Combination Crab, Salmon: $60
Call between: 5:30am-8pm
Provides: Light tackle, heavy tackle, lures, bait, rain gear, beverages, lunch
Handicapped equipped: Yes
Certifications: USCG

Capitola Boat & Bait
Capitola
Species & Seasons: Salmon Mar-Oct, Halibut Mar-Sept/Oct, Rock Cod, Ling Cod Feb-Nov
Bodies of water: Monterey Bay (North End)
Rates: Half day: $49(1) weekend, Full day: $59(1) weekend, Half day: $39(1) weekday, Full day: $49(1) weekday, pole rental $6.50

Provides: Heavy tackle
Handicapped equipped: Yes, limited

Caruso's Sportfishing Center
Sausalito 415-332-1015
Species & Seasons: Chinook Salmon Mar-Nov, Rockfish Jan-Dec, Halibut May-Sept, Albacore Aug-Oct
Bodies of water: Pacific Ocean (Farallon Islands), San Francisco Bay
Rates: 3/4 day: $45(1), Full day: $50(1)
Call between: 6:30am-5pm
Provides: Light tackle, heavy tackle, lures, bait, rain gear, beverages, lunch
Handicapped equipped: Yes

Huck Finn Sportfishing
El Granada 415-726-7133
Species & Seasons: Salmon Mar-Nov, Rockfish Jan-Dec
Bodies of water: Pacific Ocean (Pt. Reyes-Davenport, located at Half Moon Bay)
Rates: Salmon, Full day: $45(1), Rockfish: $29-$35pp
Call between: 5am-4pm
Handicapped equipped: Yes
Certifications: USCG

King Salmon Charters
Eureka 707-442-3474
Species & Seasons: Salmon May-Sept, Rockfish April-Oct, Crab Dec-July, Whale Watching Feb-April, Albacore Aug-Oct
Bodies of water: Pacific Ocean, Humboldt Bay
Rates: Half day $60(1), $120(2), Full day: $60 per hr. up to 6 people
Provides: Light tackle, heavy tackle, lures, bait
Handicapped equipped: Possible

Lovely Martha Sport Fishing
San Bruno 415-871-1691
Species & Seasons: Salmon Mar-Oct, Sturgeon Nov-Feb
Bodies of water: San Francisco Bay (Point Arena-Point St. George)
Rates: Full day: $48(1)
Call between: 6am-11pm
Provides: Light tackle, heavy tackle, lures, bait
Handicapped equipped: Yes, limited
Certifications: USCG

Patty-C Charter Fishing
Fort Bragg 707-964-0669
Species & Seasons: Salmon Feb-Nov, Rockfish, Ling Cod all year
Bodies of water: Pacific Ocean

PACIFIC OCEAN (NORTH - SOUTH) — CALIFORNIA

Rates: Half day: $55(1), 3/4 day: $65(1)
Call between: 7am-8pm
Provides: Light tackle, heavy tackle, lures, bait
Certifications: USCG

Queen of Hearts
Hayward 510-581-2628
Species & Seasons: Salmon Feb-Oct, Rock Cod all year, Whale watching Jan-Mar
Bodies of water: Pacific Ocean
Rates: 95 rates: Salmon $45, Rockcod: $35 Adults, $29 children and seniors
Call between: 8am-8pm
Handicapped equipped: Yes
Certifications: USCG

Santa Cruz Sportfishing, Inc.
Santa Cruz 408-426-4690
Species & Seasons: Salmon Mar-Aug, Rock Cod Jan-Dec, light tackle Rock Cod June-Dec, Albacore July-Nov? (when they show)
Bodies of water: Monterey Bay, Pacific Ocean
Rates: Full day: $30-$45(1) depends on trip
Call between: 3pm-6pm
Provides: Light tackle, heavy tackle, bait
Handicapped equipped: Yes
Certifications: USCG

LODGING...

Deer Lodge
Trinidad 707-677-3554
Guest Capacity: 250
Handicapped equipped: Yes
Seasons: All year
Rates: Cabins: $40-$105/day
Contact: Beverly Rolen
Guides: Yes
Species & Seasons: Salmon, Bottom Fish, Smelt May-Sept, Shellfish Dec-Aug, Steelhead Sept-Feb
Bodies of Water: Pacific Ocean, Klamath River, Trinity River, Eel River, VanDuzen River, Redwood Creek
Types of fishing: Light tackle, heavy tackle, ocean party boats
Available: Family activities

MARINAS...

Richmond Marina Bay
Richmond 510-236-1013
Hours: 9am-5pm
Bodies of water: San Francisco Bay, San Pablo Bay
Services & Products: Boat ramp, food, beverages, dry boat storage, free pump out and boat wash stations
Guides: Yes
OK to call for current conditions: No

PACIFIC OCEAN (SOUTH)

BAIT & TACKLE...

Angler's Arsenal
La Mesa 800-428-8730
Hours: 7am-4pm, closed Sat., Sun.
Carries: Lures, maps, rods, reels, mail order
Bodies of water: Pacific Ocean, San Vicente Lake, El Capitan Res., Lake Hodges
Guides: Yes
OK to call for current conditions: Yes
Contact: John Cassidy

Angler's Den
Camarillo......................... 805-388-1566
Hours: 10am-6pm, closed Sun., Mon.
Carries: Live bait, artificial, lures, maps, rods, reels, licenses
Bodies of water: Pacific Ocean, Cachuma Lake, Lake Casitas, Sespe River, Castaic Lake, Ventura River, Pyramid Lake, Lake Piru
Guides: Yes
OK to call for current conditions: Yes
Contact: Rick Graham

Bobs Bait & Tackle
Chula Vista...................... 619-420-1999
Encinitas 619-632-7051
Escondido....................... 619-741-1570
Hemet 909-658-0208
San Diego 619-222-1261
 619-278-8055
San Marcos 619-736-4077
Santee 619-562-6984
Spring Valley 619-697-2160
Vista 619-774-4317
Hours: 7am-7pm
Carries: Live bait, lures, flies, maps, rods, reels, licenses
Bodies of water: Lake Hodges, San Vicente Lake, Otay Res., El Capitan Res., Lake Morena, Lake Dixon,
Lake Wohlford, Sutherland, Pacific Ocean
Services & Products: Repair Services
Guides: Yes
OK to call for current conditions: Yes

Fisherman's Landing Tackle Shop
San Diego 619-221-8506
Hours: 8am-8pm
Carries: Lures, flies, maps, rods, reels, licenses
Bodies of water: Pacific Ocean
Services & Products: Charter boat service, repair services
OK to call for current conditions: Yes

Fishing Adventures Bait & Tackle
San Diego 619-487-1691
Hours: 5:30am-7:00pm
Carries: Live bait, lures, flies, maps, rods, reels, licenses
Bodies of water: Pacific Ocean, San Vicente Lake, El Capitan Res., Lake Hodges, Lake Miramar, Lake Wohlford, Lake Poway
Services & Products: Guide services, repair services
Guides: Yes
OK to call for current conditions: Yes
Contact: Eric or Chris

The Grant Boys
Costa Mesa 714-645-3400
Hours: 10-7 Mon.-Fri., 10-6 Sat., 10-5 Sun.
Carries: Live bait, lures, flies, maps, rods, reels, licenses
Bodies of water: Pacific Ocean, Irvine Lake, Santa Ana River Lakes, Laguna Niguel Lake
Services & Products: Camping equipment rentals
Guides: Yes
OK to call for current conditions: Yes
Contact: Fishing Department

Kimura's Fishing Tackle
Chino Hills....................... 909-393-0097
Hours: 9am-7pm, closed Sun.
Carries: Live bait, lures, rods, reels
Bodies of water: Prado Regional Park, Frank G. Bonelli Park, Pacific Ocean
Services & Products: Repair services, custom rod building
Guides: Yes
OK to call for current conditions: Yes
Contact: Gary

CALIFORNIA
PACIFIC OCEAN (SOUTH)

Lakeside Sporting Goods
Lakeside 619-443-3859
Hours: 9am-6pm, closed Sun.
Carries: Live bait, lures, flies, maps, rods, reels, licenses
Bodies of water: Pacific Ocean, San Vicente Lake, El Capitan Res., Otay Res., Lake Hodges, Barrett Lake
Services & Products: Beverages, fishing instruction, repair services, rod building
Guides: Yes
OK to call for current conditions: Yes
Contact: Richard, Jimbo or Manny

Mr. Chum
Redondo Beach 310-316-0641
Hours: 5am-5pm, closed Sun.
Carries: Chum and Charters
Bodies of water: Pacific Ocean
Services & Products: Guide services, food, beverages, fishing instruction
Guides: Yes
OK to call for current conditions: Yes
Contact: Scott Weldon

Pacific Edge, Inc.
Huntington Beach 714-840-4262
Hours: 8am-7pm Mon.-Fri., 6am-5pm Sat, Sun.
Carries: Live bait, lures, maps, rods, reels, licenses
Bodies of water: Pacific Ocean
Services & Products: Fishing instruction, repair services, marine supplies, clothing, ice
Guides: Yes
OK to call for current conditions: Yes
Contact: Mark

Port Side Marine
Avila Beach 805-595-7214
Hours: 5am-5pm
Carries: Live bait, lures, flies, maps
Bodies of water: Pacific Ocean, Port San Luis, Lopez Lake, Santa Margarita Res.
Services & Products: Charter boat service, food, beverages, gas/oil, repair services, RV parking, fishing report 805-595-2803
Guides: Yes
OK to call for current conditions: Yes
Contact: Anita Taylor

Pratt's Sporting Goods
Redlands 909-793-3278
Hours: 10am-7pm Mon.-Fri., 9am-6pm Sat.,10am-5pm Sun.
Carries: Live bait, lures, flies, maps, rods, reels, licenses
Bodies of water: Pacific Ocean, Lake Perris, Big Bear Lake, Silverwood Lake, Salton Sea
Guides: No
OK to call for current conditions: No

Skipper's 22nd St Landing
San Pedro 310-832-8304
Hours: 5am-10pm
Carries: Lures, licenses
Bodies of water: Pacific Ocean
Services & Products: Boat rentals, charter boat service, whale watching, diving
OK to call for current conditions: Yes
Contact: Anyone

Stroud Tackle
San Diego 619-276-4822
Hours: 11am-6pm, closed Sun.
Carries: Flies, maps, rods, reels
Bodies of water: Pacific Ocean, Lake Morena, Lake Cuyamaca
Services & Products: Fishing instruction, repair services, fly fishing products
Guides: Yes
OK to call for current conditions: Yes
Contact: Bill or Eileen Stroud

CHARTERS...

Bongos
Newport Beach 714-673-2810
Species & Seasons: Shark, Barracuda April-Nov, Yellowtail, Bonito Mar-Nov, Calico Bass Jan-Dec, Sand Bass May-Oct, Rock Cod Oct-Mar, White Sea Bass Dec-May, Marlin Aug-Oct
Bodies of water: Newport Beach, Pacific Ocean, Catalina Island, San Clemente Island
Call between: 8am-7pm
Provides: Light tackle, heavy tackle, lures, bait
Handicapped equipped: Yes
Certifications: USCG

Catalina Island Charter Boat
Avalon 800-296-MAKO
.... 310-510-2720
Species & Seasons: Marlin July-Oct, Sea Bass April-June, Yellowtail June-Sept, Calico Bass, Kelp Bass all year, Halibut Jan-June, Tuna Aug-Oct
Bodies of water: Pacific Ocean, Catalina Island
Call between: 9am-9pm
Provides: Light tackle, heavy tackle, lures, bait, rain gear, beverages, lunch
Handicapped equipped: Yes
Certifications: USCG

Charter Connection
Marina Del Rey 310-827-4105
Species & Seasons: Calico Bass, Sand Bass, Bonito, Barracuda, Halibut, Shark
Bodies of water: Santa Monica Bay
Rates: Varies
Call between: 9am-5pm
Provides: Light tackle, heavy tackle, lures, bait, beverages, lunch
Handicapped equipped: Yes
Certifications: USCG

Dana Wharf Sportfishing
Dana Point 714-496-5794
Species & Seasons: Calico Bass, Sand Bass, Rockfish Dec-Dec, Barracuda May-Aug, Yellowtail, Bonito June-Oct, White Sea Bass April-July, Yellowfin Tuna, Albacore July-Oct, Shark Mar-Oct
Bodies of water: Pacific Ocean, (Point Conception to Cabo San Lucas)
Rates: Half day:: $22(1-2), Full day: $32(1-2), overnight trips starting at $65
Call between: 5am-10pm
Provides: Light tackle, heavy tackle, lures, bait, rain gear, beverages, lunch
Handicapped equipped: Yes
Certifications: USCG

Islandia Sportfishing Ltd.
San Diego 619-222-1164
Species & Seasons: Barracuda Feb-Oct, Sea Bass May-Nov, Boota, Yellowtail June-Sept, Rock Cod Jan-April, Mackerel May-Oct, Albacore June-Oct, Yellowfin Tuna July-Oct
Bodies of water: Pacific Ocean (Southern California, Mexico)
Rates: Half day: $22(1), Full day: $45(1)
Call between: 5am-6pm
Provides: Light tackle, heavy tackle, lures, bait, rain gear, beverages, lunch
Handicapped equipped: Yes
Certifications: USCG

Ronald Kovach
Huntington Beach 714-840-6555
Species & Seasons: Ling Cod, Shallow Water Rockfish Nov-May, Halibut Mar-June, Calico Bass Mar-Oct, Sand Bass May-Sept, Barracuda, Yellowtail Mar-Dec
Bodies of water: Pacific Ocean: San Miguel Island, Santa Rosa Island, Catalina Island, San Nicholas Island, Coronados Islands, San Martin Island, Outer Tuna Banks, Cortez Bank, Horseshoe Kelp, Huntington Flats
Rates: Eagle Claw Fishing School Rates: 1-3 Days $99-$499
Call between: 8am-5pm

PACIFIC OCEAN (SOUTH) - PARDEE RESERVOIR — CALIFORNIA

Provides: Light tackle, heavy tackle, lures, bait
Handicapped equipped: No

Performance Yacht Charters
Newport Beach 714-673-2274
Species & Seasons: Marlin Jan-Dec
Bodies of water: Pacific Ocean (Southern California, Cabo San Lucas, Mexico)
Rates: Negotiable
Call between: 9am-6pm
Provides: Light tackle, heavy tackle, fly rod/reel, lures, bait, rain gear, beverages, lunch
Handicapped equipped: Yes

Qualifier 105 Sportfishing
San Diego 619-223-2786
Species & Seasons: Yellowfin Tuna Jan-Dec, Wahoo Sept-June, Dolphin, Yellowtail June-Dec, Marlin Sept-Nov, Albacore, Bluefin Tuna July-Sept
Bodies of water: Pacific Ocean, Revilla Gegidos Islands
Rates: Full day: $150-$250(1), includes gourmet meals
Call between: 10am-5am
Provides: Bait, lunch
Handicapped equipped: No

Sundiver Charters
Long Beach 310-493-0951
Species & Seasons: White Sea Bass, Halibut Feb-June, Yellowtail, Marlin, Tuna July-Nov, Kelp Bass Jan-Dec
Bodies of water: Pacific Ocean, Channel Islands
Rates: Charter only $500 - $2000
Call between: 9am-3pm
Provides: Beverages, lunch
Handicapped equipped: Yes
Certifications: USCG

Virg's Landing
Morro Bay 800-ROCKCOD
.... 800-762-5263
Species & Seasons: Rock Cod, Ling Cod all year, Salmon Mar-Nov, Halibut May-Nov, Albacore Aug-Dec, Whale watching Dec-May
Bodies of water: Pacific Ocean (Central coast)
Rates: Half day: $25(1), $50(2), Full day: $35(1), $70(2)
Call between: 6am-7pm
Provides: Light tackle, heavy tackle, lures, bait, rain gear, beverages, lunch
Handicapped equipped: Yes
Certifications: USCG

LODGING...

Bahia Hotel
998 W. Mission Bay Drive
San Diego 92109
Bodies of water: Misson Bay, Pacific Ocean, San Diego Bay
Services & Products: Boat rentals, lodging, food, beverages
Guides: Yes
OK to call for current conditions: No

MARINAS...

Kona Marina
San Diego 800-955-7547
Hours: 8am-5:00pm
Bodies of water: San Diego Bay, Pacific Ocean, Coronado Islands
Services & Products: Lodging, boat ramp, food, beverages, gas/oil, repair services
Guides: Yes
OK to call for current conditions: No

Marina Kona Kai
San Diego 619-224-7547
Hours: 8:30am-5pm
Bodies of water: Pacific Ocean, San Diego Bay
Services & Products: Lodging, boat ramp, food, beverages, gas/oil
Guides: Yes
OK to call for current conditions: ?
Contact: Jim Nicoletti

Seaforth Boat Rentals
San Diego 619-223-1681
Hours: 8am-6pm
Carries: Live bait, lures, rods, reels, licenses
Bodies of water: Mission Bay, Pacific Ocean, San Diego Bay
Services & Products: Boat rentals, charter boat service, boat ramp, food, beverages, fishing instruction
Guides: Yes
OK to call for current conditions: No

Shelter Cove Marina
San Diego 619-224-2471
Hours: 9am-5pm
Bodies of water: Pacific Ocean
Services & Products: Boat rentals, charter boat service, food, beverages
Guides: Yes
OK to call for current conditions: Yes
Contact: Shaun McMahon

Sunroad Resort Marina
San Diego 800-350-0736
.... 619-594-0736
Hours: 8am-5pm
Carries: Maps
Bodies of water: Pacific Ocean, San Diego Bay, Mission Bay
Services & Products: Boat rentals, charter boat service, food, beverages
Guides: Yes
OK to call for current conditions: Yes
Contact: Scott MacLaggam

Sunset Aquatic Marina
Huntington Beach 310-592-2833
Hours: 8am-5pm
Bodies of water: Huntington Harbor (Anaheim Bay), Pacific Ocean
Services & Products: Boat ramp, slips (wet and dry)
Guides: Yes
OK to call for current conditions: Yes
Contact: Larry Schwartz

PARDEE RESERVOIR

BAIT & TACKLE...

Fisherman's Friend
Lodi 209-369-0204
Hours: 5am-5:30pm
Carries: Live bait, lures, flies, maps, rods, reels, licenses
Bodies of water: Camanche Res., Pardee Res., Lake Amador, New Melones Lake, San Joaquin River, Sacramento River, Delta
Services & Products: Guide services
Guides: Yes
OK to call for current conditions: Yes
Contact: Russ or Rick

MARINAS...

New Hogan Marina
Valley Springs 209-772-1462
Hours: 7am-Dark
Carries: Live bait, lures, flies, maps, rods, reels, licenses
Bodies of water: Lake Amador, Camanche Res., Pardee Res., New Melones Lake
Services & Products: Boat rentals, boat ramp, food, beverages, gas/oil, repair services
Guides: yes
OK to call for current conditions: Yes

YOUR SILENT FISHING PARTNER

CALIFORNIA

PYRAMID LAKE - SAN VICENTE LAKE

PYRAMID LAKE

BAIT & TACKLE...

Angler's Den
Camarillo.................... 805-388-1566
Hours: 10am-6pm, closed Sun., Mon.
Carries: Live bait, artificial, lures, maps, rods, reels, licenses
Bodies of water: Pacific Ocean, Cachuma Lake, Lake Casitas, Sespe River, Castaic Lake, Ventura River, Pyramid Lake, Lake Piru
Guides: Yes
OK to call for current conditions: Yes
Contact: Rick Graham

SALTON SEA

BAIT & TACKLE...

Pratt's Sporting Goods
Redlands 909-793-3278
Hours: 10am-7pm Mon.-Fri., 9am-6pm Sat.,10am-5pm Sun.
Carries: Live bait, lures, flies, maps, rods, reels, licenses
Bodies of water: Pacific Ocean, Lake Perris, Big Bear Lake, Silverwood Lake, Salton Sea
Guides: No
OK to call for current conditions: No

CHARTERS...

Kaitlins Charter Fishing
Salton City 619-394-4175
Species & Seasons: Corvina, Tilapia April-Dec
Bodies of water: Salton Sea
Rates: Half day: $80(1), $100(2) Full day: $120(1), $140(2), up to eight $250
Call between: 7am-7pm
Provides: Light tackle, heavy tackle, lures, bait, beverages
Handicapped equipped: No
Certifications: USCG

SAN PABLO BAY

BAIT & TACKLE...

Sweeney's Sports
Napa 707-255-5544
Hours: 9am-6pm
Carries: Live bait, lures, flies, maps, rods, reels, licenses
Bodies of water: San Pablo Bay, Napa River, Lake Berryessa, Clear Lake, Putah Creek, Pacific Ocean
Services & Products: Fishing instruction, repair services
Guides: Yes
OK to call for current conditions: Yes
Contact: Mike

Western Boat & Tackle
San Rafael 415-454-4177
Hours: 7am-6:30pm Mon.-Fri., 6am-5:30 Sat., 6am-5:00 Sun.
Carries: Live bait, lures, flies, maps, rods, reels, licenses
Bodies of water: San Pablo Bay, Pacific Ocean, San Francisco Bay
Services & Products: Food, beverages, gas/oil, repair services
Guides: Yes
OK to call for current conditions: Yes

MARINAS...

Richmond Marina Bay
Richmond 510-236-1013
Hours: 9am-5pm
Bodies of water: San Francisco Bay, San Pablo Bay
Services & Products: Boat ramp, food, beverages, dry boat storage, free pump out and boat wash stations
Guides: Yes
OK to call for current conditions: No

SAN VICENTE LAKE

BAIT & TACKLE...

Angler's Arsenal
La Mesa 800-428-8730
Hours: 7am-4pm, closed Sat., Sun.
Carries: Lures, maps, rods, reels, mail order
Bodies of water: Pacific Ocean, San Vicente Lake, El Capitan Res., Lake Hodges
Guides: Yes
OK to call for current conditions: Yes
Contact: John Cassidy

Bobs Bait & Tackle
Chula Vista 619-420-1999
Encinitas 619-632-7051
Escondido 619-741-1570
Hemet 909-658-0208
San Diego 619-222-1261
                                619-278-8055
San Marcos 619-736-4077
Santee 619-562-6984
Spring Valley 619-697-2160
Vista 619-774-4317
Hours: 7am-7pm
Carries: Live bait, lures, flies, maps, rods, reels, licenses
Bodies of water: Lake Hodges, San Vicente Lake, Otay Res., El Capitan Res., Lake Morena, Lake Dixon, Lake Wohlford, Sutherland, Pacific Ocean
Services & Products: Repair Services
Guides: Yes
OK to call for current conditions: Yes

Fishing Adventures Bait & Tackle
San Diego 619-487-1691
Hours: 5:30am-7:00pm
Carries: Live bait, lures, flies, maps, rods, reels, licenses
Bodies of water: Pacific Ocean, San Vicente Lake, El Capitan Res., Lake Hodges, Lake Miramar, Lake Wohlford, Lake Poway
Services & Products: Guide services, repair services
Guides: Yes
OK to call for current conditions: Yes
Contact: Eric or Chris

Lakeside Sporting Goods
Lakeside 619-443-3859
Hours: 9am-6pm, closed Sun.
Carries: Live bait, lures, flies, maps, rods, reels, licenses
Bodies of water: Pacific Ocean, San Vicente Lake, El Capitan Res., Otay Res., Lake Hodges, Barrett Lake
Services & Products: Beverages, fishing instruction, repair services, rod building
Guides: Yes
OK to call for current conditions: Yes
Contact: Richard, Jimbo or Manny

SANTA MARGARITA RESERVOIR - SILTCOOS LAKE — CALIFORNIA

SANTA MARGARITA RESERVOIR

BAIT & TACKLE...

Port Side Marine
Avila Beach 805-595-7214
Hours: 5am-5pm
Carries: Live bait, lures, flies, maps
Bodies of water: Pacific Ocean, Port San Luis, Lopez Lake, Santa Margarita Res.
Services & Products: Charter boat service, food, beverages, gas/oil, repair services, RV parking, fishing report 805-595-2803
Guides: Yes
OK to call for current conditions: Yes
Contact: Anita Taylor

SHASTA LAKE

BAIT & TACKLE...

Hook Line & Sinker
Oakley 510-625-2441
Hours: 6am-7pm
Carries: Live bait, lures, maps, rods, reels, licenses
Bodies of water: California Delta, Clear Lake, Shasta Lake, Lake Oroville, Folsom Lake, Don Pedro Res., Camanche Res.
Services & Products: Guide services, boat ramp, food, beverages, repair services
Guides: Yes
OK to call for current conditions: Yes
Contact: Gene Buchholz

Shasta Angler
Fall River Mills 916-336-6600
Hours: 9am-5pm
Carries: Lures, flies, maps, rods, reels, licenses
Bodies of water: Fall River, Hat Creek, Pit River, Shasta Lake, McCloud River
Services & Products: Guide services, gas/oil, fishing instruction, repair services
Guides: Yes
OK to call for current conditions: Yes
Contact: Matt Nicholls

Shearms Market
Summit City 916-275-2411
Hours: 5:30am-8pm
Carries: Live bait, lures, licenses
Bodies of water: Shasta Lake, Wiskeytown Lake, Trinity Lake
Services & Products: Boat ramp, food, beverages, fishing instruction
Guides: Yes
OK to call for current conditions: Yes
Contact: Shearm

GUIDES...

Fish Tales Guide Service
Hayfork 916-628-5176
Species & Seasons: Chinook Salmon July-Dec, Steelhead Oct-April, Trout April-Nov, American Shad June-Aug, SM Bass, LM Bass Mar-July
Bodies of water: Sacramento River, Klamath River, Trinity River, Eel River, Smith River, Shasta Lake, Oregon waters: Chetco River, Rogue River
Rates: Full day: $175(1), $250(2), $300(3), $400(4)
Call between: 6am-11pm
Provides: Light tackle, lures, bait
Certifications: USCG, CPR, First aid

MARINAS...

Lakeview Marina Resort Dock
Redding 916-238-2442
Hours: 8:30am-5pm
Carries: Live bait, lures, maps, rods, reels
Bodies of water: Shasta Lake
Services & Products: Boat rentals, food, beverages, gas/oil
Guides: No
OK to call for current conditions: No

Pine Cove Marina
Lewiston 916-778-3770
Hours: 7am-7pm
Carries: Live bait, lures, flies, maps, reels
Bodies of water: Shasta Lake, Clair Engle Lake, Sacramento River, Trinity River, Lewiston Lake
Services & Products: Boat rentals, beverages, gas/oil, fishing instruction, repair services
Guides: Yes
OK to call for current conditions: Yes
Contact: Bret

SIERRA NATIONAL FOREST AREA

BAIT & TACKLE...

King's River Bait House
Sanger 209-787-2318
Hours: 5am-7pm
Carries: Live bait, lures, flies, maps, rods, reels, licenses
Bodies of water: Pine Flat Lake, Avacado Lake, Kings River
Services & Products: Food, beverages, gas/oil, fishing instruction
Guides: No
OK to call for current conditions: Yes

Shaver Lake Sports & Fishing
Shaver Lake 209-841-2740
Hours: 7am-6pm
Carries: Live bait, lures, flies, maps, rods, reels, licenses
Bodies of water: Shaver Lake, Courtright Res., Edison Lake, Florence Lake, Huntington Lake, Wishon Lake
Services & Products: Boat rentals, boat ramp, food, beverages, gas/oil, repair services
Guides: Yes
OK to call for current conditions: Yes
Contact: Dave, Mike, Bob or Ernie

SILTCOOS LAKE

LODGING...

Ada Fishing Resorts
Bakersfield 805-665-0997
Guest Capacity: 62 spaces
Handicapped equipped: No
Seasons: April to Nov
Rates: $14/day
Contact: Tony Warren
Guides: Yes
Species & Seasons: LM Bass, Bluegill, Crappie, Sturgeon, Catfish, Perch April-Oct, Rainbow Trout Mar-Nov, Salmon Oct-Dec
Bodies of Water: Siltcoos Lake
Types of fishing: Fly fishing, light tackle, heavy tackle

CALIFORNIA
SILVERWOOD LAKE - WHISKEYTOWN LAKE

SILVERWOOD LAKE

BAIT & TACKLE...

Pratt's Sporting Goods
Redlands 909-793-3278
Hours: 10am-7pm Mon.-Fri.,
9am-6pm Sat., 10am-5pm Sun.
Carries: Live bait, lures, flies, maps, rods, reels, licenses
Bodies of water: Pacific Ocean, Lake Perris, Big Bear Lake, Silverwood Lake, Salton Sea
Guides: No
OK to call for current conditions: No

SUISON BAY

BAIT & TACKLE

Tackle Shop
Benicia 707-745-4921
Hours: 6am-6pm
Carries: Live bait, lures, maps, rods, reels, licenses
Bodies of water: Carquinez Strait, Suison Bay
Services & Products: Food, beverages, fishing instruction, repair services
Guides: Yes
OK to call for current conditions: Yes
Contact: Harris or Diane Cole

WHISKEYTOWN LAKE

BAIT & TACKLE...

Shearms Market
Summit City 916-275-2411
Hours: 5:30am-8pm
Carries: Live bait, lures, licenses
Bodies of water: Shasta Lake, Wiskeytown Lake, Trinity Lake
Services & Products: Boat ramp, food, beverages, fishing instruction
Guides: Yes
OK to call for current conditions: Yes
Contact: Shearm

COLORADO

1. Arkansas River
2. Barr Lake
3. Big Thompson River
4. Blue River
5. Chatfield Reservoir
6. Colorado River
7. Crystal River
8. Elevenmile Canyon Reservoir
9. Fryingpan River
10. Horsetooth Reservoir
11. Pueblo Reservoir
12. Roaring Fork River
13. South Platte River
14. Southwestern Colorado Region
15. Spinney Mountain Reservoir
16. Standley Lake

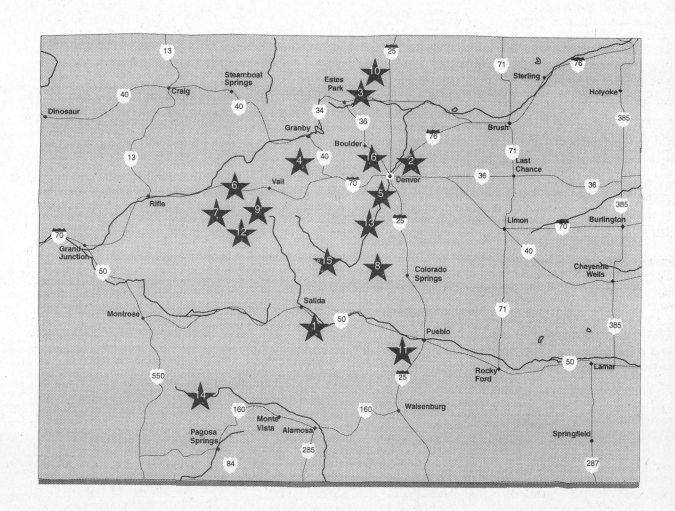

COLORADO

ARKANSAS RIVER - COLORADO RIVER

ARKANSAS RIVER

BAIT & TACKLE...

Angler's Choice
Pueblo 719-564-2671
Hours: Fisherman's Hours
Carries: Live bait, lures, flies, maps, rods, reels
Bodies of water: Pueblo Res., Arkansas River, many others
Services & Products: Boat, RV storage
Guides: Yes
OK to call for current conditions: Yes
Contact: Louis, Rosann or Bernadette

Xie's Fly Fishing Specialties
Pueblo 719-545-9540
Hours: 9am-5:30pm, closed Sun.
Carries: Flies, maps, rods, reels
Bodies of water: Arkansas River, South Platte River, Pueblo Res., Horseshoe Res., Elevenmile Canyon Res., Spinney Mountain Res.
Services & Products: Guide services, food, beverages, fishing instruction, fly tying lessons
OK to call for current conditions: Yes
Contact: Xavier Duran

LODGING...

Triple J Trout Ranch
Salida 719-539-3094
Guest Capacity: 20+
Handicapped equipped: Yes
Seasons: May to Mid Sept
Contact: Julia
Guides: Yes
Species & Seasons: Rainbow Trout, Brook Trout, Brown Trout May-Sept
Bodies of Water: Arkansas River
Types of fishing: Fly fishing, light tackle
Available: Fishing instruction, bait, tackle

BARR LAKE

BAIT & TACKLE...

Huron Bait & Tackle
Thornton 303-289-2317
Hours: 8am-6pm
Carries: Live bait, lures, flies, maps, rods, reels, licenses
Bodies of water: Standley Lake, Barbour Ponds, Barr Lake, Chatfield Res.
Services & Products: Belly boat rentals
Guides: No
OK to call for current conditions: Yes
Contact: Hank or Ann

BIG THOMPSON RIVER

BAIT & TACKLE...

Family Sports Center
1310 E Eisenhower Boulevard
Loveland 80537
Hours: 7am-7pm
Carries: Live bait, lures, flies, maps, rods, reels, licenses
Bodies of water: Boyd Lake, Big Thompson River, Horsetooth Res., Simpson Ponds, Lon Hagler Res.
Services & Products: Food, beverages, fishing instruction
Guides: Yes
OK to call for current conditions: Yes
Contact: Dave Plyter or Jim Ambrose

BLUE RIVER

GUIDES...

Fly Fishing Outfitters Inc.
Vail 970-476-3474
Species & Seasons: Trout all year
Bodies of water: Blue River, Colorado River, Eagle River, Roaring Fork River, various local lakes
Rates: Half day: $125(1), $175(2), Full day: $175(1), $225(2), Float trips: $250
Call between: 8am-8pm
Provides: fly rod/reel, lunch, float trips, rentals
Handicapped equipped: Yes
Certifications: Orvis Full Dealer

LODGING...

Elktrout Lodge
Kremmling 970-724-3343
Handicapped equipped: Yes
Seasons: May 15 to Oct 1
Rates: $450/day
Contact: Greg Cecil
Guides: Yes
Species & Seasons: Trout May-Oct
Bodies of Water: Colorado River, Blue River, ranch ponds
Types of fishing: Fly fishing, wading
Available: Fishing instruction, licenses, bait, tackle, fly fishing schools

CHATFIELD RESERVOIR

BAIT & TACKLE...

Huron Bait & Tackle
Thornton 303-289-2317
Hours: 8am-6pm
Carries: Live bait, lures, flies, maps, rods, reels, licenses
Bodies of water: Standley Lake, Barbour Ponds, Barr Lake, Chatfield Res.
Services & Products: Belly boat rentals
Guides: No
OK to call for current conditions: Yes
Contact: Hank or Ann

Uncle Milty's Tackle Box
Englewood 303-789-3775
Hours: 8am-6pm
Carries: Live bait, lures, flies, maps, rods, reels, licenses
Bodies of water: Chatfield Res., Cherry Creek Lake, South Platte River, Elevenmile Canyon Res., Spinney Mountain Res.
Services & Products: Fishing instruction, repair services
Guides: Yes
OK to call for current conditions: Yes
Contact: Milt or Ray

COLORADO RIVER

GUIDES...

Colorado Fishing Guides
Avon 970-328-5267
.... 800-461-5267
Species & Seasons: Brown Trout, Rainbow Trout, Cutthroat Trout, Brook Trout Mar-Dec
Bodies of water: Eagle River, Colorado River, Roaring Fork River, Fly Fishing School at Black Mnt. Ranch
Rates: Half day: $120(1), $150(2), Full day: $160(1), $200(2), Float trips: Half day: $190, Full day: $240, Roaring Fork River: $280
Call between: 5pm-10pm
Provides: fly rod/reel, beverages, lunch
Handicapped equipped: Yes

Fly Fishing Outfitters Inc.
Vail 970-476-3474
Species & Seasons: Trout all year
Bodies of water: Blue River, Colorado River, Eagle River, Roaring Fork River, various local lakes

COLORADO RIVER - PUEBLO RESERVOIR　　COLORADO

Rates: Half day: $125(1), $175(2),
Full day: $175(1), $225(2),
Float trips: $250
Call between: 8am-8pm
Provides: fly rod/reel, lunch,
float trips, rentals
Handicapped equipped: Yes
Certifications: Orvis Full Dealer

Roaring Fork Anglers
Glenwood Springs 970-945-0180
Species & Seasons: Trout all year,
Best times: Mar/April, July-Oct
Bodies of water: Roaring Fork River,
Fryingpan River, Colorado River,
Crystal River, private ponds
Rates: Float trip Half day: $200,
Full day: $275, Wade Half day: $125(1),
$175(2), Full day: $200(1), $225(2)
Call between: 8:30am-5:30pm
Provides: fly rod/reel, rain gear,
beverages, lunch
Handicapped equipped: Yes

LODGING...

Elktrout Lodge
Kremmling 970-724-3343
Guest Capacity:
Handicapped equipped: Yes
Seasons: May 15 to Oct 1
Rates: $450/day
Contact: Greg Cecil
Guides: Yes
Species & Seasons: Trout May-Oct
Bodies of Water: Colorado River,
Blue River, ranch ponds
Types of fishing: Fly fishing, wading
Available: Fishing instruction, licenses,
bait, tackle, fly fishing schools

CRYSTAL RIVER

GUIDES...

Aspen Trout Guides & Outfitters
Aspen 970-920-1050
Species & Seasons: Trout all year
Bodies of water: Roaring Fork River,
Fryingpan River, Maroon Creek,
Castle Creek, Crystal River
Rates: Half day: $155(1), $195(2),
Full day: $180(1), $235(2), Float trips:
Half day: $250, Full day: $300
Call between: 9am-5pm
Provides: Light tackle, fly rod/reel,
rain gear, beverages, lunch
Handicapped equipped: Yes

Roaring Fork Anglers
Glenwood Springs 970-945-0180
Species & Seasons: Trout all year,
Best times: Mar/April, July-Oct
Bodies of water: Roaring Fork River,
Fryingpan River, Colorado River,
Crystal River, private ponds
Rates: Float trip Half day: $200,
Full day: $275, Wade Half day: $125(1),
$175(2), Full day: $200(1), $225(2)
Call between: 8:30am-5:30pm
Provides: fly rod/reel, rain gear,
beverages, lunch
Handicapped equipped: Yes

ELEVENMILE CANYON RESERVOIR

BAIT & TACKLE...

Uncle Milty's Tackle Box
Englewood 303-789-3775
Hours: 8am-6pm
Carries: Live bait, lures, flies, maps, rods,
reels, licenses
Bodies of water: Chatfield Res.,
Cherry Creek Lake, South Platte River,
Elevenmile Canyon Res.,
Spinney Mountain Res.
Services & Products: Fishing instruction,
repair services
Guides: Yes
OK to call for current conditions: Yes
Contact: Milt or Ray

Xie's Fly Fishing Specialties
Pueblo 719-545-9540
Hours: 9am-5:30pm, closed Sun.
Carries: Flies, maps, rods, reels
Bodies of water: Arkansas River,
South Platte River, Pueblo Res.,
Horseshoe Res., Elevenmile Canyon
Res., Spinney Mountain Res.
Services & Products: Guide services,
food, beverages, fishing instruction,
fly tying lessons
OK to call for current conditions: Yes
Contact: Xavier Duran

FRYINGPAN RIVER

GUIDES...

Aspen Trout Guides & Outfitters
Aspen 970-920-1050
Species & Seasons: Trout all year

Bodies of water: Roaring Fork River,
Fryingpan River, Maroon Creek,
Castle Creek, Crystal River
Rates: Half day: $155(1), $195(2),
Full day: $180(1), $235(2), Float trips:
Half day: $250, Full day: $300
Call between: 9am-5pm
Provides: Light tackle, fly rod/reel,
rain gear, beverages, lunch
Handicapped equipped: Yes

Roaring Fork Anglers
Glenwood Springs 970-945-0180
Species & Seasons: Trout all year,
Best times: Mar/April, July-Oct
Bodies of water: Roaring Fork River,
Fryingpan River, Colorado River,
Crystal River, private ponds
Rates: Float trip Half day: $200,
Full day: $275, Wade Half day: $125(1),
$175(2), Full day: $200(1), $225(2)
Call between: 8:30am-5:30pm
Provides: fly rod/reel, rain gear,
beverages, lunch
Handicapped equipped: Yes

HORSETOOTH RESERVOIR

BAIT & TACKLE...

Family Sports Center
Loveland
Hours: 7am-7pm
Carries: Live bait, lures, flies, maps, rods,
reels, licenses
Bodies of water: Boyd Lake,
Big Thompson River, Horsetooth Res.,
Simpson Ponds, Lon Hagler Res.
Services & Products: Food, beverages,
fishing instruction
Guides: Yes
OK to call for current conditions: Yes
Contact: Dave Plyter or Jim Ambrose

PUEBLO RESERVOIR

BAIT & TACKLE...

Angler's Choice
Pueblo 719-564-2671
Hours: Fisherman's Hours
Carries: Live bait, lures, flies, maps,
rods, reels
Bodies of water: Pueblo Res.,
Arkansas River, many others
Services & Products: Boat, RV storage
Guides: Yes
OK to call for current conditions: Yes
Contact: Louis, Rosann or Bernadette

COLORADO
PUEBLO RESERVOIR - SOUTHWESTERN COLORADO

Xie's Fly Fishing Specialties
Pueblo 719-545-9540
Hours: 9am-5:30pm, closed Sun.
Carries: Flies, maps, rods, reels
Bodies of water: Arkansas River, South Platte River, Pueblo Res., Horseshoe Res., Elevenmile Canyon Res., Spinney Mountain Res.
Services & Products: Guide services, food, beverages, fishing instruction, fly tying lessons
OK to call for current conditions: Yes
Contact: Xavier Duran

ROARING FORK RIVER

GUIDES...

Aspen Trout Guides & Outfitters
Aspen 970-920-1050
Species & Seasons: Trout all year
Bodies of water: Roaring Fork River, Fryingpan River, Maroon Creek, Castle Creek, Crystal River
Rates: Half day: $155(1), $195(2), Full day: $180(1), $235(2), Float trips: Half day: $250, Full day: $300
Call between: 9am-5pm
Provides: Light tackle, fly rod/reel, rain gear, beverages, lunch
Handicapped equipped: Yes

Colorado Fishing Guides
Avon 970-328-5267
.... 800-461-5267
Species & Seasons: Brown Trout, Rainbow Trout, Cutthroat Trout, Brook Trout Mar-Dec
Bodies of water: Eagle River, Colorado River, Roaring Fork River, Fly Fishing School at Black Mnt. Ranch
Rates: Half day: $120(1), $150(2), Full day: $160(1), $200(2), Float trips: Half day: $190, Full day: $240, Roaring Fork River: $280
Call between: 5pm-10pm
Provides: fly rod/reel, beverages, lunch
Handicapped equipped: Yes

Fly Fishing Outfitters Inc.
Vail 970-476-3474
Species & Seasons: Trout all year
Bodies of water: Blue River, Colorado River, Eagle River, Roaring Fork River, various local lakes
Rates: Half day: $125(1), $175(2), Full day: $175(1), $225(2), Float trips: $250

Call between: 8am-8pm
Provides: fly rod/reel, lunch, float trips, rentals
Handicapped equipped: Yes
Certifications: Orvis Full Dealer

Roaring Fork Anglers
Glenwood Springs 970-945-0180
Species & Seasons: Trout all year, Best times: Mar/April, July-Oct
Bodies of water: Roaring Fork River, Fryingpan River, Colorado River, Crystal River, private ponds
Rates: Float trip Half day: $200, Full day: $275, Wade Half day: $125(1), $175(2), Full day: $200(1), $225(2)
Call between: 8:30am-5:30pm
Provides: fly rod/reel, rain gear, beverages, lunch
Handicapped equipped: Yes

The Troutfitters
Carbondale 970-963-0696
Species & Seasons: Brown Trout, Rainbow Trout all year, Cutthroat Trout July-Sept, Brook Trout June-Oct
Bodies of water: Roaring Fork River, high country lakes
Rates: Half day: $150(1), $185(2), Full day: $200(1), $250(2)
Call between:
Provides: Light tackle, fly rod/reel, rain gear, lunch, waders, shoes
Handicapped equipped: Yes

SOUTH PLATTE RIVER

BAIT & TACKLE...

Alpine Angler
Aurora 800-694-1020
Hours: 8am-7pm
Carries: Live bait, lures, flies, maps, rods, reels, licenses
Bodies of water: South Platte River, other bodies of water
Services & Products: Equipment rentals
Guides: Yes
OK to call for current conditions: Yes
Contact: Ed, George or Derek

Uncle Milty's Tackle Box
Englewood 303-789-3775
Hours: 8am-6pm
Carries: Live bait, lures, flies, maps, rods, reels, licenses
Bodies of water: Chatfield Res., Cherry Creek Lake, South Platte River, Elevenmile Canyon Res., Spinney Mountain Res.

Services & Products: Fishing instruction, repair services
Guides: Yes
OK to call for current conditions: Yes
Contact: Milt or Ray

Xie's Fly Fishing Specialties
Pueblo 719-545-9540
Hours: 9am-5:30pm, closed Sun.
Carries: Flies, maps, rods, reels
Bodies of water: Arkansas River, South Platte River, Pueblo Res., Horseshoe Res., Elevenmile Canyon Res., Spinney Mountain Res.
Services & Products: Guide services, food, beverages, fishing instruction, fly tying lessons
OK to call for current conditions: Yes
Contact: Xavier Duran

LODGING...

North Fork Guest Ranch
Shawnee 303-838-9873
.... 800-843-7895
Guest Capacity: 40
Handicapped equipped: Yes
Seasons: May 27 to Sept 16
Rates: $995-$1195/pp week, $170/pp day (3 day mininmum)
Contact: Karen May
Guides: Yes
Species & Seasons: Rainbow Trout May-Sept
Bodies of Water: North Fork of South Platte River, Cheeseman Canyon
Types of fishing: Fly fishing, light tackle
Available: Fishing instruction, bait, tackle, family activities, children's program, baby sitting, horseback riding, white water rafting

SOUTHWESTERN COLORADO REGION

BAIT & TACKLE...

Outfitter Sporting Goods
Dolores 970-882-7740
Hours: 7am-7pm
Carries: Live bait, lures, flies, maps, rods, reels, licenses
Bodies of water: Dolores River, McPhee Res.
Services & Products: Guide services, food, beverages, gas/oil, fishing instruction

SOUTHWESTERN COLORADO - STANDLEY LAKE — COLORADO

OK to call for current conditions: Yes
Contact: Bill Jones or Brooks Bennet

GUIDES...

Anderson's Guide Service
Del Norte 719-754-3376
Species & Seasons: Brook Trout, Brown Trout, Cutthroat Trout, Rainbow Trout July-Oct
Bodies of water: San Juan Mountains, La Garita, Weminuche Wilderness areas, Rio Grande Nat'l. Forest, Alpine lakes and streams, all trips via horseback
Rates: Five days, 4 nights: $995 pp
Call between: 6pm-10pm
Provides: all meals
Handicapped equipped: No

Backcountry Outfitters Inc.
Pagosa Springs 800-898-2006
.... 970-731-4630
Species & Seasons: Brown Trout May-June, Rainbow Trout, Kokanee Salmon May-Aug, Northern Pike July-Aug
Bodies of water: Navajo Res.
Rates: Full day: $240(2), $240(3), $240(4)
Call between: 7am-9pm
Provides: Light tackle, heavy tackle, lures
Handicapped equipped: Yes
Certifications: USCG

Bill Roesch
Del Norte 719-657-3117
Species & Seasons: Trout June-Oct
Bodies of water: Rio Grande River, many mountain streams in Del Norte area
Rates: Full day: $95(1), $175(2)
Call between: 9am-7pm
Provides: lunch
Handicapped equipped: Yes

LODGING...

Rivers Edge Trophy Trout Ranch
South Fork 719-873-5993
Guest Capacity: 75 RV Sites, full hook-up
Handicapped equipped: No
Seasons: May to Sept
Rates: $16/day, $95/week
Guides: Yes
Species & Seasons: Trout all year
Bodies of Water: Rio Grande River, other waters
Types of fishing: Fly fishing, wading
Available: Bait, tackle, family activities

Wetherill Ranch
Creede 719-658-2253
Guest Capacity: 60
Handicapped equipped: Yes
Seasons: May 15 to Nov 15
Rates: $42-$74/day
Guides: Yes
Species & Seasons: Rainbow Trout, Brook Trout, Brown Trout, Cutthroat Trout, May-Oct
Bodies of Water: Rio Grande River, Rio Grande Res., Ruby Lake, many creeks
Types of fishing: Fly fishing, light tackle, horse/back pack, wading, fly-out trips, float trips
Available: Fishing instruction, bait, tackle, family activities, children's program

SPINNEY MOUNTAIN RESERVOIR

BAIT & TACKLE...

Uncle Milty's Tackle Box
Englewood 303-789-3775
Hours: 8am-6pm
Carries: Live bait, lures, flies, maps, rods, reels, licenses
Bodies of water: Chatfield Res., Cherry Creek Lake, South Platte River, Elevenmile Canyon Res., Spinney Mountain Res.
Services & Products: Fishing instruction, repair services
Guides: Yes
OK to call for current conditions: Yes
Contact: Milt or Ray

Xie's Fly Fishing Specialties
Pueblo 719-545-9540
Hours: 9am-5:30pm, closed Sun.
Carries: Flies, maps, rods, reels
Bodies of water: Arkansas River, South Platte River, Pueblo Res., Horseshoe Res., Elevenmile Canyon Res., Spinney Mountain Res.
Services & Products: Guide services, food, beverages, fishing instruction, fly tying lessons
OK to call for current conditions: Yes
Contact: Xavier Duran

STANDLEY LAKE

BAIT & TACKLE...

Colorado Sports & Tackle
Commerce City 303-287-2111
Hours: 8am—?
Carries: Live bait, lures, flies, maps, rods, reels, licenses
OK to call for current conditions: Yes
Contact: Lawrence Shipman

Huron Bait & Tackle
Thornton 303-289-2317
Hours: 8am-6pm
Carries: Live bait, lures, flies, maps, rods, reels, licenses
Bodies of water: Standley Lake, Barbour Ponds, Barr Lake, Chatfield Res.
Services & Products: Belly boat rentals
Guides: No
OK to call for current conditions: Yes
Contact: Hank or Ann

Duck Creek Sporting Goods
Lafayette 303-665-8845
Hours: 10am-6pm Mon.-Thurs., 10am-7pm Fri., 9am-5pm Sat., 11am-4pm Sun.
Carries: Lures, flies, maps, rods, reels, licenses
Services & Products: Guide services, fishing instruction, repair services
OK to call for current conditions: Yes

The area maps that begin each section
are a "visual table of contents" for location headings

CONNECTICUT

1. Atlantic Ocean
2. Connecticut River
3. Fisher's Island Sound
4. Hammonasset River
5. Highland Lake
6. Housatonic River
7. Lake Candlewood
8. Long Island Sound
9. New Haven Harbor
10. Norwalk River
11. Nuagatuck River
12. Salmon River
13. Saugatuck River
14. Thames River
15. Twin Lakes
16. Wononskopomuc Lake

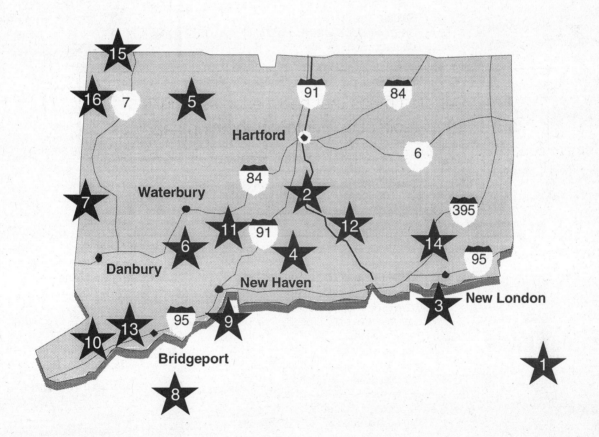

CONNECTICUT — ATLANTIC OCEAN - CONNECTICUT RIVER

ATLANTIC OCEAN

BAIT & TACKLE...

Niantic Bait & Tackle
Niantic 203-739-0269
Hours: 7am-7pm
Carries: Live bait, lures, flies, maps, rods, reels, licenses
Bodies of water: Long Island Sound, Connecticut River, Thames River, Atlantic Ocean, Niantic Bay
Services & Products: Guide services, boat ramp, fishing instruction, repair services
Guides: Yes
OK to call for current conditions: Yes
Contact: Bob

Rivers End Tackle & Bait
Old Saybrook 203-388-2283
Hours: 6am-6pm
Carries: Live bait, lures, flies, maps, rods, reels, licenses
Bodies of water: Long Island Sound, Connecticut River, Atlantic Ocean
Services & Products: Guide services, fishing instruction, repair services
Guides: Yes
OK to call for current conditions: Yes
Contact: Pat Abate or Mark Lewchik

Some-Things Fishy
West Haven 203-933-2002
Hours: 6am-8pm
Carries: Live bait, lures, rods, reels, licenses
Bodies of water: Long Island Sound, Atlantic Ocean, and a dozen Lakes
Services & Products: Repair services
Guides: Yes
OK to call for current conditions: Yes

CONNECTICUT RIVER

BAIT & TACKLE...

Fishin Factory
Middletown 203-344-9139
Hours: 7am-6pm Mon.-Fri., 6am-4pm Sat., Sun.
Carries: Live bait, lures, flies, maps, rods, reels, licenses
Bodies of water: Connecticut River
Services & Products: Fishing instruction, repair services
Guides: Yes
OK to call for current conditions: Yes

J & E Bait & Tackle
Milford
Hours: 6am-6pm
Carries: Live bait, lures, flies, maps, rods, reels, licenses
Bodies of water: Long Island Sound, Housatonic River Connecticut River
Services & Products: Fishing instruction, repair services
Guides: Yes
OK to call for current conditions: Yes
Contact: John or Elaine

Niantic Bait & Tackle
Niantic 203-739-0269
Hours: 7am-7pm
Carries: Live bait, lures, flies, maps, rods, reels, licenses
Bodies of water: Long Island Sound, Connecticut River, Thames River, Atlantic Ocean, Niantic Bay
Services & Products: Guide services, boat ramp, fishing instruction, repair services
Guides: Yes
OK to call for current conditions: Yes
Contact: Bob

Rivers End Tackle & Bait
Old Saybrook 203-388-2283
Hours: 6am-6pm
Carries: Live bait, lures, flies, maps, rods, reels, licenses
Bodies of water: Long Island Sound, Connecticut River, Atlantic Ocean
Services & Products: Guide services, fishing instruction, repair services
Guides: Yes
OK to call for current conditions: Yes
Contact: Pat Abate or Mark Lewchik

Triple T's Tackle & Variety
Torrington 203-489-8325
Hours: 6am-8pm, closed 6am-1pm Sun.
Carries: Live bait, lures, flies, maps, rods, reels, licenses
Bodies of water: Nuagatuck River, Highland Lake, Connecticut River, Westhill Pond, Dog Pond, Tyler Lake, many small streams and ponds
Services & Products: Food, beverages, fishing instruction
Guides: Yes
OK to call for current conditions: Yes
Contact: Rick or Dawn Hubbard

CHARTERS...

Knight Hawk Charters
Middletown 860-346-5030
Species & Seasons: Striped Bass, Bluefish May-Oct, Fluke May-Sept, Flounder May/June-Sept/Oct, Blackfish May/June-Sept/Nov
Bodies of water: Connecticut River, Long Island Sound, Peconic Bay (NY)
Rates: Half day: $150(2), Full day: $220(2), up to 4 people Full day: $360
Call between: 6pm-9pm
Provides: Light tackle, heavy tackle, lures, bait
Handicapped equipped: No
Certifications: USCG, Licensed Member IGFA and Fish Unlimited

KNIGHT HAWK CHARTERS
Bass Blues Fluke
1/2 Day & Night Trips Also Available
Fishing CT. River & Long Island Sound
Departing from Old Saybrook, CT
CAPT. ELI RASCATI
8 Carll Rd. • Middletown, CT. 06457
860 346-5030

MARINAS...

Damar Ltd Midway Marina
Haddam
Bodies of water: Connecticut River, Long Island Sound
Services & Products: Boat ramp, food, beverages, repair services, winter storage, summer slip rental
Guides: No
OK to call for current conditions: No

O'Hara's Landing Marina
Salisbury 203-824-7583
Hours: 6am-6pm
Carries: Live bait, lures, flies, maps, rods, reels, licenses
Bodies of water: Twin Lakes, Wononskopmuc Lake, Connecticut River
Services & Products: Boat rentals, boat ramp, food, beverages, gas/oil, repair services, dock space, boat sales
Guides: Yes
OK to call for current conditions: Yes
Contact: Barry

CONNECTICUT RIVER - LAKE CANDLEWOOD CONNECTICUT

Saybrook Marine Service
Old Saybrook 203-388-3614
Hours: 7:30am-4pm
Bodies of water: Long Island Sound, Connecticut River
Services & Products: Boat rentals, repair services, transient boat slips
Guides: No
OK to call for current conditions: No

FISHER'S ISLAND SOUND

BAIT & TACKLE...

The Fish Connection
Preston 203-885-1739
Hours: 7am-6:30pm Mon.-Thurs., 7am-7pm Fri., 6am-6pm Sat., 6am-2pm Sun. (spring and summer hrs.)
Carries: Live bait, lures, flies, maps, rods, reels, licenses
Bodies of water: Thames River, Long Island Sound, Amos Lake, Fisher's Island Sound, Long Pond
Services & Products: Guide services, charter boat service, beverages, fishing instruction, repair services, lodging, boat launch, casino
Guides: Yes
OK to call for current conditions: Yes
Contact: Jack or Joe Balint

HAMMONASSET RIVER

BAIT & TACKLE...

North Cove Outfitters
Old Saybrook 203-388-6585
Hours: 10am-8pm
Carries: Lures, flies, maps, rods, reels, licenses
Bodies of water: Long Island Sound, Salmon River, Hammonasset River, many small lakes and ponds
Services & Products: Guide services, fishing instruction
Guides: Yes
OK to call for current conditions: Yes
Contact: Brian Owens or John Prigmore

HIGHLAND LAKE

BAIT & TACKLE...

Townline Boating & Sports Accessories
Waterbury 203-596-7396
Hours: 9am-6pm Mon.-Tues.- Wed.- Fri., 9am-9pm Thurs., 6am-5pm Sat., 6am-1pm Sun.
Carries: Live bait, lures, flies, maps, rods, reels, licenses
Bodies of water: Lake Candlewood, Highland Lake, Twin Lakes and others
Services & Products: Fishing instruction, repair services
Guides: Yes
OK to call for current conditions: Yes
Contact: Doug or Linda

Triple T's Tackle & Variety
Torrington 203-489-8325
Hours: 6am-8pm, closed 6am-1pm Sun.
Carries: Live bait, lures, flies, maps, rods, reels, licenses
Bodies of water: Naugatuck River, Highland Lake, Connecticut River, Westhill Pond, Dog Pond, Tyler Lake, many small streams and ponds
Services & Products: Food, beverages, fishing instruction
Guides: Yes
OK to call for current conditions: Yes
Contact: Rick or Dawn Hubbard

HOUSATONIC RIVER

BAIT & TACKLE...

Bob's Bait & Tackle
Milford 203-876-1495
Hours: 7am-7pm Mon.-Fri., 6am-6pm Sat., 6am-4pm Sun.
Carries: Live bait, lures, flies, maps, rods, reels, licenses
Bodies of water: Long Island Sound, Housatonic River
Services & Products: Guide services, fishing instruction, repair services
OK to call for current conditions: Yes
Contact: Bob McIntosh

J & E Bait & Tackle
2 Daniel Street
Milford 06460
Hours: 6am-6pm
Carries: Live bait, lures, flies, maps, rods, reels, licenses
Bodies of water: Long Island Sound, Housatonic River, Connecticut River
Services & Products: Fishing instruction, repair services
Guides: Yes
OK to call for current conditions: Yes
Contact: John or Elaine

LAKE CANDLEWOOD

BAIT & TACKLE...

Ed's Bait & Sport Shop
Newtown 203-426-0669
Hours: 7:30am-6pm Mon.-Fri., 6am-5pm Sat., 6am-3pm Sun.
Carries: Live bait, lures, flies, maps, rods, reels, licenses
Bodies of water: Lake Lillinonan, Lake Zour, Lake Candlewood, Saugatuck Res., Lake Quassapaug
Services & Products: Fishing instruction, repair services
Guides: No
OK to call for current conditions: No

Hiller Brothers Hunting & Fish
Norwalk 203-857-3474
Hours: 6am-6pm
Carries: Live bait, lures, flies, rods, reels, licenses
Bodies of water: Long Island Sound, Lake Candlewood, Norwalk River, Saugatuck River
Services & Products: Boat ramp, beverages, fishing instruction, repair services
Guides: Yes
OK to call for current conditions: Yes
Contact: Paul or Mark

Townline Boating & Sports Accessories
Waterbury 203-596-7396
Hours: 9am-6pm Mon.-Tues.- Wed.- Fri., 9am-9pm Thurs., 6am-5pm Sat., 6am-1pm Sun.
Carries: Live bait, lures, flies, maps, rods, reels, licenses
Bodies of water: Lake Candlewood, Highland Lake, Twin Lakes and others
Services & Products: Fishing instruction, repair services
Guides: Yes
OK to call for current conditions: Yes
Contact: Doug or Linda

CONNECTICUT

LONG ISLAND SOUND

BAIT & TACKLE...

Bob's Bait & Tackle
Milford 203-876-1495
Hours: 7am-7pm Mon.-Fri.,
6am-6pm Sat., 6am-4pm Sun.
Carries: Live bait, lures, flies, maps, rods, reels, licenses
Bodies of water: Long Island Sound, Housatonic River
Services & Products: Guide services, fishing instruction, repair services
OK to call for current conditions: Yes
Contact: Bob McIntosh

The Fish Connection
Preston 203-885-1739
Hours: 7am-6:30pm Mon.-Thurs., 7am-7pm Fri., 6am-6pm Sat., 6am-2pm Sun. (spring and summer hrs.)
Carries: Live bait, lures, flies, maps, rods, reels, licenses
Bodies of water: Thames River, Long Island Sound, Amos Lake, Fisher's Island Sound, Long Pond
Services & Products: Guide services, charter boat service, beverages, fishing instruction, repair services, lodging, boat launch, casino
Guides: Yes
OK to call for current conditions: Yes
Contact: Jack or Joe Balint

Hiller Brothers Hunting & Fish
Norwalk 203-857-3474
Hours: 6am-6pm
Carries: Live bait, lures, flies, rods, reels, licenses
Bodies of water: Long Island Sound, Lake Candlewood, Norwalk River, Saugatuck River
Services & Products: Boat ramp, beverages, fishing instruction, repair services
Guides: Yes
OK to call for current conditions: Yes
Contact: Paul or Mark

Hillyer's Bait & Tackle Shop
Waterford 203-443-7615
Hours: 6am-8pm
Carries: Live bait, lures, flies, maps, rods, reels, licenses
Bodies of water: Long Island Sound
Services & Products: Boat ramp, fishing instruction, repair services
Guides: Yes
OK to call for current conditions: Yes
Contact: Anyone

J & E Bait & Tackle
Milford
Hours: 6am-6pm
Carries: Live bait, lures, flies, maps, rods, reels, licenses
Bodies of water: Long Island Sound, Housatonic River Connecticut River
Services & Products: Fishing instruction, repair services
Guides: Yes
OK to call for current conditions: Yes
Contact: John or Elaine

Niantic Bait & Tackle
Niantic 203-739-0269
Hours: 7am-7pm
Carries: Live bait, lures, flies, maps, rods, reels, licenses
Bodies of water: Long Island Sound, Connecticut River, Thames River, Atlantic Ocean, Niantic Bay
Services & Products: Guide services, boat ramp, fishing instruction, repair services
Guides: Yes
OK to call for current conditions: Yes
Contact: Bob

North Cove Outfitters
Old Saybrook 203-388-6585
Hours: 10am-8pm
Carries: Lures, flies, maps, rods, reels, licenses
Bodies of water: Long Island Sound, Salmon River, Hammonasset River, many small lakes and ponds
Services & Products: Guide services, fishing instruction
Guides: Yes
OK to call for current conditions: Yes
Contact: Brian Owens or John Prigmore

Rivers End Tackle & Bait
Old Saybrook 203-388-2283
Hours: 6am-6pm
Carries: Live bait, lures, flies, maps, rods, reels, licenses
Bodies of water: Long Island Sound, Connecticut River, Atlantic Ocean
Services & Products: Guide services, fishing instruction, repair services
Guides: Yes
OK to call for current conditions: Yes
Contact: Pat Abate or Mark Lewchik

Riverside Grocery
Waterford 203-444-0681
Hours: 8am-8pm, 6am-8pm Sat., Sun.
Carries: Live bait, lures
Bodies of water: Long Island Sound

Services & Products: Boat ramp, food, beverages
Guides: Yes
OK to call for current conditions: Yes

Some-Things Fishy
West Haven 203-933-2002
Hours: 6am-8pm
Carries: Live bait, lures, rods, reels, licenses
Bodies of water: Long Island Sound, Atlantic Ocean, and a dozen Lakes
Services & Products: Repair services
Guides: Yes
OK to call for current conditions: Yes

CHARTERS...

Connecticut Woods & Water Guide Service
Niantic 203-442-6343
Species & Seasons: Striped Bass May-Oct, Bluefish June-Oct, Little Tunny, Bonito Aug-Oct
Bodies of water: Long Island Sound
Rates: Half day: $200(1), $250(2)
Call between: 6pm-9pm
Provides: Light tackle, heavy tackle, fly rod/reel, lures, bait, rain gear, beverages
Handicapped equipped: No
Certifications: Orvis Recommended, USCG

Knight Hawk Charters
Middletown 860-346-5030
Species & Seasons: Striped Bass, Bluefish May-Oct, Fluke May-Sept, Flounder May/June-Sept/Oct, Blackfish May/June-Sept/Nov
Bodies of water: Connecticut River, Long Island Sound, Peconic Bay (NY)
Rates: Half day: $150(2), Full day: $220(2), up to 4 people Full day: $360
Call between: 6pm-9pm
Provides: Light tackle, heavy tackle, lures, bait
Handicapped equipped: No
Certifications: USCG, Licensed Member IGFA and Fish Unlimited

Saltwater Flyfishing Charters
Westport 203-226-1915
Species & Seasons: Striped Bass Mar-Dec, Bluefish June-Nov, Bonito July-Oct
Bodies of water: Norwalk Islands, Long Island Sound (western)
Rates: Half day: $375(2), Full day: $475(2)

LONG ISLAND SOUND - THAMES RIVER — CONNECTICUT

Provides: Fly rod/reel, beverages, lunch
Handicapped equipped: Yes
Certifications: USCG Masters, Orvis Endorsed

MARINAS...

Damar Ltd Midway Marina
Haddam
Bodies of water: Connecticut River, Long Island Sound
Services & Products: Boat ramp, food, beverages, repair services, winter storage, summer slip rental
Guides: No
OK to call for current conditions: No

Saybrook Marine Service
Old Saybrook 203-388-3614
Hours: 7:30am-4pm
Bodies of water: Long Island Sound, Connecticut River
Services & Products: Boat rentals, repair services, transient boat slips
Guides: No
OK to call for current conditions: No

NEW HAVEN HARBOR

MARINAS...

Shiners Cove Marina
West Haven 203-934-2182
Hours: 7am-7pm
Carries: Lures, flies, maps, rods, reels
Bodies of water: New Haven Harbor, West River
Services & Products: Food, beverages, gas/oil, repair services
Guides: Yes
OK to call for current conditions: Yes
Contact: Mike Shiner or John Izzo

NORWALK RIVER

BAIT & TACKLE...

Hiller Brothers Hunting & Fish
Norwalk 203-857-3474
Hours: 6am-6pm
Carries: Live bait, lures, flies, rods, reels, licenses
Bodies of water: Long Island Sound, Lake Candlewood, Norwalk River, Saugatuck River

Services & Products: Boat ramp, beverages, fishing instruction, repair services
Guides: Yes
OK to call for current conditions: Yes
Contact: Paul or Mark

NAUGATUCK RIVER

BAIT & TACKLE...

Triple T's Tackle & Variety
Torrington 203-489-8325
Hours: 6am-8pm, closed 6am-1pm Sun.
Carries: Live bait, lures, flies, maps, rods, reels, licenses
Bodies of water: Naugatuck River, Highland Lake, Connecticut River, Westhill Pond, Dog Pond, Tyler Lake, many small streams and ponds
Services & Products: Food, beverages, fishing instruction
Guides: Yes
OK to call for current conditions: Yes
Contact: Rick or Dawn Hubbard

SALMON RIVER

BAIT & TACKLE...

North Cove Outfitters
Old Saybrook 203-388-6585
Hours: 10am-8pm
Carries: Lures, flies, maps, rods, reels, licenses
Bodies of water: Long Island Sound, Salmon River, Hammonasset River, many small lakes and ponds
Services & Products: Guide services, fishing instruction
Guides: Yes
OK to call for current conditions: Yes
Contact: Brian Owens, John Prigmore

SAUGATUCK RIVER

BAIT & TACKLE...

Hiller Brothers Hunting & Fish
Norwalk 203-857-3474
Hours: 6am-6pm
Carries: Live bait, lures, flies, rods, reels, licenses

Bodies of water: Long Island Sound, Lake Candlewood, Norwalk River, Saugatuck River
Services & Products: Boat ramp, beverages, fishing instruction, repair services
Guides: Yes
OK to call for current conditions: Yes
Contact: Paul or Mark

THAMES RIVER

BAIT & TACKLE...

The Fish Connection
Preston 203-885-1739
Hours: 7am-6:30pm Mon.-Thurs., 7am-7pm Fri., 6am-6pm Sat., 6am-2pm Sun. (spring and summer hrs.)
Carries: Live bait, lures, flies, maps, rods, reels, licenses
Bodies of water: Thames River, Long Island Sound, Amos Lake, Fisher's Island Sound, Long Pond
Services & Products: Guide services, charter boat service, beverages, fishing instruction, repair services, lodging, boat launch, casino
Guides: Yes
OK to call for current conditions: Yes
Contact: Jack or Joe Balint

Niantic Bait & Tackle
Niantic 203-739-0269
Hours: 7am-7pm
Carries: Live bait, lures, flies, maps, rods, reels, licenses
Bodies of water: Long Island Sound, Connecticut River, Thames River, Atlantic Ocean, Niantic Bay
Services & Products: Guide services, boat ramp, fishing instruction, repair services
Guides: Yes
OK to call for current conditions: Yes
Contact: Bob

CONNECTICUT

TWIN LAKES - WONONSKOPOMUC LAKE

TWIN LAKES

BAIT & TACKLE...

Townline Boating & Sports Accessories
Waterbury 203-596-7396
Hours: 9am-6pm Mon.-Tues.- Wed.- Fri., 9am-9pm Thurs., 6am-5pm Sat., 6am-1pm Sun.
Carries: Live bait, lures, flies, maps, rods, reels, licenses
Bodies of water: Lake Candlewood, Highland Lake, Twin Lakes and others
Services & Products: Fishing instruction, repair services
Guides: Yes
OK to call for current conditions: Yes
Contact: Doug or Linda

MARINAS...

O'Hara's Landing Marina
Salisbury 203-824-7583
Hours: 6am-6pm
Carries: Live bait, lures, flies, maps, rods, reels, licenses
Bodies of water: Twin Lakes, Wononskopomuc Lake, Connecticut River
Services & Products: Boat rentals, boat ramp, food, beverages, gas/oil, repair services, dock space, boat sales
Guides: Yes
OK to call for current conditions: Yes
Contact: Barry

WONONSKOPOMUC LAKE

MARINAS...

O'Hara's Landing Marina
Salisbury 203-824-7583
Hours: 6am-6pm
Carries: Live bait, lures, flies, maps, rods, reels, licenses
Bodies of water: Twin Lakes, Wononskopomuc Lake, Connecticut River
Services & Products: Boat rentals, boat ramp, food, beverages, gas/oil, repair services, dock space, boat sales
Guides: Yes
OK to call for current conditions: Yes
Contact: Barry

DELAWARE

1. Atlantic Ocean
2. Broadkill River
3. Delaware Bay
4. Nanticoke River
5. Pocomoke River

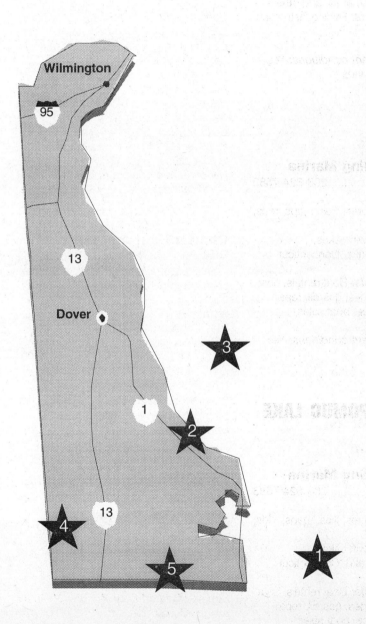

DELAWARE

ATLANTIC OCEAN - BROADKILL RIVER

ATLANTIC OCEAN

BAIT & TACKLE...

Bud & Sandy's Outdoors
Dover 302-697-9988
Hours: 7am-7pm
Carries: Live bait, lures, flies, maps, rods, reels, licenses
Bodies of water: Delaware Bay, Atlantic Ocean, Chesapeake Bay, all Tidal Rivers
Services & Products: Fishing instruction, repair services
Guides: Yes
OK to call for current conditions: Yes
Contact: Bud Faircloth

Fenwick Tackle
Fenwick Island 302-539-7766
Hours: 7am-9pm, May-Oct.
Carries: Live bait, lures, maps, rods, reels
Bodies of water: Atlantic Ocean, Assawoman Bay, Isle of Wight Bay, Sinepuxent Bay, Pocomoke River, Wicomico River
Services & Products: Repair services, crab equipment rentals
Guides: Yes
OK to call for current conditions: Yes

Hoss's Bait & Tackle
Lewes 302-645-2612
Hours: 6am-10pm
Carries: Live bait, lures, rods, reels, licenses
Bodies of water: Delaware Bay, Atlantic Ocean
Guides: Yes
OK to call for current conditions: Yes
Contact: Anyone

Kersey's Outfitters
Millsboro 302-934-7714
Hours: 8am-6pm, closed Wed.
Carries: Live bait, lures, flies, maps, rods, reels
Bodies of water: Nanticoke River, Wicomico River, Marshihope River, Pocomoke River, Broadkill River, Delaware Bay, Atlantic Ocean, area ponds
Guides: Yes
OK to call for current conditions: Yes
Contact: Anyone

R & R Sports Center
Lewes 302-645-9801
Hours: 6am-10pm
Carries: Live bait, lures, flies, maps, rods, reels, licenses
Bodies of water: Delaware Bay, Atlantic Ocean, Rehoboth Bay, Red Mill Pond
Services & Products: Charter boat service, fishing instruction, repair services
Guides: Yes
OK to call for current conditions: Yes
Contact: Anyone

CHARTERS...

Blue Lucy Charters
Lewes 302-645-5912
Species & Seasons: Bluefish May-Nov, Shark May-Sept, Tuna June-Sept, Sea Trout, Flounder May-Sept, Tautog Sept-Nov, Striped Bass Oct-Dec
Bodies of water: Delaware Bay, Atlantic Ocean
Rates: Call for free brochure-rates depend on species
Call between: 5:30am-9:30pm
Provides: Light tackle, heavy tackle, lures, bait, rain gear
Handicapped equipped: No
Certifications: USCG

Charter Boat Amethyst
Millsboro 800-999-8119
Species & Seasons: Croaker, Sea Trout, Ling, Sea Bass June-Oct
Bodies of water: Delaware Bay, Atlantic Ocean, (depart from Indian River Inlet, Rehoboth Beach)
Rates: Full day up to 6 people: Trolling $400, Bottom Fishing: $325, Tuna: $600, Shark: $500
Call between: 9am-11pm
Provides: Light tackle, heavy tackle, bait
Handicapped equipped: No
Certifications: USCG

Fatal Attraction Sportfishing
Lewes 302-945-7205
Species & Seasons: Weakfish May-Sept, Flounder May-Oct, Bluefish May-June, Mako Shark May-Sept, Yelowfin Tuna June-Oct, Bluefin Tuna July-Aug, Wahoo Aug-Sept, Dolphin, White Marlin, Blue Marlin July-Sept
Bodies of water: Delaware Bay, Atlantic Ocean
Rates: $200-$1700 (4-24hours) 6 people
Call between: 6pm-8pm
Provides: Light tackle, heavy tackle, lures, bait
Handicapped equipped: Yes
Certifications: USCG

Capt. Monty Misdom
Millsboro 302-945-5027
Species & Seasons: Mackerel Mar-April, Tautog all year, Sea Bass April-Dec, Bluefish, Mako Shark April-July, Bluefin Tuna June-Aug, Yelowfin Tuna July-Nov, Bonito, Albacore, Spanish Mackerel, Sea Trout, Croaker July-Oct
Bodies of water: Atlantic Ocean
Call between: 8pm-9pm
Provides: Light tackle, heavy tackle, lures, bait
Handicapped equipped: Yes

Miss This Charter Fishing
Newark 302-738-5081
Species & Seasons: Striped Bass Oct-Dec, Bluefish, Shark May-June, Tuna, Marlin July-Sept
Bodies of water: Atlantic Ocean
Rates: 6 people $425-$1400 day
Call between: 5pm-9:30pm
Provides: Light tackle, heavy tackle
Handicapped equipped: No
Certifications: USCG

BROADKILL RIVER

BAIT & TACKLE...

Kersey's Outfitters
Millsboro 302-934-7714
Hours: 8am-6pm, closed Wed.
Carries: Live bait, lures, flies, maps, rods, reels
Bodies of water: Nanticoke River, Wicomico River, Marshihope River, Pocomoke River, Broadkill River, Delaware Bay, Atlantic Ocean, area ponds
Guides: Yes
OK to call for current conditions: Yes
Contact: Anyone

Wilson's Sunshine Marina
Milton 302-684-3425
Hours: 6am-8:30pm
Carries: Live bait, lures, maps, rods, reels
Bodies of water: Diamond Pond, Wagmon Pond, Red Mill Pond, Broadkill River, Delaware Bay
Services & Products: Boat rentals, boat ramp
Guides: Yes
OK to call for current conditions: Yes
Contact: Russ McCann

DELAWARE BAY - NANTICOKE RIVER   DELAWARE

DELAWARE BAY

BAIT & TACKLE...

Adams Wharf
Milford 302-422-8940
Hours: 6am-8am, 1pm-5pm
Carries: Lures
Bodies of water: Delaware Bay
Services & Products: Charter boat service, head boat service
Guides: Yes
OK to call for current conditions: Yes

Bud & Sandy's Outdoors
Dover 302-697-9988
Hours: 7am-7pm
Carries: Live bait, lures, flies, maps, rods, reels, licenses
Bodies of water: Delaware Bay, Atlantic Ocean, Chesapeake Bay, all Tidal Rivers
Services & Products: Fishing instruction, repair services
Guides: Yes
OK to call for current conditions: Yes
Contact: Bud Faircloth

Hoss's Bait & Tackle
Lewes 302-645-2612
Hours: 6am-10pm
Carries: Live bait, lures, rods, reels, licenses
Bodies of water: Delaware Bay, Atlantic Ocean
Guides: Yes
OK to call for current conditions: Yes
Contact: Anyone

Kersey's Outfitters
Millsboro 302-934-7714
Hours: 8am-6pm, closed Wed.
Carries: Live bait, lures, flies, maps, rods, reels
Bodies of water: Nanticoke River, Wicomico River, Marshihope River, Pocomoke River, Broadkill River, Delaware Bay, Atlantic Ocean, area ponds
Guides: Yes
OK to call for current conditions: Yes
Contact: Anyone

R & R Sports Center
Lewes 302-645-9801
Hours: 6am-10pm
Carries: Live bait, lures, flies, maps, rods, reels, licenses
Bodies of water: Delaware Bay, Atlantic Ocean, Rehoboth Bay, Red Mill Pond
Services & Products: Charter boat service, fishing instruction, repair services
Guides: Yes
OK to call for current conditions: Yes
Contact: Anyone

Trustworthy Hardware
Millsboro 302-947-1225
Hours: 8am-6pm
Carries: Live bait, lures, flies, maps, rods, reels, licenses
Bodies of water: Indian River, Delaware Bay, Burton's Pond, Trappe Pond, Cape Henlopen
Services & Products: Fishing instruction
Guides: Yes
OK to call for current conditions: Yes
Contact: J.B.

Wilson's Sunshine Marina
Milton 302-684-3425
Hours: 6am-8:30pm
Carries: Live bait, lures, maps, rods, reels
Bodies of water: Diamond Pond, Wagmon Pond, Red Mill Pond, Broadkill River, Delaware Bay
Services & Products: Boat rentals, boat ramp
Guides: Yes
OK to call for current conditions: Yes
Contact: Russ McCann

CHARTERS...

Blue Lucy Charters
Lewes 302-645-5912
Species & Seasons: Bluefish May-Nov, Shark May-Sept, Tuna June-Sept, Sea Trout, Flounder May-Sept, Tautog Sept-Nov, Striped Bass Oct-Dec
Bodies of water: Delaware Bay, Atlantic Ocean
Rates: Call for free brochure, rates depend on species
Call between: 5:30am-9:30pm
Provides: Light tackle, heavy tackle, lures, bait, rain gear
Handicapped equipped: No
Certifications: USCG

Charter Boat Amethyst
Millsboro 800-999-8119
Species & Seasons: Croaker, Sea Trout, Ling, Sea Bass June-Oct
Bodies of water: Delaware Bay, Atlantic Ocean, (depart from Indian River Inlet, Rehoboth Beach)
Rates: Full day up to 6 people: Trolling $400, Bottom Fishing: $325, Tuna: $600, Shark: $500
Call between: 9am-11pm
Provides: Light tackle, heavy tackle, bait
Handicapped equipped: No
Certifications: USCG

Davidson Fishing Fleet
Frederica 302-335-3442
Species & Seasons: Sea Trout, Flounder May-Nov, Porgie's, Sea Bass Sept-Nov, Bluefish various times
Bodies of water: Delaware Bay
Rates: Varies
Call between: Anytime
Provides: Bait
Handicapped equipped: Yes
Certifications: USCG

Fatal Attraction Sportfishing
Lewes 302-945-7205
Species & Seasons: Weakfish May-Sept, Flounder May-Oct, Bluefish May-June, Mako Shark May-Sept, Yelowfin Tuna June-Oct, Bluefin Tuna July-Aug, Wahoo Aug-Sept, Dolphin, White Marlin, Blue Marlin July-Sept
Bodies of water: Delaware Bay, Atlantic Ocean
Rates: $200-$1700 (4-24hours) 6 people
Call between: 6pm-8pm
Provides: Light tackle, heavy tackle, lures, bait
Handicapped equipped: Yes
Certifications: USCG

NANTICOKE RIVER

BAIT & TACKLE...

Kersey's Outfitters
Millsboro 302-934-7714
Hours: 8am-6pm, closed Wed.
Carries: Live bait, lures, flies, maps, rods, reels
Bodies of water: Nanticoke River, Wicomico River, Marshihope River, Pocomoke River, Broadkill River, Delaware Bay, Atlantic Ocean, area ponds
Guides: Yes
OK to call for current conditions: Yes
Contact: Anyone

YOUR SILENT FISHING PARTNER

DELAWARE

POCOMOKE RIVER

BAIT & TACKLE...

Fenwick Tackle
Fenwick Island 302-539-7766
Hours: 7am-9pm, May-Oct.
Carries: Live bait, lures, maps, rods, reels
Bodies of water: Atlantic Ocean, Assawoman Bay, Isle of Wight Bay, Sinepuxent Bay, Pocomoke River, Wicomico River
Services & Products: Repair services, crab equipment rentals
Guides: Yes
OK to call for current conditions: Yes

Kersey's Outfitters
Millsboro 302-934-7714
Hours: 8am-6pm, closed Wed.
Carries: Live bait, lures, flies, maps, rods, reels
Bodies of water: Nanticoke River, Wicomico River, Marshihope River, Pocomoke River, Broadkill River, Delaware Bay, Atlantic Ocean, area ponds
Guides: Yes
OK to call for current conditions: Yes
Contact: Anyone

FLORIDA

1. Atlantic Ocean & Bays (North)
2. Atlantic Ocean & Bays (South)
3. Blue Cypress Lake
4. Canal Systems
5. Crescent Lake
6. Cypress Lake
7. Everglades
8. Florida Area Rivers (North)
9. Florida Area Rivers (South)
10. Florida Bay
11. Florida Keys
12. Gulf of Mexico & Bays (North)
13. Gulf of Mexico & Bays (South)
14. Indian River Lagoon
15. Intracoastal Waterway (North)
16. Intracoastal Waterway (South)
17. Lake George
18. Lake Harney
19. Lake Istokpoga
20. Lake Jackson
21. Lake Juliana
22. Lake Kerr
23. Lake Kissimmee
24. Lake Miccosukee
25. Lake Okeechobee
26. Lake Osborne
27. Lake Rousseau
28. Lake Seminole
29. Lake Talquin
30. Lake Tarpon
31. Lake Tohopekaliga
32. Lake Trafford
33. Lake Woodruff
34. Lochloosa Lake
35. Mosquito Lagoon
36. Newnan's Lake
37. Orange Lake
38. Regional Areas
39. Rodman Reservoir
40. Stick Marsh
41. Ten Thousand Islands
42. Tsala Apopka Lake

YOUR SILENT FISHING PARTNER

FLORIDA — ATLANTIC OCEAN & BAYS (NORTH)

ATLANTIC OCEAN & BAYS (NORTH)

BAIT & TACKLE...

A1A Discount Bait & Tackle
May Port 904-241-6571
Hours: 5am-8pm
Carries: Live bait, lures, flies, maps, rods, reels, licenses
Bodies of water: Atlantic Ocean, St. John's River
Services & Products: Guide services, charter boat service, boat ramp, beverages, gas/oil, fishing instruction, repair services
Guides: Yes
OK to call for current conditions: Yes
Contact: Wayne or Wendell

First Strike Marine & Tackle
New Smyrna Beach 904-427-3587
Hours: 6am-6pm
Carries: Live bait, lures, flies, maps, rods, reels, licenses
Bodies of water: Atlantic Ocean, Mosquito Lagoon, Indian River
Services & Products: Guide services, fishing instruction, repair services
Guides: Yes
OK to call for current conditions: Yes
Contact: Lou

Fishin Shack
Daytona Beach 904-788-2120
Hours: 5am-7pm
Carries: Live bait, lures, flies, maps, rods, reels
Bodies of water: Atlantic Ocean
Services & Products: Guide services, charter boat service, fishing instruction, repair services
Guides: Yes
OK to call for current conditions: Yes
Contact: Dave Rogers

Happy Fisherman Bait & Tackle
Holly Hill 904-255-1012
Hours: 6am-8pm
Carries: Live bait, lures, maps, rods, reels, licenses
Bodies of water: Atlantic Ocean, Halifax River
Services & Products: Boat ramp
Guides: Yes
OK to call for current conditions: Yes
Contact: Thomas Stone

Harold's Sport Center
New Smyrna Beach 904-428-2841
Hours: 6am-7pm
Carries: Live bait, lures, rods, reels
Bodies of water: Atlantic Ocean, Indian River, Intracoastal Waterway
Services & Products: Guide services, charter boat service, beverages, fishing instruction, repair services
Guides: Yes
OK to call for current conditions: Yes
Contact: Larry A. Ross

Hook Line & Sinker
New Smyrna Beach 904-424-9840
Hours: 6am-6pm
Carries: Live bait, lures, flies, maps, rods, reels, licenses
Bodies of water: Atlantic Ocean, Mosquito Lagoon, Indian River, Ponce Inlet
Services & Products: Boat rentals, guide services, charter boat service, boat ramp, food, beverages, fishing instruction, repair services, canoe rentals
Guides: Yes
OK to call for current conditions: Yes
Contact: Louis J. Sarlo

Satellite Bait & Tackle Inc.
Satellite Beach 407-773-6611
Hours: 6am-7pm
Carries: Live bait, lures, rods, reels, licenses
Bodies of water: Atlantic Ocean, Indian River, Banana River
Services & Products: Beverages, gas/oil, fishing instruction, repair services
Guides: Yes
OK to call for current conditions: Yes
Contact: Ed Havrila

Scotty's Bait & Tackle
Orlando 407-290-5550
Hours: 5:30am-6:30pm
Carries: Live bait, lures, flies, maps, rods, licenses
Bodies of water: Several local lakes, Lake Kissimmee, Atlantic Ocean
Services & Products: Guide services, charter boat service, food, beverages, gas/oil, fishing instruction, repair services
Guides: Yes
OK to call for current conditions: Yes

CHARTERS...

Backcountry Charter Service
DeBary 800-932-7335
Species & Seasons: Redfish, Sea Trout Dec-Jan, Tarpon May-Nov, Snook Mar-Oct, Jack Cravalle Nov-May, Ladyfish Sept-May, Striped Bass Feb-June, American Shad Jan-April, LM Bass Nov-April, Panfish April-Sept
Bodies of water: Indian River Lagoon, Mosquito Lagoon, Banana River Lagoon, St. John's River, Stick Marsh, Farm 13
Rates: Half day: $185(1-2), Full day: $275(1-2)
Call between: 24 hours
Provides: Light tackle, fly rod/reel, lures, bait, rain gear, beverages
Handicapped equipped: Yes
Certifications: USCG, FFF, IGFA

Road Runner Charters
Jacksonville 904-350-0380
Species & Seasons: King Mackerel April-Jan, Grouper, Snapper Oct-May, Barracuda June-Oct, Dolphin May-Oct, Amberjack May-Dec, Bonito Mar-Jan
Bodies of water: Atlantic Ocean
Rates: 4 hrs. $250(6 or less), 5 hrs: $300(6 or less), 3/4 day: $375(6 or less), Full day: $450(6 or less), Deep Water: $700(6or less)
Call between: 9am-5pm
Provides: Heavy tackle, lures, bait, rain gear
Handicapped equipped: Yes

Sea Venture Charter Boats
Merrit Island 407-453-6764
Species & Seasons: Dolphin, Tuna, King Mackerel, Sailfish, Wahoo, Marlin all year
Bodies of water: Atlantic Ocean (Central Coast)
Rates: $650 for boat to 6 passengers
Call between: Anytime
Provides: Light tackle, heavy tackle, lures, bait
Handicapped equipped: Yes
Certifications: USCG

L. E. Sutton
Fernandina Bch. 904-261-7509
Species & Seasons: Sea Trout, Red Bass Jan-Feb, Drum Feb-Mar, Snapper, Grouper Mar-April, Spanish Mackerel, Kingfish, Barracuda, Cobia, Sailfish, Tuna May-Sept, Sea Bass, Snapper, Trout, Red Bass Sept-Dec, Flounder April
Bodies of water: Intracoastal Waterway, Atlantic Ocean

ATLANTIC OCEAN & BAYS (NORTH - SOUTH) — FLORIDA

Rates: Half day: $100(1), $150(2),
Full day: $200(1), $250(2), $300(6)
Call between: 8am-9:30pm
Provides: Light tackle, heavy tackle, lures, bait, rain gear
Handicapped equipped: Yes

MARINAS...

Conch House Marina
St. Augustine 904-824-4347
Hours: 6am-9:30pm
Carries: Maps
Bodies of water: Salt Run, Intracoastal Waterway, Atlantic Ocean
Services & Products: Charter boat service, lodging, food, beverages, gas/oil
Guides: Yes
OK to call for current conditions: Yes
Contact: Vicki Henry

ATLANTIC OCEAN & BAYS (SOUTH)

BAIT & TACKLE...

7 Seas Bait & Tackle
Boca Raton..................... 407-392-4772
Hours: Open 7 days
Carries: Live bait, lures, flies, maps, rods, reels, licenses
Bodies of water: Atlantic Ocean, Lake Okechobee, Lake Ida
Services & Products: Guide services, fishing instruction, repair services
OK to call for current conditions: Yes
Contact: Steve Hill

Bill's Bait & Tackle Shop
Key Largo 305-451-0531
Hours: 7am-7pm M-Thrus., 7am-9pm Fri., 6am-9pm Sat., 6am-6pm Sun.
Carries: Live bait, lures, flies, maps, rods, reels, licenses
Bodies of water: Florida Bay, Atlantic Ocean
Services & Products: Guide services, charter boat service, beverages, fishing instruction, repair services, custom rod building
Guides: Yes
OK to call for current conditions: Yes

Boynton Fisherman's Supply
Boynton Beach 407-736-0568
Hours: 7am-7pm
Carries: Live bait, lures, flies, rods, reels, licenses
Bodies of water: Atlantic Ocean, Lake Ida, Lake Osborne
Services & Products: Fishing instruction, repair services
Guides: Yes
OK to call for current conditions: Yes

Capt. Harry's Fishing Supply
Miami 305-374-4661
Hours: 8:30am-5:30pm, closed Sun.
Carries: Lures, flies, maps, rods, reels, licenses
Bodies of water: Biscayne Bay, Atlantic Ocean
Services & Products: Repair services
Guides: Yes
OK to call for current conditions: Yes
Contact: Harry Vemon III

Captain's Corner
Fort Pierce 407-461-1008
Hours: 6am-8pm
Carries: Live bait, lures, rods, reels
Bodies of water: Indian River Lagoon, Intracoastal Waterway, Atlantic Ocean
Services & Products: Food, beverages
Guides: Yes
OK to call for current conditions: Yes
Contact: Jerry L. Morey

Del's Bait & Tackle
Oakland Park 305-492-1194
Hours: 6am-8pm
Carries: Live bait, lures, flies, maps, rods, reels, licenses
Bodies of water: Atlantic Ocean
Services & Products: Beverages, fishing instruction, food, repair services
Guides: Yes
OK to call for current conditions: Yes
Contact: Chris or Barb

Fancy Rods & The Reel World
Fort Pierce 407-465-6775
Hours: 6am-7pm
Bodies of water: Atlantic Ocean
Services & Products: Guide services, charter boat service, beverages, fishing instruction, repair services, custom rods
Guides: Yes
OK to call for current conditions: Yes

Iggie's Bait & Tackle
Hialeah 305-887-3929
Hours: 6:30am-8pm
Carries: Live bait, lures, flies, rods, reels, licenses
Bodies of water: Gulf of Mexico, Atlantic Ocean, Miami Airport Lake, Lake Okeechobee
Services & Products: Food, beverages, repair services
Guides: Yes

CANOE RENTALS & SALES
WEEK-END SPECIAL.....................$45.00 (Sat. & Sun.)
Daily Rate..............$30.00 (3 or more days-$25 per day)
4 Hours..$20.00)
We launch or You Launch

HOOK, LINE & SINKER
Complete Bait & Tackle
**6495 Turtle Mound Road
Bethune Beach**
904-424-9840 • Open 7 days 6 am-6pm
Fishing Licenses • Ocean & River Charters • All Credit Cards Accepted !

Kendall Bait & Tackle Inc.
Miami 305-670-FISH
Hours: 6am-6pm
Carries: Live bait, lures, flies, maps, rods, reels, licenses
Bodies of water: Atlantic Ocean, Miami Area, Biscayne Bay, Tamiami Trail Canal System, Everglades
Services & Products: Guide services, beverages, fishing instruction, repair services, fly casting lessons
Guides: Yes
OK to call for current conditions: Yes
Contact: J. Corbett or Frank

FLORIDA — ATLANTIC OCEAN & BAYS (SOUTH)

Key West Boat Rentals
Key West 305-294-2628
Hours: 8am-8pm
Carries: Lures, maps, rods, reels, licenses
Bodies of water: Carribean Sea, Atlantic Ocean, Gulf of Mexico, Straits of Florida
Services & Products: Boat rentals, guide services, charter boat service, lodging, boat ramp, food, beverages, diving
Guides: Yes
OK to call for current conditions: Yes
Contact: John or Steve

Kingsbury & Sons Tackle Inc.
Fort Lauderdale 305-467-3474
Hours: 7am-8pm
Carries: Live bait, lures, flies, maps, rods, reels, licenses
Bodies of water: Atlantic Ocean, Everglades, Intracoastal Waterway, Port Everglades Inlet
Services & Products: Guide services, charter boat service, fishing instruction, repair services
Guides: Yes
OK to call for current conditions: Yes
Contact: Dave Kingsbury or Glen

Pompano Beach Fishing Pier
Pompano Beach 305-943-1488
Hours: 24hours
Carries: Live bait, lures, flies, rods, reels
Bodies of water: Atlantic Ocean
Services & Products: Food, beverages, restaurant
Guides: Yes
OK to call for current conditions: Yes

Schulz Brothers-Fishing Headquarters
Jupiter 407-743-7335
Hours: 7am-8pm
Carries: Live bait, lures, flies, maps, rods, reels, licenses
Bodies of water: Atlantic Ocean, Intracoastal Waterway, Loxahatchee River, Lake Okeechobee
Services & Products: Guide services, charter boat service, fishing instruction, repair services
Guides: Yes
OK to call for current conditions: Yes
Contact: Anyone

Snook-Nook Discount Bait & Tackle
Jensen Beach 407-334-2145
Hours: 5:30am-8:00pm
Carries: Live bait, lures, flies, maps, rods, reels, licenses
Bodies of water: Indian River (Intracoastal Waterway), Atlantic Ocean, Fresh Water-Savanna's
Services & Products: Boat rentals, guide services, charter boat service, boat ramp, food, beverages, fishing instruction, repair services
Guides: Yes
OK to call for current conditions: Yes
Contact: Henry Calmotto or Staff

Surf Side Bait & Tackle
Melbourne Beach 407-768-7929
Hours: 6am-7pm Sun.-Thrus., 6am-9pm Fri., Sat.
Carries: Live bait, lures, flies, maps, rods, reels
Bodies of water: Atlantic Ocean, Indian River
Services & Products: Beverages, fishing instruction, repair services, custom rods
Guides: Yes
OK to call for current conditions: Yes
Contact: Victor or Danny

Watson Island Fuel & Fishing Supply
Miami 305-374-2095
Hours: 7:30am-10pm
Carries: Live bait, lures, flies, maps, rods, reels
Bodies of water: Biscayne Bay, Port of Miami, Atlantic Ocean
Services & Products: Charter boat service, boat ramp, food, beverages, gas/oil, fishing instruction
Guides: Yes
OK to call for current conditions: Yes

Whitey's Bait & Tackle
Melbourne 407-724-1440
Hours: 6am-Midnite
Carries: Live bait, lures, flies, maps, rods, reels
Bodies of water: Atlantic Ocean, Indian River
Services & Products: Guide services, food, beverages, repair services, camping supplies
Guides: Yes
OK to call for current conditions: Yes
Contact: Anyone

Willies Custom Trolling Baits
Lake Park 407-848-4484
Hours: 7am-8pm
Carries: Live bait, rods, reels
Bodies of water: Atlantic Ocean, Gulf of Mexico
Services & Products: Guide services, charter boat service, fishing instruction
Guides: Yes
OK to call for current conditions: Yes
Contact: William McDow (Willie)

CHARTERS...

Abyss Pro Dive Center
Marathon 305-743-2126
Hours: 8am-6pm
Bodies of water: Florida Keys, Gulf of Mexico, Atlantic Ocean
Services & Products: Charter boat service
Guides: Yes
OK to call for current conditions: Yes
Contact: Capt. Bill Ferrell

The Beast Fishing Charters
Miami 305-233-9996
Species & Seasons: Sailfish, Kingfish, Tuna Nov-April, Dolphin Mar-Oct, Amberjack May-Sept, Snapper, Grouper all year, Wahoo, Marlin occasionally
Bodies of water: Atlantic Ocean
Rates: Half day: $250, Full day: $350, 3 person maximum
Call between: 6pm-11pm
Provides: Light tackle, lures, bait
Handicapped equipped: No
Certifications: USCG

Bouncer's Dusky
Pembroke Pines 305-431-7530
Species & Seasons: Tarpon all year, Sailfish Nov-June, Dolphin April-Feb, Shark Mar-July, Snapper May-Dec, Grouper Dec-July, Barracuda all year, Kingfish Oct-June, Cobia Oct-April, Amberjack Feb-May
Bodies of water: Biscayne Bay, Atlantic Ocean
Rates: Full day: $450(1-2), evening 4 hrs. $250
Call between: 6pm-9pm
Provides: Light tackle, heavy tackle, fly rod/reel, lures, bait, rain gear
Handicapped equipped: Yes
Certifications: USCG

ATLANTIC OCEAN & BAYS (SOUTH) — FLORIDA

A.E. Brackett
Cudjoe Key 305-745-9478
Species & Seasons: Tarpon, Shark Mar-July, Bonefish Feb-July, Permit April-July, Barracuda Jan-July
Bodies of water: Atlantic Ocean Flats, Gulf of Mexico Backcountry, Florida Keys
Rates: Half day: $225(1-2), Full day: $300(1-2)
Call between: 6pm-8pm
Provides: Light tackle, fly rod/reel, lures, bait, rain gear
Handicapped equipped:
Certifications: USCG

Capt. Jim Brienza
Key West 305-294-6027
Species & Seasons: Tarpon Mar-July, Sailfish Jan-June, Kingfish Dec-Feb, Cobia Nov-April, Blackfin Tuna Dec-April, Dolphin May-Aug, Barracuda all year, Shark Mar-Aug, Amberjack all year, Bonito Feb-Dec
Bodies of water: Gulf of Mexico, Atlantic Ocean
Rates: Half day: $325(1-4), Full day: $450(1-4) whole boat
Call between: 6pm-10pm
Provides: Light tackle, lures, bait, rain gear, beverages
Handicapped equipped: Yes
Certifications: USCG

Captain Kidd II
Sebastian 407-589-5433
Species & Seasons: Grouper Nov-June Red Snapper, Redfish all year, Mangrove Snapper, Mutton Snapper, Dolphin Mar-Nov, Lane Snapper, Kingfish, Cobia, Sea Bass all year
Bodies of water: Sebastian Inlet, Atlantic Ocean
Rates: Half day: $25(1), Full day: $35(1)
Call between: 8am-8pm
Provides: Heavy tackle, bait
Handicapped equipped: Yes
Certifications: USCG

Charter Boat Linda D
Key West 800-299-9798
.... 305-296-9798
Species & Seasons: Sailfish, April-Dec, Wahoo, Barracuda all year, Dolphin April-Aug, Marlin April-Nov, Kingfish Dec-Mar, Tuna, Grouper Jan-Mar, Amberjack Mar-May
Bodies of water: Atlantic Ocean (Straits of Florida), Gulf of Mexico
Rates: Half day: $100(1), $200(2), $400(up to 6), Full day: $150(1), $300(2), $550(up to 6)
Call between: 8am-7pm
Provides: Light tackle, heavy tackle, lures, bait, rain gear
Handicapped equipped: Yes
Certifications: USCG

Christi Sport Fishing
Miami 305-534-5767
Species & Seasons: Sailfish Nov-May, Dolphin Feb-Sept, Wahoo Mar-July, Tuna Mar-June
Bodies of water: Atlantic Ocean
Rates: Half day: $400(1-6), Full day: $700(1-6)
Call between: 8am-10pm
Provides: Light tackle, heavy tackle, lures, bait, beverages
Handicapped equipped: Yes
Certifications: USCG

El Chino
Marathon 305-743-9280
Species & Seasons: Marlin, Wahoo, Dolphin, Tuna, Barracuda all year, Sailfish May-Feb, Tarpon April-July, Kingfish Oct-Mar
Bodies of water: Florida Key's, Gulf of Mexico, Atlantic Ocean
Rates: Half day: $450(1-6) offshore, $350(1-6) reef, Full day: $550(1-6) offshore, $450(1-6) reef
Call between: 6:30am-11pm
Provides: Light tackle, heavy tackle, lures, bait
Handicapped equipped: Yes
Certifications: USCG

Fintastic Fishing Charters
North Miami
Species & Seasons: Dolphin, Kingfish all year, Wahoo, Sailfish, Marlin, Sept-May
Bodies of water: Atlantic Ocean
Rates: 40' vessel: Half day: $465(1-6), Full day: $850(1-6), 26'-40' vessel: Half day: $375(1-4), Full day: $650(1-4)
Call between: 24 hours
Provides: Light tackle, heavy tackle, lures, bait, rain gear, beverages, lunch
Handicapped equipped: Yes
Certifications: USCG

Fishbuster & Billfisher
Key West 305-296-9969
Species & Seasons: Sailfish Nov-May, Dolphin, Marlin May-Aug
Bodies of water: Atlantic Ocean, Gulf of Mexico
Rates: Half day: $100(1), Full day: $150(1) Full boat: Half day: $400, Full day: $600
Call between: 7pm-10pm
Provides: Light tackle, heavy tackle, lures, bait, rain gear
Handicapped equipped: Yes

Fun Yet Charters
Little Torch Key 305-872-3407
Species & Seasons: Dolphin Spring-Fall, Sailfish, King Mackerel Cobia Fall-Spring, Barracuda, Grouper, Mangrove Snapper, Wahoo, Mutton Snapper all year, Tarpon Spring-Summer
Bodies of water: Gulf of Mexico, Florida Keys, Atlantic Ocean
Rates: Half day: $225(1-6), Full day: $325(1-6)
Call between: 7am-11pm
Provides: Light tackle, heavy tackle, lures, bait, rain gear
Handicapped equipped: No
Certifications: Fully licensed and Insured

Capt. Andy Griffiths
Key West 305-296-2639
Species & Seasons: Black Grouper Feb-April, Yellowtail Snapper, Mutton Snapper, Red Grouper, Porgy, Mackerel all year, Kingfish Jan-Mar, Dolphin May-Aug, Tuna, Dec-Feb
Bodies of water: Gulf of Mexico, Atlantic Ocean, Florida Keys, (Marquesas Keys, Dry Tortugas, Key West)
Rates: 3 days: $333(1), 2 days 1 night: $1300(6), 3 days 2 nights: $2000(6)
Call between: 8-8:30am-7-10pm
Provides: Light tackle, heavy tackle, lures, bait
Handicapped equipped:
Certifications: USCG

Helen C Charter Fishing Boats
N. Miami 305-947-4081
Species & Season: Sailfish Nov-May, Dolphin April-July, King Mackerel Nov-Feb, Barracuda Jan-Dec, Bonito, Shark, Wahoo
Bodies of water: Atlantic Ocean
Rates: Half day: $70, 6 people or exclusive charter: Half day: $400, Full day: $800
Call between: 7am-7pm
Provides: Light tackle, heavy tackle, lures, bait
Certifications: USCG

FLORIDA — ATLANTIC OCEAN & BAYS (SOUTH)

Hot Pursuit Charters
Marathon 800-473-4106
.... 305-743-0406
Species & Seasons: Tarpon Mar-June, Sailfish Dec-May, Dolphin April-Nov, Snapper, Grouper all year
Bodies of water: Atlantic Ocean, Straits of Florida, Gulf of Mexico
Rates: Half day: $275(1-6), Full day: $375(1-6)
Call between:
Provides: Light tackle, lures, bait
Handicapped equipped: Yes
Certifications: USCG

Joanie Fishing Charter Boat
Fort Lauderdale 305-763-6186
.... 651-9506
Species & Seasons: Sailfish, Dolphin, Tuna, Wahoo, Kingfish, Shark, Amberjack all year
Bodies of water: Atlantic Ocean
Rates: Whole boat (up to 6 people): Half day: $340, Full day: $600
Call between: 7am-9pm
Provides: Light tackle, heavy tackle, lures, bait
Handicapped equipped: Yes
Certifications: USCG

Miss Sebastian Fleet
Sebastian 407-589-3275
.... 800-298-7776
Species & Seasons: Grouper, Snapper, Marlin, Sailfish, reef fish all year
Bodies of water: Atlantic Ocean
Rates: By the person or full charter
Call between: 6am-9pm
Provides: Light tackle, heavy tackle, bait
Handicapped equipped: Yes
Certifications: USCG

Mullet Man Charters
Marathon Shores 305-289-0941
Species & Seasons: Tarpon Feb-July
Bodies of water: Alantic Ocean, Gulf of Mexico
Call between: 8am-8pm
Provides: Light tackle, heavy tackle, bait, rain gear, beverages
Handicapped equipped: No
Certifications: USCG

On the Fly
Summerland Key 800-946-6359
.... 305-745-4199
Species & Seasons: Blackfin Tuna, Yellowfin Tuna, King Mackerel, Barracuda, Cobia, Grouper, Snapper Jan-Feb, Tarpon, Permit, Sailfish, Dolphin, Cobia, Bonefish Mar-June, Tuna, Wahoo, Sailfish, Dolphin July-Dec
Bodies of water: Wreck fishing the Gulf of Mexico, Atlantic Ocean, Backcountry Florida Keys, Dry Tortugas, Marquesas Keys, Reef Fishing Key West
Rates: Half day: $350(1-2), Full day: $450(1-2)
Call between: 6am-11pm
Provides: Light tackle, heavy tackle, fly rod/reel, lures, bait, rain gear, beverages
Handicapped equipped: Yes
Certifications: USCG

The Reel Life
Key West 800-286-1855
Species & Seasons: Sailfish, Shark all year, Tarpon Mar-July, Blackfin Tuna, Cobia Oct-May, Permit April-Oct, Kingfish Nov-April, Dolphin April-Sept, Wahoo Aug-Mar, Yellowfin Tuna Jan-Mar
Bodies of water: Atlantic Ocean, Gulf of Mexico, Key West inshore areas
Rates: Half day: $300(1-4), Full day: $450(1-4)
Call between: 5:30pm-9:30pm
Provides: Light tackle, fly rod/reel, lures, bait, rain gear
Handicapped equipped: No
Certifications: USCG

Reward II
Miami 305-372-9470
Species & Seasons: Sailfish Oct-May, Dolphin Mar-Sept, African Pompano Sept-May, Kingfish, Bonito, Snapper, Grouper all year, Cobia Oct-Mar, Amberjack Feb-June
Bodies of water: Atlantic Ocean, Gulf Stream Miami to Key Biscayne
Rates: Half day: $26(1), Full day: $39(1)
Call between: 8am-8pm
Provides: Light tackle, heavy tackle, bait
Handicapped equipped: Yes
Certifications: USCG

Seven B's V
Narragansett, RI 401-789-9250
.... 407-220-0893
Species & Seasons: Snapper, Grouper, Sea Bass, Cobia, Dolphin Nov-May
Bodies of water: Ft. Pierce, Jupiter, East Coast, Gulf Stream
Rates: Full day: $25(1)

Call between: 7am-9pm
Provides: Light tackle, heavy tackle, lures, bait, beverages, lunch
Handicapped equipped: Yes
Certifications: USCG

Capt. Alan Starr
Islamorada 305-664-4373
Species & Seasons: Sailfish Nov-April, Tuna Oct-May, Cobia Jan-April, Snapper Oct-June, Dolphin April-July, Kingfish Nov-Feb
Bodies of water: Atlantic Ocean, Straits of Florida, Florida Keys, Bahamas
Rates: Half day: $450, Full day: $650, up to 6 people
Call between: Anytime
Provides: Light tackle, heavy tackle, fly rod/reel, lures, bait, rain gear
Handicapped equipped: Yes

Sun Dancer
Summerland Key 305-745-3063
Species & Seasons: Tarpon Mar-July, Sailfish Oct-May, Kingfish, Cobia Dec-Mar, Bonefish, Permit all year
Bodies of water: Atlantic Ocean, Gulf of Mexico
Rates: Half day: $350(2), Full day: $450(2), Flats Skiff: Half day: $225, Full day: $325
Call between: 7pm-9pm
Provides: Light tackle, fly rod/reel, lures, bait, rain gear
Handicapped equipped: Yes
Certifications: USCG

Tomcat Charterboat
Pompano Beach 305-946-2628
Species & Seasons: Kingfish, Dolphin, Bonito, Barracuda, Sailfish, Wahoo, Tuna, Amberjack all year
Bodies of water: Atlantic Ocean (Southeast Florida)
Rates: Half day: $85(1), $170(2), $325(6)
Call between: 7am-10pm
Provides: Light tackle, heavy tackle, lures, bait
Handicapped equipped: Yes
Certifications: USCG

Windy Day
Key West 800-831-6407
Species & Seasons: Tarpon Feb-Aug, Bonefish April-Nov, Sailfish, Snapper, Wahoo all year, Cobia Oct-June, King Mackerel Dec-Mar, Permit Feb-Dec
Bodies of water: Gulf of Mexico, Atlantic Ocean
Rates: Half day: $275(2), Ful day $400(2)
Call between: 6pm-9pm

ATLANTIC OCEAN & BAYS (SOUTH) - BLUE CYPRESS LAKE   FLORIDA

Provides: Light tackle, fly rod/reel, lures, rain gear
Handicapped equipped: Yes
Certifications: USCG Yamaha Guide

LODGING...

Breezy Palms Resort
Islamorada 305-664-2361
Guest Capacity: 39 units
Handicapped equipped: No
Seasons: All year
Rates: $45-$180/day per room
Contact: Gail M. Schaper
Guides: Yes
Species & Seasons: Marlin, Sailfish Jan-Sept, Dolphin, Tuna Mar-Sept, Bonefish Jan-Jan, Tarpon April-May
Bodies of Water: Atlantic Ocean, Gulf of Mexico, Florida Bay
Types of fishing: Fly fishing, light tackle, heavy tackle, wading
Available: Bait, tackle, boat rentals

Edgewater Lodge
PO Box 799
Long Key 33001
Guest Capacity: 40
Handicapped equipped: Yes
Seasons: All year
Rates: $60-$80/day
Contact:
Guides: Yes
Species & Seasons: Tarpon April-June, Sailfish, Kingfish Dec-April, Grouper, Snapper, Dolphin all year
Bodies of Water: Atlantic Ocean, Gulf of Mexico
Types of fishing: Fly fishing, light tackle, heavy tackle
Available: Bait, tackle

Sandalwood Lodge
12501 Overseas Hwy.
Marathon 33050
Guest Capacity: 11 rooms/efficiencies
Handicapped equipped: No
Seasons: All year
Rates: From: $40/day, $240/week
Contact: Barrie Smith
Guides: Yes
Species & Seasons: Dolphin, Wahoo, Sailfish, Marlin, Tuna, King Mackerel Grouper, Snapper
Bodies of Water: Atlantic Ocean, Florida Bay
Types of fishing: Fly fishing, light tackle, heavy tackle, wading
Available: Licenses, bait, tackle, boat rentals

MARINAS...

Dolphin Marina
Little Torch Key 800-553-0308
.... 305-872-2685
Hours: 7:30am-6pm
Carries: Live bait, lures, maps, licenses
Bodies of water: Atlantic Ocean, Gulf of Mexico
Services & Products: Boat rentals, guide services, charter boat service, lodging, boat ramp, food, beverages, gas/oil, snorkel and sunset cruises
Guides: Yes
OK to call for current conditions: Yes

Midway Tackle & Boat Sales
Lakeland 813-665-7198
Hours: 7am-5pm, closed Sat., Sun.
Carries: Lures, maps, rods, reels
Bodies of water: Winter Haven Chain of Lakes, Lake Parker, Kissimmee Chain, Gulf of Mexico, Atlantic Ocean
Services & Products: Guide services, boat ramp, beverages, Cajun and Charger boats, Suzuki and Yamaha outboards
Guides: Yes
OK to call for current conditions: Yes
Contact: Bud or Sue Rice

Sailfish Marina
Palm Beach Shores 407-844-1724
.... 800-446-4577
Hours: 6:30am-8pm
Carries: Lures, maps, licenses
Bodies of water: Atlantic Ocean, Intracoastal Waterway
Services & Products: Charter boat service, lodging, food, beverages, gas/oil, transient slips
OK to call for current conditions: Yes
Contact: Pamella Lowenhaupt

BLUE CYPRESS LAKE

BAIT & TACKLE...

Stick Marsh Bait & Tackle
Fellsmere 407-571-9855
Hours: 5:30am-5pm
Carries: Live bait, lures, flies, maps, rods, reels, licenses
Bodies of water: Blue Cypress Lake, Sebastian River & Inlet, Stick Marsh, Farm 13, Garcia Res., Lake Kissimmee

Services & Products: Guide services, food, beverages, fishing instruction
Guides: Yes
OK to call for current conditions: Yes

GUIDES...

Frank's River Fishing Tours
Vero Beach 407-562-3430
Species & Seasons: Snook, Sea Trout, Redfish, Snapper, Sea Bass, Bluegill, Crappie all year, Tarpon May-Oct
Bodies of water: Lake Okeechobee and tributaries, Blue Cypress Lake, Stick Marsh, Farm 13, Indian River, all inland waters 100 miles from Vero Beach
Rates: Half day: $100(1), $125(2), Full day: $175(1), $200(2), $25 each additional person
Call between: 6am-10pm
Provides: Light tackle, fly rod/reel, lures, rain gear, beverages
Handicapped equipped: Yes

LODGING...

Middleton's Fish Camp Inc.
21704 73rd Manor
Vero Beach 32966
Guest Capacity: 18 apartments, 30 campers
Handicapped equipped: No
Seasons: All year
Rates: $40/night
Contact: Debbie Murchie
Guides: Yes
Species & Seasons: LM Bass, Sunshine Bass all year, Crappie Sept-Mar, Bluegill, Shell Cracker Mar-Nov, Sunshine Bass Jan-Dec
Bodies of Water: Blue Cypress Lake, Garcia Block, Lake Marion, Lake Kissimmee
Types of fishing: Fly fishing, light tackle, heavy tackle
Available: Fishing instruction, licenses, bait, tackle, boat rentals

FLORIDA
CANAL SYSTEMS - EVERGLADES

CANAL SYSTEMS

BAIT & TACKLE...

Kendall Bait & Tackle Inc.
Miami 305-670-FISH
Hours: 6am-6pm
Carries: Live bait, lures, flies, maps, rods, reels, licenses
Bodies of water: Atlantic Ocean, Miami Area, Biscayne Bay, Tamiami Trail Canal System, Everglades
Services & Products: Guide services, beverages, fishing instruction, repair services, fly casting lessons
Guides: Yes
OK to call for current conditions: Yes
Contact: J. Corbett or Frank

GUIDES...

Freshwater Fishing Guide
Lake Worth 800-226-1766
Species & Seasons: LM Bass all year, Crappie Nov-May
Bodies of water: Palm Beach County Canal System, Lake Clarke, Lake Osborne, Clear Lake, Lake Ida
Rates: Half day: $150(1-2), Full day: $250(1-2), 1 additional person $25 additional
Call between: 8am-10pm
Provides: Light tackle, fly rod/reel, lures, rain gear
Handicapped equipped: Yes
Certifications: ORVIS, State of FL Emergency Medical Tec.

LODGING...

Port of the Island RV Resort
Naples 800-319-4447
Guest Capacity: 99 full service RV lots
Handicapped equipped: No
Seasons: All year
Rates: $23/day, $135/week (full hookup)
Contact: Marlene Marchand
Guides: Yes
Species & Seasons: Redfish June/Feb, Snook Sept-Dec/Feb-May, Trout, LM Bass, Mangrove Snapper, Grouper all year, Black Drum Sept-Feb
Bodies of Water: Ten Thousand Islands, Faka Union Canal System, inland water ways
Types of fishing: Fly fishing, light tackle, heavy tackle
Available: Licenses, bait, tackle, boat rentals, family activities

CRESCENT LAKE

GUIDES...

Capt. Mark "Smitty" Smith
Deland 904-738-1836
Species & Seasons: LM Bass Oct-June
Bodies of water: St. John's River, Suwannee River, Withlacoochee River, Apalachicola River, Lake Talquin, Lake George, Crescent Lake, and others
Rates: Half day: $150+(1-2), Full day: $250+(1-2), $25 additional person (limit 3)
Call between: 7pm-10pm
Provides: Light tackle, heavy tackle, rain gear
Handicapped equipped: No
Certifications: USCG

Steve Rominsky Guide Service
Welaka 904-467-2030
.... 467-8826
Species & Seasons: LM Bass all year, Striped Bass Feb-May, Panfish Mar-Sept
Bodies of water: St John's River, Crescent Lake, Rodman Res., Lake George
Rates: Full day: $175(1), $220(2)
Call between: 7am-8pm
Provides: Light tackle, heavy tackle, lures, bait, rain gear
Handicapped equipped:
Certifications: USCG

CYPRESS LAKE

GUIDES...

Southport Park
Kissimmee 407-933-5822
Species & Seasons: Bass Mar-Dec, Bluegill Feb-June, Crappie July-Oct, Perch Oct-Jan
Bodies of water: West Lake Tohopekaliga, Lake Kissimmee, Cypress Lake
Rates: Half day: $125(2), Full day: $175(2)
Call between: 6am-6pm
Provides: Light tackle, lures, bait, beverages, lunch

LODGING...

Camp Mack
Lake Wales 800-243-8013
.... 813-696-1108
Guest Capacity: 41 RV full hookup sites, 110 Park Motel RV sites, 7 rental units (fully furnished)
Seasons: All year
Rates: RV: $20/night, $120/week, Cabins: $50/day, $300/week, Park Motel Rentals: $65/night, $390/week
Contact: Jill Snively
Guides: Yes
Species & Seasons: LM Bass Nov-April, Crappie Nov-Mar, Shell Cracker, Bluegill Mar-Aug
Bodies of Water: Lake Kissimmee, Lake Hatchineha, Lake Tohopekaliga, Cypress Lake
Types of fishing: Fly fishing, light tackle
Available: Licenses, bait, tackle, family activities, campground

EVERGLADES

BAIT & TACKLE...

Denny's Bass Shop
Margate 305-968-7751
Hours: 6am-6pm, closed Wed.
Carries: Live bait, lures, flies, maps, rods, reels, licenses
Services & Products: Guide services, beverages, fishing instruction, repair services
Guides: Yes
OK to call for current conditions: Yes
Contact: Denny, Donna or Carol

Fishy Business Baits
Miramar 305-962-2273
Hours: 7:30am-7:30pm Mon.-Fri., 6am-7:30pm Sat., Sun.
Carries: Live bait, lures, maps, rods, reels, licenses
Bodies of water: Everglades, Holiday Park, Sawgrass, Alligator Alley, Snake Creek, Hollyland, Lake Okeechobee
Services & Products: Guide services, repair services
Guides: Yes
OK to call for current conditions: Yes
Contact: Jim

EVERGLADES - FLORIDA AREA RIVERS (NORTH)

FLORIDA

Kendall Bait & Tackle Inc.
Miami 305-670-FISH
Hours: 6am-6pm
Carries: Live bait, lures, flies, maps, rods, reels, licenses
Bodies of water: Atlantic Ocean, Miami Area, Biscayne Bay, Tamiami Trail Canal System, Everglades
Services & Products: Guide services, beverages, fishing instruction, repair services, fly casting lessons
Guides: Yes
OK to call for current conditions: Yes
Contact: J. Corbett or Frank

Kingsbury & Sons Tackle Inc.
Fort Lauderdale 305-467-3474
Hours: 7am-8pm
Carries: Live bait, lures, flies, maps, rods, reels, licenses
Bodies of water: Atlantic Ocean, Everglades, Intracoastal Waterway, Port Everglades Inlet
Services & Products: Guide services, charter boat service, fishing instruction, repair services
Guides: Yes
OK to call for current conditions: Yes
Contact: Dave Kingsbury or Glen

CHARTERS...

Capt. Pete Greenan's Gypsy Guide Service
Sarasota 941-923-6095
Species & Seasons: Tarpon May-Aug, Snook Mar-Dec, Redfish, Sea Trout all year, Triple Tail Oct-April
Bodies of water: Gulf of Mexico, Charlotte Harbor, Boca Grande, Sanibel, Ten Thousand Islands, Everglades Nat'l. Park
Rates: Half day: $250(1-2), Full day: $400(1-2)
Call between: 8am-10pm
Provides: Light tackle, heavy tackle, fly rod/reel, lures, bait, rain gear, beverages
Handicapped equipped: Yes
Certifications: USCG

Chokoloskee Island Charters
Chokoloskee 813-695-2286
Species & Seasons: Snook Feb-June/Sept-Dec, Redfish June-April, Tarpon Mar-Nov, Sea Trout Sept-June
Bodies of water: Everglades Nat'l. Park, Ten Thousand Islands, Gulf of Mexico
Rates: Half day: $200(1-2), $225(3), Full day: $300(1-2), $325(3)

Call between: 6pm-10pm
Provides: Light tackle, fly rod/reel, lures, bait, rain gear
Handicapped equipped: No
Certifications: USCG

Skinny Dipper
Goodland 941-642-1342
Species & Seasons: Redfish, Snook all year, Tarpon May-June
Bodies of water: Ten Thousand Islands, Everglades Nat'l Park, Marco Island
Rates: Half day: $225(1-2), Full day: $325(1-2)
Call between: Anytime
Provides: Light tackle, fly rod/reel
Handicapped equipped: No
Certifications: USCG, FFF, SAGE

GUIDES...

Capt. Brian Kelley
Everglades City 941-695-3576
.... 695-3331
Species & Seasons: Tarpon May-Oct, Snook Sept-June, Redfish June-Feb, Sea Trout, Grouper all year
Bodies of water: Everglades Nat'l. Park, Ten Thousand Islands
Rates: Half day: $175(1-2), Full day: $250(1-2)
Call between: 8am-10am/5pm-10pm
Provides: Light tackle, lures, bait, rain gear
Handicapped equipped: Yes
Certifications: USCG, Official Licensed Guide, Everglades National Park

Sawgrass Recreation Park
Ft. Lauderdale 800-457-0788
Species & Seasons: LM Bass Nov-April
Bodies of water: Everglades
Rates: Half day: $145(1-2), Full day: $195(1-2), $25 additional 3rd person
Call between: 6am-6pm
Provides: Light tackle, lures, bait, rain gear, beverages, lunch
Handicapped equipped: Yes

LODGING...

Barron River Resort
Everglades City 813-695-3331
Seasons: All year
Contact: Kathy, Larry or Johnny
Guides: Yes
Species & Seasons: Tarpon May-Oct, Snook Sept-June, Redfish June-Feb, Sea Trout, Grouper all year

Bodies of Water: Everglades Nat'l. Park, Ten Thousand Islands
Types of fishing: Fly fishing, light tackle
Available: Bait, tackle, boat rentals

MARINAS...

Everglades Holiday Park
Fort Lauderdale
Hours: 24 hours
Carries: Live bait, lures, maps, rods, reels, licenses
Bodies of water: Everglades
Services & Products: Boat rentals, guide services, boat ramp, food, beverages, gas/oil, RV sites
OK to call for current conditions: Yes

FLORIDA AREA RIVERS (NORTH)

BAIT & TACKLE...

A1A Discount Bait & Tackle
May Port 904-241-6571
Hours: 5am-8pm
Carries: Live bait, lures, flies, maps, rods, reels, licenses
Bodies of water: Atlantic Ocean, St. John's River
Services & Products: Guide services, charter boat service, boat ramp, beverages, gas/oil, fishing instruction, repair services
Guides: Yes
OK to call for current conditions: Yes
Contact: Wayne or Wendell

Bass-'N-Etc.
Salt Springs 904-685-2277
Hours: 5:30am-9pm
Carries: Live bait, lures, maps, rods, reels, licenses
Bodies of water: St. John's River, Oklawaha River, Lake George, Lake Kerr, Lake Delaney
Services & Products: Guide services, lodging, gas/oil, archery supplies
OK to call for current conditions: Yes
Contact: Dennis or Patty Rahn

FLORIDA — FLORIDA AREA RIVERS (NORTH)

Buck & Bass Sporting Goods
Pensacola 904-944-5692
Hours: 8am-6pm, closed Sun.
Carries: Live bait, lures, flies, maps, rods, reels, licenses
Bodies of water: Escambia River, Perdido River, Blackwater River, Yellow River, Hurricane Lake, Bear Lake, Stone Lake, Karrick Lake, Juniper Lake
Services & Products: Food, beverages, fishing instruction, repair services
Guides: Yes
OK to call for current conditions: Yes
Contact: Rick or Wayne

Dalkeith Road Bait & Variety
Wewahitchka
Hours: 4:30am-7pm
Carries: Live bait, lures, flies, rods, reels, licenses
Bodies of water: Apalachicola River, Chipola River, Lake Wimico, Dead Lake
Services & Products: Food, beverages, gas/oil
Guides: Yes
OK to call for current conditions: Yes
Contact: Ken or JoAnn Ardire

First Strike Marine & Tackle
New Smyrna Beach 904-427-3587
Hours: 6am-6pm
Carries: Live bait, lures, flies, maps, rods, reels, licenses
Bodies of water: Atlantic Ocean, Mosquito Lagoon, Indian River
Services & Products: Guide services, fishing instruction, repair services
Guides: Yes
OK to call for current conditions: Yes
Contact: Lou

Gray's Tackle & Guide Service
Pensacola 904-492-2666
.... 934-3151
Hours: 5:30am-8pm
Carries: Live bait, lures, flies, maps, rods, reels, licenses
Bodies of water: Gulf of Mexico, Pensacola Bay, Perdido Bay, Escambia River
Services & Products: Guide services, charter boat service, fishing instruction, repair services
OK to call for current conditions: Yes
Contact: Bob Gray or Maggie Gray

Harold's Sport Center
New Smyrna Beach 904-428-2841
Hours: 6am-7pm
Carries: Live bait, lures, rods, reels
Bodies of water: Atlantic Ocean, Indian River, Intracoastal Waterway
Services & Products: Guide services, charter boat service, beverages, fishing instruction, repair services
Guides: Yes
OK to call for current conditions: Yes
Contact: Larry A. Ross

Hook Line & Sinker
New Smyrna Beach 904-424-9840
Hours: 6am-6pm
Carries: Live bait, lures, flies, maps, rods, reels, licenses
Bodies of water: Atlantic Ocean, Mosquito Lagoon, Indian River, Ponce Inlet
Services & Products: Boat rentals, guide services, charter boat service, boat ramp, food, beverages, fishing instruction, repair services, canoe rentals
Guides: Yes
OK to call for current conditions: Yes
Contact: Louis J. Sarlo
(see ad page 89)

John's Guns & Fly Fishing
Tallahassee 904-422-1553
Hours: 9am-6:30pm
Carries: Flies, maps, rods, reels, licenses
Bodies of water: Jackson Lake, Lake Seminole, Lake Talquin, Ochlockonee River, St. Marks River, Wakulla River, Aucilla River, Econfina River, Steinhatchee River, Apalachee Bay
Services & Products: Fishing instruction, repair services, free set up and fly-casting instruction
Guides: Yes
OK to call for current conditions: Yes
Contact: John V. Underwood

Kimbrel's Bait & Grocery Store
Grand Ridge 904-592-2535
Hours: 5am-7-8pm
Carries: Live bait, lures, flies, maps, reels
Bodies of water: Lake Ocheesee, Lake Seminole, Apalachicola River
Services & Products: Guide services, food, beverages, fishing instruction
Guides: Yes
OK to call for current conditions: Yes
Contact: Irene Kimbrel

Navarre Bait & Tackle
Navarre 904-939-0734
Hours: 6am-6pm
Carries: Live bait, lures, flies, rods, reels
Bodies of water: Gulf of Mexico, Santa Rosa Sound, East River, East Bay, Yellow River
Services & Products: Beverages, fishing instruction, repair services
Guides: Yes
OK to call for current conditions: Yes
Contact: Richard or Sheila Deaton

Salty Bass Bait & Tackle
Fort Walton Beach 904-863-7999
Hours: 6am-6:30pm
Carries: Live bait, lures, flies, maps, rods, reels
Bodies of water: East River, Choctawhatchee River, Choctawhatchee Bay, Ponds, Juniper Lake, Blackwater River
Services & Products: Guide services, beverages, fishing instruction, repair services
Guides: Yes
OK to call for current conditions: Yes

Satellite Bait & Tackle Inc.
Satellite Beach 407-773-6611
Hours: 6am-7pm
Carries: Live bait, lures, rods, reels, licenses
Bodies of water: Atlantic Ocean, Indian River, Banana River
Services & Products: Beverages, gas/oil, fishing instruction, repair services
Guides: Yes
OK to call for current conditions: Yes
Contact: Ed Havrila

Snook-Nook Discount Bait & Tackle
Jensen Beach 407-334-2145
Hours: 5:30am-8:00pm
Carries: Live bait, lures, flies, maps, rods, reels, licenses
Bodies of water: Indian River (Intracoastal Waterway), Atlantic Ocean, Fresh Water-Savanna's
Services & Products: Boat rentals, guide services, charter boat service, boat ramp, food, beverages, fishing instruction, repair services
Guides: Yes
OK to call for current conditions: Yes
Contact: Henry Calmotto or Staff

FLORIDA AREA RIVERS (NORTH) — FLORIDA

Surf Side Bait & Tackle
Melbourne Beach 407-768-7929
Hours: 6am-7pm Sun.-Thrus., 6am-9pm Fri., Sat.
Carries: Live bait, lures, flies, maps, rods, reels
Bodies of water: Atlantic Ocean, Indian River
Services & Products: Beverages, fishing instruction, repair services, custom rods
Guides: Yes
OK to call for current conditions: Yes
Contact: Victor or Danny

Tarpon Fishermen's Supply Co.
Tarpon Springs 813-938-4337
Hours: 7am-6pm, closed Mon.
Carries: Live bait, lures, maps, rods, reels, licenses
Bodies of water: Gulf of Mexico, Anclote River
Services & Products: Food, beverages, fishing instruction, repair services, canoe rentals
Guides: Yes
OK to call for current conditions: Yes
Contact: Kevin Oneill

Tee Pee's Bait & Tackle Inc.
Middleburg 904-291-0309
Hours: 6am-6:30pm
Carries: Live bait, lures, rods, reels
Bodies of water: Black Creek, St. John's River, Doctors Lake
Services & Products: Food, beverages
Guides: Yes
OK to call for current conditions: Yes
Contact: Nancy Smith

Whitey's Bait & Tackle
Melbourne 407-724-1440
Hours: 6am-Midnite
Carries: Live bait, lures, flies, maps, rods, reels
Bodies of water: Atlantic Ocean, Indian River
Services & Products: Guide services, food, beverages, repair services, camping supplies
Guides: Yes
OK to call for current conditions: Yes
Contact: Anyone

CHARTERS...

Backcountry Charter Service
DeBary 800-932-7335
Species & Seasons: Redfish, Sea Trout Dec-Jan, Tarpon May-Nov, Snook Mar-Oct, Jack Cravalle Nov-May, Ladyfish Sept-May, Striped Bass Feb-June, American Shad Jan-April, LM Bass Nov-April, Panfish April-Sept
Bodies of water: Indian River Lagoon, Mosquito Lagoon, Banana River Lagoon, St. John's River, Stick Marsh, Farm 13
Rates: Half day: $185(1-2), Full day: $275(1-2)
Call between: 24 hours
Provides: Light tackle, fly rod/reel, lures, bait, rain gear, beverages
Handicapped equipped: Yes
Certifications: USCG, FFF, IGFA

Captain Blood
Panama City 904-785-6216
Species & Seasons: Redfish May-Dec, Sea Trout May-Nov, Bluefish, Cobia April-Nov, Flounder Sept-Jan, LM Bass Dec-Feb, Black Drum, Sheepshead Nov-April, Spanish Mackerel Mar-Nov, Shark Jan-Sept
Bodies of water: St. Andrew Bay, Gulf of Mexico, Apalachicola River
Rates: Saltwater: Half day: $175(1-2), Full day: $350(1-2), 6 hrs. $260
Call between: 7am-9am
Provides: Light tackle, fly rod/reel, lures
Handicapped equipped: No
Certifications: USCG

Capt. Shawn Foster
Cocoa Beach 407-784-0094
Species & Seasons: Redfish Feb-Nov, Sea Trout all year, Snook Spring-Fall, Spanish Mackerel Summer-Fall, Tarpon Spring-Summer, Cobia Mar-Sept, Triple Tail April-Aug, LM Bass Feb-Nov, Jack Cravalle, Ladyfish June-Sept
Bodies of water: Banana River, Indian River, Port Canaveral, Mosquito Lagoon, St Johns River, Stick Marsh
Rates: Half day: $200(1-2), Full day: $300(1-2), 3rd person: Half day: $25 additional, Full day: $50 additional
Call between: 5:30pm-7pm
Provides: Light tackle, heavy tackle, fly rod/reel, lures, bait, rain gear, beverages
Handicapped equipped: Yes
Certifications: USCG

GUIDES...

Bass Challenger Guide Service
Orlando 407-273-8045
.... 800-241-5314
Species & Seasons: LM Bass Oct-June
Bodies of water: Butler Chain, Clearmont Chain, Conway Chain, Disney area lakes, St. John's River (south)
Rates: Half day: $150(1-2), Full day: $200(1-2)
Call between: 24 hours
Provides: Light tackle, heavy tackle, lures, bait, rain gear, beverages
Handicapped equipped: Yes

Frank's River Fishing Tours
Vero Beach 407-562-3430
Species & Seasons: Snook, Sea Trout, Redfish, Snapper, Sea Bass, Bluegill, Crappie all year, Tarpon May-Oct
Bodies of water: Lake Okeechobee and tributaries, Blue Cypress Lake, Stick Marsh, Farm 13, Indian River, all inland waters 100 miles from Vero Beach
Rates: Half day: $100(1), $125(2), Full day: $175(1), $200(2), $25 each additional person
Call between: 6am-10pm
Provides: Light tackle, fly rod/reel, lures, rain gear, beverages
Handicapped equipped: Yes

Capt. Mark "Smitty" Smith
Deland 904-738-1836
Species & Seasons: LM Bass Oct-June
Bodies of water: St. John's River, Suwannee River, Withlacoochee River, Apalachicola River, Lake Talquin, Lake George, Crescent Lake, and others
Rates: Half day: $150+(1-2), Full day: $250+(1-2), $25 additional person (limit 3)
Call between: 7pm-10pm
Provides: Light tackle, heavy tackle, rain gear
Handicapped equipped: No
Certifications: USCG

FLORIDA

FLORIDA AREA RIVERS (NORTH)

Steve Rominsky Guide Service
Welaka 904-467-2030
.... 467-8826
Species & Seasons: LM Bass all year, Striped Bass Feb-May, Panfish Mar-Sept
Bodies of water: St John's River, Crescent Lake, Rodman Res., Lake George
Rates: Full day: $175(1), $220(2)
Call between: 7am-8pm
Provides: Light tackle, heavy tackle, lures, bait, rain gear
Handicapped equipped:
Certifications: USCG

LODGING...

Blounts Cottages
Tallassee 904-576-4301
Guest Capacity: 14-24 waterfront cottages
Handicapped equipped: No
Seasons: All year
Rates: Call for rates
Guides: Yes, recommend
Species & Seasons: LM Bass, Striped Bass, White Bass, Bream, Crappie
Bodies of Water: Lake Talquin, Ochlockonee River
Types of fishing: Fly fishing, light tackle

Hide-A-Shile
Ebro 904-535-4834
Guest Capacity: 8
Handicapped equipped: No
Seasons: All year
Rates: $25/day
Contact: Bill Mann
Guides: Yes
Species & Seasons: LM Bass, Bream, Crappie, Shell Cracker, Catfish
Bodies of Water: Choctawhatchee River
Types of fishing: Fly fishing, light tackle
Available: Bait, tackle, boat rentals

Kerr City
Ft. McCoy 904-685-2557
Guest Capacity: 30-40
Handicapped equipped: No
Seasons: All year
Rates: $275/week
Guides: Yes, recommend
Species & Seasons: LM Bass, Crappie
Bodies of Water: St. John's River, Lake Kerr, Oklawaha River, Rodman Res.

Lake Rousseau Campground & Fishing Resort
Crystal River 904-795-6336
Guest Capacity: 200
Handicapped equipped: No
Seasons: All year
Rates: $16/day
Guides: Yes
Species & Seasons: LM Bass, Catfish all year, Crappie Spring, Shell Cracker Summer
Bodies of Water: Lake Rousseau, Withlacoochee River
Types of fishing: Fly fishing, light tackle
Available: Licenses, bait, tackle, boat rentals

Lindsay's Fish Camp
PO Box 341
Geneva 32732
Guest Capacity: 100
Handicapped equipped: No
Seasons: All year
Rates: $12.50/day
Contact: George or Evelyn Griffin
Guides: Yes
Species & Seasons: LM Bass, Catfish all year, Crappie Nov-May, Shad Nov-Feb, Bream Jan-Aug
Bodies of Water: St. John's River, Econolochattchee River, Lake Harney
Types of fishing: Fly fishing, light tackle, heavy tackle, wading, float trips, airboat trips, pontoon trips
Available: Fishing instruction, licenses, bait, tackle, boat rentals, family activities

Parramore's Fish Camp & Family Resort
1675 S. Moon Road
Astor 32102
Guest Capacity: 100
Handicapped equipped: Yes
Seasons: All year
Rates: Camping: $19/night, $116.50/week, Cabins: $66/night, $396/week
Contact: Reva D. Cunningham
Guides: Yes
Species & Seasons: LM Bass, Jan-Mar, Striped Bass May-Sept, Crappie Oct-Mar, Bream May-Sept
Bodies of Water: St. John's River, Lake George, Lake Dexter, Lake Woodruff
Types of fishing: Fly fishing, light tackle
Available: Licenses, bait, tackle, boat rentals, family activities, pool, tennis court

Pine Island Fish Camp
Seville 904-749-2818
Guest Capacity: 86
Handicapped equipped: No
Seasons: All year
Rates: $40/day
Guides: Yes
Species & Seasons: LM Bass, Striped Bass, Bream, Catfish, Crappie all year
Bodies of Water: Lake George, St. John's River
Types of fishing: Fly fishing, light tackle, heavy tackle, wading
Available: Licenses, bait, tackle, boat rentals, air boat tours/rides

Riverside Lodge
Inverness 904-726-2002
Guest Capacity: Adult RV park and cabins
Handicapped equipped: Yes
Seasons: All year
Rates: Cabins: $165/week and up, RV: $15/night
Contact: Herb Goronzy
Guides: No
Bodies of Water: Withlacoochee River
Available: Adult RV spaces, cabins

Shady Oak Fish Camp
245 W. Stetson Street
Deland 32720
Handicapped equipped: No
Seasons: All year
Guides: Yes
Species & Seasons: LM Bass, Bream, Crappie, Catfish, Warmouth all year
Bodies of Water: St. John's River
Types of fishing: Fly fishing, light tackle

Trail's End Camp
Floral City 904-726-0728
Guest Capacity: 120
Handicapped equipped: No
Seasons: All year
Rates: $30-$75/day
Guides: Yes
Species & Seasons: LM Bass Nov-June, Crappie Dec-June, Bluegill Jan-June
Bodies of Water: Withlacoochee River, Tsala Apopka Lake
Types of fishing: Fly fishing, light tackle
Available: Licenses, bait, tackle, boat rentals, general store

Wynn Haven Camp
Bushnell 904-793-4744
Guest Capacity: 15 campsites
Handicapped equipped: No
Seasons: All year
Rates: $15/day
Guides: Yes

FLORIDA AREA RIVERS (SOUTH) — FLORIDA

Species & Seasons: Crappie, Bluegill, LM Bass, Warmouth Oct-April
Bodies of Water: Withlacoochee River
Types of fishing: Fly fishing, light tackle, heavy tackle
Available: Boat rentals

FLORIDA AREA RIVERS (SOUTH)

BAIT & TACKLE...

Bait Shanty
Port Charlotte 813-764-7118
Hours: 7am-5pm
Carries: Live bait, lures, flies, maps, rods, reels
Bodies of water: Gulf of Mexico, Boca Grande, Myakka River
Services & Products: Boat rentals, charter boat service, lodging, boat ramp, food, beverages, gas/oil
Guides: Yes
OK to call for current conditions: Yes

Country Store at Hidden Acres
Lorida 813-763-9532
Hours: 8am-5pm
Carries: Live bait, lures, flies, maps, rods, reels, licenses
Bodies of water: Kissimmee River, Lake Okeechobee
Services & Products: Lodging, boat ramp, food, beverages, gas/oil
Guides: No
OK to call for current conditions: No

J D's Bait & Tackle
South Venice 941-426-7443
Hours: 7am-7pm
Carries: Live bait, lures, flies, rods, reels, licenses
Bodies of water: Myakka River, Charlotte Harbor, Gulf of Mexico
Services & Products: Charter boat service, boat ramp, beverages
Guides: Yes
OK to call for current conditions: Yes
Contact: Linda or Kenneth Rennison

Perico Harbor Bait & Tackle
Bradenton 813-795-8433
Hours: 7am-6pm
Carries: Live bait, lures, maps, rods, reels, licenses
Bodies of water: Tampa Bay, Perico Bay, Manatee River, Egmont Key, Sarasota Bay, Terra Ceia Bay, Anna Maria Island
Services & Products: Guide services, charter boat service, food, beverages, gas/oil, fishing instruction, repair services
Guides: Yes
OK to call for current conditions: Yes
Contact: Lee, Libby or Carl

Tackle Box
Gainesville 904-372-1791
Hours: 7am-6pm Mon.-Fri., 6am-5pm Sat., 7am-2pm Sun.
Carries: Live bait, lures, flies, maps, rods, reels, licenses
Bodies of water: Orange Lake, Lochlossa Lake, Newman's Lake
Services & Products: Repair services
Guides: Yes
OK to call for current conditions: Yes
Contact: Recorded fishing report 904-375-FISH

CHARTERS...

Catfisher, Inc.
Cape Coral 941-574-2524
Species & Seasons: Snook, Redfish, Tarpon, Spotted Trout, Cobia, Triple Tail, Amberjack, Shark all year, Snook, Redfish during open seasons
Bodies of water: Caloosahatchee River, Pine Island Sound, Matlacha Pass, Red Fish Pass, Edison Reef, Sanibel Point, San Carlos Bay, CATCH & RELEASE!
Rates: Half day: $150(1), $200(2), Full day: $250(1), night charters +$50
Call between: 7p.m-9pm
Provides: Light tackle, lures, bait, rain gear
Handicapped equipped: No
Certifications: USCG

King Fisher Cruise Lines
Punta Gorda 941-639-0969
Species & Seasons: Tarpon May-Aug, King Mackerel, Spanish Mackerel, Amberjack Mar-Nov, Barracuda Mar-Dec, Grouper, Snapper, Snook, Redfish, Sea Trout all year
Bodies of water: Eastern Gulf of Mexico, Charlotte Harbor, Peace River, Boca Grande Pass
Rates: Deep Sea Charters: $450 Full day: per boat, $85 pp - up to 6 people. Back Bay: Full day: $250, Half day: $150, up to 4 people
Call between: 8am-6pm
Provides: Light tackle, heavy tackle, fly rod/reel, lures, bait
Handicapped equipped: Yes
Certifications: USCG, IGFA

LODGING...

Linger Lodge
Bradenton 813-755-2757
Handicapped equipped: Yes
Seasons: All year
Rates: $16.50/day
Guides: No
Species & Seasons: LM Bass, Bluegill, Catfish
Bodies of Water: Gulf of Mexico, Braden River, Manatee River
Types of fishing: Fly fishing, light tackle
Available: Restaurant

Trails End Fishing Resort
Lorida 813-655-3891
Guest Capacity: 4 cabins, sleep 16
Handicapped equipped: Yes
Seasons: All year
Rates: Cabins: $50/day, $284/week
Contact: Stan Shaw
Guides: Yes
Species & Seasons: LM Bass, Crappie, Bluegill all year, Shell Cracker Spring-Fall, Duck hunting Sept-Jan
Bodies of Water: Lake Istokpoga, Kissimmee River
Types of fishing: Fly fishing, light tackle, heavy tackle, wading
Available: Fishing instruction, licenses, bait, tackle, boat rentals, family activities

MARINAS...

Yacht Haven Park & Marina
Ft. Lauderdale 800-581-2322
.... 305-583-2322
Hours: 9am-9pm
Bodies of water: New River
Services & Products: Boat ramp, RV park
Guides: Yes
OK to call for current conditions: Yes
Contact: Ginger Backman

FLORIDA

FLORIDA BAY - FLORIDA KEYS

FLORIDA BAY

BAIT & TACKLE...

Bill's Bait & Tackle Shop
Key Largo 305-451-0531
Hours: 7am-7pm Mon-Thurs., 7am-9pm Fri., 6am-9pm Sat., 6am-6pm Sun.
Carries: Live bait, lures, flies, maps, rods, reels, licenses
Bodies of water: Florida Bay, Atlantic Ocean
Services & Products: Guide services, charter boat service, beverages, fishing instruction, repair services, custom rod building
Guides: Yes
OK to call for current conditions: Yes

CHARTERS...

Capt. Bob Dove
Islamorada 800-262-9112
Species & Seasons: Bonefish, Snook, Redfish, Sea Trout, Snapper, Barracuda, Shark all year, Tarpon Mar-Jan, Permit Mar-Dec
Bodies of water: Florida Keys (upper), Florida Bay
Rates: Half day: $225(1-2), Full day: $325(1-2), 3rd person $50 (no 3rd person bonefishing)
Call between: After 5:30 pm
Provides: Light tackle, fly rod/reel, lures, bait, rain gear
Handicapped equipped: No
Certifications: USCG and Yamaha Endorsed

LODGING...

Breezy Palms Resort
Islamorada 305-664-2361
Guest Capacity: 39 units
Handicapped equipped: No
Seasons: All year
Rates: $45-$180/day per room
Contact: Gail M. Schaper
Guides: Yes
Species & Seasons: Marlin, Sailfish Jan-Sept, Dolphin, Tuna Mar-Sept, Bonefish Jan-Jan, Tarpon April-May
Bodies of Water: Atlantic Ocean, Gulf of Mexico, Florida Bay
Types of fishing: Fly fishing, light tackle, heavy tackle, wading
Available: Bait, tackle, boat rentals

Sandalwood Lodge
12501 Overseas Hwy.
Marathon 33050
Guest Capacity: 11 rooms/efficiencies
Handicapped equipped: No
Seasons: All year
Rates: From: $40/day, $240/week
Contact: Barrie Smith
Guides: Yes
Species & Seasons: Dolphin, Wahoo, Sailfish, Marlin, Tuna, King, Grouper, Snapper
Bodies of Water: Atlantic Ocean, Florida Bay
Types of fishing: Fly fishing, light tackle, heavy tackle, wading
Available: Licenses, bait, tackle, boat rentals

FLORIDA KEYS

BAIT & TACKLE...

Bill's Bait & Tackle Shop
Key Largo 305-451-0531
Hours: 7am-7pm M-Thurs., 7am-9pm Fri., 6am-9pm Sat., 6am-6pm Sun.
Carries: Live bait, lures, flies, maps, rods, reels, licenses
Bodies of water: Florida Bay, Atlantic Ocean
Services & Products: Guide services, charter boat service, beverages, fishing instruction, repair services, custom rod building
Guides: Yes
OK to call for current conditions: Yes

Key West Boat Rentals
Key West 305-294-2628
Hours: 8am-8pm
Carries: Lures, maps, rods, reels, licenses
Bodies of water: Carribean Sea, Atlantic Ocean, Gulf of Mexico, Straits of Florida
Services & Products: Boat rentals, guide services, charter boat service, lodging, boat ramp, food, beverages, diving
Guides: Yes
OK to call for current conditions: Yes
Contact: John or Steve

CHARTERS...

Abyss Pro Dive Center
Marathon 305-743-2126
Hours: 8am-6pm
Bodies of water: Florida Keys, Gulf of Mexico, Atlantic Ocean
Services & Products: Charter boat service
Guides: Yes
OK to call for current conditions: Yes
Contact: Capt. Bill Ferrell

Bounty Hunter
Marathon 305-743-2446
Species & Seasons: Tarpon April-June, Shark June-Sept, Barracuda, Snapper, Grouper all year, Cobia Dec-Mar
Bodies of water: Florida Keys
Rates: Half day: $325(6 or less), Full day: $450(6 or less)
Call between: 6:30-7:30am/6:30-7:30pm
Provides: Light tackle, heavy tackle, bait, rain gear
Handicapped equipped: Yes
Certifications: 25 yrs. fishing

Capt. Pat Bracher
Big Pine Key 305-745-3408
Species & Seasons: Tarpon Mar-Aug, Bonefish, Permit all year, Barracuda Dec-Mar
Bodies of water: Lower Florida Keys, Key West Flats
Rates: Half day: $225(1-2), Full day: $325(1-2)
Call between: 7pm-9pm
Provides: Light tackle, fly rod/reel, lures, bait, rain gear
Handicapped equipped: No
Certifications: USCG

A.E. Brackett
Cudjoe Key 305-745-9478
Species & Seasons: Tarpon, Shark Mar-July, Bonefish Feb-July, Permit April-July, Barracuda Jan-July
Bodies of water: Atlantic Ocean Flats, Gulf of Mexico Backcountry, Florida Keys
Rates: Half day: $225(1-2), Full day: $300(1-2)
Call between: 6pm-8pm
Provides: Light tackle, fly rod/reel, lures, bait, rain gear
Certifications: USCG

FLORIDA KEYS — FLORIDA

Capt. Jim Brienza
Key West 305-294-6027
Species & Seasons: Tarpon Mar-July, Sailfish Jan-June, Kingfish Dec-Feb, Cobia Nov-April, Blackfin Tuna Dec-April, Dolphin May-Aug, Barracuda all year, Shark Mar-Aug, Amberjack all year, Bonito Feb-Dec
Bodies of water: Gulf of Mexico, Atlantic Ocean
Rates: Half day: $325(1-4), Full day: $450(1-4) whole boat
Call between: 6pm-10pm
Provides: Light tackle, lures, bait, rain gear, beverages
Handicapped equipped: Yes
Certifications: USCG

Bubba
Key West 305-296-4535
Species & Seasons: Tarpon Mar-July, Permit Mar-Aug, Cobia Nov-July, Sailfish, Barracuda, Shark all year
Bodies of water: Florida Keys, Gulf of Mexico
Rates: Half day: $325(1-4), Full day: $450(1-4)
Call between: 6:30pm-9:30pm
Provides: Light tackle, fly rod/reel, lures, bait, rain gear
Handicapped equipped: Yes

Capt. Bob Dove
Islamorada 800-262-9112
Species & Seasons: Bonefish, Snook, Redfish, Sea Trout, Snapper, Barracuda, Shark all year, Tarpon Mar-Jan, Permit Mar-Dec
Bodies of water: Florida Keys (upper), Florida Bay
Rates: Half day: $225(1-2), Full day: $325(1-2), 3rd person $50 (no 3rd person bonefishing)
Call between: After 5:30 pm
Provides: Light tackle, fly rod/reel, lures, bait, rain gear
Handicapped equipped: No
Certifications: USCG and Yamaha Endorsed

El Chino
Marathon 305-743-9280
Species & Seasons: Marlin, Wahoo, Dolphin, Tuna, Barracuda all year, Sailfish May-Feb, Tarpon April-July, Kingfish Oct-Mar
Bodies of water: Florida Keys, Gulf of Mexico, Atlantic Ocean
Rates: Half day: $450(1-6) offshore, $350(1-6) reef, Full day: $550(1-6) offshore, $450(1-6) reef
Call between: 6:30am-11pm
Provides: Light tackle, heavy tackle, lures, bait
Handicapped equipped: Yes
Certifications: USCG

Fishbuster & Billfisher
Key West 305-296-9969
Species & Seasons: Sailfish Nov-May, Dolphin, Marlin May-Aug
Bodies of water: Atlantic Ocean, Gulf of Mexico
Rates: Half day: $100(1), Full day: $150(1) Full boat: Half day: $400, Full day: $600
Call between: 7pm-10pm
Provides: Light tackle, heavy tackle, lures, bait, rain gear
Handicapped equipped: Yes

Fun Yet Charters
Little Torch Key 305-872-3407
Species & Seasons: Dolphin Spring-Fall, Sailfish, King Mackerel Cobia Fall-Spring, Barracuda, Grouper, Mangrove Snapper, Wahoo, Mutton Snapper all year, Tarpon Spring-Summer
Bodies of water: Gulf of Mexico, Florida Keys, Atlantic Ocean
Rates: Half day: $225(1-6), Full day: $325(1-6)
Call between: 7am-11pm
Provides: Light tackle, heavy tackle, lures, bait, rain gear
Handicapped equipped: No
Certifications: Fully licensed and insured

Capt. Andy Griffiths
Key West 305-296-2639
Species & Seasons: Black Grouper Feb-April, Yellowtail Snapper, Mutton Snapper, Red Grouper, Porgy, Mackerel all year, Kingfish Jan-Mar, Dolphin May-Aug, Tuna, Dec-Feb
Bodies of water: Gulf of Mexico, Atlantic Ocean, Florida Keys, (Marguesas Keys, Dry Tortugas, Key West)
Rates: 3 days: $333(1), 2 days 1 night: $1300(6), 3 days 2 nights: $2000(6)
Call between: 8-8:30am-7-10pm
Provides: Light tackle, heavy tackle, lures, bait
Certifications: USCG

Hot Pursuit Charters
Marathon 800-473-4106
.... 305-743-0406
Species & Seasons: Tarpon Mar-June, Sailfish Dec-May, Dolphin April-Nov, Snapper, Grouper all year
Bodies of water: Atlantic Ocean, Straits of Florida, Gulf of Mexico
Rates: Half day: $275(1-6), Full day: $375(1-6)
Call between:
Provides: Light tackle, lures, bait
Handicapped equipped: Yes
Certifications: USCG

Lands End Marina
Key West 305-745-4634
Species & Seasons: Tarpon April-Aug, Bonefish July-Nov, Permit July-April, Barracuda Dec-March, Shark all year
Bodies of water: Lower Florida Keys
Rates: Half day: $225(1-2), Full day: $350(1-2)
Call between: 6pm-10pm
Provides: Light tackle, fly rod/reel, lures, bait, rain gear
Handicapped equipped: No
Certifications: USCG, 20 years experience

On the Fly
Summerland Key 800-946-6359
.... 305-745-4199
Species & Seasons: Blackfin Tuna, Yellowfin Tuna, King Mackerel, Barracuda, Cobia, Grouper, Snapper Jan-Feb, Tarpon, Permit, Sailfish, Dolphin, Cobia, Bonefish Mar-June, Tuna, Wahoo, Sailfish, Dolphin July-Dec
Bodies of water: Wreck fishing the Gulf of Mexico, Atlantic Ocean, Backcountry Florida Keys, Dry Tortugas, Marquesas Keys, Reef Fishing Key West
Rates: Half day: $350(1-2), Full day: $450(1-2)
Call between: 6am-11pm
Provides: Light tackle, heavy tackle, fly rod/reel, lures, bait, rain gear, beverages
Handicapped equipped: Yes
Certifications: USCG

The Reel Life
Key West 800-286-1855
Species & Seasons: Sailfish, Shark all year, Tarpon Mar-July, Blackfin Tuna, Cobia Oct-May, Permit April-Oct, Kingfish Nov-April, Dolphin April-Sept, Wahoo Aug-Mar, Yellowfin Tuna Jan-Mar
Bodies of water: Atlantic Ocean, Gulf of Mexico, Key West inshore areas
Rates: Half day: $300(1-4), Full day: $450(1-4)
Call between: 5:30pm-9:30pm
Provides: Light tackle, fly rod/reel, lures, bait, rain gear
Handicapped equipped: No
Certifications: USCG

FLORIDA

FLORIDA KEYS - GULF OF MEXICO & BAYS (NORTH)

Capt. Alan Starr
Islamorada 305-664-4373
Species & Seasons: Sailfish Nov-April, Tuna Oct-May, Cobia Jan-April, Snapper Oct-June, Dolphin April-July Kingfish Nov-Feb
Bodies of water: Atlantic Ocean, Straits of Florida, Florida Keys, Bahamas
Rates: Half day: $450, Full day: $650, up to 6 people
Call between: Anytime
Provides: Light tackle, heavy tackle, fly rod/reel, lures, bait, rain gear
Handicapped equipped: Yes

Sun Dancer
Summerland Key 305-745-3063
Species & Seasons: Tarpon Mar-July, Sailfish Oct-May, Kingfish, Cobia Dec-Mar, Bonefish, Permit all year
Bodies of water: Atlantic Ocean, Gulf of Mexico
Rates: Half day: $350(2), Full day: $450(2), Flats Skiff: Half day: $225, Full day: $325
Call between: 7pm-9pm
Provides: Light tackle, fly rod/reel, lures, bait, rain gear
Handicapped equipped: Yes
Certifications: USCG

Ultimate Fishing Charters
Tavernier 305-852-4969
Species & Seasons: Tarpon Mar-Aug, Bonefish, Redfish all year, Permit Feb-Sept, Snook, Sea Trout Dec-June
Bodies of water: Florida Keys (Islamorada)
Rates: Half day: $200(1-2), Full day: $300(1-2), $50 additional for 3rd person
Call between: 9am-9pm
Provides: Light tackle, fly rod/reel, lures, bait, rain gear
Handicapped equipped: No
Certifications: USCG

Windy Day
Key West 800-831-6407
Species & Seasons: Tarpon Feb-Aug, Bonefish April-Nov, Sailfish, Snapper, Wahoo all year, Cobia Oct-June, King Mackerel Dec-Mar, Permit Feb-Dec
Bodies of water: Gulf of Mexico, Atlantic Ocean
Rates: Half day: $275(2), Full day $400(2)
Call between: 6pm-9pm
Provides: Light tackle, fly rod/reel, lures, rain gear
Handicapped equipped: Yes
Certifications: USCG Yamaha Guide

LODGING...

Edgewater Lodge
PO Box 799
Long Key 33001
Guest Capacity: 40
Handicapped equipped: Yes
Seasons: All year
Rates: $60-$80/day
Guides: Yes
Species & Seasons: Tarpon April-June, Sailfish, Kingfish Dec-April, Grouper, Snapper, Dolphin all year
Bodies of Water: Atlantic Ocean, Gulf of Mexico
Types of fishing: Fly fishing, light tackle, heavy tackle
Available: Bait, tackle

MARINAS...

Dolphin Marina
Little Torch Key 800-553-0308
.... 305-872-2685
Hours: 7:30am-6pm
Carries: Live bait, lures, maps, licenses
Bodies of water: Atlantic Ocean, Gulf of Mexico
Services & Products: Boat rentals, guide services, charter boat service, lodging, boat ramp, food, beverages, gas/oil, snorkel and sunset cruises
Guides: Yes
OK to call for current conditions: Yes

GULF OF MEXICO & BAYS (NORTH)

BAIT & TACKLE...

B'Jon Bait & Tackle Shop
Panama City 904-874-1982
Hours: Sunrise-Sunset
Carries: Live bait, lures, maps, rods, reels
Bodies of water: Gulf of Mexico
Services & Products: Guide services, beverages, fishing instruction, repair services
Guides: Yes
OK to call for current conditions: Yes
Contact: Tom Egan

Gray's Tackle & Guide Service
Pensacola 904-492-2666
.... 934-3151
Hours: 5:30am-8pm
Carries: Live bait, lures, flies, maps, rods, reels, licenses
Bodies of water: Gulf of Mexico, Pensacola Bay, Perdido Bay, Escambia River
Services & Products: Guide services, charter boat service, fishing instruction, repair services
OK to call for current conditions: Yes
Contact: Bob or Maggie Gray

Hernando Beach Bait & Tackle
Spring Hill 904-596-3375
Hours: 7am-5:30pm
Carries: Live bait, lures, maps, rods, reels, licenses
Bodies of water: Gulf of Mexico, Weeki Wachee River
Services & Products: Guide services, charter boat service, food, beverages, fishing instruction
OK to call for current conditions: Yes
Contact: Nancy Forshier

John's Guns & Fly Fishing
Tallahassee 904-422-1553
Hours: 9am-6:30pm
Carries: Flies, maps, rods, reels, licenses
Bodies of water: Jackson Lake, Lake Seminole, Lake Talquin, Ochlockonee River, St. Marks River, Wakulla River, Aucilla River, Econfina River, Steinhatchee River, Apalachee Bay
Services & Products: Fishing instruction, repair services, free set up and fly-casting instruction
Guides: Yes
OK to call for current conditions: Yes
Contact: John V. Underwood

Navarre Bait & Tackle
Navarre 904-939-0734
Hours: 6am-6pm
Carries: Live bait, lures, flies, rods, reels
Bodies of water: Gulf of Mexico, Santa Rosa Sound, East River, East Bay, Yellow River
Services & Products: Beverages, fishing instruction, repair services
Guides: Yes
OK to call for current conditions: Yes
Contact: Richard or Sheila Deaton

GULF OF MEXICO & BAYS (NORTH) — FLORIDA

Salty Bass Bait & Tackle
Fort Walton Beach 904-863-7999
Hours: 6am-6:30pm
Carries: Live bait, lures, flies, maps, rods, reels
Bodies of water: East River, Choctawhatchee River, Choctawhatchee Bay, Ponds, Juniper Lake, Blackwater River
Services & Products: Guide services, beverages, fishing instruction, repair services
Guides: Yes
OK to call for current conditions: Yes

Tarpon Fishermen's Supply Co.
Tarpon Springs 813-938-4337
Hours: 7am-6pm, closed Mon.
Carries: Live bait, lures, maps, rods, reels, licenses
Bodies of water: Gulf of Mexico, Anclote River
Services & Products: Food, beverages, fishing instruction, repair services, canoe rentals
Guides: Yes
OK to call for current conditions: Yes
Contact: Kevin Oneill

CHARTERS...

A Van Horn Charters
Tarpon Springs 800-757-8577
.... 813-938-8577
Species & Seasons: LM Bass, all year, Snook, Redfish Mar-Nov, Cobia Mar-June, Tarpon April-July
Bodies of water: Lake Tarpon, Gulf of Mexico Flats (from Boca Grand to Homosassa)
Rates: Half day: $250(1-2), Full day: $350(1-2), $50 additional 3rd person
Call between: Anytime
Provides: Light tackle, heavy tackle, fly rod/reel, lures, bait, rain gear
Handicapped equipped: Yes
Certifications: USCG

Absolute Flats Fishing
Palm Harbor 813-787-9830
Species & Seasons: Tarpon April-July, Snook, Redfish, Sea Trout all year, Kingfish Mar-April, Cobia May-Aug
Bodies of water: Gulf of Mexico, Tampa Bay, Clearwater, Boca Grande, Tarpon Springs
Rates: Half day: $200(2), $225(3), Full day: $300(2), $325(3)

Call between: 6pm-10pm
Provides: Light tackle, fly rod/reel, lures, bait, rain gear
Handicapped equipped: Yes
Certifications: USCG

Back Bay Fishing Charters
Destin 904-654-5566
.... 585-3321
Species & Seasons: Redfish Mar-Nov, Trout May-Oct Sheepshead all year, Flounder Sept-Nov, Pampano Mar-May
Bodies of water: Choctawatchee Bay
Rates: Half day: $225(4), Full day: $450(4)
Call between: Anytime
Provides: Light tackle, lures, bait
Certifications: USCG

Captain Blood
Panama City 904-785-6216
Species & Seasons: Redfish May-Dec, Sea Trout May-Nov, Bluefish, Cobia April-Nov, Flounder Sept-Jan, LM Bass Dec-Feb, Black Drum, Sheepshead Nov-April, Spanish Mackerel Mar-Nov, Shark Jan-Sept
Bodies of water: St. Andrew Bay, Gulf of Mexico, Apalachicola River
Rates: Saltwater: Half day: $175(1-2), Full day: $350(1-2), 6 hrs.: $260
Call between: 7am-9am
Provides: Light tackle, fly rod/reel, lures
Handicapped equipped: No
Certifications: USCG

Dolphin Bait & Tackle & AAA Charter Service
Pensacola 904-438-3242
Species & Seasons: Red Snapper, Grouper, Triggerfish, Amberjack all year, King Mackerel, Wahoo, May-Oct, Cobia April-July, Dolphin May-Nov, Marlin, Sailfish June-Oct, Red Drum June-Feb
Bodies of water: Gulf of Mexico
Rates: Half day: $400(1-6), Full day: $500(1-6), over 6 $50 additional
Call between: 7am-5pm

Provides: Light tackle, heavy tackle, lures, bait
Handicapped equipped: Yes
Certifications: USCG

Fish-N-Fool
Destin 904-837-3515
.... 865-7474
Species & Seasons: Grouper, Snapper Mar-Oct, King Mackerel, Spanish Mackerel May-Sept, Amberjack all year
Bodies of water: Gulf of Mexico
Rates: Half day: $325(up to 6 people), 8 hrs.: $625(up to 6 people), 10 hrs.: $740(up to 6 people)
Call between: 7pm-9pm
Provides: Light tackle, heavy tackle, bait
Handicapped equipped: Yes

Lo-Baby Charters
Gulf Breeze 904-934-5285
Species & Seasons: Cobia Mar-May, Mackerel, Red Snapper, Grouper, Triggerfish May-Dec
Bodies of water: Gulf of Mexico
Rates: Half day: $400(6 or less), Full day: $500(6 or less), Group rate 10 or less $600, 15 or less $700
Call between: 7am-9pm
Provides: Light tackle, heavy tackle, lures, bait
Handicapped equipped: Yes
Certifications: USCG

Quester
Pensacola 904-944-5269
.... 800-806-7889
Species & Seasons: Red Snapper, Grouper, Amberjack all year, King Mackerel June-Sept, Cobia Mar-May, Spanish Mackerel May-Sept
Bodies of water: Gulf of Mexico
Rates: Half day: $50(1), Full day: $65(1), Private charter $600, Full day: 7 people
Provides: Light tackle, heavy tackle, lures, bait
Handicapped equipped: Yes
Certifications: USCG

ABSOLUTE FLATS FISHING
SNOOK TARPON REDFISH TROUT
Capt. Rich Knox
Nearshore • Inshore • Backcountry
(813) 787-9830 Clearwater/Tampa
• Full Time Fisherman •

FLORIDA — GULF OF MEXICO & BAYS (NORTH)

Shamrock Charters
Pensacola 904-469-0609
Species & Seasons: Red Snapper Mar-Dec, King Mackerel May-Sept
Bodies of water: Gulf of Mexico
Rates: Half day: $45(1), Full day: $60(1), private charter available
Call between: 8am-9pm
Provides: Light tackle, heavy tackle, lures, bait
Handicapped equipped: Yes
Certifications: USCG

Southern Doll
Youngstown 904-722-4111
Species & Seasons: Grouper, Amberjack, Spanish Mackerel, King Mackerel, Triggerfish, Red Snapper Feb-Oct
Bodies of water: Gulf of Mexico
Rates: $60 hr. up to 6 people for half days plus
Call between: 6pm-9pm
Provides: Light tackle, heavy tackle, lures, bait, legal marriages performed
Handicapped equipped: Yes

Southern Hooker
Panama City Bch. 904-234-1308
Species & Seasons: Grouper, Snapper, Amberjack all year, King Mackerel, Spanish Mackerel Dolphin, Tuna, Wahoo, Cobia May-Nov, Marlin, Sailfish Jun-Aug
Bodies of water: Gulf of Mexico
Rates: 6 people or less $70 hour
Call between: Anytime
Provides: Light tackle, heavy tackle, lures, bait
Handicapped equipped: Yes
Certifications: USCG

Capt Sandy Ware
Panama City 904-763-8327
Species & Seasons: Red Snapper, Black Grouper, Amberjack all year, King Mackerel May-Nov, Spanish Mackerel, Cobia Mar-June, Shark May-Sept, Dolphin, Wahoo June-Oct, Marlin June-Sept, Bluefish, Redfish all year
Bodies of water: Gulf of Mexico, St. Andrews Bay
Rates: Half day: $280(6), Full day: $560(6), Additional people: Half day: $20, Full day: $40
Call between: Anytime
Provides: Light takle, heavy tackle, lures, bait
Handicapped equipped: Yes
Certifications: USCG, member FOWA, IGFA

Bob Zales
Panama City 904-763-7249
Species & Seasons: King Mackerel April-Nov, Amberjack, Grouper all year, Cobia April-Nov, Blue Marlin, White Marlin, Sailfish, Wahoo, Dolphin May-Nov, Spanish Mackerel Mar-Nov
Bodies of water: Gulf of Mexico (North East)
Rates: Half day: $50(1), $100(2), Full day: $100(1), $200(2), $65 to $90 per hour
Call between: 7am-10pm
Provides: Light tackle, heavy tackle, lures, bait
Handicapped equipped: Yes
Certifications: USCG

GUIDES...

George P. Ballard Fishing Guide
Pensacola 904-434-1001
Species & Seasons: Blue Marlin, Sailfish, Blackfin Tuna April-Nov, White Marlin, Broadbill Swordfish May-Dec, Yellowfin Tuna May-Nov, Wahoo April-Dec, Dolphin, Bonito May-Nov, King Mackerel May-Oct, Ladyfish June-Sept, Cobia Mar-April
Bodies of water: Gulf of Mexico
Rates: Half day: $100(1-2), Full day: $150(1-2)
Call between: 7am-4pm
Provides: Light tackle, heavy tackle, lures, bait
Handicapped equipped: Yes, on their boat

LODGING...

Kings Lake Campground
Route 5 Box 120
De Funiak Springs 32443
Guest Capacity: 68 RV sites(2 per site), 5 rental cabins
Handicapped equipped: Yes
Seasons: All year
Rates: RV: $15/day, Rentals: 1 bedroom $40/day, 2 bdrm $50/day (2 night min.)
Contact: Roger Roy
Guides: Yes
Species & Seasons: LM Bass Feb-Oct, Bream May-Nov, Catfish all year, Shell Cracker April-Nov
Bodies of Water: King Lake, Holley Lake, Gulf of Mexico
Types of fishing: Fly fishing, light tackle, heavy tackle
Available: Bait, tackle, boat rentals, family activities

Pat Johnson's Fish Camp
Steinhatchee 904-498-3159
Guest Capacity: 3 RVS, 8 cabins, and lodge
Seasons: All year
Rates: RV: $10/day(2), Cabins: $22, $35, $42
Contact: Alice or Pat Johnson
Guides: Yes
Species & Seasons: Speckled Trout all year, Redfish June-Feb, Mackerel April-Sept, Sheepshead April-Oct, Cobia April-Nov, Scallops July-Sept
Bodies of Water: Gulf of Mexico, Steinhatchee River
Types of fishing: Light tackle, heavy tackle
Available Fishing instruction, family activities, charter boats, licenses furnished, dock fishing

Riverside Inn Resort
Homosassa 800-442-2040
Guest Capacity: 80 rooms
Seasons: All year
Rates: $59+-$79+/day
Guides: Yes
Species & Seasons: Tarpon May-June, Redfish June-March, Trout, Grouper all year, Cobia May-Sept
Bodies of Water: Homosassa River, Crystal River, Gulf of Mexico
Types of fishing: Fly fishing, light tackle, heavy tackle
Available: Fishing istruction, licenses, bait, tackle, boat rentals, family activities

MARINAS....

East Pass Marina Fuel & Supply
Destin 904-837-2622
Hours: 7am-6pm, closed Dec.-Feb.
Carries: Live bait, lures, maps, rods, reels, licenses
Bodies of water: Gulf of Mexico, inland bays and rivers
Services & Products: Boat rentals, guide services, charter boat service, boat ramp, food, beverages, gas/oil, fishing instruction
Guides: Yes
OK to call for current conditions: Yes
Contact: Anyone

GULF OF MEXICO & BAYS (NORTH - SOUTH) — FLORIDA

Leeside Inn & Marina - Deckhands Marine Boatyard
Ft. Walton Beach 904-243-7359
.... 800-824-2747
Hours: 24hours
Bodies of water: Choctawhatchee Bay, Gulf of Mexico
Services & Products: Boat rentals, charter boat service, lodging, food, beverages, fishing instruction, repair services, marine travel lift to 30 tons
Guides: Yes
OK to call for current conditions: Yes
Contact: Rick Deckert

Weeki Wachee Marina
Spring Hill 904-596-2850
Hours: 8am-6pm
Carries: Live bait, lures, rods, reels
Bodies of water: Weeki Wachee River, Gulf of Mexico
Services & Products: Boat rentals, food, beverages, gas/oil
Guides: Yes
OK to call for current conditions: Yes

GULF OF MEXICO & BAYS (SOUTH)

BAIT & TACKLE...

Anglers Answer
Naples 813-775-7336
Hours: 6am-6pm
Carries: Live bait, lures, flies, maps, rods, reels, licenses
Bodies of water: Gulf of Mexico, Lake Okeechobee, Lake Trafford
Services & Products: Guide services, beverages, fishing instruction, repair services
Guides: Yes
OK to call for current conditions: Yes
Contact: Dan or Bill

Bait Bucket I
Tierra Verde 813-864-2108
Hours: 6am-11pm
Carries: Live bait, lures, flies, maps, rods, reels, licenses
Bodies of water: Gulf of Mexico, Intracoastal Waterways, Boca Ciega Bay, Tampa Bay, Egmont Key
Services & Products: Guide services, charter boat service, food, beverages, fishing instruction, repair services
OK to call for current conditions: Yes

Bait Shanty
Port Charlotte 813-764-7118
Hours: 7am-5pm
Carries: Live bait, lures, flies, maps, rods, reels
Bodies of water: Gulf of Mexico, Boca Grande, Myakka River
Services & Products: Boat rentals, charter boat service, lodging, boat ramp, food, beverages, gas/oil
Guides: Yes
OK to call for current conditions: Yes

Baitmasters/SeaTreats Fish Market
St. Petersburg.................. 813-321-6674
Hours: 9am-6pm, closed Sun., Mon.
Carries:
Bodies of water: Gulf of Mexico, Tampa Bay
Services & Products: Food, beverages
Guides: Yes
OK to call for current conditions: No

Golden Gate Trophy Center
Naples 813-455-1337
Hours: 6am-7pm
Carries: Live bait, lures, flies, maps, rods, reels, licenses
Bodies of water: Lake Trafford, Lake Okeechobee, Gulf of Mexico, Ten Thousand Islands, fishable fresh water canals
Services & Products: Guide services, charter boat service, beverages, repair services
OK to call for current conditions: Yes
Contact: Alec or Georgia Alexandre

Harts Landing
Sarasota 941-955-0011
Hours: 6am-10pm
Carries: Live bait, lures, maps, rods, reels, licenses
Bodies of water: Tampa Bay
Services & Products: Guide services, boat ramp, food, beverages, fishing instruction
Guides: Yes
OK to call for current conditions: Yes
Contact: Anyone

Iggie's Bait & Tackle
Hialeah 305-887-3929
Hours: 6:30am-8pm
Carries: Live bait, lures, flies, rods, reels, licenses
Bodies of water: Gulf of Mexico, Atlantic Ocean, Miami Airport Lake, Lake Okeechobee
Services & Products: Food, beverages, repair services
Guides: Yes

J D's Bait & Tackle
South Venice 941-426-7443
Hours: 7am-7pm
Carries: Live bait, lures, flies, rods, reels, licenses
Bodies of water: Myakka River, Charlotte Harbor, Gulf of Mexico
Services & Products: Charter boat service, boat ramp, beverages
Guides: Yes
OK to call for current conditions: Yes
Contact: Linda or Kenneth Rennison

Key West Boat Rentals
Key West 305-294-2628
Hours: 8am-8pm
Carries: Lures, maps, rods, reels, licenses
Bodies of water: Carribean Sea, Atlantic Ocean, Gulf of Mexico, Straits of Florida
Services & Products: Boat rentals, guide services, charter boat service, lodging, boat ramp, food, beverages, diving
Guides: Yes
OK to call for current conditions: Yes
Contact: John or Steve

Mr. C.B's Saltwater Outfitters
Sarasota 813-349-4400
Hours: 7am-6pm
Carries: Live bait, lures, flies, maps, rods, reels, licenses
Bodies of water: Gulf of Mexico, Siesta Key
Services & Products: Boat rentals, guide services, charter boat service, food, beverages, gas/oil, fishing instruction, repair services
OK to call for current conditions: Yes
Contact: Aledia or Chris

Perico Harbor Bait & Tackle
Bradenton 813-795-8433
Hours: 7am-6pm
Carries: Live bait, lures, maps, rods, reels, licenses
Bodies of water: Tampa Bay, Perico Bay, Manatee River, Egmont Key, Sarasota Bay, Terra Ceia Bay, Anna Maria Island
Services & Products: Guide services, charter boat service, food, beverages, gas/oil, fishing instruction, repair services
Guides: Yes
OK to call for current conditions: Yes
Contact: Lee, Libby or Carl

FLORIDA — GULF OF MEXICO & BAYS (SOUTH)

Rio Villa Bait & Tackle
Punta Gorda 813-639-7166
Hours: 6:30am-7pm
Carries: Live bait, lures, flies, maps, rods, reels, licenses
Bodies of water: Alligator Creek, Charlotte Harbor
Services & Products: Fishing instruction, repair services, Fishing Buddies Club
Guides: Yes
OK to call for current conditions: Yes
Contact: Becky or Jim Adkins

Tackle Box
Gainesville 904-372-1791
Hours: 7am-6pm Mon.-Fri., 6am-5pm Sat., 7am-2pm Sun.
Carries: Live bait, lures, flies, maps, rods, reels, licenses
Bodies of water: Orange Lake, Lochlossa Lake, Newman's Lake
Services & Products: Repair services
Guides: Yes
OK to call for current conditions: Yes
Contact: Recorded fishing report 904-375-FISH

Tradewinds Bait & Tackle
Port Charlotte 813-629-3118
Hours: 6am-9pm Sun.-Thrus., 6am-11pm Fri.
Carries: Live bait, lures, flies, maps, rods, reels
Bodies of water: Charlotte Harbor, Makia River, Boca Grande
Services & Products: Guide services, fishing instruction, repair services
Guides: Yes
OK to call for current conditions: Yes
Contact: Capt. George Hayden or Capt. Tony Lay

Willies Custom Trolling Baits
Lake Park 407-848-4484
Hours: 7am-8pm
Carries: Live bait, rods, reels
Bodies of water: Atlantic Ocean, Gulf of Mexico
Services & Products: Guide services, charter boat service, fishing instruction
Guides: Yes
OK to call for current conditions: Yes
Contact: William McDow (Willie)

CHARTERS...

Abyss Pro Dive Center
Marathon 305-743-2126
Hours: 8am-6pm
Bodies of water: Florida Keys, Gulf of Mexico, Atlantic Ocean
Services & Products: Charter boat service
Guides: Yes
OK to call for current conditions: Yes
Contact: Capt. Bill Ferrell

The BarHopp'R
Sarasota 800-982-9776
.... 941-925-8890
Species & Seasons: Tarpon May-July, Snook April-Dec, Redfish all year
Bodies of water: Pine Island Sound, Sarasota Bay, Charlotte Harbor, Tampa Bay
Rates: Half day: $225(2), Full day: $325(2)
Call between: 6pm-12am
Provides: Light tackle, heavy tackle, fly rod/reel, lures, bait
Handicapped equipped: Yes
Certifications: USCG

1 800 982-9776
CAPT. BUTCH RICKEY
PROFESSIONAL FISHING GUIDE
HALF DAY / FULL DAY
TAMPA BAY TO FT. MYERS
SNOOK • REDFISH • TARPON
Light-tackle back country fishing at it's best!
USCG Licensed • No License required • Fully Insured
The BarHopp'R

Blue Runner Charter Boat
Marco Island 941-642-7585
Species & Seasons: Shark Mar-Aug, Tarpon Mar-June, Grouper, Snapper, Cobia all year, Permit May-Aug
Bodies of water: Gulf of Mexico
Rates: Half day: $300(1-5), Full day: $500(1-5)
Call between: Anytime
Provides: Light tackle, heavy tackle, lures, bait
Handicapped equipped: Yes
Certifications: USCG Masters Lic.

Capt. Jim Brienza
Key West 305-294-6027
Species & Seasons: Tarpon Mar-July, Sailfish Jan-June, Kingfish Dec-Feb, Cobia Nov-April, Blackfin Tuna Dec-April, Dolphin May-Aug, Barracuda all year, Shark Mar-Aug, Amberjack all year, Bonito Feb-Dec
Bodies of water: Gulf of Mexico, Atlantic Ocean
Rates: Half day: $325(1-4), Full day: $450(1-4) whole boat
Call between: 6pm-10pm
Provides: Light tackle, lures, bait, rain gear, beverages
Handicapped equipped: Yes
Certifications: USCG

Capt. Herb Brown
Clearwater 813-797-2731
Species & Seasons: Snook April-Oct, Tarpon May-Aug, Redfish, Sea Trout all year
Bodies of water: Tarpon Springs, Tampa Bay, Gulf of Mexico
Rates: Half day: $225(1-2), Full day: $300(1-2)
Call between: 5pm-10pm
Provides: Light tackle, heavy tackle, lures, bait, rain gear
Handicapped equipped: No
Certifications: USCG

Bubba
Key West 305-296-4535
Species & Seasons: Tarpon Mar-July, Permit Mar-Aug, Cobia Nov-July, Sailfish Barracuda, Shark all year
Bodies of water: Florida Keys, Gulf of Mexico
Rates: Half day: $325(1-4), Full day: $450(1-4)
Call between: 6:30pm-9:30pm
Provides: Light tackle, fly rod/reel, lures, bait, rain gear
Handicapped equipped: Yes

Capt. Bob Smith Sport Fishing
Sarasota 813-366-2159
Species & Seasons: Tarpon, Grouper, Snook, Redfish, Sea Trout, Permit, May-June, Kingfish, Barracuda, Cobia, Snapper April-Nov
Bodies of water: Sarasota Bay, Gulf waters off Sarasota
Rates: Half day: $125(1), $150(2), Full day: $225(1), $275(2), Half day: $226(6), Full day: $425(6)
Call between: 7:30am-9:30pm
Provides: Light tackle, heavy tackle, lures, bait
Handicapped equipped: No

GULF OF MEXICO & BAYS (SOUTH) — FLORIDA

Capt. Pete Greenan's Gypsy Guide Service
Sarasota 941-923-6095
Species & Seasons: Tarpon May-Aug, Snook Mar-Dec, Redfish, Sea Trout all year, Triple Tail Oct-April
Bodies of water: Gulf of Mexico, Charlotte Harbor, Boca Grande, Sanibel, Ten Thousand Islands, Everglades Nat'l. Park
Rates: Half day: $250(1-2), Ful day: $400(1-2)
Call between: 8am-10pm
Provides: Light tackle, heavy tackle, fly rod/reel, lures, bait, rain gear, beverages
Handicapped equipped: Yes
Certifications: USCG

Catfisher, Inc.
Cape Coral 941-574-2524
Species & Seasons: Snook, Redfish, Tarpon, Spotted Trout, Cobia, Triple Tail, Amberjack, Shark all year, Snook, Redfish during open seasons
Bodies of water: Caloosahatehee River, Pine Island Sound, Matlacha Pass, Red Fish Pass, Edison Reef, Sanibel Point, San Carlos Bay, CATCH & RELEASE!
Rates: Half day: $150(1), $200(2), Full day: $250(1), night charters +$50
Call between: 7p.m-9pm
Provides: Light tackle, lures, bait, rain gear
Handicapped equipped: No
Certifications: USCG

Charter Boat Linda D
Key West 800-299-9798
.... 305-296-9798
Species & Seasons: Sailfish, April-Dec, Wahoo, Barracuda all year, Dolphin April-Aug, Marlin April-Nov, Kingfish Dec-Mar, Tuna, Grouper Jan-Mar, Amberjack Mar-May
Bodies of water: Atlantic Ocean (Straits of Florida), Gulf of Mexico
Rates: Half day: $100(1), $200(2), $400(up to 6), Full day: $150(1), $300(2), $550(up to 6)
Call between: 8am-7pm
Provides: Light tackle, heavy tackle, lures, bait, rain gear
Handicapped equipped: Yes
Certifications: USCG

Charter Boat Sweet Dee II
Marco 813-394-6000
Species & Seasons: Permit, Shark, Amberjack May-Aug, Grouper, Snapper Feb-Sept
Bodies of water: Gulf of Mexico
Rates: Half day: $300(1-6), 3/4 day: $400(1-6), Full day: $500(1-6)
Call between: Anytime
Provides: Light tackle, heavy tackle, lures, bait
Handicapped equipped: Yes
Certifications: USCG

Chokoloskee Island Charters
Chokoloskee 813-695-2286
Species & Seasons: Snook Feb-June/Sept-Dec, Redfish June-April, Tarpon Mar-Nov, Sea Trout Sept-June
Bodies of water: Everglades Nat'l. Park, Ten Thousand Islands, Gulf of Mexico
Rates: Half day: $200(1-2), $225(3), Full day: $300(1-2), $325(3)
all between: 6pm-10pm
Provides: Light tackle, fly rod/reel, lures, bait, rain gear
Handicapped equipped: No
Certifications: USCG

Daisy Mae VI
Clearwater 813-442-1502
Species & Seasons: Grouper all year, Marlin, Sailfish, Tuna, Wahoo, June-Sept, Kingfish Mar-Dec
Bodies of water: Gulf of Mexico
Rates: Half day: $100(1), $350(6), Full day: $150(1), $600(6)
Call between: 6pm-9pm
Provides: Light tackle, heavy tackle, lures, bait
Handicapped equipped: Yes
Certifications: USCG

Donna's Diamond
Lakeland 813-697-1815
Species & Seasons: Snook Jan-Sept, Tarpon May-Aug, Sea Trout, Redfish Jan-Nov
Bodies of water: Charlotte Harbor, Boca Grande
Rates: Half day: $250(1-3), Full day: $325(1-3)
Call between: 6pm-10pm
Provides: Light tackle, heavy tackle, lures, bait, rain gear
Handiapped equipped: Yes
Certifications: USCG

Capt Phil Dugger, Jr.
Boca Grande 813-629-2708
Species & Seasons: Snook, Redfish, Sea Trout Mar-Dec, Tarpon May-Aug, Kingfish seasonal
Bodies of water: Boca Grande Pass, Gasparilla Sound, Charlotte Harbor, Gulf of Mexico
Rates: Backcountry: Half day: $225, Full day: $300 Ofshore: $350-$400 (depends on size of party)
Call between: 5pm-9pm
Provides: Light tackle, heavy tackle, lures, bait, rain gear
Handicapped equipped: Yes
Certifications: USCG

El Chino
Marathon 305-743-9280
Species & Seasons: Marlin, Wahoo, Dolphin, Tuna, Barracuda all year, Sailfish May-Feb, Tarpon April-July, Kingfish Oct-Mar
Bodies of water: Florida Keys, Gulf of Mexico, Atlantic Ocean
Rates: Half day: $450(1-6) offshore, $350(1-6) reef, Full day: $550(1-6) offshore, $450(1-6) reef
Call between: 6:30am-11pm
Provides: Light tackle, heavy tackle, lures, bait
Handicapped equipped: Yes
Certifications: USCG

Capt. David J. Eimers
Naples 813-353-4828
Species & Seasons: Tarpon, Snook Mar-Dec, Redfish Sept-April, Sea Trout Nov-May
Bodies of water: Ten Thousand Islands, Marco Island
Rates: Half day: $200(2), Full day: $325(2), off season rates available
Call between: 6:30am-9pm
Provides: Ligh tackle, fly rod/reel, lures, bait, rain gear
Certifications: USCG, Yamaha and Zebco/Motor Guide

Fishbuster & Billfisher
Key West 305-296-9969
Species & Seasons: Sailfish Nov-May, Dolphin, Marlin May-Aug
Bodies of water: Atlantic Ocean, Gulf of Mexico
Rates: Half day: $100(1), Full day: $150(1) Full boat: Half day: $400, Full day: $600
Call between: 7pm-10pm
Provides: Light tackle, heavy tackle, lures, bait, rain gear
Handicapped equipped: Yes

FLORIDA — GULF OF MEXICO & BAYS (SOUTH)

Fun Yet Charters
Little Torch Key 305-872-3407
Species & Seasons: Dolphin Spring-Fall, Sailfish, King Mackerel Cobia Fall-Spring, Barracuda, Grouper, Mangrove Snapper, Wahoo, Mutton Snapper all year, Tarpon Spring-Summer
Bodies of water: Gulf of Mexico, Florida Keys, Atlantic Ocean
Rates: Half day: $225(1-6), Full day: $325(1-6)
Call between: 7am-11pm
Provides: Light tackle, heavy tackle, lures, bait, rain gear
Handicapped equipped: No
Certifications: Fully licensed and insured

Capt. Andy Griffiths
Key West 305-296-2639
Species & Seasons: Black Grouper Feb-April, Yellowtail Snapper, Mutton Snapper, Red Grouper, Porgy, Mackerel all year, Kingfish Jan-Mar, Dolphin May-Aug, Tuna Dec-Feb
Bodies of water: Gulf of Mexico, Atlantic Ocean, Florida Keys, (Marguesas Keys, Dry Tortugas, Key West)
Rates: 3 days: $333(1), 2 days 1 night: $1300(6), 3 days 2 nights: $2000(6)
Call between: 8-8:30am-7-10pm
Provides: Light tackle, heavy tackle, lures, bait
Certifications: USCG

Gulfstream II Charter Boats
Clearwater 813-442-6339
Species & Seasons: Grouper, Snapper, all year, King Mackerel, Spanish Mackerel, Cobia, Bonito, Barracuda, Tuna, Sailfish, Marlin, Wahoo Spring-Fall
Bodies of water: Gulf of Mexico
Rates: Half day: $300(6), $350(over 6), Full day: $500(6), $600(over 6), overnight and 2 day trips available
Call between: 8am-11pm
Provides: Light tackle, heavy tackle, lures, bait
Handicapped equipped: Yes
Certifications: USCG

Hot Pursuit Charters
Marathon 800-473-4106
.... 305-743-0406
Species & Seasons: Tarpon Mar-June, Sailfish Dec-May, Dolphin April-Nov, Snapper, Grouper all year
Bodies of water: Atlantic Ocean, Straits of Florida, Gulf of Mexico
Rates: Half day: $275(1-6), Full day: $375(1-6)
Provides: Light tackle, lures, bait
Handicapped equipped: Yes
Certifications: USCG

King Fisher Cruise Lines
Punta Gorda 941-639-0969
Species & Seasons: Tarpon May-Aug, King Mackerel, Spanish Mackerel, Amberjack Mar-Nov, Barracuda Mar-Dec, Grouper, Snapper, Snook, Redfish, Sea Trout all year
Bodies of water: Eastern Gulf of Mexico, Charlotte Harbor, Peace River, Boca Grande Pass
Rates: Deep Sea Charters: $450 Full day: per boat, $85 pp full day up to 6 people. ack Bay: $250 full day, $150 half day, up to 4 people
Call between: 8am-6pm
Provides: Light tackle, heavy tackle, fly rod/reel, lures, bait
Handicapped equipped: Yes
Certifications: USCG, IGFA

Absolute Flats Fishingx
Palm Harbor 813-787-9830
Species & Seasons: Tarpon April-July, Snook, Redfish, Sea Trout all year, Kingfish Mar-April, Cobia May-Aug
Bodies of water: Gulf of Mexico, Tampa Bay, Clearwater, Boca Grande, Tarpon Springs
Rates: Half day: $200(2), $225(3), Full day: $300(2),$325(3)
Call between: 6pm-10pm
Provides: Light tackle, fly rod/reel, lures, bait, rain gear
Handicapped equipped: Yes
Certifications: USCG

Lucky Strike
Key West 305-294-7988
.... 800-294-7988
Species & Seasons: Sailfish, Barracuda all year, Wahoo Oct-June, Tuna Oct-May, Dolphin Mar-Aug, King Mackerel, Cero Mackerel Dec-Mar, Grouper Jan-Mar, Snapper Oct-May, Marlin May-Oct
Bodies of water: Straits of Florida (Atlantic side of Keys), Gulf of Mexico
Rates: Half day: $95(1), $190(2), Full day: $125(1), $250(2), Boat: Half day: $375, Full day: $500
Call between: 4pm-6pm
Provides: Light tackle, bait, rain gear
Handicapped equipped: Yes
Certifications: IGFA, Billfish Foundation, FCA

Mullet Man Charters
Marathon Shores 305-289-0941
Species & Seasons: Tarpon Feb-July
Bodies of water: Alantic Ocean, Gulf of Mexico
Call between: 8am-8pm
Provides: Light tackle, heavy tackle, bait, rain gear, beverages
Handicapped equipped: No
Certifications: USCG

Niki-Joe Charters
Indian Rocks Bch. 813-595-4798
Species & Seasons: King Mackerel, Grouper, Barracuda, Redfish, Snook, Trout, Shark, Tuna, Tarpon, Snapper all year
Bodies of water: Gulf of Mexico, Tampa Bay, Boca Ciega Bay, Clearwater Bay, Tarpon Springs, (inshore flats and offshore)
Rates: Ranges $200and up
Call between: 7am-9pm
Provides: Light tackle, heavy tackle, fly rod/reel, lures, bait, rain gear, beverages, lunch
Handicapped equipped: Yes
Certifications: USCG IGFA World Record Boat, FL League of Angler Pres., FL Guides Assoc.

On the Fly
Summerland Key 800-946-6359
.... 305-745-4199
Species & Seasons: Blackfin Tuna, Yellowfin Tuna, King Mackerel, Barracuda, Cobia, Grouper, Snapper Jan-Feb, Tarpon, Permit, Sailfish, Dolphin, Cobia, Bonefish Mar-June, Tuna, Wahoo, Sailfish, Dolphin July-Dec
Bodies of water: Wreck fishing the Gulf of Mexico, Atlantic Ocean, Backcountry Florida Keys, Dry Tortugas, Marquesas Keys, Reef Fishing Key West
Rates: Half day: $350(1-2), Full day: $450(1-2)
Call between: 6am-11pm
Provides: Light tackle, heavy tackle, fly rod/reel, lures, bait, rain gear,beverages
Handicapped equipped: Yes
Certifications: USCG

The Reel Life
Key West 800-286-1855
Species & Seasons: Sailfish, Shark all year, Tarpon Mar-July, Blackfin Tuna, Cobia Oct-May, Permit April-Oct, Kingfish Nov-April, Dolphin April-Sept, Wahoo Aug-Mar, Yellowfin Tuna Jan-Mar
Bodies of water: Atlantic Ocean, Gulf of Mexico, Key West inshore areas

GULF OF MEXICO & BAYS (SOUTH) — FLORIDA

Rates: Half day: $300(1-4),
Full day: $450(1-4)
Call between: 5:30pm-9:30pm
Provides: Light tackle, fly rod/reel, lures, bait, rain gear
Handicapped equipped: No
Certifications: USCG

Skinny Dipper
Goodland 941-642-1342
Species & Seasons: Redfish, Snook all year, Tarpon May-June
Bodies of water: Ten Thousand Islands, Everglades Nat'l Park, Marco Island
Rates: Half day: $225(1-2),
Full day: $325(1-2)
Call between: Anytime
Provides: Lighttackle, fly rod/reel
Handicapped equipped: No
Certifications: USCG, FFF, SAGE

Sportfishing Guide Services, Inc.
Tampa 813-962-1435
Species & Seasons: Snook Mar-Dec, Tarpon, Cobia April-Nov, King Mackerel April-May/Nov-Dec, Speckled Trout, Redfish, LM Bass all year, Permit Nov-Feb, Alligators Sept
Bodies of water: Tampa Bay Estuary System, Gulf of Mexico Coastal Flats, (Boca Grande to Homosassa), Lake Tarpon
Rates: Half day: $250(1-2),
Fll day: $350(1-2), $50 additional 3rd person
Call between: 7am-9pm
Provides: Light tackle, heavy tackle, fly rod/reel, lures, bait, rain gear, beverages, licenses
Handicapped equipped: Yes
Certifications: International Fishing Hall of Fame, USCG, Nat'l Ass. Charter Operators, FOWA, FL Guides Assoc., OWAA

Sun Dancer
Summerland Key 305-745-3063
Species & Seasons: Tarpon Mar-July, Sailfish Oct-May, Kingfish, Cobia Dec-Mar, Bonefish, Permit all year
Bodies of water: Atlantic Ocean, Gulf of Mexico
Rates: Half day: $350(2),
Full day: $450(2), Flats Skiff:
Half day: $225, Full day: $325
Call between: 7pm-9pm
Provides: Light tackle, fly rod/reel, lures, bait, rain gear
Handicapped equipped: Yes
Certifications: USCG

GUIDES...

A.E. Brackett
Cudjoe Key 305-745-9478
Species & Seasons: Tarpon, Shark Mar-July, Bonefish Feb-July, Permit April-July, Barracuda Jan-July
Bodies of water: Atlantic Ocean Flats, Gulf of Mexico Backcountry, Florida Keys
Rates: Half day: $225(1-2),
Full day: $300(1-2)
Call between: 6pm-8pm
Provides: Light tackle, fly rod/reel, lures, bait, rain gear
Certifications: USCG

Earl Budd
Chokoloskee 941-695-4035
Species & Seasons: Snook Jan-May/Sept-Dec, Sea Trout all year, Redfish June-Feb, Cobia Mar-June, Tarpon April-June
Bodies of water: Ten Thousand Islands in Everglades, Gulf of Mexico
Rates: Half day: $200(1-2),
Full day: $275(1-2)
Call between: 4pm-10pm
Provides: ight tackle, heavy tackle, lures, bait, rain gear
Handicapped equipped: No
Certifications: USCG

Capt. Rick Grassett
Sarasota 813-923-7799
Species & Seasons: Snook, Redfish, Sea Trout all year, Tarpon May-Oct, Spanish Mackerel, Bluefish, Cobia Spring and Fall, Triple Tail Nov-Mar
Bodies of water: Tampa Bay, Charlotte Harbor, Sarasota Bay
Rates: Half day: $200(1-2)
Full day: $350(1-2), maximum 3 people, Evening Snook trip (4 hrs.): $225
Call between: 8am-9pm
Provides: Light tackle, fly rod/reel, lures, bait, beverages, lunch
Handicapped equipped: No
Certifications: ORVIS Endorsed Guide, USCG

Van Hubbard
Englewood
Species & Seasons: Snook Mar-Dec, Tarpon May-July, Redfish all year, King Mackerel Oct-Nov/Mar-May
Bodies of water: Charlotte Harbor, Gulf of Mexico
Rates: Half day: $200(1), $250(2),
Full day: $350(1-2)
Call between: 5pm-9pm

Provides: Light tackle, havy tackle, fly rod/reel, lures, bait
Handicapped equipped: Yes
Certifications: USCG, FL Guides Assoc., M.E.T., A.P.C.A., I.G.F.A., Boca Grande Fishing Guides Assoc., SEOPA, FOWA

Capt. Tim McOster
Englewood 813-475-5908
Species & Seasons: Tarpon April-July, Snook, Redfish, Sea Trout all year, Kingfish, Mackerel Spring-Fall
Bodies of water: Boca Grande, Charlotte Harbor, Gasparilla Sound
Rates: Half day: $250(1-2),
Full day: $350(1-2), up to 3 people same price
all between: 5pm-10pm
Provides: Light tackle, heavy tackle, fly rod/reel, lures, bait, beverages
Handicapped equipped: Yes
Certifications: USCG, G Loomis sponsored

Capt. Brian Mowatt
Port Charlotte 813-624-4920
Species & Seasons: Tarpon April-July, Snook, Redfish Mar-Dec
Bodies of water: Boca Grande, Charlotte Harbor
Rates: Half day: $275(1-2),
Full day: $350(1-2), 3rd person $50 additional
Call between: 7pm-9pm
Provides: Light tackle, fly rod/reel, lues, bait, rain gear
Certifications: USCG, FFF Casting Instructor

Tom & Jerry's Pro Guide Service
Leesburg 800-328-5686
Species & Seasons: LM Bass all year, Tarpon April-Nov, Snook April-Sept
Bodies of water: Lake Kissimmee Chain, Clermont Chain, Lake Okeechobee, Stick Marsh, any Central Florida lakes, Boca Grande
Rates: Fresh water: Half day: $150(1-2), Full day: $225(1-2), Salt water:
Half day: $275(1-2), Full day: $350(1-2)
Provides: Light tackle, heavy tackle, lures, rain gear
Handicapped equipped: Depends on handicap
Certifications: USCG

FLORIDA
GULF OF MEXICO & BAYS (SOUTH) - INDIAN RIVER LAGOON

Capt. Johnnie Weeks
Naples 800-774-4713
Species & Seasons: Redfish, Sea Trout all year, Snook April-Dec, Tarpon April-Sept, Grouper May-Oct
Bodies of water: Ten Thousand Islands, Marco Island, Gulf of Mexico
Rates: Half day: $250(1-4), Full day: $350(1-4), offshore $450
Call between: 6pm-10pm
Provides: Light tackle, heavy tackle, lures, bait
Handicapped equipped: Yes
Certifications: USCG

LODGING...

Breezy Palms Resort
Islamorada 305-664-2361
Guest Capacity: 39 units
Handicapped equipped: No
Seasons: All year
Rates: $45-$180/day per room
Contact: Gail M. Schaper
Guides: Yes
Species & Seasons: Marlin, Sailfish Jan-Sept, Dolphin, Tuna Mar-Sept, Bonefish Jan-Jan, Tarpon April-May
Bodies of Water: Atlantic Ocean, Gulf of Mexico, Florida Bay
Types of fishing: Fly fishing, light tackle, heavy tackle, wading
Available: Bait, tackle, boat rentals

Chokoloskee Island Park & Camp
Chokoloskee 941-695-2414
Guest Capacity: 150
Handicapped equipped: Yes
Seasons: All year
Rates: $20/day
Guides: Yes
Species & Seasons: Snook Mar-June/Sept-Dec, Redfish June-Feb, Trout Nov-April, Shark April-Dec
Bodies of Water: Ten Thousand Islands, Gulf of Mexico
Types of fishing: Light tackle, heavy tackle, salt water
Available: Fishing instruction, bait, takle, boat rentals, family activities

Edgewater Lodge
PO Box 799
Long Key 33001
Guest Capacity: 40
Handicapped equipped: Yes
Seasons: All year
Rates: $60-$80/day
Guides: Yes

Species & Seasons: Tarpon April-June, Sailfish, Kingfish Dec-April, Grouper, Snapper, Dolphin all year
Bodies of Water: Atlantic Ocean, Gulf of Mexico
Types of fishing: Fly fishing, light tackle, heavy tackle
Available: Bait, tackle

Linger Lodge
Bradenton 813-755-2757
Handicapped equipped: Yes
Seasons: All year
Rates: $16.50/day
Guides: No
Species & Seasons: LM Bass, Bluegill, Catfish
Bodies of Water: Gulf of Mexico, Braden River, Manatee River
Types of fishing: Fly fishing, light tackle
Available: Restaurant

MARINAS...

City of Gulfport Marina
St. Petersburg 813-893-1071
Hours: 7am-7pm
Carries: Live bait, lures, maps, rods, reels
Bodies of water: Gulf of Mexico
Services & Products: Boat ramp, food, beverages, gas/oil
Guides: Yes
OK to call for current conditions: Yes
Contact: Denis Frain

Dolphin Marina
Little Torch Key 800-553-0308
.... 305-872-2685
Hours: 7:30am-6pm
Carries: Live bait, lures, maps, licenses
Bodies of water: Atlantic Ocean, Gulf of Mexico
Services & Products: Boat rentals, guide services, charter boat service, lodging, boat ramp, food, beverages, gas/oil, snorkel and sunset cruises
Guides: Yes
OK to call for current conditions: Yes

Landings Marina Inc.
Sarasota 813-922-6100
Hours: 8am-5pm
Bodies of water: Gulf of Mexico
Services & Products: Boat rentals, boat ramp, beverages, gas/oil, repair services
Guides: Yes
OK to call for current conditions: No
Contact: Jaime, Bob or Janelle

Midway Tackle & Boat Sales
Lakeland 813-665-7198
Hours: 7am-5pm, closed Sat., Sun.
Carries: Lures, maps, rods, reels
Bodies of water: Winter Haven Chain of Lakes, Lake Parker, Kissimmee Chain, Gulf of Mexico, Atlantic Ocean
Services & Products: Guide services, boat ramp, beverages, Cajun and Charger boats, Suzuki and Yamaha outboards
Guides: Yes
OK to call for current conditions: Yes
Contact: Bud or Sue Rice

INDIAN RIVER LAGOON

BAIT & TACKLE...

Captain's Corner
Fort Pierce 407-461-1008
Hours: 6am-8pm
Carries: Live bait, lures, rods, reels
Bodies of water: Indian River Lagoon, Intracoastal Waterway, Atlantic Ocean
Services & Products: Food, beverages
Guides: Yes
OK to call for current conditions: Yes
Contact: Jerry L. Morey

CHARTERS...

Backcountry Charter Service
DeBary 800-932-7335
Species & Seasons: Redfish, Sea Trout Dec-Jan, Tarpon May-Nov, Snook Mar-Oct, Jack Cravalle Nov-May, Ladyfish Sept-May, Striped Bass Feb-June, American Shad Jan-April, LM Bass Nov-April, Panfish April-Sept
Bodies of watr: Indian River Lagoon, Mosquito Lagoon, Banana River Lagoon, St. John's River, Stick Marsh, Farm 13
Rates: Half day: $185(1-2), Full day: $275(1-2)
Call between: 24 hours
Provides: Light tackle, fly rod/reel, lures, bait, rain gear, beverages
Handicapped equipped: Yes
Certifications: USCG, FFF, IGFA

INTRACOASTAL WATERWAY - LAKE GEORGE — FLORIDA

INTRACOASTAL WATERWAY (NORTH)

BAIT & TACKLE...

Harold's Sport Center
New Smyrna Beach 904-428-2841
Hours: 6am-7pm
Carries: Live bait, lures, rods, reels
Bodies of water: Atlantic Ocean, Indian River, Intracoastal Waterway
Services & Products: Guide services, charter boat service, beverages, fishing instruction, repair services
Guides: Yes
OK to call for current conditions: Yes
Contact: Larry A. Ross

CHARTERS...

L. E. Sutton
Fernandina Bch. 904-261-7509
Species & Seasons: Sea Trout, Red Bass Jan-Feb, Drum Feb-Mar, Snapper, Grouper Mar-April, Spanish Mackerel, Kingfish, Barracuda, Cobia, Sailfish, Tuna May-Sept, Sea Bass, Snapper, Trout, Red Bass Sept-Dec, Flounder April
Bodies of water: Intracoastal Waterway, Atlantic Ocean
Rates: Half day: $100(1), $150(2), Full day: $200(1), $250(2), $300(6)
Call between: 8am-9:30pm
Provides: Light tackle, heavy tackle, lures, bait, rain gear
Handicapped equipped: Yes

MARINAS...

Conch House Marina
St. Augustine 904-824-4347
Hours: 6am-9:30pm
Carries: Maps
Bodies of water: Salt Run, Intracoastal Waterway, Atlantic Ocean
Services & Products: Charter boat service, lodging, food, beverages, gas/oil
Guides: Yes
OK to call for current conditions: Yes
Contact: Vicki Henry

INTRACOASTAL WATERWAY (SOUTH)

BAIT & TACKLE...

Captain's Corner
Fort Pierce 407-461-1008
Hours: 6am-8pm
Carries: Live bait, lures, rods, reels
Bodies of water: Indian River Lagoon, Intracoastal Waterway, Atlantic Ocean
Services & Products: Food, beverages
Guides: Yes
OK to call for current conditions: Yes
Contact: Jerry L. Morey

Kingsbury & Sons Tackle Inc.
Fort Lauderdale................ 305-467-3474
Hours: 7am-8pm
Carries: Live bait, lures, flies, maps, rods, reels, licenses
Bodies of water: Atlantic Ocean, Everglades, Intracoastal Waterway, Port Everglades Inlet
Services & Products: Guide services, charter boat service, fishing instruction, repair services
Guides: Yes
OK to call for current conditions: Yes
Contact: Dave Kingsbury or Glen

Schulz Brothers - Fishing Headquarters
Jupiter 407-743-7335
Hours: 7am-8pm
Carries: Live bait, lures, flies, maps, rods, reels, licenses
Bodies of water: Atlantic Ocean, Intracoastal Waterway, Loxahatchee River, Lake Okeechobee
Services & Products: Guide services, charter boat service, fishing instruction, repair services
Guides: Yes
OK to call for current conditions: Yes
Contact: Anyone

MARINAS...

Sailfish Marina
Palm Beach Shores 407-844-1724
.... 800-446-4577
Hours: 6:30am-8pm
Carries: Lures, maps, licenses
Bodies of water: Atlantic Ocean, Intracoastal Waterway
Services & Products: Charter boat service, lodging, food, beverages, gas/oil, transient slips
OK to call for current conditions: Yes
Contact: Pamella Lowenhaupt

LAKE GEORGE

BAIT & TACKLE...

Bass-'N-Etc.
Salt Springs 904-685-2277
Hours: 5:30am-9pm
Carries: Live bait, lures, maps, rods, reels, licenses
Bodies of water: St. John's River, Oklawaha River, Lake George, Lake Kerr, Lake Delaney
Services & Products: Guide services, lodging, gas/oil, archery supplies
OK to call for current conditions: Yes
Contact: Dennis or Patty Rahn

GUIDES...

Capt. Mark "Smitty" Smith
Deland 904-738-1836
Species & Seasons: LM Bass Oct-June
Bodies of water: St. John's River, Suwannee River, Withlacoochee River, Apalachicola River, Lake Talquin, Lake George, Crescent Lake, and others
Rates: Half day: $150+(1-2), Full day: $250+(1-2), $25 additional person (limit 3)
Call between: 7pm-10pm
Provides: Light tackle, heavy tackle, rain gear
Handicapped equipped: No
Certifications: USCG

Steve Rominsky Guide Service
Welaka 904-467-2030
.... 467-8826
Species & Seasons: LM Bass all year, Striped Bass Feb-May, Panfish Mar-Sept
Bodies of water: St John's River, Crescent Lake, Rodman Res., Lake George
Rates: Full day: $175(1), $220(2)
Call between: 7am-8pm
Provides: Light tackle, heavy tackle, lures, bait, rain gear
Certifications: USCG

FLORIDA

LAKE GEORGE - LAKE JULIANA

LODGING...

Parramore's Fish Camp & Family Resort
1675 S. Moon Road
Astor 32102
Guest Capacity: 100
Handicapped equipped: Yes
Seasons: All year
Rates: Camping: $19/night, $116.50/week, Cabins: $66/night, $396/week
Contact: Reva D. Cunningham
Guides: Yes
Species & Seasons: LM Bass, Jan-Mar, Striped Bass May-Sept, Crappie Oct-Mar, Bream May-Sept
Bodies of Water: St. John's River, Lake George, Lake Dexter, Lake Woodruff
Types of fishing: Fly fishing, light tackle
Available: Licenses, bait, tackle, boat rentals, family activities, pool, tennis court

Pine Island Fish Camp
Seville 904-749-2818
Guest Capacity: 86
Handicapped equipped: No
Seasons: All year
Rates: $40/day
Guides: Yes
Species & Seasons: LM Bass, Striped Bass, Bream, Catfish, Crappie all year
Bodies of Water: Lake George, St. John's River
Types of fishing: Fly fishing, light tackle, heavy tackle, wading
Available: Licenses, bait, tackle, boat rentals, air boat tours/rides

LAKE HARNEY

LODGING...

Lindsay's Fish Camp
PO Box 341
Geneva 32732
Guest Capacity: 100
Handicapped equipped: No
Seasons: All year
Rates: $12.50/day
Contact: George or Evelyn Griffin
Guides: Yes
Species & Seasons: LM Bass, Catfish all year, Crappie Nov-May, Shad Nov-Feb, Bream Jan-Aug
Bodies of Water: St. John's River, Econolochattchee River, Lake Harney

Types of fishing: Fly fishing, light tackle, heavy tackle, wading, float trips, airboat trips, pontoon trips
Available: Fishing instruction, licenses, bait, tackle, boat rentals, family activities

LAKE ISTOKPOGA

LODGING...

Trails End Fishing Resort
Lorida 813-655-3891
Guest Capacity: 4 cabins, sleep 16
Handicapped equipped: Yes
Seasons: All year
Rates: Cabins: $50/day, $284/week
Contact: Stan Shaw
Guides: Yes
Species & Seasons: LM Bass, Crappie, Bluegill all year, Shell Cracker Spring-Fall, Duck hunting Sept-Jan
Bodies of Water: Lake Istokpoga, Kissimmee River
Types of fishing: Fly fishing, light tackle, heavy tackle, wading
Available: Fishing instruction, licenses, bait, tackle, boat rentals, family activities

LAKE JACKSON

BAIT & TACKLE...

John's Guns & Fly Fishing
Tallahassee 904-422-1553
Hours: 9am-6:30pm
Carries: Flies, maps, rods, reels, licenses
Bodies of water: Jackson Lake, Lake Seminole, Lake Talquin, Ochlockonee River, St. Marks River, Wakulla River, Aucilla River, Econfina River, Steinhatchee River, Apalachee Bay
Services & Products: Fishing instruction, repair services, free set up and fly-casting instruction
Guides: Yes
OK to call for current conditions: Yes
Contact: John V. Underwood

LODGING...

Gaineys Talquin Lodge
Quincy 904-627-3822
Guest Capacity: 40
Handicapped equipped: No
Seasons: All year
Rates: $40/day double occupancy

Guides: Yes
Species & Seasons: LM Bass, Black Crappie, White Bass all year, Shell Cracker, Bream all summer
Bodies of Water: Lake Talquin, Lake Jackson, Lake Lamonia, Lake Seminole
Types of fishing: Fly fishing, light tackle
Available: Licenses, bait, tackle

LAKE JULIANA

BAIT & TACKLE...

Bait Shop
Polk City 813-984-3138
Hours: 5:30am-9pm
Carries: Live bait, lures, flies, maps, rods, reels, licenses
Bodies of water: Lake Agnes, Lake Mud, Lake Mattie, Lake Julaina
Services & Products: Food, beverages, repair services
Guides: Yes
OK to call for current conditions: Yes
Contact: Ronald Carroll

LODGING...

Fish Haven Lodge
1 Fish Haven Road
Auburndale 33823
Seasons: All year
Rates: $50-$270
Contact: Lin Chipman
Species & Seasons: LM Bass, Crappie
Bodies of Water: Lake Julianna
Types of fishing: Light tackle
Available: Bait, tackle, boat rentals, family activities

Lake Juliana Boating & Lodging
Auburndale 813-984-1144
Guest Capacity: 16 cottages 1, 2, and 3 bedrooms
Seasons: All year
Rates: Ranges from: $30-$60
Contact: Darleana D. Preast
Guides: No
Species & Seasons: Crappie Aug-Mar, Bass, Bluegill, Catfish all year
Bodies of Water: Lake Juliana, Lake Mattee
Available: Licenses, bait, tackle, boat rentals, family activities

LAKE KERR - LAKE KISSIMMEE
FLORIDA

LAKE KERR

BAIT & TACKLE...

Bass-'N-Etc.
Salt Springs 904-685-2277
Hours: 5:30am-9pm
Carries: Live bait, lures, maps, rods, reels, licenses
Bodies of water: St. John's River, Oklawaha River, Lake George, Lake Kerr, Lake Delaney
Services & Products: Guide services, lodging, gas/oil, archery supplies
OK to call for current conditions: Yes
Contact: Dennis or Patty Rahn

LODGING...

Kerr City
Ft. McCoy 904-685-2557
Guest Capacity: 30-40
Handicapped equipped: No
Seasons: All year
Rates: $275/week
Guides: Yes, recommend
Species & Seasons: LM Bass, Crappie
Bodies of Water: St. John's River, Lake Kerr, Oklawaha River, Rodman Res.

LAKE KISSIMMEE

BAIT & TACKLE...

Buck's Bayou
Lake Wales 813-696-1421
Hours: 5am-8pm
Carries: Live bait, lures, flies, maps, rods, reels, licenses
Bodies of water: Lake Kissimmee Chain
Services & Products: Lodging, boat ramp, food, beverages, gas/oil
Guides: Yes
OK to call for current conditions: Yes
Contact: John W. Buck

Scotty's Bait & Tackle
Orlando
Hours: 5:30am-6:30pm
Carries: Live bait, lures, flies, maps, rods, licenses
Bodies of water: Several local lakes, Lake Kissimmee, Atlantic Ocean
Services & Products: Guide services, charter boat service, food, beverages, gas/oil, fishing instruction, repair services
Guides: Yes
OK to call for current conditions: Yes

Stick Marsh Bait & Tackle
Fellsmere 407-571-9855
Hours: 5:30am-5pm
Carries: Live bait, lures, flies, maps, rods, reels, licenses
Bodies of water: Blue Cypress Lake, Sebastian River & Inlet, Stick Marsh, Farm 13, Garcia Res., Lake Kissimmee
Services & Products: Guide services, food, beverages, fishing instruction
Guides: Yes
OK to call for current conditions: Yes

GUIDES...

Bass Buddies Guide Service
Orlando 800-328-0022
Species & Seasons: LM Bass
Bodies of water: East Lake Tohopekaliga, West Lake Tohopekaliga, Lake Okeechobee, Kissimmee Chain, Stick Marsh, Farm 13, all Central Florida
Rates: Half day: $125(1-2), Full day: $175(1-2), $25 additional 3rd person
Call between: 24 hours
Provides: Light tackle, heavy tackle, lures, rain gear, beverages, lunch
Handicapped equipped: Yes

Bear's Bass Guide Service
Dundee 941-439-3769
Species & Seasons: LM Bass all year
Bodies of water: Stick March, Private Pits, Kissimmee Chain, other areas
Rates: Half day: $125(1), $175(2), Full day: same
Call between: 7am-10pm
Provides: Light tackle, heavy tackle, lures, bait, rain gear, beverages, lunch
Handicapped equipped: Yes

Florida Fishmasters Pro Guide
St. Cloud 407-892-5962
.... 800-424-5090
Species & Seasons: Bass all year
Bodies of water: Kissimmee Chain of Lakes, Stick Marsh
Rates: Half day: $125(1-2), Full day: $175(1-2), 3rd person $25 additional
Call between: 5am-6pm
Provides: Light tackle, heavy tackle, lures, rain gear
Handicapped equipped: Yes

Southport Park
Kissimmee 407-933-5822
Species & Seasons: Bass Mar-Dec, Bluegill Feb-June, Crappie July-Oct, Perch Oct-Jan
Bodies of water: West Lake Tohopekaliga, Lake Kissimmee, Cypress Lake
Rates: Half day: $125(2), Full day: $175(2)
Call between: 6am-6pm
Provides: Light tackle, lures, bait, beverages, lunch

Tom & Jerry's Pro Guide Service
Leesburg 800-328-5686
Species & Seasons: LM Bass all year, Tarpon April-Nov, Snook April-Sept
Bodies of water: Lake Kissimmee Chain, Clermont Chain, Lake Okeechobee, Stick Marsh, any Central Florida lakes, Boca Grande
Rates: Fresh water: Half day: $150(1-2), Full day: $225(1-2), Salt water: Half day: $275(1-2), Full day: $350(1-2)
Call between:
Provides: Light tackle, heavy tackle, lures, rain gear
Handicapped equipped: Depends on handicap
Certifications: USCG

LODGING...

Camp Mack
Lake Wales 800-243-8013
.... 813-696-1108
Guest Capacity: 41 RV full hookup sites, 110 Park Motel RV sites, 7 rental units (fully furnished)
Seasons: All year
Rates: RV: $20/night, $120/week, Cabins: $50/day, $300/week, Park Motel Rentals: $65/night, $390/week
Contact: Jill Snively
Guides: Yes
Species & Seasons: LM Bass Nov-April, Crappie Nov-Mar, Shell Cracker, Bluegill Mar-Aug
Bodies of Water: Lake Kissimmee, Lake Hatchineha, Lake Tohopekaliga, Cypress Lake
Types of fishing: Fly fishing, light tackle
Available: Licenses, bait, tackle, family activities, campground

FLORIDA
LAKE KISSIMMEE - LAKE OKEECHOBEE

Middleton's Fish Camp Inc.
21704 73rd Manor
Vero Beach 32966
Guest Capacity: 18 apartments, 30 campers
Handicapped equipped: No
Seasons: All year
Rates: $40/night
Contact: Debbie Murchie
Guides: Yes
Species & Seasons: LM Bass, Sunshine Bass all year, Crappie Sept-Mar, Bluegill, Shell Cracker Mar-Nov
Bodies of Water: Blue Cypress Lake, Garcia Block, Lake Marion, Lake Kissimmee
Types of fishing: Fly fishing, light tackle, heavy tackle
Available: Fishing instruction, licenses, bait, tackle, boat rentals

MARINAS...

Midway Tackle & Boat Sales
Lakeland 813-665-7198
Hours: 7am-5pm, closed Sat., Sun.
Carries: Lures, maps, rods, reels
Bodies of water: Winter Haven Chain of Lakes, Lake Parker, Kissimmee Chain, Gulf of Mexico, Atlantic Ocean
Services & Products: Guide services, boat ramp, beverages, Cajun and Charger boats, Suzuki and Yamaha outboards
Guides: Yes
OK to call for current conditions: Yes
Contact: Bud or Sue Rice

LAKE MICCOSUKEE

LODGING...

Reeves Fish Camp
Tallahassee 904-893-9940
Guest Capacity: 8 full hookup RV sites, 6 mobile homes(rentals), tent camping
Handicapped equipped: Yes
Seasons: All year
Rates: RV: $10, Rental unit: $35/day double occupancy
Contact: Eli Reeves
Guides: Yes
Species & Seasons: Crappie, Pickerel, LM Bass Fall-Spring, Bream, Shell Cracker Spring-Summer, Catfish Fall-Winter
Bodies of Water: Lake Miccosukee

Types of fishing: Fly fishing, light tackle, heavy tackle
Available: Licenses, bait, tackle, boat rentals, game room, pool tables, video games

LAKE OKEECHOBEE

BAIT & TACKLE...

7 Seas Bait & Tackle
Boca Raton 407-392-4772
Hours: Open 7 days
Carries: Live bait, lures, flies, maps, rods, reels, licenses
Bodies of water: Atlantic Ocean, Lake Okechobee, Lake Ida
Services & Products: Guide services, fishing instruction, repair services
OK to call for current conditions: Yes
Contact: Steve Hill

ALVIN'S BAIT & TACKLE
Home of Big "O" Tour & Guide Service
Bass Pro Shops
Tackle • Lures • Shiners • Worms
Minnows • Crickets • Nightcrawlers
Rod/Reel Trolling Motor Repair
A Loomis/Star Rod Dealer
Custom Rod Builder • Beverages
Ice • Snacks • Marine Supplies
Firearms/Ammo
INSURED GUIDE SERVICE
Ed & Libby Bedell-Owners
(800) 733-3189   100 Florida Ave.
Moore Haven, Fl 33471

Alvin's Bait & Tackle Shop
Moore Haven 800-733-3189
Hours: 6am-6pm
Carries: Live bait, lures, flies, maps, rods, reels, licenses
Bodies of water: Lake Okeechobee and adjacent area in S. FL
Services & Products: Guide services, charter boat service, food, beverages, gas/oil, fishing instruction, repair services
OK to call for current conditions: Yes
Contact: Ed Bedell

Anglers Answer
Naples 813-775-7336
Hours: 6am-6pm
Carries: Live bait, lures, flies, maps, rods, reels, licenses
Bodies of water: Gulf of Mexico, Lake Okeechobee, Lake Trafford
Services & Products: Guide services, beverages, fishing instruction, repair services
Guides: Yes
OK to call for current conditions: Yes
Contact: Dan or Bill

Country Store at Hidden Acres
Lorida 813-763-9532
Hours: 8am-5pm
Carries: Live bait, lures, flies, maps, rods, reels, licenses
Bodies of water: Kissimmee River, Lake Okeechobee
Services & Products: Lodging, boat ramp, food, beverages, gas/oil
Guides: No
OK to call for current conditions: No

Fishy Business Baits
Miramar 305-962-2273
Hours: 7:30am-7:30pm Mon.-Fri., 6am-7:30pm Sat., Sun.
Carries: Live bait, lures, maps, rods, reels, licenses
Bodies of water: Everglades, Holiday Park, Sawgrass, Alligator Alley, Snake Creek, Hollyland, Lake Okeechobee
Services & Products: Guide services, repair services
Guides: Yes
OK to call for current conditions: Yes
Contact: Jim

Golden Gate Trophy Center
Naples 813-455-1337
Hours: 6am-7pm
Carries: Live bait, lures, flies, maps, rods, reels, licenses
Bodies of water: Lake Trafford, Lake Okeechobee, Gulf of Mexico, Ten Thousand Islands, fishable fresh water canals
Services & Products: Guide services, charter boat service, beverages, repair services
OK to call for current conditions: Yes
Contact: Alec or Georgia Alexandre

LAKE OKEECHOBEE — FLORIDA

Iggie's Bait & Tackle
Hialeah 305-887-3929
Hours: 6:30am-8pm
Carries: Live bait, lures, flies, rods, reels, licenses
Bodies of water: Gulf of Mexico, Atlantic Ocean, Miami Airport Lake, Lake Okeechobee
Services & Products: Food, beverages, repair services
Guides: Yes

Juno Bait & Tackle
North Palm Beach 407-694-2797
Hours: 7-7 Mon.-Fri., 6-8 Sat., Sun.
Carries: Live bait, lures, flies, maps, rods, reels, licenses
Bodies of water: Singer Island, Lake Worth, Lake Okeechobee
Services & Products: Guide services, beverages, fishing instruction, repair services
Guides: No
OK to call for current conditions: Yes
Contact: Roy Best

R & C Bait & Tackle
Fort Lauderdale 305-572-6774
Hours: 6:30am-6pm Mon.-Fri., 5:30am-6pm Sat., 5:30am-4:30pm Sun.
Carries: Live bait, lures, flies, maps, rods, reels
Bodies of water: Alligator Alley, Lake Okeechobee, Sawgrass
Services & Products: Repair services
Guides: Yes
OK to call for current conditions: Yes
Contact: Richard Crist

Schulz Brothers - Fishing Headquarters
Jupiter 407-743-7335
Hours: 7am-8pm
Carries: Live bait, lures, flies, maps, rods, reels, licenses
Bodies of water: Atlantic Ocean, Intracoastal Waterway, Loxahatchee River, Lake Okeechobee
Services & Products: Guide services, charter boat service, fishing instruction, repair services
Guides: Yes
OK to call for current conditions: Yes
Contact: Anyone

GUIDES...

Bass Buddies Guide Service
Orlando 800-328-0022
Species & Seasons: LM Bass
Bodies of water: East Lake Tohopekaliga, West Lake Tohopekaliga, Lake Okeechobee, Kissimmee Chain, Stick Marsh, Farm 13, all Central Florida
Rates: Half day: $125(1-2), Full day: $175(1-2), $25 additional 3rd person
Call between: 24 hours
Provides: Light tackle, heavy tackle, lures, rain gear, beverages, lunch
Handicapped equipped: Yes

Chet Douthit
Clewiston 800-473-6766
Species & Seasons: Bass Nov-Mar
Bodies of water: Lake Okeechobee
Rates: Half day: $150(2), Full day: $200(2)
Call between: 6pm-9pm
Provides: Light tackle, heavy tackle
Handicapped equipped: Yes

Fargo's
Clewiston 813-983-5741
Species & Seasons: LM Bass all year, Crappie Dec-April, Bluegill Mar-June
Bodies of water: Lake Okeechobee
Rates: Half day: $150(1-2), Full day: $200(1-2)
Call between: Anytime
Provides: Light tackle, heavy tackle, fly rod/reel, rain gear
Handicapped equipped: Yes
Certifications: USCG

Frank's River Fishing Tours
Vero Beach 407-562-3430
Species & Seasons: Snook, Sea Trout, Redfish, Snapper, Sea Bass, Bluegill, Crappie all year, Tarpon May-Oct
Bodies of water: Lake Okeechobee and tributaries, Blue Cypress Lake, Stick Marsh, Farm 13, Indian River, all inland waters 100 mile from Vero Beach
Rates: Half day: $100(1), $125(2), Full day: $175(1), $200(2), $25 each additional person
Call between: 6am-10pm
Provides: Light tackle, fly rod/reel, lures, rain gear, beverages
Handicapped equipped: Yes

Capt. Steve Junkermann
Sebring 800-303-FISH
.... 813-655-2014
Species & Seasons: LM Bass all year
Bodies of water: Lake Okeechobee
Rates: Half day: $150(1-2), Full day: $200(1-2), plus bait, split day $25 extra
Call between: 6pm-11pm
Provides: Heavy tackle
Certifications: USPS, USCG

Lake Okeechobee Guide Association
Okeechobee 800-284-2446
Species & Seasons: LM Bass all year, Crappie Nov-April
Bodies of water: Lake Okeechobee
Rates: Half day: $160(1-2), Full day: $225(1-2), May-Sept. Half day: $135, Full day: $200
Call between: 8am-3pm
Provides: Light tackle, heavy tackle, rain gear
Handicapped equipped: Yes
Certifications: USCG

Nix's Fishing Headquarters
Okeechobee 813-763-2248
Species & Seasons: LM Bass all year, Crappie Nov-April, Sh Cllcrackrs May-Sept, Bluegill April-Oct
Bodies of water: Lake Okeechobee
Rates: Half day: $160(1-2), Full day: $225(1-2), May-Sept. Half day: $135, Full day: $200
Call between: 7am-3pm
Provides: Light tackle, heavy tackle, rain gear
Handicapped equipped: Yes
Certifications: USCG

Tom & Jerry's Pro Guide Service
Leesburg 800-328-5686
Species & Seasons: LM Bass all year, Tarpon April-Nov, Snook April-Sept
Bodies of water: Lake Kissimmee Chain, Clermont Chain, Lake Okeechobee, Stick Marsh, any Central Florida lakes, Boca Grande
Rates: Fresh water: Half day: $150(1-2), Full day: $225(1-2), Salt water: Half day: $275(1-2), Full day: $350(1-2)
Provides: Light tackle, heavy tackle, lures, rain gear
Handicapped equipped: Depends on handicap
Certifications: USCG

FLORIDA
LAKE OKEECHOBEE - LAKE TALQUIN

Wet Dreams Peacock Bass Service
Hollywood 305-435-0486
Species & Seasons: LM Bass, Peacock Bass, Snook, Panfish all year, Oscar May-Oct
Bodies of water: Lake Okeechobee, all canal systems in Dade and Broward Counties
Rates: Half day: $150(1), $175(2), $250(3), Full day: $200(1-2), $250(3)
Call between: 8am-10pm
Provides: Light tackle, fly rod/reel, lures, bait, rain gear, beverages, lunch
Handicapped equipped: No

LODGING...

Uncle Joe's Marina & Motel
RR 3 Box 221
Moore Haven 33471
Seasons: All year
Species & Seasons: LM Bass Dec-May, Crappie Nov-April, Bluegill Feb-July, Shell Cracker Mar-July, Catfish all year
Bodies of Water: Lake Okeechobee
Types of fishing: Fly fishing, light tackle, heavy tackle, wading
Available: Licenses, bait, tackle, boat rentals

LAKE OSBORNE

BAIT & TACKLE...

Boynton Fisherman's Supply
Boynton Beach 407-736-0568
Hours: 7am-7pm
Carries: Live bait, lures, flies, rods, reels, licenses
Bodies of water: Atlantic Ocean, Lake Ida, Lake Osborne
Services & Products: Fishing instruction, repair services
Guides: Yes
OK to call for current conditions: Yes

GUIDES...

Freshwater Fishing Guide
Lake Worth 800-226-1766
Species & Seasons: LM Bass all year, Crappie Nov-May
Bodies of water: Palm Beach County Canal System, Lake Clarke, Lake Osborne, Clear Lake, Lake Ida
Rates: Half day: $150(1-2), Full day: $250(1-2), 1 additional person $25 additional

Call between: 8am-10pm
Provides: Light tackle, fly rod/reel, lures, rain gear
Handicapped equipped: Yes
Certifications: ORVIS, State of FL Emergency Medical Tec.

LAKE ROUSSEAU

LODGING...

Lake Rousseau Campground & Fishing Resort
Crystal River 904-795-6336
Guest Capacity: 200
Handicapped equipped: No
Seasons: All year
Rates: $16/day
Guides: Yes
Species & Seasons: LM Bass, Catfish all year, Crappie Spring, Shell Cracker Summer
Bodies of Water: Lake Rousseau, Withlacoochee River
Types of fishing: Fly fishing, light tackle
Available: Licenses, bait, tackle, boat rentals

LAKE SEMINOLE

BAIT & TACKLE...

John's Guns & Fly Fishing
Tallahassee 904-422-1553
Hours: 9am-6:30pm
Carries: Flies, maps, rods, reels, licenses
Bodies of water: Jackson Lake, Lake Seminole, Lake Talquin, Ochlockonee River, St. Marks River, Wakulla River, Aucilla River, Econfina River, Steinhatchee River, Apalachee Bay
Services & Products: Fishing instruction, repair services, free set up and fly-casting instruction
Guides: Yes
OK to call for current conditions: Yes
Contact: John V. Underwood

Kimbrel's Bait & Grocery Store
Grand Ridge 904-592-2535
Hours: 5am-7-8pm
Carries: Live bait, lures, flies, maps, reels
Bodies of water: Lake Ocheesee, Lake Seminole, Apalachicola River
Services & Products: Guide services, food, beverages, fishing instruction

Guides: Yes
OK to call for current conditions: Yes
Contact: Irene Kimbrel

LODGING...

Gaineys Talquin Lodge
Quincy 904-627-3822
Guest Capacity: 40
Handicapped equipped: No
Seasons: All year
Rates: $40/day double occupancy
Guides: Yes
Species & Seasons: LM Bass, Black Crappie, White Bass all year, Shell Cracker, Bream all summer
Bodies of Water: Lake Talquin, Lake Jackson, Lake Lamonia, Lake Seminole
Types of fishing: Fly fishing, light tackle
Available: Licenses, bait, tackle

LAKE TALQUIN

BAIT & TACKLE...

John's Guns & Fly Fishing
Tallahassee 904-422-1553
Hours: 9am-6:30pm
Carries: Flies, maps, rods, reels, licenses
Bodies of water: Jackson Lake, Lake Seminole, Lake Talquin, Ochlockonee River, St. Marks River, Wakulla River, Aucilla River, Econfina River, Steinhatchee River, Apalachee Bay
Services & Products: Fishing instruction, repair services, free set up and fly-casting instruction
Guides: Yes
OK to call for current conditions: Yes
Contact: John V. Underwood

GUIDES...

Capt. Mark "Smitty" Smith
Deland 904-738-1836
Species & Seasons: LM Bass Oct-June
Bodies of water: St. John's River, Suwannee River, Withlacoochee River, Apalachicola River, Lake Talquin, Lake George, Crescent Lake and others
Rates: Half day: $150+(1-2), Full day: $250+(1-2), $25 additional person (limit 3)
Call between: 7pm-10pm
Provides: Light tackle, heavy tackle, rain gear

LAKE TALQUIN - LAKE TRAFFORD — FLORIDA

Handicapped equipped: No
Certifications: USCG

LODGING...

Blounts Cottages
Tallassee 904-576-4301
Guest Capacity: 14-24 waterfront cottages
Handicapped equipped: No
Seasons: All year
Rates: Call for rates
Guides: Yes, recommend
Species & Seasons: LM Bass, Striped Bass, White Bass, Bream, Crappie
Bodies of Water: Lake Talquin, Ochlockonee River
Types of fishing: Fly fishing, light tackle

Gaineys Talquin Lodge
Quincy 904-627-3822
Guest Capacity: 40
Handicapped equipped: No
Seasons: All year
Rates: $40/day double occupancy
Guides: Yes
Species & Seasons: LM Bass, Black Crappie, White Bass all year, Shell Cracker, Bream all summer
Bodies of Water: Lake Talquin, Lake Jackson, Lake Lamonia, Lake Seminole
Types of fishing: Fly fishing, light tackle
Available: Licenses, bait, tackle

LAKE TARPON

CHARTERS...

A Van Horn Charters
Tarpon Springs 800-757-8577
.... 813-938-8577
Species & Seasons: LM Bas, all year, Snook, Redfish Mar-Nov, Cobia Mar-June, Tarpon April-July
Bodies of water: Lake Tarpon, Gulf of Mexico Flats (from Boca Grand to Homosassa)
Rates: Half day: $250(1-2), Full day: $350(1-2), $50 additional 3d person
Call between: Anytime
Provides: Light tackle, heavy tackle, fly rod/reel, lures, bait, rain gear
Handicapped equipped: Yes
Certifications: USCG

Sportfishing Guide Services, Inc.
Tampa 813-962-1435
Species & Seasons: Snook Mar-Dec, Tarpon, Cobia April-Nov, King Mackerel April-May/Nov-Dec, Speckled Trout, Redfish LM Bass all year, Permit Nov-Feb, Alligators Sept
Bodies of water: Tampa Bay Estuary System, Gulf of Mexico Coastal Flats, (Boca Grande to Homosassa), Lake Tarpon
Rates: Half day: $250(1-2), Ful day: $350(1-2), $50 additional 3rd person
Call between: 7am-9pm
Provides: Light tackle, heavy tackle, fly rod/reel, lures, bait, rain gear, beverages, licenses
Handicapped equipped: Yes
Certifications: International Fishing Hall of Fame, USCG, Nat'l Ass. Charter Operators, FOWA, FL Guides Assoc., OWAA

LAKE TOHOPEKALIGA

GUIDES...

Bass Buddies Guide Service
Orlando 800-328-0022
Species & Seasons: LM Bass
Bodies of water: East Lake Tohopekaliga, West Lake Tohopekaliga, Lake Okeechobee, Kissimmee Chain, Stick Marsh, Farm 13, all Central Florida
Rates: Half day: $125(1-2), Full day: $175(1-2), $25 additional 3rd person
Call between: 24 hours
Provides: Light tackle, heavy tackle, lures, rain gear, beverages, lunch
Handicapped equipped: Yes

LODGING...

Camp Mack
Lake Wales 800-243-8013
.... 813-696-1108
Guest Capacity: 41 RV full hookup sites, 110 Park Motel RV sites, 7 rental units (fully furnished)
Seasons: All year
Rates: RV: $20/night, $120/week, Cabins: $50/day, $300/week, Park Motel Rentals: $65/night, $390/week
Contact: Jill Snively
Guides: Yes

Species & Seasons: LM Bass Nov-April, Crappie Nov-Mar, Shell Cracker, Bluegill Mar-Aug
Bodies of Water: Lake Kissimmee, Lake Hatchineha, Lake Tohopekaliga, Cypress Lake
Types of fishing: Fly fishing, light tackle
Available: Licenses, bait, tackle, family activities, campground

Southport Park
Kissimmee 407-933-5822
Species & Seasons: Bass Mar-Dec, Bluegill Feb-June, Crappie July-Oct, Perch Oct-Jan
Bodies of water: West Lake Tohopekaliga, Lake Kissimmee, Cypress Lake
Rates: Half day: $125(2), Full day: $175(2)
Call between: 6am-6pm
Provides: Light tackle, lures, bait, beverages, lunch

LAKE TRAFFORD

BAIT & TACKLE...

Anglers Answer
Naples 813-775-7336
Hours: 6am-6pm
Carries: Live bait, lures, flies, maps, rods, reels, licenses
Bodies of water: Gulf of Mexico, Lake Okeechobee, Lake Trafford
Services & Products: Guide services, beverages, fishing instruction, repair services
Guides: Yes
OK to call for current conditions: Yes
Contact: Dan or Bill

Golden Gate Trophy Center
Naples 813-455-1337
Hours: 6am-7pm
Carries: Live bait, lures, flies, maps, rods, reels, licenses
Bodies of water: Lake Trafford, Lake Okeechobee, Gulf of Mexico, Ten Thousand Islands, fishable fresh water canals
Services & Products: Guide services, charter boat service, beverages, repair services
OK to call for current conditions: Yes
Contact: Alec or Georgia Alexandre

FLORIDA
LAKE WOODRUFF - ORANGE LAKE

LAKE WOODRUFF

LODGING...

Parramore's Fish Camp & Family Resort
1675 S. Moon Road
Astor 32102
Guest Capacity: 100
Handicapped equipped: Yes
Seasons: All year
Rates: Camping: $19/night, $116.50/week, Cabins: $66/night, $396/week
Contact: Reva D. Cunningham
Guides: Yes
Species & Seasons: LM Bass, Jan-Mar, Striped Bass May-Sept, Crappie Oct-Mar, Bream May-Sept
Bodies of Water: St. Johns River, Lake George, Lake Dexter, Lake Woodruff
Types of fishing: Fly fishing, light tackle
Available: Licenses, bait, tackle, boat rentals, family activities, pool, tennis court

LOCHLOOSA LAKE

BAIT & TACKLE...

Tackle Box
Gainesville 904-372-1791
Hours: 7am-6pm Mon.-Fri., 6am-5pm Sat., 7am-2pm Sun.
Carries: Live bait, lures, flies, maps, rods, reels, licenses
Bodies of water: Orange Lake, Lochloosa Lake, Newnan's Lake
Services & Products: Repair services
Guides: Yes
OK to call for current conditions: Yes
Contact: Recorded fishing report
904-375-FISH

MOSQUITO LAGOON

BAIT & TACKLE...

First Strike Marine & Tackle
New Smyrna Beach 904-427-3587
Hours: 6am-6pm
Carries: Live bait, lures, flies, maps, rods, reels, licenses
Bodies of water: Atlantic Ocean, Mosquito Lagoon, Indian River
Services & Products: Guide services, fishing instruction, repair services
Guides: Yes
OK to call for current conditions: Yes
Contact: Lou

Hook Line & Sinker
New Smyrna Beach 904-424-9840
Hours: 6am-6pm
Carries: Live bait, lures, flies, maps, rods, reels, licenses
Bodies of water: Atlantic Ocean, Mosquito Lagoon, Indian River, Ponce Inlet
Services & Products: Boat rentals, guide services, charter boat service, boat ramp, food, beverages, fishing instruction, repair services, canoe rentals
Guides: Yes
OK to call for current conditions: Yes
Contact: Louis J. Sarlo
(see ad page 89)

CHARTERS...

Backcountry Charter Service
DeBary 800-932-7335
Species & Seasons: Redfish, Sea Trout Dec-Jan, Tarpon May-Nov, Snook Mar-Oct, Jack Crevalle Nov-May, Ladyfish Sept-May, Striped Bass Feb-June, Ameican Shad Jan-April, LM Bass No-April, Panfish pril-Sept
Bodies of water: Indian River Lagoon, Mosquito Lagoon, Banana River Lagoon, St. Johns River, Stick Marsh, Farm 13
Rates: Half day: $185(1-2), Full day: $275(1-2)
Call between: 24 hours
Provides: Light tackle, fly rod/reel, lures, bait, rain gear, beverages
Handicapped equipped: Yes
Certifications: USCG, FFF, IGFA

Capt. Shawn Foster
Cocoa Beach 407-784-0094
Species & Seasons: Redfish Feb-Nov, Sea Trout all year, Snook Spring-Fall, Spanish Mackerel Summer-Fall, Tarpon Spring-Summer, Cobia Mar-Sept, Triple Tail Aprl-Aug, LM Bass Feb-Nov, Jack Crevalle, Ladyfish June-Sept
Bodies of water: Banna River, Indian River, Port Canaveral, Mosquito Lagoon, St. Johns River, Stick Marsh
Rates: Half day: $200(1-2), Full day: $300(1-2), 3rd person: Half day: $25 additional, Full day: $50 additional
Call between: 5:30pm-7pm
Provides: Light tackle, heavy tackle, fly rod/reel, lures, bait, rain gear, beverages
Handicapped equipped: Yes
Certifications: USCG

NEWNAN'S LAKE

BAIT & TACKLE...

Tackle Box
Gainesville 904-372-1791
Hours: 7am-6pm Mon.-Fri., 6am-5pm Sat., 7am-2pm Sun.
Carries: Live bait, lures, flies maps, rods, reels, licenses
Bodies of water: Orange Lake, Lochloosa Lake, Newnan's Lake
Services & Products: Repair services
Guides: Yes
OK to call for current conditions: Yes
Contact: Recorded fishing report
904-375-FISH

ORANGE LAKE

BAIT & TACKLE...

Tackle Box
Gainesville 904-372-1791
Hours: 7am-6pm Mon.-Fri., 6am-5pm Sat., 7am-2pm Sun.
Carries: Live bait, lures, flies, maps, rods, reels, licenses
Bodies of water: Orange Lake, Lochloosa Lake, Newnan's Lake
Services & Products: Repair services
Guides: Yes
OK to call for current condition: Yes
Contact Recorded fishing report
904-375-FISH

GUIDES...

Sunrise Charters
Albion, NY 716-682-5563
Species & Seasons: Bass Nov-April
Bodies of water: Orange Lake, St. Johns River
Rates: $440 per day
Call between: 7am-9pm
Provides: Light tackle, lures, bait
Certifications: USCG

REGIONAL AREAS

GUIDES...

Capt. Ken Daubert's Fantasy Flats Fishing
Silver Springs 904-625-3562
Species & Seasons: LM Bass, Redfish, Striped Bass all year, Tarpon, Snook May-Oct, Cobia April-Oct, Sea Trout Mar-Dec
Bodies of water: Central Florida including both coasts
Call between: 8pm-10pm
Provides: Light tackle, heavy tackle, fly rod/reel, lures, rain gear
Handicapped equipped: Yes

Pro Bass Guide Service
Winter Garden 407-877-9676
Species & Seasons: LM Bass all year
Bodies of water: Central Florida lakes and rivers
Rates: Half day: $150(1-2), Full day: $200(1-2), $50 additional for 3rd person
Call between: 8am-8pm
Provides: Light tackle, heavy tackle, lures, bait, rain gear, beverages
Handicapped equipped: Yes
Certifications: USCG

RODMAN RESERVOIR

GUIDES...

Steve Rominsky Guide Service
Welaka 904-467-2030
.... 467-8826
Species & Seasons: LM Bass all year, Striped Bass Feb-May, Panfish Mar-Sept
Bodies of water: St John's River, Crescent Lake, Rodman Res., Lake George
Rates: Full day: $175(1), $220(2)
Call between: 7am-8pm
Provides: Light tackle, heavy tackle, lures, bait, rain gear
Certifications: USCG

"BEAR'S" BASS GUIDE SERVICE
Private Pits & Stick Marsh • 1000 + Fish over 10 lbs • 10 lb. Plus guar. Trips
"Bear" & Shirley Weaver
PO Box 549, Dundee,
Florida 33838-05949
1/2 hr. from Disney
1 941 439-3769
1 800 218-3351

LODGING...

Kerr City
Ft. McCoy 904-685-2557
Guest Capacity: 30-40
Handicapped equipped: No
Seasons: All year
Rates: $275/week
Guides: Yes, recommend
Species & Seasons: LM Bass, Crappie
Bodies of Water: St. John's River, Lake Kerr, Ocklawaha River, Rodman Res.

STICK MARSH

BAIT & TACKLE...

Stick Marsh Bait & Tackle
Fellsmere 407-571-9855
Hours: 5:30am-5pm
Carries: Live bait, lures, flies, maps, rods, reels, licenses
Bodies of water: Blue Cypress Lake, Sebastian River and Inlet, Stick Marsh, Farm 13, Garcia Res., Lake Kissimmee
Services & Products: Guide services, food, beverages, fishing instruction
Guides: Yes
OK to call for current conditions: Yes

GUIDES...

Backcountry Charter Service
DeBary 800-932-7335
Species & Seasons: Redfish, Sea Trout Dec-Jan, Tarpon May-Nov, Snook Mar-Oct, Jack Crevelle Nov-May, Ladyfish Sept-May, Striped Bass Feb-June, American Shad Jan-April, LM Bass Nov-April, Panfish April-Sept
Bodies of water: Indian River Lagoon, Mosquito Lagoon, Banana River Lagoon, St. John's River, Stick Marsh, Farm 13
Rates: Half day: $185(1-2), Full day: $275(1-2)
Call between: 24 hours
Provides: Light tackle, fly rod/reel, lures, bait, rain gear, beverages
Handicapped equipped: Yes
Certifications: USCG, FFF, IGFA

Bass Buddies Guide Service
Orlando 800-328-0022
Species & Seasons: LM Bass
Bodies of water: East Lake Tohopekaliga, West Lake Tohopekaliga, Lake Okeechobee, Kissimmee Chain, Stick Marsh, Farm 13, all Central Florida
Rates: Half day: $125(1-2), Full day: $175(1-2), $25 additional 3rd person
Call between: 24 hours
Provides: Light tackle, heavy tackle, lures, rain gear, beverages, lunch
Handicapped equipped: Yes

Bear's Bass Guide Service
Dundee 941-439-3769
Species & Seasons: LM Bass all year
Bodies of water: Stick March, Private Pits, Kissimmee Chain, other areas
Rates: Half day: $125(1), $175(2), Full day: same
Call between: 7am-10pm
Provides: Light tackle, heavy tackle, lures, bait, rain gear, beverages, lunch
Handicapped equipped: Yes

Florida Fishmasters Pro Guide
St. Cloud 407-892-5962
.... 800-424-5090
Species & Seasons: Bass all year
Bodies of water: Kissimmee Chain of Lakes, Stick Marsh
Rates: Half day: $125(1-2), Full day: $175(1-2), 3rd person $25 additional
Call between: 5am-6pm
Provides: Light tackle, heavy tackle, lures, rain gear
Handicapped equipped: Yes

FLORIDA
STICK MARSH - TEN THOUSAND ISLANDS

Capt. Shawn Foster
Cocoa Beach 407-784-0094
Species & Seasons: Redfish Feb-Nov, Sea Trout all year, Snook Spring-Fall, Spanish Mackerel Summer-Fall, Tarpon Spring-Summer, Cobia Mar-Sept, Triple Tail April-Aug, LM Bass Feb-Nov, Jack Cravalle, Ladyfish June-Sept
Bodies of water: Banana River, Indian River, Port Canaveral, Mosquito Lagoon, St Johns River, Stick Marsh
Rates: Half day: $200(1-2), Full day: $300(1-2), 3rd person: Half day: $25 additional, Full day: $50 additional
Call between: 5:30pm-7pm
Provides: Light tackle, heavy tackle, fly rod/reel, lures, bait, rain gear, beverages
Handicapped equipped: Yes
Certifications: USCG

Frank's River Fishing Tours
Vero Beach 407-562-3430
Species & Seasons: Snook, Sea Trout, Redfish, Snapper, Sea Bass, Bluegill, Crappie all year, Tarpon May-Oct
Bodies of water: Lake Okeechobee and tributaries, Blue Cypress Lake, Stick Marsh, Farm 13, Indian River, all inland waters 100 miles from Vero Beach
Rates: Half day: $100(1), $125(2), Full day: $175(1), $200(2), $25 each additional person
Call between: 6am-10pm
Provides: Light tackle, fly rod/reel, lures, rain gear, beverages
Handicapped equipped: Yes

Tom & Jerry's Pro Guide Service
Leesburg 800-328-5686
Species & Seasons: LM Bas all year, Tarpon April-Nov, Snook April-Sept
Bodies of water: Lake Kissimmee Chain, Clermont Chain, Lake Okeechobee, Stick Marsh, any Central Florida lakes, Boca Grande
Rates: Fresh water: Half day: $150(1-2), Full day: $225(1-2), Salt water: Half day: $275(1-2), Full day: $350(1-2)
Provides: Light tackle, heavy tackle, lures, rain gear
Handicapped equipped: Depends on handicap
Certifications: USCG

TEN THOUSAND ISLANDS

BAIT & TACKLE...

Golden Gate Trophy Center
Naples 813-455-1337
Hours: 6am-7pm
Carries: Live bait, lures, flies, maps, rods, reels, licenses
Bodies of water: Lake Trafford, Lake Okeechobee, Gulf of Mexico, Ten ThousandIslands, fishable fresh water canals
Services & Products: Guide services, charter boat service, beverages, repair services
OK to call for current conditions: Yes
Contact: Alec or Georgia Alexandre

CHARTERS...

Capt. Earl Budd
Chokoloskee 941-695-4035
Species & Seasons: Snook Jan-May/Sept-Dec, Sea Trout all year, Redfish June-Feb, Cobia Mar-June, Tarpon April-June
Bodies of water: Ten Thousand Islands in Everglades, Gulf of Mexico
Rates: Half day: $200(1-2), Full day: $275(1-2)
Call between: 4pm-10pm
Provides: Light tackle, heavy tackle, lures, bait, rain gear
Handicapped equipped: No
Certifications: USCG

Capt. Pete Greenan's Gypsy Guide Service
Sarasota 941-923-6095
Species & Seasons: Tarpon May-Aug, Snook Mar-Dec, Redfish, Sea Trout all year, Triple Tail Oct-April
Bodies of water: Gulf of Mexico, Charlotte Harbor, Boca Grande, Sanibel, Ten Thousand Islands, Everglades Nat'l. Park
Rates: Half day: $250(1-2), Full day: $400(1-2)
Call between: 8am-10pm
Provides: Light tackle, heavy tackle, fly rod/reel, lures, bait, rain gear, beverages
Handicapped equipped: Yes
Certifications: USCG

Chokoloskee Island Charters
Chokoloskee 813-695-2286
Species & Seasons: Snook Feb-June/Sept-Dec, Redfish June-April, Tarpon Mar-Nov, Sea Trout Sept-June
Bodies of water: Everglades Nat'l. Park, Ten Thousand Islands, Gulf of Mexico
Rates: Half day: $200(1-2), $225(3), Full day: $300(1-2), $325(3)
Call between: 6pm-10pm
Provides: Light tackle, fly rod/reel, lures, bait, rain gear
Hndicapped equipped: No
Certifications: USCG

Capt. David J. Eimers
Naples 813-353-4828
Species & Seasons: Tarpon, Snook Mar-Dec, Redfish Sept-April, Sea Trout Nov-May
Bodies of water: Ten Thousand Islands, Marco Island
Rates: Half day: $200(2), Full day: $325(2), off season rates available
Call between: 6:30am-9pm
Provides: Light tackle, fly rod/reel, lures, bait, rain gear
Certifications: USCG, Yamaha and Zbco/Motor Guide

Skinny Dipper
Goodland 941-642-1342
Species & Seasons: Redfish, Snook all year, Tarpon May-June
Bodies of water: Ten Thousand Islands, Everglades Nat'l Park, Marco Island
Rates: Half day: $225(1-2), Full day: $325(1-2)
Call between: Anytime
Provides: Light tackle, fly rod/reel
Handicapped equipped: No
Certifications: USCG, FFF, SAGE

Capt. Johnnie Weeks
Naples 800-774-4713
Species & Seasons: Redfish, Sea Trout all year, Snook April-Dec, Tarpon Aprl-Sept, Grouper May-Oct
Bodies of water: Ten Thousand Islands, Marco Island, Gulf of Mexico
Rates: Half day: $250(1-4), Full day: $350(1-4), off shore $450
Call between: 6pm-10pm
Provides: Light tackle, heavy tackle, lures, bait
Handicapped equipped: Yes
Certifications: USCG

TEN THOUSAND ISLANDS - TSALA APOPKA LAKE   FLORIDA

Capt. Brian Kelley
Everglades City 941-695-3576
.... 695-3331
Species & Seasons: Tarpon May-Oct,
Snook Sept-June, Redfish June-Feb
Sea Trout, Grouper all year
Bodies of water: Everglades Nat'l. Park,
Ten Thousand Islands
Rates: Half day: $175(1-2),
Full day: $250(1-2)
Call between: 8am-10am/5pm-10pm
Provides: Light tackle, lures, bait,
rain gear
Handicapped equipped: Yes
Certifications: USCG, Official Licensed
Guide, Everglades National Park

LODGING...

Barron River Resort
Evergades City 813-695-3331
Seasons: All year
Contact: Kathy, Larry or Johnny
Guides: Yes
Species & Seasons: Tarpon May-Oct,
Snook Sept-Ju,ne Redfish June-Feb,
Sea Trout, Grouper all year
Bodies of Water: Everglades Nat'l. Park,
Ten Thousand Isalnds
Types of fishing: Fly fishing, light tackle
Available: Bait, tackle, boat rentals

ChokoloskeeIsland Park & Camp
Chokoloskee 941-695-2414
Guest Capacity: 150
Handicapped equipped: Yes
Seasons: All year
Rates: $20/day
Guides: Yes
Species & Seasons: Snook Mar-June/
Sept-Dec, Redfish June-Feb, Trout
Nov-April, Shark April-Dec
Bodies of Water: Ten Thousand Islands,
Gulf of Mexico
Types of fishing: Light tackle, heavy
tackle, salt water
Available: Fishing instruction, bait, tackle,
boat rentals, family activities

Port of the Island RV Resort
Naples 800319-4447
Guest Capacity: 99 full service RV lots
Handicapped equipped: No
Seasons: All year
Rates: $23/day, $135/week (full hookup)
Contact: Marlene Marchand
Guides: Yes

Species & Seasons Redfish June/Feb,
Snook Sept-Dec/Feb-May, Trout,
LM Bass, Mangrove Snappers, Grouper
all year, Black Drum Sept-Feb
Bodies of Water: Ten Thousand Islands,
Faka Union Canal System, inland
water ways
Types of fishing: Fly fishing, light tackle,
heavy tackle
Available: Licenses, bait, tackle,
boat rentals, family activities

TSALA APOPKA LAKE

BAIT & TACKLE...

Happy's Bait & Tackle
Inverness 904-726-2281
Hours: 6:30am-5:30pm
Carries: Live bait, lures, flies, maps,
rods, reels
Bodies of water: Tsala Apopka Chain of
Lakes, Floral City Pool, Inverness Pool,
Hernando Pool
Services & Products: Guide services,
food, beverages, repair services
Guides: Yes
OK to call for current conditions: Yes
Contact: BobBaum

LODGING...

Trail's End Camp
Floral City 904-726-0728
Guest Capacity: 120
Handicapped equipped: No
Seasons: All year
Rates: $30-$75/day
Guides: Yes
Species & Seasons: LM Bass Nov-June,
Crappie Dec-June, Bluegill Jan-June
Bodies of Water: Withlacoochee River,
Tsala Apopka Lake
Types of fishing: Fly fishing, light tackle
Available: Licenses, bait, tackle,
boat rentals, general store

YOUR SILENT FISHING PARTNER

The business listings in the Angler's Yellow Pages are full of valuable information.
"Know before you go…"

GEORGIA

1. Atlantic Ocean
2. Chattahoochee River
3. Coosa River
4. Hartwell Lake
5. Jackson Lake
6. Lake Allatoona
7. Lake Blackshear
8. Lake Juliette
9. Lake Oconee
10. Lake Sidney Lanier
11. Lake Sinclair
12. Little River
13. North Mountain Regions
    Chattooga River
    Chatuge Lake
14. Russell Lake
15. Savannah River
16. Strom Thurmond Lake (Clarks Hill)
17. Weiss Lake
18. West Point Lake

GEORGIA

ATLANTIC OCEAN — LAKE ALLATOONA

ATLANTIC OCEAN

CHARTERS...

A A Atlantic Coast Charters
Savannah 912-897-4705
Species & Seasons: Sea Bass all Jan-Jan, Grouper, Snapper Mar-Dec, King Mackerel May-Oct, Dolphin April-Oct, Bluefish April-June, Marlin, Cobia April-Oct, Tarpon June-Sept, Shark May-Oct
Bodies of water: Atlantic Ocean, and up to 100 miles offshore
Rates: Up to 6 people: 4 hrs: $250, 11 hrs: $595, Gulfstream 15 hrs: $950
Call between: 7am-9pm
Provides: Light tackle, heavy tackle, lures, bait
Handicapped equipped: Yes
Certifications: USCG

Salt Water Charters
Savannah 912-598-1814
Species & Seasons: Red Snapper, Grouper, Black Sea Bass all year, King Mackerel April-Nov, Dolphin, Wahoo, Marlin, Amberjack April-Sept, Spanish Mackerel May-Sept, Sheepshead Dec-May
Bodies of water: South Atlantic Ocean out to the Gulf Stream
Rates: Up to 6 people: Half day: $325, Full day: $600
Call between: 7pm-9pm
Provides: Light tackle, heavy tackle, lures, bait
Handicapped equipped: No
Certifications: USCG

Tybee Island Charters
Tybee Island 912-786-4801
Species & Seasons: Grouper, Snappr, all year, King Mackerel, Dolphin May-Oct, Tarpon July-Aug, Redfish Fall-Spring, Sea Trout Spring/Summer, Shark Mar-Oct, Tuna April-May
Bodies of water: Atlantic Ocean from Hilton Head, SC to Sapello, GA Inland creeks and marshes from Hilton Head, SC to Ossabow, GA
Rates: Inshore: 4 hrs. $180(1-2), 6hrs. $270(1-2). Deep Sea Fishing: (up to 6 people) 4 hrs. $300, 6 hrs. $390, 8 hrs. $450, 11 hrs. $540, 15 hrs. $780
Call between: Anytime
Provides: Light tackle, heavy tackle, bait, beverages, lunch
Handicapped equipped: Yes
Certifications: USCG, member USPS

MARINAS...

Golden Isles Yachts
St. Simons Island 912-638-5678
Hours: 9am-5pm, closed Sun.
Bodies of water: Atlantic Ocean, St. Simons Island
Services & Products: Boat rentals, guide services, charter boat service, fishing instruction, repair services, boat storage
Guides: Yes
OK to call for current conditions: Yes
Contact: Cap Fendig

CHATTAHOOCHEE RIVER

GUIDES...

Chattahoochee Guide Service
Gainesville 404-536-7986
Species & Seasons: LM Bass Feb-Nov, Spotted Bass, Striped Bass all year, Crappie Feb.-May
Bodies of water: Lake Sidney Lanier, Chestatee River, Chattahoochee River
Rates: Half day: $100(1), $120(2), Full day: $140(1), $150(2)
Call between: Anytime
Provides: Light tackle, heavy tackle, lures, bait, rain gear, beverages
Handicapped equipped: No

COOSA RIVER

BAIT & TACKLE...

Coosa River Trading Post
Rome 706-234-5000
Hours: 7am-7pm
Carries: Live bait, lures, maps, rods, reels, licenses
Bodies of water: Coosa River, Weiss Lake
Services & Products: Boat ramp, food, beverages, gas/oil, repair services, campground
Guides: Yes
OK to call for current conditions: Yes
Contact: Al

HARTWELL LAKE

GUIDES...

Wilson's Guide Service
Elberton 706-283-3336
Species & Seasons: LM Bass, Hybrids, Striped Bass all year, Coosa Bass Mar-June, Crappie Jan-May/Sept-Nov
Bodies of water: Hartwell Lake, Russell Lake, Strom Thurmond Lake (Clarks Hill)
Rates: Full day: $150(1-2)
Call between: Anytime
Provides: Light tackle, heavy tackle, lures, bait
Handicapped equipped: Yes

JACKSON LAKE

GUIDES...

John Copeland
Covington 404-787-0762
Species & Seasons: LM Bass Feb-Dec
Bodies of water: Jackson Lake, Lake Oconee, Lake Sinclair, Russell Lake
Rates: Half day: $100(1-2), Full day: $150(1-2), Russell Lake: Full day only $225(1-3)
Call between: 7pm-10:30pm
Provides: Light tackle, lures, bait, beverages
Handicapped equipped: No

LAKE ALLATOONA

MARINAS...

Holiday Marina
Acworth 404-974-2575
Hours: 8am-7pm
Carries: Live bait, maps, rods, reels, licenses
Bodies of water: Lake Allatoona
Services & Products: Boat rentals, lodging, boat ramp, food, beverages, gas/oil, restaurant
Guides: Yes
OK to call for current conditions: No

LAKE BLACKSHEAR - LAKE SINCLAIR

GEORGIA

LAKE BLACKSHEAR

BAIT & TACKLE...

82E Sports Center
Tifton 912-382-8979
Hours: 6am-7pm
Carries: Live bait, lures, flies, rods, reels, licenses
Bodies of water: Paradise Fishing Park, Little River, Alapaha River, Willacoochee River, Lake Blackshear
Services & Products: Beverages
Guides: Yes
OK to call for current conditions: Yes
Contact: James Weldon

LAKE JULIETTE

BAIT & TACKLE...

Curly's Bait & Tackle
Macon 912-788-6948
Hours: 6am-7pm
Carries: Live bait, lures, flies, rods, reels, licenses
Bodies of water: Ocmulgee River, Oconee River, Lake Sinclair, Lake Juliette, Lake Joy, Lake Tobesofkee
Guides: No
OK to call for current conditions: Yes
Contact: Anyone

LAKE OCONEE

GUIDES...

Bill Vanderford's Guide Service
Lawrenceville 404-962-1241
Species & Seasons: Spotted Bass all year, Striped Bass Oct-June, White Bass Feb-Mar, Crappie Feb-April
Bodies of water: Lake Sidney Lanier, Lake Oconee
Rates: Half day: $125(1-2), $30 additional 3rd person, Full day: $200(1-2), $50 additional 3rd person
Call between: Anytime
Provides: Light tackle, heavy tackle, lures, bait, rain gear
Handicapped equipped: Yes

John Copeland
Covington 404-787-0762
Species & Seasons: LM Bass Feb-Dec
Bodies of water: Jackson Lake, Lake Oconee, Lake Sinclair, Russell Lake
Rates: Half day: $100(1-2), Full day: $150(1-2), Russell Lake: Full day only $225(1-3)
Call between: 7pm-10:30pm
Provides: Light tackle, lures, bait, beverages
Handicapped equipped: No

Peeble's Guide Service
Eatonton 706-485-6494
Species & Seasons: LM Bass all year, Crappie Feb-May
Bodies of water: Lake Sinclair, Lake Oconee
Rates: Half day: $125(1), $150(2), Full day: $150(1), $200(2), Lake Tours: $40 per hr.
Call between: 7pm-10pm
Provides: Light tackle, heavy tackle, lures, bait, rain gear, beverages

Tony Couch Guide Service
Buckhead 706-342-0194
Species & Seasons: LM Bass all year, Crappie Jan-Apr, Hybrids April-Jan
Bodies of water: Lake Oconee, Lake Sinclair
Rates: Half day: $150(1-2), Full day: $225(1-2)
Call between: 6pm-10:30pm
Provides: Light tackle, heavy tackle, lures, bait, beverages
Handicapped equipped: No

LAKE SIDNEY LANIER

GUIDES...

Bill Vanderford's Guide Service
Lawrenceville 404-962-1241
Species & Seasons: Spotted Bass all year, Striped Bass Oct-June, White Bass Feb-Mar, Crappie Feb-April
Bodies of water: Lake Sidney Lanier, Lake Oconee
Rates: Half day: $125(1-2), $30 additional 3rd person, Full day: $200(1-2), $50 additional 3rd person
Call between: Anytime
Provides: Light tackle, heavy tackle, lures, bait, rain gear
Handicapped equipped: Yes

Chattahoochee Guide Service
Gainesville 404-536-7986
Species & Seasons: LM Bass Feb-Nov, Spotted Bass, Striped Bass all year, Crappie Feb,-May
Bodies of water: Lake Sidney Lanier, Chestatee River, Chattahoochee River
Rates: Half day: $100(1), $120(2), Full day: $140(1), $150(2)
Call between: Anytime
Provides: Light tackle, heavy tackle, lures, bait, rain gear, beverages
Handicapped equipped: No

Dean Durham Outdoors
Dawsonville 706-864-8818
Species & Seasons: LM Bass, Spotted Bass all year
Bodies of water: Lake Sidney Lanier
Call between: 8am-9pm
Provides: Light tackle, heavy tackle, lures, bait, beverages, lunch
Certifications: USCG

Lake Lanier Fishing Guide Service
Stone Mountain 404-921-4530
Species & Seasons: Striped Bass, Spotted Bass all year
Bodies of water: Lake Sidney Lanier
Rates: Half day: $150(1-2), Full day: $250(1-2)
Call between: 3pm-8pm
Provides: Light tackle, heavy tackle, lures, bait
Handicapped equipped: No

LAKE SINCLAIR

BAIT & TACKLE...

Curly's Bait & Tackle
Macon 912-788-6948
Hours: 6am-7pm
Carries: Live bait, lures, flies, rods, reels, licenses
Bodies of water: Ocmulgee River, Oconee River, Lake Sinclair, Lake Juliette, Lake Joy, Lake Tobesofkee
Guides: No
OK to call for current conditions: Yes
Contact: Anyone

GEORGIA

LAKE SINCLAIR - SAVANNAH RIVER

GUIDES...

John Copeland
Covington 404-787-0762
Species & Seasons: LM Bass Feb-Dec
Bodies of water: Jackson Lake, Lake Oconee, Lake Sinclair, Russell Lake
Rates: Half day: $100(1-2), Full day: $150(1-2), Russell Lake: Full day only $225(1-3)
Call between: 7pm-10:30pm
Provides: Light tackle, lures, bait, beverages
Handicapped equipped: No

Peeble's Guide Service
Eatonton 706-485-6494
Species & Seasons: LM Bass all year, Crappie Feb-May
Bodies of water: Lake Sinclair, Lake Oconee
Rates: Half day: $125(1), $150(2), Full day: $150(1), $200(2), Lake Tours: $40 per hr.
Call between: 7pm-10pm
Provides: Light tackle, heavy tackle, lures, bait, rain gear, beverages

Tony Couch Guide Service
Buckhead 706-342-0194
Species & Seasons: LM Bass all year, Crappie Jan-Apr, Hybrids Apr-Jan
Bodies of water: Lake Oconee, Lake Sinclair
Rates: Half day: $150(1-2), Full day: $225(1-2)
Call between: 6pm-10:30pm
Provides: Light tackle, heavy tackle, lures, bait, beverages
Handicapped equipped: No

LITTLE RIVER

BAIT & TACKLE...

82E Sports Center
Tifton 912-382-8979
Hours: 6am-7pm
Carries: Live bait, lures, flies, rods, reels, licenses
Bodies of water: Paradise Fishing Park, Little River, Alapaha River, Willacoochee River, Lake Blackshear
Services & Products: Beverages
Guides: Yes
OK to call for current conditions: Yes
Contact: James Weldon

NORTH MOUNTAIN REGIONS

GUIDES...

Cohutta Guide Service
Mineral Bluff 706-374-5060
Species & Seasons: Rainbow Trout, Brown Trout, Brook Trout all year
Bodies of water: Hiawassee River, Chattooga River, Toccoa River, Cooper Creek, Rock Creek, Noontootla Creek, and others
Rates: Half day: $50(1-2), Full day: $100(1), $160(2), also monthly discounts and senior citizens discounts
Call between: Anytime
Provides: Light tackle, fly rod/reel, lures, bait, beverages, lunch
Handicapped equipped: Yes

LODGING...

Shady Rest Cabins
Hiawassee 706-896-2240
Guest Capacity: 7 Cabins, sleeps up to 6 people
Handicap equipped: Some cabins
Seasons: All year
Rates: $55/day double occupancy
Contact: Anyone
Guides: Yes
Species & Seasons: LM Bass, Panfish, Striped Bass, Hybrids, Catfish all year
Bodies of Water: Chatuge Lake
Types of fishing: Fly fishing, light tackle, heavy tackle
Available: Fishing instruction, licenses, bait, tackle, boat rentals

RUSSELL LAKE

GUIDES...

John Copeland
Covington 404-787-0762
Species & Seasons: LM Bass Feb-Dec
Bodies of water: Jackson Lake, Lake Oconee, Lake Sinclair, Russell Lake
Rates: Half day: $100(1-2), Full day: $150(1-2), Russell Lake: Full day only $225(1-3)
Call between: 7pm-10:30pm
Provides: Light tackle, lures, bait, beverages
Handicapped equipped: No

Wilson's Guide Service
Elberton 706-283-3336
Species & Seasons: LM Bass, Hybrids, Striped Bass all year, Coosa Bass Mar-June, Crappie Jan-May/Sept-Nov
Bodies of water: Hartwell Lake, Russell Lake, Strom Thurmond Lake (Clarks Hill)
Rates: Full day: $150(1-2)
Call between: Anytime
Provides: Light tackle, heavy tackle, lures, bait
Handicapped equipped: Yes

LODGING....

Lazy L Hunting & Fishing Resort
Elberton 706-283-8163
Guest Capacity: 50
Handicap equipped: No
Seasons: All year
Rates: $45/day
Contact: Jack Story
Guides: Yes
Species & Seasons: LM Bass Mar-May, Striped Bass April-June, Crappie Feb-April
Bodies of Water: Strom Thurmond Lake (Clarks Hill), Savannah River, Russell Lake
Types of fishing: Fly fishing, light tackle, heavy tackle
Available: Fishing instruction, licenses, bait, tackle, family activities

SAVANNAH RIVER

BAIT & TACKLE...

Allen's Kuntry Store
Evans 706-860-1493
Hours: 24 hours
Carries: Live bait, lures, flies, maps, rods, reels, licenses
Bodies of water: Savannah River, Strom Thurmond Lake
Services & Products: Food, beverages, gas/oil
Guides: Yes
OK to call for current conditions: Yes

Harrisburg Bait & Tackle
Augusta 706-736-3946
Hours: 5am-7pm
Carries: Live bait, lures, rods, reels,
Bodies of water: Strom Thurmond Lake, Savannah River, Lake Olmested

SAVANNAH RIVER - WEST POINT LAKE — GEORGIA

Services & Products: Food, beverages, repair services
Guides: Yes
OK to call for current conditions: Yes

LODGING...

Lazy L Hunting & Fishing Resort
Elberton 706-283-8163
Guest Capacity: 50
Handicap equipped: No
Seasons: All year
Rates: $45/day
Contact: Jack Story
Guides: Yes
Species & Seasons: LM Bass Mar-May, Striped Bass April-June, Crappie Feb-April
Bodies of Water: Strom Thurmond Lake (Clarks Hill), Savannah River, Russell Lake
Types of fishing: Fly fishing, light tackle, heavy tackle
Available: Fishing instruction, licenses, bait, tackle, family activities

STROM THURMOND LAKE (CLARKS HILL)

BAIT & TACKLE...

Allen's Kuntry Store
Evans 706-860-1493
Hours: 24 hours
Carries: Live bait, lures, flies, maps, rods, reels, licenses
Bodies of water: Savannah River, Strom Thurmond Lake
Services & Products: Food, beverages, gas/oil
Guides: Yes
OK to call for current conditions: Yes

Harrisburg Bait & Tackle
Augusta 706-736-3946
Hours: 5am-7pm
Carries: Live bait, lures, rods, reels,
Bodies of water: Strom Thurmond Lake, Savannah River, Lake Olmested
Services & Products: Food, beverages, repair services
Guides: Yes
OK to call for current conditions: Yes

GUIDES...

Wilson's Guide Service
Elberton 706-283-3336
Species & Seasons: LM Bass, Hybrids, Striped Bass all year, Coosa Bass Mar-June, Crappie Jan-May/Sept-Nov
Bodies of water: Hartwell Lake, Russell Lake, Strom Thurmond Lake (Clarks Hill)
Rates: Full day: $150(1-2)
Call between: Anytime
Provides: Light tackle, heavy tackle, lures, bait
Handicapped equipped: Yes

LODGING...

Lazy L Hunting & Fishing Resort
Elberton 706-283-8163
Guest Capacity: 50
Handicap equipped: No
Seasons: All year
Rates: $45/day
Contact: Jack Story
Guides: Yes
Species & Seasons: LM Bass Mar-May, Striped Bass April-June, Crappie Feb-April
Bodies of Water: Strom Thurmond Lake (Clarks Hill), Savannah River, Russell Lake
Types of fishing: Fly fishing, light tackle, heavy tackle
Available: Fishing instruction, licenses, bait, tackle, family activities

WEISS LAKE

BAIT & TACKLE...

Brushy Branch Bait & Tackle
Cave Springs 706-777-8545
Hours: 6am-9pm
Carries: Live bait, lures, maps, rods, reels, licenses
Bodies of water: Weiss Lake, Etowah River, Brushy Branch
Services & Products: Boat rentals, guide services, charter boat service, food, beverages, gas/oil, fishing instruction, repair services, survival supplies and books
OK to call for current conditions: Yes
Contact: Jackie

Coosa River Trading Post
Rome 706-234-5000
Hours: 7am-7pm
Carries: Live bait, lures, maps, rods, reels, licenses
Bodies of water: Coosa River, Weiss Lake
Services & Products: Boat ramp, food, beverages, gas/oil, repair services, campground
Guides: Yes
OK to call for current conditions: Yes
Contact: Al

WEST POINT LAKE

MARINAS...

Highland Marina & Resort
LaGrange 706-882-3437
Hours: Daylight-Dark
Carries: Live bait, lures, maps, rods, reels, licenses
Bodies of water: West Point Lake
Services & Products: Boat rentals, guide services, lodging, boat ramp, food, beverages, gas/oil, repair services
Guides: Yes
OK to call for current conditions: Yes
Contact: Fishing report #706-845-2968

OTHER LOCATIONS

BAIT & TACKLE...

Blackstock Bait & Tackle
Fairburn 706-964-7038
Hours: 7am-7pm
Carries: Live bait, lures, flies, maps, rods, reels, licenses
Bodies of water: Local fishing lakes
Guides: No
OK to call for current conditions: Yes
Contact: Tommy Blackstock

Look in the Location Index
for a complete list of fishing areas

HAWAII

1. Hawaii
2. Kauai
3. Maui
4. Molokai

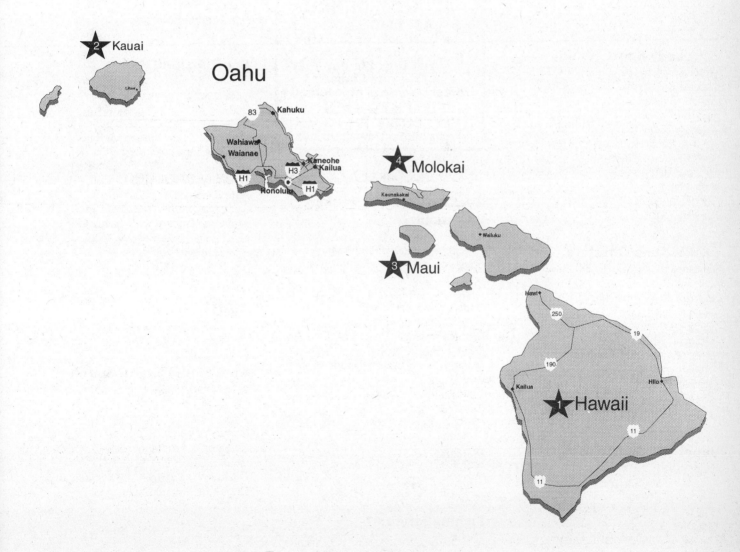

HAWAII

HAWAII

CHARTERS...

Catchem One Sports Fishing
Kailua-Kona 808-329-2670
.... 987-7871
Species & Seasons: Blue Marlin, Striped Marlin, Short Nose Spearfish, Dolphin, Yellowfin Tuna, Wahoo, Skip Jack Tuna all year
Bodies of water: Pacific Ocean, Kona Coast of "The Big Island"
Rates: Fare for Boat: Half day: $295, Full day: $395, Max 6 people
Call between: 7am-9pm
Provides: Light tackle, heavy tackle, lures, bait, rain gear (fly fishing with customer's tackle)
Handicapped equipped: Yes
Certifications: USCG

Foxy Lady Sport Fishing
Kailua-Kona 808-325-5552
Species & Seasons: Marlin, Dolphin, Wahoo, Tuna all year
Bodies of water: Pacific Ocean
Rates: Half day: $350(1-6) + tax, Full day: $575(1-6) +tax
Call between: 8am-8pm
Provides: Light tackle, heavy tackle, lures, bait
Handicapped equipped: Yes
Certifications: USCG

Jack's Kona Charters
Kealakekua 808-325-7558
.... 800-545-KONA
Species & Seasons: Marlin all year, Tuna seasonal, Dolphin winter months, Wahoo Jan-April
Bodies of water: Pacific Ocean
Rates: Varies: $300-$500 up to 6 people
Call between: 24 hours
Provides: Light tackle, heavy tackle
Handicapped equipped: Yes
Certifications: USCG

Janet "B" Sportfishing
Kailua-Kona 808-325-6374
.... 800-658-8624
Species & Seasons: YellowfinTuna, Aku, Blue Marlin, Striped Marlin, Spearfish, Black Marlin, Wahoo, Dolphin
Bodies of water: Pacific Ocean, Kona Coast, Big Island of Hawaii
Rates: Half day: $245, Full day: $375, Exclusive up to 6 people
Call between: 24 hours
Provides: Light tackle, heavy tackle, lures

Notorious Sportfishing
Kealakekua 808-325-7558
.... 800-545-KONA
Species & Seasons: Marlin, Wahoo all year, Tuna seasonal, Mahi-Mahi
Bodies of water: Pacific Ocean
Rates: Half day: $85(1), Full day: $125(1), Exclusive from: $250-$475
Call between: Anytime
Provides: Light tackle, heavy tackle, lures, bait, rain gear
Handicapped equipped: Yes
Certifications: USCG

NOTORIOUS SPORTSFISHING
35' BERTRAM
Largest Marlin to date a 1,229 lb. Pacific Blue!
Full Day, 1/2 day or Overnite Charters
Direct bookings discounted
808 325-7558
PO Box 1018
Kealakekua, Hawaii 96750

Reel Action Light Tackle Sportfishing
Kailua-Kona 808-325-6811
Species & Seasons: Marlin, Tuna, Trevally, Snapper May-Sept, Wahoo April-July, Dolphin Feb-June, Amberjack Jan-May, Shark all year
Bodies of water: Pacific Ocean, Hawaiian Waters Kona Coast
Rates: Private Charters: $150-$400
Call between: 7am-10pm
Provides: Light tackle, fly rod/reel, lures, bait
Handicapped equipped: No
Certifications: USCG

KAUAI

CHARTERS...

Fishing for Fun
Kapaa 808-822-3899
Species & Seasons: Blue Marlin, Striped Marlin, Dolphin, Wahoo, Skipjack Tuna all year, Yellowfin Tuna May-July
Bodies of water: Pacific Ocean around the Island of Kauai and Niihau
Rates: Half day: $80(1), $450(6), Full day: $120, $700(6)
Call between: 8am-10-pm
Provides: Light tackle, heavy tackle, lures, bait
Handicapped equipped: Yes, limited

Hanalei Sport Fishing & Tours
Kanalei 808-826-6114
Species & Seasons: Yellowfin Tuna May-Aug, Blue Marlin June-Oct, Wahoo, Dolphin, Amberjack all year, New Zealand: Rainbow Trout Jan-April
Bodies of water: Pacific Ocean
Rates: Hawaii Only: Half day: $110(1) Exclusive: $750
Call between: 7am-5pm (HawaiianTime)
Provides: Light tackle, heavy tackle, fly rod/reel, lures, bait, rain gear, beverages, lunch
Handicapped equipped: No

Sport Fishing Kauai
Koloa 808-742-7013
Species & Seasons: Blue Marlin, Black Marlin, Dolphin, Yellowfin Tuna under 30#, Shark Jan-Dec, Striped Marlin Dec-April, Wahoo May-Oct, Yellowfin Tuna over 100# May-Sept
Bodies of water: Pacific Ocean, Hawaiian Islands: off island of Kauai
Rates: Half day: $450(up to 6)
Call between: 6am-9pm
Provides: Light tackle, heavy tackle, lures, bait, rain gear, beverages
Handicapped equipped: Yes

MAUI

BAIT & TACKLE...

New Maui Fishing Supply
Wailuku 808-244-3449
Hours: 8am-5:30pm
Carries: Lures, flies, rods, reels
Bodies of water: Pacific Ocean
Services & Products: Repair services
Guides: Yes
OK to call for current conditions: Yes
Contact: Raymond Saito

MOLOKAI

CHARTERS...

Alyce C Sport Fishing
Kaunakakai 808-558-8377
Species & Seasons: Yellowfin Tuna May-July, Blue Marlin April-Sept, Dolphin Feb-May, Wahoo April-Aug, Striped Marlin Dec-Mar, most species caught all year
Bodies of water: Pacific Ocean, waters between Maui, Lanai and Molokai
Rates: Fare for Boat: Half day: $300, 3/4 day: $350, Full day: $400, Shares available
Call between: 6pm-9pm
Provides: Light tackle, heavy tackle, lures, bait, rain gear
Handicapped equipped: Yes
Certifications: USCG

Thank you for using the Angler's Yellow Pages

IDAHO

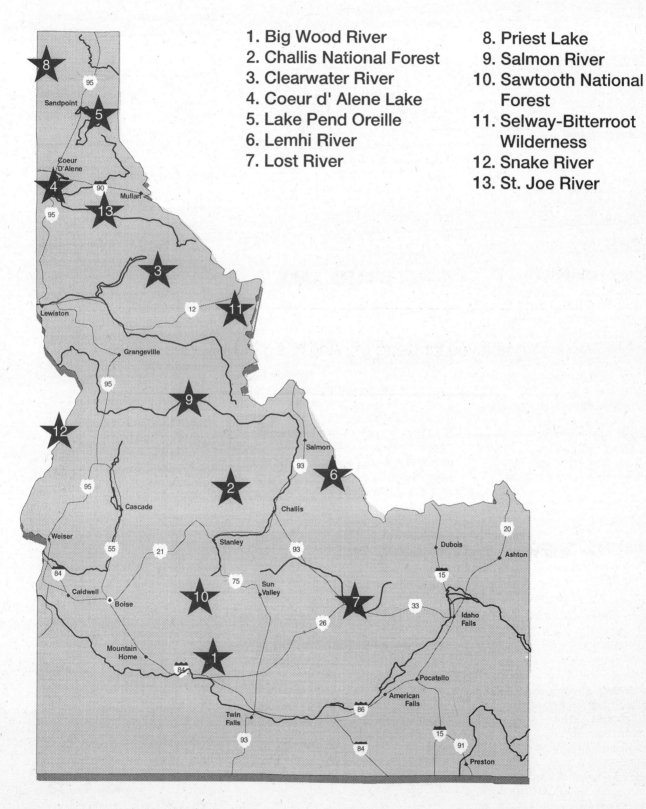

1. Big Wood River
2. Challis National Forest
3. Clearwater River
4. Coeur d' Alene Lake
5. Lake Pend Oreille
6. Lemhi River
7. Lost River
8. Priest Lake
9. Salmon River
10. Sawtooth National Forest
11. Selway-Bitterroot Wilderness
12. Snake River
13. St. Joe River

IDAHO

BIG WOOD RIVER - LEMHI RIVER

BIG WOOD RIVER

GUIDES...

Sun Valley Outfitters, Inc.
Sun Valley 208-622-3400
Species & Seasons: Rainbow Trout, Brown Trout, Brook Trout June-Oct
Bodies of water: Silver Creek, Big Wood River, Lost River, Warm Springs, Trail Creek, Little Wood River
Rates: Half day: $175(1-2),
Full day: $220(1-2)
Call between: 9am-6pm
Provides: Fly rod/reel, beverages, lunch
Handicapped equipped: Yes

CHALLIS NATIONAL FOREST

GUIDES...

White Cloud Outfitters
Challis 208-879-4574
Species & Seasons: Steelhead Mar-April, Rainbow Trout, Cutthroat Trout July-Sept
Bodies of water: Main Salmon River, High Mt. Lakes on the Challis Nat'l. Forest, Sawtooth Nat'l. recreation areas
Rates: Half day: $150(1-2),
Full day: $200(1-2), call for Horseback Lake fishing rates
Call between: 8am-Noon
Provides: Lures, bait, beverages, lunch
Handicapped equipped: Yes
Certifications: Licensed and Bonded Outfitter & Guide

CLEARWATER RIVER

GUIDES...

Beamers Hells Canyon Tours
Lewiston 509-758-4800
Species & Seasons: SM Bass, Rainbow Trout April-Sept, Sturgeon Jan-Dec, Steelhead Oct-Feb
Bodies of water: Snake River, Salmon River, Clearwater River
Rates: Full day: $150(1)
Call between: 8am-5pm
Provides: Heavy tackle, lures, beverages, lunch
Handicapped equipped: Yes
Certifications: USCG, ID Outfitters & Guides Assn., OR Packers & Guides Assn.

Jeff Carr
Eugene, OR 503-344-7331
Species & Seasons: Steelhead all year, Trout April-Oct
Bodies of water: Clearwater River
Rates: Half day: $150(1), $200(2),
Full day: $250(1), $250(2)
Call between: 5pm-9pm
Provides: Fly rod/reel, beverages, lunch
Handicapped equipped: Yes
Certifications: Oregon Guides & Packers

Clearwater Drifters & Guide Shop
Orofino 208-476-3531
Species & Seasons: Steelhead Oct-April
Bodies of water: Clearwater River
Rates: Full day: $125(1)
Provides: Light tackle, lures, bait, beverages, lunch
Handicapped equipped: No

COEUR D'ALENE LAKE

CHARTERS...

Inland Charter Service Sports Fishing
Coeur d'Alene 208-667-8025
Species & Seasons: Chinook Salmon June-Nov, Mackinaw April-Nov, Kamloop May-Nov
Bodies of water: Coeur d'Alene Lake, Lake Pend Oreille, Priest Lake
Rates: Half day: $75, Custom built trips
Call between: After 5pm
Provides: Light tackle, heavy tackle, lures, bait
Handicapped equipped: Yes
Certifications: USCG, State (First aid, Radio)

FLY SHOPS...

Castaway Fly Fishing Shop
Couer d' Alene 208-667-5441
Hours: 10am-9pm
Carries: Flies, maps, rods, reels, licenses
Bodies of water: Coeur d' Alene Lake, Coeur d' Alene River, St. Joe River, Spokane River, Clark Fork River
Services & Products: Guide Services, fly fishing instruction
OK to call for current conditions: Yes

LAKE PEND OREILLE

CHARTERS...

Diamond Charter Fishing
Hope 209-265-2565
.... 661-2470
Species & Seasons: 25# Rainbow Trout, Bull Trout May-Dec, Cutthroat Trout, Lake Trout all year
Bodies of water: Lake Pend Orielle
Rates: Half day: $225(1-4),
Full day $325(1-4)
Call between: 6am-9pm
Provides: Light tackle, heavy tackle, lures
Handicapped equipped: No
Certifications: USCG, ID Outfitters & Guides
(see ad page 135)

Eagle Charters
Hope 208-264-5274
.... 800-513-2926
Species & Seasons: Rainbow Trout, Lake Trout May-Nov
Bodies of water: Lake Pend Oreille
Rates: Half day: $275(6),
Full day: $375(6), June-Sept. $100pp
Call between: 6am-10pm
Provides: Light tackle, lures
Handicapped equipped: No
Certifications: USCG, ID Outfitters & Guides

Inland Charter Service Sports Fishing
Coeur d'Alene 208-667-8025
Species & Seasons: Chinook Salmon June-Nov, Mackinaw April-Nov, Kamloop May-Nov
Bodies of water: Coeur d'Alene Lake, Lake Pend Oreille, Priest Lake
Rates: Half day: $75, Custom built trips
Call between: After 5pm
Provides: Light tackle, heavy tackle, lures, bait
Handicapped equipped: Yes
Certifications: USCG, State (First aid, Radio)

LEMHI RIVER

BAIT & TACKLE...

North Fork Store & Cafe
North Fork 208-865-2412
Hours: 6:30am-10pm
Carries: Live bait, lures, flies, maps, rods, reels, licenses

LEMHI RIVER - SALMON RIVER

IDAHO

Bodies of water: Main Salmon River, River of No Return, North Fork Salmon River, Lemhi River
Services & Products: Guide services, charter boat service, lodging, food, beverages, gas/oil
OK to call for current conditions: Yes
Contact: Ken Hill

Provides: Light tackle, heavy tackle, lures, bait
Handicapped equipped: Yes
Certifications: USCG, State (First aid, Radio)

OK to call for current conditions: Yes
Contact: Ken Hill

GUIDES...

Beamers Hells Canyon Tours
Lewiston 509-758-4800
Species & Seasons: SM Bass, Rainbow Trout April-Sept, Sturgeon Jan-Dec, Steelhead Oct-Feb
Bodies of water: Snake River, Salmon River, Clearwater River
Rates: Full day: $150(1)
Call between: 8am-5pm
Provides: Heavy tackle, lures, beverages, lunch
Handicapped equipped: Yes
Certifications: USCG, ID Outfitters & Guides Assn., OR Packers & Guides Assn.

To Catch The BIG ONES! Fish with Diamond Charters on Lake Pend Oreille
Ed Dickson
P.O. Box 153 • Hope ID 83836
(208) 265-2565 • Cellular Phone 661-2470
Home of world record Rainbow Trout 25lbs & Mackinaw (lake trout) to 40 lbs...Year Round Fishing!

Castle Creek Outfitters & Guest Ranch
Salmon 208-756-2548
Species & Seasons: Cutthroat Trout, Rainbow Trout July-Sept
Bodies of water: Salmon River, central Idaho high mountain lakes and stream fly fishing, guest ranch or horse pack trips
Rates: Pack trip: $150/day, Ranch: $100/day
Call between: 5pm-9pm
Provides: Light tackle, fly rod/reel, lures, rain gear, beverages, lunch
Handicapped equipped: No
Certifications: Member ID Outfitters & Guides Assoc.

LOST RIVER

GUIDES...

Sun Valley Outfitters, Inc.
Sun Valley 208-622-3400
Species & Seasons: Rainbow Trout, Brown Trout, Brook Trout June-Oct
Bodies of water: Silver Creek, Big Wood River, Lost River, Warm Springs, Trail Creek, Little Wood River
Rates: Half day: $175(1-2), Full day: $220(1-2)
Call between: 9am-6pm
Provides: Fly rod/reel, beverages, lunch
Handicapped equipped: Yes

GUIDES...

Priest Lake Outdoor Adventures
Nordman 208-443-5601
Species & Seasons: Lake Trout all year
Bodies of water: Priest Lake
Rates: Half day: $155(1-2), Full day: $350(1-2), $60 additional each person
Call between: 6pm-9pm
Provides: Light tackle, lures, bait
Handicapped equipped: Yes
Certifications: USCG, ID Licensed Outfitter

Ridge Runner Outfitters
Kamiah 208-935-0757
Species & Seasons: SM Bass, Rainbow Trout July-Sept, Steelhead, Salmon Oct
Bodies of water: Salmon River
Rates: Full day: $75(1) minimum 4 people
Call between: 8am-10pm
Provides: Beverages, lunch
Handicapped equipped: Depends on handicap

PRIEST LAKE

CHARTERS...

Inland Charter Service Sports Fishing
Coeur d'Alene 208-667-8025
Species & Seasons: Chinook Salmon June-Nov, Mackinaw April-Nov, Kamloop May-Nov
Bodies of water: Coeur d'Alene Lake, Lake Pend Oreille, Priest Lake
Rates: Half day: $75, Custom built trips
Call between: after 5pm

SALMON RIVER

BAIT & TACKLE...

North Fork Store & Cafe
North Fork 208-865-2412
Hours: 6:30am-10pm
Carries: Live bait, lures, flies, maps, rods, reels, licenses
Bodies of water: Main Salmon River, River of No Return, North Fork Salmon River, Lemhi River
Services & Products: Guide services, charter boat service, lodging, food, beverages, gas/oil

YOUR SILENT FISHING PARTNER

PAGE 135

IDAHO
SALMON RIVER - SELWAY-BITTERROOT WILDERNESS

River Odysseys West
Coeur d'Alene 208-765-0841
Species & Seasons: Cutthroat Trout June-Sept, SM Bass, Rainbow Trout, Sturgeon May-Oct
Bodies of water: Snake River in Hells Canyon Idaho, Middle Fork of the Salmon River
Rates: Snake River (Hell's Canyon): 3 days: $610, 4 days: $720, 5 days: $900, Middle Fork Salmon River: $1200/6 days
Call between: 9am-5pm
Provides: Beverages, lunch
Handicapped equipped: No
Certifications: Member ID Outfitters & Guides Assoc.

Solitude River Trips
Merlin, OR 800-396-1776
Species & Seasons: Cutthroat Trout June-Sept
Bodies of water: Middle Fork of the Salmon River
Rates: $1685 pp 6 days
Call between: 8am-8pm
Provides: Light tackcl, heavy tackle, fly rod/reel, lures, bait, rain gear, beverages, lunch
Handicapped equipped: No
Certifications: Orvis, USCG, US Forest Service State of Idaho

Sun Valley Outfitters, Inc.
Sun Valley 208-622-3400
Species & Seasons: Rainbow Trout, Brown Trout, Brook Trout June-Oct
Bodies of water: Silver Creek, Big Wood River, Lost River, Warm Springs, Trail Creek, Little Wood River
Rates: Half day: $175(1-2), Full day: $220(1-2)
Call between: 9am-6pm
Provides: Fly rod/reel, beverages, lunch
Handicapped equipped: Yes

Wapiti River Guides
Riggins 800-488-9872
Species & Seasons: Steelhead Jan-April/Sept-Dec, Trout Mar-Oct, Bass April-Aug
Bodies of water: Salmon River, Grande Ronde River (Oregon)
Rates: Full day: From $125-$250
Call between: 6am-10pm
Provides: Light tackle, lures, rain gear, beverages, lunch
Handicapped equipped: Yes
Certifications: Licensed in OR and ID

White Cloud Outfitters
Challis 208-879-4574
Species & Seasons: Steelhead Mar-April, Rainbow Trout, Cutthroat Trout July-Sept
Bodies of water: Main Salmon River, High Mt. Lakes on the Challis Nat'l. Forest and Sawtooth Nat'l. recreation areas
Rates: Half day: $150(1-2), Full day: $200(1-2), call for Horseback Lake fishing rates
Call between: 8am-Noon
Provides: Lures, bait, beverages, lunch
Handicapped equipped: Yes
Certifications: Licensed and Bonded Outfitter & Guide

Wilderness River Outfitters
Springfield, OR 503-726-9471
Species & Seasons: Trout May-Oct, SM Bass June-Sept, Steelhead May-Oct, Salmon Oct-Nov/May-June
Bodies of water: Lower main Salmon River, Oregon: McKenzie River, Willamette River, Umpqua River
Rates: Full day: $225(1-2), Salmon: $250
Call between: 8am-4:30pm
Provides: Light tackle, heavy tackle, fly rod/reel, lures, bait, lunch
Handicapped equipped: Yes
Certifications: OSMB

LODGES...

Mystic Saddle Ranch
Stanley 208-774-3591
Guest Capacity: Groups of 17 maximum
Handicap equipped: No
Seasons: May 31 to Nov 1
Rates: $159/day
Guides: Yes
Species & Seasons: Trout May-Oct
Bodies of Water: Middle Fork of Salmon River, Main Salmon River, 200 high mountain lakes
Types of fishing: Fly fishing, light tackle, horse/back pack, wading
Available: Fishing instruction, family activities

Salmon River Lodge, Inc.
Salmon 208-756-6622
.... 800-635-4717
Guest Capacity: 30
Handicap equipped: No
Seasons: Mar to Nov
Rates: $80-$100/day
Contact: Jim Dartt

Guides: Yes
Species & Seasons: Trout May-Aug, Steelhead Sept-Nov/Mar-April
Bodies of Water: Main Salmon River, high mountain lakes
Types of fishing: Fly fishing, light tackle, heavy tackle, horse/back pack, wading, float trips
Available: Licenses, bait, tackle, boat rentals, family activities

SAWTOOTH NATIONAL FOREST

GUIDES...

Sawtooth Wilderness Outfitters
Garden Valley 208-462-3416
Species & Seasons: Brook Trout, Rainbow Trout, Cutthroat Trout July-Sept
Bodies of water: Sawtooth Wilderness area, 180 high alpine lakes
Rates: Full day: $140 pp per day
Call between: 8am-8pm
Handicapped equipped: Yes

White Cloud Outfitters
Challis 208-879-4574
Species & Seasons: Steelhead Mar-April, Rainbow Trout, Cutthroat Trout July-Sept
Bodies of water: Main Salmon River, High Mt. Lakes on the Challis Nat'l. Forest and Sawtooth Nat'l. recreation areas
Rates: Half day: $150(1-2), Full day: $200(1-2), call for Horseback Lake fishing rates
Call between: 8am-Noon
Provides: Lures, bait, beverages, lunch
Handicapped equipped: Yes
Certifications: Licensed and Bonded Outfitter & Guide

SELWAY-BITTERROOT WILDERNESS

GUIDES...

Renshaw Outfitting, Inc.
Kamiah 800-452-2567
Species & Seasons: Cutthroat Trout, Native Rainbow Trout June-Sept
Bodies of water: Selway-Bitterroot Wilderness, Weitas Creek

SELWAY BITTERROOT WILDERNESS - ST. JOE RIVER

Call between: 6am-10pm
Provides: Light tackle, fly rod/reel, lures, bait, rain gear
Handicapped equipped: No

SNAKE RIVER

GUIDES...

Beamers Hells Canyon Tours
Lewiston 509-758-4800
Species & Seasons: SM Bass, Rainbow Trout April-Sept, Sturgeon Jan-Dec, Steelhead Oct-Feb
Bodies of water: Snake River, Salmon River, Clearwater River
Rates: Full day: $150(1)
Call between: 8am-5pm
Provides: Heavy tackle, lures, beverages, lunch
Handicapped equipped: Yes
Certifications: USCG, ID Outfitters & Guides Assn., OR Packers & Guides Assn

River Odysseys West
Coeur d'Alene 208-765-0841
Species & Seasons: Cutthroat Trout June-Sept, SM Bass, Rainbow Trout, Sturgeon May-Oct
Bodies of water: Snake River in Hells Canyon Idaho, Middle Fork of the Salmon River
Rates: Snake River (Hell's Canyon): 3 days: $610, 4 days: $720, 5 days: $900, Middle Fork Salmon River: $1200/6 days
Call between: 9am-5pm
Provides: Beverages, lunch
Handicapped equipped: No
Certifications: Member ID Outfitters & Guides Assoc.

River Quest Excursions
Lewiston 800-589-1129
Species & Seasons: Steelhead Oct-Feb, Sturgeon April-Nov
Bodies of water: Snake River
Rates: Steelhead: $85-$110pp, 4person minimum, Sturgeon: $460 a day for boat and guide, 5 person maximum
Call between: 11am-9pm
Provides: Light tackle, heavy tackle, fly rod/reel, lures, bait
Certifications: ID State Outfitters, OR Marine Board, USCG, US Forest Service Permit

ST. JOE RIVER

FLY SHOPS...

Castaway Fly Fishing Shop
Coeur d'Alene 208-667-5441
Hours: 10am-9pm
Carries: Flies, maps, rods, reels, licenses
Bodies of water: Coeur d'Alene Lake, Coeur d'Alene River, St. Joe River, Spokane River, Clark Fork River
Services & Products: Guide Services, fly fishing instruction
OK to call for current conditions: Yes

The area maps that begin each section
are a "visual table of contents" for location headings

ILLINOIS

1. Braidwood Lake
2. Carlyle lake
3. Cedar Lake
4. Chain O'Lakes
5. Clinton Lake
6. Crab Orchard Lake
7. Des Plaines River
8. Devil's Kitchen Lake
9. Du Page River
10. Fox River
11. Illinois River
12. Kankakee River
13. Kinkaid Lake
14. Lake Egypt
15. Lake Michigan
16. Lake Murphysboro
17. Lake Springfield
18. Little Grassy Lake
19. Mississippi River
20. Newton Lake
21. Pierce Lake
22. Rend Lake
23. Rice Lake
24. Rock River
25. Sangamon River
26. Sangchris Lake
27. Wabash River

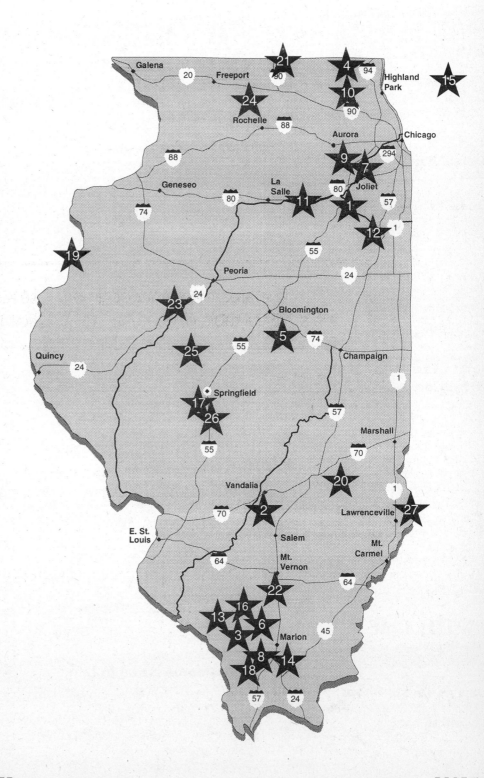

YOUR SILENT FISHING PARTNER

ILLINOIS

BRAIDWOOD LAKE - CHAIN O' LAKES

BRAIDWOOD LAKE

BAIT & TACKLE...

All Seasons Fishing & Sports
Sauk Village 708-757-5769
Hours: 5am-6pm, closed Mon.
Carries: Live bait, lures, flies, maps, rods, reels, licenses
Bodies of water: Kankakee River, Lake Michigan, numerous forest preserve's, Braidwood Lake, LaSalle Lake, Heideike Lake
Services & Products: Charter boat service, fishing instruction, repair services, taxidermy
Guides: Yes
OK to call for current conditions: Yes
Contact: Tim Baker

Pete's Bait Shop
Joliet 815-726-8828
Hours: 5:30am-5pm, closed Tues.
Carries: Live bait, lures, flies, maps, rods, reels, licenses
Bodies of water: Du Page River, Des Plaines River, Heideike Lake, Braidwood Lake, Hickory Creek
Services & Products: Beverages, fishing instruction, repair services
Guides: Yes
OK to call for current conditions: Yes
Contact: Tony

Smith Taxidermy Tank & Tackle
Joliet 815-723-0760
Hours: 7 days a week
Carries: Live bait, lures, flies, maps, rods, reels, licenses
Bodies of water: Kankakee River, Fox River, Du Page River, Illinois River, Heideike Lake, Braidwood Lake, LaSalle Lake, Lake Michigan, Jackson Creek, Spring Creek, Hickory Creek
Services & Products: Beverages, gas/oil
Guides: Yes
OK to call for current conditions: Yes
Contact: Bill Smith

CARLYLE LAKE

BAIT & TACKLE...

Jerry's Tackle Shop
Highland 618-654-3235
Hours: 7am-7pm
Carries: Live bait, lures, flies, maps, rods, reels, licenses
Bodies of water: Mississippi River, Carlyle Lake
Services & Products: Fishing instruction
Guides: Yes
OK to call for current conditions: Yes
Contact: Jerry or Lloyd

North Fork Outlet
Shattuc 618-432-5458
Hours: 8am-9pm
Carries: Live bait, lures, maps, licenses
Bodies of water: Carlyle Lake
Services & Products: Food, beverages
Guides: Yes
OK to call for current conditions: Yes

MARINAS...

Carlyle Lake Marina Keyesport
PO Box 70 62253
Keyesport
Hours: 6am-9pm
Carries: Live bait, lures, flies, maps, rods, reels, licenses
Bodies of water: Carlyle Lake, Greenville Lake
Services & Products: Boat rentals, guide services, boat ramp, food, beverages, gas/oil, repair services
Guides: Yes
OK to call for current conditions: Yes
Contact: Jim Bedrosian

CEDAR LAKE

GUIDES...

Jay's Southern Illinois Guide Service
Carbondale 314-529-1194
Species & Seasons: LM Bass, Crappie, Bluegill Jan-Dec
Bodies of water: Crab Orchard Lake, Kinkaid Lake, Cedar Lake, Little Grassy Lake, Devil's Kitchen Lake
Rates: $12 per hour
Provides: Light tackle, fly rod/reel, lures, rain gear
Handicapped equipped: Yes

Reel People Lured to Life, Inc.
Carbondale 618-529-1140
Species & Seasons: LM Bass, Crappie, Bluegill all year, White Bass Nov-Mar, Catfish June-Oct
Bodies of water: Cedar Lake, Little Grassy Lake, Devil's Kitchen Lake, Murphysboro Lake, Kinkaid Lake, Crab Orchard Lake
Rates: $13 per hour
Call between: Anytime
Provides: Light tackle, heavy tackle, lures, rain gear
Handicapped equipped: Yes (specialty)

CHAIN O'LAKES

BAIT & TACKLE...

Algonquin Bait & Tackle
Algonquin 708-854-4868
Hours: 8am-9pm
Carries: Live bait, lures, flies, maps, rods, reels, licenses
Bodies of water: Fox River, Chain O' Lakes
Services & Products: Repair services
Guides: Yes
OK to call for current conditions: Yes
Contact: Bill, Ken, Adam

Chuck's Tackle World
Hainesville 708-223-1233
Hours: 6am-7pm weekdays, 4am-9pm weekends
Carries: Live bait, lures, flies, maps, rods, reels, licenses
Bodies of water: Chain O' Lakes, Lake Michigan, Grays Lake, Round Lake, Forth Lake, Long Lake
Services & Products: Repair services
Guides: Yes
OK to call for current conditions: Yes
Contact: Chuck Wilson

Dave's Bait Tackle & Taxidermy
Crystal Lake 815-455-2040
Hours: 5am-8pm Mon.-Sat., 5am-6pm Sun.
Carries: Live bait, lures, flies, maps, rods, reels, licenses
Bodies of water: Fox River, Chain O' Lakes, Crystal Lake, Bangs Lake
Services & Products: Guide services, beverages
Guides: Yes
OK to call for current conditions: Yes
Contact: Dave Kranz

Eagle Rod & Reel Repair
So. Elgin 708-742-1557
Hours: 9am-9pm
Carries: Lures, maps, rods, reels

CHAIN O' LAKES - DES PLAINES RIVER — ILLINOIS

Bodies of water: Fox River, Chain O' Lakes, Lake Michigan
Services & Products: Repair services
OK to call for current conditions: Yes
Contact: Warren W. West

Old Man Rivers Bait Shop
Elgin 708-888-1212
Hours: 6am-6pm, 6am-4pm Sun.
Carries: Live bait, lures, rods, reels, licenses
Bodies of water: Chain O' Lakes, Fox River, Area Forest Preserves
Services & Products: Guide services, beverages, fishing instruction
OK to call for current conditions: Yes
Contact: Don

The Salmon Stop, Inc.
Waukegan 708-244-2525
Hours: 5am-7pm
Carries: Live bait, lures, flies, rods, reels, licenses
Bodies of water: Lake Michigan, Chain O' Lakes
Services & Products: Boat rentals, guide services, charter boat service, beverages, repair services
Guides: Yes
OK to call for current conditions: Yes
Contact: Anyone

GUIDES...

Jim Saric Outdoors Inc.
Deerfield 708-267-0034
Species & Seasons: Muskellunge May-Dec, Walleye Mar-May, Salmon Feb.-May
Bodies of water: Chain O'Lakes, Illinois River, Lake Michigan, Vilas County Wisconsin Lakes
Rates: Full day: $275(1-2)
Call between: 10am-9pm
Provides: Light tackle, heavy tackle, lures
Handicapped equipped: No
Certifications: USCG

CLINTON LAKE

BAIT & TACKLE...

Angel Haven Bait & Tackle
DeWitt 217-935-9737
Hours: 5am-6pm
Carries: Live bait, lures, flies, maps, rods, reels, licenses
Bodies of water: Clinton Lake, Salt Creek, Sangamon River
Services & Products: Guide services, food, beverages, fishing instruction, repair services
Guides: Yes
OK to call for current conditions: Yes
Contact: Joe

CRAB ORCHARD LAKE

BAIT & TACKLE...

Cookseys Marine Sales & Bait Shop
Marion 618-993-3366
Hours: 5:30am-7pm
Carries: Live bait, lures, flies, rods, reels, licenses
Bodies of water: Crab Orchard Wildlife Refuge, Devil's Kitchen Lake, Little Grassy Lake, Lake Egypt
Services & Products: Beverages, fishing instruction
Guides: Yes
OK to call for current conditions: Yes
Contact: Ron or Carol Reed

GUIDES...

Jay's Southern Illinois Guide Service
Carbondale 314-529-1194
Species & Seasons: LM Bass, Crappie, Bluegill Jan-Dec
Bodies of water: Crab Orchard Lake, Kinkaid Lake, Cedar Lake, Little Grassy Lake, Devil's Kitchen Lake
Rates: $12 per hour
Provides: Light tackle, fly rod/reel, lures, rain gear
Handicapped equipped: Yes

Reel People Lured to Life, Inc.
Carbondale 618-529-1140
Species & Seasons: LM Bass, Crappie, Bluegill all year, White Bass Nov-Mar, Catfish June-Oct
Bodies of water: Cedar Lake, Little Grassy Lake, Devil's Kitchen Lake, Murphysboro Lake, Kinkaid Lake, Crab Orchard Lake
Rates: $13 per hour
Call between: Anytime
Provides: Light tackle, heavy tackle, lures, rain gear
Handicapped equipped: Yes (specialty)

MARINAS...

Crab Orchard Playport
Carbondale 618-457-8668
Hours: 6am-5pm, closed Wed.
Carries: Live bait, maps, licenses
Bodies of water: Crab Orchard Lake
Services & Products: Boat rentals, boat ramp, food, beverages, gas/oil, repair services
Guides: No
OK to call for current conditions: No

DES PLAINES RIVER

BAIT & TACKLE...

Feed Loft Bait & Tackle
Channahon 815-467-9040
Hours: 6am-5pm Mon.-Fri., 5am-5pm Sat., Sun. (summer)
Carries: Live bait, lures, flies, maps, rods, reels, licenses
Services & Products: Food, beverages, fishing instruction
Guides: No
OK to call for current conditions: Yes
Contact: Bill Brown

Pete's Bait Shop
Joliet 815-726-8828
Hours: 5:30am-5pm, closed Tues.
Carries: Live bait, lures, flies, maps, rods, reels, licenses
Bodies of water: Du Page River, Des Plaines River, Heideike Lake, Braidwood Lake, Hickory Creek
Services & Products: Beverages, fishing instruction, repair services
Guides: Yes
OK to call for current conditions: Yes
Contact: Tony

MARINAS...

Three Rivers Marine Service Inc.
Wilmington 815-476-2324
Hours: 8am-7pm
Carries: Maps
Bodies of water: Des Plaines River, Gran Creek, Kankakee River
Services & Products: Boat ramp, beverages, gas/oil, repair services
Guides: Yes
OK to call for current conditions: Yes
Contact: Mary

ILLINOIS

DEVIL'S KITCHEN LAKE

BAIT & TACKLE...

Cookseys Marine Sales & Bait Shop
Marion 618-993-3366
Hours: 5:30am-7pm
Carries: Live bait, lures, flies, rods, reels, licenses
Bodies of water: Crab Orchard Wildlife Refuge, Devil's Kitchen Lake, Little Grassy Lake, Lake Egypt
Services & Products: Beverages, fishing instruction
Guides: Yes
OK to call for current conditions: Yes
Contact: Ron or Carol Reed

GUIDES...

Jay's Southern Illinois Guide Service
Carbondale 314-529-1194
Species & Seasons: LM Bass, Crappie, Bluegill Jan-Dec
Bodies of water: Crab Orchard Lake, Kinkaid Lake, Cedar Lake, Little Grassy Lake, Devil's Kitchen Lake
Rates: $12 per hour
Provides: Light tackle, fly rod/reel, lures, rain gear
Handicapped equipped: Yes

Reel People Lured to Life, Inc.
Carbondale 618-529-1140
Species & Seasons: LM Bass, Crappie, Bluegill all year, White Bass Nov-Mar, Catfish June-Oct
Bodies of water: Cedar Lake, Little Grassy Lake, Devil's Kitchen Lake, Murphysboro Lake, Kinkaid Lake, Crab Orchard Lake
Rates: $13 per hour
Call between: Anytime
Provides: Light tackle, heavy tackle, lures, rain gear
Handicapped equipped: Yes (specialty)

DU PAGE RIVER

BAIT & TACKLE...

Pete's Bait Shop
Joliet 815-726-8828
Hours: 5:30am-5pm, closed Tues.
Carries: Live bait, lures, flies, maps, rods, reels, licenses
Bodies of water: Du Page River, Des Plaines River, Heideike Lake, Braidwood Lake, Hickory Creek
Services & Products: Beverages, fishing instruction, repair services
Guides: Yes
OK to call for current conditions: Yes
Contact: Tony

Smith Taxidermy Tank & Tackle
Joliet 815-723-0760
Hours: 7 days a week
Carries: Live bait, lures, flies, maps, rods, reels, licenses
Bodies of water: Kankakee River, Fox River, Du Page River, Illinois River, Heideike Lake, Braidwood Lake, LaSalle Lake, Lake Michigan, Jackson Creek, Spring Creek, Hickory Creek
Services & Products: Beverages, gas/oil
Guides: Yes
OK to call for current conditions: Yes
Contact: Bill Smith

FOX RIVER

BAIT & TACKLE...

Algonquin Bait & Tackle
Algonquin 708-854-4868
Hours: 8am-9pm
Carries: Live bait, lures, flies, maps, rods, reels, licenses
Bodies of water: Fox River, Chain O' Lakes
Services & Products: Repair services
Guides: Yes
OK to call for current conditions: Yes
Contact: Bill, Ken, or Adam

Dave's Bait Tackle & Taxidermy
Crystal Lake 815-455-2040
Hours: 5am-8pm Mon.-Sat., 5am-6pm Sun.
Carries: Live bait, lures, flies, maps, rods, reels, licenses
Bodies of water: Fox River, Chain O' Lakes, Crystal Lake, Bangs Lake
Services & Products: Guide services, beverages
Guides: Yes
OK to call for current conditions: Yes
Contact: Dave Kranz

Eagle Rod & Reel Repair
So. Elgin 708-742-1557
Hours: 9am-9pm
Carries: Lures, maps, rods, reels
Bodies of water: Fox River, Chain O' Lakes, Lake Michigan
Services & Products: Repair services
OK to call for current conditions: Yes
Contact: Warren W West

Old Man Rivers Bait Shop
Elgin 708-888-1212
Hours: 6am-6pm, 6am-4pm Sun.
Carries: Live bait, lures, rods, reels, licenses
Bodies of water: Chain O' Lakes, Fox River, area Forest Preserves
Services & Products: Guide services, beverages, fishing instruction
OK to call for current conditions: Yes
Contact: Don

Smith Taxidermy Tank & Tackle
Joliet 815-723-0760
Hours: 7 days a week
Carries: Live bait, lures, flies, maps, rods, reels, licenses
Bodies of water: Kankakee River, Fox River, Du Page River, Illinois River, Heideike Lake, Braidwood, LaSalle Lake, Lake Michigan, Jackson Creek, Spring Creek, Hickory Creek
Services & Products: Beverages, gas/oil
Guides: Yes
OK to call for current conditions: Yes
Contact: Bill Smith

W & W Variety & Sports
Ottawa 815-434-1555
Hours: 6:30am-7pm Mon.-Fri.
Carries: Live bait, lures, flies, maps, rods, reels, licenses
Bodies of water: Illinois River, Fox River, Lasalle Lake
Services & Products: Guide services, food, beverages, repair services
OK to call for current conditions: Yes
Contact: Anyone at store

ILLINOIS RIVER - LAKE EGYPT ILLINOIS

ILLINOIS RIVER

BAIT & TACKLE...

Anderson's Outdoor Supplies
Middlegrove 309-245-4990
Hours: 6am-6pm
Carries: Live bait
Bodies of water: Illinois River, Mississippi River, Banner Marsh, Rice Lake, 100's of Strip Mine Lakes
Services & Products: Guide services, food, beverages, gas/oil, fishing instruction, repair services
Guides: Yes
OK to call for current conditions: Yes
Contact: David Anderson

Fox's Bait & Tackle
Springfield 217-528-7004
Hours: 6am-8pm
Carries: Live bait, lures, rods, reels, licenses
Bodies of water: Lake Springfield, Sangchris Lake, Sangamon River, Illinois River
Services & Products: Food, beverages
Guides: No
OK to call for current conditions: Yes
Contact: Anyone

Smith Taxidermy Tank & Tackle
Joliet 815-723-0760
Hours: 7 days a week
Carries: Live bait, lures, flies, maps, rods, reels, licenses
Bodies of water: Kankakee River, Fox River, Du Page River, Illinois River, Heideike Lake, Braidwood, LaSalle Lake, Lake Michigan, Jackson Creek, Spring Creek, Hickory Creek
Services & Products: Beverages, gas/oil
Guides: Yes
OK to call for current conditions: Yes
Contact: Bill Smith

W & W Variety & Sports
Ottawa 815-434-1555
Hours: 6:30am-7pm Mon.-Fri.
Carries: Live bait, lures, flies, maps, rods, reels, licenses
Bodies of water: Illinois River, Fox River, Lasalle Lake
Services & Products: Guide services, food, beverages, repair services
OK to call for current conditions: Yes
Contact: Anyone at store

GUIDES...

Jim Saric Outdoors Inc.
Deerfield 708-267-0034
Species & Seasons: Muskellunge May-Dec, Walleye Mar-May, Salmon Feb-May
Bodies of water: Chain O'Lakes, Illinois River, Lake Michigan, Vilas County Wisconsin Lakes
Rates: Full day: $275(1-2)
Call between: 10am-9pm
Provides: Light tackle, heavy tackle, lures
Handicapped equipped: No
Certifications: USCG

KANKAKEE RIVER

BAIT & TACKLE...

All Seasons Fishing & Sports
Sauk Village 708-757-5769
Hours: 5am-6pm, closed Mon.
Carries: Live bait, lures, flies, maps, rods, reels, licenses
Bodies of water: Kankakee River, Lake Michigan, numerous forest preserve's Braidwood Lake, LaSalle Lake, Heideike Lake
Services & Products: Charter boat service, fishing instruction, repair services, taxidermy
Guides: Yes
OK to call for current conditions: Yes
Contact: Tim Baker

Smith Taxidermy Tank & Tackle
Joliet 815-723-0760
Hours: 7 days a week
Carries: Live bait, lures, flies, maps, rods, reels, licenses
Bodies of water: Kankakee River, Fox River, Du Page River, Illinois River, Heideike Lake, Braidwood Lake, LaSalle Lake, Lake Michigan, Jackson Creek, Spring Creek, Hickory Creek
Services & Products: Beverages, gas/oil
Guides: Yes
OK to call for current conditions: Yes
Contact: Bill Smith

MARINAS...

Three Rivers Marine Service Inc.
Wilmington 815-476-2324
Hours: 8am-7pm
Carries: Maps
Bodies of water: Des Plaines River, Gran Creek, Kankakee River
Services & Products: Boat ramp, beverages, gas/oil, repair services
Guides: Yes

KINKAID LAKE

GUIDES...

Jay's Southern Illinois Guide Service
Carbondale 314-529-1194
Species & Seasons: LM Bass, Crappie, Bluegill Jan-Dec
Bodies of water: Crab Orchard Lake, Kinkaid Lake, Cedar Lake, Little Grassy Lake, Devil's Kitchen Lake
Rates: $12 per hour
Provides: Light tackle, fly rod/reel, lures, rain gear
Handicapped equipped: Yes

Reel People Lured to Life, Inc.
Carbondale 618-529-1140
Species & Seasons: LM Bass, Crappie, Bluegill all year, White Bass Nov-Mar, Catfish June-Oct
Bodies of water: Cedar Lake, Little Grassy Lake, Devil's Kitchen Lake, Murphysboro Lake, Kinkaid Lake, Crab Orchard Lake
Rates: $13 per hour
Call between: Anytime
Provides: Light tackle, heavy tackle, lures, rain gear
Handicapped equipped: Yes (specialty)

LAKE EGYPT

BAIT & TACKLE...

Cookseys Marine Sales & Bait Shop
Marion 618-993-3366
Hours: 5:30am-7pm
Carries: Live bait, lures, flies, rods, reels, licenses
Bodies of water: Crab Orchard Wildlife Refuge, Devil's Kitchen Lake, Little Grassy Lake, Lake Egypt
Services & Products: Beverages, fishing instruction
Guides: Yes
OK to call for current conditions: Yes
Contact: Ron or Carol Reed

ILLINOIS — LAKE MICHIGAN

LAKE MICHIGAN

BAIT & TACKLE...

All Seasons Fishing & Sports
Sauk Village 708-757-5769
Hours: 5am-6pm, closed Mon.
Carries: Live bait, lures, flies, maps, rods, reels, licenses
Bodies of water: Kankakee River, Lake Michigan, numerous forest preserve's Braidwood Lake, LaSalle Lake, Heideike Lake
Services & Products: Charter boat service, fishing instruction, repair services, taxidermy
Guides: Yes
OK to call for current conditions: Yes
Contact: Tim Baker

Chuck's Tackle World
Hainesville 708-223-1233
Hours: 6am-7pm weekdays, 4am-9pm weekends
Carries: Live bait, lures, flies, maps, rods, reels, licenses
Bodies of water: Chain O' Lakes, Lake Michigan, Grays Lake, Round Lake, Forth Lake, Long Lake
Services & Products: Repair services
Guides: Yes
OK to call for current conditions: Yes
Contact: Chuck Wilson

Eagle Rod & Reel Repair
So. Elgin 708-742-1557
Hours: 9am-9pm
Carries: Lures, maps, rods, reels
Bodies of water: Fox River, Chain O' Lakes, Lake Michigan
Services & Products: Repair services
OK to call for current conditions: Yes
Contact: Warren W West

Henry's Sports & Bait Shop
Chicago 312-225-8538
Hours: 4am-10pm
Carries: Live bait, lures, flies, maps, rods, reels, licenses
Bodies of water: Lake Michigan
Services & Products: Fishing instruction, repair services
Guides: Yes
OK to call for current conditions: Yes
Contact: Henry's Fishing Hotline 312-225-FISH

Jim's Bait Store
Chicago 312-978-6596
Hours: 5am-7pm
Carries: Live bait, lures, rods, reels, licenses
Bodies of water: Lake Michigan
OK to call for current conditions: Yes
Contact: Billy Winters

The Salmon Stop, Inc.
Waukegan 708-244-2525
Hours: 5am-7pm
Carries: Live bait, lures, flies, rods, reels, licenses
Bodies of water: Lake Michigan, Chain O' Lakes
Services & Products: Boat rentals, guide services, charter boat service, beverages, repair services
Guides: Yes
OK to call for current conditions: Yes
Contact: Anyone

Smith Taxidermy Tank & Tackle
Joliet 815-723-0760
Hours: 7 days a week
Carries: Live bait, lures, flies, maps, rods, reels, licenses
Bodies of water: Kankakee River, Fox River, Du Page River, Illinois River, Heideike Lake, Braidwood, LaSalle Lake, Lake Michigan, Jackson Creek, Spring Creek, Hickory Creek
Services & Products: Beverages, gas/oil
Guides: Yes
OK to call for current conditions: Yes
Contact: Bill Smith

CHARTERS...

Capt. Al's Charter Boat Fleet
Chicago 312-565-0104
Hours: 7am-9pm
Carries: Live bait, lures, flies, rods, reels, licenses
Bodies of water: Lake Michigan
Services & Products: Boat rentals, charter boat service, food, beverages, fishing instruction
Guides: Yes
OK to call for current conditions: Yes
Contact: Capt. Al

Big Bird Charters
Danville 800-355-BAIT
Species & Seasons: Lake Trout May-Sept, Coho Salmon, Chinook Salmon, Steelhead, Brown Trout April-Sept
Bodies of water: Lake Michigan out of St. Joseph
Rates: 8 hr.: $360(6)
Call between: 3pm-10pm
Provides: Light tackle, lures
Handicapped equipped: Yes
Certifications: USCG, MI
DNR Inspected

Jim Saric Outdoors Inc.
Deerfield 708-267-0034
Species & Seasons: Muskellunge May-Dec, Walleye Mar-May, Salmon Feb-May
Bodies of water: Chain O'Lakes, Illinois River, Lake Michigan, Vilas County Wisconsin Lakes
Rates: Full day: $275(1-2)
Call between: 10am-9pm
Provides: Light tackle, heavy tackle, lures
Handicapped equipped: No
Certifications: USCG

SPORT FISHING AT IT'S BEST FOR SALMON AND TROUT
ON BEAUTIFUL LAKE MICHIGAN

BIG BIRD CHARTERS
FULLY EQUIPPED, LICENSED AND INSURED
OPERATING OUT OF ST. JOSEPH, MI

CAPT. JIM CONDER
1-217-443-5327 or
800-355-BAIT
2246

312 E. ROSELAWN
DANVILLE, IL 61832
IN SEASON BOAT PHONE
616-470-4149

LAKE MICHIGAN - MISSISSIPPI RIVER — ILLINOIS

Fish Trap Charters
Watseka 815-432-2307
Species & Seasons: Chinook Salmon April-Oct, Coho Salmon Mar-June, Steelhead Mar-Aug, Lake Trout May-Oct, Brown Trout Mar-Nov
Bodies of water: Lake Michigan
Rates: 6 hrs.: $390(1-6), 9 hrs.: $540(1-6)
Call between: 5:30am-11pm
Provides: Med. light tackle, lures, bait
Handicapped equipped: Yes-Limited
Certifications: USCG Licensed-IL, IN & MI Licensed

Waukegan's Rainbow Charter
Dundee 708-428-8978
Species & Seasons: Chinook Salmon, Lake Trout, Brown Trout, Rainbow Trout, Coho Salmon April-Nov
Bodies of water: Lake Michigan
Rates: Half day: $80(1), $160(2), Full day: $160(1), $230(2)
Call between: 6am-10pm
Provides: Light tackle, heavy tackle, lures, bait, beverages, lunch
Handicapped equipped: Yes
Certifications: USCG

LAKE MURPHYSBORO

GUIDES...

Reel People Lured to Life, Inc.
Carbondale 618-529-1140
Species & Seasons: LM Bass, Crappie, Bluegill all year, White Bass Nov-Mar, Catfish June-Oct
Bodies of water: Cedar Lake, Little Grassy Lake, Devil's Kitchen Lake, Murphysboro Lake, Kinkaid Lake, Crab Orchard Lake
Rates: $13 per hour
Call between: Anytime
Provides: Light tackle, heavy tackle, lures, rain gear
Handicapped equipped: Yes (specialty)

LAKE SPRINGFIELD

BAIT & TACKLE...

Fox's Bait & Tackle
Springfield 217-528-7004
Hours: 6am-8pm
Carries: Live bait, lures, rods, reels, licenses
Bodies of water: Lake Springfield, Sangchris Lake, Sangamon River, Illinois River
Services & Products: Food, beverages
Guides: No
OK to call for current conditions: Yes
Contact: Anyone

LITTLE GRASSY LAKE

BAIT & TACKLE...

Cookseys Marine Sales & Bait Shop
Marion 618-993-3366
Hours: 5:30am-7pm
Carries: Live bait, lures, flies, rods, reels, licenses
Bodies of water: Crab Orchard Wildlife Refuge, Devil's Kitchen Lake, Little Grassy Lake, Lake Egypt
Services & Products: Beverages, fishing instruction
Guides: Yes
OK to call for current conditions: Yes
Contact: Ron or Carol Reed

GUIDES...

Jay's Southern Illinois Guide Service
Carbondale 314-529-1194
Species & Seasons: LM Bass, Crappie, Bluegill Jan-Dec
Bodies of water: Crab Orchard Lake, Kinkaid Lake, Cedar Lake, Little Grassy Lake, Devil's Kitchen Lake
Rates: $12 per hour
Call between:
Provides: Light tackle, fly rod/reel, lures, rain gear
Handicapped equipped: Yes

Reel People Lured to Life, Inc.
Carbondale 618-529-1140
Species & Seasons: LM Bass, Crappie, Bluegill all year, White Bass Nov-Mar, Catfish June-Oct
Bodies of water: Cedar Lake, Little Grassy Lake, Devil's Kitchen Lake, Murphysboro Lake, Kinkaid Lake, Crab Orchard Lake
Rates: $13 per hour
Call between: Anytime
Provides: Light tackle, heavy tackle, lures, rain gear
Handicapped equipped: Yes (specialty)

MISSISSIPPI RIVER

BAIT & TACKLE...

Anderson's Outdoor Supplies
Middlegrove 309-245-4990
Hours: 6am-6pm
Carries: Live bait
Bodies of water: Illinois River, Mississippi River, Banner Marsh, Rice Lake, 100's of Strip Mine Lakes
Services & Products: Guide services, food, beverages, gas/oil, fishing instruction, repair services
Guides: Yes
OK to call for current conditions: Yes
Contact: David Anderson

Curve Fishing Shop
Loves Park 815-877-0637
Hours: 6am-7pm
Carries: Live bait, lures, flies, maps, rods, reels, licenses
Bodies of water: Rock River, Mississippi River, (Wisconsin Lakes, Kosknog, Wabeasua, Mendota)
Services & Products: Fishing instruction, repair services
Guides: Yes
OK to call for current conditions: Yes
Contact: Norman W Devers

Dick's Bait Shop
Fulton 815-589-4949
Hours: 5am-4pm
Carries: Live bait, lures, maps, rods, reels
Bodies of water: Mississippi River
Services & Products: Food, beverages
Guides: Yes
OK to call for current conditions: Yes
Contact: Dick or Don

E Z Livin' Sports Center, Inc.
Milan 309-787-2244
Hours: 6am-9pm
Carries: Live bait, lures, flies, maps, rods, reels, licenses
Bodies of water: Mississippi River, Rock River, Lake George, Mill Creek, Lake Storey
Services & Products: Food, beverages, fishing instruction, repair services, archery sales
Guides: Yes
OK to call for current conditions: Yes
Contact: Kathy Hughes

ILLINOIS — MISSISSIPPI RIVER - ROCK RIVER

Gun Room
Hillsdale 309-658-2719
Hours: 6am-10pm
Carries: Live bait, lures, flies, maps, rods, reels, licenses
Bodies of water: Mississippi River, Rock River, Farm Ponds
Services & Products: Beverages, repair services
Guides: No
OK to call for current conditions: Yes
Contact: Anyone

Jerry's Tackle Shop
Highland 618-654-3235
Hours: 7am-7pm
Carries: Live bait, lures, flies, maps, rods, reels, licenses
Bodies of water: Mississippi River, Carlyle Lake
Services & Products: Fishing instruction
Guides: Yes
OK to call for current conditions: Yes
Contact: Jerry or Lloyd

Ron's Bait Shop
Washington Park 618-874-5317
Hours: 5am-7pm
Carries: Live bait, lures, rods, reels, licenses
Bodies of water: Mississippi River, Frank Holten Lake, Gordon F. More Park Lake, Highland Old City Lake, Horseshoe Lake
Services & Products: Food, fishing instruction
Guides: Yes
OK to call for current conditions: Yes
Contact: Ronnie Watson

Savage Tackle Box
Hamilton 217-847-3252
Hours: 6:30am-6pm
Carries: Live bait, lures, flies, maps, rods, reels
Bodies of water: Mississippi River
Services & Products: Snacks, soda
Guides: No
OK to call for current conditions: Yes
Contact: C "Doc" Savage

Toads Bait Shop
New Boston 309-587-8369
Hours: 6am-6pm
Carries: Live bait, lures, flies, maps, rods, reels
Bodies of water: Mississippi River
Services & Products: Food, beverages, fishing instruction
Guides: No
OK to call for current conditions: Yes
Contact: Kenneth or Sharon Wilkens

NEWTON LAKE

BAIT & TACKLE...

Long's Tackle Box
Robinson 618-544-2709
Hours: 7am-5pm
Carries: Live bait, lures, flies, rods, reels, licenses
Bodies of water: Wabash River, Newton Lake, Sam Parr Lake, Red Hills (State Park), Lincoln Trail Lake, Mill Creek, Turtle Creek
Services & Products: Beverages, repair services
Guides: No
OK to call for current conditions: Yes
Contact: Sharon or Scott Long

PIERCE LAKE

BAIT & TACKLE...

Outlaws Bait & Archery Shop
Loves Park 815-282-2810
Hours: 9am-5pm Mar 1.-May 1, 7am-7pm May 1-Sept. 1 (closed Dec.-Feb.)
Carries: Live bait, lures, flies, maps, rods, reels, licenses
Bodies of water: Rock River, Kishwaukee River, Pierce Lake
Services & Products: Beverages, archery supplies
Guides: No
OK to call for current conditions: Yes
Contact: Darwin Dant

Rockford Bait
Rockford 815-226-2515
Carries: Live bait, lures, flies, maps, rods, reels, licenses
Bodies of water: Rock River, Pierce Lake
Guides: No
OK to call for current conditions: Yes
Contact: Bob Rhodes

REND LAKE

LODGES...

Rend Lake Resort
Wittington 618-629-2211
Guest Capacity: 168
Handicapped equipped: Yes
Seasons: All year
Rates: $61/day
Contact: Susan Joy
Guides: Yes
Species & Seasons: LM Bass April-Nov, Crappie Spring-Fall
Bodies of Water: Rend Lake, Big Muddy River
Types of fishing: Light tackle, heavy tackle
Available: Fishing instruction, licenses, bait, tackle, boat rentals, family activities, restaurant, pool, tennis

RICE LAKE

BAIT & TACKLE...

Anderson's Outdoor Supplies
Middlegrove 309-245-4990
Hours: 6am-6pm
Carries: Live bait
Bodies of water: Illinois River, Mississippi River, Banner Marsh, Rice Lake, 100's of Strip Mine Lakes
Services & Products: Guide services, food, beverages, gas/oil, fishing instruction, repair services
Guides: Yes
OK to call for current conditions: Yes
Contact: David Anderson

ROCK RIVER

BAIT & TACKLE...

Curve Fishing Shop
Loves Park 815-877-0637
Hours: 6am-7pm
Carries: Live bait, lures, flies, maps, rods, reels, licenses
Bodies of water: Rock River, Mississippi River, (Wisconsin Lakes, Kosknog, Wabeasua, Mendota)
Services & Products: Fishing instruction, repair services
Guides: Yes
OK to call for current conditions: Yes
Contact: Norman W. Devers

E Z Livin' Sports Center, Inc.
Milan 309-787-2244
Hours: 6am-9pm
Carries: Live bait, lures, flies, maps, rods, reels, licenses
Bodies of water: Mississippi River, Rock River, Lake George, Mill Creek, Lake Storey

ROCK RIVER - WABASH RIVER

ILLINOIS

Services & Products: Food, beverages, fishing instruction, repair services, archery sales
Guides: Yes
OK to call for current conditions: Yes
Contact: Kathy Hughes

Gun Room
Hillsdale 309-658-2719
Hours: 6am-10pm
Carries: Live bait, lures, flies, maps, rods, reels, licenses
Bodies of water: Mississippi River, Rock River, Farm Ponds
Services & Products: Beverages, repair services
Guides: No
OK to call for current conditions: Yes
Contact: Anyone

Outlaws Bait & Archery Shop
Loves Park 815-282-2810
Hours: 9am-5pm Mar 1.-May 1, 7am-7pm May 1-Sept. 1 (closed Dec.-Feb.)
Carries: Live bait, lures, flies, maps, rods, reels, licenses
Bodies of water: Rock River, Kishwaukee River, Pierce Lake
Services & Products: Beverages, archery supplies
Guides: No
OK to call for current conditions: Yes
Contact: Darwin Dant

Rockford Bait
Rockford 815-226-2515
Carries: Live bait, lures, flies, maps, rods, reels, licenses
Bodies of water: Rock River, Pierce Lake
Guides: No
OK to call for current conditions: Yes
Contact: Bob Rhodes

SANGAMON RIVER

BAIT & TACKLE...

Angel Haven Bait & Tackle
DeWitt 217-935-9737
Hours: 5am-6pm
Carries: Live bait, lures, flies, maps, rods, reels, licenses
Bodies of water: Clinton Lake, Salt Creek, Sangamon River
Services & Products: Guide services, food, beverages, fishing instruction, repair services

Guides: Yes
OK to call for current conditions: Yes
Contact: Joe

Fox's Bait & Tackle
Springfield 217-528-7004
Hours: 6am-8pm
Carries: Live bait, lures, rods, reels, licenses
Bodies of water: Lake Springfield, Sangchris Lake, Sangamon River, Illinois River
Services & Products: Food, beverages
Guides: No
OK to call for current conditions: Yes
Contact: Anyone

SANGCHRIS LAKE

BAIT & TACKLE...

Fox's Bait & Tackle
Springfield 217-528-7004
Hours: 6am-8pm
Carries: Live bait, lures, rods, reels, licenses
Bodies of water: Lake Springfield, Sangchris Lake, Sangamon River, Illinois River
Services & Products: Food, beverages
Guides: No
OK to call for current conditions: Yes
Contact: Anyone

WABASH RIVER

BAIT & TACKLE...

Long's Tackle Box
Robinson 618-544-2709
Hours: 7am-5pm
Carries: Live bait, lures, flies, rods, reels, licenses
Bodies of water: Wabash River, Newton Lake, Sam Parr Lake, Red Hills (State Park), Lincoln Trail Lake, Mill Creek, Turtle Creek
Services & Products: Beverages, repair services
Guides: No
OK to call for current conditions: Yes
Contact: Sharon or Scott Long

The Angler's Yellow Pages saves you time and money. You can compare rates and services quickly and easily.

INDIANA

1. Bischoff Reservoir
2. Brookville Lake
3. Cecil M. Harden Lake
4. Geist Reservoir
5. Huntington Lake
6. Kankakee River
7. Lake Michigan
8. Lake Sullivan
9. Mississinewa Reservoir
10. Monroe Lake
11. Morse Reservoir
12. Northeast Indiana
    - Adams Lake
    - Barbee Chain of Lakes
    - Clear Lake
    - Crooked Lake
    - James Lake Chain
    - Lake Tippecanoe
    - Lake Wawasee
    - Oliver Lake
    - Sylvan Lake
    - Webster Lake
13. Salamonie Lake
14. Shakamak Lake
15. St. Joseph River
16. Summit Lake
17. Sugar Creek
18. Wabash River
19. White River

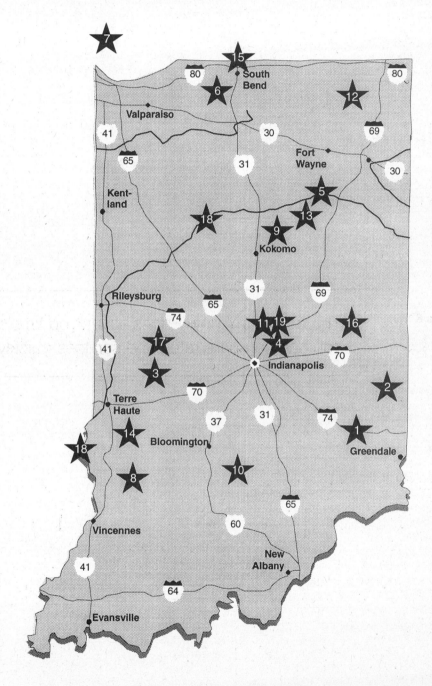

INDIANA
BISCHOFF RESERVOIR - LAKE MICHIGAN

BISCHOFF RESERVOIR

BAIT & TACKLE...

Stirn's Bait & Tackle
Batesville 812-934-6393
Hours: 6am-6pm
Carries: Live bait, lures, flies, rods, reels, licenses
Bodies of water: Bischoff Res.
Services & Products: Beverages, clothing, boots
OK to call for current conditions: Yes
Contact: Joe

BROOKVILLE LAKE

BAIT & TACKLE...

Willits Fishing & Tackle
Greenfield 317-462-0715
Hours: 7am-7pm
Carries: Live bait, lures, flies, maps, rods, reels, licenses
Bodies of water: Monroe Lake, Ohio River, Brookville Lake, Geist Res., Summit Lake
Services & Products: Fishing instruction
Guides: No
OK to call for current conditions: Yes
Contact: Tim Willits or Bob Willits

CECIL M. HARDEN LAKE

MARINAS...

Racoon Boat Rental
Rockville 317-344-1989
Hours: 8am-6pm, closed Nov.-Mar.
Carries: Live bait, lures, rods, reels, licenses
Bodies of water: Cecil M. Harden Lake
Services & Products: Boat rentals, boat ramp, food, beverages, gas/oil
Guides: No
OK to call for current conditions: Yes
Contact: Linda, Dave or Ehren

GEIST RESERVOIR

BAIT & TACKLE...

Willits Fishing & Tackle
Greenfield 317-462-0715
Hours: 7am-7pm
Carries: Live bait, lures, flies, maps, rods, reels, licenses
Bodies of water: Monroe Lake, Ohio River, Brookville Lake, Geist Res., Summit Lake
Services & Products: Fishing instruction
Guides: No
OK to call for current conditions: Yes
Contact: Tim or Bob Willits

HUNTINGTON LAKE

BAIT & TACKLE...

Bait & Hook Store
Fort Wayne 219-747-4883
Hours: 8am-6pm
Carries: Live bait, lures, flies, maps, rods, reels, licenses
Bodies of water: Huntington Lake, Salamonie Lake, many others
Services & Products: Repair services, tournament and club information
Guides: Yes
OK to call for current conditions: Yes
Contact: Ed, Jim or Matt

KANKAKEE RIVER

BAIT & TACKLE...

Kasst Bait & Tackle
La Porte 219-362-2497
Hours: 5am-9pm
Carries: Live bait, lures, flies, maps, rods, reels, licenses
Bodies of water: Pine Lake, Stone Lake, Lake Michigan, Kankakee River, St. Joseph River
Services & Products: Guide services, food, beverages, fishing instruction, repair services
Guides: Yes
OK to call for current conditions: Yes
Contact: Steve or Kay Hardwicke

LAKE MICHIGAN

BAIT & TACKLE...

Al's Bait Shop
Walkerton 219-586-2446
Hours: 7am-6pm
Carries: Live bait, lures, flies, maps, rods, reels, licenses
Bodies of water: Koontz Lake, Lake Michigan
Services & Products: Fishing instruction
Guides: No
OK to call for current conditions: Yes
Contact: Al

Great Lake Sportsman Supply
Mishawaka 219-259-8967
Hours: 9am-6pm, closed Sun.
Carries: Lures, flies, maps, rods, reels, licenses
Bodies of water: St. Joseph River, Lake Michigan
Services & Products: Fishing instruction
Guides: Yes
OK to call for current conditions: Yes
Contact: Kenneth A. McCormack

Kasst Bait & Tackle
La Porte 219-362-2497
Hours: 5am-9pm
Carries: Live bait, lures, flies, maps, rods, reels, licenses
Bodies of water: Pine Lake, Stone Lake, Lake Michigan, Kankakee River, St. Joseph River
Services & Products: Guide services, food, beverages, fishing instruction, repair services
Guides: Yes
OK to call for current conditions: Yes
Contact: Steve or Kay Hardwicke

Pic-A-Spot Campground
Warsaw 219-594-2635
Hours: 8am-8/10pm
Carries: Live bait, lures, maps, rods, reels, licenses
Bodies of water: Lake Michigan, Barbee Chain of Lakes, Lake Tippecanoe
Services & Products: Boat rentals, lodging, boat ramp, food, beverages, gas/oil
Guides: Yes
OK to call for current conditions: Yes
Contact: Anyone

LAKE MICHIGAN - NORTHEAST INDIANA — INDIANA

CHARTERS...

B & B Fishing Charters
Kouts 219-766-2801
Species & Seasons: Coho Salmon, Brown Trout Mar-May, Steelhead June-Aug, Lake Trout May-Aug, Chinook Salmon Aug-Oct
Bodies of water: Lake Michigan
Rates: 6 hrs.: $210(1-3), $330(4-6)
Call between: Anytime
Provides: Light tackle, heavy tackle, lures
Handicapped equipped: Yes
Certifications: USCG, IN, DNR

LAKE SULLIVAN

BAIT & TACKLE...

Tackett's Sports Depot
Sullivan 812-268-6603
Hours: 5am-8pm
Carries: Live bait, lures, flies, maps, rods, reels, licenses
Bodies of water: Merom (Turtle Creek), Wabash River, Lake Sullivan, Greene-Sullivan State Forest, Minehaha Fish & Wildlife, Shakamak Lake
Services & Products: Food, beverages
Guides: Yes
OK to call for current conditions: Yes
Contact: Kermit (Butch) Tackett

MISSISSINEWA RESERVOIR

BAIT & TACKLE...

Alley Tackle
Kokomo 317-459-4459
Hours: 6am-7pm
Carries: Live bait, lures, flies, maps, rods, reels, licenses
Bodies of water: Kokomo Res., Mississinewa Res., Wabash River, Wildcat Creek, Salamonie Lake
Services & Products: Fishing instruction, repair services
Guides: No
OK to call for current conditions: Yes
Contact: Terry D. Thor

Chippewa Service
Wabash 219-563-3592
Hours: 7am-5pm
Carries: Live bait, lures, flies, rods, reels, licenses
Bodies of water: Salamonie Lake, Mississinewa Res., many others
Guides: No
OK to call for current conditions: Yes
Contact: Harold

MONROE LAKE

BAIT & TACKLE...

Willits Fishing & Tackle
Greenfield 317-462-0715
Hours: 7am-7pm
Carries: Live bait, lures, flies, maps, rods, reels, licenses
Bodies of water: Monroe Lake, Ohio River, Brookville Lake, Geist Res., Summit Lake
Services & Products: Fishing instruction
Guides: No
OK to call for current conditions: Yes
Contact: Tim Willits or Bob Willits

MORSE RESERVOIR

BAIT & TACKLE...

Schwartz's Bait & Tackle
Noblesville 317-776-0129
Hours: 7am-6pm
Carries: Live bait, lures, flies, maps, rods, reels, licenses
Bodies of water: White River, Morse Res.
Services & Products: Boat rentals, boat ramp, food, beverages, gas/oil, fishing instruction, repair services
Guides: No
OK to call for current conditions: Yes

NORTHEAST INDIANA

BAIT & TACKLE...

Fremont Bait Supply
Fremont 219-495-5701
Hours: 24hours
Carries: Live bait, lures, flies, maps, rods, reels, licenses
Bodies of water: Clear Lake, James Lake Chain of Lakes, Crooked Lake, Lake George, many others
Services & Products: Beverages, fishing instruction, firewood, camping supplies, snacks
Guides: Yes
OK to call for current conditions: Yes
Contact: Marsha

Hefty's Lake Mart
Rome City 219-854-3221
Hours: 4am-10pm
Carries: Live bait, lures, flies, maps, rods, reels, licenses
Bodies of water: Sylvan Lake, Adams Lake, Dallas Lake, Waldron Lake, Jones Lake, Whitmer Lake, Atwood Lake, Oliver Lake, Steinbarger Lake
Services & Products: Food, beverages, gas/oil
Guides: No
OK to call for current conditions: Yes
Contact: Mike Hefty

Parkside Deli
Syracuse 219-457-8911
Hours: 24 hours in season
Carries: Live bait, lures, flies, maps, rods, reels, licenses
Bodies of water: Lake Wawasee, Lake Tippecanoe, Webster Lake, Barbee Chain of Lakes
Services & Products: Food, beverages, gas/oil
Guides: No
OK to call for current conditions: No

Pic-A-Spot Campground
Warsaw 219-594-2635
Hours: 8am-8/10pm
Carries: Live bait, lures, maps, rods, reels, licenses
Bodies of water: Lake Michigan, Barbee Chain of Lakes, Lake Tippecanoe
Services & Products: Boat rentals, lodging, boat ramp, food, beverages, gas/oil
Guides: Yes
OK to call for current conditions: Yes
Contact: Anyone

Tri State Bait & Tackle
Fremont 219-833-1283
Hours: 6am-6pm
Carries: Live bait, lures, flies, maps, rods, reels, licenses
Bodies of water: James Lake Chain of Lakes
Services & Products: Boat rentals, boat ramp, food, beverages, gas/oil, fishing instruction, repair services
OK to call for current conditions: Yes
Contact: Bob or Karen Bell

INDIANA
SALAMONIE LAKE - WABASH RIVER

SALAMONIE LAKE

BAIT & TACKLE...

Alley Tackle
Kokomo 317-459-4459
Hours: 6am-7pm
Carries: Live bait, lures, flies, maps, rods, reels, licenses
Bodies of water: Kokomo Res., Mississinewa Res., Wabash River, Wildcat Creek, Salamonie Lake
Services & Products: Fishing instruction, repair services
Guides: No
OK to call for current conditions: Yes
Contact: Terry D. Thor

Bait & Hook Store
Fort Wayne 219-747-4883
Hours: 8am-6pm
Carries: Live bait, lures, flies, maps, rods, reels, licenses
Bodies of water: Huntington Lake, Salamonie Lake, many others
Services & Products: Repair services, tournament and club information
Guides: Yes
OK to call for current conditions: Yes
Contact: Ed, Jim or Matt

Chippewa Service
Wabash 219-563-3592
Hours: 7am-5pm
Carries: Live bait, lures, flies, rods, reels, licenses
Bodies of water: Salamonie Lake, Mississinewa Res., many others
Guides: No
OK to call for current conditions: Yes

SHAKAMAK LAKE

BAIT & TACKLE...

Tackett's Sports Depot
Sullivan 812-268-6603
Hours: 5am-8pm
Carries: Live bait, lures, flies, maps, rods, reels, licenses
Bodies of water: Merom (Turtle Creek), Wabash River, Lake Sullivan, Greene-Sullivan State Forest, Minehaha Fish & Wildlife, Shakamak Lake
Services & Products: Food, beverages
Guides: Yes
OK to call for current conditions: Yes
Contact: Kermit (Butch) Tackett

ST. JOSEPH RIVER

BAIT & TACKLE...

Great Lake Sportsman Supply
Mishawaka 219-259-8967
Hours: 9am-6pm, closed Sun.
Carries: Lures, flies, maps, rods, reels, licenses
Bodies of water: St. Joseph River, Lake Michigan
Services & Products: Fishing instruction
Guides: Yes
OK to call for current conditions: Yes
Contact: Kenneth A. McCormack

Kasst Bait & Tackle
La Porte 219-362-2497
Hours: 5am-9pm
Carries: Live bait, lures, flies, maps, rods, reels, licenses
Bodies of water: Pine Lake, Stone Lake, Lake Michigan, Kankakee River, St. Joseph River
Services & Products: Guide services, food, beverages, fishing instruction, repair services
Guides: Yes
OK to call for current conditions: Yes
Contact: Steve or Kay Hardwicke

SUMMIT LAKE

BAIT & TACKLE...

Massengale Bait Tackle Store
New Castle 317-766-5264
Hours: 5am-7pm
Carries: Live bait, lures, flies, maps, rods, reels, licenses
Bodies of water: Summit Lake State Park
Services & Products: Food, beverages, gas/oil
Guides: Yes
OK to call for current conditions: Yes
Contact: Ed or Wilma

Willits Fishing & Tackle
Greenfield 317-462-0715
Hours: 7am-7pm
Carries: Live bait, lures, flies, maps, rods, reels, licenses
Bodies of water: Monroe Lake, Ohio River, Brookville Lake, Geist Res., Summit Lake
Services & Products: Fishing instruction
Guides: No
OK to call for current conditions: Yes

SUGAR CREEK

BAIT & TACKLE...

Pearson Sports
Marshall 317-597-2011
Hours: 8am-6pm, closed Sun.
Carries: Live bait, lures, flies, rods, reels, licenses
Bodies of water: Sugar Creek, Waveland Lake, Rockville Lake, Raccoon Lake
Services & Products: Beverages, fishing instruction, repair services
Guides: No
OK to call for current conditions: Yes
Contact: Duane Pearson

WABASH RIVER

BAIT & TACKLE...

Alley Tackle
Kokomo 317-459-4459
Hours: 6am-7pm
Carries: Live bait, lures, flies, maps, rods, reels, licenses
Bodies of water: Kokomo Res., Mississinewa Res., Wabash River, Wildcat Creek, Salamonie Lake
Services & Products: Fishing instruction, repair services
Guides: No
OK to call for current conditions: Yes
Contact: Terry D. Thor

Chippewa Service
Wabash 219-563-3592
Hours: 7am-5pm
Carries: Live bait, lures, flies, rods, reels, licenses
Bodies of water: Salamonie Lake, Mississinewa Res., many others
Guides: No
OK to call for current conditions: Yes
Contact: Harold

WHITE RIVER — INDIANA

WHITE RIVER

BAIT & TACKLE...

Indy Lake
Indianapolis 317-888-6006
Hours: 24 hours
Carries: Live bait, rods, reels, licenses
Bodies of water: White River, Le-An-Wa Lake
Services & Products: Food, beverages, 3 stocked lakes
Guides: No
OK to call for current conditions: Yes
Contact: Jon Diepering or James Page

Jim Page
Indianapolis 317-888-6006
Hours: Daylight hours-24 hours in season
Carries: Live bait, lures, flies, rods, reels, licenses
Bodies of water: White River
Services & Products: Food, beverages, fishing pay-lakes
Guides: Yes
OK to call for current conditions: Yes
Contact: Jim Page

Schwartz's Bait & Tackle
Noblesville 317-776-0129
Hours: 7am-6pm
Carries: Live bait, lures, flies, maps, rods, reels, licenses
Bodies of water: White River, Morse Res.
Services & Products: Boat rentals, boat ramp, food, beverages, gas/oil, fishing instruction, repair services
Guides: No
OK to call for current conditions: Yes

YOUR SILENT FISHING PARTNER

Know before you go...

Look in the Angler's Yellow Pages

IOWA

1. Cedar River
2. Clear Lake
3. Coralville Reservoir
4. Des Moines River
5. Iowa River
6. Lake Icaria
7. Lake Macbride
8. Lake Okoboji
9. Mississippi River
10. Nodaway River
11. Rathbun Lake
12. Red Rock Reservoir
13. Saylorville Reservoir
14. Silver Lake
15. Spirit Lake
16. Storm Lake

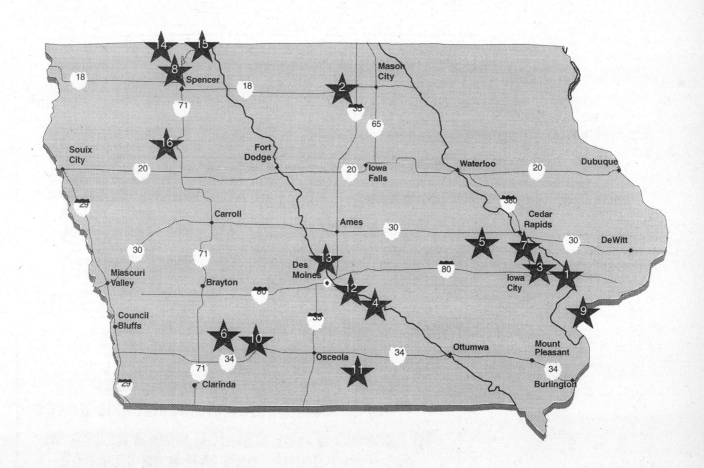

IOWA
CEDAR RIVER - DES MOINES RIVER

CEDAR RIVER

BAIT & TACKLE...

Barclay's Bait Shop
Wilton 319-732-3803
Hours: 6am-6pm, closed Thurs. and Sun. afternoons
Carries: Live bait, lures, flies, maps, rods, reels, licenses
Bodies of water: Mississippi River, Cedar River
Guides: No
OK to call for current conditions: Yes
Contact: Thomas Barclay

Fin & Feather
Cedar Rapids 319-364-4396
Iowa City 354-2200
Iowa Ciity 364-4396
Hours: 8am-9pm Mon., Thurs., 8am-5:30pm Tues.-Wed.-Fri.-Sat., 9am-5pm Sun.
Carries: Live bait, lures, flies, maps, rods, reels, licenses
Bodies of water: Iowa River, Cedar River, Lake Macbride
Services & Products: Fishing instruction, camping, hunting, archery, clothing, footwear, seminars
Guides: No
OK to call for current conditions: No

Five Seasons Bait Shop
Cedar Rapids 319-362-0544
Hours: 8am-4:30pm
Carries: Live bait, lures, maps, rods, reels, licenses
Bodies of water: Cedar River, Iowa River, Lake Macbride, Coralville Res., Pleasant Creek Lake
Services & Products: Fishing instruction, repair services, bulk soft plastic sales
Guides: Yes
OK to call for current conditions: Yes
Contact: John Zaspal

Harry's Bait & Tackle
Marion 319-377-0511
Hours: 7am-9pm
Carries: Live bait, lures
Bodies of water: Cedar River, Wapsipinicon River, Coralville Res., Lake Macbride, Pleasant Creek Lake, Mississippi River
Services & Products: Food, beverages, gas/oil, fishing instruction, repair services
Guides: Yes
OK to call for current conditions: Yes
Contact: Harry

CLEAR LAKE

BAIT & TACKLE...

Lake Sport Shop
Clear Lake 515-357-7350
Hours: 8am-6pm
Carries: Live bait, lures, maps, rods, reels, licenses
Bodies of water: Clear Lake
Services & Products: Beverages
Guides: Yes

CORALVILLE RESERVOIR

BAIT & TACKLE...

Five Seasons Bait Shop
Cedar Rapids 319-362-0544
Hours: 8am-4:30pm
Carries: Live bait, lures, maps, rods, reels, licenses
Bodies of water: Cedar River, Iowa River, Lake Macbride, Coralville Res., Pleasant Creek Lake
Services & Products: Fishing instruction, repair services, bulk soft plastic sales
Guides: Yes
OK to call for current conditions: Yes
Contact: John Zaspal

Harry's Bait & Tackle
Marion 319-377-0511
Hours: 7am-9pm
Carries: Live bait, lures
Bodies of water: Cedar River, Wapsipinicon River, Coralville Res., Lake Macbride, Pleasant Creek Lake, Mississippi River
Services & Products: Food, beverages, gas/oil, fishing instruction, repair services
Guides: Yes
OK to call for current conditions: Yes
Contact: Harry

DES MOINES RIVER

BAIT & TACKLE...

Lollipop Bait Shop
Ottumwa 515-683-1917
Hours: 7am-8:30pm April 1- Sept. 30, 9am-4pm Oct. 1- Mar. 31
Carries: Live bait, lures, maps, rods, reels, licenses
Bodies of water: Des Moines River, Lake Wapello, Rathbun Lake
Services & Products: Repair services
Guides: No
OK to call for current conditions: Yes
Contact: George or Anna Marie

Five Seasons Bait Tackle

Wholesale & Retail
Call Today !
1 800 586-5906

We Have:
- Bulk plastics & jigs
- Large quantities of closeout items
- Rods, reels & lures at special sale prices

To receive a free catalog and a listing of closeout items, call toll free today !

DES MOINES RIVER - LAKE OKOBOJI — IOWA

The Tacklebox
Des Moines 515-288-8309
Hours: 6am-10pm
Carries: Live bait, lures, maps, rods, reels, licenses
Bodies of water: Saylorville Res., Red Rock Res., Lake Easter, Des Moines River, Raccoon River
Services & Products: Food, beverages, fishing instruction, repair services
Guides: Yes
OK to call for current conditions: Yes
Contact: Anyone

Thode Sporting Goods
Des Moines 515-277-0997
Hours: 9am-6pm, closed Sun.
Carries: lures, flies, maps, rods, reels, licenses
Bodies of water: Big Creek, Saylorville Res., Des Moines River, Lake Ahquabi
Guides: No
OK to call for current conditions: Yes

IOWA RIVER

BAIT & TACKLE...

Fin & Feather
Cedar Rapids 319-364-4396
Iowa City 354-2200
Iowa Ciity 364-4396
Hours: 8am-9pm Mon., Thurs., 8am-5:30pm Tues.-Wed.-Fri.-Sat., 9am-5pm Sun.
Carries: Live bait, lures, flies, maps, rods, reels, licenses
Bodies of water: Iowa River, Cedar River, Lake Macbride
Services & Products: Fishing instruction, camping, hunting, archery, clothing, footwear, seminars
Guides: No
OK to call for current conditions: No

Five Seasons Bait Shop
Cedar Rapids 319-362-0544
Hours: 8am-4:30pm
Carries: Live bait, lures, maps, rods, reels, licenses
Bodies of water: Cedar River, Iowa River, Lake Macbride, Coralville Res., Pleasant Creek Lake
Services & Products: Fishing instruction, repair services, bulk soft plastic sales
Guides: Yes
OK to call for current conditions: Yes
Contact: John Zaspal

LAKE ICARIA

BAIT & TACKLE...

Eddie's Bait & Sport
Corning 515-322-3649
Carries: Live bait, lures, flies, maps, rods, reels, licenses
Bodies of water: Lake Icaria, Lake Binder, Nodaway River, Corning Res.
Services & Products: Guide services, fishing instruction, repair services
OK to call for current conditions: Yes
Contact: Eddie Kaufman

LAKE MACBRIDE

BAIT & TACKLE...

Fin & Feather
Cedar Rapids 319-364-4396
Iowa City 354-2200
Iowa Ciity 364-4396
Hours: 8am-9pm Mon., Thurs., 8am-5:30pm Tues.-Wed.-Fri.-Sat., 9am-5pm Sun.
Carries: Live bait, lures, flies, maps, rods, reels, licenses
Bodies of water: Iowa River, Cedar River, Lake Macbride
Services & Products: Fishing instruction, camping, hunting, archery, clothing, footwear, seminars
Guides: No
OK to call for current conditions: No

Five Seasons Bait Shop
Cedar Rapids 319-362-0544
Hours: 8am-4:30pm
Carries: Live bait, lures, maps, rods, reels, licenses
Bodies of water: Cedar River, Iowa River, Lake Macbride, Coralville Res., Pleasant Creek Lake
Services & Products: Fishing instruction, repair services, bulk soft plastic sales
Guides: Yes
OK to call for current conditions: Yes
Contact: John Zaspal

Harry's Bait & Tackle
Marion 319-377-0511
Hours: 7am-9pm
Carries: Live bait, lures
Bodies of water: Cedar River, Wapsipinicon River, Coralville Res., Lake Macbride, Pleasant Creek Lake, Mississippi River
Services & Products: Food, beverages, gas/oil, fishing instruction, repair services
Guides: Yes
OK to call for current conditions: Yes
Contact: Harry

LAKE OKOBOJI

BAIT & TACKLE...

Vick's Corner
Spirit Lake 712-336-5602
Hours: 7am-11pm
Carries: Live bait, lures, flies, maps, rods, reels
Bodies of water: Big Spirit Lake, East Okoboji Lake, West Okoboji Lake, Center Lake, Silver Lake, Little Spirit Lake
Services & Products: Food, beverages, gas/oil, fishing instruction
Guides: Yes
OK to call for current conditions: Yes
Contact: Vick or Dee

GUIDES...

Jim McDonnell
Royal 712-933-5532
Species & Seasons: SM Bass April-Oct, Walleye May-Oct, Muskellunge July-Oct, LM Bass, Northern Pike May-Oct, Perch, Crappie May-Dec, Catfish June-Oct
Bodies of water: West Okoboji, East Okoboji, Big Spirit Lake, Storm Lake, Little Sioux River, other border lakes
Rates: Half day: $110(1-2), Full day: $180(1-2), 6hr: $140, $15 each additional person
Call between: 6pm-10pm
Provides: Light tackle, heavy tackle, lures, bait, rain gear
Handicapped equipped: Depends on Handicap
Certifications: Iowa

IOWA
LAKE OKOBOJI - RED ROCK RESERVOIR

LODGING...

Four Seasons Resort
Arnolds Park 712-332-2103
Guest Capacity: 33 rooms (2-8 people per room)
Handicapped equipped: No
Seasons: All year
Rates: $35-$135/day
Contact: Mike Mitchell
Guides: Yes
Species & Seasons: Walleye, LM Bass, Muskellunge, Perch, Bluegill, Catfish
Bodies of Water: West Lake Okoboji, East Lake Okoboji, Big Spirit Lake
Types of fishing: Light tackle, heavy tackle, wading
Available: Fishing instruction, boat rentals

Northland Inn
Spirit Lake 712-336-1450
.... 800-846-8812
Guest Capacity: 48
Handicapped equipped: No
Seasons: All year
Rates: Oct-April: $20-$30/day, May-Sept.: $20-40/day
Guides: Yes, recommend
Species & Seasons: Perch, Walleye, Northern Pike, LM Bass, Muskellunge, Bluegill, Crappie, Bullhead all year
Bodies of Water: West Lake Okoboji, East Lake Okoboji, Spirit Lake, Silver Lake, Center Lake
Types of fishing: Fly fishing, light tackle, heavy tackle, wading
Available: Licenses, bait, tackle (within walking distance)

MISSISSIPPI RIVER
BAIT & TACKLE...

The Bait Shack
Dubuque 319-582-9395
Hours: 6am-8pm
Carries: Live bait, lures, flies, maps, rods, reels, licenses
Bodies of water: Mississippi River
Services & Products: Guide services, fishing instruction, repair services
Guides: Yes
OK to call for current conditions: Yes
Contact: Jim, Dave, Rob

Barclay's Bait Shop
Wilton 319-732-3803
Hours: 6am-6pm, closed Thurs. and Sun. afternoons
Carries: Live bait, lures, flies, maps, rods, reels, licenses
Bodies of water: Mississippi River, Cedar River
Guides: No
OK to call for current conditions: Yes
Contact: Thomas Barclay

Harry's Bait & Tackle
Marion 319-377-0511
Hours: 7am-9pm
Carries: Live bait, lures
Bodies of water: Cedar River, Wapsipinicon River, Coralville Res., Lake Macbride, Pleasant Creek Lake, Mississippi River
Services & Products: Food, beverages, gas/oil, fishing instruction, repair services
Guides: Yes
OK to call for current conditions: Yes
Contact: Harry

Keil's Bait & Tackle
Bellevue 319-872-3225
Hours: 7am-5pm, closed Tues.
Carries: Live bait, lures, maps, rods, reels, licenses
Bodies of water: Mississippi River Pools 12 and 13
Guides: Yes
OK to call for current conditions: Yes
Contact: John or Jill Ruggeberg

Landing 615
Guttenberg
Hours: 6am-6pm, closed Dec.-Feb.
Carries: Live bait, lures, rods, reels, licenses
Bodies of water: Mississippi River
Services & Products: Boat rentals, boat ramp, food, beverages, gas/oil, barge fishing
Guides: Yes
OK to call for current conditions: Yes
Contact: Rose Kann

NODAWAY RIVER
BAIT & TACKLE...

Eddie's Bait & Sport
Corning 515-322-3649
Carries: Live bait, lures, flies, maps, rods, reels, licenses
Bodies of water: Lake Icaria, Lake Binder, Nodaway River, Corning Res.
Services & Products: Guide services, fishing instruction, repair services
OK to call for current conditions: Yes
Contact: Eddie Kaufman

RATHBUN LAKE
BAIT & TACKLE...

Lollipop Bait Shop
Ottumwa 515-683-1917
Hours: 7am-8:30pm April 1-Sept. 30, 9am-4pm Oct. 1-Mar.31
Carries: Live bait, lures, maps, rods, reels, licenses
Bodies of water: Des Moines River, Lake Wapello, Rathbun Lake
Services & Products: Repair services
Guides: No
OK to call for current conditions: Yes
Contact: George or Anna Marie

Old Favorite Bait Co
Corydon 515-872-2755
Hours: 8am-5pm, closed Sun.
Carries: Live bait, lures, rods, reels, licenses
Bodies of water: Rathbun Lake, Little River, Bobwhite State Park Lake
Guides: No
OK to call for current conditions: Yes
Contact: Janis Thatcher

Rathbun Dam Site Depot
Moravia 515-724-3300
Hours: 6am-9pm
Carries: Live bait, lures, flies, maps, rods, reels, licenses
Bodies of water: Rathbun Lake
Services & Products: RV & boat storage, convenience store
Guides: Yes
OK to call for current conditions: Yes
Contact: Tom Ackert

RED ROCK RESERVOIR
BAIT & TACKLE...

The Tacklebox
Des Moines 515-288-8309
Hours: 6am-10pm
Carries: Live bait, lures, maps, rods, reels, licenses
Bodies of water: Saylorville Res., Red Rock Res., Lake Easter, Des Moines River, Raccoon River
Services & Products: Food, beverages, fishing instruction, repair services

RED ROCK RESERVOIR - STORM LAKE   IOWA

Guides: Yes
OK to call for current conditions: Yes
Contact: Anyone

SAYLORVILLE RESERVOIR

BAIT & TACKLE...

The Tacklebox
Des Moines 515-288-8309
Hours: 6am-10pm
Carries: Live bait, lures, maps, rods, reels, licenses
Bodies of water: Saylorville Res., Red Rock Res., Lake Easter, Des Moines River, Raccoon River
Services & Products: Food, beverages, fishing instruction, repair services
Guides: Yes
OK to call for current conditions: Yes
Contact: Anyone

Thode Sporting Goods
Des Moines 515-277-0997
Hours: 9am-6pm, closed Sun.
Carries: lures, flies, maps, rods, reels, licenses
Bodies of water: Big Creek, Saylorville Res., Des Moines River, Lake Ahquabi
Guides: No
OK to call for current conditions: Yes

SILVER LAKE

BAIT & TACKLE...

Vick's Corner
Spirit Lake 712-336-5602
Hours: 7am-11pm
Carries: Live bait, lures, flies, maps, rods, reels
Bodies of water: Big Spirit Lake, East Okoboji Lake, West Okoboji Lake, Center Lake, Silver Lake, Little Spirit Lake
Services & Products: Food, beverages, gas/oil, fishing instruction
Guides: Yes
OK to call for current conditions: Yes
Contact: Vick or Dee

LODGING...

Northland Inn
Spirit Lake 712-336-1450
.... 800-846-8812
Guest Capacity: 48
Handicapped equipped: No
Seasons: All year

Rates: Oct-April: $20-$30/day, May-Sept.: $20-40/day
Guides: Yes, recommend
Species & Seasons: Perch, Walleye, Northern Pike, LM Bass, Muskellunge, Bluegill, Crappie, Bullhead all year
Bodies of Water: West Lake Okoboji, East Lake Okoboji, Spirit Lake, Silver Lake, Center Lake
Types of fishing: Fly fishing, light tackle, heavy tackle, wading
Available: Licenses, bait, tackle (within walking distance)

SPIRIT LAKE

BAIT & TACKLE...

Vick's Corner
Spirit Lake 712-336-5602
Hours: 7am-11pm
Carries: Live bait, lures, flies, maps, rods, reels
Bodies of water: Big Spirit Lake, East Okoboji Lake, West Okoboji Lake, Center Lake, Silver Lake, Little Spirit Lake
Services & Products: Food, beverages, gas/oil, fishing instruction
Guides: Yes
OK to call for current conditions: Yes
Contact: Vick or Dee

GUIDES...

Jim McDonnell
Royal 712-933-5532
Species & Seasons: SM Bass April-Oct, Walleye May-Oct, Muskellunge July-Oct, LM Bass, Northern Pike May-Oct, Perch, Crappie May-Dec, Catfish June-Oct
Bodies of water: West Okoboji, East Okoboji, Big Spirit Lake, Storm Lake, Little Sioux River, other border lakes
Rates: Half day: $110(1-2), Full day: $180(1-2), 6hr: $140, $15 each additional person
Call between: 6pm-10pm
Provides: Light tackle, heavy tackle, lures, bait, rain gear
Handicapped equipped: Depends
Certifications: Iowa

LODGING...

Four Seasons Resort
Arnolds Park 712-332-2103
Guest Capacity: 33 rooms (2-8 people per room)

Handicapped equipped: No
Seasons: All year
Rates: $35-$135/day
Contact: Mike Mitchell
Guides: Yes
Species & Seasons: Walleye, LM Bass, Muskellunge, Perch, Bluegill, Catfish
Bodies of Water: West Lake Okoboji, East Lake Okoboji, Big Spirit Lake
Types of fishing: Light tackle, heavy tackle, wading
Available: Fishing instruction, boat rentals

Northland Inn
Spirit Lake 712-336-1450
.... 800-846-8812
Guest Capacity: 48
Handicapped equipped: No
Seasons: All year
Rates: Oct-April: $20-$30/day, May-Sept.: $20-40/day
Guides: Yes, recommend
Species & Seasons: Perch, Walleye, Northern Pike, LM Bass, Muskellunge, Bluegill, Crappie, Bullhead all year
Bodies of Water: West Lake Okoboji, East Lake Okoboji, Spirit Lake, Silver Lake, Center Lake
Types of fishing: Fly fishing, light tackle, heavy tackle, wading
Available: Licenses, bait, tackle (within walking distance)

STORM LAKE

GUIDES...

Jim McDonnell
Royal 712-933-5532
Species & Seasons: SM Bass April-Oct, Walleye May-Oct, Muskellunge July-Oct, LM Bass, Northern Pike May-Oct, Perch, Crappie May-Dec, Catfish June-Oct
Bodies of water: West Okoboji, East Okoboji, Big Spirit Lake, Storm Lake, Little Sioux River, other border lakes
Rates: Half day: $110(1-2), Full day: $180(1-2), 6hr: $140, $15 each additional person
Call between: 6pm-10pm
Provides: Light tackle, heavy tackle, lures, bait, rain gear
Handicapped equipped: Depends on handicap
Certifications: Iowa

Everything in the Angler's Yellow Pages is
alphabetically arranged for ease of reference

KANSAS

1. Arkansas River
2. Big Hill Lake
3. Cedar Bluff Reservoir
4. Cheney Reservoir
5. Clinton Lake
6. John Redmond Reservoir
7. Kanopolis Lake
8. Kansas River
9. Little Arkansas River
10. Marais des Cygnes River
11. Melvern Lake
12. Neosho River
13. Perry Lake
14. Pomona Lake

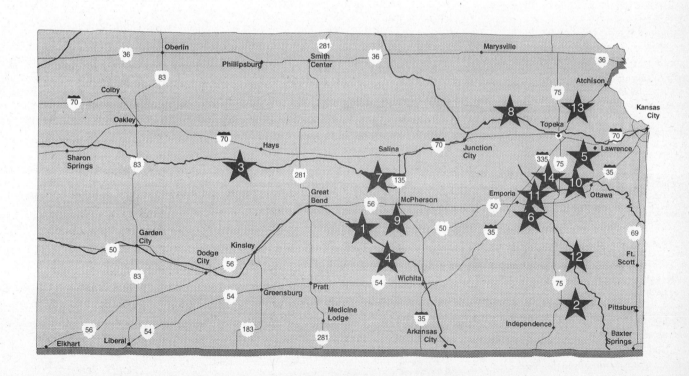

KANSAS
ARKANSAS RIVER - LITTLE ARKANSAS RIVER

ARKANSAS RIVER

BAIT & TACKLE...

Ski's Bait Shop
Hutchinson 316-669-8678
Hours: 7am-7pm summer,
10am-6pm winter
Carries: Live bait, lures, maps,
rods, reels
Bodies of water: Cheney Res.,
Kanopolis Lake, Little Arkansas River,
Arkansas River, Cour Creek,
Spring Creek
Services & Products: Beverages,
antique shop
Guides: Yes
OK to call for current conditions: Yes
Contact: Paul

BIG HILL LAKE

BAIT & TACKLE...

Osage Prairie Enterprise
Parsons 316-421-2493
Hours: 7am-7pm
Carries: Live bait, lures, flies, maps, rods,
reels, licenses
Bodies of water: Neosho River,
Big Hill Lake, Lake Parsons,
Neosho County State Fishing Lake,
Mined Land Area
Services & Products: Food, beverages
Guides: Yes
OK to call for current conditions: Yes
Contact: Jon K. Trout

CEDAR BLUFF RESERVOIR

BAIT & TACKLE...

A & M Bait & Tackle
La Crosse 913-222-3474
Hours: 7am-7pm, closed Mon.-Tues.
Carries: Live bait, lures, flies, maps, rods,
reels, licenses
Bodies of water: Cedar Bluff Res.
Services & Products: Repair services
Guides: Yes
OK to call for current conditions: Yes
Contact: A. L. Hergenreder

CHENEY RESERVOIR

BAIT & TACKLE...

Ski's Bait Shop
Hutchinson 316-669-8678
Hours: 7am-7pm summer,
10am-6pm winter
Carries: Live bait, lures, maps,
rods, reels
Bodies of water: Cheney Res.,
Kanopolis Lake, Little Arkansas River,
Arkansas River, Cour Creek,
Spring Creek
Services & Products: Beverages,
antique shop
Guides: Yes
OK to call for current conditions: Yes
Contact: Paul

CLINTON LAKE

BAIT & TACKLE...

Fishin' Hole
Topeka 913-862-0312
Hours: 7am-7:30pm
Carries: Live bait, lures, flies, maps, rods,
reels, licenses
Bodies of water: Clinton Lake,
Kansas River, Melvern Lake,
Lake Shawnee, Pomona Lake, Osage
State Lake, Perry Lake, Cabondale City
Lake, Wakarusa River, others
Services & Products: Beverages,
bow fishing
Guides: Yes
OK to call for current conditions: Yes
Contact: Anyone

JOHN REDMOND RESERVOIR

BAIT & TACKLE...

Rainbolt & Son Bait Center
Burlington 316-364-2385
Hours: 8am-6pm
Carries: Live bait, lures, maps, rods,
reels, licenses
Bodies of water: Neosho River,
John Redmond Res., Wolf Creek Nuclear
Plant Lake
Guides: No
OK to call for current conditions: Yes

KANOPOLIS LAKE

BAIT & TACKLE...

Ski's Bait Shop
Hutchinson 316-669-8678
Hours: 7am-7pm summer,
10am-6pm winter
Carries: Live bait, lures, maps,
rods, reels
Bodies of water: Cheney Res.,
Kanopolis Lake, Little Arkansas River,
Arkansas River, Cour Creek,
Spring Creek
Services & Products: Beverages,
antique shop
Guides: Yes
OK to call for current conditions: Yes
Contact: Paul

KANSAS RIVER

BAIT & TACKLE...

Fishin' Hole
Topeka 913-862-0312
Hours: 7am-7:30pm
Carries: Live bait, lures, flies, maps, rods,
reels, licenses
Bodies of water: Clinton Lake,
Kansas River, Melvern Lake,
Lake Shawnee, Pomona Lake, Osage
State Lake, Perry Lake, Cabondale City
Lake, Wakarusa River, others
Services & Products: Beverages,
bow fishing
Guides: Yes
OK to call for current conditions: Yes
Contact: Anyone

LITTLE ARKANSAS RIVER

BAIT & TACKLE...

Ski's Bait Shop
Hutchinson 316-669-8678
Hours: 7am-7pm summer,
10am-6pm winter
Carries: Live bait, lures, maps,
rods, reels
Bodies of water: Cheney Res.,
Kanopolis Lake, Little Arkansas River,
Arkansas River, Cour Creek,
Spring Creek
Services & Products: Beverages,
antique shop
Guides: Yes
OK to call for current conditions: Yes
Contact: Paul

MARAIS DES CYGNES RIVER - POMONA LAKE — KANSAS

MARAIS DES CYGNES RIVER

BAIT & TACKLE...

Melvern Lake Marina, Inc.
Melvern 316-256-6566
Hours: 6am-9pm
Carries: Live bait, lures, maps, rods, reels, licenses
Bodies of water: Melvern Lake, Marais des Cygnes River
Services & Products: Boat rentals, boat ramp, food, beverages, gas/oil, repair services
Guides: No
OK to call for current conditions: Yes

MELVERN LAKE

BAIT & TACKLE...

Fishin' Hole
Topeka 913-862-0312
Hours: 7am-7:30pm
Carries: Live bait, lures, flies, maps, rods, reels, licenses
Bodies of water: Clinton Lake, Kansas River, Melvern Lake, Lake Shawnee, Pomona Lake, Osage State Lake, Perry Lake, Cabondale City Lake, Wakarusa River, others
Services & Products: Beverages, bow fishing
Guides: Yes
OK to call for current conditions: Yes
Contact: Anyone

Melvern Lake Marina, Inc.
Melvern 316-256-6566
Hours: 6am-9pm
Carries: Live bait, lures, maps, rods, reels, licenses
Bodies of water: Melvern Lake, Marais des Cygnes River
Services & Products: Boat rentals, boat ramp, food, beverages, gas/oil, repair services
Guides: No
OK to call for current conditions: Yes

NEOSHO RIVER

BAIT & TACKLE...

Osage Prairie Enterprise
Parsons 316-421-2493
Hours: 7am-7pm
Carries: Live bait, lures, flies, maps, rods, reels, licenses
Bodies of water: Neosho River, Big Hill Lake, Lake Parsons, Neosho County State Fishing Lake, Mined Land Area
Services & Products: Food, beverages
Guides: Yes
OK to call for current conditions: Yes
Contact: Jon K. Trout

Rainbolt & Son Bait Center
Burlington 316-364-2385
Hours: 8am-6pm
Carries: Live bait, lures, maps, rods, reels, licenses
Bodies of water: Neosho River, John Redmond Res., Wolf Creek Nuclear Plant Lake
Guides: No
OK to call for current conditions: Yes

PERRY LAKE

BAIT & TACKLE...

Fishin' Hole
Topeka 913-862-0312
Hours: 7am-7:30pm
Carries: Live bait, lures, flies, maps, rods, reels, licenses
Bodies of water: Clinton Lake, Kansas River, Melvern Lake, Lake Shawnee, Pomona Lake, Osage State Lake, Perry Lake, Cabondale City Lake, Wakarusa River, others
Services & Products: Beverages, bow fishing
Guides: Yes
OK to call for current conditions: Yes
Contact: Anyone

The Tackle Box
Olathe 918-829-5586
Hours: 9am-6pm, closed Sun.
Carries: Live bait, lures, flies, maps, rods, reels, licenses
Bodies of water: Hills Lake, Smithville Res., Perry Lake, Pomona Lake
Services & Products: Beverages, gas/oil, fishing instruction, repair services
Guides: Yes
OK to call for current conditions: Yes

POMONA LAKE

BAIT & TACKLE...

Fishin' Hole
Topeka 913-862-0312
Hours: 7am-7:30pm
Carries: Live bait, lures, flies, maps, rods, reels, licenses
Bodies of water: Clinton Lake, Kansas River, Melvern Lake, Lake Shawnee, Pomona Lake, Osage State Lake, Perry Lake, Cabondale City Lake, Wakarusa River, others
Services & Products: Beverages, bow fishing
Guides: Yes
OK to call for current conditions: Yes
Contact: Anyone

The Tackle Box
Olathe 918-829-5586
Hours: 9am-6pm, closed Sun.
Carries: Live bait, lures, flies, maps, rods, reels, licenses
Bodies of water: Hills Lake, Smithville Res., Perry Lake, Pomona Lake
Services & Products: Beverages, gas/oil, fishing instruction, repair services
Guides: Yes
OK to call for current conditions: Yes

To order additional copies of the Angler's Yellow Pages
call 1-800-242-9722

KENTUCKY

1. Barren River
2. Cumberland River
3. Dale Hollow Lake
4. Green River Lake
5. Kentucky Lake
6. Kentucky River
7. Lake Barkley
8. Lake Cumberland
9. Nolin River Lake
10. Ohio River
11. Rough River
12. Rough River Lake
13. Taylorsville Lake
14. Tennessee River

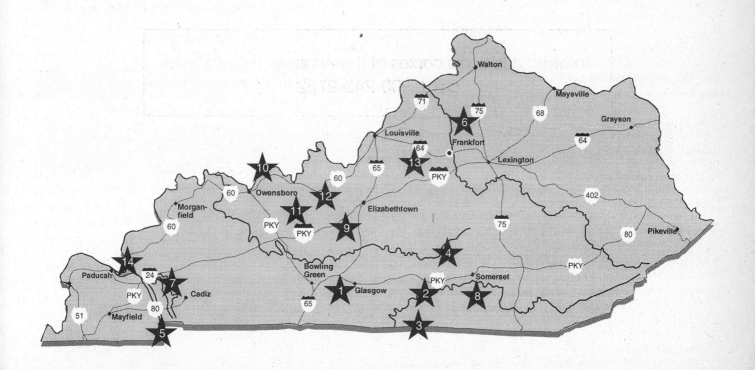

YOUR SILENT FISHING PARTNER

KENTUCKY

BARREN RIVER - KENTUCKY LAKE

BARREN RIVER

BAIT & TACKLE...

KOA Kampgrounds
Bowling Green 502-843-1919
Hours: 7am-9pm
Carries: Live bait, lures, rods, reels, licenses
Bodies of water: Barrenn River, Pay Lake
Services & Products: Lodging, food, beverages
Guides: Yes
OK to call for current conditions: Yes
Contact: Jim

CUMBERLAND RIVER

GUIDES...

Bob "Big Bass" Beals Guide Service
Gilbertsville 502-395-5533
Species & Seasons: Crappie, LM Bass, SM Bass, Sauger, Bluegill, White Bass, Yellow Bass, Rockfish, Catfish all year
Bodies of water: Lake Barkley, Tennessee River, Cumberland River, Ohio River, Kentucky Lake
Rates: 5 hrs.: $125(1-2), Full day: $200(1-2), $25 additional 3rd person
Call between: 6pm-10:30pm
Provides: Light tackle, heavy tackle, lures, bait, rain gear
Handicapped equipped: Yes
Certifications: KY Dept. of Fish & Game

Gene Collins
Nancy 606-636-6531
Species & Seasons: Striped Bass all year, Walleye Mar-Sept, Trout July-Nov
Bodies of water: Lake Cumberland, Cumberland River tailwaters
Rates: Full day: $175(1), $225(2), $275(3), $325(4)
Call between: 7am-11pm
Provides: Light tackle, heavy tackle, lures, bait
Handicapped equipped: Yes
Certifications: CPR, First aid

Fred McClintock
Celina, TN 6615-243-2142
Species & Seasons: Striped Bass May-Oct, SM Bass Nov-April
Bodies of water: Cumberland River, Dale Hollow Lake

Rates: Half day: $150(2), Full day: $250(2), SM Bass: $125, $200
Call between: 4pm-10pm
Provides: Heavy tackle, bait
Handicapped equipped: No
Certifications: KY licensed guide

Jimmie Quinn
Murray 502-762-3615
.... 753-5583
Species & Seasons: LM Bass, SM Bass Mar-Jan, Crappie Mar-May, Sauger Oct-Feb, Striped Bass all year, White Bass
Bodies of water: Kentucky Lake, Lake Barkley, Tennessee River (below Kentucky Lake Dam), Cumberland River (below Cumberland Dam), Ohio River (below Smithland Dam)
Rates: Half day: $100(1-2), Full day: $165(1-2)
Call between: Anytime
Provides: Light tackle, heavy tackle, lures, bait, rain gear, beverages
Handicapped equipped: Yes, limited
Certifications: KY State Guide

Sheltowee Trace Outfitters
Whitley 800-541-7238
Species & Seasons: SM Bass May-June/Sept-Oct
Bodies of water: Big South Fork of Cumberland River
Rates: $50 per, $100 total (raft trips)
Call between: 8:30am-5pm
Handicapped equipped: Yes

DALE HOLLOW LAKE

GUIDES...

Wise Guide Service
Cambellsville 502-465-8920
Species & Seasons: SM Bass Nov-May, LM Bass Mar-Dec, Walleye April-Sept
Bodies of water: Dale Hollow Lake, Lake Cumberland, Green River Lake
Rates: Full day: $175(1), $200(2)
Call between: 7pm-10pm

GREEN RIVER LAKE

GUIDES...

Wise Guide Service
Cambellsville 502-465-8920
Species & Seasons: SM Bass Nov-May, LM Bass Mar-Dec, Walleye April-Sept
Bodies of water: Dale Hollow Lake, Lake Cumberland, Green River Lake
Rates: Full day: $175(1), $200(2)
Call between: 7pm-10pm

KENTUCKY LAKE

BAIT & TACKLE...

Frank Miller & Son Bait & Sporting
Owensboro 502-683-3479
Hours: 7am-7pm Mon.-Thurs., 7am-8pm Fri., 6am-8pm Sat., 6am-4pm Sun.
Carries: Live bait, lures, flies, maps, rods, reels, licenses
Bodies of water: Ohio River, Green River, Rough River Lake, Kentucky Lake, Lake Barkley
Services & Products: Beverages, fishing instruction, repair services, archery supplies, gun supplies
OK to call for current conditions: Yes
Contact: Frank or Chris Miller

T & G Bait Shop
Frankfort 502-223-7219
Hours: Varies
Carries: Live bait, lures, flies, maps, rods, reels, licenses
Bodies of water: Kentucky River, Taylorsville Lake, Kentucky State Game Farm Lakes, Kentucky Lake, Lake Barkley
Services & Products: Food, beverages, gas/oil, fishing instruction
Guides: Yes
OK to call for current conditions: Yes
Contact: J.R. Thurman

GUIDES...

Bill's Guide Service
Eddyville 502-388-2520
Species & Seasons: LM Bass Mar-Nov, SM Bass Feb-Dec, Crappie Mar-May/Sept-Nov, White Bass Mar-Aug
Bodies of water: Lake Barkley, Kentucky Lake
Rates: Half day: $100(1-2), Full day: $160(1-2), $25 additional 3rd person
Call between: 7am-9pm
Provides: Light tackle, heavy tackle, lures, bait, rain gear, beverages
Handicapped equipped: No
Certifications: KY Dept of Fish & Wildlife

KENTUCKY LAKE - KENTUCKY RIVER   KENTUCKY

Bob "Big Bass" Beals Guide Service
Gilbertsville 502-395-5533
Species & Seasons: Crappie, LM Bass, SM Bass, Sauger, Bluegill, White Bass, Yellow Bass, Rockfish, Catfish all year
Bodies of water: Lake Barkley, Tennessee River, Cumberland River, Ohio River, Kentucky Lake
Rates: 5 hrs.: $125(1-2), Full day: $200(1-2), $25 additional 3rd person
Call between: 6pm-10:30pm
Provides: Light tackle, heavy tackle, lures, bait, rain gear
Handicapped equipped: Yes
Certifications: KY Dept. of Fish & Game

Gregory Freeman
Eddyville 502-388-9403
Species & Seasons: Crappie Nov-June, LM Bass Feb-Nov, Striped Bass June-Sept
Bodies of water: Lake Barkley, Kentucky Lake
Rates: Half day: $100(1-2), Full day: $175(1-2)
Call between: 7am-10pm
Provides: Light tackle, fly rod/reel, lures, bait, rain gear
Handicapped equipped: No

William Harl
Herod, IL 618-264-5129
Species & Seasons: LM Bass Mar-Nov, Crappie Mar-June, White Bass June-Sept, Bluegill May
Bodies of water: Northern section Kentucky Lake (Edgar Ferry Bridge to Dam)
Rates: Half day: $100(1-2), Full day: $160(1-2), $30 per hour
Call between: 5pm-10pm
Provides: Light tackle, lures, bait
Handicapped equipped: Yes
Certifications: KY Fish & Wildlife licensed guide

Howard's Guide Service
Paducah 502-898-2536
Species & Seasons: Crappie Feb-June/Sept-Dec, LM Bass April-Nov, White Bass July-Sept, Bluegill May-July, Sauger May-Aug, Striped Bass June-Nov
Bodies of water: Kentucky Lake, Lake Barkley
Rates: 5 hrs.: $140(1-2), 8 hrs.: $175(1-2)
Call between: 6pm-9pm
Provides: Light tackle, bait
Handicapped equipped: No

Jimmie Quinn
Murray 502-762-3615
.... 753-5583
Species & Seasons: LM Bass, SM Bass Mar-Jan, Crappie Mar-May, Sauger Oct-Feb, Striped Bass all year, White Bass
Bodies of water: Kentucky Lake, Lake Barkley, Tennessee River (below Kentucky Lake Dam), Cumberland River (below Cumberland Dam), Ohio River (below Smithland Dam)
Rates: Half day: $100(1-2), Full day: $165(1-2)
Call between: Anytime
Provides: Light tackle, heavy tackle, lures, bait, rain gear, beverages
Handicapped equipped: Yes, limited
Certifications: KY State Guide

LAKESIDE CAMPGROUND & MARINA
On Beautiful Kentucky Lake
Campsites at Waters Edge
• Full Service Marina •
Boats • Showers • Pool
Hwy 68 at Jonathan's Creek
12363 US Hwy 68 East
Benton, Kentucky 42025
502 354-8157
For Reservations: 800 842-9018

Eddie Wynn
Eddyville 502-388-2981
Species & Seasons: LM Bass Mar-Nov, Crappie March-Dec
Bodies of water: Kentucky Lake, Lake Barkley
Rates: Half day: $80(2), Full day: $150(2)
Call between: 5pm-10pm
Provides: beverages
Handicapped equipped: No
Certifications: KY Dept of Fish & Wildlife

LODGES...

Paradise Resort
Murray 800-340-2767
Guest Capacity: 72
Handicapped equipped: Yes
Seasons: All year
Rates: $40-$110/day
Guides: Yes
Species & Seasons: Crappie Mar-April, LM Bass, SM Bass, Bluegill, Catfish

May-Nov
Bodies of Water: Kentucky Lake
Available: Licenses, bait, tackle, boat rentals

MARINAS...

Lakeside Campground & Marina
Benton 502-354-8157
Hours: 6am-5pm
Carries: Live bait, lures, maps, rods, reels, licenses
Bodies of water: Kentucky Lake
Services & Products: Boat rentals, guide services, boat ramp, food, beverages, gas/oil, fishing instruction, campground
Guides: Yes

KENTUCKY RIVER

BAIT & TACKLE...

T & G Bait Shop
Frankfort 502-223-7219
Hours: Varies
Carries: Live bait, lures, flies, maps, rods, reels, licenses
Bodies of water: Kentucky River, Taylorsville Lake, Kentucky State Game Farm Lakes, Kentucky Lake, Lake Barkley
Services & Products: Food, beverages, gas/oil, fishing instruction
Guides: Yes
OK to call for current conditions: Yes
Contact: J.R. Thurman

KENTUCKY

LAKE BARKLEY - LAKE CUMBERLAND

LAKE BARKLEY

BAIT & TACKLE...

Frank Miller & Son Bait & Sporting
Owensboro 502-683-3479
Hours: 7am-7pm Mon.-Thurs.,
7am-8pm Fri., 6am-8pm Sat.,
6am-4pm Sun.
Carries: Live bait, lures, flies, maps, rods, reels, licenses
Bodies of water: Ohio River, Green River, Rough River Lake, Kentucky Lake, Lake Barkley
Services & Products: Beverages, fishing instruction, repair services, archery supplies, gun supplies
OK to call for current conditions: Yes
Contact: Frank or Chris Miller

T & G Bait Shop
Frankfort 502-223-7219
Hours: Varies
Carries: Live bait, lures, flies, maps, rods, reels, licenses
Bodies of water: Kentucky River, Taylorsville Lake, Kentucky State Game Farm Lakes, Kentucky Lake, Lake Barkley
Services & Products: Food, beverages, gas/oil, fishing instruction
Guides: Yes
OK to call for current conditions: Yes
Contact: J.R. Thurman

GUIDES...

Bill's Guide Service
Eddyville 502-388-2520
Species & Seasons: LM Bass Mar-Nov, SM Bass Feb-Dec, Crappie Mar-May/Sept-Nov, White Bass Mar-Aug
Bodies of water: Lake Barkley, Kentucky Lake
Rates: Half day: $100(1-2), Full day: $160(1-2), $25 additional 3rd person
Call between: 7am-9pm
Provides: Light tackle, heavy tackle, lures, bait, rain gear, beverages
Handicapped equipped: No
Certifications: KY Dept of Fish & Wildlife

LODGES...

Bob "Big Bass" Beals Guide Service
Gilbertsville 502-395-5533
Species & Seasons: Crappie, LM Bass, SM Bass, Sauger, Bluegill, White Bass, Yellow Bass, Rockfish, Catfish all year
Bodies of water: Lake Barkley, Tennessee River, Cumberland River, Ohio River, Kentucky Lake
Rates: 5 hrs.: $125(1-2), Full day: $200(1-2), $25 additional 3rd person
Call between: 6pm-10:30pm
Provides: Light tackle, heavy tackle, lures, bait, rain gear
Handicapped equipped: Yes
Certifications: KY Dept. of Fish & Game

Gregory Freeman
Eddyville 502-388-9403
Species & Seasons: Crappie Nov-June, LM Bass Feb-Nov, Striped Bass June-Sept
Bodies of water: Lake Barkley, Kentucky Lake
Rates: Half day: $100(1-2), Full day: $175(1-2)
Call between: 7am-10pm
Provides: Light tackle, fly rod/reel, lures, bait, rain gear
Handicapped equipped: No

Howard's Guide Service
Paducah 502-898-2536
Species & Seasons: Crappie Feb-June/Sept-Dec, LM Bass April-Nov, White Bass July-Sept, Bluegill May-July, Sauger May-Aug, Striped Bass June-Nov
Bodies of water: Kentucky Lake, Lake Barkley
Rates: 5 hrs.: $140(1-2), 8 hrs.: $175(1-2)
Call between: 6pm-9pm
Provides: Light tackle, bait
Handicapped equipped: No

Jimmie Quinn
Murray 502-762-3615
.... 753-5583
Species & Seasons: LM Bass, SM Bass Mar-Jan, Crappie Mar-May, Sauger Oct-Feb, Striped Bass all year, White Bass
Bodies of water: Kentucky Lake, Lake Barkley, Tennessee River (below Kentucky Lake Dam), Cumberland River (below Cumberland Dam), Ohio River (below Smithland Dam)
Rates: Half day: $100(1-2), Full day: $165(1-2)

Call between: Anytime
Provides: Light tackle, heavy tackle, lures, bait, rain gear, beverages
Handicapped equipped: Yes, limited
Certifications: KY State Guide

Eddie Wynn
Eddyville 502-388-2981
Species & Seasons: LM Bass Mar-Nov, Crappie March-Dec
Bodies of water: Kentucky Lake, Lake Barkley
Rates: Half day: $80(2), Full day: $150(2)
Call between: 5pm-10pm
Provides: beverages
Handicapped equipped: No
Certifications: KY Dept of Fish & Wildlife

A. J.'s Striper Guide Service on Lake Cumberland, Ky

Live Bait, Top Water, Down Rigging

ALL EQUIPMENT FURNISHED

502 866-3022

LAKE CUMBERLAND

GUIDES...

A J's Striper Guide Service
Russel Springs 502-866-3022
Species & Seasons: Striped Bass all year
Bodies of water: Lake Cumberland
Rates: Half day: $140(1), $175(2), Full day: $175(1), $225(2)
Call between: Anytime
Provides: Light tackle, heavy tackle, lures, bait, rain gear
Handicapped equipped: Yes

Gene Collins
Nancy 606-636-6531
Species & Seasons: Striped Bass all year, Walleye Mar-Sept, Trout July-Nov
Bodies of water: Lake Cumberland, Cumberland River tailwaters
Rates: Full day: $175(1), $225(2), $275(3), $325(4)

LAKE CUMBERLAND - ROUGH RIVER   KENTUCKY

Call between: 7am-11pm
Provides: Light tackle, heavy tackle, lures, bait
Handicapped equipped: Yes
Certifications: CPR, First aid

Wise Guide Service
Cambellsville 502-465-8920
Species & Seasons: SM Bass Nov-May, LM Bass Mar-Dec, Walleye April-Sept
Bodies of water: Dale Hollow Lake, Lake Cumberland, Green River Lake
Rates: Full day: $175(1), $200(2)
Call between: 7pm-10pm
Provides: Light tackle, heavy tackle, lures, bait
Handicapped equipped: No

NOLIN RIVER LAKE

BAIT & TACKLE...

Smyrna Bait & Tackle Shop
Louisville 502-964-9213
Hours: 6am-9pm
Carries: Live bait, lures, flies, maps, rods, reels, licenses
Bodies of water: Taylorsville Lake, Laurel Lake, Nolin River Lake, Rough River
Services & Products: Food, beverages, repair services
Guides: Yes
OK to call for current conditions: Yes
Contact: Freada Witt

LODGES...

Ponderosa Fishing Camp
865 Ponderosa
Clarkson 42726
Guest Capacity: 500
Handicapped equipped: Some
Seasons: April 1 to Oct 31
Rates: Varies
Contact: Kerry McKinley
Guides: No
Species & Seasons: Crappie, White Bass, LM Bass, SM Bass, Walleye
Bodies of Water: Nolin River Lake
Types of fishing: Fly fishing, light tackle
Available: Licenses, bait, tackle, boat rentals, family activities

OHIO RIVER

BAIT & TACKLE...

Frank Miller & Son Bait & Sporting
Owensboro 502-683-3479
Hours: 7am-7pm Mon.-Thurs., 7am-8pm Fri., 6am-8pm Sat., 6am-4pm Sun.
Carries: Live bait, lures, flies, maps, rods, reels, licenses
Bodies of water: Ohio River, Green River, Rough River Lake, Kentucky Lake, Lake Barkley
Services & Products: Beverages, fishing instruction, repair services, archery supplies, gun supplies
OK to call for current conditions: Yes
Contact: Frank or Chris Miller

Pit Stop
Hawesville 502-927-8942
Hours: 6am-7pm
Carries: Live bait, lures, flies, rods, reels, licenses
Bodies of water: Ohio River, Rough River Dam Resort
Services & Products: Food, beverages, gas/oil, fishing instruction
Guides: No
OK to call for current conditions: Yes
Contact: Wm A Stewart (Bill)

GUIDES...

Bob "Big Bass" Beals Guide Service
Gilbertsville 502-395-5533
Species & Seasons: Crappie, LM Bass, SM Bass, Sauger, Bluegill, White Bass, Yellow Bass, Rockfish, Catfish all year
Bodies of water: Lake Barkley, Tennessee River, Cumberland River, Ohio River, Kentucky Lake
Rates: 5 hrs.: $125(1-2), Full day: $200(1-2), $25 additional 3rd person
Call between: 6pm-10:30pm
Provides: Light tackle, heavy tackle, lures, bait, rain gear
Handicapped equipped: Yes
Certifications: KY Dept. of Fish & Game

Jimmie Quinn
Murray 502-762-3615
.... 753-5583
Species & Seasons: LM Bass, SM Bass Mar-Jan, Crappie Mar-May, Sauger Oct-Feb, Striped Bass all year, White Bass
Bodies of water: Kentucky Lake, Lake Barkley, Tennessee River (below Kentucky Lake Dam), Cumberland River (below Cumberland Dam), Ohio River (below Smithland Dam)
Rates: Half day: $100(1-2), Full day: $165(1-2)
Call between: Anytime
Provides: Light tackle, heavy tackle, lures, bait, rain gear, beverages
Handicapped equipped: Yes, limited
Certifications: KY State Guide

ROUGH RIVER

BAIT & TACKLE...

Pit Stop
Hawesville 502-927-8942
Hours: 6am-7pm
Carries: Live bait, lures, flies, rods, reels, licenses
Bodies of water: Ohio River, Rough River Dam Resort
Services & Products: Food, beverages, gas/oil, fishing instruction
Guides: No
OK to call for current conditions: Yes
Contact: Wm A Stewart (Bill)

Smyrna Bait & Tackle Shop
Louisville 502-964-9213
Hours: 6am-9pm
Carries: Live bait, lures, flies, maps, rods, reels, licenses
Bodies of water: Taylorsville Lake, Laurel Lake, Nolin River Lake, Rough River
Services & Products: Food, beverages, repair services
Guides: Yes
OK to call for current conditions: Yes
Contact: Freada Witt

KENTUCKY

ROUGH RIVER LAKE - TENNESSEE RIVER

ROUGH RIVER LAKE

BAIT & TACKLE...

Frank Miller & Son Bait & Sporting
Owensboro 502-683-3479
Hours: 7am-7pm Mon.-Thurs., 7am-8pm Fri., 6am-8pm Sat., 6am-4pm Sun.
Carries: Live bait, lures, flies, maps, rods, reels, licenses
Bodies of water: Ohio River, Green River, Rough River Lake, Kentucky Lake, Lake Barkley
Services & Products: Beverages, fishing instruction, repair services, archery supplies, gun supplies
OK to call for current conditions: Yes
Contact: Frank or Chris Miller

MARINAS...

Nick Bronger's Boat Dock
Mc Daniels 502-257-8955
Hours: 6am-8pm
Carries: Live bait, lures, maps, rods, reels, licenses
Bodies of water: Rough River Lake
Services & Products: Boat rentals, boat ramp, food, beverages, gas/oil
Guides: No
OK to call for current conditions: Yes

TAYLORSVILLE LAKE

BAIT & TACKLE...

Pumpkin Patch General Store
Taylorsville 502-477-9363
Hours: 7am-10pm
Carries: Live bait, lures, maps, rods, reels, licenses
Bodies of water: Taylorsville Lake, Salt River, Beech Fork River
Services & Products: Food, beverages, fishing instruction
Guides: Yes
OK to call for current conditions: Yes
Contact: Don Terry

Smyrna Bait & Tackle Shop
Louisville 502-964-9213
Hours: 6am-9pm
Carries: Live bait, lures, flies, maps, rods, reels, licenses
Bodies of water: Taylorsville Lake, Laurel Lake, Nolin River Lake, Rough River
Services & Products: Food, beverages, repair services
Guides: Yes
OK to call for current conditions: Yes
Contact: Freada Witt

T & G Bait Shop
Frankfort 502-223-7219
Hours: Varies
Carries: Live bait, lures, flies, maps, rods, reels, licenses
Bodies of water: Kentucky River, Taylorsville Lake, Kentucky State Game Farm Lakes, Kentucky Lake, Lake Barkley
Services & Products: Food, beverages, gas/oil, fishing instruction
Guides: Yes
OK to call for current conditions: Yes
Contact: J.R. Thurman

TENNESSEE RIVER

GUIDES...

Bob "Big Bass" Beals Guide Service
Gilbertsville 502-395-5533
Species & Seasons: Crappie, LM Bass, SM Bass, Sauger, Bluegill, White Bass, Yellow Bass, Rockfish, Catfish all year
Bodies of water: Lake Barkley, Tennessee River, Cumberland River, Ohio River, Kentucky Lake
Rates: 5 hrs.: $125(1-2), Full day: $200(1-2), $25 additional 3rd person
Call between: 6pm-10:30pm
Provides: Light tackle, heavy tackle, lures, bait, rain gear
Handicapped equipped: Yes
Certifications: KY Dept. of Fish & Game

Jimmie Quinn
Murray 502-762-3615
.... 753-5583
Species & Seasons: LM Bass, SM Bass Mar-Jan, Crappie Mar-May, Sauger Oct-Feb, Striped Bass all year, White Bass
Bodies of water: Kentucky Lake, Lake Barkley, Tennessee River (below Kentucky Lake Dam), Cumberland River (below Cumberland Dam), Ohio River (below Smithland Dam)
Rates: Half day: $100(1-2), Full day: $165(1-2)
Call between: Anytime
Provides: Light tackle, heavy tackle, lures, bait, rain gear, beverages
Handicapped equipped: Yes, limited
Certifications: KY State Guide

LOUISIANA

1. Barataria Bay
2. Breton Sound
3. Caddo Lake
4. Calcasieu Lake
5. Gulf of Mexico
6. Lake Bistineau
7. Lake Borgne
8. Lake Mechant
9. Little Lake
10. Mississippi Delta
11. Mississippi River
12. Toledo Bend Reservoir
13. Vermilion Bay

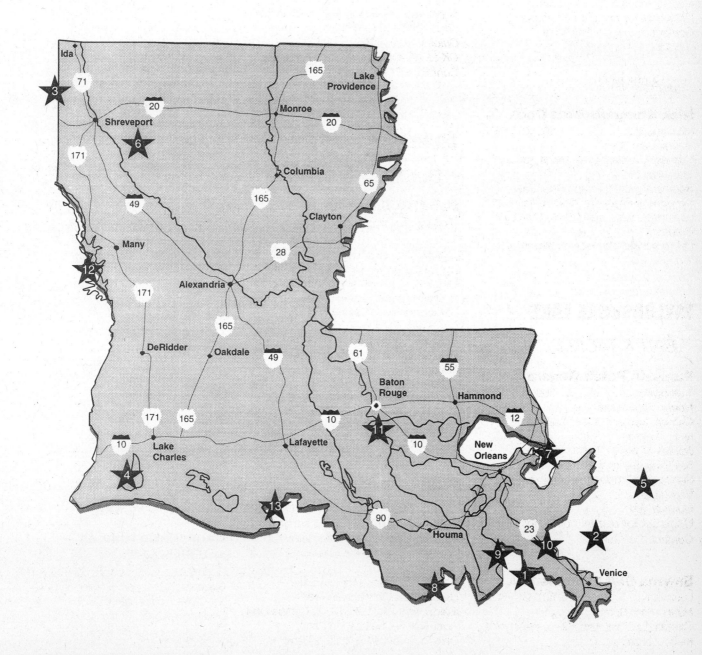

LOUISIANA

BARATARIA BAY - GULF OF MEXICO

BARATARIA BAY

CHARTERS...

Captain Crickett's Charters
Marrero 504-340-7521
Species & Seasons: Speckled Trout, Redfish April-Jan, Bass Feb-Mar
Bodies of water: Barataria Bay, Little Lake, Grand Isle
Rates: Half day: $200(2), Full day: $250(2), $75 additional pp for a total of 4
Call between: 8am-8pm
Provides: Light tackle, lures, bait
Handicapped equipped: Yes
Certifications: USCG

BRETON SOUND

CHARTERS...

Capt. Joe McDonald Charters
Delacroix Is. 504-684-3442
Species & Seasons: Speckled Trout, Redfish, Flounder Jan-Dec, Red Snapper, Cobia, Grouper June-Sept
Bodies of water: Louisiana Marsh, Black Bay, BretonSound
Rates: Full day: $200(1), $250(2), $300(3-4) + fuel and bait
Call between: 5am-6pm
Provides: Light tackle
Handicapped equipped: No

Escape Fishing charters
Slidell 504-643-5905
Species & Seasons: Speckled Trout, Redfish May-April
Bodies of water: Black Bay, Breton Sound and surrounding marshes, Delacroix Island
Rates: Full day: $250(2), $335(3), $495(4)
Call between: 8am-10pm
Provides: Light tackle, lures, bait, rain gear
Handicapped equipped: Yes
Certifications: USCG

CADDO LAKE

BAIT & TACKLE...

Tackle Masters
Bossier City 318-747-0815
Hours: 10am-6pm, closed Sun., Mon.
Carries: Live bait, lures, maps, rods, reels, licenses
Bodies of water: Caddo Lake, Toledo Bend Res., Lake Bistineau, Caney Lake
Services & Products: Repair services
Guides: Yes
OK to call for current conditions: Yes
Contact: Darrel Phillips

CALCASIEU LAKE

CHARTERS...

Calcasieu Charter Service
Lake Charles 318-478-2734
Species & Seasons: Speckled Trout Mar-Dec, Redfish Feb-Dec, Red Snapper Jan-Dec, Cobia May-Oct, King Mackerel, Spanish Mackerel April-Oct
Bodies of water: Calcasieu Lake, Gulf of Mexico
Rates: Full day: $275(1-2)
Call between: 4pm-9pm
Provides: Light tackle, heavy tackle, lures, bait, beverages, lunch
Handicapped equipped: No
Certifications: USCG

GUIDES...

Atwell's Guide Service
Lake Charles 318-598-2990
Species & Seasons: Speckled Trout, Redfish, Flounder Mar-Dec
Bodies of water: Calcasieu Lake, Gulf of Mexico
Rates: $275 per boat (1-3 people per boat)
Provides: Light tackle, rain gear

GULF OF MEXICO

BAIT & TACKLE...

Country Station's Tackle Shop
Broussard 318-837-5159
Hours: 6am-9pm
Carries: Live bait, lures, maps, rods, reels, licenses
Bodies of water: Vermilion Bay, Gulf of Mexico
Services & Products: Food, beverages, gas/oil, fishing instruction, repair services
Guides: Yes
OK to call for current conditions: Yes
Contact: Larry or Laurie

CHARTERS...

Calcasieu Charter Service
Lake Charles 318-478-2734
Species & Seasons: Speckled Trout Mar-Dec, Redfish Feb-Dec, Red Snapper Jan-Dec, Cobia May-Oct, King Mackerel, Spanish Mackerel April-Oct
Bodies of water: Calcasieu Lake, Gulf of Mexico
Rates: Full day: $275(1-2)
Call between: 4pm-9pm
Provides: Light tackle, heavy tackle, lures, bait, beverages, lunch
Handicapped equipped: No
Certifications: USCG

Cherece IV Charters
Grand Isle 504-787-2200
Species & Seasons: Snapper, Tuna, Wahoo, Cobia, Triggerfish, Speckled Trout Jan-Dec
Bodies of water: Gulf of Mexico
Rates: Full day: $650(6)
Call between: 8am-9pm
Provides: Heavy tackle, lures, bait
Handicapped equipped: Yes
Certifications: USCG

Coup Platte Hunting and Fishing
Houma 504-868-7940
Species & Seasons: Redfish Jan-Jan, Speckled Trout April-Oct
Bodies of water: Gulf of Mexico, Lake Mechant, Sister Lake, Lost Lake

GULF OF MEXICO - MISSISSIPPI DELTA — LOUISIANA

Rates: *Fishing: $85 one day, $150, one day/one night,
$235 two days/one night,
$300 pp two days/two nights.
Hunting/Fishing: $225 per day.
*Fishing rates based upon a minimum of 3 people
Provides: Light tackle
Handicapped equipped: No
Certifications: USCG

The Charter Boat Teaser
Marrero 504-341-4245
Species & Seasons: Wahoo Dec-May, Marlin, Dolphin May-Sept, Tarpon July-Sept, Cobia June-Nov, Tuna, Snapper, Redfish all year, Trout May-Oct, Bass
Bodies of water: Gulf of Mexico
Rates: Up to 3 people: Starts at $350-$1125(6 people) per boat
Call between: 9am-10pm
Provides: Light tackle, heavy tackle, bait
Handicapped equipped: Yes
Certifications: USCG

GUIDES...

Atwell's Guide Service
Lake Charles 318-598-2990
Species & Seasons: Speckled Trout, Redfish, Flounder Mar-Dec
Bodies of water: Calcasieu Lake, Gulf of Mexico
Rates: $275 per boat
(1-3 people per boat)
Provides: Light tackle, rain gear

Great Outdoors Guide Service
Slidell 504-583-3101
Species & Seasons: Trout, Redfish, Flounder Jan-Jan, LM Bass Feb-Nov
Bodies of water: Lake Borgne, Rigolets, Gulf of Mexico, all surrounding waters
Rates: Half day: $150(1-2),
Full day: $200(1-2)
Call between: 4pm
Provides: Light tackle, lures, bait
Handicapped equipped: No
Certifications: USCG

LAKE BISTINEAU

BAIT & TACKLE...

Tackle Masters
Bossier City 318-747-0815
Hours: 10am-6pm, closed Sun., Mon.
Carries: Live bait, lures, maps, rods, reels, licenses
Bodies of water: Caddo Lake, Toledo Bend Res., Lake Bistineau, Caney Lake
Services & Products: Repair services
Guides: Yes
OK to call for current conditions: Yes
Contact: Darrel Phillips

LAKE BORGNE

GUIDES...

Great Outdoors Guide Service
Slidell 504-583-3101
Species & Seasons: Trout, Redfish, Flounder Jan-Jan, LM Bass Feb-Nov
Bodies of water: Lake Borgne, Rigolets, Gulf of Mexico, all surrounding waters
Rates: Half day: $150(1-2),
Full day: $200(1-2)
Call between: 4pm
Provides: Light tackle, lures, bait
Handicapped equipped: No
Certifications: USCG

LAKE MERCHANT

CHARTERS...

Coup Platte Hunting and Fishing
Houma 504-868-7940
Species & Seasons: Redfish Jan-Jan, Speckled Trout April-Oct
Bodies of water: Gulf of Mexico, Lake Mechant, Sister Lake, Lost Lake
Rates: *Fishing: $85 one day,
$150, one day/one night,
$235 two days/one night,
$300 pp two days/two nights.
Hunting/Fishing: $225 per day.
*Fishing rates based upon a minimum of 3 people
Provides: Light tackle
Handicapped equipped: No
Certifications: USCG

LITTLE LAKE

CHARTERS...

Captain Crickett's Charters
Marrero 504-340-7521
Species & Seasons: Speckled Trout, Redfish April-Jan, Bass Feb-Mar
Bodies of water: Barataria Bay, Little Lake, Grand Isle
Rates: Half day: $200(2),
Full day: $250(2), $75 additional pp for a total of 4
Call between: 8am-8pm
Provides: Light tackle, lures, bait
Handicapped equipped: Yes
Certifications: USCG

MISSISSIPPI DELTA

CHARTERS...

Cajun Fishing Adventures
Luling 504-785-9833
Species & Seasons: Redfish, Speckled Trout Jan-Dec
Bodies of water: Mississippi River Delta
Rates: Full day: $250(2), $75 additional pp up to 4 per boat
Call between: 8am-10pm
Provides: Light tackle, fly rod/reel, lures, rain gear
Handicapped equipped: No
Certifications: USCG

Captain Crickett's Charters
Marrero 504-340-7521
Species & Seasons: Speckled Trout, Redfish April-Jan, Bass Feb-Mar
Bodies of water: Barataria Bay, Little Lake, Grand Isle
Rates: Half day: $200(2),
Full day: $250(2), $75 additional pp for a total of 4
Call between: 8am-8pm
Provides: Light tackle, lures, bait
Handicapped equipped: Yes
Certifications: USCG

LOUISIANA
MISSISSIPPI DELTA - VERMILLION BAY

GUIDES...

Mississippi Delta Guide Service
Avondale 504-436-0511
Species & Seasons: Speckled Trout, Redfish, LM Bass, Flounder, Striped Bass all year
Bodies of water: Lower Mississippi Delta
Rates: Full day: $220(1), $275(2), $325(3)
Call between: 8am-8pm
Provides: Light tackle, lures, bait, rain gear
Handicapped equipped: No
Certifications: USCG

Southern Safaris Inc.
Westwego 800-966-4868
Species & Seasons: Redfish, Speckled Trout, LM Bass all year
Bodies of water: Lafitte area, Myrtle Grove area (lower Mississippi River area)
Rates: Spin-light tackle: Half day: $175(1), $230(2), Full Day $250(1), $350(2) Fly: Full day: $300(1-2) includes lunch, drink and tackle
Call between: 24 hours
Provides: Light tackle, fly rod/reel
Handicapped equipped: Yes
Certifications: USCG

MISSISSIPPI RIVER

BAIT & TACKLE...

Sportsman's Haven
Baton Rouge 504-355-9807
Hours: 4am-7pm
Carries: Live bait, lures, flies, maps, rods, reels, licenses
Bodies of water: Louisiana Coast (fresh and salt water), False River, Atchafalaya Basin, Mississippi River
Services & Products: Food, beverages, gas/oil
Guides: Yes
OK to call for current conditions: Yes
Contact: Joe Husser or David Mincin

TOLEDO BEND RESERVOIR

BAIT & TACKLE...

Tackle Masters
Bossier City 318-747-0815
Hours: 10am-6pm, closed Sun., Mon.
Carries: Live bait, lures, maps, rods, reels, licenses
Bodies of water: Caddo Lake, Toledo Bend Res., Lake Bistineau, Caney Lake
Services & Products: Repair services
Guides: Yes
OK to call for current conditions: Yes
Contact: Darrel Phillips

GUIDES...

Toledo Bend Guide Service
Zwolle 318-645-4415
Species & Seasons: LM Bass Jan-Dec, Striped Bass, Bluegill May-July, Crappie April-Oct
Bodies of water: Toledo Bend Res.
Rates: Half day: $100(1-2), Full day: $200(1-2)
Call between: 6pm-9pm
Provides: Light tackle, lures, bait
Handicapped equipped: No

LODGES...

Wildwood Resort
Zwolle 318-645-6114
Guest Capacity: 66
Handicapped equipped: Yes
Seasons: All year
Rates: Varies
Contact: Helga Donald
Guides: Yes
Species & Seasons: LM Bass, White Perch, Bream, Striped Bass
Bodies of Water: Toledo Bend Res.
Types of fishing: Fly fishing, light tackle, heavy tackle
Available: Family activities (3 stocked ponds for guests only)

MARINAS...

Cozy Point
Zwolle 318-645-9847
Hours: 6am-8pm
Carries: Live bait, lures, maps
Bodies of water: Toledo Bend Res.

Services & Products: Lodging, boat ramp, beverages, gas/oil, fishing instruction
Guides: Yes
OK to call for current conditions: Yes
Contact: Jerrie

Jolly Roger Marina
Converse 318-567-2547
Hours: 6am-7pm
Carries: Live bait, lures, maps, rods, reels, licenses
Bodies of water: Toledo Bend Res.
Services & Products: Boat rentals, guide services, lodging, boat ramp, food, beverages, gas/oil, fishing instruction
Guides: Yes
OK to call for current conditions: Yes
Contact: David K. Rogers

Pendleton Bridge Resort & Marina
Many 318-256-2958
Hours: Seasonal
Carries: Live bait, lures, maps, licenses
Bodies of water: Toledo Bend Res.
Services & Products: Boat rentals, guide services, lodging, boat ramp, food, beverages, gas/oil
Guides: Yes
OK to call for current conditions: Yes
Contact: Mitch or Sue Griffith

VERMILION BAY

BAIT & TACKLE...

Country Station's Tackle Shop
Broussard 318-837-5159
Hours: 6am-9pm
Carries: Live bait, lures, maps, rods, reels, licenses
Bodies of water: Vermilion Bay, Gulf of Mexico
Services & Products: Food, beverages, gas/oil, fishing instruction, repair services
Guides: Yes
OK to call for current conditions: Yes
Contact: Larry or Laurie

MAINE

1. Atlantic Ocean
2. Big Lake
3. Casco Bay
4. Kennebago Lake
5. Kennebec River
6. Kezar Lake
7. Moosehead Lake
8. Penobscot River
9. Private Lakes
10. Sebago Lake
11. South Branch Lake
12. West Grand Lake

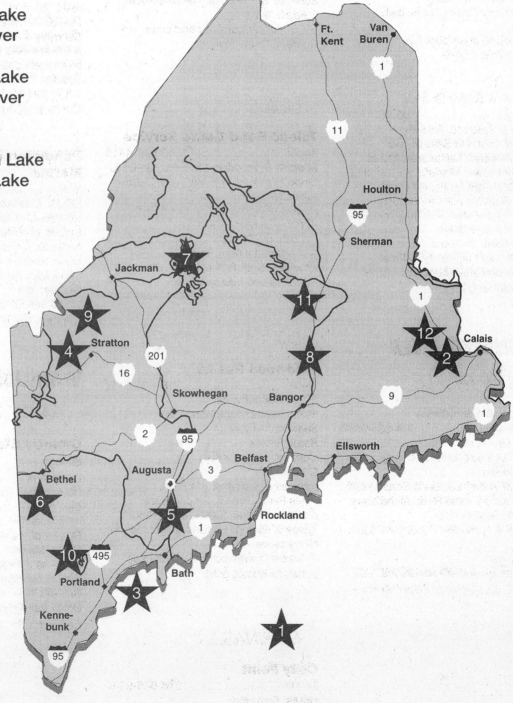

YOUR SILENT FISHING PARTNER

MAINE

ATLANTIC OCEAN - KENNEBEC RIVER

ATLANTIC OCEAN

BAIT & TACKLE...

Eddie's Files & Tackle
Bangor 207-947-1648
Hours: 10am-5pm, closed Sun.
Carries: Lures, flies, maps, rods, reels
Bodies of water: Penobscot River, Atlantic Ocean, Moosehead Lake
Services & Products: Guide services
Guides: Yes
OK to call for current conditions: Yes
Contact: Ed Reif

CHARTERS...

Bingo Deep Sea Fishing
Edgecomb 207-882-9309
Species & Seasons: Striped Bass, Bluefish July-Oct, Cok May-Dec, Mackerel May-Nov
Bodies of water: Mid-coast Maine rivers, Atlantic Ocean
Rates: Half day: $25(1) Boat $150, Full day: $50(1) Boat $300, private parties $300
Call between: 6pm-10pm
Provides: Light tackle, heavy tackle, lures, bait
Handicapped equipped: No
Certifications: USCG

BIG LAKE

LODGING...

Long Lake Camps
Princeton 207-796-2051
Guest Capacity: 35
Handicapped equipped: No
Seasons: April 27 to Oct 30
Rates: Varies
Contact: Kyle Staples
Guides: Yes
Species & Seasons: SM Bass May-Sept, Salmon April-June/Sept-Oct, Pickerel, Perch April-Oct
Bodies of Water: Long Lake, Grand Falls Lake, Big Lake, West Grand Lake
Types of fishing: Fly fishing, light tackle, wading, trolling, spin casting
Available: Licenses, bait, tackle, boat rentals, family activities

CASCO BAY

BOAT RENTALS...

Portland Boat Rental
Portland 207-773-5522
Bodies of water: Casco Bay
Services & Products: Boat rentals
Guides: Yes
OK to call for current conditions: Yes
Contact: Raymond Taylor

CHARTERS...

Obsession Charters
Topsham 207-729-3997
Species & Seasons: Striped Bass June-Sept, Bluefish July-Sept, Blue Shark Aug-Sept
Bodies of water: Kennebec River, Casco Bay, Gulf of Maine
Rates: Half day: $185(1-4), Full day: $285(1-4)
Call between: 7pm-9pm
Provides: Light tackle, fly rod/reel, lures, bait, rain gear
Handicapped equipped: No
Certifications: USCG

MARINAS...

New Meadows Marina
Brunswick 207-443-6277
Hours: 8am-5pm, closed 8-12 Sun.
Bodies of water: Casco Bay, Kennebec River
Services & Products: Boat rentals, beverages, gas/oil, repair services, dockage rental
Guides: Yes
OK to call for current conditions: Yes
Contact: Michelle

KENNEBAGO LAKE

LODGING...

Grant's Kennebago Camps
Rangeley 207-864-3608
Guest Capacity: 60
Handicapped equipped: Yes
Seasons: May 18 to Oct 1
Rates: $100/day
Contact: John Blunt
Guides: Yes
Species & Seasons: Brook Trout, Brown Trout, Salmon June-Sept

Bodies of Water: Kennebago Lake, Kennebago River, Flat Iron Pond, Little Kennebago Lake
Types of fishing: Fly fishing, wading, fly-out trips, float trips
Available: Fishing instruction, licenses, bait, tackle, boat rentals, family activities, baby sitting

KENNEBEC RIVER

CHARTERS...

Breakaway Sportfishing Inc.
East Booth Bay 207-633-6990
Species & Seasons: Mackerel May-Oct, Striped Bass June-Oct, Bluefish, Shark, Bluefin Tuna July-Oct
Bodies of water: Kennebec River, Sheepscot River, Gulf of Maine
Rates: Half day: $30(1), Private Charter: Half day: $350(1-12), Full day: $600(1-12)
Call between: 7am-10pm
Provides: Light tackle, heavy tackle, lures, bait
Handicapped equipped: Yes
Certifications: USCG

Kayla D
Bath 207-443-3316
Species & Seasons: Striped Bass June-Sept, Bluefish July-Aug, Shark July-Sept
Bodies of water: Gulf of Maine, Kennibec River
Rates: Half day: $295(1-6), Full day: $395(1-6)
Call between: 7-10am/7-10 pm
Provides: Light tackle, heavy tackle, lures, bait, rain gear
Certifications: USCG

Obsession Charters
Topsham 207-729-3997
Species & Seasons: Striped Bass June-Sept, Bluefish July-Sept, Blue Shark Aug-Sept
Bodies of water: Kennebec River, Casco Bay, Gulf of Maine
Rates: Half day: $185(1-4), Full day: $285(1-4)
Call between: 7pm-9pm
Provides: Light tackle, fly rod/reel, lures, bait, rain gear
Handicapped equipped: No
Certifications: USCG

KENNEBEC RIVER - PRIVATE LAKES — MAINE

GUIDES...

Penobscot Drift Boats
Bangor 207-942-3234
Species & Seasons: Landlocked Salmon, Brook Trout May-Oct
Bodies of water: West Branch of Penobscot River, East Outlet of the Kennebec River
Rates: Half day: $150(1), $175(2), Full day: $250(1), $275(2)
Call between: Anytime
Provides: Fly rod/reel, beverages, lunch
Certifications: Licensed ME Whitewater and Fishing Guide

MARINAS...

New Meadows Marina
Brunswick 207-443-6277
Hours: 8am-5pm, closed 8-12 Sun.
Carries:
Bodies of water: Casco Bay, Kennebec River
Services & Products: Boat rentals, beverages, gas/oil, repair services, dockage rental
Guides: Yes
OK to call for current conditions: Yes
Contact: Michelle

KEZAR LAKE

BAIT & TACKLE...

Lovell Bait & Tackle
Lovell 207-925-3001
Hours: 7am-6pm
Carries: Live bait, lures, flies, maps, rods, reels, licenses
Bodies of water: Kezar Lake, Moose Pond, Sebago Lake
Services & Products: Guide services, fishing instruction
OK to call for current conditions: Yes
Contact: Carl or Alice

GUIDES...

Rocky Ridge Guide Service
Lovell 207-925-6262
Species & Seasons: SM Bass, LM Bass May-Sept, Salmon, Lake Trout April-Sept
Bodies of water: Kezar Lake, Sebago Lake, Thomson Lake, Moose Pond and others

Rates: Half day: $150(1-2), Full day: $200(1-2) $50 additional 3rd person
Call between: 9am-9pm
Provides: Light tackle, lures, bait, beverages, lunch
Handicapped equipped:
Certifications: Reg. ME Master Guide, NAFC approved Guide, Daiwa Advisory Staff

MOOSEHEAD LAKE

BAIT & TACKLE...

Eddie's Files & Tackle
Bangor 207-947-1648
Hours: 10am-5pm, closed Sun.
Carries: Lures, flies, maps, rods, reels
Bodies of water: Penobscot River, Atlantic Ocean, Moosehead Lake
Services & Products: Guide services
Guides: Yes
OK to call for current conditions: Yes
Contact: Ed Reif

PENOBSCOT RIVER

BAIT & TACKLE...

Eddie's Files & Tackle
Bangor 207-947-1648
Hours: 10am-5pm, closed Sun.
Carries: Lures, flies, maps, rods, reels
Bodies of water: Penobscot River, Atlantic Ocean, Moosehead Lake
Services & Products: Guide services
Guides: Yes
OK to call for current conditions: Yes
Contact: Ed Reif

GUIDES...

Penobscot Drift Boats
Bangor 207-942-3234
Species & Seasons: Landlocked Salmon, Brook Trout May-Oct
Bodies of water: West Branch of Penobscot River, East Outlet of the Kennebec River
Rates: Half day: $150(1), $175(2), Full day: $250(1), $275(2)
Call between: Anytime
Provides: Fly rod/reel, beverages, lunch
Handicapped equipped:
Certifications: Licensed ME Whitewater and Fishing Guide

LODGING...

Matagamon Wilderness Camps
Patten 207-528-2448
Guest Capacity: 25
Handicapped equipped: No
Seasons: All year
Rates: $30/day
Contact: Don Dudley
Guides: Yes
Species & Seasons: Brook Trout, Salmon, Lake Trout, Whitefish April-Sept
Bodies of Water: Grand Lake Matagamon, East Branch Penobscot River, Fowler Ponds, Hay Lake
Types of fishing: Fly fishing, wading, back packing

South Branch Lake Camps
Seboils 207-732-3446
.... 800-248-0554
Guest Capacity: 30
Handicapped equipped: No
Seasons: May 15 to Oct 30
Rates: $65/day
Guides: Yes
Species & Seasons: SM Bass May-Oct
Bodies of Water: South Branch Lake, Penobscot River, Piscataquis River
Types of fishing: Fly fishing, light tackle,
Available: Licenses, bait, tackle, boat rentals

PRIVATE LAKES

LODGING...

King and Barlett Fish & Game Club
Eustis 207-243-2956
Guest Capacity: 35
Handicapped equipped: No
Seasons: May 15 to Dec 1
Rates: $175/day
Contact: Todd Wallace
Guides: Yes
Species & Seasons: Brook Trout, Lake Trout, Salmon April-Sept
Bodies of Water: King Lake, Bartlett Lake, other ponds
Types of fishing: Fly fishing, light tackle, wading, float trips
Available: Fishing instruction, licenses, bait, tackle, boats(included), family activities, children's program

MAINE

SEBAGO LAKE - WEST GRAND LAKE

SEBAGO LAKE

BAIT & TACKLE...

Lovell Bait & Tackle
Lovell 207-925-3001
Hours: 7am-6pm
Carries: Live bait, lures, flies, maps, rods, reels, licenses
Bodies of water: Kezar Lake, Moose Pond, Sebago Lake
Services & Products: Guide services, fishing instruction
OK to call for current conditions: Yes
Contact: Carl or Alice

GUIDES...

Rocky Ridge Guide Service
Lovell 207-925-6262
Species & Seasons: SM Bass, LM Bass May-Sept, Salmon, Lake Trout April-Sept
Bodies of water: Kezar Lake, Sebago Lake, Thomson Lake, Moose Pond and others
Rates: Half day: $150(1-2), Full day: $200(1-2) $50 additional 3rd person
Call between: 9am-9pm
Provides: Light tackle, lures, bait, beverages, lunch
Handicapped equipped:
Certifications: Reg. ME Master Guide, NAFC approved Guide, Daiwa Advisory Staff

LODGING...

Sebago Lake Camps & Cottages
North Sebago 207-787-3211
Hours: 8am-7pm
Carries: Licenses
Bodies of water: Sebago Lake
Services & Products: Boat rentals and lodging
Guides: Yes
OK to call for current conditions: Yes
Contact: Ray Nelson

SOUTH BRANCH LAKE

LODGING...

South Branch Lake Camps
Seboils 207-732-3446
.... 800-248-0554
Guest Capacity: 30
Handicapped equipped: No
Seasons: May 15 to Oct 30
Rates: $65/day
Guides: Yes
Species & Seasons: SM Bass May-Oct
Bodies of Water: South Branch Lake, Penobscot River, Piscataquis River
Types of fishing: Fly fishing, light tackle,
Available: Licenses, bait, tackle, boat rentals

WEST GRAND LAKE

LODGING...

Long Lake Camps
Princeton 207-796-2051
Guest Capacity: 35
Handicapped equipped: No
Seasons: April 27 to Oct 30
Rates: Varies
Contact: Kyle Staples
Guides: Yes
Species & Seasons: SM Bass May-Sept, Salmon April-June/Sept-Oct, Pickerel, Perch April-Oct
Bodies of Water: Long Lake, Grand Falls Lake, Big Lake, West Grand Lake
Types of fishing: Fly fishing, light tackle, wading, trolling, spin casting
Available: Licenses, bait, tackle, boat rentals, family activities

MARYLAND

1. Atlantic Ocean
2. Chesapeake Bay
3. Choptank River
4. Cunningham Lake
5. Deep Creek Lake
6. Elk River
7. Gunpowder River
8. Jennings Randolph Lake
9. Liberty Lake
10. Loch Raven Reservoir
11. Monocacy River
12. Patuxent River
13. Potomac River
14. Prettyboy Reservoir
15. Rocky Gorge Reservoir
16. Savage River Reservoir
17. Susquehanna River
18. Tridelphia Reservoir

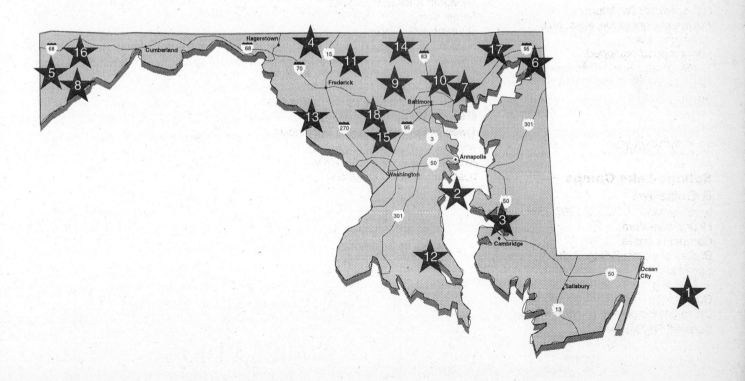

MARYLAND

ATLANTIC OCEAN - CHESAPEAKE BAY

ATLANTIC OCEAN

BAIT & TACKLE...

Tochterman's
Baltimore 410-327-6942
.... 800-533-3474
Hours: 8am-9pm
Carries: Live bait, lures, flies, maps, rods, reels, licenses
Bodies of water: Atlantic Ocean, Chesapeake Bay, Loch Raven Res., Liberty Res., Gunpowder River
Services & Products: Fishing instruction, repair services
Guides: Yes
OK to call for current conditions: Yes
Contact: Tony Tochterman or Jeff Devon

CHESAPEAKE BAY

BAIT & TACKLE...

Annapolis City Marina
Annapolis 410-268-0660
Hours: Sun up-Sun down
Carries: Live bait, lures, maps, rods, reels
Bodies of water: Chesapeake Bay
Services & Products: Boat rentals, guide services, charter boat service, boat ramp, food, beverages, gas/oil, fishing instruction
Guides: Yes
OK to call for current conditions: Yes

Bunky's Charterboats
Solomons Island 410-326-3241
Hours: 6am-7pm
Carries: Live bait, lures, maps, rods, reels, licenses
Bodies of water: Chesapeake Bay, Patuxent River
Services & Products: Boat rentals, guide services, charter boat service, food, beverages, gas/oil, fishing instruction
OK to call for current conditions: Yes
Contact: Kathy Conner

Fisherman's Edge
Baltimore 800-338-0053
Hours: 10am-5pm, closed Sun.
Carries: Lures, flies, rods, reels, licenses
Bodies of water: Chesapeake Bay, Potomac River, Susquehanna River
Services & Products: Guide services, fishing instruction
Guides: Yes
OK to call for current conditions: Yes
Contact: Joe Bruce

Gibson Island Marina
Pasadena 410-360-2500
Hours: 8am-5pm
Bodies of water: Chesapeake Bay, Magothy River
Services & Products: Beverages, gas/oil, repair services
Guides: Yes
OK to call for current conditions: Yes
Contact: Bill Egge

H M Woodburn & Co
Solomons 410-326-3241
Hours: 6am-7pm
Carries: Live bait, lures, maps, rods, reels, licenses
Bodies of water: Chesapeake Bay, Patuxent River, Potomac River
Services & Products: Boat rentals, charter boat service, food, beverages, gas/oil, head boat
OK to call for current conditions: Yes
Contact: Kathy or Karen

Herb's Tackle Shop
North East 410-287-5490
Hours: 6am-6pm
Carries: Live bait, lures, flies, maps, rods, reels, licenses
Bodies of water: Chesapeake Bay, North East River, Elk River, Susquehanna River
Services & Products: Guide services, charter boat service, fishing instruction, repair services
OK to call for current conditions: Yes
Contact: Herb, Mike or Eleanore

Inner Harbor Marina of Baltimore Inc.
Baltimore 410-837-5339
Hours: 24 hour service
Bodies of water: Chesapeake Bay
Services & Products: Food, beverages, gas/oil
Guides: Yes
OK to call for current conditions: Yes
Contact: Steve McBride

Laurel Fishing & Hunting Ltd.
Laurel 301-725-5527
Hours: 9am-8:30pm Mon-Thurs., 6am-8:30pm Fri.-Sat., 6am-4pm Sun.
Carries: Live bait, lures, flies, maps, rods, reels, licenses
Bodies of water: Chesapeake Bay, Potomac River, Rocky Gorge Res., Tridelphia Res.
Services & Products: Guide services, repair services
Guides: Yes
OK to call for current conditions: Yes
Contact: Larry or Steve Coburn

Markel's Boat Yard
Baltimore 410-477-3445
Hours: 9am-6pm
Carries: Maps
Bodies of water: Chesapeake Bay, North Point Creek, Patapsco River
Services & Products: Beverages, gas/oil, repair services, tank pump out
Guides: Yes

On The Fly
Monkton 410-329-6821
Hours: 10am-7pm
Carries: Flies, rods, reels, licenses
Bodies of water: Chesapeake Bay, Gunpowder River
Services & Products: Guide services, fishing instruction
OK to call for current conditions: Yes
Contact: Anyone

Set's Sport Shop
Baltimore 410-823-1367
Hours: 10am-9pm, closed Sun.
Carries: Live bait, lures, flies, maps, rods, reels, licenses
Bodies of water: Chesapeake Bay, Loch Raven Res., Prettyboy Res., Liberty Lake, Gunpowder River, Conowingo Lake, Susquehanna River, Tidal Rivers

---

CHESAPEAKE BAY FISHING

MISS LINDA

CHARTER BOAT

CAPT. JIM GASCH
(301) 855-5381

8668 BRAEBURN CT.
CHESAPEAKE BEACH, MD 20732

CHESAPEAKE BAY — MARYLAND

Services & Products: Guide services, fishing instruction, repair services
Guides: Yes
OK to call for current conditions: Yes
Contact: Harry L. Leister

Shore Sportsman
Trappe 410-820-5599
Hours: 5am-8pm
Carries: Live bait, lures, flies, maps, rods, reels, licenses
Bodies of water: Chesapeake Bay, Choptank River, Tred Avon River
Services & Products: Repair services
Guides: Yes
OK to call for current conditions: Yes
Contact: Ed Spear

Tochterman's
Baltimore 410-327-6942
.... 800-533-3474
Hours: 8am-9pm
Carries: Live bait, lures, flies, maps, rods, reels, licenses
Bodies of water: Chesapeake Bay, Atlantic Ocean, Loch Raven Res., Liberty Res., Gunpowder River
Services & Products: Fishing instruction, repair services
Guides: Yes
OK to call for current conditions: Yes
Contact: Tony Tochterman, Jeff Devon

Weavers Marine Service Inc.
Baltimore 410-686-4944
Hours: 8am-4:30pm, closed Sun.
Bodies of water: Chesapeake Bay, Back River
Services & Products: Boat ramp, beverages, gas/oil, repair services, towing
Guides: No
OK to call for current conditions: Yes
Contact: Samuel J. Weaver

CHARTERS...

Annapolis Sport Fishing Center
Annapolis 410-263-0990
Species & Seasons: Striped Bass May-Nov, Bluefish May-Oct, White Perch May-Sept
Bodies of water: Chesapeake Bay and Tributaries
Rates: Half day: $200(1), $250(2), Full day: $300(1), $350(2), up to 6 capacity
Call between: 7am-7pm
Provides: Light tackle, heavy tackle, fly rod/reel, lures, bait, rain gear
Handicapped equipped: Yes
Certifications: USCG

Associated Bay Captains
Deale 301-261-5353
410-269-1115
Species & Seasons: Striped Bass April-July/Sept-Nov, Black Drum, Bluefish, White Perch, Spot, Croaker, Flounder June-Nov, Spanish Mackerel July-Nov
Bodies of water: Chesapeake Bay
Rates: Half day: $275(1-6), Full day: $330(1-6), Over 6 Full day: $430, $25 additional pp over 10
Call between: Evenings
Provides: Light tackle, heavy tackle, lures
Handicapped equipped: Yes

Capt. Norm Bartlett
Joppa 410-679-8790
Species & Seasons: Striped Bass Mar-Dec, SM Bass, LM Bass June-Oct
Bodies of water: Chesapeake Bay and Tributaries
Rates: Full day: $300(2)
Call between: 8am-9:30pm
Provides: Light tackle, fly rod/reel
Handicapped equipped: No
Certifications: USCG, MD State Guide

Chesapeake Bay Sport Fishing & Charters
Deale 800-394-4101
.... 410-867-4101
Species & Seasons: Striped Bass May-July/Sept-Nov, Bluefish June-Oct, Spanish Mackerel July-Oct, Black Drum May-Sept, Spot, Croaker June-Oct, Perch June-July, Weakfish, Flounder June-Oct
Bodies of water: Chesapeake Bay
Rates: Half day: $375(1-6), $425(7-10), Full day: $400(1-6), $500(7-10), $30 additinal pp over 10
Call between: 9am-5pm
Provides: Light tackle, heavy tackle, fly rod/reel, lures, bait, beverages, lunch
Handicapped equipped: Yes
Certifications: USCG, MD State Fishing Guide

Chesapeake Sport Charters Inc.
Piney Point 301-994-0240
Species & Seasons: Striped Bass April-Dec, Bluefish May-Oct, Flounder, Weakfish June-Oct
Bodies of water: Chesapeake Bay and Tributaries
Rates: $360(6), $30 additional pp, max. 18 people (rates subject to change each year)

Call between: 8am-7pm
Provides: Light tackle, heavy tackle, lures, bait
Handicapped equipped: Yes
Certifications: USCG

James Sport Fishing Charters
Annapolis 800-322-4039
Species & Seasons: Striped Bass May-Nov, Bluefish, Croaker, Weakfish, Spot June-Sept, Flounder, Spanish Mackerel July-Sept, Black Drum June-June
Bodies of water: Chesapeake Bay
Rates: Half day: $275(6), over 6 $40pp, Full day: $385(6), over 6 $40pp
Call between: 5pm-10pm
Provides: Light tackle, heavy tackle, lures, bait
Handicapped equipped: Yes
Certifications: Licensed 49 passengers

Mary Lou II
Chesapeake Bch. 301-855-0784
Species & Seasons: Striped Bass May-July/Sept-Nov, Bluefish May-Oct, Spot, Croaker June-Oct, Black Drum June-July, Catfish July-Sept, Flounder, Weakfish June-Oct
Bodies of water: Chesapeake Bay (Rt. 50/301 Bridge to Cove Point)
Rates: Half day: $275(1-6), Full day: $350(1-6)
Call between: 7pm-10pm
Provides: Light tackle, heavy tackle, lures
Handicapped equipped: Yes
Certifications: USCG

JAMES SPORTFISHING CHARTERS
Professional Chesapeake Bay Services
Charters • Tours • Rentals
On the
"BOUNTY HUNTER"
Capt. Glenn A. James
1 800 322-4039
55' Licensed • 49 Passengers

MARYLAND
CHESAPEAKE BAY - ELK RIVER

Miss Linda
Chesapeake Bch. 301-855-5381
Species & Seasons: Striped Bass May-Nov, Bluefish May-Oct, Spot, Croaker June-Oct, Drum June-July, Flounder July-Sept, Spanish Mackerel July-Sept, Weakfish June-Sept, White Perch June-Oct
Bodies of water: Chesapeake Bay, Choptank River, Eastern Bay, Herring Bay
Rates: Half day: $275(6), Full day: $350(6), $30 additional pp over 6
Call between: 8am-9pm
Provides: Light tackle, heavy tackle
Handicapped equipped: No
Certifications: USCG
(see ad page 180)

Relative
Friendship 301-855-5454
Species & Seasons: Striped Bass April-July/Sept-Nov, Black Drum May-July, Bluefish April-Nov, Croaker June-Sept, Weakfish June-Nov, Spot June-Sept
Bodies of water: Chesapeake Bay (Bay Bridge to Potomac River)
Rates: Half day: $275(6), Full day: $350(6), make-up parties arranged, 4 hrs. afternoon/evenings "special rate"
Call between: 5pm-9pm
Provides: Light tackle, heavy tackle, lures. Bait additional cost.
Handicapped equipped: Yes
Certifications: USCG

Capt. Gary Sacks
Ridge 800-984-2008
Species & Seasons: Striped Bass May-Dec, Bluefish May-Oct, Croaker, Spot, Flounder, Sea Trout June-Oct, Spanish Mackerel July-Sept, Cobia Aug-Sept
Bodies of water: Chesapeake Bay, Potomac River
Rates: Full day: $330(1-6)
Call between: 5pm-9pm
Provides: Light tackle, heavy tackle, lures, bait
Handicapped equipped: No
Certifications: USCG, MD Guide

Sea Dux Outfitters
Chestertown 410-778-4362
Species & Seasons: Striped Bass April-Nov, Black Drum May-July, White Perch June-Sept, Bluefish, Spot, Catfish July-Sept, duck hunting also available
Bodies of water: Chesapeake Bay, middle, upper area
Rates: Half day: $300(1-6), Full day: $420(1-6)
Call between: 6pm-11pm
Provides: Light tackle, heavy tackle, lures, bait
Handicapped equipped: Yes
Certifications: USCG, MCBA

CHOPTANK RIVER

BAIT & TACKLE...

Shore Sportsman
Trappe 410-820-5599
Hours: 5am-8pm
Carries: Live bait, lures, flies, maps, rods, reels, licenses
Bodies of water: Choptank River, Chesapeake Bay, Tred Avon River
Services & Products: Repair services
Guides: Yes
OK to call for current conditions: Yes
Contact: Ed Spear

CHARTERS...

Miss Linda
Chesapeake Bch. 301-855-5381
Species & Seasons: Striped Bass May-Nov, Bluefish May-Oct, Spot, Croaker June-ct, Drum June-July, Flounder July-Sept, Spanish Mackerel July-Sept, Weakfish June-Sept, White Perch June-Oct
Bodies of water: Choptank River, Chesapeake Bay, Eastern Bay, Herring Bay
Rates: Half day: $275(6), Full day: $350(6), $30 additional pp over 6
Call between: 8am-9pm
Provides: Light tackle, heavy tackle
Handicapped equipped: No
Certifications: USCG

CUNNINGHAM LAKE

BAIT & TACKLE...

Fox Sport, Beer, & Wine Store
Frederick 301-663-FOXS
Hours: 6am-9pm
Carries: Live bait, lures, flies, maps, rods, reels, licenses
Bodies of water: Cunningham Lake, Monocacy River, Potomac River, Shenandoah River, Catoctin Mtn. trout streams, Frank Bentz Pond
Services & Products: Food, beverages, fishing instruction, repair services, knife sharpening
Guides: Yes
OK to call for current conditions: Yes
Contact: Bill or Todd Offutt

Thurmont Sporting Goods
Thurmont 301-271-7404
Hours: 8am-6pm
Carries: Live bait, lures, flies, maps, rods, reels, licenses
Bodies of water: Cunningham Lake, Bilhunting Creek, Monocacy River
Services & Products: Guide services
Guides: Yes
OK to call for current conditions: Yes
Contact: Richard

DEEP CREEK LAKE

BAIT & TACKLE...

Swanton Grocery Gas & Liquor
Swanton 301-387-5701
Hours: 6am-9pm
Carries: Live bait, lures, rods, reels, licenses
Bodies of water: Deep Creek Lake, Jennings Randolph Lake, Savage River Res.
Services & Products: Food, beverages, gas/oil
Guides: Yes
OK to call for current conditions: Yes
Contact: Robert McBee

ELK RIVER

BAIT & TACKLE...

Herb's Tackle Shop
North East 410-287-5490
Hours: 6am-6pm
Carries: Live bait, lures, flies, maps, rods, reels, licenses
Bodies of water: Elk River, North East River, Susquehanna River, Chesapeake Bay
Services & Products: Guide services, charter boat service, fishing instruction, repair services
OK to call for current conditions: Yes
Contact: Herb, Mike or Eleanore

GUNPOWDER RIVER - LOCH RAVEN RESERVOIR — MARYLAND

GUNPOWDER RIVER

BAIT & TACKLE...

On The Fly
Monkton 410-329-6821
Hours: 10am-7pm
Carries: Flies, rods, reels, licenses
Bodies of water: Gunpowder River, Chesapeake Bay
Services & Products: Guide services, fishing instruction
OK to call for current conditions: Yes
Contact: Anyone

Set's Sport Shop
Baltimore 410-823-1367
Hours: 10am-9pm, closed Sun.
Carries: Live bait, lures, flies, maps, rods, reels, licenses
Bodies of water: Gunpowder River, Loch Raven Res., Prettyboy Res., Liberty Lakes, Conowingo Lake, Susquehanna River, Chesapeake Bay, Tidal Rivers
Services & Products: Guide services, fishing instruction, repair services
Guides: Yes
OK to call for current conditions: Yes
Contact: Harry L. Leister

Tochterman's
Baltimore 410-327-6942
.... 800-533-3474
Hours: 8am-9pm
Carries: Live bait, lures, flies, maps, rods, reels, licenses
Bodies of water: Gunpowder River, Atlantic Ocean, Chesapeake Bay, Loch Raven Res., Liberty Res.
Services & Products: Fishing instruction, repair services
Guides: Yes
OK to call for current conditions: Yes
Contact: Tony Tochterman, Jeff Devon

JENNINGS RANDOLPH LAKE

BAIT & TACKLE...

Swanton Grocery Gas & Liquor
Swanton 301-387-5701
Hours: 6am-9pm
Carries: Live bait, lures, rods, reels, licenses
Bodies of water: Jennings Randolph Lake, Deep Creek Lake, Savage River Res.
Services & Products: Food, beverages, gas/oil
Guides: Yes
OK to call for current conditions: Yes
Contact: Robert McBee

LIBERTY LAKE

BAIT & TACKLE...

Beck's Gunsmithing
Parkton 410-357-5767
Hours: 9am-7pm
Carries: Live bait, lures, flies, maps, rods, reels, licenses
Bodies of water: Liberty Lake, Loch Raven Res., Prettyboy Res.
Services & Products: Fishing instruction, repair services
Guides: No
OK to call for current conditions: Yes
Contact: Michael or Sharon Beck

Set's Sport Shop
Baltimore 410-823-1367
Hours: 10am-9pm, closed Sun.
Carries: Live bait, lures, flies, maps, rods, reels, licenses
Bodies of water: Liberty Lake, Loch Raven Res., Prettyboy Res., Gunpowder River, Conowingo Lake, Susquehanna River, Chesapeake Bay, Tidal Rivers
Services & Products: Guide services, fishing instruction, repair services
Guides: Yes
OK to call for current conditions: Yes
Contact: Harry L. Leister

Tochterman's
Baltimore 410-327-6942
.... 800-533-3474
Hours: 8am-9pm
Carries: Live bait, lures, flies, maps, rods, reels, licenses
Bodies of water: Liberty Lake, Atlantic Ocean, Chesapeake Bay, Loch Raven Res., Gunpowder River
Services & Products: Fishing instruction, repair services
Guides: Yes
OK to call for current conditions: Yes
Contact: Tony Tochterman, Jeff Devon

LOCH RAVEN RESERVOIR

BAIT & TACKLE...

Beck's Gunsmithing
Parkton 410-357-5767
Hours: 9am-7pm
Carries: Live bait, lures, flies, maps, rods, reels, licenses
Bodies of water: Loch Raven Res., Liberty Res., Prettyboy Res.
Services & Products: Fishing instruction, repair services
Guides: No
OK to call for current conditions: Yes
Contact: Michael or Sharon Beck

Set's Sport Shop
Baltimore 410-823-1367
Hours: 10am-9pm, closed Sun.
Carries: Live bait, lures, flies, maps, rods, reels, licenses
Bodies of water: Loch Raven Res., Prettyboy Res., Liberty Lakes, Gunpowder River, Conowingo Lake, Susquehanna River, Chesapeake Bay, Tidal Rivers
Services & Products: Guide services, fishing instruction, repair services
Guides: Yes
OK to call for current conditions: Yes
Contact: Harry L. Leister

Tochterman's
Baltimore 410-327-6942
.... 800-533-3474
Hours: 8am-9pm
Carries: Live bait, lures, flies, maps, rods, reels, licenses
Bodies of water: Loch Raven Res., Atlantic Ocean, Chesapeake Bay, Liberty Res., Gunpowder River
Services & Products: Fishing instruction, repair services
Guides: Yes
OK to call for current conditions: Yes
Contact: Tony Tochterman, Jeff Devon

YOUR SILENT FISHING PARTNER

MARYLAND

MONOCACY RIVER - POTOMAC RIVER

MONOCACY RIVER

BAIT & TACKLE...

Fox Sport, Beer, & Wine Store
Frederick 301-663-FOXS
Hours: 6am-9pm
Carries: Live bait, lures, flies, maps, rods, reels, licenses
Bodies of water: Monocacy River, Potomac River, Shenandoah River, Catoctin Mtn. trout streams, Cunningham Falls, Frank Bentz Pond
Services & Products: Food, beverages, fishing instruction, repair services, knife sharpening
Guides: Yes
OK to call for current conditions: Yes
Contact: Bill or Todd Offutt

Thurmont Sporting Goods
Thurmont 301-271-7404
Hours: 8am-6pm
Carries: Live bait, lures, flies, maps, rods, reels, licenses
Bodies of water: Monocacy River, Bilhunting Creek, Cunningham Lake,
Services & Products: Guide services
Guides: Yes
OK to call for current conditions: Yes
Contact: Richard

PATUXENT RIVER

BAIT & TACKLE...

Bunky's Charterboats
Solomons Island 410-326-3241
Hours: 6am-7pm
Carries: Live bait, lures, maps, rods, reels, licenses
Bodies of water: Patuxent River, Chesapeake Bay
Services & Products: Boat rentals, guide services, charter boat service, food, beverages, gas/oil, fishing instruction
OK to call for current conditions: Yes
Contact: Kathy Conner

H M Woodburn & Co
Solomons 410-326-3241
Hours: 6am-7pm
Carries: Live bait, lures, maps, rods, reels, licenses
Bodies of water: Patuxent River, Chesapeake Bay, Potomac River
Services & Products: Boat rentals, charter boat service, food, beverages, gas/oil, head boat

OK to call for current conditions: Yes
Contact: Kathy or Karen

POTOMAC RIVER

BAIT & TACKLE...

Adrian's Market
Germantown 301-963-7552
Hours: 5:30am-9pm, closed Sun.
Carries: Live bait, lures, flies, rods, reels, licenses
Bodies of water: Potomac River, Seneca Creek
Services & Products: Food, beverages
Guides: No
OK to call for current conditions: No

Fisherman's Edge
Baltimore 800-338-0053
Hours: 10am-5pm, closed Sun.
Carries: Lures, flies, rods, reels, licenses
Bodies of water: Potomac River, Chesapeake Bay, Susquehanna River
Services & Products: Guide services, fishing instruction
Guides: Yes
OK to call for current conditions: Yes
Contact: Joe Bruce

Fox Sport, Beer, & Wine Store
Frederick 301-663-FOXS
Hours: 6am-9pm
Carries: Live bait, lures, flies, maps, rods, reels, licenses
Bodies of water: Potomac River, Monocacy River, Shenandoah River, Catoctin Mtn. trout streams, Cunningham Falls, Frank Bentz Pond
Services & Products: Food, beverages, fishing instruction, repair services, knife sharpening
Guides: Yes
OK to call for current conditions: Yes
Contact: Bill or Todd Offutt

H M Woodburn & Co
Solomons 410-326-3241
Hours: 6am-7pm
Carries: Live bait, lures, maps, rods, reels, licenses
Bodies of water: Potomac River, Chesapeake Bay, Patuxent River
Services & Products: Boat rentals, charter boat service, food, beverages, gas/oil, head boat
OK to call for current conditions: Yes
Contact: Kathy or Karen

Laurel Fishing & Hunting Ltd.
Laurel 301-725-5527
Hours: 9am-8:30pm Mon-Thurs., 6am-8:30pm Fri.-Sat., 6am-4pm Sun.
Carries: Live bait, lures, flies, maps, rods, reels, licenses
Bodies of water: Potomac River, Chesapeake Bay, Rocky Gorge Res., Tridelphia Res.
Services & Products: Guide services, repair services
Guides: Yes
OK to call for current conditions: Yes
Contact: Larry or Steve Coburn

CHARTERS...

Capt. Andy Andrzejewski
La Plata 301-932-1509
Species & Seasons: LM Bass, Striped Bass all year
Bodies of water: Potomac River, In Virginia: Rappahanock River, Chickahominy River, Lake Anna, Lake Gaston, Buggs Island
Rates: Half day: $150(1-2), Full day: $225(1-2)
Call between: 6pm-10pm
Provides: Light tackle, lures, bait, rain gear, beverages, lunch (on request)
Handicapped equipped: Yes
Certifications: USCG, PRFC

Capt. Jims Charterboat Service
Cobb Island 800-44FISH1
Species & Seasons: Striped Bass May-Dec, Croaker, White Perch, Weakfish, May-Sept, Flounder, Spot, Bluefish June-Sept
Bodies of water: Potomac River (middle)
Rates: Half day: $270(6), $540(12), Full day: $330(6), $660(12)
Call between: Anytime
Provides: Light tackle, heavy tackle, lures, bait, rain gear
Handicapped equipped: Yes

Ken Penrod's Life Outdoors Unlimited
Beltsville 301-937-0010
Species & Seasons: LM Bass, SM Bass, Striped Bass Spring-Winter
Bodies of water: Tidal Potomac River, Upper Potomac River, Susquehanna River, Lake Anna
Rates: Half day: $150 (1-2) + gas, Full day: $250(1-2) + gas

POTOMAC RIVER - SUSQUEHANNA RIVER — MARYLAND

Call between: 6am-9pm
Provides: Light tackle, heavy tackle, fly rod/reel, lures
Handicapped equipped: Yes
Certifications: USCG

Mark Kovach Fishing Services
Silver Spring 301-588-8742
Species & Seasons: SM Bass April-Nov
Bodies of water: Potomac River
Rates: Full day: $330(1-2)
Call between: Anytime
Provides: Light tackle, fly rod/reel, lures, beverages, lunch
Handicapped equipped: Yes
Certifications: FFF Certified Fly Casting Instructor, MD Master Fishing Guide

Potomac Guide Service
Gaithersburg 301-840-9521
Species & Seasons: LM Bass March-Nov, SM Bass March-Dec, Striped Bass when in season
Bodies of water: Potomac River, Susquehanna River, Lake Erie, Canada trips
Rates: Half day: $150(1-2), Full day: $225(1-2)
Call between: 7pm-10pm
Provides: Light tackle, lures, rain gear, beverages, lunch
Handicapped equipped: Yes
Certifications: USCG

Capt. Gary Sacks
Ridge 800-984-2008
Species & Seasons: Striped Bass May-Dec, Bluefish May-Oct, Croaker, Spot, Flounder, Sea Trout June-Oct, Spanish Mackerel July-Sept, Cobia Aug-Sept
Bodies of water: Potomac River, Chesapeake Bay
Rates: Full day: $330(1-6)
Call between: 5pm-9pm
Provides: Light tackle, heavy tackle, lures, bait
Handicapped equipped: No
Certifications: USCG, MD Guide

PRETTY BOY RESERVOIR

BAIT & TACKLE...

Beck's Gunsmithing
Parkton 410-357-5767
Hours: 9am-7pm
Carries: Live bait, lures, flies, maps, rods, reels, licenses
Bodies of water: Prettyboy Res., Loch Raven Res., Liberty Res.
Services & Products: Fishing instruction, repair services
Guides: No
OK to call for current conditions: Yes
Contact: Michael or Sharon Beck

Set's Sport Shop
Baltimore 410-823-1367
Hours: 10am-9pm, closed Sun.
Carries: Live bait, lures, flies, maps, rods, reels, licenses
Bodies of water: Prettyboy Res., Loch Raven Res., Liberty Lake, Gunpowder River, Conowingo Lake, Susquehanna River, Chesapeake Bay, Tidal Rivers
Services & Products: Guide services, fishing instruction, repair services
Guides: Yes
OK to call for current conditions: Yes
Contact: Harry L. Leister

ROCKY GORGE RESERVOIR

BAIT & TACKLE...

Laurel Fishing & Hunting Ltd.
Laurel 301-725-5527
Hours: 9am-8:30pm Mon-Thurs., 6am-8:30pm Fri.-Sat., 6am-4pm Sun.
Carries: Live bait, lures, flies, maps, rods, reels, licenses
Bodies of water: Rocky Gorge Res., Potomac River, Chesapeake Bay, Tridelphia Res.
Services & Products: Guide services, repair services
Guides: Yes
OK to call for current conditions: Yes
Contact: Larry or Steve Coburn

SAVAGE RIVER RESERVOIR

BAIT & TACKLE...

Swanton Grocery Gas & Liquor
Swanton 301-387-5701
Hours: 6am-9pm
Carries: Live bait, lures, rods, reels, licenses
Bodies of water: Savage River Res., Deep Creek Lake, Jennings Randolph Lake
Services & Products: Food, beverages, gas/oil
Guides: Yes
OK to call for current conditions: Yes
Contact: Robert McBee

SUSQUEHANNA RIVER

BAIT & TACKLE...

Fisherman's Edge
Baltimore 800-338-0053
Hours: 10am-5pm, closed Sun.
Carries: Lures, flies, rods, reels, licenses
Bodies of water: Susquehanna River, Chesapeake Bay, Potomac River
Services & Products: Guide services, fishing instruction
Guides: Yes
OK to call for current conditions: Yes
Contact: Joe Bruce

Herb's Tackle Shop
North East 410-287-5490
Hours: 6am-6pm
Carries: Live bait, lures, flies, maps, rods, reels, licenses
Bodies of water: Susquehanna River, North East River, Elk River, Chesapeake Bay
Services & Products: Guide services, charter boat service, fishing instruction, repair services
OK to call for current conditions: Yes
Contact: Herb, Mike or Eleanore

Set's Sport Shop
Baltimore 410-823-1367
Hours: 10am-9pm, closed Sun.
Carries: Live bait, lures, flies, maps, rods, reels, licenses
Bodies of water: Susquehanna River, Loch Raven Res., Prettyboy Res., Liberty Lake, Gunpowder River, Conowingo Lake, Chesapeake Bay, Tidal Rivers
Services & Products: Guide services, fishing instruction, repair services
Guides: Yes
OK to call for current conditions: Yes
Contact: Harry L. Leister

MARYLAND
SUSQUEHANNA RIVER - TRIDELPHIA RESERVOIR

GUIDES...

Ken Penrod's Life Outdoors Unlimited
Beltsville 301-937-0010
Species & Seasons: LM Bass, SM Bass, Striped Bass Spring-Winter
Bodies of water: Susquehanna River, Tidal Potomac River, Upper Potomac River, Lake Anna
Rates: Half day: $150 (1-2) + gas, Full day: $250(1-2) + gas
Call between: 6am-9pm
Provides: Light tackle, heavy tackle, fly rod/reel, lures
Handicapped equipped: Yes
Certifications: USCG

Potomac Guide Service
Gaithersburg 301-840-9521
Species & Seasons: LM Bass March-Nov, SM Bass March-Dec, Striped Bass when in season
Bodies of water: Susquehanna River, Potomac River, Lake Erie, Canada trips
Rates: Half day: $150(1-2), Full day: $225(1-2)
Call between: 7pm-10pm
Provides: Light tackle, lures, rain gear, beverages, lunch
Handicapped equipped: Yes
Certifications: USCG

TRIDELPHIA RESERVOIR

BAIT & TACKLE...

Laurel Fishing & Hunting Ltd
Laurel 301-725-5527
Hours: 9am-8:30pm Mon-Thurs., 6am-8:30pm Fri.-Sat., 6am-4pm Sun.
Carries: Live bait, lures, flies, maps, rods, reels, licenses
Bodies of water: Tridelphia Res., Potomac River, Chesapeake Bay, Rocky Gorge Res.
Services & Products: Guide services, repair services
Guides: Yes
OK to call for current conditions: Yes
Contact: Larry or Steve Coburn

MASSACHUSETTS

1. Atlantic Ocean
2. Boston Harbor
3. Buzzards Bay
4. Cape Cod Bay
5. Cape Cod Lakes & Rivers
6. Concord River
7. Goose Pond
8. Lake Buell
9. Lake Lashaway
10. Massachusetts Bay
11. Merrimack River
12. Mystic River
13. Nantucket Sound
14. Onota Lake
15. Parker River
16. Quabbin Reservoir
17. Quincy Bay
18. Rhode Island Sound
19. Saugus River
20. Vineyard Sound
21. Wachusett Reservoir
22. Walden Pond
23. Whitings Pond
24. Whitmans Pond

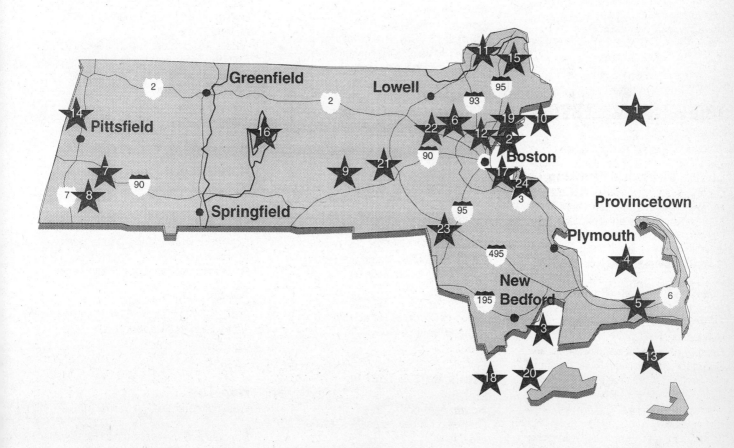

MASSACHUSETTS
ATLANTIC OCEAN

ATLANTIC OCEAN

BAIT & TACKLE...

Blackbeard Bait & Tackle
Eastham 508-240-3369
Hours: 7am-9pm
Carries: Live bait, lures, flies, maps, rods, reels
Bodies of water: Atlantic Ocean, Cape Cod Bay and many lakes and ponds
Services & Products: Fishing instruction, repair services, rod rentals
Guides: Yes
OK to call for current conditions: Yes
Contact: Bob

Bob's Bait Shack
Winthrop 617-846-5896
Hours: 8am-7pm Mon.-Fri., 7am-4pm Sat., Sun.
Carries: Live bait, lures, flies, rods, reels
Bodies of water: Massachusetts Bay, Atlantic Ocean
Services & Products: Beverages, repair services
Guides: Yes
OK to call for current conditions: Yes
Contact: Bob

Larry's Tackle Shop
Edgartown 508-627-5088
Hours: 7am-9pm
Carries: Live bait, lures, flies, maps, rods, reels
Bodies of water: Atlantic Ocean
Services & Products: Guide services, charter boat service, food, beverages, fishing instruction, repair services
Guides: Yes
OK to call for current conditions: Yes

Little John's Bait & Tackle
Saugus 617-233-9696
Hours: 7am-9pm weekdays, 5am-9pm weekends
Carries: Live bait, lures, rods, reels, licenses
Bodies of water: Saugus River, Atlantic Ocean, Mystic River, Point of Pines River, Prankers Pond, Sluice Pond, Browns Pond, Horn Pond, Golden Hills Ponds, Ipswich River
Services & Products: Boat ramp, fishing instruction, repair services, custom rods
Guides: Yes
OK to call for current conditions: Yes
Contact: Lit'l John

Mike's Bait & Tackle Box
Sandwich 508-888-6244
Hours: 24 hours, 7 days a week
Carries: Live bait, lures, flies, maps, rods, reels, licenses
Bodies of water: Wakeby Pond, Peters Pond, Spectacle Pond, Atlantic Ocean
Guides: No
OK to call for current conditions: Yes
Contact: Phillip Brennan

Ric's Bait & Tackle
Leominster 508-537-0065
Hours: 6am-7pm Mon.-Fri., 4:30am-7pm Sat., Sun.
Carries: Live bait, lures, flies, maps, rods, reels
Bodies of water: Atlantic Ocean, Wachusett Res., Quabbin Res., many more
Services & Products: Beverages, fishing instruction, repair services
Guides: Yes
OK to call for current conditions: Yes

Sea Store
Woods Hole 508-548-9108
Hours: 8am-5pm
Carries: Live bait, lures, flies, rods, reels
Bodies of water: Nantucket Sound, Vineyard Sound, Buzzards Bay, Block Island Sound, Atlantic Ocean
Services & Products: Guide services, charter boat service, fishing instruction
OK to call for current conditions: Yes
Contact: Ed Levy or J.C. Burke

Surfland Bait & Tackle
Newburyport 508-462-4202
Hours: 6am-9pm
Carries: Live bait, lures, flies, maps, rods, reels
Bodies of water: Merrimack River, Parker River, Atlantic Ocean, Plum Island River
Guides: Yes
OK to call for current conditions: Yes
Contact: Kay Moulton

Tim's Bait & Tackle
Plymouth.......................... 508-224-2009
Hours: 6am-6pm
Carries: Live bait, lures, flies, maps, rods, reels
Bodies of water: Cape Cod Bay, Cape Cod Canal, Atlantic Ocean, over 300 ponds
Services & Products: Boat rentals, repair services
Guides: Yes
OK to call for current conditions: Yes

CHARTERS...

Amethyst II
Falmouth.......................... 508-540-9651
Species & Seasons: Striped Bass, Bluefish, Porgy, Tautog May-Nov, White Marlin July-Sept, Tuna July-Oct
Bodies of water: Nantucket Sound, Atlantic Ocean
Rates: Half day: $350, Full day: $475 (prices per 6 people max.), Marlin/Tuna: $850, Overnite canyon: $1750
Call between: 8am-8pm
Provides: Light tackle, heavy tackle, fly rod/reel, lures, bait, rain gear
Handicapped equipped: Yes
Certifications: USCG

Banshee
West Chatham 508-945-0403
Species & Seasons: Striped Bass, Bluefish May-Nov
Bodies of water: Nantucket Sound, Atlantic Ocean
Rates: 1995 rates: Full day: $475(1-6)
Call between: 5pm-9pm
Provides: Light tackle, heavy tackle, lures
Handicapped equipped: No
Certifications: USCG

Day Fishing Charters Unlimited
Boston 617-328-9224
.... 800-964-9224
Species & Seasons: Bluefish, Cod, Tuna June-Sept
Bodies of water: Cape Cod to Boston, Atlantic Ocean
Rates: Private yachts 1-6 people from $200 for 4 hrs.
Call between: 9am-5pm
Provides: Light tackle, heavy tackle, bait
Handicapped equipped: No
Certifications: USCG

Hop-Tuit
West Falmouth 508-540-7642
.... 564-8086
Species & Seasons: Striped Bass, Bluefish May-Nov, Bonito, False Albacore, Spanish Mackerel Aug-Oct, Tuna, Marlin July-Oct

ATLANTIC OCEAN - BOSTON HARBOR   MASSACHUSETTS

Bodies of water: Buzzards Bay, Nantucket Sound, Vineyard Sound, Atlantic Ocean
Rates: 4 hrs.: $285(1-4), 6 hrs.: $400(1-4), Offshore: $600
Call between: 6pm-9pm
Provides: Light tackle, fly rod/reel, lures, rain gear
Handicapped equipped: Yes
Certifications: USCG

Luau
North Eastham 508-255-4527
Species & Seasons: Striped Bass, Cod May-Oct, Bluefish June-Oct, Flounder, Mackerel May-June
Bodies of water: Cape Cod Bay, Massachusetts Bay, Nantucket Sound, Atlantic Ocean
Rates: Hafl day: $326(1-6), Full day: $450(1-6)
Call between: 6pm-10pm
Provides: Light tackle, heavy tackle, lures, bait
Handicapped equipped: Yes
Certifications: USCG

Priscilla J
Nantucket 508-228-4225
Species & Seasons: Striped Bass, Bluefish May-Nov
Bodies of water: Atlantic Ocean, Nantucket Sound
Rates: Boat #1: $400/tide(1-6), Boat #2 Flats Boat: $275/tide (1-2 Flyfishing only)
Provides: Light tackle, fly rod/reel, lures
Handicapped equipped: Yes
Certifications: USCG, Loomis, Sage Guide

Reel Treat Charters
Tewksbury 508-851-9622
Species & Seasons: Cod, Mackerel May-Oct, Striped Bass, Bluefish June-Oct, Shark June-Sept
Bodies of water: Merrimack River, Atlantic Ocean
Rates: Half day: $330, Full day: $420, (prices per 6 people max.), Evenings: $210
Call between: 6am-10pm
Provides: Light tackle, heavy tackle, lures, bait
Handicapped equipped: No
Certifications: NCCA member NACCO member, USCG

Shady Lady II
Provincetown 508-487-0182
Species & Seasons: Bluefish, Striped Bass June-Sept, Bluefin Tuna July-Sept
Bodies of water: Cape Cod Bay, Atlantic Ocean
Rates: Half day: $350(1-6), Full day: $600(1-6)
Call between: 8am-9pm
Provides: Light tackle, heavy tackle, lures
Handicapped equipped: Yes
Certifications: USCG

South Shore Sport Fishing
Norwell 617-878-6731
Species & Seasons: Striped Bass, Bluefish, Mako Shark, Blue Shark, July-Sept
Bodies of water: Cape Cod Bay, Stellwagen Bank, Atlantic Ocean
Rates: Call for current rates
Call between: 8am-9pm
Provides: Light tackle, heavy tackle, fly rod/reel, lures, bait
Handicapped equipped: No
Certifications: USCG

Ralph Pratt
Canton 617-828-7797
Species & Seasons: Cod Mar-June
Bodies of water: Stellwagen Bank
Rates: $750(6)
Call between: 8am-10pm
Provides: Heavy tackle, bait
Handicapped equipped: No
Certifications: USCG

FLY SHOPS...

Bear's Den
Taunton 508-880-6226
Hours: Noon-7pm, closed Sun.
Carries: Flies, rods, reels
Bodies of water: Atlantic Ocean, Cape Cod Bay, local rivers and ponds
Services & Products: Guide services, fishing instruction
Guides: Yes
OK to call for current conditions: Yes
Contact: Bob

BOSTON HARBOR

BAIT & TACKLE...

Neponset Circle Fishing & Dart
Dorchester 617-436-9231
Hours: Open 7 days a week
Carries: Live bait, lures, flies, maps, rods, reels, licenses
Bodies of water: Boston Harbor, Jamaica Pond, Houghtons Pond, Charles River, Whitmans Pond, Porkapaog Pond
Services & Products: Fishing instruction, repair services
Guides: Yes
OK to call for current conditions: Yes
Contact: Darrell or Ralph

CHARTERS...

Applejack Charters
Scituate 617-545-9643
Species & Seasons: Cod May-Oct, Mackerel May-July, Bluefish, Striped Bass June-Oct
Bodies of water: Massachusetts Bay, Cape Cod Bay, Boston Harbor
Rates: Half day: $150(1-2), $165(3), $180(4), Full day: $250(1-2), $275(3), $300(4)
Call between: 7am-8pm
Provides: Light tackle, heavy tackle, lures, bait
Handicapped equipped: No
Certifications: USCG

Selma K Charters
Quincy 617-479-6465
Species & Seasons: Cod, Ground Fish April-July/Sept-Nov, Bluefish, Striped Bass July-Oct
Bodies of water: Boston Harbor, Massachusetts Bay, Cape Cod Bay
Rates: Half day: $225(5), Full day: $425(5)
Call between: Anytime
Provides: Heavy tackle, lures, bait
Handicapped equipped: No
Certifications: USCG

MASSACHUSETTS — BOSTON HARBOR - CAPE COD BAY

Roger Brousseau
Weymouth 617-335-3298
Species & Seasons: Cod April-June, Flounder May-June, Striped Bass, Shark June-Oct, Bluefish June-Nov
Bodies of water: Quincy Bay, Boston Harbor, Stellwagen Bank, Cape Cod Bay
Rates: Half day: $200(2), Full day: $300(2), 2 boats - 2-6 people
Call between: Anytime
Provides: Light tackle, heavy tackle, fly rod/reel, lures, bait, rain gear, beverages, lunch
Handicapped equipped: Yes
Certifications: USCG

BUZZARDS BAY

BAIT & TACKLE...

Sea Store
Woods Hole 508-548-9108
Hours: 8am-5pm
Carries: Live bait, lures, flies, rods, reels
Bodies of water: Nantucket Sound, Vineyard Sound, Buzzards Bay, Block Island Sound, Atlantic Ocean
Services & Products: Guide services, charter boat service, fishing instruction
OK to call for current conditions: Yes
Contact: Ed Levy or J.C. Burke

CHARTERS...

Frosty V
Rockland 617-878-6882
Species & Seasons: Bluefish, Striped Bass July-Sept, Cod May-June, Flounder May-Sept
Bodies of water: Cape Cod Bay, Buzzards Bay, Nantucket Sound
Rates: Half day: $190(6), Full day: $370(6)
Call between: 6pm-9pm
Provides: Heavy tackle, lures, bait
Handicapped equipped: No
Certifications: USCG

Hop-Tuit
West Falmouth 508-540-7642
.... 564-8086
Species & Seasons: Striped Bass, Bluefish May-Nov, Bonito, False Albacore, Spanish Mackerel Aug-Oct, Tuna, Marlin July-Oct
Bodies of water: Buzzards Bay, Nantucket Sound, Vineyard Sound, Atlantic Ocean

Rates: 4 hrs.: $285(1-4), 6 hrs.: $400(1-4), Offshore: $600
Call between: 6pm-9pm
Provides: Light tackle, fly rod/reel, lures, rain gear
Handicapped equipped: Yes
Certifications: USCG

Last Call
New Bedford 508-999-4999
.... 800-233-FISH
Species & Seasons: Striped Bass, Bluefish May-Oct, Tautog May-Nov, Porgy June-Oct, Fluke July-Aug
Bodies of water: Buzzards Bay, Vineyard Sound, Cuttyhunk Island
Rates: Half day: $200(4), Full day: $350(4)
Call between: 6am-10pm
Provides: Light tackle, heavy tackle, lures, bait
Certifications: USCG

Laughing Gull
Westport 508-636-2730
Species & Seasons: Bluefish, Striped Bass May-Oct, Tautog Sept-Oct, Flounder June-Sept
Bodies of water: Westport River, Buzzards Bay, Vineyard Sound, Rhode Island Sound
Rates: Half day: $175(1-4), Full day: $275(1-4)
Call between:
Provides: Light tackle, heavy tackle, lures, bait
Handicapped equipped: Yes, limited
Certifications: USCG

Patriot Party Boats
Falmouth 800-734-0088
Species & Seasons: Striped Bass, May-Nov, Bluefish, Porgy, Tautog, Sea Bass, Fluke May-Oct
Bodies of water: Vineyard Sound, Nantucket Sound, Buzzards Bay
Rates: Half day: $20(1), Full day: $30(1)
Call between: 9am-5pm
Provides: Heavy tackle, lures, bait
Handicapped equipped: Yes
Certifications: USCG

Rip Dancer
Attleboro 508-226-2462
Species & Seasons: Striped Bass June-Nov, Bluefish July-Nov
Bodies of water: Buzzards Bay, Rhode Island Sound
Rates: Half day: $300(6), Full day: $500(6)
Call between: 6pm-10pm

Provides: Light tackle, fly rod/reel, lures, bait
Handicapped equipped: I'll try to help anyway I can
Certifications: USCG

Capt. Barry Summer
South Plymouth 508-759-6597
Species & Seasons: Striped Bass May-June/Aug-Sept, Bluefish June-Sept, Yellowfin Tuna, Bluefin Tuna July-Sept, Porgy May-July/Sept-Oct, Tautog May-Oct
Bodies of water: Cape Cod Bay, Buzzards Bay, Nantucket Sound, Vineyard Sound
Rates: Varies
Call between: 8am-8pm
Provides: Light tackle, heavy tackle, lures, bait, rain gear, beverages, lunch
Handicapped equipped: No
Certifications: USCG

CAPE COD BAY

BAIT & TACKLE...

Blackbeard Bait & Tackle
Eastham 508-240-3369
Hours: 7am-9pm
Carries: Live bait, lures, flies, maps, rods, reels
Bodies of water: Atlantic Ocean, Cape Cod Bay, many lakes and ponds
Services & Products: Fishing instruction, repair services, rod rentals
Guides: Yes
OK to call for current conditions: Yes
Contact: Bob

Tim's Bait & Tackle
Plymouth 508-224-2009
Hours: 6am-6pm
Carries: Live bait, lures, flies, maps, rods, reels
Bodies of water: Cape Cod Bay, Cape Cod Canal, Atlantic Ocean, over 300 ponds
Services & Products: Boat rentals, repair services
Guides: Yes
OK to call for current conditions: Yes

CAPE COD BAY — MASSACHUSETTS

CHARTERS...

Applejack Charters
Scituate 617-545-9643
Species & Seasons: Cod May-Oct, Mackerel May-July, Bluefish, Striped Bass June-Oct
Bodies of water: Massachusetts Bay, Cape Cod Bay, Boston Harbor
Rates: Half day: $150(1-2), $165(3), $180(4),
Full day: $250(1-2), $275(3), $300(4)
Call between: 7am-8pm
Provides: Light tackle, heavy tackle, lures, bait
Handicapped equipped: No
Certifications: USCG

Banjo Charters
Oak Bluffs 508-693-3154
Species & Seasons: Striped Bass, Bluefish May-Nov, Bonito, Yellowfin Tuna July-Nov, Mako Shark, Blue Shark, Fluke June-Oct
Bodies of water: Vineyard Sound, Nantucket Sound, Cape Cod Bay, Atlantic waters south and east of Martha's Vineyard
Rates: Half day: $400(1-6),
Full day: $800(1-6)
Call between: Anytime
Provides: Light tackle, heavy tackle, fly rod/reel, lures, bait, rain gear
Handicapped equipped: Yes

Barracuda
Newburyport 508-465-8483
Species & Seasons: Striped Bass June-Oct, Bluefish July-Oct, Bluefin Tuna July-Sept, Cod, Haddock June-Sept, Mackerel June-July
Bodies of water: Gulf of Maine, Cape Cod Bay, Merrimack River
Rates: Half day: $265(6), Full day: $450(6), Night fishing (7-10:30pm): $215
Call between: 7am-8pm
Provides: Light tackle, heavy tackle, lures, bait
Handicapped equipped: No
Certifications: USCG

Bigfish II Sportfishing Charters
Green Harbor 617-834-7504
Species & Seasons: Bluefin Tuna July-Oct, Striped Bass, Bluefish June-Oct, Cod, Halibut, Pollock, Wolffish, Haddock, Monkfish Mar-Nov, Shark July-Oct
Bodies of water: Stellwagen Bank, Cape Cod Bay, Massachusetts Bay
Rates: Varies
Provides: Light tackle, heavy tackle, fly rod/reel, lures, bait
Handicapped equipped: Yes
Certifications: USCG

Bluefish
Dennis 508-385-7265
Species & Seasons: Bluefish, Striped Bass, Flounder, Mackerel
Bodies of water: Cape Cod Bay
Rates: 4 hrs.: $260, 6 hrs.: $310, 8 hrs.: $360, 6 person max.
Call between: 5pm-8pm
Provides: Light tackle, heavy tackle, lures, rain gear
Handicapped equipped: Yes

Capt. John Boats, Inc.
Plymouth 508-746-2643
.... 800-242-2469
Species & Seasons: Cod, Wolffish, Pollock, Haddock April-Dec, Flounder May-Sept, Mackerel seasonal
Bodies of water: Cape Cod Bay, Massachusetts Bay, Stellwagen Bank, Cashes Ledge
Rates: Half day: $16.50(1),
Full day: $27(1)
Call between: 8am-6pm
Provides: Light tackle & heavy tackle(rental), bait(free), beverages, lunch
Handicapped equipped: Yes
Certifications: USCG

Roger Brousseau
Weymouth 617-335-3298
Species & Seasons: Cod April-June, Flounder May-June, Striped Bass, Shark June-Oct, Bluefish June-Nov
Bodies of water: Quincy Bay, Boston Harbor, Stellwagen Bank, Cape Cod Bay
Rates: Half day: $200(2),
Full day: $300(2), 2 boats 2-6 people
Call between: Anytime
Provides: Light tackle, heavy tackle, fly rod/reel, lures, bait, rain gear, beverages, lunch
Handicapped equipped: Yes
Certifications: USCG

Day Fishing Charters Unlimited
Boston 617-328-9224
.... 800-964-9224
Species & Seasons: Bluefish, Cod, Tuna June-Sept
Bodies of water: Cape Cod to Boston, Atlantic Ocean
Rates: Private yachts 1-6 people from $200 for 4 hrs.
Call between: 9am-5pm
Provides: Light tackle, heavy tackle, bait
Handicapped equipped: No
Certifications: USCG

Frosty V
Rockland 617-878-6882
Species & Seasons: Bluefish, Striped Bass July-Sept, Cod May-June, Flounder May-Sept
Bodies of water: Cape Cod Bay, Buzzards Bay, Nantucket Sound
Rates: Half day: $190(6),
Full day: $370(6)
Call between: 6pm-9pm
Provides: Heavy tackle, lures, bait
Handicapped equipped: No
Certifications: USCG

Jazz Sport Fishing
Duxbury 617-934-5040
Species & Seasons: Striped Bass, Bluefish May-Oct, Cod, Pollock, Haddock, Wolffish April-Oct
Bodies of water: Cape Cod Bay, Duxbury, Kingston & Plymouth Harbors
Rates: Full day: $300(2), $400(3)
Call between: 4pm-9pm
Provides: Light tackle, fly rod/reel, lures, bait
Handicapped equipped: No
Certifications: USCG

Lady J
Wareham 508-295-8552
Species & Seasons: Flounder, Mackerel, Tautog, Cod, May-June, Striped Bass May-Oct, Bluefish June-Oct
Bodies of water: Cape Cod Bay
Rates: Half day(4 hrs.): $290(1-6),
Full day (8hrs.): $400(1-6)
Call between: 6-12am/1-10pm
Provides: Light tackle, heavy tackle, lures, bait
Handicapped equipped: Yes

MASSACHUSETTS
CAPE COD BAY - CONCORD RIVER

Luau
North Eastham 508-255-4527
Species & Seasons: Striped Bass, Cod May-Oct, Bluefish June-Oct, Flounder, Mackerel May-June
Bodies of water: Cape Cod Bay, Massachusetts Bay, Nantucket Sound, Atlantic Ocean
Rates: Hafl day: $326(1-6), Full day: $450(1-6)
Call between: 6pm-10pm
Provides: Light tackle, heavy tackle, lures, bait
Handicapped equipped: Yes
Certifications: USCG

Selma K Charters
Quincy 617-479-6465
Species & Seasons: Cod, Ground Fish April-July/Sept-Nov, Bluefish, Striped Bass July-Oct
Bodies of water: Boston Harbor, Massachusetts Bay, Cape Cod Bay
Rates: Half day: $225(5), Full day: $425(5)
Call between: Anytime
Provides: Heavy tackle, lures, bait
Handicapped equipped: No
Certifications: USCG

Shady Lady II
Provincetown 508-487-0182
Species & Seasons: Bluefish, Striped Bass June-Sept, Bluefin Tuna July-Sept
Bodies of water: Cape Cod Bay, Atlantic Ocean
Rates: Half day: $350(1-6), Full day: $600(1-6)
Call between: 8am-9pm
Provides: Light tackle, heavy tackle, lures
Handicapped equipped: Yes
Certifications: USCG

South Shore Sport Fishing
Norwell 617-878-6731
Species & Seasons: Striped Bass, Bluefish, Mako Shark, Blue Shark July-Sept
Bodies of water: Cape Cod Bay, Stellwagen Bank, Atlantic Ocean
Rates: Call for current rates
Call between: 8am-9pm
Provides: Light tackle, heavy tackle, fly rod/reel, lures, bait
Handicapped equipped: No
Certifications: USCG

Capt. Barry Summer
South Plymouth 508-759-6597
Species & Seasons: Striped Bass May-June/Aug-Sept, Bluefish June-Sept, Yellowfin Tuna, Bluefin Tuna July-Sept, Porgy May-July/Sept-Oct, Tautog May-Oct
Bodies of water: Cape Cod Bay, Buzzards Bay, Nantucket Sound, Vineyard Sound
Rates: Varies
Call between: 8am-8pm
Provides: Light tackle, heavy tackle, lures, bait, rain gear, beverages, lunch
Handicapped equipped: No
Certifications: USCG

FLY SHOPS...

Bear's Den
Taunton 508-880-6226
Hours: Noon-7pm, closed Sun.
Carries: Flies, rods, reels
Bodies of water: Atlantic Ocean, Cape Cod Bay, local rivers and ponds
Services & Products: Guide services, fishing instruction
Guides: Yes
OK to call for current conditions: Yes
Contact: Bob

CAPE COD LAKES & RIVERS

BAIT & TACKLE...

Mike's Bait & Tackle Box
Sandwich 508-888-6244
Hours: 24 hours, 7 days a week
Carries: Live bait, lures, flies, maps, rods, reels, licenses
Bodies of water: Wakeby Pond, Peters Pond, Spectacle Pond, Atlantic Ocean
Guides: No
OK to call for current conditions: Yes
Contact: Phillip Brennan

Sports Port
Hyannis 508-775-3096
Hours: 7am-7pm
Carries: Live bait, lures, flies, maps, rods, reels, licenses
Bodies of water: Cape Cod, Seashore - over 365 lakes
Services & Products: Guide services, charter boat service, fishing instruction, repair services
Guides: Yes
OK to call for current conditions: Yes
Contact: Karen

Tim's Bait & Tackle
Plymouth 508-224-2009
Hours: 6am-6pm
Carries: Live bait, lures, flies, maps, rods, reels
Bodies of water: Cape Cod Bay, Cape Cod Canal, Atlantic Ocean, over 300 ponds
Services & Products: Boat rentals, repair services
Guides: Yes
OK to call for current conditions: Yes

GUIDES...

Al's Fishing Guide Service
Worcester 508-797-5700
.... 800-588-5700
Species & Seasons: Landlocked Salmon April-May, Striped Bass May-Oct, Chinook Salmon, Coho Salmon Sept-Nov, Steelhead Sept-April, Brown Trout Sept-Dec
Bodies of water: Wachusett Res., Quabbin Res., Cape Cod Canal, Race Point, Salmon River (NY), Oswego River (NY)
Rates: Half day: $100(1), $200(2), Full day: $150(1), $300(2) prices vary
Call between: 5pm-10pm
Provides: Light tackle, heavy tackle, fly rod/reel, lures, bait
Handicapped equipped: Yes
Certifications: NY Licensed Guide, Certified Master Fisherman Mass.

CONCORD RIVER

BAIT & TACKLE...

Andy's Bait & Tackle Shop
Acton 508-897-0717
Hours:
Carries: Live bait, lures, flies, maps, rods, reels, licenses
Bodies of water: Assabet River, Concord River, Sudbury River, Walden Pond, White Pond
Services & Products: Repair services
Guides: Yes
OK to call for current conditions: Yes

GOOSE POND

BAIT & TACKLE...

Norm's Bait & Tackle
Great Barrington 413-528-6628
Hours: 7am-7pm
Carries: Live bait, lures, flies, rods, reels
Bodies of water: Green River, Lake Buell, Laurel Lake, Goose Pond, Stockbridge Bowl, and many more
Services & Products: Guide services, charter boat service, fishing instruction
OK to call for current conditions: Yes
Contact: Norm Sr.

MARINAS...

Onota Boat Livery
Pittsfield 413-442-1724
Hours: 7am-7pm
Carries: Live bait, lures, flies, maps, rods, reels, licenses
Bodies of water: Onota Lake, Pontoosuc Lake, Goose Pond, Lake Buell, Laurel Lake
Services & Products: Boat rentals, boat ramp, food, beverages, gas/oil, fishing instruction, repair services, boat sales
Guides: Yes
OK to call for current conditions: Yes
Contact: Tom Dailey

LAKE BUELL

BAIT & TACKLE...

Norm's Bait & Tackle
Great Barrington 413-528-6628
Hours: 7am-7pm
Carries: Live bait, lures, flies, rods, reels
Bodies of water: Green River, Lake Buell, Laurel Lake, Goose Pond, Stockbridge Bowl, and many more
Services & Products: Guide services, charter boat service, fishing instruction
OK to call for current conditions: Yes
Contact: Norm Sr.

MARINAS...

Onota Boat Livery
Pittsfield 413-442-1724
Hours: 7am-7pm
Carries: Live bait, lures, flies, maps, rods, reels, licenses
Bodies of water: Onota Lake, Pontoosuc Lake, Goose Pond, Lake Buell, Laurel Lake
Services & Products: Boat rentals, boat ramp, food, beverages, gas/oil, fishing instruction, repair services, boat sales
Guides: Yes
OK to call for current conditions: Yes
Contact: Tom Dailey

LAKE LASHAWAY

BAIT & TACKLE...

Northern Pike Trading Post
Brookfield 508-867-6264
Hours: 5:30am-9pm
Carries: Live bait, lures, flies, rods, reels
Bodies of water: South Pond, North Pond, Quaboag River, Lake Lashaway, Wickaboag Pond
Services & Products: Boat rentals, guide services, food, beverages
OK to call for current conditions: Yes
Contact: Stan Nelson

LODGES...

Copper Lantern Motor Lodge
W. Brookfield 508-867-6441
Guest Capacity: 84, some efficiencies
Handicapped equipped: No
Seasons: All year
Rates: $35-$52/day
Contact: Dan, Judy, or Millie
Guides: No
Species & Seasons: Lake Trout, LM Bass, SM Bass, Salmon, Brook Trout, Bullhead April-Oct, Northern Pike all year
Bodies of Water: Quabbin Res., Quaboag River, Quaboag Pond, Wickaboag Pond, South Pond, Lake Lashaway
Types of fishing: Fly fishing, light tackle, wading, float trips
Available: Licenses, bait, tackle, boat rentals near by

MASSACHUSETTS BAY

BAIT & TACKLE...

Bob's Bait Shack
Winthrop 617-846-5896
Hours: 8am-7pm Mon.-Fri., 7am-4pm Sat., Sun.
Carries: Live bait, lures, flies, rods, reels
Bodies of water: Massachusetts Bay, Atlantic Ocean
Services & Products: Beverages, repair services
Guides: Yes
OK to call for current conditions: Yes
Contact: Bob

CHARTERS...

Applejack Charters
Scituate 617-545-9643
Species & Seasons: Cod May-Oct, Mackerel May-July, Bluefish, Striped Bass June-Oct
Bodies of water: Massachusetts Bay, Cape Cod Bay, Boston Harbor
Rates: Half day: $150(1-2), $165(3), $180(4), Full day: $250(1-2), $275(3), $300(4)
Call between: 7am-8pm
Provides: Light tackle, heavy tackle, lures, bait
Handicapped equipped: No
Certifications: USCG

Bigfish II Sportfishing Charters
Green Harbor 617-834-7504
Species & Seasons: Bluefin Tuna July-Oct, Striped Bass, Bluefish June-Oct, Cod, Halibut, Pollock, Wolffish, Haddock, Monkfish Mar-Nov, Shark July-Oct
Bodies of water: Stellwagen Bank, Cape Cod Bay, Massachusetts Bay
Rates: Varies
Call between:
Provides: Light tackle, heavy tackle, fly rod/reel, lures, bait
Handicapped equipped: Yes
Certifications: USCG

MASSACHUSETTS

MASSACHUSETTS BAY - MYSTIC RIVER

Capt. John Boats, Inc.
Plymouth..................... 508-746-2643
.... 800-242-2469
Species & Seasons: Cod, Wolffish, Pollock, Haddock April-Dec, Flounder May-Sept, Mackerel seasonal
Bodies of water: Cape Cod Bay, Massachusetts Bay, Stellwagen Bank, Cashes Ledge
Rates: Half day: $16.50(1),
Full day: $27(1)
Call between: 8am-6pm
Provides: Light tackle & heavy tackle(rental), bait(free), beverages, lunch
Handicapped equipped: Yes
Certifications: USCG

Luau
North Eastham 508-255-4527
Species & Seasons: Striped Bass, Cod May-Oct, Bluefish June-Oct, Flounder, Mackerel May-June
Bodies of water: Cape Cod Bay, Massachusetts Bay, Nantucket Sound, Atlantic Ocean
Rates: Hafl day: $326(1-6),
Full day: $450(1-6)
Call between: 6pm-10pm
Provides: Light tackle, heavy tackle, lures, bait
Handicapped equipped: Yes
Certifications: USCG

Rainbow Chaser
Dracut 508-957-5865
Species & Seasons: Cod, Haddock, Pollock, Wolffish April-Oct, Mackerel, Flounder, Tautog, Striped Bass May-Oct, Bluefish June-Oct, Shark, Tuna, Bluefin Tuna, Tuna when open
Bodies of water: Gulf of Maine, Massachusetts Bay
Rates: Half day: $295, Full day: $495, prices per 6 people maximum, Big Game: $695 (10 hr. trip)
Call between: 7am-10pm
Provides: Light tackle, heavy tackle, lures, bait
Handicapped equipped: Yes
Certifications: USCG, IGFA

Selma K Charters
Quincy 617-479-6465
Species & Seasons: Cod, Ground Fish April-July/Sept-Nov, Bluefish, Striped Bass July-Oct
Bodies of water: Boston Harbor, Massachusetts Bay, Cape Cod Bay
Rates: Half day: $225(5),
Full day: $425(5)
Call between: Anytime
Provides: Heavy tackle, lures, bait
Handicapped equipped: No
Certifications: USCG

The Fox
Marblehead 617-631-1879
Species & Seasons: Striped Bass May-Oct, Bluefish June-Sept
Bodies of water: Massachusetts Bay, Cape Ann to Boston
Rates: Half day: $250(1-2),
Full day: $375(1-2), Early morning/Late evening 3 hrs. $180(1)
Call between: Anytime
Provides: Light tackle, fly rod/reel, lures, bait, beverages, lunch
Handicapped equipped: No
Certifications: FFF Cert. Casting Instructor, ORVIS, USCG

MERRIMACK RIVER

BAIT & TACKLE...

Surfland Bait & Tackle
Newburyport 508-462-4202
Hours: 6am-9pm
Carries: Live bait, lures, flies, maps, rods, reels
Bodies of water: Merrimack River, Parker River, Atlantic Ocean, Plum Island River
Guides: Yes
OK to call for current conditions: Yes
Contact: Kay Moulton

CHARTERS...

Barracuda
Newburyport 508-465-8483
Species & Seasons: Striped Bass June-Oct, Bluefish July-Oct, Bluefin Tuna July-Sept, Cod, Haddock June-Sept, Mackerel June-July
Bodies of water: Gulf of Maine, Cape Cod Bay, Merrimack River
Rates: Half day: $265(6),
Full day: $450(6),
Night fishing (7-10:30pm): $215
Call between: 7am-8pm
Provides: Light tackle, heavy tackle, lures, bait
Handicapped equipped: No
Certifications: USCG

Fishfinder
Rochdale 508-892-8230
.... 463-9479
Species & Seasons: Cod, Striped Bass, Bluefish May-Oct, Shark July-Oct
Bodies of water: Merrimack River, Gulf of Maine
Rates: Half day: $275(1-6),
Full day: $395(1-6)
Call between: 6pm-10pm
Provides: Light tackle, heavy tackle, lures, bait
Handicapped equipped: No
Certifications: USCG

My Mistress Too
Newburyport 508-465-5564
Species & Seasons: Bluefish July-Oct, Striped Bass May-Sept, Ground Fish May-Oct, Shark June-Sept
Bodies of water: Merrimack River, Parker River, Gulf of Maine, Stellwagen Bank
Rates: Boat Half day: $300,
Boat Full day: $475
Call between: 8am-10pm
Provides: Light tackle, heavy tackle, fly rod/reel, lures, bait
Handicapped equipped: Yes
Certifications: USCG

Reel Treat Charters
Tewksbury 508-851-9622
Species & Seasons: Cod, Mackerel May-Oct, Striped Bass, Bluefish June-Oct, Shark June-Sept
Bodies of water: Merrimack River, Atlantic Ocean
Rates: Half day: $330, Full day: $420, prices per 6 people maximum, Evenings: $210
Call between: 6am-10pm
Provides: Light tackle, heavy tackle, lures, bait
Handicapped equipped: No
Certifications: NCCA member NACCO member, USCG

MYSTIC RIVER

BAIT & TACKLE...

Little John's Bait & Tackle
Saugus 617-233-9696
Hours: 7am-9pm weekdays,
5am-9pm weekends
Carries: Live bait, lures, rods, reels, licenses

MYSTIC RIVER - NANTUCKET SOUND — MASSACHUSETTS

Bodies of water: Saugus River, Atlantic Ocean, Mystic River, Point of Pines River, Prankers Pond, Sluice Pond, Browns Pond, Horn Pond, Golden Hills Ponds, Ipswich River
Services & Products: Boat ramp, fishing instruction, repair services, custom rods
Guides: Yes
OK to call for current conditions: Yes
Contact: Lit'l John

CHARTERS...

Luau
North Eastham 508-255-4527
Species & Seasons: Striped Bass, Cod May-Oct, Bluefish June-Oct, Flounder, Mackerel May-June
Bodies of water: Cape Cod Bay, Massachusetts Bay, Nantucket Sound, Atlantic Ocean
Rates: Hafl day: $326(1-6), Full day: $450(1-6)
Call between: 6pm-10pm
Provides: Light tackle, heavy tackle, lures, bait
Handicapped equipped: Yes
Certifications: USCG

NANTUCKET SOUND

BAIT & TACKLE...

Green Pond Fish'n Gear Inc.
East Falmouth 508-548-2573
Carries: Live bait, lures, flies, rods, reels, licenses
Bodies of water: Nantucket Sound, many area ponds
Services & Products: Food, beverages, fishing instruction, repair services, fish market
Guides: Yes
OK to call for current conditions: Yes
Contact: Dick, Bob or Ellie

Sea Store
Woods Hole 508-548-9108
Hours: 8am-5pm
Carries: Live bait, lures, flies, rods, reels
Bodies of water: Nantucket Sound, Vineyard Sound, Buzzards Bay, Block Island Sound, Atlantic Ocean
Services & Products: Guide services, charter boat service, fishing instruction
OK to call for current conditions: Yes
Contact: Ed Levy or J.C. Burke

CHARTERS...

Amethyst II
Falmouth 508-540-9651
Species & Seasons: Striped Bass, Bluefish, Porgy, Tautog May-Nov, White Marlin July-Sept, Tuna July-Oct
Bodies of water: Nantucket Sound, Atlantic Ocean
Rates: Half day: $350, Full day: $475, prices per 6 people maximum, Marlin/Tuna: $850, Overnite canyon: $1750
Call between: 8am-8pm
Provides: Light tackle, heavy tackle, fly rod/reel, lures, bait, rain gear
Handicapped equipped: Yes
Certifications: USCG

Ananta Sportfishing
East Falmouth 508-548-0019
Species & Seasons: Striped Bass, Bluefish May-Oct
Bodies of water: Nantucket Sound, Vineyard Sound on Cape Cod
Rates: 6 hrs. private (1-6): $425
Call between: 6pm-9pm
Provides: Light tackle, heavy tackle, lures, bait, rain gear
Handicapped equipped: Yes
Certifications: USCG

Banjo Charters
Oak Bluffs 508-693-3154
Species & Seasons: Striped Bass, Bluefish May-Nov, Bonito, Yellowfin Tuna July-Nov, Mako Shark, Blue Shark, Fluke June-Oct
Bodies of water: Vineyard Sound, Nantucket Sound, Cape Cod Bay, Atlantic waters south and east of Martha's Vineyard
Rates: Half day: $400(1-6), Full day: $800(1-6)
Call between: Anytime
Provides: Light tackle, heavy tackle, fly rod/reel, lures, bait, rain gear
Handicapped equipped: Yes

Banshee
West Chatham 508-945-0403
Species & Seasons: Striped Bass, Bluefish May-Nov
Bodies of water: Nantucket Sound, Atlantic Ocean
Rates: 1995 rates: Full day: $475(1-6)
Call between: 5pm-9pm
Povides: Light tackle, heavy tackle, lures
Handicapped equipped: No
Certifications: USCG

East Wind
Osterville 508-420-3934
Species & Seasons: Striped Bass, Bluefish May-Nov
Bodies of water: Nantucket Sound, Vineyard Sound, Cuttyhunk Island, Monomoy Island
Rates: Boat: Half day: $375, Full day: $550
Call between: 9am-9pm
Provides: Light tackle, heavy tackle, fly rod/reel, lures, bait
Handicapped equipped: No
Certifications: USCG

Frosty V
Rockland 617-878-6882
Species & Seasons: Bluefish, Striped Bass July-Sept, Cod May-June, Flounder May-Sept
Bodies of water: Cape Cod Bay, Buzzards Bay, Nantucket Sound
Rates: Half day: $190(6), Full day: $370(6)
Call between: 6pm-9pm
Provides: Heavy tackle, lures, bait
Handicapped equipped: No
Certifications: USCG

Golden Eagle
South Harwich 508-432-5611
Species & Seasons: Porgy June-Oct, Black Sea Bass May-July, Fluke, Bluefish July-Aug, Tautog May-Oct
Bodies of water: Nantucket Sound
Rates: Half day: $17(1), $34(2), Full day: $34(1), $68(2)
Call between: 8am-12 noon/6pm-8pm
Provides: Light tackle, heavy tackle, bait
Handicapped equipped: Yes
Certifications: USCG

Hop-Tuit
West Falmouth 508-540-7642
.... 564-8086
Species & Seasons: Striped Bass, Bluefish May-Nov, Bonito, False Albacore, Spanish Mackerel Aug-Oct, Tuna, Marlin July-Oct
Bodies of water: Buzzards Bay, Nantucket Sound, Vineyard Sound, Atlantic Ocean
Rates: 4 hrs.: $285(1-4), 6 hrs.: $400 (1-4), Offshore: $600
Call between: 6pm-9pm
Provides: Light tackle, fly rod/reel, lures, rain gear
Handicapped equipped: Yes
Certifications: USCG

MASSACHUSETTS
NANTUCKET SOUND - QUABBIN RESERVOIR

Lee Marie
East Falmouth 508-548-9498
Species & Seasons: Striped Bass, Bluefish May-Oct
Bodies of water: Nantucket Sound Islands of Martha's Vineyard and Nantucket
Rates: Call for rates and availability of dates
Call between: Anytime
Provides: Light tackle, heavy tackle, lures, bait, rain gear
Handicapped equipped: No
Certifications: USCG

Patriot Party Boats
Falmouth 800-734-0088
Species & Seasons: Striped Bass, May-Nov, Bluefish, Porgy, Tautog, Sea Bass, Fluke May-Oct
Bodies of water: Vineyard Sound, Nantucket Sound, Buzzards Bay
Rates: Half day: $20(1), Full day: $30(1)
Call between: 9am-5pm
Provides: Heavy tackle, lures, bait
Handicapped equipped: Yes
Certifications: USCG

Priscilla J
Nantucket 508-228-4225
Species & Seasons: Striped Bass, Bluefish May-Nov
Bodies of water: Atlantic Ocean, Nantucket Sound
Rates: Boat #1: $400/tide(1-6), Boat #2 Flats Boat: $275/tide(1-2 Flyfishing only)
Provides: Light tackle, fly rod/reel, lures
Handicapped equipped: Yes
Certifications: USCG, Loomis, Sage Guide

Capt. Barry Summer
South Plymouth 508-759-6597
Species & Seasons: Striped Bass May-June/Aug-Sept, Bluefish June-Sept, Yellowfin Tuna, Bluefin Tuna July-Sept, Porgy May-July/Sept-Oct, Tautog May-Oct
Bodies of water: Cape Cod Bay, Buzzards Bay, Nantucket Sound, Vineyard Sound
Rates: Varies
Call between: 8am-8pm
Provides: Light tackle, heavy tackle, lures, bait, rain gear, beverages, lunch
Handicapped equipped: No
Certifications: USCG

Yankee Deep Sea Fishing
Harwich Port 508-432-2520
.... 617-329-1583(W)
Species & Seasons: Porgy, Sea Bass, Tautog May-Oct, Fluke July-Oct
Bodies of water: Nantucket Sound
Rates: Half day: $18(1), $36(2), Full day: $34(1), $68(2)
Call between: 7am-7pm
Provides: Light tackle, bait, beverages
Handicapped equipped: Yes, but no wheel chairs
Certifications: USCG

ONOTA LAKE
MARINAS...

Onota Boat Livery
Pittsfield 413-442-1724
Hours: 7am-7pm
Carries: Live bait, lures, flies, maps, rods, reels, licenses
Bodies of water: Onota Lake, Pontoosuc Lake, Goose Pond, Lake Buell, Laurel Lake
Services & Products: Boat rentals, boat ramp, food, beverages, gas/oil, fishing instruction, repair services, boat sales
Guides: Yes
OK to call for current conditions: Yes
Contact: Tom Dailey

PARKER RIVER
BAIT & TACKLE...

Surfland Bait & Tackle
Newburyport 508-462-4202
Hours: 6am-9pm
Carries: Live bait, lures, flies, maps, rods, reels
Bodies of water: Merrimack River, Parker River, Atlantic Ocean, Plum Island River
Guides: Yes
OK to call for current conditions: Yes
Contact: Kay Moulton

CHARTERS...

My Mistress Too
Newburyport 508-465-5564
Species & Seasons: Bluefish July-Oct, Striped Bass May-Sept, Ground Fish May-Oct, Shark June-Sept
Bodies of water: Merrimack River, Parker River, Gulf of Maine, Stellwagen Bank
Rates: Boat Half day: $300, Boat Full day: $475
Call between: 8am-10pm
Provides: Light tackle, heavy tackle, fly rod/reel, lures, bait
Handicapped equipped: Yes
Certifications: USCG

QUABBIN RESERVOIR
BAIT & TACKLE...

Ric's Bait & Tackle
Leominster 508-537-0065
Hours: 6am-7pm Mon.-Fri., 4:30am-7pm Sat., Sun.
Carries: Live bait, lures, flies, maps, rods, reels
Bodies of water: Atlantic Ocean, Wachusett Res., Quabbin Res., many more
Services & Products: Beverages, fishing instruction, repair services
Guides: Yes
OK to call for current conditions: Yes

GUIDES...

Al's Fishing Guide Service
Worcester 508-797-5700
.... 800-588-5700
Species & Seasons: Landlocked Salmon April-May, Striped Bass May-Oct, Chinook Salmon, Coho Salmon Sept-Nov, Steelhead Sept-April, Brown Trout Sept-Dec
Bodies of water: Wachusett Res., Quabbin Res., Cape Cod Canal, Race Point, Salmon River (NY), Oswego River (NY)
Rates: Half day: $100(1), $200(2), Full day: $150(1), $300(2) prices vary
Call between: 5pm-10pm
Provides: Light tackle, heavy tackle, fly rod/reel, lures, bait
Handicapped equipped: Yes
Certifications: NY Licensed Guide, Certified Master Fisherman Mass.

QUABBIN RESERVOIR - VINEYARD SOUND — MASSACHUSETTS

LODGES...

Copper Lantern Motor Lodge
W. Brookfield 508-867-6441
Guest Capacity: 84, some efficiencies
Handicapped equipped: No
Seasons: All year
Rates: $35-$52/day
Contact: Dan, Judy, or Millie
Guides: No
Species & Seasons: Lake Trout, LM Bass, SM Bass, Salmon, Brook Trout, Bullhead April-Oct, Northern Pike all year
Bodies of Water: Quabbin Res., Quaboag River, Quaboag Pond, Wickaboag Pond, South Pond, Lake Lashaway
Types of fishing: Fly fishing, light tackle, wading, float trips
Available: Licenses, bait, tackle, boat rentals near by

the Copper Lantern Motor Lodge
REGULAR ROOMS & EFFICIENCIES
YOUR HOSTS: THE LELANDS
P.O. Box 1138 • 184 W. MAIN ST.
ROUTE 9 & 67
WEST BROOKFIELD, MASS 01585
508 867-6441

QUINCY BAY

BAIT & TACKLE...

Fore River Fishing Tackle
Quincy 617-770-1397
Hours: 7am-6pm weekdays, 6am-6pm weekends
Carries: Live bait, lures, maps, rods, reels, licenses
Bodies of water: Fore River, Town River Bay, Weymouth Back River, Whitmans Pond, Eaton's Pond, Hingham Bay, Quincy Bay
Services & Products: Fishing instruction, repair services
Guides: Yes

OK to call for current conditions: Yes
Contact: Rick Newcomb

CHARTERS...

Roger Brousseau
Weymouth 617-335-3298
Species & Seasons: Cod April-June, Flounder May-June, Striped Bass, Shark June-Oct, Bluefish June-Nov
Bodies of water: Quincy Bay, Boston Harbor, Stellwagen Bank, Cape Cod Bay
Rates: Half day: $200(2), Full day: $300(2), 2 boats 2-6 people
Call between: Anytime
Provides: Light tackle, heavy tackle, fly rod/reel, lures, bait, rain gear, beverages, lunch
Handicapped equipped: Yes
Certifications: USCG

RHODE ISLAND SOUND

CHARTERS...

Laughing Gull
Westport 508-636-2730
Species & Seasons: Bluefish, Striped Bass May-Oct, Tautog Sept-Oct, Flounder June-Sept
Bodies of water: Westport River, Buzzards Bay, Vineyard Sound, Rhode Island Sound
Rates: Half day: $175(1-4), Full day: $275(1-4)
Call between:
Provides: Light tackle, heavy tackle, lures, bait
Handicapped equipped: Yes, limited
Certifications: USCG

Rip Dancer
Attleboro 508-226-2462
Species & Seasons: Striped Bass June-Nov, Bluefish July-Nov
Bodies of water: Buzzards Bay, Rhode Island Sound
Rates: Half day: $300(6), Full day: $500(6)
Call between: 6pm-10pm
Provides: Light tackle, fly rod/reel, lures, bait
Handicapped equipped: I'll try to help anyway I can
Certifications: USCG

SAUGUS RIVER

BAIT & TACKLE...

Little John's Bait & Tackle
Saugus 617-233-9696
Hours: 7am-9pm weekdays, 5am-9pm weekends
Carries: Live bait, lures, rods, reels, licenses
Bodies of water: Saugus River, Atlantic Ocean, Mystic River, Point of Pines River, Prankers Pond, Sluice Pond, Browns Pond, Horn Pond, Golden Hills Ponds, Ipswich River
Services & Products: Boat ramp, fishing instruction, repair services, custom rods
Guides: Yes
OK to call for current conditions: Yes
Contact: Lit'l John

VINEYARD SOUND

BAIT & TACKLE...

Sea Store
Woods Hole 508-548-9108
Hours: 8am-5pm
Carries: Live bait, lures, flies, rods, reels
Bodies of water: Nantucket Sound, Vineyard Sound, Buzzards Bay, Block Island Sound, Atlantic Ocean
Services & Products: Guide services, charter boat service, fishing instruction
OK to call for current conditions: Yes
Contact: Ed Levy or J.C. Burke

CHARTERS...

Ananta Sportfishing
East Falmouth 508-548-0019
Species & Seasons: Striped Bass, Bluefish May-Oct
Bodies of water: Nantucket Sound, Vineyard Sound on Cape Cod
Rates: 6 hrs. private: $425(1-6)
Call between: 6pm-9pm
Provides: Light tackle, heavy tackle, lures, bait, rain gear
Handicapped equipped: Yes
Certifications: USCG

MASSACHUSETTS
VINEYARD SOUND - WACHUSETT RESERVOIR

Banjo Charters
Oak Bluffs 508-693-3154
Species & Seasons: Striped Bass, Bluefish May-Nov, Bonito, Yellowfin Tuna July-Nov, Mako Shark, Blue Shark, Fluke June-Oct
Bodies of water: Vineyard Sound, Nantucket Sound, Cape Cod Bay, Atlantic waters south and east of Martha's Vineyard
Rates: Half day: $400(1-6), Full day: $800(1-6)
Call between: Anytime
Provides: Light tackle, heavy tackle, fly rod/reel, lures, bait, rain gear
Handicapped equipped: Yes

East Wind
Osterville 508-420-3934
Species & Seasons: Striped Bass, Bluefish May-Nov
Bodies of water: Nantucket Sound, Vineyard Sound, Cuttyhunk Island, Monomoy Island
Rates: Boat: Half day: $375, Full day: $550
Call between: 9am-9pm
Provides: Light tackle, heavy tackle, fly rod/reel, lures, bait
Handicapped equipped: No
Certifications: USCG

Half Fast
Randolph 617-986-4375
Species & Seasons: Cod Mar-June, Porgy May-July, Tuna, Shark July-Nov, Striped Bass, Bluefish June-Nov
Bodies of water: Stellwagen Bank, Great South Channel, Vineyard Sound
Rates: Full day 6 people: Cod: $700, Bass & Blues: $600, Porgy: $400
Call between: Anytime
Provides: Light tackle, heavy tackle, lures, bait
Handicapped equipped: No
Certifications: USCG

Hop-Tuit
West Falmouth 508-540-7642
.... 564-8086
Species & Seasons: Striped Bass, Bluefish May-Nov, Bonito, False Albacore, Spanish Mackerel Aug-Oct, Tuna, Marlin July-Oct
Bodies of water: Buzzards Bay, Nantucket Sound, Vineyard Sound, Atlantic Ocean
Rates: 4 hrs.: $285(1-4), 6 hrs.: $400 (1-4), Offshore: $600
Call between: 6pm-9pm

Provides: Light tackle, fly rod/reel, lures, rain gear
Handicapped equipped: Yes
Certifications: USCG

Last Call
New Bedford 508-999-4999
.... 800-233-FISH
Species & Seasons: Striped Bass, Bluefish May-Oct, Tautog May-Nov, Porgy June-Oct, Fluke July-Aug
Bodies of water: Buzzards Bay, Vineyard Sound, Cuttyhunk Island
Rates: Half day: $200(4), Full day: $350(4)
Call between: 6am-10pm
Provides: Light tackle, heavy tackle, lures, bait
Certifications: USCG

Laughing Gull
Westport 508-636-2730
Species & Seasons: Bluefish, Striped Bass May-Oct, Tautog Sept-Oct, Flounder June-Sept
Bodies of water: Westport River, Buzzards Bay, Vineyard Sound, Rhode Island Sound
Rates: Half day: $175(1-4), Full day: $275(1-4)
Provides: Light tackle, heavy tackle, lures, bait
Handicapped equipped: Yes, limited
Certifications: USCG

Patriot Party Boats
Falmouth 800-734-0088
Species & Seasons: Striped Bass, May-Nov, Bluefish, Porgy, Tautog, Sea Bass, Fluke May-Oct
Bodies of water: Vineyard Sound, Nantucket Sound, Buzzards Bay
Rates: Half day: $20(1), Full day: $30(1)
Call between: 9am-5pm
Provides: Heavy tackle, lures, bait
Handicapped equipped: Yes
Certifications: USCG

Capt. Barry Summer
South Plymouth 508-759-6597
Species & Seasons: Striped Bass May-June/Aug-Sept, Bluefish June-Sept, Yellowfin Tuna, Bluefin Tuna July-Sept, Porgy May-July/Sept-Oct, Tautog May-Oct
Bodies of water: Cape Cod Bay, Buzzards Bay, Nantucket Sound, Vineyard Sound
Rates: Varies
Call between: 8am-8pm

Provides: Light tackle, heavy tackle, lures, bait, rain gear, beverages, lunch
Handicapped equipped: No
Certifications: USCG

WACHUSETT RESERVOIR

BAIT & TACKLE...

Ric's Bait & Tackle
Leominster 508-537-0065
Hours: 6am-7pm Mon.-Fri., 4:30am-7pm Sat., Sun.
Carries: Live bait, lures, flies, maps, rods, reels
Bodies of water: Atlantic Ocean, Wachusett Res., Quabbin Res., many more
Services & Products: Beverages, fishing instruction, repair services
Guides: Yes
OK to call for current conditions: Yes

Wachusett Bait & Tackle
W. Boylston 508-835-2462
Hours: 6am-7pm
Carries: Live bait, lures, flies, maps, rods, reels
Bodies of water: Wachusett Res., Stillwater River, Waushaccum East and West, Mossy Pond
Services & Products: Guide services, fishing instruction, repair services
Guides: Yes
OK to call for current conditions: Yes
Contact: Bob Danico

GUIDES...

Al's Fishing Guide Service
Worcester 508-797-5700
.... 800-588-5700
Species & Seasons: Landlocked Salmon April-May, Striped Bass May-Oct, Chinook Salmon, Coho Salmon Sept-Nov, Steelhead Sept-April, Brown Trout Sept-Dec
Bodies of water: Wachusett Res., Quabbin Res., Cape Cod Canal, Race Point, Salmon River (NY), Oswego River (NY)
Rates: Half day: $100(1), $200(2), Full day: $150(1), $300(2) prices vary
Call between: 5pm-10pm
Provides: Light tackle, heavy tackle, fly rod/reel, lures, bait

WACHUSETT RESERVOIR - WHITMANS POND — MASSACHUSETTS

Handicapped equipped: Yes
Certifications: NY Licensed Guide, Certified Master Fisherman Mass.

WALDEN POND

BAIT & TACKLE...

Andy's Bait & Tackle Shop
Acton 508-897-0717
Carries: Live bait, lures, flies, maps, rods, reels, licenses
Bodies of water: Assabet River, Concord River, Sudbury River, Walden Pond, White Pond
Services & Products: Repair services
Guides: Yes
OK to call for current conditions: Yes

WHITINGS POND

BAIT & TACKLE...

Airport Sport Shop Inc.
North Attleboro 508-695-7071
Hours: 9am-7pm Mon.-Fri., 6am-5pm Sat., Sun.
Carries: Live bait, lures, flies, maps, rods, reels
Bodies of water: Turnpike Lake, Lake Mirimichi, Fales Pond, Whitings Pond, Wading River
Services & Products: Food, beverages, fishing instruction, repair services
Guides: No
OK to call for current conditions: Yes

WHITMANS POND

BAIT & TACKLE...

Fore River Fishing Tackle
Quincy 617-770-1397
Hours: 7am-6pm weekdays, 6am-6pm weekends
Carries: Live bait, lures, maps, rods, reels, licenses
Bodies of water: Fore River, Town River Bay, Weymouth Back River, Whitmans Pond, Eaton's Pond, Hingham Bay, Quincy Bay
Services & Products: Fishing instruction, repair services
Guides: Yes
OK to call for current conditions: Yes
Contact: Rick Newcomb

Neponset Circle Fishing & Dart
Dorchester 617-436-9231
Hours: Open 7 days a week
Carries: Live bait, lures, flies, maps, rods, reels, licenses
Bodies of water: Boston Harbor, Jamaica Pond, Houghtons Pond, Charles River, Whitmans Pond, Porkapaog Pond
Services & Products: Fishing instruction, repair services
Guides: Yes
OK to call for current conditions: Yes
Contact: Darrell or Ralph

The Angler's Yellow Pages is the quickest and easiest way to find what you want, when you want it

MICHIGAN

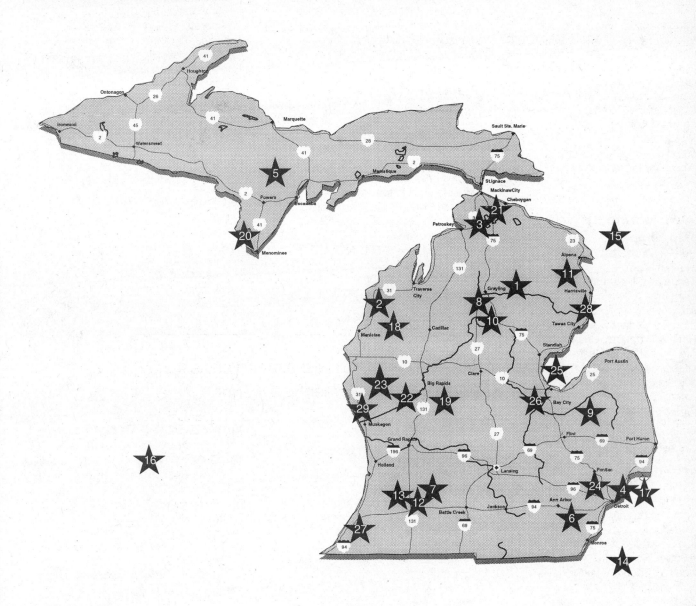

1. AuSable River
2. Betsie River
3. Burt Lake
4. Detroit River
5. Escanaba River
6. Ford Lake
7. Gull Lake
8. Higgins Lake
9. Holloway Reservoir
10. Houghton Lake
11. Hubbard Lake
12. Kalamazoo River
13. Lake Allegan
14. Lake Erie
15. Lake Huron
16. Lake Michigan
17. Lake St. Clair
18. Manistee River
19. Mantiny Lake
20. Menominee River
21. Mullet Lake
22. Muskegon River
23. Pere Marquette River
24. Pontiac Lake
25. Saginaw Bay
26. Saginaw River
27. St. Joseph River
28. Tawas Lake
29. White River

MICHIGAN

AUSABLE RIVER

BAIT & TACKLE...

Eigner Sports Outfitters
Hale 517-728-2621
Hours: 8am-6pm
Carries: Live bait, lures, flies, maps, rods, reels, licenses
Bodies of water: Lake Huron, Rifle River, AuSable River, Sage Lake
Services & Products: Boat rentals, guide services, beverages, fishing instruction, repair services, Minnkota motors
Guides: Yes
OK to call for current conditions: Yes
Contact: Bob Eigner

Fellows Marine & Tackle Shop
Oscoda 517-739-1921
Hours: 7am-9pm
Carries: Lures, flies, maps, rods, reels, licenses
Bodies of water: AuSable River, Lake Huron, Cedar Lake, Van Etten Lake
Services & Products: Charter boat service, gas/oil, fishing instruction, repair services
Guides: Yes
OK to call for current conditions: Yes
Contact: Anyone

North Star Motel & Sport Shop
Tawas City 517-362-2255
Hours: 7am-11pm
Carries: Live bait, lures, flies, maps, rods, reels, licenses
Bodies of water: Lake Huron, Tawas Lake, Sand Lake, AuSable River
Services & Products: Lodging, fishing instruction
Guides: Yes
OK to call for current conditions: Yes
Contact: Helen

GUIDES...

Bidigare's Charter Service
Oscoda .... 517-739-1342(S)
 .... 810-773-4199(W)
Species & Seasons: Chinook Salmon, Lake Trout, Brown Trout May-Sept, Steelhead Oct-Dec/Mar-May
Bodies of water: Lake Huron, AuSable River

Rates: 6 hrs: $260(1-4), $295(5), $320(6), 8 hrs.: $310(1-4), $365(5), $410(6), 10hrs: $410(1-4), $490(5), $570(6), Drift trips: Full day: $125(1), $200(2)
Call between: 5-6am-9-11pm
Provides: Light tackle, heavy tackle, lures, bait
Handicapped equipped: Yes
Certifications: USCG

Riverborne Angler
Traverse City 616-941-FISH
 929-4800
Species & Seasons: Salmon Sept-Nov, Steelhead Oct-June, Trout April-Nov, Bass May-Sept
Bodies of water: Lake Michigan, Pere Marquette River, Manistee River, AuSable River, Betsie River, Muskegon River, Platte River, Boardman River, many inland lakes
Rates: Half day: $150(1), $175(2), Full day: $200(1), $225(2)
Call between: 9am-6pm
Provides: Fly rod/reel, rain gear, beverages, lunch
Handicapped equipped: Yes
Certifications: MDNR

BETSIE RIVER

FLY SHOPS...

Backcast Fly Shop
Benzonia 616-882-5222
Hours: 9am-7pm Mon.-Thurs., 7am-8pm Fri.-Sat., 7am-5pm Sun.
Carries: Live bait, lures, flies, maps, rods, reels, licenses
Bodies of water: Lake Michigan, Crystal Lake, Betsie River, Platte River, many others
Services & Products: Guide services, fishing instruction, mail order 800-717-5222
Guides: Yes
OK to call for current conditions: Yes
Contact: Claude, Steve, Dave or Rick

GUIDES...

Riverborne Angler
Traverse City 616-941-FISH
 929-4800
Species & Seasons: Salmon Sept-Nov, Steelhead Oct-June, Trout April-Nov, Bass May-Sept

Bodies of water: Lake Michigan, Pere Marquette River, Manistee River, AuSable River, Betsie River, Muskegon River, Platte River, Boardman River, many inland lakes
Rates: Half day: $150(1), $175(2), Full day: $200(1), $225(2)
Call between: 9am-6pm
Provides: Fly rod/reel, rain gear, beverages, lunch
Handicapped equipped: Yes
Certifications: MDNR

BURT LAKE

BAIT & TACKLE...

Outdoor Adventure Store
Cheboygan 616-627-5273
Hours: 7am-7pm
Carries: Live bait, lures, flies, maps, rods, reels, licenses
Bodies of water: Mullet Lake, Black Lake, Cheboygan River, Burt Lake, Black River, Lake Huron, Indian River, many brookie streams
Services & Products: Food, beverages, fishing instruction, repair services
Guides: Yes
OK to call for current conditions: Yes
Contact: Brenda, Orval or Scottie

Young's Bait & Party Shop
Alanson 616-548-5286
Hours: 6am-12pm
Carries: Live bait, lures, flies, maps, rods, reels, licenses
Bodies of water: Lake Michigan, Crooked Lake, Burt Lake, Walloon Lake, Pickeral Lake, Round Lake
Services & Products: Food, beverages
Guides: Yes
OK to call for current conditions: Yes
Contact: David Stepanovich

DETROIT RIVER

BAIT & TACKLE...

Trenton Lighthouse
Trenton 313-675-7080
Hours: 6am-6pm
Carries: Live bait, lures, flies, maps, rods, reels, licenses
Bodies of water: Detroit River, Lake Erie
Services & Products: Charter boat service, boat ramp, food, beverages, fishing instruction

DETROIT RIVER - HOUGHTON LAKE MICHIGAN

Guides: Yes
OK to call for current conditions: Yes
Contact: Frank

Zubok's Tackle & Ski Shop
Taylor 313-295-2230
.... 295-4839
Hours: 9am-8pm
Carries: Live bait, lures, flies, maps, rods, reels, licenses
Bodies of water: Lake Erie, Detroit River, Lake St. Clair, Belleville Lake, Ford Lake
Services & Products: Guide services, charter boat service, fishing instruction, repair services
Guides: Yes
OK to call for current conditions: Yes
Contact: Paul Zubok

GUIDES...

Mark R. Martin
Twin Lake 616-744-0330
Species & Seasons: Steelhead April-May, Walleye (day) May-June, Walleye (night) July-Nov
Bodies of water: Muskegon River, Muskegon Lake, Lake White, Spring Lake, Grand River, Saginaw Bay, Saginaw River, Detroit River
Rates: 6 hrs: $200(1), $250(2)
Call between: 9am-6pm
Provides: Light tackle, heavy tackle, lures, bait
Handicapped equipped: Yes
Certifications: USCG

ESCANABA RIVER

BAIT & TACKLE...

Ludington Bait & Tackle
Escanaba 906-786-2798
Hours: 6am-7pm
Carries: Live bait, lures, flies, maps, rods, reels, licenses
Bodies of water: Escanaba River, Lake Michigan
Guides: Yes
OK to call for current conditions: Yes
Contact: Chris or Diane

FORD LAKE

BAIT & TACKLE...

Zubok's Tackle & Ski Shop
Taylor 313-295-2230
.... 295-4839
Hours: 9am-8pm
Carries: Live bait, lures, flies, maps, rods, reels, licenses
Bodies of water: Lake Erie, Detroit River, Lake St. Clair, Belleville Lake, Ford Lake
Services & Products: Guide services, charter boat service, fishing instruction, repair services
Guides: Yes
OK to call for current conditions: Yes
Contact: Paul Zubok

GULL LAKE

BAIT & TACKLE...

Shoup's Foods
Otsego 616-694-6510
Hours: 7am-11:30pm
Carries: Live bait, lures, rods, reels, licenses
Bodies of water: Gun Lake, Gull Lake, Lake Allegan, Kalamazoo River
Services & Products: Food, beverages, repair services, groceries
Guides: Yes
OK to call for current conditions: Yes
Contact: Mike Shoup

HIGGINS LAKE

BAIT & TACKLE...

Jay's Sporting Goods
Clare 517-386-3475
Hours: 9am-8pm
Carries: Live bait, lures, flies, maps, rods, reels, licenses
Bodies of water: Saginaw Bay, Houghton Lake, Higgins Lake, Bud Lake, Long Lake
Guides: Yes
OK to call for current conditions: Yes
Contact: Carl Athey

HOLLOWAY RESERVOIR

BAIT & TACKLE...

Fishing Tackle Grab Bag
5521 N State Road
Davison 48423
Hours: 9am-6pm
Carries: Live bait, lures, flies, maps, rods, reels, licenses
Bodies of water: Holloway Res., Mott Lake, Lake Fenton, Lake Nepessing
Services & Products: Fishing instruction
Guides: Yes
OK to call for current conditions: Yes
Contact: Gary, Varian or John

HOUGHTON LAKE

BAIT & TACKLE...

Jay's Sporting Goods
Clare 517-386-3475
Hours: 9am-8pm
Carries: Live bait, lures, flies, maps, rods, reels, licenses
Bodies of water: Saginaw Bay, Houghton Lake, Higgins Lake, Bud Lake, Long Lake
Guides: Yes
OK to call for current conditions: Yes
Contact: Carl Athey

Lake City Sport Shop, Inc.
Lake City 616-839-4875
Hours: 8am-5pm, closed Wed. (except summer)
Carries: Live bait, lures, flies, maps, rods, reels, licenses
Bodies of water: Lake Missaukee, Crooked Lake, Lake Sapphire, Clam River, Manistee River, Houghton Lake
Guides: No
OK to call for current conditions: Yes
Contact: John Wachowski

MICHIGAN

HUBBARD LAKE - LAKE ERIE

HUBBARD LAKE

BAIT & TACKLE...

Side Door Bait & Tackle
Spruce 517-736-6418
Hours: 7am-8pm
Carries: Live bait, lures, maps, rods, reels, licenses
Bodies of water: Hubbard Lake, Jewel Lake
Services & Products: Guide services, lodging, food, beverages, fishing instruction
OK to call for current conditions: Yes
Contact: Len Barraco

KALAMAZOO RIVER

BAIT & TACKLE...

Shoup's Foods
Otsego 616-694-6510
Hours: 7am-11:30pm
Carries: Live bait, lures, rods, reels, licenses
Bodies of water: Gun Lake, Gull Lake, Lake Allegan, Kalamazoo River
Services & Products: Food, beverages, repair services, groceries
Guides: Yes
OK to call for current conditions: Yes
Contact: Mike Shoup

LAKE ALLEGAN

BAIT & TACKLE...

Shoup's Foods
Otsego 616-694-6510
Hours: 7am-11:30pm
Carries: Live bait, lures, rods, reels, licenses
Bodies of water: Gun Lake, Gull Lake, Lake Allegan, Kalamazoo River
Services & Products: Food, beverages, repair services, groceries
Guides: Yes
OK to call for current conditions: Yes
Contact: Mike Shoup

LAKE ERIE

BAIT & TACKLE...

D & R Sports Center Inc.
Kalamazoo 616-372-2277
Hours: 9am-6pm Mon.Thrus., 9am-8pm Wed.Fri., 9am-5pm Sat.
Carries: Live bait, lures, flies, maps, rods, reels, licenses
Bodies of water: Lake Michigan, Lake Erie, large inland lakes
Services & Products: Boat rentals, food, beverages, oil, repair services
Guides: Yes
OK to call for current conditions: Yes
Contact: Anyone

Professional Fishing Center
Harrison Twp. 810-469-2070
Hours: 6am-9pm
Carries: Live bait, lures, flies, maps, rods, reels, licenses
Bodies of water: Lake St. Clair, Lake Erie, Lake Huron
Services & Products: Guide services, charter boat service, beverages, gas/oil, fishing instruction
Guides: Yes
OK to call for current conditions: Yes

Trenton Lighthouse
Trenton 313-675-7080
Hours: 6am-6pm
Carries: Live bait, lures, flies, maps, rods, reels, licenses
Bodies of water: Detroit River, Lake Erie
Services & Products: Charter boat service, boat ramp, food, beverages, fishing instruction
Guides: Yes
OK to call for current conditions: Yes
Contact: Frank

Zubok's Tackle & Ski Shop
Taylor 313-295-2230
.... 295-4839
Hours: 9am-8pm
Carries: Live bait, lures, flies, maps, rods, reels, licenses
Bodies of water: Lake Erie, Detroit River, Lake St. Clair, Belleville Lake, Ford Lake
Services & Products: Guide services, charter boat service, fishing instruction, repair services
Guides: Yes
OK to call for current conditions: Yes
Contact: Paul Zubok

CHARTERS...

Capt. Bob Bingle
Algonac 810-794-3854
Species & Seasons: SM Bass, Yellow Perch June-Oct, Chinook Salmon July-Aug, Walleye May-June, Duck Hunting Nov-Dec
Bodies of water: Lake Huron, Lake St. Clair, Lake Erie
Rates: $400(4), $450(5), $600(6)
Call between: Anytime
Provides: Light tackle, heavy tackle, lures, bait, beverages, lunch
Handicapped equipped: Yes
Certifications: USCG

Crews Inn Sportfishing Charter
Mt. Clemens 810-465-4124
Species & Seasons: Chinook Salmon April-May/Aug-Sept, Walleye May-July, Muskellunge July-Aug/Sept-Nov, Perch Sept-Nov
Bodies of water: Lake Huron (lower), Lake Erie (Breast Bay), Lake St. Clair
Rates: Half day: $350(1-5), Full day: $450(1-5), $50 additional 6th person
Call between: 9am-12noon
Provides: Light tackle, heavy tackle, lures, bait
Handicapped equipped: Yes
Certifications: USCG, MDNR inspected

LeChasseur Sport Fishing
15611 Pine Street
Monroe 48161
Species & Seasons: Walleye April-Aug, Perch Aug-Nov, Salmon Aug-Oct
Bodies of water: Lake Erie, Lake Ontario
Rates: Perch: $300, 6 maximum, Walleye:$330-$550, 6 maximum, Salmon $440(4)
Call between:
Provides: Light tackle, heavy tackle, fly rod/reel, lures, bait
Handicapped equipped: Yes
Certifications: USCG

Ronald E. Levitan Jr.
Redford 313-538-8318
Species & Seasons: Walleye April-Aug, Perch Sept-Nov
Bodies of water: Lake Erie at Monroella Salle
Rates: Half day(6hrs.): $65(1), Full day(8 hrs.): $80(1)
Call between: 6pm-11pm

LAKE ERIE - LAKE HURON
MICHIGAN

Provides: Light tackle, heavy tackle, lures, bait
Handicapped equipped: Yes
Certifications: USCG, MI and OH Guide

Luna Pier Harbour Club
Luna Pier 313-848-8777
Species & Seasons: Walleye May-July, Yellow Perch Sept-Oct
Bodies of water: Lake Erie
Rates: $240(4), $275(5), $300(6)
Call between: 7am-7pm
Provides: Light tackle, heavy tackle, lures, bait, rain gear, beverages, lunch
Handicapped equipped: Yes
Certifications: USCG, MDNR

North Bay Charters
New Baltimore 810-725-8233
Species & Seasons: Salmon April-June, Walleye May-Aug, Muskellunge, Perch, SM Bass July-Oct
Bodies of water: Lake Huron, Lake St. Clair, Lake Erie and connecting waters
Rates: Half day: $55(1), Full day: $75(1), 4 people: $250 and up
Call between: 8am-9pm
Provides: Light tackle, heavy tackle, lures, bait, rain gear, beverages, lunch
Handicapped equipped: Yes
Certifications: USCG, MDNR Inspected, insured

Capt. George Satterfield
Monroe 313-289-1505
.... 800-382-7499
Species & Seasons: Walleye May-Aug, Perch Aug-Nov
Bodies of water: Lake Erie at Monroe
Rates: $60 per person
Call between: 8am-10pm
Provides: Light tackle, lures, bait
Handicapped equipped: Yes
Certifications: USCG State of MI

Trade Winds Charter Service
LaSalle 313-243-2319
Species & Seasons: Walleye April-Aug, Perch Aug-Nov
Bodies of water: Lake Erie
Rates: Half day: $55(1), Full day: $75(1)
Call between: Anytime
Provides: Light tackle, heavy tackle, fly rod/reel, lures, bait, rain gear
Handicapped equipped: Yes
Certifications: USCG

West Sister Sport Fishing Group
Toledo, OH 800-488-3474
Species & Seasons: Walleye, Bass, Perch
Bodies of water: Lake Erie
Call between: Anytime
Provides: Light tackle, heavy tackle, fly rod/reel, lures, bait, rain gear, beverages, lunch
Handicapped equipped: Yes
Certifications: USCG

LAKE HURON
BAIT & TACKLE...

Birch Tree Resort Ltd
Drummond Island 906-493-5355
Hours: 24 hours
Carries: Live bait, lures, maps, rods, reels
Bodies of water: Lake Huron
Services & Products: Boat rentals, guide services, charter boat service, lodging, boat ramp, beverages, gas/oil, fishing instruction
Guides: Yes
OK to call for current conditions: Yes
Contact: Kim Messenger

Bubba's Bait & Tackle
Saginaw 517-752-9898
Hours: 6am-6-7pm
Carries: Live bait, lures, flies, maps, rods, reels, licenses
Bodies of water: Saginaw River, Shiawassee River, Tittabawassee River, Saginaw Bay, all tributaries, Lake Huron
Services & Products: Food, beverages, fishing instruction, repair services
Guides: Yes
OK to call for current conditions: Yes
Contact: Roger Mohl or Jan Pardon

Dick's Live Bait
Sebewaing 517-656-7275
Hours: 7am-7pm
Carries: Live bait, lures, maps, rods, reels, licenses
Bodies of water: Lake Huron
Services & Products: Boat rentals, boat ramp, food, beverages, fishing instruction, repair services
Guides: Yes
OK to call for current conditions: Yes
Contact: Dick, Cora or Keith

Eigner Sports Outfitters
Hale 517-728-2621
Hours: 8am-6pm
Carries: Live bait, lures, flies, maps, rods, reels, licenses
Bodies of water: Lake Huron, Rifle River, AuSable River, Sage Lake
Services & Products: Boat rentals, guide services, beverages, fishing instruction, repair services, Minnkota motors
Guides: Yes
OK to call for current conditions: Yes
Contact: Bob Eigner

Fellows Marine & Tackle Shop
Oscoda 517-739-1921
Hours: 7am-9pm
Carries: Lures, flies, maps, rods, reels, licenses
Bodies of water: AuSable River, Lake Huron, Cedar Lake, Van Etten Lake
Services & Products: Charter boat service, gas/oil, fishing instruction, repair services
Guides: Yes
OK to call for current conditions: Yes
Contact: Anyone

North Star Motel & Sport Shop
Tawas City 517-362-2255
Hours: 7am-11pm
Carries: Live bait, lures, flies, maps, rods, reels, licenses
Bodies of water: Lake Huron, Tawas Lake, Sand Lake, AuSable River
Services & Products: Lodging, fishing instruction
Guides: Yes
OK to call for current conditions: Yes
Contact: Helen

Outdoor Adventure Store
Cheboygan 616-627-5273
Hours: 7am-7pm
Carries: Live bait, lures, flies, maps, rods, reels, licenses
Bodies of water: Mullet Lake, Black Lake, Cheboygan River, Burt Lake, Black River, Lake Huron, Indian River, many brookie streams
Services & Products: Food, beverages, fishing instruction, repair services
Guides: Yes
OK to call for current conditions: Yes
Contact: Brenda, Orval or Scottie

MICHIGAN — LAKE HURON

Professional Fishing Center
Harrison Twp. 810-469-2070
Hours: 6am-9pm
Carries: Live bait, lures, flies, maps, rods, reels, licenses
Bodies of water: Lake St. Clair, Lake Erie, Lake Huron
Services & Products: Guide services, charter boat service, beverages, gas/oil, fishing instruction
Guides: Yes
OK to call for current conditions: Yes

See & Sea
Sebewaing 517-883-2755
Hours: 6am-10pm
Carries: Live bait, lures, maps, rods, reels, licenses
Bodies of water: Saginaw Bay, Lake Huron
Guides: Yes
OK to call for current conditions: Yes

CHARTERS...

Bidigare's Charter Service
Oscodo .... 517-739-1342(S)
.... 810-773-4199(W)
Species & Seasons: Chinook Salmon, Lake Trout, Brown Trout May-Sept, Steelhead Oct-Dec/Mar-May
Bodies of water: Lake Huron, AuSable River
Rates: 6 hrs: $260(1-4), $295(5), $320(6), 8 hrs.: $310(1-4), $365(5), $410(6), 10hrs: $410(1-4), $490(5), $570(6), Drift trips: Full day: $125(1), $200(2)
Call between: 5-6am-9-11pm
Provides: Light tackle, heavy tackle, lures, bait
Handicapped equipped: Yes
Certifications: USCG

Capt. Bob Bingle
Algonac 810-794-3854
Species & Seasons: SM Bass, Yellow Perch June-Oct, Chinook Salmon July-Aug, Walleye May-June, Duck Hunting Nov-Dec
Bodies of water: Lake Huron, Lake St. Clair, Lake Erie
Rates: $400(4), $450(5), $600(6)
Call between: Anytime
Provides: Light tackle, heavy tackle, lures, bait, beverages, lunch
Handicapped equipped: Yes
Certifications: USCG

Capt. Dale W. Brown
Gladwin 517-426-8580
Species & Seasons: Brown Trout, Steelhead, Lake Trout, Chinook Salmon June-Sept
Bodies of water: Lake Huron
Rates: Half day: $260(4)
Call between:
Provides: Light tackle, lures
Handicapped equipped: Yes

Crews Inn Sportfishing Charter
Mt. Clemens 810-465-4124
Species & Seasons: Chinook Salmon April-May/Aug-Sept, Walleye May-July, Muskellunge July-Aug/Sept-Nov, Perch Sept-Nov
Bodies of water: Lake Huron (lower), Lake Erie (Breast Bay), Lake St. Clair
Rates: Half day: $350(1-5), Full day: $450(1-5), $50 additional 6th person
Call between: 9am-12noon
Provides: Light tackle, heavy tackle, lures, bait
Handicapped equipped: Yes
Certifications: USCG, MDNR inspected

Huron Charter Service
Harbor Beach 517-479-6300
.... 479-6365
Species & Seasons: Salmon, Steelhead, Brown Trout, April-Sept, Lake Trout May-Sept, Walleye July-Sept
Bodies of water: Lake Huron
Rates: Half day: $75(1-3/$240 minimum)
Call between: 7am-9pm
Provides: Light tackle, lures, bait
Handicapped equipped: Yes

Steve Jones
Mount Clemens................ 810-463-3474
Species & Seasons: Muskellunge June-Nov Salmon April-June, Walleye April-Oct, SM Bass June-Oct, Perch Sept-Oct
Bodies of water: Lake St. Clair, Lake Huron
Rates: Half day: $80(1), Full day: $100(1)
Call between:
Provides: Light tackle, heavy tackle, lures, bait
Handicapped equipped: Yes
Certifications: USCG

Capt. John Matthews
Utica 810-731-3352
Species & Seasons: Salmon, Lake Trout May-Sept
Bodies of water: Lake Huron
Rates: Half day: $100(1), $140(2), 8 hrs: $300(4)
Call between: 4pm-10pm
Provides: Light tackle, heavy tackle, lures
Handicapped equipped: Yes

North Bay Charters
New Baltimore 810-725-8233
Species & Seasons: Salmon April-June, Walleye May-Aug, Muskellunge, Perch, SM Bass July-Oct
Bodies of water: Lake Huron, Lake St. Clair, Lake Erie and connecting waters
Rates: Half day: $55(1), Full day: $75(1), 4 people: $250 and up
Call between: 8am-9pm
Provides: Light tackle, heavy tackle, lures, bait, rain gear, beverages, lunch
Handicapped equipped: Yes
Certifications: USCG, MDNR Inspected, insured

Professional Marine Service
Ocqueoc .... 906-847-6580(S)
.... 517-733-8569(W)
Species & Seasons: Chinook Salmon, Coho Salmon, Pink Salmon July-Oct, Brown Trout June-Sept, Lake Trout June-Aug
Bodies of water: Northern Lake Huron, Northern Lake Michigan
Rates: Half day: $150(1-2)
Call between:
Provides: Light tackle, lures, bait
Handicapped equipped: Yes
Certifications: USCG, USPS

West Sister Sport Fishing Group
Toledo, OH....................... 800-488-3474
Species & Seasons: Salmon, Trout
Bodies of water: Lake Huron
Call between: Anytime
Provides: Light tackle, heavy tackle, fly rod/reel, lures, bait, rain gear, beverages, lunch
Handicapped equipped: Yes
Certifications: USCG

LAKE HURON - LAKE MICHIGAN — MICHIGAN

LODGES...

Birch Tree Resort Ltd
Drummond Island 906-493-5355
Hours: 24 hours
Carries: Live bait, lures, maps, rods, reels
Bodies of water: Lake Huron
Services & Products: Boat rentals, guide services, charter boat service, lodging, boat ramp, beverages, gas/oil, fishing instruction
Guides: Yes
OK to call for current conditions: Yes
Contact: Kim Messenger

LAKE MICHIGAN

BAIT & TACKLE...

D & R Sports Center Inc.
Kalamazoo 616-372-2277
Hours: 9am-6pm Mon.Thrus., 9am-8pm Wed.Fri., 9am-5pm Sat.
Carries: Live bait, lures, flies, maps, rods, reels, licenses
Bodies of water: Lake Michigan, Lake Erie, large inland lakes
Services & Products: Boat rentals, food, beverages, oil, repair services
Guides: Yes
OK to call for current conditions: Yes
Contact: Anyone

Ludington Bait & Tackle
Escanaba 906-786-2798
Hours: 6am-7pm
Carries: Live bait, lures, flies, maps, rods, reels, licenses
Bodies of water: Escanaba River, Lake Michigan
Services & Products:
Guides: Yes
OK to call for current conditions: Yes
Contact: Chris or Diane

Specialty Bait, Gifts & Tackle Shop
Berrien Springs 616-471-9020
Hours: 7am-10pm
Carries: Live bait, lures, flies, maps, rods, reels, licenses
Bodies of water: St. Joseph River, Lake Michigan, Indian Lake, Black Lake, Clear Lake
Services & Products: Beverages, repair services

Guides: Yes
OK to call for current conditions: Yes
Contact: Floyd

Young's Bait & Party Shop
Alanson 616-548-5286
Hours: 6am-12pm
Carries: Live bait, lures, flies, maps, rods, reels, licenses
Bodies of water: Lake Michigan, Crooked Lake, Burt Lake, Walloon Lake, Pickeral Lake, Round Lake
Services & Products: Food, beverages
Guides: Yes
OK to call for current conditions: Yes
Contact: David Stepanovich

CHARTERS...

Capt. J. Scott Anderson
Traverse City 616-941-4376
Species & Seasons: Salmon July-Sept, Lake Trout May-Sept, Steelhead June-Aug
Bodies of water: Lake Michigan
Rates: Half day: $240, Full day: $450
Call between: 7:30pm-9:30pm
Provides: Light tackle, lures, bait
Handicapped equipped: Yes
Certifications: USCG, DNR Inspected

Bolhouse Charters
Grand Rapids 616-456-7596
.... 361-0704
Species & Seasons: Coho Salmon, Lake Trout, Brown Trout, Steelhead, Chinook Salmon May-Nov
Bodies of water: Lake Michigan
Rates: Half day: $280(4), $330(6), Full day: $380(4), $430(6)
Call between: 8am-11pm
Provides: Light tackle, fly rod/reel, lures, bait
Handicapped equipped: Yes
Certifications: State inspected, USCG

Bud's Charter & Fishing Guide Service
Manistee 616-723-9414
Species & Seasons: Steelhead, Lake Trout June-Sept, Steelhead Oct-Jan, Brown Trout April-June, Coho Salmon, Chinook Salmon July-Sept
Bodies of water: Big Manistee River, Lake Michigan
Rates: Varies
Call between: 7pm-9pm

Provides: Light tackle, heavy tackle, lures, bait
Handicapped equipped: Yes

Co Hooker Charters
Holland 616-335-2076
Species & Seasons: Brown Trout, April-May, Coho Salmon, Chinook Salmon, Steelhead April-Oct, Lake Trout May-Sept, Perch April-May/July-Aug
Bodies of water: Lake Michigan
Rates: Half day: $240(1-6), Full day: $400(1-6)
Call between: 5pm-10pm
Provides: Light tackle, lures, bait
Handicapped equipped: No
Certifications: USCG, MDNR inspected

Capt. Emil Dean
Bear Lake 616-362-3760
Species & Seasons: Chinook Salmon, Coho Salmon, Lake Trout, Brown Trout May-Sept, Steelhead all year
Bodies of water: Lake Michigan, Manistee River
Rates: River: $300(4), Lake: $400(6) 8 hr. trips
Call between: 5pm-9pm
Provides: Light tackle, heavy tackle, lures, bait
Handicapped equipped: Yes

Capt. Gary Gamble
Niles 616-684-4009
Species & Seasons: Coho Salmon April-May, Chinook Salmon April-May/Aug-Oct, Steelhead Feb-April/July-Dec, Brown Trout Mar-May, Lake Trout May-Sept
Bodies of water: Lake Michigan, St. Joseph River
Rates: River: $75pp, $210 minimum, Lake: $80pp, $300 minimum
Call between: 6pm-8pm
Provides: Light tackle, heavy tackle, lures, bait
Handicapped equipped: Yes
Certifications: USCG

YOUR SILENT FISHING PARTNER

MICHIGAN — LAKE MICHIGAN

Capt. Ed Jenkins
Belding 616-794-1394
Species & Seasons: Brown Trout, Lake Trout, Coho Salmon, Chinook Salmon, Steelhead May-Oct
Bodies of water: Lake Michigan at Port Ludington
Rates: Half day: $70, Full day: $90, based on 4 people
Call between: Anytime
Provides: Light tackle, heavy tackle, lures, bait, beverages
Handicapped equipped: Yes
Certifications: USCG

Capt. Charles A. Knipschild
Benton Harbor 616-927-LURE
Species & Seasons: Perch, Chinook Salmon, Steelhead Mar-Oct, Coho Salmon Mar-June, Lake Trout, Brown Trout April-Sept
Bodies of water: Lake Michigan
Rates: $300 Minimum per trip. Includes 1-6 people
Call between: 6pm-10pm
Provides: Light tackle, lures, bait
Handicapped equipped: Yes
Certifications: USCG

Capt. Larry L. Marek
Comstock Park 616-784-5886
.... 842-5578
Species & Seasons: Steelhead, Lake Trout, Brown Trout, Salmon May-Oct
Bodies of water: Lake Michigan at Grand Haven
Rates: 6 hrs: $70pp, 4 person minimum
Call between: 8am-6pm
Provides: Light tackle, lures
Handicapped equipped: Yes

Capt. Gerald L. Murphy
Defiance, OH 419-393-2856
Species & Seasons: Steelhead, Salmon
Bodies of water: Lake Michigan
Rates: Full day: $260(4)
Call between: 5:30pm-10:30pm
Provides: Light tackle, lures
Handicapped equipped: No
Certifications: USCG

Capt. Steve Otterbein
Traverse City 616-946-2204
Species & Seasons: Lake Trout, Brown Trout, Steelhead, Salmon May-Sept
Bodies of water: Lake Michigan, Leland Area

Rates: Half day: $55pp, minimum $240, Full day: $450, up to 6 - $50 surcharge on off-shore trips beyond the Manitou Islands
Call between: Anytime
Provides: Light tackle, lures
Handicapped equipped: No
Certifications: USCG licensed, State of MI inspected

Patina Charter Service
Elberta 616-352-4434
Species & Seasons: Brown Trout May-June, Chinook Salmon June-Aug, Steelhead June-July, Lake Trout June-Sept, Coho Salmon Aug-Sept
Bodies of water: Lake Michigan at Frankfort Harbor
Rates: Half day: $65pp, 4 minimum/6 maximun, Full day: $480(1-6) 9 hrs.
Call between: Anytime
Provides: Light tackle, heavy tackle, lures
Handicapped equipped: Yes
Certifications: USCG, MDNR Inspected

Professional Marine Service
Ocqueoc .... 906-847-6580(S)
.... 517-733-8569(W)
Species & Seasons: Chinook Salmon, Coho Salmon, Pink Salmon July-Oct, Brown Trout June-Sept, Lake Trout June-Aug
Bodies of water: Northern Lake Huron, Northern Lake Michigan
Rates: Half day: $150(1-2)
Call between:
Provides: Light tackle, lures, bait
Handicapped equipped: Yes
Certifications: USCG, USPS

Rainbow Charters
Berrien Springs 616-471-3900
Species & Seasons: Steelhead, Brown Trout Jan-Dec, Lake Trout May-Sept, Chinook Salmon April-Oct, Coho Salmon Mar-Oct, Walleye April-Mar, Perch April-Oct, Catfish April-Oct
Bodies of water: Lake Michigan, St. Joseph River
Rates: River: $75pp, 3 person minimum, Lake: $80pp, 4 person minimum, $10 extra pp on weekends/holidays
Call between: 5pm-8pm
Provides: Light tackle, heavy tackle, lures, bait, rain gear
Handicapped equipped: Yes
Certifications: USCG

Rockin-N-Reelin
Ludington 616-845-5987
Species & Seasons: Lake Salmon, Brown Trout, Lake Trout, Steelhead Arpil-Oct
Bodies of water: Lake Michigan at Port of Ludington
Rates: Half day: $260(4), Full day: $360(4)
Call between: 5am-9pm
Provides: Heavy tackle, lures
Handicapped equipped: No
Certifications: USCG

Salmon Nailer Charters
Tekonsha 800-432-9468
Species & Seasons: Chinook Salmon, Lake Trout, Steelhead, Brown Trout, Coho Salmon, Perch April-Oct
Bodies of water: Lake Michigan
Rates: 5 hrs: $250(1-6), 8hrs.: $350(1-6)
Call between: 5pm-10pm
Provides: Light tackle, heavy tackle, lures, bait
Handicapped equipped: Yes
Certifications: USCG

Tammy Too Charters
Spring Lake 616-842-0893
.... 800-824-2343
Species & Seasons: Chinook Salmon, Coho Salmon, Steelhead, Lake Trout, Brown Trout May-Sept
Bodies of water: Lake Michigan at Grand Haven
Rates: Half day(6hrs): $280(1-4), Full day(8hrs): $380(1-4), maximun 6 people, $50 each additional person over 4
Call between: 8am-9pm
Provides: Light tackle, lures, bait, rain gear
Handicapped equipped: Yes
Certifications: USCG, MDNR Inspected

Capt. E.J. Thompson, Jr.
Ludington 616-843-7000
................................843-3090
................................843-3387
Species & Seasons: Lake Trout May-Sept, Chinook Salmon May-Oct, Coho Salmon June-Oct, Steelhead July-Sept, Brown Trout May-June, Yellow Perch June-July
Bodies of water: Lake Michigan, Pere Marquette Lake
Rates: Half day: $55pp(1-6) $220 minimum, Full day: $65pp(1-6) $260 minimum, $75 additional for off-shore Steelhead trips
Call between: 9am-6pm

LAKE MICHIGAN - LAKE ST. CLAIR — MICHIGAN

Provides: Heavy tackle, lures
Handicapped equipped: Yes
Certifications: USCG, NACA, LACA

Capt. Bob Ward
Belding 616-243-9721
.... 800-968-1402
Species & Seasons: Lake Trout, Steelhead, Coho Salmon, Chinook Salmon, Brown Trout May-Oct
Bodies of water: Lake Michigan at Port of Muskegon
Rates: Half day: $75pp, 4 person minimum
Call between: 8am-5pm
Provides: Heavy tackle, lures
Handicapped equipped: Yes
Certifications: USCG

West Sister Sport Fishing Group
Toledo, OH 800-488-3474
Species & Seasons: Salmon, Trout
Bodies of water: Lake Michigan
Call between: Anytime
Provides: Light tackle, heavy tackle, fly rod/reel, lures, bait, rain gear, beverages, lunch
Handicapped equipped: Yes
Certifications: USCG

Captain Chuck Wilkinson
South Haven 616-637-8007
Species & Seasons: Perch April-Oct
Bodies of water: Lake Michigan
Rates: Half day: $30
Call between: 8am-8pm
Provides: Bait
Handicapped equipped: Yes

Capt. Gordon Zuverink
Holland 616-399-5219
Species & Seasons: Lake Trout May-Sept, Steelhead, Brown Trout, Salmon May-Oct
Bodies of water: Lake Michigan
Rates: $240(1-4), $270(5), $290(6)
Call between: 8am-11pm
Provides: Light tackle, heavy tackle, bait, rain gear
Handicapped equipped: No

FLY SHOPS...

Backcast Fly Shop
Benzonia 616-882-5222
Hours: 9am-7pm Mon.-Thurs., 7am-8pm Fri.-Sat., 7am-5pm Sun.

Carries: Live bait, lures, flies, maps, rods, reels, licenses
Bodies of water: Lake Michigan, Crystal Lake, Betsie River, Platte River, many others
Services & Products: Guide services, fishing instruction, mail order 800-717-5222
Guides: Yes
OK to call for current conditions: Yes
Contact: Claude, Steve, Dave or Rick

GUIDES...

Riverborne Angler
Traverse City 616-941-FISH
.... 929-4800
Species & Seasons: Salmon Sept-Nov, Steelhead Oct-June, Trout April-Nov, Bass May-Sept
Bodies of water: Lake Michigan, Pere Marquette River, Manistee River, AuSable River, Betsie River, Muskegon River, Platte River, Boardman River, many inland lakes
Rates: Half day: $150(1), $175(2), Full day: $200(1), $225(2)
Call between: 9am-6pm
Provides: Fly rod/reel, rain gear, beverages, lunch
Handicapped equipped: Yes
Certifications: MDNR

Michael Gnatkowski
Ludington......................... 616-845-1158
Species & Seasons: Steelhead Mar-Dec, Salmon June-Oct, Brown Trout April-Oct, Walleye May-Dec
Bodies of water: Lake Michigan, Pere Marquette River, Tittabawassee River, Saginaw River
Rates: Full day: $200(1-2), Lake: Half day: $200, Full day: $300
Call between: 8am-10pm
Provides: Light tackle, heavy tackle, fly rod/reel, lures, bait
Handicapped equipped: Yes
Certifications: MI River Guides, USCG

LODGES...

Riverside Motel & Marina
Manistee 616-723-3554
Handicapped equipped: Yes
Rates: $25-$150/day
Contact: Anyone
Guides: Yes

Species & Seasons: Steelhead Nov-Mar/May-July, Brown Trout Mar-May, Lake Trout May-July, Salmon July-Oct
Bodies of Water: Lake Michigan, Manistee Lake, Tippy Dam Pond, Manistee River, Little Manistee River
Types of fishing: Fly fishing, light tackle, float trips, lake trips
Available: Fishing instruction, boat rentals

LAKE ST. CLAIR

BAIT & TACKLE...

Drayton Boat Livery
Waterford 810-673-3407
Hours: 6:30am-8pm, 6:30am-8pm Sun., closed Wed.
Carries: Live bait, lures, flies, maps, rods, reels
Bodies of water: Loon Lake, Pontiac Lake, Lake Oakland, Woodhull Lake, Lake St. Clair
Services & Products: Boat rentals, fishing instruction
Guides: Yes
OK to call for current conditions: Yes
Contact: Wendell Lee

Kelly's Outfitters Inc.
Waterford 810-666-1440
Hours: 8am-8pm Mon.-Fri., 7am-8pm Sat., 7am-5pm Sun.
Carries: Live bait, lures, flies, maps, rods, reels, licenses
Bodies of water: Pontiac Lake, Cass Lake, Kent Lake, St. Clair River, Lake St. Clair, many others
Services & Products: Canoes, hunting equipment
Guides: Yes
OK to call for current conditions: Yes
Contact: Anyone

Professional Fishing Center
Harrison Twp. 810-469-2070
Hours: 6am-9pm
Carries: Live bait, lures, flies, maps, rods, reels, licenses
Bodies of water: Lake St. Clair, Lake Erie, Lake Huron
Services & Products: Guide services, charter boat service, beverages, gas/oil, fishing instruction
Guides: Yes
OK to call for current conditions: Yes

MICHIGAN

LAKE ST. CLAIR - MANISTEE RIVER

Zubok's Tackle & Ski Shop
Taylor 313-295-2230
.... 295-4839
Hours: 9am-8pm
Carries: Live bait, lures, flies, maps, rods, reels, licenses
Bodies of water: Lake Erie, Detroit River, Lake St. Clair, Belleville Lake, Ford Lake
Services & Products: Guide services, charter boat service, fishing instruction, repair services
Guides: Yes
OK to call for current conditions: Yes
Contact: Paul Zubok

CHARTERS...

Capt. Bob Bingle
Algonac 810-794-3854
Species & Seasons: SM Bass, Yellow Perch June-Oct, Chinook Salmon July-Aug, Walleye May-June, Duck Hunting Nov-Dec
Bodies of water: Lake Huron, Lake St. Clair, Lake Erie
Rates: $400(4), $450(5), $600(6)
Call between: Anytime
Provides: Light tackle, heavy tackle, lures, bait, beverages, lunch
Handicapped equipped: Yes
Certifications: USCG

Crews Inn Sportfishing Charter
Mt. Clemens 810-465-4124
Species & Seasons: Chinook Salmon April-May/Aug-Sept, Walleye May-July, Muskellunge July-Aug/Sept-Nov, Perch Sept-Nov
Bodies of water: Lake Huron (lower), Lake Erie (Breast Bay), Lake St. Clair
Rates: Half day: $350(1-5), Full day: $450(1-5), $50 additional 6th person
Call between: 9am-12noon
Provides: Light tackle, heavy tackle, lures, bait
Handicapped equipped: Yes
Certifications: USCG, MDNR inspected

Steve Jones
Mount Clemens 810-463-3474
Species & Seasons: Muskellunge June-Nov Salmon April-June, Walleye April-Oct, SM Bass June-Oct, Perch Sept-Oct
Bodies of water: Lake St. Clair, Lake Huron
Rates: Half day: $80(1), Full day: $100(1)

Provides: Light tackle, heavy tackle, lures, bait
Handicapped equipped: Yes
Certifications: USCG

North Bay Charters
New Baltimore 810-725-8233
Species & Seasons: Salmon April-June, Walleye May-Aug, Muskellunge, Perch, SM Bass July-Oct
Bodies of water: Lake Huron, Lake St. Clair, Lake Erie and connecting waters
Rates: Half day: $55(1), Full day: $75(1), 4 people: $250 and up
Call between: 8am-9pm
Provides: Light tackle, heavy tackle, lures, bait, rain gear, beverages, lunch
Handicapped equipped: Yes
Certifications: USCG, MDNR Inspected, insured

5-19 "AT EASE"

RIVER CHARTERS

West Michigan River Fishing on the Famous Manistee & Muskegon Rivers

King Salmon : Sept.1 - Sept 30

Winter/Spring Steelhead: October 1 - May 7th

- Enclosed & heated river sled with all tackle provided...
- Licensed & Insured - references
- $20. off full day trip when mentioning this ad!
- Book NOW for best dates...
- Accommodations on request...

Call or write for free color brochure: **616 856-4589**

Terry Weiler
8988 - 36th Avenue
Newaygo, MI 49337

MANISTEE RIVER

BAIT & TACKLE...

Ed's Sport Shop
Baldwin 616-745-4974
Hours: 7am-10pm
Carries: Live bait, lures, flies, maps, rods, reels, licenses

Bodies of water: Pere Marquette River, Big Manistee River, Little Manistee River, White River, Pine River, 156 lakes
Services & Products: Guide services, beverages, fishing instruction
Guides: Yes
OK to call for current conditions: Yes
Contact: Douglas or Loretta Loomis

Lake City Sport Shop, Inc.
Lake City 616-839-4875
Hours: 8am-5pm, closed Wed. (except summer)
Carries: Live bait, lures, flies, maps, rods, reels, licenses
Bodies of water: Lake Missaukee, Crooked Lake, Lake Sapphire, Clam River, Manistee River, Houghton Lake
Guides: No
OK to call for current conditions: Yes
Contact: John Wachowski

GUIDES...

5-19 "At Ease" River Charters
Newaygo 616-856-4589
Species & Seasons: Salmon Sept-Oct, Steelhead Oct-May
Bodies of water: Manistee River, Muskegon River
Rates: Full day: $100(1), $150(2), $200(3)
Call between: 4:30pm-10pm
Provides: Light tackle, heavy tackle, fly rod/reel, lures, bait
Handicapped equipped: Yes
Certifications: Inland Pilots License

Bud's Charter & Fishing Guide Service
Manistee 616-723-9414
Species & Seasons: Steelhead, Lake Trout June-Sept, Steelhead Oct-Jan, Brown Trout April-June, Coho Salmon, Chinook Salmon July-Sept
Bodies of water: Big Manistee River, Lake Michigan
Rates: Varies
Call between: 7pm-9pm
Provides: Light tackle, heavy tackle, lures, bait
Handicapped equipped: Yes

MANISTEE RIVER - MUSKEGON RIVER — MICHIGAN

Capt. Emil Dean
Bear Lake 616-362-3760
Species & Seasons: Chinook Salmon, Coho Salmon, Lake Trout, Brown Trout May-Sept, Steelhead all year
Bodies of water: Lake Michigan, Manistee River
Rates: River: $300(4), Lake: $400(6) (8 hr. trips)
Call between: 5pm-9pm
Provides: Light tackle, heavy tackle, lures, bait
Handicapped equipped: Yes

River Haven Guide Service
Manistee 616-723-7479
Species & Seasons: Steelhead Sept-April
Bodies of water: Big Manistee River
Rates: Full day: $200(1), $250(2), $300(3)
Call between: 6pm-8pm
Provides: Light tackle, lures, bait
Handicapped equipped: No
Certifications: USCG licensed, insured, Member of MI River Guide Assoc.

Riverborne Angler
Traverse City 616-941-FISH
.... 929-4800
Species & Seasons: Salmon Sept-Nov, Steelhead Oct-June, Trout April-Nov, Bass May-Sept
Bodies of water: Lake Michigan, Pere Marquette River, Manistee River, AuSable River, Betsie River, Muskegon River, Platte River, Boardman River, many inland lakes
Rates: Half day: $150(1), $175(2), Full day: $200(1), $225(2)
Call between: 9am-6pm
Provides: Fly rod/reel, rain gear, beverages, lunch
Handicapped equipped: Yes
Certifications: MDNR

LODGES...

Branch Trout Fishing Resort
Branch 616-898-3178
Handicapped equipped: No
Seasons: Mar 1 to Nov 30
Contact: William C. Ray
Guides: Yes
Species & Seasons: Rainbow Trout Mar-Nov, Steelhead Mar-May, Salmon Sept-Nov
Bodies of Water: Pere Marquette River, Manistee River, Little Manistee River, White River, Muskegon River
Types of fishing: Fly fishing, wading, float trips, pay fishing at Branch Trout Fishing Resort
Available: Fishing instruction, bait, tackle, family activities, pay fishing (trout ponds)

Riverside Motel & Marina
Manistee 616-723-3554
Handicapped equipped: Yes
Rates: $25-$150/day
Guides: Yes
Species & Seasons: Steelhead Nov-Mar/May-July, Brown Trout Mar-May, Lake Trout May-July, Salmon July-Oct
Bodies of Water: Lake Michigan, Manistee Lake, Tippy Dam Pond, Manistee River, Little Manistee River
Types of fishing: Fly fishing, light tackle, float trips, lake trips
Available: Fishing instruction, boat rentals

MANTINY LAKE

BAIT & TACKLE...

Chippewa Lake Sports Shop
Chippewa Lake 616-867-3245
Hours: 8am-7pm
Carries: Live bait, lures, rods, reels, licenses
Bodies of water: Chippewa Lake, Mantiny Lake, Lake Mecosta, Muskegon River
Guides: No
OK to call for current conditions: Yes
Contact: Sue Troyer

MENOMINEE RIVER

BAIT & TACKLE...

Northwood Wilderness Outfitters
Iron Mountain 906-774-9009
Hours: 5:30am-7pm
Carries: Live bait, lures, flies, maps, rods, reels, licenses
Bodies of water: Menominee River, Brule River, Pine River (Wisc.), Popple River (Wisc.), Peavy Falls Flowage, Michigamme Flowage, many small lakes
Services & Products: Boat rentals, lodgin wilderness Lake Trout camps
Guides: Yes
OK to call for current conditions: Yes
Contact: Randy or Gus

MULLET LAKE

BAIT & TACKLE...

Outdoor Adventure Store
Cheboygan 616-627-5273
Hours: 7am-7pm
Carries: Live bait, lures, flies, maps, rods, reels, licenses
Bodies of water: Mullet Lake, Black Lake, Cheboygan River, Burt Lake, Black River, Lake Huron, Indian River, many brookie streams
Services & Products: Food, beverages, fishing instruction, repair services
Guides: Yes
OK to call for current conditions: Yes
Contact: Brenda, Orval or Scottie

MUSKEGON RIVER

BAIT & TACKLE...

Chippewa Lake Sports Shop
Chippewa Lake 616-867-3245
Hours: 8am-7pm
Carries: Live bait, lures, rods, reels, licenses
Bodies of water: Chippewa Lake, Mantiny Lake, Lake Mecosta, Muskegon River
Guides: No
OK to call for current conditions: Yes
Contact: Sue Troyer

The Trading Post
3000 N Wyman Road
Weidman 48893
Hours: 9am-9pm, Noon-9pm Sun.
Carries: Live bait, lures, flies, rods, reels, licenses
Bodies of water: Chippewa River, Muskegon River, Lake Isabella, Chippewa Lake, many more
Services & Products: Food, beverages, oil, guns
Guides: Yes
OK to call for current conditions: No

MICHIGAN

MUSKEGON RIVER - PONTIAC LAKE

GUIDES...

5-19 "At Ease" River Charters
Newaygo 616-856-4589
Species & Seasons: Salmon Sept-Oct, Steelhead Oct-May
Bodies of water: Manistee River, Muskegon River
Rates: Full day: $100(1), $150(2), $200(3)
Call between: 4:30pm-10pm
Provides: Light tackle, heavy tackle, fly rod/reel, lures, bait
Handicapped equipped: Yes
Certifications: Inland Pilots License

Mark R. Martin
Twin Lake 616-744-0330
Species & Seasons: Steelhead April-May, Walleye (day) May-June, Walleye (night) July-Nov
Bodies of water: Muskegon River, Muskegon Lake, Lake White, Spring Lake, Grand River, Saginaw Bay, Saginaw River, Detroit River
Rates: 6 hrs: $200(1), $250(2)
Call between: 9am-6pm
Provides: Light tackle, heavy tackle, lures, bait
Handicapped equipped: Yes
Certifications: USCG

Riverborne Angler
Traverse City 616-941-FISH
.... 929-4800
Species & Seasons: Salmon Sept-Nov, Steelhead Oct-June, Trout April-Nov, Bass May-Sept
Bodies of water: Lake Michigan, Pere Marquette River, Manistee River, AuSable River, Betsie River, Muskegon River, Platte River, Boardman River, many inland lakes
Rates: Half day: $150(1), $175(2), Full day: $200(1), $225(2)
Call between: 9am-6pm
Provides: Fly rod/reel, rain gear, beverages, lunch
Handicapped equipped: Yes
Certifications: MDNR

LODGES...

Branch Trout Fishing Resort
Branch 616-898-3178
Handicapped equipped: No
Seasons: Mar 1 to Nov 30
Contact: William C. Ray
Guides: Yes
Species & Seasons: Rainbow Trout Mar-Nov, Steelhead Mar-May, Salmon Sept-Nov
Bodies of Water: Pere Marquette River, Manistee River, Little Manistee River, White River, Muskegon River
Types of fishing: Fly fishing, wading, float trips, pay fishing at Branch Trout Fishing Resort
Available: Fishing instruction, bait, tackle, family activities, pay fishing (trout ponds)

PERE MARQUETTE RIVER

BAIT & TACKLE...

Ed's Sport Shop
Baldwin 616-745-4974
Hours: 7am-10pm
Carries: Live bait, lures, flies, maps, rods, reels, licenses
Bodies of water: Pere Marquette River, Big Manistee River, Little Manistee River, White River, Pine River, 156 lakes
Services & Products: Guide services, beverages, fishing instruction
Guides: Yes
OK to call for current conditions: Yes
Contact: Douglas or Loretta Loomis

GUIDES...

Michael Gnatkowski
Ludington 616-845-1158
Species & Seasons: Steelhead Mar-Dec, Salmon June-Oct, Brown Trout April-Oct, Walleye May-Dec
Bodies of water: Lake Michigan, Pere Marquette River, Tittabawassee River, Saginaw River
Rates: Full day: $200(1-2), Lake: Half day: $200, Full day: $300
Call between: 8am-10pm
Provides: Light tackle, heavy tackle, fly rod/reel, lures, bait
Handicapped equipped: Yes
Certifications: MI River Guides, USCG

Riverborne Angler
Traverse City 616-941-FISH
.... 929-4800
Species & Seasons: Salmon Sept-Nov, Steelhead Oct-June, Trout April-Nov, Bass May-Sept
Bodies of water: Lake Michigan, Pere Marquette River, Manistee River, AuSable River, Betsie River, Muskegon River, Platte River, Boardman River, many inland lakes
Rates: Half day: $150(1), $175(2), Full day: $200(1), $225(2)
Call between: 9am-6pm
Provides: Fly rod/reel, rain gear, beverages, lunch
Handicapped equipped: Yes
Certifications: MDNR

LODGES...

Branch Trout Fishing Resort
Branch 616-898-3178
Handicapped equipped: No
Seasons: Mar 1 to Nov 30
Contact: William C. Ray
Guides: Yes
Species & Seasons: Rainbow Trout Mar-Nov, Steelhead Mar-May, Salmon Sept-Nov
Bodies of Water: Pere Marquette River, Manistee River, Little Manistee River, White River, Muskegon River
Types of fishing: Fly fishing, wading, float trips, pay fishing at Branch Trout Fishing Resort
Available: Fishing instruction, bait, tackle, family activities, pay fishing (trout ponds)

PONTIAC LAKE

BAIT & TACKLE...

Drayton Boat Livery
Waterford 810-673-3407
Hours: 6:30am-8pm, 6:30am-8pm Sun., closed Wed.
Carries: Live bait, lures, flies, maps, rods, reels
Bodies of water: Loon Lake, Pontiac Lake, Lake Oakland, Woodhull Lake, Lake St. Clair
Services & Products: Boat rentals, fishing instruction
Guides: Yes
OK to call for current conditions: Yes
Contact: Wendell Lee

PONTIAC LAKE - ST. JOSEPH RIVER — MICHIGAN

Kelly's Outfitters Inc.
Waterford 810-666-1440
Hours: 8am-8pm Mon.-Fri.,
7am-8pm Sat., 7am-5pm Sun.
Carries: Live bait, lures, flies, maps, rods, reels, licenses
Bodies of water: Pontiac Lake, Cass Lake, Kent Lake, St. Clair River, Lake St. Clair, many others
Services & Products: Canoes, hunting equipment
Guides: Yes
OK to call for current conditions: Yes
Contact: Anyone

Lenny's Bait & Tackle
Waterford 810-623-9676
Hours: 7am-8pm
Carries: Live bait, lures, flies, maps, rods, reels
Bodies of water: Williams Lake, Woodhull Lake, Maceday Lake, Greens Lake, Lotus Lake, Huntoon Lake, Pontiac Lake, Loon Lake, Lake Oakland
Services & Products: Beverages, fishing instruction
Guides: No
OK to call for current conditions: Yes
Contact: Anyone

SAGINAW BAY

BAIT & TACKLE...

Bubba's Bait & Tackle
Saginaw 517-752-9898
Hours: 6am-6-7pm
Carries: Live bait, lures, flies, maps, rods, reels, licenses
Bodies of water: Saginaw River, Shiawassee River, Tittabawassee River, Saginaw Bay, all tributaries, Lake Huron
Services & Products: Food, beverages, fishing instruction, repair services
Guides: Yes
OK to call for current conditions: Yes
Contact: Roger Mohl or Jan Pardon

Jay's Sporting Goods
Clare 517-386-3475
Hours: 9am-8pm
Carries: Live bait, lures, flies, maps, rods, reels, licenses
Bodies of water: Saginaw Bay, Houghton Lake, Higgins Lake, Bud Lake, Long Lake
Guides: Yes
OK to call for current conditions: Yes
Contact: Carl Athey

See & Sea
Sebewaing 517-883-2755
Hours: 6am-10pm
Carries: Live bait, lures, maps, rods, reels, licenses
Bodies of water: Saginaw Bay, Lake Huron
Guides: Yes
OK to call for current conditions: Yes

GUIDES...

Mark R. Martin
Twin Lake 616-744-0330
Species & Seasons: Steelhead April-May, Walleye (day) May-June, Walleye (night) July-Nov
Bodies of water: Muskegon River, Muskegon Lake, Lake White, Spring Lake, Grand River, Saginaw Bay, Saginaw River, Detroit River
Rates: 6 hrs: $200(1), $250(2)
Call between: 9am-6pm
Provides: Light tackle, heavy tackle, lures, bait
Handicapped equipped: Yes
Certifications: USCG

LODGES...

Caseville Resort Inc.
Caseville 517-856-2323
Handicapped equipped: No
Seasons: April 1 to Oct 15
Rates: $42.40/day
Contact: Charlene Fisher
Guides: No
Species & Seasons: Perch April-Sept, Walleye July-Sept, Salmon Oct
Bodies of Water: Saginaw Bay, Pigeon River
Types of fishing:
Available: Licenses, bait, tackle, boat rentals, cottages, RV sites

SAGINAW RIVER

BAIT & TACKLE...

Bubba's Bait & Tackle
Saginaw 517-752-9898
Hours: 6am-6-7pm
Carries: Live bait, lures, flies, maps, rods, reels, licenses
Bodies of water: Saginaw River, Shiawassee River, Tittabawassee River, Saginaw Bay, all tributaries, Lake Huron
Services & Products: Food, beverages, fishing instruction, repair services
Guides: Yes
OK to call for current conditions: Yes
Contact: Roger Mohl or Jan Pardon

GUIDES...

Michael Gnatkowski
Ludington 616-845-1158
Species & Seasons: Steelhead Mar-Dec, Salmon June-Oct, Brown Trout April-Oct, Walleye May-Dec
Bodies of water: Lake Michigan, Pere Marquette River, Tittabawassee River, Saginaw River
Rates: Full day: $200(1-2), Lake: Half day: $200, Full day: $300
Call between: 8am-10pm
Provides: Light tackle, heavy tackle, fly rod/reel, lures, bait
Handicapped equipped: Yes
Certifications: MI River Guides, USCG

Mark R. Martin
Twin Lake 616-744-0330
Species & Seasons: Steelhead April-May, Walleye (day) May-June, Walleye (night) July-Nov
Bodies of water: Muskegon River, Muskegon Lake, Lake White, Spring Lake, Grand River, Saginaw Bay, Saginaw River, Detroit River
Rates: 6 hrs: $200(1), $250(2)
Call between: 9am-6pm
Provides: Light tackle, heavy tackle, lures, bait
Handicapped equipped: Yes
Certifications: USCG

ST. JOSEPH RIVER

BAIT & TACKLE...

Barron Lake Sports Center
Niles 616-684-3048
Hours: 7am-7pm
Carries: Live bait, lures, flies, maps, rods, reels, licenses
Bodies of water: St. Joseph River, Barron Lake
Services & Products: Food, beverages, gas/oil
Guides: No
OK to call for current conditions: Yes
Contact: Ron

MICHIGAN
ST. JOSEPH RIVER - WHITE RIVER

Jims Fish-N-Bait & Sharpening
Burr Oak 616-432-3986
Hours: 7am-dark, closed Thurs.
Carries: Live bait, lures, flies, maps, rods, reels, licenses
Bodies of water: St. Joseph River
Services & Products: Beverages, gas/oil, fishing instruction
Guides: No
OK to call for current conditions: Yes
Contact: Jim Lee

Prairie River Bait & Tackle
Sturgis 616-467-7903
Hours: 7am-9:30pm
Carries: Live bait, lures, flies, maps, rods, reels, licenses
Bodies of water: St. Joseph River, Lake Templene, Klinger Lake, Corey Lake
Services & Products: Boat rentals, guide services, beverages
OK to call for current conditions: Yes

Specialty Bait, Gifts & Tackle Shop
Berrien Springs 616-471-9020
Hours: 7am-10pm
Carries: Live bait, lures, flies, maps, rods, reels, licenses
Bodies of water: St. Joseph River, Lake Michigan, Indian Lake, Black Lake, Clear Lake
Services & Products: Beverages, repair services
Guides: Yes
OK to call for current conditions: Yes
Contact: Floyd

CHARTERS...

Capt. Gary Gamble
Niles 616-684-4009
Species & Seasons: Coho Salmon April-May, Chinook Salmon April-May/Aug-Oct, Steelhead Feb-April/July-Dec, Brown Trout Mar-May, Lake Trout May-Sept
Bodies of water: Lake Michigan, St. Joseph River
Rates: River: $75pp, $210 minimum, Lake: $80pp, $300 minimum
Call between: 6pm-8pm
Provides: Light tackle, heavy tackle, lures, bait
Handicapped equipped: Yes
Certifications: USCG

Rainbow Charters
Berrien Springs 616-471-3900
Species & Seasons: Steelhead, Brown Trout Jan-Dec, Lake Trout May-Sept, Chinook Salmon April-Oct, Coho Salmon Mar-Oct, Walleye April-Mar, Perch April-Oct, Catfish April-Oct
Bodies of water: Lake Michigan, St. Joseph River
Rates: River: $75pp, 3 person minimum, Lake: $80pp, 4 person minimum, $10 extra pp on weekends/holidays
Call between: 5pm-8pm
Provides: Light tackle, heavy tackle, lures, bait, rain gear
Handicapped equipped: Yes
Certifications: USCG

TAWAS LAKE

BAIT & TACKLE...

North Star Motel & Sport Shop
Tawas City 517-362-2255
Hours: 7am-11pm
Carries: Live bait, lures, flies, maps, rods, reels, licenses
Bodies of water: Lake Huron, Tawas Lake, Sand Lake, AuSable River
Services & Products: Lodging, fishing instruction
Guides: Yes
OK to call for current conditions: Yes
Contact: Helen

WHITE RIVER

BAIT & TACKLE...

Ed's Sport Shop
Baldwin 616-745-4974
Hours: 7am-10pm
Carries: Live bait, lures, flies, maps, rods, reels, licenses
Bodies of water: Pere Marquette River, Big Manistee River, Little Manistee River, White River, Pine River, 156 lakes
Services & Products: Guide services, beverages, fishing instruction
Guides: Yes
OK to call for current conditions: Yes
Contact: Douglas or Loretta Loomis

LODGES...

Branch Trout Fishing Resort
Branch 616-898-3178
Handicapped equipped: No
Seasons: Mar 1 to Nov 30
Contact: William C. Ray
Guides: Yes
Species & Seasons: Rainbow Trout Mar-Nov, Steelhead Mar-May, Salmon Sept-Nov
Bodies of Water: Pere Marquette River, Manistee River, Little Manistee River, White River, Muskegon River
Types of fishing: Fly fishing, wading, float trips, pay fishing at Branch Trout Fishing Resort
Available: Fishing instruction, bait, tackle, family activities, pay fishing (trout ponds)

MINNESOTA

1. Battle Lake
2. Belle Taine Lake
3. Big Pine Lake
4. Big Sandy Lake
5. Birch Lake
6. Bowstring Lake
7. Buttle Lake
8. Boundary Waters Canoe Area
9. Cass Lake
10. Central Region Lakes
    Antler Lake
    Benedict lake
    Big Chippewa River
    Big Lake
    Big Sand Lake
    Island Lake
    Jack the Horse Lake
    Lake Andrusia
    Lake George
    Little Boy Lake
    Lost Lake
    Spider Lake
    Thunder Lake
    Wabana Lake
    Widow Lake
11. Clitherall Lake
12. Crow Wing Chain
13. Deer Lake
14. Farm Island Lake
15. Fish Hook Lake
16. Floyd Lake
17. Forest Lake
18. Green Lake
19. Gull Lake
20. Kabetogama Lake
21. Lake Alexander
22. Lake Bemidji
23. Lake Florida
24. Lake Lida
25. Lake Miltona
26. Lake Minnetonka
27. Lake Minnewaska
28. Lake of the Woods
29. Lake Osakis
30. Lake Pepin
31. Lake Shetek
32. Lake Superior
33. Lake Winnibigoshish
34. Lax Lake
35. Leech Lake
36. Madison Lake
37. Mille Lacs
38. Minnesota River
39. Mississippi River
40. Namakan Lake
41. Nest Lake
42. North Star lake
43. Otter Tail Lake
44. Pelican Lake
45. Pokegama Lake
46. Rainy Lake
47. Rainy River
48. Rice Lake
49. Rush Lake
50. Sand Point Lake
51. Straight River
52. Swan Lake
53. Turtle Lake
54. Union Lake
55. Vermilion Lake
56. Victoria Lake
57. White Bear Lake
58. Whitefish Lake Chain
59. Woman Lake

MINNESOTA

BATTLE LAKE - BELLE TAINE LAKE

BATTLE LAKE

BAIT & TACKLE...

Koep's Clitherall Corner
Clitherall 218-864-8731
Hours: 6:45am-10pm
Carries: Live bait, lures, flies, maps, rods, reels, licenses
Bodies of water: Battle Lake, Clitherall Lake, East Battle Lake, Otter Tail Lake
Services & Products: Guide services, food, beverages, gas/oil, fishing instruction
OK to call for current conditions: Yes
Contact: Eileen, Joe, Steven or Nancy

LODGING...

Baker's Bonnie Beach Resort
Battle Lake 218-864-5534
Guest Capacity: 80
Handicapped equipped: Yes
Seasons: May 15 to Oct 1
Rates: $325-$525/week
Contact: Doug Baker
Guides: Yes
Species & Seasons: Walleye May-June, Northern Pike May-Feb, LM Bass May-Sept, Crappie, Bluegill, Bullheads all year
Bodies of Water: Battle Lake, East Battle Lake, Otter Tail Lake
Types of fishing: Light tackle, heavy tackle, wading
Available: Fishing instruction, licenses, bait, tackle, boat rentals, baby sitting

Battle View Resort
Henning 218-583-4195
Guest Capacity: 30
Handicapped equipped: Just ramps
Seasons: May 15 to Sept 15
Rates: $265/week
Guides: No
Species & Seasons: Walleye, Northern Pike, LM Bass, Bluegill, Crappie
Bodies of Water: Battle Lake, East Battle Lake
Types of fishing: Fly fishing, light tackle, heavy tackle, wading
Available: Boat rentals

Deer Lake Resort
Battle Lake 218-495-3319
Guest Capacity: 9 cabins, 9 camp sites
Handicapped equipped: Yes
Seasons: May 15 to Oct 1
Rates: $245-$$335/week
Contact: Cliff Turner
Guides: Yes
Species & Seasons: Walleye, Perch, Crappie, LM Bass, SM Bass, Bluegill, Northern Pike, Bullheads May-Oct
Bodies of Water: Otter Tail River, Otter Tail Lake, Deer Lake, East Lost Lake, East Battle Lake, Battle Lake
Types of fishing: Fly fishing, wading, float trips
Available: Fishing instruction, bait, tackle, boat rentals, family activities

Moe's Ottertail Beach Resort
Route 3 Box 122
Battle Lake 56515
Handicapped equipped: No
Seasons: May 15 to Nov 1
Rates: $390/week
Guides: Yes
Species & Seasons: Walleye, Northern Pike, Perch May-Oct
Bodies of Water: Otter Tail Lake, Battle Lake, Rush Lake, Star Lake
Types of fishing: Light tackle, wading
Available: Bait, tackle, boat rentals, family activities, children's program, baby sitting

Sunset Beach Resort & Campground
Battle Lake 218-583-2750
Guest Capacity: 32 plus campers
Handicapped equipped: No
Seasons: May 10 to Sept 30
Rates: Cabins: $310-$410/week, Camping: $15-$18/day
Contact: Fred or Rose
Guides: Yes
Species & Seasons: LM Bass, Walleye, Northern Pike May-Sept, Muskellunge June-Sept
Bodies of Water: Battle Lake, Otter Tail Lake
Types of fishing: Light tackle
Available: Bait, tackle, boat rentals

Vacationland Resort
Battle Lake 218-864-5826
.... 507-583-2548(W)
Guest Capacity: 50
Handicapped equipped: No
Seasons: May 1 to Oct 30
Rates: $365/week
Contact:
Guides: Yes
Species & Seasons: Walleye, Northern Pike, LM Bass May-Mar
Bodies of Water: Battle Lake, Otter Tail Lake
Types of fishing: Light tackle, heavy tackle
Available: Licenses, bait, tackle, boat rentals, family activities

Woodland Beach Resort - Campground
Battle Lake 800-827-3069
Handicapped equipped: No
Seasons: May to Oct
Rates: $400/week
Guides: Yes
Species & Seasons: Walleye May-Sept, Northern Pike July-Aug, Perch June-Sept, LM Bass June-Oct, Muskellunge Aug-Oct
Bodies of Water: Otter Tail Lake, Battle Lake
Types of fishing: Light tackle, heavy tackle
Available: Licenses, bait, tackle, boat rentals, baby sitting

BELLE TAINE LAKE

LODGING...

Belle Shore Resort
Nevis 800-864-3750
.... 218-652-3197
Guest Capacity: 36
Handicapped equipped: No
Seasons: May 1 to Oct 1
Rates: $300-$700/week
Contact: Wayne Johnson
Guides: Yes
Species & Seasons: LM Bass June-Oct, Northern Pike, Walleye, Crappie May-Oct
Bodies of Water: Belle Taine Lake, Mantrap Lake, Crow Wing
Types of fishing: Light tackle
Available: Licenses, boat rentals, family activities, children's program, baby sitting

Resort Content
Route 2 Box 255
Nevis 56467
Guest Capacity: 8 cabins (2 and 3 bedroom units)
Handicapped equipped: No
Seasons: May to Oct
Rates: $60-$85/day, $300-$475/week
Guides: Yes, recommend
Species & Seasons: Walleye, LM Bass, Northern Pike, Panfish, Muskellunge May-Sept
Bodies of Water: Mantrap Lake, Crow Wing Chain of Lakes, Leech Lake, Lake Belle Taine
Types of fishing: Light tackle
Available: Boat rentals, family activities, children's program, baby sitting

BIG PINE LAKE - BOWSTRING LAKE

MINNESOTA

BIG PINE LAKE

LODGING...

Waldheim Resort
Finlayson.................. 612-233-7405
Guest Capacity: 70
Handicapped equipped: No
Seasons: May to Oct
Rates: $40-$75/day
Contact: Patti or Jim Watt
Guides: No
Species & Seasons: Walleye, Northern Pike, SM Bass, LM Bass, Crappie, Bluegill
Bodies of Water: Big Pine Lake
Types of fishing: Light tackle
Available: Bait, tackle, boat rentals, family activities, snacks, launch, docks

BIG SANDY LAKE

LODGING...

Sheshebe Resort
McGregor 218-426-3441
Guest Capacity: 40
Handicapped equipped: No
Seasons: All year
Rates: $300/week
Contact: Tony or Lynda Cluett
Guides: Yes
Species & Seasons: Walleye, LM Bass, Northern Pike, Bluegill, Crappie
Bodies of Water: Lake Minnewawa, Big Sandy Lake
Types of fishing: Light tackle, heavy tackle
Available: Fishing instruction, bait, tackle, boat rentals

BIRCH LAKE

LODGING...

Nor'Wester Lodge
Grand Marais 218-388-2252
.... 800-992-4386
Guest Capacity: 75
Handicapped equipped: No
Seasons: All year
Rates: $465/week double occupancy
Contact: Carl
Guides: Yes
Species & Seasons: Walleye May-April, LM Bass, Northern Pike May-May, Trout May-Sept
Bodies of Water: Poplar Lake, Birch Lake, Caribow Lake
Types of fishing: Light tackle, heavy tackle
Available: Fishing instruction, licenses, bait, tackle, boat rentals, family activities

River Point Resort & Outfitting Co.
Ely 800-456-5580
Guest Capacity: 80
Handicapped equipped: Yes
Seasons: May to Oct
Rates: $500-$1600/week
Contact: Steve Koschak
Guides: Yes
Species & Seasons: Walleye, Northern Pike, Crappie, SM Bass May-Oct
Bodies of Water: Birch Lake, South Kawishiwi River, Basswood Lake, Boundary Waters Canoe Area
Types of fishing: Light tackle, heavy tackle, float trips, BWCA/Quetico (Canada) canoe trips
Available: Fishing instruction, licenses, bait, tackle, boat rentals, family activities, children's program, baby sitting

Shady Shores Resort
Hackensack 218-675-6540
Guest Capacity: 11 cabins, 2-4 bedrooms
Handicapped equipped: No
Seasons: May to Nov
Rates: $300-$600/week
Contact: Jim DeSignor
Guides: Yes
Species & Seasons: Walleye, Northern Pike, Crappie, Bluegill May-Nov, LM Bass June-Nov
Bodies of Water: Birch Lake, Tenmile Lake, Leech Lake
Types of fishing: Fly fishing, light tackle, heavy tackle, horse/back pack, wading
Available: Bait, tackle, boat rentals, family activities, swimming, canoeing

Timber Bay Lodge & Houseboats
Babbitt 800-846-6821
Guest Capacity: 60
Handicapped equipped: No
Seasons: Mid May to Oct 1
Rates: $600-$1400/week
Contact: John Rykken
Guides: Yes
Species & Seasons: Walleye May-July, Northern Pike, Crappie May-Oct
Bodies of Water: Birch Lake
Types of fishing: Light tackle
Available: Licenses, bait, tackle, boat rentals, family activities, children's program, houseboat rentals

Timber Wolf Lodge
Ely 218-827-3512
Guest Capacity: 64 cabins, 23 camping sites
Handicapped equipped: Yes
Seasons: All year
Rates: $90-$200/night, $550-$1,475/week
Contact: Jeff Schulze
Guides: Yes
Species & Seasons: Walleye June-Aug, SM Bass, Crappie May-June, Northern Pike May-June/Fall
Bodies of Water: Bear Island River, Birch Lake, Boundary Waters Canoe Area, Vermilion Lake
Types of fishing: Fly fishing, light tackle, heavy tackle, wading, day trips to other lakes
Available: Fishing instruction, licenses, bait, tackle, boat rentals, family activities, children's program, baby sitting

BOWSTRING LAKE

BAIT & TACKLE...

Rapids Tackle
Grand Rapids 218-326-5822
Hours: 5:30am-9pm
Carries: Live bait, lures, flies, maps, rods, reels, licenses
Bodies of water: Lake Winnibigoshish, Bowstring Lake, Pokegama Lake, Mississippi River, Bigfork River, 1200 smaller lakes
Services & Products: Guide services, beverages, repair services
Guides: Yes
OK to call for current conditions: Yes
Contact: Don Wendt

Y Bait Station
Deer River 218-246-2867
Hours: 6am-9pm
Carries: Live bait, lures, flies, maps, rods, reels, licenses
Bodies of water: Lake Winnibigoshish, Ball Club Lake, Bowstring Lake, Squaw Lake
Services & Products: Guide services, food, beverages, gas/oil, fishing instruction
OK to call for current conditions: Yes
Contact: Brett Jahn

YOUR SILENT FISHING PARTNER

MINNESOTA
BOWSTRING LAKE - BOUNDARY WATERS CANOE AREA

LODGING...

Northern Acres Resort & Camping
HCR 3 Box 446
Deer River 56636
Guest Capacity: 34 cabins, 20 campsites
Handicapped equipped: No
Seasons: All year
Rates: $60/day, $465/week
Contact: Jack Heathman
Guides: Yes
Species & Seasons: Walleye, Northern Pike May-Feb, Perch, Crappie all year
Bodies of Water: Bowstring Lake, Sand Lake, Winibigoshkish Lake, Jessie Lake
Types of fishing: Light tackle, heavy tackle
Available: Licenses, bait, tackle, boat rentals

Pine Grove Lodge
Max 218-798-2865
Guest Capacity: 30
Handicapped equipped: No
Seasons: May to Nov
Rates: $370/week
Contact: Wayne Wahlstrom
Guides: Yes
Species & Seasons: Walleye, Northern Pike, LM Bass, Crappie, Perch May-Oct
Bodies of Water: Sand Lake, Bowstring Lake, Cut Foot Sioux Lake, Lake Winnibigoshish
Types of fishing: Fly fishing, light tackle, heavy tackle, wading
Available: Fishing instruction, bait, tackle, boat rentals, family activities, children's program, baby sitting

Trail's End
Deer River 218-832-3231
Guest Capacity: 60
Handicapped equipped: No
Seasons: All year
Rates: Starting at $495/week
Guides: Yes
Species & Seasons: Walleye, Northern Pike, Perch, Crappie
Bodies of Water: Bowstring Lake, Lake Winnibigoshish, Sand Lake, Jessie Lake
Available: Bait, tackle, boat rentals, family activities, children's program, baby sitting

BUTTLE LAKE

GUIDES...

Gary Burks
Underwood 218-495-3154
Species & Seasons: LM Bass, Walleye, Northern Pike, Panfish May-Oct
Bodies of water: Otter Tail County Lakes
Rates: Half day: $75(1), $90(2),
Full day: $130(1), $150(2)
Call between: 6pm-10pm
Provides: Light tackle, heavy tackle, lures, bait
Handicapped equipped: No

BOUNDARY WATERS CANOE AREA

GUIDES...

Chip Leer
Ray 218-875-2204
Species & Seasons: Walleye, SM Bass, LM Bass, Crappie, Sturgeon, Northern Pike April-Oct
Bodies of water: Kabetogama Namakan Lake Lake, Rainy Lake, Rainy River, Sand Point Lake, Crane Lake, Voyageurs National Park, Lake of the Woods
Rates: Half day: $150(2),
Full day: $200(2)
Call between: 6am-11pm
Provides: Light tackle, heavy tackle, fly rod/reel, lures, bait, rain gear, beverages, lunch
Handicapped equipped: Yes
Certifications: USCG

Top of the Trail Outfitters & Cabins
Grand Marais 800-869-0883
Species & Seasons: SM Bass, Northern Pike, Walleye, Lake Trout May-Sept
Bodies of water: Saganaga Lake and lakes in the Eastern Boundary Waters Canoe Area, the eastern portion of the Quetico Provincial Park
Rates: Call for rate schedule
Call between: 8am-9pm
Handicapped equipped: Yes

LODGING...

Borderland Lodge & Outfitters
Crane Lake 800-777-8392
Guest Capacity: 69
Handicapped equipped: No
Seasons: All year
Rates: $357-$1,400/week
Contact: Anyone
Guides: Yes
Species & Seasons: Walleye, LM Bass, Northern Pike May-Mar, Crappie all year
Bodies of Water: Crane Lake, Sand Point Lake, Namakan Lake, Kabetogama Lake, Lac La Croix
Types of fishing: Light tackle, fly-out trips, shuttles to Boundary Waters and Quetico (Canada)
Available: Licenses, bait, tackle, boat rentals, family activities, children's program

Cabin O' Pines Resort & Campground
Orr 800-757-3122
Guest Capacity: 162
Handicapped equipped: No
Seasons: Memorial Day to Mid Sept
Rates: $24/day pp, $120/week pp
Contact: Gary or Lori
Guides: Yes
Species & Seasons: Walleye, Northern Pike May-Oct, LM Bass, SM Bass June-Oct, Bluegill June-July, Muskellunge July-Aug
Bodies of Water: Pelican Lake, Little Fork River, Lac La Croix
Types of fishing: Light tackle, heavy tackle, fly-out trips
Available: Bait, tackle, boat rentals, family activities, baby sitting

Campbell's Cabins and Trading Post
Crane Lake 218-993-2361
Guest Capacity: 70
Handicapped equipped: No
Seasons: May to Sept
Rates: $118/day
Contact: Jan Handberg
Guides: Yes
Species & Seasons: LM Bass, SM Bass, Walleye, Northern Pike, Trout May-Sept
Bodies of Water: Lac La Croix (Ontario)
Types of fishing: Light tackle, fly-out trips, canoe
Available: Licenses, bait, tackle, boat rentals

BOUNDARY WATERS CANOE AREA — MINNESOTA

Canadian Waters
111 E Sheridan
Ely 55731
Guest Capacity: 300
Handicapped equipped: Yes
Seasons: May to Sept
Rates: $75/day
Guides: No
Species & Seasons: Walleye, LM Bass, SM Bass, Northern Pike, Lake Trout May-Sept
Bodies of Water: Boundary Waters Canoe Area
Types of fishing: Fly fishing, light tackle, heavy tackle, fly-out trips, float trips
Available: Licenses, bait, tackle, boat rentals

Cedar Shores
Ely 218-365-5775
Guest Capacity: 23
Handicapped equipped: No
Seasons: May 15 to Sept 15
Rates: $500/week
Contact: Larry
Guides: Yes
Species & Seasons: Walleye, Northern Pike, SM Bass, Perch May-Sept
Bodies of Water: Shagawa Lake, Little Long, Burnside Lake, Boundary Waters Canoe Area
Types of fishing: Light tackle, heavy tackle, canoe
Available: Licenses, bait, tackle, boat rentals, family activities

Custom Cabin Rentals
Ely 218-365-6947
Guest Capacity: 50
Handicapped equipped: No
Seasons: All year
Rates: $565 2 people/week includes boat
Guides: Yes
Species & Seasons: LM Bass, SM Bass, Walleye, Northern Pike, Trout
Bodies of Water: Moose Lake, Basswood Lake
Types of fishing: Fly fishing, light tackle, wading, fly-out trips
Available: Fishing instruction, bait, tackle, boat rentals

Eagle Wing Resort
Ray 218-875-3111
Guest Capacity: 5 cabins (30 people)
Handicapped equipped: No
Seasons: May 13 to Oct 1
Rates: $295-$545/week
Contact: Russ or Marlys Kingery
Guides: Yes
Species & Seasons: Walleye, Northern Pike May-Oct
Bodies of Water: Kabetogama Lake, Namakan Lake, Crane Lake, Sand Point Lake
Types of fishing: Fly fishing, light tackle, heavy tackle
Available: Fishing instruction, licenses, bait, tackle, boat rentals, family activities

Eagle Wing Resort (advertisement)
Minnesota - Canadian Border
Lake Kabetogama
Gateway to Voyageurs National Park
Modern Cabins — 1 & 2 Bedroom — Smoke-Free
➤ Fish Cleaning & Freezer Services
➤ Playground/Paddleboats/Canoe
➤ Protected Harbor and Beach
➤ Boat & Motor Rentals
➤ Electric & Gas on Dock
Eagle Wing Resort
10042 Gappa Road
Ray, MN 56669
(218) 875-3111
Russ & Marlys Kingery
"With the Wilderness As Your Neighbor"

End of the Trail Lodge
4284 End of Trail Lane
Tower 55790
Guest Capacity: 30
Handicapped equipped: No
Seasons: May to Mar
Rates: $400-$650/week
Guides: Yes
Species & Seasons: Walleye, Northern Pike, Muskellunge May-Feb, Crappie all year, LM Bass, SM Bass May-Feb
Bodies of Water: Vermilion Lake, Trout Lake, Boundary Waters Canoe Area
Types of fishing: Light tackle, heavy tackle
Available: Bait, tackle, boat rentals

Grandview Resort
Cook 218-666-5327
Guest Capacity: 24
Handicapped equipped: No
Seasons: May 1 to Oct 1
Rates: $800+/week 6 people
Contact: Kathie Gustafson
Guides: Yes
Species & Seasons: Northern Pike, Walleye, SM Bass, LM Bass, Crappie, Bluegill, Muskellunge May-Freeze-up
Bodies of Water: Vermilion Lake, Trout Lake, Boundary Waters Canoe Area
Types of fishing: Light tackle, heavy tackle
Available: Boat rentals

Hungry Jack Lodge & Campground
Grand Marais 218-388-2265
.... 800-338-1566
Guest Capacity: 150
Handicapped equipped: Yes
Seasons: All year
Rates: Varies
Guides: Yes
Species & Seasons: SM Bass May-Oct, Walleye May-Feb, Rainbow Trout, Steelhead, Lake Trout, Splake May-Mar, Northern Pike May-Feb
Bodies of Water: Hungry Jack Lake, West Bearskin Lake, Lake Superior
Types of fishing: Fly fishing, light tackle, heavy tackle, horse/back pack, wading, fly-out trips, ice fishing
Available: Fishing instruction, licenses, bait, tackle, boat rentals, family activities, children's program, baby sitting, guided snowmobile trips, hunting

Jackpine Lodge
Ely 218-365-5700
Guest Capacity: 100
Handicapped equipped: No
Seasons: May 15 to Oct 15
Rates: $75/day
Contact: Don Stocks
Guides: Yes
Species & Seasons: Lake Trout, Walleye, Northern Pike, LM Bass, SM Bass
Bodies of Water: Snowbank Lake
Types of fishing: Light tackle
Available: Licenses, bait, tackle, boat rentals, baby sitting

MINNESOTA

BOUNDARY WATERS CANOE AREA

LaTourell's Resort & Outfitters
Ely 218-365-4531
Guest Capacity: 60
Handicapped equipped: No
Seasons: May to Oct
Rates: $375-$800/week
Guides: Yes
Species & Seasons: Walleye, SM Bass, Northern Pike, Trout May-Oct
Bodies of Water: Boundary Waters Canor Area, Basswood Lake
Types of fishing: Fly fishing, light tackle, fly-out trips
Available: Fishing instruction, licenses, bait, tackle, boat rentals

Muskego Point Resort
Cook 218-666-5696
Guest Capacity: 81
Handicapped equipped: No
Seasons: May 12 to Oct 5
Rates: $500-$1200/week 2 persons
Contact: Grant, Judy or Jenny Hughes
Guides: Yes
Species & Seasons: Walleye May-Oct, Northern Pike, Muskellunge July-Oct, LM Bass, SM Bass June-Oct
Bodies of Water: Vermilion Lake, Boundary Waters Canoe Area
Types of fishing: Fly fishing, light tackle, heavy tackle
Available: Fishing instruction, licenses, bait, tackle, boat rentals, family activities, baby sitting

Nor'Wester Lodge
Grand Marais 218-388-2252
.... 800-992-4386
Guest Capacity: 75
Handicapped equipped: No
Seasons: All year
Rates: $465/week double occupancy
Contact: Carl
Guides: Yes
Species & Seasons: Walleye May-April, LM Bass, Northern Pike May-May, Trout May-Sept
Bodies of Water: Poplar Lake, Birch Lake, Caribow Lake
Types of fishing: Light tackle, heavy tackle
Available: Fishing instruction, licenses, bait, tackle, boat rentals, family activities

Northernair Lodge
Ely 218-365-4882
Guest Capacity: 75-80
Handicapped equipped: No
Seasons: All year
Rates: $375-$595/week

Contact: Francis Fitzgerald
Guides: Yes
Species & Seasons: Walleye, SM Bass, Northern Pike, May-Mar, Panfish all year
Bodies of Water: Mitchell Lake, 500 lakes within a 20 mile radius
Types of fishing: Fly fishing, light tackle, heavy tackle, float trips
Available: Fishing instruction, bait, tackle, boat rentals, family activities, children's program, only resort on lake, no public access

Northwind Lodge
Ely 218-365-5489
Guest Capacity: 50
Handicapped equipped: No
Seasons: May to Oct
Rates: $450+/week
Contact:
Guides: Yes
Species & Seasons: Walleye May-July, Northern Pike May-Oct, SM Bass, LM Bass July-Sept
Bodies of Water: Jasper Lake, Ojibway Lake, Triangle Lake, Moose Lake, Lake One, Wood Lake, Tofte Lake, Snowbank Lake, Boundary Waters Canoe Area
Types of fishing: Fly fishing, light tackle, wilderness canoe trips
Available: Fishing instruction, licenses, bait, tackle, boat rentals, family activities, free mountain biking, kayaking, canoe tours

Olson Bay Resort
Ely 218-365-4876
Guest Capacity: 55
Handicapped equipped: No
Seasons: May 15 to Oct 1
Rates: $510/week, 4 people
Contact: Gary or Barb Detoffol
Guides: Yes
Species & Seasons: Walleye May-July, Northern Pike May-Sept, SM Bass June-July
Bodies of Water: Shagawa Lake, many others
Types of fishing: Light tackle, heavy tackle, fly-out trips, canoe trips
Available: Fishing instruction, boat rentals, family activities, children's program, baby sitting, bar, restaurant

River Point Resort & Outfitting Co.
Ely 800-456-5580
Guest Capacity: 80
Handicapped equipped: Yes
Seasons: May to Oct
Rates: $500-$1600/week

Contact: Steve Koschak
Guides: Yes
Species & Seasons: Walleye, Northern Pike, Crappie, SM Bass May-Oct
Bodies of Water: Birch Lake, South Kawishiwi River, Basswood Lake, Boundary Waters Canoe Area
Types of fishing: Light tackle, heavy tackle, float trips, BWCA/Quetico (Canada) canoe trips
Available: Fishing instruction, licenses, bait, tackle, boat rentals, family activities, children's program, baby sitting

Sherrick Wilderness Resort
Crane Lake 218-374-3531
Guest Capacity: 55
Handicapped equipped: No
Seasons: May 13 to Oct 15
Rates: Cabin: $220-$280/week double occupancy
Contact: Bill Sherrick
Guides: No
Species & Seasons: SM Bass, Northern Pike, Walleye, Perch, Panfish May-Oct
Bodies of Water: Johnson Lake, Little Johnson Lake, Spring Lake, Crane Lake
Types of fishing: Fly fishing, light tackle, heavy tackle
Available: Bait, boat rentals, out board motors, premixed gas

Smitty's on Snowbank
Ely 800-950-8310
Guest Capacity: 82
Handicapped equipped: No
Seasons: All year
Rates: $44.95/day
Guides: Yes
Species & Seasons: Lake Trout May-Sept/Jan-Mar, SM Bass, Walleye, Northern Pike May-Nov
Bodies of Water: Snowbank Lake, Moose Lake, Basswood Lake, Boundary Waters Canoe Area
Types of fishing: Fly fishing, light tackle, heavy tackle, fly-out trips
Available: Fishing instruction, licenses, bait, tackle, boat rentals

Superior Forest Lodge & Outfitters
Ely 800-777-7503
Guest Capacity: 70
Handicapped equipped: No
Seasons: Mid May to Oct 1
Rates: $69-$750
Contact: Tim or Nancy Krugman
Guides: Yes
Species & Seasons: Northern Pike, SM Bass May-Oct, Walleye, LM Bass, Panfish June-Oct

BOUNDARY WATERS CANOE AREA - CASS LAKE

MINNESOTA

Bodies of Water: Canadian and Minnesota Boundary Waters Canoe Area
Types of fishing: Fly fishing, light tackle, heavy tackle, wading, fly-out trips, float trips, canoe trips
Available: Licenses, bait, tackle, boat rentals, family activities, children's program

Timber Wolf Lodge
Ely 218-827-3512
Guest Capacity: 64 cabins, 23 camping sites
Handicapped equipped: Yes
Seasons: All year
Rates: $90-$200/night, $550-$1,475/week
Contact: Jeff Schulze
Guides: Yes
Species & Seasons: Walleye June-Aug, SM Bass, Crappie May-June, Northern Pike May-June/Fall
Bodies of Water: Bear Island River, Birch Lake, Boundary Waters Canoe Area, Vermilion Lake
Types of fishing: Fly fishing, light tackle, heavy tackle, wading, day trips to other lakes
Available: Fishing instruction, licenses, bait, tackle, boat rentals, family activities, children's program, baby sitting

Tom & Woods Moose Lake Wilderness Canoe Trips
Ely 800-322-5837
Guest Capacity: 100
Handicapped equipped: No
Seasons: May 1 to Sept 25
Rates: $88/day
Contact: Blayne Hall
Guides: Yes
Species & Seasons: Lake Trout, Northern Pike, Walleye, SM Bass, LM Bass all seasons
Bodies of Water: Boundary Waters Canoe Area, Quetico Provencial Park (Canada)
Types of fishing: Light tackle
Available: Fishing instruction, licenses, bait, tackle, boat rentals

Windigo Lodge
Grand Marais 218-388-2222
Guest Capacity: 100
Handicapped equipped: Yes
Seasons: All year
Rates: $75/day and up double occupancy
Contact: Bob or Char
Guides: Yes
Species & Seasons: Walleye, Lake Trout, Brook Trout, LM Bass, Splake May-Oct

Bodies of Water: Poplar Lake, Saganaga Lake, Gunflint Lake, Sea Gull Lake, Caribow Lake, Swamp Lakes, Boundary Waters Canoe Area
Types of fishing: Fly fishing, light tackle, heavy tackle, wading
Available: Fishing instruction, licenses, bait, tackle, boat rentals, family activities, children's program(near), baby sitting(near)

CASS LAKE

LODGING...

Big Wolf Lake Resort & Campground
Bemidji 800-322-0281
Guest Capacity: 18 cottages 1-9 bdrm, 40 campsites
Seasons: All year
Rates: $450
Guides: Yes
Species & Seasons: Walleye, Northern Pike, Crappie, LM Bass, Muskellunge
Bodies of Water: Mississippi River, Cass Lake
Types of fishing: Light tackle, heavy tackle, canoe trips
Available: Licenses, bait, tackle, boat rentals, family activities, children's program, heated pool, lodge, whirpool, sauna

Judds Resort
Bena 218-665-2216
Guest Capacity: 160 cabins
Handicapped equipped: Yes
Seasons: All year
Rates: $80/day and up, $380/week & up
Contact: Ron or Sharon Hunter
Guides: Yes
Species & Seasons: Walleye, Northern Pike, Muskellunge May-Feb, Perch all year

Bodies of Water: Lake Winnibigoshish, Cass Lake, Leech Lake
Types of fishing: Light tackle, heavy tackle, wading, launch
Available: Fishing instruction, licenses, bait, tackle, boat rentals, family activities, children's program, baby sitting, camping (27 sites)

Little Wolf Resort
Cass Lake 218-335-2138
Guest Capacity: 40
Handicapped equipped: No
Seasons: May to Oct
Rates: $345/week, daily rates available
Contact: Ralph or Karen
Guides: Yes
Species & Seasons: Walleye, Muskellunge, LM Bass, Northern Pike, Panfish
Bodies of Water: Leech Lake, Cass Lake
Types of fishing: Light tackle, heavy tackle
Available: Bait, tackle, boat rentals, family activities

Lost Acres Resort
Blackduck 800-835-6414
.... 218-835-6414
Guest Capacity: 60
Handicapped equipped: Yes, partially
Seasons: May 10 to April 5
Rates: $58-$100/day, $290-$500/week
Guides: Yes
Species & Seasons: Walleye, Northern Pike May-Feb, Panfish all year, Muskellunge, LM Bass June-Feb
Bodies of Water: Mississippi River Chain of lakes, Little Rice Lake, Rice Lake, Cass Lake, Lake Andrusia, Wolf Lake
Types of fishing: Fly fishing, light tackle, heavy tackle
Available: Fishing instruction, licenses, bait, tackle, boat rentals, family activities, motor rentals, pontoon with fishfinder

800-892-1192
218-335-2138

LITTLE WOLF RESORT
On Little Wolf Lake
Where Dreams Are Made

RALPH & KAREN PHILLIPS

Rt. 2, Box 270
Cass Lake, MN 56633

MINNESOTA

CASS LAKE - CENTRAL REGION LAKES

Pike Point Resort & Lodge
Tenstrike 218-586-2810
Guest Capacity: 43
Handicapped equipped: No
Seasons: May to Oct
Rates: $58-$92/day, $290-$460/week
Contact: Ron or Joan Yearling
Guides: Yes
Species & Seasons: Walleye, Northern Pike May-Oct, LM Bass, Bluegill June-Sept, Crappie May-Sept
Bodies of Water: Lake Bemidji, Cass Lake, Mississippi River, Chain Lakes, Leech Lake, Winnibigoshish, Red Lake
Types of fishing: Fly fishing, light tackle, heavy tackle
Available: Fishing instruction, licenses, bait, tackle, boat rentals, family activities, baby sitting

View Point Resort
Cass Lake 218-335-6746
Guest Capacity: 6 Cabins (2, 3 bed)
Handicapped equipped: Yes
Seasons: May 15 to Oct 1
Rates:
Contact: L. R. Grunwald
Guides: Yes
Species & Seasons: Muskellunge, Northern Pike June-Sept, Walleye, LM Bass May-July, Crappie, Bluegill
Bodies of Water: Little Wolf Lake, Wolf Lake, Cass Lake, Leech Lake, many more
Types of fishing: Fly fishing, light tackle, heavy tackle, wading
Available: Licenses, bait, tackle, boat rentals, family activities, baby sitting, sand beach, walking trails

(MORE) CENTRAL REGION LAKES

BAIT & TACKLE...

Pierce's Country Store
Remer 218-566-2334
Hours: 6am-9pm
Carries: Live bait, lures, maps, licenses
Bodies of water: Leech Lake, Thunder Lake, Rice Lake, Little Thunder Lake
Services & Products: Lodging, food, beverages, gas/oil
Guides: No
OK to call for current conditions: Yes
Contact: Dean Pierce

GUIDES...

Duane Lobbins
New London 612-354-4289
Species & Seasons: Walleye, Northern Pike May-Jan, LM Bass, SM Bass June-Oct, Panfish all year
Bodies of water: All central Minnesota lakes
Rates: Half day: $50(1), $85(2), $110(3), Full day: $100(1), $150(2), $200(3)
Call between: 6pm-10pm
Provides: Light tackle, heavy tackle, fly rod/reel, lures, bait, rain gear
Handicapped equipped: Yes

Gary Stay
Longville 218-363-2308
Species & Seasons: Muskellunge June-Oct, LM Bass, SM Bass, Walleye, Northern Pike May-Oct, Panfish April-Oct
Bodies of water: Leech Lake, Woman Lake, Little Boy Lake, Wabedo Lake, Lake Winnibigoshish, many other area waters
Rates: Half day: $110(1-3), Full day: $175(1-3)
Call between: 6pm-10pm
Provides: Light tackle, heavy tackle, lures, bait
Handicapped equipped: Yes

LODGING...

Antler Lodge
Bigfork 218-245-1136
Guest Capacity: 74
Handicapped equipped: No
Seasons: All year
Rates: $49/day, $425/week
Contact: Pat Berzins
Guides: Yes
Species & Seasons: LM Bass, Walleye, Northern Pike May-Feb, Crappie, Bluegill all year
Bodies of Water: Antler Lake, Eagle Lake, Long Lake
Types of fishing: Fly fishing, light tackle
Available: Licenses, bait, tackle, boat rentals

Balsam Bay Resort
Remer 800-952-7098
.... 218-566-2346
Handicapped equipped: No
Seasons: May 12 to Nov 15
Rates: $300/week 2 people
Guides: No
Species & Seasons: Northern Pike, Walleye, LM Bass May-Feb, Bluegill, Crappie all year
Bodies of Water: Big Sand Lake, Leech Lake, Winnibigoshish
Types of fishing: Light tackle, heavy tackle
Available: Boat rentals

Berndt's Kamp Kappy Resort- Campgrounds & Hobby Land
Brandon 612-524-2225
Handicapped equipped: Yes
Seasons: May to Oct
Rates: Cabin: $65-$90/day, $335-$465/week, camping also
Contact: Sharalyn Berndt
Guides: No
Species & Seasons: Crappie, Bluegill, Walleye, Northern Pike, LM Bass May-Oct
Bodies of Water: Chippewa River, Little Chippewa River
Available: Licenses, bait, tackle, boat rentals, family activities

Big Springs Resort & Campground
Remer 218-566-2322
Handicapped equipped: No
Seasons: May to Mid Oct
Rates: $65-up/day, $390-up/week
Guides: Yes, on availability
Species & Seasons: Walleye, LM Bass, SM Bass, Northern Pike, Crappie, Bluegill May-Oct
Bodies of Water: Thunder Lake
Types of fishing: Fly fishing, light tackle
Available: Fishing instruction, bait, tackle, boat rentals, family activities, outboard motors, gas, convenience store

Birch Bay Resort
Grand Rapids 218-326-2370
Guest Capacity: 29
Handicapped equipped: No
Seasons: May 15 to Oct 1
Rates: $380/week
Guides: No
Species & Seasons: Walleye May-Oct, LM Bass, SM Bass, Northern Pike, Crappie, Bluegill, Perch June-Oct
Bodies of Water: Wabana Lake, Trout Lake, Little Trout Lake
Available: Licenses, bait (some), tackle(some), boat rentals

Camp Jack the Horse
Marcell 218-832-3421
Handicapped equipped: No
Seasons: May to Nov
Rates: $350/week and up
Contact: M. Youngdahl
Guides: Yes
Species & Seasons: LM Bass, Northern Pike, Crappie, Bluegill

CENTRAL REGION LAKES — MINNESOTA

Bodies of Water: Jack the Horse Lake
Types of fishing: Fly-fishing, light tackle
Available: Licenses, boat rentals, naturalist program

Cedar Bay Resort
Hackensack 218-682-2431
Guest Capacity: 25
Handicapped equipped: No
Seasons: May 15 to Oct 1
Rates: $250-$400/week
Contact: Kris or Fern Kahlson
Guides: No
Species & Seasons: Northern Pike, LM Bass, Bluegill, Crappie
Bodies of Water: Widow Lake
Available: Boat rentals

Conway's Sandy Beach Resort
Bemidji 218-335-8894
Guest Capacity: 90
Handicapped equipped: No
Seasons: May 15 to Oct 15
Rates: $500/week
Contact: Jan Conway
Guides: Yes
Species & Seasons: Walleye May-June, Northern Pike, Crappie May-Oct, LM Bass June-Oct, Muskellunge July-Sept
Bodies of Water: Big Lake
Types of fishing: Light tackle, heavy tackle
Available: Bait, tackle, boat rentals, family activities

Deer Lake Resort
Battle Lake 218-495-3319
Guest Capacity: 9 cabins, 9 camp sites
Handicapped equipped: Yes
Seasons: May 15 to Oct 1
Rates: $245-$$335/week
Contact: Cliff Turner
Guides: Yes
Species & Seasons: Walleye, Perch, Crappie, LM Bass, SM Bass, Bluegill, Northern Pike, Bullheads May-Oct
Bodies of Water: Otter Tail River, Otter Tail Lake, Deer Lake, East Lost Lake, East Battle Lake, Battle Lake
Types of fishing: Fly fishing, wading, float trips
Available: Fishing instruction, bait, tackle, boat rentals, family activities

Great Escape Resort
Bemidji 218-335-8834
Guest Capacity: 20
Handicapped equipped: No
Seasons: May to Oct
Rates: $300-$450/week
Contact: Jim or Midge Drebing
Guides: No
Species & Seasons: Walleye, Perch, Northern Pike, Muskellunge, LM Bass May-Oct
Bodies of Water: Lake Andrusia
Types of fishing: Fly fishing, light tackle, heavy tackle
Available: Licenses, bait, tackle, boat rentals

Home Bay Resort
Park Rapids 800-553-4072
Guest Capacity: 52
Handicapped equipped: No
Seasons: All year
Rates: $80-$90/day, $345-$625/week
Contact: Robert Davidson
Guides: Yes
Species & Seasons: Walleye, Northern Pike, LM Bass, Crappie, Bluegill, Perch
Bodies of Water: Big Sand Lake
Types of fishing: Light tackle
Available: Licenses, bait, tackle, boat rentals, baby sitting

Interlachen Resort
Hackensack 218-682-2490
Guest Capacity: 48
Handicapped equipped: No
Seasons: May 1 to Oct 1
Rates: $325-$450/week, daily rates also available
Contact: Gary or Connie Erickson
Guides: Yes
Species & Seasons: Walleye, LM Bass, Northern Pike, Crappie, Bluegill, Muskellunge May-Oct
Bodies of Water: Kid Lake, Lost Lake, 127 other lakes in 10 mile radius
Available: Motor rental

Little Boy Resort & Campground
Longville 218-363-2188
.... 800-592-0024
Handicapped equipped: No
Seasons: May 1 to Oct 25
Rates: $70-$125/day, $350-$625/week, Campground: $15-$18/day
Contact: Doug or Laura Mayer
Guides: Yes, recommend
Species & Seasons: Muskellunge, Walleye, Northern Pike, SM Bass, LM Bass, Crappie, Bluegill, Rock Bass, Suckers
Bodies of Water: Little Boy Lake, Wabedo Lake
Types of fishing: Light tackle, heavy tackle
Available: Bait, tackle, boat rentals

Lost Acres Resort
Blackduck 800-835-6414
.... 218-835-6414
Guest Capacity: 60
Handicapped equipped: Yes, partially
Seasons: May 10 to April 5
Rates: $58-$100/day, $290-$500/week
Guides: Yes
Species & Seasons: Walleye, Northern Pike May-Feb, Panfish all year, Muskellunge, LM Bass June-Feb
Bodies of Water: Mississippi River Chain of lakes, Little Rice Lake, Rice Lake, Cass Lake, Lake Andrusia, Wolf Lake
Types of fishing: Fly fishing, light tackle, heavy tackle
Available: Fishing instruction, licenses, bait, tackle, boat rentals, family activities, motor rentals, pontoon w/fishfinder

Miller's Resort
Deer River 218-246-8951
Guest Capacity: 13
Handicapped equipped: No
Seasons: May 13 to Oct 1
Rates: Cabin: $250/week
Guides: Not necessary, small lake
Species & Seasons: Walleye, Northern Pike, Crappie, Bluegill, LM Bass May-Oct
Bodies of Water: Island Lake
Types of fishing: Fly fishing, light tackle
Available: Fishing instruction, boat rentals, family activities, fish cleaning instructions

Pinehurst Lodge Resort
Benedict 800-359-2567
.... 218-224-2577
Guest Capacity: 7 quality cabins
Bodies of Water: Benedict Lake
Available: Swimming, tennis, boats

Taviani's Wagon Wheel Resort
Lake George 218-266-3664
Guest Capacity: 10 housekeeping cabins
Handicapped equipped: No
Seasons: May to Nov
Rates: $435/week for 4
Contact: Norm or Penny
Guides: Yes, but not needed on our lake
Species & Seasons: Panfish, Crappie, Walleye, Northern Pike May-Oct, LM Bass June-Oct
Bodies of Water: Lake George
Types of fishing: Fly fishing, light tackle, heavy tackle, fish from dock, troll in lake
Available: Bait, tackle, boat rentals, family activities, swim-fish-relax

MINNESOTA
CENTRAL REGION LAKES - DEER LAKE

Timber Lane Resort
Alexandria 612-846-7153
Guest Capacity: 40
Handicapped equipped: No
Seasons: May 1 to Nov 1
Rates: $75-$120/day, $450-$750/week
Contact: Terry Rinehart
Guides: Yes
Species & Seasons: Walleye, Northern Pike May-Feb, LM Bass, SM Bass June-Feb, Crappie, Bluegill all year
Bodies of Water: Area of many lakes
Types of fishing: Light tackle
Available: Licenses, bait, tackle, boat rentals, family activities, baby sitting, pontoon rental, paddleboat rental

Wildview Lodge
Marcell 218-326-8406
.... 326-5124
Guest Capacity: 8 cabins
Handicapped equipped: No
Seasons: May 15 to Oct 1
Rates: $300/week
Guides: No
Species & Seasons: Northern Pike, Panfish, Perch May-Oct, LM Bass June-Oct, Walleye June-?
Bodies of Water: Spider Lake, Ruby Lake, Burnt Shanty Lake, Black Island Lake
Types of fishing: Light tackle
Available: Fishing instruction, licenses, bait, tackle, boat rentals, family activities, baby sitting

CLITHERALL LAKE

BAIT & TACKLE...

Koep's Clitherall Corner
Clitherall 218-864-8731
Hours: 6:45am-10pm
Carries: Live bait, lures, flies, maps, rods, reels, licenses
Bodies of water: Battle Lake, Clitherall Lake, East Battle Lake, Otter Tail Lake
Services & Products: Guide services, food, beverages, gas/oil, fishing instruction
OK to call for current conditions: Yes
Contact: Eileen, Joe, Steven or Nancy

GUIDES...

Gary Burks
Underwood 218-495-3154
Species & Seasons: LM Bass, Walleye, Northern Pike, Panfish May-Oct

Bodies of water: Otter Tail County Lakes
Rates: Half day $75(1), $90(2), Full day $130(1), $150(2)
Call between: 6pm-10pm
Provides: Light tackle, heavy tackle, lures, bait
Handicapped equipped: No

LODGING...

Old Town Resort
Clitherall 800-545-4062
Guest Capacity: 56
Handicapped equipped: No
Seasons: April to Dec
Rates: $55/day
Contact: Pauline or Jack Plantin
Guides: Yes
Species & Seasons: Crappie May-July, Walleye, Northern Pike May-Oct, LM Bass June-Sept
Bodies of Water: Clitherall Lake
Types of fishing: Light tackle, wading
Available: Fishing instruction, bait, tackle, boat rentals

CROW WING CHAIN

LODGING...

Belle Shore Resort
Nevis 800-864-3750
.... 218-652-3197
Guest Capacity: 36
Handicapped equipped: No
Seasons: May 1 to Oct 1
Rates: $300-$700/week
Contact: Wayne Johnson
Guides: Yes
Species & Seasons: LM Bass June-Oct, Northern Pike, Walleye, Crappie May-Oct
Bodies of Water: Belle Taine Lake, Mantrap Lake, Crow Wing
Types of fishing: Light tackle
Available: Licenses, boat rentals, family activities, children's program, baby sitting

Eagles Landing Resort
Nevis 218-732-4211
Handicapped equipped: No
Seasons: May to Oct
Rates: $300-$500/week, $60-$100/day
Contact: Bill or Darlene Hopkins
Guides: No
Species & Seasons: Walleye, Northern Pike, Crappie, Bluegill May-Oct, LM Bass June-Oct
Bodies of Water: Crow Wing

Types of fishing: Fly fishing, light tackle
Available: Fishing instruction, licenses, bait, tackle, boat rentals, family activities, children's program, weekly fishing contest

In-We-Go-Resort & Motel
Nevis 218-652-3536
.... 800-347-2480
Guest Capacity: 75
Handicapped equipped: Yes
Seasons: All year
Rates: $39.50-$150/day
Contact: John Olson
Guides: No
Species & Seasons: Walleye, Northern Pike, LM Bass May-Feb, Crappie, Bluegill, Perch all year
Bodies of Water: 8th, 9th and 10th Crow Wing Lakes
Types of fishing: Light tackle
Available: Licenses, bait, tackle, boat rentals, family activities, children's program, baby sitting

Resort Content
Route 2 Box 255
Nevis 56467
Guest Capacity: 8 cabins
(2 and 3 bedroom units)
Handicapped equipped: No
Seasons: May to Oct
Rates: $60-$85/day, $300-$475/week
Guides: Yes, recommend
Species & Seasons: Walleye, LM Bass, Northern Pike, Panfish, Muskellunge May-Sept
Bodies of Water: Mantrap Lake, Crow Wing Chain of Lakes, Leech Lake, Lake Belle Taine
Types of fishing: Light tackle
Available: Boat rentals, family activities, children's program, baby sitting

DEER LAKE

LODGING...

Back O' the Moon
Grand Rapids 218-326-8648
Guest Capacity: 36
Handicapped equipped: No
Seasons: All year
Rates: $70/day, $350/week
Contact: Ron or Shirley
Guides: No
Species & Seasons: Walleye May-June, Northern Pike May-Oct, LM Bass June-Aug, Bluegill July-Sept
Bodies of Water: Bass Lake, Deer Lake, Moose Lake, Mississippi River

DEER LAKE - FLOYD LAKE

MINNESOTA

Types of fishing: Light tackle, heavy tackle
Available: Bait, tackle, boat rentals

Breezy Portage Resort & Store
Deer River 218-246-8688
Guest Capacity: 20
Handicapped equipped: No
Rates: $300-$350/week
Guides: Yes, recommend
Species & Seasons: Walleye May-Oct, Muskellunge June-Oct, SM Bass June-Sept, Perch all year
Bodies of Water: Moose Lake, Little Moose Lake, Deer Lake
Types of fishing: Light tackle, heavy tackle
Available: Fishing instruction, licenses, bait, tackle, boat rentals, family activities, billards, video games, beer, pizza, groceries

Deer Lake Resort
Battle Lake 218-495-3319
Guest Capacity: 9 cabins, 9 camp sites
Handicapped equipped: Yes
Seasons: May 15 to Oct 1
Rates: $245-$$335/week
Contact: Cliff Turner
Guides: Yes
Species & Seasons: Walleye, Perch, Crappie, LM Bass, SM Bass, Bluegill, Northern Pike, Bullheads May-Oct
Bodies of Water: Otter Tail River, Otter Tail Lake, Deer Lake, East Lost Lake, East Battle Lake, Battle Lake
Types of fishing: Fly fishing, wading, float trips
Available: Fishing instruction, bait, tackle, boat rentals, family activities

FARM ISLAND LAKE

BAIT & TACKLE...

Tutt's Bait & Tackle
Garrison 612-692-4341
Hours: 7am-9pm
Carries: Live bait, lures, flies, maps, rods, reels, licenses
Bodies of water: Mille Lacs, Mississippi River, Bay Lake, Farm Island Lake, Borden Lake
Guides: Yes
OK to call for current conditions: Yes
Contact: Orrin Tutt

LODGING...

Bill's Resort & Campground
Aitkin 218-927-3841
Handicapped equipped: No
Seasons: All year
Contact: Babs
Guides: Yes
Species & Seasons: Walleye, Northern Pike, Crappie, LM Bass, SM Bass, Bluegill, Catfish all year
Bodies of Water: Farm Island Lake, Little Pine Lake
Available: Boat rentals, new playground

Bradley's Farm Island Resort & RV Park
Aitkin 218-678-2881
Guest Capacity: 50
Handicapped equipped: No
Seasons: May 15 to Oct 1
Rates: $50-$150/day, $265-$610/week
Contact: Lorrie or Dick
Guides: Yes
Species & Seasons: Walleye, Northern Pike, Crappie, Bluegill May-Oct, LM Bass June-Oct
Bodies of Water: Farm Island Lake, Mille Lacs
Types of fishing: Boat and motor only
Available: Bait, boat rentals

Whitewood Resort
Aitkin 218-927-3804
Guest Capacity: 50
Handicapped equipped: No
Seasons: May to Oct
Rates: $250-$450/week
Contact: Mike or Mavis McGuire
Guides: No
Species & Seasons: Walleye, Northern Pike, Crappie, Bluegill, LM Bass all summer long
Bodies of Water: Mille Lacs, Cedar Lake, Farm Island Lake
Types of fishing: Fly fishing, light tackle, heavy tackle
Available: Fishing instruction, boat rentals, family activities

FISH HOOK LAKE

GUIDES...

Kelly Condiff
Park Rapids 218-732-7796
Species & Seasons: LM Bass, Northern Pike May-Oct, Crappie April-Oct, Walleye May-Oct, Trout April-Sept, Muskellunge June-Oct

Bodies of water: Leech Lake, Fish Hook Lake Chain, Mantrap Lake
Rates: Half day: $100(1-2), Full day: $150(1-2)
Call between: 9am-9pm
Provides: Light tackle, heavy tackle, lures, bait
Handicapped equipped: No

LODGING...

Loon's Nest Resort
Park Rapids 800-531-3477
Guest Capacity: 13 cabins
Handicapped equipped: No
Seasons: May to Oct
Rates: $295-$495/week
Contact: Louie or Rickie
Guides: Yes
Species & Seasons: Walleye, Northern Pike May-July, LM Bass June-Oct, Crappie, Bluegill April-July
Bodies of Water: Fish Hook Lake
Types of fishing: Fly fishing, light tackle, heavy tackle
Available: Bait, tackle, boat rentals, family activities, children's program, baby sitting

FLOYD LAKE

LODGING...

Blue Sky Resort
Detroit Lakes 218-847-5521
Guest Capacity: 50 +rollaways and cribs
Handicapped equipped: No
Seasons: May 15 to Oct 31
Rates: $350/2 people per week, $630/6 people per week
Contact: Serene Flanagan
Guides: No
Species & Seasons: Bluegill, Crappie all year, LM Bass, Northern Pike, Walleye May-Feb
Bodies of Water: Little Floyd Lake, Floyd Lake, 412 other lakes within 40 miles
Types of fishing: Fly fishing, light tackle
Available: Boat rentals, baby sitting, pontoon, motor rentals

MINNESOTA

FOREST LAKE - GULL LAKE

FOREST LAKE

BAIT & TACKLE...

Forest Lake Sports & Tackle & Taxidermy
Forest Lake 612-464-1200
Hours: 5am-9pm
Carries: Live bait, lures, flies, maps, rods, reels, licenses
Bodies of water: Mississippi River, St. Croix River, Forest Lake, Clear Lake, many others
Services & Products: Guide services, food, beverages, gas/oil, fishing instruction
Guides: Yes
OK to call for current conditions: Yes
Contact: Clay Zimmerman

Mike's Sporting Goods
Forest Lake 612-464-1557
Hours: 6am-8pm
Carries: Live bait, lures, flies, maps, rods, reels, licenses
Bodies of water: Forest Lake, Chisago Lake, Greer Lake, Lindstrom Lake
Services & Products: Food, beverages, hunting products, clothing, propane
Guides: Yes
OK to call for current conditions: Yes
Contact: Tim O'Brien

GREEN LAKE

LODGING...

Indian Beach Resort
13412 Indian Beach Road
Spicer 56288
Guest Capacity: 110
Handicapped equipped: No
Seasons: May to Oct
Guides: Yes
Species & Seasons: Walleye May-June/Sept-Oct, SM Bass May-June
Bodies of Water: Green Lake
Types of fishing: Light tackle, heavy tackle, wading
Available: Fishing instruction, licenses, bait, tackle, boat rentals, family activities

Willow Bay Resort
Spicer 612-796-5517
Guest Capacity: 8 cabins
Handicapped equipped: No
Seasons: May 1 to Oct 1
Rates: Varies
Contact: Joanne

Guides: Yes, recommend
Species & Seasons: SM Bass, LM Bass, May-Nov, Walleye, Northern Pike, Panfish May-Mar
Bodies of Water: Nest Lake, Green Lake, Crow River, Lake Florida
Types of fishing: Light tackle, heavy tackle
Available: Licenses, bait, tackle, boat rentals, family activities

GULL LAKE

(also see Crow Wing Chain of Lakes)

BAIT & TACKLE...

Koep's Bait & Tackle
Nisswa 218-963-2547
Hours: 6:30am-9pm Summer, 9am-5pm Winter
Carries: Live bait, lures, flies, maps, rods, reels, licenses
Bodies of water: Mississippi River, Gull Lake, Pelican Lake, Long Lake, Pine Mountain Lake, Whitefish Lake Chain, Lake Hubert
Services & Products: Guide services, beverages, fishing instructio,] repair services
Guides: Yes
OK to call for current conditions: Yes
Contact: Dave, Ryan or Marv

GUIDES...

Paul Coventry
Brainerd 218-829-1846
Species & Seasons: Walleye, Northern Pike, LM Bass, Trout May-Nov, Muskellunge June-Nov, Panfish April-Nov
Bodies of water: Gull Lake, Whitefish Lake Chain, Pelican Lake, North Long Lake, Mille Lacs, Leech Lake, Lake Winnibigoshish
Rates: Half day: $150(Maximun 3), Full day: $300(Maximum 3)
Call between: 7am-10pm
Provides: Light tackle, heavy tackle, lures, bait, rain gear
Handicapped equipped: Yes
Certifications: USCG

Koeps Bait & Tackle
Nisswa 218-963-2547
Species & Seasons: Walleye, Bass, Northern Pike, Crappie, Sunfish
Bodies of water: Mississippi River, Gull Lake, Pelican Lake, North Long Lake, Whitefish Lake Chain
Rates: Half day: $150(1-3), Full day: $300(1-3)
Call between: 8am-6pm
Provides: Light tackle, heavy tackle, fly rod/reel, lures, bait, rain gear
Handicapped equipped: Yes
Certifications: USCG

LODGING...

Gilbert Lake Resort
Brainerd 218-829-4652
Guest Capacity: 3 cabins (15 people)
Handicapped equipped: No
Seasons: May 1 to Oct 1
Rates: $350/week
Guides: Yes
Species & Seasons: LM Bass, Northern Pike, Crappie, Bluegill
Bodies of Water: Gilbert Lake, Gull Lake, Whitefish Lake Chain, Mille Lacs, many others
Types of fishing: Light tackle
Available: Fishing instruction, bait, tackle, boat rentals, Brainerd City activities 2 miles

Little Pine Resort & Campground
3734 Little Pine Road W
Brainerd 56401
Guest Capacity: 40
Handicapped equipped: No
Seasons: All year
Rates: $350-$800/week
Guides: Yes
Species & Seasons: Panfish all year, Northern Pike, LM Bass May-Feb
Bodies of Water: Gull Lake
Types of fishing: Fly fishing, light tackle, wading
Available: Licenses, bait, tackle, boat rentals, baby sitting

Quarterdeck Resort & Restaurant
Nisswa 800-950-5596
.... 218-963-2482
Guest Capacity: 160
Seasons: All year
Rates: Cabins: $74-$120/day, $340-$767/week
Contact: Allan C. Gunsbury
Guides: Yes
Species & Seasons: Walleye, Northern Pike May-Feb, LM Bass May-Feb, Bluegill all year
Bodies of Water: Gull Lake of Gull Lake
Types of fishing: Light tackle

GULL LAKE - LAKE BEMIDJI

Available: Fishing instruction, licenses, bait, tackle, boat rentals, family activities, children's program, baby sitting, full service restaurant

Sandy Beach Resort
Nisswa 218-963-4458
Guest Capacity: 186
Handicapped equipped: No
Seasons: May 12 to Oct 2
Rates: $690/week
Guides: Yes
Species & Seasons: Walleye, Northern Pike May-Feb, LM Bass May-?, Bluegill all year
Bodies of Water: Gull Lake
Types of fishing: Light tackle
Available: Licenses, boat rentals, family activities

KABETOGAMA LAKE

GUIDES...

Chip Leer
Ray 218-875-2204
Species & Seasons: Walleye, SM Bass, LM Bass, Crappie, Sturgeon, Northern Pike April-Oct
Bodies of water: Kabetogama Namakan Lake Lake, Rainy Lake, Rainy River, Sand Point Lake, Crane Lake, Voyageurs National Park, Lake of the Woods
Rates: Half day: $150(2), Full day: $200(2)
Call between: 6am-11pm
Provides: Light tackle, heavy tackle, fly rod/reel, lures, bait, rain gear, beverages, lunch
Handicapped equipped: Yes
Certifications: USCG

LODGING...

Borderland Lodge & Outfitters
Crane Lake 800-777-8392
Guest Capacity: 69
Handicapped equipped: No
Seasons: All year
Rates: $357-$1,400/week
Guides: Yes
Species & Seasons: Walleye, LM Bass, Northern Pike May-Mar, Crappie all year
Bodies of Water: Crane Lake, Sand Point Lake, Namakan Lake, Kabetogama Lake, Lac La Croix
Types of fishing: Light tackle, fly-out trips, shuttles to Boundary Waters and Quetico (Canada)

Available: Licenses, bait, tackle, boat rentals, family activities, children's program

Eagle Wing Resort
Ray 218-875-3111
Guest Capacity: 5 cabins (30 people)
Handicapped equipped: No
Seasons: May 13 to Oct 1
Rates: $295-$545/week
Contact: Russ or Marlys Kingery
Guides: Yes
Species & Seasons: Walleye, Northern Pike May-Oct
Bodies of Water: Kabetogama Lake, Namakan Lake, Crane Lake, Sand Point Lake
Types of fishing: Fly fishing, light tackle, heavy tackle
Available: Fishing instruction, licenses, bait, tackle, boat rentals, family activities

Four Winds Resort
Ray 218-875-2821
Guest Capacity: 50
Handicapped equipped: No
Seasons: May 15 to Oct 1
Rates: $150/pp/week
Guides: Yes
Species & Seasons: Walleye, Northern Pike, SM Bass, Crappie May-Oct
Bodies of Water: Kabetogama Lake, Namakan Lake
Types of fishing: Light tackle
Available: Licenses, bait, tackle, boat rentals, baby sitting

Moosehorn Resort
Ray 218-875-3491
.... 800-777-7968
Guest Capacity: 50
Handicapped equipped: No
Seasons: May to Winter
Rates: From $450/week, 2 people, $1300/week, 6 people
Guides: Yes
Species & Seasons: Walleye, Northern Pike, LM Bass, Crappie May-Oct, Whitefish Oct-Nov
Bodies of Water: Kabetogama Lake, Namakan Lake, Sand Point Lake, Rainy Lake
Types of fishing: Light tackle
Available: Fishing instruction, licenses, bait, tackle, boat rentals

Park Point Resort
Ray 800-272-4533
Guest Capacity: 45
Handicapped equipped: No
Seasons: May to Oct 30
Rates: $450/week

Guides: Yes
Species & Seasons: Walleye Sept-Oct/May-June, Northern Pike July-Sept, SM Bass, LM Bass July-Aug, Crappie May
Bodies of Water: Kabetogama Lake, Rainy Lake, Namakan Lake
Types of fishing: Light tackle, heavy tackle
Available: Fishing instruction, licenses, bait, tackle, boat rentals, beach, waterskiing

LAKE ALEXANDER

BAIT & TACKLE...

T J Snell's Bait & Groceries
Cushing 218-575-2923
Hours: 7am-9pm (Summer)
Carries: Live bait, lures, flies, maps, rods, reels, licenses
Bodies of water: Lake Alexander, Shamineau Lake, Fish Trap Lake, Crow Wing River
Services & Products: Boat rentals, food, beverages, gas/oil, propane, groceries
Guides: Yes
OK to call for current conditions: Yes
Contact: Tina or John Snell

LAKE BEMIDJI

LODGING...

Frontier Resort
Pinewood 800-872-6621
Guest Capacity: 36
Handicapped equipped: No
Seasons: All year
Rates: $495/week
Contact: Jane or Gary McCollom
Guides: Yes
Species & Seasons: Northern Pike, Walleye May-Feb, LM Bass June-Feb, Crappie, Bluegill all year
Bodies of Water: Balm Lake, Clearwater Lake, Lake Bemidji, many small lakes
Types of fishing: Light tackle, heavy tackle
Available: Fishing instruction, licenses, bait, tackle, boat rentals, family activities, children's program, baby sitting

MINNESOTA

LAKE BEMIDJI - LAKE MINNETONKA

Pike Point Resort & Lodge
Tenstrike 218-586-2810
Guest Capacity: 43
Handicapped equipped: No
Seasons: May to Oct
Rates: $58-$92/day, $290-$460/week
Contact: Ron or Joan Yearling
Guides: Yes
Species & Seasons: Walleye, Northern Pike May-Oct, LM Bass, Bluegill June-Sept, Crappie May-Sept
Bodies of Water: Lake Bemidji, Cass Lake, Mississippi River, Chain Lakes, Leech Lake, Winnibigoshish, Red Lake
Types of fishing: Fly fishing, light tackle, heavy tackle
Available: Fishing instruction, licenses, bait, tackle, boat rentals, family activities, baby sitting

LAKE FLORIDA

LODGING...

Lake Florida Resort
Spicer 612-354-4272
Guest Capacity: 67
Handicapped equipped: Yes, partial
Seasons: May 15 to Oct 1
Rates: $79-$209/day, $395-$1045/week
Contact: Bob or Connie Dickerson
Guides: Yes
Species & Seasons: Walleye, Northern Pike, LM Bass, Bluegill, Perch seasons vary
Bodies of Water: Lake Florida with 15 other fishing lakes within 15 minute drive
Types of fishing: Fly fishing, light tackle, heavy tackle, wading
Available: Licenses, bait, tackle, boat rentals, family activities, children's program, baby sitting

Willow Bay Resort
Spicer 612-796-5517
Guest Capacity: 8 cabins
Handicapped equipped: No
Seasons: May 1 to Oct 1
Rates: Varies
Contact: Joanne
Guides: Yes, recommend
Species & Seasons: SM Bass, LM Bas, May-Nov, Walleye, Northern Pike, Panfish May-Mar
Bodies of Water: Nest Lake, Green Lake, Crow River, Lake Florida
Types of fishing: Light tackle, heavy tackle
Available: Licenses, bait, tackle, boat rentals, family activities

LAKE LIDA

LODGING...

Maple Beach Resort
Pelican Rapids 218-863-5248
Guest Capacity: 50
Handicapped equipped: Some
Seasons: May 15 to Sept 30
Rates: $42.50-$65/day, $215-$395/week
Contact: Ann
Guides: Yes
Species & Seasons: Walleye May-Sept, Northern Pike, Bluegill all year, Crappie May-April, LM Bass May-Feb, Trout May-Sept
Bodies of Water: Lake Lida
Types of fishing: Fly fishing, light tackle
Available: Fishing instruction, licenses, bait, tackle, boat rentals, fenced-in playground, swimming, lawn games, table tennis, burger grill serving 7 days a week

LAKE MILTONA

GUIDES...

T J's Guide Service
Osakis 612-859-3392
Species & Seasons: Walleye, Northern Pike May-Feb, LM Bass June-Nov, Crappie, Sunfish Jan-Jan
Bodies of water: Lake Osakis, Alexandria Chain of Lakes, Lake Reno, Lake Ida, Lake Miltona
Rates: Half day: $90(2), Full day: $175(2), $40 additional 3rd person
Call between: 5pm-9pm
Provides: Light tackle, heavy tackle, lures, bait
Handicapped equipped: Yes

Viking Land Guide Service
Osakis 800-267-9326
Species & Seasons: Walleye, Muskellunge, Northern Pike, LM Bass, SM Bass May-Feb, Perch, Sunfish, Crappie all year, Sturgeon April-Dec
Bodies of water: Mille Lacs, Leech Lake, Rainy River, Lake Osakis, Alexandria Chain of Lakes, Lake Miltona, Lake Ida, Lake Minnewaska
Rates: Half day: $50(1), $75(2), $110(3), Full day: $85(1), $110(2), $175(3), Children welcomed
Call between: Anytime
Provides: Light tackle, heavy tackle, lures, bait, rain gear, beverages, lunch
Handicapped equipped: Yes
Certifications: USCG

LODGING...

Surfside Resort
Alexandria 612-886-5438
Guest Capacity: 34
Handicapped equipped: No
Seasons: May 1 to Oct 30
Rates: $70/day
Contact: Rick
Guides: Yes
Species & Seasons: Walleye May-July, LM Bass June-Oct, Northern Pike, Panfish May-Oct, Walleye Sept-Oct
Bodies of Water: Lake Mary, Lake Carlos, Lake Ida, Lake Miltona, Lake Osakis
Types of fishing: Fly fishing, light tackle, heavy tackle, wading
Available: Fishing instruction, licenses, bait, tackle, boat rentals, family activities, children's program

Viking Bay Resort
Miltona 218-943-2104
Guest Capacity: 60
Handicapped equipped: No
Seasons: All year
Rates: From $70/day
Guides: Yes
Species & Seasons: Walleye, Northern Pike, LM Bass, SM Bass May-Feb, Bluegill all year, Muskellunge June-Feb
Bodies of Water: Lake Miltona
Types of fishing: Light tackle
Available: Licenses, bait, tackle, boat rentals, family activities

LAKE MINNETONKA

BAIT & TACKLE...

B & D Bait and Tackle
Richfield 612-866-5640
Hours: 9am-6pm
Carries: Live bait, lures, flies, maps, rods, reels, licenses
Bodies of water: Mississippi River, Minnesota River, Lake Minnetonka
Services & Products: Beverages, repair services
Guides: Yes
OK to call for current conditions: Yes
Contact: Pat Buchanan

LAKE MINNETONKA - LAKE OF THE WOODS
MINNESOTA

Shoreline Bait & Tackle
Spring Park 612-471-7876
Hours: 7am-9pm
Carries: Live bait, lures, flies, maps, rods, reels, licenses
Bodies of water: Lake Minnetonka
Services & Products: Guide services, beverages
Guides: Yes
OK to call for current conditions: Yes
Contact: Ron or Steve

Thorne Brothers Fishing Specialist
Fridley 612-572-3782
Hours: 9:30am-8:30pm Mon.-Fri., 9am-5pm Sat., 11am-3pm Sun.
Carries: Lures, flies, maps, rods, reels, licenses
Bodies of water: Mississippi River, Mille Lacs, Lake Minnetonka, Leech Lake
Services & Products: Repair services
Guides: Yes
OK to call for current conditions: Yes
Contact: Anyone

LAKE MINNEWASKA

BAIT & TACKLE...

Minnewaska Bait and Tackle
Starbuck 612-239-2239
Hours: 6am-9pm
Carries: Live bait, lures, maps, rods, reels, licenses
Bodies of water: Lake Minnewaska, Pelican Lake, Lake Emily
Services & Products: Food, beverages, gas/oil, fishing instruction
Guides: Yes
OK to call for current conditions: Yes
Contact: Larry Jensen

GUIDES...

Viking Land Guide Service
Osakis 800-267-9326
Species & Seasons: Walleye, Muskellunge, Northern Pike, LM Bass, SM Bass May-Feb, Perch, Sunfish, Crappie all year, Sturgeon April-Dec
Bodies of water: Mille Lacs, Leech Lake, Rainy River, Lake Osakis, Alexandria Chain of Lakes, Lake Miltona, Lake Ida, Lake Minnewaska
Rates: Half day: $50(1), $75(2), $110(3), Full day: $85(1), $110(2), $175(3), Children welcomed
Call between: Anytime

Provides: Light tackle, heavy tackle, lures, bait, rain gear, beverages, lunch
Handicapped equipped: Yes
Certifications: USCG

LODGING...

Bayside Resort & RV Park
Glenwood 612-634-3233
Guest Capacity: 70
Handicapped equipped: No
Seasons: May to Oct
Rates: $320/week 2 bedrooms
Contact: Kyle Nestor
Guides: Yes
Species & Seasons: Walleye, Northern Pike May-Feb, Crappie May-Dec, SM Bass, LM Bass June-Aug, Bluegill all year
Bodies of Water: Lake Minnewaska
Types of fishing: Light tackle, heavy tackle
Available: Licenses, bait, tackle, boat rentals, baby sitting, gas, store

El Reno Resort & Campground
Glenwood 800-291-5616
.... 612-283-5594
Guest Capacity: 40+
Handicapped equipped: No
Seasons: May to Oct 1
Rates: $12.50/night
Contact: Kathie
Guides: No
Species & Seasons: Walleye, Northern Pike, LM Bass, SM Bass May-Oct
Bodies of Water: Lake Reno, Lake Minnewaska, Alexandria Chain of Lakes
Available: Licenses, bait, tackle, grocery store, boat ramp

LAKE OF THE WOODS

GUIDES...

Chip Leer
Ray 218-875-2204
Species & Seasons: Walleye, SM Bass, LM Bass, Crappie, Sturgeon, Northern Pike April-Oct
Bodies of water: Kabetogama Lake, Namakan Lake, Rainy Lake, Rainy River, Sand Point Lake, Crane Lake, Voyageurs National Park, Lake of the Woods
Rates: Half day: $150(2), Full day: $200(2)

Call between: 6am-11pm
Provides: Light tackle, heavy tackle, fly rod/reel, lures, bait, rain gear, beverages, lunch
Handicapped equipped: Yes
Certifications: USCG

LODGING...

Angle Outpost
Angle Inlet 800-441-5014
Guest Capacity: 65
Handicapped equipped: No
Seasons: All year
Contact: Diane Edman
Guides: Yes
Species & Seasons: Walleye May-April, Muskellunge June-Nov, SM Bass, Northern Pike all year
Bodies of Water: Lake of the Woods
Types of fishing: Light tackle, heavy tackle
Available: Fishing instruction, licenses, bait, tackle, boat rentals

Ballard's Resort
Baudette 218-634-1849
Guest Capacity: 77
Handicapped equipped: No
Seasons: All year
Rates: $150/week pp
Contact: Gary Moeller
Guides: Yes
Species & Seasons: Walleye, Sauger May-April, Northern Pike, SM Bass, Perch all year
Bodies of Water: Lake of the Woods, Rainy River
Types of fishing: Light tackle, heavy tackle, guided charter boat fishing
Available: Licenses, bait, tackle, boat rentals, guided trips from Lund Pro-V's

Bayview Lodge
Baudette 218-634-2194
Handicapped equipped: No
Seasons: All year
Rates: $38/day double occupancy
Contact: Randee
Guides: Yes
Species & Seasons: Walleye, Sauger, Northern Pike
Bodies of Water: Rainy River, Lake of the Woods
Types of fishing: Light tackle and downrigging
Available: Licenses, bait, tackle, boat rentals

MINNESOTA
LAKE OF THE WOODS - LAKE OSAKIS

Jake's Northwest Angle
Angle Inlet 218-223-8181
Guest Capacity: 33 beds(resort), 15 campsites
Handicapped equipped: No
Seasons: Memorial Day to Oct 25 - Dec 15 to Mar 20
Contact: Celeste Colson
Guides: Yes
Species & Seasons: Walleye June-Oct/Dec-Mar, Muskellunge June-Oct, SM Bass June-July, Sauger June-Sept/Dec-Mar, Yellow Perch Feb-Mar
Bodies of Water: Lake of the Woods
Types of fishing: Light tackle, heavy tackle, fly-out trips
Available: Fishing instruction, licenses, bait, tackle, boat rentals

Zippel Bay Resort
Williams 800-222-2537
Guest Capacity: 50
Handicapped equipped: No
Seasons: All year
Rates: $340-$540/week
Contact: Nick Painovich
Guides: Yes
Species & Seasons: Walleye, May-Oct, Sauger Dec-Apr, Northern Pike April-May, SM Bass July-Aug, Perch April-May
Bodies of Water: Lake of the Woods
Types of fishing: Light tackle
Available: Fishing instruction, licenses, bait, tackle, boat rentals, baby sitting

LAKE OSAKIS

GUIDES...

T J's Guide Service
Osakis 612-859-3392
Species & Seasons: Walleye, Northern Pike May-Feb, LM Bass June-Nov, Crappie, Sunfish Jan-Jan
Bodies of water: Lake Osakis, Alexandria Chain of lakes, Lake Reno, Lake Ida, Lake Miltona
Rates: Half day: $90(2), Full day: $175(2), $40 additional 3rd person
Call between: 5pm-9pm
Provides: Light tackle, heavy tackle, lures, bait
Handicapped equipped: Yes

Viking Land Guide Service
Osakis 800-267-9326
Species & Seasons: Walleye, Muskellunge, Northern Pike, LM Bass, SM Bass May-Feb, Perch, Sunfish, Crappie all year, Sturgeon April-Dec

Bodies of water: Mille Lacs, Leech Lake, Rainy River, Lake Osakis, Alexandria Chain of lakes, Lake Miltona, Lake Ida, Lake Minnewaska
Rates: Half day: $50(1), $75(2), $110(3), Full day: $85(1), $110(2), $175(3), Children welcomed
Call between: Anytime
Provides: Light tackle, heavy tackle, lures, bait, rain gear, beverages, lunch
Handicapped equipped: Yes
Certifications: USCG

LODGING...

Black's Crescent Beach Resort
Osakis 800-535-2790
Guest Capacity: 130
Handicapped equipped: No
Seasons: May 1 to Oct 3
Rates: $60-$75/day $300-$465/week
Contact: Jerry or Deanna
Guides: Yes
Species & Seasons: Walleye, Bluegill, LM Bass May-June, Crappie Sept-Oct, Northern Pike all season
Bodies of Water: Lake Osakis
Types of fishing: Fly fishing, light tackle
Available: Fishing instruction, licenses, bait, tackle, boat rentals, family activities, baby sitting, pontoon rentals

Early Inn Resort & Campground
Osakis 612-859-2149
.... 800-258-2149
Guest Capacity: 80
Handicapped equipped: No
Seasons: May 1 to Oct 1
Rates: $250/week to $500/week

Contact: Doug & Karla Dagel
Guides: Yes
Species & Seasons: Walleye, Northern Pike, Bluegill, Crappie, LM Bass May-Oct
Bodies of Water: Lake Osakis
Types of fishing: Light tackle
Available: Fishing instruction, licenses, bait, tackle, boat rentals, family activities, baby sitting, boat lifts, lodge with gameroom

Red Barn Resort
Sauk Centre 612-352-5112
Guest Capacity: 40
Handicapped equipped: No
Seasons: May 1 to Oct 31
Rates: $200-$500
Contact: Dale or Pat
Guides: No
Species & Seasons: Sunfish, Crappie, Northern Pike, LM Bass, Walleye all season
Bodies of Water: Sauk Lake, Lake Osakis
Types of fishing: Light tackle, heavy tackle
Available: Bait, tackle

Surfside Resort
Alexandria 612-886-5438
Guest Capacity: 34
Handicapped equipped: No
Seasons: May 1 to Oct 30
Rates: $70/day
Contact: Rick
Guides: Yes
Species & Seasons: Walleye May-July, LM Bass June-Oct, Northern Pike, Panfish May-Oct, Walleye Sept-Oct
Bodies of Water: Lake Mary, Lake Carlos, Lake Ida, Lake Miltona, Lake Osakis

Minnesota's Lake of the Woods
ZIPPEL BAY Resort
Trophy, Walleye Northern and Smallmouth!
Great Shoreline Fishing!
• Cabins • Camping • Dining & Lounge
• Guided Charter Boat Fishing
• Boat & Motor Rentals
• Ice Fishing & Spearing
• Guided Duck Hunting
• Whitetail Bow & Rifle Hunting
Call for a Color Brochure!
1 800 222-2537
See Zippel Bay's Location on Minnesota Road Map

LAKE OSAKIS - LAKE WINNIBIGOSHISH   MINNESOTA

Types of fishing: Fly fishing, light tackle, heavy tackle, wading
Available: Fishing instruction, licenses, bait, tackle, boat rentals, family activities, children's program

LAKE PEPIN

BAIT & TACKLE...

B & M Bait & Tackle
Rochester 507-282-4982
Hours: Open 7 days
Carries: Live bait, lures, flies, maps, rods, reels, licenses
Bodies of water: Lake Zumbro, Mississippi River, Zumbro River, Root River, Lake Pepin
Services & Products: Guide services, beverages, fishing instruction, repair services
Guides: Yes
OK to call for current conditions: Yes
Contact: Bob or Brad Benike

LODGING...

Sunset Motel & Resort
Lake City..................... 612-345-5331
.... 800-945-0192
Guest Capacity: 25 rooms, kitchenettes, cabins
Handicapped equipped: Yes
Seasons: All year
Rates: $42/day
Contact: Darlene Roland
Guides: Yes
Species & Seasons: Northern Pike, Walleye, Crappie, Sauger May-Nov, Striped Bass July-Oct
Bodies of Water: Mississippi River, Lake Pepin
Types of fishing: Fly fishing, light tackle, heavy tackle
Available: Baby sitting and boat rental(2blocks)

LAKE SHETEK

BAIT & TACKLE...

Outdoor Inn Sports Headquarters
Pipestone..................... 507-825-3673
Hours: 6am-8pm
Carries: Live bait, lures, flies, maps, rods, reels, licenses
Bodies of water: Lake Benton, Lake Sarah, Lake Shetek, Twin Lakes, Sioux River, Lake Hendricks, Lake Thompson, Lake Madison
Services & Products: Repair services
Guides: Yes
OK to call for current conditions: Yes
Contact: Dick Wieme

LAKE SUPERIOR

BAIT & TACKLE...

Nature's Trophies Taxidermy
Eveleth 218-744-4885
Hours: 5am-8pm
Carries: Live bait, lures, flies, licenses
Bodies of water: Lake Superior, Whiteface Res., Vermilion Lake
Services & Products: Taxidermy
Guides: Yes
OK to call for current conditions: Yes
Contact: Mario Spampinato

LODGING...

Hungry Jack Lodge & Campground
Grand Marais 218-388-2265
.... 800-338-1566
Guest Capacity: 150
Handicapped equipped: Yes
Seasons: All year
Rates: Varies
Guides: Yes
Species & Seasons: SM Bass May-Oct, Walleye May-Feb, Rainbow Trout, Steelhead, Lake Trout, Splake May-Mar, Northern Pike May-Feb
Bodies of Water: Hungry Jack Lake, West Bearskin Lake, Lake Superior
Types of fishing: Fly fishing, light tackle, heavy tackle, horse/back pack, wading, fly-out trips, ice fishing
Available: Fishing instruction, licenses, bait, tackle, boat rentals, family activities, children's program, baby sitting, guided snowmobile trips, hunting

Park Lake Resort & Campground
Mahtowa..................... 218-389-6935
Handicapped equipped: Yes
Seasons: All year
Rates: $460/week
Contact: Patrick Pierzynowski
Guides: Yes
Species & Seasons: Panfish all year, Walleye, Northern Pike, LM Bass, SM Bass May-Feb
Bodies of Water: Park Lake, Lake Superior
Types of fishing: Fly fishing, light tackle, heavy tackle
Available: Licenses, bait, tackle, boat rentals, family activities

LAKE WINNIBIGOSHISH

BAIT & TACKLE...

Ben's Bait & Tackle
Grand Rapids 800-897-8281
Hours: 6am-6pm
Carries: Live bait, lures, flies, maps, rods, reels, licenses
Bodies of water: Mississippi River, Leech Lake, Lake Winnibigoshish
Services & Products: Guide services, food, beverages, fishing instruction
Guides: Yes
OK to call for current conditions: Yes
Contact: Ben

Rapids Tackle
Grand Rapids 218-326-5822
Hours: 5:30am-9pm
Carries: Live bait, lures, flies, maps, rods, reels, licenses
Bodies of water: Lake Winnibigoshish, Bowstring Lake, Pokegama Lake, Mississippi River, Bigfork River, 1200 smaller lakes
Services & Products: Guide services, beverages, repair services
Guides: Yes
OK to call for current conditions: Yes
Contact: Don Wendt

Y Bait Station
Deer River 218-246-2867
Hours: 6am-9pm
Carries: Live bait, lures, flies, maps, rods, reels, licenses
Bodies of water: Lake Winnibigoshish, Ball Club Lake, Bowstring Lake, Squaw Lake
Services & Products: Guide services, food, beverages, gas/oil, fishing instruction
OK to call for current conditions: Yes
Contact: Brett Jahn

MINNESOTA
LAKE WINNIBIGOSHISH

GUIDES...

Bill Broberg
Coleraine 218-245-1765
Species & Seasons: Walleye, Northern Pike, LM Bass, Crappie, Perch May-Oct
Bodies of water: Lake Winnibigoshish, Mississippi River, Trout Lake
Rates: Half day: $100(1-2), Full day: $140(1-2)
Call between: 5:30pm-9pm
Provides: Light tackle, lures, bait, rain gear
Handicapped equipped: No

Paul Coventry
Brainerd 218-829-1846
Species & Seasons: Walleye, Northern Pike, LM Bass, Trout May-Nov, Muskellunge June-Nov, Panfish April-Nov
Bodies of water: Gull Lake, Whitefish Lake Chain, Pelican Lake, North Long Lake, Mille Lacs, Leech Lake, Lake Winnibigoshish
Rates: Half day: $150(Maximun 3), Full day: $300(Maximum 3)
Call between: 7am-10pm
Provides: Light tackle, heavy tackle, lures, bait, rain gear
Handicapped equipped: Yes
Certifications: USCG

Gary Stay
Longville 218-363-2308
Species & Seasons: Muskellunge June-Oct, LM Bass, SM Bass, Walleye, Northern Pike May-Oct, Panfish April-Oct
Bodies of water: Leech Lake, Woman Lake, Little Boy Lake, Wabedo Lake, Lake Winibigoshish, many other area waters
Rates: Half day: $110(1-3), Full day: $175(1-3)
Call between: 6pm-10pm
Provides: Light tackle, heavy tackle, lures, bait
Handicapped equipped: Yes

LODGING...

Balsam Bay Resort
Remer 800-952-7098
.... 218-566-2346
Guest Capacity:
Handicapped equipped: No
Seasons: May 12 to Nov 15
Rates: $300/week 2 people
Guides: No
Species & Seasons: Northern Pike, Walleye, LM Bass May-Feb, Bluegill, Crappie all year
Bodies of Water: Big Sand Lake, Leech Lake, Lake Winnibigoshis
Types of fishing: Light tackle, heavy tackle
Available: Boat rentals

Four Seasons Resort
Bena 218-665-2231
Guest Capacity: 120
Handicapped equipped: Yes
Seasons: All year
Rates: $50-$120/day, $365-$700/week
Contact: Joe
Guides: Yes
Species & Seasons: Walleye May-Oct, Northern Pike, Muskellunge July-Nov, Perch all year
Bodies of Water: Lake Winnibigoshish
Types of fishing: Light tackle, heavy tackle
Available: Fishing instruction, licenses, bait, tackle, boat rentals, family activities, heated pool, covered ocks with electricity

Hunters Point
Isle 612-676-3227
Guest Capacity: 100
Handicapped equipped: No
Seasons: All year
Guides: Yes
Species & Seasons: Walleye May-Feb, Muskellunge, SM Bass Jun-Sept, Crappie Mar-May, Perch Dec-Mar
Bodies of Water: Mille Lacs, Leech Lake, Lake Winnibigoshish
Types of fishing: Light tackle, heavy tackle, float trips
Available: Fishing insruction, licenses, bait, tackle, boat rentals, family activities

Judds Resort
Bena 218-665-2216
Guest Capacity: 160 cabins
Handicapped equipped: Yes
Seasons: All year
Rates: $80/day and up, $380/week and up
Contact: Ron or Sharon Hunter
Guides: Yes
Species & Seasons: Walleye, Northern Pike, Muskellunge May-Feb, Perch all year
Bodies of Water: Lake Winnibigoshish, Cass Lake, Leech Lake
Types of fishing: Ligh tackle, heavy tackle, wading, launch
Available: Fishing instruction, licenses, bait, tackle, boat rentals, family activities, children's program, baby sitting, camping (27 sites)

McArdle's Resort
Bena 218-665-2212
Guest Capacity: 160
Handicapped equipped: No
Seasons: May 12 to April 1
Rates: $65-$145/day, $350-$735/week
Guides: Yes
Species & Seasons: Walleye, Northern Pike May-Feb, Perch all season
Bodies of Water: Lake Winnibigoshish
Types of fishing: Light tackle, heavy tackle
Avilable: Fishing instruction, licenses, bait, tackle, boat rentals, family activities, children's program, baby sitting, private guide, launches, gas, playground, RV camping

North Star Resort
Bena 218-654-3330
Guest Capacity: 62-65
Handicapped equipped: Yes, some cabins
Seasons: May 1 to Feb 25
Rates: $220-$440/week
Contact: Tom or Karen Legro
Guides: Yes
Species & Seasons: Perch, Crappie, Bluegill all year, Northern Pike, Walleye May-Feb, Muskellunge June-Feb
Bodies of Water: Leech Lake, Lake innibigoshish, Tenmile Lake
Types of fishing: Fly fishing, light tackle, heavy tackle
Available: Bait, tackle, boat rentals, family activities

Northern Acres Resort & Camping
HCR 3 Box 446
Deer River 56636
Guest Capacity: 34 cabins, 20 campsites
Handicapped equipped: No
Seasons: All year
Rates: $60/day, $465/week
Contact: Jack Heathman
Guides: Yes
Species & Seasons: Walleye, Northern Pike May-Feb, Perch, Crappie all year
Bodies of Water: Bowstring Lake, Sand Lake, Winibigoshkish Lake, Jessie Lake
Types of fishing: Light tackle, heavy tackle
Available: Licenses, bait, tackle, boat rentals

LAKE WINNIBIGOSHISH - LEECH LAKE — MINNESOTA

Pike Point Resort & Lodge
Tenstrike 218-586-2810
Guest Capacity: 43
Handicapped equipped: No
Seasons: May to Oct
Rates: $58-$92/day, $290-$460/week
Contact: Ron or Joan Yearling
Guides: Yes
Species & Seasons: Walleye, Northern Pike May-Oct, LM Bass, Bluegill June-Sept, Crappie May-Sept
Bodies of Water: Lake Bemidji, Cass Lake, Mississippi River, Chain Lakes, Leech Lake, Winnibigoshish, Red Lake
Type of fishing: Fly fishing, light tackle, heavy tackle
Available: Fishing instruction, licenses, bait, tackle, boat rentals, family activities, baby sitting

Pine Grove Lodge
Max 218-798-2865
Guest Capacity: 30
Handicapped equipped: No
Seasons: May to Nov
Rates: $370/week
Contact: Wayne Wahlstrom
Guides: Yes
Species & Seasons: Walleye, Northern Pike, LM Bass, Crappie, Perch May-Oct
Bodies of Water: Sand Lake, Bowstring Lake, Cut Foot ioux Lake, Lake Winnibigoshish
Types of fishing: Fly fishing, light tackle, heavy tackle, wading
Available: Fishing instruction, bait, tackle, boat rentals, family activities, children's program, baby sitting

Trail's End
Deer River 218-832-3231
Guest Capacity: 60
Handicapped equipped: No
Seasons: All year
Rates: Starting at $495/week
Guides: Yes
Species & Seasons: Walleye, Northern Pike, Perch, Crappie
Bodies of Water: Bowstring Lake, Lake Winnibigoshish, Sand Lake, Jessie Lake
Available: Bait, tackle, boat rental, family activities, children's program, baby sitting

LAX LAKE

LODGING...

Lax Lake Resort & Campgrounds
Silver Bay 218-353-7424
Guest Capacity: 46 lodging, 16 campsites with electricity
Handicapped equipped: No
Seasons: May 15 to Oct 15
Rates: $46-$142/night - $15/camping
Contact: Dean or Jan
Guides: No
Species & Seasons: Walleye, Northern Pike, SM Bass, LM Bass, Crappie, Bluegill, June-Aug, also ice fishing
Bodies of Water: Lax Lake, Beaver River, Baptism River, Tettegouche Lake
Types of fishing: Fly fishing, light tackle
Available: Fishing instruction, bait, tackle, boat rentals, family activities

LEECH LAKE

BAIT & TACKLE...

Ben's Bait & Tackle
Grand Rapids 800-897-8281
Hours: 6am-6pm
Carries: Live bait, lures, flies, maps, rods, reels, licenses
Bodies of water: Mississippi River, Leech Lake, Lake Winnibigoshish
Services & Products: Guide services, food, beverages, fishing instruction
Guides: Yes
OK to call for current conditions: Yes
ontact: Ben

Pierce's Country Store
Remer 218-566-2334
Hours: 6am-9pm
Carries: Live bait, lures, maps, licenses
Bodies of water: Leech Lake, Thunder Lake, Rice Lake, Little Thunder Lake
Services & Products: Lodging, food, beverages, gas/oil
Guides: No
OK to call for current conditions: Yes
Contact: Dean Pierce

Thorne Brothers Fishing Specialist
Fridley 612-572-3782
Hours: 9:30am-8:30pm Mon.-Fri., 9am-5pm Sat., 11am-3pm Sun.
Carries: Lures, flies, maps, rods, reels, licenses
Bodies of water: Mississippi River, Mille Lacs Lake, Lake Minnetonka, Leech Lake
Services & Products: Repair services
Guides: Yes
OK to call for current conditions: Yes
Contact: Anyone

GUIDES...

Kelly Condiff
Park Rapids 218-732-7796
Species & Seasons: LM Bass, Northern Pike May-Oct, Crappie April-Oct, Walleye May-Oct, Trout April-Sept, Muskellunge June-Oct
Bodies of water: Leech Lake, Fish Hook Lake Chain, Mantrap Lake
Rates: Half day: $100(1-2), Full day: $150(1-2)
Call between: 9am-9pm
Provides: Light tackle, heavy tackle, lures, bait
Handicapped equipped: No

Paul Coventry
Brainerd 218-829-1846
Species & Seasons: Walleye, Northern Pike, LM Bass, Trout May-Nov, Muskellunge June-Nov, Panfish April-Nov
Bodies of water: Gull Lake, Whitefish Lake Chain, Pelican Lake, North Long Lake, Mille Lacs, Leech Lake, Lake Winnibigoshish
Rates: Half day: $150, maximum 3, Full day: $300, maximum 3
Call between: 7am-10pm
Provide: Light tackle, heavy tackle, lures, bait, rain gear
Handicapped equipped: Yes
Certifications: USCG

Ted Gwinn
St. Paul .... 218-547-3514(S)
.... 612-688-0338(W)
Species & Seasons: Muskellunge, Northern Pike July-Sept, Walleye May-Sept, LM Bass, SM Bass June-Sept
Bodies of water: Leech Lake
Rates: Full days only: $175(1-2), everthing provided
Call between: 6pm-10pm
Provides: Light tackle, heavy tackle, lures, bait
Certifications: USCG & State of MN Pilots license

MINNESOTA — LEECH LAKE

Gary Stay
Longville 218-363-2308
Species & Seasons: Muskellunge June-Oct, LM Bass, SM Bass, Walleye, Northern Pike May-Oct, Panfish April-Oct
Bodies of water: Leech Lake, Woman Lake, Little Boy Lake, Wabedo Lake, Lake Winnibigoshish, many other area waters
Rates: Half day: $110(1-3), Full day: $175(1-3)
Call between: 6pm-10pm
Provides: Light tackle, heavy tackle, ures, bait
Handicapped equipped: Yes

Viking Land Guide Service
Osakis 800-267-9326
Species & Seasons: Walleye, Muskellunge, Northern Pike, LM Bass, SM Bass May-Feb, Perch, Sunfish, Crappie all year, Sturgeon April-Dec
Bodies of water: Mille Lacs, Leech Lake, Rainy River, Lake Osakis, Alexandria Chain of Lakes, Lake Miltona, Lake Ida, Lake Minnewaska
Rats: Half day: $50(1), $75(2), $110(3), Full day: $85(1), $110(2), $175(3), Children welcomed
Call between: Anytime
Provides: Light tackle, heavy tackle, lures, bait, rain gear, beverages, lunch
Handicapped equipped: Yes
Certifications: USCG

LODGING...

Balsam Bay Resort
Remer 800-952-7098
.... 218-566-2346
Guest Capacity:
Handicapped equipped: No
Seasons: May 12 to Nov 15
Rates: $300week 2 people
Guides: No
Species & Seasons: Northern Pike, Walleye, LM Bass May-Feb, Bluegill, Crappie all year
Bodies of Water: Big Sand Lake, Leech Lake, Winnibigoshish
Types of fishing: Light tackle, heavy tackle
Available: Boat rentals

Birchwood Resort
Walker 218-547-1454
Guest Capacity: 58
Handicapped equipped: No
Seasons: May 10 to Oct 15
Rates: $66-$97/night, $330-$485/week
Contact: Gene Alderson
Guides: Yes
Species & Seasons: Walleye, Northern Pike all year, Perch Spring-Fall, Muskellunge, LM Bass Summer
Bodies of Water: Leech Lake
Types of fishing: Light tackle
Available: Licenses, bait, tackle, boat rentals, family activities, launch service

Cedar Springs Lodge
Walker 28-836-2248
Guest Capacity: 65
Handicapped equipped: Yes
Seasons: May 10 to Oct 15
Contact: Elwood Marion
Guides: Yes
Species & Seasons: Walleye, Northern Pike, Muskellunge, Perch, Panfish
Bodies of Water: Leech Lake
Types of fishing: Fly fishing, light tackle, heavy tackle, wading
Available: Fishing instruction, bait, tackle, boat rentals, family activities

Chase on the Lake
Wlker 218-547-1531
Guest Capacity: 50
Handicapped equipped: No
Seasons: All year
Rates: Summer: $56-$126/day double occupancy, Winter: $36-$86/day double occupancy
Contact: Mark Shimer
Guides: Yes, recommend
Species & Seasons: Walleye, Muskellunge, Northern Pike, Perch, Crappie
Bodies of Water: Leech Lake
Available: Boat rentals, baby sitting

Hunters Point
Isle 612-676-3227
Guest Capcity: 100
Handicapped equipped: No
Seasons: All year
Guides: Yes
Species & Seasons: Walleye May-Feb, Muskellunge, SM Bass Jun-Sept, Crappie Mar-May, Perch Dec-Mar
Bodies of Water: Mille Lacs, Leech Lake, Lake Winnibigoshish
Types of fishing: Light tackle, heavy tackle, float trips
Available: Fishing instruction, licenses, bait, tackle, boat rentals, family activities

Judds Resort
Bena 218-665-2216
Guest Capacity: 160 cabins
Handicapped equipped: Yes
Seasons: All yer
Rates: $80/day and up, $380/week and up
Contact: Ron or Sharon Hunter
Guides: Yes
Species & Seasons: Walleye, Northern Pike, Muskellunge May-Feb, Perch all year
Bodies of Water: Lake Winnibigoshish, Cass Lake, Leech Lake
Types of fishing: Liht tackle, heavy tackle, wading, launch
Available: Fishing instruction, licenses, bait, tackle, boat rentals, family activities, children's program, baby sitting, camping (27 sites)

Little Wolf Resort
Cass Lake 218-335-2138
Guest Capacity: 40
Handicapped equipped: No
Seasons: May to Oct
Rates: $345/week, daily rates available
Contact: Ralph or Karen
Guides: Yes
Species & Seasons: Walleye, Muskellunge, LM Bass, Northern Pike, Panfish
Bodies of Water: Leech Lake, Cass Lake
Types of fishig: Light tackle, heavy tackle
Available: Bait, tackle, boat rentals, family activities

Maple Trails Resort
Boy River 218-889-2258
Guest Capacity: 30
Handicapped equipped: No
Seasons: Mid May to Mid Oct
Rates: $65-$75/day, $295-$395/week
Contact: Daniel Flaherty
Guides: Yes
Species & Seasons: Walleye, Northern Pike, Crappie, Bluegill, Muskellunge May-Oct, LM Bass June-Oct
Bodies of Water: Boy Lake, Boy River, Leech Lake
Types of fishing: Light tackle
Available: Licenses, bait, tackle, boat rentals (pontoons), baby stting, cabins with swimming pool

LEECH LAKE   MINNESOTA

North Star Resort
Bena 218-654-3330
Guest Capacity: 62-65
Handicapped equipped: Yes, some cabins
Seasons: May 1 to Feb 25
Rates: $220-$440/week
Contact: Tom or Karen Legro
Guides: Yes
Species & Seasons: Perch, Crappie, Bluegill all year, Northern Pike, Walleye May-Feb, Muskellunge June-Feb
Bodies of Water: Leech Lake, Lake Winnebegoshish, Tenmile Lake
Types of fishig: Fly fishing, light tackle, heavy tackle
Available: Bait, tackle, boat rentals, family activities

O'Neills Red Wing Lodge
Walker 800-862-1272
Guest Capacity: 70
Handicapped equipped: No
Seasons: May 12 to Oct 10
Rates: from $405/week
Contact: Marlene O'Neill
Guides: Yes
Species & Seasons: Walleye, Northern Pike May-Oct, Muskellunge June-Oct, Perch, Panfish all year
Bodies of Water: Leech Lake
Types of fishing: Light tackle
Available: Fishing instruction, licenses, bait, tackle, boat rentals

Pike Point Resort &Lodge
Tenstrike 218-586-2810
Guest Capacity: 43
Handicapped equipped: No
Seasons: May to Oct
Rates: $58-$92/day, $290-$460/week
Contact: Ron or Joan Yearling
Guides: Yes
Species & Seasons: Walleye, Northern Pike May-Oct, LM Bass, Bluegill June-Sept, Crappie May-Sept
Bodies of Water: Lake Bemidji, Cass Lake, Mississippi River, Chain Lakes, Leech Lake, Winnibigoshish, Red Lake
Types of fishing: Fly fishin, light tackle, heavy tackle
Available: Fishing instruction, licenses, bait, tackle, boat rentals, family activities, baby sitting

Quietwoods Campground & Resort
Hackensack 218-675-6240
Guest Capacity: 3 cabins, 20 lakeside campsites
Seasons: May 1 to Oct 1
Rates: Cabins: $495/week, Camping: $19.50/day
Guides: No
Species & Seasons: Walleye May-June, Northern Pike July-Oct, LM Bass June-Oct, Panfish, Crappi, Whitefish May-Oct
Bodies of Water: Tenmile Lake, Leech Lake
Types of fishing: Fly fishing, light tackle, wading, float trips, fishing off docks for resort guests
Available: Bait, tackle, boat rentals, children's program, swimming beach, rec room, playground

Resort Content
Route 2 Box 255
Nevis 56467
Guest Capacity: 8 cabins (2 and 3 bedroom units)
Handicapped equipped: No
Seasons: May to Oct
Rates: $60-$85/day, $300-$475/week
Guides: Yes, recommend
Species & Seasons: Walleye, LM Bass, Northern Pike, Panfish, Muskellunge May-Sept
Bodies of Water: Matrap Lake, Crow Wing Chain of Lakes, Leech Lake, Lake Belle Taine
Types of fishing: Light tackle
Available: Boat rentals, family activities, children's program, baby sitting

Shady Shores Resort
Hackensack 218-675-6540
Guest Capacity: 11 cabins, 2-4 bedrooms
Handicapped equipped: No
Seasons: May to Nov
Rates: $300-$600/week
Contact: Jim DeSignor
Guides: Yes
Species & Seasons: Walleye, Northern Pike, Crappie, Bluegill May-Nov, LM Bass June-Nov
Bodies of Water: Birch Lake, Tenmile Lake, Leech Lake
Types of fishing: Fly fishing, light tackle, heay tackle, horse/back pack, wading
Available: Bait, tackle, boat rentals, family activities, swimming, canoeing

Timber Trails Resort
Remer 800-283-2889
Guest Capacity: 70 (approximately)
Handicapped equipped: No
Seasons: Mid May to Mid Nov
Rates: $300-$490/week
Contact: Pat or Toni Dysart
Guides: Yes
Species & Seasons: Walleye May-Feb, Muskellunge June-Feb, Northern Pike May, Crappie all year, SM Bass, LM Bass May-Feb
Bodies of Water: Big Boy Lake, Leech Lak, Boy River
Types of fishing: Light tackle
Available: Fishing instruction, licenses, bait, tackle, boat rentals

Tonga's Launch Service & Cabins
Federal Dam 218-654-3715
Guest Capacity: 50
Handicapped equipped: No
Seasons: Cabins all year, fishing May to April
Rates: $50/day
Guides: Yes
Species & Seasons: Walleye, Perch, Northern Pike May-April, Muskellunge, LM Bass June-Oct
Bodies of Water: Leech Lake
Types of fishing: Light tackle, launch fishing
Available: Fishing instruction, licenss, bait, tackle, boat rentals

Tri-Birches Resort & Campground
Hackensack 800-450-6524
Guest Capacity: 40
Handicapped equipped: No
Seasons: May to Oct
Rates: $299-$390/week
Contact: Dan or Gail Watters
Guides: Yes
Species & Seasons: Crappie May-June, Bluegill, Northern Pike, Walleye, LM Bass all season
Bodies of Water: 4 Point Lake, Leech Lake, Woman Lake, 127 lakes within a 10 mile radius
Types of fishing: Fly fishing, light tackle
Available: ait, tackle, boat rentals, cabins, camping

MINNESOTA

LEECH LAKE - MILLE LACS

View Point Resort
Cass Lake 218-335-6746
Guest Capacity: 6 Cabins (2, 3 bed)
Handicapped equipped: Yes
Seasons: May 15 to Oct 1
Contact: L. R. Grunwald
Guides: Yes
Species & Seasons: Muskellunge, Northern Pike June-Sept, Walleye, LM Bass May-July, Crappie, Bluegill
Bodies of Water: Little Wolf Lake, Wolf Lake, Cass Lake, Leech Lake, many more
Types of fishing: Fly fishing, light tackle, heavy takle, wading
Available: Licenses, bait, tackle, boat rentals, family activities, baby sitting, sand beach, walking trails

Woodland Resort
Walker 218-547-1080
Guest Capacity: 1-4 bdrm cabins, 12 units, small campground
Handicapped equipped: No
Seasons: May 12 to Sept 30
Rates: $265-$455/week
Contact: Mike or Kelly
Guides: Yes
Species & Seasons: Walleye, Perch May-Sept, Northern Pike July-Sept, Muskellunge Aug-Sept
Bodies of Water: Leech Lake
Types of ishing: Fly fishing, light tackle, heavy tackle, wading
Available: Bait, tackle, boat rentals

MADISON LAKE

BAIT & TACKLE...

Lake Sports
Madison Lake 507-243-3838
Carries: Live bait, lures, flies, maps, rods, reels, licenses
Bodies of water: Madison Lake, Lake Washington, Lake Jefferson, Lake George, Lake Frances, Tetonka Lake, Lake Elysian, Eagle Lake
Services & Products: Boat rentals, guide services, food, beverages, fishing instruction
OK to call for current conditions: Yes
Contact: Ron Guappone

MILLE LACS

BAIT & TACKLE...

Thorne Brothers Fishing Specialist
Fridley 612-572-3782
Hours: 9:30am-8:30pm Mon.-Fri., 9am-5pm Sat., 11am- 3pm Sun.
Carries: Lures, flies, maps, rods, reels, licenses
Bodies of water: Mississippi River, Mille Lacs, Lake Minnetonka, Leech Lake
Services & Products: Repair services
Guides: Yes
OK to call for current conditions: Yes
Contact: Anyone

Tutt's Bait & Tackle
Garrison 612-692-4341
Hours: 7am-9pm
Carries: Live bait, lures, flies, maps, rods, reels, licenses
Bodies of water: Mille Lacs, Mississippi River, Bay Lake, Farm Island Lake, Borden Lake
Guides: Yes
OK to call for current conditions: Yes
Contact: Orrin Tutt

GUIDES...

Paul Coventry
Brainerd 218-829-1846
Species & Seasons: Walleye, Northern Pike, LM Bass, Trout May-Nov, Muskellunge June-Nov, Panfish April-Nov
Bodies of water: Gull Lake, Whitefish Lake Chain, Pelican Lake, North Long Lake, Mille Lacs, Leech Lake, Lake Winnibigoshish
Rates: Half day: $150(Maximun 3), Full day: $300(Maximum 3)
Call between: 7am-10pm
Provides: Light tackle, heavy tackle, lures, bait, rain gear
Handicapped equipped: Yes
Certifications: USCG

Viking Land Guide Service
Osakis 800-267-9326
Species & Seasons: Walleye, Muskellunge, Northern Pike, LM Bass, SM Bass May-Feb, Perch, Sunfish, Crappie all year, Sturgeon April-Dec

Bodies of water: Mille Lacs, Leech Lake, Rainy River, Lake Osakis, Alexandria Chain of Lakes, Lake Miltona, Lake Ida, Lake Minnewaska
Rates: Half day: $50(1), $75(2), $110(3), Full day: $85(1), $110(2), $175(3), Children welcomed
Call between: Anytime
Provides: Light tackle, heavy tackle, lures, bait, rain gear, beverages, lunch
Handicapped equipped: Yes
Certifications: USCG

LODGING...

Bradley's Farm Island Resort & RV Park
Aitkin 218-678-2881
Guest Capacity: 50
Handicapped equipped: No
Seasons: May 15 to Oct 1
Rates: $50-$150/day, $265-$610/week
Contact: Lorrie or Dick
Guides: Yes
Species & Seasons: Walleye, Northern Pike, Crappie, Bluegill May-Oct, LM Bass June-Oct
Bodies of Water: Farm Island Lake, Mille Lacs
Types of fishing: Boat and motor only
Available: Bait, boat rentals

Camp Holiday Resort & Campground
Route 1 Box 170
Deerwood 56444
Guest Capacity: 100
Handicapped equipped: No
Seasons: May 1 to Oct 15
Rates: $50-$80/day
Contact: Ann M. Erickson
Guides: Yes
Species & Seasons: Walleye, Northern Pike May-Feb, LM Bass June-Feb, Bluegill, Crappie all year
Bodies of Water: Mille Lacs, Pine Lake, Round Lake
Types of fishing: Light tackle
Available: Licenses, bait, tackle, boat rentals, family activities, children's rogram, baby sitting

Fairhaven Resort & Restaurant
Wahkon 612-495-3325
.... 800-235-5435
Guest Capacity: 35 cabins, 9 camping sites
Handicapped equipped: No
Seasons: May to Oct

MILLE LACS - MISSISSIPPI RIVER MINNESOTA

Rates: $39/night 2 adults
Guides: Yes
Species & Seasons: Walleye May-Feb, Perch all year
Bodies of Water: Mille Lacs
Types of fishing: Fly fishing, light tackle, heavy tackle
Available: Bait, tackle, boatrentals, family activities, restaurant with home cooking

Flagship Inn & Marina
HC 69 Box 204
Isle 56342
Guest Capacity: 44 plus 27 RV sites (full), 130 RV sites electric
Handicapped equipped: Yes
Seasons: All year
Contact: Ruby Tenhoff
Guides: Yes
Species & Seasons: Walley Northene, Pike, Muskellunge, Crappie, SM Bass May-Feb
Bodies of Water: Mille Lacs
Types of fishing: Light tackle, heavy tackle, float trips, ice fishing packages
Available: Fishing instruction, licenses, bait, tackle, boa rentals, family activities, 2 full service restaurants

Gilbert Lake Resort
Brainerd 218-829-4652
Guest Capacity: 3 cabins (15 people)
Handicapped equipped: No
Seasons: May 1 to Oct 1
Rates: $350/week
Guides: Yes
Species & Seasons: LM Bass, Northern Pike, Crappie, Bluegill
Bodies of Water: Gilbert Lake, Gull Lake, Whitefish Lake Chain, Mille Lacs, many others
Types of fishing: Light tackle
Available: Fishing istruction, bait, tackle, boat rentals, Brainerd City activities 2 miles

Hunters Point
Isle 612-676-3227
Guest Capacity: 100
Handicapped equipped: No
Seasons: All year
Guides: Yes
Species & Seasons: Walleye May-Feb, Muskellunge, SM Bass Jun-Sept, Crappie Mar-May, Perch Dec-Mar
Bodies of Water: Mille Lacs, Leech Lake, Lake Winnibigoshish
Types of fishing: Light tackle, heavy tackle, float trips
Available: Fishing instruction, licenses, bait, tackle, boat rentals, family activities

McQuoid's Inn on Mille Lacs
Isle 800-862-3535
.... 612-676-3535
Guest Capacity: 120-180
Handicapped equipped: Yes
Seasons: All year
Rates: Weekdays: $54.95/day, Weekends: $64.95/day
Guides: Yes
Species & Seasons: Walleye May-Sept, Northern Pike, Muskellunge June-Sept, Walleye Dec-Feb
Bodies of Water: Mille Lacs
Types of fishing: Light tackle, heavy ackle
Available: Boat rentals, deluxe fish house rentals, snowmobile rentals

St. Albans Bay Lodge
HCR 1 Box 40
Garrison 56450
Guest Capacity: 30
Handicapped equipped: Yes
Seasons: May 1 to Oct 30
Rates: $39-$59/day
Contact: Darlene or Steve
Guides: Yes
Species & Seasons: Walleye May-Oct, Northern Pike Sept-Oct, Muskellunge, Crappie May-?
Bodies of Water: Mille Lacs
Types of fishing: Light tackle, heavy tackle
Available: Boat rentals, family activities

Sunset Bay Resort
Aitkin 218-927-269
Guest Capacity: 30
Handicapped equipped: No
Seasons: May 1 to Sept 30
Rates: From $500/week
Contact: Jim Spaeth
Guides: Yes
Species & Seasons: Northern Pike, Walleye May-Nov, LM Bass June-Nov, Crappie, Bluegill all season
Bodies of Water: Cedar Lake, Mille Lacs, Mississippi River
Types of fishing: Light tackle
Available: Boat rentals

Whitewood Resort
Aitkin 218-927-3804
Guest Capacity: 50
Handicapped equipped: No
Seasons: May to Oct
Rates: $250-$450/week
Contact: Mike or Mavis McGuire
Guides: No
Species & Seasons: Walleye, Northern Pike, Crappie, Bluegill, LM Bass all summer long

Bodies of Water: Mille Lacs, Cedar Lake, Farm Island Lake
Types of fishing: Fly fishing, light tackle, heavy tackle
Available: Fishing instruction, boat rentals, family activities

MINNESOTA RIVER

BAIT TACKLE...

B & D Bait and Tackle
Richfield 612-866-5640
Hours: 9am-6pm
Carries: Live bait, lures, flies, maps, rods, reels, licenses
Bodies of water: Mississippi River, Minnesota River, Lake Minnetonka
Services & Products: Beverages, repair services
Guides: Yes
OK to call for current conditions: Yes
Contact: Pat Buchanan

Bobber Shop
Mankato 507-625-8228
Hours: 7am-7pm
Carries: Live bait, lures, flies, maps, rods, reels, licenses
Bodies of water: Minnesota River, 14 lakes within 15 miles
Services & Products: Guide services
Guides: Yes
OK to call for current conditions: Yes
Contact: Ron or Steve Robb

MISSISSIPPI RIVER

BAIT & TACKLE...

B & D Bait and Tackle
Richfield 612-866-5640
Hours: 9am-6pm
Carries: Live bait, lures, flies, maps, rods, reels, licenses
Bodies of water: Mississippi River, Minnesota River, Lake Minnetonka
Services & Products: Beverages, repair services
Guides: Yes
OK to call for current conditions: Yes
Contact: Pat Buchanan

MINNESOTA — MISSISSIPPI RIVER

B & M Bait & Tackle
Rochester 507-282-4982
Hours: Open 7 days
Carries: Live bait, lures, flies, maps, rods, reels, licenses
Bodies of water: Lake Zumbro, Mississippi River, Zumbro River, Root River, Lake Pepin
Services & Products: Guide services, beverages, fishing instruction, repair services
Guides: Yes
OK to call for current conditions: Yes
Contact: Bob or Brad Benike

Ben's Bait & Tackle
Grand Rapids 800-897-8281
Hours: 6am-6pm
Carries: Live bait, lures, flies, maps, rods, reels, licenses
Bodies of water: Mississippi River, Leech Lake, Lake Winnibigoshish
Services & Products: Guide services, food, beverages, fishing instruction
Guides: Yes
OK to call for current conditions: Yes
Contact: Ben

Bryn Mawr Conoco Auto Bait Center
Minneapolis 612-377-4743
.... 377-1068
Hours: 6:30am-8:30pm
Carries: Live bait, lures, maps, rods, reels, licenses
Bodies of water: Mississippi River, Wirth Lake, Cedar Lake, Lake of the Isles, Lake Calhoun, Lake Harriet
Services & Products: Food, beverages, gas/oil, repair services
Guides: No
OK to call for current conditions: Yes
Contact: Joe Anders

Dave's Sales & Service
Hibbing 218-262-5405
Hours: 6am-8pm
Carries: Live bait, lures, flies, maps, rods, reels, licenses
Bodies of water: Swan Lake, Mississippi River, Side Lake
Services & Products: Guide services, repair services
Guides: Yes
OK to call for current conditions: Yes
Contact: David Boettcher

Forest Lake Sports & Tackle & Taxidermy
Forest Lake 612-464-1200
Hours: 5am-9pm
Carries: Live bait, lures, flies, maps, rods, reels, licenses
Bodies of water: Mississippi River, St. Croix River, Forest Lake, Clear Lake, many others
Services & Products: Guide services, food, beverages, gas/oil, fishing instruction
Guides: Yes
OK to call for current conditions: Yes
Contact: Clay Zimmerman

Koep's Bait & Tackle
Nisswa 218-963-2547
Hours: 6:30am-9pm Summer, 9am-5pm Winter
Carries: Live bait, lures, flies, maps, rods, reels, licenses
Bodies of water: Mississippi River, Gull Lake, Pelican Lake, Long Lake, Pine Mountain Lake, Whitefish Lake Chain, Lake Hubert
Services & Products: Guide services, beverages, fishing instruction, repair services,
Guides: Yes
OK to call for current conditions: Yes
Contact: Dave, Ryan or Marv

Rapids Tackle
Grand Rapids 218-326-5822
Hours: 5:30am-9pm
Carries: Live bait, lures, flies, maps, rods, reels, licenses
Bodies of water: Lake Winnibigoshish, Bowstring Lake, Pokegama Lake, Mississippi River, Bigfork River, 1200 smaller lakes
Services & Products: Guide services, beverages, repair services
Guides: Yes
OK to call for current conditions: Yes
Contact: Don Wendt

Thorne Brothers Fishing Specialist
Fridley 612-572-3782
Hours: 9:30am-8:30pm Mon.-Fri., 9am-5pm Sat., 11am-3pm Sun.
Carries: Lures, flies, maps, rods, reels, licenses
Bodies of water: Mississippi River, Mille Lacs Lake, Lake Minnetonka, Leech Lake
Services & Products: Repair services
Guides: Yes
OK to call for current conditions: Yes
Contact: Anyone

Trading Post Inc.
Crosby 218-546-6228
Hours: 6am-9pm
Carries: Live bait, lures, flies, maps, rods, reels, licenses
Bodies of water: Cuyuna Range Mine Pits, Mississippi River, Serpent Lake, Rabbit Lake, over 50 other lakes
Services & Products: Boat rentals, guide services, fishing instruction
OK to call for current conditions: Yes
Contact: Bob or Cindy

Tutt's Bait & Tackle
Garrison 612-692-4341
Hours: 7am-9pm
Carries: Live bait, lures, flies, maps, rods, reels, licenses
Bodies of water: Mille Lacs, Mississippi River, Bay Lake, Farm Island Lake, Borden Lake
Guides: Yes
OK to call for current conditions: Yes
Contact: Orrin Tutt

GUIDES...

Bill Broberg
Coleraine 218-245-1765
Species & Seasons: Walleye, Northern Pike, LM Bass, Crappie, Perch May-Oct
Bodies of water: Lake Winnibigoshish, Mississippi River, Trout Lake
Rates: Half day: $100(1-2), Full day: $140(1-2)
Call between: 5:30pm-9pm
Provides: Light tackle, lures, bait, rain gear
Handicapped equipped: No

Koeps Bait & Tackle
Nisswa 218-963-2547
Species & Seasons: Walleye, Bass, Northern Pike, Crappie, Sunfish
Bodies of water: Mississippi River, Gull Lake, Pelican Lake, North Long Lake, Whitefish Lake Chain
Rates: Half day: $150(1-3), Full day: $300(1-3)
Call between: 8am-6pm
Provides: Light tackle, heavy tackle, fly rod/reel, lures, bait, rain gear
Handicappd equipped: Yes
Certifications: USCG

MISSISSIPPI RIVER - NAMAKAN LAKE

MINNESOTA

LODGING...

Back O' the Moon
Grand Rapids 218-326-8648
Guest Capacity: 36
Handicapped equipped: No
Seasons: All year
Rates: $70/day, $350/week
Contact: Ron or Shirley
Guides: No
Species & Seasons: Walleye May-June, Northern Pike May-Oct, LM Bass June-Aug, Bluegill July-Sept
Bodies of Water: Bass Lke, Deer Lake, Moose Lake, Mississippi River
Types of fishing: Light tackle, heavy tackle
Available: Bait, tackle, boat rentals

Big Wolf Lake Resort & Campground
Bemidji 800-322-0281
Guest Capacity: 18 cottages 1-9 bdrm, 40 campsites
Seasons: All year
Rates: $450
Guides: Yes
Species & Seasons: Walleye, Northern Pike, Crappie, LM Bass, Muskellunge
Bodies of Water: Mississippi River, Cass Lake
Types of fishing: Light tackle, heavy tackle, canoe trips
Available: Licenses, bait, tackle, boat rentals, family activities, cildren's program, heated pool, lodge, whirpool, sauna

Kozy Kove Resort
1450 Wonderland Park Road NE
Brainerd 56401
Seasons: Mid May to Early Oct
Rates: $265-$295/week (1995 rates, will increase in '96), also weekend rates and day rates
Contact: Jeannine or Rick Zetah
Guides: No
Species & Seasons: Bluegill, Northern Pike, LM Bass, Walleye, Crappie May-Sept
Bodies of Water: Rice Lake, Mississippi Rivr
Available: Boat rentals, play area, pontoon rentals, canoes, paddleboat

Pike Point Resort & Lodge
Tenstrike 218-586-2810
Guest Capacity: 43
Handicapped equipped: No
Seasons: May to Oct
Rates: $58-$92/day, $290-$460/week
Contact: Ron or Joan Yearling
Guides: Yes
Species & Seasons: Walleye, Northern Pike May-Oct, LM Bass, Bluegill June-Sept, Crappie May-Sept
Bodies of Water: Lake Bemidji, Cass Lake, Mississippi River, Chain Lakes, Leech Lake, Winnibigoshish, Red Lake
Types of fishing: Fly fishing, light tackle, heavy tackle
Available: Fishing instruction, lienses, bait, tackle, boat rentals, family activities, baby sitting

Sunset Bay Resort
Aitkin 218-927-2691
Guest Capacity: 30
Handicapped equipped: No
Seasons: May 15 to Sept 30
Rates: From $500/week
Contact: Jim Spaeth
Guides: Yes
Species & Seasons: Northern Pike, Walleye May-Nov, LM Bass June-Nov, Crappie, Bluegill all season
Bodies of Water: Cedar Lke, Mille Lacs, Mississippi River
Types of fishing: Light tackle
Available: Boat rentals

Sunset Motel & Resort
Lake City 612-345-5331
.... 800-945-0192
Guest Capacity: 25 rooms, kitchenettes, cabins
Handicapped equipped: Yes
Seasons: All year
Rates: $42/day
Contact: Darlene Roland
Guides: Yes
Species & Seasons: Northern Pike, Walleye, Crappie, Sauger May-Nov, Striped Bass July-Oct
Bodies of Water: Mississippi River, Lake Pepin
Types of fishing: Fly fishing, light tackle, heavy tackle
Available: Baby sitting, boat rental(2blocks)

NAMAKAN LAKE

GUIDES...

Chip Leer
Ray 218-875-2204
Species & Seasons: Walleye, SM Bass, LM Bass, Crappie, Sturgeon, Northern Pike April-Oct
Bodies of water: Kabetogama Namakan Lake Lake, Rainy Lake, Rainy River, Sand Point Lake, Crane Lake, Voyageurs National Park, Lake of the Woods
Rates: Half day: $150(2), Full day: $200(2)
Call between: 6am-11pm
Provides: Light tackle, heavy tackle, fly rod/reel, lures, bait, ran gear, beverages, lunch
Handicapped equipped: Yes
Certifications: USCG

LODGING...

Borderland Lodge & Outfitters
Crane Lake 800-777-8392
Guest Capacity: 69
Handicapped equipped: No
Seasons: All year
Rates: $357-$1,400/week
Guides: Yes
Species & Seasons: Walleye, LM Bass, Norther Pike May-Mar, Crappie all year
Bodies of Water: Crane Lake, Sand Point Lake, Namakan Lake, Kabetogama Lake, Lac La Croix
Types of fishing: Light tackle, fly-out trips, shuttles to Boundary Waters and Quetico (Canada)
Available: Licenses, bait, tackle, boat rentals, family activities, children's program

Eagle Wing Resort
Ray 218-875-3111
Guest Capacity: 5 cabins (30 people)
Handicapped equipped: No
Seasons: May 13 to Oct 1
Rates: $295-$545/week
Contact: Russ or Marlys Kingery
Guides: Yes
Species & Seasons: Walleye, Northern Pike May-Oct
Bodies of Water: Kabetogama Lake, Namakan Lake, Crane Lake, and Point Lake
Types of fishing: Fly fishing, light tackle, heavy tackle
Available: Fishing instruction, licenses, bait, tackle, boat rentals, family activities

MINNESOTA

NAMAKAN LAKE - OTTER TAIL LAKE

Four Winds Resort
Ray 218-875-2821
Guest Capacity: 50
Handicapped equipped: No
Seasons: May 15 to Oct 1
Rates: $150/pp/week
Guides: Yes
Species & Seasons: Walleye, Northern Pike, SM Bass, Crappie May-Oct
Bodies of Water: Kabetogama Lake, Namakan Lake
Types of fishing: Light tackle
Available: Licenses, bait, tackle, boat rentals, baby sitting

Moosehorn Resort
Ray 218-75-3491
.... 800-777-7968
Guest Capacity: 50
Handicapped equipped: No
Seasons: May to Winter
Rates: From $450/week, 2 people - $1300/week, 6 people
Guides: Yes
Species & Seasons: Walleye, Northern Pike, LM Bass, Crappie May-Oct, Whitefish Oct-Nov
Bodies of Water: Kabetogama Lake, Namakan Lake, Sand Point Lake, Rainy Lake
Types of fishing: Light tackle
Available: Fishing instruction, licenses, bait, tackle, boat rentls

Park Point Resort
Ray 800-272-4533
Guest Capacity: 45
Handicapped equipped: No
Seasons: May to Oct 30
Rates: $450/week
Guides: Yes
Species & Seasons: Walleye Sept-Oct/May-June, Northern Pike July-Sept, SM Bass, LM Bass July-Aug, Crappie May
Bodies of Water: Kabetogama Lake, Rainy Lake, Namakan Lake
Types of fishing: Light tackle, heavy tackle
Available: Fishing instruction, license, bait, tackle, boat rentals, beach, waterskiing

NEST LAKE

LODGING...

North Shore Resort
Spicer 612-796-5150
Guest Capacity: 85
Handicapped equipped: No
Seasons: May 1 to Oct 15
Rates: $300-$650/week
Contact: Bob Peterson
Guides: No
Species & Seasons: Northern Pike, Walleye, LM Bass May-Oct, Bluegill, Crappie all year
Bodies of Water: Nest Lake
Types of fishing: Fly fishing, light tackle
Aailable: Bait, tackle, boat rentals, family activities

Willow Bay Resort
Spicer 612-796-5517
Guest Capacity: 8 cabins
Handicapped equipped: No
Seasons: May 1 to Oct 1
Rates: Varies
Contact: Joanne
Guides: Yes, recommend
Species & Seasons: SM Bass, LM Bass, May-Nov, Walleye, Northern Pike, Panfish May-Mar
Bodies of Water: Nest Lake, Green Lake, Crow River, Lake Florida
Types of fishing: Light tackle, heavy tackle
Available: Licenses, bait, tackle, boat rentals, family activities

NORTH STAR LAKE

LODING...

Cedar Point Resort
Marcell 218-832-3808
Guest Capacity: 60
Handicapped equipped: No
Seasons: May to Oct
Rates: $55/day and up, $295/week and up
Contact: Pete or Maria May
Guides: Yes
Species & Seasons: Walleye, Northern Pike, Crappie, Bluegill, LM Bass May-Oct, Muskellunge June-Oct
Bodies of Water: North Star Lake
Types of fishing: Fly fishing, light tackle, heavy tackle, wading
vailable: Bait, tackle, boat rentals, family activities, children's program, baby sitting, swimming pool

Kokomo Resort
Marcell 218-832-3774
Guest Capacity: 36
Handicapped equipped: Yes, some
Seasons: May 15 to Nov 30
Rates: $50-$80/day, $300-$460/week
Guides: Yes, recommend
Species & Seasons: Northern Pike, SM Bass, LM Bass May-Oct, Walleye June-Sept, Crappie, Bluegill May-Sept
Bodies of Water: North Star Lake
Types of fishing: Fly fishing, light takle
Available: Fishing instruction, licenses, boat rentals

OTTER TAIL LAKE

BAIT & TACKLE...

Koep's Clitherall Corner
Clitherall 218-864-8731
Hours: 6:45am-10pm
Carries: Live bait, lures, flies, maps, rods, reels, licenses
Bodies of water: Battle Lake, Clitherall Lake, East Battle Lake, Otter Tail Lake
Services & Products: Guide services, food, beverages, gas/oil, fishing instruction
OK to call for current conditions: Yes
Contact: Eileen, Joe, Steven or Nancy

GUIDES...

Gary Burks
Underwood 218-495-315
Species & Seasons: LM Bass, Walleye, Northern Pike, Panfish May-Oct
Bodies of water: Otter Tail County Lakes
Rates: Half day: $75(1), $90(2), Full day: $130(1), $150(2)
Call between: 6pm-10pm
Provides: Light tackle, heavy tackle, lures, bait
Handicapped equipped: No

LODGING...

Baker's Bonnie Beach Resort
Battle Lake 218-864-5534
Guest Capacity: 80
Handicapped equipped: Yes
Seasons: May 15 to Oct 1
Rates: $325-$525/week
Contact: Doug Baker
Guides: Yes
Species & Seasons: Walleye May-June, Northern Pike May-Feb, LM Bass May-Sept, Crappie, Bluegill, Bullheads all year

OTTER TAIL LAKE - PELICAN LAKE — MINNESOTA

Bodies of Water: Battle Lake, East Battle Lake, Otter Tail Lake
Types of fishing: Light tackle, heavy tackle, wading
Available: Fishing instruction, licenses, bait, tackle, boat rentals, baby sitting

Deer Lake Resort
Battle Lake 218-495-3319
Guest Capacity: 9 cabins, 9 camp sites
Handicapped equipped: Yes
Seasons: May 15 to Oct 1
Rates: $245-$$335/week
Contact: Cliff Turner
Guides: Yes
Species & Seasons: Walleye, Perch, Crappie, LM Bass, SM Bass, Bluegill, Northern Pike, Bullheads May-Oct
Bodies of Water: Otter Tail River, OtterTail Lake, Deer Lake, East Lost Lake, East Battle Lake, Battle Lake
Types of fishing: Fly fishing, wading, float trips
Available: Fishing instruction, bait, tackle, boat rentals, family activities

Moe's Ottertail Beach Resort
Route 3 Box 122
Battle Lake 56515
Handicapped equipped: No
Seasons: May 15 to Nov 1
Rates: $390/week
Guides: Yes
Species & Seasons: Walleye, Northern Pike, Perch May-Oct
Bodies of Water: Otter Tail Lake, Battle Lake, Rush Lake, Star Lake
Types of fishing: Light tackle, wading
Available: Bait, tackle, boat rentals, family activities, children's program, baby sitting

Stoller's Nifty Nook Resort
Battle Lake 218-495-3479
Guest Capacity: 30
Handicapped equipped: No
Seasons: May 10 to Oct 1
Rates: $75/day, $350/week
Contact: Mary Stoller
Guides: Yes
Species & Seasons: Walleye, Northern Pike May-Feb, LM Bass May, Perch all seasons
Bodies of Water: Otter Tail Lake
Types of fishing: Light tackle
Available: Licenses, bait, tackle, boat rentals, baby sitting

Sunset Beach Resort & Campground
Battle Lake 218-583-2750
Guest Capacity: 32 plus campers
Handicapped equipped: No
Seasons: May 10 to Sept 30
Rates: Cabins: $310-$410/week, Camping: $15-$18/day
Contact: Fred or Rose
Guides: Yes
Species & Seasons: LM Bass, Walleye, Northern Pike May-Sept, Muskellunge June-Sept
Bodies of Water: Battle Lake, Otter Tail Lake
Types of fishing: Light tackle
Available: Bait, tackle, boat rentals

Swan Lake Resort
Fergus Falls 218-736-4626
Guest Capacity: 65
Handicapped equipped: No
Seasons: May 6 to Oct 1
Rates: $415/week
Contact: Denny or Steph
Guides: No
Species & Seasons: Bluegill, LM Bass, Northern Pike, Walleye May-Oct, Crappie May-June
Bodies of Water: Swan Lake, Otter Tail Lake, Rush Lake
Types of fishing: Light tackle
Available: Licenses, bait, tackle, boat rentals, family activities, children's program, campground

Vacationland Resort
BattleLake 218-864-5826
.... 507-583-2548(W)
Guest Capacity: 50
Handicapped equipped: No
Seasons: May 1 to Oct 30
Rates: $365/week
Guides: Yes
Species & Seasons: Walleye, Northern Pike, LM Bass May-Mar
Bodies of Water: Battle Lake, Otter Tail Lake
Types of fishing: Light tackle, heavy tackle
Available: Licenses, bait, tackle, boat rentals, family activities

Weslake Resort & Conerence Center
Underwood 218-826-6523
Guest Capacity: 8-2 BR cabins, 1-5 BR cabin
Seasons: All year
Rates: $80-$120/day 4 persons, $350-$775/week
Contact: Gary Nelson
Guides: Yes
Species & Seasons: Walleye, Northern Pike May-Feb, LM Bass June-Feb, Crappie, Bluegill all year
Bodies of Water: West Lost Lake, Otter Tail River, Otter Tail Lake
Types of fishing: Fly fishing, light tackle, wading
Available: Fishing instruction, bait, tackle, boat rentals, family activities, children's program, baby sitting, executive lodge (16 people)

Woodland Beach Resort - Campground
Battle Lake 800-827-3069
Handicapped equipped: No
Seasons: May to Oct
Rates: $400/week
Guides: Yes
Species & Seasons: Walleye May-Sept, Northern Pike July-Aug, Perch June-Sept, LM Bass June-Oct, Muskellunge Aug-Oct
Bodies of Water: Otter Tail Lake, Battle Lake
Types of fishing: Light tackle, heavy tackle
Available: Licenses, bait, tackle, boat rentals, baby sitting

PELICAN LAKE
(also see Crow Wing Chain)

BAIT & TACKLE...

Koep's Bait & Tackle
Nisswa 218-963-2547
Hours: 6:30am-9pm Summer, 9am-5pm Winter
Carries: Live bait, lures, flies, maps, rods, reels, licenses
Bodies of water: Mississippi River, Gull Lake, Pelican Lake, Long Lake, Pine Mountain Lake, Whitefish Lake Chain, Lake Hubert
Services & Products: Guide services, beverages, fishing instruction, repair services
Guides: Yes
OK to call for current conditions: Yes
Contact: Dave, Ryan or Marv

MINNESOTA

PELICAN LAKE - RAINY LAKE

GUIDES...

Paul Coventry
Brainerd 218-829-1846
Species & Seasons: Walleye, Northern Pike, LM Bass, Trout May-Nov, Muskellunge June-Nov, Panfish April-Nov
Bodies of water: Gull Lake, Whitefish Lake Chain, Pelican Lake, North Long Lake, Mille Lacs, Leech Lake, Lake Winnibigoshish
Rates: Half day: $150 maximun 3, Full day: $300 maximum 3
Call between: 7am-10pm
Provides: Light tackle, heavy tackle, lures, bait, rain gear
Handicapped equipped: Yes
Certifications: USCG

Koeps Bait & Tackle
Nisswa 218-963-2547
Species & Seasons: Walleye, Bass, Northern Pike, Crappie, Sunfish
Bodies of water: Mississippi River, Gull Lake, Pelican Lake, North Long Lake, Whitefish Lake Chain
Rates: Half day: $15(1-3), Full day: $300(1-3)
Call between: 8am-6pm
Provides: Light tackle, heavy tackle, fly rod/reel, lures, bait, rain gear
Handicapped equipped: Yes
Certifications: USCG

LODGING...

Black Pine Beach Resort
Pequot Lakes 800-543-4714
.... 218-543-4714
Guest Capacity: 100
Handicapped equipped: Yes
Seasons: All year
Rates: $65-$125/day (until June 3, and after Aug. 26), $385-$1185/week
Guides: Yes
Species & Seasons: Walleye, Northern Pike, LM Bass May-Feb, Crappie, luegill all year
Bodies of Water: Whitefish Lake Chain, Ossawinnamakee Chain of Lakes, Pelican Lake
Types of fishing: Light tackle
Available: Bait, tackle, boat rentals, family activities, swimming, game room, play ground

POKEGAMA LAKE

BAIT & TACKLE...

Rapids Tackle
Grand Rapids 218-326-5822
Hours: 5:30am-9pm
Carries: Live bait, lures, flies, maps, rods, reels, licenses
Bodies of water: Lake Winnibigoshish, Bowstring Lake, Pokegama Lake, Mississippi River, Bigfork River, 1200 smaller lakes
Services & Products: Guide services, beverages, repair services
Guides: Yes
OK to all for current conditions: Yes
Contact: Don Wendt

LODGING...

Birch Cove Resort & Campground
Grand Rapids 218-326-8754
Guest Capacity: 78
Handicapped equipped: No
Seasons: May 15 to Oct 15
Rates: Cabin: $550/week, Camp: $17/day
Guides: Yes
Species & Seasons: Walleye, Northern Pike May-Oct, LM Bass, Panfish June-Oct
Bodies of Water: Pokegama Lake
Types of fishing: Fly fishing, light tackle, heavy tackle, wading
Available: Bait, tackle, boat rentals

RAINY LAKE

GUIDES...

Chip Leer
Ray 218-875-2204
Species & Seasons: Walleye, SM Bass, LM Bass, Crappie, Sturgeon, Northern Pike April-Oct
Bodies of water: Kabetogama Namakan Lake Lake, Rainy Lake, Rainy River, Sand Point Lake, Crane Lake, Voyageurs National Park, Lake of the Woods
Rates: Half day: $150(2), Full day: $200(2)
Call between: 6am-11pm
Provides: Light tackle, heavy tackle, fly rod/reel, lures, bait, rain gear, beverges, lunch
Handicapped equipped: Yes
Certifications: USCG

Viking Land Guide Service
Osakis 800-267-9326
Species & Seasons: Walleye, Muskellunge, Northern Pike, LM Bass, SM Bass May-Feb, Perch, Sunfish, Crappie all year, Sturgeon April-Dec
Bodies of water: MilleLacs, Leech Lake, Rainy River, Lake Osakis, Alexandria Chain of Lakes, Lake Miltona, Lake Ida, Lake Minnewaska
Rates: Half day: $50(1), $75(2), $110(3), Full day: $85(1), $110(2), $175(3), Children welcomed
Call between: Anytime
Provides: Light tackle, heavy tackle, lures, bait, rain gear, beverages, lunch
Handicapped equipped: Yes
Certifications: USCG

Woody's Fairly Reliable Guide Service
Ranier 218-286-5001
Species & Seasons: Sturgeon April-May, Northern Pike, Walleye, SM Bass May-Oct Crappie May-June/Sept-Oct, Muskellunge Sept-Oct
Bodies of water: Rainy Lake and tributaries, Rainy River and tributaries
Rates: Half day: $150(1-2), Full day: $195(1-2) +bait and gas ($30pp "follow" boats)
Call between: 9am-6pm
Provides: Light tackle, lures
Certifications: USCG

LODGING...

Island View Lodge
International Falls 218-286-3511
Guest Capacity: 120
Handicapped equipped: Yes
Seasons: Dec 1 to Oct 31
Rates: $60/day
Guides: Yes
Species & Seasons: Walleye, Northern Pike, SM Bass May-Oct, Crappie May-June
Bodies of Water: Rainy Lake
Types of fishing: Fly fishing, light tackle
Available: Fishig instruction, licenses, bait, tackle, boat rentals, baby sitting

Moosehorn Resort
Ray 218-875-3491
800-777-7968
Guest Capacity: 50
Handicapped equipped: No
Seasons: May to Winter
Rates: From $450/week, 2 people - $1300/week, 6 people
Guides: Yes

RAINY LAKE - RICE LAKE — MINNESOTA

Species & Seasons: Walleye, Northern Pike, LM Bass, Crappie May-Oct, Whitefish Oct-Nov
Bodies of Water: Kabetogama Lake, Namakan Lake, Sand Point Lake, Rainy Lake
Types of fishing: Light tackle
Available: Fishing instruction, licenses, bait, tackle, boat rentals

Park Point Resort
Ray 800-272-4533
Guest Capacity: 45
Handicapped equipped: No
Seasons: May to Oct 30
Rates: $450/week
Guides: Yes
Species & Seasons: Walleye Sept-Oct/May-June, Northern Pike July-Sept, SM Bass, LM Bass July-Aug, Crappie May
Bodies of Water: Kabetogama Lake, Rainy Lake, Namakan Lake
Types of fishing: Light tackle, heavy tackle
Available: Fishing instruction, license, bait, tackle, boat rentals, beach, waterskiing

RAINY RIVER

GUIDES...

Chip Leer
Ray 218-875-2204
Species & Seasons: Walleye, SM Bass, LM Bass, Crappie, Sturgeon, Northern Pike April-Oct
Bodies of water: Kabetogama Namakan Lake Lake, Rainy Lake, Rainy River, Sand Point Lake, Crane Lake, Voyageurs National Park, Lake of the Woods
Rates: Half day: $150(2), Full day: $200(2)
Call between: 6am-11pm
Provides: Light tackle, heavy tackle, fly rod/reel, lures, bait, rain gear, beverages, lunch
Handicapped equipped: Yes
Certifications: USCG

Woody's Fairly Reliable Guide Service
Ranier 218-286-5001
Species & Seasons: Sturgeon April-May, Northern Pike, Walleye, SM Bass May-Oct, Crappie May-June/Sept-Oct, Muskellunge Sept-Oct
Bodies of water: Rain Lake and tributaries, Rainy River and tributaries

Rates: Half day: $150(1-2), Full day: $195(1-2) +bait and gas ($30pp "follow" boats)
Call between: 9am-6pm
Provides: Light tackle, lures
Certifications: USCG

LODGING...

Ballard's Resort
Baudette 218-634-1849
Guest Capacity: 77
Handicapped equipped: No
Seasons: All year
Rates: $150/pp week
Contact: Gary Moeller
Guides: Yes
Species & Seasons: Walleye, Sauger May-April, Northern Pike, SM Bass, Perch all year
Bodies of Water: Lake of the Woods, Rainy River
Types of fishing: Light ackle, heavy tackle, guided charter boat fishing
Available: Licenses, bait, tackle, boat rentals, guided trips from Lund Pro-V's

Bayview Lodge
Baudette 218-634-2194
Handicapped equipped: No
Seasons: All year
Rates: $38/day double occupancy
Contact: Randee
Guides: Yes
Species & Seasons: Walleye, Sauger, Northern Pike
Bodies of Water: Rainy River, Lake of the Woods
Types of fishing: Light tackle, downrigging
Available: Licenses, bait, tackle, boat rentals

RICE LAKE

BAIT & TACKLE..

Mike's Bait & Tackle
Eden Valley 612-453-2248
Carries: Live bait, lures, flies, maps, rods, reels, licenses
Bodies of water: Rice Lake, Lake Koronis, Horseshoe Chain
Services & Products: Food, beverages, fishing instruction
Guides: Yes
OK to call for current conditions: Yes
Contact: Michael

Pierce's Country Store
Remer 218-566-2334
Hours: 6am-9pm
Carries: Live bait, lures, maps, licenses
Bodies of water: Leech Lake, Thunder Lake, Rie Lake, Little Thunder Lake
Services & Products: Lodging, food, beverages, gas/oil
Guides: No
OK to call for current conditions: Yes
Contact: Dean Pierce

LODGING...

Anchor Inn Resort
Spring Lake 218-798-2718
Guest Capacity: 70
Handicapped equipped: No
Seasons: May to Nov 15
Rates: From $350-$575/week
Contact: Charles T. Kitterman
Guides: No
Species & Seasons: Walleye, Northern Pike, LM Bass May-Mar, Crappie, Panfish, Perch all year
Bodies of Water: Bowstring River, Little Sand Lake, Sand Lake, Rice Lake
Types of fishing: Fly fishing, light tackle, heavy tackle
Available: Licenses, bait, tackle, boat rentals

Kozy Kove Resort
1450 Wonderland Park Road NE
Brainerd 56401
Seasons: Mid May to Early Oct
Rates: $265-$295/week (1995 rates, will increase in '96), also weekend rates and day rates
Contact: Jeannine or Rick Zetah
Guides: No
Species & Seasons: Bluegill, Northern Pike, LM Bass, Walleye, Crappie May-Sept
Bodies of Water: Rice Lake, Mississippi River
Available: Boatrentals, play area, pontoon rentals, canoes, paddleboat

MINNESOTA

RICE LAKE - STRAIGHT RIVER

Lost Acres Resort
Blackduck 800-835-6414
.... 218-835-6414
Guest Capacity: 60
Handicapped equipped: Yes, partially
Seasons: May 10 to April 5
Rates: $58-$100/day, $290-$500/week
Guides: Yes
Species & Seasons: Walleye, Northern Pike May-Feb, Panfish all year, Muskellunge, LM Bass June-Feb
Bodies of Water: Mississippi River Chain of lakes, Little Rice Lake, Rice Lake, Cass Lake, Lake Andrusia, Wolf Lake
Types of fishing: Fly fishing, light tackle, heavy tackle
Available: Fishing instructin, licenses, bait, tackle, boat rentals, family activities, motor rentals, pontoon w/fishfinder

RUSH LAKE

LODGING...

Limmer's Resort
Ottertail .... 612-646-4707(W)
.... 218-367-2790(S)
Guest Capacity: 34+
Handicapped equipped: Yes
Seasons: May to Oct
Rates: $50/day
Contact: Kathy or Howard
Guides: Yes
Species & Seasons: Walleye, Northern Pike, LM BassMay-Oct, Crappie, Bluegill all year
Bodies of Water: Rush Lake, Otter Tail River
Types of fishing: Light tackle, heavy tackle
Available: Fishing instruction, licenses, bait, tackle, boat rentals

Moe's Ottertail Beach Resort
Route 3 Box 122
Battle Lake 56515
Handicapped equipped: No
Seasons: May 15 to Nov 1
Rates: $390/week
Guides: Yes
Species & Seasons: Walleye, Northern Pike, Perch May-Oct
Bodies of Water: Otter Tail Lake, Battle Lake, Rush Lake, Star Lake
Types of fishing: Light tackle, wading
Available: Bait, tackle, boat rentals, family activities, children's program, baby sitting

Swan Lake Resort
Fergus Falls 218-736-4626
Guest Capacity: 65
Handicapped equipped: No
Seasons: May 6 to Oct 1
Rates: $415/week
Contact: Denny or Steph
Guides: No
Species & Seasons: Bluegill, LM Bass, Northern Pike, Walleye May-Oct, Crappie May-June
Bodies of Water: Swan Lake, Otter Tail Lake, Rush Lake
Types of fishing: Light tackle
Available: Licenses, bait, tackle, boat rentals, family actvities, children's program, campground

SAND POINT LAKE

GUIDES...

Chip Leer
Ray 218-875-2204
Species & Seasons: Walleye, SM Bass, LM Bass, Crappie, Sturgeon, Northern Pike April-Oct
Bodies of water: Kabetogama Lake, Namakan Lake, Rainy Lake, Rainy River, Sand Point Lake, Crane Lake, Voyageurs National Park, Lake of the Woods
Rates: Half day: $150(2),
Full day: $200(2)
Call between: 6am-11pm
Provides: Light tackle, heavy tackle, fly rod/reel, lures, bait, rain gear, beverages, lunch
Handicapped equipped: Yes
Certifications: USCG

LODGING...

Borderland Lodge & Outfitters
Crane Lake 800-777-8392
Guest Capacity: 69
Handicapped equipped: No
Seasons: All year
Rates: $357-$1,400/week
Guides: Yes
Species & Seasons: Walleye, LM Bass, Northrn Pike May-Mar, Crappie all year
Bodies of Water: Crane Lake, Sand Point Lake, Namakan Lake, Kabetogama Lake, Lac La Croix
Types of fishing: Light tackle, fly-out trips, shuttles to Boundary Waters and Quetico (Canada)

Available: Licenses, bait, tackle, boat rentals, family activities, children's program

Eagle Wing Resort
Ray 218-875-3111
Guest Capacity: 5 cabins (30 people)
Handicapped equipped: No
Seasons: May 13 to Oct 1
Rates: $295-$545/week
Contact: Russ or Marlys Kingery
Guides: Yes
Species & Seasons: Walleye, Northern Pike May-Oct
Bodies of Water: Kabetogama Lake, Namakan Lake, Crane Lake, and Point Lake
Types of fishing: Fly fishing, light tackle, heavy tackle
Available: Fishing instruction, licenses, bait, tackle, boat rentals, family activities

Moosehorn Resort
Ray 218-875-3491
.... 800-777-7968
Guest Capacity: 50
Handicapped equipped: No
Seasons: May to Winter
Rates: From $450/week, 2 people - $1300/week, 6 people
Guides: Yes
Species & Seasons: Walleye, Northern Pike, LM Bass, Crappie May-Oct, Whitefish Oct-Nov
Bodies of Water: Kabetogama Lake, Namakan Lake, Sand Point Lake, Rainy Lake
Types of fishing: Light tackle
vailable: Fishing instruction, licenses, bait, tackle, boat rentals

STRAIGHT RIVER

BAIT & TACKLE...

Summy's Bait Tackle & Rod Reel
Owatonna 507-451-5312
Hours: 8am-8pm
Carries: Live bait, lures, flies
Bodies of water: Straight River, Crane Creek
Services & Products: Repair services
Guides: No
OK to call for current conditions: Yes
Contact: John Summy

STRAIGHT RIVER - VERMILION LAKE

MINNESOTA

LODGING...

Bass Bay Resort & Campground
Osage 800-952-1592
Guest Capacity: 60
Handicapped equiped: No
Seasons: May 15 to Oct 1
Rates: $350-$375/week,
Camping: $15.50, seasonal rates "call"
Contact: Bill, Ben, or Chris
Guides: Yes
Species & Seasons: Walleye, LM Bass, Bluegill, Crappie, Trout May-Oct
Bodies of Water: Straight Lake
Types of fishing: Fly fishing, light tackle, wading
Available: Fishing instruction, boat rentals

SWAN LAKE

BAIT & TACKLE...

Dave's Sales & Service
Hibbing 218-262-5405
Hours: 6am-8pm
Carries: Live bait, lures, flies, maps, rods, reels, licenses
Bodies of water: Swan Lake, Mississippi River, Side Lake
Services & Products: Guide services, repair services
Guides: Yes
OK to call for current conditions: Yes
Contact: David Boettcher

LODGING...

Swan Lake Resort
Fergus Falls 218-736-4626
Guest Capacity: 65
Handicapped equipped: No
Seasons: May to Oct 1
Rates: $415/week
Contact: Denny or Steph
Guides: No
Species & Seasons: Bluegill, LM Bass, Northern Pike, Walleye May-Oct, Crappie May-June
Bodies of Water: Swan Lake, Otter Tail Lake, Rush Lake
Types of fishing: Light tackle
Available: Licenses, bait, tackle, boat rentals, family activities, children's program, campground

TURTLE LAKE

LODGING...

Kohl's Resort
Bemidji 218-243-2131
Guest Capacity: 76+
Handicapped equipped: No
Seasons: All year
Rates: In season: $625-$1045/week, Off season: $394-$730/week
Contact: Loye Felix
Guides: Yes
Species & Seasons: Crappie, Northern Pike, Bluegill Spring and Fall, Walleye May-Fall, LM Bass Spring-Aug
Bodies of Water: Located on Turtle Lake
Available: Bait, tackle, family activities, bab sitting, boat comes with cabin

Sletten Resort
Bemidji 218-586-2518
Guest Capacity: 26
Handicapped equipped: No
Seasons: May 29 to Sept 15
Rates: $295-$400/week
Guides: Yes
Species & Seasons: Walleye May-July, Panfish, Northern Pike, Crappie, LM Bass May-Sept
Bodies of Water: Fox Lake, Movil Lake, Turtle Lake
Available: Boat rentals

UNION LAKE

BAIT & TACKLE...

Union Lake Sarah Campground
Erskine 218-687-5155
Hours: 6am-10pm
Carries: Live bait, lures, flies, maps, rods, reels, licenses
Bodies of ater: Union Lake, Lake Sarah
Services & Products: Boat rentals, boat ramp, food, beverages, gas/oil, fishing instruction, repair services
Guides: No
OK to call for current conditions: Yes
Contact: Jason Carlson

VERMILION LAKE

BAIT & TACKLE...

Nature's Trophies Taxidermy
Eveleth 218-744-4885
Hours: 5am-8pm
Caries: Live bait, lures, flies, licenses
Bodies of water: Lake Superior, Whiteface Res., Vermilion Lake
Services & Products: Taxidermy
Guides: Yes
OK to call for current conditions: Yes
Contact: Mario Spampinato

LODGING...

End of the Trail Lodge
4284 End of Trail Lane
Tower 55790
Guest Capacity: 30
Handicapped equipped: No
Seasons: May to Mar
Rates: $400-$650/week
Guides: Yes
Species & Seasons: Walleye, Northern Pike, Muskellunge May-Feb, Crappie all year, LM Bass, SM Bass May-Feb
Bodies of Water: Vermilion Lake, Trout Lake, Boundary Waters Canoe Area
Types of fishing: Light tackle, heavy tackle
Available: Bait, tackle, boat rentals

Grandview Resort
Cook 218-666-5327
Guest Capacity: 24
Handicapped equipped: No
Seasons: May 1 to Oct 1
Rates: $800+/week 6 people
Contact: Kathie Gustafson
Guides: Yes
Species & Seasons: Northern Pike, Walleye, SM Bass, LM Bass, Crappie, Bluegill, Muskellunge May-Freeze-Up
Bodies of Water: Vermilion Lake, Trout Lake, Boundary Waters Canoe Area
Types of fishing: Light tackle, heav tackle
Available: Boat rentals

MINNESOTA
VERMILION LAKE - WHITEFISH LAKE CHAIN

Life of Riley Resort
Cook 218-666-5453
Guest Capacity: 60
Handicapped equipped: Yes, limited
Seasons: Mid May to Oct 1
Rates: $410/week 2 adults
Contact: Rock or Lee
Guides: Yes
Species & Seasons: Walleye May-June/Fall, Northern Pike June-Oct, LM Bass, SM Bass June-July/Fall, Crappie May-June, Panfish July-Sept
Bodies of Water: Vermilion Lake, Vermilion River
Types of fishing: Fly fishing, light tackle, heavy tackle
vailable: Fishing instruction(seminar), licenses, bait, tackle, boat rentals, family activities, children's program, baby sitting

Muskego Point Resort
Cook 218-666-5696
Guest Capacity: 81
Handicapped equipped: No
Seasons: May 12 to Oct 5
Rates: $500-$1200/week 2 persons
Contact: Grant, Judy or Jenny Hughes
Guides: Yes
Species & Seasons: Walleye May-Oct, Northern Pike, Muskellunge July-Oct, LM Bass, SM Bas June-Oct
Bodies of Water: Vermilion Lake, Boundary Waters Canoe Area
Types of fishing: Fly fishing, light tackle, heavy tackle
Available: Fishing instruction, licenses, bait, tackle, boat rentals, family activities, baby sitting

Pehrson Lodge Resort
Cook 800-543-9937
Guest Capacity: 140
Handicapped equipped: No
Seasons: May 15 to Sept 25
Rates: $76-$162/day
Contact: Steve Raps
Guides: Yes
Species & Seasons:
Bodies of Water: Vermilion Lake
Types of fishing: Fly fishing, light tackle
Available: Fishing instruction, licenses, bait, tackle, boat rentals, familyactivities, children's program

Retreat Lodge & Resort
Cook 218-666-2330
Guest Capacity: 24 (approximately)
Handicapped equipped: No
Seasons: May 13 to Oct 1
Rates: $110/night, $550/week
Guides: Yes
Species & Seasons: Walleye, Northern Pike May-Feb, Crappie, Bluegill all year, Muskellunge June-Feb
Bodies of Water: Vermilion Lake
Types of fishing: Light tackle
Available: Peace, privacy, we sell only gas to our clients

Timber Wolf Lodge
Ely 218-827-3512
Guest Capacity: 64 cabins, 23 camping sites
Handicapped equipped: Yes
Seasons: All year
Rates: $90-$200/night, $550-$1,475/week
Contact: Jeff Schulze
Guides: Yes
Species & Seasons: Walleye June-Aug, SM Bass, Crappie May-June, Northern Pike May-June/Fall
Bodies of Water: Bear Island River, Birch Lake, Boundary Waters Canoe Area, Vermilion Lake
Types of fishing: Fly fishing, light tackle, havy tackle, wading, day trips to other lakes
Available: Fishing instruction, licenses, bait, tackle, boat rentals, family activities, children's program, baby sitting

Vermilion Beach Village Resort
Cook 218-666-5440
Guest Capacity: 140
Handicapped equipped: No
Seasons: May 10 to Oct 1
Rates: $625/week
Contact: Beverly J. Stinson
Guides: Yes
Species & Seasons: Walleye, Northern Pike, SM Bass May-Feb, Muskellunge Jun-Feb, Crappie, Bluegill all season
Bodies of Water: Vermilion Lake
Types of fishing: Light tackle, heavy tackle
Available: Licenses, bait, boat rentals, family activities, children's program, baby sitting, restaurant, lounge

VICTORIA LAKE

LODGING...

Broken Arrow Resort & Campground
Alexandria 612-763-4646
Handicapped equipped: Yes
Seasons: May 1 to Sept 31
Rates: $350-$675/week
Guides: Yes
Species & Seasons: Walleye, Northern Pike, LM Bass May, Panfish all season
Bodies of Water: Lake Victoria
Types of fishing: Fly fishing, light tackle
Available: Fishing instruction, bait, tackle, boat rentals, family activities

WHITE BEAR LAKE

BAIT & TACKLE...

Hansen's Sporting Goods
White Bear Lake 612-770-4120
Hours: 6:30am-7pm
Carries: Live bait, lures, flies, maps, rods, reels, licenses
Bodies of water: St. Croix River, White Bear Lake, Bald Eagle Lake, Silver Lake, Long Lake
Services & Products: Food, beverages, gas/oil, fishing instruction, repair services
Guides: Yes
OK to call for current conditions: Yes

WHITEFISH LAKE CHAIN
(also see Crow Wing Chain)

BAIT & TACKLE...

Koep's Bait & Tackle
Nisswa 218-963-2547
Hours: 6:30am-9pm Summer, 9am-5pm Winter
Carries: Live bait, lures, flies, maps, rods, reels, licenses
Bodies of water: Mississippi River, Gull Lake, Pelican Lake, Long Lake, Pine Mountain Lake, Whitefish Lake Chain, Lake Hubert
Services & Products: Guide services, beverages, fishing instruction, repair services
Guides: Yes
OK to call for current conditions: Yes
Contact: Dave, Ryan or Marv

GUIDES...

Paul Coventry
Brainerd 218-829-1846
Species & Seasons: Walleye, Northern Pike, LM Bass, Trout May-Nov, Muskellunge June-Nov, Panfish April-Nov

WHITEFISH LAKE CHAIN - WOMAN LAKE — MINNESOTA

Bodies of water: Gull Lake, Whitefish Lake Chain, Pelican Lake, North Long Lake, Mille Lacs, Leech Lake, Lake Winnibigoshish
Rates: Half day: $150 maximun 3, Full day: $300 maximum 3
Call between: 7am-10pm
Provides: Light tackle, heavy tackle, lures, bait, rain gear
Handicapped equipped: Yes
Certifications: USCG

Koeps Bait & Tackle
Nisswa 218-963-2547
Species & Seasons: Walleye, Bass, Northern Pike, Crappie, Sunfish
Bodies of water: Mississippi River, Gull Lake, Pelican Lake, North Long Lake, Whitefish Lake Chain
Rates: Half day: $10(1-3), Full day: $300(1-3)
Call between: 8am-6pm
Provides: Light tackle, heavy tackle, fly rod/reel, lures, bait, rain gear
Handicapped equipped: Yes
Certifications: USCG

LODGING...

Bay View Lodge
Crosslake 218-543-4182
Guest Capacity: 92
Handicapped equipped: No
Seasons: May to Oct
Rates: $900/week
Contact: Jim or Mary Ann Berg
Guides: Yes
Species & Seasons: Crappie May-June, Walleye, LM Bass, Northern Pike May-Oct, Lake Trout June-Oct
Bodies of Water: Whiteish Lake Chain, 14 lakes all accessible by boat
Types of fishing: Fly fishing, light tackle, heavy tackle, wading
Available: Fishing instruction, bait, tackle, boat rentals, baby sitting

Black Pine Beach Resort
Pequot Lakes.................... 800-543-4714
.... 218-543-4714
Guest Capacity: 100
Handicapped equipped: Yes
Seasons: All year
Rates: $65-$125/day (until June 3, and after Aug. 26), $385-$1185/week
Guides: Yes
Species & Seasons: Walleye, Northern Pike, LM Bass May-Feb, Crappie, Bluegill all year
Bodies of Water: Whitefish Lake Chain, Ossawinnamakee Chain of Lakes, Pelican Lake
Types of fishing: Light tackle
Available: Bait, tackle, boat rentals, family activities, swimming, game room, play ground

Gilbert Lake Resort
Brainerd 218-829-4652
Guest Capacity: 3 cabins (15 people)
Handicapped equipped: No
Seasons: May 1 to Oct 1
Rates: $350/week
Guides: Yes
Species & Seasons: LM Bass, Northern Pike, Crappie, Bluegill
Bodies of Water: Gilbert Lake, Gull Lake, Whitefish Lake Chain, Mille Lacs, many others
Types of fishing: Light tackle
Available: Fishing intruction, bait, tackle, boat rentals, Brainerd City activities 2 miles

Heath's Resort
Pine River 218-587-2286
Handicapped equipped: Yes
Seasons: All year
Rates: $500/week
Contact: Dave or Carole Heath
Guides: Yes
Bodies of Water: Whitefish Lake Chain
Available: Licenses, bait, tackle, boat rentals, family activities, baby sitting

Silver Sands Resort
Pequot Lakes................... 218-568-7837
Guest Capacity: 47
Handicapped equipped: No
Seasons: May to Oct
Rates: $300-$700/week
Contact: Dan Sigan
Guides: Yes
Species & Seasons: Walleye, Northern Pike, Crappie, Trout, LM Bass
Bodies of Water: Hay Lake, Whitefish Lake Chain
Types of fishing: Light tackle
Available: Bait, tackle, boat rentals, family activities

MARINAS...

Bait Box & Marina
Crosslake 218-692-3850
Hours: 7:30am-9:30pm Summer, 8am-8pm Winter
Carries: Live bait, lures, flies, maps, rods, reels, licenses
Bodies of water: Whitefish Lake Chain
Services & Products: Boat rentals, beverages, gas/oil
Guides: Yes
OK to call for current conditions: Yes

WOMAN LAKE

GUIDES...

Gary Stay
Longville 218-363-2308
Species & Seasons: Muskellunge June-Oct, LM Bass, SM Bass, Walleye, Northern Pike My-Oct, Panfish April-Oct
Bodies of water: Leech Lake, Woman Lake, Little Boy Lake, Wabedo Lake, Lake Winnibigoshish, many other area waters
Rates: Half day: $110(1-3), Full day: $175(1-3)
Call between: 6pm-10pm
Provides: Light tackle, heavy tackle, lures, bait
Handicapped equipped: Yes

LODGING...

Holiday Haven Resort
Longville 218-363-2473
Guest Capacity:
Handicapped equipped: No
Seasons: May to Oct
Rates: $380/week
Guides: Yes
Species & Seasons: Walleye, Northern Pike Spring-Fall, SM Bass May-Fall, Panfish Summer, Perch Fall
Bodies of Water: Woman Lake
Types of fishing: Light tackle
Available: Bait, tackle, boat rentals, baby sitting

Tri-Birches Resort & Campground
Hackensack 800-450-6524
Guest Capacity: 40
Handicapped equipped: No
Seasons: May to Oct
Rates: $299-$390/week
Contact: Dan or Gail Watters
Guides: Yes
Species & Seasons: Crappie May-June, Bluegill, Northern Pike, Walleye, LM Bass all season
Bodies of Water: 4 Point Lake, Leech Lake, Woman Lake, 127 lakes within a 10 mile radius
Types of fishing: Fly fishing, light tackle
Available: Bait, tackle, boat rentals, cabins, camping

Keep an eye out for new, updated editions
of the Angler's Yellow Pages

MISSISSIPPI

1. Arkabutla Lake
2. Chandeleur Sound
3. Eagle Lake
4. Enid Lake
5. Flower Lake
6. Grenada Lake
7. Gulf of Mexico
8. Lake Washington
9. Mississippi River
10. Pearl River
11. Ross Barnett Reservoir
12. Sardis Lake
13. St. Louis Bay
14. Tallahatchie River
15. Yazoo River

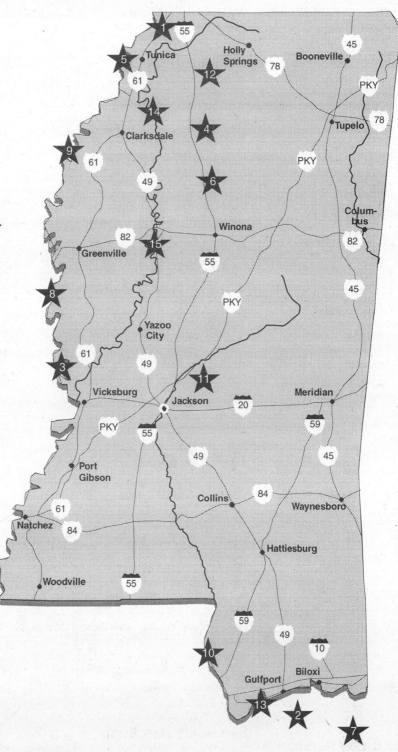

MISSISSIPPI
ARKABUTLA LAKE - GULF OF MEXICO

ARKABUTLA LAKE

BAIT & TACKLE...

Senatobia Bait Shop
Senatobia 601-562-5885
Hours: 5am-6pm
Carries: Live bait, lures, flies, maps, rods, reels, licenses
Bodies of water: Sardis Lake, Tallahatchie River, Enid Lake, Arkabutla Lake, Moon Lake, Flower Lake, Tunica Cuttoff, Coldwater River
Services & Products: Food, beverages, oil, fishing instruction
Guides: Yes
OK to call for current conditions: Yes
Contact: Dave or Gerrie

CHANDELEUR SOUND

CHARTERS...

Chandeleur Guide Fishing Inc.
Ocean Springs 601-875-9055
Species & Seasons: Speckled Trout, Redfish, Flounder Mar-Nov
Bodies of water: Chandeleur Islands off Louisiana, Gulf of Mexico, Seaplane to 50 foot houseboat on Chandeleur Sound
Rates: $3800 6 people, $633pp-3 full days and nights
Call between: 6pm-10pm
Provides: Beverages, lunch
Handicapped equipped: No

Kingfish Charter Boat
Biloxi 601-392-3448
Species & Seasons: Redfish, Speckled Trout, Flounder, Shark April-Nov
Bodies of water: Chandeleur Sound
Rates: 3-4 day fishing trips only
Call between: 8am-5pm
Provides: Beverages, lunch
Handicapped equipped: No
Certifications: USCG

EAGLE LAKE

GUIDES...

Central Delta Guide Service
Belzoni 601-247-2732
Species & Seasons: LM Bass, Crappie Mar-Dec, Bluegill May-Nov
Bodies of water: Mississippi River/Oxbow lakes: Ferguson, Lee, Chotard, Albermarie, Whittington; Lake Washington, Eagle Lake, Wasp Lake, Wolf Lake, Jackson Lake, Bee Lake, Belzoni River
Rates: Half day: $70(1), $110(2), Full day: $120(1), $200(2), Half prices for children 10-16 yrs. old
Call between: 7am-10pm
Provides: Light tackle, lures, bait, rain gear
Handicapped equipped: Depends on hanidcap

ENID LAKE

BAIT & TACKLE...

Senatobia Bait Shop
Senatobia 601-562-5885
Hours: 5am-6pm
Carries: Live bait, lures, flies, maps, rods, reels, licenses
Bodies of water: Sardis Lake, Tallahatchie River, Enid Lake, Arkabutla Lake, Moon Lake, Flower Lake, Tunica Cuttoff, Coldwater River
Services & Products: Food, beverages, oil, fishing instruction
Guides: Yes
OK to call for current conditions: Yes
Contact: Dave or Gerrie

FLOWER LAKE

BAIT & TACKLE...

JT's Bait Joint
Tunica 601-363-3946
Hours: 6am-?
Carries: Live bait, lures, flies, maps, rods, reels, licenses
Bodies of water: Mississippi River, Tunica Cuttoff, Flower Lake, Moon Lake
Services & Products: Boat ramp, food, beverages, gas/oil, fishing instruction
Guides: Yes
OK to call for current conditions: Yes
Contact: J.T. Smith

Senatobia Bait Shop
Senatobia 601-562-5885
Hours: 5am-6pm
Carries: Live bait, lures, flies, maps, rods, reels, licenses
Bodies of water: Sardis Lake, Tallahatchie River, Enid Lake, Arkabutla Lake, Moon Lake, Flower Lake, Tunica Cuttoff, Coldwater River
Services & Products: Food, beverages, oil, fishing instruction
Guides: Yes
OK to call for current conditions: Yes
Contact: Dave or Gerrie

GRENADA LAKE

BAIT & TACKLE...

Delta Bait Shop
Greenwood 601-455-5442
Hours: 5am-6pm
Carries: Live bait, lures, flies, rods, reels, licenses
Bodies of water: Yazoo River, Yalobusha River, Tallahatchie River, Little Eagle, Grenada Lake, many more
Services & Products: Guide services, charter boat service, boat ramp, beverages, fishing instruction, repair services
OK to call for current conditions: Yes
Contact: Ray, Lewy or James

GULF OF MEXICO

BAIT & TACKLE...

Biloxi Rod & Tackle
Biloxi 601-432-5411
Hours: 8am-7pm, closed Sun., Mon.
Carries: Lures, flies, maps, rods, reels, licenses
Bodies of water: Gulf of Mexico
Services & Products: Guide services, charter boat service, fishing instruction, repair services
Guides: Yes
OK to call for current conditions: Yes
Contact: Danny Bledsoe

Thigpen Bait & Tackle Shop
Picayune 601-798-3474
Hours: 6am-6pm
Carries: Live bait, lures, flies, maps, rods, reels, licenses
Bodies of water: Pearl River, Jordan River, Gulf of Mexico, Lake Pontchartrain
Services & Products: Repair services
Guides: Yes
OK to call for current conditions: Yes
Contact: Robert Thigpen

GULF OF MEXICO - ROSS BARNETT RESERVOIR MISSISSIPPI

CHARTERS...

Chandeleur Guide Fishing Inc.
Ocean Springs 601-875-9055
Species & Seasons: Speckled Trout, Redfish, Flounder Mar-Nov
Bodies of water: Chandeleur Islands off Louisiana, Gulf of Mexico, Seaplane to 50 foot houseboat on Chandeleur Sound
Rates: $3800 6 people, $633pp-3 full days and nights
Call between: 6pm-10pm
Provides: Beverages, lunch
Handicapped equipped: No

P.J. Charter Boat
Long Beach 601-863-2362
.... 800-377-3630
Species & Seasons: King Mackerel, June-Oct, Red Snapper, Red Drum, Spanish Mackerel April-Oct, Jack Cravalle, Cobia, Shark May-Oct, Bluefish June-Oct
Bodies of water: Mississippi Sound, Gulf of Mexico
Rates: Whole boat: $485 per day (8hrs.)
Call between: 6pm-10pm
Provides: Light tackle, heavy tackle, lures, bait
Handicapped equipped: Yes
Certifications: USCG

Skipper
D'Iberville 601-385-2910
Species & Seasons: Snapper Nov-Mar, Spanish Mackerel Mar-Oct, King Mackerel, Dolphin June-Oct, Red Drum June-Sept, Cobia May-Oct
Bodies of water: Gulf of Mexico
Rates: Half day: $350(1-6), $35 additional each person over 6
Full day: $450(1-6) $45 additional each person over 6
Call between: 7am-10pm
Provides: Light tackle, heavy tackle, lures, bait

MARINAS...

Bay Marina
Bay St. Louis 601-466-4970
Hours: 7am-7pm
Carries: Live bait, lures, maps, rods, reels, licenses
Bodies of water: St. Louis Bay, Gulf of Mexico, Louisiana Marsh, Cat Island, Ship Island

Services & Products: Boat rentals, guide services, charter boat service, lodging, boat ramp, food, beverages, gas/oil, fishing instruction, repair services, boat slips
OK to call for current conditions: Yes
Contact: Mickey Demoran

Wolf River Canoes & Kayaks
Long Beach 601-452-7666
Hours: 7am-8pm
Bodies of water: Wolf River, St. Louis Bay, Gulf of Mexico, Jordan River
Services & Products: Boat rentals
Guides: Yes
OK to call for current conditions: No

LAKE WASHINGTON

GUIDES...

Central Delta Guide Service
Belzoni 601-247-2732
Species & Seasons: LM Bass, Crappie Mar-Dec, Bluegill May-Nov
Bodies of water: Mississippi River/ Oxbow lakes: Ferguson, Lee, Chotard, Albermarie, Whittington; Lake Washington, Eagle Lake, Wasp Lake, Wolf Lake, Jackson Lake, Bee Lake and Belzoni River
Rates: Half day: $70(1), $110(2), Full day: $120(1), $200(2), Half prices for children 10-16 yrs. old
Call between: 7am-10pm
Provides: Light tackle, lures, bait, rain gear
Handicapped equipped: Depends on hanidcap

MISSISSIPPI RIVER

BAIT & TACKLE...

JT's Bait Joint
Tunica 601-363-3946
Hours: 6am-?
Carries: Live bait, lures, flies, maps, rods, reels, licenses
Bodies of water: Mississippi River, Tunica Cuttoff, Flower Lake, Moon Lake
Services & Products: Boat ramp, food, beverages, gas/oil, fishing instruction
Guides: Yes
OK to call for current conditions: Yes
Contact: J.T. Smith

GUIDES...

Central Delta Guide Service
Belzoni 601-247-2732
Species & Seasons: LM Bass, Crappie Mar-Dec, Bluegill May-Nov
Bodies of water: Mississippi River/ Oxbow lakes: Ferguson, Lee, Chotard, Albermarie, Whittington; Lake Washington, Eagle Lake, Wasp Lake, Wolf Lake, Jackson Lake, Bee Lake and Belzoni River
Rates: Half day: $70(1), $110(2), Full day: $120(1), $200(2), Half prices for children 10-16 yrs. old
Call between: 7am-10pm
Provides: Light tackle, lures, bait, rain gear
Handicapped equipped: Depends on hanidcap

PEARL RIVER

BAIT & TACKLE...

Thigpen Bait & Tackle Shop
Picayune 601-798-3474
Hours: 6am-6pm
Carries: Live bait, lures, flies, maps, rods, reels, licenses
Bodies of water: Pearl River, Jordan River, Gulf of Mexico, Lake Pontchartrain
Services & Products: Repair services
Guides: Yes
OK to call for current conditions: Yes
Contact: Robert Thigpen

ROSS BARNETT RESERVOIR

BAIT & TACKLE...

Reservoir Shell
Brandon 601-992-2257
Hours: 5am-9pm
Carries: Live bait, lures, flies, maps, rods, reels, licenses
Bodies of water: Ross Barnett Reservoir
Services & Products: Food, beverages, gas/oil
Guides: Yes
OK to call for current conditions: Yes

MISSISSIPPI

SARDIS LAKE — YAZOO RIVER

SARDIS LAKE

BAIT & TACKLE...

Senatobia Bait Shop
Senatobia 601-562-5885
Hours: 5am-6pm
Carries: Live bait, lures, flies, maps, rods, reels, licenses
Bodies of water: Sardis Lake, Tallahatchie River, Enid Lake, Arkabutla Lake, Moon Lake, Flower Lake, Tunica Cuttoff, Coldwater River
Services & Products: Food, beverages, oil, fishing instruction
Guides: Yes
OK to call for current conditions: Yes
Contact: Dave or Gerrie

GUIDES...

North Delta Guide Service
Clarksdale 601-627-1402
Species & Seasons: LM Bass Mar-Nov
Bodies of water: Sardis Lake, Desoto Lake
Rates: Half day: $75(1), $100(2), Full day: $125(1), $150(2)
Call between: 5pm-10pm
Provides: Light tackle, heavy tackle, lures, bait, rain gear, beverages, lunch
Handicapped equipped: Yes
Certifications: Guide School, Tournament Fisherman

ST. LOUIS BAY

MARINAS...

Bay Marina
Bay St. Louis 601-466-4970
Hours: 7am-7pm
Carries: Live bait, lures, maps, rods, reels, licenses
Bodies of water: St. Louis Bay, Gulf of Mexico, Louisiana Marsh, Cat Island, Ship Island
Services & Products: Boat rentals, guide services, charter boat service, lodging, boat ramp, food, beverages, gas/oil, fishing instruction, repair services, boat slips
OK to call for current conditions: Yes
Contact: Mickey Demoran

Wolf River Canoes & Kayaks
Long Beach 601-452-7666
Hours: 7am-8pm
Bodies of water: Wolf River, St. Louis Bay, Gulf of Mexico, Jordan River
Services & Products: Boat rentals
Guides: Yes
OK to call for current conditions: No

TALLAHATCHIE RIVER

BAIT & TACKLE...

Delta Bait Shop
Greenwood 601-455-5442
Hours: 5am-6pm
Carries: Live bait, lures, flies, rods, reels, licenses
Bodies of water: Yazoo River, Yalobusha River, Tallahatchie River, Little Eagle, Grenada Lake, many more
Services & Products: Guide services, charter boat service, boat ramp, beverages, fishing instruction, repair services
OK to call for current conditions: Yes
Contact: Ray, Lewy or James

Senatobia Bait Shop
Senatobia 601-562-5885
Hours: 5am-6pm
Carries: Live bait, lures, flies, maps, rods, reels, licenses
Bodies of water: Sardis Lake, Tallahatchie River, Enid Lake, Arkabutla Lake, Moon Lake, Flower Lake, Tunica Cuttoff, Coldwater River
Services & Products: Food, beverages, oil, fishing instruction
Guides: Yes
OK to call for current conditions: Yes
Contact: Dave or Gerrie

YAZOO RIVER

BAIT & TACKLE...

Delta Bait Shop
Greenwood 601-455-5442
Hours: 5am-6pm
Carries: Live bait, lures, flies, rods, reels, licenses
Bodies of water: Yazoo River, Yalobusha River, Tallahatchie River, Little Eagle, Grenada Lake, many more
Services & Products: Guide services, charter boat service, boat ramp, beverages, fishing instruction, repair services
OK to call for current conditions: Yes
Contact: Ray, Lewy or James

Thank you for using the Angler's Yellow Pages

To order additional copies of the Angler's Yellow Pages
call 1-800-242-9722

MISSOURI

1. Bull Shoals Lake
2. Grand River
3. Harry S Truman Reservoir
4. Lake Jacomo
5. Lake of the Ozarks
6. Lake Taneycomo
7. Longview Reservoir
8. Mark Twain Lake
9. Meramec River
10. Mississippi River
11. Missouri River
12. Pomme de Terre Lake
13. Smithville Reservoir
14. Stockton Lake
15. Table Rock Lake
16. White River

MISSOURI

BULL SHOALS LAKE - HARRY S TRUMAN RESERVOIR

BULL SHOALS LAKE

LODGES...

Antlers Resort & Campground
Branson 417-338-2331
Guest Capacity: Resort: 122, Camp: 10 full hookup sites, 6 tent sites
Handicapped equipped: No
Seasons: All year
Rates: Varies
Contact: Barbara Johnson
Guides: Yes
Species & Seasons: Crappie, LM Bass Mar-April/Sept-Oct, Bluegill April/May-Sept/Oct/Nov, Channel Catfish, Flathead Catfish April/May-Sept/Oct, Rainbow Trout, Brown Trout Jan-Dec
Bodies of Water: Table Rock Lake, Lake Taneycomo, Bull Shoals Lake
Types of fishing: Fly fishing, light tackle, heavy tackle, wading
Available: Licenses, bait, tackle, boat rentals, recreation room

Big Creek Lakefront Resort
Theodosia 800-597-4887
Guest Capacity: 30
Handicapped equipped: No
Seasons: All year
Rates: $35/day double occupancy
Contact: Jim or Nancy Heintz
Guides: Yes
Species & Seasons: White Bass Mar-April/Oct-Nov, Crappie, Trout, SM Bass April-June, LM Bass all year, Catfish June-Sept
Bodies of Water: Bull Shoals Lake
Types of fishing: Light tackle, heavy tackle
Available: Licenses, bait, tackle, boat rentals, family activities, in ground pool, covered dock w/elec.

Carte Court
Theodosia 417-273-4434
.... 800-609-6711
Guest Capacity: 40
Handicapped equipped: Yes, somewhat
Seasons: All year
Rates: From $35/day double occupancy
Contact: Mary Ann
Guides: Yes
Species & Seasons: LM Bass, Crappie, Catfish, Trout
Bodies of Water: Bull Shoals Lake, Norfork Lake, White River, Lake Taneycomo
Types of fishing: Fly fishing, light tackle, wading, float trips

Available: Family activities, pool, hot tub Within 1 mile: Fishing instruction, licenses, bait, tackle, boat rentals

Cedar Creek Cove Resort
Theodosia 417-273-4927
Guest Capacity: 7 cabins
Handicapped equipped: Yes
Seasons: All year
Rates: $40-$55/day, $240-$330/week
Contact: Ron or Gail Misek
Guides: Yes
Species & Seasons: LM Bass, SM Bass, Walleye all year, Spotted Bass Feb-Nov, Crappie April-Oct
Bodies of Water: Bull Shoals Lake(located on), Norfork Lake, Lake Taneycomo
Types of fishing: Light tackle, heavy tackle
Available: Licenses, bait, tackle, boat rentals, family activities, baby sitting, rec. room, pizzas, soda, candy

Shore Acres Resort
HCR 4 Box 2010
Reeds Spring 65737
Guest Capacity: 110
Handicapped equipped: No
Seasons: All year
Rates: $50/day
Contact: Pat McEvoy
Guides: Yes
Species & Seasons: LM Bass, Crappie April is best, Catfish, Bluegill all year
Bodies of Water: Table Rock Lake, Lake Taneycomo, Bull Shoals Lake, Beaver Lake(AR)
Types of fishing: Light tackle, wading
Available: Licenses, bait, tackle, boat rentals, family activities

Stormy Point Camp & Resort
Branson 417-338-2255
Guest Capacity: 90 units, 55 campsites
Handicapped equipped: Yes
Seasons: April 1 to Dec 15
Rates: Camping: $22/day, Lodging: $65/day double occupancy
Contact: Ron or Karen Holloway
Guides: Yes
Species & Seasons: SM Bass, LM Bass, Crappie, Perch April-Oct
Bodies of Water: Lake Taneycomo, Bull Shoals Lake, Beaver Lake(AR)
Types of fishing: Fly fishing, light tackle, heavy tackle, wading
Available: Fishing instruction, licenses, bait, tackle, boat rentals

GRAND RIVER

BAIT & TACKLE...

Cleta's Bait Shop
Lock Springs 816-772-3297
Hours: 8am-8pm
Carries: Live bait, lures, flies, maps, rods, reels
Bodies of water: Indian Creek Conservation Lake, Grand River, Thompson River
Services & Products: Food, beverages, fishing instruction
Guides: Yes
OK to call for current conditions: Yes
Contact: Cleta Ahlstedt

HARRY S TRUMAN RESERVOIR

BAIT & TACKLE...

Devil's Backbone Store
Warsaw 816-438-7563
Hours: 5am-11pm
Carries: Live bait, lures, maps, rods, reels
Bodies of water: Stockton Lake, Pomme de Terre Lake, Lake of the Ozarks, Harry S. Truman Res.
Services & Products: Guide services, lodging, boat ramp, food, beverages, fishing instruction
Guides: Yes
OK to call for current conditions: Yes
Contact: Jim Tyre

Laurie Bait & Tackle Bass Pro
Laurie 314-374-6065
Hours: 8am-6pm, closed Sun.
Carries: Live bait, lures, flies, maps, rods, reels, licenses
Bodies of water: Lake of the Ozarks, Harry S. Truman Res.
Services & Products: Oil, repair services
Guides: Yes
OK to call for current conditions: Yes
Contact: Larry, Sharon or Don

LODGES...

Angler's Resort
Wheatland 417-282-5507
Guest Capacity: 50
Handicapped equipped: No

HARRY S TRUMAN RESERVOIR - LAKE OF THE OZARKS - MISSOURI

Seasons: Mar 1 to Nov 30
Rates: $30-$50/day
Contact: Darrell or Laura Guinn
Guides: Yes
Species & Seasons: Crappie Feb-Dec, LM Bass Mar-Dec, Muskellunge, Walleye April-Nov, White Bass Mar-Nov
Bodies of Water: Pomme de Terre Lake, Truman Res., Stockton Lake, Lake of the Ozarks, Niangua River (Bennett Springs), Pomme de Terre River
Types of fishing: Fly fishing, light tackle, heavy tackle, float trips
Available: Bait, tackle, boat rentals, family activities, baby sitting, kitchenettes, canoe float trips, playground

Empire Resort
Camdenton 314-346-2177
Guest Capacity: 85
Handicapped equipped: Yes
Seasons: All year
Rates: $38-$58/day double occupancy
Contact: Jim Redman
Guides: Yes
Species & Seasons: Crappie, LM Bass Dec-June, LM Bass, White Bass, Wallleye Mar-Sept, White Bass, Hybrids Walleye Aug-Nov, Bluegill, Catfish all year, Striped Bass Aug-Oct
Bodies of Water: Lake of the Ozarks, Truman Res
Types of fishing: Fly fishing, light tackle, heavy tackle, float trips
Available: Fishing instruction, licenses, bait, tackle, boat rentals, family activities, baby sitting

Russ T Lake Shore Resort
Wheatland 417-282-6241
Guest Capacity: 38
Handicapped equipped: Yes, 1 unit
Seasons: April to Nov
Rates: $38/day
Guides: Yes, recommend
Species & Seasons: Muskellunge, LM Bass, Crappie, White Bass, Walleye March-Nov
Bodies of Water: Pomme de Terre Lake, Truman Res., Bennett Spring
Types of fishing: Light tackle, heavy tackle, float trips
Available: Boat rentals, family activities, golf (18 hole)

Southwood Shores
Lake Ozark 314-365-4644
Guest Capacity: 300
Handicapped equipped: Yes, some
Seasons: All year
Rates: Varies
Contact: Sharon Flint
Guides: Yes
Species & Seasons: Crappie Mar-Arpil, LM Bass, White Bass, Striped Bass May-Sept, Catfish June-Sept
Bodies of Water: Lake of the Ozarks, Truman Res., Osage River, Missourii River
Types of fishing: Light tackle, heavy tackle
Available: Indoor, outdoor pools, hot tub

Tebo Creek Lodge
Clinton 816-477-3516
Guest Capacity: 80
Seasons: Mar to Nov
Rates: $37.50/night double occupancy
Guides: Yes
Species & Seasons: LM Bass, Crappie, Walleye, Catfish
Bodies of Water: Truman Res., Lake of the Ozarks
Types of fishing: Light tackle, heavy tackle
Available: Licenses, bait, tackle

Willow Winds Resort
Wheatland 800-556-5591
Guest Capacity: 11 units, 4 sleeps 10, 6 sleeps 6, 1 sleeps 3
Handicapped equipped: No
Seasons: Mar 15 to Sept 15
Rates: $32.95-$42.95-$54.95/day
Guides: Yes, recommend
Species & Seasons: Muskellunge Spring and Fall, LM Bass, Crappie, White Bass all year, Walleye Spring
Bodies of Water: Pomme de Terre Lake, Truman Res., Lake of the Ozarks, Stockton Lake
Types of fishing: Light tackle, heavy tackle, float trips
Available: Boat rentals, family activities, swimming pool

LAKE JACOMO

MARINAS...

Longview Lake Marina
Kansas City 816-966-0131
Hours: 7am-sunset
Carries: Live bait, lures, maps, rods, reels, licenses
Bodies of water: Little Blue River, Longview Res., Lake Jacomo
Services & Products: Boat rentals, boat ramp, food, beverages, gas/oil, fishing instruction, repair services
Guides: Yes
OK to call for current conditions: Yes
Contact: Sam Diamond

LAKE OF THE OZARKS

BAIT & TACKLE...

Devil's Backbone Store
Warsaw 816-438-7563
Hours: 5am-11pm
Carries: Live bait, lures, maps, rods, reels
Bodies of water: Stockton Lake, Pomme de Terre Lake, Lake of the Ozarks, Harry S. Truman Res.
Services & Products: Guide services, lodging, boat ramp, food, beverages, fishing instruction
Guides: Yes
OK to call for current conditions: Yes
Contact: Jim Tyre

Laurie Bait & Tackle Bass Pro
Laurie 314-374-6065
Hours: 8am-6pm, closed Sun.
Carries: Live bait, lures, flies, maps, rods, reels, licenses
Bodies of water: Lake of the Ozarks, Harry S. Truman Res.
Services & Products: Oil, repair services
Guides: Yes
OK to call for current conditions: Yes
Contact: Larry, Sharon or Don

LODGES...

Angler's Resort
Wheatland 417-282-5507
Guest Capacity: 50
Handicapped equipped: No
Seasons: Mar 1 to Nov 30
Rates: $30-$50/day
Contact: Darrell or Laura Guinn
Guides: Yes
Species & Seasons: Crappie Feb-Dec, LM Bass Mar-Dec, Muskellunge, Walleye April-Nov, White Bass Mar-Nov
Bodies of Water: Pomme de Terre Lake, Truman Res., Stockton Lake, Lake of the Ozarks, Niangua River (Bennett Springs), Pomme de Terre River
Types of fishing: Fly fishing, light tackle, heavy tackle, float trips
Available: Bait, tackle, boat rentals, family activities, baby sitting, kitchenettes, canoe float trips, playground

MISSOURI — LAKE OF THE OZARKS

Cedar Green Resort
Camdenton 314-346-2849
Guest Capacity: 66
Handicapped equipped: No
Seasons: April 1 to Oct 15
Rates: $34-$95/day
Contact: Gary or Shirley Myers
Guides: Yes
Species & Seasons: White Bass July-Oct, LM Bass, Crappie April-Oct
Bodies of Water: Lake of the Ozarks
Types of fishing: Light tackle
Available: Fishing instruction, bait, tackle, boat rentals, family activities

Digger O'Dells Resort & Motel
Camdenton 314-873-5380
Guest Capacity: 75-80
Seasons: April 1 to Nov 1
Rates: $35.-$125/day
Contact: Tom or Joyce
Guides: Available outside resort
Species & Seasons: Crappie, LM Bass, White Bass, Catfish, Walleye all year
Bodies of Water: Lake of the Ozarks
Types of fishing: Light tackle
Available: Licenses, bait, tackle, boat rentals, family activities, baby sitting

Empire Resort
Camdenton 314-346-2177
Guest Capacity: 85
Handicapped equipped: Yes
Seasons: All year
Rates: $38-$58/day double occupancy
Contact: Jim Redman
Guides: Yes
Species & Seasons: Crappie, LM Bass Dec-June, LM Bass, White Bass, Wallleye Mar-Sept, White Bass, Hybrids Walleye Aug-Nov, Bluegill, Catfish all year, Striped Bass Aug-Oct
Bodies of Water: Lake of the Ozarks, Harry S. Truman Res.
Types of fishing: Fly fishing, light tackle, heavy tackle, float trips
Available: Fishing instruction, licenses, bait, tackle, boat rentals, family activities, baby sitting

Lakeview Resort
Sunrise Beach 800-936-5655
.... 314-374-5555
Guest Capacity: 300
Handicapped equipped: Yes
Seasons: All year
Rates: $39.95-$254.95/day
Guides: Yes

Species & Seasons: Crappie Mar-Nov, LM Bass, Bluegill, White Bass April-Oct, Catfish May-Sept
Bodies of Water: Lake of the Ozarks
Types of fishing: Fly fishing, light tackle, heavy tackle, wading, float trips
Available: Licenses, bait, tackle, boat rentals, family activities, baby sitting

Lodge of the Ozarks
Lake Ozark 314-365-6729
Guest Capacity: 100+
Handicapped equipped: No
Seasons: Mar to Nov
Rates: Upon request
Contact: Rick
Guides: Yes
Species & Seasons: LM Bass, Bluegill, Striped Bass Mar-Dec, Crappie all year, Spoonbill Mar-April
Bodies of Water: Lake of the Ozarks
Types of fishing: Light tackle
Available: Fishing instruction, licenses (close by), bait (close by), tackle (close by), boat rentals, family activities

Mallard Point Resort
Lake Ozark 314-365-2623
Guest Capacity: 100
Handicapped equipped: No
Seasons: Mar to Nov 15
Contact: Bruce Thomson
Guides: Yes
Species & Seasons: LM Bass, Crappie, White Bass, Catfish
Bodies of Water: Lake of the Ozarks
Types of fishing: Light tackle

Marina Bay Resort
Osage Beach 314-348-2200
Guest Capacity: 300+rooms
Handicapped equipped: Yes
Seasons: All year
Rates: Hotel: $59-$109/day, Condo's: $139-$149/day
Contact: Victor Dollar
Guides: Yes
Bodies of Water: Lake of the Ozarks
Types of fishing: Light tackle, heavy tackle
Available: Fishing instruction, bait, tackle, boat rentals, family activities, children's program

Ozark Village Resort
Lake Ozark 314-365-2805
Guest Capacity: 150
Handicapped equipped: Yes
Seasons: Mar 1 to Nov 1
Rates: Off season: $37-$48/day, In season: $47-$70/day
Contact: Joe or Steve Pollock
Guides: Yes
Species & Seasons: Crappie Mar-June, LM Bass June-Aug, White Bass Aug-Nov
Bodies of Water: Lake of the Ozarks
Types of fishing: Fly fishing, light tackle, heavy tackle
Available: Bait, tackle, boat rentals, family activities, children's program

---

Robin's Resort
LAKE OF THE OZARKS

On the Grand Glaize Arm...Robin's Resort is noted for it's modern, clean facilities at the water's edge, gentle sloping grounds & location by land & water in the heart of Osage Beach, Missouri.

- 1 and 2 BR Lakefront Units
- 3 and 4 BR Lakeview Homes
- Boat Rentals - Fishing, Pontoon
- Covered Boat Stalls - 20', 24', 28'
- Concrete Launching Ramp
- Heated & Baited Fishing Docks
- 1200' Private Shoreline Fishing
- Live Bait - Minnows, Worms
- Recreation Room - Snacks
- Heated Pool - Floating Sun Deck

COLOR BROCHURE:
Robin's Resort
Lake Road 54-29
Rt. 3 Box 7310
Osage Beach, MO 65065

FOR RESERVATIONS CALL:
1 (573) 348-2275
Operators: Mark & Amy Baker

OFF-SEASON FISHING:
March, April - Crappie
April, May - Stripped Bass
May, June - White Bass
October - Variety

LAKE OF THE OZARKS — MISSOURI

Paradise Cove Resort
Osage Beach 314-348-2526
Guest Capacity: 70
Handicapped equipped: No
Seasons: Mar to Nov
Rates: $32-$80/day
Contact: Jack Board
Guides: Yes, recommend
Species & Seasons: Crappie, LM Bass, White Bass, Catfish
Bodies of Water: Lake of the Ozarks
Types of fishing: Light tackle
Available: Boat rentals

Robin's Resort
Osage Beach 573-348-2275
Guest Capacity: 125
Handicapped equipped: Yes, a few units
Seasons: Mar 1 to Nov 15
Rates: Off season: $39-$60/day, In season: $54-$79/day
Contact: Mark Baker
Guides: Yes
Species & Seasons: Crappie, Striped Bass, White Bass, Catfish
Bodies of Water: Lake of the Ozarks
Types of fishing: Light tackle, heavy tackle, heated fishing dock
Available: Bait, tackle, boat rentals, family activities, baby sitting, boat dock, pool, rec. room, laundry, horseshoes, shuffleboard
(see ad page 258)

Rock Harbor Resort
Sunrise Beach 314-374-5586
Guest Capacity: 150
Handicapped equipped: No
Seasons: Mar 1 to Dec 1
Rates: On request
Guides: Yes
Species & Seasons: Crappie, LM Bass, Catfish
Bodies of Water: Lake of the Ozarks
Types of fishing: Fly fishing, light tackle
Available: Licenses, boat rentals, family activities

Southwood Shores
Lake Ozark 314-365-4644
Guest Capacity: 300
Handicapped equipped: Yes, some
Seasons: All year
Rates: Varies
Contact: Sharon Flint
Guides: Yes
Species & Seasons: Crappie Mar-Arpil, LM Bass, White Bass, Striped Bass May-Sept, Catfish June-Sept
Bodies of Water: Lake of the Ozarks, Truman Res., Osage River, Missourii River

Types of fishing: Light tackle, heavy tackle
Available: Indoor, outdoor pools, hot tub

Tebo Creek Lodge
Clinton 816-477-3516
Guest Capacity: 80
Seasons: Mar to Nov
Rates: $37.50/night double occupancy
Guides: Yes
Species & Seasons: LM Bass, Crappie, Walleye, Catfish
Bodies of Water: Truman Res., Lake of the Ozarks
Types of fishing: Light tackle, heavy tackle
Available: Licenses, bait, tackle

The Ponderosa Resort
Osage Beach 314-348-2171
Guest Capacity: 60
Handicapped equipped: No
Seasons: April 1 to Oct 31
Rates: $44-$52/day
Contact: Glenn Kaffenberger
Guides: No
Species & Seasons: Crappie Mar-June, LM Bass Feb-Nov, Catfish, Bluegill Feb-Dec
Bodies of Water: Lake of the Ozarks
Types of fishing: Fly fishing, light tackle
Available: Boat rentals, family activities

Whispering Woods Resort
Kimberling City 800-226-4951
Guest Capacity: 72
Handicapped equipped: No
Seasons: All year
Rates: $40-$70/day
Contact: Gary or Lorene Watson
Guides: Yes
Species & Seasons: LM Bass, Crappie, Walleye, Bluegill all year
Bodies of Water: Table Rock Lake, Lake Taneycomo, James River, White River
Types of fishing: Fly fishing, light tackle, heavy tackle
Available: Fishing instruction, bait, tackle, boat rentals, family activities, children's program, baby sitting

Willow Winds Resort
Wheatland 800-556-5591
Guest Capacity: 11 units, 4 sleeps 10, 6 sleeps 6, 1 sleeps 3
Handicapped equipped: No
Seasons: Mar 15 to Sept 15
Rates: $32.95-$42.95-$54.95/day
Guides: Yes, recommend

Species & Seasons: Muskellunge Spring and Fall, LM Bass, Crappie, White Bass all year, Walleye Spring
Bodies of Water: Pomme de Terre Lake, Truman Res., Lake of the Ozarks, Stockton Lake
Types of fishing: Light tackle, heavy tackle, float trips
Available: Boat rentals, family activities, swimming pool

Wilson's Resort
Camdenton 314-873-5178
Guest Capacity: 40
Handicapped equipped: No
Seasons: All year
Rates: $36-$89/day
Contact: Joan or Mike Lawson
Guides: Yes
Species & Seasons: Crappie all year, LM Bass Mar-Nov, Catfish May-Oct, Walleye, Panfish April-Oct
Bodies of Water: Lake of the Ozarks
Types of fishing: Light tackle
Available: Licenses, bait, tackle, boat rentals, family activities

MARINAS...

Cutty's Wharf
Route 2 Box 3781 A
Osage Beach 65065
Bodies of water: Lake of the Ozarks

G & G Marina, Inc.
Roach 314-346-2433
Hours: 9am-5pm, closed Tues.
Carries: Lures, maps
Bodies of water: Lake of the Ozarks
Services & Products: Boat ramp, gas/oil, repair services
Guides: Yes

Run About Marina
Osage Beach 314-348-5268
Hours: 8am-8pm (winter)
Carries: Live bait, lures, maps, rods, reels
Bodies of water: Lake of the Ozarks
Services & Products: Boat rentals, guide services, boat ramp, food, beverages, gas/oil
Guides: Yes
OK to call for current conditions: Yes
Contact: Jim

MISSOURI — LAKE TANEYCOMO

LAKE TANEYCOMO

LODGES...

Antlers Resort & Campground
Branson 417-338-2331
Guest Capacity: Resort: 122,
Camp: 10 full hookup sites, 6 tent sites
Handicapped equipped: No
Seasons: All year
Rates: Varies
Contact: Barbara Johnson
Guides: Yes
Species & Seasons: Crappie, LM Bass Mar-April/Sept-Oct, Bluegill April/May-Sept/Oct/Nov, Channel Catfish, Flathead Catfish April/May-Sept/Oct, Rainbow Trout, Brown Trout Jan-Dec
Bodies of Water: Table Rock Lake, Lake Taneycomo, Bull Shoals Lake
Types of fishing: Fly fishing, light tackle, heavy tackle, wading
Available: Licenses, bait, tackle, boat rentals, recreation room

Big Cedar Lodge
Ridgedale 417-335-2777
Guest Capacity: 450-500
Handicapped equipped: Yes
Seasons: All year
Rates: $79-$849/day
Guides: Yes
Species & Seasons: LM Bass Mar-May, Crappie April-May, Trout Sept-Jan
Bodies of Water: Table Rock Lake, Lake Taneycomo
Types of fishing: Fly fishing, light tackle
Available: Fishing instruction, licenses, bait, tackle, boat rentals, family activities, children's program

Carte Court
Theodosia 417-273-4434
.... 800-609-6711
Guest Capacity: 40
Handicapped equipped: Yes, somewhat
Seasons: All year
Rates: From $35/day double occupancy
Contact: Mary Ann
Guides: Yes
Species & Seasons: LM Bass, Crappie, Catfish, Trout
Bodies of Water: Bull Shoals Lake, Norfork Lake, White River, Lake Taneycomo
Types of fishing: Fly fishing, light tackle, wading, float trips
Available: Family activities, pool, hot tub
Within 1 mile: Fishing instruction, licenses, bait, tackle, boat rentals

Cedar Creek Cove Resort
Theodosia 417-273-4927
Guest Capacity: 7 cabins
Handicapped equipped: Yes
Seasons: All year
Rates: $40-$55/day, $240-$330/week
Contact: Ron or Gail Misek
Guides: Yes
Species & Seasons: LM Bass, SM Bass, Walleye all year, Spotted Bass Feb-Nov, Crappie April-Oct
Bodies of Water: Bull Shoals Lake(located on), Norfork Lake, Lake Taneycomo
Types of fishing: Light tackle, heavy tackle
Available: Licenses, bait, tackle, boat rentals, family activities, baby sitting, rec. room, pizzas, soda, candy

Fish Camp Co.
Rockaway Beach 417-561-4213
Handicapped equipped: No
Seasons: All year
Contact: Scotty Hill
Guides: Yes
Species & Seasons: Trout all year
Bodies of Water: Lake Taneycomo
Types of fishing: Light tackle
Available: Fishing instruction, bait, tackle, boat rentals

Shore Acres Resort
HCR 4 Box 2010
Reeds Spring 65737
Guest Capacity: 110
Handicapped equipped: No
Seasons: All year
Rates: $50/day
Contact: Pat McEvoy
Guides: Yes
Species & Seasons: LM Bass, Crappie April is best, Catfish, Bluegill all year
Bodies of Water: Table Rock Lake, Lake Taneycomo, Bull Shoals Lake, Beaver Lake(AR)
Types of fishing: Light tackle, wading
Available: Licenses, bait, tackle, boat rentals, family activities

Stormy Point Camp & Resort
Branson 417-338-2255
Guest Capacity: 90 units, 55 campsites
Handicapped equipped: Yes
Seasons: April 1 to Dec 15
Rates: Camping: $22/day, Lodging: $65/day double occupancy
Contact: Ron or Karen Holloway
Guides: Yes
Species & Seasons: SM Bass, LM Bass, Crappie, Perch April-Oct
Bodies of Water: Lake Taneycomo, Bull Shoals Lake, Beaver Lake(AR)
Types of fishing: Fly fishing, light tackle, heavy tackle, wading
Available: Fishing instruction, licenses, bait, tackle, boat rentals

Whispering Woods Resort
Kimberling City 800-226-4951
Guest Capacity: 72
Handicapped equipped: No
Seasons: All year
Rates: $40-$70/day
Contact: Gary or Lorene Watson
Guides: Yes
Species & Seasons: LM Bass, Crappie, Walleye, Bluegill all year
Bodies of Water: Table Rock Lake, Lake Taneycomo, James River, White River
Types of fishing: Fly fishing, light tackle, heavy tackle
Available: Fishing instruction, bait, tackle, boat rentals, family activities, children's program, baby sitting

Wildwood Inn
Kimberling City 800-641-4083
Guest Capacity: 160
Handicapped equipped: No
Seasons: All year
Rates: In-season: $49.95 and up/day
Guides: Yes
Species & Seasons: Spotted Bass, LM Bass, SM Bass, Crappie, Catfish
Bodies of Water: Table Rock Lake, Lake Taneycomo
Types of fishing:
Available: Fishing instruction, boat rentals, family activities, baby sitting

MARINAS...

State Park Marina
Branson 417-334-3069
Hours: 7am-8pm (Memorial-Labor Day)
Carries: Live bait, lures, flies, maps, licenses
Bodies of water: Table Rock Lake, Lake Taneycomo
Services & Products: Boat rentals, guide services, boat ramp, food, beverages, gas/oil, scuba, camping
Guides: Yes
OK to call for current conditions: Yes
Contact: Craig Walls

LONGVIEW RESERVOIR - POMME DE TERRE LAKE
MISSOURI

LONGVIEW RESERVOIR

MARINAS...

Longview Lake Marina
Kansas City 816-966-0131
Hours: 7am-sunset
Carries: Live bait, lures, maps, rods, reels, licenses
Bodies of water: Little Blue River, Longview Res., Lake Jacomo
Services & Products: Boat rentals, boat ramp, food, beverages, gas/oil, fishing instruction, repair services
Guides: Yes
OK to call for current conditions: Yes
Contact: Sam Diamond

MARK TWAIN LAKE

BAIT & TACKLE...

The Hobbie Hut
Perry 314-565-3150
Hours: 5am-9pm Fri., Sat., 5am-6:30pm Sun.-Thrus.
Carries: Live bait, lures, flies, maps, rods, reels, licenses
Bodies of water: Mark Twain Lake, Mississippi River
Services & Products: Food, beverages, fishing instruction
Guides: Yes
OK to call for current conditions: Yes

MERAMEC RIVER

LODGES...

Bird's Nest Lodge & River Resort
Steelville 314-775-2606
Guest Capacity: 300
Handicapped equipped: No
Seasons: All year
Rates: $13-$25/pp day
Guides: Yes
Species & Seasons: SM Bass May-Feb, Trout Mar-Oct, Rock Bass, LM Bass all year
Bodies of Water: Upper Meramec River
Types of fishing: Fly fishing, light tackle, wading, float trips, jet boat guides
Available: Bait, tackle, boat rentals, family activities, camping seasonal

MISSISSIPPI RIVER

BAIT & TACKLE...

Della's Live Bait & Sporting
St. Louis 314-544-2266
Hours: 8am-9pm
Carries: Live bait, lures, flies, maps, rods, reels, licenses
Bodies of water: Mississippi River
Services & Products: Beverages, archery supplies
Guides: Yes
OK to call for current conditions: No

The Hobbie Hut
Perry 314-565-3150
Hours: 5am-9pm Fri., Sat., 5am-6:30pm Sun.-Thrus.
Carries: Live bait, lures, flies, maps, rods, reels, licenses
Bodies of water: Mark Twain Lake, Mississippi River
Services & Products: Food, beverages, fishing instruction
Guides: Yes
OK to call for current conditions: Yes

Village Market
Clarksville 314-242-3511
Hours: 6am-10pm
Carries: Live bait, lures, flies, maps, rods, reels, licenses
Bodies of water: Mississippi River, Salt River, creeks
Services & Products: Boat ramp, food, beverages, gas/oil, groceries
Guides: Yes
OK to call for current conditions: Yes
Contact: Bill, Sandi, Mike or Linda

MISSOURI RIVER

BAIT & TACKLE...

Clock Bait Shop
Kansas City 816-436-0612
Hours: 6am-7pm Mon.-Thurs., 6am-8pm Fri., Sat., 6am-5pm Sun.
Carries: Live bait, lures, flies, maps, rods, reels
Bodies of water: Little Platte River, Big Platte River, Missourii River, Smithville Res.
Services & Products: Beverages, fishing instruction, repair services, snacks, ice
Guides: Yes
OK to call for current conditions: Yes
Contact: Thora Habelitz

LODGES...

Southwood Shores
Lake Ozark 314-365-4644
Guest Capacity: 300
Handicapped equipped: Yes, some
Seasons: All year
Rates: Varies
Contact: Sharon Flint
Guides: Yes
Species & Seasons: Crappie Mar-Arpil, LM Bass, White Bass, Striped Bass May-Sept, Catfish June-Sept
Bodies of Water: Lake of the Ozarks, Truman Res., Osage River, Missourii River
Types of fishing: Light tackle, heavy tackle
Available: Indoor, outdoor pools, hot tub

MARINAS...

Nemo Landing Marina
Pittsburg 417-993-5160
Hours: 7am-7pm
Carries: Live bait, lures, maps, licenses
Bodies of water: Missourii River
Services & Products: Boat rentals, boat ramp, food, beverages, gas/oil
Guides: Yes
OK to call for current conditions: Yes
Contact: Brenda Vaughan

POMME DE TERRE LAKE

BAIT & TACKLE...

Devil's Backbone Store
Warsaw 816-438-7563
Hours: 5am-11pm
Carries: Live bait, lures, maps, rods, reels
Bodies of water: Stockton Lake, Pomme de Terre Lake, Lake of the Ozarks, Harry S. Truman Res.
Services & Products: Guide services, lodging, boat ramp, food, beverages, fishing instruction
Guides: Yes
OK to call for current conditions: Yes
Contact: Jim Tyre

The Trading Post
Hermitage 417-745-6432
Bodies of water: Pomme de Terre Lake
Guides: Yes
Contact: Pat Miller

YOUR SILENT FISHING PARTNER

MISSOURI
POMME DE TERRE LAKE - STOCKTON LAKE

GUIDES...

Charlie's Guide Service
Hermitage 800-243-6883
Species & Seasons: Muskellunge, LM Bass, Crappie Mar-Dec
Bodies of water: Pomme de Terre Lake
Rates: Half day: $70(1-2), Full day: $120(1-2)
Handicapped equipped: Yes

LODGES...

Angler's Resort
Wheatland 417-282-5507
Guest Capacity: 50
Handicapped equipped: No
Seasons: Mar 1 to Nov 30
Rates: $30-$50/day
Contact: Darrell or Laura Guinn
Guides: Yes
Species & Seasons: Crappie Feb-Dec, LM Bass Mar-Dec, Muskellunge, Walleye April-Nov, White Bass Mar-Nov
Bodies of Water: Pomme de Terre Lake, Truman Res., Stockton Lake, Lake of the Ozarks, Niangua River (Bennett Springs), Pomme de Terre River
Types of fishing: Fly fishing, light tackle, heavy tackle, float trips
Available: Bait, tackle, boat rentals, family activities, baby sitting, kitchenettes, canoe float trips, playground

Russ T Lake Shore Resort
Wheatland 417-282-6241
Guest Capacity: 38
Handicapped equipped: Yes, 1 unit
Seasons: April to Nov
Rates: $38/day
Guides: Yes, recommend
Species & Seasons: Muskellunge, LM Bass, Crappie, White Bass, Walleye March-Nov
Bodies of Water: Pomme de Terre Lake, Truman Res., Bennett Spring
Types of fishing: Light tackle, heavy tackle, float trips
Available: Boat rentals, family activities, golf (18 hole)

Sunflower Resort
Wheatland 800-258-5260
Guest Capacity: 50
Handicapped equipped: No
Seasons: Mar to Nov
Rates: $40/day
Contact: Tony or Sandy
Guides: Yes
Species & Seasons: Muskellunge, LM Bass, Crappie, Walleye, Catfish all year
Bodies of Water: Pomme de Terre Lake
Types of fishing: Fly fishing, light tackle, heavy tackle, wading
Available: Boat rentals, family activities

Willow Winds Resort
Wheatland 800-556-5591
Guest Capacity: 11 units, 4 sleeps 10, 6 sleeps 6, 1 sleeps 3
Handicapped equipped: No
Seasons: Mar 15 to Sept 15
Rates: $32.95-$42.95-$54.95/day
Guides: Yes, recommend
Species & Seasons: Muskellunge Spring and Fall, LM Bass, Crappie, White Bass all year, Walleye Spring
Bodies of Water: Pomme de Terre Lake, Truman Res., Lake of the Ozarks, Stockton Lake
Types of fishing: Light tackle, heavy tackle, float trips
Available: Boat rentals, family activities, swimming pool

SMITHVILLE RESERVOIR

BAIT & TACKLE...

Burton's Bait & Tackle
Smithville 816-532-4659
Hours: 6am-8pm
Carries: Live bait, lures, flies, maps, rods, reels, licenses
Bodies of water: Smithville Res., Platte River
Services & Products: Guide services, food, beverages
Guides: Yes
OK to call for current conditions: Yes
Contact: Gary Burton

MARINAS...

Camp Branch Marina
Smithville 816-532-4984
Hours: 7am-8pm
Carries: Live bait, lures, maps, rods, reels
Bodies of water: Smithville Res.
Services & Products: Boat rentals, guide services, boat ramp, food, beverages, gas/oil, fishing instruction, repair services, camp supplies, groceries
OK to call for current conditions: Yes
Contact: David George

STOCKTON LAKE

BAIT & TACKLE...

Devil's Backbone Store
Warsaw 816-438-7563
Hours: 5am-11pm
Carries: Live bait, lures, maps, rods, reels
Bodies of water: Stockton Lake, Pomme de Terre Lake, Lake of the Ozarks, Harry S. Truman Res.
Services & Products: Guide services, lodging, boat ramp, food, beverages, fishing instruction
Guides: Yes
OK to call for current conditions: Yes
Contact: Jim Tyre

LODGES...

Angler's Resort
Wheatland 417-282-5507
Guest Capacity: 50
Handicapped equipped: No
Seasons: Mar 1 to Nov 30
Rates: $30-$50/day
Contact: Darrell or Laura Guinn
Guides: Yes
Species & Seasons: Crappie Feb-Dec, LM Bass Mar-Dec, Muskellunge, Walleye April-Nov, White Bass Mar-Nov
Bodies of Water: Pomme de Terre Lake, Truman Res., Stockton Lake, Lake of the Ozarks, Niangua River (Bennett Springs), Pomme de Terre River
Types of fishing: Fly fishing, light tackle, heavy tackle, float trips
Available: Bait, tackle, boat rentals, family activities, baby sitting, kitchenettes, canoe float trips, playground

Willow Winds Resort
Wheatland 800-556-5591
Guest Capacity: 11 units, 4 sleeps 10, 6 sleeps 6, 1 sleeps 3
Handicapped equipped: No
Seasons: Mar 15 to Sept 15
Rates: $32.95-$42.95-$54.95/day
Guides: Yes, recommend
Species & Seasons: Muskellunge Spring and Fall, LM Bass, Crappie, White Bass all year, Walleye Spring
Bodies of Water: Pomme de Terre Lake, Truman Res., Lake of the Ozarks, Stockton Lake
Types of fishing: Light tackle, heavy tackle, float trips
Available: Boat rentals, family activities, swimming pool

TABLE ROCK LAKE — MISSOURI

TABLE ROCK LAKE

BAIT & TACKLE...

Cape Fair Bait & Tackle
Cape Fair 417-538-4242
Hours: 7am-8pm
Carries: Live bait, lures, maps, rods, reels, licenses
Bodies of water: Table Rock Lake
Services & Products: Guide services, food, beverages, fishing instruction
Guides: Yes
OK to call for current conditions: Yes
Contact: Al Bergman

Outback Emporium
Lampe 417-779-4020
Hours: 7am-7pm
Carries: Live bait, lures, flies, maps, rods, reels
Bodies of water: Table Rock Lake
Services & Products: Food, beverages, gas/oil, fishing instruction
Guides: Yes
OK to call for current conditions: Yes
Contact: Glenn or Ann Parsons

GUIDES...

Hook's Guide Service
Reeds Springs 417-338-2277
Species & Seasons: LM Bass, SM Bass, Kentucky Bass all year
Bodies of water: Table Rock Lake
Rates: Half day: $145(2), Full day: $195(2) $50 additional 3rd person
Call between: 7pm-10pm
Provides: Light tackle, lures, beverages
Handicapped equipped: Yes, limited
Certifications: USCG Licensed, insured

LODGES...

Antlers Resort & Campground
Branson 417-338-2331
Guest Capacity: Resort: 122, Camp: 10 full hookup sites, 6 tent sites
Handicapped equipped: No
Seasons: All year
Rates: Varies
Contact: Barbara Johnson
Guides: Yes
Species & Seasons: Crappie, LM Bass Mar-April/Sept-Oct, Bluegill April/May-Sept/Oct/Nov, Channel Catfish, Flathead Catfish April/May-Sept/Oct, Rainbow Trout, Brown Trout Jan-Dec
Bodies of Water: Table Rock Lake, Lake Taneycomo, Bull Shoals Lake
Types of fishing: Fly fishing, light tackle, heavy tackle, wading
Available: Licenses, bait, tackle, boat rentals, recreation room

Aunts Creek Resort
Reeds Spring 417-739-4411
Guest Capacity: 60
Handicapped equipped: Yes
Seasons: All year
Rates: $45-$56/2 days
Contact: Bill or Jane
Guides: Yes
Species & Seasons: LM Bass, SM Bass, Spotted Bass all year
Bodies of Water: Table Rock Lake
Types of fishing: Light tackle, heavy tackle
Available: Licenses, bait, tackle, boat rentals

Big Cedar Lodge
Ridgedale 417-335-2777
Guest Capacity: 450-500
Handicapped equipped: Yes
Seasons: All year
Rates: $79-$849/day
Guides: Yes
Species & Seasons: LM Bass Mar-May, Crappie April-May, Trout Sept-Jan
Bodies of Water: Table Rock Lake, Lake Taneycomo
Types of fishing: Fly fishing, light tackle
Available: Fishing instruction, licenses, bait, tackle, boat rentals, family activities, children's program

Boomerang Resort
Reeds Spring 417-338-2358
Guest Capacity: 86
Handicapped equipped: No
Seasons: All year
Rates: $37-$122/day, weekly discount packages available
Contact: Debbie Lindsey
Guides: Yes
Species & Seasons: SM Bass, LM Bass, Bluegill, Catfish
Bodies of Water: Table Rock Lake
Types of fishing: Light tackle, heavy tackle
Available: Licenses, bait, tackle, boat rentals, family activities

Bridgeport Resort
Cape Fair 417-538-2500
Handicapped equipped: No
Seasons: All year
Rates: $40-$65/day, 7th day free
Contact: Bob or Teresa Ramsell
Guides: Yes
Species & Seasons: LM Bass Mar-Nov, Crappie Mar-June, Flathead Catfish, Channel Catfish, Bluegill, Feb-Nov, White Bass Mar-May, Spoonbill Mar-April
Bodies of Water: Table Rock Lake
Types of fishing: Light tackle, float trips
Available: Fishing instruction, licenses, bait, tackle, boat rentals, family activities

Butter Milk Spring Resort
Galena 417-538-2899
Handicapped equipped: No
Seasons: All year
Rates: Spring/Fall: $40/day, $240/week
Contact: Frank Szot
Guides: Yes
Species & Seasons: LM Bass, Crappie, Catfish, Bluegill, Walleye all year
Bodies of Water: Table Rock Lake
Types of fishing: Light tackle
Available: Fishing instruction, licenses, bait, tackle, boat rentals, family activities

Crest Lodge Resort
Reeds Spring 417-739-4456
Guest Capacity: 90-100
Handicapped equipped: No
Seasons: April to Nov
Rates: $54-$92
Guides: Yes
Species & Seasons: LM Bass, Catfish, Crappie, White Bass, Panfish April-Nov
Bodies of Water: Table Rock Lake
Types of fishing: Fly fishing, light tackle, heavy tackle
Available: Boat rentals, family activities

Double Oak Resort
Galena 417-538-2553
.... 800-525-3625
Guest Capacity: 56
Handicapped equipped: No
Seasons: Mar 1 to Nov 15
Rates: $30-$74/day
Contact: Dave Williams
Guides: Yes
Species & Seasons: LM Bass, Catfish April-Nov, Crappie April-June, Bluegill June-Nov
Bodies of Water: Table Rock Lake
Types of fishing: Light tackle
Available: Licenses, bait, tackle, boat rentals, family activities
(see ad page 264)

MISSOURI — TABLE ROCK LAKE

Edgewater Villa Resort
Reeds Spring 417-739-4585
Guest Capacity: 60
Handicapped equipped: Yes
Seasons: Mar 1 to Nov 1
Guides: Yes
Species & Seasons: Spotted Bass, LM Bass, SM Bass all season, Crappie Mar-June, Catfish Summer
Bodies of Water: Table Rock Lake
Types of fishing: Fly fishing, light tackle, heavy tackle
Available: Fishing instruction, boat rentals

Fishermen's Luck Resort
Reeds Spring 417-739-4485
Guest Capacity: 86
Handicapped equipped: No
Seasons: Mar 15 to Oct 31
Rates: $46-$56/day double occupancy
Contact: Dee Tinnes
Guides: Yes
Species & Seasons: LM Bass, Catfish, Bluegill all year, Crappie Mar-May, White Bass Spring
Bodies of Water: Table Rock Lake
Types of fishing: Fly fishing, light tackle, heavy tackle
Available: Licenses, bait, tackle, boat rentals, family activities

Gobbler's Mountain Resort
Reeds Spring 417-338-2304
Guest Capacity: 25
Handicapped equipped: No
Seasons: All year
Rates: $38-$78/day
Contact: Al Morton
Guides: Yes
Species & Seasons: LM Bass, SM Bass, Mar-June, White Bass May-July, Catfish May-Oct
Bodies of Water: Table Rock Lake
Types of fishing: Light tackle, heavy tackle
Available: Licenses, bait, tackle, boat rentals

Happy Hollow Resort
Blue Eye 417-779-4360
Guest Capacity: 70
Handicapped equipped: Ramp available
Seasons: All year
Rates: $38-$75/day
Contact: Mike or Brenda Kossmann
Guides: Yes
Species & Seasons: LM Bass, April-June, Catfish June-Sept, Crappie Mar-May, Bluegill May-Aug
Bodies of Water: Table Rock Lake
Types of fishing: Fly fishing, light tackle
Available: Licenses, bait, tackle, boat rentals, family activities, pool, playground, fish and swim ramp

Hide-Away Resort
Galena 417-538-2992
Guest Capacity: 50
Handicapped equipped: No
Seasons: Mar to Dec
Rates: Varies
Contact: Sue Deems
Guides: Yes
Species & Seasons: LM Bass all year, Panfish, Catfish May-Sept, Crappie Spring
Bodies of Water: Table Rock Lake
Types of fishing: Light tackle
Available: Licenses, bait, tackle, boat rentals

Double Oak Resort
Table Rock Lake
- Perfect for entire family fun
- 100 yrds from your room to lake
- Fishing on James River Arm
- All rooms efficiency units
- 4 types of boats available
- Weekly Summer rentals
- Spring/Fall by day or week

1 800 525-3625
In Ozark Mountains Near Branson

Holiday Hideaway Resort
Reeds Spring 417-739-4542
Guest Capacity: 14 cabins
Handicapped equipped: No
Seasons: All year
Rates: $43-$111/day
Contact: R.D. Van Horn
Guides: Yes
Species & Seasons: LM Bass, Crappie, Catfish all year
Bodies of Water: Table Rock Lake
Types of fishing: Light tackle
Available: Licenses, bait, tackle, boat rentals, family activities, childern's playground, pool, dock fishing

Lucky 13 Resort
Reeds Spring 417-739-4414
Guest Capacity: 100
Handicapped equipped: No
Seasons: April 1 to Oct 31
Rates: $50/2 days
Guides: Yes
Species & Seasons: LM Bass Mar-Dec, Crappie Mar-Oct, Perch all year
Bodies of Water: Table Rock Lake
Types of fishing: Fly fishing, light tackle
Available: Boat rentals, private dock facilities

Oak Hill Resort
Reeds Spring 417-739-4566
Guest Capacity: 75
Handicapped equipped: No
Seasons: Mar to Nov
Rates: $50-$140/day
Contact: Dick Stewart
Guides: Yes
Species & Seasons: Spotted Bass, LM Bass, SM Bass all year, Channel Catfish, Bluegill May-Sept
Bodies of Water: Table Rock Lake
Types of fishing: Light tackle, heavy tackle
Available: Licenses, boat rentals, family activities

Shore Acres Resort
HCR 4 Box 2010
Reeds Spring 65737
Guest Capacity: 110
Handicapped equipped: No
Seasons: All year
Rates: $50/day
Contact: Pat McEvoy
Guides: Yes
Species & Seasons: LM Bass, Crappie April is best, Catfish, Bluegill all year
Bodies of Water: Table Rock Lake, Lake Taneycomo, Bull Shoals Lake, Beaver Lake(AR)
Types of fishing: Light tackle, wading
Available: Licenses, bait, tackle, boat rentals, family activities

The Timbers Resort
Shell Knob 417-858-2723
Guest Capacity: 75
Handicapped equipped: Yes
Seasons: All year
Rates: Depends on season and size of group
Contact: Paula Baird
Guides: Yes, recommend
Species & Seasons: LM Bass, Crappie, Walleye, Catfish, Bluegill
Bodies of Water: Table Rock Lake
Types of fishing: Light tackle
Available: Boat rentals

TABLE ROCK LAKE - WHITE RIVER
MISSOURI

Whispering Woods Resort
Kimberling City 800-226-4951
Guest Capacity: 72
Handicapped equipped: No
Seasons: All year
Rates: $40-$70/day
Contact: Gary or Lorene Watson
Guides: Yes
Species & Seasons: LM Bass, Crappie, Walleye, Bluegill all year
Bodies of Water: Table Rock Lake, Lake Taneycomo, James River, White River
Types of fishing: Fly fishing, light tackle, heavy tackle
Available: Fishing instruction, bait, tackle, boat rentals, family activities, children's program, baby sitting

White Wing Resort
Branson 417-338-2318
Guest Capacity: 220
Handicapped equipped: No
Seasons: Mar to Nov
Rates: $45-$104/day
Contact: Ron Thomas
Guides: Yes
Species & Seasons: LM Bass, Catfish, Crappie, White Bass Mar-Nov
Bodies of Water: Table Rock Lake
Types of fishing: Light tackle
Available: Bait, tackle, boat rentals, family activities

Wildwood Inn
Kimberling City 800-641-4083
Guest Capacity: 160
Handicapped equipped: No
Seasons: All year
Rates: In-season: $49.95/day and up
Guides: Yes
Species & Seasons: Spotted Bass, LM Bass, SM Bass, Crappie, Catfish
Bodies of Water: Table Rock Lake, Lake Taneycomo
Available: Fishing instruction, boat rentals, family activities, baby sitting

MARINAS...

State Park Marina
Branson 417-334-3069
Hours: 7am-8pm (Memorial-Labor Day)
Carries: Live bait, lures, flies, maps, licenses
Bodies of water: Table Rock Lake, Lake Taneycomo
Services & Products: Boat rentals, guide services, boat ramp, food, beverages, gas/oil, scuba, camping

Guides: Yes
OK to call for current conditions: Yes
Contact: Craig Walls

WHITE RIVER

LODGES...

Carte Court
Theodosia 417-273-4434
.... 800-609-6711
Guest Capacity: 40
Handicapped equipped: Yes, somewhat
Seasons: All year
Rates: From $35/day double occupancy
Contact: Mary Ann
Guides: Yes
Species & Seasons: LM Bass, Crappie, Catfish, Trout
Bodies of Water: Bull Shoals Lake, Norfork Lake, White River, Lake Taneycomo
Types of fishing: Fly fishing, light tackle, wading, float trips
Available: Family activities, pool, hot tub
Within 1 mile: Fishing instruction, licenses, bait, tackle, boat rentals

Whispering Woods Resort
Kimberling City 800-226-4951
Guest Capacity: 72
Handicapped equipped: No
Seasons: All year
Rates: $40-$70/day
Contact: Gary or Lorene Watson
Guides: Yes
Species & Seasons: LM Bass, Crappie, Walleye, Bluegill all year
Bodies of Water: Table Rock Lake, Lake Taneycomo, James River, White River
Types of fishing: Fly fishing, light tackle, heavy tackle
Available: Fishing instruction, bait, tackle, boat rentals, family activities, children's program, baby sitting

Look in the Species Index
to find service providers by species of fish

MONTANA

1. Absaroka Beartooth Wilderness
2. Beaverhead River
3. Big Hole River
4. Bighorn River
5. Bitterroot River
6. Blackfeet Indian Reservation
7. Blackfoot River
8. Bob Marshall Wilderness
9. Boulder River
10. Canyon Ferry Lake
11. Clark Canyon Reservoir
12. Clark Fork River
13. Dearborn River
14. Flathead Lake
15. Flathead River
16. Fort Peck Lake
17. Gallatin River
18. Hebgen Lake
19. Jefferson River
20. Lake Koocanusa
21. Madison River
22. Missouri River
23. Private Waters
24. Regional Areas
    High Country Lakes
    High Mountain Lakes
    Lee Metcalf
     Wilderness Area
    Lewis & Clark
     National Forest
    Lo Lo National Forest
    Madison Mountain
     Ranges
25. Smith River
26. Stillwater River
27. Thompson Lakes
28. Whitefish Lake
29. Yellowstone National Park
30. Yellowstone River

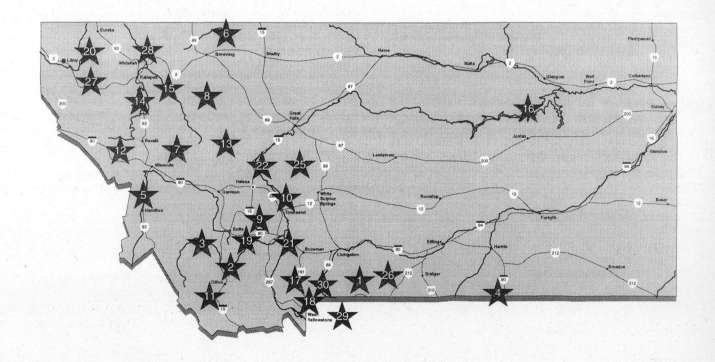

YOUR SILENT FISHING PARTNER

MONTANA
ABSAROKA BEARTOOTH WILDERNESS - BIG HOLE RIVER

ABSAROKA BEARTOOTH WILDERNESS

GUIDES...

Beartooth Plateau Outfitters
Cooke City 800-253-8545
Species & Seasons: Cutthroat Trout, Brook Trout, Rainbow Trout, Arctic Grayling June-Oct, Golden Trout July-Oct
Bodies of water: Yellowstone Nat'l. Park, (Lamar River, Slough Creek, Miller Creek, Pebble Creek, Cache Creek), High Alpine Mountain Lakes in Absaroka Beartooth Wilderness Area
Rates: Full day: $180pp,
7 day package: $1200pp includes 5 day horseback pack trip, lodging, meals, airport pick-up
Call between: 7am-7pm
Provides: Lunch, horses, camp, tents, sleeping bags
Handicapped equipped: No
Certifications: Endorsed ORVIS Outfitter

Seven C Quarter Circle Outfitters
Red Lodge 406-445-2280
Species & Seasons: Rainbow Trout, Cutthroat Trout, Brook Trout, Golden Trout, Brown Trout July-Sept
Bodies of water: Absaroka Beartooth Wilderness, Alpine Lakes, Stillwater River
Rates: Full day: $180(1), $360(2)
Call between: 6pm-10pm
Provides: Lunch
Handicapped equipped: No

BEAVERHEAD RIVER

GUIDES...

Anglers Afloat, Inc.
Stevensville 406-777-3421
Species & Seasons: Rainbow Trout, Brown Trout, Cutthroat Trout, Brook Trout Mar-Oct
Bodies of water: Bitterroot River, Blackfoot River, Big Hole River, Rock Creek, Beaverhead River, Clark Fork River
Rates: Half day: $250(1-2),
Full day: $285(1-2)
Call between: 8-10am/8-10pm
Provides: Fly rod/reel, beverages, lunch
Handicapped equipped: Yes
Certifications: Licensed MT Outfitter

East Fork Outfitters
Sula 406-821-4946
.... 800-763-3688
Species & Seasons: Brown Trout, Rainbow Trout, Cutthroat Trout June-Sept, ALL CATCH & RELEASE!
Bodies of water: Bitterroot River, Big Hole River, Clark Fork River, Beaverhead River
Rates: Wade fishing: Half day: $65(2), Full day: $125(2), Boat: Bitterroot River: $275(2), Big Hole River: $310(2), Clark Fork River: $330(2), Beaverhead River: $330(2)
Call between: 8am-10pm
Provides: Beverages, lunch
Handicapped equipped: No

Great Divide Outfitters
Divide 406-267-3346
Species & Seasons: Brown Trout, Rainbow Trout, Brook Trout, Arctic Grayling April-Oct
Bodies of water: Big Hole River, Beaverhead River, Jefferson River, Clark Fork River
Rates: Half day: $150(1), $175(2), Full day: $200(1), $250(2)
Call between: 7am-9pm
Provides: Fly rod/reel, rain gear, beverages, lunch
Handicapped equipped: Yes

Pioneer Outfitters
Wise River 406-832-3128
Species & Seasons: Trout May-Oct
Bodies of water: Big Hole River, Beaverhead River, High Mountain Lakes, Clark Canyon Res.
Call between: 8am-8pm
Provides: Fly rod/reel, lunch
Handicapped equipped: Yes

Trout Fishing Only
Hamilton 800-363-2408
Species & Seasons: Trout June-Nov
Bodies of water: Bitterroot River, Big Hole River, Beaverhead River, Madison River, Yellowstone River, Clark Fork River
Rates: Half day: $200(1-2), Full day: $270(1-2)
Call between: 7pm-10pm
Provides: Fly rod/reel, lunch
Handicapped equipped: Yes

LODGES...

Rush's Lakeview Guest Ranch
Butte 406-276-3300
Guest Capacity: 50
Handicapped equipped: No
Seasons: All year
Rates: $695/7 days, 6 nights
Guides: Yes
Species & Seasons: Brown Trout, Brook Trout, Rainbow Trout, Golden Trout, Grayling, Cutthroat, May-Nov
Bodies of Water: Madison River, Jefferson River, Ruby River, Beaverhead River, Red Rock River, Big Hole River, Elk River
Types of fishing: Fly fishing, light tackle, horse/back pack, wading, float trips
Available: Fishing instruction, family activities, baby sitting

BIG HOLE RIVER

GUIDES...

Anglers Afloat, Inc.
Stevensville 406-777-3421
Species & Seasons: Rainbow Trout, Brown Trout, Cutthroat Trout, Brook Trout Mar-Oct
Bodies of water: Bitterroot River, Blackfoot River, Big Hole River, Rock Creek, Beaverhead River, Clark Fork River
Rates: Half day: $250(1-2),
Full day: $285(1-2)
Call between: 8-10am/8-10pm
Provides: Fly rod/reel, beverages, lunch
Handicapped equipped: Yes
Certifications: Licensed MT Outfitter

Canoeing House Rentals & Riverboat Fly Fishing
Three Forks 406-285-3488
Species & Seasons: Trout April-Nov
Bodies of water: Jefferson River, Madison River, Gallatin River, Yellowstone River, Big Hole River
Rates: Half day: $150(2), Full day: $225(2)
Call between: 7am-9pm
Handicapped equipped: No
Certifications: Licensed Fishing Outfitter State of MT, Professional Guides Assoc.

BIG HOLE RIVER - BIGHORN RIVER — MONTANA

East Fork Outfitters
Sula 406-821-4946
.... 800-763-3688
Species & Seasons: Brown Trout, Rainbow Trout, Cutthroat Trout June-Sept, ALL CATCH & RELEASE!
Bodies of water: Bitterroot River, Big Hole River, Clark Fork River, Beaverhead River
Rates: Wade fishing: Half day: $65(2), Full day: $125(2), Boat: Bitterroot River: $275(2), Big Hole River: $310(2), Clark Fork River: $330(2), Beaverhead River: $330(2)
Call between: 8am-10pm
Provides: Beverages, lunch
Handicapped equipped: No

Great Divide Outfitters
Divide 406-267-3346
Species & Seasons: Brown Trout, Rainbow Trout, Brook Trout, Arctic Grayling April-Oct
Bodies of water: Big Hole River, Beaverhead River, Jefferson River, Clark Fork River
Rates: Half day: $150(1), $175(2), Full day: $200(1), $250(2)
Call between: 7am-9pm
Provides: Fly rod/reel, rain gear, beverages, lunch
Handicapped equipped: Yes

Jack River Outfitters
Ennis 406-682-4948
Species & Seasons: Brown Trout, Rainbow Trout April-Nov
Bodies of water: Madison River, Big Hole River, Yellowstone River, Jefferson River, Missouri River, Hebgen Lake, Ennis Lake
Rates: Half day: $170(2), Full day: $250(2), $50 additional 3rd person
Call between: 7-9pm
Provides: Light tackle, fly rod/reel, rain gear, beverages, lunch
Handicapped equipped: Yes, limited

Pioneer Outfitters
Wise River 406-832-3128
Species & Seasons: Trout May-Oct
Bodies of water: Big Hole River, Beaverhead River, High Mountain Lakes, Clark Canyon Res.
Call between: 8am-8pm
Provides: Fly rod/reel, lunch
Handicapped equipped: Yes

Trout Fishing Only
Hamilton 800-363-2408
Species & Seasons: Trout June-Nov
Bodies of water: Bitterroot River, Big Hole River, Beaverhead River, Madison River, Yellowstone River, Clark Fork River
Rates: Half day: $200(1-2), Full day: $270(1-2)
Call between: 7pm-10pm
Provides: Fly rod/reel, lunch
Handicapped equipped: Yes

LODGES...

Rush's Lakeview Guest Ranch
Butte 406-276-3300
Guest Capacity: 50
Handicapped equipped: No
Seasons: All year
Rates: $695/7 days, 6 nights
Guides: Yes
Species & Seasons: Brown Trout, Brook Trout, Rainbow Trout, Golden Trout, Grayling, Cutthroat, May-Nov
Bodies of Water: Madison River, Jefferson River, Ruby River, Beaverhead River, Red Rock River, Big Hole River, Elk River
Types of fishing: Fly fishing, light tackle, horse/back pack, wading, float trips
Available: Fishing instruction, family activities, baby sitting

BIGHORN RIVER

BAIT & TACKLE...

Scheels Sport Shop
Billings 406-656-9220
Hours: 9am-9pm
Carries: Live bait, artificial lures, flies, maps, rods, reels, licenses
Bodies of water: Bighorn River, Fort Peck Lake, Stillwater River, Cooney Res., Rock Creek, Yellowstone Nat'l. Park
Guides: Yes
OK to call for current conditions: Yes
Contact: Mike Johnston

Shell Shack
Laurel 406-628-8986
Hours: 9am-5pm, closed Sun.
Carries: Live bait, artificial lures, flies, maps, rods, reels,
Bodies of water: Yellowstone River, Bighorn River, Stillwater River, Boulder River, Yellowtail Res.
Services & Products: Fishing instruction, repair services
Guides: Yes
OK to call for current conditions: Yes
Contact: Tom Brown

GUIDES...

Big Timber Guides
Big Timber 406-932-4080
.... 930-4080
Species & Seasons: Rainbow Trout, Brown Trout Mar-Nov, Cutthroat Trout June-Sept, Brook Trout June-Oct, Walleye Mar-Oct, Lake Trout Mar-Aug, Paddlefish April-June
Bodies of water: Yellowstone River, Boulder River, Bighorn River, Madison River, Missouri River, Canyon Ferry Lake, Hauser Lake, Holter Lake
Rates: Half day: $100(1), $200(2), Full day: $200(1), $250(2), Weekly rates
Call between: 7am-10:30pm
Provides: Light tackle, heavy tackle, fly rod/reel, rain gear, beverages, lunch
Handicapped equipped: Yes
Certifications: Licensed MT Outfitter

George Kelly's Bighorn Country Outfitters
Fort Smith 406-666-2326
Species & Seasons: Rainbow Trout Mar-Nov, Brown Trout Mar-Dec
Bodies of water: Bighorn River
Rates: Full day: $250(1-2)
Call between: Anytime
Provides: Beverages, lunch
Handicapped equipped: Yes

MONTANA
BIGHORN RIVER - BLACKFOOT RIVER

Montana Adventures in Angling
Billings 406-248-2995
Species & Seasons: Rainbow Trout, Brown Trout, Cutthroat Trout Mar-Dec, Lake Trout June-Nov, Whitefish Mar-Dec, Northern Pike, Arctic Grayling April-Nov
Bodies of water: Bighorn River, Yellowstone River, Boulder River, Missouri River Stillwater River, other streams in eastern Montana, Blackfeet Indian Res.
Rates: Full day: $200(1), $270(2)
Provides: Light tackle, fly rod/reel, lures, rain gear, beverages, lunch
Handicapped equipped: Yes
Certifications: ORVIS Endorsed and ORVIS Guide of yr 1992, Licensed MT Outfitter, Blackeet Tribal Outfitter

Stillwaters Outfitting
Billings 406-652-8111
Species & Seasons: Rainbow Trout, Brown Trout April-Nov
Bodies of water: Bighorn River, Yellowstone River, Rock Creek, Yellowstone Nat'l. Park
Rates: Float trips: Full day: $210(1), $275(2), Fly fishing instruction
Call between: 6pm-10pm
Provides: Fly rod/reel, beverages, lunch
Handicapped equipped: Yes
Certifications: Licensed MT Outfitter, Certified CPR, First aid

BITTERROOT RIVER

GUIDES...

Allaman's Montana Adventure Trips
Darby 406-821-3763
Species & Seasons: Rainbow Trout, Cutthroat Trout, Brook Trout, Brown Trout, June-Oct
Bodies of water: Bitterroot River, High Mt. Lakes
Rates: Half day: $200(1), $300(2), Full day: $400(1), $600(2)
Call between: 10pm-8am
Provides: Beverages, lunch
Certifications: Licensed MT Outfitter

Anglers Afloat, Inc.
Stevensville 406-777-3421
Species & Seasons: Rainbow Trout, Brown Trout, Cutthroat Trout, Brook Trout Mar-Oct
Bodies of water: Bitterroot River, Blackfoot River, Big Hole River, Rock Creek, Beaverhead River, Clark Fork River
Rates: Half day: $250(1-2), Full day: $285(1-2)
Call between: 8-10am/8-10pm
Provides: Fly rod/reel, beverages, lunch
Handicapped equipped: Yes
Certifications: Licensed MT Outfitter

East Fork Outfitters
Sula 406-821-4946
.... 800-763-3688
Species & Seasons: Brown Trout, Rainbow Trout, Cutthroat Trout June-Sept, ALL CATCH & RELEASE!
Bodies of water: Bitterroot River, Big Hole River, Clark Fork River, Beaverhead River
Rates: Wade fishing: Half day: $65(2), Full day: $125(2), Boat: Bitterroot River: $275(2), Big Hole River: $310(2), Clark Fork River: $330(2), Beaverhead River: $330(2)
Call between: 8am-10pm
Provides: Beverages, lunch
Handicapped equipped: No

Trout Fishing Only
Hamilton 800-363-2408
Species & Seasons: Trout June-Nov
Bodies of water: Bitterroot River, Big Hole River, Beaverhead River, Madison River, Yellowstone River, Clark Fork River
Rates: Half day: $200(1-2), Full day: $270(1-2)
Call between: 7pm-10pm
Provides: Fly rod/reel, lunch
Handicapped equipped: Yes

Wildlife Adventures, Inc.
Victor 406-642-3262
Species & Seasons: Rainbow Trout, Cutthroat Trout, Brook Trout June-Oct
Bodies of water: Bitterroot River, Big Creek, Bear Creek, Storm Creek, White Sand Creek, White Sand Lake, Siah Lake
Rates: Half day: $125(1), $150(2), Full day: $175(1), $200(2)
Call between: 8am-8pm
Provides: Light tackle, fly rod/reel, lures, bait, beverages, lunch
Handicapped equipped: Yes

BLACKFEET INDIAN RESERVATION

GUIDES...

Montana Adventures in Angling
Billings 406-248-2995
Species & Seasons: Rainbow Trout, Brown Trout, Cutthroat Trout Mar-Dec, Lake Trout June-Nov, Whitefish Mar-Dec, Northern Pike, Arctic Grayling April-Nov
Bodies of water: Bighorn River, Yellowstone River, Boulder River, Missouri River Stillwater River, other streams in eastern Montana, Blackfeet Indian Res.
Rates: Full day: $200(1), $270(2)
Provides: Light tackle, fly rod/reel, lures, rain gear, beverages, lunch
Handicapped equipped: Yes
Certifications: ORVIS Endorsed and ORVIS Guide of yr 1992, Licensed MT Outfitter, Blackeet Tribal Outfitter

Northern High Plains Outfitters
Browning 800-231-3825
.... 406-338-7413
Species & Seasons: Trout, April-June, Rainbow Trout Sept-Nov, Brown Trout, Cutthroat Trout, Brook Trout Sept-Oct
Bodies of water: Blackfeet Indian Reservation, Lewis & Clark Nat'l Forest, Bob Marshall Wilderness, private Alberta Canada Spring Creek
Rates: Half day: $100(1), Full day: $200(1)
Call between: 8am-5pm
Provides: Light tackle, fly rod/reel, lures, rain gear, beverages, lunch
Handicapped equipped: Yes

BLACKFOOT RIVER

FLY SHOPS...

Paul Roos Outfitters
Helena 800-858-3497
Hours: 7am-6pm, closed Sun.
Carries: Flies, maps, rods, reels, licenses
Bodies of water: Missouri River, Blackfoot River, Smith River, Boulder River
Services & Products: Guide services, lodging, food, beverages, fishing instruction

BLACKFOOT RIVER - BOB MARSHALL WILDERNESS — MONTANA

Guides: Yes
OK to call for current conditions: Yes
Contact: Michael or Geoff

GUIDES...

Anglers Afloat, Inc.
Stevensville 406-777-3421
Species & Seasons: Rainbow Trout, Brown Trout, Cutthroat Trout, Brook Trout Mar-Oct
Bodies of water: Bitterroot River, Blackfoot River, Big Hole River, Rock Creek, Beaverhead River, Clark Fork River
Rates: Half day: $250(1-2), Full day: $285(1-2)
Call between: 8-10am/8-10pm
Provides: Fly rod/reel, beverages, lunch
Handicapped equipped: Yes
Certifications: Licensed MT Outfitter

Copenhaver Outfitters
Ovando 406-793-5547
Species & Seasons: Cutthroat Trout, Trout, Brown Trout July-Aug
Bodies of water: North Fork Blackfoot River; Youngs Creek, South Fork Flathead River (Bob Marshall Wilderness Area - pack trips)
Rates: Full day: $150(1), call for pack trip rates
Call between: 7-8am/6-10pm
Provides: Beverages, lunch
Handicapped equipped: Depends on handicap - must be able to ride horse

Montana River Outfitters
Wolf Creek 406-761-1677
Species & Seasons: Rainbow Trout, Brown Trout Mar-Nov, Cutthroat Trout May-Sept
Bodies of water: Smith River, South Fork Flathead River, Missouri River, Blackfoot River
Rates: Half day: $215(1-2), Full day: $225(1), $290(2)
Call between: Anytime
Provides: Light tackle, fly rod/reel, rain gear, beverages, lunch
Certifications: Mastery

Montana River Outfitters
Great Falls 406-761-1677
.... 235-4350(S)
Species & Seasons: Rainbow Trout, Brown Trout Jan-Dec, Cutthroat Trout June-Sept
Bodies of water: Missouri River, Smith River, Blackfoot River, Yellowstone River, Clark Fork River, South Fork of the Flathead River
Rates: Half day: $215(1-2), Full day: $255(1), $290(2), $340(3)
Call between: 10am-5pm
Provides: Beverages, lunch
Handicapped equipped: Yes
Certifications: MOGA, FOAM, Licensed MT Outfitter

Paul Roos Outfitters, Inc.
Helena 800-858-3497
Species & Seasons: Cutthroat Trout, Rainbow Trout, Brown Trout
Bodies of water: Missouri River, Smith River, Big Blackfoot, Rock Creek, many other rivers and streams
Rates: Full day: $290(1) and up
Call between: 8am-5pm
Provides: Fly rod/reel(rental), beverages, lunch
Handicapped equipped: No
Certifications: ORVIS

LODGES...

White Tail Ranch Outfitters, Inc.
Ovando 406-793-5666
Guest Capacity: 32
Handicapped equipped: Yes, depending on requirements
Seasons: All year
Rates: Varies, $80/day pp
Guides: Yes, recommend
Species & Seasons: Cutthroat Trout, Bull Trout Summer-Fall
Bodies of Water: Blackfoot River, Seeley Lake, Clearwater River, Cooper Lake, N. Fork Blackfoot River, Bob Marshall Wilderness, Nevada Lake
Types of fishing: Fly fishing, horse/back pack, wading
Available: Fishing instruction, family activities, baby sitting

BOB MARSHALL WILDERNESS

GUIDES...

Bartlett Creek Outfitters
Deer Lodge 406-693-2433
Species & Seasons: Rainbow Trout, Cutthroat Trout June-Sept
Bodies of water: South Fork of Flathead River, Bob Marshall Wilderness
Rates: 7-14 day trips: $150 a day pp
Call between: 7pm-10:30pm
Provides: Light tackle
Handicapped equipped: No

Big Salmon Outfitters
Ronan 406-676-3999
Species & Seasons: Cutthroat Trout July-Aug
Bodies of water: Bob Marshall Wilderness, So. Fork of Flathead River, Big Salmon Lake, White River
Rates: Full day: $150(1)
Call between: 7am-8pm
Provides: Fly rod/reel, beverages, lunch

Copenhaver Outfitters
Ovando 406-793-5547
Species & Seasons: Cutthroat Trout, Trout, Brown Trout July-Aug
Bodies of water: North Fork Blackfoot River; Youngs Creek, South Fork Flathead River (Bob Marshall Wilderness Area - pack trips)
Rates: Full day: $150(1), call for pack trip rates
Call between: 7-8am/6-10pm
Provides: Beverages, lunch
Handicapped equipped: Depends on handicap - must be able to ride horse

Northern High Plains Outfitters
Browning 800-231-3825
.... 406-338-7413
Species & Seasons: Trout, April-June, Rainbow Trout Sept-Nov, Brown Trout, Cutthroat Trout, Brook Trout Sept-Oct
Bodies of water: Blackfeet Indian Reservation, Lewis & Clark Nat'l Forest, Bob Marshall Wilderness, private Alberta Canada Spring Creek
Rates: Half day: $100(1), Full day: $200(1)
Call between: 8am-5pm
Provides: Light tackle, fly rod/reel, lures, rain gear, beverages, lunch
Handicapped equipped: Yes

MONTANA
BOB MARSHALL WILDERNESS - BOULDER RIVER

LODGES...

White Tail Ranch Outfitters, Inc.
Ovando 406-793-5666
Guest Capacity: 32
Handicapped equipped: Yes, depending on requirements
Seasons: All year
Rates: Varies, $80/day pp
Guides: Yes, recommend
Species & Seasons: Cutthroat Trout, Bull Trout Summer-Fall
Bodies of Water: Blackfoot River, Seeley Lake, Clearwater River, Cooper Lake, N. Fork Blackfoot River, Bob Marshall Wilderness, Nevada Lake
Types of fishing: Fly fishing, horse/back pack, wading
Available: Fishing instruction, family activities, baby sitting

BOULDER RIVER

BAIT & TACKLE...

Shell Shack
Laurel 406-628-8986
Hours: 9am-5pm, closed Sun.
Carries: Live bait, artificial lures, flies, maps, rods, reels,
Bodies of water: Yellowstone River, Bighorn River, Stillwater River, Boulder River, Yellowtail Res.
Services & Products: Fishing instruction, repair services
Guides: Yes
OK to call for current conditions: Yes
Contact: Tom Brown

FLY SHOPS...

Paul Roos Outfitters
Helena 800-858-3497
Hours: 7am-6pm, closed Sun.
Carries: Flies, maps, rods, reels, licenses
Bodies of water: Missouri River, Blackfoot River, Smith River, Boulder River
Services & Products: Guide services, lodging, food, beverages, fishing instruction
Guides: Yes
OK to call for current conditions: Yes
Contact: Michael or Geoff

GUIDES...

Big Timber Guides
Big Timber 406-932-4080
.... 930-4080
Species & Seasons: Rainbow Trout, Brown Trout Mar-Nov, Cutthroat Trout June-Sept, Brook Trout June-Oct, Walleye Mar-Oct, Lake Trout Mar-Aug, Paddlefish April-June
Bodies of water: Yellowstone River, Boulder River, Bighorn River, Madison River, Missouri River, Canyon Ferry Lake, Hauser Lake, Holter Lake
Rates: Half day: $100(1), $200(2), Full day: $200(1), $250(2), Weekly rates
Call between: 7am-10:30pm
Provides: Light tackle, heavy tackle, fly rod/reel, rain gear, beverages, lunch
Handicapped equipped: Yes
Certifications: Licensed MT Outfitter

Fly Fishing Montana Co., Inc.
Bozeman 406-585-9066
Species & Seasons: Trout, Brown Trout, Rainbow Trout, Cutthroat Trout Feb-Nov
Bodies of water: Yellowstone River, Missouri River, Madison River, Gallatin River, Boulder River, Paradise Valley Spring Creeks (float and wade trips)
Rates: Half day: $110(1), $120(2), Full day: $200(1), $225(2)
Call between: 8am-8pm
Provides: Fly rod/reel, beverages, lunch
Handicapped equipped: Yes
Certifications: Licensed MT Outfitters

Montana Adventures in Angling
Billings 406-248-2995
Species & Seasons: Rainbow Trout, Brown Trout, Cutthroat Trout Mar-Dec, Lake Trout June-Nov, Whitefish Mar-Dec, Northern Pike, Arctic Grayling April-Nov
Bodies of water: Bighorn River, Yellowstone River, Boulder River, Missouri River Stillwater River, other streams in eastern Montana, Blackfeet Indian Res.
Rates: Full day: $200(1), $270(2)
Provides: Light tackle, fly rod/reel, lures, rain gear, beverages, lunch
Handicapped equipped: Yes
Certifications: ORVIS Endorsed and ORVIS Guide of yr 1992, Licensed MT Outfitter, Blackeet Tribal Outfitter

Running M Outfitters
Big Timber 406-932-6121
Species & Seasons: Rainbow Trout, Cutthroat Trout, Brook Trout all year, Golden Trout July-Aug
Bodies of water: Yellowstone River, Boulder River, Stillwater River, High Country Lakes, various other streams and private ponds
Rates: Ranch style trips(cost per day pp): $150(2-4), $100(5-6) Children under 6 free, many options available
Call between: Before 9am-After 9pm
Provides: Beverages, lunch
Handicapped equipped: Yes, depends on handicap
Certifications: FOAM, MOGA, USFS, DSL, BLM, MBO - licensed, insured

LODGES...

Fly Fisherman's Lodge
Livingston 406-222-7437
Seasons: Closed Nov to Feb
Guides: Yes
Bodies of Water: Yellowstone River, Boulder River, Gallatin River, Madison River, Stillwater River
Types of fishing: Fly fishing
Available: Guide services, food

Hawley Mountain Ranch
McLeod 406-932-5791
Guest Capacity: 20
Handicapped equipped: No
Seasons: May to Nov
Rates: $1200-$1300/week
Contact: Cathy Johnson
Guides: Yes
Species & Seasons: Rainbow Trout, Cutthroat Trout, Brook Trout all year
Bodies of Water: Boulder River, Private lake, back country streams, lakes
Types of fishing: Fly fishing, light tackle, horse/back pack, wading, float trips
Available: Fishing instruction, family activities, baby sitting

CANYON FERRY LAKE - DEARBORN RIVER — MONTANA

CANYON FERRY LAKE

GUIDES...

Big Timber Guides
Big Timber 406-932-4080
.... 930-4080
Species & Seasons: Rainbow Trout, Brown Trout Mar-Nov, Cutthroat Trout June-Sept, Brook Trout June-Oct, Walleye Mar-Oct, Lake Trout Mar-Aug, Paddlefish April-June
Bodies of water: Yellowstone River, Boulder River, Bighorn River, Madison River, Missouri River, Canyon Ferry Lake, Hauser Lake, Holter Lake
Rates: Half day: $100(1), $200(2), Full day: $200(1), $250(2), Weekly rates
Call between: 7am-10:30pm
Provides: Light tackle, heavy tackle, fly rod/reel, rain gear, beverages, lunch
Handicapped equipped: Yes
Certifications: Licensed MT Outfitter

CLARK CANYON RESERVOIR

GUIDES...

Pioneer Outfitters
Wise River 406-832-3128
Species & Seasons: Trout May-Oct
Bodies of water: Big Hole River, Beaverhead River, High Mountain Lakes, Clark Canyon Res.
Call between: 8am-8pm
Provides: Fly rod/reel, lunch
Handicapped equipped: Yes

CLARK FORK RIVER

GUIDES...

Anglers Afloat, Inc.
Stevensville 406-777-3421
Species & Seasons: Rainbow Trout, Brown Trout, Cutthroat Trout, Brook Trout Mar-Oct
Bodies of water: Bitterroot River, Blackfoot River, Big Hole River, Rock Creek, Beaverhead River, Clark Fork River
Rates: Half day: $250(1-2), Full day: $285(1-2)
Call between: 8-10am/8-10pm
Provides: Fly rod/reel, beverages, lunch
Handicapped equipped: Yes
Certifications: Licensed MT Outfitter

East Fork Outfitters
Sula 406-821-4946
.... 800-763-3688
Species & Seasons: Brown Trout, Rainbow Trout, Cutthroat Trout June-Sept, ALL CATCH & RELEASE!
Bodies of water: Bitterroot River, Big Hole River, Clark Fork River, Beaverhead River
Rates: Wade fishing: Half day: $65(2), Full day: $125(2), Boat: Bitterroot River: $275(2), Big Hole River: $310(2), Clark Fork River: $330(2), Beaverhead River: $330(2)
Call between: 8am-10pm
Provides: Beverages, lunch
Handicapped equipped: No

Flat Iron Outfitting
Thompson Falls 406-827-3666
Species & Seasons: Rainbow Trout, Cutthroat Trout June-Sept
Bodies of water: Thompson River, Clark Fork River, Mountain Lakes in the Lo Lo Nat'l. Forest
Rates: Half day: $75(1), $125(2), Full day: $125(1), $200(2)
Call between: 8am-8pm
Provides: Light tackle, fly rod/reel, lures, bait, beverages, lunch
Handicapped equipped: Yes

Great Divide Outfitters
Divide 406-267-3346
Species & Seasons: Brown Trout, Rainbow Trout, Brook Trout, Arctic Grayling April-Oct
Bodies of water: Big Hole River, Beaverhead River, Jefferson River, Clark Fork River
Rates: Half day: $150(1), $175(2), Full day: $200(1), $250(2)
Call between: 7am-9pm
Provides: Fly rod/reel, rain gear, beverages, lunch
Handicapped equipped: Yes

Montana River Outfitters
Great Falls 406-761-1677
.... 235-4350(S)
Species & Seasons: Rainbow Trout, Brown Trout Jan-Dec, Cutthroat Trout June-Sept
Bodies of water: Missouri River, Smith River, Blackfoot River, Yellowstone River, Clark Fork River, South Fork of the Flathead River
Rates: Half day: $215(1-2), Full day $255(1), $290(2), $340(3)
Call between: 10am-5pm
Provides: Beverages, lunch
Handicapped equipped: Yes
Certifications: MOGA, FOAM, Licensed MT Outfitter

Simpson Outfitters, Inc.
East Helena 406-227-5277
Species & Seasons: Brown Trout, Rainbow Trout May-Oct
Bodies of water: Missouri River, Upper Smith River, Madison River, Jefferson River, Clark Fork River, Gallatin River
Rates: Half day: $125(1), $150(2), Full day: $250(1), $275(2)
Call between: 3pm-9pm
Provides: Light tackle, fly rod/reel, bait

Trout Fishing Only
Hamilton 800-363-2408
Species & Seasons: Trout June-Nov
Bodies of water: Bitterroot River, Big Hole River, Beaverhead River, Madison River, Yellowstone River, Clark Fork River
Rates: Half day: $200(1-2), Full day: $270(1-2)
Call between: 7pm-10pm
Provides: Fly rod/reel, lunch
Handicapped equipped: Yes

DEARBORN RIVER

GUIDES...

Lass & Ron Mills Outfitting Inc.
Augusta 406-562-3335
Species & Seasons: Rainbow Trout, Cutthroat Trout, Brown Trout July-Aug
Bodies of water: North Fork of Sun River, South Fork of Flathead River, Dearborn River, South Fork of Sun River
Rates: Pack trips (5-8 days): $185 per day
Call between: 7-9am/5-10pm
Provides: Lunch
Handicapped equipped: Yes, depends handicap

MONTANA

FLATHEAD LAKE - GALLATIN RIVER

FLATHEAD LAKE

GUIDES...

Rach Outfitters Inc.
Kalispell 406-857-3439
Species & Seasons: Lake Trout all year
Bodies of water: Flathead Lake
Rates: Half day: $225(1-4),
Full day: $395(1-2)
Call between: 6am-11pm
Provides: Light tackle, lures, bait, rain gear, beverages, lunch (on full days)
Handicapped equipped: Yes

FLATHEAD RIVER

GUIDES...

Bartlett Creek Outfitters
Deer Lodge 406-693-2433
Species & Seasons: Rainbow Trout, Cutthroat Trout June-Sept
Bodies of water: South Fork of Flathead River, Bob Marshall Wilderness
Rates: 7-14 day trips: $150 a day pp
Call between: 7pm-10:30pm
Provides: Light tackle
Handicapped equipped: No

Big Salmon Outfitters
Ronan 406-676-3999
Species & Seasons: Cutthroat Trout July-Aug
Bodies of water: Bob Marshall Wilderness, So. Fork of Flathead River, Big Salmon Lake, White River
Rates: Full day: $150(1)
Call between: 7am-8pm
Provides: Fly rod/reel, beverages, lunch

Copenhaver Outfitters
Ovando 406-793-5547
Species & Seasons: Cutthroat Trout, Trout, Brown Trout July-Aug
Bodies of water: North Fork Blackfoot River; Youngs Creek, South Fork Flathead River (Bob Marshall Wilderness Area - pack trips)
Rates: Full day: $150(1), call for pack trip rates
Call between: 7-8am/6-10pm
Provides: Beverages, lunch
Handicapped equipped: Depends on handicap - must be able to ride horse

Lass & Ron Mills Outfitting Inc.
Augusta 406-562-3335
Species & Seasons: Rainbow Trout, Cutthroat Trout, Brown Trout July-Aug
Bodies of water: North Fork of Sun River, South Fork of Flathead River, Dearborn River, South Fork of Sun River
Rates: Pack trips (5-8 days): $185 per day
Call between: 7-9am/5-10pm
Provides: Lunch
Handicapped equipped: Yes, depends handicap

Montana River Outfitters
Wolf Creek 406-761-1677
Species & Seasons: Rainbow Trout, Brown Trout Mar-Nov, Cutthroat Trout May-Sept
Bodies of water: Smith River, South Fork Flathead River, Missouri River, Blackfoot River
Rates: Half day: $215(1-2), Full day: $225(1), $290(2)
Call between: Anytime
Provides: Light tackle, fly rod/reel, rain gear, beverages, lunch
Certifications: Mastery

Montana River Outfitters
Great Falls 406-761-1677
.... 235-4350(S)
Species & Seasons: Rainbow Trout, Brown Trout Jan-Dec, Cutthroat Trout June-Sept
Bodies of water: Missouri River, Smith River, Blackfoot River, Yellowstone River, Clark Fork River, South Fork of the Flathead River
Rates: Half day: $215(1-2), Full day: $255(1), $290(2), $340(3)
Call between: 10am-5pm
Provides: Beverages, lunch
Handicapped equipped: Yes
Certifications: MOGA, FOAM, Licensed MT Outfitter

Wild River Adventures
West Glacier 800-826-2724
Species & Seasons: Cutthroat Trout June-Oct
Bodies of water: North Fork Flathead River, Middle Fork Flathead River
Call between: 9am-8pm
Provides: Light tackle, fly rod/reel, lures, rain gear, beverages, lunch
Handicapped equipped: Yes

FORT PECK LAKE

BAIT & TACKLE...

Minnow Bucket
Huntley 406-348-2440
Hours: 6am-8pm, closed Tues.
Carries: Live bait, artificial lures, rods, reels, licenses
Bodies of water: Yellowstone River, Fort Peck Lake, Yellowtail Res., Tongue River Res.
Services & Products: Fishing instruction
Guides: Yes
OK to call for current conditions: Yes
Contact: Will

Scheels Sport Shop
Billings 406-656-9220
Hours: 9am-9pm
Carries: Live bait, artificial lures, flies, maps, rods, reels, licenses
Bodies of water: Bighorn River, Fort Peck Lake, Stillwater River, Cooney Res., Rock Creek, Yellowstone Nat'l. Park
Guides: Yes
OK to call for current conditions: Yes
Contact: Mike Johnston

GALLATIN RIVER

GUIDES...

Canoeing House Rentals & Riverboat Fly Fishing
Three Forks 406-285-3488
Species & Seasons: Trout April-Nov
Bodies of water: Jefferson River, Madison River, Gallatin River, Yellowstone River, Big Hole River
Rates: Half day: $150(2), Full day: $225(2)
Call between: 7am-9pm
Handicapped equipped: No
Certifications: Licensed Fishing Outfitter State of MT, Professional Guides Assoc.

Diamond K Outfitters
Big Sky 406-580-0928
Species & Seasons: Rainbow Trout, Brown Trout, Cutthroat Trout, Arctic Grayling June-Oct
Bodies of water: Alpine Lakes and streams in backcountry of Yellowstone Nat'l. Park, Gallatin River, Lee Metcalf Wilderness Area, Madison Mtn. Ranges

GALLATIN RIVER - JEFFERSON RIVER — MONTANA

Rates: Full day: $240(1-2)
Provides: Fly rod/reel
Handicapped equipped: Yes

East Slope Anglers
PO Box 160249
Big Sky 59716
Species & Seasons: Trout all year
Bodies of water: Madison River, Yellowstone Rover, Gallatin River, Missouri River, Jefferson River, Yellowstone Nat'l. Park, Alpine Lakes
Rates: Half day: $100(1), $125(2),
Full day: $200(1), $225(2),
Float trips: $255(2)
Provides: Fly rod/reel, beverages, lunch
Certifications: MT Outfitter

Fly Fishing Montana Co., Inc.
Bozeman 406-585-9066
Species & Seasons: Trout, Brown Trout, Rainbow Trout, Cutthroat Trout Feb-Nov
Bodies of water: Yellowstone River, Missouri River, Madison River, Gallatin River, Boulder River, Paradise Valley Spring Creeks (float and wade trips)
Rates: Half day: $110(1), $120(2),
Full day: $200(1), $225(2)
Call between: 8am-8pm
Provides: Fly rod/reel, beverages, lunch
Handicapped equipped: Yes
Certifications: Licensed MT Outfitters

Hawkridge Outfitters & Rod Builders
Bozeman 406-585-9608
Species & Seasons: Brown Trout, Rainbow Trout, Cutthroat Trout Mar-Nov, Arctic Grayling June-Sept
Bodies of water: Gallatin River, Yellowstone Nat'l. Park
Call between: 7am-9am/5pm-9pm
Provides: Beverages, lunch
Handicapped equipped: No

Montana Rivers to Ridges
Big Sky 406-995-2298
Species & Seasons: Trout Jan-Dec
Bodies of water: Madison River, Gallatin River, Yellowstone Nat'l. Park Missouri River, Hebgen Lake, Earthquake Lake
Rates: Full day: $240(1-2)
Call between: 6pm-9pm
Provides: Fly rod/reel, beverages, lunch
Handicapped equipped: Yes
Certifications: Gallatin Nat'l. Forest Permitee

Simpson Outfitters, Inc.
East Helena 406-227-5277
Species & Seasons: Brown Trout, Rainbow Trout May-Oct
Bodies of water: Missouri River, Upper Smith River, Madison River, Jefferson River, Clark Fork River, Gallatin River
Rates: Half day: $125(1), $150(2),
Full day: $250(1), $275(2)
Call between: 3pm-9pm
Provides: Light tackle, fly rod/reel, bait

Tite Line Fishing
Townsend 406-266-3225
Species & Seasons: Trout Mar-Oct
Bodies of water: Missouri River, Yellowstone River, Gallitan River, Jefferson River, Madison River
Rates: Full day: $190(1), $265(2)
Provides: Fly rod/reel, rain gear, beverages, lunch

LODGES...

Fly Fisherman's Lodge
Livingston 406-222-7437
Seasons: Closed Nov to Feb
Guides: Yes
Bodies of Water: Yellowstone River, Boulder River, Gallatin River, Madison River, Stillwater River
Types of fishing: Fly fishing
Available: Guide services, food

HEBGEN LAKE

GUIDES...

Jack River Outfitters
Ennis 406-682-4948
Species & Seasons: Brown Trout, Rainbow Trout April-Nov
Bodies of water: Madison River, Big Hole River, Yellowstone River, Jefferson River, Missouri River, Hebgen Lake, Ennis Lake
Rates: Half day: $170(2),
Full day: $250(2), $50 additional 3rd person
Call between: 7-9pm
Provides: Light tackle, fly rod/reel, rain gear, beverages, lunch
Handicapped equipped: Yes, limited

Montana Rivers to Ridges
Big Sky 406-995-2298
Species & Seasons: Trout Jan-Dec
Bodies of water: Madison River, Gallatin River, Yellowstone Nat'l. Park Missouri River, Hebgen Lake, Earthquake Lake
Rates: Full day: $240(1-2)
Call between: 6pm-9pm
Provides: Fly rod/reel, beverages, lunch
Handicapped equipped: Yes
Certifications: Gallatin Nat'l. Forest Permitee

JEFFERSON RIVER

GUIDES...

Canoeing House Rentals & Riverboat Fly Fishing
Three Forks 406-285-3488
Species & Seasons: Trout April-Nov
Bodies of water: Jefferson River, Madison River, Gallatin River, Yellowstone River, Big Hole River
Rates: Half day: $150(2),
Full day: $225(2)
Call between: 7am-9pm
Handicapped equipped: No
Certifications: Licensed Fishing Outfitter State of MT, Professional Guides Assoc.

East Slope Anglers
PO Box 160249
Big Sky 59716
Species & Seasons: Trout all year
Bodies of water: Madison River, Yellowstone Rover, Gallatin River, Missouri River, Jefferson River, Yellowstone Nat'l. Park, Alpine Lakes
Rates: Half day: $100(1), $125(2),
Full day: $200(1), $225(2),
Float trips: $255(2)
Provides: Fly rod/reel, beverages, lunch
Certifications: MT Outfitter

Great Divide Outfitters
Divide 406-267-3346
Species & Seasons: Brown Trout, Rainbow Trout, Brook Trout, Arctic Grayling April-Oct
Bodies of water: Big Hole River, Beaverhead River, Jefferson River, Clark Fork River
Rates: Half day: $150(1), $175(2),
Full day: $200(1), $250(2)
Call between: 7am-9pm
Provides: Fly rod/reel, rain gear, beverages, lunch
Handicapped equipped: Yes

MONTANA

JEFFERSON RIVER - MADISON RIVER

Jack River Outfitters
Ennis 406-682-4948
Species & Seasons: Brown Trout, Rainbow Trout April-Nov
Bodies of water: Madison River, Big Hole River, Yellowstone River, Jefferson River, Missouri River, Hebgen Lake, Ennis Lake
Rates: Half day: $170(2), Full day: $250(2), $50 additional 3rd person
Call between: 7-9pm
Provides: Light tackle, fly rod/reel, rain gear, beverages, lunch
Handicapped equipped: Yes, limited

Simpson Outfitters, Inc.
East Helena 406-227-5277
Species & Seasons: Brown Trout, Rainbow Trout May-Oct
Bodies of water: Missouri River, Upper Smith River, Madison River, Jefferson River, Clark Fork River, Gallatin River
Rates: Half day: $125(1), $150(2), Full day: $250(1), $275(2)
Call between: 3pm-9pm
Provides: Light tackle, fly rod/reel, bait

Tite Line Fishing
Townsend 406-266-3225
Species & Seasons: Trout Mar-Oct
Bodies of water: Missouri River, Yellowstone River, Gallitan River, Jefferson River, Madison River
Rates: Full day: $190(1), $265(2)
Provides: Fly rod/reel, rain gear, beverages, lunch

LODGES...

Rush's Lakeview Guest Ranch
Butte 406-276-3300
Guest Capacity: 50
Handicapped equipped: No
Seasons: All year
Rates: $695/7 days, 6 nights
Guides: Yes
Species & Seasons: Brown Trout, Brook Trout, Rainbow Trout, Golden Trout, Grayling, Cutthroat, May-Nov
Bodies of Water: Madison River, Jefferson River, Ruby River, Beaverhead River, Red Rock River, Big Hole River, Elk River
Types of fishing: Fly fishing, light tackle, horse/back pack, wading, float trips
Available: Fishing instruction, family activities, baby sitting

LAKE KOOCANUSA

GUIDES...

Fowler Charter
Eureka 406-296-3274
Species & Seasons: Salmon, Rainbow Trout, Cutthroat Trout June-Oct
Bodies of water: Lake Koocanusa
Rates: 26 ft. boat with guide: Half day: $120(2-4), Full day $200(2-4), 18 ft. boat with guide Half day: $80(2), Full day: $150(2)
Call between: 7am-10pm
Certifications: Licensed Guide

Lazy JR Outfitters
Libby 406-293-6820
Species & Seasons: Trout June-Oct, LM Bass July-Sept, King Salmon Jan-Dec
Bodies of water: Kootenai River, Lake Koocanusa, McGregor Lake, Thompson Lakes
Rates: Half day: $75(1), $140(2), Full day: $120(1), $220(2)
Call between: 6am-10pm
Provides: Light tackle, bait, lunch
Handicapped equipped: No
Certifications: MOGA

MADISON RIVER

FLY SHOPS...

Bud Lilly's Trout Shop
PO Box 698
W. Yellowstone 59758
Hours: 7am-9pm June 15-Sept. 15, 8:30am-5:30pm Sept.16-June 14
Carries: Lures, flies, maps, rods, reels, licenses
Bodies of water: Yellowstone Nat'l. Park, Madison River
Services & Products: Guide services, fishing instruction, camping equipment
Guides: Yes
OK to call for current conditions: Yes
Contact: Dick Greene

GUIDES...

Big Timber Guides
Big Timber 406-932-4080
.... 930-4080
Species & Seasons: Rainbow Trout, Brown Trout Mar-Nov, Cutthroat Trout June-Sept, Brook Trout June-Oct, Walleye Mar-Oct, Lake Trout Mar-Aug, Paddlefish April-June
Bodies of water: Yellowstone River, Boulder River, Bighorn River, Madison River, Missouri River, Canyon Ferry Lake, Hauser Lake, Holter Lake
Rates: Half day: $100(1), $200(2), Full day: $200(1), $250(2), Weekly rates
Call between: 7am-10:30pm
Provides: Light tackle, heavy tackle, fly rod/reel, rain gear, beverages, lunch
Handicapped equipped: Yes
Certifications: Licensed MT Outfitter

Canoeing House Rentals & Riverboat Fly Fishing
Three Forks 406-285-3488
Species & Seasons: Trout April-Nov
Bodies of water: Jefferson River, Madison River, Gallatin River, Yellowstone River, Big Hole River
Rates: Half day: $150(2), Full day: $225(2)
Call between: 7am-9pm
Handicapped equipped: No
Certifications: Licensed Fishing Outfitter State of MT, Professional Guides Assoc.

East Slope Anglers
PO Box 160249
Big Sky 59716
Species & Seasons: Trout all year
Bodies of water: Madison River, Yellowstone Rover, Gallatin River, Missouri River, Jefferson River, Yellowstone Nat'l. Park, Alpine Lakes
Rates: Half day: $100(1), $125(2), Full day: $200(1), $225(2), Float trips: $255(2)
Provides: Fly rod/reel, beverages, lunch
Certifications: MT Outfitter

Fly Fishing Montana Co., Inc.
Bozeman 406-585-9066
Species & Seasons: Trout, Brown Trout, Rainbow Trout, Cutthroat Trout Feb-Nov
Bodies of water: Yellowstone River, Missouri River, Madison River, Gallatin River, Boulder River, Paradise Valley Spring Creeks (float and wade trips)

MADISON RIVER - MISSOURI RIVER — MONTANA

Rates: Half day: $110(1), $120(2),
Full day: $200(1), $225(2)
Call between: 8am-8pm
Provides: Fly rod/reel, beverages, lunch
Handicapped equipped: Yes
Certifications: Licensed MT Outfitters

Jack River Outfitters
Ennis 406-682-4948
Species & Seasons: Brown Trout, Rainbow Trout April-Nov
Bodies of water: Madison River, Big Hole River, Yellowstone River, Jefferson River, Missouri River, Hebgen Lake, Ennis Lake
Rates: Half day: $170(2),
Full day: $250(2), $50 additional 3rd person
Call between: 7-9pm
Provides: Light tackle, fly rod/reel, rain gear, beverages, lunch
Handicapped equipped: Yes, limited

Montana Rivers to Ridges
Big Sky 406-995-2298
Species & Seasons: Trout Jan-Dec
Bodies of water: Madison River, Gallatin River, Yellowstone Nat'l. Park Missouri River, Hebgen Lake, Earthquake Lake
Rates: Full day: $240(1-2)
Call between: 6pm-9pm
Provides: Fly rod/reel, beverages, lunch
Handicapped equipped: Yes
Certifications: Gallatin Nat'l. Forest Permitee

Simpson Outfitters, Inc.
East Helena 406-227-5277
Species & Seasons: Brown Trout, Rainbow Trout May-Oct
Bodies of water: Missouri River, Upper Smith River, Madison River, Jefferson River, Clark Fork River, Gallatin River
Rates: Half day: $125(1), $150(2),
Full day: $250(1), $275(2)
Call between: 3pm-9pm
Provides: Light tackle, fly rod/reel, bait

Tite Line Fishing
Townsend 406-266-3225
Species & Seasons: Trout Mar-Oct
Bodies of water: Missouri River, Yellowstone River, Gallitan River, Jefferson River, Madison River
Rates: Full day: $190(1); $265(2)
Provides: Fly rod/reel, rain gear, beverages, lunch

Trout Fishing Only
Hamilton 800-363-2408
Species & Seasons: Trout June-Nov
Bodies of water: Bitterroot River, Big Hole River, Beaverhead River, Madison River, Yellowstone River, Clark Fork River
Rates: Half day: $200(1-2),
Full day: $270(1-2)
Call between: 7pm-10pm
Provides: Fly rod/reel, lunch
Handicapped equipped: Yes

LODGES...

Fly Fisherman's Lodge
Livingston 406-222-7437
Seasons: Closed Nov to Feb
Guides: Yes
Bodies of Water: Yellowstone River, Boulder River, Gallatin River, Madison River, Stillwater River
Types of fishing: Fly fishing
Available: Guide services, food

Rush's Lakeview Guest Ranch
Butte 406-276-3300
Guest Capacity: 50
Handicapped equipped: No
Seasons: All year
Rates: $695/7 days, 6 nights
Guides: Yes
Species & Seasons: Brown Trout, Brook Trout, Rainbow Trout, Golden Trout, Grayling, Cutthroat, May-Nov
Bodies of Water: Madison River, Jefferson River, Ruby River, Beaverhead River, Red Rock River, Big Hole River, Elk River
Types of fishing: Fly fishing, light tackle, horse/back pack, wading, float trips
Available: Fishing instruction, family activities, baby sitting

MISSOURI RIVER

FLY SHOPS...

Paul Roos Outfitters, Inc.
Helena 800-858-3497
Species & Seasons: Cutthroat Trout, Rainbow Trout, Brown Trout
Bodies of water: Missouri River, Smith River, Big Blackfoot, Rock Creek, many other rivers and streams

Rates: Full day: $290(1) and up
Call between: 8am-5pm
Provides: Fly rod/reel(rental), beverages, lunch
Handicapped equipped: No
Certifications: ORVIS

GUIDES...

Big Timber Guides
Big Timber 406-932-4080
.... 930-4080
Species & Seasons: Rainbow Trout, Brown Trout Mar-Nov, Cutthroat Trout June-Sept, Brook Trout June-Oct, Walleye Mar-Oct, Lake Trout Mar-Aug, Paddlefish April-June
Bodies of water: Yellowstone River, Boulder River, Bighorn River, Madison River, Missouri River, Canyon Ferry Lake, Hauser Lake, Holter Lake
Rates: Half day: $100(1), $200(2),
Full day: $200(1), $250(2), Weekly rates
Call between: 7am-10:30pm
Provides: Light tackle, heavy tackle, fly rod/reel, rain gear, beverages, lunch
Handicapped equipped: Yes

East Slope Anglers
PO Box 160249
Big Sky 59716
Species & Seasons: Trout all year
Bodies of water: Madison River, Yellowstone Rover, Gallatin River, Missouri River, Jefferson River, Yellowstone Nat'l. Park, Alpine Lakes
Rates: Half day: $100(1), $125(2),
Full day: $200(1), $225(2),
Float trips: $255(2)
Provides: Fly rod/reel, beverages, lunch
Certifications: MT Outfitter

Fly Fishing Montana Co., Inc.
Bozeman 406-585-9066
Species & Seasons: Trout, Brown Trout, Rainbow Trout, Cutthroat Trout Feb-Nov
Bodies of water: Yellowstone River, Missouri River, Madison River, Gallatin River, Boulder River, Paradise Valley Spring Creeks (float and wade trips)
Rates: Half day: $110(1), $120(2),
Full day: $200(1), $225(2)
Call between: 8am-8pm
Provides: Fly rod/reel, beverages, lunch
Handicapped equipped: Yes
Certifications: Licensed MT Outfitters

MONTANA

MISSOURI RIVER - REGIONAL AREAS

Jack River Outfitters
Ennis 406-682-4948
Species & Seasons: Brown Trout, Rainbow Trout April-Nov
Bodies of water: Madison River, Big Hole River, Yellowstone River, Jefferson River, Missouri River, Hebgen Lake, Ennis Lake
Rates: Half day: $170(2), Full day: $250(2), $50 additional 3rd person
Call between: 7-9pm
Provides: Light tackle, fly rod/reel, rain gear, beverages, lunch
Handicapped equipped: Yes, limited

Montana Adventures in Angling
Billings 406-248-2995
Species & Seasons: Rainbow Trout, Brown Trout, Cutthroat Trout Mar-Dec, Lake Trout June-Nov, Whitefish Mar-Dec, Northern Pike, Arctic Grayling April-Nov
Bodies of water: Bighorn River, Yellowstone River, Boulder River, Missouri River Stillwater River, other streams in eastern Montana, Blackfeet Indian Res.
Rates: Full day: $200(1), $270(2)
Provides: Light tackle, fly rod/reel, lures, rain gear, beverages, lunch
Handicapped equipped: Yes
Certifications: ORVIS Endorsed and ORVIS Guide of yr 1992, Licensed MT Outfitter, Blackeet Tribal Outfitter

Montana River Outfitters
Wolf Creek 406-761-1677
Species & Seasons: Rainbow Trout, Brown Trout Mar-Nov, Cutthroat Trout May-Sept
Bodies of water: Smith River, South Fork Flathead River, Missouri River, Blackfoot River
Rates: Half day: $215(1-2), Full day: $225(1), $290(2)
Call between: Anytime
Provides: Light tackle, fly rod/reel, rain gear, beverages, lunch
Certifications: Mastery

Montana River Outfitters
Great Falls....................... 406-761-1677
.... 235-4350(S)
Species & Seasons: Rainbow Trout, Brown Trout Jan-Dec, Cutthroat Trout June-Sept
Bodies of water: Missouri River, Smith River, Blackfoot River, Yellowstone River, Clark Fork River, South Fork of the Flathead River

Rates: Half day: $215(1-2), Full day: $255(1), $290(2), $340(3)
Call between: 10am-5pm
Provides: Beverages, lunch
Handicapped equipped: Yes
Certifications: MOGA, FOAM, Licensed MT Outfitter

Montana Rivers to Ridges
Big Sky 406-995-2298
Species & Seasons: Trout Jan-Dec
Bodies of water: Madison River, Gallatin River, Yellowstone Nat'l. Park Missouri River, Hebgen Lake, Earthquake Lake
Rates: Full day: $240(1-2)
Call between: 6pm-9pm
Provides: Fly rod/reel, beverages, lunch
Handicapped equipped: Yes
Certifications: Gallatin Nat'l. Forest Permitee

Paul Roos Outfitters, Inc.
Helena 800-858-3497
Species & Seasons: Cutthroat Trout, Rainbow Trout, Brown Trout
Bodies of water: Missouri River, Smith River, Big Blackfoot, Rock Creek, many other rivers and streams
Rates: Full day: $290(1) and up
Call between: 8am-5pm
Provides: Fly rod/reel(rental), beverages, lunch
Handicapped equipped: No
Certifications: ORVIS

Simpson Outfitters, Inc.
East Helena 406-227-5277
Species & Seasons: Brown Trout, Rainbow Trout May-Oct
Bodies of water: Missouri River, Upper Smith River, Madison River, Jefferson River, Clark Fork River, Gallatin River
Rates: Half day: $125(1), $150(2), Full day: $250(1), $275(2)
Call between: 3pm-9pm
Provides: Light tackle, fly rod/reel, bait

Tite Line Fishing
Townsend 406-266-3225
Species & Seasons: Trout Mar-Oct
Bodies of water: Missouri River, Yellowstone River, Gallitan River, Jefferson River, Madison River
Rates: Full day: $190(1), $265(2)
Provides: Fly rod/reel, rain gear, beverages, lunch

LODGES...

Fly Fishers' Inn
Cascade 406-468-2529
Guest Capacity: 14
Handicapped equipped: No
Seasons: All year
Rates: $125/day, including meals
Contact: Rick Pasquale
Guides: Yes
Species & Seasons: Trout June-Nov
Bodies of Water: Missouri River
Types of fishing: Fly fishing, wading, float trips
Available: Fishing instruction, licenses

PRIVATE WATERS

LODGES...

Hill Country Expeditions
Geyser 800-531-4484
Guest Capacity: 10
Handicapped equipped: No
Seasons: April to Nov
Rates: $200/day, board, room and guide included
Guides: Yes
Species & Seasons: Rainbow Trout April-Nov
Bodies of Water: Private Pond
Types of fishing: Fly fishing, light tackle
Available: Fishing instruction, family activities, will pick up guest from airport

REGIONAL AREAS

GUIDES...

Allaman's Montana Adventure Trips
Darby 406-821-3763
Species & Seasons: Rainbow Trout, Cutthroat Trout, Brook Trout, Brown Trout, June-Oct
Bodies of water: Bitterroot River, High Mt. Lakes
Rates: Half day: $200(1), $300(2), Full day: $400(1), $600(2)
Call between: 10pm-8am
Provides: Beverages, lunch
Certifications: Licensed MT Outfitter

REGIONAL AREAS - SMITH RIVER

MONTANA

Buffalo Horn Outfitters
Gallatin Gateway 406-763-4388
Species & Seasons: Rainbow Trout, Cutthroat Trout, Brook Trout, Arctic Grayling May-Sept, Golden Trout July-Aug
Bodies of water: Tributaries and lakes of Southwestern Montana and Yellowstone Nat'l. Park Backcountry
Rates: Full day: $175(1), $300(2), Pack trips overnight to 6 days
Call between: 7am-9pm
Provides: Fly rod/reel, beverages, lunch
Handicapped equipped: Yes
Certifications: Licensed MT Outfitter, Yellowstone Park LCP

Diamond K Outfitters
Big Sky 406-580-0928
Species & Seasons: Rainbow Trout, Brown Trout, Cutthroat Trout, Arctic Grayling June-Oct
Bodies of water: Alpine Lakes and streams in backcountry of Yellowstone Nat'l. Park, Gallatin River, Lee Metcalf Wilderness Area, Madison Mtn. Ranges
Rates: Full day: $240(1-2)
Provides: Fly rod/reel
Handicapped equipped: Yes

Flat Iron Outfitting
Thompson Falls 406-827-3666
Species & Seasons: Rainbow Trout, Cutthroat Trout June-Sept
Bodies of water: Thompson River, Clark Fork River, Mountain Lakes in the Lo Lo Nat'l. Forest
Rates: Half day: $75(1), $125(2), Full day: $125(1), $200(2)
Call between: 8am-8pm
Provides: Light tackle, fly rod/reel, lures, bait, beverages, lunch
Handicapped equipped: Yes

Lucky Day Outfitter
Livingston 406-686-4402
Species & Seasons: Cutthroat Trout, Trout June-Sept
Bodies of water: High Mountain Lakes
Rates: Half day: $110(1), $150(2), Full day: $200(1), $250(2), Over night camp trips: $250
Call between: 5-8am/10pm
Provides: Lunch
Handicapped equipped: No

Northern High Plains Outfitters
Browning 800-231-3825
.... 406-338-7413
Species & Seasons: Trout, April-June, Rainbow Trout Sept-Nov, Brown Trout, Cutthroat Trout, Brook Trout Sept-Oct
Bodies of water: Blackfeet Indian Reservation, Lewis & Clark Nat'l Forest, Bob Marshall Wilderness, private Alberta Canada Spring Creek
Rates: Half day: $100(1), Full day: $200(1)
Call between: 8am-5pm
Provides: Light tackle, fly rod/reel, lures, rain gear, beverages, lunch
Handicapped equipped: Yes

Pioneer Outfitters
Wise River 406-832-3128
Species & Seasons: Trout May-Oct
Bodies of water: Big Hole River, Beaverhead River, High Mountain Lakes, Clark Canyon Res.
Call between: 8am-8pm
Provides: Fly rod/reel, lunch
Handicapped equipped: Yes

Running M Outfitters
Big Timber 406-932-6121
Species & Seasons: Rainbow Trout, Cutthroat Trout, Brook Trout all year, Golden Trout July-Aug
Bodies of water: Yellowstone River, Boulder River, Stillwater River, High Country Lakes, various other streams and private ponds
Rates: Ranch style trips(cost per day pp): $150(2-4), $100(5-6) Children under 6 free, many options available
Call between: Before 9am-After 9pm
Provides: Beverages, lunch
Handicapped equipped: Yes, depends on handicap
Certifications: FOAM, MOGA, USFS, DSL, BLM, MBO licensed, insured

Z-J Outfitters
Bozeman 406-586-3196
.... 222-5464
Species & Seasons: Trout Mar-Dec, Walleye May-Sept, Northern Pike May-Nov, Paddlefish Mar-June, Sauger May-June
Bodies of water: Montana Lakes in Central, Southern, & Eastern portions, all South Central and Eastern Rivers
Rates: Varies (custom trips)
Call between: 6am-8pm
Provides: Light tackle, heavy tackle, fly rod/reel, lures, bait, beverages, lunch

Handicapped equipped: Yes
Certifications: MT Outfitter & Guides Assoc.

LODGES...

Montana High Country Tours, Inc.
Dillon 406-683-4920
Guest Capacity: 12
Handicapped equipped: No
Seasons: All year
Rates: From $130/day
Contact: Russ Kipp
Guides: Yes
Species & Seasons: Rainbow Trout, Brown Trout, Cutthroat Trout, Brook Trout, Grayling April-Nov
Bodies of Water: All Southwest Montana Rivers
Types of fishing: Fly fishing, horse/back pack, wading, float trips, float tubes
Available: Fishing instruction, licenses, family activities, children's program, baby sitting, all inclusive packages

SMITH RIVER

FLY SHOPS...

Paul Roos Outfitters
Helena 800-858-3497
Hours: 7am-6pm, closed Sun.
Carries: Flies, maps, rods, reels, licenses
Bodies of water: Missouri River, Blackfoot River, Smith River, Boulder River
Services & Products: Guide services, lodging, food, beverages, fishing instruction
Guides: Yes
OK to call for current conditions: Yes
Contact: Michael or Geoff

MONTANA

SMITH RIVER - THOMPSON LAKES

GUIDES...

Montana River Outfitters
Wolf Creek 406-761-1677
Species & Seasons: Rainbow Trout, Brown Trout Mar-Nov, Cutthroat Trout May-Sept
Bodies of water: Smith River, South Fork Flathead River, Missouri River, Blackfoot River
Rates: Half day: $215(1-2), Full day: $225(1), $290(2)
Call between: Anytime
Provides: Light tackle, fly rod/reel, rain gear, beverages, lunch
Certifications: Mastery

Montana River Outfitters
Great Falls 406-761-1677
.... 235-4350(S)
Species & Seasons: Rainbow Trout, Brown Trout Jan-Dec, Cutthroat Trout June-Sept
Bodies of water: Missouri River, Smith River, Blackfoot River, Yellowstone River, Clark Fork River, South Fork of the Flathead River
Rates: Half day: $215(1-2), Full day: $255(1), $290(2), $340(3)
Call between: 10am-5pm
Provides: Beverages, lunch
Handicapped equipped: Yes
Certifications: MOGA, FOAM, Licensed MT Outfitter

Paul Roos Outfitters, Inc.
Helena 800-858-3497
Species & Seasons: Cutthroat Trout, Rainbow Trout, Brown Trout
Bodies of water: Missouri River, Smith River, Big Blackfoot, Rock Creek, many other rivers and streams
Rates: Full day: $290(1) and up
Call between: 8am-5pm
Provides: Fly rod/reel(rental), beverages, lunch
Handicapped equipped: No
Certifications: ORVIS

Simpson Outfitters, Inc.
East Helena 406-227-5277
Species & Seasons: Brown Trout, Rainbow Trout May-Oct
Bodies of water: Missouri River, Upper Smith River, Madison River, Jefferson River, Clark Fork River, Gallatin River
Rates: Half day: $125(1), $150(2), Full day: $250(1), $275(2)
Call between: 3pm-9pm
Provides: Light tackle, fly rod/reel, bait

STILLWATER RIVER

BAIT & TACKLE...

Scheels Sport Shop
Billings 406-656-9220
Hours: 9am-9pm
Carries: Live bait, artificial lures, flies, maps, rods, reels, licenses
Bodies of water: Bighorn River, Fort Peck Lake, Stillwater River, Cooney Res., Rock Creek, Yellowstone Nat'l. Park
Guides: Yes
OK to call for current conditions: Yes
Contact: Mike Johnston

Shell Shack
Laurel 406-628-8986
Hours: 9am-5pm, closed Sun.
Carries: Live bait, artificial lures, flies, maps, rods, reels,
Bodies of water: Yellowstone River, Bighorn River, Stillwater River, Boulder River, Yellowtail Res.
Services & Products: Fishing instruction, repair services
Guides: Yes
OK to call for current conditions: Yes
Contact: Tom Brown

GUIDES...

Montana Adventures in Angling
Billings 406-248-2995
Species & Seasons: Rainbow Trout, Brown Trout, Cutthroat Trout Mar-Dec, Lake Trout June-Nov, Whitefish Mar-Dec, Northern Pike, Arctic Grayling April-Nov
Bodies of water: Bighorn River, Yellowstone River, Boulder River, Missouri River Stillwater River, other streams in eastern Montana, Blackfeet Indian Res.
Rates: Full day: $200(1), $270(2)
Provides: Light tackle, fly rod/reel, lures, rain gear, beverages, lunch
Handicapped equipped: Yes
Certifications: ORVIS Endorsed and ORVIS Guide of year 1992, Licensed MT Outfitter, Blackeet Tribal Outfitter

Running M Outfitters
Big Timber 406-932-6121
Species & Seasons: Rainbow Trout, Cutthroat Trout, Brook Trout all year, Golden Trout July-Aug
Bodies of water: Yellowstone River, Boulder River, Stillwater River, High Country Lakes, various other streams and private ponds
Rates: Ranch style trips(cost per day pp): $150(2-4), $100(5-6) Children under 6 free, many options available
Call between: Before 9am-After 9pm
Provides: Beverages, lunch
Handicapped equipped: Yes, depends on handicap
Certifications: FOAM, MOGA, USFS, DSL, BLM, MBO - licensed, insured

Seven C Quarter Circle Outfitters
Red Lodge 406-445-2280
Species & Seasons: Rainbow Trout, Cutthroat Trout, Brook Trout, Golden Trout, Brown Trout July-Sept
Bodies of water: Absaroka Beartooth Wilderness, Alpine Lakes, Stillwater River
Rates: Full day: $180(1), $360(2)
Call between: 6pm-10pm
Provides: Lunch
Handicapped equipped: No

LODGES...

Fly Fisherman's Lodge
Livingston 406-222-7437
Seasons: Closed Nov to Feb
Guides: Yes
Bodies of Water: Yellowstone River, Boulder River, Gallatin River, Madison River, Stillwater River
Types of fishing: Fly fishing
Available: Guide services, food

THOMPSON LAKES

GUIDES...

Bear Paw Outfitters
Livingston 406-222-6642
Species & Seasons: Cutthroat Trout July-Oct
Bodies of water: Slough Creek Yellowstone Nat'l. Park), Elbow Lake, Thompson Lakes
Call between: 6am-11pm
Provides: Beverages, lunch
Handicapped equipped: No

THOMPSON LAKES - YELLOWSTONE NATIONAL PARK — MONTANA

Lazy JR Outfitters
Libby 406-293-6820
Species & Seasons: Trout June-Oct, LM Bass July-Sept, King Salmon Jan-Dec
Bodies of water: Kootenai River, Lake Koocanusa, McGregor Lake, Thompson Lakes
Rates: Half day: $75(1), $140(2), Full day: $120(1), $220(2)
Call between: 6am-10pm
Provides: Light tackle, bait, lunch
Handicapped equipped: No
Certifications: MOGA

WHITEFISH LAKE

GUIDES...

Whitefish Lake Fishing
Whitefish 406-862-5313
Species & Seasons: Lake Trout May-Oct
Bodies of water: Whitefish Lake
Rates: Half day: $125(1), $140(2), $150(3), $160(4)
Call between: 10am-10pm
Provides: Light tackle, lures, bait, rain gear
Handicapped equipped: Yes
Certifications: MT Outfitter

YELLOWSTONE NATIONAL PARK

BAIT & TACKLE...

Scheels Sport Shop
Billings 406-656-9220
Hours: 9am-9pm
Carries: Live bait, artificial lures, flies, maps, rods, reels, licenses
Bodies of water: Bighorn River, Fort Peck Lake, Stillwater River, Cooney Res., Rock Creek, Yellowstone Nat'l. Park
Guides: Yes
OK to call for current conditions: Yes
Contact: Mike Johnston

FLY SHOPS...

Bud Lilly's Trout Shop
PO Box 160249
W. Yellowstone 59716
Hours: 7am-9pm June 15-Sept. 15, 8:30am-5:30pm Sept.16-June 14
Carries: Lures, flies, maps, rods, reels, licenses
Bodies of water: Yellowstone Nat'l. Park, Madison River
Services & Products: Guide services, fishing instruction, camping equipment
Guides: Yes
OK to call for current conditions: Yes
Contact: Dick Greene

Park's Fly Shop
Gardiner 406-848-7314
Hours: 9am-5pm
Carries: Lures, flies, maps, rods, reels, licenses
Bodies of water: Yellowstone River, Yellowstone Nat'l. Park
Services & Products: Guide services, fishing instruction
OK to call for current conditions: Yes

GUIDES...

Bear Paw Outfitters
Livingston 406-222-6642
Species & Seasons: Cutthroat Trout July-Oct
Bodies of water: Slough Creek Yellowstone Nat'l. Park), Elbow Lake, Thompson Lakes
Call between: 6am-11pm
Provides: Beverages, lunch
Handicapped equipped: No

Beartooth Plateau Outfitters
Cooke City 800-253-8545
Species & Seasons: Cutthroat Trout, Brook Trout, Rainbow Trout, Arctic Grayling June-Oct, Golden Trout July-Oct
Bodies of water: Yellowstone Nat'l. Park, (Lamar River, Slough Creek, Miller Creek, Pebble Creek, Cache Creek), High Alpine Mountain Lakes in Absaroka Beartooth Wilderness Area
Rates: Full day: $180pp,
7 day package: $1200pp includes 5 day horseback pack trip, lodging, meals, airport pick-up
Call between: 7am-7pm
Provides: Lunch, horses, camp, tents, sleeping bags
Handicapped equipped: No
Certifications: Endorsed ORVIS Outfitter

Blue Ribbon Fishing Tours
Livingston 406-222-7714
Species & Seasons: Rainbow Trout, Brown Trout, Cutthroat Trout June-Oct
Bodies of water: Upper Yellowstone River, Yellowstone Nat'l. Park, Spring Creeks in Paradise Valley, Mountain Lakes
Rates: Half day: $185(1), $195(2), Full day: $250(1), $265(2)
Call between: 6pm-10pm
Provides: Beverages, lunch
Handicapped equipped: Yes
Certifications: Trout Unlimited, FOAM

Buffalo Horn Outfitters
Gallatin Gateway 406-763-4388
Species & Seasons: Rainbow Trout, Cutthroat Trout, Brook Trout, Arctic Grayling May-Sept, Golden Trout July-Aug
Bodies of water: Tributaries and lakes of Southwestern Montana and Yellowstone Nat'l. Park Backcountry
Rates: Full day: $175(1), $300(2),
Pack trips overnight to 6 days
Call between: 7am-9pm
Provides: Fly rod/reel, beverages, lunch
Handicapped equipped: Yes
Certifications: Licensed MT Outfitter, Yellowstone Park LCP

Diamond K Outfitters
Big Sky 406-580-0928
Species & Seasons: Rainbow Trout, Brown Trout, Cutthroat Trout, Arctic Grayling June-Oct
Bodies of water: Alpine Lakes and streams in backcountry of Yellowstone Nat'l. Park, Gallatin River, Lee Metcalf Wilderness Area, Madison Mtn. Ranges
Rates: Full day: $240(1-2)
Provides: Fly rod/reel
Handicapped equipped: Yes

East Slope Anglers
PO Box 160249
Big Sky 59716
Species & Seasons: Trout all year
Bodies of water: Madison River, Yellowstone Rover, Gallatin River, Missouri River, Jefferson River, Yellowstone Nat'l. Park, Alpine Lakes
Rates: Half day: $100(1), $125(2), Full day: $200(1), $225(2), Float trips: $255(2)
Provides: Fly rod/reel, beverages, lunch
Certifications: MT Outfitter

MONTANA — YELLOWSTONE NATIONAL PARK - YELLOWSTONE RIVER

Hawkridge Outfitters & Rod Builders
Bozeman 406-585-9608
Species & Seasons: Brown Trout, Rainbow Trout, Cutthroat Trout Mar-Nov, Arctic Grayling June-Sept
Bodies of water: Gallatin River, Yellowstone Nat'l. Park
Call between: 7am-9am/5pm-9pm
Provides: Beverages, lunch
Handicapped equipped: No

Montana Rivers to Ridges
Big Sky 406-995-2298
Species & Seasons: Trout Jan-Dec
Bodies of water: Madison River, Gallatin River, Yellowstone Nat'l. Park, Missouri River, Hebgen Lake, Earthquake Lake
Rates: Full day: $240(1-2)
Call between: 6pm-9pm
Provides: Fly rod/reel, beverages, lunch
Handicapped equipped: Yes
Certifications: Gallatin Nat'l. Forest Permitee

Montana's Master Angler
Livingston 406-222-2273
Species & Seasons: Rainbow Trout, Brown Trout, Cutthroat Trout Mar-Nov
Bodies of water: Yellowstone River, Yellowstone Nat'l. Park, Paradise Valley Spring Creeks, Paradise Valley Lakes
Rates: Full day: $250(1-2)
Call between: 8am-9pm
Provides: Beverages, lunch
Handicapped equipped: Yes

Skyline Guide Service
Cooke City 406-838-2380
Species & Seasons: Trout June-Oct
Bodies of water: Yellowstone Nat'l. Park, (Slough Creek, Pebble Creek, Cache Creek, Lamar River), Yellowstone River
Rates: Full day: $125(1), $250(2)
Call between: Anytime
Provides: Beverages, lunch
Handicapped equipped:
Certifications: MOGA, licensed, insured

Stillwaters Outfitting
Billings 406-652-8111
Species & Seasons: Rainbow Trout, Brown Trout April-Nov
Bodies of water: Bighorn River, Yellowstone River, Rock Creek, Yellowstone Nat'l. Park
Rates: Float trips: Full day: $210(1), $275(2), Fly fishing instruction

Call between: 6pm-10pm
Provides: Fly rod/reel, beverages, lunch
Handicapped equipped: Yes
Certifications: Licensed MT Outfitter, Certified CPR, First aid

YELLOWSTONE RIVER

BAIT & TACKLE...

Minnow Bucket
Huntley 406-348-2440
Hours: 6am-8pm, closed Tues.
Carries: Live bait, artificial lures, rods, reels, licenses
Bodies of water: Yellowstone River, Fort Peck Lake, Yellowtail Res., Tongue River Res.
Services & Products: Fishing instruction
Guides: Yes
OK to call for current conditions: Yes
Contact: Will

Shell Shack
Laurel 406-628-8986
Hours: 9am-5pm, closed Sun.
Carries: Live bait, artificial lures, flies, maps, rods, reels,
Bodies of water: Yellowstone River, Bighorn River, Stillwater River, Boulder River, Yellowtail Res.
Services & Products: Fishing instruction, repair services
Guides: Yes
OK to call for current conditions: Yes
Contact: Tom Brown

FLY SHOPS...

Park's Fly Shop
Gardiner 406-848-7314
Hours: 9am-5pm
Carries: Lures, flies, maps, rods, reels, licenses
Bodies of water: Yellowstone River, Yellowstone Nat'l. Park
Services & Products: Guide services, fishing instruction
OK to call for current conditions: Yes

GUIDES...

Big Timber Guides
Big Timber 406-932-4080
.... 930-4080
Species & Seasons: Rainbow Trout, Brown Trout Mar-Nov, Cutthroat Trout June-Sept, Brook Trout June-Oct, Walleye Mar-Oct, Lake Trout Mar-Aug, Paddlefish April-June
Bodies of water: Yellowstone River, Boulder River, Bighorn River, Madison River, Missouri River, Canyon Ferry Lake, Hauser Lake, Holter Lake
Rates: Half day: $100(1), $200(2), Full day: $200(1), $250(2), Weekly rates
Call between: 7am-10:30pm
Provides: Light tackle, heavy tackle, fly rod/reel, rain gear, beverages, lunch
Handicapped equipped: Yes
Certifications: Licensed MT Outfitter

Blue Ribbon Fishing Tours
Livingston 406-222-7714
Species & Seasons: Rainbow Trout, Brown Trout, Cutthroat Trout June-Oct
Bodies of water: Upper Yellowstone River, Yellowstone Nat'l. Park, Spring Creeks in Paradise Valley, Mountain Lakes
Rates: Half day: $185(1), $195(2), Full day: $250(1), $265(2)
Call between: 6pm-10pm
Provides: Beverages, lunch
Handicapped equipped: Yes
Certifications: Trout Unlimited, FOAM

Canoeing House Rentals & Riverboat Fly Fishing
Three Forks 406-285-3488
Species & Seasons: Trout April-Nov
Bodies of water: Jefferson River, Madison River, Gallatin River, Yellowstone River, Big Hole River
Rates: Half day: $150(2), Full day: $225(2)
Call between: 7am-9pm
Handicapped equipped: No
Certifications: Licensed Fishing Outfitter State of MT, Professional Guides Assoc.

Cudney Guide Service
Emigrant 406-333-4057
Species & Seasons: Rainbow Trout, Cutthroat Trout, Brown Trout May-Sept
Bodies of water: Yellowstone River, private lakes
Rates: Half day: $200(1-2), Full day: $250(1-2)

YELLOWSTONE RIVER — MONTANA

Call between: 7am-7pm
Provides: Beverages, lunch
Handicapped equipped: Yes
Certifications: FOAM

East Slope Anglers
PO Box 160249
Big Sky 59716
Species & Seasons: Trout all year
Bodies of water: Madison River, Yellowstone River, Gallatin River, Missouri River, Jefferson River, Yellowstone Nat'l. Park, Alpine Lakes
Rates: Half day: $100(1), $125(2), Full day: $200(1), $225(2), Float trips: $255(2)
Provides: Fly rod/reel, beverages, lunch
Certifications: MT Outfitter

Fly Fishing Montana Co., Inc.
Bozeman 406-585-9066
Species & Seasons: Trout, Brown Trout, Rainbow Trout, Cutthroat Trout Feb-Nov
Bodies of water: Yellowstone River, Missouri River, Madison River, Gallatin River, Boulder River, Paradise Valley spring creeks (float and wade trips)
Rates: Half day: $110(1), $120(2), Full day: $200(1), $225(2)
Call between: 8am-8pm
Provides: Fly rod/reel, beverages, lunch
Handicapped equipped: Yes
Certifications: Licensed MT Outfitter

Jack River Outfitters
Ennis 406-682-4948
Species & Seasons: Brown Trout, Rainbow Trout April-Nov
Bodies of water: Madison River, Big Hole River, Yellowstone River, Jefferson River, Missouri River, Hebgen Lake, Ennis Lake
Rates: Half day: $170(2), Full day: $250(2), $50 additional 3rd person
Call between: 7-9pm
Provides: Light tackle, fly rod/reel, rain gear, beverages, lunch
Handicapped equipped: Yes, limited

Lone Willow Creek Guide Service
Livingston 406-222-7584
Species & Seasons: Rainbow Trout, Cutthroat Trout, Brown Trout, Whitefish June-Oct
Bodies of water: Yellowstone River, mountain lakes
Rates: Half day: $200(1-2), Full day: $250(1-2)

Call between: 5am-10pm
Provides: Light tackle, beverages, lunch
Handicapped equipped: Yes

Montana Adventures in Angling
Billings 406-248-2995
Species & Seasons: Rainbow Trout, Brown Trout, Cutthroat Trout Mar-Dec, Lake Trout June-Nov, Whitefish Mar-Dec, Northern Pike, Arctic Grayling April-Nov
Bodies of water: Bighorn River, Yellowstone River, Boulder River, Missouri River Stillwater River, other streams in eastern Montana, Blackfeet Indian Res.
Rates: Full day: $200(1), $270(2)
Provides: Light tackle, fly rod/reel, lures, rain gear, beverages, lunch
Handicapped equipped: Yes
Certifications: ORVIS endorsed and ORVIS guide of year 1992, Licensed MT Outfitter, Blackeet Tribal Outfitter

Montana Guide Service, Inc.
Gardiner 406-848-7265
Species & Seasons: Trout April-Oct
Bodies of water: Yellowstone River (upper)
Rates: Half day: $150(1), $200(2), Full day: $250(1), $350(2)
Call between: 8am-4pm
Handicapped equipped: Yes

Montana River Outfitters
Great Falls................ 406-761-1677
.... 235-4350(S)
Species & Seasons: Rainbow Trout, Brown Trout Jan-Dec, Cutthroat Trout June-Sept
Bodies of water: Missouri River, Smith River, Blackfoot River, Yellowstone River, Clark Fork River, south fork of the Flathead River
Rates: Half day: $215(1-2), Full day: $255(1), $290(2), $340(3)
Call between: 10am-5pm
Provides: Beverages, lunch
Handicapped equipped: Yes
Certifications: MOGA, FOAM, Licensed MT Outfitter

Montana's Master Angler
Livingston 406-222-2273
Species & Seasons: Rainbow Trout, Brown Trout, Cutthroat Trout Mar-Nov
Bodies of water: Yellowstone River, Yellowstone Nat'l. Park, Paradise Valley spring creeks, Paradise Valley lakes
Rates: Full day: $250(1-2)

Call between: 8am-9pm
Provides: Beverages, lunch
Handicapped equipped: Yes

Running M Outfitters
Big Timber 406-932-6121
Species & Seasons Rainbow Trout, Cutthroat Trout, Brook Trout all year, Golden Trout July-Aug
Bodies of water: Yellowstone River, Boulder River, Stillwater River, High Country Lakes, various other streams and private ponds
Rates: Ranch style trips(cost per day pp): $150(2-4), $100(5-6) Children under 6 free, many options available
Call between: Before 9am-After 9pm
Provides: Beverages, lunch
Handicapped equipped: Yes, depends on handicap
Certifications: FOAM, MOG, USFS, DSL, BLM, MBO licensed, insured

Roy Senter
Livingston 406-222-3775
.... 222-0904
Species & Seasons: Trout Jan-Dec
Bodies of water: Yellowstone River
Rates: Full day: $250(1-2)
Call between: 6pm-9pm
Provides: Fly rod/reel, rain gear, beverages, lunch
Handicapped equipped: No

Skyline Guide Service
Cooke City 406-838-2380
Species & Seasons: Trout June-Oct
Bodies of water: Yellowstone Nat'l. Park, (Slough Creek, Pebble Creek, Cache Creek, Lamar River), Yellowstone River
Rates: Full day: $125(1), $250(2)
Call between: Anytime
Provides: Beverages, lunch
Handicapped equipped:
Certifications: MOGA, licensed, insured

Stillwaters Outfitting
Billings 406-652-8111
Species & Seasons: Rainbow Trout, Brown Trout April-Nov
Bodies of water: Bighorn River, Yellowstone River, Rock Creek, Yellowstone Nat'l. Park
Rates: Float trips: Full day: $210(1), $275(2), Fly fishing instruction
Call between: 6pm-10pm
Provides: Fly rod/reel, beverages, lunch
Handicapped equipped: Yes
Certifications: Licensed MT Outfitter, Certified CPR, First aid

YOUR SILENT FISHING PARTNER

MONTANA — YELLOWSTONE RIVER

Tite Line Fishing
Townsend 406-266-3225
Species & Seasons: Trout Mar-Oct
Bodies of water: Missouri River, Yellowstone River, Gallitan River, Jefferson River, Madison River
Rates: Full day: $190(1), $265(2)
Provides: Fly rod/reel, rain gear, beverages, lunch

Trout Fishing Only
Hamilton 800-363-2408
Species & Seasons: Trout June-Nov
Bodies of water: Bitterroot River, Big Hole River, Beaverhead River, Madison River, Yellowstone River, Clark Fork River
Rates: Half day: $200(1-2), Full day: $270(1-2)
Call between: 7pm-10pm
Provides: Fly rod/reel, lunch
Handicapped equipped: Yes

LODGES...

Fly Fisherman's Lodge
Livingston 406-222-7437
Seasons: Closed Nov to Feb
Guides: Yes
Bodies of Water: Yellowstone River, Boulder River, Gallatin River, Madison River, Stillwater River
Types of fishing: Fly fishing
Available: Guide services, food

Mountain Sky Guest Ranch
Bozeman 800-548-3392
Guest Capacity: 75
Handicapped equipped: Yes
Seasons: End of May to Oct 1
Rates: Starting $1,715/week (1995 rates)
Contact: Laura Asbell
Guides: Yes
Bodies of Water: Yellowstone River, Spring Creeks
Types of fishing: Fly fishing
Available: Fishing instruction, family activities, children's program

NEBRASKA

1. Conestoga Lake
2. Elkhorn River
3. Elwood Reservoir
4. Harlan County Lake
5. Jeffrey Reservoir
6. Johnson Reservoir
7. Lake McConaughy
8. Loup River
9. Maloney Reservoir
10. Merritt Reservoir
11. Missouri River
12. Pawnee Lake
13. Platte River
14. Sherman Reservoir
15. Sutherland Reservoir
16. Valentine NWR Lakes

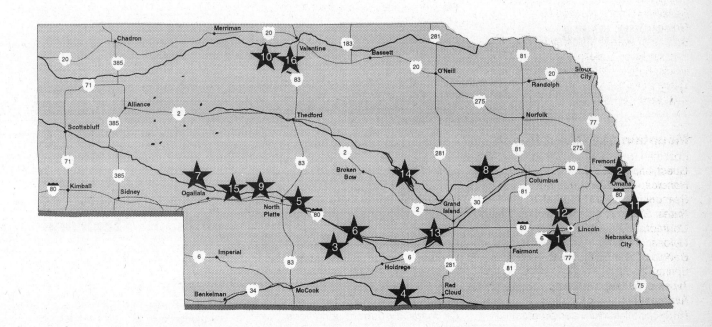

NEBRASKA

CONESTOGA LAKE — JOHNSON RESERVOIR

CONESTOGA LAKE

BAIT & TACKLE...

Fish Tackle & Supply
Lincoln 402-476-1710
Hours: 7am-7pm
Carries: Live bait, lures, flies, maps, rods, reels, licenses
Bodies of water: Conestoga Lake, Pawnee Lake
Guides: No
OK to call for current conditions: Yes
Contact: O.J. or Quintin Fish

Wolf Tackle Supply
Lincoln 402-464-4265
Hours: 9:30am-6pm, closed Sun.
Carries: Lures, flies, maps, rods, reels, licenses
Bodies of water: Missouri River, Branched Oak Lake, Conestoga Lake, Pawnee Lake, Stagecoach Lake, Wagon Trail Lake, Twin Lakes
Guides: Yes
OK to call for current conditions: Yes
Contact: Roger Wolf

ELKHORN RIVER

BAIT & TACKLE...

The Bait Dock
Omaha 402-697-9730
Hours: 7:30am-7pm Tues.-Thrus., 7:30am-8pm Fri., 6am-8pm Sat., 6am-6pm Sun., closed Mon. (summer hours)
Carries: Live bait, lures, flies, maps, rods, reels, licenses
Bodies of water: Missouri River, Platte River, Elkhorn River, Cunningham Lake, Standing Bear Lake
Services & Products: Food, beverages, oil, repair services, fishing consultation, line winding, special orders
Guides: No
OK to call for current conditions: Yes
Contact: Mack Robertson

ELWOOD RESERVOIR

BAIT & TACKLE...

Krazy Dicks
728 8th Street
Gothenburg 69138
Hours: 6am-10pm
Carries: Live bait, lures, rods, reels, licenses
Bodies of water: Jeffery Res., Johnson Res., Midway Lake, Elwood Res.
Services & Products: Food, beverages, gas/oil
Guides: Yes
OK to call for current conditions: Yes

Randy Steward's Collectibles Bait & Tackle Shop
Lexington 308-324-5873
Hours: 8am-8pm, closed Mon.
Carries: Live bait, lures, flies, maps, rods, reels, licenses
Bodies of water: Johnson Res., Elwood Res., Plum Creek, Gallagher Cayon State Rec. Area
Services & Products: Guide services, food, beverages, fishing instruction
Guides: Yes
OK to call for current conditions: Yes
Contact: Randy Seward

HARLAN COUNTY LAKE

BAIT & TACKLE...

L & N Live Bait Farm
Grand Island 308-384-3159
Hours: 7am-8pm
Carries: Live bait, lures, flies, maps, rods, reels, licenses
Bodies of water: Sherman Res., Harlan County Lake, Platte River, Loup River
Services & Products: Beverages, fishing instruction
Guides: No
OK to call for current conditions: Yes
Contact: Larry L. Pollock

MARINAS...

Patterson Harbor, Inc.
Republican City 308-799-4600
Hours: 7am-10pm, closed Nov.-Mar.
Carries: Live bait, lures, maps, rods, reels, licenses
Bodies of water: Harlan County Lake
Services & Products: Boat rentals, lodging, boat ramp, food, beverages, gas/oil, fishing instruction, repair services
Guides: Yes
OK to call for current conditions: Yes

JEFFERY RESERVOIR

BAIT & TACKLE...

Krazy Dicks
728 8th Street
Gothenburg 69138
Hours: 6am-10pm
Carries: Live bait, lures, rods, reels, licenses
Bodies of water: Jeffery Res., Johnson Res., Midway Lake, Elwood Res.
Services & Products: Food, beverages, gas/oil
Guides: Yes
OK to call for current conditions: Yes
Contact: Larry Nichols

Minnow Bucket
North Platte 308-532-2676
Hours: 6am-10pm
Carries: Live bait, lures, maps, rods, reels, licenses
Bodies of water: Lake McConaughy, Maloney Res., Sutherland Res., Jeffrey Res., Johnson Res.
Services & Products: Food, beverages, fishing instruction
Guides: Yes
OK to call for current conditions: Yes
Contact: Don Garrick

JOHNSON RESERVOIR

BAIT & TACKLE...

Krazy Dicks
728 8th Street
Gothenburg 69138
Hours: 6am-10pm
Carries: Live bait, lures, rods, reels, licenses
Bodies of water: Jeffery Res., Johnson Res., Midway Lake, Elwood Res.
Services & Products: Food, beverages, gas/oil
Guides: Yes
OK to call for current conditions: Yes
Contact: Larry Nichols

JOHNSON RESERVOIR - MERRITT RESERVOIR — NEBRASKA

Minnow Bucket
North Platte 308-532-2676
Hours: 6am-10pm
Carries: Live bait, lures, maps, rods, reels, licenses
Bodies of water: Lake McConaughy, Maloney Res., Sutherland Res., Jeffrey Res., Johnson Res.
Services & Products: Food, beverages, fishing instruction
Guides: Yes
OK to call for current conditions: Yes
Contact: Don Garrick

Randy Steward's Collectibles Bait & Tackle Shop
Lexington 308-324-5873
Hours: 8am-8pm, closed Mon.
Carries: Live bait, lures, flies, maps, rods, reels, licenses
Bodies of water: Johnson Res., Elwood Res., Plum Creek, Gallagher Cayon State Rec. Area
Services & Products: Guide services, food, beverages, fishing instruction
Guides: Yes
OK to call for current conditions: Yes
Contact: Randy Seward

LAKE MCCONAUGHY

BAIT & TACKLE...

Minnow Bucket
North Platte 308-532-2676
Hours: 6am-10pm
Carries: Live bait, lures, maps, rods, reels, licenses
Bodies of water: Lake McConaughy, Maloney Res., Sutherland Res., Jeffrey Res., Johnson Res.
Services & Products: Food, beverages, fishing instruction
Guides: Yes
OK to call for current conditions: Yes
Contact: Don Garrick

Northriver Bait Tackle & Trade
Sutherland 308-386-2550
Hours: 8am-10pm
Carries: Live bait, lures, flies, maps, rods, reels, licenses
Bodies of water: Sutherland Res., Lake McConaughy, Diamond Bar Lake, Platte River, public power canals
Services & Products: Food, beverages, fishing instruction, repair services
Guides: Yes
OK to call for current conditions: Yes
Contact: Steve or Deb Smith

Spahn Marine
Big Springs 308-889-3531
Hours: 8am-5:30pm, closed Sun.
Carries: Live bait, lures, maps, rods, reels, licenses
Bodies of water: Lake McConaughy, Sutherland Res., North Platte River, Lake Ogallala
Services & Products: Fishing instruction, repair services, boat sales
OK to call for current conditions: Yes

LODGES...

North Shore Lodge
Lemoyne 308-355-2222
Guest Capacity: 64+ (44 extra large campsites)
Handicapped equipped: No
Seasons: Memorial Day to Labor Day
Rates: $40-$130/day
Contact: Sue or Gayle
Guides: Yes
Species & Seasons: Trout, LM Bass, Walleye, Catfish, Striped Bass all year
Bodies of Water: Lake McConaughy
Types of fishing: Fly fishing, light tackle, wading
Available: Licenses, bait, tackle, boat rentals

LOUP RIVER

BAIT & TACKLE...

Bobbers Bait & Camp Supply
Columbus 402-564-6773
Hours: 6am-10:30pm
Carries: Live bait, lures, flies, maps, rods, reels, licenses
Bodies of water: Loup Canal, Loup River, Platte River, several lakes
Services & Products: Guide services (airboat), food, beverages, fishing instruction, repair services, camp supplies
Guides: Yes
OK to call for current conditions: Yes
Contact: James or Bobber Kaspar

L & N Live Bait Farm
Grand Island 308-384-3159
Hours: 7am-8pm
Carries: Live bait, lures, flies, maps, rods, reels, licenses
Bodies of water: Sherman Res., Harlan County Lake, Platte River, Loup River
Services & Products: Beverages, fishing instruction
Guides: No
OK to call for current conditions: Yes
Contact: Larry L. Pollock

MALONEY RESERVOIR

BAIT & TACKLE...

Minnow Bucket
North Platte 308-532-2676
Hours: 6am-10pm
Carries: Live bait, lures, maps, rods, reels, licenses
Bodies of water: Lake McConaughy, Maloney Res., Sutherland Res., Jeffrey Res., Johnson Res.
Services & Products: Food, beverages, fishing instruction
Guides: Yes
OK to call for current conditions: Yes
Contact: Don Garrick

MERRITT RESERVOIR

LODGES...

Merritt Resort
Valentine 402-376-3437
Guest Capacity: 15 cabins
Handicapped equipped: Yes, partially
Seasons: All year
Rates: $61-$91/night
Contact: Jon T. Davenport
Guides: Yes
Species & Seasons: Walleye May-Aug, LM Bass April-Sept, Muskellunge, Crappie May-Sept, Perch, Bluegill June-Sept, Catfish May-Oct
Bodies of Water: Merritt Reservoir, Valentine NWR Lakes (Hackberry lake, Dads Lake, Big Alkali Lake, Pelican Lake), Snake River
Types of fishing: Fly fishing, light tackle, heavy tackle, wading
Available: Fishing instruction, licenses, bait, tackle, boat rentals, family activities

NEBRASKA

MISSOURI RIVER - PLATTE RIVER

MISSOURI RIVER

BAIT & TACKLE...

The Bait Dock
Omaha 402-697-9730
Hours: 7:30am-7pm Tues.-Thrus., 7:30am-8pm Fri., 6am-8pm Sat., 6am-6pm Sun., closed Mon. (summer hours)
Carries: Live bait, lures, flies, maps, rods, reels, licenses
Bodies of water: Missouri River, Platte River, Elkhorn River, Cunningham Lake, Standing Bear Lake
Services & Products: Food, beverages, oil, repair services, fishing consultation, line winding, special orders
Guides: No
OK to call for current conditions: Yes
Contact: Mack Robertson

Genes Service & Sports Center
Plattsmouth 402-296-4190
Hours: 6am-8pm
Carries: Live bait, lures, flies, rods, reels, licenses
Bodies of water: Platte River, Missouri River
Services & Products: Food, beverages, gas/oil, fishing instruction, repair services
OK to call for current conditions: Yes
Contact: Gene Meier

Tackle Box
Omaha 402-571-3304
Hours: 8am-8pm
Carries: Live bait, lures, maps, rods, reels, licenses
Bodies of water: Cunningham Lake, Standing Bear Lake, Missouri River, Summit Lake, DeSoto Bend NWR
Services & Products: Beverages, fishing instruction, repair services, archery
Guides: Yes
OK to call for current conditions: Yes
Contact: Anyone

Wolf Tackle Supply
Lincoln 402-464-4265
Hours: 9:30am-6pm, closed Sun.
Carries: Lures, flies, maps, rods, reels, licenses
Bodies of water: Missouri River, Branched Oak Lake, Conestoga Lake, Pawnee Lake, Stagecoach Lake, Wagon Trail Lake, Twin Lakes
Guides: Yes
OK to call for current conditions: Yes
Contact: Roger Wolf

PAWNEE LAKE

BAIT & TACKLE...

Fish Tackle & Supply
Lincoln 402-476-1710
Hours: 7am-7pm
Carries: Live bait, lures, flies, maps, rods, reels, licenses
Bodies of water: Conestoga Lake, Pawnee Lake
Guides: No
OK to call for current conditions: Yes
Contact: O.J. or Quintin Fish

Wolf Tackle Supply
Lincoln 402-464-4265
Hours: 9:30am-6pm, closed Sun.
Carries: Lures, flies, maps, rods, reels, licenses
Bodies of water: Missouri River, Branched Oak Lake, Conestoga Lake, Pawnee Lake, Stagecoach Lake, Wagon Trail Lake, Twin Lakes
Guides: Yes
OK to call for current conditions: Yes
Contact: Roger Wolf

PLATTE RIVER

BAIT & TACKLE...

The Bait Dock
Omaha 402-697-9730
Hours: 7:30am-7pm Tues.-Thrus., 7:30am-8pm Fri., 6am-8pm Sat., 6am-6pm Sun., closed Mon. (summer hours)
Carries: Live bait, lures, flies, maps, rods, reels, licenses
Bodies of water: Missouri River, Platte River, Elkhorn River, Cunningham Lake, Standing Bear Lake
Services & Products: Food, beverages, oil, repair services, fishing consultation, line winding, special orders
Guides: No
OK to call for current conditions: Yes
Contact: Mack Robertson

Bait Shack
Hastings 402-463-7065
Hours: 7am-8pm
Carries: Live bait, lures, flies, maps, rods, reels
Bodies of water: Sand Pits, Platte River, Blue River, Republican River
Services & Products: Fishing instruction, repair services
Guides: Yes
OK to call for current conditions: Yes
Contact: Red or Daren Aldrich

Bobbers Bait & Camp Supply
Columbus 402-564-6773
Hours: 6am-10:30pm
Carries: Live bait, lures, flies, maps, rods, reels, licenses
Bodies of water: Loup Canal, Loup River, Platte River, several lakes
Services & Products: Guide services (airboat), food, beverages, fishing instruction, repair services, camp supplies
Guides: Yes
OK to call for current conditions: Yes
Contact: James or Bobber Kaspar

Genes Service & Sports Center
Plattsmouth 402-296-4190
Hours: 6am-8pm
Carries: Live bait, lures, flies, rods, reels, licenses
Bodies of water: Platte River, Missouri River
Services & Products: Food, beverages, gas/oil, fishing instruction, repair services
OK to call for current conditions: Yes
Contact: Gene Meier

L & N Live Bait Farm
Grand Island 308-384-3159
Hours: 7am-8pm
Carries: Live bait, lures, flies, maps, rods, reels, licenses
Bodies of water: Sherman Res., Harlan County Lake, Platte River, Loup River
Services & Products: Beverages, fishing instruction
Guides: No
OK to call for current conditions: Yes
Contact: Larry L. Pollock

Northriver Bait Tackle & Trade
Sutherland 308-386-2550
Hours: 8am-10pm
Carries: Live bait, lures, flies, maps, rods, reels, licenses
Bodies of water: Sutherland Res., Lake McConaughy, Diamond Bar Lake, Platte River, public power canals
Services & Products: Food, beverages, fishing instruction, repair services
Guides: Yes
OK to call for current conditions: Yes
Contact: Steve or Deb Smith

PLATTE RIVER - VALENTINE NWR   NEBRASKA

Spahn Marine
Big Springs 308-889-3531
Hours: 8am-5:30pm, closed Sun.
Carries: Live bait, lures, maps, rods, reels, licenses
Bodies of water: Lake McConaughy, Sutherland Res., North Platte River, Lake Ogallala
Services & Products: Fishing instruction, repair services, boat sales
OK to call for current conditions: Yes

SHERMAN RESERVOIR

BAIT & TACKLE...

Dub's Sports
Grand Island 308-382-5467
Hours: 9am-8pm
Carries: Live bait, lures, flies, maps, rods, reels, licenses
Bodies of water: Sherman Res., Johnson Res., Harlan County Lake, Platte River, Loup River
Guides: No
OK to call for current conditions: Yes
Contact: Dick Dubas

L & N Live Bait Farm
Grand Island 308-384-3159
Hours: 7am-8pm
Carries: Live bait, lures, flies, maps, rods, reels, licenses
Bodies of water: Sherman Res., Harlan County Lake, Platte River, Loup River
Services & Products: Beverages, fishing instruction
Guides: No
OK to call for current conditions: Yes
Contact: Larry L. Pollock

SUTHERLAND RESERVOIR

BAIT & TACKLE...

Minnow Bucket
North Platte 308-532-2676
Hours: 6am-10pm
Carries: Live bait, lures, maps, rods, reels, licenses
Bodies of water: Lake McConaughy, Maloney Res., Sutherland Res., Jeffrey Res., Johnson Res.
Services & Products: Food, beverages, fishing instruction
Guides: Yes
OK to call for current conditions: Yes
Contact: Don Garrick

Northriver Bait Tackle & Trade
Sutherland 308-386-2550
Hours: 8am-10pm
Carries: Live bait, lures, flies, maps, rods, reels, licenses
Bodies of water: Sutherland Res., Lake McConaughy, Diamond Bar Lake, Platte River, public power canals
Services & Products: Food, beverages, fishing instruction, repair services
Guides: Yes
OK to call for current conditions: Yes
Contact: Steve or Deb Smith

Spahn Marine
Big Springs 308-889-3531
Hours: 8am-5:30pm, closed Sun.
Carries: Live bait, lures, maps, rods, reels, licenses
Bodies of water: Lake McConaughy, Sutherland Res., North Platte River, Lake Ogallala
Services & Products: Fishing instruction, repair services, boat sales
OK to call for current conditions: Yes

VALENTINE NWR

LODGES...

Merritt Resort
Valentine 402-376-3437
Guest Capacity: 15 cabins
Handicapped equipped: Yes, partially
Seasons: All year
Rates: $61-$91/night
Contact: Jon T. Davenport
Guides: Yes
Species & Seasons: Walleye May-Aug, LM Bass April-Sept, Muskellunge, Crappie May-Sept, Perch, Bluegill June-Sept, Catfish May-Oct
Bodies of Water: Merritt Reservoir, Valentine NWR Lakes (Hackberry lake, Dads Lake, Big Alkali Lake, Pelican Lake), Snake River
Types of fishing: Fly fishing, light tackle, heavy tackle, wading
Available: Fishing instruction, licenses, bait, tackle, boat rentals, family activities

YOUR SILENT FISHING PARTNER

The Angler's Yellow Pages lets you
tap the fishing information grapevine

NEVADA

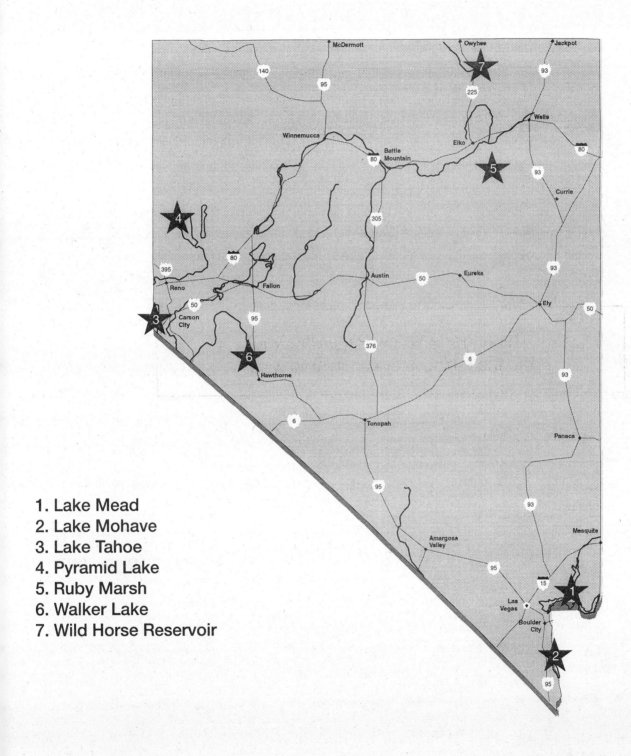

1. Lake Mead
2. Lake Mohave
3. Lake Tahoe
4. Pyramid Lake
5. Ruby Marsh
6. Walker Lake
7. Wild Horse Reservoir

NEVADA

LAKE MEAD - WILD HORSE RESERVOIR

LAKE MEAD

BAIT & TACKLE...

Blue Lake Bait & Tackle
Las Vegas 702-452-8299
Hours: 4am-8pm
Carries: Live bait, lures, flies, maps, rods, reels, licenses
Bodies of water: Lake Mead, Lake Mojave, Lake Havasu (AZ)
Services & Products: Guide services, food, beverages, fishing instruction, repair services
Guides: Yes
OK to call for current conditions: Yes
Contact: Don Sollberger

LAKE MOJAVE

BAIT & TACKLE...

Blue Lake Bait & Tackle
Las Vegas 702-452-8299
Hours: 4am-8pm
Carries: Live bait, lures, flies, maps, rods, reels, licenses
Bodies of water: Lake Mead, Lake Mojave, Lake Havasu (AZ)
Services & Products: Guide services, food, beverages, fishing instruction, repair services
Guides: Yes
OK to call for current conditions: Yes
Contact: Don Sollberger

LAKE TAHOE

CHARTERS...

Pyramid-Tahoe Fishing Charters
Reno 702-852-FISH
Species & Seasons: Cutthroat Trout Oct-June, Mackinaw, Rainbow Trout, Brown Trout, Kakanee Salmon June-Sept
Bodies of water: Pyramid Lake, Lake Tahoe (north shore)
Rates: Half day: $60(1), $120(2), Full day: $90(1), $180(2), up to 6 people
Call between: 7am-9pm
Provides: Light tackle, fly rod/reel, lures, bait, rain gear, 1 day fishing license, I bring the coffee!
Handicapped equipped: Yes
Certifications: ORVIS, USCG

PYRAMID LAKE

BAIT & TACKLE...

Fish Connection
Gardnerville 702-782-4734
Hours: 8:30am-6pm, closed Sun.
Carries: Live bait, lures, flies, maps, rods, reels
Bodies of water: Pyramid Lake, Walker Lake, Lake Tahoe, East Fork Walker River, West Fork Walker River, East Fork Carson River, West Fork Carson River
Services & Products: Guide services, fishing instruction, repair services, rod building, full line fly shop
Guides: Yes
OK to call for current conditions: Yes
Contact: Mike or Sue Solgat

CHARTERS...

Pyramid-Tahoe Fishing Charters
Reno 702-852-FISH
Species & Seasons: Cutthroat Trout Oct-June, Mackinaw, Rainbow Trout, Brown Trout, Kakanee Salmon June-Sept
Bodies of water: Pyramid Lake, Lake Tahoe (north shore)
Rates: Half day: $60(1), $120(2), Full day: $90(1), $180(2), up to 6 people
Call between: 7am-9pm
Provides: Light tackle, fly rod/reel, lures, bait, rain gear, 1 day fishing license, I bring the coffee!
Handicapped equipped: Yes
Certifications: ORVIS, USCG

RUBY MARSH

BAIT & TACKLE...

Nevada Jim's Outdoor Sports
Elko 702-753-5467
Hours: 9:30am-6pm Mon.-Thurs., 9:30am-7pm Fri., 8am-5pm Sat., closed Sun.
Carries: Live bait, lures, flies, maps, rods, reels
Bodies of water: Wild Horse Res., South Fork Res., Ruby Marsh, Ruby High Lakes
Guides: No
OK to call for current conditions: Yes
Contact: Jim

GUIDES...

Elko Guide Service
Elko 702-738-7539
Species & Seasons: LM Bass May-Oct, SM Bass April-Oct, Rainbow Trout all year, Brook Trout July-Sept, Brown Trout April-Oct
Bodies of water: Ruby Marsh, Ruby Mountain High Lakes, Wildhorse Res., Wilson Res., Southfork Res., Crittenden Res.
Rates: Full day: $150(1), $300(2), pack trips, cabin rentals
Call between: Anytime
Provides: Fly rod/reel, lures, beverages, lunch
Handicapped equipped: No

WALKER LAKE

BAIT & TACKLE...

Fish Connection
Gardnerville 702-782-4734
Hours: 8:30am-6pm, closed Sun.
Carries: Live bait, lures, flies, maps, rods, reels
Bodies of water: Pyramid Lake, Walker Lake, Lake Tahoe, East Fork Walker River, West Fork Walker River, East Fork Carson River, West Fork Carson River
Services & Products: Guide services, fishing instruction, repair services, rod building, full line fly shop
Guides: Yes
OK to call for current conditions: Yes
Contact: Mike or Sue Solgat

WILD HORSE RESERVOIR

BAIT & TACKLE...

Nevada Jim's Outdoor Sports
Elko 702-753-5467
Hours: 9:30am-6pm Mon.-Thurs., 9:30am-7pm Fri., 8am-5pm Sat., closed Sun.
Carries: Live bait, lures, flies, maps, rods, reels
Bodies of water: Wild Horse Res., South Fork Res., Ruby Marsh, Ruby High Lakes
Guides: No
OK to call for current conditions: Yes
Contact: Jim

WILD HORSE RESERVOIR
NEVADA

GUIDES...

Elko Guide Service
Elko 702-738-7539
Species & Seasons: LM Bass May-Oct, SM Bass April-Oct, Rainbow Trout all year, Brook Trout July-Sept, Brown Trout April-Oct
Bodies of water: Ruby Marsh, Ruby Mountain High Lakes, Wildhorse Res., Wilson Res., Southfork Res., Crittenden Res.
Rates: Full day: $150(1), $300(2), pack trips, cabin rentals
Call between: Anytime
Provides: Fly rod/reel, lures, beverages, lunch
Handicapped equipped: No

Know before you go...

Look in the Angler's Yellow Pages

NEW HAMPSHIRE

1. Atlantic Ocean
2. Contoocook River
3. Gulf of Maine
4. Lake Winnipesaukee
5. Lake Winnisquam
6. Newfound Lake
7. Squam Lake

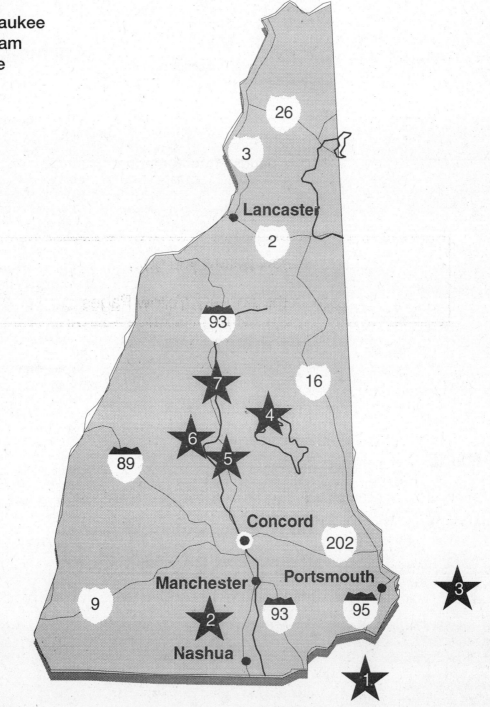

NEW HAMPSHIRE

ATLANTIC OCEAN - SQUAM LAKE

ATLANTIC OCEAN

CHARTERS...

Cap'n Sav's Charters
Rye 603-964-6967
Species & Seasons: Striped Bass June-Sept, Bluefish July-Sept, Mackerel May-June
Bodies of water: Atlantic Ocean
Rates: Half day: $150(4), Full day: $300(4)
Call between: 8am-6pm
Provides: Light tackle, heavy tackle, bait
Handicapped equipped: No
Certifications: USCG

CONTOOCOOK RIVER

LODGES...

Woodbound Inn
Woodbound Road Route 202
Jaffrey 03452
Guest Capacity: 100
Handicapped equipped: Yes
Seasons: All year
Rates: $69-$99/day
Contact: Rick Kuhlmorgen
Guides: Yes
Bodies of Water: Lake Contoocook, Woodbound Inn's Trout Pond, Gilmore Pond, Contoocook River
Types of fishing: Light tackle
Available: Tackle, family activities, meeting banquet facilities, lake front cabins, 9 hole golf course

GULF OF MAINE

CHARTERS...

Capt. Raymond Maimone
Rye 603-926-0264
Species & Seasons: Codfish April-June, Mackerel May-July, Striped Bass May-Oct, Bluefish June-Oct
Bodies of water: Gulf of Maine, from Rye Harbor N.H.
Rates: Full day: $300(6)
Call between: 5am-8pm
Provides: Light tackle, heavy tackle, fly rod/reel, lures, bait
Handicapped equipped: Yes
Certifications: Merchant Marine Captain

LAKE WINNIPESAUKEE

BAIT & TACKLE...

Waldron's Live Bait & Sport
Meredith 603-279-3152
Hours: 5:30am-8pm
Carries: Live bait, lures, flies, maps, rods, reels, licenses
Bodies of water: Lake Winnipesaukee, Squam Lake, Lake Winnisquam
Services & Products: Guide services, food, beverages, fishing instruction, repair services
Guides: Yes
OK to call for current conditions: Yes
Contact: Paul Belville or Justin Morton

MARINAS...

Silver Sands Motel & Marina
Gilford 603-293-7200
Hours: Varies
Bodies of water: Lake Winnipesaukee, Lake Winnisquam, Squam Lake, Newfound Lake
Services & Products: Boat rentals, lodging, boat ramp, gas/oil
Guides: Yes
OK to call for current conditions: No

LAKE WINNISQUAM

BAIT & TACKLE...

Sarge's Country Store
Winnisquam 603-542-4329
Hours: 4am-10pm
Carries: Live bait, lures, maps, rods, reels, licenses
Bodies of water: Lake Winnisquam
Services & Products: Boat ramp, food, beverages, fishing instruction
OK to call for current conditions: Yes

Waldron's Live Bait & Sport
Meredith 603-279-3152
Hours: 5:30am-8pm
Carries: Live bait, lures, flies, maps, rods, reels, licenses
Bodies of water: Lake Winnipesaukee, Squam Lake, Lake Winnisquam
Services & Products: Guide services, food, beverages, fishing instruction, repair services
Guides: Yes
OK to call for current conditions: Yes
Contact: Paul Belville or Justin Morton

MARINAS...

Silver Sands Motel & Marina
Gilford 603-293-7200
Hours: Varies
Bodies of water: Lake Winnipesaukee, Lake Winnisquam, Squam Lake, Newfound Lake
Services & Products: Boat rentals, lodging, boat ramp, gas/oil
Guides: Yes
OK to call for current conditions: No

NEWFOUND LAKE

MARINAS...

Silver Sands Motel & Marina
Gilford 603-293-7200
Hours: Varies
Bodies of water: Lake Winnipesaukee, Lake Winnisquam, Squam Lake, Newfound Lake
Services & Products: Boat rentals, lodging, boat ramp, gas/oil
Guides: Yes
OK to call for current conditions: No

SQUAM LAKE

BAIT & TACKLE...

Waldron's Live Bait & Sport
Meredith 603-279-3152
Hours: 5:30am-8pm
Carries: Live bait, lures, flies, maps, rods, reels, licenses
Bodies of water: Lake Winnipesaukee, Squam Lake, Lake Winnisquam
Services & Products: Guide services, food, beverages, fishing instruction, repair services
Guides: Yes
OK to call for current conditions: Yes
Contact: Paul Belville or Justin Morton

SQUAM LAKE
NEW HAMPSHIRE

MARINAS...

Silver Sands Motel & Marina
Gilford 603-293-7200
Hours: Varies
Bodies of water: Lake Winnipesaukee, Lake Winnisquam, Squam Lake, Newfound Lake
Services & Products: Boat rentals, lodging, boat ramp, gas/oil
Guides: Yes
OK to call for current conditions: No

Look in the Location Index
for a complete list of fishing areas

NEW JERSEY

1. Absecon Inlet
2. Atlantic Ocean
3. Barnegat Bay
4. Barnegat Inlet
5. Cape May
6. Delaware Bay
7. Delaware River
8. Great Bay
9. Greenwood Lake
10. Lake Hopatcong
11. Maurice River
12. Pay Lake
13. Raritan Bay
14. Round Valley Reservoir
15. Sandy Hook Bay
16. Shark River
17. Spruce Run Reservoir
18. Toms River
19. Union Lake

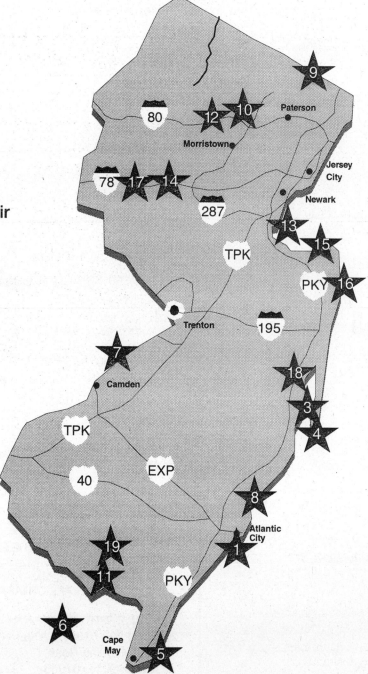

NEW JERSEY
ABSECON INLET - ATLANTIC OCEAN

ABSECON INLET

MARINAS...

Bayside Bait & Tackle
Brigantine 609-266-2819
Hours: 6am-6pm
Carries: Live bait, lures, flies, maps, rods, reels
Bodies of water: Absecon Inlet, Atlantic Ocean
Services & Products: Charter boat service, food, beverages, gas/oil, repair services, waverunner rentals
Guides: Yes
OK to call for current conditions: Yes
Contact: Sam Lionelli

Kammerman's Atlantic City Marina
Atlantic City 609-348-8418
Hours: 7am-7pm
Carries: Live bait, lures, maps, rods, reels
Bodies of water: Absecon Inlet, Absecon Bar, Great Bay, Atlantic Ocean
Services & Products: Charter boat service, beverages, gas/oil
Guides: Yes
OK to call for current conditions: Yes
Contact: Butch or Judy

ATLANTIC OCEAN

BAIT & TACKLE...

Art Beck's Star Auto
Irvington 201-372-7827
Hours: 8am-6pm, 6am-6pm Sat.
Carries: Live bait, lures, flies, maps, rods, reels, licenses
Bodies of water: Atlantic Ocean, Essex Lakes
Guides: Yes
OK to call for current conditions: Yes
Contact: Art Beck, Jr.

Brigantine Bait & Tackle
Brigantine 609-266-7011
Hours: 6am-6pm (May-Oct.)
Carries: Live bait, lures, maps, rods, reels
Bodies of water: Atlantic Ocean
Services & Products: Boat ramp, food, beverages, gas/oil, fishing instruction, repair services, marine supplies
Guides: Yes
OK to call for current conditions: Yes
Contact: Paula Martin

Downe's Bait & Tackle
Bayville 908-269-0137
Hours: 5:30am-9pm (seasonal)
Carries: Live bait, lures, flies, maps, rods, reels, licenses
Bodies of water: Barnegat Bay, Atlantic Ocean
Services & Products: Boat rentals, boat ramp, food, beverages
Guides: Yes
OK to call for current conditions: Yes

Fishermen's Headquarters Inc.
Ship Bottom 609-494-5739
Hours:
Carries: Live bait, lures, flies, maps, rods, reels, licenses
Bodies of water: Atlantic Ocean, Barnegat Light Inlet, Little Egg Inlet
Services & Products: Beverages, fishing instruction, repair services, frozen baits
Guides: Yes
OK to call for current conditions: Yes

Jim's Bait & Tackle
Cape May 609-884-3900
Hours: 5am-9pm
Carries: Live bait, lures, flies, maps, rods, reels
Bodies of water: Delaware Bay, Atlantic Ocean, Cape May Canal, Cape May Harbor
Services & Products: Guide services, charter boat service, beverages, fishing instruction, repair services
Guides: Yes
OK to call for current conditions: Yes
Contact: Jim or Cheri Wallace

Nautical Shop
Toms River 908-270-1030
Hours: 6am-6pm
Carries: Live bait, lures, flies, maps, rods, reels
Bodies of water: Toms River, Atlantic Ocean, Barnegat Bay
Services & Products: Block ice, cube ice
Guides: Yes
OK to call for current conditions: Yes
Contact: Robert S. Oehme

Schupp's Landing
Highlands 908-872-1479
Hours: 6am-8pm
Carries: Live bait, lures
Bodies of water: Shrewsbury River, Atlantic Ocean
Services & Products: Boat rentals, food, beverages, gas/oil
Guides: Yes
OK to call for current conditions: Yes
Contact: Al Schupp

CHARTERS...

Atlantic Star
Atl. Highlands 908-291-5508
Species & Seasons: Flounder Mar-May, Fluke May-Oct, Tautog, Sea Bass, Porgies, Ling Oct-Dec
Bodies of water: Shrewsbury River, Sandy Hook Bay, Raritan Bay, Atlantic Ocean
Rates: Open party fishing boat, reservations not required, but accepted. Mar-Oct: Half day: $20 pp, Oct-Dec: 3/4 day: $30 pp
Call between: 6pm-10pm
Provides: Bait, tackle available for rent
Handicapped equipped: Yes
Certifications: USCG

FISH P.T. GUIDE SERVICE
CAPT. PETE KELLEY
UPPER NY STATE AREA
LAKE CHAMPLAIN • ADIRONDACKS
LAKE ONTARIO

• For Information •
Call (201) 226-8380 or Write:
15 Gladding Road
Caldwell, NJ 07006

NEW YORK STATE

Ps. 107

ATLANTIC OCEAN — NEW JERSEY

Autumn Mist Charter
Fords 516-668-2661
Species & Seasons: Cod April-Nov, Striped Bass May-Nov, Shark, Tuna June-Oct, Bonito, Albacore July-Oct Dolphin July-Sept
Bodies of water: Atlantic Ocean
Rates: Half day: $350(1-6) inshore, Full day: $600(1-6) inshore, $800(1-6) offshore
Call between: 6pm-10pm
Provides: Light tackle, heavy tackle, fly rod/reel, lures, bait
Handicapped equipped: Yes
Certifications: USCG

Avalon Sportfishing Center
Avalon 609-861-5951
Species & Seasons: Bluefish May-October, Shark June-July, Tuna July-Sept, King Mackerel, Spanish Mackerel July-Oct, Striped Bass Oct-Nov
Bodies of water: Atlantic Ocean from Avalon N.J.
Rates: Inshore trolling: Half day: $350 (1-6), Full day: $450(1-6), Call for Offshore prices
Call between: 6 pm 10 pm
Provides: Light tackle, heavy tackle, lures, bait
Handicapped equipped: Yes
Certifications: USCG

Big Bill II
Croydon, PA 215-785-2567
Species & Seasons: Tuna, Fluke July-Oct, Bluefish May-Nov, Shark June-Oct, Sea Bass May-Nov
Bodies of water: Atlantic Ocean at Barnegat Light
Rates: Half day: $225(1), Full day: $315 and up
Call between: 9am-10pm
Provides: Light tackle, heavy tackle, lures, bait
Handicapped equipped: No
Certifications: USCG

Big Marie-S II
Avon 908-776-9354
Species & Seasons: Fluke May-Oct, Bluefish Oct-Dec
Bodies of water: Atlantic Ocean
Rates: Half day: $20(1)
Call between: 9am-7pm
Provides: Bait
Handicapped equipped: Yes

Bluefin Sportfishing
Jackson 908-367-6952
Species & Seasons: Shark June-July, Bluefin Tuna June-Aug, Yellowfin Tuna July-Oct, White Marlin, Blue Marlin July-Sept, Sea Bass April-Nov, Tautog Nov-July, Striped Bass Nov-Dec, Cod Nov-Jan
Bodies of water: Atlantic Ocean - Mud Hole, Hudson Canyon to Wilmington Canyon
Rates: Call for rates
Call between: 7pm-9:30pm
Provides: Light tackle, heavy tackle, lures, bait
Certifications: USCG

Catherine II
Wall 908-681-6577
Species & Seasons: Mackerel Jan-May, Blackfish May-June, Sea Bass June-Sept, Bluefish May-Nov, Fluke May-Oct, Bonito July-Sept, Albacore Sept-Oct, Blackfish Oct-Jan, Striped Bass Nov-Dec
Bodies of water: Atlantic Ocean
Rates: Varies
Call between: 9am-10pm
Provides: Light tackle, heavy tackle, bait
Handicapped equipped: Yes
Certifications: USCG

Christina II Charters
Tuckerton 609-296-0066
Species & Seasons: Striped Bass April-July/Oct-Jan, Fluke, Weakfish June-Oct, Mako Shark June-Aug
Bodies of water: Delaware Bay, Cape May, Atlantic Ocean, Great Bay
Rates: Full day: $300(1-3) Striped Bass
Call between: 7pm-10pm
Provides: Light tackle, heavy tackle, lures, bait

Connie Claire
Barnegat Light 609-494-6787
Species & Seasons: Sea Bass, Tague April-Dec, Bluefish May-Dec, Weakfish July-Nov, Tuna June-Sept, Albacore Sept-Nov, Bonito July-Sept, Fluke June-Oct
Bodies of water: Barnegat Bay, Barnegat Inlet, Atlantic Ocean
Rates: Full day: $450(8), $35 additional pp up to 15
Call between: 11am-11pm
Provides: Light tackle, heavy tackle, lures, bait
Handicapped equipped: Yes
Certifications: USCG

Crack-A-Dawn II
Cedar Grove 201-239-5821
.... 908-229-7096
Species & Seasons: Bluefish May-Oct, Striped Bass April-Dec, Fluke, Tautog May-Sept, Tautog, Tuna, Flounder, Sea Bass, Weakfish Aug-Oct, Shark June-Aug
Bodies of water: Sandy Hook area, Atlantic Ocean (to 20 miles offshore)
Rates: Charters to 21 people
Call between: 6pm-10pm
Provides: Light tackle, heavy tackle, lures, bait
Handicapped equipped: Yes
Certifications: USCG/FCC

Elixir Sportfishing Charters
Red Bank 908-741-9296
Species & Seasons: Fluke June-Sept, Bluefish June-Oct, Shark June-Aug, Tuna June-Oct, Wreck/Bottom May-Oct
Bodies of water: Atlantic Ocean, Mansaquan River, Barnegat Bay, Sandy Hook Bay, Raritan Bay
Rates: Varies: $350 and up
Call between: 9am-5pm
Provides: Light tackle, heavy tackle, fly rod/reel, lures, bait, rain gear
Handicapped equipped: Yes
Certifications: USCG

Finaddict
Edison 908-985-5275
Species & Seasons: Flounder April-May, Fluke May-Sept, Bluefish May-Nov, Shark June-Oct, Tuna July-Oct
Bodies of water: Mansaquan River, Raritan Bay, Atlantic Ocean
Rates: Full day: $250-$800(4)
Call between: 6pm-9pm
Provides: Light tackle, heavy tackle, fly rod/reel, lures, bait
Handicapped equipped: No

Hook-Up
Point Pleasant 908-899-1780
Species & Seasons: Tautog, Sea Bass April-Nov, Flounder April-May, Mackerel April-April, Bluefish May-Oct, Shark June-Oct, Bonito Aug-Oct, Tuna, Dolphin Aug-Nov
Bodies of water: Atlantic Ocean, Mansaquan Inlet
Rates: Call for rates
Call between: 8am-10pm
Provides: Light tackle, heavy tackle, lures, bait
Handicapped equipped: No

NEW JERSEY — ATLANTIC OCEAN

Jersey Bounce
Brighton Beach 609-494-0249
Species & Seasons: Mackerel April-May, Wreck Fishing May-June, Bluefish June-Oct, Shark June-Sept, Tuna, Marlin July-Sept, Fluke May-Oct
Bodies of water: Little Egg Harbor Bay, Atlantic Ocean
Rates: Call for rates
Call between: 6pm-9pm
Provides: Light tackle, heavy tackle, lures, bait, ice
Handicapped equipped: Yes
Certifications: USCG

Jersey Devil
Barnegat Light 609-494-0022
Species & Seasons: Wreck Fishing all year, Bluefish May-Dec, Flounder May-Oct, Tuna Aug-Nov
Bodies of water: Atlantic Ocean
Rates: Full day: $30(1)
Provides: Light tackle, heavy tackle, bait, beverages, lunch
Handicapped equipped: Yes
Certifications: USCG

June Bug
Moorestown 609-778-4257
Species & Seasons: Bluefish, Striped Bass, Wreck fishing May-Nov, Marlin, Tuna June-Sept
Bodies of water: Atlantic Ocean
Rates: Inshore: $500, Offshore: Day: $1000, Overnight: $1300
Call between: 9am-5pm
Provides: Light tackle, heavy tackle, lures, bait, ice
Handicapped equipped: No
Certifications: USCG

Leyte-Jo
Tuckerton 609-296-5322
Species & Seasons: Mackerel April-May, Bluefish May-Dec, Bonito June-Aug, Flounder June-Oct, Sea Bass May-Oct, Striped Bass Oct-Dec
Bodies of water: Atlantic Ocean, Great Bay, Lett Bay
Rates: Full day: $270(1-6)
Call between: 6pm-9pm
Provides: Light tackle, heavy tackle, lures, bait
Handicapped equipped: Yes
Certifications: USCG

Miss Michele III
Brick 908-899-4984
Species & Seasons: Flounder Mar-May, Mackerel Mar-April, Sea Bass, Tautog Mar-July, Fluke, Bluefish, Striped Bass, Tuna May-Oct
Bodies of water: Atlantic Ocean
Rates: Call for rates
Call between: Anytime
Provides: Light tackle, heavy tackle, lures, bait
Handicapped equipped: Yes
Certifications: USCG

No Limit
Holgate 609-492-1896
.... 730-1439
Species & Seasons: Tuna, Marlin, Dolphin, Swordfish, Shark June-Oct./ June-July, Bluefish May-Oct, Sea Bass, Tautog May-Nov, Fluke July-Oct
Bodies of water: Atlantic Ocean
Rates: Varies, all trips up to 6 people
Call between: 6pm-10pm
Provides: Light tackle, heavy tackle, lures, bait, beverages, lunch
Handicapped equipped: No
Certifications: USCG

Penguin
Phillipsburg 908-859-4384
Species & Seasons: Tautog, Sea Bass, Lingall year, Bluefish Summer, Mackerel Spring
Bodies of water: Atlantic Ocean, Barnegat Light area
Rates: Full day: $50(1)
Call between: 5pm-10pm
Provides: Heavy tackle, bait
Handicapped equipped: No
Certifications: USCG

Sportsfishing Charters:
"Jersey Bounce"
Shark • Marlin • Tuna • Fluke • Blues
Luhrs 290 Open SF
1-4 People • All tackle provided
Half Day/Full Day
CAPT. VIC BERTOTTI
Clean ○ Full Electronics
For Rates & Available dates:
609 494-0249
3rd & the Bay, Beach Haven, NJ

Phantom II
Leonardo 908-291-5688
Species & Seasons: Striped Bass May-Dec, Bluefish May-Oct, Fluke June-Oct
Bodies of water: Raritan Bay, Atlantic Ocean
Rates: Varies
Call between: Anytime
Provides: Light tackle, heavy tackle, lures, bait
Handicapped equipped: No
Certifications: USCG

Queen Mary
Point Pleasant 908-899-3766
Species & Seasons: Mackerel April-May, Bluefish May-Dec, Fluke June-Sept
Bodies of water: Atlantic Ocean
Rates: 3/4 day: $31(1), Fluke: Half day: $18
Call between: 5pm-7pm
Provides: Heavy tackle, lures, bait
Handicapped equipped: No
Certifications: USCG

Rambunctious
Riverton 609-829-1813
Species & Seasons: Striped Bass April-June/Oct-Dec, Fluke, Weakfish May-Oct, Bluefish May-Nov, Sea Bass April-Nov, Shark May-Oct, Tuna, Marlin, Dolphin June-Oct
Bodies of water: Delaware Bay out of Cape May, Atlantic Ocean inshore to Wilmington, Baltimore Canyons
Rates: Varies: $450 and up
Call between: 8:30am-10pm
Provides: Light tackle, heavy tackle, lures, bait
Handicapped equipped: Yes

Sandi Pearl
Leesburg 609-785-2836
Species & Seasons: Drum May-June, Shark June-Oct, Sea Trout, Bluefish, Fluke May-Oct, Striped Bass Aug-Nov, Tuna July-Sept
Bodies of water: Atlantic Ocean, Delaware Bay, Maurice River
Rates: 8 hrs: $320(8)
Call between: 9am-9pm
Provides: Light tackle, heavy tackle, lures, bait
Handicapped equipped: Yes
Certifications: USCG

ATLANTIC OCEAN — NEW JERSEY

Shari Lynn
Sayreville 908-613-8307
Species & Seasons: Striped Bass, Flounder April-June, Bluefish, Fluke May-Nov, Shark June-Aug, Tuna June-Nov, Marlin July-Sept, Weakfish Sept-Nov, Tautog May-Jan, Cod Sept-Jan
Bodies of water: Sandy Hook Bay, Atlantic Ocean
Rates: Charter groups to 40
Call between: 7am-7pm
Provides: Light tackle, heavy tackle, lures, bait
Handicapped equipped: Yes
Certifications: USCG

Starlight
Cape May 609-729-7776
.... 305-743-8436(W)
Species & Seasons: Sea Bass April-Dec, Flounder, Bluefish May-Oct, Yellowtail, Snapper, Grouper Dec-April
Bodies of water: Atlantic Ocean, Delaware Bay
Rates: Half day: $20-$22(1), Full day: $30-$35
Call between:
Provides: Light tackle, heavy tackle, bait
Handicapped equipped: Yes
Certifications: USCG

Thriller Charter Inc.
N. Cape May 215-674-5690
Species & Seasons: Striped Bass April-May, Weakfish May-Sept, Bluefish May-July, Flounder May-Sept, Shark June-Sept, Sea Bass May-Oct, Tuna July-Oct, Striped Bass Oct-Nov, Marlin July-Sept
Bodies of water: Atlantic Ocean, South Jersey Coast, Delaware Bay
Rates: $300-$600(1-6)
Call between: 6pm-10pm
Provides: Light tackle, heavy tackle, lures, bait, rain gear
Handicapped equipped: Yes
Certifications: USCG

Trophy Striped Bass
Bricktown 908-458-1772
.... 295-1437
Species & Seasons: Striped Bass, Bluefish May-Nov, Weakfish June-Nov, Bonito, Albacore July-Oct, Bluefin Tuna Sept-Oct
Bodies of water: Atlantic Ocean, rivers from Sandy Hook to Barnegat Inlet
Rates: Full day: $450(2)
Call between: 6pm-9pm
Provides: Light tackle, heavy tackle, fly rod/reel, lures, bait
Handicapped equipped: No
Certifications: USCG, Yamaha Elite Guide

Ursula
Hammonton 609-561-0827
Species & Seasons: Mackerel Mar-April, Bluefish, Sea Bass May-Nov, Tuna July-Nov, Marlin, Swordfish, Dolphin July-Oct, Tautog Mar-Dec, Flounder May-Sept, Striped Bass, May-Nov
Bodies of water: Atlantic Ocean
Rates: Varies, 6-22 people
Call between: 7pm-9pm
Provides: Light tackle, heavy tackle, lures, bait
Handicapped equipped: Yes

FLY SHOPS...

The Fly Hatch
Red Bank 908-530-6784
Hours: 10am-6pm Mon.-Wed., 10am-8pm Thurs., Fri., 10am-5pm Sat., closed Sun
Carries: Flies, rods, reels
Bodies of water: Atlantic Ocean, Delaware River, Raritan Bay
Services & Products: Guide services, fishing instruction, repair services
Guides: Yes
OK to call for current conditions: Yes
Contact: Dave

MARINAS...

Bayside Bait & Tackle
Brigantine 609-266-2819
Hours: 6am-6pm
Carries: Live bait, lures, flies, maps, rods, reels
Bodies of water: Absecon Inlet, Atlantic Ocean
Services & Products: Charter boat service, food, beverages, gas/oil, repair services, waverunner rentals
Guides: Yes
OK to call for current conditions: Yes
Contact: Sam Lionelli

Kammerman's Atlantic City Marina
Atlantic City 609-348-8418
Hours: 7am-7pm
Carries: Live bait, lures, maps, rods, reels
Bodies of water: Absecon Inlet, Absecon Bar, Great Bay, Atlantic Ocean
Services & Products: Charter boat service, beverages, gas/oil
Guides: Yes
OK to call for current conditions: Yes
Contact: Butch or Judy

Moran's Dockside
Avalon 609-368-1321
Hours: 6am-6pm
Carries: Live bait, lures, maps, rods, reels
Bodies of water: Atlantic Ocean, Intercoastal waterway
Services & Products: Charter boat service, food, beverages
OK to call for current conditions: Yes
Contact: Ernie Venafro

Smuggler's Cove
Stone Harbor 609-368-1700
Hours: 7am-7pm
Carries: Live bait, lures, flies, maps, rods, reels
Bodies of water: Atlantic Ocean, Delaware Bay
Services & Products: Boat rentals, boat ramp, food, beverages, gas/oil, fishing instruction
Guides: Yes
OK to call for current conditions: Yes
Contact: Lou

Sportsman's Outpost
2517 Fries Mill Road
Williamstown 08094
Carries: Live bait, lures, flies, maps, rods, reels, licenses
Bodies of water: Delaware River, Delaware Bay, Atlantic Ocean, Maurice River, Union Lake
Services & Products: Repair services
Guides: Yes
OK to call for current conditions: Yes
Contact: Lou

Sterling Harbor Ship's Store
Wildwood 609-729-1425
Hours: 6am-6pm
Carries: Live bait, lures, flies, maps, rods, reels
Bodies of water: Atlantic Ocean, Delaware Bay
Services & Products: Boat rentals, guide services, charter boat service, lodging, boat ramp, beverages, fishing instruction, repair services
Guides: Yes
OK to call for current conditions: Yes
Contact: George or Paul

NEW JERSEY
BARNEGAT BAY - CAPE MAY

BARNEGAT BAY

BAIT & TACKLE...

Downe's Bait & Tackle
Bayville 908-269-0137
Hours: 5:30am-9pm (seasonal)
Carries: Live bait, lures, flies, maps, rods, reels, licenses
Bodies of water: Barnegat Bay, Atlantic Ocean
Services & Products: Boat rentals, boat ramp, food, beverages
Guides: Yes
OK to call for current conditions: Yes

Nautical Shop
Toms River 908-270-1030
Hours: 6am-6pm
Carries: Live bait, lures, flies, maps, rods, reels
Bodies of water: Toms River, Atlantic Ocean, Barnegat Bay
Services & Products: Block ice, cube ice
Guides: Yes
OK to call for current conditions: Yes
Contact: Robert S. Oehme

CHARTERS...

Connie Claire
Barnegat Light 609-494-6787
Species & Seasons: Sea Bass, Tague April-Dec, Bluefish May-Dec, Weakfish July-Nov, Tuna June-Sept, Albacore Sept-Nov, Bonito July-Sept, Fluke June-Oct
Bodies of water: Barnegat Bay, Barnegat Inlet, Altantic Ocean
Rates: Full day: $450(8), $35 additional pp up to 15
Call between: 11am-11pm
Provides: Light tackle, heavy tackle, lures, bait
Handicapped equipped: Yes
Certifications: USCG

Elixir Sportfishing Charters
Red Bank 908-741-9296
Species & Seasons: Fluke June-Sept, Bluefish June-Oct, Shark June-Aug, Tuna June-Oct, Wreck/Bottom May-Oct
Bodies of water: Atlantic Ocean, Mansaquan River, Barnegat Bay, Sandy Hook Bay, Raritan Bay
Rates: Varies: $350 and up

Call between: 9am-5pm
Provides: Light tackle, heavy tackle, fly rod/reel, lures, bait, rain gear
Handicapped equipped: Yes
Certifications: USCG

MARINAS...

Baywood Marina
Brick Town 908-477-3322
Hours: 8am-5pm
Bodies of water: Barnegat Bay
Services & Products: Boat ramp, beverages, gas/oil, repair services
Guides: Yes
OK to call for current conditions: Yes
Contact: Ed Harrison

BARNEGAT INLET

BAIT & TACKLE...

Fishermen's Headquarters Inc.
Ship Bottom 609-494-5739
Carries: Live bait, lures, flies, maps, rods, reels, licenses
Bodies of water: Atlantic Ocean, Barnegat Light Inlet, Little Egg Inlet
Services & Products: Beverages, fishing instruction, repair services, frozen baits
Guides: Yes
OK to call for current conditions: Yes

CHARTERS...

Connie Claire
Barnegat Light 609-494-6787
Species & Seasons: Sea Bass, Tague April-Dec, Bluefish May-Dec, Weakfish July-Nov, Tuna June-Sept, Albacore Sept-Nov, Bonito July-Sept, Fluke June-Oct
Bodies of water: Barnegat Bay, Barnegat Inlet, Altantic Ocean
Rates: Full day: $450(8), $35 additional pp up to 15
Call between: 11am-11pm
Provides: Light tackle, heavy tackle, lures, bait
Handicapped equipped: Yes
Certifications: USCG

Penguin
Phillipsburg 908-859-4384
Species & Seasons: Tautog, Sea Bass, Lingall year, Bluefish Summer, Mackerel Spring
Bodies of water: Atlantic Ocean, Barnegat Light area
Rates: Full day: $50(1)
Call between: 5pm-10pm
Provides: Heavy tackle, bait
Handicapped equipped: No
Certifications: USCG

Trophy Striped Bass
Bricktown 908-458-1772
.... 295-1437
Species & Seasons: Striped Bass, Bluefish May-Nov, Weakfish June-Nov, Bonito, Albacore July-Oct, Bluefin Tuna Sept-Oct
Bodies of water: Atlantic Ocean, rivers from Sandy Hook to Barnegat Inlet
Rates: Full day: $450(2)
Call between: 6pm-9pm
Provides: Light tackle, heavy tackle, fly rod/reel, lures, bait
Handicapped equipped: No
Certifications: USCG, Yamaha Elite Guide

CAPE MAY

BAIT & TACKLE...

Jim's Bait & Tackle
Cape May 609-884-3900
Hours: 5am-9pm
Carries: Live bait, lures, flies, maps, rods, reels
Bodies of water: Delaware Bay, Atlantic Ocean, Cape May Canal, Cape May Harbor
Services & Products: Guide services, charter boat service, beverages, fishing instruction, repair services
Guides: Yes
OK to call for current conditions: Yes
Contact: Jim or Cheri Wallace

CHARTERS...

Christina II Charters
Tuckerton 609-296-0066
Species & Seasons: Striped Bass April-July/Oct-Jan, Fluke, Weakfish June-Oct, Mako Shark June-Aug

CAPE MAY - DELAWARE RIVER   NEW JERSEY

Bodies of water: Delaware Bay, Cape May, Atlantic Ocean, Great Bay
Rates: Full day: $300(1-3) Stripers
Call between: 7pm-10pm
Provides: Light tackle, heavy tackle, lures, bait

DELAWARE BAY

BAIT & TACKLE...

Jim's Bait & Tackle
Cape May 609-884-3900
Hours: 5am-9pm
Carries: Live bait, lures, flies, maps, rods, reels
Bodies of water: Delaware Bay, Atlantic Ocean, Cape May Canal, Cape May Harbor
Services & Products: Guide services, charter boat service, beverages, fishing instruction, repair services
Guides: Yes
OK to call for current conditions: Yes
Contact: Jim or Cheri Wallace

CHARTERS...

Christina II Charters
Tuckerton 609-296-0066
Species & Seasons: Striped Bass April-July/Oct-Jan, Fluke, Weakfish June-Oct, Mako Shark June-Aug
Bodies of water: Delaware Bay, Cape May, Atlantic Ocean, Great Bay
Rates: Full day: $300(1-3) Striped Bass
Call between: 7pm-10pm
Provides: Light tackle, heavy tackle, lures, bait

Rambunctious
Riverton 609-829-1813
Species & Seasons: Striped Bass April-June/Oct-Dec, Fluke, Weakfish May-Oct, Bluefish May-Nov, Sea Bass April-Nov, Shark May-Oct, Tuna, Marlin, Dolphin June-Oct
Bodies of water: Delaware Bay out of Cape May, Atlantic Ocean inshore to Wilmington, Baltimore Canyons
Rates: Varies: $450 and up
Call between: 8:30am-10pm
Provides: Light tackle, heavy tackle, lures, bait
Handicapped equipped: Yes

Sandi Pearl
Leesburg 609-785-2836
Species & Seasons: Drum May-June, Shark June-Oct, Sea Trout, Bluefish, Fluke May-Oct, Striped Bass Aug-Nov, Tuna July-Sept
Bodies of water: Atlantic Ocean, Delaware Bay, Maurice River
Rates: 8 hrs: $320(8)
Call between: 9am-9pm
Provides: Light tackle, heavy tackle, lures, bait
Handicapped equipped: Yes
Certifications: USCG

Starlight
Cape May 609-729-7776
.... 305-743-8436(W)
Species & Seasons: Sea Bass April-Dec, Flounder, Bluefish May-Oct, Yellowtail, Snapper, Grouper Dec-April
Bodies of water: Atlantic Ocean, Delaware Bay
Rates: Half day: $20-$22(1), Full day: $30-$35
Call between:
Provides: Light tackle, heavy tackle, bait
Handicapped equipped: Yes
Certifications: USCG

Thriller Charter Inc.
N. Cape May 215-674-5690
Species & Seasons: Striped Bass April-May, Weakfish May-Sept, Bluefish May-July, Flounder May-Sept, Shark June-Sept, Sea Bass May-Oct, Tuna July-Oct, Striped Bass Oct-Nov, Marlin July-Sept
Bodies of water: Atlantic Ocean, South Jersey Coast, Delaware Bay
Rates: $300-$600(1-6)
Call between: 6pm-10pm
Provides: Light tackle, heavy tackle, lures, bait, rain gear
Handicapped equipped: Yes
Certifications: USCG

MARINAS...

Smuggler's Cove
Stone Harbor 609-368-1700
Hours: 7am-7pm
Carries: Live bait, lures, flies, maps, rods, reels
Bodies of water: Atlantic Ocean, Delaware Bay
Services & Products: Boat rentals, boat ramp, food, beverages, gas/oil, fishing instruction

Guides: Yes
OK to call for current conditions: Yes
Contact: Lou

Sportsman's Outpost
2517 Fries Mill Road
Williamstown 08094
Carries: Live bait, lures, flies, maps, rods, reels, licenses
Bodies of water: Delaware River, Delaware Bay, Atlantic Ocean, Maurice River, Union Lake
Services & Products: Repair services
Guides: Yes
OK to call for current conditions: Yes
Contact: Lou

Sterling Harbor Ship's Store
Wildwood 609-729-1425
Hours: 6am-6pm
Carries: Live bait, lures, flies, maps, rods, reels
Bodies of water: Atlantic Ocean, Delaware Bay
Services & Products: Boat rentals, guide services, charter boat service, lodging, boat ramp, beverages, fishing instruction, repair services
Guides: Yes
OK to call for current conditions: Yes
Contact: George or Paul

DELAWARE RIVER

BAIT & TACKLE...

Ramsey Outdoor
Ramsey 201-261-5000
Hours: 9am-9:30pm, closed Sun.
Carries: Live bait, lures, flies, maps, rods, reels, licenses
Bodies of water: Hudson River, Delaware River, Greenwood Lake, Lake Hopatcong
Guides: Yes
OK to call for current conditions: Yes
Contact: Joe Keegan

NEW JERSEY — DELAWARE RIVER - MAURICE RIVER

FLY SHOPS...

The Fly Hatch
Red Bank 908-530-6784
Hours: 10am-6pm Mon.-Wed., 10am-8pm Thurs., Fri., 10am-5pm Sat., closed Sun
Carries: Flies, rods, reels
Bodies of water: Atlantic Ocean, Delaware River, Raritan Bay
Services & Products: Guide services, fishing instruction, repair services
Guides: Yes
OK to call for current conditions: Yes
Contact: Dave

MARINAS...

Sportsman's Outpost
2517 Fries Mill Road
Williamstown 08094
Carries: Live bait, lures, flies, maps, rods, reels, licenses
Bodies of water: Delaware River, Delaware Bay, Atlantic Ocean, Maurice River, Union Lake
Services & Products: Repair services
Guides: Yes
OK to call for current conditions: Yes
Contact: Lou

GREAT BAY

CHARTERS...

Christina II Charters
Tuckerton 609-296-0066
Species & Seasons: Striped Bass April-July/Oct-Jan, Fluke, Weakfish June-Oct, Mako Shark June-Aug
Bodies of water: Delaware Bay, Cape May, Atlantic Ocean, Great Bay
Rates: Full day: $300(1-3) Striped Bass
Call between: 7pm-10pm
Provides: Light tackle, heavy tackle, lures, bait

Leyte-Jo
Tuckerton 609-296-5322
Species & Seasons: Mackerel April-May, Bluefish May-Dec, Bonito June-Aug, Flounder June-Oct, Sea Bass May-Oct, Striped Bass Oct-Dec
Bodies of water: Atlantic Ocean, Great Bay, Lett Bay
Rates: Full day: $270(1-6)
Call between: 6pm-9pm

Provides: Light tackle, heavy tackle, lures, bait
Handicapped equipped: Yes
Certifications: USCG

MARINAS...

Kammerman's Atlantic City Marina
Atlantic City 609-348-8418
Hours: 7am-7pm
Carries: Live bait, lures, maps, rods, reels
Bodies of water: Absecon Inlet, Absecon Bar, Great Bay, Atlantic Ocean
Services & Products: Charter boat service, beverages, gas/oil
Guides: Yes
OK to call for current conditions: Yes
Contact: Butch or Judy

GREENWOOD LAKE

BAIT & TACKLE...

Ramsey Outdoor
Ramsey 201-261-5000
Hours: 9am-9:30pm, closed Sun.
Carries: Live bait, lures, flies, maps, rods, reels, licenses
Bodies of water: Hudson River, Delaware River, Greenwood Lake, Lake Hopatcong
Guides: Yes
OK to call for current conditions: Yes
Contact: Joe Keegan

LAKE HOPATCONG

BAIT & TACKLE...

Ramsey Outdoor
Ramsey 201-261-5000
Hours: 9am-9:30pm, closed Sun.
Carries: Live bait, lures, flies, maps, rods, reels, licenses
Bodies of water: Hudson River, Delaware River, Greenwood Lake, Lake Hopatcong
Guides: Yes
OK to call for current conditions: Yes
Contact: Joe Keegan

MARINAS...

Lake's End Marina
Landing 201-398-5707
Hours: 6am-8pm
Carries: Live bait, lures, maps, rods, reels, licenses
Bodies of water: Lake Hopatcong, Lake Musconetcong, Cranberry Lake, Bear Pond
Services & Products: Boat rentals, guide services, boat ramp, gas/oil, repair services
Guides: Yes
OK to call for current conditions: Yes

MAURICE RIVER

CHARTERS...

Sandi Pearl
Leesburg 609-785-2836
Species & Seasons: Drum May-June, Shark June-Oct, Sea Trout, Bluefish, Fluke May-Oct, Striped Bass Aug-Nov, Tuna July-Sept
Bodies of water: Atlantic Ocean, Delaware Bay, Maurice River
Rates: 8 hrs: $320(8)
Call between: 9am-9pm
Provides: Light tackle, heavy tackle, lures, bait
Handicapped equipped: Yes
Certifications: USCG

MARINAS...

Sportsman's Outpost
2517 Fries Mill Road
Williamstown 08094
Carries: Live bait, lures, flies, maps, rods, reels, licenses
Bodies of water: Delaware River, Delaware Bay, Atlantic Ocean, Maurice River, Union Lake
Services & Products: Repair services
Guides: Yes
OK to call for current conditions: Yes
Contact: Lou

PAY LAKE - SANDY HOOK BAY

NEW JERSEY

PAY LAKE

BAIT & TACKLE...

Go Fish
Newton 201-579-6633
Hours: 8am
Carries: Live bait, lures
Bodies of water: Pay Lake
Services & Products: Boat rentals
Guides: Yes
OK to call for current conditions: Yes

RARITAN BAY

CHARTERS...

Atlantic Star
Atl. Highlands................... 908-291-5508
Species & Seasons: Flounder Mar-May, Fluke May-Oct, Tautog, Sea Bass, Porgies, Ling Oct-Dec
Bodies of water: Shrewsbury River, Sandy Hook Bay, Raritan Bay, Atlantic Ocean
Rates: Open party fishing boat, reservations not required, but accepted. Mar-Oct: Half day: $20 pp, Oct-Dec: 3/4 day: $30 pp
Call between: 6pm-10pm
Provides: Bait, tackle available for rent
Handicapped equipped: Yes
Certifications: USCG

Elixir Sportfishing Charters
Red Bank 908-741-9296
Species & Seasons: Fluke June-Sept, Bluefish June-Oct, Shark June-Aug, Tuna June-Oct, Wreck/Bottom May-Oct
Bodies of water: Atlantic Ocean, Mansaquan River, Barnegat Bay, Sandy Hook Bay, Raritan Bay
Rates: Varies: $350 and up
Call between: 9am-5pm
Provides: Light tackle, heavy tackle, fly rod/reel, lures, bait, rain gear
Handicapped equipped: Yes
Certifications: USCG

Finaddict
Edison 908-985-5275
Species & Seasons: Flounder April-May, Fluke May-Sept, Bluefish May-Nov, Shark June-Oct, Tuna July-Oct
Bodies of water: Mansaquan River, Raritan Bay, Atlantic Ocean
Rates: Full day: $250-$800(4)

Call between: 6pm-9pm
Provides: Light tackle, heavy tackle, fly rod/reel, lures, bait
Handicapped equipped: No

FLY SHOPS...

The Fly Hatch
Red Bank 908-530-6784
Hours: 10am-6pm Mon.-Wed., 10am-8pm Thurs., Fri., 10am-5pm Sat., closed Sun
Carries: Flies, rods, reels
Bodies of water: Atlantic Ocean, Delaware River, Raritan Bay
Services & Products: Guide services, fishing instruction, repair services
Guides: Yes
OK to call for current conditions: Yes
Contact: Dave

ROUND VALLEY RESERVOIR

BAIT & TACKLE...

Les Shannon's Fly & Tackle Shop
Califon 908-832-5736
Hours: 8am-4pm, closed Tues.
Carries: Live bait, flies, maps, rods, reels, licenses
Bodies of water: Round Valley Res., Spruce Run Res., So. Branch of Raritan River, Musconetcong River
Services & Products: Fishing instruction
OK to call for current conditions: Yes
Contact: Les Shannon

SANDY HOOK BAY

CHARTERS...

Atlantic Star
Atl. Highlands................... 908-291-5508
Species & Seasons: Flounder Mar-May, Fluke May-Oct, Tautog, Sea Bass, Porgy, Ling Oct-Dec
Bodies of water: Shrewsbury River, Sandy Hook Bay, Raritan Bay, Atlantic Ocean
Rates: Open party fishing boat, reservations not required, but accepted. Mar-Oct: Half day: $20 pp, Oct-Dec: 3/4 day: $30 pp

Call between: 6pm-10pm
Provides: Bait, tackle available for rent
Handicapped equipped: Yes
Certifications: USCG

Crack-A-Dawn II
Cedar Grove 201-239-5821
.... 908-229-7096
Species & Seasons: Bluefish May-Oct, Striped Bass April-Dec, Fluke, Tautog May-Sept, Tautog, Tuna, Flounder, Sea Bass, Weakfish Aug-Oct, Shark June-Aug
Bodies of water: Sandy Hook area, Atlantic Ocean (to 20 miles offshore)
Rates: Charters to 21 people
Call between: 6pm-10pm
Provides: Light tackle, heavy tackle, lures, bait
Handicapped equipped: Yes
Certifications: USCG/FCC

Elixir Sportfishing Charters
Red Bank 908-741-9296
Species & Seasons: Fluke June-Sept, Bluefish June-Oct, Shark June-Aug, Tuna June-Oct, Wreck/Bottom May-Oct
Bodies of water: Atlantic Ocean, Mansaquan River, Barnegat Bay, Sandy Hook Bay, Raritan Bay
Rates: Varies: $350 and up
Call between: 9am-5pm
Provides: Light tackle, heavy tackle, fly rod/reel, lures, bait, rain gear
Handicapped equipped: Yes
Certifications: USCG

Shari Lynn
Sayreville 908-613-8307
Species & Seasons: Striped Bass, Flounder April-June, Bluefish, Fluke May-Nov, Shark June-Aug, Tuna June-Nov, Marlin July-Sept, Weakfish Sept-Nov, Tautog May-Jan, Cod Sept-Jan
Bodies of water: Sandy Hook Bay, Atlantic Ocean
Rates: Charter groups to 40
Call between: 7am-7pm
Provides: Light tackle, heavy tackle, lures, bait
Handicapped equipped: Yes
Certifications: USCG

NEW JERSEY
SANDY HOOK BAY - UNION LAKE

Trophy Striped Bass
Bricktown 908-458-1772
.... 295-1437
Species & Seasons: Striped Bass, Bluefish May-Nov, Weakfish June-Nov, Bonito, Albacore July-Oct, Bluefin Tuna Sept-Oct
Bodies of water: Atlantic Ocean, rivers from Sandy Hook to Barnegat Inlet
Rates: Full day: $450(2)
Call between: 6pm-9pm
Provides: Light tackle, heavy tackle, fly rod/reel, lures, bait
Handicapped equipped: No
Certifications: USCG, Yamaha Elite Guide

SHARK RIVER

MARINAS...

Bry's Marine
Neptune 908-775-7364
Hours: 8:30am-5:30pm, 9am-4pm Sun.
Bodies of water: Shark River
Services & Products: Boat ramp, repair services
Guides: Yes
OK to call for current conditions: Yes

SPRUCE RUN RESERVOIR

BAIT & TACKLE...

Les Shannon's Fly & Tackle Shop
Califon 908-832-5736
Hours: 8am-4pm, closed Tues.
Carries: Live bait, flies, maps, rods, reels, licenses
Bodies of water: Round Valley Res., Spruce Run Res., So. Branch of Raritan River, Musconetcong River
Services & Products: Fishing instruction
OK to call for current conditions: Yes
Contact: Les Shannon

TOMS RIVER

BAIT & TACKLE...

Nautical Shop
Toms River 908-270-1030
Hours: 6am-6pm
Carries: Live bait, lures, flies, maps, rods, reels
Bodies of water: Toms River, Atlantic Ocean, Barnegat Bay
Services & Products: Block ice, cube ice
Guides: Yes
OK to call for current conditions: Yes
Contact: Robert S. Oehme

UNION LAKE

MARINAS...

Sportsman's Outpost
2517 Fries Mill Road
Williamstown 08094
Carries: Live bait, lures, flies, maps, rods, reels, licenses
Bodies of water: Delaware River, Delaware Bay, Atlantic Ocean, Maurice River, Union Lake
Services & Products: Repair services
Guides: Yes
OK to call for current conditions: Yes
Contact: Lou

NEW MEXICO

1. Avalon Reservoir
2. Brantley Reservoir
3. Caballo Reservoir
4. Cimarron River
5. Conchas Lake
6. Eagle Nest Lake
7. El Vado Lake
8. Elephant Butte Reservoir
9. Navajo Reservoir
10. Pecos River
11. Rio Chama River
12. Rio Grande River
13. Ute Reservoir

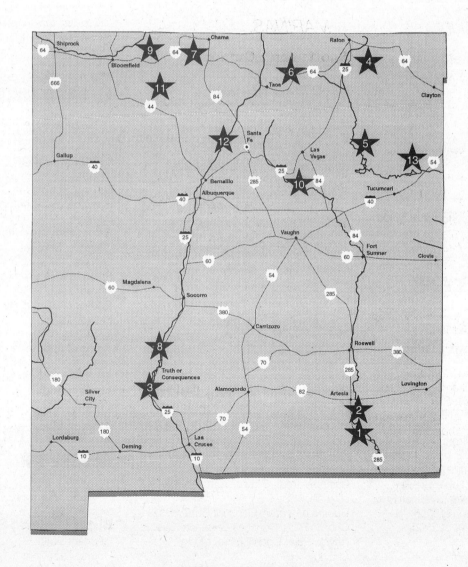

NEW MEXICO
AVALON RESERVOIR - ELEPHANT BUTTE RESERVOIR

AVALON RESERVOIR

BAIT & TACKLE...

Bailey's Bait & Tackle Shop
Carlsbad 505-885-8503
Hours: 7am-7pm Mon.-Thurs., 7am-8pm Fri.-Sat., 7am-5pm Sun.
Carries: Live bait, lures
Bodies of water: Brantley Res., Avalon Res., Red Bluff Lake (TX), Pecos River
Services & Products: Live bait, frozen bait
Guides: No
OK to call for current conditions: Yes
Contact: Harry Bailey or Dennis Munson

BRANTLEY RESERVOIR

BAIT & TACKLE...

Bailey's Bait & Tackle Shop
Carlsbad 505-885-8503
Hours: 7am-7pm Mon.-Thurs., 7am-8pm Fri.-Sat., 7am-5pm Sun.
Carries: Live bait, lures
Bodies of water: Brantley Res., Lake Avalon Res., Red Bluff Lake (TX), Pecos River
Services & Products: Live bait, frozen bait
Guides: No
OK to call for current conditions: Yes
Contact: Harry Bailey or Dennis Munson

CABALLO RESERVOIR

GUIDES...

Desert Bass Fishing Guide Services
Elephant Butte 505-744-5314
.... 800-9-GET-BIT
Species & Seasons: Striped Bass, LM Bass, SM Bass, White Bass, Catfish, Rainbow Trout, Brown Trout, Walleye all year
Bodies of water: Elephant Butte Res., Caballo Res., Conchas Lake, Ute Res., Navajo Res., Cochiti Lake, San Juan River
Rates: Half day: $125(1), $150(2), $175(3) Full day: $175(1), $225(2), $275(3)
Call between: 6am-10pm
Provides: Light tackle, heavy tackle, lures, bait
Handicapped equipped: Yes

CIMARRON RIVER

GUIDES...

Santa Fe Flyfishing School
Santa Fe 505-986-3913
.... 800-555-7707
Species & Seasons: Rainbow Trout, Brown Trout, Cutthroat Trout Mar-Nov
Bodies of water: Rio Grande River, Rio Chama River, Pecos River, Vermejo River Park Ranch, San Juan River, Cimarron River, all of northern New Mexico waters
Rates: Half day: $185(1-2), Full day: $225(1-2), $275(3), 1995 rates
Provides: Flies, rain gear, beverages, lunch
Handicapped equipped: Yes
Certifications: Permitted VSFS, State Park & Rec CPR, First aid

MARINAS...

Eagle Nest Marina
Eagle Nest 505-377-6941
Hours: 6am-6pm
Carries: Live bait, lures, flies, maps, rods, reels, licenses
Bodies of water: Eagle Nest Lake, Cimarron River, Red River, Coyote Creek
Services & Products: Boat rentals, guide services, charter boat service, lodging, food, beverages, gas/oil, fishing instruction, repair services
OK to call for current conditions: Yes
Contact: Sue or Moe Finley

CONCHAS LAKE

GUIDES...

Desert Bass Fishing Guide Services
Elephant Butte 505-744-5314
.... 800-9-GET-BIT
Species & Seasons: Striped Bass, LM Bass, SM Bass, White Bass, Catfish, Rainbow Trout, Brown Trout, Walleye all year
Bodies of water: Elephant Butte Res., Caballo Res., Conchas Lake, Ute Res., Navajo Res., Cochiti Lake, San Juan River
Rates: Half day: $125(1), $150(2), $175(3) Full day: $175(1), $225(2), $275(3)
Call between: 6am-10pm
Provides: Light tackle, heavy tackle, lures, bait
Handicapped equipped: Yes

EAGLE NEST LAKE

MARINAS...

Eagle Nest Marina
Eagle Nest 505-377-6941
Hours: 6am-6pm
Carries: Live bait, lures, flies, maps, rods, reels, licenses
Bodies of water: Eagle Nest Lake, Cimarron River, Red River, Coyote Creek
Services & Products: Boat rentals, guide services, charter boat service, lodging, food, beverages, gas/oil, fishing instruction, repair services
OK to call for current conditions: Yes
Contact: Sue or Moe Finley

EL VADO LAKE

LODGING...

Spruce Lodge
Chama 505-756-2593
Guest Capacity: 44
Handicapped equipped: No
Seasons: May to Nov
Rates: $55/day double occupancy
Contact: Don
Guides: Yes, recommend
Species & Seasons: Trout, Lake Trout all year
Bodies of Water: Heron Lake, El Vado Lake, Chama River, other rivers and lakes in the High Country
Types of fishing: Fly fishing, light tackle, heavy tackle
Available: River fishing

ELEPHANT BUTTE RESERVOIR

BAIT & TACKLE

Butte General Store & Marina
Elephant Butte 505-744-5427
Hours: 7am-7pm
Carries: Live bait, lures, maps, rods, reels
Bodies of water: Elephant Butte Lake

ELEPHANT BUTTE RESERVOIR - RIO CHAMA RIVER — NEW MEXICO

Services & Products: Guide services, food, beverages, gas/oil, repair services, storage
OK to call for current conditions: Yes
Contact: Chester Connor, Jr.

GUIDES...

Buddy's Guide Service
Elephant Butte 505-894-6156
Species & Seasons: Striped Bass all year
Bodies of water: Elephant Butte Res.
Rates: Half day: $200(1-2), Full day: $325(1-2), $400(3)
Provides: Heavy tackle, lures, bait
Handicapped equipped: Yes

Desert Bass Fishing Guide Services
Elephant Butte 505-744-5314
.... 800-9-GET-BIT
Species & Seasons: Striped Bass, LM Bass, SM Bass, White Bass, Catfish, Rainbow Trout, Brown Trout, Walleye all year
Bodies of water: Elephant Butte Res., Caballo Res., Conchas Lake, Ute Res., Navajo Res., Cochiti Lake, San Juan River
Rates: Half day: $125(1), $150(2), $175(3) Full day: $175(1), $225(2), $275(3)
Call between: 6am-10pm
Provides: Light tackle, heavy tackle, lures, bait
Handicapped equipped: Yes

NAVAJO RESERVOIR

GUIDES...

Desert Bass Fishing Guide Services
Elephant Butte 505-744-5314
.... 800-9-GET-BIT
Species & Seasons: Striped Bass, LM Bass, SM Bass, White Bass, Catfish, Rainbow Trout, Brown Trout, Walleye all year
Bodies of water: Elephant Butte Res., Caballo Res., Conchas Lake, Ute Res., Navajo Res., Cochiti Lake, San Juan River
Rates: Half day: $125(1), $150(2), $175(3) Full day: $175(1), $225(2), $275(3)
Call between: 6am-10pm

Provides: Light tackle, heavy tackle, lures, bait
Handicapped equipped: Yes

PECOS RIVER

BAIT & TACKLE...

Bailey's Bait & Tackle Shop
Carlsbad 505-885-8503
Hours: 7am-7pm Mon.-Thurs., 7am-8pm Fri.-Sat., 7am-5pm Sun.
Carries: Live bait, lures
Bodies of water: Brantley Res., Lake Avalon Res., Red Bluff Lake (TX), Pecos River
Services & Products: Live bait, frozen bait
Guides: No
OK to call for current conditions: Yes
Contact: Harry Bailey or Dennis Munson

GUIDES...

Santa Fe Flyfishing School
Santa Fe 505-986-3913
.... 800-555-7707
Species & Seasons: Rainbow Trout, Brown Trout, Cutthroat Trout Mar-Nov
Bodies of water: Rio Grande River, Rio Chama River, Pecos River, Vermejo River Park Ranch, San Juan River, Cimarron River, all of northern New Mexico waters
Rates: Half day: $185(1-2), Full day: $225(1-2), $275(3), 1995 rates
Provides: Flies, rain gear, beverages, lunch
Handicapped equipped: Yes
Certifications: Permitted VSFS, State Park & Rec CPR, First aid

PRIVATE LAKES & STREAMS

LODGING...

The Lodge at Chama
Chama 505-756-2133
Guest Capacity: 22 (11 rms.)
Handicapped equipped: Yes
Seasons: All year
Rates: $375/day includes lodging, meals, bar, guided activities
Contact: Frank Simms
Guides: Yes

Species & Seasons: Rainbow Trout, Brook Trout, Brown Trout, Cutthroat Trout May-Oct
Bodies of Water: 14 ranch lakes, 3 streams, San Juan River 1.5 hrs away
Types of fishing: Fly fishing, light tackle, wading, float trips
Available: Fishing instruction, tackle, boat, family activities

RIO CHAMA RIVER

GUIDES...

Santa Fe Flyfishing School
Santa Fe 505-986-3913
.... 800-555-7707
Species & Seasons: Rainbow Trout, Brown Trout, Cutthroat Trout Mar-Nov
Bodies of water: Rio Grande River, Rio Chama River, Pecos River, Vermejo River Park Ranch, San Juan River, Cimarron River, all of northern New Mexico waters
Rates: Half day: $185(1-2), Full day: $225(1-2), $275(3), 1995 rates
Call between:
Provides: Flies, rain gear, beverages, lunch
Handicapped equipped: Yes
Certifications: Permitted VSFS, State Park & Rec CPR, First aid

Pat Smith
Tierra Amarilla 505-588-7899
Species & Seasons: Brown Trout, Rainbow Trout all year
Bodies of water: Upper Rio Chama (fly fishing only), lower Rio Chama (horseback fishing-a quality trip.)
Rates: Call for rates
Call between: 8am-9pm
Provides: Light tackle, bait, beverages, lunch, horses
Handicapped equipped: No
Certifications: CPR

NEW MEXICO
RIO CHAMA RIVER - UTE RESERVOIR

Taylor Streit
Taos 505-751-1312
Species & Seasons: Trout June-Nov (all species)
Bodies of water: Rio Grande River, Rio Chama River, all northern New Mexico
Rates: Full day: $275(1), $325(2), $375(3)
Call between: 7am-8pm
Provides: Fly rod/reel, beverages, lunch
Handicapped equipped: No

LODGING...

Spruce Lodge
Chama 505-756-2593
Guest Capacity: 44
Handicapped equipped: No
Seasons: May to Nov
Rates: $55/day double occupancy
Contact: Don
Guides: Yes, recommend
Species & Seasons: Trout, Lake Trout all year
Bodies of Water: Heron Lake, El Vado Lake, Chama River, other rivers and lakes in the High Country
Types of fishing: Fly fishing, light tackle, heavy tackle
Available: River fishing

RIO GRANDE RIVER

GUIDES...

Santa Fe Flyfishing School
Santa Fe 505-986-3913
.... 800-555-7707
Species & Seasons: Rainbow Trout, Brown Trout, Cutthroat Trout Mar-Nov
Bodies of water: Rio Grande River, Rio Chama River, Pecos River, Vermejo River Park Ranch, San Juan River, Cimarron River, all of northern New Mexico waters
Rates: Half day: $185(1-2), Full day: $225(1-2), $275(3), 1995 rates
Provides: Flies, rain gear, beverages, lunch
Handicapped equipped: Yes
Certifications: Permitted VSFS, State Park & Rec CPR, First aid

Taylor Streit
Taos 505-751-1312
Species & Seasons: Trout June-Nov (all species)
Bodies of water: Rio Grande River, Rio Chama River, all northern New Mexico
Rates: Full day: $275(1), $325(2), $375(3)
Call between: 7am-8pm
Provides: Fly rod/reel, beverages, lunch
Handicapped equipped: No

UTE RESERVOIR

GUIDES...

Desert Bass Fishing Guide Services
Elephant Butte 505-744-5314
.... 800-9-GET-BIT
Species & Seasons: Striped Bass, LM Bass, SM Bass, White Bass, Catfish, Rainbow Trout, Brown Trout, Walleye all year
Bodies of water: Elephant Butte Res., Caballo Res., Conchas Lake, Ute Res., Navajo Res., Cochiti Lake, San Juan River
Rates: Half day: $125(1), $150(2), $175(3) Full day: $175(1), $225(2), $275(3)
Call between: 6am-10pm
Provides: Light tackle, heavy tackle, lures, bait
Handicapped equipped: Yes

NEW YORK

1. Adirondacks
2. Ashokan Reservoir
3. Atlantic Ocean
4. Beaverkill River
5. Black Lake
6. Black River
7. Block Island Sound
8. Canadarago Lake
9. Chautauqua Lake
10. Chenango River
11. Delaware River
12. Finger Lakes
13. Great South Bay
14. Greenwood Lake
15. Hudson River
16. Lake Champlain
17. Lake Erie
18. Lake George
19. Lake Ontario
20. Lake Ronkonkoma
21. Long Island Sound
22. Mohawk River
23. Niagara River
24. Oneida Lake
25. Onondaga Lake
26. Oswego River
27. Otsego Lake
28. Otselic River
29. Pepacton Reservoir
30. Salmon River
31. Saratoga Lake
32. St. Lawrence River
33. Swinging Bridge Reservoir
34. Tioughnioga River
35. Whitney Point Lake

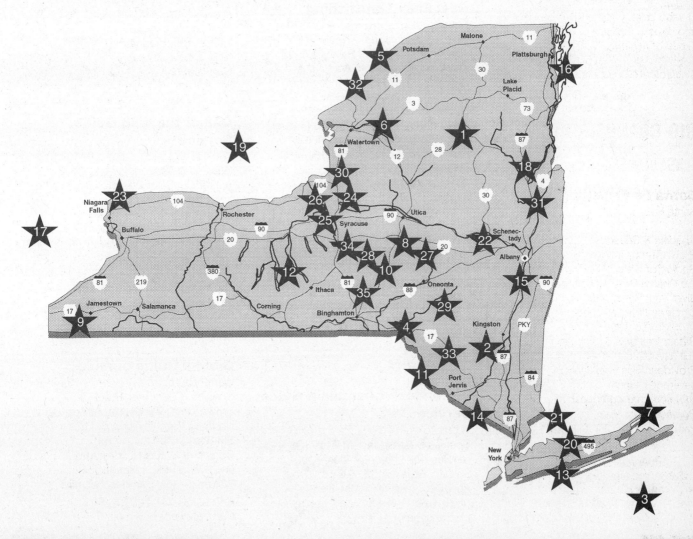

YOUR SILENT FISHING PARTNER — PAGE 313

NEW YORK

ADIRONDACKS

BAIT & TACKLE...

Gordon's Marine Tackle & Archery
W. Plattsburgh 518-561-2109
Hours: 8:30am-6/8pm, closed Sun.
Carries: Live bait, lures, flies, maps, rods, reels
Bodies of water: Lake Champlain, Saranac River, Chazy Lake, Chateauguay Lake, Adirondacks area
Services & Products: Charter boat service
Guides: Yes
OK to call for current conditions: Yes

Outdoorsman Sport Shop
Diamond Point 518-668-3910
Hours: 5am-9pm, (closed Mon. in winter)
Carries: Live bait, lures, flies, maps, rods, reels, licenses
Bodies of water: Lake George, Hudson Rver, Schroon River, Schroon Lake, Brandt Lake, Loon Lake, Lake Champlain, Lake Luzern, Glen Lake, Trout Lake
Services & Products: Guide services, charter boat service, lodging, fishing instruction
Guides: Yes
OK to call for current conditions: Yes
Contact: Garry or Sally Nelson

CHARTERS...

Naughty Lady Charters
Adirondack 518-532-7305
Species & Seasons: Salmon, Lake Trout, Walleye, Northern Pike May/Sept-Oct
Bodies of water: Lake Champlain, Lake George, Schroon Lake
Rates: Half day: $120(1), Full day: $230(1)
Call between: 5am-10pm
Provides: Light tackle, lures, bait
Handicapped equipped: No
Certifications: USCG, NYOGA

Old Troll Sportfishing Charters
Hudson Falls 518-747-3378
Species & Seasons: Atlantic Salmon, Lake Trout April-Nov, SM Bass, LM Bass June-Nov, Northern Pike, Panfish April-Nov
Rates: Half day: $120(1), $150(2), $175(4), Full day: $300(1-4)

Call between: 7am-9pm
Provides: Light tackle, lures, bait, rain gear
Handicapped equipped: No

Placid Bay Ventures Guide & Charter
Lake Placid 518-523-1744
..............................523-2001
Species & Seasons: Lake Trout, Brook Trout April-Nov, Salmon April-June, Chinook Salmon, Atlantic Salmon Aug-Oct, SM Bass June-Nov, Northern Pike May-Mar, Muskellunge Sept-Nov, Walleye, Rainbow Trout, Brown Trout April-Nov
Bodies of water: Lake Placid, Adirondack Lakes and steams, Lake Champlain, Lake Ontario
Rates: Full day: $200(1-2)
Provides: Light tackle, heavy tackle, fly rod/reel, lures, lodging also available
Handicapped equipped: Yes, large boat, some limitations
Certifications: USCG, NYSOGA

Reel Easy Sportfishing
Scotia 518-399-5336
Species & Seasons: Atlantic Salmon April-Nov, Lake Trout, Rainbow Trout May-Nov, Brown Trout April-Oct, SM Bass June-Sept, Northern Pike May-Sept, Walleye May-Oct
Bodies of water: Lake Champlain, Great Sacandaga Lake, Mohawk River, Barge Canal, Saranac Lake Region
Rates: Reel Easy I (local lakes-rivers): 4hrs: $120(1-3), 6hrs: $175(1-3) 8hrs: $225(1-3), Reel Easy II (Lake Ontario-Champlain): 6hrs: $240(1-4), 8hrs: $300(1-4), Ice fishing (Jan-Mar): $75(1)
Call between: 7am-9pm
Provides: Light tackle, heavy tackle, lures, bait
Handicapped equipped: Yes, no wheelchairs
Certifications: USCG, NY State Licensed

GUIDES...

Adirondack Champlain Guide Service
Willsboro 518-963-7351
Species & Seasons: SM Bass June-Nov, LM Bass, Northern Pike June-Oct, Salmon, Brown Trout, Rainbow Trout April-Dec, Lake Trout May-Dec, Brook Trout April-Oct, Walleye May-Sept, Muskellunge Aug-Oct

Bodies of water: Lake Champlain, Ausable River, Boquet River, Saranac River, Saranac Lake Chain, St.Regis Chain of Lakes
Rates: Full day: $165(1), $210(2), 1 day fishing with guide, 2 nights lodging, 4 meals $185pp
Call between: 8am-9pm
Provides: Light tackle, fly rod/reel, lures, bait, rain gear, beverages, lunch
Handicapped equipped: Yes
Certifications: New York State, USCG

Bear Cub Adventure Tours
Lake Placid 518-523-4339
Species & Seasons: Brook Trout, Brown Trout, Rainbow Trout, April-Sept, Northern Pike May-Sept, LM Bass, SM Bass June-Nov
Bodies of water: Ausable River, Chubb River, Saranac River, Saranac Lake Chain, Adirondack Park(ponds)
Rates: Half day: $100(1), $150(2), Full day: $150(1), $200(2), children and group discounts
Call between: 8am-9pm
Provides: Light tackle, bait, beverages, lunch
Handicapped equipped: Yes, limited access
Certifications: NY State Licensed Guide

Call of the Wild Guide Service
Wallkill 914-895-3097
Species & Seasons: Brook Trout April-June, Salmon Sept-June, Lake Trout May-May
Bodies of water: Lake George, Fulton Chain Lakes, Salmon River, Lake Champlain, Pharroah Lake, Hudson River
Call between: 8am-9pm
Provides: Light tackle, heavy tackle, fly rod/reel, lures, bait, rain gear, beverages, lunch
Handicapped equipped: Yes

Gibaldi Guide Service
Warrensburg
Species & Seasons: Brook Trout, Brown Trout, Rainbow Trout April-Sept, Northern Pike May-Dec, LM Bass, SM Bass June-Nov
Bodies of water: Hundreds lakes, ponds and rivers in the Adirondack Mtns., Warren, Essex, Hamilton Counties
Rates: Full day: $200(1), $300(2)
Call between: Anytime

ADIRONDACKS - ATLANTIC OCEAN NEW YORK

Provides: Light tackle, heavy tackle, lures, bait
Handicapped equipped: Yes
Certifications: NY State Licensed, ADK Wilderness Guide, All Red Cross First aid, CPR, Guide School Cert.

Peaked Hill Guide Service
Severance 518-532-7953
Species & Seasons: LM Bass, SM Bass June-Nov, Tiger Muskellunge, Northern Pike May-Mar
Bodies of water: Paradox Lake, Eagle Lake, Schroon Lake, Schroon River, Lake Champlain, Lake George, Lake Durant and several back water ponds for Bass and Pike
Rates: Half day: $65(1), $115(2), Full day: $95(1), $185(2)
Call between: 5pm-9pm
Provides: Light tackle, heavy tackle, lures, bait, rain gear, beverages
Handicapped equipped: No
Certifications: NY State Guide

Singing Wolf Guide Service
PO Box 14782
Albany 12212
Species & Seasons: Trout all year
Bodies of water: Ashokan Res., Esopas Creek, Thompson's Lake, Delaware River, Big Pond, Little Pond, Beaverkill River, Kinderhook Creek, Boquet River, East Branch Ausable River, Batten Kill, remote ponds and streams
Rates: Full day: $125, lunch additional, various groups and trips negotiable with situation
Provides: Light tackle, lures, beverages, lunch
Handicapped equipped: Yes, certain areas only
Certifications: NY State DEC License, Member NYOGA

Tahawus Guide Service, Ltd.
Lake Placid 518-891-4334
Species & Seasons: Trout Arpil-Sept, Salmon, Panfish April-Nov, LM Bass June-Nov, Northern Pike May-Nov
Bodies of water: Ausable River, Boquet River, Saranac River, remote Adirondack Ponds, Lake Placid, Saranac Lake Chain
Rates: Full day: $200(1), $250(2), overnight rates on request
Call between: 8pm-11pm
Provides: Light tackle, fly rod/reel, lures, bait, rain gear, beverages, lunch
Handicapped equipped: Yes
Certifications: NY State Licensed Guide

Whiteface Guide Service
Wilmington 518-946-7258
Species & Seasons: Rainbow Trout, Brown Trout, Lake Trout, Brook Trout, Salmon April-Sept
Bodies of water: Lake Placid, Upper Saranac Lake, Taylor Pond, remote wilderness ponds, west branch Ausable River
Rates: Half day: $100(1-2), Full day: $175(1-2)
Call between: 8am-9pm
Provides: Light tackle, fly rod/reel, lures, bait
Handicapped equipped: Yes
Certifications: NY State Licensed Guide

LODGING...

Long Pond Lodge
Willsboro 518-963-7351
Guest Capacity: 16 people
Handicapped equipped: No
Seasons: All year
Rates: $90/pp: 3 days fishing/2 nights lodging, 4 meals
Contact: Pete Casamento
Guides: Yes
Species & Seasons: LM Bass, Northern Pike June-Oct, SM Bass June-Nov, Salmon April-Dec, Brown Trout, Brook Trout, Rainbow Trout, Lake Trout April-Dec
Bodies of Water: Lake Champlain, Ausable River, Boquet River, Saranac Lake, Lake Placid
Types of fishing: Fly fishing, light tackle, wading, float trips
Available: Fishing instruction, licenses, bait, tackle, boat rentals

McIntyre's Campground Cabins Marina
Au Sable Forks 518-647-5492
Handicapped equipped: No
Seasons: May 1 to Oct 15
Rates: Camping: $15/day, Housekeeping Unit: $30/day
Contact: Don McIntyre
Guides: Yes
Species & Seasons: SM Bass, LM Bass June-Oct, Northern Pike, Walleye, Trout May-Oct
Bodies of Water: Union Falls Pond, Saranac River, Au Sable River
Types of fishing: Fly fishing, light tackle, wading
Available: Bait, tackle, boat rentals

ASHOKAN RESERVOIR

BAIT & TACKLE...

The Tackle Shack
Phoenicia 914-688-7780
Hours: 7am-8pm
Carries: Live bait, lures, flies, maps, rods, reels, licenses
Bodies of water: Esodus Creek, Ashokan Res., Pepacton Res., Hudson River
Guides: Yes
OK to call for current conditions: Yes
Contact: Frank

GUIDES...

Singing Wolf Guide Service
PO Box 14782
Albany 12212
Species & Seasons: Trout all year
Bodies of water: Ashokan Res., Esopas Creek, Thompson's Lake, Delaware River, Big Pond, Little Pond, Beaverkill River, Kinderhook Creek, Boquet River, East Branch Ausable River, Batten Kill, remote ponds and streams
Rates: Full day: $125, lunch additional, various groups and trips negotiable with situation
Provides: Light tackle, lures, beverages, lunch
Handicapped equipped: Yes, certain areas only
Certifications: NY State DEC License, Member NYOGA

ATLANTIC OCEAN

BAIT & TACKLE...

Chester's Hunting & Fishing West Ltd.
Farmingville 516-696-3800
Hours: 9:30am-9pm
Carries: Live bait, lures, flies, rods, reels, licenses
Bodies of water: Long Island Sound, Atlantic Ocean, Great South Bay, Lake Ronkonkoma, Connetquot River
Services & Products: Repair services
Guides: Yes
OK to call for current conditions: Yes
Contact: Fred Laager

NEW YORK — ATLANTIC OCEAN

Freddie's of Montauk
Montauk 516-668-5520
Hours: 7am-6pm, closed Dec.-April
Carries: Live bait, lures, flies, maps, rods, reels
Bodies of water: Block Island Sound, Atlantic Ocean (south shore)
Services & Products: Beverages, fishing instruction, repair services, surfcasting tournaments
Guides: Yes
OK to call for current conditions: Yes
Contact: Bill or John

Scag's Bait & Tackle
Staten Island 718-727-7373
Hours: 7am-7:30pm
Carries: Live bait, lures, flies, rods, reels
Bodies of water: Atlantic Ocean, Raritan Bay, New Jersey Bay, New York Harbor, local ponds and lakes
Services & Products: Beverages, fishing instruction, repair services
Guides: Yes
OK to call for current conditions: Yes
Contact: Pat Scaglione

CHARTERS...

3-Sea-Sons Sport Fishing
Lindenhurst 516-888-4010
Species & Seasons: Mako Shark June-Oct, Tuna July-Oct, Bluefin Tuna Sept-Oct, Bluefish May-Dec, Fluke May-Sept
Bodies of water: Atlantic Ocean
Rates: $375-$700(1-6)
Call between: 8pm-10pm
Provides: Light tackle, heavy tackle, fly rod/reel, lures, bait
Handicapped equipped: Yes
Certifications: USCG

Alyssa Ann
Commack 516-543-4529
Species & Seasons: Tuna July-Oct, Shark June-Nov, Striped Bass, Bluefish May-Dec, Cod Mar-Dec
Bodies of water: Atlantic Ocean, Block Island Sound, Eastern Long Island Sound, waters surrounding Montauk PT, NY
Rates: Half day: $350(6), Full day: $600(6), Tuna, Shark, Marlin: $800
Call between: 6pm-10pm
Provides: Light tackle, heavy tackle, lures, bait
Handicapped equipped: Yes
Certifications: USCG

Awesome Fishing Charters
Freeport 516-546-0695
Species & Seasons: Striped Bass May-Nov, Fluke May-Sept, Bluefish, Shark June-Oct, Flounder April-May
Bodies of water: Atlantic Ocean waters off of Jones Beach
Rates: Half day: $50-$90(1), $175(2), Full day: $75-$125(1), $275(2)
Call between: 8am-5pm
Provides: Light tackle, heavy tackle, lures, bait, beverages, lunch
Handicapped equipped: Yes
Certifications: USCG

Blue Fin IV
Montauk 516-668-9323
Species & Seasons: Cod Mar-June, Striped Bass May-Dec, Bluefish May-Nov, Fluke, Shark June-Oct, Tuna June-Sept, other species too
Bodies of water: Block Island Sound, Atlantic Ocean
Rates: Local: Half day: $350(1-6), Full day: $595(1-6), Offshore: Full day: $795(1-6)
Call between: 6pm-9pm
Provides: Light tackle, heavy tackle, fly rod/reel, lures, bait, rain gear
Handicapped equipped: Yes
Certifications: USCG, IGFA

John Botting
Cape Vincent 315-654-2634
.... 743-6683
Species & Seasons: SM Bass, Perch, Lake Trout, Salmon June-Oct
Bodies of water: Lake Ontario, Atlantic Ocean, Gulf of Mexico
Rates: Full day: $200(1), $250-$300(2-4), $50 additional pp up to 6
Call between: Anytime
Provides: Light tackle, heavy tackle, lures, bait
Handicapped equipped: yes
Certifications: USCG

Fishooker Charters
Montauk 516-668-3821
Species & Seasons: Shark, Bluefish June-Nov, Tuna July-Oct, Striped Bass June-Dec, Cod April-June, Fluke July-Sept
Bodies of water: Block Island Sound, Atlantic Ocean
Rates: Boat: Half day: $350(1-6), Full day: $600-$800(1-6)
Call between: 9am-10pm
Provides: Light tackle, heavy tackle, fly rod/reel, lures, bait
Handicapped equipped: Yes, except wheelchairs
Certifications: USCG
(see ad page 317)

Capt Barry Kohlus
Montauk 516-668-5405
Species & Seasons: Cod all year, Flounder May-June, Striped Bass, Bluefish, June-Nov, Shark, Tuna June-Oct, Marlin July-Aug, Fluke July-Sept, Tautog Oct-Nov, Sea Bass May-July
Bodies of water: Atlantic Ocean, Block Island Sound
Rates: Inshore: Half day: $350(6), Full day: $600(6), Offshore: Full day: $800(6), Spring special $600
Call between: 7pm-10pm
Provides: Light tackle, heavy tackle, lures, bait, rain gear
Handicapped equipped: Yes
Certifications: USCG

Montauk Sportfishing
Montauk 516-668-2019
Species & Seasons: Shark, Tuna, Marlin, Striped Bass, Bluefish, Fluke, Flounder, Cod
Bodies of water: Atlantic Ocean, Long Island Sound
Rates: $350-$1800
Certifications: USCG

MONTAUK, L.I.
41' Custom Built - BLUE FIN IV
Over 25 Species - Fly to 130lb.
50 Years Family Experience
Capt. Michael Potts 516 668-9323

ATLANTIC OCEAN - BLACK RIVER — NEW YORK

Charterboat 'FISHOOKER'
Shark • Tuna • Bass • Blues
MONTAUK'S Finest Sports Fishing
Capt. Otto Haselman
136 Greenwich St.
Montauk, N.Y.
516 668-3821
Call for reservations & brochure!

MARINAS...

Burnett's Marina
Bay Shore 516-665-9050
Hours: 6am-8pm
Carries: Live bait, lures, maps, rods, reels
Bodies of water: Great South Bay, Atlantic Ocean
Services & Products: Charter boat service, beverages, repair services
Guides: Yes
OK to call for current conditions: Yes
Contact: Tony Contarino

BEAVERKILL RIVER

BAIT & TACKLE...

Al's Sport Store
Downsville 607-363-7740
Hours: 6am-6pm
Carries: Live bait, lures, flies, maps, rods, reels, licenses
Bodies of water: Delaware River, Beaverkill River, Pepacton Res.
Services & Products: Canoe rentals, lodging, canoe ramp
Guides: Yes
OK to call for current conditions: Yes
Contact: Al Carpenter

The Beaverkill Angler
Roscoe 607-498-5194
Hours: 9am-5:30pm
Carries: Flies, maps, rods, reels
Bodies of water: Beaverkill River, Delaware River, East & West Branches
Services & Products: Guide services, fishing instruction
Guides: Yes
OK to call for current conditions: Yes

Donegal Inc.
Roscoe 607-498-5911
Hours: 8am-6pm
Carries: Flies, maps, rods, reels
Bodies of water: Beaverkill River, Willowemac River, Delaware River, East West Branch, Neversink River
Services & Products: Guide services, fishing instruction
OK to call for current conditions: Yes
Contact: Paul

The Little Store
Roscoe 607-498-5553
Hours: 9am-5:30pm
Carries: Live bait, lures, flies, maps, rods, reels, licenses
Bodies of water: Beaverkill River, Willowemac River
Guides: Yes
OK to call for current conditions: Yes

Manor Sport Shop
Livingston Manor 914-439-3002
Hours: 8am-6pm
Carries: Live bait, lures, flies, maps, rods, reels, licenses
Bodies of water: Beaverkill River, Willowemac River, Pepacton Res.
Services & Products: Fishing instruction, repair services, custom rods, guns, ammo, camping supplies
Guides: Yes
OK to call for current conditions: Yes
Contact: Joe Dimilte

GUIDES...

Singing Wolf Guide Service
PO Box 14782
Albany 12212
Species & Seasons: Trout all year
Bodies of water: Ashokan Res., Esopas Creek, Thompson's Lake, Delaware River, Big Pond, Little Pond, Beaverkill River, Kinderhook Creek, Boquet River, East Branch Ausable River, Batten Kill, remote ponds and streams
Rates: Full day: $125, lunch additional, various groups and trips negotiable with situation
Provides: Light tackle, lures, beverages, lunch
Handicapped equipped: Yes, certain areas only
Certifications: NY State DEC License, Member NYOGA

BLACK LAKE

LODGING...

Golden Horseshoe Camps
Hammond 315-375-6395
Guest Capacity: 50
Handicapped equipped: Yes
Seasons: May 1 to Sept 30
Rates: $40/day, $170/week double occupancy
Contact: Lois Rockefeller
Guides: No
Species & Seasons: Crappie all year, Northern Pike May-Sept-Dec, LM Bass, SM Bass June-Oct
Bodies of Water: Black Lake, St. Lawrence River
Types of fishing: Light tackle, heavy tackle
Available: Boat rentals

Pinehurst on the St. Lawrence Inc.
Alexandria Bay 315-482-9452
Guest Capacity: 190
Handicapped equipped: No
Seasons: May to Oct
Rates: $36-$150/day, $280-$800/week
Guides: Yes
Species & Seasons: Northern Pike, Walleye, Muskellunge May, LM Bass, SM Bass May-June
Bodies of Water: St Lawrence River, Lake Ontario, Black Lake
Types of fishing: Light tackle, heavy tackle
Available: Boat rentals

BLACK RIVER

BAIT & TACKLE...

The Green Drake
Utica 315-735-6679
Hours: 9am-7pm
Carries: Flies, rods, reels
Bodies of water: West Canada Creek, Black River, Salmon River, Lake Ontario, Oriskany Creek, Delaware River
Services & Products: Guide services, fishing instruction, repair services, custom rods
Guides: Yes
OK to call for current conditions: Yes
Contact: George Massoud

NEW YORK

BLACK RIVER - CANADARAGO LAKE

GUIDES...

Alex Atchie's Guide Service
Watertown 315-782-3904
Species & Seasons: Chinook Salmon Sept-Oct, Atlantic Salmon Aug-Oct, Steelhead Oct-Nov/Feb-April
Bodies of water: Black River, Salmon River
Rates: Full day: $120(1), $240(2)
Call between: 6pm-10pm
Provides: Light tackle, heavy tackle, lures, bait
Handicapped equipped: Yes, depending on handicap
Certifications: NY Licensed Guide, Member of Oswego Cty River Guides Assoc.

Tightlines Guide Service
Pulaski 800-452-1176
Species & Seasons: Chinook Salmon, Coho Salmon Sept-Nov, Steelhead Nov-May, Brown Trout Oct-Nov
Bodies of water: Lake Ontario, Salmon River, Black River, Oswego River, Little Salmon River, and eastern Lake Ontario Tributaries
Rates: Float trips: Half day: $150(1), $175(2), Full day: $180(1), $220(2), Wade trips: $135pp
Call between: 6pm-10pm
Provides: Light tackle, heavy tackle, fly rod/reel, lures, bait
Handicapped equipped: No
Certifications: NY Registered Guide

Wild River Inn Lodge & Guide Service
Pulaski 315-298-4195
Species & Seasons: Salmon Aug-Nov, Steelhead Oct-May, Lake Trout May-Aug, Brown Trout Oct-July, Walleye May-July, SM Bass June-Sept
Bodies of water: Salmon River, Lake Ontario, Black River, Oswego River, and other Lake Ontario Tributaries
Rates: Full day (starting at): $160(1), $220(2), Lodge (starting at): $22.50/pp
Call between: 9am-9pm
Provides: Light tackle, heavy tackle, fly rod/reel, lures, bait
Handicapped equipped: Yes, on the lake, river no
Certifications: NY State Licensed Guide, USCG

MARINAS...

Grunert's Marina & Cottages
Sackets Harbor 315-646-2003
Hours: 7am-7pm
Carries: Maps
Bodies of water: Black River, Black River Bay, Lake Ontario
Services & Products: Lodging, boat ramp, beverages, gas/oil
Guides: Yes
OK to call for current conditions: Yes
Contact: Charles L. Grunert

BLOCK ISLAND SOUND

BAIT & TACKLE...

Freddie's of Montauk
Montauk 516-668-5520
Hours: 7am-6pm, closed Dec.-April
Carries: Live bait, lures, flies, maps, rods, reels
Bodies of water: Block Island Sound, Atlantic Ocean (south shore)
Services & Products: Beverages, fishing instruction, repair services, surfcasting tournaments
Guides: Yes
OK to call for current conditions: Yes
Contact: Bill or John

CHARTERS...

Alyssa Ann
Commack 516-543-4529
Species & Seasons: Tuna July-Oct, Shark June-Nov, Striped Bass, Bluefish May-Dec, Cod Mar-Dec
Bodies of water: Atlantic Ocean, Block Island Sound, Eastern Long Island Sound, waters surrounding Montauk PT, NY
Rates: Half day: $350(6), Full day: $600(6), Tuna, Shark, Marlin: $800
Call between: 6pm-10pm
Provides: Light tackle, heavy tackle, lures, bait
Handicapped equipped: Yes
Certifications: USCG

Blue Fin IV
Montauk 516-668-9323
Species & Seasons: Cod Mar-June, Striped Bass May-Dec, Bluefish May-Nov, Fluke, Shark June-Oct, Tuna June-Sept, other species too
Bodies of water: Block Island Sound, Atlantic Ocean
Rates: Local: Half day: $350(1-6), Full day: $595(1-6), Offshore: Full day: $795(1-6)
Call between: 6pm-9pm
Provides: Light tackle, heavy tackle, fly rod/reel, lures, bait, rain gear
Handicapped equipped: Yes
Certifications: USCG, IGFA

Fishooker Charters
Montauk 516-668-3821
Species & Seasons: Shark, Bluefish June-Nov, Tuna July-Oct, Striped Bass June-Dec, Cod April-June, Fluke July-Sept
Bodies of water: Block Island Sound, Atlantic Ocean
Rates: Boat: Half day: $350(1-6), Full day: $600-$800(1-6)
Call between: 9am-10pm
Provides: Light tackle, heavy tackle, fly rod/reel, lures, bait
Handicapped equipped: Yes, except wheelchairs
Certifications: USCG

Capt Barry Kohlus
Montauk 516-668-5405
Species & Seasons: Cod all year, Flounder May-June, Striped Bass, Bluefish, June-Nov, Shark, Tuna June-Oct, Marlin July-Aug, Fluke July-Sept, Tautog Oct-Nov, Sea Bass May-July
Bodies of water: Atlantic Ocean, Block Island Sound
Rates: Inshore: Half day: $350(6), Full day: $600(6), Offshore: Full day: $800(6), Spring special $600
Call between: 7pm-10pm
Provides: Light tackle, heavy tackle, lures, bait, rain gear
Handicapped equipped: Yes
Certifications: USCG

CANADARAGO LAKE

GUIDES...

Michael Empey, Sr.
Richfield Springs 315-858-2286
Species & Seasons: Lake Trout, Salmon April-Sept, Walleye, Tiger Muskellunge May-Oct
Bodies of water: Otsego lake, Canadarago Lake
Rates: Varies: $75-$$200 per day

CANADARAGO LAKE - DELAWARE RIVER

NEW YORK

Call between: Anytime
Provides: Light tackle, lures, bait
Handicapped equipped: No
Certifications: NY State DEC Licensed

CHAUTAUQUA LAKE

BAIT & TACKLE...

Nellie's Bait Farm
Kennedy 716-267-2248
Hours: 8:30am-6pm, closed Sun.
Carries: Live bait
Bodies of water: Lake Erie, Chautauqua Lake
Services & Products:
Guides: Yes
OK to call for current conditions: Yes
Contact: Nelson Nord

GUIDES...

Allegheny Outdoors
Bradford, PA 814-368-8608
Species & Seasons: Trout, Walleye, Muskellunge, Northern Pike, SM Bass, Steelhead
Bodies of water: Chautauqua Lake
Rates: Half day: $75(1), $100(2)
Full day: $125(1), $150(2), prices vary with type of fishing
Call between: 5pm-11pm
Provides: Light tackle, heavy tackle, lures, bait
Certifications: NYS DEC licensed

CHANANGO RIVER

GUIDES...

A J's Outdoor Services
Courtland 607-758-7533
Species & Seasons: SM Bass, LM Bass June-Sept, Rainbow Trout, Brown Trout, Brook Trout April-Sept, Walleye, Bullhead, Pickerel, Northern Pike June-Sept, Yellow Perch all year
Bodies of water: Tioughnioga River, Otselic River, Chanango River
Rates: Full day: $75+(1-2), $24 additional pp
Call between: 5pm-9pm
Provides: Bait, beverages, lunch
Handicapped equipped: Some
Certifications: NYSDEC Licensed Guide

DELAWARE RIVER

BAIT & TACKLE...

Al's Sport Store
Downsville 607-363-7740
Hours: 6am-6pm
Carries: Live bait, lures, flies, maps, rods, reels, licenses
Bodies of water: Delaware River, Beaverkill River, Pepacton Res.
Services & Products: Canoe rentals, lodging, canoe ramp
Guides: Yes
OK to call for current conditions: Yes
Contact: Al Carpenter

The Beaverkill Angler
Roscoe 607-498-5194
Hours: 9am-5:30pm
Carries: Flies, maps, rods, reels
Bodies of water: Beaverkill River, Delaware River, East and West Branches
Services & Products: Guide services, fishing instruction
Guides: Yes
OK to call for current conditions: Yes

Donegal Inc.
Roscoe 607-498-5911
Hours: 8am-6pm
Carries: Flies, maps, rods, reels
Bodies of water: Beaverkill River, Willowemac River, Delaware River, East West Branch, Neversink River
Services & Products: Guide services, fishing instruction
OK to call for current conditions: Yes
Contact: Paul

The Green Drake
Utica 315-735-6679
Hours: 9am-7pm
Carries: Flies, rods, reels
Bodies of water: West Canada Creek, Black River, Salmon River, Lake Ontario, Oriskany Creek, Delaware River
Services & Products: Guide services, fishing instruction, repair services, custom rods
Guides: Yes
OK to call for current conditions: Yes
Contact: George Massoud

Tom's Bait & Tackle Shop
Narrowsburg 914-252-7445
Hours: 8am-6pm
Carries: Live bait, lures, flies, rods, reels, licenses

Bodies of water: Delaware River, Lake Huntington, Swinging Bridge Res., Lake Superior, Crystal Lake
Services & Products: Rod & reel rentals
Guides: Yes
OK to call for current conditions: Yes
Contact: Tom or Cecilia

CAMPS...

Catskill Fly Fishing Center & Museum
Livingston Manor 914-439-4810
Educational & Recreational Programs: Stream ecology, angling, fly tying, rod building, ages 8-18
Other interesting points: Gift shop, visitor's center, exhibits on rods, files, reels and the evolution of fly fishing,

GUIDES...

Don Brown Guide Service
Jefferson 607-652-7844
Species & Seasons: Brown Trout, Rainbow Trout, Brook Trout April-Jee
Bodies of water: Schoharie River, West Branch Delaware River & Tributaries
Rates: Half day: $100(1-2),
Full day: $150(1-2)
Call between: 6pm-9pm
Handicapped equipped: No
Certifications: NY State Licensed Hunting & Fishing Guide 27 years

Singing Wolf Guide Service
PO Box 14782
Albany 12212
Species & Seasons: Trout all year
Bodies of water: Ashokan Res., Esopas Creek, Thompson's Lake, Delaware River, Big Pond, Little Pond, Beaverkill River, Kinderhook Creek, Boquet River, East Branch Ausable River, Batten Kill, remote ponds and streams
Rates: Full day: $125, lunch additional, various groups & trips negotiable with situation
Provides: Light tackle, lures, beverages, lunch
Handicapped equipped: Yes, certain areas only
Certifications: NY State DEC License, Member NYOGA

NEW YORK
DELAWARE RIVER - FINGER LAKES

Upper Delaware Outfitters
Hankins 914-887-4853
Species & Seasons: Trout April-July/Sept, SM Bass July-Oct, Shad May-July
Bodies of water: Delaware River (Drift boat)
Rates: Full day: $135(1-2)
Call between: 6pm-10pm
Provides: Beverages, lunch
Handicapped equipped: No
Certifications: NY State Licensed Guide

LODGING...

Eldred Preserve
Eldred 914-557-8316
Guest Capacity: 60
Handicapped equipped: No
Seasons: All year
Rates: $85/day
Contact: Bonnie or Lou
Guides: Yes
Species & Seasons: Trout, Catfish, Panfish, Pickerel all year, LM Bass, SM Bass June-Oct
Bodies of Water: Sunrise Lake, Delaware River, Lake Wallenpaupack (PA)
Types of fishing: Fly fishing, light tackle, float trips, bass boat rentals
Available: Fishing instruction, licenses, bait, tackle, boat rentals, sporting clays, restaurant

Green Acres Motel
Hancock 607-467-3620
Guest Capacity: 11 units, 12 rooms
Handicapped equipped: No, but easily accessible
Seasons: All year
Rates: $35/day single + tax, $40/day double occupancy + tax, $50/day (2 double beds) + tax
Contact: Maria Bacon
Guides: Yes
Species & Seasons: Trout April-Oct, Shad Spring
Bodies of Water: Delaware River
Types of fishing: Fly fishing, wading
Available: In-room coffee, golf course and restaurants nearby

Timberline Motel
Hancock 607-467-2042
Guest Capacity: 30
Handicapped equipped: No
Seasons: April 1 to Dec 30
Rates: $30-$75/day (per room)
Contact: Jerry

Guides: No
Species & Seasons: Trout, SM Bass, Muskellunge, Walleye, American Shad April-Nov
Bodies of Water: West Branch of Delaware River
Types of fishing: Fly fishing
Available: Fishing instruction, licenses, bait, tackle, boat rentals, family activities all near by
(see ad page 321)

GREEN ACRES MOTEL
RR1, Box 111, Rt. 17 • Hancock, NY 13783
607 467-3620
Moderately priced, clean comfortable rooms, private baths, air conditioning and in room coffee. Scenically located on Rt 17 West Branch of the Delaware. Restaurants, golf course, fishing & hunting nearby. *Open All Year!*

Your Hosts:
Ken & Maria Bacon

FINGER LAKES

BAIT & TACKLE...

Fishermen's Friend
Waterloo 315-539-3847
Hours: 6am-6pm
Carries: Live bait, lures, maps, rods, reels, licenses
Bodies of water: Seneca Lake, Heart of the Finger Lakes
Services & Products: Guide services, repair services
Guides: Yes
OK to call for current conditions: Yes
Contact: Walt or Mina

CHARTERS...

Captain Ron's Charters
Romulus 315-585-6408
.... 727-5507
Species & Seasons: Salmon, Lake Trout, Rainbow Trout, Brown Trout April-Oct, Perch, Northern Pike May-Oct
Bodies of water: Lake Ontario, Seneca Lake
Rates: Half day: $225(1-3), Full day: $300(1-3)
Call between: 6pm-8pm
Provides: Light tackle, heavy tackle, lures, bait
Handicapped equipped: Yes
Certifications: USCG

Expediter Charters
Montour Falls 607-535-7558
Species & Seasons: Brown Trout, Coho Salmon April-Oct, Steelhead May-Oct, Chinook Salmon June-Oct
Bodies of water: Lake Ontario, Seneca Lake
Rates: Half day: $250(1-2), Full day: $450(1-2)
Call between: 6am-10pm
Provides: Light tackle, heavy tackle, lures, bait
Handicapped equipped: Yes
Certifications: USCG

Loon-A-Sea Charter Service
Trumansburg 607-387-5474
Species & Seasons: LM Bass, SM Bass June-Nov, Walleye May-Aug, Sightseeing May-Nov
Bodies of water: Cayuga Lake, Seneca Lake, Lake Ontario
Rates: Cayuga, Seneca Lakes: $35 pp hr., Lake Ontario: $35pp hr. + expenses
Call between: 3pm-9pm
Provides: Light tackle, lures, bait, rain gear
Handicapped equipped: Yes
Certifications: USCG

Vitamin Sea Charters
Waterloo 315-539-8184
Species & Seasons: Lake Trout, Rainbow Trout, Brown Trout, Atlantic Salmon, Chinook Salmon April-Oct, SM Bass June-Oct, Northern Pike, Walleye May-Oct
Bodies of water: Lake Ontario, Seneca Lake
Rates: Half day: $180(1-2), $220(3), Full day: $250(1-2), $300(3)

FINGER LAKES - GREENWOOD LAKE — NEW YORK

Call between: 6pm-9:30pm
Provides: Light tackle, lures, bait
Handicapped equipped: Yes
Certifications: USCG, NY State

GUIDES...

Finger Lakes Outfitters
Fairport 716-223-8236
Species & Seasons: Chinook Salmon Aug-Nov, Brown Trout Oct-Dec, Steelhead Oct-May, Brown Trout April-Sept, Rainbow Trout Oct-May
Bodies of water: Lake Ontario Tributaries, Salmon River, Maxwell Creek, Irondequoit Creek, Oak Orchard Creek, Finger Lakes Tributaries, Naples Creek, Catherine's Creek, Salmon Creek and more
Rates: Half day: $75(1), $100(2), Full day: $150(1), $200(2)
Call between: 7am-10pm
Provides: Fly rod/reel, lures(flies), beverages, lunch
Handicapped equipped: No
Certifications: NY State Guide, Red Cross First aid, CPR, Water Safety, fully insured

Let's Go Fishing
Syracuse 315-478-7231
Species & Seasons: Trout April-Sept, Northern Pike May-Mar, LM Bass June-Nov, Salmon depends on waters and species, Panfish all year
Bodies of water: Central New York region, Finger Lakes, Lake Ontario, Whitney Point Lake, Oneida Lake
Call between: 6pm-9pm
Provides: Light tackle, heavy tackle, fly rod/reel, lures, bait
Handicapped equipped: No
Certifications: NY State Licensed Guide

M-R Bass Outfitters
35 14th Street
Troy 12180
Species & Seasons: Shad April-June, Striped Bass April-July, Northern Pike, Muskellunge May-Nov, LM Bass June-Nov, Walleye May-Nov
Bodies of water: Hudson River, Mohawk River, Lake Champlain, Saratoga Lake, Finger Lakes, Onieda Lake and any body of water in New York State
Rates: Half day: $50-$75(1), $75-$100(2), Full day: $100-$175(1), $150-$200(2)
Call between: Anytime
Provides: Light tackle, heavy tackle, fly rod/reel, lures, bait, rain gear, beverages, lunch, photos

Handicapped equipped: No
Certifications: NYSOGA, ENCON, USCG

MARINAS..

Jansen Marina, Inc.
Conesus 716-346-2060
Hours: 9am-8pm
Carries: Maps
Bodies of water: Conesus Lake, Hemlock Lake
Services & Products: Boat rentals, gas/oil, repair services
Guides: No
OK to call for current conditions: No

Roy's Marina
Geneva 315-789-3094
Hours: 8am-5pm
Carries: Live bait, lures, maps, licenses
Bodies of water: Seneca Lake
Services & Products: Boat rentals, boat ramp, gas/oil, fishing instruction, repair services
Guides: Yes
OK to call for current conditions: Yes
Contact: Roy Japp

GREAT SOUTH BAY

BAIT & TACKLE...

Chester's Hunting & Fishing West Ltd.
Farmingville 516-696-3800
Hours: 9:30am-9pm
Carries: Live bait, lures, flies, rods, reels, licenses

TIMBERLINE MOTEL
Route 17, Hancock, NY • 607 467-2042
Located on the West Branch of the Delaware River
Located within walking distance of the excellent fishing at the Hale Eddy Bridge and only minutes from the special regs section with its fine year-round fishing.

Bodies of water: Long Island Sound, Atlantic Ocean, Great South Bay, Lake Ronkonkoma, Connetquot River
Services & Products: Repair services
Guides: Yes
OK to call for current conditions: Yes
Contact: Fred Laager

MARINAS...

Burnett's Marina
Bay Shore 516-665-9050
Hours: 6am-8pm
Carries: Live bait, lures, maps, rods, reels
Bodies of water: Great South Bay, Atlantic Ocean
Services & Products: Charter boat service, beverages, repair services
Guides: Yes
OK to call for current conditions: Yes
Contact: Tony Contarino

GREENWOOD LAKE

BAIT & TACKLE...

O & H Bait Shop
Chester 914-469-2566
Hours: 6am-6pm
Carries: Live bait, lures, flies, maps, rods, reels, licenses
Bodies of water: Walton Lake, Hudson River, Round Lake, Greenwood Lake
Services & Products: Repair services
Guides: No
OK to call for current conditions: Yes
Contact: Jim

GUIDES...

Pete Traina
Ridgewood 718-821-6367
Species & Seasons: Bluefish, Flounder, Fluke, Trout, plus other species
Bodies of water: Long Island Sound, White Lake, Highland Lake, Greenwood Lake, all Sullivan County lakes and streams
Rates: Varies,
(also Bodyguard and Escort Service)
Call between: 8am-11pm
Provides: Light tackle, heavy tackle, lures, bait, rain gear, beverages, lunch
Handicapped equipped: Yes
Certifications: USCG, NY State Licensed Guide

NEW YORK
HUDSON RIVER - LAKE CHAMPLAIN

HUDSON RIVER

BAIT & TACKLE...

O & H Bait Shop
Chester 914-469-2566
Hours: 6am-6pm
Carries: Live bait, lures, flies, maps, rods, reels, licenses
Bodies of water: Walton Lake, Hudson River, Round Lake, Greenwood Lake
Services & Products: Repair services
Guides: No
OK to call for current conditions: Yes
Contact: Jim

Outdoorsman Sport Shop
Diamond Point 518-668-3910
Hours: 5am-9pm, (closed Mon. in winter)
Carries: Live bait, lures, flies, maps, rods, reels, licenses
Bodies of water: Lake George, Hudson Rver, Schroon River, Schroon Lake, Brandt Lake, Loon Lake, Lake Champlain, Lake Luzern, Glen Lake, Trout Lake
Services & Products: Guide services, charter boat service, lodging, fishing instruction
Guides: Yes
OK to call for current conditions: Yes
Contact: Garry or Sally Nelson

The Tackle Shack
Phoenicia 914-688-7780
Hours: 7am-8pm
Carries: Live bait, lures, flies, maps, rods, reels, licenses
Bodies of water: Esodus Creek, Ashokan Res., Pepacton Res., Hudson River
Guides: Yes
OK to call for current conditions: Yes
Contact: Frank

CHARTERS...

Trophy Seeker Charters
Verbank 914-677-9071
Species & Seasons: Brown Trout April-Aug, Chinook Salmon July-Sept, Coho Salmon, Lake Trout April-Sept, Steelhead April-Oct, Striped Bass April-June
Bodies of water: Hudson River, Lake Ontario
Rates: Lake Ontario: 6 hrs: $300(1-4), 8 hrs: $375(1-4), Hudson River: 6 hrs: $250(1-3)
Call between: Anytime
Provides: Light tackle, heavy tackle, lures, bait
Handicapped equipped: Yes
Certifications: USCG, Licensed NY State

GUIDES...

Call of the Wild Guide Service
Wallkill 914-895-3097
Species & Seasons: Brook Trout April-June, Salmon Sept-June, Lake Trout May-May
Bodies of water: Lake George, Fulton Chain Lakes, Salmon River, Lake Champlain, Pharroah Lake, Hudson River
Call between: 8am-9pm
Provides: Light tackle, heavy tackle, fly rod/reel, lures, bait, rain gear, beverages, lunch
Handicapped equipped: Yes

M-R Bass Outfitters
35 14th Street
Troy 12180
Species & Seasons: Shad April-June, Striped Bass April-July, Northern Pike, Muskellunge May-Nov, LM Bass June-Nov, Walleye May-Nov
Bodies of water: Hudson River, Mohawk River, Lake Champlain, Saratoga Lake, Finger Lakes, Onieda Lake and any body of water in New York State
Rates: Half day: $50-$75(1), $75-$100(2), Full day: $100-$175(1), $150-$200(2)
Call between: Anytime
Provides: Light tackle, heavy tackle, fly rod/reel, lures, bait, rain gear, beverages, lunch, photos
Handicapped equipped: No
Certifications: NYSOGA, ENCON, USCG

Reel Action Guide Service
Glenmont 518-434-1133
Species & Seasons: LM Bass, SM Bass June-Nov, Walleye, Northern Pike, Panfish May-Nov
Bodies of water: Saratoga Lake, Mohawk River, Hudson River
Rates: Half day: $125(2), Full day: $175(2)
Call between: 8am-10pm
Provides: Light tackle, heavy tackle, lures, beverages
Handicapped equipped: No
Certifications: NY State Licensed

LODGING...

Garnet Hill Lodge
North River 518-251-2821
Guest Capacity: 70
Handicapped equipped: Yes
Seasons: All year
Rates: $75/day (European plan)
Contact: George Heim
Guides: Yes
Species & Seasons: Brown Trout, Salmon, Rainbow Trout, Brook Trout April-Nov
Bodies of Water: Hudson River, Siamese Ponds (Wilderness)
Types of fishing: Fly fishing, light tackle, horse/back pack, wading, float trips
Available: Fishing instruction, boat rentals, family activities, baby sitting

LAKE CHAMPLAIN

BAIT & TACKLE...

Gordon's Marine Tackle & Archery
W. Plattsburgh 518-561-2109
Hours: 8:30am-6/8pm, closed Sun.
Carries: Live bait, lures, flies, maps, rods, reels
Bodies of water: Lake Champlain, Saranac River, Chazy Lake, Chateauguay Lake, Adirondacks area
Services & Products: Charter boat service
Guides: Yes
OK to call for current conditions: Yes

Outdoorsman Sport Shop
Diamond Point 518-668-3910
Hours: 5am-9pm, (closed Mon. in winter)
Carries: Live bait, lures, flies, maps, rods, reels, licenses
Bodies of water: Lake George, Hudson Rver, Schroon River, Schroon Lake, Brandt Lake, Loon Lake, Lake Champlain, Lake Luzern, Glen Lake, Trout Lake
Services & Products: Guide services, charter boat service, lodging, fishing instruction
Guides: Yes
OK to call for current conditions: Yes
Contact: Garry or Sally Nelson

LAKE CHAMPLAIN — NEW YORK

CHARTERS...

Fish P.T. Guide Service
Caldwell, NJ 201-226-8380
Species & Seasons: Trout, Salmon April-June, SM Bass May-Oct, King Salmon Aug-Sept Landlocked Atlantic Salmon, Lake Trout Sept-Nov
Bodies of water: Lake Champlain, Adirondacks, Lake Ontario
Rates: Lake Ontario weekend, 3 days/2nights: $325pp(minimum 3), Lake Champlain-Adirondacks, 2 days/2 nights: $225(minimum 2)
Call between: Before 8am-After 7pm
Provides: Light tackle, medium tackle, fly rod/reel, lures, beverages, lunch
Handicapped equipped: Yes

Justy-Joe Sportfishing Charters
Gansevoort 518-798-0336
Species & Seasons: Salmon, Lake Trout April-Dec
Bodies of water: Lake George, Lake Champlain
Rates: Half day: $160(1-2), $180(3-4), Full day: $280(1-2), $300(3-4)
Provides: Light tackle
Handicapped equipped: Yes
Certifications: USCG, NY State Licensed Guide

Naughty Lady Charters
Adirondack 518-532-7305
Species & Seasons: Salmon, Lake Trout, Walleye, Northern Pike May/Sept-Oct
Bodies of water: Lake Champlain, Lake George, Schroon Lake
Rates: Half day: $120(1), Full day: $230(1)
Call between: 5am-10pm
Provides: Light tackle, lures, bait
Handicapped equipped: No
Certifications: USCG, NYOGA

Placid Bay Ventures Guide & Charter
Lake Placid 518-523-1744
.... 518-523-2001
Species & Seasons: Lake Trout, Brook Trout April-Nov, Salmon April-June, Chinook Salmon, Atlantic Salmon Aug-Oct, SM Bass June-Nov, Northern Pike May-Mar, Muskellunge Sept-Nov, Walleye, Rainbow Trout, Brown Trout April-Nov
Bodies of water: Lake Placid, Adirondack lakes and steams, Lake Champlain, Lake Ontario
Rates: Full day: $200(1-2)

Provides: Light tackle, heavy tackle, fly rod/reel, lures, lodging also available
Handicapped equipped: Yes, large boat, some limitations
Certifications: USCG, NYSOGA

Reel Easy Sportfishing
Scotia 518-399-5336
Species & Seasons: Atlantic Salmon April-Nov, Lake Trout, Rainbow Trout May-Nov, Brown Trout April-Oct, SM Bass June-Sept, Northern Pike May-Sept, Walleye May-Oct
Bodies of water: Lake Champlain, Great Sacandaga Lake, Mohawk River, Barge Canal, Saranac Lake Region
Rates: Reel Easy I (local lakes-rivers): 4hrs: $120(1-3), 6hrs: $175(1-3) 8hrs: $225(1-3), Reel Easy II (Lake Ontario-Champlain): 6hrs: $240(1-4), 8hrs: $300(1-4), Ice fishing (Jan-Mar): $75(1)
Call between: 7am-9pm
Provides: Light tackle, heavy tackle, lures, bait
Handicapped equipped: Yes, no wheelchairs
Certifications: USCG, NY State Licensed

GUIDES...

Adirondack Champlain Guide Service
Willsboro 518-963-7351
Species & Seasons: SM Bass June-Nov, LM Bass, Northern Pike June-Oct, Salmon, Brown Trout, Rainbow Trout April-Dec, Lake Trout May-Dec, Brook Trout April-Oct, Walleye May-Sept, Muskellunge Aug-Oct
Bodies of water: Lake Champlain, Ausable River, Boquet River, Saranac River, Saranac Lake Chain, St. Regis Chain of Lakes
Rates: Full day: $165(1), $210(2), 1 day fishing with guide, 2 nights lodging, 4 meals: $185pp
Call between: 8am-9pm
Provides: Light tackle, fly rod/reel, lures, bait, rain gear, beverages, lunch
Handicapped equipped: Yes
Certifications: New York State, USCG

Call of the Wild Guide Service
Wallkill 914-895-3097
Species & Seasons: Brook Trout April-June, Salmon Sept-June, Lake Trout May-May
Bodies of water: Lake George, Fulton Chain Lakes, Salmon River, Lake Champlain, Pharroah Lake, Hudson River
Call between: 8am-9pm
Provides: Light tackle, heavy tackle, fly rod/reel, lures, bait, rain gear, beverages, lunch
Handicapped equipped: Yes

M-R Bass Outfitters
35 14th Street
Troy 12180
Species & Seasons: Shad April-June, Striped Bass April-July, Northern Pike, Muskellunge May-Nov, LM Bass June-Nov, Walleye May-Nov
Bodies of water: Hudson River, Mohawk River, Lake Champlain, Saratoga Lake, Finger Lakes, Onieda Lake and any body of water in New York State
Rates: Half day: $50-$75(1), $75-$100(2), Full day: $100-$175(1), $150-$200(2)
Call between: Anytime
Provides: Light tackle, heavy tackle, fly rod/reel, lures, bait, rain gear, beverages, lunch, photos
Handicapped equipped: No
Certifications: NYSOGA, ENCON, USCG

FISH P.T. GUIDE SERVICE
CAPT. PETE KELLEY
UPPER NY STATE AREA
LAKE CHAMPLAIN • ADIRONDACKS
LAKE ONTARIO

• For Information •
Call (201) 226-8380 or Write:
15 Gladding Road
Caldwell, NJ 07006

NEW YORK STATE

Ps. 107

NEW YORK

LAKE CHAMPLAIN - LAKE GEORGE

Peaked Hill Guide Service
Severance 518-532-7953
Species & Seasons: LM Bass, SM Bass June-Nov, Tiger Muskellunge, Northern Pike May-Mar
Bodies of water: Paradox Lake, Eagle Lake, Schroon Lake, Schroon River, Lake Champlain, Lake George, Lake Durant and several back water ponds for Bass and Pike
Rates: Half day: $65(1), $115(2), Full day: $95(1), $185(2)
Call between: 5pm-9pm
Provides: Light tackle, heavy tackle, lures, bait, rain gear, beverages
Handicapped equipped: No
Certifications: NY State Guide

LODGING...

Long Pond Lodge
Willsboro 518-963-7351
Guest Capacity: 16 people
Handicapped equipped: No
Seasons: All year
Rates: $90/pp: 3 days fishing/2 nights lodging, 4 meals
Contact: Pete Casamento
Guides: Yes
Species & Seasons: LM Bass, Northern Pike June-Oct, SM Bass June-Nov, Salmon April-Dec, Brown Trout, Brook Trout, Rainbow Trout, Lake Trout April-Dec
Bodies of Water: Lake Champlain, Ausable River, Boquet River, Saranac Lake, Lake Placid
Types of fishing: Fly fishing, light tackle, wading, float trips
Available: Fishing instruction, licenses, bait, tackle, boat rentals

LAKE ERIE

BAIT & TACKLE...

Big Catch Bait & Tackle
Buffalo 716-877-0971
Hours: 6am-9pm
Carries: Live bait, lures, rods, reels, licenses
Bodies of water: Lake Erie, Niagara River
Services & Products: Bulk worms packaged for entry into Canada
Guides: Yes
OK to call for current conditions: Yes

Captain Bill's
Niagara Falls 716-283-3487
Hours: 10am-6pm, closed Mon.
Carries: Live bait, lures, flies, maps, rods, reels
Bodies of water: Niagara River, Lake Erie, Lake Ontario
Services & Products: Boat rentals, guide services, charter boat service, boat ramp, food, beverages, gas/oil, scuba diving, snorkel trips
OK to call for current conditions: Yes
Contact: Steve Cornell

Mark's Tackle
Niagara Falls 716-285-7255
Hours: 6am-6pm, 6am-12pm Sun.
Carries: Live bait, lures, flies, maps, rods, reels, licenses
Bodies of water: Lake Erie, Niagara River, Lake Ontario
Guides: Yes
OK to call for current conditions: Yes
Contact: Anyone

Nellie's Bait Farm
Kennedy 716-267-2248
Hours: 8:30am-6pm, closed Sun.
Carries: Live bait
Bodies of water: Lake Erie, Chautauqua Lake
Guides: Yes
OK to call for current conditions: Yes
Contact: Nelson Nord

Niagara Outdoors
N. Tonawanda 716-695-LURE
Hours: 7:30am-7:30pm
Carries: Live bait, lures, flies, maps, rods, reels, licenses
Bodies of water: Lake Ontario, Lake Erie, Niagara River (upper and lower)
Services & Products: Fishing instruction, repair services
Guides: Yes
OK to call for current conditions: Yes
Contact: Anyone

Rainbow Sports
N. Tonawanda 716-692-7510
.... 691-6860
Hours: 9am-7pm, closed Sun.
Carries: Live bait, lures, flies, maps, rods, reels, licenses
Bodies of water: Lake Erie, Niagara River, Lake Ontario, Erie Canal
Services & Products: Fishing instruction, repair services, archery
Guides: Yes
OK to call for current conditions: Yes
Contact: Paul Tessuer

CHARTERS...

Sunrise Charters
Albion 716-682-5563
Species & Seasons: Salmon, Trout, Steelhead April-Oct, Walleye May-July, SM Bass Nov-April
Bodies of water: Lake Ontario, Lake Erie, North Central FL: Orange Lake, Rodman Res., St Johns River
Rates: Full day: $440(5)
Call between: 7am-9pm
Provides: Light tackle, lures, bait
Handicapped equipped: Yes
Certifications: USCG

GUIDES...

Jim Hanley
Derby 716-549-2232
Species & Seasons: SM Bass May-Nov, Walleye July-Sept, Muskellunge Sept-Nov
Bodies of water: Lake Erie, Niagara River, Lake Ontario
Rates: Half day: $175(1-2), $200(3), Full day: $250(1-2), $300(3)
Call between: 9am-8pm
Provides: Light tackle, heavy tackle, fly rod/reel, lures, bait
Handicapped equipped: Yes
Certifications: USCG

MARINAS...

Small Boat Harbor Marina
Buffalo 716-828-0027
Hours: 24 hours, 7 days a week (May-Oct.)
Carries: Live bait, lures, rods, reels
Bodies of water: Lake Erie
Services & Products: Charter boat service, boat ramp, food, beverages, gas/oil, repair services
Guides: No
OK to call for current conditions: No
Contact: Anthony LaRusso

LAKE GEORGE

BAIT & TACKLE...

Outdoorsman Sport Shop
Diamond Point 518-668-3910
Hours: 5am-9pm, (closed Mon. in winter)
Carries: Live bait, lures, flies, maps, rods, reels, licenses

LAKE GEORGE - LAKE ONTARIO — NEW YORK

Bodies of water: Lake George, Hudson Rver, Schroon River, Schroon Lake, Brandt Lake, Loon Lake, Lake Champlain, Lake Luzern, Glen Lake, Trout Lake
Services & Products: Guide services, charter boat service, lodging, fishing instruction
Guides: Yes
OK to call for current conditions: Yes
Contact: Garry or Sally Nelson

CHARTERS...

E & R Sport Fishing Charters
Hudson Falls 800-336-6987
Species & Seasons: Lake Trout, Atlantic Salmon April-Dec, SM Bass, LM Bass June-Nov
Bodies of water: Lake George
Rates: Half day: $175(1),
Full day: $300(1), Lodging also available
Call between: Anytime
Provides: Light tackle, fly rod/reel, lures, bait
Handicapped equipped: Yes
Certifications: USCG, NY State Licensed Guide

Justy-Joe Sportfishing Charters
Gansevoort 518-798-0336
Species & Seasons: Salmon, Lake Trout April-Dec
Bodies of water: Lake George, Lake Champlain
Rates: Half day: $160(1-2), $180(3-4), Full day: $280(1-2), $300(3-4)
Provides: Light tackle
Handicapped equipped: Yes
Certifications: NY State Licensed Guide, USCG

Naughty Lady Charters
Adirondack 518-532-7305
Species & Seasons: Salmon, Lake Trout, Walleye, Northern Pike May/Sept-Oct
Bodies of water: Lake Champlain, Lake George, Schroon Lake
Rates: Half day: $120(1), Full day: $230(1)
Call between: 5am-10pm
Provides: Light tackle, lures, bait
Handicapped equipped: No
Certifications: USCG, NYOGA

Sand N'Surf Charter Service & Motel
Daimont Point 800-903-4622
.... 518-668-4622
Species & Seasons: Lake Trout, Salmon May-Nov, LM Bass, SM Bass June-Fall

Bodies of water: Lake George
Rates: Half day: $175(1-2), $200(4), Full day: $350(1-2), $400(4), free room with spring and fall charters
Call between: 9am-8pm
Provides: Light tackle, lures, bait, rain gear
Handicapped equipped: Yes
Certifications: USCG, NY State Guide

GUIDES...

Call of the Wild Guide Service
Wallkill 914-895-3097
Species & Seasons: Brook Trout April-June, Salmon Sept-June, Lake Trout May-May
Bodies of water: Lake George, Fulton Chain Lakes, Salmon River, Lake Champlain, Pharroah Lake, Hudson River
Call between: 8am-9pm
Provides: Light tackle, heavy tackle, fly rod/reel, lures, bait, rain gear, beverages, lunch
Handicapped equipped: Yes

Peaked Hill Guide Service
Severance 518-532-7953
Species & Seasons: LM Bass, SM Bass June-Nov, Tiger Muskellunge, Northern Pike May-Mar
Bodies of water: Paradox Lake, Eagle Lake, Schroon Lake, Schroon River, Lake Champlain, Lake George, Lake Durant and several back water ponds for Bass and Pike
Rates: Half day: $65(1), $115(2), Full day: $95(1), $185(2)
Call between: 5pm-9pm
Provides: Light tackle, heavy tackle, lures, bait, rain gear, beverages
Handicapped equipped: No
Certifications: NY State Guide

LAKE ONTARIO

BAIT & TACKLE...

Ace Trading Post & Taxidermy
Oswego 315-342-3244
Hours: Sunrise-Sunset
Carries: Live bait, lures, flies, maps, rods, reels, licenses
Bodies of water: Lake Ontario (eastern basin), Oswego River, Oneida Lake

Services & Products: Guide services, charter boat service, lodging, food, beverages, fishing instruction, taxidermy
OK to call for current conditions: Yes
Contact: Anyone

B-E Fshing Tackle Inc.
Ontario 800-356-2921
Carries: Live bait, lures, flies, maps, rods, reels, licenses
Bodies of water: Lake Ontario, Sodus Bay, Oneida Lake
Services & Products: Repair services
Guides: Yes
OK to call for current conditions: Yes
Contact: Anyone

Braddock Bait & Tackle
Hilton 716-392-6600
Hours: 7am-8pm
Carries: Live bait, lures, flies, maps, rods, reels, licenses
Bodies of water: Lake Ontario
Services & Products: Boat rentals, charter boat service, boat ramp, food, beverages, gas/oil, fishing instruction
Guides: Yes
OK to call for current conditions: Yes
Contact: Bob Manville

Captain Bill's
Niagara Falls 716-283-3487
Hours: 10am-6pm, closed Mon.
Carries: Live bait, lures, flies, maps, rods, reels
Bodies of water: Niagara River, Lake Erie, Lake Ontario
Services & Products: Boat rentals, guide services, charter boat service, boat ramp, food, beverages, gas/oil, scuba diving, snorkel trips
OK to call for current conditions: Yes
Contact: Steve Cornell

The Green Drake
Utica 315-735-6679
Hours: 9am-7pm
Carries: Flies, rods, reels
Bodies of water: West Canada Creek, Black River, Salmon River, Lake Ontario, Oriskany Creek, Delaware River
Services & Products: Guide services, fishing instruction, repair services, custom rods
Guides: Yes
OK to call for current conditions: Yes
Contact: George Massoud

NEW YORK — LAKE ONTARIO

Mark's Tackle
Niagara Falls 716-285-7255
Hours: 6am-6pm, 6am-12pm Sun.
Carries: Live bait, lures, flies, maps, rods, reels, licenses
Bodies of water: Lake Erie, Niagara River, Lake Ontario
Guides: Yes
OK to call for current conditions: Yes
Contact: Anyone

Niagara Outdoors
N. Tonawanda 716-695-LURE
Hours: 7:30am-7:30pm
Carries: Live bait, lures, flies, maps, rods, reels, licenses
Bodies of water: Lake Ontario, Lake Erie, Niagara River (upper and lower)
Services & Products: Fishing instruction, repair services
Guides: Yes
OK to call for current conditions: Yes
Contact: Anyone

Rainbow Sports
N. Tonawanda 716-692-7510
.... 691-6860
Hours: 9am-7pm, closed Sun.
Carries: Live bait, lures, flies, maps, rods, reels, licenses
Bodies of water: Lake Erie, Niagara River, Lake Ontario, Erie Canal
Services & Products: Fishing instruction, repair services, archery
Guides: Yes
OK to call for current conditions: Yes
Contact: Paul Tessuer

The Rivers Edge Tackle Shop
Mexico 315-963-3327
Hours: 5am-11pm
Carries: Live bait, lures, flies, rods, reels, licenses
Bodies of water: Little Salmon River, Lake Ontario
Services & Products: Fishing instruction
Guides: Yes
OK to call for current conditions: Yes
Contact: Clarence or Sally Blunt

Salmon River Sports Shop
Pulaski 315-298-4343
Hours: 5-6am-7-9pm
Carries: Live bait, lures, flies, maps, rods, reels
Bodies of water: Salmon River, Lake Ontario, Oneida Lake, Sandy Creek, Grindstone, Little Salmon River

Services & Products: Guide services, charter boat service, lodging, fishing instruction, repair services, custom rods
OK to call for current conditions: Yes
Contact: Ron or Tyler Gervaise

Scheffler's Hardware
Wilson 716-751-9374
Hours: 8am-6pm
Carries: Live bait, maps
Bodies of water: Lake Ontario
Services & Products: Food, beverages, oil, hardware, restaurant
Guides: Yes
OK to call for current conditions: Yes
Contact: Larry Scheffler, Jr.

Thousand Island Bait Store
Alexandria Bay 315-482-9903
Hours: 6am-9pm
Carries: Live bait, lures, flies, maps, rods, reels, licenses
Bodies of water: St. Lawrence River, Lake Ontario
Services & Products: Food, beverages, gas/oil, repair services
Guides: Yes
OK to call for current conditions: Yes
Contact: Greg Coon

CHARTERS...

Albatross Charters
Hannibal 315-626-6051
Species & Seasons: Trout, Salmon April-Oct
Bodies of water: Lake Ontario
Rates: Half day: $50(1), $100(2), Full day: $60(1), $120(2)
Call between: 7am-11pm
Provides: Light tackle, heavy tackle, lures, bait
Handicapped equipped: No
Certifications: USCG

Amicus Charters
North Greece 315-654-3404
.... 392-6393
Species & Seasons: Trout, Salmon, Northern Pike May-Oct, Walleye May-Sept, SM Bass June-Oct
Bodies of water: Lake Ontario, Thousand Islands, St Lawrence River, Cape Vincent
Rates: 8 hrs: $240-$290(4)
Call between: 6pm-10pm
Provides: Light tackle, lures, bait
Handicapped equipped: No

AV Charters
Lafayette 315-677-3713
Species & Seasons: Brown Trout, Lake Trout, Steelhead, Atlantic Salmon, Skamania April-Oct, Coho Salmon, Chinook Salmon June-Oct, Walleye May-Oct
Bodies of water: Mexico Bay, Sandy Pond, Lake Ontario
Rates: Half day: $200(4), Full day: $325(4)
Call between: 10am-9pm
Provides: Light tackle, heavy tackle, lures, bait
Handicapped equipped: Yes
Certifications: USCG

Blue Nose Sportfishing Charters
Newton, NJ 201-948-4992
.... 315-676-7571
Species & Seasons: Brown Trout, Coho Salmon, Steelhead, Lake Trout, Rainbow Trout, Chinook Salmon, Atlantic Salmon April-Nov, Walleye, Northern Pike May-Nov, LM Bass, SM Bass June-Nov
Bodies of water: Oswego River, Lake Ontario
Rates: Full day: $225(1-2), $87.50 additional pp (1995 rates)
Call between: 8am-7pm
Provides: Light tackle, lures, bait, rain gear
Handicapped equipped: No
Certifications: USCG

Buc-A-Roo Charters
Kent
Species & Seasons: Brown Trout, Lake Trout, Rainbow Trout, Chinook Salmon, Coho Salmon, Atlantic Salmon April-Oct
Bodies of water: Lake Ontario
Rates: Half day: $370(1-4), Full day: $470(1-4)
Call between: 9am-9pm
Provides: Light tackle, lures, bait
Handicapped equipped: Yes
Certifications: USCG

C-Frog Charters/Lodging
Clifton Springs 315-462-9860
Species & Seasons: Brown Trout, Rainbow Trout April-July, Lake Trout May-Aug, Chinook Salmon July-Oct, SM Bass July-Aug
Bodies of water: Lake Ontario, Sodus Bay
Rates: Half day: $300(1), Full day: $400(1)
Call between: PM

LAKE ONTARIO — NEW YORK

Provides: Light tackle, lures, bait, rain gear
Handicapped equipped: Yes
Certifications: USCG

Captain Ron's Charters
Romulus 315-585-6408
.... 727-5507
Species & Seasons: Salmon, Lake Trout, Rainbow Trout, Brown Trout April-Oct, Perch, Northern Pike May-Oct
Bodies of water: Lake Ontario, Seneca Lake
Rates: Half day: $225(1-3), Full day: $300(1-3)
Call between: 6pm-8pm
Provides: Light tackle, heavy tackle, lures, bait
Handicapped equipped: Yes
Certifications: USCG

Cinelli Sportfishing Service
Olcott 716-433-5210
Species & Seasons: Chinook Salmon, Coho Salmon, Lake Trout, Brown Trout, Steelhead April-Nov, SM Bass June-Nov
Bodies of water: Western Lake Ontario, Niagara River
Rates: Half day: $95(1), Full day: $125(1), River: $330(3), Lake: $460(4)
Call between: 7pm-10pm
Provides: Light tackle, heavy tackle, lures, bait
Handicapped equipped: Yes
Certifications: USCG

Deep Six Charters
Lockport 716-433-0583
Species & Seasons: Trout, Salmon April-Sept
Bodies of water: Lower Niagara River, Lake Ontario
Rates: Half day: $75(1), Full day: $150(1)
Call between: Anytime
Provides: Light tackle, heavy tackle, lures
Handicapped equipped: Yes
Certifications: USCG

Empress Charter Service
Lockport 716-751-6280
Species & Seasons: Chinook Salmon, Brown Trout, Coho Salmon, Rainbow Trout, Lake Trout April-Oct
Bodies of water: Lake Ontario
Rates: Half day: $360, Full day: $450
Call between: 5am-11pm
Provides: Light tackle, lures, bait
Handicapped equipped: No
Certifications: USCG

Expediter Charters
Montour Falls 607-535-7558
Species & Seasons: Brown Trout, Coho Salmon April-Oct, Steelhead May-Oct, Chinook Salmon June-Oct
Bodies of water: Lake Ontario, Seneca Lake
Rates: Half day: $250(1-2), Full day: $450(1-2)
Call between: 6am-10pm
Provides: Light tackle, heavy tackle, lures, bait
Handicapped equipped: Yes
Certifications: USCG

Farr-Out Charters
Webster 716-671-6924
Species & Seasons: Salmon, Steelhead, Brown Trout, April-Oct, Lake Trout April-Sept, SM Bass June-Sept
Bodies of water: Lake Ontario
Rates: $450(1-4), $500(5-6)
Call between: 5pm-10pm
Provides: Light tackle, heavy tackle, lures, bait
Handicapped equipped: Yes
Certifications: USCG

Fish P.T. Guide Service
Caldwell, NJ 201-226-8380
Species & Seasons: Trout, Salmon April-June, SM Bass May-Oct, King Salmon Aug-Sept Landlocked Atlantic Salmon, Lake Trout Sept-Nov
Bodies of water: Lake Champlain, Adirondacks, Lake Ontario
Rates: Lake Ontario weekend, 3 days/2nights: $325pp(minimum 3), Lake Champlain-Adirondacks, 2 days/2 nights: $225(minimum 2)
Call between: Before 8am-After 7pm
Provides: Light tackle, medium tackle, fly rod/reel, lures, beverages, lunch
Handicapped equipped: Yes

Fish Taxi Charters
Dexter 315-639-3632
Species & Seasons: Lake Trout, Brown Trout, Walleye May-Sept, Steelhead, SM Bass June-Sept, Salmon July-Sept
Bodies of water: Lake Ontario
Rates: Full day: $400(4)
Call between: 7am-7pm
Provides: Light tackle, lures
Handicapped equipped: No

Grover Moore
Henderson Harbor 315-938-7239
Species & Seasons: Lake Trout, Brown Trout, Steelhead May-Sept, Salmon July-Sept, Walleye May-June, SM Bass June-Sept
Bodies of water: Eastern Lake Ontario
Rates: Half day: $270(1-4), Full day: $400(1-4)
Call between: 6pm-10pm
Provides: Light tackle, heavy tackle, lures, bait
Handicapped equipped: Yes, depending on handicap
Certifications: USCG

Jerry's Sport Fish & Charters
Henderson Harbor 802-658-6107
.... 315-938-5128
Species & Seasons: Brown Trout April-June, Walleye May-July, Steelhead April-July, Lake Trout April-Sept, Chinook Salmon, Coho Salmon July-Sept
Bodies of water: Lake Ontario and streams
Rates: Mon-Thurs: $699(4) charter package + lodging 2 days, 8hrs: $375(4)
Call between: 7am-9pm
Provides: Light tackle, lures, bait
Handicapped equipped: Yes
Certifications: USCG, NY State Licensed Guide

Just 4 Fun Charters
Kent 716-682-5512
Species & Seasons: Brown Trout April-May, Salmon, Steelhead, Lake Trout April-Oct
Bodies of water: Lake Ontario, Oak Orchard River
Rates: Half day: $250(1), Full day: $400(1), River Fishing: $100 per day
Call between: 6pm-9am
Provides: Light tackle, heavy tackle, fly rod/reel, lures
Handicapped equipped: Yes

YOUR SILENT FISHING PARTNER

NEW YORK — LAKE ONTARIO

K & G Sportfishing Charter Fleet & Lodge
Oswego 800-346-6533
Species & Seasons: Walleye May-July, LM Bass, SM Bass June-Sept, Salmon July-Oct, Brown Trout Mar-Aug, Steelhead Jan-Dec, Lake Trout April-Sept, Atlantic Salmon April-Dec
Bodies of water: Lake Ontario, Oswego River, Salmon River
Rates: Half day: $110, Full day: $200 (rates are based on party of 4 includes lodging)
Call between: 8am-10pm
Provides: Light tackle, fly rod/reel, lures, licenses, lodging
Handicapped equipped: Yes
Certifications: USCG, NY State Guide, North American Fishing Club

Capt. Art Larkin
Elbridge 315-689-9095
.... 649-2917
Species & Seasons: Brown Trout April-May, Walleye May-June, Lake Trout, Salmon, SM Bass June-Oct
Bodies of water: Lake Ontario
Rates: Half day: $225(1-4), Full day: $340(1-4)
Call between: 9:30am-1pm/8pm-10pm
Provides: Heavy tackle, lures, bait, rain gear
Handicapped equipped: No
Certifications: USCG

Little Whip Fishing Charters
Oswego 315-343-4852
Species & Seasons: Brown Trout April-June, Walleye May-June, Steelhead, Lake Trout April-Aug, Salmon July-Sept
Bodies of water: Lake Ontario, Oswego River
Rates: Half day: $200(2-4), Full day: $350(2-4), Walleye: Full day: $225(2)
Call between: Anytime
Provides: Light tackle, heavy tackle, lures, bait
Handicapped equipped: Depends on handicap
Certifications: USCG

Loon-A-Sea Charter Service
Trumansburg 607-387-5474
Species & Seasons: LM Bass, SM Bass June-Nov, Walleye May-Aug, Sightseeing May-Nov
Bodies of water: Cayuga Lake, Seneca Lake, Lake Ontario
Rates: Cayuga, Seneca Lakes: $35 pp hr., Lake Ontario: $35pp hr. + expenses
Call between: 3pm-9pm
Provides: Light tackle, lures, bait, rain gear
Handicapped equipped: Yes
Certifications: USCG

Lucky Dutchman Charters
Pulaski 800-368-4467
Species & Seasons: Brown Trout Mar-June, Lake Trout May-July, Salmon Aug-Oct, Steelhead Sept-Dec
Bodies of water: Lake Ontario, Salmon River
Call between: 8am-10pm
Provides: Light tackle, heavy tackle, lures
Handicapped equipped: Yes
Certifications: USCG, SRGA

Milky Way Fishing Charters
Mannsville 315-846-5077
Species & Seasons: SM Bass, Lake Trout, Walleye June-Sept, Salmon July-Sept
Bodies of water: Lake Ontario (Henderson Harbor region)
Rates: Bass: Half day: $225(1-4), Full day: $340(1-4), + bait, additional $75pp, Trout, Salmon: Half day: $200, Full day: $275
Call between: 7am-9pm
Provides: Light tackle, heavy tackle, lures, bait, rain gear
Handicapped equipped: No
Certifications: USCG

Octavius M&M Charters
Parish 315-625-7100
.... 625-7064
Species & Seasons: Brown Trout April-June, Lake Trout May-Sept, Salmon July-Oct, Steelhead Oct-April, SM Bass June-July
Bodies of water: Salmon River, Lake Ontario, Oswego River
Rates: Call for rates
Call between: Noon-11pm
Provides: Light tackle, lures, bait
Handicapped equipped: Yes

Pequod I Charters
Rochester 800-858-8618
Species & Seasons: Trout, Salmon April-Sept
Bodies of water: Lake Ontario
Rates: Half day: $225(1-6), Full day: $425(1-6)
Call between: 4pm-10pm
Provides: Light tackle, lures, rain gear
Handicapped equipped: Yes
Certifications: USCG

Placid Bay Ventures Guide & Charter
Lake Placid 518-523-1744
.... 523-2001
Species & Seasons: Lake Trout, Brook Trout April-Nov, Salmon April-June, Chinook Salmon, Atlantic Salmon Aug-Oct, SM Bass June-Nov, Northern Pike May-Mar, Muskellunge Sept-Nov, Walleye, Rainbow Trout, Brown Trout April-Nov
Bodies of water: Lake Placid, Adirondack Lakes and steams, Lake Champlain, Lake Ontario
Rates: Full day: $200(1-2)
Provides: Light tackle, heavy tackle, fly rod/reel, lures, lodging also available
Handicapped equipped: Yes, large boat, some limitations
Certifications: USCG, NYSOGA

Port Ontario Charters
Pulaski 315-298-6751
Species & Seasons: Brown Trout April-Aug, Lake Trout May-Sept, Steelhead May-June, Chinook Salmon July-Oct
Bodies of water: Eastern Lake Ontario
Rates: Half day: $325(4), Full day: $475(4)
Call between: 5pm-9pm
Provides: Light tackle, lures, bait
Handicapped equipped: Yes
Certifications: USCG

Prime Time Charters
Sodus Point 315-483-8600
Species & Seasons: Brown Trout, Lake Trout, Rainbow Trout, Coho Salmon, Chinook Salmon April-Oct
Bodies of water: Lake Ontario
Rates: Half day: $125(3), $150(4), Full day: $250(3), $300(4)
Call between: 4pm-8pm
Provides: Light tackle, heavy tackle, lures, bait
Certifications: USCG

Proteus Sportfishing
Cazenovia 315-655-2531
Species & Seasons: Brown Trout April-June, Rainbow Trout May-Nov, Lake Trout April-Sept, Chinook Salmon July-Sept
Bodies of water: Lake Ontario from Port of Oswego
Rates: Half day: $330(1-4)
Call between: 9am-9pm

LAKE ONTARIO — NEW YORK

Provides: Light tackle, heavy tackle, lures, bait
Handicapped equipped: Yes
Certifications: USCG

Reel Pleasure Charters
Lewiston 716-754-2022
Species & Seasons: Chinook Salmon Sept-Oct, Steelhead, Lake Trout Nov-April, Coho Salmon, Brown Trout April-May, SM Bass July-Aug
Bodies of water: Lower Niagara River, Lake Ontario
Rates: Full day: $175(1), $260(2), $330(3)
Call between: 8am-9am
Provides: Light tackle, heavy tackle, lures, bait
Handicapped equipped: Yes

Scout'Em Out Charters
Mexico 201-875-1697
.... 315-963-0681
Species & Seasons: Brown Trout April-July, Lake Trout April-Aug, Steelhead May-Aug, Atlantic Salmon April-Sept, Coho Salmon, Chinook Salmon July-Oct
Bodies of water: Lake Ontario, Mexico Bay Area
Rates: Half day: $240(1-2), Full day: $300(1-2)
Call between: 6pm-10pm
Provides: Light tackle, heavy tackle, lures, bait
Handicapped equipped: Yes
Certifications: USCG

Sea Fury Charters
Pulaski 315-298-2446
Species & Seasons: Brown Trout, Lake Trout April-Aug, Chinook Salmon July-Oct, Steelhead Trout, April-Aug
Bodies of water: Lake Ontario
Rates: Half day (6hrs): $320(1-4), Full day (9hrs): $470(1-4)
Call between: Anytime
Provides: Light tackle, lures, bait
Handicapped equipped: No
Certifications: USCG

Dave Shaban
Watertown 315-788-6843
Species & Seasons: Trout, Salmon April-Sept, Walleye, Northern Pike May-Sept, SM Bass June-Sept
Bodies of water: Eastern Lake Ontario, St. Lawrence River
Rates: Half day: $280(4), Full day: $380(4)
Call between: 10am-8pm
Provides: Light tackle, heavy tackle, lures, bait

Handicapped equipped: Yes
Certifications: USCG

Strike Zone Charters
Pulaski 315-298-2074
Species & Seasons: Steelhead Nov-May, Brown Trout April-Oct, Lake Trout May-Sept, Salmon July-Nov
Bodies of water: Lake Ontario, Salmon River
Rates: Half day: $320(4), Full day: $480(4)
Call between: 9am-5pm
Provides: Light tackle, lures, bait
Handicapped equipped: Yes

Sunrise Charters
Albion 716-682-5563
Species & Seasons: Salmon, Trout, Steelhead April-Oct, Walleye May-July, SM Bass Nov-April
Bodies of water: Lake Ontario, Lake Erie, North Central FL: Orange Lake, Rodman Res., St Johns River
Rates: Full day: $440(5)
Call between: 7am-9pm
Provides: Light tackle, lures, bait
Handicapped equipped: Yes
Certifications: USCG

Triple Deuce Charters
Pulaski 800-874-3478
Species & Seasons: Brown Trout April-Sept, Lake Trout May-Sept, Salmon July-Sept, SM Bass June-Sept
Bodies of water: Lake Ontario
Rates: 6 hrs: $300(1-4), 8hrs: $400(1-4)
Call between: 6pm-10pm
Provides: Light tackle, lures, bait
Handicapped equipped: Yes
Certifications: USCG

Trophy Seeker Charters
Verbank 914-677-9071
Species & Seasons: Brown Trout April-Aug, Chinook Salmon July-Sept, Coho Salmon, Lake Trout April-Sept, Steelhead April-Oct, Striped Bass April-June
Bodies of water: Hudson River, Lake Ontario
Rates: Lake Ontario: 6 hrs: $300(1-4), 8 hrs: $375(1-4),
Hudson River: 6 hrs: $250(1-3)
Call between: Anytime
Provides: Light tackle, heavy tackle, lures, bait
Handicapped equipped: Yes
Certifications: USCG, Licensed NY State

Vitamin Sea Charters
Waterloo 315-539-8184
Species & Seasons: Lake Trout, Rainbow Trout, Brown Trout, Atlantic Salmon, Chinook Salmon April-Oct, SM Bass June-Oct, Northern Pike, Walleye May-Oct
Bodies of water: Lake Ontario, Seneca Lake
Rates: Half day: $180(1-2), $220(3), Full day: $250(1-2), $300(3)
Call between: 6pm-9:30pm
Provides: Light tackle, lures, bait
Handicapped equipped: Yes
Certifications: USCG, NY State

Zip's Charter Service
Wilson 716-751-9932
Species & Seasons: Chinook Salmon April-Oct, Steelhead, Rainbow Trout, Dec-Sept, Brown Trout April-June, Lake Trout Jan-Oct
Bodies of water: Lake Ontario, Niagara River
Rates: River boat: Full day: $110(1), $220(2), Lake boat: 8 hrs: $350(1-4)
Call between: 7pm-1pm
Provides: Light tackle, heavy tackle, lures, bait
Handicapped equipped: No
Certifications: USCG

GUIDES...

John Botting
Cape Vincent 315-654-2634
.... 743-6683
Species & Seasons: SM Bass, Perch, Lake Trout, Salmon June-Oct
Bodies of water: Lake Ontario, Atlantic Ocean, Gulf of Mexico
Rates: Full day: $200(1), $250-$300(2-4), $50 additional pp up to 6
Call between: Anytime
Provides: Light tackle, heavy tackle, lures, bait
Handicapped equipped: yes
Certifications: USCG

NEW YORK — LAKE ONTARIO

Excellent Guide Service
Hastings 315-676-3475
Species & Seasons: Pacific Salmon Sept-Nov, Coho Salmon Sept-Oct, Brown Trout Oct-Nov, Steelhead Oct-April
Bodies of water: Salmon River, and tributaries of Lake Ontario
Rates: Stream Side: Full day: $125(1), $240(2), Drift boat trips: Full day: $250
Call between: 7pm-9pm
Provides: Light tackle, fly rod/reel, lures, bait
Handicapped equipped: Yes

Russ Finehout
Clayton 315-686-5201
Species & Seasons: Lake Trout, Walleye May-Sept, Salmon July-Sept, Northern Pike May-Nov, SM Bass June-Nov
Bodies of water: Lake Ontario, St. Lawrence River
Rates: Half day: $135(1), $150(2), Full day: $270(1), $285(2)
Call between: 7am-10pm
Provides: Light tackle, heavy tackle, lures, bait, rain gear, beverages, lunch
Certifications: USCG

Finger Lakes Outfitters
Fairport 716-223-8236
Species & Seasons: Chinook Salmon Aug-Nov, Brown Trout Oct-Dec, Steelhead Oct-May, Brown Trout April-Sept, Rainbow Trout Oct-May
Bodies of water: Lake Ontario Tributaries, Salmon River, Maxwell Creek, Irondequoit Creek, Oak Orchard Creek, Finger Lakes Tributaries, Naples Creek, Catherine's Creek, Salmon Creek and more
Rates: Half day: $75(1), $100(2), Full day: $150(1), $200(2)
Call between: 7am-10pm
Provides: Fly rod/reel, lures(flies), beverages, lunch
Handicapped equipped: No
Certifications: NY State Guide, Red Cross First aid, CPR, Water Safety, fully insured

Jim Hanley
Derby 716-549-2232
Species & Seasons: SM Bass May-Nov, Walleye July-Sept, Muskellunge Sept-Nov
Bodies of water: Lake Erie, Niagara River, Lake Ontario
Rates: Half day: $175(1-2), $200(3), Full day: $250(1-2), $300(3)
Call between: 9am-8pm

Provides: Light tackle, heavy tackle, fly rod/reel, lures, bait
Handicapped equipped: Yes
Certifications: USCG

High Adventure Guide Service
Pulaski 315-298-2410
Species & Seasons: Salmon Sept-Nov, Steelhead Nov-May, Brown Trout Oct-April
Bodies of water: Lake Ontario Tributaries
Rates: Half day: $150(1-2), Full day: $240(1-2)
Call between: 6pm-9pm
Provides: Light tackle, heavy tackle, fly rod/reel, lures, bait
Handicapped equipped: Yes
Certifications: USCG, New York State, First aid, CPR

LeClair's Guiding Service
Clay 315-699-3319
Species & Seasons: Salmon, Steelhead Aug-May, Brown Trout (Lake) Oct-Nov, Rainbow Trout, Brown Trout May-Aug, SM Bass, Panfish July-Aug, Northern Pike April-Aug, Walleye Sept-Nov
Bodies of water: Salmon River Tributaries of Lake Ontario, West Canada Creek, French Creek, Big Bay Creek
Rates: Full day: $110(1), $240(2) (prices are for Salmon, Steelhead, other prices vary)
Call between: 8am-9pm
Provides: Light tackle, fly rod/reel, lures, bait, rain gear
Handicapped equipped: Yes
Certifications: NY State Licensed Guide

Let's Go Fishing
Syracuse 315-478-7231
Species & Seasons: Trout April-Sept, Northern Pike May-Mar, LM Bass June-Nov, Salmon depends on waters and species, Panfish all year
Bodies of water: Central New York region, Finger Lakes, Lake Ontario, Whitney Point Lake, Oneida Lake
Call between: 6pm-9pm
Provides: Light tackle, heavy tackle, fly rod/reel, lures, bait
Handicapped equipped: No
Certifications: NY State Licensed Guide

Roger Moyse
Alexandria Bay 315-482-5248
Species & Seasons: Lake Trout April-June, Northern Pike, Walleye May-Nov, SM Bass June-Oct, LM Bass June-Sept, Muskellunge Sept-Nov
Bodies of water: Lake Ontario, St. Lawrence River
Rates: Half day: $150(1-2), Full day: $225(1-2), Walleye, Trout, Muskellunge rates higher
Call between: 8am-9pm
Provides: Light tackle, lures, bait, beverages, lunch
Handicapped equipped: Yes
Certifications: USCG

Tightlines Guide Service
Pulaski 800-452-1176
Species & Seasons: Chinook Salmon, Coho Salmon Sept-Nov, Steelhead Nov-May, Brown Trout Oct-Nov
Bodies of watr: Lake Ontario, Salmon River, Black River, Oswego River, Little Salmon River, and eastern Lake Ontario Tributaries
Rates: Float trips: Half day: $150(1), $175(2), Full day: $180(1), $220(2), Wade trips: $135pp
Call between: 6pm-10pm
Provides: Light tackle, heavy tackle, fly rod/reel, lures, bait
Handicapped equipped: No
Certifications: NY Registered Guide

Wicked Will Fishing Services
Cazenovia 315-655-3908
Species & Seasons: Brown Trout, Lake Trout, Rainbow Trout, Steelhead April-Nov, Coho Salmon, Chinook Salmon July-Nov, Atlantic Salmon June-Nov
Bodies of water: Lake Ontario, Salmon River
Rates: 6 hrs. $250(1-4)
Call between:
Provides: Heavy tackle, lures, bait
Handicapped equipped: Limited

Wild River Inn Lodge & Guide Service
Pulaski 315-298-4195
Species & Seasons: Salmon Aug-Nov, Steelhead Oct-May, Lake Trout May-Au, Brown Trout Oct-July, Walleye May-July, SM Bass June-Sept
Bodies of water: Salmon River, Lake Ontario, Black River, Oswego River, and other Lake Ontario Tributaries
Rates: Full day (starting at): $160(1), $220(2), Lodge (starting at): $22.50/pp
Call between: 9am-9pm

LAKE ONTARIO — NEW YORK

Provides: Light tackle, heavy tackle, fly rod/reel, lures, bait
Handicapped equipped: Yes, on the lake, river no
Certifications: NY State Licensed Guide, USCG

LODGING...

"All Season" Lodge
Sandy Creek 315-387-5850
Guest Capacity: 20
Handicapped equipped: No
Seasons: All year
Rates: $22/pp day +tax
Contact: Rose
Guides: Yes
Species & Seasons: SM Bass June-Nov, Northern Pike, Walleye May-Mar, Lake Trout Jan-Sept, Salmon all year, Ice fishing Nov-April, Brook Trout April-Sept
Bodies of Water: Lake Ontario, Salmon River
Types of fishing: Fly fishing, light tackle, heavy tackle, wading, boat
Available: Licenses

Angler's Roost Campgrounds, Bed & Breakfast
Pulaski 315-387-5690
Guest Capacity: 50
Handicapped equipped: Yes, campgrounds are, not B&B
Seasons: Camp: May to Nov, B&B: all year
Rates: Camp: $17/day, $90/week, B&B: $20-$25/day
Contact: Richard M. Machemer
Guides: Yes
Species & Seasons: LM Bass, SM Bass June-Nov, Brown Trout April-June, Lake Trout June-Sept, Lake Salmon July-Sept, River Salmon Sept-Oct, ice fishing Dec-Mar, Steelhead Oct-April
Bodies of Water: Lake Ontario, Little Sandy Creek, Salmon River
Types of fishing: Fly fishing, light tackle, heavy tackle, wading, float trips, charter on lake
Available: Fishing instruction, licenses, bait, tackle, family activities, fish cleaning and freezing

Barracks Club
Penfield 315-654-2327
.... 716-671-2708
Guest Capacity: 22
Handicapped equipped: No
Seasons: May 14 to Sept 30
Rates: Lodge: $22/day
Cabins: $250/$275/$300/week
Contact: John F Grieco, Jr.
Guides: Yes, recommend
Species & Seasons: Black Bass June-Oct, Pike May-Oct, Perch, Walleye May-Mar
Bodies of Water: St. Lawrence River, Lake Ontario
Types of fishing: Light tackle, heav tackle

Cannon's Place Motel
Altmar 315-298-5054
Guest Capacity: 65
Handicapped equipped: Yes
Seasons: All year
Rates: $15/pp day
Guides: Yes
Species & Seasons: Steelhead Oct-May, Brown Trout April-June, Lake Trout April-Sept, Coho Salmon, Chinook Salmon July-Nov
Bodies of Water: Lake Ontario, Salmon River, Oneida Lake, Sandy Pond
Types of fishing: Fly fishing, light tackle, heavy tackle, wading, float trips
Available: Fishing instruction, licenses, bait, tackle, family activities

Crew Quarters Lodging
Oswego 315-342-6285
.... 343-6856
Guest Capacity: 13
Handicapped equipped: Yes, restaurant and lounge
Seasons: All year
Rates: $40dbl/day
Contact: Tom, Sandy or Sharon
Guides: Yes
Species & Seasons:
Bodies of Water: Lake Ontario, Salmon River
Types of fishing: Light tackle, heavy tackle, wading

Feeder Creek Lodge
Pulaski 315-298-4467
Guest Capacity: 14
Seasons: All year
Rates: $30/day
Contact: Barbara Van Wormer
Guides: Yes
Species & Seasons: Brown Trout, Mar-June, Lake Trout May-July, Salmon Aug-Oct, Steelhead Sept-Dec
Bodies of Water: Lake Ontario, Salmon River
Types of fishing: Fly fishing, light tackle, heavy tackle, wading, float trips, lake charters
Available: Licenses

Jefferson Street Lodge
Pulaski 315-298-6247
Guest Capacity: 9
Handicapped equipped: No
Seasons: Aug to Nov
Rates: $15/day pp
Contact: Sandy Althouse
Guides: Yes, recommend
Species & Seasons: Coho Salmon, Steelhead, King Salmon
Bodies of Water: Salmon River, Lake Ontario
Types of fishing: Wading

Laurdon Heights
Pulaski 315-298-6091
Guest Capacity: 36
Handicapped equipped: Yes
Seasons: All year
Rates: Varies
Guides: Yes
Species & Seasons: Salmon River: Steelhead Oct-May, Salmon Sept-Oct, Brown Trout Oct-Nov, Lake Ontario: Steelhead, Salmon May-Oct, Brown Trout April-Oct
Bodies of Water: Lake Ontario, Salmon River
Types of fishing: Fly fishing, light tackle, heavy tackle, wading, float trips
Available: Condo units, full kitchens

Log Cabin Inn & Motel
PO Box 24
Pulaski, 13142
Guest Capacity: 60
Handicapped equipped: No
Seasons: All year
Rates: $25/pp day
Contact: J. Gonger
Guides: Yes
Species & Seasons: Steelhead Nov-April, Brown Trout Mar-May, Lake Trout Arpil-Oct, Salmon April-Nov, SM Bass June-Aug
Bodies of Water: Lake Ontario, Salmon River
Types of fishing: Fly fishing, light tackle, heavy tackle, float trips
Available: Licenses

NEW YORK — LAKE ONTARIO

Montclair Motel
Parish 315-625-7100
.... 625-7064
Guest Capacity: 20-40
Handicapped equipped: Yes
Seasons: All year
Rates: Call for rates
Guides: Yes
Species & Seasons: Brown Trout April-June, Lake Trout May-Sept, Salmon July-Oct, Steelhead Oct-April, SM Bass June-July
Bodies of Water: Lake Ontario, Oneida Lake, Salmon River, Oswego River
Types of fishing: Fly fishing, light tackle, wading, float trips, charter boat
Available: Licenses

Oswego Days Inn
Oswego 315-343-3136
Guest Capacity: 44 rooms
Handicapped equipped: No
Seasons: All year
Rates: $64/day, weekly rates available
Contact: Alice Blum
Guides: Yes, recommend
Species & Seasons: LM Bass, SM Bass June-Nov, Walleye June-Aug, Steelhead Nov-May, Chinook Salmon Aug-Nov, Lake Trout Jan-April, Atlantic Salmon Sept-Nov/April-May, Brown Trout Oct-May, Chinook Salmon Sept-Nov
Bodies of Water: Lake Ontario, Oswego River, Salmon River, Salmon Reservoir, Oneida Lake
Types of fishing: Fly fishing, light tackle, heavy tackle, wading

Pinehurst on the St. Lawrence Inc.
Alexandria Bay 315-482-9452
Guest Capacity: 190
Handicapped equipped: No
Seasons: May to Oct
Rates: $36-$150/day, $280-$800/week
Guides: Yes
Species & Seasons: Northern Pike, Walleye, Muskellunge May, LM Bass, SM Bass May-June
Bodies of Water: St Lawrence River, Lake Ontario, Black Lake
Types of fishing: Light tackle, heavy tackle
Available: Boat rentals

Port Lodge Motel
Pulaski 315-298-6876
Guest Capacity: 34 rooms
Handicapped equipped: Yes
Seasons: All year
Rates: $39-$59/day
Contact: Free Martin
Guides: Yes
Species & Seasons: Chinook Salmon July-Nov, Steelhead Nov-Mar, Brown Trout Mar-May, Walleye, Salmon, Trout all year
Bodies of Water: Lake Ontario, Salmon River, Oneida Lake, Sandy Pond, Oswego River
Types of fishing: Fly fishing, light tackle, heavy tackle, wading, float trips
Available: Licenses, family acticvities, Within 100 yards: Fishing instruction, bait, tackle, boat rentals, children's program

The Portly Angler Lodge
Pulaski 315-298-4773
Guest Capacity: 250
Handicapped equipped: Yes
Seasons: July 14 to May 14
Rates: Varies
Guides: Yes
Species & Seasons: Steelhead Oct-May, Chinook Salmon, Coho Salmon Aug-Nov, Brown Trout April-Nov, Lake Trout May-Sept, SM Bass June-Sept
Bodies of Water: Salmon River, Lake Ontario
Types of fishing: Fly fishing, light tackle, wading, float trips, charter boats
Available: Licenses, bar, lounge

Schoolhouse Inn
Altmar 315-298-5293
.... 298-3367
Guest Capacity: 32
Handicapped equipped: No
Seasons: All year
Rates: Nov.-Aug: $15/day + tax
Spt.-Oct: $20/day + tax
Contact: Capt Bill Lillie or Lori
Guides: Yes
Species & Seasons: Salmon Sept-Oct, Steelhead Nov-April, Walleye, LM Bass, SM Bass, Northern Pike, Lake Trout June-Sept, Brown Trout April-July
Bodies of Water: Lake Ontario and Tributaries, Salmon River, Oswego River, Oneida Lake
Types of fishing: Fly fishing, light tackle, heavy tackle, wading, float trips, lake charters
Available: Bait, tackle

Shangri-La Campground & Marina
Three Mile Bay 315-649-2979
Guest Capacity: 100+
Handicapped equipped: Yes
Seasons: May 1 to Oct 1
Rates: $70/day
Contact: Joan Coughlin
Guides: Yes
Species & Seasons: Walleye, Salmon, Trout May-Oct, SM Bass June-Oct
Bodies of Water: Lake Ontario
Types of fishing: Fly fishing, light tackle, heavy tackle
Available: Licenses, bait, tackle, boat rentals, family activities, restaurant

Shillelaghs & Shamrocks
Port Ontario 315-298-7040
Guest Capacity: 22
Handicapped equipped: Yes
Seasons: Mar 1 to Nov 15
Rates: $30/day with full breakfast
Contact: Sue or Bill
Guides: Yes
Species & Seasons: Salmon, Northern Pike, Walleye, SM Bass May-Nov, Lake Trout April-Sept, Brown Trout Mar-June, Steelhead Oct-May
Bodies of Water: Lake Ontario, Salmon River, various feeder streams to Lake Ontario
Types of fishing: Fly fishing, light tackle, heavy tackle, wading, float trips
Available: Fishing instruction, boat rentals, family activities, tavern, restaurant

Strike King Lodge
Mexico 315-963-7826
Guest Capacity: 24-32
Handicapped equipped: No
Seasons: Mar to De
Rates: $65/day
Guides: Yes
Bodies of Water: Lake Ontario, Oswego River, Salmon River, Little Salmon River
Types of fishing: Fly fishing, light tackle, heavy tackle, float trips
Available: Fishing instruction, baby sitting, charters, float trips

Sunset Cabins & RV Park
Oswego 315-343-2166
Guest Capacity: 150
Handicapped equipped: No
Seasons: May 1 to Oct 20
Rates: Tents: $10, Cabins: $40, RV: $18, Cottages: $100
Guides: Yes, Charter boats

LAKE ONTARIO - LAKE RONKONKOMA — NEW YORK

Species & Seasons: Trout, Perch, Salmon, SM Bass, Steelhead April-Nov
Bodies of Water: Lake Ontario, Oswego River
Types of fishing: Fly fishing, light tackle, heavy tackle, wading, float trips
Available: In town: Licenses, bait, tackle, boat rentals, auto races Saturday nights, tennis, horseshoes, swimming

The Stone House Inn
Altmar 315-298-6028
Guest Capacity: 36
Handicapped equipped: Yes, it is accessible
Seasons: All year
ates: $15-$30/pp day
Contact: Charlotte or Howard Bennett
Guides: Yes
Species & Seasons: Salmon Sept-Oct, Steelhead Nov-April, Brown Trout June-Oct
Bodies of Water: Salmon River, Lake Ontario, Salmon River Res.
Types of fishing: Fly fishing, light tackle, heavy tackle, wading, float trips

The Thomas Inn
Oswego 315-343-4900
Guest Capacity: 47 rooms
Seasons: All year
Rates: $54/day, weekly rates available
Contact: Brenda Reed
Guides: Yes, recommend
Species & Seasons: LM Bass, SM Bass June-Nov, Walleye June-Aug, Steelhead Nov-May, Chinook Salmon Aug-Nov, Lake Trout Jan-April, Brown Trout Oct-May, Chinook Salmon Sept-Nov, Atlantic Salmon April-May
Bodies of Water: Lake Ontario, Oswego River, Salmon River, Salmon Reservoir, Oneida Lake
Types of fishing: Fly fishing, light tackle, wading

MARINAS...

Braddock Bay Marina Inc.
Rochester 716-227-1579
Hours: 7am-9pm, closed Nov.-Feb.
Carries: Lures, maps, rods, reels
Bodies of water: Lake Ontario, Braddock Bay, Genesee River
Services & Products: Boat rentals, charter boat service, boat ramp, gas/oil, repair services
Guides: Yes
OK to call for current conditions: Yes
Contact: Red Gray

Chinook Harbor Marina
Fair Haven 315-947-5599
Hours: 5am-10pm
Carries: Live bait, lures, maps, rods, reels, licenses
Bodies of water: Lake Ontario, Little Sodus Bay
Services & Products: Charter boat service, lodging, boat ramp, food, beverages, gas/oil, restaurant
Guides: Yes
OK to call for current conditions: Yes
Contact: Lori Campbell

Clark's Marina
Pulaski 315-298-5832
Hours: 7am-7pm
Carries:
Bodies of water: Salmon River, Lake Ontario
Services & Products: Boat rentals, lodging, boat ramp, boat dockage
Guides: Yes
OK to call for current conditions: Yes
Contact: Don Clark

Green Harbor Campground & Marina
Lyndonville 716-682-9780
Carries: Live bait, rods, reels, licenses
Bodies of water: Lake Ontario, Perch Creek
Services & Products: Lodging, boat ramp, food, beverages, gas/oil, repair services
Guides: Yes
OK to call for current conditions: Yes
Contact: Anne Marie Holland

Grunert's Marina & Cottages
Sackets Harbor 315-646-2003
Hours: 7am-7pm
Carries: Maps
Bodies of water: Black River, Black River Bay, Lake Ontario
Services & Products: Lodging, boat ramp, beverages, gas/oil
Guides: Yes
OK to call for current conditions: Yes
Contact: Charles L. Grunert

Kitto's Marina
Dexter 315-639-6043
.... 639-6922
Hours: 7am-8:30pm
Carries: Live bait
Bodies of water: Chaumont Bay, Lake Ontario
Services & Products: Boat rentals, boat ramp, beverages

Guides: Yes
OK to call for current conditions: Yes
Contact: Duff or Eddie

McDonough Marine
Olcott 716-778-7665
.... 778-2048
Hours: 8am-5pm
Carries: Live bait, lures, rods, reels
Bodies of water: 18 Mile Creek, Lake Ontario
Services & Products: Boat rentals, lodging, food, beverages
OK to call for current conditions: Yes
Contact: Jim McDonough

Wilson Boatyard & Marina
Wilson 716-751-9202
Hours: 6am-8pm
Carries: Live bait, lures, maps, rods, reels, licenses
Bodies of water: Lake Ontario, 12 Mile Creek, Niagara River
Services & Products: Charter boat service, boat ramp, food, beverages, gas/oil
Guides: Yes
OK to call for current conditions: Yes
Contact: Marge, Steve or Duane

LAKE RONKONKOMA

BAIT & TACKLE...

Chester's Hunting & Fishing West Ltd.
Farmingville 516-696-3800
Hours: 9:30am-9pm
Carries: Live bait, lures, flies, rods, reels, licenses
Bodies of water: Long Island Sound, Atlantic Ocean, Great South Bay, Lake Ronkonkoma, Connetquot River
Services & Products: Repair services
Guides: Yes
OK to call for current conditions: Yes
Contact: Fred Laager

NEW YORK
LONG ISLAND SOUND - NIAGARA RIVER

LONG ISLAND SOUND

BAIT & TACKLE...

Chester's Hunting & Fishing West Ltd.
Farmingville 516-696-3800
Hours: 9:30am-9pm
Carries: Live bait, lures, flies, rods, reels, licenses
Bodies of water: Long Island Sound, Atlantic Ocean, Great South Bay, Lake Ronkonkoma, Connetquot River
Services & Products: Repair services
Guides: Yes
OK to call for current conditions: Yes
Contact: Fred Laager

CHARTER...

Alyssa Ann
Commack 516-543-4529
Species & Seasons: Tuna July-Oct, Shark June-Nov, Striped Bass, Bluefish May-Dec, Cod Mar-Dec
Bodies of water: Atlantic Ocean, Block Island Sound, Eastern Long Island Sound, waters surrounding Montauk PT, NY
Rates: Half day: $350(6), Full day: $600(6), Tuna, Shark, Marlin: $800
Call between: 6pm-10pm
Provides: Light tackle, heavy tackle, lures, bait
Handicapped equipped: Yes
Certifications: USCG

Montauk Sportfishing
Montauk 516-668-2019
Species & Seasons: Shark, Tuna, Marlin, Striped Bass, Bluefish, Fluke, Flounder, Cod
Bodies of water: Atlantic Ocean, Long Island Sound
Rates: $350-$1800
Certifications: USCG

GUIDES...

Pete Traina
Ridgewood 718-821-6367
Species & Seasons: Bluefish, Flounder, Fluke, Trout, plus other species
Bodies of water: Long Island Sound, White Lake, Highland Lake, Greenwood Lake, all Sullivan County lakes and streams
Rates: Varies, Bodyguard/Escort Service
Call between: 8am-11pm
Provides: Light tackle, heavy tackle, lures, bait, rain gear, beverages, lunch
Handicapped equipped: Yes
Certifications: USCG, NY State Licensed Guide

MARINAS...

Gone Fishing Marina
Montauk 516-668-3232
Hours: 6am-7pm
Carries: Live bait, lures, maps, rods, reels
Bodies of water: Long Island Sound
Services & Products: Charter boat service, boat ramp, food, beverages, gas/oil, fishing instruction, repair services
OK to call for current conditions: Yes
Contact: T.J. Jordan

MOHAWK RIVER

CHARTERS...

Reel Easy Sportfishing
Scotia 518-399-5336
Species & Seasons: Atlantic Salmon April-Nov, Lake Trout, Rainbow Trout May-Nov, Brown Trout April-Oct, SM Bass June-Sept, Northern Pike May-Sept, Walleye May-Oct
Bodies of water: Lake Champlain, Great Sacandaga Lake, Mohawk River, Barge Canal, Saranac Lake Region
Rates: Reel Easy I (local lakes-rivers): 4hrs: $120(1-3), 6hrs: $175(1-3) 8hrs: $225(1-3), Reel Easy II (Lake Ontario-Champlain): 6hrs: $240(1-4), 8hrs: $300(1-4), Ice fishing (Jan-Mar): $75(1)
Call between: 7am-9pm
Provides: Light tackle, heavy tackle, lures, bait
Handicapped equipped: Yes, no wheelchairs
Certifications: USCG, NY State Licensed

GUIDES...

M-R Bass Outfitters
35 14th Street
Troy 12180
Species & Seasons: Shad April-June, Striped Bass April-July, Northern Pike, Muskellunge May-Nov, LM Bass June-Nov, Walleye May-Nov
Bodies of water: Hudson River, Mohawk River, Lake Champlain, Saratoga Lake, Finger Lakes, Onieda Lake and any body of water in New York State
Rates: Half day: $50-$75(1), $75-$100(2), Full day: $100-$175(1), $150-$200(2)
Call between: Anytime
Provides: Light tackle, heavy tackle, fly rod/reel, lures, bait, rain gear, beverages, lunch, photos
Handicapped equipped: No
Certifications: NYSOGA, ENCON, USCG

Reel Action Guide Service
Glenmont 518-434-1133
Species & Seasons: LM Bass, SM Bass June-Nov, Walleye, Northern Pike, Panfish May-Nov
Bodies of water: Saratoga Lake, Mohawk River, Hudson River
Rates: Half day: $125(2), Full day: $175(2)
Call between: 8am-0pm
Provides: Light tackle, heavy tackle, lures, beverages
Handicapped equipped: No
Certifications: NY State Licensed

NIAGARA RIVER

BAIT & TACKLE...

Big Catch Bait & Tackle
Buffalo 716-877-0971
Hours: 6am-9pm
Carries: Live bait, lures, rods, reels, licenses
Bodies of water: Lake Erie, Niagara River
Services & Products: Bulk worms packaged for entry into Canada
Guides: Yes
OK to call for current conditions: Yes

Captain Bill's
Niagara Falls 716-283-3487
Hours: 10am-6pm, closed Mon.
Carries: Live bait, lures, flies, maps, rods, reels
Bodies of water: Niagara River, Lake Erie, Lake Ontario
Services & Producs: Boat rentals, guide services, charter boat service, boat ramp, food, beverages, gas/oil, scuba diving, snorkel trips
OK to call for current conditions: Yes
Contact: Steve Cornell

NIAGARA RIVER - ONEIDA LAKE NEW YORK

Mark's Tackle
Niagara Falls 716-285-7255
Hours: 6am-6pm, 6am-12pm Sun.
Carries: Live bait, lures, flies, maps, rods, reels, licenses
Bodies of water: Lake Erie, Niagara River, Lake Ontario
Guides: Yes
OK to call for current conditions: Yes
Contact: Anyone

Niagara Outdoors
N. Tonawanda 716-695-LURE
Hours: 7:30am-7:30pm
Carries: Live bait, lures, flies, maps, rods, reels, licenses
Bodies of water: Lake Ontario, Lake Erie, Niagara River (upper and lower)
Services & Products: Fishing instruction, repair services
Guides: Yes
OK to call for current conditions: Yes
Contact: Anyone

Rainbow Sports
N. Tonawanda 716-692-7510
.... 691-6860
Hours: 9am-7pm, closed Sun.
Carries: Live bait, lures, flies, maps, rods, reels, licenses
Bodies of water: Lake Erie, Niagara River, Lake Ontario, Erie Canal
Services & Products: Fishing instruction, repair services, archery
Guides: Yes
OK to call for current conditions: Yes
Contact: Paul Tessuer

CHARTERS...

Cinelli Sportfishing Service
Olcott 716-433-5210
Species & Seasons: Chinook Salmon, Coho Salmon, Lake Trout, Brown Trout, Steelhead April-Nov, SM Bass June-Nov
Bodies of water: Western Lake Ontario, Niagara River
Rates: Half day: $95(1), Full day: $125(1), River: $330(3), Lake: $460(4)
Call between: 7pm-10pm
Provides: Light tackle, heavy tackle, lures, bait
Handicapped equipped: Yes
Certifications: USCG

Deep Six Charters
Lockport 716-433-0583
Species & Seasons: Trout, Salmon April-Sept
Bodies of water: Lower Niagara River, Lake Ontario
Rates: Half day: $75(1), Full day: $150(1)
Call between: Anytime
Provides: Light tackle, heavy tackle, lures
Handicapped equipped: Yes
Certifications: USCG

Reel Pleasure Charters
Lewiston 716-754-2022
Species & Seasons: Chinook Salmon Sept-Oct, Steelhead, Lake Trout Nov-April, Coho Salmon, Brown Trout April-May, SM Bass July-Aug
Bodies of water: Lower Niagara River, Lake Ontario
Rates: Full day: $175(1), $260(2), $330(3)
Call between: 8am-9am
Provides: Light tackle, heavy tackle, lures, bait
Handicapped equipped: Yes

Zip's Charter Service
Wilson 716-751-9932
Species & Seasons: Chinook Salmon April-Oct, Steelhead, Rainbow Trout, Dec-Sept, Brown Trout April-June, Lake Trout Jan-Oct
Bodies of water: Lake Ontario, Niagara River
Rates: River boat: Full day: $110(1), $220(2), Lake boat: 8 hrs: $350(1-4)
Call between: 7pm-1pm
Provides: Light tackle, heavy tackle, lures, bait
Handicapped equipped: No
Certifications: USCG

GUIDES...

Jim Hanley
Derby 716-549-2232
Species & Seasons: SM Bass May-Nov, Walleye July-Sept, Muskellunge Sept-Nov
Bodies of water: Lake Erie, Niagara River, Lake Ontario
Rates: Half day: $175(1-2), $200(3), Full day: $250(1-2), $300(3)
Call between: 9am-8pm
Provides: Light tackle, heavy tackle, fly rod/reel, lures, bait
Handicapped equipped: Yes
Certifications: USCG

MARINAS...

Wilson Boatyard & Marina
Wilson 716-751-9202
Hours: 6am-8pm
Carries: Live bait, lures, maps, rods, reels, licenses
Bodies of water: Lake Ontario, 12 Mile Creek, Niagara River
Services & Products: Charter boat service, boat ramp, food, beverages, gas/oil
Guides: Yes
OK to call for current conditions: Yes
Contact: Marge, Steve or Duane

ONEIDA LAKE

BAIT & TACKLE...

Ace Trading Post & Taxidermy
Oswego 315-342-3244
Hours: Sunrise-Sunset
Carries: Live bait, lures, flies, maps, rods, reels, licenses
Bodies of water: Lake Ontario (eastern basin), Oswego River, Oneida Lake
Services & Products: Guide services, charter boat service, lodging, food, beverages, fishing instruction, taxidermy
OK to call for current conditions: Yes
Contact: Anyone

B-E Fshing Tackle Inc.
Ontario 800-356-2921
Carries: Live bait, lures, flies, maps, rods, reels, licenses
Bodies of water: Lake Ontario, Sodus Bay, Oneida Lake
Services & Products: Repair services
Guides: Yes
OK to call for current conditions: Yes
Contact: Anyone

Mickey's
N. Syracuse 315-358-7998
Hours: 7am-8pm
Carries: Live bait, lures, flies, maps, rods, reels, licenses
Bodies of water: Oneida Lake, Salmon River, Onondaga Lake
Services & Products: Beverages, fishing instruction
Guides: Yes
OK to call for current conditions: Yes
Contact: Fran, Jim or Al Daher

NEW YORK — ONEIDA LAKE

Salmon River Sports Shop
Pulaski 315-298-4343
Hours: 5-6am-7-9pm
Carries: Live bait, lures, flies, maps, rods, reels
Bodies of water: Salmon River, Lake Ontario, Oneida Lake, Sandy Creek, Grindstone, Little Salmon Riiver
Services & Products: Guide services, charter boat service, lodging, fishing instruction, repair services, custom rods
OK to call for current conditions: Yes
Contact: Ron or Tyler Gervaise

GUIDES...

Let's Go Fishing
Syracuse 315-478-7231
Species & Seasons: Trout April-Sept, Northern Pike May-Mar, LM Bass June-Nov, Salmon depends on waters and species, Panfish all year
Bodies of water: Central New York region, Finger Lakes, Lake Ontario, Whitney Point Lake, Oneida Lake
Call between: 6pm-9pm
Provides: Light tackle, heavy tackle, fly rod/reel, lures, bait
Handicapped equipped: No
Certifications: NY State Licensed Guide

M-R Bass Outfitters
35 14th Street
Troy 12180
Species & Seasons: Shad April-June, Striped Bass April-July, Northern Pike, Muskellunge May-Nov, LM Bass June-Nov, Walleye May-Nov
Bodies of water: Hudson River, Mohawk River, Lake Champlain, Saratoga Lake, Finger Lakes, Onieda Lake and any body of water in New York State
Rates: Half day: $50-$75(1), $75-$100(2), Full day: $100-$175(1), $150-$200(2)
Call between: Anytime
Provides: Light tackle, heavy tackle, fly rod/reel, lures, bait, rain gear, beverages, lunch, photos
Handicapped equipped: No
Certifications: NYSOGA, ENCON, USCG

LODGING...

Cannon's Place Motel
Altmar 315-298-5054
Guest Capacity: 65
Handicapped equipped: Yes
Seasons: All year
Rates: $15/pp day
Guides: Yes
Species & Seasons: Steelhead Oct-May, Brown Trout April-June, Lake Trout April-Sept, Coho Salmon, Chinook Salmon July-Nov
Bodies of Water: Lake Ontario, Salmon River, Oneida Lake, Sandy Pond
Types of fishing: Fly fishing, light tackle, heavy tackle, wading, floa trips
Available: Fishing instruction, licenses, bait, tackle, family activities

Kirchner's Fishing Kamp
Cleveland 315-675-3662
Guest Capacity: 35
Handicapped equipped: No
Seasons: May 1 to Oct 15
Jan 15 to Mar 15
Rates: $320-$420/week
Contact: Bill or Nancy Kirchner
Guides: Yes
Species & Seasons: Walleye May-Oct, Perch Sept-Oct/Jan-Mar, LM Bass, SM Bass June-Oct
Bodies of Water: Oneida Lake
Types of fishing: Light tackle
Available: Fishing instruction, licenses, bit, tackle, boat rentals

Montclair Motel
Parish 315-625-7100
.... 625-7064
Guest Capacity: 20-40
Handicapped equipped: Yes
Seasons: All year
Rates: Call for rates
Guides: Yes
Species & Seasons: Brown Trout April-June, Lake Trout May-Sept, Salmon July-Oct, Steelhead Oct-April, SM Bass June-July
Bodies of Water: Lake Ontario, Oneida Lake, Salmon River, Oswego River
Types of fishing: Fly fishing, light tackle, wading, float trips, charter boat
Available: Licenses

Oswego Days Inn
Oswego 315-343-3136
Guest Capacity: 44 rooms
Handicapped equipped: No
Seasons: All year
Rates: $64/day, weekly rates available
Contact: Alice Blum
Guides: Yes, recommend
Species & Seasons: LM Bass, SM Bass June-Nov, Walleye June-Aug, Steelhead Nov-May, Chinook Salmon Aug-Nov, Lake Trout Jan-April, Atlantic Salmon Sept-Nov/April-May, Brown Trout Oct-May, Chinook Salmon Sept-Nov
Bodies of Water: Lake Ontario, Oswego River, Salmon River, Salmon Reservoir, Oneida Lake
Types of fishing: Fly fishing, light tackle, heavy tackle, wading

Port Lodge Motel
Pulaski 315-298-6876
Guest Capacity: 34 rooms
Handicapped equipped: Yes
Seasons: All year
Rates: $39-$59/day
Contact: Free Martin
Guides: Yes
Species & Seasons: Chinook Salmon July-Nov, Steelhead Nov-Mar, Brown Trout Mar-May, Walleye, Salmon, Trout all year
Bodies of Water: Lake Ontario, Salmon River, Oneida Lake, Sandy Pond, Oswego River
Types of fishing: Fly fishing, light tackle, heavy tackle, wading, float trips
Available: Licenses, family acticvities, Within 100 yards: Fishing instruction, bait, tackle, boat rentals, children's program

Schoolhouse Inn
Altmar 315-298-5293
.... 298-3367
Guest Capacity: 32
Handicapped equipped: No
Seasons: All year
Rates: Nov.-Aug: $15/day + tax
Sept.-Oct: $20/day + tax
Contact: Capt Bill Lillie or Lori
Guides: Yes
Species & Seasons: Salmon Sept-Oct, Steelhead Nov-April, Walleye, LM Bass, SM Bass, Northern Pike, Lake Trout June-Sept, Brown Trout April-July
Bodies of Water: Lake Ontario and Tributaries, Salmon River, Oswego River, Oneida Lake
Types of fishing: Fly fishing, light tackle, heavy tackle, wading, float trips, lake charters
Available: Bait, tackle

The Thomas Inn
Oswego 315-343-4900
Guest Capacity: 47 rooms
Seasons: All year
Rates: $54/day, weekly rates available
Contact: Brenda Reed
Guides: Yes, recommend
Species & Seasons: LM Bass, SM Bass June-Nov, Walleye June-Aug, Steelhead Nov-May, Chinook Salmon Aug-Nov, Lake Trout Jan-April, Brown Trout Oct-May, Chinook Salmon Sept-Nov, Atlantic Salmon April-May

ONEIDA LAKE - OSWEGO RIVER   NEW YORK

Bodies of Water: Lake Ontario, Oswego River, Salmon River, Salmon Reservoir, Oneida Lake
Types of fishing: Fly fishing, light tackle, wading

ONONDAGA LAKE

BAIT & TACKLE...

Mickey's
N. Syracuse 315-358-7998
Hours: 7am-8pm
Carries: Live bait, lures, flies, maps, rods, reels, licenses
Bodies of water: Oneida Lake, Salmon River, Onondaga Lake
Services & Products: Beverages, fishing instruction
Guides: Yes
OK to call for current conditions: Yes
Contact: Fran, Jim or Al Daher

OSWEGO RIVER

BAIT & TACKLE...

Ace Trading Post & Taxidermy
Oswego 315-342-3244
Hours: Sunrise-Sunset
Carries: Live bait, lures, flies, maps, rods, reels, licenses
Bodies of water: Lake Ontario (eastern basin), Owego River, Oneida Lake
Services & Products: Guide services, charter boat service, lodging, food, beverages, fishing instruction, taxidermy
OK to call for current conditions: Yes
Contact: Anyone

CHARTERS...

Blue Nose Sportfishing Charters
Newton, NJ 201-948-4992
 315-676-7571
Species & Seasons: Brown Trout, Coho Salmon, Steelhead, Lake Trout, Rainbow Trout, Chinook Salmon, Atlantic Salmon April-Nov, Walleye, Northern Pike May-Nov, LM Bass, SM Bass June-Nov
Bodies of water: Oswego River, Lake Ontario
Rates: Full day: $225(1-2), $87.50 additional pp (1995 rates)

Call between: 8am-7pm
Provides: Light tackle, lures, bait, rain gear
Handicapped equipped: No
Certifications: USCG

K & G Sportfishing Charter Fleet & Lodge
Oswego 800-346-6533
Species & Seasons: Walleye May-July, LM Bass, SM Bass June-Sept, Salmon July-Oct, Brown Trout Mar-Aug, Steelhead Jan-Dec, Lake Trout April-Sept, Atlantic Salmon April-Dec
Bodies of water: Lake Ontario, Oswego River, Salmon River
Rates: Half day: $110, Full day: $200 (rates are based on party of 4 includes lodging)
Call between: 8am-10pm
Provides: Light tackle, fly rod/reel, lures, licenses, lodging
Handicapped equipped: Yes
Certifications: USCG, NY State Guide, North American Fishing Club

Little Whip Fishing Charters
Oswego 315-343-4852
Species & Seasons: Brown Trout April-June, Walleye May-June, Steelhead, Lake Trout April-Aug, Salmon July-Sept
Bodies of water: Lake Ontario, Oswego River
Rates: Half day: $200(2-4), Full day: $350(2-4), Walleye: Full day: $225(2)
Call between: Anytime
Provides: Light tackle, heavy tackle, lures, bait
Handicapped equipped: Depends on handicap
Certifications: USCG

Octavius M&M Charters
Parish 315-625-7100
 625-7064
Species & Seasons: Brown Trout April-June, Lake Trout May-Sept, Salmon July-Oct, Steelhead Oct-April, SM Bass June-July
Bodies of water: Salmon River, Lake Ontario, Oswego River
Rates: Call for rates
Call between: Noon-11pm
Provides: Light tackle, lures, bait
Handicapped equipped: Yes

GUIDES...

Al's Fishing Guide Service
Worcester, MA 800-588-5700
 508-797-570
Species & Seasons: Chinook Salmon, Coho Salmon Sept-Nov, Steelhead Sept-April, Brown Trout Sept-Dec, Landlocked Salmon April-May, Striped Bass May-Oct
Bodies of water: Salmon River, Oswego River,
Rates: Half day: $100(1), $200(2), Full day: $150(1), $300(2), prices vary
Call between: 5pm-10pm
Provides: Light tackle, heavy tackle, fly rod/reel, lures, bait
Handicapped equipped: Yes
Certifications: NY Licensed Guide

Tightlines Guide Service
Pulaski 800-452-1176
Species & Seasons: Chinook Salmon, Coho Salmon Sept-Nov, Steelhead Nov-May, Brown Trout Oct-Nov
Bodies of water: Lake Ontario, Salmon River, Black River, Oswego River, Little Salmon River, and eastern Lake Ontario Tributaries
Rates: Float trips: Half day: $150(1), $175(2), Full day: $180(1), $220(2), Wade trips: $135pp
Call between: 6pm-10pm
Provides: Light tackle, heavy tackle, fly rod/reel, lures, bait
Handicapped equipped: No
Certifications: NY Registered Guide

Wild River Inn Lodge & Guide Service
Pulaski 315-298-4195
Species & Seasons: Salmon Aug-Nov, Steelhead Oct-May, Lake Trout May-Aug, Brown Trout Oct-July, Walleye May-July, SM Bass June-Sept
Bodies of water: Salmon River, Lake Ontario, Black River, Oswego River, and other Lake Ontario Tributaries
Rates: Full day (starting at): $160(1), $220(2), Lodge (starting at): $22.50/pp
Call between: 9am-9pm
Provides: Light tackle, heavy tackle, fly rod/reel, lures, bait
Handicapped equipped: Yes, on the lake, river no
Certifications: USCG, NY State Licensed Guide

NEW YORK

OSWEGO RIVER - OTSELIC RIVER

LODGING...

Holly Drive Motel
901 Holly Drive
Fulton 13069
Guest Capacity: 68
Handicapped equipped: No
Seasons: All year
Rates: $35/pp day
Contact: Nick

Montclair Motel
Parish 315-625-7100
.... 625-7064
Guest Capacity: 20-40
Handicapped equipped: Yes
Seasons: All year
Rates: Call for rates
Guides: Yes
Species & Seasons: Brown Trout April-June, Lake Trout May-Sept, Salmon July-Oct, Steelhead Oct-April, SM Bass June-July
Bodies of Water: Lake Ontario, Oneida Lake, Salmon River, Oswego River
Types of fishing: Fly fishing, light tackle, wading, float trips, charter boat
Available: Licenses

Oswego Days Inn
Oswego 315-343-3136
Guest Capacity: 44 rooms
Handicapped equipped: No
Seasons: All year
Rates: $64/day, weekly rates available
Contact: Alice Blum
Guides: Yes, recommend
Species & Seasons: LM Bass, SM Bass June-Nov, Walleye June-Aug, Steelhead Nov-May, Chinook Salmon Aug-Nov, Lake Trout Jan-April, Atlantic Salmon Sept-Nov/April-May, Brown Trout Oct-May, Chinook Salmon Sept-Nov
Bodies of Water: Lake Ontario, Oswego River, Salmon River, Salmon Reservoir, Oneida Lake
Types of fishing: Fly fishing, light tackle, heavy tackle, wading

Port Lodge Motel
Pulaski 315-298-6876
Guest Capacity: 34 rooms
Handicapped equipped: Yes
Seasons: All year
Rates: $39-$59/day
Contact: Free Martin
Guides: Yes
Species & Seasons: Chinook Salmon July-Nov, Steelhead Nov-Mar, Brown Trout Mar-May, Walleye, Salmon, Trout all year
Bodies of Water: Lake Ontario, Salmon River, Oneida Lake, Sandy Pond, Oswego River
Types of fishing: Fly fishing, light tackle, heavy tackle, wading, float trips
Available: Licenses, family acticvities, Within 100 yards: Fishing instruction, bait, tackle, boat rentals, children's program

Schoolhouse Inn
Altmar 315-298-5293
.... 298-3367
Guest Capacity: 32
Handicapped equipped: No
Seasons: All year
Rates: Nov.-Aug: $15/day + tax
Sept.-Oct: $20/day + tax
Contact: Capt Bill Lillie or Lori
Guides: Yes
Species & Seasons: Salmon Sept-Oct, Steelhead Nov-April, Walleye, LM Bass, SM Bass, Northern Pike, Lake Trout June-Sept, Brown Trout April-July
Bodies of Water: Lake Ontario and Tributaries, Salmon River, Oswego River, Oneida Lake
Types of fishing: Fly fishing, light tackle, heavy tackle, wading, float trips, lake charters
Available: Bait, tackle

Strike King Lodge
Mexico 315-963-7826
Guest Capacity: 24-32
Handicapped equipped: No
Seasons: Mar to Dec
Rates: $65/day
Guides: Yes
Species & Seasons:
Bodies of Water: Lake Ontario, Oswego River, Salmon River, Little Salmon River
Types of fishing: Fly fishing, light tackle, heavy tackle, float trips
Available: Fishing instruction, baby sitting, charters, float trips

Sunset Cabins & RV Park
Oswego 315-343-2166
Guest Capacity: 150
Handicapped equipped: No
Seasons: May 1 to Oct 20
Rates: Tents: $10, Cabins: $40, RV: $18, Cottages: $100
Guides: Yes, Charter boats
Species & Seasons: Trout, Perch, Salmon, SM Bass, Steelhead April-Nov
Bodies of Water: Lake Ontario, Oswego River
Types of fishing: Fly fishing, light tackle, heavy tackle, wading, float trips
Available: In town: Licenses, bait, tackle, boat rentals, auto races Saturday nights, tennis, horseshoes, swimming

The Thomas Inn
Oswego 315-343-4900
Guest Capacity: 47 rooms
Handicapped equipped:
Seasons: All year
Rates: $54/day, weekly rates available
Contact: Brenda Reed
Guides: Yes, recommend
Species & Seasons: M Bass, SM Bass June-Nov, Walleye June-Aug, Steelhead Nov-May, Chinook Salmon Aug-Nov, Lake Trout Jan-April, Brown Trout Oct-May, Chinook Salmon Sept-Nov, Atlantic Salmon April-May
Bodies of Water: Lake Ontario, Oswego River, Salmon River, Salmon Res., Oneida Lake
Types of fishing: Fly fishing, light tackle, wading

OTSEGO LAKE

GUIDES...

Michael Empey, Sr.
Richfield Springs 315-858-2286
Species & Seasons: Lake Trout, Salmon April-Sept, Walleye, Tiger Muskellunge May-Oct
Bodies of water: Otsego lake, Canadarago Lake
Rates: Varies: $75-$$200 per day
Call between: Anytime
Provides: Light tackle, lures, bait
Handicapped equipped: No
Certifications: NY State DEC Licensed

OTSELIC RIVER

GUIDES...

A J's Outdoor Services
Courtland 607-758-7533
Species & Seasons: SM Bass, LM Bass June-Sept, Rainbow Trout, Brown Trout, Brook Trout April-Sept, Walleye, Bullhead, Pickerel, Northern Pike June-Sept, Yellow Perch all year
Bodies of water: Tioughnioga River, Otselic River, Chanango River
Rates: Full day: $75+(1-2), $24 additional pp

OTSELIC RIVER - SALMON RIVER / NEW YORK

Call between: 5pm-9pm
Provides: Bait, beverages, lunch
Handicapped equipped: Some
Certifications: NYSDEC Licensed Guide

PEPACTON RESERVOIR

BAIT & TACKLE...

Al's Sport Store
Downsville 607-363-7740
Hours: 6am-6pm
Carries: Live bait, lures, flies, maps, rods, reels, licenses
Bodies of water: Delaware River, Beaverkill River, Pepacton Res.
Services & Products: Canoe rentals, lodging, canoe ramp
Guides: Yes
OK to call for current conditions: Yes
Contact: Al Carpenter

Manor Sport Shop
Livingston Manor 914-439-3002
Hours: 8am-6pm
Carries: Live bait, lures, flies, maps, rods, reels, licenses
Bodies of water: Beaverkill River, Willowemac River, Pepacton Res.
Services & Products: Fishing instruction, repair services, custom rods, guns, ammo, camping supplies
Guides: Yes
OK to call for current conditions: Yes
Contact: Joe Dimilte

The Tackle Shack
Phoenicia 914-688-7780
Hours: 7am-8pm
Carries: Live bait, lures, flies, maps, rods, reels, licenses
Bodies of water: Esodus Creek, Ashokan Res., Pepacton Res., Hudson River
Services & Products:
Guides: Yes
OK to call for current conditions: Yes
Contact: Frank

SALMON RIVER

BAIT & TACKLE...

The Green Drake
Utica 315-735-6679
Hours: 9am-7pm
Carries: Flies, rods, reels
Bodies of water: West Canada Creek, Black River, Salmon River, Lake Ontario, Oriskany Creek, Delaware River

Services & Products: Guide services, fishing instruction, repair services, custom rods
Guides: Yes
OK to call for current conditions: Yes
Contact: George Massoud

Les Maynard's Fly Shop
Waterloo 315-539-3236
Hours: 8am-9pm, closed Sun.
Carries: Flies, rods, reels
Bodies of water: Salmon River, Maxwell Creek, Owosco Inlet, Fall Creek, Keuka Outlet
Services & Products: Fly casting, fly tying lessons, private stocked pond
Guides: Yes
OK to call for current conditions: Yes
Contact: Les Maynard

Mickey's
N. Syracuse 315-358-7998
Hours: 7am-8pm
Carries: Live bait, lures, flies, maps, rods, reels, licenses
Bodies of water: Oneida Lake, Salmon River, Onondaga Lake
Services & Products: Beverages, fishing instruction
Guides: Yes
OK to call for current conditions: Yes
Contact: Fran, Jim or Al Daher

Salmon River Sports Shop
Pulaski 315-298-4343
Hours: 5-6am-7-9pm
Carries: Live bait, lures, flies, maps, rods, reels
Bodies of water: Salmon River, Lake Ontario, Oneida Lake, Sandy Creek, Grindstone, Little Salmon Riiver
Services & Products: Guide services, charter boat service, lodging, fishing instruction, repair services, custom rods
OK to call for current conditions: Yes
Contact: Ron or Tyler Gervaise

CHARTERS...

K & G Sportfishing Charter Fleet & Lodge
Oswego 800-346-6533
Species & Seasons: Walleye May-July, LM Bass, SM Bass June-Sept, Salmon July-Oct, Brown Trout Mar-Aug, Steelhead Jan-Dec, Lake Trout April-Sept, Atlantic Salmon April-Dec
Bodies of water: Lake Ontario, Oswego River, Salmon River

Rates: Half day: $110, Full day: $200 (rates are based on party of 4 includes lodging)
Call between: 8am-10pm
Provides: Light tackle, fly rod/reel, lures, licenses, lodging
Handicapped equipped: Yes
Certifications: USCG, NY State Guide, North American Fishing Club

Lucky Dutchman Charters
Pulaski 800-368-4467
Species & Seasons: Brown Trout Mar-June, Lake Trout May-July, Salmon Aug-Oct, Steelhead Sept-Dec
Bodies of water: Lake Ontario, Salmon River
Call between: 8am-10pm
Provides: Light tackle, heavy tackle, lures
Handicapped equipped: Yes
Certifications: USCG, SRGA

Aj's OUTDOOR SERVICES
A WEEKEND FISHING?
What better way to unwind & relax than a weekend spent in the outdoors!
We Can Make It Happen For You!
(607) 758-7533
Or write: P.O. Box 466, Cortland, N.Y. 13045

We also provide:
Camping, hiking, & hunting trips
N.Y.S. Lic. Outdoor Guide   Member: N.Y.S.O.G.A.

NEW YORK — SALMON RIVER

Octavius M&M Charters
Parish 315-625-7100
.... 625-7064
Species & Seasons: Brown Trout April-June, Lake Trout May-Sept, Salmon July-Oct, Steelhead Oct-April, SM Bass June-July
Bodies of water: Salmon River, Lake Ontario, Oswego River
Rates: Call for rates
Call between: Noon-11pm
Provides: Light tackle, lures, bait
Handicapped equipped: Yes

Strike Zone Charters
Pulaski 315-298-2074
Species & Seasons: Steelhead Nov-May, Brown Trout April-Oct, Lake Trout May-Sept, Salmon July-Nov
Bodies of water: Lake Ontario, Salmon River
Rates: Half day: $320(4), Full day: $480(4)
Call between: 9am-5pm
Provides: Light tackle, lures, bait
Handicapped equipped: Yes

GUIDES...

Alex Atchie's Guide Service
Watertown 315-782-3904
Species & Seasons: Chinook Salmon Sept-Oct, Atlantic Salmon Aug-Oct, Steelhead Oct-Nov/Feb-April
Bodies of water: Black River, Salmon River
Rates: Full day: $120(1), $240(2)
Call between: 6pm-10pm
Provides: Light tackle, heavy tackle, lures, bait
Handicapped equipped: Yes, depending on handicap
Certifications: NY Licensed Guide, Member of Oswego Cty River Guides Assoc.

Al's Fishing Guide Service
Worcester, MA 800-588-5700
.... 508-797-570
Species & Seasons: Chinook Salmon, Coho Salmon Sept-Nov, Steelhead Sept-April, Brown Trout Sept-Dec, Landlocked Salmon April-May, Striped Bass May-Oct
Bodies of water: Salmon River, Oswego River,
Rates: Half day: $100(1), $200(2), Full day: $150(1), $300(2), prices vary
Call between: 5pm-10pm
Provides: Light tackle, heavy tackle, fly rod/reel, lures, bait
Handicapped equipped: Yes
Certifications: NY Licensed Guide

Call of the Wild Guide Service
Wallkill 914-895-3097
Species & Seasons: Brook Trout April-June, Salmon Sept-June, Lake Trout May-May
Bodies of water: Lake George, Fulton Chain Lakes, Salmon River, Lake Champlain, Pharroah Lake, Hudson River
Call between: 8am-9pm
Provides: Light tackle, heavy tackle, fly rod/reel, lures, bait, rain gear, beverages, lunch
Handicapped equipped: Yes

Excellent Guide Service
Hastings 315-676-3475
Species & Seasons: Pacific Salmon Sept-Nov, Coho Salmon Sept-Oct, Brown Trout Oct-Nov, Steelhead Oct-April
Bodies of water: Salmon River, and tributaries of Lake Ontario
Rates: Stream Side: Full day: $125(1), $240(2), Drift boat trips: Full day: $250
Call between: 7pm-9pm
Provides: Light tackle, fly rod/reel, lures, bait
Handicapped equipped: Yes

Finger Lakes Outfitters
Fairport 716-223-8236
Species & Seasons: Chinook Salmon Aug-Nov, Brown Trout Oct-Dec, Steelhead Oct-May, Brown Trout April-Sept, Rainbow Trout Oct-May
Bodies of water: Lake Ontario Tributaries, Salmon River, Maxwell Creek, Irondequoit Creek, Oak Orchard Creek, Finger Lakes Tributaries, Naples Creek, Catherine's Creek, Salmon Creek and more
Rates: Half day: $75(1), $100(2), Full day: $150(1), $200(2)
Call between: 7am-10pm
Provides: Fly rod/reel, lures(flies), beverages, lunch
Handicapped equipped: No
Certifications: NY State Guide, Red Cross First aid, CPR, Water Safety, fully insured

LeClair's Guiding Service
Clay 315-699-3319
Species & Seasons: Salmon, Steelhead Aug-May, Brown Trout (Lake) Oct-Nov, Rainbow Trout, Brown Trout May-Aug, SM Bass, Panfish July-Aug, Northern Pike April-Aug, Walleye Sept-Nov
Bodies of water: Salmon River Tributaries of Lake Ontario, West Canada Creek, French Creek, Big Bay Creek
Rates: Full day: $110(1), $240(2) (prices are for Salmon, Steelhead, other prices vary)
Call between: 8am-9pm
Provides: Light tackle, fly rod/reel, lures, bait, rain gear
Handicapped equipped: Yes
Certifications: NY State Licensed Guide

Tightlines Guide Service
Pulaski 800-452-1176
Species & Seasons: Chinook Salmon, Coho Salmon Sept-Nov, Steelhead Nov-May, Brown Trout Oct-Nov
Bodies of water: Lake Ontario, Salmon River, Black River, Oswego River, Little Salmon River, and eastern Lake Ontario Tributaries
Rates: Float trips: Half day: $150(1), $175(2), Full day: $180(1), $220(2), Wade trips: $135pp
Call between: 6pm-10pm
Provides: Light tackle, heavy tackle, fly rod/reel, lures, bait
Handicapped equipped: No
Certifications: NY Registered Guide

Wicked Will Fishing Services
Cazenovia 315-655-3908
Species & Seasons: Brown Trout, Lake Trout, Rainbow Trout, Steelhead April-Nov, Coho Salmon, Chinook Salmon July-Nov, Atlantic Salmon June-Nov
Bodies of water: Lake Ontario, Salmon River
Rates: 6 hrs. $250(1-4)
Call between:
Provides: Heavy tackle, lures, bait
Handicapped equipped: Limited

Wild River Inn Lodge & Guide Service
Pulaski 315-298-4195
Species & Seasons: Salmon Aug-Nov, Steelead Oct-May, Lake Trout May-Aug, Brown Trout Oct-July, Walleye May-July, SM Bass June-Sept
Bodies of water: Salmon River, Lake Ontario, Black River, Oswego River, and other Lake Ontario Tributaries

SALMON RIVER   NEW YORK

Rates: Full day (starting at): $160(1), $220(2), Lodge (starting at): $22.50/pp
Call between: 9am-9pm
Provides: Light tackle, heavy tackle, fly rod/reel, lures, bait
Handicapped equipped: Yes, on the lake, river no
Certifications: USCG, NY State Licensed Guide

LODGING...

"All Season" Lodge
Sandy Creek 315-387-5850
Guest Capacity: 20
Handicapped equipped: No
Seasons: All year
Rates: $22/pp day +tax
Contact: Rose
Guides: Yes
Species & Seasons: SM Bass June-Nov, Northern Pike, Walleye May-Mar, Lake Trout Jan-Sept, Salmon all year, Ice fishing Nov-April, Brook Trout April-Sept
Bodies of Water: Lake Ontario, Salmon River
Types of fishing: Fly fishing, light tackle, heavy tackle, wading, boat
Available: Licenses

Angler's Roost Campgrounds, Bed & Breakfast
Pulaski 315-387-5690
Guest Capacity: 50
Handicapped equipped: Yes, campgrounds are, not B&B
Seasons: Camp: May to Nov, B&B: all year
Rates: Camp: $17/day, $90/week, B&B: $20-$25/day
Contact: Richard M. Machemer
Guides: Yes
Species & Seasons: LM Bass, SM Bass June-Nov, Brown Trout April-June, Lake Trout June-Sept, Lake Salmon July-Sept, River Salmon Sept-Oct, ice fishing Dec-Mar, Steelhead Oct-April
Bodies of Water: Lake Ontario, Little Sandy Creek, Salmon River
Types of fishing: Fly fishing, light tackle, heavy tackle, wading, float trips, charter on lake
Available: Fishing instruction, licenses, bait, tackle, family activities, fish cleaning and freezing

Cannon's Place Motel
Altmar 315-298-5054
Guest Capacity: 65
Handicapped equipped: Yes
Seasons: All year
Rates: $15/pp day
Guides: Yes
Species & Seasons: Steelhead Oct-May, Brown Trout April-June, Lake Trout April-Sept, Coho Salmon, Chinook Salmon July-Nov
Bodies of Water: Lake Ontario, Salmon River, Oneida Lake, Sandy Pond
Types of fishing: Fly fishing, light tackle, heavy tckle, wading, float trips
Available: Fishing instruction, licenses, bait, tackle, family activities

Crew Quarters Lodging
Oswego 315-342-6285
.... 343-6856
Guest Capacity: 13
Handicapped equipped: Yes, restaurant and lounge
Seasons: All year
Rates: $40db/day
Contact: Tom, Sandy or Sharon
Guides: Yes
Bodies of Water: Lake Ontario, Salmon River
Types of fishing: Light tackle, heavy tackle, wading

Feeder Creek Lodge
Pulaski 315-298-4467
Guest Capacity: 14
Seasons: All year
Rates: $30/day
Contact: Barbara Van Wormer
Guides: Yes
Species & Seasons: Brown Trout, Mar-June, Lake Trout May-July, Salmon Aug-Oct, Steelhead Sept-Dec
Bodies of Water: Lake Ontario, Salmon River
Types of fishing: Fly fishing, light tackle, heavy tackle, wading, float trips, lake charters
Available: Licenses

Jefferson Street Lodge
Pulaski 315-298-6247
Guest Capacity: 9
Handicapped equipped: No
Seasons: Aug to Nov
Rates: $15/day pp
Contact: Sandy Althouse
Guides: Yes, recommend
Species & Seasons: Coho Salmon, Steelhead, King Salmon
Bodies of Water: Salmon River, Lake Ontario
Types of fishing: Wading

Laurdon Heights
Pulaski 315-298-6091
Guest Capacity: 36
Handicapped equipped: Yes
Seasons: All year
Rates: Varies
Guides: Yes
Species & Seasons: Salmon River: Steelhead Oct-May, Salmon Sept-Oct, Brown Trout Oct-Nov, Lake Ontario: Steelhead, Salmon May-Oct, Brown Trout April-Oct
Bodies of Water: Lake Ontario, Salmon River
Types of fishing: Fly fishing, light tackle, heavy tackle, wading, float trips
Available: Condo units, full kitchens

Log Cabin Inn & Motel
PO Box 24
Pulaski 13142
Guest Capacity: 60
Handicapped equipped: No
Seasons: All year
Rates: $25/pp day
Contact: J. Gonger
Guides: Yes
Species & Seasons: Steelhead Nov-April, Brown Trout Mar-May, Lake Trout Arpil-Oct, Salmon April-Nov, SM Bass June-Aug
Bodies of Water: Lake Ontario, Salmon River
Types of fishing: Fly fishing, light tackle, heavy tackle, float trips
Available: Licenses

Montclair Motel
Parish 315-625-7100
.... 625-7064
Guest Capacity: 20-40
Handicapped equipped: Yes
Seasons: All year
Rates: Call for rates
Guides: Yes
Species & Seasons: Brown Trout April-June, Lake Trout May-Sept, Salmon July-Oct, Steelhead Oct-April, SM Bass June-July
Bodies of Water: Lake Ontario, Oneida Lake, Salmon River, Oswego River
Types of fishing: Fly fishing, light tackle, wading, float trips, charter boat
Available: Licenses

NEW YORK

SALMON RIVER - SARATOGA LAKE

Oswego Days Inn
Oswego 315-343-3136
Guest Capacity: 44 rooms
Handicapped equipped: No
Seasons: All year
Rates: $64/day, weekly rates available
Contact: Alice Blum
Guides: Yes, recommend
Species & Seasons: LM Bass, SM Bass June-Nov, Walleye June-Aug, Steelhead Nov-May, Chinook Salmon Aug-Nov, Lake Trout Jan-April, Atlantic Salmon Sept-Nov/April-May, Brown Trout Oct-May, Chinook Salmon Sept-Nov
Bodies of Water: Lake Ontario, Oswego River, Salmon River, Salmon Reservoir, Oneida Lake
Types of fishing: Fly fishing, light tackle, heavy tackle, wading

Port Lodge Motel
Pulaski 315-298-6876
Guest Capacity: 34 rooms
Handicapped equipped: Yes
Seasons: All year
Rates: $39-$59/day
Contact: Free Martin
Guides: Yes
Species & Seasons: Chinook Salmon July-Nov, Steelhead Nov-Mar, Brown Trout Mar-May, Walleye, Salmon, Trout all year
Bodies of Water: Lake Ontario, Salmon River, Oneida Lake, Sandy Pond, Oswego River
Types of fishing: Fly fishing, light tackle, heavy tackle, wading, float trips
Available: Licenses, family acticvities, Within 100 yards: Fishing instruction, bait, tackle, boat rentals, children's program

The Portly Angler Lodge
Pulaski 315-298-4773
Guest Capacity: 250
Handicapped equipped: Yes
Seasons: July 14 to May 14
Rates: Varies
Guides: Yes
Species & Seasons: Steelhead Oct-May, Chinook Salmon, Coho Salmon Aug-Nov, Brown Trout April-Nov, Lake Trout May-Sept, SM Bass June-Sept
Bodies of Water: Salmon River, Lake Ontario
Types of fishing: Fly fishing, light tackle, wading, float trips, charter boats
Available: Licenses, bar, lounge

Schoolhouse Inn
Altmar 315-298-5293
.... 298-3367
Guest Capacity: 32
Handicapped equipped: No
Seasons: All year
Rates: Nov.-Aug: $15/day + tax
Sept.-Oct: $20/day + tax
Contact: Capt Bill Lillie or Lori
Guides: Yes
Species & Seasons: Salmon Sept-Oct, Steelhead Nov-April, Walleye, LM Bass, SM Bass, Northern Pike, Lake Trout June-Sept, Brown Trout April-July
Bodies of Water: Lake Ontario and Tributaries, Salmon River, Oswego River, Oneida Lake
Types of fishing: Fly fishing, light tackle, heavy tackle, wading, float trips, lake charters
Available: Bait, tackle

Shillelaghs & Shamrocks
Port Ontario 315-298-7040
Guest Capacity: 22
Handicapped equipped: Yes
Seasons: Mar 1 to Nov 15
Rates: $30/day with full breakfast
Contact: Sue or Bill
Guides: Yes
Species & Seasons: Salmon, Northern Pike, Walleye, SM Bass May-Nov, Lake Trout April-Sept, Brown Trout Mar-June, Steelhead Oct-May
Bodies of Water: Lake Ontario, Salmon River, various feeder streams to Lake Ontario
Types of fishing: Fly fishing, light tackle, heavy tackle, wading, float trips
Available: Fishing instruction, boat rentals, family activities, tavern, restaurant

The Stone House Inn
Altmar 315-298-6028
Guest Capacity: 36
Handicapped equipped: Yes, it is accessible
Seasons: All year
Rates: $15-$30/pp day
Contact: Charlotte or Howard Bennett
Guides: Yes
Species & Seasons: Salmon Sept-Oct, Steelhead Nov-April, Brown Trout June-Oct
Bodies of Water: Salmon River, Lake Ontario, Salmon River Res.
Types of fishing: Fly fishing, light tackle, heavy tackle, wading, float trips

Strike King Lodge
Mexico 315-963-7826
Guest Capacity: 24-32
Handicapped equipped: No
Seasons: Mar to Dec **Rates:** $65/day
Guides: Yes
Bodies of Water: Lake Ontario, Oswego River, Salmon River, Little Salmon River
Types of fishing: Fly fishing, light tackle, heavy tackle, float trips
Available: Fishing instruction, baby sitting, charters, float trips

The Thomas Inn
Oswego 315-343-4900
Guest Capacity: 47 rooms
Seasons: All year
Rates: $54/day, weekly rates available
Contact: Brenda Reed
Guides: Yes, recommend
Species & Seasons: LM Bass, SM Bass June-Nov, Walleye June-Aug, Steelhead ov-May, Chinook Salmon Aug-Nov, Lake Trout Jan-April, Brown Trout Oct-May, Chinook Salmon Sept-Nov, Atlantic Salmon April-May
Bodies of Water: Lake Ontario, Oswego River, Salmon River, Salmon Reservoir, Oneida Lake
Types of fishing: Fly fishing, light tackle, wading

MARINAS...

Clark's Marina
Pulaski 315-298-5832
Hours: 7am-7pm
Bodies of water: Salmon River, Lake Ontario
Services & Products: Boat rentals, lodging, boat ramp, boat dockage
Guides: Yes
OK to call for current conditions: Yes
Contact: Don Clark

SARATOGA LAKE

GUIDES...

M-R Bass Outfitters
35 14th Street
Troy 12180
Species & Seasons: Shad April-June, Striped Bass April-July, Northern Pike, Muskellunge May-Nov, LM Bass June-Nov, Walleye May-Nov
Bodies of water: Hudson River,

SARATOGA LAKE - ST. LAWRENCE RIVER — NEW YORK

Bodies of water: Hudson River, Mohawk River, Lake Champlain, Saratoga Lake, Finger Lakes, Onieda Lake and any body of water in New York State
Rates: Half day: $50-$75(1), $75-$100(2), Full day: $100-$175(1), $150-$200(2)
Call between: Anytime
Provides: Light tackle, heavy tackle, fly rod/reel, lures, bait, rain gear, beverages, lunch, photos
Handicapped equipped: No
Certifications: NYSOGA, ENCON, USCG

Reel Action Guide Service
Glenmont 518-434-1133
Species & Seasons: LM Bass, SM Bass June-Nov, Walleye, Northern Pike, Panfish May-Nov
Bodies of water: Saratoga Lake, Mohawk River, Hudson River
Rates: Half day: $125(2), Full day: $175(2)
Call between: 8am-10pm
Provides: Light tackle, heavy tackle, lures, beverages
Handicapped equipped: No
Certifications: NY State Licensed

ST. LAWRENCE RIVER

BAIT & TACKLE...

Thousand Island Bait Store
Alexandria Bay 315-482-9903
Hours: 6am-9pm
Carries: Live bait, lures, flies, maps, rods, reels, licenses
Bodies of water: St. Lawrence River, Lake Ontario
Services & Products: Food, beverages, gas/oil, repair services
Guides: Yes
OK to call for current conditions: Yes
Contact: Greg Coon

CHARTERS...

1000 Islands Fishing Charters
Clayton 800-544-4241
Species & Seasons: Northern Pike, Walleye May-Nov, LM Bass June-Nov, Muskellunge Sept-Nov
Bodies of water: St. Lawrence River
Rates: From $35pp up to 15
Call between: 9am-9pm
Provides: Light tackle, bait, rain gear
Handicapped equipped: Yes

Amicus Charters
North Greece 315-654-3404
.... 716-392-6393
Species & Seasons: Trout, Salmon, Northern Pike May-Oct, Walleye May-Sept, SM Bass June-Oct
Bodies of water: Lake Ontario, Thousand Islands, St Lawrence River, Cape Vincent
Rates: 8 hrs: $240-$290(4)
Call between: 6pm-10pm
Provides: Light tackle, lures, bait
Handicapped equipped: No

Riverguide Charters
Clayton 315-686-2415
Species & Seasons: Northern Pike, Walleye May-Nov, LM Bass, SM Bass June-Oct, Muskellunge Sept-Oct
Bodies of water: St. Lawrence River, Thousand Islands
Rates: Half day: $150(1-2), Full day: $250(1-2), 3-6 people, rates quoted
Call between: 5pm-9pm
Provides: Light tackle, bait, beverages
Handicapped equipped: Yes, sight/hearing impaired only
Certifications: USCG

Dave Shaban
Watertown 315-788-6843
Species & Seasons: Trout, Salmon April-Sept, Walleye, Northern Pike May-Sept, SM Bass June-Sept
Bodies of water: Eastern Lake Ontario, St. Lawrence River
Rates: Half day: $280(4), Full day: $380(4)
Call between: 10am-8pm
Provides: Light tackle, heavy tackle, lures, bait
Handicapped equipped: Yes
Certifications: USCG

GUIDES...

Clay Ferguson
LaFargeville 315-686-3100
Species & Seasons: Walleye, Northern Pike May-Nov, LM Bass June-Oct, Muskellunge July-Dec
Bodies of water: St Lawrence River
Rates: Half day: $75(1), $150(2), Full day: $200(1), $280(2), $20 additional pp
Call between: 5pm-10pm
Provides: Light tackle, heavy tackle, lures, bait, beverages, lunch
Handicapped equipped: No
Certifications: USCG

Let's Go Fishing With Amicus Charters

Captain Herb Park

SportFishing

★ Bass
★ Pike
★ Trout & Salmon
★ Walleye

1000 Island Area Cape Vincent, NY

27' Sportcraft, Fully equipped & insured

USCG License
All tackle furnished

FOR ADDITIONAL INFORMATION CALL:
(716) 392-6393
or
(315) 654-3404
or write:
P. O. Box 282 • North Greece, N.Y. 14515

NEW YORK — ST. LAWRENCE RIVER

Russ Finehout
Clayton 315-686-5201
Species & Seasons: Lake Trout, Walleye May-Sept, Salmon July-Sept, Northern Pike May-Nov, SM Bass June-Nov
Bodies of water: Lake Ontario, St. Lawrence River
Rates: Half day: $135(1), $150(2), Full day: $270(1),$285(2)
Call between: 7am-10pm
Provides: Light tackle, heavy tackle, lures, bait, rain gear, beverages, lunch
Certifications: USCG

Larry Kernehan
Alexandria Bay 315-482-9368
Species & Seasons: Northern Pike May-Nov, LM Bass, SM Bass June-Nov
Bodies of water: St Lawrence River
Rates: Half day: $175(2), Full day: $225(2)
Call between: Anytime
Provides: Light tackle, bait, rain gear
Handicapped equipped:
Certifications: USCG

Roger oyse
Alexandria Bay 315-482-5248
Species & Seasons: Lake Trout April-June, Northern Pike, Walleye May-Nov, SM Bass June-Oct, LM Bass June-Sept, Muskellunge Sept-Nov
Bodies of water: Lake Ontario, St. Lawrence River
Rates: Half day: $150(1-2), Full day: $225(1-2), Walleye, Trout, Muskellunge rates higher
Call between: 8am-9pm
Provides: Light tckle, lures, bait, beverages, lunch
Handicapped equipped: Yes
Certifications: USCG

Pat Snyder
Alexandria Bay 315-482-3750
Species & Seasons: Northern Pike May-Mar, SM Bass June-Nov, Walleye July-Sept, Muskellunge Aug-Dec
Bodies of water: St Lawrence River, Thousand Islands, Alexandria Bay area
Rates: Half day: $175(1-2), Full day: $225(1-2), $25 additional pp
Call between: 8am-10pm
Provides: Light tackle, bai, rain gear
Handicapped equipped: Yes
Certifications: USCG

LODGING...

Barracks Club
Penfield 315-654-2327
.... 716-671-2708
Guest Capacity: 22
Handicapped equipped: No
Seasons: May 14 to Sept 30
Rates: Lodge: $22/day
Cabins: $250/$275/$300/week
Contact: John F Grieco, Jr.
Guides: Yes, recommend
Species & Seasons: LM Bass June-Oct, Northern PikeMay-Oct, Perch, Walleye May-Mar
Bodies of Water: St Lawrence River, Lake Ontario
Types of fishing: Light tackle, heavy tackle

Golden Horseshoe Camps
Hammond 315-375-6395
Guest Capacity: 50
Handicapped equipped: Yes
Seasons: May 1 to Sept 30
Rates: $40/day, $170/week double occupancy
Contact: Lois Rockefeller
Guides: No*Species & Seasons:* Crappie all year, Northern Pike May-Sept-Dec, LM Bass, SM Bass June-Oct
Bodies of Water: Black Lake, St. Lawrence River
Types of fishing: Light tackle, heavy tackle
Available: Boat rentals

Hill's Motor Court
Alexandria Bay 315-482-2741
Guest Capacity: 36
Handicapped equipped: No
Seasons: May 15 to Oct 1
Rates: Off season: $40-$60/day, On season: $62-$90/day
Guides: Yes
Bodies of Water: St Lawrece River

Pinehurst on the St. Lawrence Inc.
Alexandria Bay 315-482-9452
Guest Capacity: 190
Handicapped equipped: No
Seasons: May to Oct
Rates: $36-$150/day, $280-$800/week
Guides: Yes
Species & Seasons: Northern Pike, Walleye, Muskellunge May, LM Bass, SM Bass May-June
Bodies of Water: St Lawrence River, Lake Ontario, Black Lake
Types of fishing: Light tackle, heavy tackle
Available: Boat rentals

Sojourn Cottages
Chippewa Bay
May1-Oct.1: 315-324-5229
Oct.-April: 716-586-1369
Guest Capacity: 40
Handicapped equipped: No
Seasons: May 1 to Sept 30
Rates: Cottage: $55-$85/day
Contact: Gail Wolfe
Guides: Yes
Species & Seasons: Northern Pike, Walleye May-Sept, Perch all year, SM Bass, LM Bass June-?
Bodies of Water: St Lawrence River
Types of fishing: Light tackle
Available: Bait, boat rentals

MARINAS...

Bill & Jacks Marina
Fishers Landing 315-686-3592
Hours: 7am-8pm
Carries: Live bait, lures, flies, maps, rods, reels, licenses
Bodies of water: St. LawrenceRiver
Services & Products: Boat rentals, guide services, charter boat service, lodging, boat ramp, food, beverages, gas/oil, fishing instruction, repair services
Guides: Yes
OK to call for current conditions: Yes
Contact: Mark W. Kellogg

French Creek Marina
Clayton 315-686-3621
Hours: 8am-dark
Carries: Live bait, lures, maps, rods, reels
Bodies of water: St Lawrence River
Services & Products: Boat rentals, guide services, charter boat service, boat ramp, beverages, gas/oil, repair services, parts
Guides: Yes
OK to call for current conditions: Yes
Contact: Wilburt Wahl Jr.

SWINGING BRIDGE RESERVOIR - WHITNEY POINT LAKE — NEW YORK

SWINGING BRIDGE RESERVOIR

BAIT & TACKLE...

Tom's Bait & Tackle Shop
Narrowsburg 914-252-7445
Hours: 8am-6pm
Carries: Live bait, lures, flies, rods, reels, licenses
Bodies of water: Delaware River, Lake Huntington, Swinging Bridge Res., Lake Superior, Crystal Lake
Services & Products: Rod, reel rentals
Guides: Yes
OK to call for current conditions: Yes
Contact: Tom or Cecilia

TIOUGHNIOGA RIVER

GUIDES...

A J's Outdoor Service
Courtland 607-758-7533
Species & Seasons: SM Bass, LM Bass June-Sept, Rainbow Trout, Brown Trout, Brook Trout April-Sept, Walleye, Bullhead, Pickerel, Northern Pike June-Sept, Yellow Perch all year
Bodies of water: Tioughnioga River, Otselic River, Chanango River
Rates: Full day: $75+(1-2), $24 additional pp
Call between: 5pm-9pm
Provides: Bait, beverages, lunch
Handicapped equipped: Some
Certifications: NYSDEC Licensed Guide

WHITNEY POINT LAKE

GUIDES...

Let's Go Fishing
Syracuse 315-478-7231
Species & Seasons: Trout April-Sept, Northern Pike May-Mar, LM Bass June-Nov, Salmon depends on waters and species, Panfish all year
Bodies of water: Central New York region, Finger Lakes, Lake Ontario, Whitney Point Lake, Oneida Lake
Call between: 6pm-9pm
Provides: Light tackle, heavy tackle, fly rod/reel, lures, bait
Handicapped equipped: No
Certifications: NY State Licensed Guide

The Angler's Yellow Pages saves you time and money.
You can compare rates and services quickly and easily.

NORTH CAROLINA

1. Albemarle Sound
2. Atlantic Ocean
3. Badin Lake
4. Bogue Sound
5. Cape Fear River
6. Falls Lake
7. Jordan Lake
8. Kerr Reservoir
9. Lake Gaston
10. Lake Norman
11. Lake Tillery
12. Lake Townsend
13. Lake Upchurch
14. Lake Wylie
15. Neuse River
16. Oak Hollow Lake
17. Pamilco Sound
18. Pasquotank River
19. Sharon Harris Lake
20. Western North Carolina Lakes & Rivers
    Big Creek
    Catalochee Creek
    Davidson River
    Fontana Lake
    Great Smoky Mtns. Nat'l. Park
    Nanthala Nat'l. Forest
    Oconaluttee River
    Pisgah Nat'l. Forest
21. White Oak River

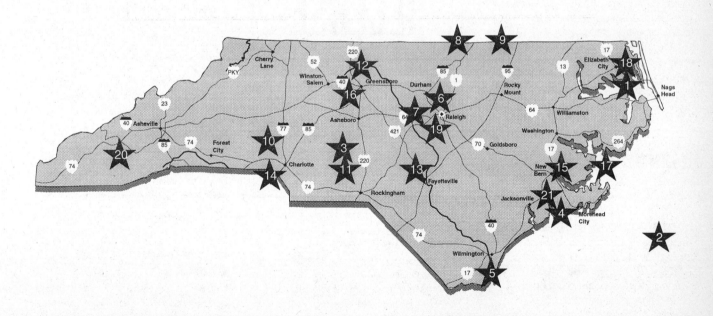

NORTH CAROLINA
ALBEMARLE SOUND - ATLANTIC OCEAN

ALBEMARLE SOUND

MARINAS...

Manteo Waterfront Marina
Manteo 919-473-3320
Hours: 7am-11pm
Bodies of water: Atlantic Ocean, Albemarle Sound, Pamlico Sound, Roanoke Sound, Croatan Sound
Services & Products: Charter boat service, lodging, boat ramp, food, beverages, repair services
OK to call for current conditions: No

Pembroke Fishing Center
Edenton 919-482-5343
Hours: 5:30am-?
Carries: Live bait, lures, flies, rods, reels
Bodies of water: Albemarle Sound, Roanoke River, Chowan River, Pasquotank River
Services & Products: Boat rentals, boat ramp, food, beverages, gas/oil
Guides: Yes
OK to call for current conditions: Yes
Contact: Jerry or Irene

Salty Dawg Marina
Manteo 919-473-3405
Hours: 8am-6pm
Carries: Lures, maps, rods, reels
Bodies of water: Atlantic Ocean, Oregon Inlet, Roanoke Sound, Croatan Sound, Pamlico Sound, Albemarle Sound
Services & Products: Charter boat service, gas/oil, repair services
Contact: Jennie O'Neal

ATLANTIC OCEAN

BAIT & TACKLE...

Emerald Isle Mini Mart
Emerald Isle 919-354-3446
Hours: 7am-12pm
Carries: Lures, maps, rods, reels
Bodies of water: Atlantic Ocean, Bogue Sound, Pamilco Sound
Services & Products: Charter boat service, food, beverages, gas/oil
Guides: Yes
OK to call for current conditions: Yes
Contact: Rick Smith

Tex's Tackle & Bait
Wilmington 910-791-1763
Hours: 8am-7pm, closed Mon.
Carries: Lures, flies, maps, rods, reels
Bodies of water: Atlantic Ocean, Sutton Lake, Cape Fear River, North East Cape Fear River
Services & Products: Fishing instruction
Guides: Yes
OK to call for current conditions: Yes
Contact: Tex Grissom

CHARTERS...

Big Eye Fisheries
Hatteras 919-995-6890
Species & Seasons: Yellowfin Tuna April-Sept, Bluefin Tuna Jan-Mar, Dolphin May-Sept, Wahoo April-Oct, King Mackerel Oct-Nov, Blue Marlin May-Aug, White Marlin June-Aug, Sailfish July-Sept
Bodies of water: Atlantic Ocean
Rates: Boat: $750 a day (6 people)
Call between: 5:30pm-9:30pm
Provides: Light tackle, heavy tackle, lures, bait
Handicapped equipped: Yes
Certifications: USCG

"RELEASE"
OFFSHORE
SPORTFISHING CHARTERS
47' CAROLINA SPORTSFISHERMEN
MARLIN • TUNA • WAHOO • DOLPHIN
EXCELLENT...
GIANT BLUEFIN TUNA FISHING
DECEMBER THRU MARCH
CAPT. ROM WHITAKER
BOX 150, HATTERAS, NC 27943
919 995-4570

Capt. Jim's Marina
Calabash.......................... 910-579-3660
Species & Seasons: Dolphin, Tuna, Wahoo May-Sept, King Mackerel April-Dec, Marlin May-Sept, Snapper, Grouper all year
Bodies of water: Atlantic Ocean
Rates: $60-$150pp
Call between: 7am-6pm
Provides: Light tackle, heavy tackle, lures, bait, beverages, lunch
Handicapped equipped: Yes
Certifications: USCG

Carolina Princess
Morehead City 919-726-5479
.... 800-682-3456
Species & Seasons: Red Snapper, Silver Snapper, Grouper, Triggerfish, Amberjack all year
Bodies of water: Atlantic Ocean, Gulf Stream waters
Rates: Full day: $55(1), $110(2)
Call between: 8am-9pm
Provides: Heavy tackle, bait
Handicapped equipped: Yes
Certifications: USCG

Charter Boat Booking Service
Atlantic Beach.................. 919-726-2273
Species & Seasons: Tuna Mar-July, Dolphin Mar-Oct, Wahoo Mar-Dec, King Mackerel all year, Spanish Mackerel May-Oct, Grouper Mar-Dec, Red Snapper April-Oct, Sea Bass Mar-Dec, Blue Marlin April-Oct, Cobia Mar-Dec
Bodies of water: Atlantic Ocean
Rates: Boat: Half day: $250, 3/4 day: $550 Full day: $700
Call between: Anytime
Provides: Light tackle, heavy tackle, fly rod/reel, lures, bait
Handicapped equipped: Yes
Certifications: Licensed Charter Captain

Nancy Lee Fishing Charter
Emerald Isle 919-354-FISH
Species & Seasons: Bass, Snapper, Grouper, Grunts April-Dec, King Mackerel, Spanish Mackerel, Dolphin, Tuna April-Dec
Bodies of water: Atlantic Ocean
Rates: Half day: $350(1-8), Full day: $750(1-8), Party Boat: Half day: $35pp
Call between: 7am-11pm
Provides: Light tackle, heavy tackle, lures, bait
Handicapped equipped: Yes
Certifications: USCG

Release Sportfishing Charters
Hatteras 919-995-4570
Species & Seasons: Bluefin Tuna Dec-Mar, Blue Marlin April-Sept, White Marlin, Dolphin May-Sept, Sailfish June-Sept, Yellowfin Tuna Mar-Dec, Wahoo April-Nov, King Mackerel Sept-Nov
Bodies of water: Atlantic Ocean (Gulf Stream)
Rates: Full day: $750(6)

ATLANTIC OCEAN - BOGUE SOUND

Call between: 7pm-10pm
Provides: Light tackle, heavy tackle, lures, bait
Handicapped equipped: Yes
Certifications: USCG

Still Serchin Charter Fishing
Holden Beach 910-842-8372
Species & Seasons: King Mackerel, Reeffish, Cobia May-Nov Snapper, Grouper, Dolphin Mar-Nov
Bodies of water: Atlantic Ocean
Rates: Half day: $50(1),
Full day: $100(1), $600(1-6)
Call between: 7pm-9pm
Provides: Light tackle, heavy tackle, lures, bait
Handicapped equipped: Yes
Certifications: USCG

Tuna Duck
Hatteras 919-986-7257
Species & Seasons: Blue Marlin, White Marlin, Dolphin April-Oct, Yellowfin Tuna Mar-Mar, Bluefin Tuna, Bluefish Dec-April, Wahoo all year, King Mackerel Sept-Feb, Sailfish June-Oct, Spearfish April-June
Bodies of water: Atlantic Ocean
Rates: Full day: $750(6)
Call between: 6pm-10pm
Provides: Heavy tackle, lures, bait
Certifications: USCG

LODGES...

Cedar Creek Campground
Sea Level 919-225-9571
Guest Capacity: 68 camp sites
Handicapped equipped: Some
Seasons: All year
Rates: $12-$16.50/day double occupancy
Contact: Catherine Nelson
Guides: Yes
Species & Seasons: Flounder, Trout Spring-Fall
Bodies of Water: Atlantic Ocean, Core Sound, Pamlico Sound, Drum Inlet
Types of fishing: Fly fishing, light tackle, heavy tackle, wading
Available: Fishing instruction, bait, tackle

MARINAS...

Anchorage Marina
Atlantic Beach 919-726-4423
Hours: daylight-dark
Carries: Lures, maps, rods, reels
Bodies of water: Bogue Sound Onslon Bay, Atlantic Ocean
Services & Products: Boat ramp, food, beverages, gas/oil, fishing instruction, repair services
Guides: Yes
OK to call for current conditions: Yes
Contact: Anyone

Cedar Creek Campground & Marina
Sea Level 919-225-9571
Hours: 6:30am-9pm
Carries: Live bait, lures, flies, maps, rods, reels
Bodies of water: Core Sound, Drum Inlet, Pamlico Sound, Atlantic Ocean
Services & Products: Boat ramp, food, beverages, gas/oil, fishing instruction, campgrounds
Guides: Yes
OK to call for current conditions: Yes
Contact: Jerry Nelson

Dudley's Marina
Swansboro 919-393-2204
Hours: 6am-8pm
Carries: Live bait, lures, maps, rods, reels
Bodies of water: Atlantic Ocean, Bogue Inlet, Bogue Sound, White Oak River
Services & Products: Charter boat service, boat ramp, food, beverages, gas/oil, fishing instruction, repair services
Guides: Yes
OK to call for current conditions: Yes

Harbor Master
Morehead City 919-726-2541
Hours: 8am-4:30pm
Bodies of water: Bogue Sound, Atlantic Ocean
Services & Products: Beverages, repair services, railway and travel lift, propeller reconditioning and rehubbing
Guides: Yes
OK to call for current conditions: No

Island Harbor Marina
Emerald Island 919-354-3106
Hours: 5:30am-8:30pm
Carries: Live bait, lures, maps, rods, reels
Bodies of water: Atlantic Ocean, Bouge Sound, White Oak River
Services & Products: Boat rentals, charter boat service, boat ramp, food, beverages, gas/oil, fishing instruction, repair services
Guides: Yes

NORTH CAROLINA

OK to call for current conditions: Yes
Contact: Eric or Ken

Manteo Waterfront Marina
Manteo 919-473-3320
Hours: 7am-11pm
Bodies of water: Atlantic Ocean, Albemarle Sound, Pamlico Sound, Roanoke Sound, Croatan Sound
Services & Products: Charter boat service, lodging, boat ramp, food, beverages, repair services
OK to call for current conditions: No

Salty Dawg Marina
Manteo 919-473-3405
Hours: 8am-6pm
Carries: Lures, maps, rods, reels
Bodies of water: Atlantic Ocean, Oregon Inlet, Roanoke Sound, Croatan Sound, Pamlico Sound, Albemarle Sound
Services & Products: Charter boat service, gas/oil, repair services
Contact: Jennie O'Neal

BADIN LAKE

BAIT & TACKLE...

Wilgrove Express Bait & Tackle
Charlotte 704-545-1228
Hours: 6am-8pm, closed Sun.
Carries: Live bait, lures, flies, maps, rods, reels, licenses
Bodies of water: Lake Norman, Lake Wylie, Lake Tillery, Badin Lake
Services & Products: Food, beverages, gas/oil
Guides: Yes
OK to call for current conditions: Yes
Contact: Sally Newman

BOGUE SOUND

BAIT & TACKLE...

Emerald Isle Mini Mart
Emerald Isle 919-354-3446
Hours: 7am-12pm
Carries: Lures, maps, rods, reels
Bodies of water: Atlantic Ocean, Bogue Sound, Pamilco Sound
Services & Products: Charter boat service, food, beverages, gas/oil
Guides: Yes
OK to call for current conditions: Yes
Contact: Rick Smith

YOUR SILENT FISHING PARTNER

NORTH CAROLINA
BOGUE SOUND - KERR RESERVOIR

MARINAS...

Anchorage Marina
Atlantic Beach.................. 919-726-4423
Hours: daylight-dark
Carries: Lures, maps, rods, reels
Bodies of water: Bogue Sound Onslon Bay, Atlantic Ocean
Services & Products: Boat ramp, food, beverages, gas/oil, fishing instruction, repair services
Guides: Yes
OK to call for current conditions: Yes
Contact: Anyone

Dudley's Marina
Swansboro 919-393-2204
Hours: 6am-8pm
Carries: Live bait, lures, maps, rods, reels
Bodies of water: Atlantic Ocean, Bogue Inlet, Bogue Sound, White Oak River
Services & Products: Charter boat service, boat ramp, food, beverages, gas/oil, fishing instruction, repair services
Guides: Yes
OK to call for current conditions: Yes

Harbor Master
Morehead City 919-726-2541
Hours: 8am-4:30pm
Bodies of water: Bogue Sound, Atlantic Ocean
Services & Products: Beverages, repair services, railway and travel lift, propeller reconditioning and rehubbing
Guides: Yes
OK to call for current conditions: No

Island Harbor Marina
Emerald Island 919-354-3106
Hours: 5:30am-8:30pm
Carries: Live bait, lures, maps, rods, reels
Bodies of water: Atlantic Ocean, Bouge Sound, White Oak River
Services & Products: Boat rentals, charter boat service, boat ramp, food, beverages, gas/oil, fishing instruction, repair services
Guides: Yes
OK to call for current conditions: Yes
Contact: Eric or Ken

CAPE FEAR RIVER

BAIT & TACKLE...

Tex's Tackle & Bait
Wilmington 910-791-1763
Hours: 8am-7pm, closed Mon.
Carries: Lures, flies, maps, rods, reels
Bodies of water: Atlantic Ocean, Sutton Lake, Cape Fear River, North East Cape Fear River
Services & Products: Fishing instruction
Guides: Yes
OK to call for current conditions: Yes
Contact: Tex Grissom

FALLS LAKE

BAIT & TACKLE...

Buck & Bass
Graham 910-227-5993
Hours: 8am-6pm
Carries: Live bait, lures, flies, maps, rods, reels, licenses
Bodies of water: Kerr Res., Jordan Lake, Falls Lake, Sharon Harris Lake
Services & Products: Food, beverages, fishing instruction
Guides: Yes
OK to call for current conditions: Yes
Contact: Jack

Welcome Bait & Tackle Shop
Oxford 919-693-2503
Hours: 7am-7pm
Carries: Live bait, lures, flies, rods, reels
Bodies of water: Kerr Res., Falls Lake, Tar River
Services & Products: Beverages, fishing instruction
Guides: No
OK to call for current conditions: Yes
Contact: Wayne

GUIDES...

Capt. Ronald W. Ellis
Pittsboro 919-542-5047
Species & Seasons: Crappie(day) Jan-June, Crappie(night), Catfish April-Nov, LM Bass Feb-Nov, Bluegill, Hybrids, Striped Bass Mar-Nov
Bodies of water: Jordan Lake, Falls Lake, Sharon Harris Lake
Rates: Half day: $50(1), $75(2), Full day: $100(1), $150(2), Night crappie fishing $25pp
Call between: 9pm-11pm
Provides: Light tackle, heavy tackle, fly rod/reel, lures, bait, rain gear
Handicapped equipped: Yes
Certifications: Licensed by the State

JORDAN LAKE

BAIT & TACKLE...

Buck & Bass
Graham 910-227-5993
Hours: 8am-6pm
Carries: Live bait, lures, flies, maps, rods, reels, licenses
Bodies of water: Kerr Res., Jordan Lake, Falls Lake, Sharon Harris Lake
Services & Products: Food, beverages, fishing instruction
Guides: Yes
OK to call for current conditions: Yes
Contact: Jack

GUIDES...

Capt. Ronald W. Ellis
Pittsboro 919-542-5047
Species & Seasons: Crappie(day) Jan-June, Crappie(night), Catfish April-Nov, LM Bass Feb-Nov, Bluegill, Hybrids, Striped Bass Mar-Nov
Bodies of water: Jordan Lake, Falls Lake, Sharon Harris Lake
Rates: Half day: $50(1), $75(2), Full day: $100(1), $150(2), Night crappie fishing $25pp
Call between: 9pm-11pm
Provides: Light tackle, heavy tackle, fly rod/reel, lures, bait, rain gear
Handicapped equipped: Yes
Certifications: Licensed by the State

KERR RESERVOIR

BAIT & TACKLE...

Buck & Bass
Graham 910-227-5993
Hours: 8am-6pm
Carries: Live bait, lures, flies, maps, rods, reels, licenses
Bodies of water: Kerr Res., Jordan Lake, Falls Lake, Sharon Harris Lake
Services & Products: Food, beverages, fishing instruction

KERR RESERVOIR - LAKE WYLIE

NORTH CAROLINA

Guides: Yes
OK to call for current conditions: Yes
Contact: Jack

Welcome Bait & Tackle Shop
Oxford 919-693-2503
Hours: 7am-7pm
Carries: Live bait, lures, flies, rods, reels
Bodies of water: Kerr Res., Falls Lake, Tar River
Services & Products: Beverages, fishing instruction
Guides: No
OK to call for current conditions: Yes
Contact: Wayne

GUIDES...

Randy Howell's Professional Guide Service
Littleton 919-586-3396
Species & Seasons: LM Bass Feb-Nov, Crappie Mar-May, Striped Bass all year
Bodies of water: Lake Gaston, Kerr Res.
Rates: Half day: $150(1-2), Full day: $250(1-2)
Call between: 8pm-10pm
Provides: Light tackle, heavy tackle, lures, bait, beverages
Handicapped equipped: Yes
Certifications: ORVIS

LAKE GASTON

GUIDES...

Randy Howell's Professional Guide Service
Littleton 919-586-3396
Species & Seasons: LM Bass Feb-Nov, Crappie Mar-May, Striped Bass all year
Bodies of water: Lake Gaston, Kerr Res.
Rates: Half day: $150(1-2), Full day: $250(1-2)
Call between: 8pm-10pm
Provides: Light tackle, heavy tackle, lures, bait, beverages
Handicapped equipped: Yes
Certifications: ORVIS

LAKE NORMAN

BAIT & TACKLE...

Wilgrove Express Bait & Tackle
Charlotte 704-545-1228
Hours: 6am-8pm, closed Sun.
Carries: Live bait, lures, flies, maps, rods, reels, licenses
Bodies of water: Lake Norman, Lake Wylie, Lake Tillery, Badin Lake
Services & Products: Food, beverages, gas/oil
Guides: Yes
OK to call for current conditions: Yes
Contact: Sally Newman

GUIDES...

Tony Key
Mooresville 704-664-9232
Species & Seasons: Striped Bass Sept-May, Catfish May-Sept
Bodies of water: Lake Norman
Rates: Half day: $150(1-2), Full day: $300(1-2), $75 additional 3rd person
Call between: Noon-8pm
Provides: Light tackle, heavy tackle, lures, bait
Handicapped equipped: Yes

LAKE TILLERY

BAIT & TACKLE...

Wilgrove Express Bait & Tackle
Charlotte 704-545-1228
Hours: 6am-8pm, closed Sun.
Carries: Live bait, lures, flies, maps, rods, reels, licenses
Bodies of water: Lake Norman, Lake Wylie, Lake Tillery, Badin Lake
Services & Products: Food, beverages, gas/oil
Guides: Yes
OK to call for current conditions: Yes
Contact: Sally Newman

LAKE TOWNSEND

BAIT & TACKLE...

Reed's Mart
Greensboro 910-282-6612
Hours: 6am-7pm
Carries: Live bait, lures, flies, rods, reels
Bodies of water: Lake Brandt, Lake Higgins, Lake Jeanette, Belews Lake, Lake Townsend
Services & Products: Food, beverages, gas/oil
Guides: No
OK to call for current conditions: No

LAKE UPCHURCH

MARINAS...

Lake View Park
Cumberland 910-424-4814
Hours: 6am-8pm, closed Dec.-Feb.
Carries: Live bait, lures, rods, reels
Bodies of water: Lake Upchurch
Services & Products: Boat rentals, boat ramp, snacks
Guides: No
OK to call for current conditions: Yes

LAKE WYLIE

BAIT & TACKLE...

Wilgrove Express Bait & Tackle
Charlotte .:....................... 704-545-1228
Hours: 6am-8pm, closed Sun.
Carries: Live bait, lures, flies, maps, rods, reels, licenses
Bodies of water: Lake Norman, Lake Wylie, Lake Tillery, Badin Lake
Services & Products: Food, beverages, gas/oil
Guides: Yes
OK to call for current conditions: Yes
Contact: Sally Newman

NORTH CAROLINA

LAKE WYLIE - PAMLICO SOUND

GUIDES...

Mark Goss
Lake Wylie, SC 803-831-2285
Species & Seasons: LM Bass Jan-Dec
Bodies of water: Lake Wylie
Rates: Half day: $125(1), !150(2),
Full day: $175(1), $200(2)
Call between: 8pm-9pm
Provides: Light tackle, lures, beverages
Handicapped equipped: Yes

NEUSE RIVER

BAIT & TACKLE...

Shorebird Boat Rentals, Inc.
New Bern.......................... 919-638-7075
Hours: 8am-8pm
Carries: Lures, rods, reels
Bodies of water: Neuse River, Trent River
Services & Products: Boat rentals, guide services, charter boat service, food, beverages
OK to call for current conditions: Yes
Contact: Rob

MARINAS...

Northwest Creek Marina
New Bern.......................... 919-637-7442
Hours: 8am-5pm
Carries: Lures, maps
Bodies of water: Neuse River, Trent River
Services & Products: Boat rentals, boat ramp, food, beverages, gas/oil, fishing instruction
Guides: Yes
OK to call for current conditions: Yes
Contact: Dockmaster

Ramada Marina & Hotel
New Bern.......................... 919-636-2888
Hours: 9am-6pm
Bodies of water: Trent River, Neuse River, Pamlico Sound
Services & Products: Boat rentals, lodging, food, beverages
Guides: Yes
OK to call for current conditions: Yes

OAK HOLLOW LAKE

BAIT & TACKLE...

Northwood Oil Co.
High Point 910-887-1960
Hours: 7am-8pm, closed Sun.
Carries: Live bait, licenses
Bodies of water: Oak Hollow Lake, Lake Tom-A-Lex, High Point City Lake
Services & Products: Beverages, gas/oil
Guides: No
OK to call for current conditions: Yes
Contact: Bill Carroll

PAMLICO SOUND

BAIT & TACKLE...

Emerald Isle Mini Mart
Emerald Isle 919-354-3446
Hours: 7am-12pm
Carries: Lures, maps, rods, reels
Bodies of water: Atlantic Ocean, Bogue Sound, Pamilco Sound
Services & Products: Charter boat service, food, beverages, gas/oil
Guides: Yes
OK to call for current conditions: Yes
Contact: Rick Smith

LODGES...

Cedar Creek Campground
Sea Level 919-225-9571
Guest Capacity: 68 camp sites
Handicapped equipped: Some
Seasons: All year
Rates: $12-$16.50/day double occupancy
Contact: Catherine Nelson
Guides: Yes
Species & Seasons: Flounder, Trout Spring-Fall
Bodies of Water: Atlantic Ocean, Core Sound, Pamlico Sound, Drum Inlet
Types of fishing: Fly fishing, light tackle, heavy tackle, wading
Available: Fishing instruction, bait, tackle

MARINAS...

Cedar Creek Campground & Marina
Sea Level 919-225-9571
Hours: 6:30am-9pm
Carries: Live bait, lures, flies, maps, rods, reels
Bodies of water: Core Sound, Drum Inlet, Pamlico Sound, Atlantic Ocean
Services & Products: Boat ramp, food, beverages, gas/oil, fishing instruction, campgrounds
Guides: Yes
OK to call for current conditions: Yes
Contact: Jerry Nelson

Manteo Waterfront Marina
Manteo 919-473-3320
Hours: 7am-11pm
Bodies of water: Atlantic Ocean, Albemarle Sound, Pamlico Sound, Roanoke Sound, Croatan Sound
Services & Products: Charter boat service, lodging, boat ramp, food, beverages, repair services
OK to call for current conditions: No

Ramada Marina & Hotel
New Bern.......................... 919-636-2888
Hours: 9am-6pm
Bodies of water: Trent River, Neuse River, Pamlico Sound
Services & Products: Boat rentals, lodging, food, beverages
Guides: Yes
OK to call for current conditions: Yes

Salty Dawg Marina
Manteo 919-473-3405
Hours: 8am-6pm
Carries: Lures, maps, rods, reels
Bodies of water: Atlantic Ocean, Oregon Inlet, Roanoke Sound, Croatan Sound, Pamlico Sound, Albemarle Sound
Services & Products: Charter boat service, gas/oil, repair services
Contact: Jennie O'Neal

PASQUOTANK RIVER - WHITE OAK RIVER
NORTH CAROLINA

PASQUOTANK RIVER

MARINAS...

The Pelican
Elizabeth City 919-335-5108
Hours: 8am-6pm
Carries: Live bait, lures, flies, rods, reels
Bodies of water: Pasquotank River
Services & Products: Boat ramp, food, beverages, gas/oil
Guides: No
OK to call for current conditions: No

Pembroke Fishing Center
Edenton 919-482-5343
Hours: 5:30am-?
Carries: Live bait, lures, flies, rods, reels
Bodies of water: Albemarle Sound, Roanoke River, Chowan River, Pasquotank River
Services & Products: Boat rentals, boat ramp, food, beverages, gas/oil
Guides: Yes
OK to call for current conditions: Yes
Contact: Jerry or Irene

SHARON HARRIS LAKE

BAIT & TACKLE...

Buck & Bass
Graham 910-227-5993
Hours: 8am-6pm
Carries: Live bait, lures, flies, maps, rods, reels, licenses
Bodies of water: Kerr Res., Jordan Lake, Falls Lake, Sharon Harris Lake
Services & Products: Food, beverages, fishing instruction
Guides: Yes
OK to call for current conditions: Yes
Contact: Jack

GUIDES...

Capt. Ronald W. Ellis
Pittsboro 919-542-5047
Species & Seasons: Crappie(day) Jan-June, Crappie(night), Catfish April-Nov, LM Bass Feb-Nov, Bluegill, Hybrids, Striped Bass Mar-Nov
Bodies of water: Jordan Lake, Falls Lake, Sharon Harris Lake
Rates: Half day: $50(1), $75(2), Full day: $100(1), $150(2), Night crappie fishing $25pp
Call between: 9pm-11pm
Provides: Light tackle, heavy tackle, fly rod/reel, lures, bait, rain gear
Handicapped equipped: Yes
Certifications: Licensed by the State

WESTERN NORTH CAROLINA LAKES & RIVERS

BAIT & TACKLE...

JHLP Inc.
Hendersonville 704-697-2200
Hours: 9am-6pm
Carries: Live bait, lures, flies, maps, rods, reels, licenses
Bodies of water: Hartwell Lake (SC), Lake Keowee (SC), Fontana Lake
Guides: Yes
OK to call for current conditions: Yes
Contact: Jim Hart

FLY SHOPS...

Lowe Fly Shop & Outfitters
Waynesville 704-452-0039
Hours: 6am-6pm, closed Sun.
Carries: Live bait, lures, flies, maps, rods, reels, licenses
Bodies of water: Catalochee Creek, Oconaluftee River, Deep Creek, Davidson River, Big Creek, Fontana Lake
Services & Products: Fishing instruction, repair services
Guides: Yes
OK to call for current conditions: Yes
Contact: Roger Lowe

GUIDES...

Highland Fly Fishing
Bryson City 800-258-9840
.... 704-488-8975
Species & Seasons: Rainbow Trout, Brown Trout, Brook Trout Mar-Dec
Bodies of water: Great Smokey Mtns. Nat'l. Park, Pisgah Nat'l. Forest, Nanthala Nat'l. Forest, New Zealand packages, Montana Trips
Rates: Full day: $195(1), $245(2)
Call between: Anytime
Provides: Fly rod/reel, beverages, lunch
Handicapped equipped: Yes
Certifications: 26 yrs. experience

WHITE OAK RIVER

MARINAS...

Dudley's Marina
Swansboro 919-393-2204
Hours: 6am-8pm
Carries: Live bait, lures, maps, rods, reels
Bodies of water: Atlantic Ocean, Bogue Inlet, Bogue Sound, White Oak River
Services & Products: Charter boat service, boat ramp, food, beverages, gas/oil, fishing instruction, repair services
Guides: Yes
OK to call for current conditions: Yes

Island Harbor Marina
Emerald Island 919-354-3106
Hours: 5:30am-8:30pm
Carries: Live bait, lures, maps, rods, reels
Bodies of water: Atlantic Ocean, Bouge Sound, White Oak River
Services & Products: Boat rentals, charter boat service, boat ramp, food, beverages, gas/oil, fishing instruction, repair services
Guides: Yes
OK to call for current conditions: Yes
Contact: Eric or Ken

Look in the Location Index
for a complete list of fishing areas

NORTH DAKOTA

1. Devil's Lake
2. Lake Oahe
3. Lake Sakakawea
4. Lake Tschida
5. Missouri River
6. Powers Lake

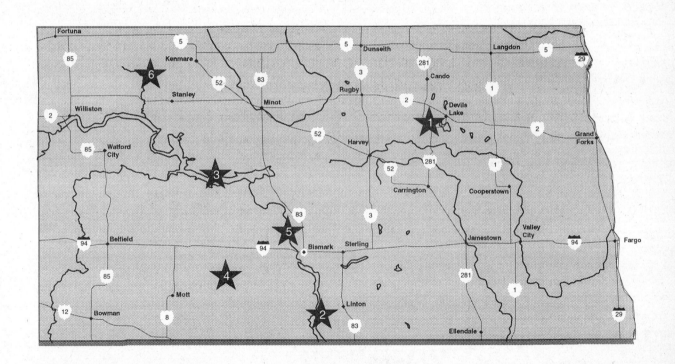

NORTH DAKOTA
DEVIL'S LAKE - LAKE SAKAKAWEA

DEVIL'S LAKE

BAIT & TACKLE...

Dry Dock Bait & Tackle
Carrington 701-652-2421
Hours: 7am-6pm, closed Sun.
Carries: Live bait, lures, flies, rods, reels, licenses
Bodies of water: Devils Lake, Pipestem Res., Jim Lake, Missouri River, Lake Sakakawea
Services & Products: Food, beverages, gas/oil, fishing instruction
Guides: No
OK to call for current conditions: Yes
Contact: Duane Klien

J'S Reel and Rod Repair
Martin 701-693-2856
Hours: 9am-1am, Closed Sun.
Carries: Live bait, lures, rods, reels, licenses
Bodies of water: Lake Sakakawea, Devils Lake, Harvey Res., Coal Mine Lake
Services & Products: Food, beverages, fishing instruction, repair services, custom rods
Guides: Yes
OK to call for current conditions: Yes
Contact: Jess or Bonita

Super America
Devils Lake 701-662-5185
Hours: 6am-11pm
Carries: Live bait, lures, maps, licenses
Bodies of water: Devils Lake, Sheyenne River
Services & Products: Food, beverages, gas/oil
Guides: No
OK to call for current conditions: No

GUIDES...

Tim's Guide Service
Devil's Lake 701-662-5688
Species & Seasons: Northern Pike, Walleye, Perch, White Bass all year
Bodies of water: Devils Lake, we also provide ice fishing which includes heated ice shacks, meals, tackle, holes drilled, tackle and bait
Rates: Half day: $50(1), Full day: $100(1), Group rates are negotiable
Call between: 8am-5pm
Provides: Light tackle, heavy tackle, lures, bait
Certifications: Licensed Guide

LAKE OAHE

GUIDES...

Terry Focke
Bismarck 701-258-2989
Species & Seasons: Walleye, Salmon, Northern Pike April-Nov
Bodies of water: Lake Sakakawea, Missouri River, upper Lake Oahe
Rates: Full day: $110(1), $175(2), call for other rates
Call between: 8am-10pm
Provides: Light tackle, lures, bait
Handicapped equipped: No
Certifications: USCG, ND License

Hap's Guide Service
Garrison 701-463-2084
Species & Seasons: Walleye, Sauger all year, Chinook Salmon Aug-Oct, Combo: Goose Hunt (am) Walleye (pm) Oct-Dec
Bodies of water: Lake Sakakawea, Lake Oahe, Missouri River
Rates: Walleye/Sauger:
Full Day: $160(2), $200(3), Salmon:
Half day: $120(2),
Full day: $200(2), Combo: Goose Hunt/Walleye $100pp day
Call between: 7am-10pm
Provides: Light tackle, heavy tackle
Handicapped equipped: Yes
Certifications: USCG, ND License

Northland Charter
Bismarck 701-222-4162
.... 654-7640(S)
Species & Seasons: Walleye May-Oct, Salmon, Trout Ice-out to end of Oct
Bodies of water: Lake Sakakawea, Missouri River, upper Lake Oahe
Rates: Full day: $130(1), $185(2)
Call between: 6pm-10pm
Provides: Light tackle, heavy tackle, lures, bait
Handicapped equipped: Yes
Certifications: USCG

LAKE SAKAKAWEA

BAIT & TACKLE...

Dry Dock Bait & Tackle
Carrington 701-652-2421
Hours: 7am-6pm, closed Sun.
Carries: Live bait, lures, flies, rods, reels, licenses
Bodies of water: Devils Lake, Pipestem Res., Jim Lake, Missouri River, Lake Sakakawea
Services & Products: Food, beverages, gas/oil, fishing instruction
Guides: No
OK to call for current conditions: Yes
Contact: Duane Klien

General Store
New Town 701-627-3939
Hours: 6am-12pm
Carries: Live bait, lures, maps, rods, reels, licenses
Bodies of water: Lake Sakakawea
Services & Products: Food, beverages, gas/oil
Guides: Yes
OK to call for current conditions: Yes
Contact: Karen

Gil's Bait Shop
Mott 701-824-2456
Hours: 7am-9pm
Carries: Live bait
Bodies of water: Lake Sakakawea, Indian Creek, Lake Tschida
OK to call for current conditions: Yes
Contact: Gilbert Mehrer

J'S Reel and Rod Repair
Martin 701-693-2856
Hours: 9am-1am, Closed Sun.
Carries: Live bait, lures, rods, reels, licenses
Bodies of water: Lake Sakakawea, Devils Lake, Harvey Res., Coal Mine Lake
Services & Products: Food, beverages, fishing instruction, repair services, custom rods
Guides: Yes
OK to call for current conditions: Yes
Contact: Jess or Bonita

Jim's Sales and Service
New Town 701-627-3212
Hours: 7am-7pm
Carries: Live bait, lures, maps, rods, reels, licenses
Bodies of water: Lake Sakakawea
Services & Products: Gas/oil
Guides: Yes
OK to call for current conditions: Yes
Contact: Jim

LAKE SAKAKAWEA - MISSOURI RIVER — NORTH DAKOTA

Scenic Sports & Liquor
Williston 701-572-8696
Hours: 6am-9pm
Carries: Live bait, lures, flies, maps, rods, reels, licenses
Bodies of water: Missouri River, Yellowstone River, Lake Sakakawea
Services & Products: Food, beverages, gas/oil, fishing instruction, hunting and archery equipment
Guides: Yes
OK to call for current conditions: Yes
Contact: John Salvevold

Tobacco Gardens Recreation
Waterford City 701-842-6931
Hours: 8am-8/10pm
Carries: Live bait, lures, maps
Bodies of water: Lake Sakakawea
Services & Products: Lodging, boat ramp, food, beverages, gas/oil, cafe
Guides: Yes
OK to call for current conditions: Yes
Contact: Brad

GUIDES...

Chris Cove
Epping 701-859-4201
Species & Seasons: Walleye, Northern Pike May-Oct
Bodies of water: Lake Sakakawea
Rates: Half day: $100(1), $150(2), Full day: $150(1), $200(2), weekly rates available
Call between: 6pm-11pm
Provides: Light tackle, bait
Handicapped equipped: No
Certifications: USCG, ND License

Terry Focke
Bismarck 701-258-2989
Species & Seasons: Walleye, Salmon, Northern Pike April-Nov
Bodies of water: Lake Sakakawea, Missouri River, upper Lake Oahe
Rates: Full day: $110(1), $175(2), call for other rates
Call between: 8am-10pm
Provides: Light tackle, lures, bait
Handicapped equipped: No
Certifications: USCG, ND License

Hap's Guide Service
Garrison 701-463-2084
Species & Seasons: Walleye, Sauger all year, Chinook Salmon Aug-Oct, Combo: Goose Hunt (am) Walleye (pm) Oct-Dec
Bodies of water: Lake Sakakawea, Lake Oahe, Missouri River
Rates: Walleye/Sauger: Full Day: $160(2), $200(3), Salmon: Half day: $120(2), Full day: $200(2), Combo: Goose Hunt/Walleye $100pp day
Call between: 7am-10pm
Provides: Light tackle, heavy tackle
Handicapped equipped: Yes
Certifications: USCG, ND License

Ko-No-Ko Charters
Highway 200 Box 149
Pick City 58545
Species & Seasons: Walleye Mar-Oct, Salmon July-Oct
Bodies of water: Lake Sakakawea, Missouri River
Rates: Half day: $60(1), $120(2), Full day: $120(1), $200(2)
Call between: 7am-10pm
Provides: Light tackle, lures, bait
Handicapped equipped: No
Certifications: NDSGF

Tom McKinven
Harvey 701-324-2793
.... 324-3933
Species & Seasons: Walleye June-Sept
Bodies of water: Lake Sakakawea
Rates: Half day: $75(1-2), Full day: $75(1), $150(2)
Call between: Before 8am-After 10pm
Provides: Light tackle, lures, bait, rain gear
Handicapped equipped: No
Certifications: USCG

Northland Charter
Bismarck 701-222-4162
.... 654-7640(S)
Species & Seasons: Walleye May-Oct, Salmon, Trout Ice-out to end of Oct
Bodies of water: Lake Sakakawea, Missouri River, upper Lake Oahe
Rates: Full day: $130(1), $185(2)
Call between: 6pm-10pm
Provides: Light tackle, heavy tackle, lures, bait
Handicapped equipped: Yes
Certifications: USCG

Rodger's Guide Service
Garrison 701-337-5572
Species & Seasons: Walleye, Sauger, Saugeye April-Nov, Northern Pike Mar-June
Bodies of water: Lake Sakakawea, Missouri River
Rates: Full day: $160(1-2) + gas, bait, $210(3) + gas, bait
Call between: 7pm-11pm
Provides: Light tackle, lures, rain gear
Certifications: USCG

LODGING...

Chris Cove
Epping 701-859-4201
Guest Capacity: 15
Handicap equipped: Yes
Seasons: All year
Rates: $20-$35/day
Guides: Yes
Species & Seasons: Walleye, Northern Pike May-Oct
Bodies of Water: Lake Sakakawea
Types of fishing: Light tackle, float trips
Available: Licenses, bait, tackle

LAKE TSCHIDA

BAIT & TACKLE...

Gil's Bait Shop
Mott 701-824-2456
Hours: 7am-9pm
Carries: Live bait
Bodies of water: Lake Sakakawea, Indian Creek, Lake Tschida
OK to call for current conditions: Yes
Contact: Gilbert Mehrer

MISSOURI RIVER

BAIT & TACKLE...

Dry Dock Bait & Tackle
Carrington 701-652-2421
Hours: 7am-6pm, closed Sun
Carries: Live bait, lures, flies, rods, reels, licenses
Bodies of water: Devils Lake, Pipestem Res., Jim Lake, Missouri River, Lake Sakakawea
Services & Products: Food, beverages, gas/oil, fishing instruction
Guides: No
OK to call for current conditions: Yes
Contact: Duane Klien

NORTH DAKOTA

MISSOURI RIVER - POWERS LAKE

John's Bait Shop
Powers Lake 701-464-5519
Hours: 12am-11:59pm
Carries: Live bait
Bodies of water: Missouri River, Powers Lake, Smishek Lake
Services & Products: Fishing instruction
Guides: No
OK to call for current conditions: Yes
Contact: John Kulstad

Scenic Sports & Liquor
Williston 701-572-8696
Hours: 6am-9pm
Carries: Live bait, lures, flies, maps, rods, reels, licenses
Bodies of water: Missouri River, Yellowstone River, Lake Sakakawea
Services & Products: Food, beverages, gas/oil, fishing instruction, hunting and archery equipment
Guides: Yes
OK to call for current conditions: Yes
Contact: John Salvevold

GUIDES...

Terry Focke
Bismarck 701-258-2989
Species & Seasons: Walleye, Salmon, Northern Pike April-Nov
Bodies of water: Lake Sakakawea, Missouri River, upper Lake Oahe
Rates: Full day: $110(1), $175(2), call for other rates
Call between: 8am-10pm
Provides: Light tackle, lures, bait
Handicapped equipped: No
Certifications: USCG, ND License

Hap's Guide Service
Garrison 701-463-2084
Species & Seasons: Walleye, Sauger all year, Chinook Salmon Aug-Oct, Combo: Goose Hunt (am) Walleye (pm) Oct-Dec
Bodies of water: Lake Sakakawea, Lake Oahe, Missouri River
Rates: Walleye/Sauger: Full Day: $160(2), $200(3), Salmon: Half day: $120(2), Full day: $200(2), Combo: Goose Hunt/Walleye $100pp day
Call between: 7am-10pm
Provides: Light tackle, heavy tackle
Handicapped equipped: Yes
Certifications: USCG, ND License

Ko-No-Ko Charters
Highway 200 Box 149
Pick City 58545
Species & Seasons: Walleye Mar-Oct, Salmon July-Oct
Bodies of water: Lake Sakakawea, Missouri River
Rates: Half day: $60(1), $120(2), Full day: $120(1), $200(2)
Call between: 7am-10pm
Provides: Light tackle, lures, bait
Handicapped equipped: No
Certifications: NDSGF

Northland Charter
Bismarck 701-222-4162
.... 654-7640(S)
Species & Seasons: Walleye May-Oct, Salmon, Trout Ice-out to end of Oct
Bodies of water: Lake Sakakawea, Missouri River, upper Lake Oahe
Rates: Full day: $130(1), $185(2)
Call between: 6pm-10pm
Provides: Light tackle, heavy tackle, lures, bait
Handicapped equipped: Yes
Certifications: USCG

Rodger's Guide Service
Garrison 701-337-5572
Species & Seasons: Walleye, Sauger, Saugeye April-Nov, Northern Pike Mar-June
Bodies of water: Lake Sakakawea, Missouri River
Rates: Full day: $160(1-2) + gas, bait, $210(3) + gas, bait
Call between: 7pm-11pm
Provides: Light tackle, lures, rain gear
Certifications: USCG

POWERS LAKE

BAIT & TACKLE...

John's Bait Shop
Powers Lake 701-464-5519
Hours: 12am-11:59pm
Carries: Live bait
Bodies of water: Missouri River, Powers Lake, Smishek Lake
Services & Products: Fishing instruction
Guides: No
OK to call for current conditions: Yes
Contact: John Kulstad

OHIO

1. Alum Creek Lake
2. Caesar Creek Lake
3. Cowan Lake
4. Deer Creek Lake
5. Delaware Lake
6. Dillon Lake
7. East Fork Lake
8. Grand River
9. Great Miami River
10. Hoover Reservoir
11. Lake Erie
12. Leesville Lake
13. Maumee River
14. Monroe Lake
15. Ohio River
16. Paint Creek Lake
17. Portage River
18. Pymatuning Reservoir
19. Rocky Fork Lake
20. Sandusky Bay
21. Sandusky River
22. Scioto River
23. Tappan Lake

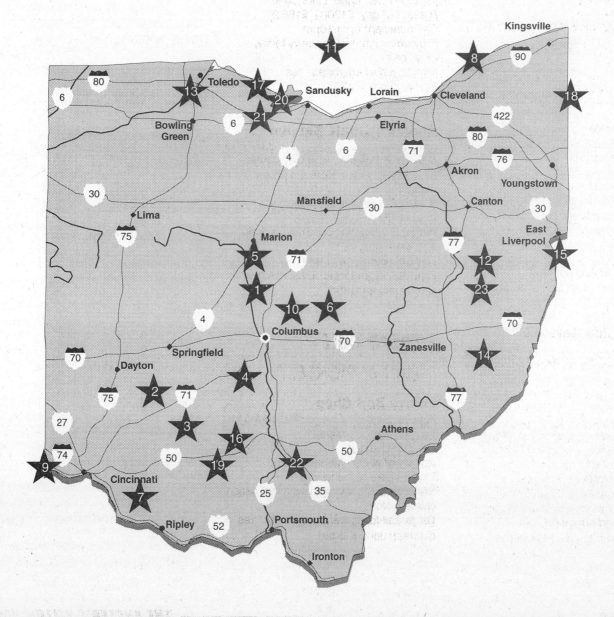

OHIO
ALUM CREEK LAKE - EAST FORK LAKE

ALUM CREEK LAKE

BAIT & TACKLE...

Somethin's Fishy
Delaware 614-369-3812
Hours: 6am-9pm
Carries: Live bait, lures, flies, maps, rods, reels, licenses
Bodies of water: Delaware Lake, Alum Creek Lake, Hoover Res., Olentangy River
Services & Products: Food, beverages, wholesale bait and tackle
Guides: Yes
OK to call for current conditions: Yes
Contact: Rich Gillette

CAESAR CREEK LAKE

BAIT & TACKLE...

Afield
Cincinnati 513-353-3536
Hours: Mixed hours
Carries: Live bait, lures, flies, maps, rods, reels, licenses
Bodies of water: Ohio River, Brookville Lake, East Fork Lake, Caesar Creek Lake, Rocky Fork Lake
Services & Products: Fishing instruction, repair services
Guides: Yes
OK to call for current conditions: Yes
Contact: Harold

Fehrmann's Bait & Tackle
Cincinnati 513-542-1300
Hours: 6am-5pm, 5:30am-1pm Sun. (seasonal)
Carries: Live bait, lures, flies, maps, rods, reels, licenses
Bodies of water: Ohio River, Little Miami River, Great Miami River, Licking River, East Fork Lake, Caesar Creek Lake, Brookville Lake
Guides: Yes
OK to call for current conditions: Yes
Contact: Mickey Abt or Ron Robinson

Tackle Town
Wilmington 513-382-7627
Hours: 6:30am-8pm Weekdays, 7am-7pm Weekends
Carries: Live bait, lures, maps, rods, reels, licenses
Bodies of water: Caesar Creek Lake, Cowan Lake, Rocky Fork Lake, Paint Creek Lake, East Fork Lake

Services & Products: Food, beverages, repair services, custom rods, camping goods
Guides: Yes
OK to call for current conditions: Yes
Contact: Paul C. Long

COWAN LAKE

BAIT & TACKLE...

Tackle Town
Wilmington 513-382-7627
Hours: 6:30am-8pm weekdays, 7am-7pm weekends
Carries: Live bait, lures, maps, rods, reels, licenses
Bodies of water: Caesar Creek Lake, Cowan Lake, Rocky Fork Lake, Paint Creek Lake, East Fork Lake
Services & Products: Food, beverages, repair services, custom rods, camping goods
Guides: Yes
OK to call for current conditions: Yes
Contact: Paul C. Long

DEER CREEK LAKE

BAIT & TACKLE...

Boyer Outdoor Supply
Circleville 614-474-4185
Hours: 9am-8pm
Carries: Live bait, lures, flies, maps, rods, reels, licenses
Bodies of water: Hargus Lake, Deer Creek Lake, Ross Lake, Scioto River, Darby Creek
Services & Products: Fishing instruction
Guides: Yes
OK to call for current conditions: Yes

DELAWARE LAKE

BAIT & TACKLE...

Somethin's Fishy
Delaware 614-369-3812
Hours: 6am-9pm
Carries: Live bait, lures, flies, maps, rods, reels, licenses
Bodies of water: Delaware Lake, Alum Creek Lake, Hoover Res., Olentangy River

Services & Products: Food, beverages, wholesale bait and tackle
Guides: Yes
OK to call for current conditions: Yes
Contact: Rich Gillette

DILLON LAKE

BAIT & TACKLE...

Sportsmans One Stop Inc.
Zanesville 614-452-6140
Hours: 7am-8pm
Carries: Live bait, lures, maps, rods, reels, licenses
Bodies of water: Dillon Lake, Licking River, Muskingum River, Ohio Power Reacreation Area
Services & Products: Food, beverages, repair services
OK to call for current conditions: Yes
Contact: Mike

EAST FORK LAKE

BAIT & TACKLE...

Afield
Cincinnati 513-353-3536
Hours: Mixed hours
Carries: Live bait, lures, flies, maps, rods, reels, licenses
Bodies of water: Ohio River, Brookville Lake, East Fork Lake, Caesar Creek Lake, Rocky Fork Lake
Services & Products: Fishing instruction, repair services
Guides: Yes
OK to call for current conditions: Yes
Contact: Harold

Fehrmann's Bait & Tackle
Cincinnati 513-542-1300
Hours: 6am-5pm, 5:30am-1pm Sun. (seasonal)
Carries: Live bait, lures, flies, maps, rods, reels, licenses
Bodies of water: Ohio River, Little Miami River, Great Miami River, Licking River, East Fork Lake, Caesar Creek Lake, Brookville Lake
Guides: Yes
OK to call for current conditions: Yes
Contact: Mickey Abt or Ron Robinson

EAST FORK LAKE - LAKE ERIE — OHIO

Tackle Town
Wilmington 513-382-7627
Hours: 6:30am-8pm Weekdays, 7am-7pm Weekends
Carries: Live bait, lures, maps, rods, reels, licenses
Bodies of water: Caesar Creek Lake, Cowan Lake, Rocky Fork Lake, Paint Creek Lake, East Fork Lake
Services & Products: Food, beverages, repair services, custom rods, camping goods
Guides: Yes
OK to call for current conditions: Yes
Contact: Paul C. Long

GRAND RIVER

BAIT & TACKLE...

Grand River Tackle
Grand River 216-352-7222
Hours: 6am-8pm
Carries: Live bait, lures, flies, maps, rods, reels, licenses
Bodies of water: Lake Erie, Grand River, Chagrin River, Conneaut Creek
Services & Products: Guide services, food, beverages, fishing instruction, repair services
OK to call for current conditions: Yes
Contact: Bruce or Chris

Hoplins Bait & Tackle
Mentor 216-257-9487
Hours: 6am-9pm
Carries: Live bait, lures, rods, reels, licenses
Bodies of water: Lake Erie, Grand River, Chagrin River
Services & Products: Guide services, charter boat service, lodging, beverages
Guides: Yes
OK to call for current conditions: Yes
Contact: Ron Burlingham

GREAT MIAMI RIVER

BAIT & TACKLE...

Fehrmann's Bait & Tackle
Cincinnati 513-542-1300
Hours: 6am-5pm, 5:30am-1pm Sun. (seasonal)
Carries: Live bait, lures, flies, maps, rods, reels, licenses
Bodies of water: Ohio River, Little Miami River, Great Miami River, Licking River, East Fork Lake, Caesar Creek Lake, Brookville Lake
Guides: Yes
OK to call for current conditions: Yes
Contact: Mickey Abt or Ron Robinson

Lake Gloria Golf & Fishing Center
10511 Pippin Road
Cincinnati 45231
Hours: 6:30am-dark
Carries: Live bait, lures, rods, reels
Bodies of water: Ohio River, Great Miami River, Lake Gloria
Services & Products: Food, beverages
Guides: No
OK to call for current conditions: Yes

HOOVER RESERVOIR

BAIT & TACKLE...

Somethin's Fishy
Delaware 614-369-3812
Hours: 6am-9pm
Carries: Live bait, lures, flies, maps, rods, reels, licenses
Bodies of water: Delaware Lake, Alum Creek Lake, Hoover Res., Olentangy River
Services & Products: Food, beverages, wholesale bait and tackle
Guides: Yes
OK to call for current conditions: Yes
Contact: Rich Gillette

LAKE ERIE

BAIT & TACKLE...

Alvin Bait
Port Clinton 419-732-2846
Hours: 6am-10pm
Carries: Live bait, lures, maps, rods, licenses
Bodies of water: Lake Erie, Portage River, Sandusky Bay
Services & Products: Guide services, boat ramp, food, beverages, fishing instruction
Guides: Yes
OK to call for current conditions: Yes
Contact: Alvin

Bay View Center
Sandusky 419-684-9449
Hours: 6am-10pm
Carries: Live bait, lures, flies, maps, rods, reels, licenses
Bodies of water: Lake Erie, Sandusky Bay, Sandusky River, Cold Creek
Services & Products: Food, beverages, fishing instruction, repair services
Guides: Yes
OK to call for current conditions: Yes
Contact: Jim or Bob

George's Bait & Carryout
Lorain 216-282-2660
Hours: 7am-8pm
Carries: Live bait, lures, flies, maps, rods, reels, licenses
Bodies of water: Lake Erie
Services & Products: Charter boat service, food, beverages, fishing instruction, repair services
Guides: Yes
OK to call for current conditions: Yes
Contact: George Garwell

Grand River Tackle
Grand River 216-352-7222
Hours: 6am-8pm
Carries: Live bait, lures, flies, maps, rods, reels, licenses
Bodies of water: Lake Erie, Grand River, Chagrin River, Conneaut Creek
Services & Products: Guide services, food, beverages, fishing instruction, repair services
OK to call for current conditions: Yes
Contact: Bruce or Chris

Hi Way Bait Store
Lakeside Marblhd 419-734-3601
Hours: 5:30am-10pm, closed Dec.-Feb.
Carries: Live bait, lures, maps, rods, reels, licenses
Bodies of water: Lake Erie western basin, Island area
Services & Products: Guide services, charter boat service, lodging, food, beverages, repair services
Guides: Yes
OK to call for current conditions: Yes
Contact: Don Mitchell

OHIO — LAKE ERIE

Hoplins Bait & Tackle
Mentor 216-257-9487
Hours: 6am-9pm
Carries: Live bait, lures, rods, reels, licenses
Bodies of water: Lake Erie, Grand River, Chagrin River
Services & Products: Guide services, charter boat service, lodging, beverages
Guides: Yes
OK to call for current conditions: Yes
Contact: Ron Burlingham

Jack's Deli
Sandusky 419-626-3354
Hours: 6am-2am, closed Oct.-Mar.
Carries: Live bait, lures, maps, rods, reels, licenses
Bodies of water: Lake Erie, Huron River, Cold Creek
Services & Products: Food, beverages, gas/oil
Guides: Yes
OK to call for current conditions: Yes
Contact: Adam, Jonathon

Junior's Bait & Tackle
Ashtabula 216-964-6580
Hours: 5:30am-9pm
Carries: Live bait, lures, flies, maps, rods, reels, licenses
Bodies of water: Lake Erie
Services & Products: Charter boat service, lodging, boat ramp, food, beverages, fishing instruction, paddle boats
Guides: Yes
OK to call for current conditions: Yes
Contact: Junior Dioneff

Kelly's Bait & Tackle
Andover 216-293-7272
Hours: 5am-late pm
Carries: Live bait, lures, flies, maps, rods, reels, licenses
Bodies of water: Pymatuning Lake, Lake Erie
Services & Products: Guide services
Guides: Yes
OK to call for current conditions: Yes
Contact: Dolly or Gary Lewis

Sandy Shore Variety Store
Sandusky 419-626-1291
Hours: 6am-6pm
Carries: Live bait, lures, flies, maps, rods, reels, licenses
Bodies of water: Sandusky Bay, Lake Erie

Services & Products: Food, beverages, fishing instruction, repair services
Guides: Yes
OK to call for current conditions: Yes
Contact: Mike Spisak

CHARTERS...

Baltic Charters
Madison 800-879-8025
Species & Seasons: SM Bass May-June, Walleye June-Sept, Perch Sept-Oct
Bodies of water: Central Lake Erie
Rates: 6 hrs: $200(4-6), 8 hrs(Walleye): $300(4), $400(6)
Call between: 8pm-10pm
Provides: Light tackle, heavy tackle, lures, bait, rain gear
Handicapped equipped: Yes

Capt. Art & Capt. Kevin Bellman
Toledo 419-691-3103
Species & Seasons: SM Bass April-May, Walleye April-Nov, Yellow Perch Aug-Nov, Catfish June-Nov
Bodies of water: Lake Erie, western basin
Rates: Full day: $200(2), $375(6)
Call between: 5pm-10pm
Provides: Light tackle, lures, bait, beverages, lunch
Handicapped equipped: Yes
Certifications: USCG

BC Charters
Martin 419-855-7555
Species & Seasons: Walleye April-Aug, SM Bass June-Oct, Yellow Perch Aug-Oct
Bodies of water: Lake Erie, western basin

Rates: Boat: $350 up (maximun 6)
Call between: 7pm-11pm
Provides: Light tackle, lures, bait
Certifications: USCG

Bounty Hunter Charters
Glenwillow 216-439-2332
Species & Seasons: Walleye April-Sept, SM Bass May-Oct
Bodies of water: Lake Erie
Rates: Full day: $60(1)
Call between:
Provides: Light tackle, heavy tackle, lures, bait
Handicapped equipped: Yes
Certifications: USCG, OH Guide License

Break Time Charters
Toledo 419-698-8301
.... 351-3117
Species & Seasons: Walleye April-Nov, Yellow Perch Aug-Nov
Bodies of water: Lake Erie
Rates: 7 hrs: $300(6)
Call between: 9am-12pm
Provides: Light tackle, lures, bait
Handicapped equipped: Yes
Certifications: USCG, OH DNR licensed guide

C-Cat Sportsfishing Charters
Sandusky 419-626-9342
Species & Seasons: Walleye May-July, Perch Sept-Nov, SM Bass all summer
Bodies of water: Lake Erie
Rates: 4 hrs. (Walleye): $250, 6 hrs.(Perch): $250, 8 hrs. (Walleye): $360, can accommodate up to 6 people
Call between: Anytime
Provides: Bait
Handicapped equipped: Yes, no wheelchairs
Certifications: USCG
(see ad page 363)

CAPT. BOB HOUSTON
(419) 698-8301
Mobile (419) 351-3117

440 Whitlock
Toledo, Ohio 43605

BREAKTIME CHARTERS
Lake Erie Walleye, Perch, Small Mouth

U.S.C.G. Licensed
Wildlife Div. Lic. Guide

Fully Equipped
Fully Insured

LAKE ERIE — OHIO

DB Sport Fishing Charters
Perry 800-769-1750
Species & Seasons: SM Bass May-June, Walleye June-Oct, Perch Oct-Nov, Walleye April-May
Bodies of water: Mosquito Creek Lake, Lake Erie, Central Basin
Rates: Bass/Perch: $180(1-4), Walleye: $280(1-4)
Call between: 4pm-10pm
Provides: Light tackle, heavy tackle, lures, bait
Handicapped equipped: Yes
Certifications: USCG, OH Liscenced Guide

Double-O-Seven Charters
Mentor 216-974-8970
Species & Seasons: Walleye April-June, Perch Aug-Oct
Bodies of water: Lake Erie
Rates: Half day: $300(1-6), Full day: $370(1-6)
Call between: Anytime
Provides: Light tackle, heavy tackle, lures, bait
Handicapped equipped: Yes
Certifications: USCG, OH Guide Lic., NCCBA

Eagle Eye Charters
Euclid 216-731-7948
Species & Seasons: Walleye April-Nov, SM Bass May-Nov, Perch, Steelhead June-Nov
Bodies of water: Lake Erie, western and central basin
Rates: $360-$390(6), call for free brochure
Provides: Heavy tackle, lures
Certifications: USCG, State of OH

Erie Pro Guide Group
Oregon .... 800-6 FISH-US
Species & Seasons: Walleye Mar-Nov, SM Bass May-Nov, Yellow Perch Aug-Nov
Bodies of water: Lake Erie
Rates: Full day: $390(1-6)
Call between: 9am-9pm
Provides: Light tackle, lures, bait
Handicapped equipped: Yes
Certifications: USCG

Fish-Erie Charters
Huron 419-433-4746
Species & Seasons: Walleye April-Oct, Perch, SM Bass Aug-Oct
Bodies of water: Lake Erie, western and central basins
Rates: Full day: $360(6)
Call between: 5pm-10pm
Provides: Light tackle, lures, bait, rain gear
Handicapped equipped: No
Certifications: USCG, OH Guide

Fishin Magician
Grand River 216-639-8437
Species & Seasons: Walleye June-Aug, Perch Sept-Oct
Bodies of water: Lake Erie
Rates: 8 hrs: $300(1-4)
Provides: Light tackle, heavy tackle, lures
Handicapped equipped: No
Certifications: USCG, OH License Guide

The Hoaky
Huron 419-433-5004
Species & Seasons: Walleye, SM Bass, Yellow Perch May-Nov
Bodies of water: Lake Erie, western and central basins
Rates: Half day: $250(6), Full day: $330(6)
Call between: 6pm-10pm
Provides: Light tackle, lures, bait
Handicapped equipped: No
Certifications: USCG

Capt. Ernie James
Huron 419-433-7369
.... 626-3260
Species & Seasons: Walleye, LM Bass, Yellow Perch April-Nov
Bodies of water: Lake Erie
Rates: Call for rates
Call between: 7am-11pm
Provides: Light tackle, lures, bait, ice
Handicapped equipped: No
Certifications: USCG

J.I.L. Charters
2318 E Harbor Road
Port Clinton 43452
Species & Seasons: Walleye April-Oct, SM Bass July-Oct
Bodies of water: Lake Erie
Rates: Full day: $390(6)
Call between: 7pm-9pm
Provides: Lures, bait, beverages, lunch
Handicapped equipped: No
Certifications: USCG, OH Licensed Guide

Lakeland Charter Service
Port Clinton 419-734-2101
Species & Seasons: Walleye April-Oct, SM Bass Aug-Oct
Bodies of water: Lake Erie
Rates: $420(6), Walk-ons: $35pp (both include bait, ice)
Call between: 7am-9pm
Provides: Light tackle, lures, bait, beverages, lunch
Handicapped equipped: No

Majestic Fishing Fleet
Lorain 216-244-2621
Species & Seasons: Walleye May-Nov, Perch Aug-Nov
Bodies of water: Lake Erie
Rates: Half day: $25(1), $50(2), Full day: $50(1), $100(2), Private: $350-$800(1-80)
Call between: 6pm-9pm
Provides: Light tackle, bait, beverages
Handicapped equipped: No
Certifications: USCG, full insurance, Licensed Guide OH

Matta Charter Fishing
4905 E Court Drive
Port Clinton 43452
Species & Seasons: Walleye April-Nov, Perch, SM Bass May-Nov
Bodies of water: Lake Erie
Rates: Full day: $375(1-6)
Provides: Light tackle, lures, bait, ice
Handicapped equipped: Yes
Certifications: USCG

C-CAT
Sportsfishing Charters
Sandusky, Ohio
Capt. Chuck Catri
U.S.C.G. Licensed
419 626-9342

OHIO — LAKE ERIE

Osprey Charter Service
Castalia 419-684-7435
Species & Seasons: Walleye April-Nov, SM Bass May-Nov, Perch Aug-Nov
Bodies of water: Lake Erie
Rates: Full day: $360(6)
Call between: 5pm-10pm
Provides: Light tackle, lures, bait, beverages, lunch
Handicapped equipped: Yes
Certifications: USCG, Erie Dearie Fishing Team

Reel-Eye-Deal Charters
Mentor Lake 800-203-3201
Species & Seasons: Walleye May-Oct, Steelhead June-Oct, SM Bass July-Sept, Yellow Perch Sept-Nov
Bodies of water: Lake Erie
Rates: Walleye, Trout, SM Bass: $360(1-6), Yellow Perch: $250, Walleye (evening-5hrs) $280
Call between: 6am-11pm
Provides: Light tackle, heavy tackle, lures, bait
Handicapped equipped: Yes
Certifications: USCG, OH Licensed Guide

The Release Charter Service
Barberton 800-432-0709
Species & Seasons: Brown Trout, Coho Salmon, Steelhead April-May, Walleye June-July, Chinook Salmon, Rainbow Trout, Steelhead, Lake Trout, Atlantic Salmon Aug-Oct
Bodies of water: Lake Erie, Lake Ontario
Rates: Lake Erie: Half day: $240(group), Full day: $390(group), Lake Ontario: Half day: $240(group), Full day: $425(group)
Call between: Anytime
Provides: Light tackle, heavy tackle, lures, bait, lodging also available
Handicapped equipped: Yes
Certifications: USCG, OH Licensed Guide

Sandpiper Fishing Charter
Parma 216-267-8960
Species & Seasons: Walleye, SM Bass April-Oct, Yellow Perch Aug-Oct
Bodies of water: Lake Erie, western basin
Rates: Full day: $60(1), $200(2), $330(6)
Call between: 9am-11pm
Provides: Light tackle, bait
Handicapped equipped: Yes
Certifications: USCG, OH Guide

Saucy Tomato Charters
Sandusky 419-626-3103
Species & Seasons: Walleye, Yellow Perch April-Nov, SM Bass May-Oct
Bodies of water: Lake Erie
Rates: 4 hrs: $220(6), Full day: $330(6)
Call between: Anytime
Provides: Light tackle, lures, bait
Handicapped equipped: No
Certifications: OH Fishing Guide, USCG

Capt. Tom Schofield
Huron 800-819-8100
.... 419-433-5671
Species & Seasons: Walleye, SM Bass April-Nov, Perch Spring-Fall
Bodies of water: Western Lake Erie
Rates: Half day: $240(6), Full day: $330(6)
Call between: 8am-10pm
Provides: Light tackle, lures, bait
Handicapped equipped: Yes
Certifications: USCG

Speerfish Charters
Sandusky 419-627-8340
Species & Seasons: Walleye, SM Bass April-Oct, Yellow Perch Sept-Nov
Bodies of water: Lake Erie
Rates: Half day: $270(1-6), Full day: $340(1-6)
Call between: 6pm-9pm
Provides: Light tackle, lures, bait
Handicapped equipped: Yes
Certifications: USCG, OH Licensed Guide

Sportsman Charter Service
Marblehead 800-546-3474
Species & Seasons: Walleye April-Oct, SM Bass May-Oct, Yellow Perch April/Sept-Oct
Bodies of water: Lake Erie, western and central basins
Rates: Full day: $390(6)
Call between: 9am-9pm
Provides: Light tackle, lures, bait, beverages, lunch
Handicapped equipped: Yes
Certifications: USCG

Strike Zone Sport Fishing
Kent 800-627-3474
Species & Seasons: Walleye, SM Bass April-Nov, Steelhead July-Oct, Perch Sept-Nov
Bodies of water: Lake Erie
Rates: $360-$400(1-6)
Call between: Anytime
Provides: Light tackle, heavy tackle, lures, bait, beverages, lunch
Handicapped equipped: Yes
Certifications: USCG

Taylor Charters
Huron 419-433-4693
Species & Seasons: Walleye, SM Bass, Yellow Perch April-Oct
Bodies of water: Lake Erie, central and western basins
Call between: 11am-8pm
Provides: Light tackle
Handicapped equipped: No
Certifications: USCG, OH Licensed Guide

Thumper Charters
7278 Jackson Street
Mentor 44060
Species & Seasons: Walleye May-Oct, Steelhead June-Oct, Perch Sept-Nov
Bodies of water: Lake Erie
Rates: Half day: $290(6), Full day: $390(6)
Call between: 8am-6pm
Provides: Light tackle, lures, bait
Handicapped equipped: Yes
Certifications: USCG

Trophy Charters
Andover 216-293-7249
Species & Seasons: Walleye April-Sept, Yellow Perch Oct, SM Bass May-Oct
Bodies of water: Lake Erie
Rates: April-May: Full day: $390(1-6), June-Sept: Full day: $420(1-6), Oct: Full day: $300(1-6)
Call between: Anytime
Provides: Light tackle, heavy tackle, lures, bait, rain gear
Handicapped equipped: Yes
Certifications: USCG, OH Licensed Guide

Trophy Runner Charters
Mentor 216-951-4012
Species & Seasons: SM Bass May-June/Sept-Oct, Walleye, Steelhead June-Oct, Perch Aug-Oct
Bodies of water: Lake Erie
Rates: Full day: $390(1-6)
Call between: 7am-11pm
Provides: Light tackle, heavy tackle, lures, bait
Handicapped equipped: Yes
Certifications: USCG, OH Fishing Guide Licensed

LAKE ERIE - MAUMEE RIVER — OHIO

West Sister Sport Fishing Group
Toledo 800-488-FISH
Species & Seasons: SM Bass, Steelhead Spring-Fall, Walleye April-Sept, Yellow Perch Aug-Oct, Muskellunge June-Aug, Chinook Salmon April-Sept, Coho Salmon May-Aug, Brown Trout Spring-Summer
Bodies of water: Lake Erie, Michigan: Lake St. Clair, Lake Michigan, Lake Huron, various inland tributaries
Call between: Anytime
Provides: Light tackle, heavy tackle, fly rod/reel, lures, bait, rain gear, beverages, lunch
Handicapped equipped: Yes
Certifications: USCG, Licensed Taxidermist

Winke Guide Service
Port Clinton 800-274-9255
.... 419-798-4140
Species & Seasons: Walleye April-Nov, SM Bass May-Oct
Bodies of water: Lake Erie
Rates: 8 hrs: $360(6), Lodging available
Call between: 6pm-10pm
Provides: Light tackle, lures, bait, beverages, lunch
Handicapped equipped: Yes
Certifications: USCG, OH Licensed Guide

Capt. Denny & Lynn Zukowski
Willowick 216-942-1909
Species & Seasons: Walleye May-Aug, Yellow Perch Aug-Dec
Bodies of water: Lake Erie (Cleveland)
Rates: Half day: $18(1), Full day: $25(1), 6 hrs: $550(30)
Call between: Anytime
Provides: Light tackle, lures, bait, beverages, lunch
Handicapped equipped: Yes
Certifications: USCG

LODGES...

Teal Pt. Lodge & Charters
Oak Harbor 419-898-5106
Guest Capacity: 9 units
Handicapped equipped: No
Seasons: All year hunting and fishing
Rates: $24/pp day
Contact: Bob or John Les
Guides: Yes

Species & Seasons: Walleye all year, SM Bass May-Oct, Perch Aug-Nov, Catfish June-Aug
Bodies of Water: Western Basin of Lake Erie, Toussiant River, Turtle Creek, Portage River, Maumee Bay, Lake Erie Islands
Types of fishing: Light tackle, Lake Erie charter boats
Available: Fishing instruction, family activities, bird and wildlife observation

MARINAS...

Harrison Marina Inc.
Toledo 419-729-1676
Hours: 6am-8pm
Carries: Live bait, lures, maps, rods, reels, licenses
Bodies of water: Lake Erie, Maumee River
Services & Products: Charter boat service, food, beverages, gas/oil
Guides: Yes
OK to call for current conditions: Yes

Holiday Harbor Marina
Huron 419-433-2140
Hours: 8am-5pm
Carries: Maps
Bodies of water: Huron River, Lake Erie
Services & Products: Boat ramp, gas/oil, repair services, boat lift
Guides: Yes
OK to call for current conditions: No

Martins Marina
Sandusky 419-625-4703
Hours: 7am-10:30pm
Carries:
Bodies of water: Sandusky Bay, Lake Erie, Cold Creek
Services & Products: Boat rentals, boat ramp, campsites, RV sites
Guides: Yes
OK to call for current conditions: Yes
Contact: L. M. Martin

Sunset Point Marina
Kelleys Island 419-746-2373
Hours: April-Nov.
Carries: Live bait
Bodies of water: Lake Erie
Services & Products: Lodging, boat ramp, gas/oil, ice, freezer space
Guides: Yes
OK to call for current conditions: Yes
Contact: Mary or Theresa

Tibbel's Marina
Marblehead 419-734-1143
Hours: 6am-11pm
Carries: Live bait, lures, maps, rods, reels, licenses
Bodies of water: Lake Erie, Maumee River, Fremont River, Sandusky River, Portage River
Services & Products: Guide services, charter boat service, lodging, boat ramp, food, beverages, gas/oil, fishing instruction, repair services, dockage, motels
OK to call for current conditions: Yes
Contact: Jack, Guy or John Tibbels

LEESVILLE LAKE

BAIT & TACKLE...

Bill's Bait & Tackle
Wellsville 216-532-1727
Hours: 6am-7pm
Carries: Live bait, lures, flies, maps, rods, reels, licenses
Bodies of water: Ohio River, Highlandtown State Lake, Pymatuning Lake, Tappan Lake, Leesville Lake
Services & Products: Custom made lures, jigs, spinners, flies
Guides: Yes
OK to call for current conditions: Yes
Contact: Bill

MAUMEE RIVER

MARINAS...

Harrison Marina Inc.
Toledo 419-729-1676
Hours: 6am-8pm
Carries: Live bait, lures, maps, rods, reels, licenses
Bodies of water: Lake Erie, Maumee River
Services & Products: Charter boat service, food, beverages, gas/oil
Guides: Yes
OK to call for current conditions: Yes

OHIO — MAUMEE RIVER - PAINT CREEK LAKE

Tibbel's Marina
Marblehead 419-734-1143
Hours: 6am-11pm
Carries: Live bait, lures, maps, rods, reels, licenses
Bodies of water: Lake Erie, Maumee River, Fremont River, Sandusky River, Portage River
Services & Products: Guide services, charter boat service, lodging, boat ramp, food, beverages, gas/oil, fishing instruction, repair services, dockage, motels
OK to call for current conditions: Yes
Contact: Jack, Guy or John Tibbels

MONROE LAKE

BAIT & TACKLE...

Crawford's Crawdads
Clarington 614-458-0206
Hours: 7am-11pm
Carries: Live bait, lures, maps, rods, reels, licenses
Bodies of water: Ohio River, Monroe Lake, Sunfish Creek, Opossum Creek, Captina Creek
Services & Products: Boat rentals, guide services, boat ramp, beverages, fishing instruction, camping facilities
Guides: Yes
OK to call for current conditions: Yes
Contact: Vicki Crawford

OHIO RIVER

BAIT & TACKLE...

Afield
Cincinnati 513-353-3536
Hours: Mixed hours
Carries: Live bait, lures, flies, maps, rods, reels, licenses
Bodies of water: Ohio River, Brookville Lake, East Fork Lake, Caeser Creek Lake, Rocky Fork Lake
Services & Products: Fishing instruction, repair services
Guides: Yes
OK to call for current conditions: Yes
Contact: Harold

Bass Shaq
East Liverpool 216-385-1311
Hours: 7am-7pm
Carries: Live bait, lures, flies, maps, rods, reels, licenses
Bodies of water: Ohio River, Beaver Creek, Highlandtown Lake
Services & Products: Charter boat service, food, beverages, gas/oil, fishing instruction, repair services
Guides: Yes
OK to call for current conditions: Yes
Contact: Mike Karcher

Big Boys Water Toys
Cheshire 614-367-7802
Hours: 8am-5pm, closed Sun.
Carries: Live bait, lures, flies, maps, rods, reels
Bodies of water: Ohio River, Tycoon Lake
Services & Products: Repair services, boat sales
Guides: No
OK to call for current conditions: Yes
Contact: Del, Chad or Keith

Bill's Bait & Tackle
Wellsville 216-532-1727
Hours: 6am-7pm
Carries: Live bait, lures, flies, maps, rods, reels, licenses
Bodies of water: Ohio river, Highlandtown State Lake, Pymatuning Lake, Tappan Lake, Leesville Lake
Services & Products: Custom made lures, jigs, spinners, flies
Guides: Yes
OK to call for current conditions: Yes
Contact: Bill

Crawford's Crawdads
Clarington 614-458-0206
Hours: 7am-11pm
Carries: Live bait, lures, maps, rods, reels, licenses
Bodies of water: Ohio River, Monroe Lake, Sunfish Creek, Opossum Creek, Captina Creek
Services & Products: Boat rentals, guide services, boat ramp, beverages, fishing instruction, camping facilities
Guides: Yes
OK to call for current conditions: Yes
Contact: Vicki Crawford

Fehrmann's Bait & Tackle
Cincinnati 513-542-1300
Hours: 6am-5pm, 5:30am-1pm Sun. (seasonal)
Carries: Live bait, lures, flies, maps, rods, reels, licenses
Bodies of water: Ohio River, Little Miami River, Great Miami River, Licking River, East Fork Lake, Caesar Creek Lake, Brookville Lake
Guides: Yes
OK to call for current conditions: Yes
Contact: Mickey Abt or Ron Robinson

Lake Gloria Golf & Fishing Center
10511 Pippin Road
Cincinnati 45231
Hours: 6:30am-dark
Carries: Live bait, lures, rods, reels
Bodies of water: Ohio River, Great Miami River, Lake Gloria
Services & Products: Food, beverages
Guides: No
OK to call for current conditions: Yes

Liberty Rental
Waverly 614-947-4214
Carries: Live bait, rods, reels, licenses
Bodies of water: Sunfish Creek, Scioto River, Ohio River, Paint Creek Lake, Pee Pee Creek
Guides: No
OK to call for current conditions: Yes

PAINT CREEK LAKE

BAIT & TACKLE...

Cole's Bait & Tackle
Bainbridge 513-365-1436
Hours: 7am-7pm
Carries: Live bait, lures, maps, rods, reels, licenses
Bodies of water: Paint Creek Lake, Rocky Fork Lake
Services & Products: Food, beverages, fishing instruction
Guides: No
OK to call for current conditions: Yes
Contact: Leon Cole

Liberty Rental
Waverly 614-947-4214
Carries: Live bait, rods, reels, licenses
Bodies of water: Sunfish Creek, Scioto River, Ohio River, Paint Creek Lake, Pee Pee Creek
Guides: No
OK to call for current conditions: Yes

PAINT CREEK LAKE - ROCKY FORK LAKE

OHIO

Tackle Town
Wilmington 513-382-7627
Hours: 6:30am-8pm Weekdays, 7am-7pm Weekends
Carries: Live bait, lures, maps, rods, reels, licenses
Bodies of water: Caesar Creek Lake, Cowan Lake, Rocky Fork Lake, Paint Creek Lake, East Fork Lake
Services & Products: Food, beverages, repair services, custom rods, camping goods
Guides: Yes
OK to call for current conditions: Yes
Contact: Paul C. Long

PORTAGE RIVER

BAIT & TACKLE...

Alvin Bait
Port Clinton 419-732-2846
Hours: 6am-10pm
Carries: Live bait, lures, maps, rods, licenses
Bodies of water: Lake Erie, Portage River, Sandusky Bay
Services & Products: Guide services, boat ramp, food, beverages, fishing instruction
Guides: Yes
OK to call for current conditions: Yes
Contact: Alvin

LODGES...

Teal Pt. Lodge & Charters
Oak Harbor 419-898-5106
Guest Capacity: 9 units
Handicapped equipped: No
Seasons: All year hunting and fishing
Rates: $24/pp day
Contact: Bob or John Les
Guides: Yes
Species & Seasons: Walleye all year, SM Bass May-Oct, Perch Aug-Nov, Catfish June-Aug
Bodies of Water: Western Basin of Lake Erie, Toussiant River, Turtle Creek, Portage River, Maumee Bay, Lake Erie Islands
Types of fishing: Light tackle, Lake Erie charter boats
Available: Fishing instruction, family activities, bird and wildlife observation

MARINAS...

Tibbel's Marina
Marblehead 419-734-1143
Hours: 6am-11pm
Carries: Live bait, lures, maps, rods, reels, licenses
Bodies of water: Lake Erie, Maumee River, Fremont River, Sandusky River, Portage River
Services & Products: Guide services, charter boat service, lodging, boat ramp, food, beverages, gas/oil, fishing instruction, repair services, dockage, motels
OK to call for current conditions: Yes
Contact: Jack, Guy or John Tibbels

PYMATUNING RESERVOIR

BAIT & TACKLE...

Bill's Bait & Tackle
Wellsville 216-532-1727
Hours: 6am-7pm
Carries: Live bait, lures, flies, maps, rods, reels, licenses
Bodies of water: Ohio river, Highlandtown State Lake, Pymatuning Lake, Tappan Lake, Leesville Lake
Services & Products: Custom made lures, jigs, spinners, flies
Guides: Yes
OK to call for current conditions: Yes
Contact: Bill

Gateway Bait & Tackle
Andover 216-293-7227
Carries: Live bait, lures, flies, maps, rods, reels, licenses
Bodies of water: Pymatuning Lake
Services & Products: Beverages
Guides: Yes
OK to call for current conditions: Yes
Contact: Gretta Williams

Kelly's Bait & Tackle
Andover 216-293-7272
Hours: 5am-late pm
Carries: Live bait, lures, flies, maps, rods, reels, licenses
Bodies of water: Pymatuning Lake, Lake Erie
Services & Products: Guide services
Guides: Yes
OK to call for current conditions: Yes
Contact: Dolly or Gary Lewis

ROCKY FORK LAKE

BAIT & TACKLE...

Afield
Cincinnati 513-353-3536
Hours: Mixed hours
Carries: Live bait, lures, flies, maps, rods, reels, licenses
Bodies of water: Ohio River, Brookville Lake, East Fork Lake, Caesar Creek Lake, Rocky Fork Lake
Services & Products: Fishing instruction, repair services
Guides: Yes
OK to call for current conditions: Yes
Contact: Harold

Cole's Bait & Tackle
Bainbridge 513-365-1436
Hours: 7am-7pm
Carries: Live bait, lures, maps, rods, reels, licenses
Bodies of water: Paint Creek Lake, Rocky Fork Lake
Services & Products: Food, beverages, fishing instruction
Guides: No
OK to call for current conditions: Yes
Contact: Leon Cole

Tackle Town
Wilmington 513-382-7627
Hours: 6:30am-8pm Weekdays, 7am-7pm Weekends
Carries: Live bait, lures, maps, rods, reels, licenses
Bodies of water: Caesar Creek Lake, Cowan Lake, Rocky Fork Lake, Paint Creek Lake, East Fork Lake
Services & Products: Food, beverages, repair services, custom rods, camping goods
Guides: Yes
OK to call for current conditions: Yes
Contact: Paul C. Long

YOUR SILENT FISHING PARTNER

OHIO

SANDUSKY BAY - TAPPAN LAKE

SANDUSKY BAY

BAIT & TACKLE...

Alvin Bait
Port Clinton 419-732-2846
Hours: 6am-10pm
Carries: Live bait, lures, maps, rods, licenses
Bodies of water: Lake Erie, Portage River, Sandusky Bay
Services & Products: Guide services, boat ramp, food, beverages, fishing instruction
Guides: Yes
OK to call for current conditions: Yes
Contact: Alvin

Bay View Center
Sandusky 419-684-9449
Hours: 6am-10pm
Carries: Live bait, lures, flies, maps, rods, reels, licenses
Bodies of water: Lake Erie, Sandusky Bay, Sandusky River, Cold Creek
Services & Products: Food, beverages, fishing instruction, repair services
Guides: Yes
OK to call for current conditions: Yes
Contact: Jim or Bob

Sandy Shore Variety Store
Sandusky 419-626-1291
Hours: 6am-6pm
Carries: Live bait, lures, flies, maps, rods, reels, licenses
Bodies of water: Sandusky Bay, Lake Erie
Services & Products: Food, beverages, fishing instruction, repair services
Guides: Yes
OK to call for current conditions: Yes
Contact: Mike Spisak

MARINAS...

Martins Marina
Sandusky 419-625-4703
Hours: 7am-10:30pm
Carries:
Bodies of water: Sandusky Bay, Lake Erie, Cold Creek
Services & Products: Boat rentals, boat ramp, campsites, RV sites
Guides: Yes
OK to call for current conditions: Yes
Contact: L. M. Martin

SANDUSKY RIVER

BAIT & TACKLE...

Bay View Center
Sandusky 419-684-9449
Hours: 6am-10pm
Carries: Live bait, lures, flies, maps, rods, reels, licenses
Bodies of water: Lake Erie, Sandusky Bay, Sandusky River, Cold Creek
Services & Products: Food, beverages, fishing instruction, repair services
Guides: Yes
OK to call for current conditions: Yes
Contact: Jim or Bob

U.S. Marathon
Upper Sandusky 419-294-2850
Hours: 24 hours 6 days, closed 12pm-8am Sun.
Carries: Live bait, lures, maps, licenses
Bodies of water: Sandusky River, Marseilles Resevoir
Services & Products: Food, beverages, gas/oil
Guides: Yes
OK to call for current conditions: Yes
Contact: Steve Seitz

MARINAS...

Tibbel's Marina
Marblehead 419-734-1143
Hours: 6am-11pm
Carries: Live bait, lures, maps, rods, reels, licenses
Bodies of water: Lake Erie, Maumee River, Fremont River, Sandusky River, Portage River
Services & Products: Guide services, charter boat service, lodging, boat ramp, food, beverages, gas/oil, fishing instruction, repair services, dockage, motels
OK to call for current conditions: Yes
Contact: Jack, Guy or John Tibbels

SCIOTO RIVER

BAIT & TACKLE...

Boyer Outdoor Supply
Circleville 614-474-4185
Hours: 9am-8pm
Carries: Live bait, lures, flies, maps, rods, reels, licenses
Bodies of water: Hargus Lake, Deer Creek Lake, Ross Lake, Scioto River, Darby Creek
Services & Products: Fishing instruction
Guides: Yes
OK to call for current conditions: Yes

Liberty Rental
Waverly 614-947-4214
Carries: Live bait, rods, reels, licenses
Bodies of water: Sunfish Creek, Scioto River, Ohio River, Paint Creek Lake, Pee Pee Creek
Guides: No
OK to call for current conditions: Yes

TAPPAN LAKE

BAIT & TACKLE...

Bill's Bait & Tackle
Wellsville 216-532-1727
Hours: 6am-7pm
Carries: Live bait, lures, flies, maps, rods, reels, licenses
Bodies of water: Ohio River, Highlandtown State Lake, Pymatuning Lake, Tappan Lake, Leesville Lake
Services & Products: Custom made lures, jigs, spinners, flies
Guides: Yes
OK to call for current conditions: Yes
Contact: Bill

OKLAHOMA

1. Arcadia Lake
2. Arkansas River
3. Broken Bow Lake
4. Eufaula Lake
5. Foss Lake
6. Ft. Cobb Lake
7. Grand Lake O' The Cherokees
8. Kaw Lake
9. Lake Eucha
10. Lake Texoma
11. Lake Thunderbird
12. Robert S. Kerr Lake
13. Skiatook Lake
14. Tenkiller Lake
15. Webber Falls Reservoir

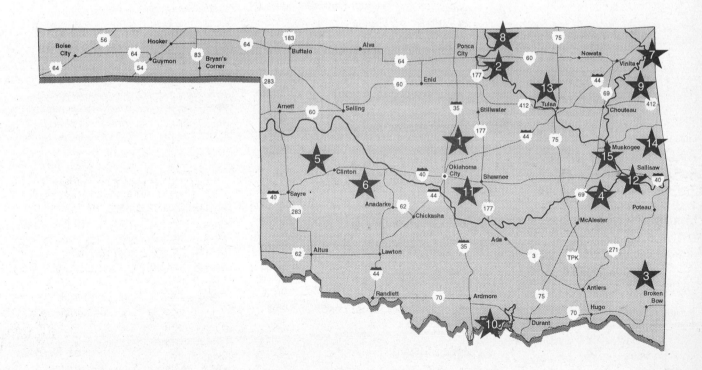

OKLAHOMA
ARCADIA LAKE - GRAND LAKE 'O CHEROKEES

ARCADIA LAKE

BAIT & TACKLE...

V C's Quick Mart
Arcadia 405-396-8990
Hours: 6am-11pm
Carries: Live bait, lures, maps, rods, reels, licenses
Bodies of water: Arcadia Lake, Deep Fork River
Services & Products: Food, beverages, gas/oil
OK to call for current conditions: Yes

ARKANSAS RIVER

BAIT & TACKLE...

Mack's Bait
RR 1 Box 111
Burbank 74633
Hours: 6:30am-7pm, closed Mon.
Carries: Live bait, lures, maps, rods, reels, licenses
Bodies of water: Arkansas River, Kaw Lake
Services & Products: Guide services, food, beverages, gas/oil, free advice on fishing
Guides: Yes
OK to call for current conditions: Yes
Contact: Mack

BROKEN BOW LAKE

BAIT & TACKLE...

Lakeside Grocery Bait & Tackle
Broken Bow 405-494-6540
Hours: 6am-8pm, 6am-4pm Sun.
Carries: Live bait, lures, maps, rods, reels, licenses
Bodies of water: Broken Bow Lake
Services & Products: Guide services, beverages, gas/oil, fishing instruction, repair services
Guides: Yes
OK to call for current conditions: Yes
Contact: Mike or Glenda Ward

EUFAULA LAKE

BAIT & TACKLE...

Frisbie's Fishing & Sporting
Checotah 918-473-5625
Hours: 8am-5pm, closed Sun.
Carries: Live bait, lures, maps, rods, reels, licenses
Bodies of water: Eufaula Lake, Webber Falls Res., Robert S. Kerr Lake
Guides: No
OK to call for current conditions: Yes
Contact: Jeanette Frisbie

FOSS LAKE

BAIT & TACKLE...

B & K Bait House
Foss 405-592-4518
Hours: Daylight-Dark
Carries: Live bait, lures, maps, rods, reels, licenses
Bodies of water: Foss Lake, Lugert Lake, Ft. Cobb Lake
Services & Products: Food, beverages, gas/oil, boat storage
Guides: Yes
OK to call for current conditions: Yes

FT. COBB LAKE

BAIT & TACKLE...

B & K Bait House
Foss 405-592-4518
Hours: daylite-dark
Carries: Live bait, lures, maps, rods, reels, licenses
Bodies of water: Foss Lake, Lugert Lake, Ft. Cobb Lake
Services & Products: Food, beverages, gas/oil, boat storage
Guides: Harry
OK to call for current conditions: Yes

GRAND LAKE O' THE CHEROKEES

GUIDES...

Lonnie Johnson
Commerce 918-675-4465
Species & Seasons: LM Bass Mar-Nov, Crappie, White Bass, Hybrid Bass Jan-Jan, Catfish Dec-Dec, Perch Mar-Oct
Bodies of water: Grand Lake O' The Cherokees, Lake Eucha
Rates: Half day: $100(1-2), Full day: $185(1-2)
Call between: 7am-7pm
Provides: Light tackle, heavy tackle, fly rod/reel, lures, bait, rain gear, beverages, lunch
Handicapped equipped: Yes
Certifications: Guiding since 1973, CPR course

Joy Swartz
Commerce 918-675-9985
Species & Seasons: LM Bass Mar-Dec, White Bass Feb-Dec, Crappie April-May, Catfish May, Bluegill May-June
Bodies of water: Grand Lake O' The Cherokees
Rates: Half day: $100(1-2), Full day: $185(1-2)
Call between: 6pm-10pm
Provides: Light tackle, heavy tackle, lures, bait, rain gear, beverages, lunch
Handicapped equipped: No

MARINAS...

Ballerina Pier 59
Grove 918-786-5357
Hours: 4:30am-5pm
Carries: Live bait, lures, licenses
Bodies of water: Grand Lake O' The Cherokees
Services & Products: Boat rentals, lodging, boat ramp, food, beverages, gas/oil, repair services, heated fishing dock
Guides: Yes
OK to call for current conditions: Yes
Contact: Raymond Horak

KAW LAKE - WEBBER FALLS RESERVOIR

OKLAHOMA

KAW LAKE

BAIT & TACKLE...

Mack's Bait
RR 1 Box 111
Burbank 74633
Hours: 6:30am-7pm, closed Mon.
Carries: Live bait, lures, maps, rods, reels, licenses
Bodies of water: Arkansas River, Kaw Lake
Services & Products: Guide services, food, beverages, gas/oil, free advice on fishing
Guides: Yes
OK to call for current conditions: Yes
Contact: Mack

LAKE EUCHA

GUIDES...

Lonnie Johnson
Commerce 918-675-4465
Species & Seasons: LM Bass Mar-Nov, Crappie, White Bass, Hybrid Bass Jan-Jan, Catfish Dec-Dec, Perch Mar-Oct
Bodies of water: Grand Lake O' The Cherokees, Lake Eucha
Rates: Half day: $100(1-2), Full day: $185(1-2)
Call between: 7am-7pm
Provides: Light tackle, heavy tackle, fly rod/reel, lures, bait, rain gear, beverages, lunch
Handicapped equipped: Yes
Certifications: Guiding since 1973, CPR course

LAKE TEXOMA

LODGING...

Caney Creek Resort
Kingston 800-772-4927
.... 405-564-4351
Guest Capacity: 60
Handicapped equipped: Yes
Seasons: All year
Rates: $55/day
Guides: Yes
Species & Seasons: Striped Bass, LM Bass, Catfish
Bodies of Water: Lake Texoma
Types of fishing: Fly fishing, light tackle, heavy tackle
Available: Fishing instruction, licenses, bait, tackle, family activities, restaurant, store, guide service

Lake Texoma Resort
Kingston 405-564-2311
Guest Capacity: 800
Handicapped equipped: Yes, semi
Seasons: All year
Rates: $40-$99
Contact: Kristi Putman
Guides: Yes
Species & Seasons: Striped Bass, Crappie, Catfish Mar-June, Sand Bass Sept-Nov
Bodies of Water: Lake Texoma
Types of fishing: Fly fishing, light tackle, heavy tackle
Available: Licenses, bait, tackle, boat rentals, family activities, children's program, baby sitting, bicycle rental, Go-Cart track, bumper boats

LAKE THUNDERBIRD

BAIT & TACKLE...

Jak's Feed Bag
Mc Loud 405-964-2800
Hours: 8am-Midnight
Carries: Live bait, lures, flies, rods, reels
Bodies of water: Shawnee ResLake Stanley, Dappke, Lake Thunderbird
Services & Products: Food, beverages
Guides: No
OK to call for current conditions: No

ROBERT S. KERR LAKE

BAIT & TACKLE...

Frisbie's Fishing & Sporting
Checotah 918-473-5625
Hours: 8am-5pm, closed Sun.
Carries: Live bait, lures, maps, rods, reels, licenses
Bodies of water: Eufaula Lake, Webber Falls Res., Robert S. Kerr Lake
Guides: No
OK to call for current conditions: Yes
Contact: Jeanette Frisbie

SKIATOOK LAKE

BAIT & TACKLE...

Greenwood Fishing Center & Motor Lodge
Skiatook 918-396-2626
Hours: 24hours
Carries: Live bait, lures, flies, maps, rods, reels, licenses
Bodies of water: Skiatook Lake
Services & Products: Guide services, lodging, food, beverages, gas/oil, fishing instruction, RV sites
Guides: Yes
OK to call for current conditions: Yes
Contact: Paul Greenwood

TENKILLER LAKE

MARINAS...

Sixshooter Resort & Marina
Cookson 918-457-5152
Hours: 8am-8pm
Carries: Live bait, licenses
Bodies of water: Tenkiller Lake
Services & Products: Boat rentals, lodging, boat ramp, food, beverages, gas/oil
Guides: Yes
OK to call for current conditions: Yes
Contact: Anyone

WEBBER FALLS RESERVOIR

BAIT & TACKLE...

Frisbie's Fishing & Sporting
Checotah 918-473-5625
Hours: 8am-5pm, closed Sun.
Carries: Live bait, lures, maps, rods, reels, licenses
Bodies of water: Eufaula Lake, Webber Falls Res., Robert S. Kerr Lake
Guides: No
OK to call for current conditions: Yes
Contact: Jeanette Frisbie

Look in the Species Index
to find service providers by species of fish

OREGON

1. Alsea River
2. Applegate Lake
3. Chetco River
4. Columbia River
5. Coquille River
6. Crane Prairie Reservoir
7. Deschutes River
8. Elk River
9. John Day River
10. Klamath Lake
11. McKenzie River
12. Nehalem River
13. Pacific Ocean
14. Prineville Reservoir
15. Regional Lakes & Rivers
16. Rogue River
17. Salmon River
18. Santiam River
19. Siletz River
20. Siltcoos Lake
21. Smith River
22. Tillamook Bay
23. Trask River
24. Tualatin River
25. Umpqua River
26. Willamette River

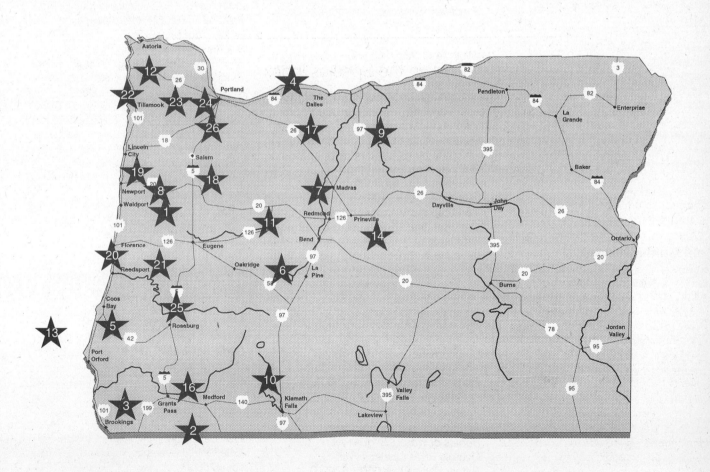

OREGON — ALSEA RIVER - CHETCO RIVER

ALSEA RIVER

GUIDES...

Oregon/Alaskan Outfitter & River Guide
Philomath 503-929-6955
Species & Seasons: Salmon May-Nov, Trout April-Sept, Steelhead Feb-Dec, SM Bass May-Oct
Bodies of water: Deschutes River, Umpqua River, John Day River, Nestucca River, Willamette River, Santiam River, Alsea River, Siletz Riverr, Rogue River, Alaskan trips also available
Rates: Call for rates
Provides: Light tackle, fly rod/reel, lunch
Handicapped equipped: Yes
Certifications: USCG

Roaring Fork Guide Service
Springfield 503-726-7234
Species & Seasons: Steelhead April-Oct/Oct-Mar, Chinook Salmon April-July/Sept-Dec, Trout April-Oct
Bodies of water: McKenzie River, Willamette River, Santiam River, Nestucca River, Alsea River, Siuslaw River, Smith River, Umpqua River, Coquille River, Rogue River, Elk River, Sixes River
Rates: Half day: $100(1), $175(2), Full day: $175(1), $250(2), multi-day discounts available
Call between: 6am-10pm
Provides: Light tackle, heavy tackle, fly rod/reel, lures, bait, rain gear, beverages, lunch
Handicapped equipped: Depends on disability

Sehl Guide Service
Tidewater 503-528-3382
Species & Seasons: Steelhead May-July/Dec-Feb, Sturgeon April-May, Chinook Salmon May-July/Sept-Nov
Bodies of water: Alsea Bay, Alsea River, Elk River, Sixes River, Siletz Riverr, Columbia River, Umpqua River, Santiam River, Willamette River
Rates: Full day: $100 pp, Senior discount
Call between: 7:30-8am/6-8pm
Provides: Light tackle, heavy tackle, lures, bait, beverages, lunch
Handicapped equipped: Yes
Certifications: USCG

Bob Zagorin
Eugene 503-344-9252
Species & Seasons: Trout May-Oct, Steelhead May-Dec/Nov-Mar
Bodies of water: McKenzie River, Willamette River, Smith River, Siletz Riverr, Alsea River, Siuslaw River
Rates: Half day: $125(1), $150(2), Full day: $175(1), $200(2)
Call between:
Provides: Light tackle, heavy tackle, fly rod/reel, lures, bait, rain gear, beverages, lunch
Handicapped equipped: Yes
Certifications: OSMB, OOA, McKenzie Guides Assoc.

APPLEGATE LAKE

GUIDES...

Jim Pringle Guide Service
Medford 503-535-3509
Species & Seasons: Salmon April-Dec, LM Bass, SM Bass, Crappie May-Sept, Rainbow Trout, Steelhead all year, Brook Trout May-Oct
Bodies of water: Rogue River, Hyatt Res., Chetco River, Emigrant Lake, Umpqua River, Klamath Lake, Lost Creek Res., Fish Lake, Applegate Lake, Lake of the Woods, Howard Prairie Lake
Rates: Half day: $75(2), Full day: $200(2), Chetco River: $250, Lake fishing: $50 pp
Call between: 8am-10pm
Provides: Light tackle, heavy tackle, fly rod/reel, lures, bait
Handicapped equipped: Yes
Certifications: USCG, O.S. Marine Board, Member & Past President of Rogue River Guides Assoc.

CHETCO RIVER

GUIDES...

Ross Bell
Gold Beach 503-247-2149
Species & Seasons: Chinook Salmon April-Nov, Steelhead Dec-Mar
Bodies of water: Rogue River, Coquille River, Chetco River
Rates: Half day: $100(1), $200(2), Full day: $125(1), $250(2)
Call between: Anytime
Provides: Light tackle, heavy tackle, lures, bait
Handicapped equipped: Yes
Certifications: USCG, OR Outfitter/Guide License

Gary and Val Early
Brookings 503-469-0525
.... 907-262-6132
Species & Seasons: Chinook Salmon Aug-Dec, Steelhead Sept-Mar, Salmon April-Aug
Bodies of water: Rogue River, Chetco River, Coquille River, Umpqua River, Smith River (California), Kenai River (Alaska)
Rates: Full day: $125(1), $250(2),
Call between: 5pm-9pm
Provides: Light tackle, heavy tackle, fly rod/reel, lures, bait
Handicapped equipped: Yes
Certifications: ORVIS, USCG, Red Cross

Jim Pringle Guide Service
Medford 503-535-3509
Species & Seasons: Salmon April-Dec, LM Bass, SM Bass, Crappie May-Sept, Rainbow Trout, Steelhead all year, Brook Trout May-Oct
Bodies of water: Rogue River, Hyatt Res., Chetco River, Emigrant Lake, Umpqua River, Klamath Lake, Lost Creek Res., Fish Lake, Applegate Lake, Lake of the Woods, Howard Prairie Lake
Rates: Half day: $75(2), Full day: $200(2), Chetco River: $250, Lake fishing: $50 pp
Call between: 8am-10pm
Provides: Light tackle, heavy tackle, fly rod/reel, lures, bait
Handicapped equipped: Yes
Certifications: USCG, O.S. Marine Board, Member and past President of Rogue River Guides Assoc.

Kern Grieve Guide Service
Trail 800-645-1624
Species & Seasons: Chinook Salmon May-Aug/July-Sept, Steelhead Aug-Nov/Nov-April
Bodies of water: Rogue River, South Umpqua River, Chetco River
Rates: Half day: $100(1), $200(2), Full day: $125(1), $250(2), 4day trip: $900 pp
Call between: 7am-9pm
Provides: Light tackle, heavy tackle, lures, bait, (beverages, lunch on some trips)
Handicapped equipped: Yes
Certifications: USCG, OSMB, BLM, USFS

Otter River Trips
Merlin 800-443-8590
Species & Seasons: Steelhead Nov-April, Coho Salmon May-Oct
Bodies of water: Chetco River, Rogue River
Rates: Half day: $80(1), $110(2), Full day: $90(1), $180(2)
Call between: 6am-9pm
Provides: Light tackle, fly rod/reel, lures, bait, rain gear
Handicapped equipped: No

Terry O'Conners Rogue Excursions
White City 503-826-6222
Species & Seasons: Salmon May-July/Aug/Nov-Dec, Steelhead Sept-Nov/Jan-April
Bodies of water: Rogue River, Chetco River, Elk River
Rates: Full day: $250(2)
Call between: 6pm-10pm
Provides: Light tackle, heavy tackle, fly rod/reel, lures, bait
Handicapped equipped: Yes
Certifications: USCG, OR Guides and Packers

COLUMBIA RIVER

GUIDES...

Columbia River Guide Service
Hermiston 800-821-2119
Species & Seasons: Walleye Feb-April/June-Oct, Sturgeon May-June, Steelhead Aug-Nov
Bodies of water: Columbia River, John Day River
Rates: Full day: $125(1), $250(2), $500(4)
Call between: Anytime
Provides: Light tackle, lures, bait, beverages
Handicapped equipped: No
Certifications: OR Guide License, USCG

Dean's Guide Service
Netarts 503-842-7107
.... 800-842-7107
Species & Seasons: Chinook Salmon April-June/Sept-Nov, Steelhead April-July, Sturgeon all year
Bodies of water: Trask River, Tillamook River, Wilson River, Nestucca River, Columbia River, Nehalem Bay, Nehalem River, Tillamook Bay

Rates: Full day: $115(1), $230(2)
Call between: 9am-9pm
Provides: Light tackle, heavy tackle, lures, bait
Handicapped equipped: Yes
Certifications: USCG/OSMB

Diamond D Guide Service
Sweet Home 800-347-4072
Species & Seasons: Chinook Salmon Sept-Nov/April-June, Steelhead all year, Walleye July-Sept, SM Bass May-Oct
Bodies of water: Columbia River, Willamette River, Tillamook Bay, Siletz River, Santiam River, coastal river systems
Rates: Half day: $75(1), $150(2), Full day: $125(1), $240(2)
Call between: 6-6:30am/8-11pm
Provides: Light tackle, heavy tackle
Certifications: USCG

Driftwood Enterprises
Sandy 503-668-5816
Species & Seasons: Chinook Salmon April-May, Sturgeon Feb-April/May-July/Oct-Nov, Shad May-July, Walleye July-Sept, Steelhead, Salmon Aug-Oct
Bodies of water: Columbia River
Rates: Half day: $35(1), Full day: $65(1)
Call between: 6pm-9pm
Provides: Light tackle, heavy tackle, fly rod/reel, lures, bait
Handicapped equipped: Yes

Fly By Nyte Guide Service
Hines 541-739-2770
Species & Seasons: Walleye Feb-Nov, SM Bass May-Nov, Steelhead Oct-Feb, Sturgeon May-Nov
Bodies of water: Columbia River, John Day River (Lower Arm)
Rates: Half day: $120(2) Full day: $115(1), $230(2)
Call between: 7am-9pm
Provides: Light tackle, heavy tackle, lures, bait, rain gear, beverages, lunch
Handicapped equipped: Yes
Certifications: USCG, fully insured

Terry Johnson
The Dalles 800-831-4107
Species & Seasons: Walleye Feb-Dec, Salmon April-Oct, Steelhead July-Nov
Bodies of water: Columbia River
Rates: Full day: $200(1)
Call between: 5pm-9:30pm
Provides: Light tackle, heavy tackle, lures, bait, beverages, lunch
Handicapped equipped: No
Certifications: USCG

Northwest River Guides
Beaverton 503-626-0829
Species & Seasons: Chinook Salmon April-June/Sept-Dec, Steelhead July-Sept/Dec-Mar, Trout June-July
Bodies of water: Tillamook Bay, Wilson River, Trask River, Nestucca River, Nehalem River, Willamette River, Columbia River, Clackamas River, Sandy River, Deschutes River, North Santiam River
Rates: Half day: $65(1), $130(2), Full day: $125(1), $250(2)
Call between: 5pm-9pm
Provides: Light tackle, fly rod/reel, lures, bait, rain gear, lunch
Handicapped equipped: Yes
Certifications: USCG, Swiftwater Rescue

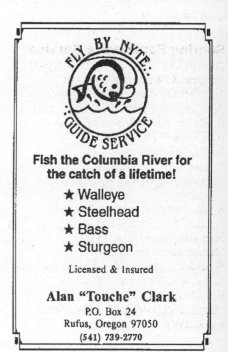

Fish the Columbia River for the catch of a lifetime!
★ Walleye
★ Steelhead
★ Bass
★ Sturgeon

Licensed & Insured

Alan "Touche" Clark
P.O. Box 24
Rufus, Oregon 97050
(541) 739-2770

Oregon Alaska Sportfishing
Tillamook 503-842-5171
Species & Seasons: Sturgeon Sept-June, Salmon April-June/Sept-Dec, Steelhead Dec-April
Bodies of water: Columbia River, North Coast of Oregon, North and South Coast of Oregon, Alaskan trips also available
Rates: Full day: $125(1), $250(2), multiple day charters by arrangement
Call between: 8am-8pm
Provides: Light tackle, heavy tackle, lures, bait
Handicapped equipped: Yes
Certifications: USCG, First aid/CPR Trained

OREGON

COLUMBIA RIVER - DESCHUTES RIVER

River's Bend Outfitters
The Dalles 503-296-5949
Species & Seasons: Walleye, Sturgeon Jan-Dec, Salmon Aug-Oct, Steelhead July-Feb, SM Bass May-Nov
Bodies of water: Columbia River, Deschutes River, John Day River
Rates: Full day: $125(1), $250(2), $450(4)
Call between: 6pm-12pm
Provides: Light tackle, heavy tackle, lures, bait, rain gear, beverages, lunch
Handicapped equipped: Yes

Sehl Guide Service
Tidewater 503-528-3382
Species & Seasons: Steelhead May-July/Dec-Feb, Sturgeon April-May, Chinook Salmon May-July/Sept-Nov
Bodies of water: Alsea Bay, Alsea River, Elk River, Sixes River, Siletz Riverr, Columbia River, Umpqua River, Santiam River, Willamette River
Rates: Full day: $100 pp, Senior discount
Call between: 7:30-8am/6-8pm
Provides: Light tackle, heavy tackle, lures, bait, beverages, lunch
Handicapped equipped: Yes
Certifications: USCG

Weston Charters
The Dalles 503-296-5776
Species & Seasons: Walleye all year, Salmon, Steelhead Aug-Oct, Sturgeon Summer-Fall
Bodies of water: Columbia River
Rates: Half day: $95(1), $190(2), Full day: $125(1), $250(2), up to 4 people, minimum 2
Call between: Anytime
Provides: Light tackle, heavy tckle, lures, bait, beverages, lunch
Handicapped equipped: No

COQUILLE RIVER

GUIDES...

Ross Bell
Gold Beach 503-247-2149
Species & Seasons: Chinook Salmon April-Nov, Steelhead Dec-Mar
Bodies of water: Rogue River, Coquille River, Chetco River
Rates: Half day: $100(1), $200(2), Full day: $125(1), $250(2)
Call between: Anytime
Provides: Light tackle, heavy tackle, lures, bait

Handicapped equipped: Yes
Certifications: USCG, OR Outfitter and Guide License

Gary and Val Early
Brookings 503-469-0525
.... 907-262-6132
Species & Seasons: Chinook Salmon Aug-Dec, Steelhead Sept-Mar, Salmon April-Aug
Bodies of water: Rogue River, Chetco River, Coquille River, Umpqua River, Smith River (California), Kenai River (Alaska)
Rates: Full day: $125(1), $250(2),
Call between: 5pm-9pm
Provides: Light tackle, heavy tackle, fly rod/reel, lures, bait
Handicapped equipped: Yes
Certifications: ORVIS, USCG, Red Cross

Larry's Guide Service
Roseburg 503-673-3099
Species & Seasons: Steelhead Dec-April/May-Nov, Salmon April-June/Oct-Jan, SM Bass June-Oct, Striped Bass April-June, Sturgeon May-July/Jan-Feb, Shad May-June, Trout April-July
Bodies of water: Rogue River, Umpqua River, Coquille River, Smith River, Sixes River, Elk River
Rates: Half day: $125(1-2), Full day: $125(1), $200(2), Sturgeon, Striped Bass: $125 pp
Call between: 5pm-10pm
Provides: Light tackle, heavy tackle, lures, bait, beverages
Handicapped equipped: Yes
Certifications: USCG, First aid, CPR

Michael's Guide Service
Glide 503-496-3627
Species & Seasons: Steelhead Jan-Dec, Salmon May-June/Aug-Dec, SM Bass May-Sept, Shad May-June
Bodies of water: Umpqua River, Coquille River, Elk River, Sixes River, Rogue River, Smith River
Rates: Full day: $125(1), $200(2), can take 3rd person
Call between: 8am-8pm
Provides: Light tackle, lures, bait
Handicapped equipped: No
Certifications: USCG

Roaring Fork Guide Service
Springfield 503-726-7234
Species & Seasons: Steelhead April-Oct/Oct-Mar, Chinook Salmon April-July/Sept-Dec, Trout April-Oct

Bodies of water: McKenzie River, Willamette River, Santiam River, Nestucca River, Alsea River, Siuslaw River, Smith River, Umpqua River, Coquille River, Rogue River, Elk River, Sixes River
Rates: Half day: $100(1), $175(2), Full day: $175(1), $250(2), multi-day discounts available
Call between: 6am-10pm
Provides: Light tackle, heavy tackle, fly rod/reel, lures, bait, rain gear, beverages, lunch
Handicapped equipped: Depends on disability

CRANE PRAIRIE RESERVOIR

GUIDES...

High Cascade Descent
Bend 503-389-0562
Species & Seasons: Trout April-Oct
Bodies of water: Deschutes River, Cascade Lakes, Crane Prairie Res., East Lake
Rates: Half day: $80(1), $160(2), Full day: $130(1), $200(2)
Call between: 6am-10pm
Provides: Light tackle, heavy tackle, fly rod/reel, lures, bait, rain gear, beverages, lunch
Handicapped equipped: Yes
Certifications: OR Outfitter/Guide

DESCHUTES RIVER

GUIDES...

Al's Wild Water Adventures
Creswell 800-289-4534
.... 503-895-4465
Species & Seasons: SM Bass Mar-Oct, Salmon, Steelhead all year, Rainbow Trout April-Oct
Bodies of water: John Day River, Rogue River, Owyhee River, Crooked River, Deschutes River, Grande Ronde River, McKenzie River, North Umpqua River, Main Umpqua River, South Umpqua River
Rates: Full day: $125(1) (average)
Call between: 9am-1pm
Provides: Light tackle, lures, rain gear, beverages, lunch
Handicapped equipped: Yes
Certifications: OR State Marine Board

DESCHUTES RIVER - ELK RIVER — OREGON

Jeff Carr
Eugene 503-344-7331
Species & Seasons: Steelhead all year, Trout April-Oct
Bodies of water: McKenzie River, Umpqua River, Deschutes River, Clearwater River (Idaho)
Rates: Half day: $150(1), $200(2), Full day: $250(1), $250(1-2)
Call between: 5pm-9pm
Provides: Fly rod/reel, beverages, lunch
Handicapped equipped: Yes
Certifications: OR Guides and Packers

High Cascade Descent
Bend 503-389-0562
Species & Seasons: Trout April-Oct
Bodies of water: Deschutes River, Cascade Lakes, Crane Prairie Res., East Lake
Rates: Half day: $80(1), $160(2), Full day: $130(1), $200(2)
Call between: 6am-10pm
Provides: Light tackle, heavy tackle, fly rod/reel, lures, bait, rain gear, beverages, lunch
Handicapped equipped: Yes
Certifications: OR Outfitter/Guide

High Desert Drifters Guides & Outfitters
Bend 503-389-0607
Species & Seasons: Rainbow Trout May-Oct, Brown Trout Feb-May, Steelhead Aug-Jan
Bodies of water: Deschutes River
Rates: Full day: $250(1), $300(2), 3-4 day trips: $200 pp
Call between: 8am-6pm
Provides: Fly rod/reel, beverages, lunch
Handicapped equipped: Yes
Certifications: OSMB, BLM

Lacy's Whitewater & Wild Fish
Bend 503-389-2434
.... 800-896-6157
Species & Seasons: SM Bass April-Oct, Steelhead July-Dec, Trout all year
Bodies of water: John Day River, Deschutes River, Cascade Lakes
Rates: Full day: $275(1), $325(2), Extended trips (2-6 days): $225 pp per day
Provides: Fly rod/reel, beverages, lunch
Handicapped equipped: Yes

Northwest River Guides
Beaverton 503-626-0829
Species & Seasons: Chinook Salmon April-June/Sept-Dec, Steelhead July-Sept/Dec-Mar, Trout June-July
Bodies of water: Tillamook Bay, Wilson River, Trask River, Nestucca River, Nehalem River, Willamette River, Columbia River, Clackamas River, Sandy River, Deschutes River, North Santiam River
Rates: Half day: $65(1), $130(2), Full day: $125(1), $250(2)
Call between: 5pm-9pm
Provides: Light tackle, fly rod/reel, lures, bait, rain gear, lunch
Handicapped equipped: Yes
Certifications: USCG, Swiftwater Rescue

Oregon/Alaskan Outfitter & River Guide
Philomath 503-929-6955
Species & Seasons: Salmon May-Nov, Trout April-Sept, Steelhead Feb-Dec, SM Bass May-Oct
Bodies of water: Deschutes River, Umpqua River, John Day River, Nestucca River, Willamette River, Santiam River, Alsea River, Siletz Riverr, Rogue River, Alaskan trips also available
Rates: Call for rates
Provides: Light tackle, fly rod/reel, lunch
Handicapped equipped: Yes
Certifications: USCG

River's Bend Outfitters
The Dalles 503-296-5949
Species & Seasons: Walleye, Sturgeon Jan-Dec, Salmon Aug-Oct, Steelhead July-Feb, SM Bass May-Nov
Bodies of water: Columbia River, Deschutes River, John Day River
Rates: Full day: $125(1), $250(2), $450(4)
Call between: 6pm-12pm
Provides: Light tackle, heavy tackle, lures, bait, rain gear, beverages, lunch
Handicapped equipped: Yes

Rodger Carbone's Fly-fishing Guide Service
Bend 503-389-7599
Species & Seasons: Rainbow Trout April-Nov, Steelhead Sept-Dec
Bodies of water: Deschutes River
Rates: 1 day trips: 2 or more people $145 pp, Multiple day trips: 4 or more people $205 pp per day, 2 people $245 pp per day
Call between: 7:30am-10pm

Provides: Beverages, lunch
Handicapped equipped: No
Certifications: BLM, OR Guides & Packers, OSMB

ELK RIVER
GUIDES...

Larry's Guide Service
Roseburg 503-673-3099
Species & Seasons: Steelhead Dec-April/May-Nov, Salmon April-June/Oct-Jan, SM Bass June-Oct, Striped Bass April-June, Sturgeon May-July/Jan-Feb, Shad May-June, Trout April-July
Bodies of water: Rogue River, Umpqua River, Coquille River, Smith River, Sixes River, Elk River
Rates: Half day: $125(1-2), Full day: $125(1), $200(2), Sturgeon, Striped Bass: $125 pp
Call between: 5pm-10pm
Provides: Light tackle, heavy tackle, lures, bait, beverages
Handicapped equipped: Yes
Certifications: USCG, First aid, CPR

Michael's Guide Service
Glide 503-496-3627
Species & Seasons: Steelhead Jan-Dec, Salmon May-June/Aug-Dec, SM Bass May-Sept, Shad May-June
Bodies of water: Umpqua River, Coquille River, Elk River, Sixes River, Rogue River, Smith River
Rates: Full day: $125(1), $200(2), can take 3rd person
Call between: 8am-8pm
Provides: Light tackle, lures, bait
Handicapped equipped: No
Certifications: USCG

Steve Neverick
Noti 503-935-4623
Species & Seasons: Steelhead Dec-Mar/July-Sept, Chinook Salmon April-June/July-Dec, Sturgeon Feb-July
Bodies of water: Umpqua River, Willamette River, Smith River, Sixes River, Elk River, Rogue River, Siuslaw River, McKenzie River
Rates: Half day: $125(1), $150(2), Full day: $200-$250(2)
Call between: 6pm-9pm
Provides: Light tackle, heavy tackle, fly rod/reel, lures, bait
Handicapped equipped: Depends
Certifications: USCG, OSMB

OREGON
ELK RIVER - JOHN DAY RIVER

Roaring Fork Guide Service
Springfield 503-726-7234
Species & Seasons: Steelhead April-Oct/Oct-Mar, Chinook Salmon April-July/Sept-Dec, Trout April-Oct
Bodies of water: McKenzie River, Willamette River, Santiam River, Nestucca River, Alsea River, Siuslaw River, Smith River, Umpqua River, Coquille River, Rogue River, Elk River, Sixes River
Rates: Half day: $100(1), $175(2), Full day: $175(1), $250(2), multi-day discounts available
Call between: 6am-10pm
Provides: Light tackle, heavy tackle, fly rod/reel, lures, bait, rain gear, beverages, lunch
Handicapped equipped: Depends on disability

Sehl Guide Service
Tidewater 503-528-3382
Species & Seasons: Steelhead May-July/Dec-Feb, Sturgeon April-May, Chinook Salmon May-July/Sept-Nov
Bodies of water: Alsea Bay, Alsea River, Elk River, Sixes River, Siletz Riverr, Columbia River, Umpqua River, Santiam River, Willamette River
Rates: Full day: $100 pp, Senior discount
Call between: 7:30-8am/6-8pm
Provides: Light tackle, heavy tackle, lures, bait, beverages, lunch
Handicapped equipped: Yes
Certifications: USCG

Terry O'Conners Rogue Excursions
White City 503-826-6222
Species & Seasons: Salmon May-July/Aug/Nov-Dec, Steelhead Sept-Nov/Jan-April
Bodies of water: Rogue River, Chetco River, Elk River
Rates: Full day: $250(2)
Call between: 6pm-10pm
Provides: Light tackle, heavy tackle, fly rod/reel, lures, bait
Handicapped equipped: Yes
Certifications: USCG, OR Guides and Packers

LODGES...

Hannah Fishing Camp
Elkton 800-459-2525
.... 503-459-2575
Guest Capacity: 8
Handicapped equipped: No
Seasons: All year
Rates: $150/day
Contact: Denny Hannah
Guides: Yes
Species & Seasons: Steelhead Jan-Mar, Striped Bass April-June, Sturgeon May-Aug, SM Bass May-Oct, Salmon Sept-Jan, Shad April-July
Bodies of Water: Umpqua River, Rogue River, John Day River, Elk River, Sixes River
Types of fishing: Fly fishing, light tackle, big fish
Available: Fishing instruction, bait, tackle, family activities

JOHN DAY RIVER

GUIDES...

Al's Wild Water Adventures
Creswell 800-289-4534
.... 503-895-4465
Species & Seasons: SM Bass Mar-Oct, Salmon, Steelhead all year, Rainbow Trout April-Oct
Bodies of water: John Day River, Rogue River, Owyhee River, Crooked River, Deschutes River, Grande Ronde River, McKenzie River, North Umpqua River, Main Umpqua River, South Umpqua River
Rates: Full day: $125(1) (average)
Call between: 9am-1pm
Provides: Light tackle, lures, rain gear, beverages, lunch
Handicapped equipped: Yes
Certifications: OR State Marine Board

Columbia River Guide Service
Hermiston 800-821-2119
Species & Seasons: Walleye Feb-April/June-Oct, Sturgeon May-June, Steelhead Aug-Nov
Bodies of water: Columbia River, John Day River
Rates: Full day: $125(1), $250(2), $500(4)
Call between: Anytime
Provides: Light tackle, lures, bait, beverages
Handicapped equipped: No
Certifications: OR Guide License, USCG

Fly By Nyte Guide Service
Hines 541-739-2770
Species & Seasons: Walleye Feb-Nov, SM Bass May-Nov, Steelhead Oct-Feb, Sturgeon May-Nov
Bodies of water: Columbia River, John Day River (Lower Arm)
Rates: Half day: $120(2), Full day: $115(1), $230(2)
Call between: 7am-9pm
Provides: Light tackle, heavy tackle, lures, bait, rain gear, beverages, lunch
Handicapped equipped: Yes
Certifications: USCG, fully insured

Lacy's Whitewater & Wild Fish
Bend 503-389-2434
.... 800-896-6157
Species & Seasons: SM Bass April-Oct, Steelhead July-Dec, Trout all year
Bodies of water: John Day River, Deschutes River, Cascade Lakes
Rates: Full day: $275(1), $325(2), Extended trips (2-6 days): $225 pp per day
Provides: Fly rod/reel, beverages, lunch
Handicapped equipped: Yes

Oregon/Alaskan Outfitter & River Guide
Philomath 503-929-6955
Species & Seasons: Salmon May-Nov, Trout April-Sept, Steelhead Feb-Dec, SM Bass May-Oct
Bodies of water: Deschutes River, Umpqua River, John Day River, Nestucca River, Willamette River, Santiam River, Alsea River, Siletz Riverr, Rogue River, Alaskan trips also available
Rates: Call for rates
Provides: Light tackle, fly rod/reel, lunch
Handicapped equipped: Yes
Certifications: USCG

River's Bend Outfitters
The Dalles 503-296-5949
Species & Seasons: Walleye, Sturgeon Jan-Dec, Salmon Aug-Oct, Steelhead July-Feb, SM Bass May-Nov
Bodies of water: Columbia River, Deschutes River, John Day River
Rates: Full day: $125(1), $250(2), $450(4)
Call between: 6pm-12pm
Provides: Light tackle, heavy tackle, lures, bait, rain gear, beverages, lunch
Handicapped equipped: Yes

JOHN DAY RIVER - MCKENZIE RIVER — OREGON

LODGES...

Hannah Fishing Camp
Elkton 800-459-2525
.... 503-459-2575
Guest Capacity: 8
Handicapped equipped: No
Seasons: All year
Rates: $150/day
Contact: Denny Hannah
Guides: Yes
Species & Seasons: Steelhead Jan-Mar, Striped Bass April-June, Sturgeon May-Aug, SM Bass May-Oct, Salmon Sept-Jan, Shad April-July
Bodies of Water: Umpqua River, Rogue River, John Day River, Elk River, Sixes River
Types of fishing: Fly fishing, light tackle, big fish
Available: Fishing instruction, bait, tackle, family activities

KLAMATH LAKE

GUIDES...

Jim Pringle Guide Service
Medford 503-535-3509
Species & Seasons: Salmon April-Dec, LM Bass, SM Bass, Crappie May-Sept, Rainbow Trout, Steelhead all year, Brook Trout May-Oct
Bodies of water: Rogue River, Hyatt Res., Chetco River, Emigrant Lake, Umpqua River, Klamath Lake, Lost Creek Res., Fish Lake, Applegate Lake, Lake of the Woods, Howard Prairie Lake
Rates: Half day: $75(2), Full day: $200(2), Chetco River: $250, Lake fishing: $50 pp
Call between: 8am-10pm
Provides: Light tackle, heavy tackle, fly rod/reel, lures, bait
Handicapped equipped: Yes
Certifications: USCG, O.S. Marine Board, Member and past President of Rogue River Guides Assoc.

MCKENZIE RIVER

GUIDES...

Al's Wild Water Adventures
Creswell 800-289-4534
.... 503-895-4465
Species & Seasons: SM Bass Mar-Oct, Salmon, Steelhead all year, Rainbow Trout April-Oct
Bodies of water: John Day River, Rogue River, Owyhee River, Crooked River, Deschutes River, Grande Ronde River, McKenzie River, North Umpqua River, Main Umpqua River, South Umpqua River
Rates: Full day: $125(1) (average)
Call between: 9am-1pm
Provides: Light tackle, lures, rain gear, beverages, lunch
Handicapped equipped: Yes
Certifications: OR State Marine Board

Brad Edwards River Outfitter
Leaburg 503-896-3547
Species & Seasons: Salmon May-July, Trout April-Oct, Steelhead April-Dec
Bodies of water: McKenzie River
Rates: Full day: $200(2)
Call between: 5pm-9pm
Provides: Light tackle, heavy tackle, fly rod/reel, lures, bait, lunch
Handicapped equipped: Yes
Certifications: OSMB

Jeff Carr
Eugene 503-344-7331
Species & Seasons: Steelhead all year, Trout April-Oct
Bodies of water: McKenzie River, Umpqua River, Deschutes River, Clearwater River (Idaho)
Rates: Half day: $150(1), $200(2), Full day: $250(1), $250(1-2)
Call between: 5pm-9pm
Provides: Fly rod/reel, beverages, lunch
Handicapped equipped: Yes
Certifications: OR Guides and Packers

Helfrich River Outfitter, Inc.
Vida 503-896-3786
Species & Seasons: Rainbow Trout May-Nov, Cutthroat Trout June-Sept, Steelhead Sept-Dec
Bodies of water: McKenzie River, Middle Fork of Salmon River, Lower Main Salmon River, Rogue River
Rates: Full day: $150(1), $200(2), 4 days: $880, 6 days: $1800
Call between: 8am-10pm
Provides: Fly rod/reel, lures, beverages, lunch
Handicapped equipped: Yes

Steve Neverick
Noti 503-935-4623
Species & Seasons: Steelhead Dec-Mar/July-Sept, Chinook Salmon April-June/July-Dec, Sturgeon Feb-July
Bodies of water: Umpqua River, Willamette River, Smith River, Sixes River, Elk River, Rogue River, Siuslaw River, McKenzie River
Rates: Half day: $125(1), $150(2), Full day: $200-$250(2)
Call between: 6pm-9pm
Provides: Light tackle, heavy tackle, fly rod/reel, lures, bait
Handicapped equipped: Depends
Certifications: USCG, OSMB

Chris Olsen
Vida 503-953-6453
Species & Seasons: Trout April-June, Native Trout June-Aug, Steelhead Sept-Oct/Dec-April
Bodies of water: McKenzie River, Middle Fork of the Salmon River, Rogue River
Rates: Half day: $175(2), Full day: $210(2), rates vary with different rivers
Call between: 6pm-9pm
Provides: Light tackle, heavy tackle, fly rod/reel, lures, bait, beverages, lunch
Handicapped equipped: No
Certifications: License and Insured OR, WA, ID

Roaring Fork Guide Service
Springfield 503-726-7234
Species & Seasons: Steelhead April-Oct/Oct-Mar, Chinook Salmon April-July/Sept-Dec, Trout April-Oct
Bodies of water: McKenzie River, Willamette River, Santiam River, Nestucca River, Alsea River, Siuslaw River, Smith River, Umpqua River, Coquille River, Rogue River, Elk River, Sixes River
Rates: Half day: $100(1), $175(2), Full day: $175(1), $250(2), multi-day discounts available
Call between: 6am-10pm
Provides: Light tackle, heavy tackle, fly rod/reel, lures, bait, rain gear, beverages, lunch
Handicapped equipped: Depends on disability

OREGON
MCKENZIE RIVER - PACIFIC OCEAN

Wilderness River Outfitters
Springfield 503-726-9471
Species & Seasons: Trout May-Oct, SM Bass June-Sept, Steelhead May-Oct, Salmon Oct-Nov/May-June
Bodies of water: McKenzie River, Willamette River, Umpqua River, Lower Main Salmon River
Rates: Full day: $225(1-2), Salmon: $250
Call between: 8am-4:30pm
Provides: Light tackle, heavy tackle, fly rod/reel, lures, bait, lunch
Handicapped equipped: Yes
Certifications: OSMB

Bob Zagorin
Eugene 503-344-9252
Species & Seasons: Trout May-Oct, Steelhead May-Dec/Nov-Mar
Bodies of water: McKenzie River, Willamette River, Smith River, Siletz Riverr, Alsea River, Siuslaw River
Rates: Half day: $125(1), $150(2), Full day: $175(1), $200(2)
Call between:
Provides: Light tackle, heavy tackle, fly rod/reel, lures, bait, rain gear, beverages, lunch
Handicapped equipped: Yes
Certifications: OSMB, OOA, McKenzie Guides Assoc.

NEHALEM RIVER

GUIDES...

Dean's Guide Service
Netarts 503-842-7107
.... 800-842-7107
Species & Seasons: Chinook Salmon April-June/Sept-Nov, Steelhead April-July, Sturgeon all year
Bodies of water: Trask River, Tillamook River, Wilson River, Nestucca River, Columbia River, Nehalem Bay, Nehalem River, Tillamook Bay
Rates: Full day: $115(1), $230(2)
Call between: 9am-9pm
Provides: Light tackle, heavy tackle, lures, bait
Handicapped equipped: Yes
Certifications: USCG/OSMB

Northwest River Guides
Beaverton 503-626-0829
Species & Seasons: Chinook Salmon April-June/Sept-Dec, Steelhead July-Sept/Dec-Mar, Trout June-July

Bodies of water: Tillamook Bay, Wilson River, Trask River, Nestucca River, Nehalem River, Willamette River, Columbia River, Clackamas River, Sandy River, Deschutes River, North Santiam River
Rates: Half day: $65(1), $130(2), Full day: $125(1), $250(2)
Call between: 5pm-9pm
Provides: Light tackle, fly rod/reel, lures, bait, rain gear, lunch
Handicapped equipped: Yes
Certifications: USCG, Swiftwater Rescue

MARINAS...

Old Mill Marina
Garibaldi 503-322-0324
Carries: Live bait, lures, flies, maps, rods, reels, licenses
Bodies of water: Pacific Ocean, Wilson River, Nehalem River, Trask River
Services & Products: Boat rentals, guide services, lodging, boat ramp, food, beverages, gas/oil, fishing instruction
Guides: Yes
OK to call for current conditions: Yes
Contact: Steve, Rick or Terry

PACIFIC OCEAN

CHARTERS...

Bobs Sportfishing
Charleston 800-628-9633
.... 503-888-4241
Species & Seasons: Halibut May-June, Bottom Fish Mar-Sept, Salmon June-Aug, Tuna Aug
Bodies of water: Pacific Ocean
Rates: 6 hrs: $55(pp), 12 hrs: $110(pp)
Call between: 8am-8pm
Provides: Light tackle, heavy tackle, fly rod/reel, bait
Handicapped equipped: Yes
Certifications: USCG

Garibaldi/D & D Charters
Garibaldi 800-900-4665
.... 503-322-0381
Species & Seasons: Bottom Fish April-Oct, Coho Salmon July-?, Chinook Salmon Sept-Nov, Halibut Aug-?
Bodies of water: Pacific Ocean, Tillamook Bay
Rates: Half day: $45(1), Full day: $60-$70(1), rates vary with type of trip taken
Call between: 6am-9pm

Provides: Light tackle, heavy tackle, lures, bait, beverages (coffee only)
Handicapped equipped: Yes
Certifications: USCG

Tradewinds Ocean Sportfishing
Depoe Bay 800-445-8730
.... 503-765-2345
Species & Seasons: Halibut May-Sept, Bottom Fish, Rockfish all year, Salmon May-July/Sept-Nov, Tuna, Albacore Aug-Nov
Bodies of water: Depoe Bay, Pacific Ocean
Rates: Half day: $45(1-2), Full day: $70(1-2), other options available, group rates
Call between: Anytime
Provides: Light tackle, heavy tackle, lures, bait, rain gear, coffee
Handicapped equipped: Yes
Certifications: 12 vessels all USCG certified

LODGES...

Elkqua Lodge
Elkton 503-584-2161
Guest Capacity: 8-10
Handicapped equipped: No
Seasons: All year
Rates: $50-$75/day
Guides: Yes
Species & Seasons: Chinook Salmon Spring-Fall, SM Bass May-Oct, Shad April-July, Sturgeon, Striped Bass, Steelhead all year
Bodies of Water: Umpqua River, coastal lakes, Pacific Ocean
Types of fishing: Fly fishing, light tackle, heavy tackle, float trips
Available: Fishing instruction, licenses, bait, tackle, family activities, baby sitting

MARINAS...

Old Mill Marina
Garibaldi 503-322-0324
Carries: Live bait, lures, flies, maps, rods, reels, licenses
Bodies of water: Pacific Ocean, Wilson River, Nehalem River, Trask River
Services & Products: Boat rentals, guide services, lodging, boat ramp, food, beverages, gas/oil, fishing instruction
Guides: Yes
OK to call for current conditions: Yes
Contact: Steve, Rick or Terry

PRINEVILLE RESERVOIR - ROGUE RIVER OREGON

PRINEVILLE RESERVOIR

LODGES...

Prineville Reservoir Resort, Inc.
Prineville 503-447-7468
Handicapped equipped: Yes
Seasons: Mar 1 to Oct 15
Rates: Varies
Contact: Laura Hawes
Guides: No
Species & Seasons: Crappie May-Aug, Trout April-June, LM Bass, SM Bass May-Aug, Catfish Mar-Sept
Bodies of Water: Prineville Reservoir
Types of fishing: Fly fishing, light tackle, heavy tackle
Available: Licenses, bait, tackle, boat rentals, family activities

REGIONAL LAKES & RIVERS

GUIDES...

Cornucopia Wilderness Pack Station
Richland 503-893-6400
.... 742-5400
Species & Seasons: Brook Trout, Bull Trout July-Oct, Crappie, SM Bass, Catfish April-Oct, Sturgeon Mar-Oct
Bodies of water: Snake River, Hells Canyon Res., Highland Lakes by horse
Rates: Half day: $125(1), $200(2), Full day: $225(1), $400(2)
Call between: 6am-7pm
Provides: Bait, rain gear, lunch
Handicapped equipped: No

Mike Laverty Professional River Guide
Forest Grove 503-357-5732
Species & Seasons: Chinook Salmon April-June/Sept-Dec, Steelhead April-Oct/Dec-April
Bodies of water: Oregon's premier Central and North Coast rivers
Rates: Full day: $125(1), $225(2)
Call between: 8am-9pm
Provides: Light tackle, heavy tackle, lures, bait
Handicapped equipped: Yes
Certifications: First aid, CPR Certified

Wapiti River Guides
Riggins, ID 800-488-9872
Species & Seasons: Steelhead Jan-April, Trout Mar-Oct, Bass April-Aug
Bodies of water: Grande Ronde River (OR), Salmon River (ID)
Rates: From: $125-$250/day
Call between: 6am-10pm
Provides: Light tackle, lures, rain gear, beverages, lunch
Handicapped equipped: Yes
Certifications: Licensed in Oregon and Idaho

ROGUE RIVER

GUIDES...

Al's Wild Water Adventures
Creswell 800-289-4534
.... 503-895-4465
Species & Seasons: SM Bass Mar-Oct, Salmon, Steelhead all year, Rainbow Trout April-Oct
Bodies of water: John Day River, Rogue River, Owyhee River, Crooked River, Deschutes River, Grande Ronde River, McKenzie River, North Umpqua River, Main Umpqua River, South Umpqua River
Rates: Full day: $125(1) (average)
Call between: 9am-1pm
Provides: Light tackle, lures, rain gear, beverages, lunch
Handicapped equipped: Yes
Certifications: OR State Marine Board

Beaver State Adventures
Klamath Falls 800-644-2920
Species & Seasons: Steelhead July-April, Salmon April-Nov
Bodies of water: Rogue River
Rates: Half day: $100, Full day: $150 pp up to 4
Call between: Anytime
Provides: Light tackle, fly rod/reel, lures, bait
Handicapped equipped: Yes
Certifications: OR Guide/Outfitter, USCG

Ross Bell
Gold Beach 503-247-2149
Species & Seasons: Chinook Salmon April-Nov, Steelhead Dec-Mar
Bodies of water: Rogue River, Coquille River, Chetco River
Rates: Half day: $100(1), $200(2), Full day: $125(1), $250(2)
Call between: Anytime
Provides: Light tackle, heavy tackle, lures, bait
Handicapped equipped: Yes
Certifications: USCG, OR Outfitter and Guide License

Gary and Val Early
Brookings 503-469-0525
.... 907-262-6132
Species & Seasons: Chinook Salmon Aug-Dec, Steelhead Sept-Mar, Salmon April-Aug
Bodies of water: Rogue River, Chetco River, Coquille River, Umpqua River, Smith River (California), Kenai River (Alaska)
Rates: Full day: $125(1), $250(2),
Call between: 5pm-9pm
Provides: Light tackle, heavy tackle, fly rod/reel, lures, bait
Handicapped equipped: Yes
Certifications: ORVIS, USCG, Red Cross

Helfrich River Outfitter, Inc.
Vida 503-896-3786
Species & Seasons: Rainbow Trout May-Nov, Cutthroat Trout June-Sept, Steelhead Sept-Dec
Bodies of water: McKenzie River, Middle Fork of Salmon River, Lower Main Salmon River, Rogue River
Rates: Full day: $150(1), $200(2), 4 days: $880, 6 days: $1800
Call between: 8am-10pm
Provides: Fly rod/reel, lures, beverages, lunch
Handicapped equipped: Yes

Jim Pringle Guide Service
Medford 503-535-3509
Species & Seasons: Salmon April-Dec, LM Bass, SM Bass, Crappie May-Sept, Rainbow Trout, Steelhead all year, Brook Trout May-Oct
Bodies of water: Rogue River, Hyatt Res., Chetco River, Emigrant Lake, Umpqua River, Klamath Lake, Lost Creek Res., Fish Lake, Applegate Lake, Lake of the Woods, Howard Prairie Lake
Rates: Half day: $75(2), Full day: $200(2), Chetco River: $250, Lake fishing: $50 pp
Call between: 8am-10pm
Provides: Light tackle, heavy tackle, fly rod/reel, lures, bait
Handicapped equipped: Yes
Certifications: USCG, O.S. Marine Board, Member and past President of Rogue River Guides Assoc.

OREGON — ROGUE RIVER

Kern Grieve Guide Service
Trail 800-645-1624
Species & Seasons: Chinook Salmon May-Aug/July-Sept, Steelhead Aug-Nov/Nov-April
Bodies of water: Rogue River, South Umpqua River, Chetco River
Rates: Half day: $100(1), $200(2), Full day: $125(1), $250(2), 4day trip: $900 pp
Call between: 7am-9pm
Provides: Light tackle, heavy tackle, lures, bait, (beverages, lunch on some trips)
Handicapped equipped: Yes
Certifications: USCG, OSMB, BLM, USFS

Larry's Guide Service
Roseburg 503-673-3099
Species & Seasons: Steelhead Dec-April/May-Nov, Salmon April-June/Oct-Jan, SM Bass June-Oct, Striped Bass April-June, Sturgeon May-July/Jan-Feb, Shad May-June, Trout April-July
Bodies of water: Rogue River, Umpqua River, Coquille River, Smith River, Sixes River, Elk River
Rates: Half day: $125(1-2), Full day: $125(1), $200(2), Sturgeon, Striped Bass: $125 pp
Call between: 5pm-10pm
Provides: Light tackle, heavy tackle, lures, bait, beverages
Handicapped equipped: Yes
Certifications: USCG, First aid, CPR

Michael's Guide Service
Glide 503-496-3627
Species & Seasons: Steelhead Jan-Dec, Salmon May-June/Aug-Dec, SM Bass May-Sept, Shad May-June
Bodies of water: Umpqua River, Coquille River, Elk River, Sixes River, Rogue River, Smith River
Rates: Full day: $125(1), $200(2), can take 3rd person
Call between: 8am-8pm
Provides: Light tackle, lures, bait
Handicapped equipped: No
Certifications: USCG

Steve Neverick
Noti 503-935-4623
Species & Seasons: Steelhead Dec-Mar/July-Sept, Chinook Salmon April-June/July-Dec, Sturgeon Feb-July
Bodies of water: Umpqua River, Willamette River, Smith River, Sixes River, Elk River, Rogue River, Siuslaw River, McKenzie River

Rates: Half day: $125(1), $150(2), Full day: $200-$250(2)
Call between: 6pm-9pm
Provides: Light tackle, heavy tackle, fly rod/reel, lures, bait
Handicapped equipped: Depends
Certifications: USCG, OSMB

Chris Olsen
Vida 503-953-6453
Species & Seasons: Trout April-June, Native Trout June-Aug, Steelhead Sept-Oct/Dec-April
Bodies of water: McKenzie River, Middle Fork of the Salmon River, Rogue River
Rates: Half day: $175(2), Full day: $210(2), rates vary with different rivers
Call between: 6pm-9pm
Provides: Light tackle, heavy tackle, fly rod/reel, lures, bait, beverages, lunch
Handicapped equipped: No
Certifications: License and Insured OR, WA, ID

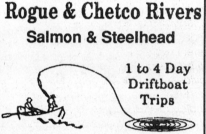

Rogue & Chetco Rivers
Salmon & Steelhead
1 to 4 Day Driftboat Trips
Lodging & Meals at Historic Lodges
1 (800) 336-1647
1 (541) 479-9554
ROGUE WILDERNESS, INC.
PO Box 1110 • Merlin, OR 97532

Oregon/Alaskan Outfitter & River Guide
Philomath 503-929-6955
Species & Seasons: Salmon May-Nov, Trout April-Sept, Steelhead Feb-Dec, SM Bass May-Oct
Bodies of water: Deschutes River, Umpqua River, John Day River, Nestucca River, Willamette River, Santiam River, Alsea River, Siletz River, Rogue River, Alaskan trips also available
Rates: Call for rates
Provides: Light tackle, fly rod/reel, lunch
Handicapped equipped: Yes
Certifications: USCG

Otter River Trips
Merlin 800-443-8590
Species & Seasons: Steelhead Nov-April, Coho Salmon May-Oct
Bodies of water: Chetco River, Rogue River
Rates: Half day: $80(1), $110(2), Full day: $90(1), $180(2)
Call between: 6am-9pm
Provides: Light tackle, fly rod/reel, lures, bait, rain gear
Handicapped equipped: No

Roaring Fork Guide Service
Springfield 503-726-7234
Species & Seasons: Steelhead April-Oct/Oct-Mar, Chinook Salmon April-July/Sept-Dec, Trout April-Oct
Bodies of water: McKenzie River, Willamette River, Santiam River, Nestucca River, Alsea River, Siuslaw River, Smith River, Umpqua River, Coquille River, Rogue River, Elk River, Sixes River
Rates: Half day: $100(1), $175(2), Full day: $175(1), $250(2), multi-day discounts available
Call between: 6am-10pm
Provides: Light tackle, heavy tackle, fly rod/reel, lures, bait, rain gear, beverages, lunch
Handicapped equipped: Depends on disability

Rogue Wilderness Inc.
Merlin 800-336-1647
Species & Seasons: Chinook Salmon May-June/Aug-Oct, Steelhead, Coho Salmon, Aug-Oct
Bodies of water: Rogue River
Rates: Full day: $206(minimum 2), 3-4 days with lodging: $750 and $875
Call between: 8am-8pm
Provides: Fly rod/reel, lures, bait, beverages, lunch
Handicapped equipped: Yes

Terry O'Conners Rogue Excursions
White City 503-826-6222
Species & Seasons: Salmon May-July/Aug/Nov-Dec, Steelhead Sept-Nov/Jan-April
Bodies of water: Rogue River, Chetco River, Elk River
Rates: Full day: $250(2)
Call between: 6pm-10pm
Provides: Light tackle, heavy tackle, fly rod/reel, lures, bait
Handicapped equipped: Yes
Certifications: USCG, OR Guides and Packers

ROGUE RIVER - SANTIAM RIVER — OREGON

Umpqua River Adventures
Roseburg 503-673-6355
Species & Seasons: Chinook Salmon April-July/Aug-Sept, Steelhead May-Sept/Dec-Mar, Coho Salmon Sept-Dec, Shad May-July
Bodies of water: Umpqua River, Rouge River
Rates: Umpqua River: $75 (6hrs), Rogue River: Half day: $125(1), $250(2)
Call between: Anytime
Provides: Light tackle, heavy tackle, lures, bait
Handicapped equipped: No
Certifications: OSMB, USCG

LODGES...

Hannah Fishing Camp
Elkton 800-459-2525
.... 503-459-2575
Guest Capacity: 8
Handicapped equipped: No
Seasons: All year
Rates: $150/day
Contact: Denny Hannah
Guides: Yes
Species & Seasons: Steelhead Jan-Mar, Striped Bass April-June, Sturgeon May-Aug, SM Bass May-Oct, Salmon Sept-Jan, Shad April-July
Bodies of Water: Umpqua River, Rogue River, John Day River, Elk River, Sixes River
Types of fishing: Fly fishing, light tackle, big fish
Available: Fishing instruction, bait, tackle, family activities

Morrison's Rogue River Lodge
Merlin 503-476-3825
Handicapped equipped: No
Seasons: May 1 to Nov 15
Rates: Summer: $80/pp day, Fall: $120/pp day
Contact: Michelle Hanten
Guides: Yes
Species & Seasons: Steelhead Sept-Nov, Salmon May-June, Salmon Sept
Bodies of Water: Rogue River
Types of fishing: Fly fishing, light tackle, wading, float trips
Available: Licenses, family activities, rafting

SALMON RIVER

GUIDES...

Helfrich River Outfitter, Inc.
Vida 503-896-3786
Species & Seasons: Rainbow Trout May-Nov, Cutthroat Trout June-Sept, Steelhead Sept-Dec
Bodies of water: McKenzie River, Middle Fork of Salmon River, Lower Main Salmon River, Rogue River
Rates: Full day: $150(1), $200(2), 4 days: $880, 6 days: $1800
Call between: 8am-10pm
Provides: Fly rod/reel, lures, beverages, lunch
Handicapped equipped: Yes

Chris Olsen
Vida 503-953-6453
Species & Seasons: Trout April-June, Native Trout June-Aug, Steelhead Sept-Oct/Dec-April
Bodies of water: McKenzie River, Middle Fork of the Salmon River, Rogue River
Rates: Half day: $175(2), Full day: $210(2), rates vary with different rivers
Call between: 6pm-9pm
Provides: Light tackle, heavy tackle, fly rod/reel, lures, bait, beverages, lunch
Handicapped equipped: No
Certifications: License and Insured OR, WA, ID

Solitude River Trips
Merlin 800-396-1776
Species & Seasons: Cutthroat Trout June-Sept
Bodies of water: Middle Fork of the Salmon River
Rates: 6 days: $1685 pp
Call between: 8am-8pm
Provides: Light tackle, heavy tackle, fly rod/reel, lures, bait, rain gear, beverages, lunch
Handicapped equipped: No
Certifications: ORVIS, USCG, US Forest Service, State of Idaho

Wilderness River Outfitters
Springfield 503-726-9471
Species & Seasons: Trout May-Oct, SM Bass June-Sept, Steelhead May-Oct, Salmon Oct-Nov/May-June
Bodies of water: McKenzie River, Willamette River, Umpqua River, Lower Main Salmon River

Rates: Full day: $225(1-2), Salmon: $250
Call between: 8am-4:30pm
Provides: Light tackle, heavy tackle, fly rod/reel, lures, bait, lunch
Handicapped equipped: Yes
Certifications: OSMB

SANTIAM RIVER

GUIDES...

Diamond D Guide Service
Sweet Home 800-347-4072
Species & Seasons: Chinook Salmon Sept-Nov/April-June, Steelhead all year, Walleye July-Sept, SM Bass May-Oct
Bodies of water: Columbia River, Willamette River, Tillamook Bay, Siletz Riverr, Santiam River, coastal river systems
Rates: Half day: $75(1), $150(2), Full day: $125(1), $240(2)
Call between: 6-6:30am/8-11pm
Provides: Light tackle, heavy tackle
Certifications: USCG

Northwest River Guides
Beaverton 503-626-0829
Species & Seasons: Chinook Salmon April-June/Sept-Dec, Steelhead July-Sept/Dec-Mar, Trout June-July
Bodies of water: Tillamook Bay, Wilson River, Trask River, Nestucca River, Nehalem River, Willamette River, Columbia River, Clackamas River, Sandy River, Deschutes River, North Santiam River
Rates: Half day: $65(1), $130(2), Full day: $125(1), $250(2)
Call between: 5pm-9pm
Provides: Light tackle, fly rod/reel, lures, bait, rain gear, lunch
Handicapped equipped: Yes
Certifications: USCG, Swiftwater Rescue

Oregon/Alaskan Outfitter & River Guide
Philomath 503-929-6955
Species & Seasons: Salmon May-Nov, Trout April-Sept, Steelhead Feb-Dec, SM Bass May-Oct
Bodies of water: Deschutes River, Umpqua River, John Day River, Nestucca River, Willamette River, Santiam River, Alsea River, Siletz Riverr, Rogue River, Alaskan trips also available
Rates: Call for rates
Provides: Light tackle, fly rod/reel, lunch
Handicapped equipped: Yes
Certifications: USCG

OREGON
SANTIAM RIVER - SMITH RIVER

Roaring Fork Guide Service
Springfield 503-726-7234
Species & Seasons: Steelhead April-Oct/Oct-Mar, Chinook Salmon April-July/Sept-Dec, Trout April-Oct
Bodies of water: McKenzie River, Willamette River, Santiam River, Nestucca River, Alsea River, Siuslaw River, Smith River, Umpqua River, Coquille River, Rogue River, Elk River, Sixes River
Rates: Half day: $100(1), $175(2), Full day: $175(1), $250(2), multi-day discounts available
Call between: 6am-10pm
Provides: Light tackle, heavy tackle, fly rod/reel, lures, bait, rain gear, beverages, lunch
Handicapped equipped: Depends on disability

Sehl Guide Service
Tidewater 503-528-3382
Species & Seasons: Steelhead May-July/Dec-Feb, Sturgeon April-May, Chinook Salmon May-July/Sept-Nov
Bodies of water: Alsea Bay, Alsea River, Elk River, Sixes River, Siletz Riverr, Columbia River, Umpqua River, Santiam River, Willamette River
Rates: Full day: $100 pp, Senior discount
Call between: 7:30-8am/6-8pm
Provides: Light tackle, heavy tackle, lures, bait, beverages, lunch
Handicapped equipped: Yes
Certifications: USCG

SILETZ RIVER
GUIDES...

Joe Bergh
Myrtle Creek 503-863-6152
Species & Seasons: SM Bass June-Sept, Steelhead June-Nov/Jan-April, Coho Salmon Sept-Oct, Shad May-July
Bodies of water: Umpqua River, Siletz Riverr, Smith River
Rates: Half day: $125(2), Full day: $125(1), $200(2)
Call between: 6pm-10pm
Provides: Light tackle, heavy tackle, lures, bait
Handicapped equipped: Yes
Certifications: Guide License, Red Cross Card

Diamond D Guide Service
Sweet Home 800-347-4072
Species & Seasons: Chinook Salmon Sept-Nov/April-June, Steelhead all year, Walleye July-Sept, SM Bass May-Oct
Bodies of water: Columbia River, Willamette River, Tillamook Bay, Siletz Riverr, Santiam River, coastal river systems
Rates: Half day: $75(1), $150(2), Full day: $125(1), $240(2)
Call between: 6-6:30am/8-11pm
Provides: Light tackle, heavy tackle
Certifications: USCG

Oregon/Alaskan Outfitter & River Guide
Philomath 503-929-6955
Species & Seasons: Salmon May-Nov, Trout April-Sept, Steelhead Feb-Dec, SM Bass May-Oct
Bodies of water: Deschutes River, Umpqua River, John Day River, Nestucca River, Willamette River, Santiam River, Alsea River, Siletz Riverr, Rogue River, Alaskan trips also available
Rates: Call for rates
Provides: Light tackle, fly rod/reel, lunch
Handicapped equipped: Yes
Certifications: USCG

Sehl Guide Service
Tidewater 503-528-3382
Species & Seasons: Steelhead May-July/Dec-Feb, Sturgeon April-May, Chinook Salmon May-July/Sept-Nov
Bodies of water: Alsea Bay, Alsea River, Elk River, Sixes River, Siletz Riverr, Columbia River, Umpqua River, Santiam River, Willamette River
Rates: Full day: $100 pp, Senior discount
Call between: 7:30-8am/6-8pm
Provides: Light tackle, heavy tackle, lures, bait, beverages, lunch
Handicapped equipped: Yes
Certifications: USCG

Bob Zagorin
Eugene 503-344-9252
Species & Seasons: Trout May-Oct, Steelhead May-Dec/Nov-Mar
Bodies of water: McKenzie River, Willamette River, Smith River, Siletz Riverr, Alsea River, Siuslaw River
Rates: Half day: $125(1), $150(2), Full day: $175(1), $200(2)
Call between:
Provides: Light tackle, heavy tackle, fly rod/reel, lures, bait, rain gear, beverages, lunch

Handicapped equipped: Yes
Certifications: OSMB, OOA, McKenzie Guides Assoc.

SILTCOOS LAKE
LODGES...

Nightingale's Fish Camp
83130 Siltcoos Station Road
Westlake 97493
Handicapped equipped: Yes
Seasons: All year
Rates: $14/day
Contact: Anita Chasco
Guides: No
Species & Seasons: SM Bass, Crappie, Perch, Catfish, Trout May-Oct
Bodies of Water: Siltcoos Lake
Types of fishing: Light tackle
Available: Licenses, bait, tackle, boat rentals

Westlake Resort
Westlake 503-997-3722
Guest Capacity: 9 cabins
Handicapped equipped: No
Seasons: All year
Rates: $40-$60/week
Guides: Yes, recommend
Species & Seasons: SM Bass, Perch, Catfish, Bluegill, Trout May-Nov
Bodies of Water: Silkoos Lake
Types of fishing: Fly fishing, light tackle, wading
Available: Licenses, bait, tackle, boat rentals

SMITH RIVER
GUIDES...

Joe Bergh
Myrtle Creek 503-863-6152
Species & Seasons: SM Bass June-Sept, Steelhead June-Nov/Jan-April, Coho Salmon Sept-Oct, Shad May-July
Bodies of water: Umpqua River, Siletz Riverr, Smith River
Rates: Half day: $125(2), Full day: $125(1), $200(2)
Call between: 6pm-10pm
Provides: Light tackle, heavy tackle, lures, bait
Handicapped equipped: Yes
Certifications: Guide License, Red Cross Card

SMITH RIVER - TILLAMOOK BAY   OREGON

Gary and Val Early
Brookings 503-469-0525
.... 907-262-6132
Species & Seasons: Chinook Salmon Aug-Dec, Steelhead Sept-Mar, Salmon April-Aug
Bodies of water: Rogue River, Chetco River, Coquille River, Umpqua River, Smith River (California), Kenai River (Alaska)
Rates: Full day: $125(1), $250(2),
Call between: 5pm-9pm
Provides: Light tackle, heavy tackle, fly rod/reel, lures, bait
Handicapped equipped: Yes
Certifications: ORVIS, USCG, Red Cross

Larry's Guide Service
Roseburg 503-673-3099
Species & Seasons: Steelhead Dec-April/May-Nov, Salmon April-June/Oct-Jan, SM Bass June-Oct, Striped Bass April-June, Sturgeon May-July/Jan-Feb, Shad May-June, Trout April-July
Bodies of water: Rogue River, Umpqua River, Coquille River, Smith River, Sixes River, Elk River
Rates: Half day: $125(1-2), Full day: $125(1), $200(2), Sturgeon, Striped Bass: $125 pp
Call between: 5pm-10pm
Provides: Light tackle, heavy tackle, lures, bait, beverages
Handicapped equipped: Yes
Certifications: USCG, First aid, CPR

Michael's Guide Service
Glide 503-496-3627
Species & Seasons: Steelhead Jan-Dec, Salmon May-June/Aug-Dec, SM Bass May-Sept, Shad May-June
Bodies of water: Umpqua River, Coquille River, Elk River, Sixes River, Rogue River, Smith River
Rates: Full day: $125(1), $200(2), can take 3rd person
Call between: 8am-8pm
Provides: Light tackle, lures, bait
Handicapped equipped: No
Certifications: USCG

Steve Neverick
Noti 503-935-4623
Species & Seasons: Steelhead Dec-Mar/July-Sept, Chinook Salmon April-June/July-Dec, Sturgeon Feb-July
Bodies of water: Umpqua River, Willamette River, Smith River, Sixes River, Elk River, Rogue River, Siuslaw River, McKenzie River

Rates: Half day: $125(1), $150(2), Full day: $200-$250(2)
Call between: 6pm-9pm
Provides: Light tackle, heavy tackle, fly rod/reel, lures, bait
Handicapped equipped: Depends
Certifications: USCG, OSMB

Roaring Fork Guide Service
Springfield 503-726-7234
Species & Seasons: Steelhead April-Oct/Oct-Mar, Chinook Salmon April-July/Sept-Dec, Trout April-Oct
Bodies of water: McKenzie River, Willamette River, Santiam River, Nestucca River, Alsea River, Siuslaw River, Smith River, Umpqua River, Coquille River, Rogue River, Elk River, Sixes River
Rates: Half day: $100(1), $175(2), Full day: $175(1), $250(2), multi-day discounts available
Call between: 6am-10pm
Provides: Light tackle, heavy tackle, fly rod/reel, lures, bait, rain gear, beverages, lunch
Handicapped equipped: Depends

Bob Zagorin
Eugene 503-344-9252
Species & Seasons: Trout May-Oct, Steelhead May-Dec/Nov-Mar
Bodies of water: McKenzie River, Willamette River, Smith River, Siletz Riverr, Alsea River, Siuslaw River
Rates: Half day: $125(1), $150(2), Full day: $175(1), $200(2)
Call between:
Provides: Light tackle, heavy tackle, fly rod/reel, lures, bait, rain gear, beverages, lunch
Handicapped equipped: Yes
Certifications: OSMB, OOA, McKenzie Guides Assoc.

TILLAMOOK BAY

CHARTERS...

Garibaldi/D & D Charters
Garibaldi 800-900-4665
.... 503-322-0381
Species & Seasons: Bottom Fish April-Oct, Coho Salmon July-?, Chinook Salmon Sept-Nov, Halibut Aug-?
Bodies of water: Pacific Ocean, Tillamook Bay
Rates: Half day: $45(1), Full day: $60-$70(1), rates vary with type of trip taken

Call between: 6am-9pm
Provides: Light tackle, heavy tackle, lures, bait, beverages (coffee only)
Handicapped equipped: Yes
Certifications: USCG

GUIDES...

Dean's Guide Service
Netarts 503-842-7107
.... 800-842-7107
Species & Seasons: Chinook Salmon April-June/Sept-Nov, Steelhead April-July, Sturgeon all year
Bodies of water: Trask River, Tillamook River, Wilson River, Nestucca River, Columbia River, Nehalem Bay, Nehalem River, Tillamook Bay
Rates: Full day: $115(1), $230(2)
Call between: 9am-9pm
Provides: Light tackle, heavy tackle, lures, bait
Handicapped equipped: Yes
Certifications: USCG/OSMB

Diamond D Guide Service
Sweet Home 800-347-4072
Species & Seasons: Chinook Salmon Sept-Nov/April-June, Steelhead all year, Walleye July-Sept, SM Bass May-Oct
Bodies of water: Columbia River, Willamette River, Tillamook Bay, Siletz Riverr, Santiam River, coastal river systems
Rates: Half day: $75(1), $150(2), Full day: $125(1), $240(2)
Call between: 6-6:30am/8-11pm
Provides: Light tackle, heavy tackle
Certifications: USCG

Northwest River Guides
Beaverton 503-626-0829
Species & Seasons: Chinook Salmon April-June/Sept-Dec, Steelhead July-Sept/Dec-Mar, Trout June-July
Bodies of water: Tillamook Bay, Wilson River, Trask River, Nestucca River, Nehalem River, Willamette River, Columbia River, Clackamas River, Sandy River, Deschutes River, North Santiam River
Rates: Half day: $65(1), $130(2), Full day: $125(1), $250(2)
Call between: 5pm-9pm
Provides: Light tackle, fly rod/reel, lures, bait, rain gear, lunch
Handicapped equipped: Yes
Certifications: USCG, Swiftwater Rescue

OREGON
TRASK RIVER - UMPQUA RIVER

TRASK RIVER

GUIDES...

Dean's Guide Service
Netarts 503-842-7107
.... 800-842-7107
Species & Seasons: Chinook Salmon April-June/Sept-Nov, Steelhead April-July, Sturgeon all year
Bodies of water: Trask River, Tillamook River, Wilson River, Nestucca River, Columbia River, Nehalem Bay, Nehalem River, Tillamook Bay
Rates: Full day: $115(1), $230(2)
Call between: 9am-9pm
Provides: Light tackle, heavy tackle, lures, bait
Handicapped equipped: Yes
Certifications: USCG/OSMB

Northwest River Guides
Beaverton 503-626-0829
Species & Seasons: Chinook Salmon April-June/Sept-Dec, Steelhead July-Sept/Dec-Mar, Trout June-July
Bodies of water: Tillamook Bay, Wilson River, Trask River, Nestucca River, Nehalem River, Willamette River, Columbia River, Clackamas River, Sandy River, Deschutes River, North Santiam River
Rates: Half day: $65(1), $130(2), Full day: $125(1), $250(2)
Call between: 5pm-9pm
Provides: Light tackle, fly rod/reel, lures, bait, rain gear, lunch
Handicapped equipped: Yes
Certifications: USCG, Swiftwater Rescue

MARINAS...

Old Mill Marina
Garibaldi 503-322-0324
Carries: Live bait, lures, flies, maps, rods, reels, licenses
Bodies of water: Pacific Ocean, Wilson River, Nehalem River, Trask River
Services & Products: Boat rentals, guide services, lodging, boat ramp, food, beverages, gas/oil, fishing instruction
Guides: Yes
OK to call for current conditions: Yes
Contact: Steve, Rick or Terry

TUALATIN RIVER

BAIT & TACKLE...

Hank's Super Center
Cornelius 503-359-0333
Hours: 8am-9pm
Carries: Live bait, lures, flies, maps, rods, reels, licenses
Bodies of water: Hagg Lake, Tualatin River, Gales Creek, Dairy Creek
Services & Products: Food, beverages
Guides: No
OK to call for current conditions: Yes
Contact: Richard or Ruben

UMPQUA RIVER

BAIT & TACKLE...

Northwest Outdoors Supply
Roseburg 503-440-3042
Hours: 9am-5:30pm Mon.-Fri., 10am-4pm Sat., closed Sun.
Carries: Lures, flies, maps, rods, reels, licenses
Bodies of water: North Umpqua River, South Umpqua River, Main Umpqua River, Diamond Lake, Lemolo Lake, Ben Irving Res., Cooper Creek Res., Tokette Lake
Services & Products: Fishing instruction, repair services
Guides: Yes
OK to call for current conditions: Yes
Contact: Alex or John

GUIDES...

Al's Wild Water Adventures
Creswell 800-289-4534
.... 503-895-4465
Species & Seasons: SM Bass Mar-Oct, Salmon, Steelhead all year, Rainbow Trout April-Oct
Bodies of water: John Day River, Rogue River, Owyhee River, Crooked River, Deschutes River, Grande Ronde River, McKenzie River, North Umpqua River, Main Umpqua River, South Umpqua River
Rates: Full day: $125(1) (average)
Call between: 9am-1pm
Provides: Light tackle, lures, rain gear, beverages, lunch
Handicapped equipped: Yes
Certifications: OR State Marine Board

Jeff Carr
Eugene 503-344-7331
Species & Seasons: Steelhead all year, Trout April-Oct
Bodies of water: McKenzie River, Umpqua River, Deschutes River, Clearwater River (Idaho)
Rates: Half day: $150(1), $200(2), Full day: $250(1), $250(1-2)
Call between: 5pm-9pm
Provides: Fly rod/reel, beverages, lunch
Handicapped equipped: Yes
Certifications: OR Guides and Packers

Joe Bergh
Myrtle Creek 503-863-6152
Species & Seasons: SM Bass June-Sept, Steelhead June-Nov/Jan-April, Coho Salmon Sept-Oct, Shad May-July
Bodies of water: Umpqua River, Siletz Riverr, Smith River
Rates: Half day: $125(2), Full day: $125(1), $200(2)
Call between: 6pm-10pm
Provides: Light tackle, heavy tackle, lures, bait
Handicapped equipped: Yes
Certifications: Guide License, Red Cross Card

Gary and Val Early
Brookings 503-469-0525
.... 907-262-6132
Species & Seasons: Chinook Salmon Aug-Dec, Steelhead Sept-Mar, Salmon April-Aug
Bodies of water: Rogue River, Chetco River, Coquille River, Umpqua River, Smith River (California), Kenai River (Alaska)
Rates: Full day: $125(1), $250(2)
Call between: 5pm-9pm
Provides: Light tackle, heavy tackle, fly rod/reel, lures, bait
Handicapped equipped: Yes
Certifications: ORVIS, USCG, Red Cross

Jim Pringle Guide Service
Medford 503-535-3509
Species & Seasons: Salmon April-Dec, LM Bass, SM Bass, Crappie May-Sept, Rainbow Trout, Steelhead all year, Brook Trout May-Oct
Bodies of water: Rogue River, Hyatt Res., Chetco River, Emigrant Lake, Umpqua River, Klamath Lake, Lost Creek Res., Fish Lake, Applegate Lake, Lake of the Woods, Howard Prairie Lake

UMPQUA RIVER — OREGON

Rates: Half day: $75(2), Full day: $200(2), Chetco River: $250, Lake fishing: $50 pp
Call between: 8am-10pm
Provides: Light tackle, heavy tackle, fly rod/reel, lures, bait
Handicapped equipped: Yes
Certifications: USCG, O.S. Marine Board, Member and past President of Rogue River Guides Assoc.

Kern Grieve Guide Service
Trail 800-645-1624
Species & Seasons: Chinook Salmon May-Aug/July-Sept, Steelhead Aug-Nov/Nov-April
Bodies of water: Rogue River, South Umpqua River, Chetco River
Rates: Half day: $100(1), $200(2), Full day: $125(1), $250(2), 4day trip: $900 pp
Call between: 7am-9pm
Provides: Light tackle, heavy tackle, lures, bait, (beverages, lunch on some trips)
Handicapped equipped: Yes
Certifications: USCG, OSMB, BLM, USFS

Larry's Guide Service
Roseburg 503-673-3099
Species & Seasons: Steelhead Dec-April/May-Nov, Salmon April-June/Oct-Jan, SM Bass June-Oct, Striped Bass April-June, Sturgeon May-July/Jan-Feb, Shad May-June, Trout April-July
Bodies of water: Rogue River, Umpqua River, Coquille River, Smith River, Sixes River, Elk River
Rates: Half day: $125(1-2), Full day: $125(1), $200(2), Sturgeon, Striped Bass: $125 pp
Call between: 5pm-10pm
Provides: Light tackle, heavy tackle, lures, bait, beverages
Handicapped equipped: Yes
Certifications: USCG, First aid, CPR

Michael's Guide Service
Glide 503-496-3627
Species & Seasons: Steelhead Jan-Dec, Salmon May-June/Aug-Dec, SM Bass May-Sept, Shad May-June
Bodies of water: Umpqua River, Coquille River, Elk River, Sixes River, Rogue River, Smith River
Rates: Full day: $125(1), $200(2), can take 3rd person
Call between: 8am-8pm
Provides: Light tackle, lures, bait
Handicapped equipped: No
Certifications: USCG

Steve Neverick
Noti 503-935-4623
Species & Seasons: Steelhead Dec-Mar/July-Sept, Chinook Salmon April-June/July-Dec, Sturgeon Feb-July
Bodies of water: Umpqua River, Willamette River, Smith River, Sixes River, Elk River, Rogue River, Siuslaw River, McKenzie River
Rates: Half day: $125(1), $150(2), Full day: $200-$250(2)
Call between: 6pm-9pm
Provides: Light tackle, heavy tackle, fly rod/reel, lures, bait
Handicapped equipped: Depends
Certifications: USCG, OSMB

Oregon/Alaskan Outfitter & River Guide
Philomath 503-929-6955
Species & Seasons: Salmon May-Nov, Trout April-Sept, Steelhead Feb-Dec, SM Bass May-Oct
Bodies of water: Deschutes River, Umpqua River, John Day River, Nestucca River, Willamette River, Santiam River, Alsea River, Siletz Riverr, Rogue River, Alaskan trips also available
Rates: Call for rates
Provides: Light tackle, fly rod/reel, lunch
Handicapped equipped: Yes
Certifications: USCG

Roaring Fork Guide Service
Springfield 503-726-7234
Species & Seasons: Steelhead April-Oct/Oct-Mar, Chinook Salmon April-July/Sept-Dec, Trout April-Oct
Bodies of water: McKenzie River, Willamette River, Santiam River, Nestucca River, Alsea River, Siuslaw River, Smith River, Umpqua River, Coquille River, Rogue River, Elk River, Sixes River
Rates: Half day: $100(1), $175(2), Full day: $175(1), $250(2), multi-day discounts available
Call between: 6am-10pm
Provides: Light tackle, heavy tackle, fly rod/reel, lures, bait, rain gear, beverages, lunch
Handicapped equipped: Depends on disability

Sehl Guide Service
Tidewater 503-528-3382
Species & Seasons: Steelhead May-July/Dec-Feb, Sturgeon April-May, Chinook Salmon May-July/Sept-Nov
Bodies of water: Alsea Bay, Alsea River, Elk River, Sixes River, Siletz Riverr, Columbia River, Umpqua River, Santiam River, Willamette River
Rates: Full day: $100 pp, Senior discount
Call between: 7:30-8am/6-8pm
Provides: Light tackle, heavy tackle, lures, bait, beverages, lunch
Handicapped equipped: Yes
Certifications: USCG

Umpqua River Adventures
Roseburg 503-673-6355
Species & Seasons: Chinook Salmon April-July/Aug-Sept, Steelhead May-Sept/Dec-Mar, Coho Salmon Sept-Dec, Shad May-July
Bodies of water: Umpqua River, Rouge River
Rates: Umpqua River: $75 (6hrs), Rogue River: Half day: $125(1), $250(2)
Call between: Anytime
Provides: Light tackle, heavy tackle, lures, bait
Handicapped equipped: No
Certifications: OSMB, USCG

Wilderness River Outfitters
Springfield 503-726-9471
Species & Seasons: Trout May-Oct, SM Bass June-Sept, Steelhead May-Oct, Salmon Oct-Nov/May-June
Bodies of water: McKenzie River, Willamette River, Umpqua River, Lower Main Salmon River
Rates: Full day: $225(1-2), Salmon: $250
Call between: 8am-4:30pm
Provides: Light tackle, heavy tackle, fly rod/reel, lures, bait, lunch
Handicapped equipped: Yes
Certifications: OSMB

OREGON
UMPQUA RIVER - WILLAMETTE RIVER

LODGES...

Elkqua Lodge
Elkton 503-584-2161
Guest Capacity: 8-10
Handicapped equipped: No
Seasons: All year
Rates: $50-$75/day
Guides: Yes
Species & Seasons: Chinook Salmon Spring-Fall, SM Bass May-Oct, Shad April-July, Sturgeon, Striped Bass, Steelhead all year
Bodies of Water: Umpqua River, coastal lakes, Pacific Ocean
Types of fishing: Fly fishing, light tackle, heavy tackle, float trips
Available: Fishing instruction, licenses, bait, tackle, family activities, baby sitting

Hannah Fishing Camp
Elkton 800-459-2525
.... 503-459-2575
Guest Capacity: 8
Handicapped equipped: No
Seasons: All year
Rates: $150/day
Contact: Denny Hannah
Guides: Yes
Species & Seasons: Steelhead Jan-Mar, Striped Bass April-June, Sturgeon May-Aug, SM Bass May-Oct, Salmon Sept-Jan, Shad April-July
Bodies of Water: Umpqua River, Rogue River, John Day River, Elk River, Sixes River
Types of fishing: Fly fishing, light tackle, big fish
Available: Fishing instruction, bait, tackle, family activities

WILLAMETTE RIVER
GUIDES...

Diamond D Guide Service
Sweet Home 800-347-4072
Species & Seasons: Chinook Salmon Sept-Nov/April-June, Steelhead all year, Walleye July-Sept, SM Bass May-Oct
Bodies of water: Columbia River, Willamette River, Tillamook Bay, Siletz Riverr, Santiam River, coastal river systems
Rates: Half day: $75(1), $150(2), Full day: $125(1), $240(2)
Call between: 6-6:30am/8-11pm
Provides: Light tackle, heavy tackle
Certifications: USCG

Steve Neverick
Noti 503-935-4623
Species & Seasons: Steelhead Dec-Mar/July-Sept, Chinook Salmon April-June/July-Dec, Sturgeon Feb-July
Bodies of water: Umpqua River, Willamette River, Smith River, Sixes River, Elk River, Rogue River, Siuslaw River, McKenzie River
Rates: Half day: $125(1), $150(2), Full day: $200-$250(2)
Call between: 6pm-9pm
Provides: Light tackle, heavy tackle, fly rod/reel, lures, bait
Handicapped equipped: Depends
Certifications: USCG, OSMB

Northwest River Guides
Beaverton 503-626-0829
Species & Seasons: Chinook Salmon April-June/Sept-Dec, Steelhead July-Sept/Dec-Mar, Trout June-July
Bodies of water: Tillamook Bay, Wilson River, Trask River, Nestucca River, Nehalem River, Willamette River, Columbia River, Clackamas River, Sandy River, Deschutes River, North Santiam River
Rates: Half day: $65(1), $130(2), Full day: $125(1), $250(2)
Call between: 5pm-9pm
Provides: Light tackle, fly rod/reel, lures, bait, rain gear, lunch
Handicapped equipped: Yes
Certifications: USCG, Swiftwater Rescue

Oregon/Alaskan Outfitter & River Guide
Philomath 503-929-6955
Species & Seasons: Salmon May-Nov, Trout April-Sept, Steelhead Feb-Dec, SM Bass May-Oct
Bodies of water: Deschutes River, Umpqua River, John Day River, Nestucca River, Willamette River, Santiam River, Alsea River, Siletz Riverr, Rogue River, Alaskan trips also available
Rates: Call for rates
Provides: Light tackle, fly rod/reel, lunch
Handicapped equipped: Yes
Certifications: USCG

Roaring Fork Guide Service
Springfield 503-726-7234
Species & Seasons: Steelhead April-Oct/Oct-Mar, Chinook Salmon April-July/Sept-Dec, Trout April-Oct
Bodies of water: McKenzie River, Willamette River, Santiam River, Nestucca River, Alsea River, Siuslaw River, Smith River, Umpqua River, Coquille River, Rogue River, Elk River, Sixes River
Rates: Half day: $100(1), $175(2), Full day: $175(1), $250(2), multi-day discounts available
Call between: 6am-10pm
Provides: Light tackle, heavy tackle, fly rod/reel, lures, bait, rain gear, beverages, lunch
Handicapped equipped: Depends on disability

Sehl Guide Service
Tidewater 503-528-3382
Species & Seasons: Steelhead May-July/Dec-Feb, Sturgeon April-May, Chinook Salmon May-July/Sept-Nov
Bodies of water: Alsea Bay, Alsea River, Elk River, Sixes River, Siletz Riverr, Columbia River, Umpqua River, Santiam River, Willamette River
Rates: Full day: $100 pp, Senior discount
Call between: 7:30-8am/6-8pm
Provides: Light tackle, heavy tackle, lures, bait, beverages, lunch
Handicapped equipped: Yes
Certifications: USCG

Wilderness River Outfitters
Springfield 503-726-9471
Species & Seasons: Trout May-Oct, SM Bass June-Sept, Steelhead May-Oct, Salmon Oct-Nov/May-June
Bodies of water: McKenze River, Willamette River, Umpqua River, Lower Main Salmon River
Rates: Full day: $225(1-2), Salmon: $250
Call between: 8am-4:30pm
Provides: Light tackle, heavy tackle, fly rod/reel, lures, bait, lunch
Handicapped equipped: Yes
Certifications: OSMB

WILLAMETTE RIVER

OREGON

Bob Zagorin
Eugene 503-344-9252
Species & Seasons: Trout May-Oct, Steelhead May-Dec/Nov-Mar
Bodies of water: McKenzie River, Willamette River, Smith River, Siletz Riverr, Alsea River, Siuslaw River
Rates: Half day: $125(1), $150(2), Full day: $175(1), $200(2)
Call between:
Provides: Light tackle, heavy tackle, fly rod/reel, lures, bait, rain gear, beverages, lunch
Handicapped equipped: Yes
Certifications: OSMB, OOA, McKenzie Guides Assoc.

Everything in the Angler's Yellow Pages is
alphabetically arranged for ease of reference

PENNSYLVANIA

1. Allegheny Reservoir
2. Beltzville Lake
3. Blue Marsh Lake
4. Crooked Creek Reservoir
5. Delaware Bay
6. Eastern Pennsylvania
   Rivers & Streams
   Delaware River
   Fishing Creek
   French Creek
   Juniata River
   Lehigh River
   Little Lehigh Creek
   Loyalsock Creek
   Penns Creek
   Pine Creek
   Schuylkill River
   Susquehanna River
   Tulpehocken Creek
   Yellow Breeches Creek
7. Harveys Lake
8. Keystone Lake
9. Lake Arthur
10. Lake Erie
11. Lake Marburg
12. Lake Nockamixon
13. Lake Wallenpaupack
14. Muddy Run Reservoir
15. Private Waters
16. Pymatuning Reservoir
17. Raystown Lake
18. Shawnee Lake
19. Stillwater Lake
20. Western Pennsylvania
    Rivers & Streams
    Allegheny River
    Bushkill Creek
    Conococheague Creek
    Laurel Hill Creek
    Neshannock Creek
    Youghiogheny River

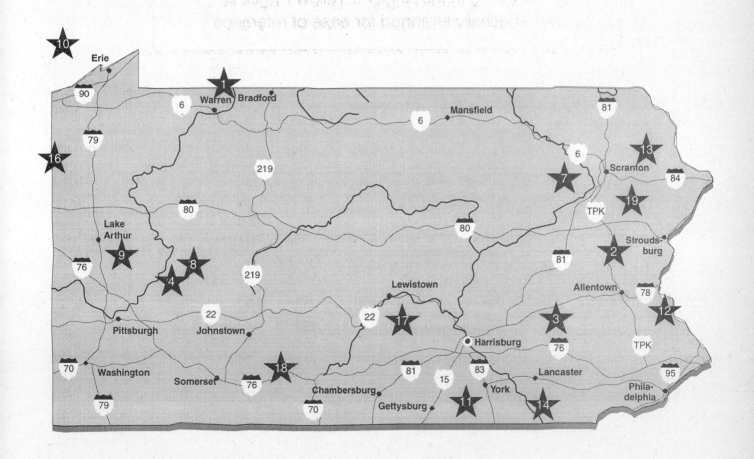

PENNSYLVANIA

ALLEGHENY RESERVOIR - EASTERN PENNSYLVANIA

ALLEGHENY RESERVOIR

BAIT & TACKLE...

Bac Inc.
Erie 814-838-2850
Hours: 5am-9pm
Carries: Live bait, lures, flies, maps, rods, reels, licenses
Bodies of water: Lake Erie, Chataqua Lake, Conneaut Lake, Pymatuning Res., Allegheny Res.
Services & Products: Guide services, food, beverages, fishing instruction
Guides: Yes
OK to call for current conditions: Yes

GUIDES...

Allegheny Outdoors
Bradford 814-368-8608
Species & Seasons: Trout April-Sept, Walleye May-Mar, Muskellunge June-Sept, Northern Pike Dec-Sept, SM Bass June-Oct, Steelhead Oct-April, Crappie, White Bass May-June, Yellow Perch Dec-Mar, Perch, Northern Pike, Walleye(ice fishing) Dec-Mar
Bodies of water: Allegheny Nat'l. Forest, Allegheny River, Allegheny Res., Cattaraugus Creek, (NY), Chautauqua Lake (NY)
Rates: Half day: $75(1), $100(2), Full day: $125(1), $150(2) different kinds of fishing, different prices
Call between: 5pm-11pm
Provides: Light tackle, heavy tackle, lures, bait
Certifications: NYS DEC Licensed Fishing Guide

BELTZVILLE LAKE

BAIT & TACKLE...

Beltzville Pro Fishing
Lehighton 610-377-9115
Hours: 6am-6:30pm
Carries: Live bait, lures, flies, maps, rods, reels, licenses
Bodies of water: Beltzville Lake, Mauch Chunk Lake, Lehigh River, Delaware River
Guides: No
OK to call for current conditions: Yes
Contact: Ernie or Neil

Chris's Bait & Tackle
Mertztown 610-682-4129
Hours: 6:30am-9pm Mon.-Fri., 6:30am-4pm Sat., 6:30-1pm Sun.
Carries: Live bait, lures, flies, maps, rods, reels, licenses
Bodies of water: Blue Marsh Lake, Beltzville Lake, Lake Nockamixon, Schuylkill River, Green Lane Res., Lehigh River, Little Lehigh Creek
Services & Products: Repair services
Guides: Yes
OK to call for current conditions: Yes
Contact: Chris Mohry

BLUE MARSH LAKE

BAIT & TACKLE...

Chris's Bait & Tackle
Mertztown 610-682-4129
Hours: 6:30am-9pm Mon.-Fri., 6:30am-4pm Sat., 6:30-1pm Sun.
Carries: Live bait, lures, flies, maps, rods, reels, licenses
Bodies of water: Blue Marsh Lake, Beltzville Lake, Lake Nockamixon, Schuylkill River, Green Lane Res., Lehigh River, Little Lehigh Creek
Services & Products: Repair services
Guides: Yes
OK to call for current conditions: Yes
Contact: Chris Mohry

R & R Sporting Goods
Reading 610-376-3004
Hours: 8am-6pm
Carries: Live bait, lures, flies, maps, rods, reels, licenses
Bodies of water: Blue Marsh Lake, Ontelaunee Lake, Schuylkill River, Tulpehocken Creek
Guides: No
OK to call for current conditions: Yes
Contact: Ron Strunk

CROOKED CREEK RESERVOIR

BAIT & TACKLE...

Allegheny Bait & Tackle
Tarentum 412-224-6888
Hours: 7am-9pm
Carries: Live bait, flies, maps, rods, reels, licenses
Bodies of water: Allegheny River, Crooked Creek Res., Moraine State Park
Services & Products: Boat ramp, repair services
Guides: No
OK to call for current conditions: Yes
Contact: Joe, Rick or Ronie

Frailey Sporting Goods
Shelcota 412-354-3478
Hours: 6am-7:30pm
Carries: Live bait, lures, flies, maps, rods, reels, licenses
Bodies of water: Keystone Power Dam, Mahoning Creek Lake, Allegheny River, Crooked Creek Lake Park
Services & Products: Beverages
Guides: No
OK to call for current conditions: Yes
Contact: Sally

DELAWARE BAY

BAIT & TACKLE...

Al's Rainbow Sporting Goods
Philadelphia 215-465-7842
Hours: 10am-7pm Mon-Tues-Thurs, 10am-9pm Wed.-Fri., 10am-6pm Sat., closed Sun.
Carries: Live bait, lures, flies, maps, rods, reels, licenses
Bodies of water: Atlantic Ocean, Delaware Bay, area streams, lakes, rivers
Services & Products: Fishing instruction, repair services
Guides: Yes
OK to call for current conditions: Yes
Contact: Al Hannan

EASTERN PENNSYLVANIA RIVERS & STREAMS

BAIT & TACKLE...

Beltzville Pro Fishing
Lehighton 610-377-9115
Hours: 6am-6:30pm
Carries: Live bait, lures, flies, maps, rods, reels, licenses
Bodies of water: Beltzville Lake, Mauch Chunk Lake, Lehigh River, Delaware River
Guides: No
OK to call for current conditions: Yes
Contact: Ernie or Neil

EASTERN PENNSYLVANIA

Chris's Bait & Tackle
Mertztown........................ 610-682-4129
Hours: 6:30am-9pm Mon.-Fri., 6:30am-4pm Sat., 6:30-1pm Sun.
Carries: Live bait, lures, flies, maps, rods, reels, licenses
Bodies of water: Blue Marsh Lake, Beltzville Lake, Lake Nockamixon, Schuylkill River, Green Lane Res., Lehigh River, Little Lehigh Creek
Services & Products: Repair services
Guides: Yes
OK to call for current conditions: Yes
Contact: Chris Mohry

Dave's Sports Center
Doylestown 215-766-8000
Hours: 9am-6pm, closed Mon.
Carries: Live bait, lures, flies, maps, rods, reels, licenses
Bodies of water: Delaware River, Lake Nockamixon, Tohickon Creek, Neshaminy Creek
Services & Products: Repair services (Minnkota, OMC, Cannon)
Guides: Yes
OK to call for current conditions: Yes
Contact: Lynn

Dave's Taxidermy & Tackle Shop
Shamokin........................... 717-644-1547
Hours: 8am-6pm, closed Sun., Mon.
Carries: Live bait, lures, flies, maps, rods, reels, licenses
Bodies of water: Susquehanna River, Roaring Creek
Services & Products: Fishing instruction, fly tying materials and classes, taxidermy
Guides: Yes
OK to call for current conditions: Yes
Contact: Dave

Don's Tackle Shop
Lebanon 717-272-0270
Hours: 9am-8pm
Carries: Live bait, lures, flies, rods, reels, licenses
Bodies of water: Susquehanna River
Services & Products: Fishing instruction, repair services
Guides: No
OK to call for current conditions: Yes
Contact: Don Weise

Dunmore Bait & Tackle
Dunmore 717-344-1666
Hours: 6am-7pm
Carries: Live bait, lures, flies, maps, rods, reels, licenses
Bodies of water: Roaring Brook, Lackawanna River, Susquehanna River, Lake Wallenpaupack, Elmhurst Res.
Services & Products: Fishing instruction, repair services, knife sharpening
Guides: Yes
OK to call for current conditions: Yes
Contact: Double J.

Elly's Bait & Tackle
Saegertown 814-398-2468
Hours: 8am-9pm Mon.-Fri., 7am-6pm Sat., Sun.
Carries: Live bait, lures, flies, maps, rods, reels, licenses
Bodies of water: Lake Erie, Pymatuning Res., French Creek
Services & Products: Repair services
Guides: Yes
OK to call for current conditions: Yes
Contact: John Dudley

Jeff's Bait Shop
Millerstown....................... 717-589-3422
Hours: 7am-9pm, closed Nov.-Mar.
Carries: Live bait, lures, rods, reels, licenses
Bodies of water: Juniata River
Services & Products: Lodging, boat ramp, beverages
Guides: No
OK to call for current conditions: Yes
Contact: Jeff Pittman

Jim's Service
Lewistown 717-248-2795
Hours: 10am-8pm, closed Wed.
Carries: Live bait, lures, rods, reels
Bodies of water: Juniata River, Raystown Lake, Whipples Dam, Little Buffalo River, other streams, lakes
Guides: Yes
OK to call for current conditions: Yes
Contact: Larry W. Fink

Londonderry Bait & Tackle Shop
Middletown 717-944-2463
Hours: 7am-6pm
Carries: Live bait, lures, rods, reels, licenses
Bodies of water: Susquehanna River, Pinchot Lake, Juniata River
Services & Products: Beverages
Guides: No
OK to call for current conditions: Yes
Contact: Woody or Richard

Nestors Rod & Bow Pro Shop
Whitehall 610-433-6051
Hours: 10am-9pm
Carries: Live bait, lures, flies, maps, rods, reels, licenses
Bodies of water: Little Lehigh Creek, Monocacy Creek, Bushkill Creek, Lehigh River
Services & Products: Fishing instruction, fly tying classes
Guides: No
OK to call for current conditions: Yes
Contact: Dan Buss

North Park Bait & Tackle
Allison Park 412-367-7959
Hours: 7am-9pm
Carries: Live bait, lures, flies, rods, reels, licenses
Bodies of water: North Park Lake, Pine Creek, Allegheny River, Ohio River
Services & Products: Food, beverages
Guides: No
OK to call for current conditions: Yes
Contact: Dwight or Glenn Yingling

Out-N-About Sporting Goods
Lewisburg 717-524-7977
Hours: 8am-6pm, closed Sun.
Carries: Live bait, lures, flies, maps, rods, reels, licenses
Bodies of water: Susquehanna River, Penns Creek, Raystown Lake, Walker Lake, Rose Valley Lake
Services & Products: Guide services, fishing instruction, repair services
OK to call for current conditions: Yes

Pleasant Hill Bait Co
Cogan Station 800-451-3931
.... 717-494-1292
Hours: 7am-7pm, closed Sun.
Carries: Live bait, maps
Bodies of water: Susquehanna River, Pine Creek, Lycoming Creek, Loyalsock Creek, Rose Valley Lake
Services & Products: Live bait in bulk
Guides: No
OK to call for current conditions: Yes
Contact: Dick Sunderlin

PENNSYLVANIA — EASTERN PENNSYLVANIA

R & R Sporting Goods
Reading 610-376-3004
Hours: 8am-6pm
Carries: Live bait, lures, flies, maps, rods, reels, licenses
Bodies of water: Blue Marsh Lake, Ontelaunee Lake, Schuylkill River, Tulpehocken Creek
Guides: No
OK to call for current conditions: Yes
Contact: Ron Strunk

Raystown Fishing & Hunting Supplies
RR 3 Box 294 A
Huntingdon 16652
Hours: 9am-6pm
Carries: Live bait, lures, flies, maps, rods, reels, licenses
Bodies of water: Juniata River, Raystown Lake
Services & Products: Guide services, fishing instruction, repair services
Guides: Yes
OK to call for current conditions: Yes
Contact: Robert Mort

Susquehanna Fishing Tackle
Lancaster 717-397-1399
Hours: 9am-5pm Mon., Tue., 9am-9pm Wed-Thurs-Fri., 5am-4pm Sat., closed Sun.
Carries: Live bait, lures, flies, maps, rods, reels, licenses
Bodies of water: Susquehanna River, Octoraro Res., Muddy Run Res., Lake Redman
Services & Products: Guide services, fishing instruction, repair services
OK to call for current conditions: Yes
Contact: Anyone

The Sportsmans Shop
New Holland 717-354-4311
Hours: 9am-9pm, closed Sun.
Carries: Live bait, lures, flies, maps, rods, reels, licenses
Bodies of water: Susquehanna River, French Creek, Conestoga River, Middle Creek
Guides: No
OK to call for current conditions: No

FLY SHOPS...

Eyler's Inc. Fly & Tackle
Bryn Mawr 610-527-3388
Hours: Closed Sun., Mon.
Carries: Live bait, lures, flies, maps, rods, reels, licenses
Bodies of water: Valley Creek, Valley Forge Nat'l. Park, Schuylkill River
Guides: Yes
OK to call for current conditions: No

Falling Spring Outfitters, Inc.
Scotland 717-263-7811
Hours: 10am-6pm, closed Mon.
Carries: Flies, maps, rods, reels
Bodies of water: Falling Spring Branch, Letort Spring Run, Conococheague Creek, Potomac River, Yellow Breeches Creek
Services & Products: Guide services, fishing instruction, instruction in fly tying
OK to call for current conditions: Yes
Contact: Mark Sturtevant

Pennsylvania Outdoor Warehouse
Williamsport 717-322-4739
Hours: 9am-9pm Mon-Tues-Thurs-Fri., 9am-5:30pm Wed., Sat., 12-4pm Sun.
Carries: Live bait, lures, flies, maps, rods, reels, licenses
Bodies of water: Pine Creek, Loyalsock Creek, Lycoming Creek, Fishing Creek, Slate Run, Cedar Run
Services & Products: Fly fishing guide service
Guides: Yes
OK to call for current conditions: Yes
Contact: Chuck Mahen

The Sporting Gentleman
Media 610-565-6140
Hours: 10am-5:30pm, closed Sun.
Carries: Flies, maps, rods, reels, licenses
Bodies of water: Streams, rivers, lakes in SE PA
Services & Products: Guide services, fly fishing schools, fly tying schools
Guides: Yes
OK to call for current conditions: Yes
Contact: Barry Staats

Tulpehocken Creek Outfitters
West Lawn 610-678-1899
Hours: 10am-7pm, closed Sun., Mon.
Carries: Flies, maps, rods, reels, licenses
Bodies of water: Tulpehocken Creek, Little Lehigh Creek, Letort Spring Run, Yellow Breeches Creek
Services & Products: Guide services, fly fishing schools (fly tying, rod building)
OK to call for current conditions: Yes
Contact: Tony Gehman

GUIDES...

Susquehanna River Guides
New Cumberland 717-774-2307
Species & Seasons: SM Bass Mar-April/June-Oct
Bodies of water: Susquehanna River, Juniata River
Rates: Half day: $100(1), $150(2), Full day: $200(1), $225(2)
Call between: 4pm-10pm
Provides: Beverages, lunch
Handicapped equipped: No

Ray Serfass
Pocono Summit 717-839-7736
Species & Seasons: Shad April-May, SM Bass, LM Bass June-Nov, Channel Catfish April-Nov, Striped Bass June-Sept
Bodies of water: Delaware River, Stillwater Lake, Gouldsboro Lake
Rates: Half day: $125(1-2), $175(3), Full day: $200(1-2), $275(3)
Call between: Anytime
Provides: Light tackle, heavy tackle, fly rod/reel, lures, bait
Handicapped equipped: Yes
Certifications: PA Guide Permit

LODGES...

Feathered Hook
Coburn 814-349-8757
Hours: 8am-8pm, closed in winter
Carries: Flies, rods, reels
Bodies of water: Penns Creek, Elk Creek, Big Fishing Creek
Services & Products: Guide services and lodging
OK to call for current conditions: Yes

Indian Springs Fly Fishing Camp
Pennsburg .... 215-679-5022 (home)
.... 717-224-2708 (camp)
Guest Capacity: 8
Seasons: April 21 to Oct 21
Rates: $295/day
Contact: Lee Hartman
Guides: Yes
Species & Seasons: Trout April-Sept, Shad May-June
Bodies of Water: Upper Delaware River
Types of fishing: Fly fishing, wading, float trips
Available: Fishing instruction, lodging, food, package trips

EASTERN PENNSYLVANIA - LAKE ERIE / PENNSYLVANIA

MARINAS...

Tri State Canoe Rentals
Matamoras 717-491-4948
Hours: Daily, all year
Carries: Lures, licenses
Bodies of water: Delaware River
Services & Products: Boat rentals, guide services, boat ramp
OK to call for current conditions: Yes
Contact: Charlie Shay

HARVEYS LAKE

GUIDES...

Down Rigger Charter Fishing
Wilkes Barre 717-825-3076
Species & Seasons: Brown Trout, Rainbow Trout, Striped Bass April-Nov
Bodies of water: Harveys Lake, Lake Wallenpaupack
Rates: 4 hrs: $100-$125(1-3)
Call between: 5pm-9pm
Provides: Light tackle, lures, bait
Handicapped equipped: No
Certifications: PA Guide Permit

KEYSTONE LAKE

BAIT & TACKLE...

Frailey Sporting Goods
Shelcota 412-354-3478
Hours: 6am-7:30pm
Carries: Live bait, lures, flies, maps, rods, reels, licenses
Bodies of water: Keystone Power Dam, Mahoning Creek Lake, Allegheny River, Crooked Creek Lake Park
Services & Products: Beverages
Guides: No
OK to call for current conditions: Yes
Contact: Sally

Transue's Tackle
W. Kittanning 412-543-2971
Hours: 7am-9pm
Carries: Live bait, lures, flies, rods, reels, licenses
Bodies of water: Allegheny River, Keystone Lake
Services & Products: Beverages, gas/oil, repair services
Guides: Yes
OK to call for current conditions: Yes
Contact: Mark Transue

LAKE ARTHUR

BAIT & TACKLE...

Allegheny Bait & Tackle
Tarentum 412-224-6888
Hours: 7am-9pm
Carries: Live bait, flies, maps, rods, reels, licenses
Bodies of water: Allegheny River, Crooked Creek Res., Moraine State Park
Services & Products: Boat ramp, repair services
Guides: No
OK to call for current conditions: Yes
Contact: Joe, Rick or Ronie

Anderson's Appalachian Trails
Prospect 412-865-2178
Hours: 8am-8pm Mon.-Fri., 8am-7pm Sat, Sun.
Carries: Live bait, lures, flies, maps, rods, reels, licenses
Bodies of water: Moraine State Park
Services & Products: Food, beverages, gas/oil
Guides: Yes
OK to call for current conditions: Yes

Moraine Fishing & Camping Center
Prospect 412-865-9318
Hours: 7am-7pm
Carries: Live bait, lures, flies, maps, rods, reels
Bodies of water: Lake Arthur, Moraine State Park
Services & Products: Beverages
Guides: Yes
OK to call for current conditions: Yes
Contact: Jim Bohrer

FLY SHOPS...

Fly Tyers "Vice"
Pittsburgh 412-276-2831
Hours: 9am-6pm, closed Fri, Sat., Sun.
Carries: Flies, rods, reels
Bodies of water: Lake Erie, Lake Arthur, Lake Wilhelm, Neshonnick Creek, Slippery Rock, Laurel Hill Creek, Loyalhanna Creek
Services & Products: Guide services, fishing instruction, repair services
Guides: Yes
OK to call for current conditions: Yes
Contact: Tony Marasco

LAKE ERIE

BAIT & TACKLE...

Bac Inc.
Erie 814-838-2850
Hours: 5am-9pm
Carries: Live bait, lures, flies, maps, rods, reels, licenses
Bodies of water: Lake Erie, Chataqua Lake, Conneaut Lake, Pymatuning Res., Allegheny Res.
Services & Products: Guide services, food, beverages, fishing instruction
Guides: Yes
OK to call for current conditions: Yes

Elly's Bait & Tackle
Saegertown 814-398-2468
Hours: 8am-9pm Mon.-Fri., 7am-6pm Sat., Sun.
Carries: Live bait, lures, flies, maps, rods, reels, licenses
Bodies of water: Lake Erie, Pymatuning Res., French Creek
Services & Products: Repair services
Guides: Yes
OK to call for current conditions: Yes
Contact: John Dudley

CHARTERS...

Debi Duz Custom Charters
Pittsburgh 412-366-3270
Species & Seasons: Walleye July-Aug, Trout, Salmon May-Sept, Perch, SM Bass May-June/Sept-Oct
Bodies of water: Lake Erie, Lake Ontario
Rates: Salmon, Trout: Full day: $460 (1-6), Walleye: Full day: $360(1-4)
Call between: Anytime
Provides: Light tackle, heavy tackle, lures, bait
Handicapped equipped: Yes

La-Gre-Le Charters
Sharpsville 800-214-0690
Species & Seasons: Walleye June-Sept, SM Bass May-June, Perch Sept-Oct
Bodies of water: Central Basin Lake Erie
Rates: Varies
Call between: 8am-4:30pm
Provides: Heavy tackle, lures
Handicapped equipped: Yes
Certifications: USCG

PENNSYLVANIA
LAKE ERIE - PRIVATE WATERS

Reel Time Charters
Saegertown 814-763-5172
Species & Seasons: SM Bass, Perch May-July/Sept-Oct, Walleye July-Sept
Bodies of water: Central Basin of Lake Erie from Geneva to the PA Line
Rates: Bass, Perch: Full day: $220(1-4), Walleye: Full day: $400(6)
Call between: 6pm-10pm
Provides: Light tackle, heavy tackle, lures
Handicapped equipped: Yes
Certifications: USCG

Wallhanger Fishing Charters
Waterford 814-796-6461
Species & Seasons: Walleye, SM Bass, Salmon, Trout April-Oct
Bodies of water: Lake Erie at Erie, PA
Rates: Half day: (from) $220-$330(1-6), Full day: (from) $320-$460(1-6)
Call between: 8am-10:30pm
Provides: Light tackle, heavy tackle, lures, bait
Certifications: USCG

FLY SHOPS...

Fly Tyers "Vice"
Pittsburgh 412-276-2831
Hours: 9am-6pm, closed Fri, Sat., Sun.
Carries: Flies, rods, reels
Bodies of water: Lake Erie, Lake Arthur, Lake Wilhelm, Neshonnick Creek, Slippery Rock, Laurel Hill Creek, Loyalhanna Creek
Services & Products: Guide services, fishing instruction, repair services
Guides: Yes
OK to call for current conditions: Yes
Contact: Tony Marasco

LAKE MARBURG

BAIT & TACKLE...

Shearer's Bait & Tackle
Glenville 717-227-0771
Hours: 7am-7pm
Carries: Live bait, lures, flies, maps, rods, reels, licenses
Bodies of water: Lake Redman, Codorus State Park, Lake Williams, local stocked trout streams
Services & Products: Boat rentals, food, beverages, repair services

Guides: Yes
OK to call for current conditions: Yes
Contact: Linda Spangler

Sowers Marine
Highway 116, West 2 Miles
Spring Grove 17362
Hours: 8am-5pm Mon.-Fri., 8am-1pm Sat., Sun.
Carries: Live bait, lures, flies, rods, reels
Bodies of water: Lake Marburg, Codorus State Park
Guides: Yes
OK to call for current conditions: Yes

LAKE NOCKAMIXON

BAIT & TACKLE...

Chris's Bait & Tackle
Mertztown 610-682-4129
Hours: 6:30am-9pm Mon.-Fri., 6:30am-4pm Sat., 6:30-1pm Sun.
Carries: Live bait, lures, flies, maps, rods, reels, licenses
Bodies of water: Blue Marsh Lake, Beltzville Lake, Lake Nockamixon, Schuylkill River, Green Lane Res., Lehigh River, Little Lehigh Creek
Services & Products: Repair services
Guides: Yes
OK to call for current conditions: Yes
Contact: Chris Mohry

Dave's Sports Center
Doylestown 215-766-8000
Hours: 9am-6pm, closed Mon.
Carries: Live bait, lures, flies, maps, rods, reels, licenses
Bodies of water: Delaware River, Lake Nockamixon, Tohickon Creek, Neshaminy Creek
Services & Products: Repair services (Minnkota, OMC, Cannon)
Guides: Yes
OK to call for current conditions: Yes
Contact: Lynn

LAKE WALLENPAUPACK

BAIT & TACKLE...

Dunmore Bait & Tackle
Dunmore 717-344-1666
Hours: 6am-7pm
Carries: Live bait, lures, flies, maps, rods, reels, licenses

Bodies of water: Roaring Brook, Lackawanna River, Susquehanna River, Lake Wallenpaupack, Elmhurst Res.
Services & Products: Fishing instruction, repair services, knife sharpening
Guides: Yes
OK to call for current conditions: Yes
Contact: Double J.

GUIDES...

Down Rigger Charter Fishing
Wilkes Barre 717-825-3076
Species & Seasons: Brown Trout, Rainbow Trout, Striped Bass April-Nov
Bodies of water: Harveys Lake, Lake Wallenpaupack
Rates: 4 hrs: $100-$125(1-3)
Call between: 5pm-9pm
Provides: Light tackle, lures, bait
Handicapped equipped: No
Certifications: PA Guide Permit

MUDDY RUN RESERVOIR

BAIT & TACKLE...

Susquehanna Fishing Tackle
Lancaster 717-397-1399
Hours: 9am-5pm Mon., Tue., 9am-9pm Wed-Thurs-Fri., 5am-4pm Sat., closed Sun.
Carries: Live bait, lures, flies, maps, rods, reels, licenses
Bodies of water: Susquehanna River, Octoraro Res., Muddy Run Res., Lake Redman
Services & Products: Guide services, fishing instruction, repair services
OK to call for current conditions: Yes
Contact: Anyone

PRIVATE WATERS

LODGES...

Big Moores Run Lodge
Coudersport 814-647-5300
Guest Capacity: 12
Handicapped equipped: No
Seasons: Mar to Jan
Rates: Varies
Guides: Yes
Species & Seasons: Brook Trout, Brown Trout, Rainbow Trout all year
CATCH AND RELEASE!

PRIVATE WATERS - WESTERN PENNSYLVANIA   PENNSYLVANIA

Bodies of Water: Private water, and over 800 miles of public streams, fly fishing only
Types of fishing: Fly fishing, wading
Available: Fishing instruction, family activities

PYMATUNING RESERVOIR

(also see Ohio listings)

BAIT & TACKLE...

Bac Inc.
Erie 814-838-2850
Hours: 5am-9pm
Carries: Live bait, lures, flies, maps, rods, reels, licenses
Bodies of water: Lake Erie, Chataqua Lake, Conneaut Lake, Pymatuning Res., Allegheny Res.
Services & Products: Guide services, food, beverages, fishing instruction
Guides: Yes
OK to call for current conditions: Yes

Elly's Bait & Tackle
Saegertown 814-398-2468
Hours: 8am-9pm Mon.-Fri., 7am-6pm Sat., Sun.
Carries: Live bait, lures, flies, maps, rods, reels, licenses
Bodies of water: Lake Erie, Pymatuning Res., French Creek
Services & Products: Repair services
Guides: Yes
OK to call for current conditions: Yes
Contact: John Dudley

RAYSTOWN LAKE

BAIT & TACKLE...

Jim's Service
Lewistown 717-248-2795
Hours: 10am-8pm, closed Wed.
Carries: Live bait, lures, rods, reels
Bodies of water: Juniata River, Raystown Lake, Whipples Dam, Little Buffalo River, other streams, lakes
Guides: Yes
OK to call for current conditions: Yes
Contact: Larry W. Fink

Out-N-About Sporting Goods
Lewisburg 717-524-7977
Hours: 8am-6pm, closed Sun.
Carries: Live bait, lures, flies, maps, rods, reels, licenses
Bodies of water: Susquehanna River, Penns Creek, Raystown Lake, Walker Lake, Rose Valley Lake
Services & Products: Guide services, fishing instruction, repair services
OK to call for current conditions: Yes

Raystown Fishing & Hunting Supplies
RR 3 Box 294 A
Huntingdon 16652
Hours: 9am-6pm
Carries: Live bait, lures, flies, maps, rods, reels, licenses
Bodies of water: Juniata River, Raystown Lake
Services & Products: Guide services, fishing instruction, repair services
Guides: Yes
OK to call for current conditions: Yes
Contact: Robert Mort

SHAWNEE LAKE

BAIT & TACKLE...

White Horse Trading Co
Berlin 814-267-5552
Hours: 9am-5pm, closed Sun.
Carries: Live bait, lures, flies, rods, reels, licenses
Bodies of water: Shawnee Lake, Brush Creek, Wills Creek, Stoney Creek
Services & Products: Beverages
Guides: No
OK to call for current conditions: Yes
Contact: Debbie Custer

STILLWATER LAKE

GUIDES...

Ray Serfass
Pocono Summit 717-839-7736
Species & Seasons: Shad April-May, SM Bass, LM Bass June-Nov, Channel Catfish April-Nov, Striped Bass June-Sept
Bodies of water: Delaware River, Stillwater Lake, Gouldsboro Lake
Rates: Half day: $125(1-2), $175(3), Full day: $200(1-2), $275(3)

Call between: Anytime
Provides: Light tackle, heavy tackle, fly rod/reel, lures, bait
Handicapped equipped: Yes
Certifications: PA Guide Permit

WESTERN PENNSYLVANIA RIVERS & STREAMS

BAIT & TACKLE...

Allegheny Bait & Tackle
Tarentum 412-224-6888
Hours: 7am-9pm
Carries: Live bait, flies, maps, rods, reels, licenses
Bodies of water: Allegheny River, Crooked Creek Res., Moraine State Park
Services & Products: Boat ramp, repair services
Guides: No
OK to call for current conditions: Yes
Contact: Joe, Rick or Ronie

Frailey Sporting Goods
Shelcota 412-354-3478
Hours: 6am-7:30pm
Carries: Live bait, lures, flies, maps, rods, reels, licenses
Bodies of water: Keystone Power Dam, Mahoning Creek Lake, Allegheny River, Crooked Creek Lake Park
Services & Products: Beverages
Guides: No
OK to call for current conditions: Yes
Contact: Sally

Lock 3 Bait & Tackle
Cheswick 412-274-7710
Hours: 7am-9pm
Carries: Live bait, lures, flies, rods, reels, licenses
Bodies of water: Allegheny River
Services & Products: Guide services, beverages, repair services
Guides: Yes
OK to call for current conditions: Yes
Contact: Lee Murray

PENNSYLVANIA

WESTERN PENNSYLVANIA

Nestors Rod & Bow Pro Shop
Whitehall 610-433-6051
Hours: 10am-9pm
Carries: Live bait, lures, flies, maps, rods, reels, licenses
Bodies of water: Little Lehigh Creek, Monocacy Creek, Bushkill Creek, Lehigh River
Services & Products: Fishing instruction, fly tying classes
Guides: No
OK to call for current conditions: Yes
Contact: Dan Buss

North Park Bait & Tackle
Allison Park 412-367-7959
Hours: 7am-9pm
Carries: Live bait, lures, flies, rods, reels, licenses
Bodies of water: North Park Lake, Pine Creek, Allegheny River, Ohio River
Services & Products: Food, beverages
Guides: No
OK to call for current conditions: Yes
Contact: Dwight or Glenn Yingling

Rega's Bait Shop
Connellsville 412-628-4410
Hours: 7am-9pm
Carries: Live bait, lures, flies, rods, reels, licenses
Bodies of water: Youghiogheny River
Services & Products: Repair services
Guides: Yes
OK to call for current conditions: Yes
Contact: Ralph Rega

Transue's Tackle
W. Kittanning 412-543-2971
Hours: 7am-9pm
Carries: Live bait, lures, flies, rods, reels, licenses
Bodies of water: Allegheny River, Keystone Lake
Services & Products: Beverages, gas/oil, repair services
Guides: Yes
OK to call for current conditions: Yes
Contact: Mark Transue

FLY SHOPS...

Falling Spring Outfitters, Inc.
Scotland 717-263-7811
Hours: 10am-6pm, closed Mon.
Carries: Flies, maps, rods, reels
Bodies of water: Falling Spring Branch, Letort Spring Run, Conococheague Creek, Potomac River, Yellow Breeches Creek
Services & Products: Guide services, fishing instruction, instruction in fly tying
OK to call for current conditions: Yes
Contact: Mark Sturtevant

Fly Tyers "Vice"
Pittsburgh 412-276-2831
Hours: 9am-6pm, closed Fri, Sat., Sun.
Carries: Flies, rods, reels
Bodies of water: Lake Erie, Lake Arthur, Lake Wilheim, Neshonnick Creek, Slippery Rock, Laurel Hill Creek, Loyalhanna Creek
Services & Products: Guide services, fishing instruction, repair services
Guides: Yes
OK to call for current conditions: Yes
Contact: Tony Marasco

Outdoor Shop
Volant 412-533-3212
Hours: 9am-6pm
Carries: Lures, flies, maps, rods, reels, licenses
Bodies of water: Neshannock Creek
Services & Products: Guide services, fishing instruction, fly fishing lessons
Guides: Yes
OK to call for current conditions: Yes
Contact: Anyone

GUIDES...

Allegheny Outdoors
Bradford 814-368-8608
Species & Seasons: Trout April-Sept, Walleye May-Mar, Muskellunge June-Sept, Northern Pike Dec-Sept, SM Bass June-Oct, Steelhead Oct-April, Crappie, White Bass May-June, Yellow Perch Dec-Mar, Perch, Northern Pike, Walleye(ice fishing) Dec-Mar
Bodies of water: Allegheny Nat'l. Forest, Allegheny River, Allegheny Res., Cattaraugus Creek, (NY), Chautauqua Lake (NY)
Rates: Half day: $75(1), $100(2), Full day: $125(1), $150(2) different kinds of fishing, different prices
Call between: 5pm-11pm
Provides: Light tackle, heavy tackle, lures, bait
Certifications: NYS DEC Licensed Fishing Guide

RHODE ISLAND

1. Atlantic Ocean
2. Block Island Sound
3. Narragansett Bay
4. Pascoag Reservoir
5. Point Judith Pond
6. Slatersville Reservoir
7. Watchaug Pond
8. Wilson Reservoir
9. Worden Pond

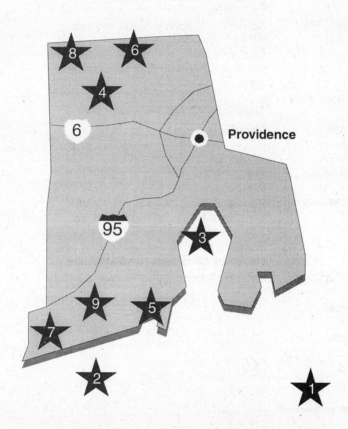

RHODE ISLAND

ATLANTIC OCEAN - BLOCK ISLAND SOUND

ATLANTIC OCEAN

BAIT & TACKLE...

Main Street Bait & Tackle
Bradford 401-377-2220
Hours: 6am-7pm
Carries: Live bait, lures, flies, rods, reels, licenses
Bodies of water: Wood River, Pawcatuck River, Watchaug Pond, Wordens Pond, Atlantic Ocean
Services & Products: Beverages, fishing instruction, canoe rentals
Guides: Yes
OK to call for current conditions: Yes
Contact: Dave or Bert

CHARTERS...

Cayenne Cay
W. Kingston 401-792-3581
Species & Seasons: Striped Bass May-Dec, Bluefish June-Dec, Fluke, June-Sept, Tautog, Cod April-Dec, Tuna July-Sept, Bonito July-Oct
Bodies of water: Narragansett Bay, Block Island Sound, Atlantic Ocean
Rates: Half day: $50(pp),
Full day: $75(pp), 4 person minimum, 6 maximum
Call between: 8am-8pm
Provides: Light tackle, heavy tackle, fly rod/reel, lures, bait
Handicapped equipped: Yes
Certifications: USCG

Lil Toot
Saunderstown.................. 401-294-1132
Species & Seasons: Cod April-Nov, Bluefish June-Oct, Striped Bass May-Nov, Shark June-Oct, Tuna July-Oct, Tautog Oct-Dec, Fluke June-Aug, Bonito July-Oct, Marlin July-Aug
Bodies of water: Atlantic Ocean, Block Island Sound, Narragansett Bay
Rates: Half day: $300(6),
Full day: $450(6), Tuna: $750
Call between: Anytime
Provides: Light tackle, heavy tackle, lures, bait
Handicapped equipped: Yes
Certifications: USCG

Poseidon
Narragansett 401-789-1444
Species & Seasons: Cod May-Oct, Bluefish June-Nov, Striped Bass, Tuna, Shark June-Oct, Bonito, Tuna July-Sept
Bodies of water: Narragansett Bay, Block Island Sound, Atlantic Ocean
Rates: $350-$650(6)
Call between: 8am-10pm
Provides: Light tackle, heavy tackle, lures, bait, rain gear
Handicapped equipped: Yes

MARINAS...

Long Cove Marina & Campground
Narragansett 401-783-4902
Hours: 9am-10pm, May 1-Oct 15
Bodies of water: Point Judith Pond, Atlantic Ocean
Services & Products: Boat ramp, camp sites, RV sites
Guides: Yes
OK to call for current conditions: No

BLOCK ISLAND SOUND

CHARTERS...

Cayenne Cay
W. Kingston 401-792-3581
Species & Seasons: Striped Bass May-Dec, Bluefish June-Dec, Fluke, June-Sept, Tautog, Cod April-Dec, Tuna July-Sept, Bonito July-Oct
Bodies of water: Narragansett Bay, Block Island Sound, Atlantic Ocean
Rates: Half day: $50(pp),
Full day: $75(pp), 4 person minimum, 6 maximum
Call between: 8am-8pm
Provides: Light tackle, heavy tackle, fly rod/reel, lures, bait
Handicapped equipped: Yes
Certifications: USCG

Hot Pursuit
Warwick 401-738-2427
Species & Seasons: Tuna June-Nov, Bluefish June-Oct, Striped Bass, Cod May-Nov, White Marlin July-Sept, Fluke June-Sept
Bodies of water: Block Island Sound and further
Rates: Inshore: Full day: $575(1-6), Offshore: Full day: $750(1-6)
Provides: Light tackle, heavy tackle, lures, bait
Handicapped equipped: Depends
Certifications: USCG

Lil Toot
Saunderstown.................. 401-294-1132
Species & Seasons: Cod April-Nov, Bluefish June-Oct, Striped Bass May-Nov, Shark June-Oct, Tuna July-Oct, Tautog Oct-Dec, Fluke June-Aug, Bonito July-Oct, Marlin July-Aug
Bodies of water: Atlantic Ocean, Block Island Sound, Narragansett Bay
Rates: Half day: $300(6),
Full day: $450(6), Tuna: $750
Call between: Anytime
Provides: Light tackle, heavy tackle, lures, bait
Handicapped equipped: Yes
Certifications: USCG

Poseidon
Narragansett 401-789-1444
Species & Seasons: Cod May-Oct, Bluefish June-Nov, Striped Bass, Tuna, Shark June-Oct, Bonito, Tuna July-Sept
Bodies of water: Narragansett Bay, Block Island Sound, Atlantic Ocean
Rates: $350-$650(6)
Call between: 8am-10pm
Provides: Light tackle, heavy tackle, lures, bait, rain gear
Handicapped equipped: Yes

Sakarak
Narragansett 401-789-8801
Species & Seasons: Cod April-July, Striped Bass June-Nov, Tuna, Bonito, Dolphin July-Sept
Bodies of water: Block Island Sound
Rates: Half day: $325((6),
Full day: $425-$800(6), Flyfishing: Half day: $275, Full day: $325, maximum 3 people
Call between: 6-8 pm
Provides: Light tackle, heavy tackle, fly rod/reel, lures, bait
Handicapped equipped: Yes
Certifications: USCG

Seven B's V
Narragansett 401-789-9250
.... 407-220-0893
Species & Seasons: Sea Bass, Cod, Pollock, Hake, Tuna, Tautog, Fluke, Flounder May-Nov
Bodies of water: Block Island Sound to Nantucket shoals

BLOCK ISLAND SOUND - POINT JUDITH POND — RHODE ISLAND

Rates: Half day: $20(1), Full day: $40(1)
Call between: 7am-9pm
Provides: Light tackle, heavy tackle, lures, bait, beverages, lunch
Handicapped equipped: Yes
Certifications: USCG

MARINAS...

Snug Harbor Marina
Wakefield 401-783-7766
Hours: 5am-9pm
Carries: Live bait, lures, flies, maps, rods, reels
Bodies of water: Block Island Sound, Narragansett Bay, Point Judith Pond
Services & Products: Canoe rentals, charter boat service, food, beverages, gas/oil, fishing instruction, repair services
OK to call for current conditions: Yes
Contact: Elisa Conti

NARRAGANSETT BAY

BAIT & TACKLE...

Sportsmans Bate & Tackle
Warwick 401-737-7393
Hours: 5:30am-8pm
Carries: Live bait, lures, maps, rods, reels, licenses
Bodies of water: Greenwich Bay, Narragansett Bay
Services & Products: Beverages, fishing instruction, repair services
Guides: Yes
OK to call for current conditions: Yes

CHARTERS...

Cayenne Cay
W. Kingston 401-792-3581
Species & Seasons: Striped Bass May-Dec, Bluefish June-Dec, Fluke, June-Sept, Tautog, Cod April-Dec, Tuna July-Sept, Bonito July-Oct
Bodies of water: Narragansett Bay, Block Island Sound, Atlantic Ocean
Rates: Half day: $50(pp),
Full day: $75(pp), 4 person minimum, 6 maximum
Call between: 8am-8pm
Provides: Light tackle, heavy tackle, fly rod/reel, lures, bait
Handicapped equipped: Yes
Certifications: USCG

Lil Toot
Saunderstown 401-294-1132
Species & Seasons: Cod April-Nov, Bluefish June-Oct, Striped Bass May-Nov, Shark June-Oct, Tuna July-Oct, Tautog Oct-Dec, Fluke June-Aug, Bonito July-Oct, Marlin July-Aug
Bodies of water: Atlantic Ocean, Block Island Sound, Narragansett Bay
Rates: Half day: $300(6),
Full day: $450(6), Tuna: $750
Call between: Anytime
Provides: Light tackle, heavy tackle, lures, bait
Handicapped equipped: Yes
Certifications: USCG

Poseidon
Narragansett 401-789-1444
Species & Seasons: Cod May-Oct, Bluefish June-Nov, Striped Bass, Tuna, Shark June-Oct, Bonito, Tuna July-Sept
Bodies of water: Narragansett Bay, Block Island Sound, Atlantic Ocean
Rates: $350-$650(6)
Call between: 8am-10pm
Provides: Light tackle, heavy tackle, lures, bait, rain gear
Handicapped equipped: Yes

MARINAS...

Snug Harbor Marina
Wakefield 401-783-7766
Hours: 5am-9pm
Carries: Live bait, lures, flies, maps, rods, reels
Bodies of water: Block Island Sound, Narragansett Bay, Point Judith Pond
Services & Products: Canoe rentals, charter boat service, food, beverages, gas/oil, fishing instruction, repair services
OK to call for current conditions: Yes
Contact: Elisa Conti

Warwick Cove Marina
Warwick 401-737-2446
Hours: 7am-8pm
Carries: Live bait, lures, maps
Bodies of water: Narragansett Bay
Services & Products: Food, beverages, gas/oil, slip rentals
Guides: Yes
OK to call for current conditions: Yes
Contact: John Williams

PASCOAG RESERVOIR

BAIT & TACKLE...

Fishin's Stuff
Pascoag 401-568-4748
Hours: 7am-7pm
Carries: Live bait, lures, flies, maps, rods, reels, licenses
Bodies of water: Pascoag Res., Wilson Res., Echo Lake, Round Top, Slatersville Res.
Services & Products: Repair services
Guides: Yes
OK to call for current conditions: Yes
Contact: Bob

POINT JUDITH POND

MARINAS...

Long Cove Marina & Campground
Narragansett 401-783-4902
Hours: 9am-10pm, May 1-Oct 15
Bodies of water: Point Judith Pond, Atlantic Ocean
Services & Products: Boat ramp, camp sites, RV sites
Guides: Yes
OK to call for current conditions: No

Snug Harbor Marina
Wakefield 401-783-7766
Hours: 5am-9pm
Carries: Live bait, lures, flies, maps, rods, reels
Bodies of water: Block Island Sound, Narragansett Bay, Point Judith Pond
Services & Products: Canoe rentals, charter boat service, food, beverages, gas/oil, fishing instruction, repair services
OK to call for current conditions: Yes
Contact: Elisa Conti

RHODE ISLAND
SLATERSVILLE RESERVOIR - WORDENS POND

SLATERSVILLE RESERVOIR

BAIT & TACKLE...

Fishin's Stuff
Pascoag 401-568-4748
Hours: 7am-7pm
Carries: Live bait, lures, flies, maps, rods, reels, licenses
Bodies of water: Pascoag Res., Wilson Res., Echo Lake, Round Top, Slatersville Res.
Services & Products: Repair services
Guides: Yes
OK to call for current conditions: Yes
Contact: Bob

WATCHAUG POND

BAIT & TACKLE...

Main Street Bait & Tackle
Bradford 401-377-2220
Hours: 6am-7pm
Carries: Live bait, lures, flies, rods, reels, licenses
Bodies of water: Wood River, Pawcatuck River, Watchaug Pond, Wordens Pond, Atlantic Ocean
Services & Products: Beverages, fishing instruction, canoe rentals
Guides: Yes
OK to call for current conditions: Yes
Contact: Dave or Bert

WILSON RESERVOIR

BAIT & TACKLE...

Fishin's Stuff
Pascoag 401-568-4748
Hours: 7am-7pm
Carries: Live bait, lures, flies, maps, rods, reels, licenses
Bodies of water: Pascoag Res., Wilson Res., Echo Lake, Round Top, Slatersville Res.
Services & Products: Repair services
Guides: Yes
OK to call for current conditions: Yes
Contact: Bob

WORDENS POND

BAIT & TACKLE...

Main Street Bait & Tackle
Bradford 401-377-2220
Hours: 6am-7pm
Carries: Live bait, lures, flies, rods, reels, licenses
Bodies of water: Wood River, Pawcatuck River, Watchaug Pond, Wordens Pond, Atlantic Ocean
Services & Products: Beverages, fishing instruction, canoe rentals
Guides: Yes
OK to call for current conditions: Yes
Contact: Dave or Bert

SOUTH CAROLINA

1. Atlantic Ocean
2. Hartwell Lake
3. Lake Greenwood
4. Lake Marion (Santee Cooper)
5. Lake Moultrie (Santee Cooper)
6. Lake Murray
7. Lake Strom Thurmond (Clarks Hill)
8. Lake Wylie
9. Regional Areas
10. Russell Lake
11. Saluda River
12. Savannah River
13. Wateree Lake

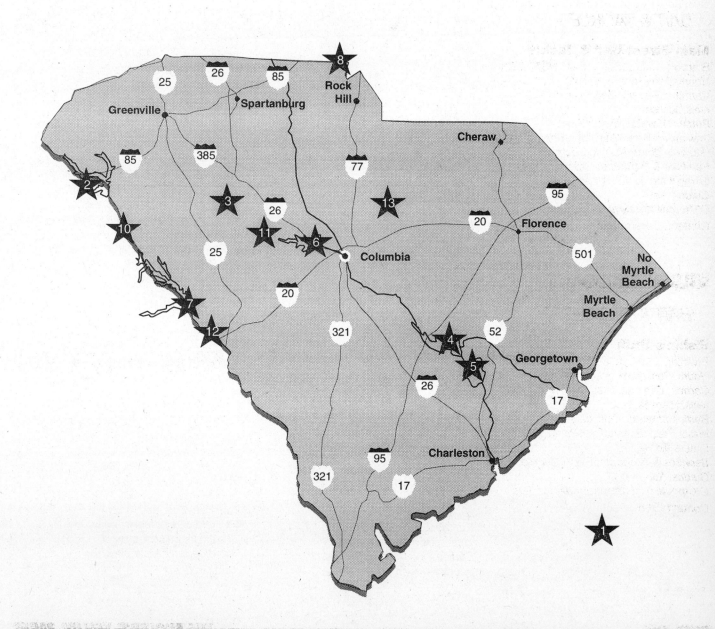

SOUTH CAROLINA

ATLANTIC OCEAN

CHARTERS...

Hurricane Fleet
N. Myrtle Beach 803-249-3571
Species & Seasons: Yellowfin Tuna, Dolphin May-Sept, King Mackerel April-Dec, Blue Marlin May-Aug, White Marlin, Sailfish June-Sept, Snapper, Grouper all year
Bodies of water: Atlantic Ocean
Rates: $60-$150 pp
Call between: 7am-9pm
Provides: Light tackle, heavy tackle, lures, bait, beverages, lunch
Handicapped equipped: Yes
Certifications: USCG

Marsh Grass Charters Inc.
Charleston 803-766-1464
Species & Seasons: Blue Marlin, White Marlin, Sailfish, Yellowfin Tuna, Wahoo, Dolphin April-Nov, King Mackerel, Grouper, Snapper all year
Bodies of water: Atlantic Ocean, off shore of Charleston, S.C.
Rates: Half day: $500(1-4), $550(5-6), Full day: $700(1-4), $750(5-6), Marlin: $800-$850
Call between: 9am-9pm
Provides: Light tackle, lures, bait, rain gear, ice
Handicapped equipped: Yes
Certifications: USCG

MARINAS...

Blue Water Marine
Hilton Head Isle 803-671-3060
Hours: 7:30am-7:30pm
Carries: Lures, rods, reels, licenses
Bodies of water: Atlantic Ocean, Calbogue Sound, Port Royal Sound
Services & Products: Charter boat service, boat ramp, repair services
OK to call for current conditions: Yes
Contact: Anyone

Captain Dicks Marina
Murrells Inlet 803-651-3676
.... 800-344-FISH
Hours: 6am-9pm
Carries: Lures, maps, licenses
Bodies of water: Attlantic Ocean, Murrells Inlet
Services & Products: Boat rentals, guide services, charter boat service, food, beverages, gas/oil, fishing instruction
OK to call for current conditions: Yes

HARTWELL LAKE

BAIT & TACKLE...

Lake Russell Bait & Tackle
Lowndesville 803-348-2947
Hours: 5am-9pm
Carries: Live bait, lures, flies, maps, rods, reels, licenses
Bodies of water: Russell Lake, Hartwell Lake, Clarks Hill Lake
Services & Products: Guide services, lodging, food, beverages, gas/oil, fishing instruction
Guides: Yes
OK to call for current conditions: Yes
Contact: George

Store & More
Pickens 803-878-2750
Hours: 6am-11pm
Carries: Live bait, lures, flies, maps, rods, reels, licenses
Bodies of water: Hartwell Lake, Lake Keowee, Lake Jocassee, White Water Lake, Lake Cherokee
Services & Products: Food, beverages, gas/oil
Guides: No
OK to call for current conditions: No

LAKE GREENWOOD

MARINAS...

Tower Point Marina
Greenwood 803-223-7332
Hours: 6am-1am
Carries: Live bait, lures, maps, rods, reels
Bodies of water: Lake Greenwood, Reedy River, Saluda River
Services & Products: Boat rentals, boat ramp, food, beverages, gas/oil
OK to call for current conditions: Yes
Contact: Brenda S. Lindley

LAKE MARION (SANTEE-COOPER)

BAIT & TACKLE...

Randolph's Landing (Lodging)
Manning 800-478-2152
Hours: 6am-8pm
Carries: Live bait, lures, flies, maps, rods, reels, licenses
Bodies of water: Lake Marion
Services & Products: Boat rentals, guide services, lodging, boat ramp, food, beverages, gas/oil, fishing instruction, repair services
Guides: Yes
OK to call for current conditions: Yes
Contact: Nathan Bristow

Sportsman Stop
Aiken 803-641-7365
Hours: 5am-6pm
Carries: Live bait, lures, flies, maps, rods, reels, licenses
Bodies of water: Lake Murray, Clarks Hill Lake, Savannah River, Lake Marion, Lake Moultrie
Services & Products: Food, beverages, gas/oil, repair services
Guides: Yes
OK to call for current conditions: Yes
Contact: Pete Day

GUIDES...

Don's Guide Service
Manning 803-478-2536
Species & Seasons: Blue Catfish Dec-April, Flathead Catfish May-June/July-Nov, Striped Bass June-July/Nov-Dec
Bodies of water: Lake Marion, Lake Moultrie, (Santee-Cooper)
Rates: Full day: $250(1-2), $40 addidtional pp over 2
Call between: 8pm-11pm
Provides: Light tackle, heavy tackle, lures, bait, gas, oil
Handicapped equipped: Yes
Certifications: USCG

LAKE MARION - LAKE MOULTRIE

Pete Pritchard
Summerton 803-478-7533
Species & Seasons: Crappie Mar-July/Sept-Dec, Catfish all year, Striped Bass Oct-Jan
Bodies of water: Lake Marion (Santee-Cooper)
Rates: Full day: $200(1-2), $35 additional pp over 2
Call between: 8pm-10pm
Provides: Light tackle, heavy tackle, lures, bait
Handicapped equipped: Yes
Certifications: USCG

Randy's Guide Service
Summerton 803-478-8184
Species & Seasons: Catfish, Striped Bass, Crappie Mar-Nov
Bodies of water: Lake Marion (Santee-Cooper)
Rates: Full day: $150(1), plus expenses
Call between: 6am-10pm
Provides: Light tackle, heavy tackle, lures, bait
Handicapped equipped: Yes

Billy Spearin
Eutawville 803-492-7017
Species & Seasons: Catfish all year
Bodies of water: Lake Marion, Lake Moultrie (Santee-Cooper)
Rates: Full day: $225(2)
Call between: 8-10am/6-7pm
Provides: Heavy tackle, bait
Handicapped equipped: Yes
Certifications: USCG

LODGES...

Cypress Pointe Condominiums
Manning 803-478-7253
.... 800-510-8760
Guest Capacity: 50
Handicapped equipped: Yes, some
Seasons: All year
Rates: $45/day, $600/week
Contact: Doug Rhodes
Species & Seasons: Crappie Spring/Fall, LM Bass, Catfish all year, Striped Bass Winter/Fall/Spring, Bluegill Spring/Summer
Bodies of Water: Lake Marion, Lake Moultrie (Santee Cooper)
Types of fishing: Light tackle, heavy tackle
Available: Licenses, bait, tackle, boat rentals, family activities

Harry's Fish Camp
Pineville 803-351-4561
Guest Capacity: 300
Handicapped equipped: No
Seasons: All year
Rates: Varies
Contact: Tom Collum
Guides: Yes
Species & Seasons: LM Bass, Striped Bass, Catfish, Crappie, Bream all year
Bodies of Water: Lake Marion, Lake Moultrie (Santee Cooper), Santee River, Cooper River
Types of fishing: Fly fishing, light tackle, heavy tackle, wading
Available: Licenses, bait, tackle

Randolph's Landing
Manning 800-BIG-CATS
.... 803-478-2152
Seasons: All year
Guides: Yes
Bodies of Water: Lake Marion (Santee Cooper)
Available: Boat rentals, restaurant, fishing pier, campsites, swimming area, boat ramp, repair services, lodging

MARINAS...

Cypress Shores Marina
Eutawville 803-492-7506
Hours: 6am-6pm
Carries: Live bait, lures, maps, rods, reels, licenses
Bodies of water: Lake Marion, Lake Moultrie
Services & Products: Boat rentals, lodging, boat ramp, food, beverages, gas/oil, fishing instruction
Guides: Yes
OK to call for current conditions: Yes
Contact: Barbara or Bryan

Lakevue Landing
Manning 803-478-2133
Hours: 7am-11pm
Carries: Live bait, lures, maps, rods, reels, licenses
Bodies of water: Lake Marion, Lake Moultrie
Services & Products: Boat rentals, lodging, boat ramp, food, beverages, gas/oil
Guides: Yes
OK to call for current conditions: Yes
Contact: Betty or Lee Caudill

SOUTH CAROLINA

LAKE MOULTRIE (SANTEE-COOPER)

BAIT & TACKLE...

Sportsman Stop
Aiken 803-641-7365
Hours: 5am-6pm
Carries: Live bait, lures, flies, maps, rods, reels, licenses
Bodies of water: Lake Murray, Clarks Hill Lake, Savannah River, Lake Marion, Lake Moultrie
Services & Products: Food, beverages, gas/oil, repair services
Guides: Yes
OK to call for current conditions: Yes
Contact: Pete Day

GUIDES...

Don's Guide Service
Manning 803-478-2536
Species & Seasons: Blue Catfish Dec-April, Flathead Catfish May-June/July-Nov, Striped Bass June-July/Nov-Dec
Bodies of water: Lake Marion, Lake Moultrie, (Santee-Cooper)
Rates: Full day: $250(1-2), $40 addidtional pp over 2
Call between: 8pm-11pm
Provides: Light tackle, heavy tackle, lures, bait, gas, oil
Handicapped equipped: Yes
Certifications: USCG

Billy Spearin
Eutawville 803-492-7017
Species & Seasons: Catfish all year
Bodies of water: Lake Marion, Lake Moultrie (Santee-Cooper)
Rates: Full day: $225(2)
Call between: 8-10am/6-7pm
Provides: Heavy tackle, bait
Handicapped equipped: Yes
Certifications: USCG

SOUTH CAROLINA

LAKE MOULTRIE - LAKE MURRAY

LODGES...

Cypress Pointe Condominiums
Manning 803-478-7253
.... 800-510-8760
Guest Capacity: 50
Handicapped equipped: Yes, some
Seasons: All year
Rates: $45/day, $600/week
Contact: Doug Rhodes
Species & Seasons: Crappie Spring/Fall, LM Bass, Catfish all year, Striped Bass Winter/Fall/Spring, Bluegill Spring/Summer
Bodies of Water: Lake Marion, Lake Moultrie (Santee Cooper)
Types of fishing: Light tackle, heavy tackle
Available: Licenses, bait, tackle, boat rentals, family activities

Harry's Fish Camp
Pineville 803-351-4561
Guest Capacity: 300
Handicapped equipped: No
Seasons: All year
Rates: Varies
Contact: Tom Collum
Guides: Yes
Species & Seasons: LM Bass, Striped Bass, Catfish, Crappie, Bream all year
Bodies of Water: Lake Marion, Lake Moultrie (Santee Cooper), Santee River, Cooper River
Types of fishing: Fly fishing, light tackle, heavy tackle, wading
Available: Licenses, bait, tackle

MARINAS...

Cypress Shores Marina
Eutawville 803-492-7506
Hours: 6am-6pm
Carries: Live bait, lures, maps, rods, reels, licenses
Bodies of water: Lake Marion, Lake Moultrie
Services & Products: Boat rentals, lodging, boat ramp, food, beverages, gas/oil, fishing instruction
Guides: Yes
OK to call for current conditions: Yes
Contact: Barbara or Bryan

Lakevue Landing
Manning 803-478-2133
Hours: 7am-11pm
Carries: Live bait, lures, maps, rods, reels, licenses
Bodies of water: Lake Marion, Lake Moultrie
Services & Products: Boat rentals, lodging, boat ramp, food, beverages, gas/oil
Guides: Yes
OK to call for current conditions: Yes
Contact: Betty or Lee Caudill

LAKE MURRAY

BAIT & TACKLE...

Dooley's Sport Shop
Lexington 803-359-6084
Hours: 6am-7pm
Carries: Live bait, lures, flies, maps, rods, reels, licenses
Bodies of water: Lake Murray
Services & Products: Guide services, beverages, fishing instruction
OK to call for current conditions: Yes
Contact: Charles, Monte or Mike

Lynnhurst Bait & Tackle
N. Augusta 803-279-7894
Hours: 7am-7pm, closed Sun.
Carries: Live bait, lures, flies, maps, rods, reels, licenses
Bodies of water: Savannah River, Stevens Creek, Clarks Hill Lake, Lake Murray
Services & Products: Food, beverages, gas/oil
Guides: Yes
OK to call for current conditions: Yes
Contact: James Cullum

Sportsman Stop
Aiken 803-641-7365
Hours: 5am-6pm
Carries: Live bait, lures, flies, maps, rods, reels, licenses
Bodies of water: Lake Murray, Clarks Hill Lake, Savannah River, Lake Marion, Lake Moultrie
Services & Products: Food, beverages, gas/oil, repair services
Guides: Yes
OK to call for current conditions: Yes
Contact: Pete Day

GUIDES...

Benny Cubitt Guide Service
Inman 803-578-4660
.... 364-4518
Species & Seasons: Striped Bass April-Jan
Bodies of water: Lake Murray
Rates: Full day: $260(2), $300 up to 4
Call between: 6pm-10pm
Provides: Light tackle, heavy tackle, lures, bait
Certifications: USCG

D. W. Eggleston
Denver, NC 704-483-5502
Species & Seasons: Striped Bass all year
Bodies of water: Lake Murray
Rates: Half day: $150(1), $200(2), Full day: $200(1), $250(2) $20 additional pp over 2, maximum 4
Call between: 8am-9pm
Provides: Light tackle, lures, bait
Handicapped equipped: No
Certifications: USCG

Just Add Water Inc.
Chapin 803-345-9682
.... 800-951-4007
Species & Seasons: Crappie, Bream, LM Bass, Striped Bass all year
Bodies of water: Lake Murray
Rates: Crappie: Full day: $200, LM Bass: Full day: $250, Striped Bass: Full day: $300
Call between: 9am-8pm
Provides: Light tackle, heavy tackle, fly rod/reel, lures, bait, lodging also available
Handicapped equipped: Yes
Certifications: USCG

Ronnie Shealy
Newberry 803-276-6496
Species & Seasons: Striped Bass April-Oct
Bodies of water: Lake Murray
Rates: Full day: $240(2), $280(4)
Call between: 6pm-10pm
Provides: Heavy tackle, bait
Handicapped equipped: No
Certifications: USCG

LAKE MURRAY - REGIONAL AREAS

Steve Wise
Prosperity 803-364-3930
Species & Seasons: Striped Bass all year but best April-Sept
Bodies of water: Lake Murray
Rates: Full day: $300(1-4)
Call between: 9pm-11pm
Provides: Light tackle, heavy tackle, lures, bait
Handicapped equipped: Yes
Certifications: USCG

LODGES...

Saluda River Resort
Silverstreet 803-276-7917
Guest Capacity: 85 sites
Handicapped equipped: No
Seasons: All year
Rates: $16/per camper
Contact: Joann or Bill Wesberry
Guides: Yes
Species & Seasons: Striped Bass Jan-May, LM Bass April-Sept, Bream May, Panfish April-Oct
Bodies of Water: Saluda River, Lake Murray
Types of fishing: Fly fishing, light tackle, heavy tackle
Available: Licenses, bait, tackle, family activities

MARINAS...

Black's Bridge Marina
Prosperity 803-364-3035
Hours: 6am-9pm
Carries: Live bait, lures, maps, rods, reels, licenses
Bodies of water: Lake Murray
Services & Products: Guide services, lodging, boat ramp, food, beverages, gas/oil
Guides: Yes
OK to call for current conditions: Yes
Contact: Michael (Buck) Bailey

Holland's Marina at Logan's Port
Prosperity 803-364-3092
.... 364-2227
Hours: 6am-8pm
Carries: Live bait, lures, flies, maps, rods, reels, licenses
Bodies of water: Lake Murray
Services & Products: Guide services, lodging, boat ramp, food, beverages, gas/oil, fishing instruction, repair services

Guides: Yes
OK to call for current conditions: Yes
Contact: Hughey Capps

Turner's Landing
Lexington 803-359-0644
Hours: 24 hours, 7 days
Carries: Live bait
Bodies of water: Lake Murray
Services & Products: Boat ramp, food, beverages
Guides: No
OK to call for current conditions: Yes
Contact: Art Turner

LAKE STROM THURMOND (CLARKS HILL)

BAIT & TACKLE...

Lake Russell Bait & Tackle
Lowndesville 803-348-2947
Hours: 5am-9pm
Carries: Live bait, lures, flies, maps, rods, reels, licenses
Bodies of water: Russell Lake, Hartwell Lake, Clarks Hill Lake
Services & Products: Guide services, lodging, food, beverages, gas/oil, fishing instruction
Guides: Yes
OK to call for current conditions: Yes
Contact: George

Lynnhurst Bait & Tackle
N. Augusta 803-279-7894
Hours: 7am-7pm, closed Sun.
Carries: Live bait, lures, flies, maps, rods, reels, licenses
Bodies of water: Savannah River, Stevens Creek, Clarks Hill Lake, Lake Murray
Services & Products: Food, beverages, gas/oil
Guides: Yes
OK to call for current conditions: Yes
Contact: James Cullum

Sportsman Stop
Aiken 803-641-7365
Hours: 5am-6pm
Carries: Live bait, lures, flies, maps, rods, reels, licenses
Bodies of water: Lake Murray, Clarks Hill Lake, Savannah River, Lake Marion, Lake Moultrie

Services & Products: Food, beverages, gas/oil, repair services
Guides: Yes
OK to call for current conditions: Yes
Contact: Pete Day

GUIDES...

Dave Willard
Clarks Hill 803-637-6379
Species & Seasons: Striped Bass, Hybrids, LM Bass all year
Bodies of water: Lake Strom Thurmond (Clarks Hill)
Rates: Full day: $225(1-2), $50 additional pp over 2
Call between: Anytime
Provides: Light tackle, lures, bait
Handicapped equipped: Yes
Certifications: USCG

LAKE WYLIE

GUIDES...

Mark Goss
Lake Wylie 803-831-2285
Species & Seasons: LM Bass all year
Bodies of water: Lake Wylie, Wateree Lake
Rates: Half day: $125(1), $150(2), Full day: $175(1), $200(2)
Call between: 8pm-9pm
Provides: Light tackle, lures, beverages
Handicapped equipped: Yes

REGIONAL AREAS

GUIDES...

Creekside Angler
Greenville 803-487-4722
Species & Seasons: Trout
Bodies of water: Smoky Mtns., Outer Banks (NC)
Rates: Full day: $150(1), $225(2)
Call between: 5am-10pm
Provides: Light tackle, fly rod/reel, lures, lunch
Handicapped equipped: Yes

SOUTH CAROLINA
RUSSELL LAKE - WATEREE LAKE

RUSSELL LAKE

BAIT & TACKLE...

Lake Russell Bait & Tackle
Lowndesville 803-348-2947
Hours: 5am-9pm
Carries: Live bait, lures, flies, maps, rods, reels, licenses
Bodies of water: Russell Lake, Hartwell Lake, Clarks Hill Lake
Services & Products: Guide services, lodging, food, beverages, gas/oil, fishing instruction
Guides: Yes
OK to call for current conditions: Yes
Contact: George

SALUDA RIVER

MARINAS...

Tower Point Marina
Greenwood 803-223-7332
Hours: 6am-1am
Carries: Live bait, lures, maps, rods, reels
Bodies of water: Lake Greenwood, Reedy River, Saluda River
Services & Products: Boat rentals, boat ramp, food, beverages, gas/oil
OK to call for current conditions: Yes
Contact: Brenda S. Lindley

LODGES...

Saluda River Resort
Silverstreet 803-276-7917
Guest Capacity: 85 sites
Handicapped equipped: No
Seasons: All year
Rates: $16/per camper
Contact: Joann or Bill Wesberry
Guides: Yes
Species & Seasons: Striped Bass Jan-May, LM Bass April-Sept, Bream May, Panfish April-Oct
Bodies of Water: Saluda River, Lake Murray
Types of fishing: Fly fishing, light tackle, heavy tackle
Available: Licenses, bait, tackle, family activities

SAVANNAH RIVER

BAIT & TACKLE...

Lynnhurst Bait & Tackle
N. Augusta 803-279-7894
Hours: 7am-7pm, closed Sun.
Carries: Live bait, lures, flies, maps, rods, reels, licenses
Bodies of water: Savannah River, Stevens Creek, Clarks Hill Lake, Lake Murray
Services & Products: Food, beverages, gas/oil
Guides: Yes
OK to call for current conditions: Yes
Contact: James Cullum

Sportsman Stop
Aiken 803-641-7365
Hours: 5am-6pm
Carries: Live bait, lures, flies, maps, rods, reels, licenses
Bodies of water: Lake Murray, Clarks Hill Lake, Savannah River, Lake Marion, Lake Moultrie
Services & Products: Food, beverages, gas/oil, repair services
Guides: Yes
OK to call for current conditions: Yes
Contact: Pete Day

WATEREE LAKE

GUIDES...

Mark Goss
Lake Wylie 803-831-2285
Species & Seasons: LM Bass all year
Bodies of water: Lake Wylie, Wateree Lake
Rates: Half day: $125(1), $150(2), Full day: $175(1), $200(2)
Call between: 8pm-9pm
Provides: Light tackle, lures, beverages
Handicapped equipped: Yes

Thank you for using the Angler's Yellow Pages

The business listings in the Angler's Yellow Pages are full of valuable information.
"Know before you go…"

SOUTH DAKOTA

1. Lake Francis Case
2. Lake Louise
3. Lake Oahe
4. Lake Sharpe
5. Missouri River
6. Richmond Lake

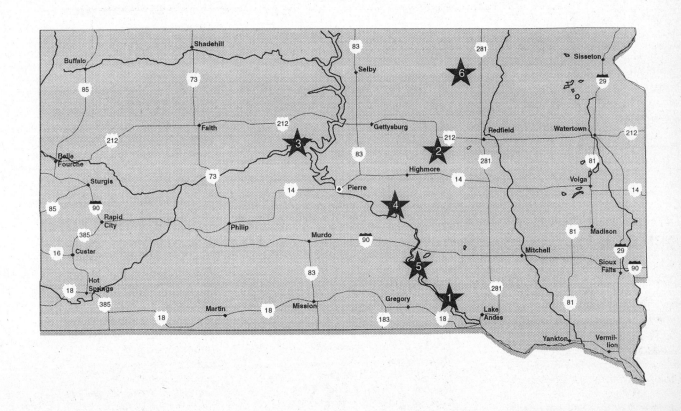

SOUTH DAKOTA

LAKE FRANCIS CASE - LAKE OAHE

LAKE FRANCIS CASE

BAIT & TACKLE...

Fort Randall Bait & Tackle
Pickstown 605-487-7760
Hours: 6:30am-11pm
Carries: Live bait, lures, maps, rods, reels, licenses
Bodies of water: Lake Francis Case, Missouri River
Services & Products: Guide services (Walleye and SM Bass Half day: $125, Full day: $175), lodging, food, beverages, gas/oil, camping supplies
OK to call for current conditions: Yes
Contact: Bryce Broyhill

LAKE LOUISE

GUIDES...

Dakota Expeditions
Miller 605-853-2545
Species & Seasons: Walleye, SM Bass May-Aug, Northern Pike April-June, LM Bass May-July
Bodies of water: Lake Louise, Lake Sharpe, Lake Oahe
Rates: Full day: $175(2) + gas, bait, refreshments
Call between: 6am-10pm
Provides: Rain gear
Handicapped equipped: No
Certifications: USCG, SD Pro Guides Association

LAKE OAHE

BAIT & TACKLE...

Bridge City Bait
Mobridge 605-845-3132
Hours: 6am-9pm
Carries: Live bait, lures, maps, rods, reels, licenses
Bodies of water: Lake Oahe, Missouri River
Services & Products: Boat rentals, guide services, charter boat service, lodging, boat ramp, food, beverages, gas/oil, taxidermy
Guides: Yes
OK to call for current conditions: Yes
Contact: Jerry, Doug or Janice

Carl's Bait Shop
Ft. Pierre 605-223-9453
Hours: 6am-10pm
Carries: Live bait, lures, flies, maps, rods, licenses
Bodies of water: Lake Oahe, Missouri River, Lake Sharp
Services & Products: Guide services, food, beverages, fishing instruction, accurate daily fishing reports
Guides: Yes
OK to call for current conditions: Yes
Contact: Ron Walker or Joan Heltzel

GUIDES...

Adventure III Guide Service
Pierre 605-224-4479
Species & Seasons: Walleye, Chinook Salmon May-Sept
Bodies of water: Lake Oahe, Lake Sharpe
Rates: Full day: $200(1-2), $240(3)
Call between: 7pm-10pm
Provides: Light tackle, heavy tackle, lures
Handicapped equipped: Yes
Certifications: USCG, CPR, First aid

Dakota Expeditions
Miller 605-853-2545
Species & Seasons: Walleye, SM Bass May-Aug, Northern Pike April-June, LM Bass May-July
Bodies of water: Lake Oahe, Lake Sharpe, Lake Louise
Rates: Full day: $175(2) + gas, bait, refreshments
Call between: 6am-10pm
Provides: Rain gear
Handicapped equipped: No
Certifications: USCG, SD Pro Guides Association

Fishing With Dave
Pierre 605-224-1186
Species & Seasons: Walleye, Salmon May-Sept, Northern Pike April-June
Bodies of water: Lake Oahe, Lake Sharpe
Rates: Half day: $150(2), Full day: $200(2), $235(3) + tax
Call between: 5pm-10pm
Provides: Light tackle, heavy tackle, lures, bait
Handicapped equipped: Yes
Certifications: USCG, CPR, FCC

Jorgenson's Guide Service
Ipswich 605-426-6524
Species & Seasons: Walleye, SM Bass May-Oct, Salmon Sept-Oct
Bodies of water: Lake Oahe
Rates: Half day: $100(1-2), Full day: $170(1-2)
Call between: 8pm-11pm
Provides: Light tackle, lures, bait
Handicapped equipped: Yes
Certifications: USCG

Scott Pitlick
Pierre 605-224-5629
Species & Seasons: Walleye all year, Northern Pike Mar-May, SM Bass, LM Bass April-Dec, Salmon ice out-freeze up
Bodies of water: Lake Oahe, Lake Sharpe
Rates: Half day: $120(2) + tax, Full day: $200(2) + tax, $25 additional pp over 2
Call between: 6pm-10pm
Provides: Light tackle, heavy tackle, lures, bait
Handicapped equipped: Yes

Vern's Guide Service
Mobridge 605-845-2516
.... 845-7394
Species & Seasons: Walleye, Northern Pike all year, Salmon Oct-Nov, SM Bass, Catfish April-Oct
Bodies of water: Lake Oahe
Rates: Half day: $75(1), $100(2), Full day: $125(1), $200(2)
Call between: 8am-11pm
Provides: Light tackle, heavy tackle, lures, bait, lunch
Handicapped equipped: Yes
Certifications: USCG

LODGING...

New Evarts Resort
Glenham 605-762-3256
Guest Capacity: 65
Handicapped equipped: No
Seasons: April 1 to Nov 25
Rates: $40/day
Contact: Val VanKley
Guides: Yes
Species & Seasons: Walleye, Sauger all year, Northern Pike May-June, Catfish, Bass, SM Bass, White Bass April-Nov, Salmon Aug-Nov
Bodies of Water: Lake Oahe
Types of fishing: Light tackle, heavy tackle
Available: Licenses, bait, tackle, boat rentals, family activities, baby sitting

LAKE OAHE - RICHMOND LAKE / SOUTH DAKOTA

South Whitlock Resort
Gettysburg 605-765-9196
Guest Capacity: 60
Handicapped equipped: Yes
Seasons: April 1 to Dec 22
Rates: $200/day
Contact: Chuck Krause
Guides: Yes
Species & Seasons: Walleye May-Oct, Salmon Sept-Oct
Bodies of Water: Lake Oahe
Types of fishing: Light tackle, heavy tackle
Available: Fishing instruction, licenses, bait, tackle, boat rentals, family activities, baby sitting

LAKE SHARPE

BAIT & TACKLE...

Carl's Bait Shop
Ft. Pierre 605-223-9453
Hours: 6am-10pm
Carries: Live bait, lures, flies, maps, rods, licenses
Bodies of water: Lake Sharpe, Missouri River, Lake Oahe
Services & Products: Guide services, food, beverages, fishing instruction, accurate daily fishing reports
Guides: Yes
OK to call for current conditions: Yes
Contact: Ron Walker or Joan Heltzel

GUIDES...

Adventure III Guide Service
Pierre 605-224-4479
Species & Seasons: Walleye, Chinook Salmon May-Sept
Bodies of water: Lake Sharpe, Lake Oahe
Rates: Full day: $200(1-2), $240(3)
Call between: 7pm-10pm
Provides: Light tackle, heavy tackle, lures
Handicapped equipped: Yes
Certifications: USCG, CPR, First aid

Dakota Expeditions
Miller 605-853-2545
Species & Seasons: Walleye, SM Bass May-Aug, Northern Pike April-June, LM Bass May-July
Bodies of water: Lake Sharpe, Lake Oahe, Lake Louise
Rates: Full day: $175(2) + gas, bait, refreshments
Call between: 6am-10pm

Provides: Rain gear
Handicapped equipped: No
Certifications: USCG, SD Pro Guides Association

Fishing With Dave
Pierre 605-224-1186
Species & Seasons: Walleye, Salmon May-Sept, Northern Pike April-June
Bodies of water: Lake Sharpe, Lake Oahe
Rates: Half day: $150(2), Full day: $200(2), $235(3) + tax
Call between: 5pm-10pm
Provides: Light tackle, heavy tackle, lures, bait
Handicapped equipped: Yes
Certifications: USCG, CPR, FCC

Scott Pitlick
Pierre 605-224-5629
Species & Seasons: Walleye all year, Northern Pike Mar-May, SM Bass, LM Bass April-Dec, Salmon ice out-freeze up
Bodies of water: Lake Sharpe, Lake Oahe
Rates: Half day: $120(2) + tax, Full day: $200(2) + tax, $25 additional pp over 2
Call between: 6pm-10pm
Provides: Light tackle, heavy tackle, lures, bait
Handicapped equipped: Yes

MISSOURI RIVER

BAIT & TACKLE...

Bridge City Bait
Mobridge 605-845-3132
Hours: 6am-9pm
Carries: Live bait, lures, maps, rods, reels, licenses
Bodies of water: Missouri River, Lake Oahe
Services & Products: Boat rentals, guide services, charter boat service, lodging, boat ramp, food, beverages, gas/oil, taxidermy
Guides: Yes
OK to call for current conditions: Yes
Contact: Jerry, Doug or Janice

Carl's Bait Shop
Ft. Pierre 605-223-9453
Hours: 6am-10pm
Carries: Live bait, lures, flies, maps, rods, licenses
Bodies of water: Missouri River, Lake Oahe, Lake Sharp

Services & Products: Guide services, food, beverages, fishing instruction, accurate daily fishing reports
Guides: Yes
OK to call for current conditions: Yes
Contact: Ron Walker or Joan Heltzel

Fort Randall Bait & Tackle
Pickstown 605-487-7760
Hours: 6:30am-11pm
Carries: Live bait, lures, maps, rods, reels, licenses
Bodies of water: Missouri River, Lake Francis Case
Services & Products: Guide services (Walleye and SM Bass Half day: $125, Full day: $175), lodging, food, beverages, gas/oil, camping supplies
OK to call for current conditions: Yes
Contact: Bryce Broyhill

RICHMOND LAKE

BAIT & TACKLE...

Mattern's Sporting Goods
Aberdeen 605-229-2787
Hours: 8am-6pm, 8am-3pm Sat., Sun.
Carries: Live bait, lures, flies, maps, rods, reels
Bodies of water: Richmond Lake, Mina Lake, Elm Lake, Elm River, James River
Services & Products: Beverages, fishing instruction, repair services
Guides: Yes

The Angler's Yellow Pages lets you
tap the fishing information grapevine

TENNESSEE

1. Cumberland River
2. Dale Hollow Lake
3. Douglas Lake
4. Ft. Loudoun Lake
5. Kentucky Lake
6. Lake Barkley
7. Lake Graham
8. Melton Hill Lake
9. Norris Lake
10. Old Hickory Lake
11. Percy Priest Lake
12. Smoky Mountains
13. Tennessee River
14. Tims Ford Lake
15. Watts Bar Lake

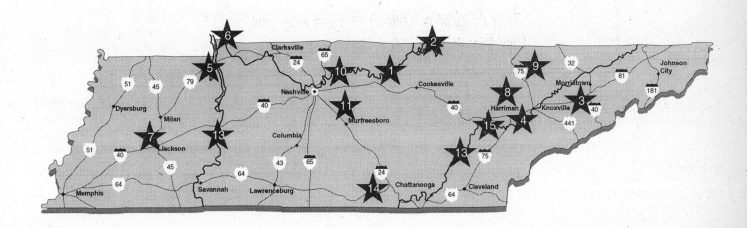

TENNESSEE

CUMBERLAND RIVER - DOUGLAS LAKE

CUMBERLAND RIVER

BAIT & TACKLE...

Cook's Shanty
Elmwood 615-897-2699
Hours: 7am-9pm, 7am-6pm Sun.
Carries: Live bait, lures, maps
Bodies of water: Cumberland River
Services & Products: Food, beverages
Guides: Yes
OK to call for current conditions: Yes
Contact: Thomas W. Culver

GUIDES...

Steve McCadams
Paris 901-642-0360
Species & Seasons: Crappie, LM Bass Mar-Nov, Bluegill April-June, Catfish June-Sept, White Bass July-Sept, Sauger June-July
Bodies of water: Tennessee River, Kentucky Lake, Cumberland River, Lake Barkley
Rates: Full day: $210(1-2), $235(3)
Call between: 7pm-10pm
Provides: Light tackle, heavy tackle
Handicapped equipped: Yes

Fred McClintock
Celina 615-243-2142
Species & Seasons: Striped Bass May-Oct, SM Bass Nov-April
Bodies of water: Cumberland River, Dale Hollow Lake
Rates: Half day: $150(2),
Full day: $250(2),
SM Bass: Half day: $125, Full day: $200
Call between: 4pm-10pm
Provides: Heavy tackle, bait
Handicapped equipped: No
Certifications: KY Licensed Guide

South Harpeth Outfitters
Nashville 615-952-4186
Species & Seasons: Rainbow Trout, Brown Trout Mar-Dec, SM Bass Feb-Nov, Striped Bass April-Nov, Brook Trout all year
Bodies of water: Cumberland River, Tennessee River and tributaries, private spring creeks, private trophy ponds
Rates: Half day: $200(1), $275(2),
Full day: $250(1), $325(2), $400(3), $500(4)
Call between: 7pm-9:30pm
Provides: Light tackle, fly rod/reel, lures, bait, beverages, lunch
Handicapped equipped: Yes
Certifications: Ande Fishing Team, AirFlo Fishing Team, Tennessee Outdoor Writers Assoc.

Don Wirth
Nashville 615-383-5044
Species & Seasons: Striped Bass July-Oct, Muskellunge Dec-Mar
Bodies of water: Cumberland River, Dale Hollow Lake
Rates: Striped Bass: Half day: $150(1-2), Full day: $250(1-2),
Muskellunge: Full day: $300
Call between: 9am-9pm
Provides: Heavy tackle, lures, bait, beverages
Handicapped equipped: No

DALE HOLLOW LAKE

GUIDES...

Fred McClintock
Celina 615-243-2142
Species & Seasons: Striped Bass May-Oct, SM Bass Nov-April
Bodies of water: Cumberland River, Dale Hollow Lake
Rates: Half day: $150(2),
Full day: $250(2), SM Bass:
Half day: $125, Full day: $200
Call between: 4pm-10pm
Provides: Heavy tackle, bait
Handicapped equipped: No
Certifications: KY Licensed Guide

Don Wirth
Nashville 615-383-5044
Species & Seasons: Striped Bass July-Oct, Muskellunge Dec-Mar
Bodies of water: Cumberland River, Dale Hollow Lake
Rates: Striped Bass: Half day: $150(1-2), Full day: $250(1-2),
Muskellunge: Full day: $300
Call between: 9am-9pm
Provides: Heavy tackle, lures, bait, beverages
Handicapped equipped: No

LODGES...

Cedar Hill Resort
Celina 615-243-3201
Guest Capacity: 325
Handicapped equipped: No
Seasons: Mar 1 to Nov 30
Rates: $35-$170/day, $200-$850/weekly
Contact: R. Roberts
Guides: Yes
Species & Seasons: SM Bass Mar-Nov, Walleye May-Aug, Trout April-Sept
Bodies of Water: Dale Hollow Lake, Obey River
Types of fishing: Light tackle
Available: Fishing instruction, licenses, bait, tackle, boat rentals, family activities

Horse Creek Dock and Resort
Celina 800-545-2595
Guest Capacity: 40 units
Seasons: All year
Rates: $120/weekend
Guides: Yes
Species & Seasons: Bass all year, Trout April-Oct
Bodies of Water: Dale Hollow Lake
Types of fishing: Light tackle
Available: Fishing instruction, licenses, bait, tackle, boat rentals, family activities

MARINAS...

East Port Marina
Alpine 615-879-7511
Hours: 6am-7pm
Carries: Live bait, lures, maps, rods, reels, licenses
Bodies of water: Dale Hollow Lake
Services & Products: Boat rentals, guide services, lodging, boat ramp, food, beverages, gas/oil, fishing instruction, repair services, houseboat rental, store, restaurant, pontoon boats
Guides: Yes
OK to call for current conditions: Yes
Contact: Clyde or Vickie Craig

DOUGLAS LAKE

GUIDES...

Old Smoky Outfitters Inc.
Gatlinburg 615-430-1936
Species & Seasons: Brook Trout, Rainbow Trout, Brown Trout Mar-Nov, SM Bass Feb-May/Sept-Nov, LM Bass Mar-Nov, Striped Bass April-Nov
Bodies of water: Great Smoky Mountains Nat'l. Park, Finger Lakes of Smokies, Douglas Lake
Rates: Half day: $135(1), $175(2),
Full day: $200(1), $240(2),
overnight trips available May-Sept.

DOUGLAS LAKE - LAKE GRAHAM / TENNESSEE

Call between: 9am-5pm
Provides: Light tackle, fly rod/reel, lures, beverages, lunch
Handicapped equipped: Yes
Certifications: ORVIS

FT. LOUDON LAKE

BAIT & TACKLE...

Minit Check-Bass Pro Shop
Oak Ridge 615-483-6211
Hours: 6am-9pm
Carries: Live bait, lures, flies, maps, rods, reels, licenses
Bodies of water: Tn. River, Watts Bar Lake, Ft. Loudon Lake, Melton Hill Lake, Norris Lake
Services & Products: Beverages, fishing instruction
Guides: Yes
OK to call for current conditions: Yes
Contact: Bobby Ford or Chris Whitson

KENTUCKY LAKE

GUIDES...

Steve McCadams
Paris 901-642-0360
Species & Seasons: Crappie, LM Bass Mar-Nov, Bluegill April-June, Catfish June-Sept, White Bass July-Sept, Sauger June-July
Bodies of water: Tennessee River, Kentucky Lake, Cumberland River, Lake Barkley
Rates: Full day: $210(1-2), $235(3)
Call between: 7pm-10pm
Provides: Light tackle, heavy tackle
Handicapped equipped: Yes

Jim Story Guide Service
Tennessee Ridge 615-721-3548
Species & Seasons: LM Bass Mar-Nov, SM Bass, Crappie Mar-June
Bodies of water: Kentucky Lake, Lake Barkley
Rates: Half day: $150(1-2), Full day: $200(1-2)
Call between: 7pm-10pm
Provides: Light tackle, heavy tackle, lures
Handicapped equipped: No
Certifications: USCG

LODGES...

Beaverdam Resort
Camden 901-584-3963
Guest Capacity: 20
Handicapped equipped: No
Seasons: All year
Rates: $36-$58/day
Contact: Will Parker
Guides: Yes
Species & Seasons: LM Bass, SM Bass, Crappie, Panfish Mar-Nov, Catfish April-Sept, Sauger Dec-Feb
Bodies of Water: Kentucky Lake
Types of fishing: Light tackle
Available: Fishing instruction, licenses, bait, tackle, boat rentals

Mansard Island Resort
Springville 800-533-5590
Guest Capacity: 120
Handicapped equipped: No
Seasons: All year
Rates: $35/day and up
Contact: Cee Koenig
Guides: Yes
Species & Seasons: Crappie Mar-May, LM Bass, SM Bass April-May
Bodies of Water: Kentucky Lake
Types of fishing: Light tackle
Available: Licenses, bait, tackle, boat rentals, family activities, full service marina

Shamrock Resort
Buchanan 901-232-8211
Guest Capacity: 200
Handicapped equipped: No
Seasons: Mar 15 to Nov 1
Rates: $50/day
Guides: Yes
Species & Seasons: Crappie Mar-June, LM Bass, SM Bass Sept-Oct, Striped Bass July-Sept
Bodies of Water: Kentucky Lake
Types of fishing: Fly fishing, light tackle, heavy tackle, wading
Available: Fishing instruction, licenses, bait, tackle, boat rentals, family activities, pool, tennis, basketball. swing

LAKE BARKLEY

GUIDES...

Steve McCadams
Paris 901-642-0360
Species & Seasons: Crappie, LM Bass Mar-Nov, Bluegill April-June, Catfish June-Sept, White Bass July-Sept, Sauger June-July
Bodies of water: Tennessee River, Kentucky Lake, Cumberland River, Lake Barkley
Rates: Full day: $210(1-2), $235(3)
Call between: 7pm-10pm
Provides: Light tackle, heavy tackle
Handicapped equipped: Yes

Jim Story Guide Service
Tennessee Ridge 615-721-3548
Species & Seasons: LM Bass Mar-Nov, SM Bass, Crappie Mar-June
Bodies of water: Kentucky Lake, Lake Barkley
Rates: Half day: $150(1-2), Full day: $200(1-2)
Call between: 7pm-10pm
Provides: Light tackle, heavy tackle, lures
Handicapped equipped: No
Certifications: USCG

LAKE GRAHAM

BAIT & TACKLE...

Daniel C-D Service Station
Jackson 901-427-0745
Hours: 7am-10pm
Carries: Live bait, lures, rods, reels, licenses
Bodies of water: Lake Graham
Services & Products: Food, beverages, gas/oil
Guides: No
OK to call for current conditions: Yes
Contact: Wayne Daniel

Lake Graham Store
Jackson 901-423-4937
Hours: 1/2 hour before sunrise-1/2 hour after sunset
Carries: Live bait, lures, flies, maps, rods, reels, licenses
Bodies of water: Lake Graham
Services & Products: Boat rentals, guide services, boat ramp, food, beverages, fishing instruction
Guides: Yes
OK to call for current conditions: Yes
Contact: Dan Foster

TENNESSEE

MELTON HILL LAKE

BAIT & TACKLE...

Minit Check-Bass Pro Shop
Oak Ridge 615-483-6211
Hours: 6am-9pm
Carries: Live bait, lures, flies, maps, rods, reels, licenses
Bodies of water: Tennessee River, Watts Bar Lake, Ft. Loudon Lake, Melton Hill Lake, Norris Lake
Services & Products: Beverages, fishing instruction
Guides: Yes
OK to call for current conditions: Yes
Contact: Bobby Ford or Chris Whitson

NORRIS LAKE

BAIT & TACKLE...

Minit Check-Bass Pro Shop
Oak Ridge 615-483-6211
Hours: 6am-9pm
Carries: Live bait, lures, flies, maps, rods, reels, licenses
Bodies of water: Tennessee River, Watts Bar Lake, Ft. Loudon Lake, Melton Hill Lake, Norris Lake
Services & Products: Beverages, fishing instruction
Guides: Yes
OK to call for current conditions: Yes
Contact: Bobby Ford or Chris Whitson

GUIDES...

T's Pleasure Guide Service
Hamilton, OH 513-868-9214
Species & Seasons: Striped Bass Nov-May
Bodies of water: Norris Lake
Rates: 2 day trips: $525, up to 4 people
Call between: After 1pm week days
Provides: Heavy tackle, lures, bait
Handicapped equipped: No

MARINAS...

Andersonville Marina & Boat Dock
Andersonville 615-494-9649
Hours: 24 hours Mar.-Oct., 7am-7pm Nov.-Feb.
Carries: Live bait, lures, flies, maps, rods, reels, licenses
Bodies of water: Norris Lake
Services & Products: Boat rentals, guide services, lodging, boat ramp, food, beverages, gas/oil, fishing instruction
Guides: Yes
OK to call for current conditions: Yes
Contact: Ike Vanderpool

OLD HICKORY LAKE

BAIT & TACKLE...

Nort's Drive In
Nashville 615-361-1818
Hours: 4:30am-10pm
Carries: Live bait, lures, flies, maps, rods, reels, licenses
Bodies of water: Percy Priest Lake, Old Hickory Lake
Services & Products: Guide services, food, beverages, fishing instruction
Guides: Yes
OK to call for current conditions: Yes

GUIDES...

Professional Guide Service
Smyrna 615-459-0567
Species & Seasons: LM Bass, SM Bass all year, Crappie Nov-May
Bodies of water: Percy Priest Lake, Old Hickory Lake
Rates: Half day: $125(1-2), Full day: $200(1-2)
Call between: Anytime
Provides: Light tackle, lures, rain gear
Handicapped equipped: No

PERCY PRIEST LAKE

BAIT & TACKLE...

Nort's Drive In
Nashville 615-361-1818
Hours: 4:30am-10pm
Carries: Live bait, lures, flies, maps, rods, reels, licenses
Bodies of water: Percy Priest Lake, Old Hickory Lake
Services & Products: Guide services, food, beverages, fishing instruction
Guides: Yes
OK to call for current conditions: Yes

GUIDES...

Jack Christian Guide Service
Goodlettsville 615-672-0194
Species & Seasons: SM Bass Mar-May/Oct-Dec, LM Bass Mar-May, Striped Bass, Hybrid Bass May-June/Dec, Bass (night) July-Sept
Bodies of water: Percy Priest Lake
Rates: Half day: $150(1-2), Full day: $225(1-2)
Call between: 7pm-9pm
Provides: Light tackle, heavy tackle, lures, bait
Handicapped equipped: Yes

Professional Guide Service
Smyrna 615-459-0567
Species & Seasons: LM Bass, SM Bass all year, Crappie Nov-May
Bodies of water: Percy Priest Lake, Old Hickory Lake
Rates: Half day: $125(1-2), Full day: $200(1-2)
Call between: Anytime
Provides: Light tackle, lures, rain gear
Handicapped equipped: No

MARINAS...

Four Corners Marina
Antioch 615-641-9523
Hours: 7am-9pm
Carries: Live bait, lures, maps, rods, licenses
Bodies of water: Percy Priest Lake
Services & Products: Boat rentals, guide services, boat ramp, food, beverages, gas/oil, repair services
Guides: Yes
OK to call for current conditions: Yes

SMOKY MOUNTAINS

GUIDES...

Creekside Angler
Greenville, SC 803-487-4722
Species & Seasons: Trout
Bodies of water: Smoky Mountains
Rates: Full day: $150(1), $225(2)
Call between: 5-10
Provides: Light tackle, fly rod/reel, lures, lunch
Handicapped equipped: Yes

TENNESSEE RIVER - WATTS BAR LAKE
TENNESSEE

TENNESSEE RIVER

BAIT & TACKLE...

Minit Check-Bass Pro Shop
Oak Ridge 615-483-6211
Hours: 6am-9pm
Carries: Live bait, lures, flies, maps, rods, reels, licenses
Bodies of water: Tn. River, Watts Bar Lake, Ft. Loudon Lake, Melton Hill Lake, Norris Lake
Services & Products: Beverages, fishing instruction
Guides: Yes
OK to call for current conditions: Yes
Contact: Bobby Ford or Chris Whitson

GUIDES...

Steve McCadams
Paris 901-642-0360
Species & Seasons: Crappie, LM Bass Mar-Nov, Bluegill April-June, Catfish June-Sept, White Bass July-Sept, Sauger June-July
Bodies of water: Tennessee River, Kentucky Lake, Cumberland River, Lake Barkley
Rates: Full day: $210(1-2), $235(3)
Call between: 7pm-10pm
Provides: Light tackle, heavy tackle
Handicapped equipped: Yes

South Harpeth Outfitters
Nashville 615-952-4186
Species & Seasons: Rainbow Trout, Brown Trout Mar-Dec, SM Bass Feb-Nov, Striped Bass April-Nov, Brook Trout all year
Bodies of water: Cumberland River, Tennessee River and tributaries, private spring creeks, private trophy ponds
Rates: Half day: $200(1), $275(2), Full day: $250(1), $325(2), $400(3), $500(4)
Call between: 7pm-9:30pm
Provides: Light tackle, fly rod/reel, lures, bait, beverages, lunch
Handicapped equipped: Yes
Certifications: Ande Fishing Team, AirFlo Fishing Team, Tennessee Outdoor Writers Assoc.

LODGES...

Cottonport Fish N' Camp
Decatur 334-4999
Guest Capacity: 100
Handicapped equipped: Yes
Seasons: Mid Mar to Mid Oct
Rates: Varies
Contact: Karen Armstrong
Guides: Yes
Species & Seasons: LM Bass, SM Bass, Sauger, Walleye, Crappie, Bream, Perch, Catfish
Bodies of Water: Tennessee River
Types of fishing: Light tackle, float trips
Available: Licenses, bait, tackle, cabins, camping, RV hook-ups

MARINAS...

Cherokee Shores Marina & Campground
Ten Mile 615-334-5620
Hours: 8am-whenever pm
Carries: Live bait, lures, flies, maps, rods, reels, licenses
Bodies of water: Tennessee River
Services & Products: Lodging, boat ramp, food, beverages, gas/oil, fishing instruction, campground
Guides: Yes
OK to call for current conditions: Yes

TIMS FORD

LODGES...

Holiday Landing and Resort
PO Box 1556, 912 Old Awalt Road
Tullahoma 37388
Handicapped equipped: No
Seasons: All year
Rates: $39.50/day
Guides: Yes, recommend
Species & Seasons: Striped Bass, SM Bass, LM Bass, Walleye, Crappie
Bodies of Water: Tims Ford
Available: Licenses, bait, tackle, boat rentals, restaurant

WATTS BAR LAKE

BAIT & TACKLE...

Minit Check-Bass Pro Shop
Oak Ridge 615-483-6211
Hours: 6am-9pm
Carries: Live bait, lures, flies, maps, rods, reels, licenses
Bodies of water: Tn. River, Watts Bar Lake, Ft. Loudon Lake, Melton Hill Lake, Norris Lake
Services & Products: Beverages, fishing instruction
Guides: Yes
OK to call for current conditions: Yes
Contact: Bobby Ford or Chris Whitson

MARINAS...

Bayside Marina
Ten Mile 615-376-7031
Hours: 7am-9pm, closed Nov. 15-Mar. 15
Carries: Live bait, lures, maps, rods, reels, licenses
Bodies of water: Watts Bar Lake
Services & Products: Boat rentals, lodging, boat ramp, food, beverages, gas/oil
Guides: Yes
OK to call for current conditions: Yes
Contact: Anyone

The Angler's Yellow Pages is the quickest and easiest way to find what you want, when you want it

TEXAS

1. Amistad Reservoir
2. Aransas Bay
3. B.A. Steinhagen Lake
4. Baffin Bay
5. Belton Lake
6. Brazos River
7. Caddo Lake
8. Calaveras Lake
9. Canyon Lake
10. Cedar Reservoir
11. Choke Canyon Lake
12. Coleto Creek Reservoir
13. Copano Bay
14. Corpus Christi Bay
15. Falcon Reservoir
16. Galveston Bay
17. Guadalupe River
18. Gulf of Mexico
19. Hubbard Creek Reservoir
20. Intracoastal Waterway
21. Ivie Reservoir
22. Laguna Madre
23. Lake Buchanan
24. Lake Fork
25. Lake Ft. Phantom Hill
26. Lake Livingston
27. Lake Lyndon B. Johnson
28. Lake O' The Pines
29. Lake Palestine
30. Lake Ray Roberts
31. Lake Tawakoni
32. Lake Texoma
33. Lake Travis
34. Lake Waco
35. Lake Whitney
36. Lake Worth
37. Navasota River
38. O.C. Fisher Lake
39. Pat Mayse Lake
40. Possum Kingdom Lake
41. Private & Pay Lakes
42. Red River
43. Redfish Bay
44. Richland Cr. Reservoir
45. Rio Grande River
46. Sam Rayburn Reservoir
47. San Antonio Bay
48. Somerville Lake
49. Stillhouse Hollow Lake
50. Toledo Bend Reservoir
51. Twin Buttes Reservoir

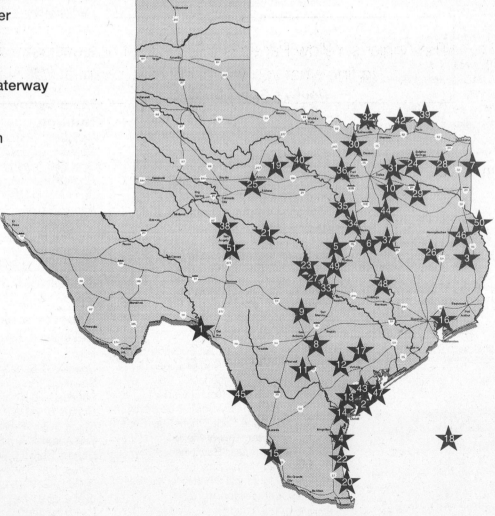

YOUR SILENT FISHING PARTNER

PAGE 421

TEXAS

AMISTAD RESERVOIR

LODGES...

American RV Resort Campground
Del Rio 210-775-6484
Guest Capacity: 200+
Handicapped equipped: Yes
Seasons: All year
Rates: RV site: $14.75/night
Contact: Bob Perry or Sara Sutton
Guides: Yes
Species & Seasons: LM Bass, Striped Bass, Catfish all year, White Bass Nov-May
Bodies of Water: Lake Amistad
Types of fishing: Light tackle, heavy tackle
Available: Licenses, boat rentals, family activities

Lakeview Inn
Del Rio 210-775-9521
Guest Capacity: 34 rooms
Handicapped equipped: No
Seasons: All year
Rates: Ask for fisherman rate
Guides: Yes
Species & Seasons: LM Bass, SM Bass, Walleye, Yellow/Blue Catfish, White Bass, Striped Bass all year
Bodies of Water: Lake Amistad
Available: Boat hookups

Ramada Inn
Del Rio 210-775-1511
Guest Capacity: 127
Handicapped equipped: Yes
Seasons: All year
Rates: $47.25/day, ask for fisherman rate
Contact: Terra Van Gorkon
Guides: Yes
Species & Seasons: LM Bass, SM Bass, Walleye, Catfish, White Bass, Striped Bass all year
Bodies of Water: Lake Amistad
Types of fishing: Fly fishing, light tackle, heavy tackle, wading
Available: Boat hookups, restaurant

Remington Inn
Del Rio 210-775-0585
Guest Capacity: 95 rooms
Handicapped equipped: Yes
Seasons: All year
Guides: Yes
Species & Seasons: LM Bass, SM Bass, Walleye, Catfish, Yellow/Blue Catfish, White Bass, Striped Bass all year
Bodies of Water: Lake Amistad
Available: Boat hookups

ARANSAS BAY

BAIT & TACKLE...

Fisherman's Wharf
Port Aransas 800-605-5448
Hours: 5:30am-10pm
Carries: Live bait, lures, maps, rods, reels, licenses
Bodies of water: Gulf of Mexico, Nueces Bay, Red Fish Bay, Aransas Bay, Intracoastal waterway
Services & Products: Guide services, charter boat service, food, beverages, gas/oil, fishing instruction
Guides: Yes
OK to call for current conditions: Yes
Contact: Carl Moore

Woody's Sport Center
Port Aransas 512-749-5252
Hours: 6am-8-10pm
Carries: Live bait, lures, maps, rods, reels, licenses
Bodies of water: Gulf of Mexico, Inland Bay, Aransas Bay, Redfish Bay, Corpus Christi Bay, Laguna Madre
Services & Products: Guide services, charter boat service, boat ramp, food, beverages, gas/oil, fishing instruction
OK to call for current conditions: Yes

CHARTERS...

Fisherman's Wharf
Port Aransas 800-605-5448
Species & Seasons: Red Snapper, Redfish Jan-Dec, Amberjack ?-July, Speckled Trout April-Oct, Flounder Sept-Jan, Sailfish July-Sept, Blue Marlin, White Marlin June-Sept, Shark May-Sept
Bodies of water: Gulf of Mexico, Redfish Bay, Aransas Bay, Nueces Bay
Call between: 7am-7pm
Provides: Light tackle, heavy tackle, bait
Handicapped equipped: Yes
Certifications: USCG

Mickey's Fishing Charters
Rockport 572-729-0113
Species & Seasons: Spotted Sea Trout, Red Drum, Black Drum, Flounder all year
Bodies of water: Coastal Bend, Red Fish Bay, Aransas Bay
Rates: Half day: $200(1-2), Full day: $250(1-2)
Call between: 8am-8pm
Provides: Light tackle, lures, bait
Handicapped equipped: Yes

Red Fish Charters
Fulton 800-862-7987
.... 512-729-8220
Species & Seasons: Redfish, Trout, all year Flounder Oct-Dec, Black Drum Feb-April
Bodies of water: Estes Flats, Aransas Bay, California Hole, Redfish Bay, Copano Bay
Rates: Your boat weekdays: $150(2), Your boat or mine: Full day: $250(1-2), $300(3), $350(4)
Call between: Anytime
Provides: Light tackle, bait
Handicapped equipped: No
Certifications: USCG, TP & W Guide

GUIDES...

Mike Sydows Fishing & Hunting
Rockport 512-729-7212
Species & Seasons: Redfish, Speckled Trout all year
Bodies of water: Aransas Bay, San Antonio Bay, Corpus Christi Bay
Rates: Full day: $350(1-2), $425(4)
Call between: Anytime
Provides: Light tackle, lures, bait, rain gear
Handicapped equipped: No
Certifications: USCG

Robert Brooks Fishing Guide Service
Fulton 512-729-7170
Species & Seasons: Red Drum, Speckled Trout, Flounder, Black Drum, Sheepshead all year
Bodies of water: Aransas Bay, Copano Bay, Carlos Bay, Mesquite Bay, San Antonio Bay, Redfish Bay, Corpus Christi Bay, Nueces Bay
Rates: Half day: Negotiable(1-2), Full day: $300(1-2), $50 additional pp over 2 up to 4
Call between: 6pm-10pm

ARANSAS BAY - BAFFIN BAY — TEXAS

Provides: Light tackle, heavy tackle, fly rod/reel, lures, bait, rain gear
Handicapped equipped: Yes
Certifications: USCG

Saltwater Safaris
Rockport 512-729-4131
Species & Seasons: Redfish July-Jan, Speckled Trout April-Jan, Black Drum Jan-April, Flounder Sept-Nov
Bodies of water: Corpus Christi Bay, Aransas Bay, Rf Fish Bay, Copano Bay, Mid TX Coast Line
Rates: Half day: $250(1-2), Full day: $300(1-2), $50 additional pp over 2
Call between: 6pm-9pm
Provides: Light tackle, fly rod/reel, lures, bait, beverages, caps, ice
Handicapped equipped: No
Certifications: USCG, TX Parks & Wildlife License

LODGES...

Mickey's RV Park
Rockport 512-729-0113
Guest Capacity: 100 RV campers
Handicapped equipped: No
Seasons: All year
Rates: $16/day
Contact: Jerry Mickey
Guides: Yes
Species & Seasons: Spotted Sea Trout, Red Drum, Flounder all year
Bodies of Water: Redfish Bay, Aransas Bay
Types of fishing: Light tackle, wading
Available: Fishing instruction, family activities

Rod & Reel Motel
Rockport 512-729-2028
.... 800-667-3570
Hours: 24 hours
Carries: Lures, maps, rods, reels
Bodies of water: Aransas Bay, Copano Bay, Gulf of Mexico
Services & Products: Guide services, lodging, fishing instruction, hunting guide service
OK to call for current conditions: Yes
Contact: Eugene Morel

MARINAS...

Fin & Feather Marina & RV Park
Aransas Pass 512-758-7414
Hours: 6am-11pm
Carries: Live bait, lures, maps, rods, reels, licenses
Bodies of water: Gulf of Mexico, Corpus Christi Bay, Aransas Bay
Services & Products: Boat rentals, guide services, charter boat service, boat ramp, food, beverages, fishing instruction
Guides: Yes
OK to call for current conditions: Yes
Contact: Rich

B. A. STEINHAGEN LAKE

BAIT & TACKLE...

Ann's Tackle Shop
Jasper 409-384-7685
Hours: 8am-5:30pm, closed Sun.
Carries: Lures, maps, rods, reels, licenses
Bodies of water: Sam Rayburn Res., Toledo Bend Res., B.A. Steinhagen Lake
Services & Products: Guide services
Guides: Yes
OK to call for current conditions: Yes
Contact: Ann or Debra

The "Reel Doctor"
Jasper 800-704-REEL
Hours: 9am-9pm
Carries: Maps, rods, reels
Bodies of water: Sam Rayburn Res., Toledo Bend Res., B.A. Steinhagen Lake, Lake Livingston
Services & Products: Repair services
Guides: Yes
OK to call for current conditions: Yes
Contact: Don Leidig

BAFFIN BAY

GUIDES...

Capt. Carl's Fish Guide Service
Corpus Christi 800-368-8175
Species & Seasons: Speckled Trout, Redfish all year
Bodies of water: Corpus Christi Bay, Laguna Madre, Baffin Bay
Rates: Half day: $200(1), $225(2), Full day: $300(1), $325(2), $50 additional pp up to 6
Call between: 8am-8pm
Provides: Light tackle, lures, bait
Handicapped equipped: Yes
Certifications: USCG

David Green's Guide Service
Corpus Christi 512-939-9912
Species & Seasons: Speckled Trout Mar-Nov, Redfish May-Oct
Bodies of water: Laguna Madre, Baffin Bay
Rates: Full day: $300(1), $325(2), $400(3), $475(4)
Call between: 5pm-9pm
Provides: Light tackle, lures, bait
Handicapped equipped: No
Certifications: TPWD Licensed Guide, USCG Licensed Captain

High Tide Fishing & Hunting Adventures
Corpus Christi 512-851-1161
Species & Seasons: Speckled Trout April-June, Redfish June-Sept
Bodies of water: Laguna Madre, Baffin Bay
Rates: Full day: $325(2), $50 additional pp up to 4
Call between: 10am-10pm
Provides: Light tackle, lures, bait
Handicapped equipped: No
Certifications: USCG, TX Parks & Wildlife Dept.

Phyllis Ingram's Guide Service
Corpus Christi 512-857-0702
Species & Seasons: Speckled Trout Mar-Dec, Redfish June-Nov
Bodies of water: Laguna Madre, Baffin Bay
Rates: Half day: $225(2), Full day: $325(2), special rates available Oct-Feb
Call between: 8am-8pm
Provides: Light tackle, lures, bait, rain gear
Certifications: USCG

TEXAS

BAFFIN BAY - CEDAR RESERVOIR

LODGES...

Wild Horse Lodge and Charters
Bishop 512-584-3098
Guest Capacity: 12 beds
Handicapped equipped: No
Seasons: All year
Rates: $100/night(1-2) $25 additional pp
Contact: Jan or Calvin Canamore
Guides: Yes
Species & Seasons: Speckled Trout, Redfish, Drum Jan-Dec
Bodies of Water: Baffin Bay, Laguna Madre
Types of fishing: Fly fishing, light tackle, heavy tackle, wading
Available: Fishing instruction, bait, tackle, family activities, Dove hunting, skeet, lighted pier

BELTON LAKE

BAIT & TACKLE...

B&P Minnow Farm
Milano 512-455-3222
Hours: 11am-9pm
Carries: Live bait, lures, flies, rods, reels
Bodies of water: Somerville Lake, Belton Lake, Brazos River
Guides: Yes
OK to call for current conditions: Yes
Contact: Jimann Jones

BRAZOS RIVER

BAIT & TACKLE...

B&P Minnow Farm
Milano 512-455-3222
Hours: 11am-9pm
Carries: Live bait, lures, flies, rods, reels
Bodies of water: Somerville Lake, Belton Lake, Brazos River
Guides: Yes
OK to call for current conditions: Yes
Contact: Jimann Jones

Bosqueville Fastime
Waco 817-756-1656
Hours: 5:30am-10pm
Carries: Live bait, lures, flies, maps, rods, reels, licenses
Bodies of water: Lake Waco, Lake Whitney, Brazos River, Bosque River

Services & Products: Food, beverages, gas/oil
Guides: Yes
OK to call for current conditions: Yes
Contact: Gary Harvick

GUIDES...

Little Rocky Lodge & Guide Service
Laguna Park 817-622-3010
Species & Seasons: Striped Bass, SM Bass Oct-July, Spotted Bass, LM Bass May-Oct
Bodies of water: Lake Whitney, Brazos River
Rates: Half day: $125(2),
Full day: $200(2), up to 4 people
Call between: 8pm-10pm
Provides: Light tackle, heavy tackle, lures, bait

Sportfishing Unlimited
Whitney 817-694-3974
Species & Seasons: Striped Bass Dec-May, SM Bass, LM Bass all year
Bodies of water: Lake Whitney, Stillhouse Hollow Lake, Brazos River (Whitney Dam to Waco)
Rates: Half day: $200(1), $300(2),
Full day: $200(1), $300(2),
4 day package: $1000
Call between: Anytime
Provides: Light tackle, heavy tackle, lures, beverages
Certifications: USCG, State of TX

CADDO LAKE

LODGES...

Pine Needle Lodge
Jefferson 903-665-2911
Guest Capacity: 20
Seasons: All year
Rates: $40-$50/day
Contact: Barry or Ann Bennick
Guides: Yes, recommend
Species & Seasons: LM Bass, Crappie, White Bass, Hybrids, Bluegill, Cftffish all year
Bodies of Water: Caddo Lake, Lake 'O The Pines
Types of fishing: Fly fishing, light tackle, trout lines
Available: Boat rentals, family activities, canoe rental, boat ramp

CALAVERAS LAKE

BAIT & TACKLE...

Canyon Bait House
Canyon Lake 210-899-9747
Hours: Closed Wed.
Carries: Live bait, lures, flies, maps, rods, reels
Bodies of water: Calaveras Lake, Guadalupe River
Services & Products: Guide services, food, beverages, fishing instruction
OK to call for current conditions: Yes
Contact: Chris Davis

CANYON LAKE

BAIT & TACKLE...

River Valley Campground
Canyon Lake 210-964-3613
Hours: 8:30am-6pm
Carries: Lures, flies
Bodies of water: Guadalupe River, Canyon Lake
Services & Products: Boat rentals, lodging, food, beverages, RV sites
Guides: Yes
OK to call for current conditions: Yes
Contact: Michael Strange

CEDAR RESERVOIR

LODGES...

Sunny Glen Resort Motel & Camp
Malakoff 903-489-0715
Guest Capacity: 1000+
Handicapped equipped: No
Seasons: All year
Contact: Grace Janke
Guides: Yes
Species & Seasons: Bass, Sandies, Crappie, April-June, Catfish, Hybrids all year
Bodies of Water: Cedar Creek Lake
Types of fishing: Light tackle, heavy tackle
Available: Bait, tackle, family activities, paddle boat rentals, jet ski, camping, motel, cabins, marina, boat ramps

CHOKE CANYON LAKE - CORPUS CHRISTI BAY   TEXAS

CHOKE CANYON LAKE

GUIDES...

Choke Canyon Bassin Guide Service
Gonzales.......................... 210-672-3109
Species & Seasons: LM Bass all year
Bodies of water: Choke Canyon Lake
Rates: Half day: $175(1-2),
Full day: $250(1-2)
Call between: 6pm-10pm
Provides: Heavy tackle, rain gear, beverages
Handicapped equipped: No
Certifications: TX Licensed Guide

Elroy's Guide Service
Three Rivers 512-786-4775
Species & Seasons: LM Bass, Catfish, Crappie all year
Bodies of water: Choke Canyon Lake
Rates: Half day: $140(1-2),
Full day: $240(1-2)
Call between: 6am-8pm
Handicapped equipped: Yes

James Glenn
Three Rivers 512-786-4762
Species & Seasons: LM Bass, Catfish, Crappie all year, Alligator Gar Mar-Oct
Bodies of water: Choke Canyon Lake
Rates: Half day: $150(1-2),
Full day: $250(1-2)
Call between: Anytime
Provides: Bait (Catfish, Gar)
Handicapped equipped: Yes

COLETO CREEK RESERVOIR

BAIT & TACKLE...

Dam Store
Victoria 512-576-4086
Hours: 7am-9pm
Carries: Live bait, lures, rods, reels
Bodies of water: Coleto Creek Res., Guadalupe River, San Antonio River
Services & Products: Boat rentals, guide services, food, beverages, gas/oil
Guides: Yes
OK to call for current conditions: Yes
Contact: Jim King

COPANO BAY

CHARTERS...

Red Fish Charters
Fulton 800-862-7987
.... 512-729-8220
Species & Seasons: Redfish, Trout, all year Flounder Oct-Dec, Black Drum Feb-April
Bodies of water: Estes Flats, Aransas Bay, California Hole, Redfish Bay, Copano Bay
Rates: Your boat weekdays: $150(2), Your boat or mine: Full day: $250(1-2), $300(3), $350(4)
Call between: Anytime
Provides: Light tackle, bait
Handicapped equipped: No
Certifications: USCG, TP & W Guide

GUIDES...

Robert Brooks Fishing Guide Service
Fulton 512-729-7170
Species & Seasons: Red Drum, Speckled Trout, Flounder, Black Drum, Sheepshead all year
Bodies of water: Aransas Bay, Copano Bay, Carlos Bay, Mesquite Bay, San Antonio Bay, Redfish Bay, Corpus Christi Bay, Nueces Bay
Rates: Half day: Negotiable(1-2), Full day: $300(1-2), $50 additional pp over 2 up to 4
Call between: 6pm-10pm
Provides: Light tackle, heavy tackle, fly rod/reel, lures, bait, rain gear
Handicapped equipped: Yes
Certifications: USCG

Saltwater Safaris
Rockport.......................... 512-729-4131
Species & Seasons: Redfish July-Jan, Speckled Trout April-Jan, Black Drum Jan-April, Flounder Sept-Nov
Bodies of water: Corpus Christi Bay, Aransas Bay, Red Fish Bay, Copano Bay, Mid-TX Coast Line
Rates: Half day: $250(1-2),
Full day: $300(1-2), $50 additional pp over 2
Call between: 6pm-9pm
Provides: Light tackle, fly rod/reel, lures, bait, beverages, caps, ice
Handicapped equipped: No
Certifications: USCG, TX Parks & Wildlife License

LODGES...

Rod & Reel Motel
Rockport.......................... 512-729-2028
.... 800-667-3570
Hours: 24 hours
Carries: Lures, maps, rods, reels
Bodies of water: Aransas Bay, Copano Bay, Gulf of Mexico
Services & Products: Guide services, lodging, fishing instruction, hunting guide service
OK to call for current conditions: Yes
Contact: Eugene Morel

CORPUS CHRISTI BAY

BAIT & TACKLE...

Woody's Sport Center
Port Aransas 512-749-5252
Hours: 6am-8-10pm
Carries: Live bait, lures, maps, rods, reels, licenses
Bodies of water: Gulf of Mexico, Inland Bay, Aransas Bay, Redfish Bay, Corpus Christi Bay, Laguna Madre
Services & Products: Guide services, charter boat service, boat ramp, food, beverages, gas/oil, fishing instruction
OK to call for current conditions: Yes

GUIDES...

Capt. Carl's Fish Guide Service
Corpus Christi 800-368-8175
Species & Seasons: Speckled Trout, Redfish all year
Bodies of water: Corpus Christi Bay, Laguna Madre, Baffin Bay
Rates: Half day: $200(1), $225(2),
Full day: $300(1), $325(2), $50 additional pp up to 6
Call between: 8am-8pm
Provides: Light tackle, lures, bait
Handicapped equipped: Yes
Certifications: USCG

YOUR SILENT FISHING PARTNER

TEXAS

CORPUS CHRISTI BAY - GALVESTON BAY

Mike Sydows Fishing & Hunting
Rockport 512-729-7212
Species & Seasons: Redfish, Speckled Trout all year
Bodies of water: Aransas Bay, San Antonio Bay, Corpus Christi Bay
Rates: Full day: $350(1-2), $425(4)
Call between: Anytime
Provides: Light tackle, lures, bait, rain gear
Handicapped equipped: No
Certifications: USCG

Robert Brooks Fishing Guide Service
Fulton 512-729-7170
Species & Seasons: Red Drum, Speckled Trout, Flounder, Black Drum, Sheepshead all year
Bodies of water: Aransas Bay, Copano Bay, Carlos Bay, Mesquite Bay, San Antonio Bay, Redfish Bay, Corpus Christi Bay, Nueces Bay
Rates: Half day: Negotiable(1-2), Full day: $300(1-2), $50 additional pp over 2 up to 4
Call between: 6pm-10pm
Provides: Light tackle, heavy tackle, fly rod/reel, lures, bait, rain gear
Handicapped equipped: Yes
Certifications: USCG

Saltwater Safaris
Rockport 512-729-4131
Species & Seasons: Redfish July-Jan, Speckled Trout April-Jan, Black Drum Jan-April, Flounder Sept-Nov
Bodies of water: Corpus Christi Bay, Aransas Bay, Red Fish Bay, Copano Bay, Mid TX Coast Line
Rates: Half day: $250(1-2), Full day: $300(1-2), $50 additional pp over 2
Call between: 6pm-9pm
Provides: Light tackle, fly rod/reel, lures, bait, beverages, caps, ice
Handicapped equipped: No
Certifications: USCG, TX Parks & Wildlife License

MARINAS...

Fin & Feather Marina & RV Park
Aransas Pass 512-758-7414
Hours: 6am-11pm
Carries: Live bait, lures, maps, rods, reels, licenses
Bodies of water: Gulf of Mexico, Corpus Christi Bay, Aransas Bay
Services & Products: Boat rentals, guide services, charter boat service, boat ramp, food, beverages, fishing instruction
Guides: Yes
OK to call for current conditions: Yes
Contact: Rich

FALCON RESERVOIR

MARINAS...

San Ygnacio RV Park & Mobile
San Ygnacio 210-765-5182
Hours: Sunrise-Sunset
Carries: Maps
Bodies of water: Rio Grande River, Falcon Res.
Services & Products: Boat rentals, guide services, charter boat service, boat ramp, fishing instruction
Guides: Yes
OK to call for current conditions: Yes
Contact: Capt. Joel Ruiz

GALVESTON BAY

BAIT & TACKLE...

Fifty-Fifty Dock
Texas City 409-948-3453
Hours: 5am-9pm
Carries: Live bait, lures, rods, reels, licenses
Bodies of water: Galveston Bay, Gulf of Mexico
Services & Products: Boat ramp, food, beverages
Guides: Yes
OK to call for current conditions: Yes
Contact: James Priest

CHARTERS...

Clear Lake Charter Boats Inc.
League City 713-334-4858
Species & Seasons: Redfish Mar-Dec, Speckled Trout, Sand Trout, Red Snapper all year, Ling, Black Tipped Shark Mar-Sept
Bodies of water: Clear Lake, Galveston Bay, Gulf of Mexico
Rates: Varies
Call between: 8:30am-6:30pm
Provides: Light tackle, heavy tackle, lures, bait, rain gear, beverages, lunch
Handicapped equipped: Yes

GUIDES...

Tarpon Adventures of Galveston
Houston 713-667-8034
Species & Seasons: Trout, Redfish Oct-June, Tarpon, Shark June-Sept
Bodies of water: Galveston Bay, East Bay, West Bay, Trinity Bay, Matagorda Bay, near shore
Rates: Half day: $275, Full day: $375
Call between: Anytime
Provides: Light tackle, heavy tackle, lures, bait
Handicapped equipped: Yes
Certifications: TP&W, USCG

MARINAS...

Way Out Marina
PO Box 1493
Crystal Beach 77650
Hours: 5am-8pm
Carries: Live bait, lures, maps
Bodies of water: Galveston Bay, Gulf of Mexico
Services & Products: Boat ramp, food, beverages, gas/oil
Guides: Yes
OK to call for current conditions: Yes
Contact: Sarah Hargrove

GUADALUPE RIVER - GULF OF MEXICO — TEXAS

GUADALUPE RIVER

BAIT & TACKLE...

Canyon Bait House
Canyon Lake.................... 210-899-9747
Hours: Closed Wed.
Carries: Live bait, lures, flies, maps, rods, reels
Bodies of water: Calaveras Lake, Guadalupe River
Services & Products: Guide services, food, beverages, fishing instruction
OK to call for current conditions: Yes
Contact: Chris Davis

Dam Store
Victoria 512-576-4086
Hours: 7am-9pm
Carries: Live bait, lures, rods, reels
Bodies of water: Coleto Creek Res., Guadalupe River, San Antonio River
Services & Products: Boat rentals, guide services, food, beverages, gas/oil
Guides: Yes
OK to call for current conditions: Yes
Contact: Jim King

River Valley Campground
Canyon Lake.................... 210-964-3613
Hours: 8:30am-6pm
Carries: Lures, flies
Bodies of water: Guadalupe River, Canyon Lake
Services & Products: Boat rentals, lodging, food, beverages, RV sites
Guides: Yes
OK to call for current conditions: Yes
Contact: Michael Strange

GULF OF MEXICO

BAIT & TACKLE...

Adams Bait & Tackle
Galveston......................... 409-740-4282
Hours: 6am-12pm
Carries: Live bait, lures, maps, rods, reels
Bodies of water: Gulf of Mexico
Services & Products: Beverages, repair services
Guides: Yes
OK to call for current conditions: Yes
Contact: David Hartt

Bridge Bait
Freeport 409-239-2248
Hours: 6am-9pm
Carries: Live bait, lures, maps, rods, reels, licenses
Bodies of water: Christmas Bay, Drum Bay, Salt Lake, Nicks Lake, Swan Lake, Gulf of Mexico
Services & Products: Boat ramp, food, beverages, fishing instruction
Guides: Yes
OK to call for current conditions: Yes
Contact: Anyone

Fifty-Fifty Dock
Texas City 409-948-3453
Hours: 5am-9pm
Carries: Live bait, lures, rods, reels, licenses
Bodies of water: Galveston Bay, Gulf of Mexico
Services & Products: Boat ramp, food, beverages
Guides: Yes
OK to call for current conditions: Yes
Contact: James Priest

Fisherman's Wharf
Port Aransas 800-605-5448
Hours: 5:30am-10pm
Carries: Live bait, lures, maps, rods, reels, licenses
Bodies of water: Gulf of Mexico, Nueces Bay, Red Fish Bay, Aransas Bay, Intracoastal waterway
Services & Products: Guide services, charter boat service, food, beverages, gas/oil, fishing instruction
Guides: Yes
OK to call for current conditions: Yes
Contact: Carl Moore

Jabo's Tacklebox
Freeport 409-251-2058
Hours: 5am-12pm
Carries: Live bait, lures, flies, maps
Bodies of water: Bastrop Bay, Intracoastal waterway, Christmas Bay, Lost Lake, Cox Lake, Gulf of Mexico
Services & Products: Boat ramp, food, beverages, gas/oil, fishing instruction
Guides: Yes
OK to call for current conditions: Yes
Contact: Jabo or Ann

Trainers Bait & Tackle
Corpus Christi 512-937-5347
Hours: 5am-11pm
Carries: Live bait, lures, maps, rods, reels
Bodies of water: Laguna Madre, Gulf of Mexico
Services & Products: Guide services, boat ramp, food, beverages, fishing instruction
Guides: Yes
OK to call for current conditions: Yes
Contact: Ray Trainer

Woody's Sport Center
Port Aransas 512-749-5252
Hours: 6am-8-10pm
Carries: Live bait, lures, maps, rods, reels, licenses
Bodies of water: Gulf of Mexico, Inland Bay, Aransas Bay, Redfish Bay, Corpus Christi Bay, Laguna Madre
Services & Products: Guide services, charter boat service, boat ramp, food, beverages, gas/oil, fishing instruction
OK to call for current conditions: Yes

CHARTERS...

Action Charters
Clute 409-265-0999
Species & Seasons: Red Snapper, Shark, King Mackerel, Amberjack all year, Dolphin May-Oct, Tuna Sept-April, Ling May-Nov
Bodies of water: Gulf of Mexico off Freeport, TX
Rates: $100-$75(6-30) private charter
Call between: 6am-9pm
Provides: Light tackle
Handicapped equipped: Yes
Certifications: USCG

Aqua Safari Charters
Galveston 800-759-4547
Species & Seasons: Blackfin Tuna Nov-April, Red Snapper all year, Kingfish May-Nov, Ling, Dolphin May-Oct, Marlin May-Sept, Shark April-Nov, Gulf Trout Dec-Mar, Amberjack April-October
Bodies of water: Gulf of Mexico
Rates: Half day: $45(1), Full day: $75(1), 32 hr. Tuna trip: $200 pp
Call between: Noon-5pm
Provides: Light tackle, heavy tackle, lures, bait
Handicapped equipped: Yes
Certifications: USCG

TEXAS — GULF OF MEXICO

Clear Lake Charter Boats Inc.
League City 713-334-4858
Species & Seasons: Redfish Mar-Dec, Speckled Trout, Sand Trout, Red Snapper all year, Ling, Black Tipped Shark Mar-Sept
Bodies of water: Clear Lake, Galveston Bay, Gulf of Mexico
Rates: Varies
Call between: 8:30am-6:30pm
Provides: Light tackle, heavy tackle, lures, bait, rain gear, beverages, lunch
Handicapped equipped: Yes

Easy Going Charters
Freeport 800-293-2947
Species & Seasons: King Mackerel, Dolphin May-Oct, Red Snapper, Shark, Bonito all year, Tuna Mar-Oct
Bodies of water: Gulf of Mexico
Rates: Half day: $300(6), Full day: $600(6)
Call between: Anytime
Provides: Light tackle, heavy tackle, lures, bait
Handicapped equipped: Yes
Certifications: USCG

Fisherman's Wharf
Port Aransas 800-605-5448
Species & Seasons: Red Snapper, Redfish Jan-Dec, Amberjack ?-July, Speckled Trout April-Oct, Flounder Sept-Jan, Sailfish July-Sept, Blue Marlin, White Marlin June-Sept, Shark May-Sept
Bodies of water: Gulf of Mexico, Redfish Bay, Aransas Bay, Nueces Bay
Call between: 7am-7pm
Provides: Light tackle, heavy tackle, bait
Handicapped equipped: Yes
Certifications: USCG

Galveston Charter Service
Houston 409-935-7777
Species & Seasons: Red Snapper, Kingfish, Ling, Dolphin April-April
Bodies of water: Galveston offshore May/Oct., Puerto Escondido Mexico Nov/April
Rates: $750-$975 (6 maximum) depending what day of the week
Call between: 7pm-9pm
Provides: Light tackle, heavy tackle, lures, bait
Handicapped equipped: Yes
Certifications: USCG, insured

Island Sea Sports
Port Aransas 800-GO2DIVE
.... 512-749-4167
Species & Seasons: Kingfish May-Oct, Redfish, Speckled Trout Mar-Oct, Black Drum Oct-April, Snapper, Grouper, Amberjack all year, Barracuda May-Sept
Bodies of water: Gulf of Mexico, Inland water surrounding Corpus Christi
Rates: 8 hrs: $400(3), $50 additional pp over 3
Call between: 10am-6pm
Provides: Light tackle, heavy tackle, fly rod/reel, bait, beverages
Handicapped equipped: Yes
Certifications: USCG

Jim's Guide Service
Port Mansfield 210-944-3474
Species & Seasons: Speckled Trout, Redfish all year (Bay), Tuna May-Sept, Snapper all year, Kingfish April-Oct, Sailfish, Marlin, Dolphin May-Oct
Bodies of water: Lower Laguna Madre Bay, Gulf of Mexico
Rates: Bay fishing: Full day: $300(1), $345(2), Near shore (Gulf): Full day: $475(4), Offshore (Gulf): $650(4)
Call between: Anytime
Provides: Light tackle, heavy tackle, lures, bait, beverages
Handicapped equipped: Yes, mild
Certifications: USCG, TPWD Licensed

Jim's Pier
S. Padre Island 210-761-2865
Species & Seasons: Redfish, Speckled Trout, Red Snapper all year, King Mackerel, Dolphin, Wahoo, Tuna, Sailfish, Blue Marlin May-Oct, Tarpon July-Nov
Bodies of water: Laguna Madre, Gulf of Mexico
Rates: Bay fishing: Half day: $200, Full day: $400, Deep Sea: Half day: $350, Full day: $700, Bay Party boat: $18 pp, Snapper Party boat: $60 pp
Call between: 6am-9pm
Provides: Light tackle, heavy tackle, fly rod/reel, lures, bait
Handicapped equipped: Yes
Certifications: USCG

Johnston's Sportfishing
Freeport 800-460-1312
Species & Seasons: Snapper, King, Ling, Dolphin Sailfish, Marlin May-Oct
Bodies of water: Gulf of Mexico out of Freeport
Rates: $1000(6)
Call between: 5pm-9:30pm
Provides: Light tackle, heavy tackle, lures, bait
Handicapped equipped: Yes

Padre Island Safaris
Corpus Christi 512-937-8446
Species & Seasons: Shark Mar-Nov, Tarpon June-Oct, Jack Crevalle Mar-Oct, Speckled Trout, Redfish all year
Bodies of water: Padre Island Surf., Gulf of Mexico, Padre Island Nat'l Seashore
Rates: Full day: $300(2), $50 additional pp over 2, maximum 5
Call between:
Provides: Light tackle, heavy tackle, lures, bait
Handicapped equipped: No
Certifications: Dept. of Interior license

Sidon Gulf Charter Inc.
Sabine Pass 409-724-6536
Species & Seasons: Red Snapper, King Mackerel, Cobia, Dolphin June-Sept
Bodies of water: Offshore Gulf of Mexico
Rates: 1-6 people, 12 hour trips
Call between: 7am-10pm
Provides: Heavy tackle, lures, bait
Handicapped equipped: Yes
Certifications: USCG

Sun Chaser Charter Fishing
Port Aransas 800-460-0217
Species & Seasons: Red Snapper Jan-Nov, Amberjack April-June, Shark, King Mackerel, Dolphin, Spanish Mackerel April-Sept
Bodies of water: Gulf of Mexico
Rates: $550(1-3), $50 additional pp up to 6
Call between: 8am-10pm
Provides: Light tackle, heavy tackle, lures, bait
Certifications: USCG

LODGES...

Rod & Reel Motel
Rockport 512-729-2028
.... 800-667-3570
Hours: 24 hours
Carries: Lures, maps, rods, reels
Bodies of water: Aransas Bay, Copano Bay, Gulf of Mexico
Services & Products: Guide services, lodging, fishing instruction, hunting guide service
OK to call for current conditions: Yes
Contact: Eugene Morel

GULF OF MEXICO - LAGUNA MADRE — TEXAS

MARINAS...

Fin & Feather Marina & RV Park
Aransas Pass 512-758-7414
Hours: 6am-11pm
Carries: Live bait, lures, maps, rods, reels, licenses
Bodies of water: Gulf of Mexico, Corpus Christi Bay, Aransas Bay
Services & Products: Boat rentals, guide services, charter boat service, boat ramp, food, beverages, fishing instruction
Guides: Yes
OK to call for current conditions: Yes
Contact: Rich

Island Moorings Marina
Port Aransas 512-749-4100
Hours: 8am-6pm, 8am-8pm Sat., Sun.
Bodies of water: Gulf of Mexico
Services & Products: Guide services, charter boat service, food, beverages, gas/oil, repair services, swimming pool/hot tub, laundry, showers, tennis courts
Guides: Yes
OK to call for current conditions: Yes
Contact: Sherrill Spink

Way Out Marina
PO Box 1493
Crystal Beach 77650
Hours: 5am-8pm
Carries: Live bait, lures, maps
Bodies of water: Galveston Bay, Gulf of Mexico
Services & Products: Boat ramp, food, beverages, gas/oil
Guides: Yes
OK to call for current conditions: Yes
Contact: Sarah Hargrove

White Sands Marina & Charter
Port Isabel 210-943-2414
Hours: 6am-7pm
Carries: Live bait, lures, maps, rods, reels, licenses
Bodies of water: Laguna Madre Bay, Gulf of Mexico
Services & Products: Boat rentals, guide services, charter boat service, lodging, boat ramp, food, beverages, gas/oil, boat slips
OK to call for current conditions: Yes
Contact: Luis or Mario

HUBBARD CREEK RESERVOIR

BAIT & TACKLE...

J and J Bait & Tackle Shop
Abilene 915-676-4796
Hours: 6am-8pm
Carries: Live bait, lures, maps, rods, reels, licenses
Bodies of water: Ivie Res., Hubbard Creek Res., Lake Ft. Phantom Hill, Kirby, Abilene Lake
Services & Products: Repair services
OK to call for current conditions: Yes

INTRACOASTAL WATERWAY

BAIT & TACKLE...

Fisherman's Wharf
Port Aransas 800-605-5448
Hours: 5:30am-10pm
Carries: Live bait, lures, maps, rods, reels, licenses
Bodies of water: Gulf of Mexico, Nueces Bay, Red Fish Bay, Aransas Bay, Intracoastal waterway
Services & Products: Guide services, charter boat service, food, beverages, gas/oil, fishing instruction
Guides: Yes
OK to call for current conditions: Yes
Contact: Carl Moore

Jabo's Tacklebox
Freeport 409-251-2058
Hours: 5am-12pm
Carries: Live bait, lures, flies, maps
Bodies of water: Bastrop Bay, Intracoastal waterway, Christmas Bay, Lost Lake, Cox Lake, Gulf of Mexico
Services & Products: Boat ramp, food, beverages, gas/oil, fishing instruction
Guides: Yes
OK to call for current conditions: Yes
Contact: Jabo or Ann

IVIE RESERVOIR

BAIT & TACKLE...

J and J Bait & Tackle Shop
Abilene 915-676-4796
Hours: 6am-8pm
Carries: Live bait, lures, maps, rods, reels, licenses
Bodies of water: Ivie Res., Hubbard Creek Res., Lake Ft. Phantom Hill, Kirby, Abilene Lake
Services & Products: Repair services
OK to call for current conditions: Yes

Texas Fishing
San Angelo 915-949-0319
Hours: 6am-10pm
Carries: Live bait, lures, flies, maps, rods, reels
Bodies of water: O.C. Fisher Lake, Lake Nasworthy, Twin Buttes Res., Ivie Res., Concho River, Colorado River
Services & Products: Beverages, fishing instruction, repair services
Guides: Yes
OK to call for current conditions: Yes
Contact: Don or Carolyn Carter

LAGUNA MADRE

BAIT & TACKLE...

Trainers Bait & Tackle
Corpus Christi 512-937-5347
Hours: 5am-11pm
Carries: Live bait, lures, maps, rods, reels
Bodies of water: Laguna Madre, Gulf of Mexico
Services & Products: Guide services, boat ramp, food, beverages, fishing instruction
Guides: Yes
OK to call for current conditions: Yes
Contact: Ray Trainer

Woody's Sport Center
Port Aransas 512-749-5252
Hours: 6am-8-10pm
Carries: Live bait, lures, maps, rods, reels, licenses
Bodies of water: Gulf of Mexico, Inland Bay, Aransas Bay, Redfish Bay, Corpus Christi Bay, Laguna Madre
Services & Products: Guide services, charter boat service, boat ramp, food, beverages, gas/oil, fishing instruction
OK to call for current conditions: Yes

TEXAS

LAGUNA MADRE - LAKE FORK

CHARTERS...

Jim's Guide Service
Port Mansfield 210-944-3474
Species & Seasons: Speckled Trout, Redfish all year (Bay), Tuna May-Sept, Snapper all year, Kingfish April-Oct, Sailfish, Marlin, Dolphin May-Oct
Bodies of water: Lower Laguna Madre Bay, Gulf of Mexico
Rates: Bay fishing: Full day: $300(1), $345(2), Near shore (Gulf): Full day: $475(4), Offshore (Gulf): $650(4)
Call between: Anytime
Provides: Light tackle, heavy tackle, lures, bait, beverages
Handicapped equipped: Yes, mild
Certifications: USCG, TPWD Licensed

Jim's Pier
S. Padre Island 210-761-2865
Species & Seasons: Redfish, Speckled Trout, Red Snapper all year, King Mackerel, Dolphin, Wahoo, Tuna, Sailfish, Blue Marlin May-Oct, Tarpon July-Nov
Bodies of water: Laguna Madre, Gulf of Mexico
Rates: Bay fishing: Half day: $200, Full day: $400, Deep Sea: Half day: $350, Full day: $700, Bay Party boat: $18 pp, Snapper Party boat: $60 pp
Call between: 6am-9pm
Provides: Light tackle, heavy tackle, fly rod/reel, lures, bait
Handicapped equipped: Yes
Certifications: USCG

GUIDES...

Capt. Carl's Fish Guide Service
Corpus Christi 800-368-8175
Species & Seasons: Speckled Trout, Redfish all year
Bodies of water: Corpus Christi Bay, Laguna Madre, Baffin Bay
Rates: Half day: $200(1), $225(2), Full day: $300(1), $325(2), $50 additional pp up to 6
Call between: 8am-8pm
Provides: Light tackle, lures, bait
Handicapped equipped: Yes
Certifications: USCG

David Green's Guide Service
Corpus Christi 512-939-9912
Species & Seasons: Speckled Trout Mar-Nov, Redfish May-Oct
Bodies of water: Laguna Madre, Baffin Bay
Rates: Full day: $300(1), $325(2), $400(3), $475(4)
Call between: 5pm-9pm
Provides: Light tackle, lures, bait
Handicapped equipped: No
Certifications: TPWD Licensed Guide, USCG Licensed Captain

High Tide Fishing & Hunting Adventures
Corpus Christi 512-851-1161
Species & Seasons: Speckled Trout April-June, Redfish June-Sept
Bodies of water: Laguna Madre, Baffin Bay
Rates: Full day: $325(2), $50 additional pp up to 4
Call between: 10am-10pm
Provides: Light tackle, lures, bait
Handicapped equipped: No
Certifications: USCG, TX Parks & Wildlife Dept.

Phyllis Ingram's Guide Service
Corpus Christi 512-857-0702
Species & Seasons: Speckled Trout Mar-Dec, Redfish June-Nov
Bodies of water: Laguna Madre, Baffin Bay
Rates: Half day: $225(2), Full day: $325(2), special rates available Oct-Feb
Call between: 8am-8pm
Provides: Light tackle, lures, bait, rain gear
Certifications: USCG

LODGES...

Wild Horse Lodge and Charters
Bishop ....,.......... 512-584-3098
Guest Capacity: 12 beds
Handicapped equipped: No
Seasons: All year
Rates: $100/night(1-2) $25 additional pp
Contact: Jan or Calvin Canamore
Guides: Yes
Species & Seasons: Speckled Trout, Redfish, Drum Jan-Dec
Bodies of Water: Baffin Bay, Laguna Madre

Types of fishing: Fly fishing, light tackle, heavy tackle, wading
Available: Fishing instruction, bait, tackle, family activities, Dove hunting, skeet, lighted pier

MARINAS...

White Sands Marina & Charter
Port Isabel 210-943-2414
Hours: 6am-7pm
Carries: Live bait, lures, maps, rods, reels, licenses
Bodies of water: Laguna Madre Bay, Gulf of Mexico
Services & Products: Boat rentals, guide services, charter boat service, lodging, boat ramp, food, beverages, gas/oil, boat slips
OK to call for current conditions: Yes
Contact: Luis or Mario

LAKE BUCHANAN

GUIDES...

Ed Rutledge
Buchanan Dam 800-373-1072
.... 515-793-6473
Species & Seasons: Striped Bass all year
Bodies of water: Lake Buchanan, Ink's Lake, Lake Lyndon B. Johnson
Rates: Half day: $220(4), Full day: $300(4)
Call between: 8pm-10pm
Provides: All tackle, bait
Handicapped equipped: Yes

LAKE FORK

BAIT & TACKLE...

Fishin' World
Dallas 214-358-4941
Hours: 9am-6pm, closed Sun.
Carries: Lures, flies, maps, rods, reels, licenses
Bodies of water: Lake Fork, Lake Ray Roberts, Lake Texoma, Tri-Lakes, Possum Kingdom Lake, "Amazon River-Brazil"
Guides: Yes
OK to call for current conditions: Yes
Contact: Rob Cooper

LAKE FORK - LAKE O' THE PINES — TEXAS

Minnow Bucket
Quitman 903-878-2500
Hours: 5:30am-10pm
Carries: Live bait, lures, maps, rods, reels, licenses
Bodies of water: Lake Fork
Services & Products: Guide services, lodging, boat ramp, food, beverages, gas/oil, fishing instruction, RV sites
Guides: Yes
OK to call for current conditions: Yes
Contact: Martin, Melody, Tony or Chris

GUIDES...

C C's Lake Fork Guide Servie
Quitman 903-878-2799
Species & Seasons: LM Bass all year, Crappie Dec-Mar, Bluegill June-Sept
Bodies of water: Lake Fork
Rates: 6 hrs: $150(1-2), 10 hrs: $225(1-2)
Call between: 7pm-9pm
Provides: Can furnish tackle on request at extra charge
Handicapped equipped: No

Jim Kirpatrick
Golden 903-768-2083
Species & Seasons: LM Bass, Crappie Jan-June
Bodies of water: Lake Fork, Sam Rayburn Res., private lakes
Rates: Half day: $250(1-2), Full day: $325(1-2)
Call between: 7pm-9pm
Provides: Rain gear, beverages, lunch
Handicapped equipped: Yes
Certifications: Cert. TX Licensed Guide

Lake Fork Professional Guide Service
Rowlett 800-475-9380
Species & Seasons: LM Bass Feb-Dec
Bodies of water: Lake Fork
Rates: Half day: $150(1-2), Full day: $225(1-2)
Call between: 9am-8pm
Provides: Heavy tackle, beverages
Handicapped equipped: No
Certifications: Licensed TX Parks & Wildlife

Mattern Guide Service
Palestine 903-723-2847
Species & Seasons: LM Bass Feb-Aug, Crappie May-Aug
Bodies of water: Richland Chambers, Lake Fork, Lake Palestine

Rates: Half day: $150(1), $175(2), Full day: $200(1), $225(2), weekend packages on request
Call between: 8am-10pm
Provides: Light tackle, heavy tackle, lures, bait, beverages
Handicapped equipped: No
Certifications: TWPD licensed

Tony Parker's Guide Service
Wills Point 903-873-2892
Species & Seasons: LM Bass Feb-Jan, Striped Bass June-Jan, White Bass April-Jan
Bodies of water: Lake Fork, Lake Tawakoni
Rates: Half day: $150(1-2), Full day: $225(1-2)
Call between: 7pm-10pm
Provides: Light tackle, heavy tackle, lures, bait
Handicapped equipped: Yes
Certifications: State licensed

LAKE FT. PHANTOM HILL

BAIT & TACKLE...

J and J Bait & Tackle Shop
Abilene 915-676-4796
Hours: 6am-8pm
Carries: Live bait, lures, maps, rods, reels, licenses
Bodies of water: Ivie Res., Hubbard Creek Res., Lake Ft. Phantom Hill, Kirby, Abilene Lake
Services & Products: Repair services
OK to call for current conditions: Yes

LAKE LIVINGSTON

BAIT & TACKLE...

The "Reel Doctor"
Jasper 800-704-REEL
Hours: 9am-9pm
Carries: Maps, rods, reels
Bodies of water: Sam Rayburn Res., Toledo Bend Res., B.A. Steinhagen Lake, Lake Livingston
Services & Products: Repair services
Guides: Yes
OK to call for current conditions: Yes
Contact: Don Leidig

LAKE LYNDON B. JOHNSON

GUIDES...

Ed Rutledge
Buchanan Dam 800-373-1072
      515-793-6473
Species & Seasons: Striped Bass all year
Bodies of water: Lake Buchanan, Ink's Lake, Lake Lyndon B. Johnson
Rates: Half day: $220(4), Full day: $300(4)
Call between: 8pm-10pm
Provides: All tackle, bait
Handicapped equipped: Yes

LAKE O' THE PINES

LODGES...

Pine Needle Lodge
Jefferson 903-665-2911
Guest Capacity: 20
Seasons: All year
Rates: $40-$50/day
Contact: Barry or Ann Bennick
Guides: Yes, recommend
Species & Seasons: LM Bass, Crappie, White Bass, Hybrids, Bluegill, Catffish all year
Bodies of Water: Caddo Lake, Lake 'O The Pines
Types of fishing: Fly fishing, light tackle, trout lines
Available: Boat rentals, family activities, canoe rental, boat ramp

MARINAS...

Bullfrog Marina
Jefferson 903-755-2712
Carries: Live bait, lures, rods, reels, licenses
Bodies of water: Lake O' The Pines
Services & Products: Boat rentals, lodging, boat ramp, food, beverages, gas/oil, boat slips
Guides: Yes
OK to call for current conditions: Yes
Contact: Larry

TEXAS
LAKE O' THE PINES - LAKE TEXOMA

Scenic View Motel & Marina
Lone Star 903-656-2272
Hours: 7am-8pm, closed Mon.
Carries: Live bait, lures, licenses
Bodies of water: Lake O' The Pines
Services & Products: Lodging, boat ramp, beverages, gas/oil, fishing instruction
Guides: Yes
OK to call for current conditions: Yes

LAKE PALESTINE

GUIDES...

Mattern Guide Service
Palestine 903-723-2847
Species & Seasons: LM Bass Feb-Aug, Crappie May-Aug
Bodies of water: Richland Chambers, Lake Fork, Lake Palestine
Rates: Half day: $150(1), $175(2), Full day: $200(1), $225(2), weekend packages on request
Call between: 8am-10pm
Provides: Light tackle, heavy tackle, lures, bait, beverages
Handicapped equipped: No
Certifications: TWPD licensed

LAKE RAY ROBERTS

BAIT & TACKLE...

Fishin' World
Dallas 214-358-4941
Hours: 9am-6pm, closed Sun.
Carries: Lures, flies, maps, rods, reels, licenses
Bodies of water: Lake Fork, Lake Ray Roberts, Lake Texoma, Tri-Lakes, Possum Kingdom Lake, "Amazon River-Brazil"
Guides: Yes
OK to call for current conditions: Yes
Contact: Rob Cooper

The Tackle Box
Pottsboro 903-786-9072
Hours: 5:30am-7pm, 5:30-9pm Fri., Sat.
Carries: Live bait, lures, flies, maps, rods, reels, licenses
Bodies of water: Lake Texoma, Lake Murray, Lake Ray Roberts, Red River
Services & Products: Guide services, lodging, food, beverages, gas/oil, fishing instruction, repair services
Guides: Yes
OK to call for current conditions: Yes
Contact: Steve Dunkle

GUIDES...

Charlie Steed
Gainesville 817-665-6416
Species & Seasons: LM Bass Mar-May, Crappie April-Nov, Catfish June-July
Bodies of water: Lake Ray Roberts, Moss Lake
Rates: Half day: $150(1), $175(2), Full day: $175(1), $200(2)
Call between: 7pm-10pm
Provides: Heavy tackle, bait
Handicapped equipped: No
Certifications: CPR, First aid

LAKE TAWAKONI

GUIDES...

Tony Parker's Guide Service
Wills Point 903-873-2892
Species & Seasons: LM Bass Feb-Jan, Striped Bass June-Jan, White Bass April-Jan
Bodies of water: Lake Fork, Lake Tawakoni
Rates: Half day: $150(1-2), Full day: $225(1-2)
Call between: 7pm-10pm
Provides: Light tackle, heavy tackle, lures, bait
Handicapped equipped: Yes
Certifications: State licensed

LAKE TEXOMA

BAIT & TACKLE...

Damsite Bait Shop
Denison 903-465-0165
Hours: day light-dark
Carries: Live bait, lures, flies, maps, rods, reels, licenses
Bodies of water: Red River, Lake Texoma
Services & Products: Food, beverages
Guides: No
OK to call for current conditions: Yes
Contact: Calvin Evans

Dave's Ski & Tackle Inc.
Denison 903-465-6110
Hours: 5am-10pm
Carries: Live bait, lures, flies, maps, rods, reels, licenses
Bodies of water: Lake Texoma, Red River, Randall Lake, Baker Lake
Services & Products: Guide services, food, beverages, gas/oil
Guides: Yes
OK to call for current conditions: Yes
Contact: Dave Parkey

Fishin' World
Dallas 214-358-4941
Hours: 9am-6pm, closed Sun.
Carries: Lures, flies, maps, rods, reels, licenses
Bodies of water: Lake Fork, Lake Ray Roberts, Lake Texoma, Tri-Lakes, Possum Kingdom Lake, "Amazon River-Brazil"
Guides: Yes
OK to call for current conditions: Yes
Contact: Rob Cooper

The Tackle Box
Pottsboro 903-786-9072
Hours: 5:30am-7pm, 5:30-9pm Fri., Sat.
Carries: Live bait, lures, flies, maps, rods, reels, licenses
Bodies of water: Lake Texoma, Lake Murray, Lake Ray Roberts, Red River
Services & Products: Guide services, lodging, food, beverages, gas/oil, fishing instruction, repair services
Guides: Yes
OK to call for current conditions: Yes
Contact: Steve Dunkle

GUIDES...

Striper Express Guide Service
Pottsboro 903-786-4477
Species & Seasons: Striped Bass, White Bass all year
Bodies of water: Lake Texoma
Rates: All private charters: $285(1-3), $375(4), $450(5)
Call between: 4pm-9pm
Provides: Light tackle, lures, bait, rain gear, fish cleaning
Handicapped equipped: Yes
Certifications: USCG

LAKE TEXOMA - LAKE WORTH   TEXAS

Striper Guide Service
Pottsboro 903-786-8400
Species & Seasons: Striped Bass all year
Bodies of water: Lake Texoma
Rates: Full day: $200(1-2), $50 additional pp over 2 up to 4
Call between: Anytime
Provides: Heavy tackle, lures, bait, rain gear
Handicapped equipped: Yes
Certifications: TX Licensed Guide

LODGES...

The Inn at Preston Bend
Pottsboro 903-786-2448
Guest Capacity: 30-36
Handicapped equipped: No
Seasons: All year
Rates: Non-Cooking: $42/day, Cooking: $60/day
Contact: Lee Safford
Guides: Yes
Species & Seasons: Catfish, Black Bass, Striped Bass, Crappie all year
Bodies of Water: Lake Texoma
Types of fishing: Light tackle
Available: Licenses, family activities

MARINAS...

Cedar Bayou Marina
Gordonville 903-523-4248
Hours: 7am, closed Mon.
Carries: Lures, licenses
Bodies of water: Lake Texoma
Services & Products: Boat rentals, guide services, lodging, boat ramp, food, beverages, gas/oil, repair services
Guides: Yes
OK to call for current conditions: Yes
Contact: Ron

LAKE TRAVIS

MARINAS...

Lakeway Marina
Austin 512-261-7511
Hours: 8am-8pm
Carries: Live bait, maps, licenses
Bodies of water: Lake Travis
Services & Products: Boat rentals, guide services, charter boat service, lodging, boat ramp, food, beverages, gas/oil, fishing instruction, repair services
OK to call for current conditions: Yes

LAKE WACO

BAIT & TACKLE...

Bosqueville Fastime
Waco 817-756-1656
Hours: 5:30am-10pm
Carries: Live bait, lures, flies, maps, rods, reels, licenses
Bodies of water: Lake Waco, Lake Whitney, Brazos River, Bosque River
Services & Products: Food, beverages, gas/oil
Guides: Yes
OK to call for current conditions: Yes
Contact: Gary Harvick

LAKE WHITNEY

BAIT & TACKLE...

Bosqueville Fastime
Waco 817-756-1656
Hours: 5:30am-10pm
Carries: Live bait, lures, flies, maps, rods, reels, licenses
Bodies of water: Lake Waco, Lake Whitney, Brazos River, Bosque River
Services & Products: Food, beverages, gas/oil
Guides: Yes
OK to call for current conditions: Yes
Contact: Gary Harvick

GUIDES...

Little Rocky Lodge & Guide Service
Laguna Park 817-622-3010
Species & Seasons: Striped Bass, SM Bass Oct-July, Spotted Bass, LM Bass May-Oct
Bodies of water: Lake Whitney, Brazos River
Rates: Half day: $125(2), Full day: $200(2), up to 4 people
Call between: 8pm-10pm
Provides: Light tackle, heavy tackle, lures, bait

Sportfishing Unlimited
Whitney 817-694-3974
Species & Seasons: Striped Bass Dec-May, SM Bass, LM Bass all year
Bodies of water: Lake Whitney, Stillhouse Hollow Lake, Brazos River (Whitney Dam to Waco)
Rates: Half day: $200(1), $300(2), Full day: $200(1), $300(2), 4 day package: $1000
Call between: Anytime
Provides: Light tackle, heavy tackle, lures, beverages
Certifications: USCG, State of TX

Striper Specialty Guide Service
Waco 817-848-5136
Species & Seasons: Striped Bass Mar-Sept
Bodies of water: Lake Whitney
Rates: Half day: $150(1-4), Full day: $250(1-4)
Call between: 5pm-10pm
Provides: Heavy tackle, lures, bait
Handicapped equipped: No
Certifications: TPWD License

LAKE WORTH

MARINAS...

Lake Worth Marina
Fort Worth 817-237-2997
Hours: 6am-12pm
Carries: Live bait, lures, rods, reels
Bodies of water: Lake Worth
Guides: Yes
OK to call for current conditions: Yes

YOUR SILENT FISHING PARTNER

TEXAS
NAVASOTA RIVER - RED RIVER

NAVASOTA RIVER

BAIT & TACKLE...

Ronning's Bait & Tackle
Madisonville 409-348-2570
Hours: 7:30am-5:30pm, closed Wed.
Carries: Live bait, lures, rods, reels
Bodies of water: Lake Madisonville, Trinity River, Navasota River
Services & Products: Beverages
Guides: No
OK to call for current conditions: No

O. C. FISHER LAKE

BAIT & TACKLE...

Texas Fishing
San Angelo 915-949-0319
Hours: 6am-10pm
Carries: Live bait, lures, flies, maps, rods, reels
Bodies of water: O.C. Fisher Lake, Lake Nasworthy, Twin Buttes Res., Ivie Res., Concho River, Colorado River
Services & Products: Beverages, fishing instruction, repair services
Guides: Yes
OK to call for current conditions: Yes
Contact: Don or Carolyn Carter

PAT MAYSE LAKE

BAIT & TACKLE...

Brannan's Bass Shop
Powderly 800-725-3422
Hours: 6am-8pm
Carries: Live bait, lures, flies, maps, rods, reels, licenses
Bodies of water: Pat Mayse Lake

Services & Products: Repair services (Minnkota)
Guides: Yes
OK to call for current conditions: Yes
Contact: Gleen or Kathy Brannan

POSSUM KINGDOM LAKE

BAIT & TACKLE...

Fishin' World
Dallas 214-358-4941
Hours: 9am-6pm, closed Sun.
Carries: Lures, flies, maps, rods, reels, licenses
Bodies of water: Lake Fork, Lake Ray Roberts, Lake Texoma, Tri-Lakes, Possum Kingdom Lake, "Amazon River-Brazil"
Guides: Yes
OK to call for current conditions: Yes
Contact: Rob Cooper

GUIDES...

Tom Ranft
Graford 817-779-2158
Species & Seasons: Striped Bass all year, Catfish, Crappie Summer
Bodies of water: Possum Kingdom Lake
Rates: 4-6 hrs: $200(2), $50 pp to 6 people, fishing morning or evenings
Call between: Anytime
Provides: Light tackle, heavy tackle, bait
Handicapped equipped: Yes

HC 52 BOX 755 • GRAFORD, TX 76449

TOM RANFT
Licensed Fishing Guide
(817) 779-2438

Answering Machine (817) 779-2158
Possum Kingdom Lake

PRIVATE & PAY LAKES

BAIT & TACKLE...

Fishing Hole
Tyler 903-531-2301
Hours: 8am-til?
Carries: Live bait, rods, reels
Bodies of water: Private lakes (pay)
Services & Products: Food, beverages, fishing instruction, restaurant
Guides: No
OK to call for current conditions: Yes
Contact: Jiim Barrow

GUIDES...

Southwest Safaris
Campbellton 210-579-4808
Species & Seasons: LM Bass, Hybrid Striped Bass, Coppernose Bluegill, Catfish Mar-Sept
Bodies of water: Private ponds and lakes (12)
Rates: Full day: $200, minimum 2
Call between: 8am-10pm
Provides: Light tackle, lures, bait, beverages, lunch
Handicapped equipped: No

RED RIVER

BAIT & TACKLE...

Damsite Bait Shop
Denison 903-465-0165
Hours: day light-dark
Carries: Live bait, lures, flies, maps, rods, reels, licenses
Bodies of water: Red River, Lake Texoma
Services & Products: Food, beverages
Guides: No
OK to call for current conditions: Yes
Contact: Calvin Evans

Dave's Ski & Tackle Inc.
Denison 903-465-6110
Hours: 5am-10pm
Carries: Live bait, lures, flies, maps, rods, reels, licenses
Bodies of water: Lake Texoma, Red River, Randall Lake, Baker Lake
Services & Products: Guide services, food, beverages, gas/oil
Guides: Yes
OK to call for current conditions: Yes
Contact: Dave Parkey

RED RIVER - RICHLAND CR. RESERVOIR — TEXAS

The Tackle Box
Pottsboro 903-786-9072
Hours: 5:30am-7pm, 5:30-9pm Fri., Sat.
Carries: Live bait, lures, flies, maps, rods, reels, licenses
Bodies of water: Lake Texoma, Lake Murray, Lake Ray Roberts, Red River
Services & Products: Guide services, lodging, food, beverages, gas/oil, fishing instruction, repair services
Guides: Yes
OK to call for current conditions: Yes
Contact: Steve Dunkle

REDFISH BAY

BAIT & TACKLE...

Fisherman's Wharf
Port Aransas 800-605-5448
Hours: 5:30am-10pm
Carries: Live bait, lures, maps, rods, reels, licenses
Bodies of water: Gulf of Mexico, Nueces Bay, Red Fish Bay, Aransas Bay, Intracoastal waterway
Services & Products: Guide services, charter boat service, food, beverages, gas/oil, fishing instruction
Guides: Yes
OK to call for current conditions: Yes
Contact: Carl Moore

Woody's Sport Center
Port Aransas 512-749-5252
Hours: 6am-8-10pm
Carries: Live bait, lures, maps, rods, reels, licenses
Bodies of water: Gulf of Mexico, Inland Bay, Aransas Bay, Redfish Bay, Corpus Christi Bay, Laguna Madre
Services & Products: Guide services, charter boat service, boat ramp, food, beverages, gas/oil, fishing instruction
OK to call for current conditions: Yes

CHARTERS...

Fisherman's Wharf
Port Aransas 800-605-5448
Species & Seasons: Red Snapper, Redfish Jan-Dec, Amberjack ?-July, Speckled Trout April-Oct, Flounder Sept-Jan, Sailfish July-Sept, Blue Marlin, White Marlin June-Sept, Shark May-Sept
Bodies of water: Gulf of Mexico, Redfish Bay, Aransas Bay, Nueces Bay

Call between: 7am-7pm
Provides: Light tackle, heavy tackle, bait
Handicapped equipped: Yes
Certifications: USCG

Mickey's Fishing Charters
Rockport 572-729-0113
Species & Seasons: Spotted Sea Trout, Red Drum, Black Drum, Flounder all year
Bodies of water: Coastal Bend, Red Fish Bay, Aransas Bay
Rates: Half day: $200(1-2), Full day: $250(1-2)
Call between: 8am-8pm
Provides: Light tackle, lures, bait
Handicapped equipped: Yes

Red Fish Charters
Fulton 800-862-7987
.... 512-729-8220
Species & Seasons: Redfish, Trout, all year Flounder Oct-Dec, Black Drum Feb-April
Bodies of water: Estes Flats, Aransas Bay, California Hole, Redfish Bay, Copano Bay
Rates: Your boat weekdays: $150(2), Your boat or mine: Full day: $250(1-2), $300(3), $350(4)
Call between: Anytime
Provides: Light tackle, bait
Handicapped equipped: No
Certifications: USCG, TP & W Guide

GUIDES...

Robert Brooks Fishing Guide Service
Fulton 512-729-7170
Species & Seasons: Red Drum, Speckled Trout, Flounder, Black Drum, Sheepshead all year
Bodies of water: Aransas Bay, Copano Bay, Carlos Bay, Mesquite Bay, San Antonio Bay, Redfish Bay, Corpus Christi Bay, Nueces Bay
Rates: Half day: Negotiable(1-2), Full day: $300(1-2), $50 additional pp over 2up to 4
Call between: 6pm-10pm
Provides: Light tackle, heavy tackle, fly rod/reel, lures, bait, rain gear
Handicapped equipped: Yes
Certifications: USCG

Saltwater Safaris
Rockport 512-729-4131
Species & Seasons: Redfish July-Jan, Speckled Trout April-Jan, Black Drum Jan-April, Flounder Sept-Nov
Bodies of water: Corpus Christi Bay, Aransas Bay, Red Fish Bay, Copano Bay, Mid TX Coast Line
Rates: Half day: $250(1-2), Full day: $300(1-2), $50 additional pp over 2
Call between: 6pm-9pm
Provides: Light tackle, fly rod/reel, lures, bait, beverages, caps, ice
Handicapped equipped: No
Certifications: USCG, TX Parks & Wildlife License

LODGES...

Mickey's RV Park
Rockport 512-729-0113
Guest Capacity: 100 RV campers
Handicapped equipped: No
Seasons: All year
Rates: $16/day
Contact: Jerry Mickey
Guides: Yes
Species & Seasons: Spotted Sea Trout, Red Drum, Flounder all year
Bodies of Water: Redfish Bay, Aransas Bay
Types of fishing: Light tackle, wading
Available: Fishing instruction, family activities

RICHLAND CR. RESERVOIR

BAIT & TACKLE...

Malakoff Bait & Tackle
Malakoff 903-489-0223
Hours: Varies
Carries: Live bait, lures, maps, rods, reels
Bodies of water: Cedar Creek, Richland-Chambers, Lake Athens
Services & Products: Repair services
Guides: Yes
OK to call for current conditions: Yes

TEXAS
RICHLAND CR. RESERVOIR - SAM RAYBURN RESERVOIR

GUIDES...

Mattern Guide Service
Palestine 903-723-2847
Species & Seasons: LM Bass Feb-Aug, Crappie May-Aug
Bodies of water: Richland Chambers, Lake Fork, Lake Palestine
Rates: Half day: $150(1), $175(2), Full day: $200(1), $225(2), weekend packages on request
Call between: 8am-10pm
Provides: Light tackle, heavy tackle, lures, bait, beverages
Handicapped equipped: No
Certifications: TWPD licensed

MARINAS...

Clearview Marina
Corsicana 903-872-1442
Hours: 5:30am-8:30pm
Carries: Live bait, lures, maps, licenses
Bodies of water: Richland-Chambers
Services & Products: Guide services, boat ramp, food, beverages, gas/oil, RV sites
Guides: Yes
OK to call for current conditions: Yes
Contact: Sonny Collins

RIO GRANDE RIVER

MARINAS...

San Ygnacio RV Park & Mobile
San Ygnacio 210-765-5182
Hours: Sunrise-Sunset
Carries: Maps
Bodies of water: Rio Grande River, Falcon Res.
Services & Products: Boat rentals, guide services, charter boat service, boat ramp, fishing instruction
Guides: Yes
OK to call for current conditions: Yes
Contact: Capt. Joel Ruiz

SAM RAYBURN RESERVOIR

BAIT & TACKLE...

Ann's Tackle Shop
Jasper 409-384-7685
Hours: 8am-5:30pm, closed Sun.
Carries: Lures, maps, rods, reels, licenses
Bodies of water: Sam Rayburn Res., Toledo Bend Res., B.A. Steinhagen Lake
Services & Products: Guide services
Guides: Yes
OK to call for current conditions: Yes
Contact: Ann or Debra

The "Reel Doctor"
Jasper 800-704-REEL
Hours: 9am-9pm
Carries: Maps, rods, reels
Bodies of water: Sam Rayburn Res., Toledo Bend Res., B.A. Steinhagen Lake, Lake Livingston
Services & Products: Repair services
Guides: Yes
OK to call for current conditions: Yes
Contact: Don Leidig

GUIDES...

Jim Kirpatrick
Golden 903-768-2083
Species & Seasons: LM Bass, Crappie Jan-June
Bodies of water: Lake Fork, Sam Rayburn Res., private lakes
Rates: Half day: $250(1-2), Full day: $325(1-2)
Call between: 7pm-9pm
Provides: Rain gear, beverages, lunch
Handicapped equipped: Yes
Certifications: Cert. TX Licensed Guide

Will Kirkpatrick
Broaddus 409-584-3177
Species & Seasons: LM Bass all year
Bodies of water: Sam Rayburn Res.
Rates: Half day: $110(1-2), Full day: $175(1-2)
Call between: 6pm-9pm
Provides: Light tackle, lures, rain gear, beverages, lunch (upon request, small charge)
Handicapped equipped: Yes, limited mobility only
Certifications: TX Licensed Guide

David Walker
Brookeland 409-698-9905
Species & Seasons: LM Bass, Spotted Bass, Crappie, Catfish all year
Bodies of water: Sam Rayburn Res., Toledo Bend Res., Angelina River
Rates: Half day: $125(1-2), Full day: $175(1-2)
Call between: 8am-10pm
Provides: Light tackle(some), heavy tackle, lures(some), bait
Handicapped equipped: No
Certifications: State of TX licensed

LODGES...

Hollywood Creek Motel & Marina
Huntington 409-897-2300
Guest Capacity: 100
Handicapped equipped: No
Seasons: All year
Rates: $35-$50/day, weekly rates available
Contact: Manager
Guides: Yes
Species & Seasons: LM Bass, Crappie, Channel Catfish, Blue Catfish, Opesoulas Catfish
Bodies of Water: Sam Rayburn Res.
Types of fishing: Fly fishing, light tackle, heavy tackle, fly-in, airport transportation
Available: Bait, tackle, boat rentals, restaurant, kitchenette apartments, marina, launch ramp, RV park

Rayburn Country Resort
Sam Rayburn 800-882-1442
.... 409-698-2444
Guest Capacity: 400
Handicapped equipped: Yes
Seasons: All year
Rates: $40-$200/day
Contact: Bob Almand
Guides: Yes
Species & Seasons: LM Bass Feb-June/Sept-Dec, Hybrid Striped Bass Feb-May, Crappie Mar-June
Bodies of Water: Sam Rayburn Res.
Types of fishing: Light tackle, heavy tackle
Available: Family activities, children's program

SAN ANTONIO BAY

GUIDES...

Mike Sydows Fishing & Hunting
Rockport 512-729-7212
Species & Seasons: Redfish, Speckled Trout all year
Bodies of water: Aransas Bay, San Antonio Bay, Corpus Christi Bay
Rates: Full day: $350(1-2), $425(4)
Call between: Anytime
Provides: Light tackle, lures, bait, rain gear
Handicapped equipped: No
Certifications: USCG

Robert Brooks Fishing Guide Service
Fulton 512-729-7170
Species & Seasons: Red Drum, Speckled Trout, Flounder, Black Drum, Sheepshead all year
Bodies of water: Aransas Bay, Copano Bay, Carlos Bay, Mesquite Bay, San Antonio Bay, Redfish Bay, Corpus Christi Bay, Nueces Bay
Rates: Half day: Negotiable(1-2), Full day: $300(1-2), $50 additional pp over 2up to 4
Call between: 6pm-10pm
Provides: Light tackle, heavy tackle, fly rod/reel, lures, bait, rain gear
Handicapped equipped: Yes
Certifications: USCG

SOMERVILLE LAKE

BAIT & TACKLE...

B&P Minnow Farm
Milano 512-455-3222
Hours: 11am-9pm
Carries: Live bait, lures, flies, rods, reels
Bodies of water: Somerville Lake, Belton Lake, Brazos River
Guides: Yes
OK to call for current conditions: Yes
Contact: Jimann Jones

STILLHOUSE HOLLOW LAKE

GUIDES...

Sportfishing Unlimited
Whitney 817-694-3974
Species & Seasons: Striped Bass Dec-May, SM Bass, LM Bass all year
Bodies of water: Lake Whitney, Stillhouse Hollow Lake, Brazos River (Whitney Dam to Waco)
Rates: Half day: $200(1), $300(2), Full day: $200(1), $300(2), 4 day package: $1000
Call between: Anytime
Provides: Light tackle, heavy tackle, lures, beverages
Certifications: USCG, State of TX

TOLEDO BEND RESERVOIR

BAIT & TACKLE...

Ann's Tackle Shop
Jasper 409-384-7685
Hours: 8am-5:30pm, closed Sun.
Carries: Lures, maps, rods, reels, licenses
Bodies of water: Sam Rayburn Res., Toledo Bend Res., B.A. Steinhagen Lake
Services & Products: Guide services
Guides: Yes
OK to call for current conditions: Yes
Contact: Ann or Debra

The "Reel Doctor"
Jasper 800-704-REEL
Hours: 9am-9pm
Carries: Maps, rods, reels
Bodies of water: Sam Rayburn Res., Toledo Bend Res., B.A. Steinhagen Lake, Lake Livingston
Services & Products: Repair services
Guides: Yes
OK to call for current conditions: Yes
Contact: Don Leidig

GUIDES...

David Walker
Brookeland 409-698-9905
Species & Seasons: LM Bass, Spotted Bass, Crappie, Catfish all year
Bodies of water: Sam Rayburn Res., Toledo Bend Res., Angelina River

Rates: Half day: $125(1-2), Full day: $175(1-2)
Call between: 8am-10pm
Provides: Light tackle(some), heavy tackle, lures(some), bait
Handicapped equipped: No
Certifications: State of TX licensed

TWIN BUTTES RESERVOIR

BAIT & TACKLE...

Texas Fishing
San Angelo 915-949-0319
Hours: 6am-10pm
Carries: Live bait, lures, flies, maps, rods, reels
Bodies of water: O.C. Fisher Lake, Lake Nasworthy, Twin Buttes Res., Ivie Res., Concho River, Colorado River
Services & Products: Beverages, fishing instruction, repair services
Guides: Yes
OK to call for current conditions: Yes
Contact: Don or Carolyn Carter

Know before you go...

Look in the Angler's Yellow Pages

UTAH

1. Boulder Mountains
2. Fishlake National Forest
3. Flaming Gorge Reservoir
4. Green River
5. Jordanelle Reservoir
6. Panguitch Lake
7. Provo River
8. Strawberry Reservoir
9. Uinta Mountains
10. Utah Lake
11. Weber River

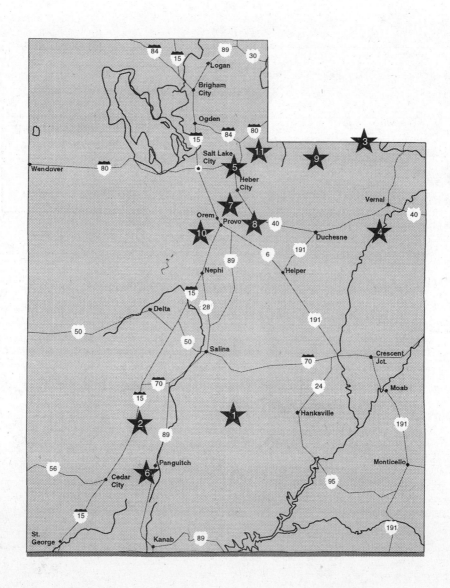

UTAH — BOULDER MOUNTAINS - GREEN RIVER

BOULDER MOUNTAINS

GUIDES...

The Outdoor Source
Salt Lake City 801-836-2372
Species & Seasons: Brook Trout, Cutthroat Trout, Tiger Trout May-Nov
Bodies of water: Boulder Mtns. (80 alpine lakes), Fremont River
Rates: Full day: $155(1), $195(2)
Call between: 7am-10pm
Provides: Light tackle, fly rod/reel, beverages, lunch
Handicapped equipped: Yes

LODGES...

Road Creek Ranch
Loa 801-836-2485
.... 836-2000
Guest Capacity: 35
Handicapped equipped: Yes
Seasons: All year
Rates: $75/day
Contact: Brian Draper or Mark Leavitt
Guides: Yes
Species & Seasons: Rainbow Trout, Brook Trout, Brown Trout, Steelhead, Cutthroat Trout all year
Bodies of Water: 270 natural lakes of Boulder Mountains
Types of fishing: Fly fishing, wading
Available: Fishing instruction, family activities, lodging, pheasant hunting, cattle drives

FISHLAKE NATIONAL FOREST

LODGES...

Elk Meadows Resort
Beaver 800-248-7669
Guest Capacity: 300+
Handicapped equipped: No
Seasons: All year
Rates: $54-$118/day
Contact: Penny Anfinson
Guides: Yes
Bodies of Water: Puffer Lake, Fishlake National Forest
Types of fishing: Fly fishing, light tackle, heavy tackle, horse/back pack, wading
Available: Family activities

FLAMING GORGE RESERVOIR

LODGES...

Red Canyon Lodge
Dutch John 801-889-3759
Guest Capacity: 35
Handicapped equipped: Yes
Seasons: April to Oct
Rates: $30-$95/day
Contact: Mark Wilson
Guides: Yes
Species & Seasons: Rainbow Trout, Brown Trout, Cutthroat Trout, Lake Trout all year, Kokanee Salmon, SM Bass April-Sept, Golden Trout June-Sept
Bodies of Water: Green River, Flaming Gorge Res.
Types of fishing: Fly fishing, light tackle, horse/back pack, wading, float trips
Available: Fishing instruction, licenses, bait, tackle, boat rentals, family activities, horseback riding, private lakes, free children's fishing pond

MARINAS...

Lucerne Valley Marina
Manila 801-784-3483
Hours: 6am-9pm
Carries: Live bait, lures, flies, maps, rods, reels, licenses
Bodies of water: Green River, Flaming Gorge Res.
Services & Products: Boat rentals, guide services, boat ramp, food, beverages, gas/oil, repair services, and campground
Guides: Yes
OK to call for current conditions: Yes

GREEN RIVER

FLY SHOPS...

Western Rivers Flyfisher
867 E 900 South
Salt Lake City 84105
Carries: Flies, maps, rods, reels, licenses
Bodies of water: Green River, Provo River, Strawberry Res.
Services & Products: Guide services, fishing instruction
Guides: Yes
OK to call for current conditions: Yes
Contact: Steve, Andy, Todd or Jon

GUIDES...

Flaming Gorge Flying Service
Dutch John 801-885-3338
.... 885-3370
Species & Seasons: Rainbow Trout, Cutthroat Trout, Brown Trout all year
Bodies of water: Green River, below Flaming Gorge Lake
Rates: Full day: $200(1), $275(2)
Call between: 8am-8pm
Provides: Fly rod/reel, rain gear, beverages, lunch
Handicapped equipped: Yes
Certifications: State of Utah guide permit, Permitee Ashley National Forest

Trout Creek Flies
Dutch John 800-835-4551
Species & Seasons: Rainbow Trout, Brown Trout, Cutthroat Trout all year
Bodies of water: Green River, Flaming Gorge Tailwater
Rates: Full day: $250(1) + tax, $275(2) + tax, Overnight river fish/camp trips 3 days 2 nights: $1275 + tax
Call between: 10am-8pm
Provides: Fly rod/reel, beverages, lunch
Handicapped equipped: Yes

LODGES...

Red Canyon Lodge
Dutch John 801-889-3759
Guest Capacity: 35
Handicapped equipped: Yes
Seasons: April to Oct
Rates: $30-$95/day
Contact: Mark Wilson
Guides: Yes
Species & Seasons: Rainbow Trout, Brown Trout, Cutthroat Trout, Lake Trout all year, Kokanee Salmon, SM Bass April-Sept, Golden Trout June-Sept
Bodies of Water: Green River, Flaming Gorge Res.
Types of fishing: Fly fishing, light tackle, horse/back pack, wading, float trips
Available: Fishing instruction, licenses, bait, tackle, boat rentals, family activities, horseback riding, private lakes, free children's fishing pond

GREEN RIVER - STRAWBERRY RESERVOIR — UTAH

MARINAS...

Lucerne Valley Marina
Manila 801-784-3483
Hours: 6am-9pm
Carries: Live bait, lures, flies, maps, rods, reels, licenses
Bodies of water: Green River, Flaming Gorge Res.
Services & Products: Boat rentals, guide services, boat ramp, food, beverages, gas/oil, repair services, and campground
Guides: Yes
OK to call for current conditions: Yes

JORDANELLE RESERVOIR

GUIDES...

Wasatch Adventures
Salt Lake City 801-596-1536
Species & Seasons: Trout Jan-Jan, Salmon June-Sept, Walleye, White Bass April-Oct, LM Bass, SM Bass, Channel Catfish May-Sept
Bodies of water: Strawberry Res., Jordanelle Res., Deer Creek Res., East Canyon Res., Utah Lake, Provo River, Weber River
Rates: Half day: $150(1-2), Full day: $200(1-2), hourly rates available
Call between: 8am-9pm
Provides: Light tackle, heavy tackle, lures, bait
Handicapped equipped: No

PANGUITCH LAKE

LODGES...

Beaver Dam Lodge
Panguitch 801-676-8339
Guest Capacity: 56
Handicapped equipped: No
Seasons: All year
Rates: $65-$85/day
Guides: No
Species & Seasons: Rainbow Trout all year
Bodies of Water: Panguitch Lake
Types of fishing: Fly fishing, light tackle, wading
Available: Licenses, bait, tackle, boat rentals

Deer Trail Lodge
Panguitch 801-676-2211
Guest Capacity: 75
Handicapped equipped: No
Seasons: All year
Rates: $25-$125/room or cabin
Contact: Al Olthof
Guides: No
Species & Seasons: Rainbow Trout Jan-Oct
Bodies of Water: Panguitch Lake, Panguitch Creek, Mammoth Creek, Sevier River
Types of fishing: Fly fishing, light tackle, horse/back pack, wading
Available: Licenses, bait, tackle, boat rentals, family activities

PROVO RIVER

FLY SHOPS...

Western Rivers Flyfisher
867 E 900 South
Salt Lake City 84105
Carries: Flies, maps, rods, reels, licenses
Bodies of water: Green River, Provo River, Strawberry Res.
Services & Products: Guide services, fishing instruction
Guides: Yes
OK to call for current conditions: Yes
Contact: Steve, Andy, Todd or Jon

GUIDES...

Jan's Mountain Outfitters
Park City 801-649-4949
.... 800-745-1020
Species & Seasons: Rainbow Trout, Brown Trout May-Oct, Cutthroat Trout, Brook Trout July-Sept
Bodies of water: Weber River, Provo River, Currant Creek, Strawberry Res., Private Trophy Ponds
Rates: Half day: $180(1-2), $85 (add on fee 3rd person), Full day: $250(1-2), $105 (add on fee 3rd person)
Call between: 9am-7pm
Provides: Fly rod/reel, beverages, lunch
Handicapped equipped: No

Passage to Utah
Salt Lake City 801-582-1896
Species & Seasons: Rainbow Trout, Brown Trout, Cutthroat Trout, Brook Trout May-Oct
Bodies of water: Provo River and several small streams
Rates: Full day: $250(1-2)
Call between: Anytime
Provides: Fly rod/reel, rain gear, beverages, lunch
Handicapped equipped: Yes

Wasatch Adventures
Salt Lake City 801-596-1536
Species & Seasons: Trout Jan-Jan, Salmon June-Sept, Walleye, White Bass April-Oct, LM Bass, SM Bass, Channel Catfish May-Sept
Bodies of water: Strawberry Res., Jordanelle Res., Deer Creek Res., East Canyon Res., Utah Lake, Provo River, Weber River
Rates: Half day: $150(1-2), Full day: $200(1-2), hourly rates available
Call between: 8am-9pm
Provides: Light tackle, heavy tackle, lures, bait
Handicapped equipped: No

STRAWBERRY RESERVOIR

FLY SHOPS...

Western Rivers Flyfisher
867 E 900 South
Salt Lake City 84105
Carries: Flies, maps, rods, reels, licenses
Bodies of water: Green River, Provo River, Strawberry Res.
Services & Products: Guide services, fishing instruction
Guides: Yes
OK to call for current conditions: Yes
Contact: Steve, Andy, Todd or Jon

GUIDES...

Jan's Mountain Outfitters
Park City 801-649-4949
.... 800-745-1020
Species & Seasons: Rainbow Trout, Brown Trout May-Oct, Cutthroat Trout, Brook Trout July-Sept
Bodies of water: Weber River, Provo River, Currant Creek, Strawberry Res., Private Trophy Ponds
Rates: Half day: $180(1-2), $85 (add on fee 3rd person), Full day: $250(1-2), $105 (add on fee 3rd person)
Call between: 9am-7pm
Provides: Fly rod/reel, beverages, lunch
Handicapped equipped: No

UTAH — STRAWBERRY RESERVOIR - WEBER RIVER

Wasatch Adventures
Salt Lake City 801-596-1536
Species & Seasons: Trout Jan-Jan, Salmon June-Sept, Walleye, White Bass April-Oct, LM Bass, SM Bass, Channel Catfish May-Sept
Bodies of water: Strawberry Res., Jordanelle Res., Deer Creek Res., East Canyon Res., Utah Lake, Provo River, Weber River
Rates: Half day: $150(1-2), Full day: $200(1-2), hourly rates available
Call between: 8am-9pm
Provides: Light tackle, heavy tackle, lures, bait
Handicapped equipped: No

UINTA MOUNTAINS

GUIDES...

Quarter Circle E Outfitters
Lapoint 801-247-2749
Species & Seasons: Trout, Catfish May-Nov
Bodies of water: Lakes and streams in High Uintas Mountains
Rates: Pack trips, lodge, cabins, horses
Call between: 9am-8pm
Provides: Light tackle, bait, rain gear, beverages, lunch
Certifications: USFS

UTAH LAKE

GUIDES...

Wasatch Adventures
Salt Lake City 801-596-1536
Species & Seasons: Trout Jan-Jan, Salmon June-Sept, Walleye, White Bass April-Oct, LM Bass, SM Bass, Channel Catfish May-Sept
Bodies of water: Strawberry Res., Jordanelle Res., Deer Creek Res., East Canyon Res., Utah Lake, Provo River, Weber River
Rates: Half day: $150(1-2), Full day: $200(1-2), hourly rates available
Call between: 8am-9pm
Provides: Light tackle, heavy tackle, lures, bait
Handicapped equipped: No

WEBER RIVER

GUIDES...

Jan's Mountain Outfitters
Park City 801-649-4949
.... 800-745-1020
Species & Seasons: Rainbow Trout, Brown Trout May-Oct, Cutthroat Trout, Brook Trout July-Sept
Bodies of water: Weber River, Provo River, Currant Creek, Strawberry Res., Private Trophy Ponds
Rates: Half day: $180(1-2), $85 (add on fee 3rd person), Full day: $250(1-2), $105 (add on fee 3rd person)
Call between: 9am-7pm
Provides: Fly rod/reel, beverages, lunch
Handicapped equipped: No

Wasatch Adventures
Salt Lake City 801-596-1536
Species & Seasons: Trout Jan-Jan, Salmon June-Sept, Walleye, White Bass April-Oct, LM Bass, SM Bass, Channel Catfish May-Sept
Bodies of water: Strawberry Res., Jordanelle Res., Deer Creek Res., East Canyon Res., Utah Lake, Provo River, Weber River
Rates: Half day: $150(1-2), Full day: $200(1-2), hourly rates available
Call between: 8am-9pm
Provides: Light tackle, heavy tackle, lures, bait
Handicapped equipped: No

VERMONT

1. Black River
2. Crystal Lake
3. Lake Champlain
4. Lake Memphremagog
5. Lake Willoughby
6. Lamoille River
7. Seymour Lake
8. White River
9. Winooski River

VERMONT
BLACK RIVER - LAKE WILLOUGHBY

BLACK RIVER

LODGES...

Craftsbury Center
Craftsbury Common 800-729-7751
Guest Capacity: 90
Handicapped equipped: No
Seasons: All year
Rates: From $52.50/day pp double occupancy, all meals included
Contact: Reservation Desk
Guides: Yes
Species & Seasons: Brook Trout, Rainbow Trout, Brown Trout, SM Bass, Northern Pike May-Oct, Perch Dec-Mar (ice fishing)
Bodies of Water: Hosmer Pond, Black River, Lamoille River
Types of fishing: Fly fishing, light tackle, wading, float trips
Available: Fishing instruction, boat rentals, family activities, baby sitting
Nearby: licenses, bait, tackle

CRYSTAL LAKE

GUIDES...

Possible Tours Charters
Greensboro Bend 802-533-7063
Species & Seasons: Lake Trout, Rainbow Trout, Steelhead, Salmon, Brown Trout April-Oct
Bodies of water: Lake Memphremagog, Seymour Lake, Lake Willoughby, Crystal Lake, Echo Lake, Shadow Lake, Caspian Lake
Rates: Half day: $90(2), Full day: $175(2)
Call between: 6pm-9pm
Provides: Light tackle, lures/flies
Handicapped equipped: Yes
Certifications: VT Registered Guide

LAKE CHAMPLAIN

CHARTERS...

Blue Chip II Charters
Burlington 802-862-8235
Species & Seasons: Trout, Salmon April-Oct, Northern Pike May-Oct
Bodies of water: Lake Champlain
Rates: 4 hrs: $200(1-6), 6 hrs: $300(1-6)
Call between: 5pm-9pm
Provides: Light tackle, lures
Handicapped equipped: Yes
Certifications: USCG, insured

Buck Horn Charters
Essex Junction 802-878-2365
Species & Seasons: Atlantic Salmon, Lake Trout, Brown Trout, Steelhead April-Aug
Bodies of water: Lake Champlain, Lake Ontario trips also available
Rates: Half day: $140(4), Full day: $200(4)
Call between: Anytime
Provides: Light tackle, lures
Handicapped equipped: Yes, limited
Certifications: USCG

Mission Fishin' Sportfishing
S. Londonderry 802-824-6031
Species & Seasons: Salmon, Brown Trout, Steelhead, Lake Trout, Walleye April-Oct
Bodies of water: Lake Champlain and select Tributaries
Rates: 26' boat (Salmon, Trout): 4 hrs: $225(1-4), 6 hrs: $300(1-4), 8 hrs: $350(1-4)
Call between: 8am-9pm
Provides: Light tackle, lures, bait
Handicapped equipped: No
Certifications: USCG

Sure Strike Charters
Essex Junction 802-878-5074
Species & Seasons: Lake Trout April-Sept, Salmon May-July, Brown Trout April-July, Rainbow Trout, Steelhead June-Aug, LM Bass, SM Bass, Walleye, Northern Pike May-Oct
Bodies of water: Lake Champlain Port of Burlington Vermont
Rates: 28' boat: 6 hrs: $300(1-4), 8 hrs: $400(1-4), Bass boat: 6 hrs: $240(1-2)
Call between: 6pm-9pm
Provides: Light tackle, lures
Handicapped equipped: Yes
Certifications: USCG

FLY SHOPS...

Schirmer's Fly Shop
S. Burlington 802-863-6105
Hours: 10am-6pm, closed Sun.
Carries: Flies, maps, rods, reels, licenses
Bodies of water: Lake Champlain, trout streams, lakes, rivers
Services & Products: Guide services, lodging, fishing instruction, back packing, camping guides
Guides: Yes
OK to call for current conditions: Yes
Contact: Ed

GUIDES...

Champ Guide Service
Jericho .... 802-899-3104(W)
.... 372-4730(S)
Species & Seasons: Lake Trout April-Oct, Atlantic Salmon June-Oct, Brown Trout April-Aug, Chinook Salmon Aug-Oct, Walleye, June-Aug, LM Bass, SM Bass May-Oct, Northern Pike June-Oct, Panfish Jan-Dec
Bodies of water: Lake Champlain and Tributaries, Lake Ontario trips also available
Rates: 6 hrs: $300(4), 8 hrs: $375(4), $50 additional pp over 4 up to 6
Call between: 3pm-10pm
Provides: Light tackle, fly rod/reel, lures, bait
Handicapped equipped: Yes
Certifications: USCG

LAKE MEMPHREMAGOG

GUIDES...

Possible Tours Charters
Greensboro Bend 802-533-7063
Species & Seasons: Lake Trout, Rainbow Trout, Steelhead, Salmon, Brown Trout April-Oct
Bodies of water: Lake Memphremagog, Seymour Lake, Lake Willoughby, Crystal Lake, Echo Lake, Shadow Lake, Caspian Lake
Rates: Half day: $90(2), Full day: $175(2)
Call between: 6pm-9pm
Provides: Light tackle, lures/flies
Handicapped equipped: Yes
Certifications: VT Registered Guide

LAKE WILLOUGHBY

GUIDES...

Possible Tours Charters
Greensboro Bend 802-533-7063
Species & Seasons: Lake Trout, Rainbow Trout, Steelhead, Salmon, Brown Trout April-Oct
Bodies of water: Lake Memphremagog, Seymour Lake, Lake Willoughby, Crystal Lake, Echo Lake, Shadow Lake, Caspian Lake
Rates: Half day: $90(2), Full day: $175(2)
Call between: 6pm-9pm
Provides: Light tackle, lures/flies
Handicapped equipped: Yes
Certifications: VT Registered Guide

LAMOILLE RIVER - WINOOSKI RIVER

VERMONT

LAMOILLE RIVER

LODGES...

Craftsbury Center
Craftsbury Common 800-729-7751
Guest Capacity: 90
Handicapped equipped: No
Seasons: All year
Rates: From $52.50/day pp double occupancy, all meals included
Contact: Reservation Desk
Guides: Yes
Species & Seasons: Brook Trout, Rainbow Trout, Brown Trout, SM Bass, Northern Pike May-Oct, Perch Dec-Mar (ice fishing)
Bodies of Water: Hosmer Pond, Black River, Lamoille River
Types of fishing: Fly fishing, light tackle, wading, float trips
Available: Fishing instruction, boat rentals, family activities, baby sitting
Nearby: licenses, bait, tackle

SEYMOUR LAKE

GUIDES...

Possible Tours Charters
Greensboro Bend 802-533-7063
Species & Seasons: Lake Trout, Rainbow Trout, Steelhead, Salmon, Brown Trout April-Oct
Bodies of water: Lake Memphremagog, Seymour Lake, Lake Willoughby, Crystal Lake, Echo Lake, Shadow Lake, Caspian Lake
Rates: Half day: $90(2), Full day: $175(2)
Call between: 6pm-9pm
Provides: Light tackle, lures/flies
Handicapped equipped: Yes
Certifications: VT Registered Guide

The Vermont Sportsman
Morgan 802-895-4209
Species & Seasons: Lake Trout, Brown Trout, Salmon, Brook Trout May-Oct
Bodies of water: Seymour Lake, Connecticut River
Rates: Full day: $150(1)
Call between: 6pm-9pm
Provides: Light tackle, fly rod/reel, lures, lunch
Handicapped equipped: No
Certifications: Registered VT State Guide

WHITE RIVER

GUIDES...

Steamline
Waitsfield 802-496-5463
Species & Seasons: Brown Trout, Rainbow Trout, Brook Trout May-Oct
Bodies of water: Winooski River, White River, Dog River, Little River
Rates: Half day: $85(1), $125(2)
Call between: 8am-8pm
Handicapped equipped: No

WINOOSKI RIVER

GUIDES...

Steamline
Waitsfield 802-496-5463
Species & Seasons: Brown Trout, Rainbow Trout, Brook Trout May-Oct
Bodies of water: Winooski River, White River, Dog River, Little River
Rates: Half day: $85(1), $125(2)
Call between: 8am-8pm
Handicapped equipped: No

YOUR SILENT FISHING PARTNER

Look in the Location Index
for a complete list of fishing areas

VIRGINIA

1. Atlantic Ocean
2. Chesapeake Bay
3. James River
4. Kerr Reservoir (Buggs Island)
5. Lake Anna
6. Lake Gaston
7. Leesville Lake
8. Potomac River
9. Roanoke/Staunton River
10. Shenandoah River
11. Smith Mountain Lake

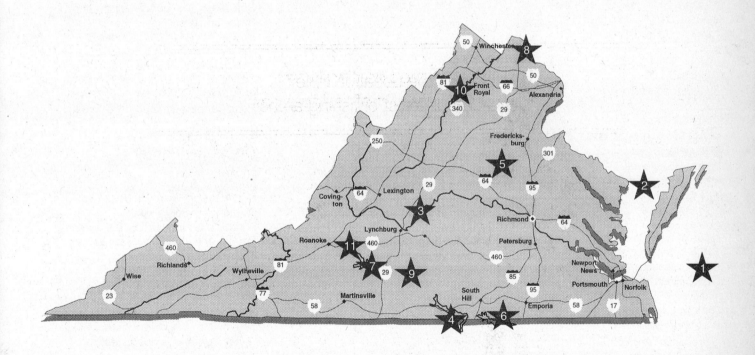

VIRGINIA

ATLANTIC OCEAN - CHESAPEAKE BAY

ATLANTIC OCEAN

BAIT & TACKLE...

Virginia Beach Fishing Center
Virginia Beach 804-491-8000
Hours: 5:30am-8pm
Carries: Live bait, lures, flies, maps, rods, reels, licenses
Bodies of water: Atlantic Ocean, Rudee Inlet
Services & Products: Boat rentals, charter boat service, food, beverages, gas/oil
OK to call for current conditions: Yes
Contact: John Crowling

CHARTERS...

Capt. Donald Cherrix
Chincoteague 804-336-6865
Species & Seasons: Marlin, Tuna June-Oct, Dolphin July-Sept
Bodies of water: Atlantic Ocean
Rates: Full day: $695(6)
Provides: Light tackle, heavy tackle, lures, bait
Handicapped equipped: Yes

Capt. George Garner
Chincoteague 804-336-5931
Species & Seasons: Bluefin Tuna June-July, Yellowfin Tuna, Dolphin July-Oct, Shark May-Oct, Bluefish Spring-Fall, False Albacore June-Sept, Flounder April-Oct
Bodies of water: Atlantic Ocean Inshore and Offshore, Chincoteague Bay, Chincoteague Island, VA
Rates: Half day: $350(6), Full day: $600(6), Overnight 24 hrs: $1100 (4), 36 hrs: $1600(4)
Call between: Anytime
Provides: Light tackle, heavy tackle, lures, bait
Handicapped equipped: No
Certifications: USCG

Capt. Ray Parker
Wachapreague 804-787-1040
Species & Seasons: Tautog Sept-Mar, Flounder April-Nov, Sea Bass Sept-Dec, Dolphin July-Sept Skipjack, Tuna, Bonito June-Sept, Drum May-June
Bodies of water: Atlantic Ocean inland waters of Eastern Shore of VA and out to 50 miles, Chesapeake Bay
Rates: Full day: $350-$650(6)
Call between: 9am-9pm
Provides: Light tackle, heavy tackle, lures, bait
Handicapped equipped: Yes

Capt. Sam Parker
Wachapreague 804-787-3070
Species & Seasons: Flounder April-Oct, Yellowfin Tuna, Dolphin June-Aug, Wahoo July-Aug, Sea Bass May-Sept, Trout Sept-Nov
Bodies of water: Atlantic Ocean, inlets leading to the Atlantic Ocean around the Barrier Islands off Virginia
Rates: Bottom fishing: Full day: $330(6), Offshore: Full day: $650(6)
Call between: 4pm-10pm
Provides: Light tackle, heavy tackle, lures, bait
Handicapped equipped: Yes
Certifications: USCG

Four Winds Charter
Virginia Beach 804-464-4680
Species & Seasons: Sea Bass April-June/Oct-Dec, Tautog Mar-May, Trout May-June, Spot, Croaker May-Sept/Oct, Striped Bass May-June/Oct-Dec, Flounder May-Oct
Bodies of water: Atlantic Ocean, Chesapeake Bay
Rates: Competitive to group rates
Call between: 9am-5pm
Provides: Light tackle, heavy tackle, fly reel, bait
Handicapped equipped: Yes
Certifications: USCG

Live Bait Deep Sea Fishing
Virginia Beach 804-474-4471
Species & Seasons: Tautog, Sea Bass, Bluefish, Trout, Striped Bass April-June, Flounder, Channel Bass, Black Drum May-June, Cobia, Amberjack, Spanish Mackerel, Bluefish July-Sept, Striped Bass, Tautog Oct-Dec
Bodies of water: Atlantic Ocean and off shore to 30 mi of VA Beach, lower Chesapeake Bay
Rates: Half day: $300, Full day: $500, 6 people maximum
Provides: Heavy tackle, lures, bait
Handicapped equipped: Limited
Certifications: USCG

Patty Wagon Charters
Chincoteague 410-437-2287
.... 804-336-1459
Species & Seasons: Tuna, Marlin June-Oct, Shark, Flounder May-Oct, Bluefish May-June, King Mackerel, Spanish Mackerel June-Sept, Dolphin July-Oct
Bodies of water: Atlantic Ocean off Chincoteague, VA
Rates: $600(5), chunking or trolling
Call between: 4pm-9pm
Provides: Light tackle, heavy tackle, lures, bait, rain gear
Handicapped equipped: No
Certifications: USCG, CPR, First aid

CHESAPEAKE BAY

CHARTERS...

Al Hart's Charter Service
Hampton 804-868-6968
Species & Seasons: Bluefish, Striped Bass, Trout April-Nov
Bodies of water: Chesapeake Bay
Rates: Minimum 6, $180
Call between: Anytime
Provides: Light tackle, heavy tackle, lures, bait
Handicapped equipped: No

Capt. Ray Parker
Wachapreague 804-787-1040
Species & Seasons: Tautog Sept-Mar, Flounder April-Nov, Sea Bass Sept-Dec, Dolphin July-Sept Skipjack, Tuna, Bonito June-Sept, Drum May-June
Bodies of water: Chesapeake Bay, Atlantic Ocean inland waters of Eastern Shore of VA and out to 50 miles
Rates: Full day: $350-$650(6)
Call between: 9am-9pm
Provides: Light tackle, heavy tackle, lures, bait
Handicapped equipped: Yes

Four Winds Charter
Virginia Beach 804-464-4680
Species & Seasons: Sea Bass April-June/Oct-Dec, Tautog Mar-May, Trout May-June, Spot, Croaker May-Sept/Oct, Striped Bass May-June/Oct-Dec, Flounder May-Oct
Bodies of water: Chesapeake Bay, Atlantic Ocean
Rates: Competitive to group rates
Call between: 9am-5pm

CHESAPEAKE BAY - LAKE ANNA — VIRGINIA

Provides: Light tackle, heavy tackle, fly reel, bait
Handicapped equipped: Yes
Certifications: USCG

Live Bait Deep Sea Fishing
Virginia Beach 804-474-4471
Species & Seasons: Tautog, Sea Bass, Bluefish, Trout, Striped Bass April-June, Flounder, Channel Bass, Black Drum May-June, Cobia, Amberjack, Spanish Mackerel, Bluefish July-Sept, Striped Bass, Tautog Oct-Dec
Bodies of water: Lower Chesapeake Bay, Atlantic Ocean and off shore to 30 mi of VA Beach
Rates: Half day: $300, Full day: $500, 6 people maximum
Provides: Heavy tackle, lures, bait
Handicapped equipped: Limited
Certifications: USCG

JAMES RIVER

BAIT & TACKLE ...

Timberlake Sporting Goods
Lynchburg 804-239-3474
Hours: 9am-6pm, 9am-5pm Sat., Sun.
Carries: Live bait, lures, flies, maps, rods, reels, licenses
Bodies of water: James River, Smith Mountain Lake, Leesville Lake
Services & Products: Canoe rentals
Guides: Yes
OK to call for current conditions: Yes

FLY SHOPS...

Murray's Fly Shop
Edinburg 703-984-4212
Hours: 8am-6pm, closed Sun.
Carries: Lures, flies, maps, rods, reels
Bodies of water: James River, Shenandoah River, Potomac River, Shenandoah National Park trout streams
Services & Products: Guide services, fishing instruction
Guides: Yes
OK to call for current conditions: Yes
Contact: Anyone

KERR RESERVOIR (BUGGS ISLAND)

GUIDES...

Capt. Andy Andrzejewski
La Plata 301-932-1509
Species & Seasons: LM Bass, Striped Bass all year
Bodies of water: Buggs Island, Potomac River, In Virginia: Rappahannock River, Chickahominy River, Lake Anna, Lake Gaston
Rates: Half day: $150(1-2), Full day: $225(1-2)
Call between: 6pm-10pm
Provides: Light tackle, lures, bait, rain gear, beverages, lunch (on request)
Handicapped equipped: Yes
Certifications: USCG, PRFC

Jim's Guide Service
Boydton 804-372-3557
Species & Seasons: LM Bass Mar-Oct
Bodies of water: Kerr Reservoir (Buggs Island), Lake Gaston
Rates: Half day: $150(1-2), Full day: $225(1-2)
Call between: 7pm-10pm
Handicapped equipped: No
Certifications: USCG

LODGING...

Days Inn
Bracey 800-897-7801
Guest Capacity: 50 rooms
Handicapped equipped: Yes
Seasons: All year
Rates: $45-65/day
Contact: Bill McCauley
Guides: No, but several in the area
Species & Seasons: Striped Bass, Channel Catfish all year, LM Bass, Crappie, Bream Mar-Nov
Bodies of Water: Kerr Res. (Buggs Island), Lake Gaston
Types of fishing: Fly fishing, light tackle, heavy tackle
Available: Within 10 miles: Fishing instruction, licenses, bait, tackle, boat rentals, family activities, children's program, baby sitting

LAKE ANNA

MARINAS...

Anna Point Marina & Inn
Mineral 703-895-5900
Hours: 5am-9pm
Carries: Live bait, lures, maps, rods, reels, licenses
Bodies of water: Lake Anna
Services & Products: Boat rentals, guide services, lodging, boat ramp, food, beverages, gas/oil, fishing instruction, repair services, boat sales, para sailing
OK to call for current conditions: Yes
Contact: Dave Fauntleroy

GUIDES...

Capt. Andy Andrzejewski
La Plata 301-932-1509
Species & Seasons: LM Bass, Striped Bass all year
Bodies of water: Lake Anna, Potomac River, In Virginia: Rappahannock River, Chickahominy River, Lake Gaston, Buggs Island
Rates: Half day: $150(1-2), Full day: $225(1-2)
Call between: 6pm-10pm
Provides: Light tackle, lures, bait, rain gear, beverages, lunch (on request)
Handicapped equipped: Yes
Certifications: USCG, PRFC

Glenn Briggs Guide Service
Bumpass 703-895-5307
Species & Seasons: LM Bass Feb-Dec, Striped Bass Oct-June
Bodies of water: Lake Anna
Rates: Half day: $100(2), Full day: $175(2), $30 additional pp
Provides: Heavy tackle
Handicapped equipped: Yes
Certifications: USCG, Master Angler's Award

VIRGINIA

LAKE ANNA - POTOMAC RIVER

Ken Penrod's Life Outdoors Unlimited
Beltsville 301-937-0010
Species & Seasons: LM Bass, SM Bass, Striped Bass Spring-Winter
Bodies of water: Lake Anna, Tidal Potomac River, Upper Potomac River, Susquehanna River
Rates: Half day: $150 (1-2) + gas, Full day: $250(1-2) + gas
Call between: 6am-9pm
Provides: Light tackle, heavy tackle, fly rod/reel, lures
Handicapped equipped: Yes
Certifications: USCG

LAKE GASTON

GUIDES...

Capt. Andy Andrzejewski
La Plata 301-932-1509
Species & Seasons: LM Bass, Striped Bass all year
Bodies of water: Lake Gaston, Potomac River, In Virginia: Rappahanock River, Chickahominy River, Lake Anna, Buggs Island
Rates: Half day: $150(1-2), Full day: $225(1-2)
Call between: 6pm-10pm
Provides: Light tackle, lures, bait, rain gear, beverages, lunch (on request)
Handicapped equipped: Yes
Certifications: USCG, PRFC

Jim's Guide Service
Boydton 804-372-3557
Species & Seasons: LM Bass Mar-Oct
Bodies of water: Lake Gaston, Kerr Reservoir (Buggs Island)
Rates: Half day: $150(1-2), Full day: $225(1-2)
Call between: 7pm-10pm
Handicapped equipped: No
Certifications: USCG

LODGING...

Days Inn
Bracey 800-897-7801
Guest Capacity: 50 rooms
Handicapped equipped: Yes
Seasons: All year
Rates: $45-65/day
Contact: Bill McCauley
Guides: No, but several in the area

Species & Seasons: Striped Bass, Channel Catfish all year, LM Bass, Crappie, Bream Mar-Nov
Bodies of Water: Lake Gaston, Kerr Res. (Buggs Island)
Types of fishing: Fly fishing, light tackle, heavy tackle
Available: Within 10 miles: Fishing instruction, licenses, bait, tackle, boat rentals, family activities, children's program, baby sitting

LEESVILLE LAKE

BAIT & TACKLE...

Timberlake Sporting Goods
Lynchburg 804-239-3474
Hours: 9am-6pm, 9am-5pm Sat., Sun.
Carries: Live bait, lures, flies, maps, rods, reels, licenses
Bodies of water: Leesville Lake, Smith Mountain Lake, James River
Services & Products: Canoe rentals
Guides: Yes
OK to call for current conditions: Yes

MARINAS...

Crazy Horse Marina
Moneta 540-721-1587
Hours: 8am-8pm
Carries: Live bait, lures, maps, rods, reels
Bodies of water: Leesville Lake, Smith Mountain Lake, Roanoke/Staunton River
Services & Products: Boat rentals, lodging, boat ramp, food, beverages, gas/oil, fishing instruction
Guides: Yes
OK to call for current conditions: Yes
Contact: Wayne Dunford

POTOMAC RIVER

FLY SHOPS...

Murray's Fly Shop
Edinburg 540-984-4212
Hours: 8am-6pm, closed Sun.
Carries: Lures, flies, maps, rods, reels
Bodies of water: Potomac River, Shenandoah River, James River, Shenandoah National Park trout streams
Services & Products: Guide services, fishing instruction

Guides: Yes
OK to call for current conditions: Yes
Contact: Anyone

GUIDES...

Capt. Andy Andrzejewski
La Plata 301-932-1509
Species & Seasons: LM Bass, Striped Bass all year
Bodies of water: Potomac River, In Virginia: Rappahanock River, Chickahominy River, Lake Anna, Lake Gaston, Buggs Island
Rates: Half day: $150(1-2), Full day: $225(1-2)
Call between: 6pm-10pm
Provides: Light tackle, lures, bait, rain gear, beverages, lunch (on request)
Handicapped equipped: Yes
Certifications: USCG, PRFC

Ken Penrod's Life Outdoors Unlimited
Beltsville 301-937-0010
Species & Seasons: LM Bass, SM Bass, Striped Bass Spring-Winter
Bodies of water: Tidal Potomac River, Upper Potomac River, Susquehanna River, Lake Anna
Rates: Half day: $150 (1-2) + gas, Full day: $250(1-2) + gas
Call between: 6am-9pm
Provides: Light tackle, heavy tackle, fly rod/reel, lures
Handicapped equipped: Yes
Certifications: USCG

Mark Kovach Fishing Services
Silver Spring 301-588-8742
Species & Seasons: SM Bass April-Nov
Bodies of water: Potomac River
Rates: Full day: $330(1-2)
Call between: Anytime
Provides: Light tackle, fly rod/reel, lures, beverages, lunch
Handicapped equipped: Yes
Certifications: FFF Certified Fly Casting Instructor, MD Master Fishing Guide

Potomac Guide Service
Gaithersburg 301-840-9521
Species & Seasons: LM Bass March-Nov, SM Bass March-Dec, Striped Bass when in season
Bodies of water: Potomac River, Susquehanna River, Lake Erie, Canada trips

POTOMAC RIVER - SMITH MOUNTAIN LAKE · VIRGINIA

Rates: Half day: $150(1-2), Full day: $225(1-2)
Call between: 7pm-10pm
Provides: Light tackle, lures, rain gear, beverages, lunch
Handicapped equipped: Yes
Certifications: USCG

ROANOKE/STAUNTON RIVER

MARINAS...

Crazy Horse Marina
Moneta 540-721-1587
Hours: 8am-8pm
Carries: Live bait, lures, maps, rods, reels
Bodies of water: Roanoke/Staunton River, Smith Mountain Lake, Leesville Lake
Services & Products: Boat rentals, lodging, boat ramp, food, beverages, gas/oil, fishing instruction
Guides: Yes
OK to call for current conditions: Yes
Contact: Wayne Dunford

SHENANDOAH RIVER

BAIT & TACKLE...

River Rental Outfitters
Bentonville 540-635-5050
Hours: 9am-6pm Mon.-Fri., 7am-7pm Sat., Sun.
Carries: Live bait, lures, flies, rods, reels, licenses
Bodies of water: Shenandoah River (south fork), Lake Frederick, Passage Creek
Services & Products: Boat rentals, lodging, food, beverages
Guides: Yes
OK to call for current conditions: Yes
Contact: Trace Noel

FLY SHOPS...

Murray's Fly Shop
Edinburg 540-984-4212
Hours: 8am-6pm, closed Sun.
Carries: Lures, flies, maps, rods, reels
Bodies of water: Shenandoah River, Potomac River, James River, Shenandoah National Park trout streams
Services & Products: Guide services, fishing instruction
Guides: Yes
OK to call for current conditions: Yes
Contact: Anyone

SMITH MOUNTAIN LAKE

BAIT & TACKLE...

Timberlake Sporting Goods
Lynchburg 804-239-3474
Hours: 9am-6pm, 9am-5pm Sat., Sun.
Carries: Live bait, lures, flies, maps, rods, reels, licenses
Bodies of water: Smith Mountain Lake, James River, Leesville Lake
Services & Products: Canoe rentals
Guides: Yes
OK to call for current conditions: Yes

GUIDES...

My Time Striper Guide Service
Moneta 800-817-5007
Species & Seasons: Striped Bass April-Dec
Bodies of water: Smith Mountain Lake
Rates: Half day: $135(2), $160(3), $185(4), Full day: $225(2), $275(3), $325(4)
Call between: 8am-10pm
Provides: Light tackle, heavy tackle, lures, bait
Handicapped equipped: Yes
Certifications: USCG

MARINAS...

Campers Paradise Marina
Moneta 540-297-6109
Hours: 7am-9pm
Carries: Live bait, lures, maps, rods, reels, licenses
Bodies of water: Smith Mountain Lake
Guides: Yes
OK to call for current conditions: Yes
Contact: Wendell Walton

Crazy Horse Marina
Moneta 540-721-1587
Hours: 8am-8pm
Carries: Live bait, lures, maps, rods, reels
Bodies of water: Smith Mountain Lake, Leesville Lake, Roanoke/Staunton River
Services & Products: Boat rentals, lodging, boat ramp, food, beverages, gas/oil, fishing instruction
Guides: Yes
OK to call for current conditions: Yes
Contact: Wayne Dunford

The Angler's Yellow Pages is the quickest and easiest way to find what you want, when you want it

WASHINGTON

1. Bogachiel River
2. Columbia River
3. Cowlitz River
4. Curlew Lake
5. Franklin D. Roosevelt Lake
6. Hoh River
7. Lewis River
8. Nisqually River
9. Pacific Ocean
10. Puget Sound
11. Regional Areas
12. Satsop River
13. Silver Lake
14. Snake River
15. Snohomish River
16. Sol Duc River
17. Stillaguamish River
18. Strait of Juan de Fuca
19. Wenatchee River

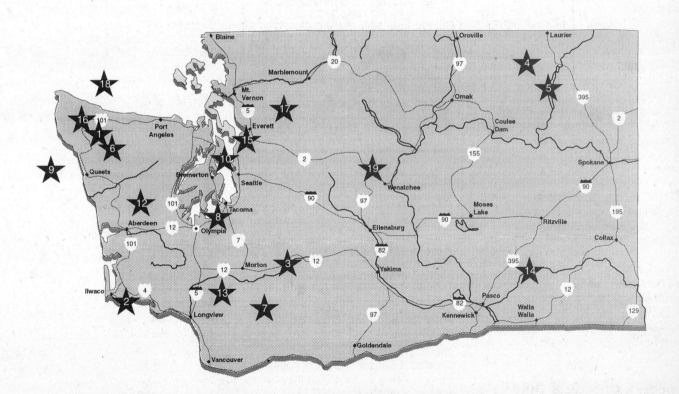

WASHINGTON
BOGACHIEL RIVER - COLUMBIA RIVER

BOGACHIEL RIVER

GUIDES...

Bob Pigott Guide Service
Port Angeles 360-327-3554
Species & Seasons: Steelhead all year, Chinook Salmon May-Nov, Coho Salmon Aug-Nov, Sockeye Salmon June-Nov, Cutthroat Trout April-Nov, Rainbow Trout June-July
Bodies of water: Sol Duc River, Bogachiel River, Hoh River, Calawha River, Queets River, Elwah River, Olympic National Park
Rates: Full day: $190(1), $270(2)
Call between: 7pm-9pm
Provides: Fly rod/reel
Certifications: Olympic National Park Concession, WA State Dept. of Wildlife

Jeff Sahar Guide Service
Kent 206-631-4611
Species & Seasons: Steelhead Dec-Aug, Salmon Mar-Nov
Bodies of water: Sol Duc River, Bogachiel River, Quillayute River, Hoh River
Rates: Call for rates
Call between: 7am-9pm
Provides: All bait and tackle, heated boat
Handicapped equipped: No

Mr. Steelhead Guide Service
Silvana 360-652-6850
Species & Seasons: Steelhead Jan-Jan, Salmon June-Jan, Trout June-April
Bodies of water: Sauk River Skykomish River, Skagit River, Stilliguamish River, Snohomish River, Cowlitz River, Kalama River, Satsop River, Bogachiel River, Sol Duc River, Hoh River, Wenatchee River
Rates: Half day: $80(1), Full day: $125(1), $250(2), 5 days: $1000 + gratuities
Call between: 7am-10pm
Provides: Light tackle, fly rod/reel, lures, bait, lunch
Handicapped equipped: Yes
Certifications: CPR, First aid

Woodie's Charter & Guide Service
Clallam Bay 360-963-2421
Species & Seasons: Steelhead June-Oct/Nov-April, Chinook Salmon June-Aug/Aug-Oct, Salmon, Bottomfish June-Sept, Halibut June-July
Bodies of water: River Float Trips: Bogachiel River, Sol Duc River, Hoh River, Saltwater Charters: Strait of Juan de Fuca from Sekiu, WA
Rates: River trips (8 hrs.): $150(1), $250(2), Saltwater Charters (6 hrs.): Salmon: $70(1), Halibut, Bottomfish: $80(1)
Call between: After 6pm or leave message
Provides: Light tackle, heavy tackle, lures, bait
Handicapped equipped: Yes
Certifications: USCG, Quantum, Cannon, Gamakatsu

WASHINGTON STEELHEAD & SALMON RIVER TRIPS
SUMMER & WINTER STEELHEAD
SPRING & FALL SALMON
CALL OR WRITE:
CLAUDE C. ANDERSON
P.O. BOX 3973
FEDERAL WAY, WA 98063-3973
206 839-3584
STATE & U.S. COAST GUARD LICENSED
MEMBER, WA. OUTFITTERS & GUIDES ASSOC.

COLUMBIA RIVER

CHARTERS...

Pacific Salmon Charters
PO Box 519
Ilwaco 98624
Species & Seasons: Salmon July-Aug, Sturgeon all year, Bottomfish May-Sept
Bodies of water: Columbia River, Pacific Ocean
Rates: Full day: $58-$85(1)
Call between: 8am-9pm
Provides: Light tackle, heavy tackle, lures, bait
Handicapped equipped: Yes

FLY SHOPS...

Angler's Workshop
Woodland 360-225-9445
Hours: 9am-5pm, closed Sun.
Carries: Flies, maps, rods, reels
Bodies of water: Columbia River, Lewis River (north fork, east fork)
Services & Products: Rod building, fly tying
Guides: Yes
OK to call for current conditions: No

GUIDES...

C.C. Anderson Guide Service
Federal Way 206-839-3584
Species & Seasons: Steelhead June-Oct/Nov-Mar, Chinook Salmon April-May/Sept-Oct, Coho Salmon Sept-Nov
Bodies of water: Southwest Washington State Rivers: Cowlitz River, Lewis River, Columbia River
Rates: Full day: $175(1), $250(2), day trips only up to 10 hrs.
Call between: 6am-8pm
Provides: Light tackle, lures, bait, rain gear
Handicapped equipped: No
Certifications: USCG, CPR, First aid, fully licensed and insured

Clancy's Guided Sportfishing
Chehallis 360-262-9549
.... 800-871-9549
Species & Seasons: Steelhead June-Nov/Nov-April, Chinook Salmon Mar-June/Aug-Nov, Sturgeon Feb-Sept
Bodies of water: Lewis River, Chehalis River, Cowlitz river, Wynoochee River, Willapa Bay, Snake River, Satsop River, Columbia River
Rates: Full day: $150(1) + tax, $250(2) + tax
Call between: Anytime
Provides: Light tackle, lures, bait
Handicapped equipped: Yes
Certifications: USCG, CPR

LODGES...

Silver Lake Resort
Silver Lake 360-274-6141
Guest Capacity: Cabins/Motel: 11 rooms, RV: 23 sites, Tents: 14 sites
Handicapped equipped: No

COLUMBIA RIVER - FRANKLIN D. ROOSEVELT LAKE — WASHINGTON

Seasons: All year
Rates: Cabins/Motel: $45-$75/day, Tent/RV: $11-$16/day
Contact: Pat Hill
Guides: Yes
Species & Seasons: LM Bass, Crappie Mar-Nov, Bluegill, Perch April-Oct, Catfish May-Nov, Trout Feb-Oct
Bodies of Water: Silver Lake, Toutle River, Cowlitz River, Columbia River
Types of fishing: Fly fishing, light tackle, heavy tackle, wading
Available: Fishing instruction, licenses, bait, tackle, boat rentals, playground, boat launch, moorage, convenience store

MARINAS...

Columbia Park Marina
Richland 509-736-1493
Hours: 10am-7pm
Carries:
Bodies of water: Columbia River, Snake River
Services & Products: Boat rentals, boat ramp, food, beverages, gas/oil
OK to call for current conditions: No

COWLITZ RIVER

GUIDES...

C.C. Anderson Guide Service
Federal Way 206-839-3584
Species & Seasons: Steelhead June-Oct/Nov-Mar, Chinook Salmon April-May/Sept-Oct, Coho Salmon Sept-Nov
Bodies of water: Southwest Washington State Rivers: Cowlitz River, Lewis River, Columbia River
Rates: Full day: $175(1), $250(2), day trips only up to 10 hrs.
Call between: 6am-8pm
Provides: Light tackle, lures, bait, rain gear
Handicapped equipped: No
Certifications: USCG, CPR, First aid, fully licensed and insured

Clancy's Guided Sportfishing
Chehallis 360-262-9549
.... 800-871-9549
Species & Seasons: Steelhead June-Nov/Nov-April, Chinook Salmon Mar-June/Aug-Nov, Sturgeon Feb-Sept
Bodies of water: Lewis River, Chehalis River, Cowlitz river, Wynoochee River, Willapa Bay, Snake River, Satsop River, Columbia River
Rates: Full day: $150(1) + tax, $250(2) + tax
Call between: Anytime
Provides: Light tackle, lures, bait
Handicapped equipped: Yes
Certifications: USCG, CPR

Mr. Steelhead Guide Service
Silvana 360-652-6850
Species & Seasons: Steelhead Jan-Jan, Salmon June-Jan, Trout June-April
Bodies of water: Sauk River Skykomish River, Skagit River, Stillaguamish River, Snohomish River, Cowlitz River, Kalama River, Satsop River, Bogachiel River, Sol Duc River, Hoh River, Wenatchee River
Rates: Half day: $80(1), Full day: $125(1), $250(2), 5 days: $1000 + gratuities
Call between: 7am-10pm
Provides: Light tackle, fly rod/reel, lures, bait, lunch
Handicapped equipped: Yes
Certifications: CPR, First aid

LODGES...

Silver Lake Resort
Silver Lake 360-274-6141
Guest Capacity: Cabins/Motel: 11 rooms, RV: 23 sites, Tents: 14 sites
Handicapped equipped: No
Seasons: All year
Rates: Cabins/Motel: $45-$75/day, Tent/RV: $11-$16/day
Contact: Pat Hill
Guides: Yes
Species & Seasons: LM Bass, Crappie Mar-Nov, Bluegill, Perch April-Oct, Catfish May-Nov, Trout Feb-Oct
Bodies of Water: Silver Lake, Toutle River, Cowlitz River, Columbia River
Types of fishing: Fly fishing, light tackle, heavy tackle, wading
Available: Fishing instruction, licenses, bait, tackle, boat rentals, playground, boat launch, moorage, convenience store

CURLEW LAKE

LODGES...

Fisherman's Cove Resort
1157 Fisherman's Cove Road
Republic 99166
Guest Capacity: 100
Handicapped equipped: No
Seasons: All year
Rates: $14-$65/day
Contact: Sandra Beck
Guides: No
Species & Seasons: Rainbow Trout April-Nov, SM Bass June-Oct
Bodies of Water: Curlew Lake
Types of fishing: Fly fishing, light tackle
Available: Bait, tackle, boat rentals, family activities, restaurant, horseback riding

FRANKLIN D. ROOSEVELT LAKE

GUIDES...

White Stone Fishing Guide
PO Box 296
Wilbur 99185
Species & Seasons: Silver Trout April-Aug, Rainbow Trout April-Oct, SM Bass, Walleye, Perch June-Oct
Bodies of water: Franklin D. Roosevelt Lake
Rates: Full day: $75(1), $150(2)
Call between: 8am-9pm
Provides: Light tackle, heavy tackle, lures, bait
Handicapped equipped: No

WASHINGTON

HOH RIVER - PACIFIC OCEAN

HOH RIVER

GUIDES...

Bob Pigott Guide Service
Port Angeles 360-327-3554
Species & Seasons: Steelhead all year, Chinook Salmon May-Nov, Coho Salmon Aug-Nov, Sockeye Salmon June-Nov, Cutthroat Trout April-Nov, Rainbow Trout June-July
Bodies of water: Sol Duc River, Bogachiel River, Hoh River, Calawha River, Queets River, Elwah River, Olympic National Park
Rates: Full day: $190(1), $270(2)
Call between: 7pm-9pm
Provides: Fly rod/reel
Certifications: Olympic National Park Concession, WA State Dept. of Wildlife

Jeff Sahar Guide Service
Kent 206-631-4611
Species & Seasons: Steelhead Dec-Aug, Salmon Mar-Nov
Bodies of water: Sol Duc River, Bogachiel River, Quillayute River, Hoh River
Rates: Call for rates
Call between: 7am-9pm
Provides: All bait and tackle, heated boat
Handicapped equipped: No

Mr. Steelhead Guide Service
Silvana 360-652-6850
Species & Seasons: Steelhead Jan-Jan, Salmon June-Jan, Trout June-April
Bodies of water: Sauk River Skykomish River, Skagit River, Stillaguamish River, Snohomish River, Cowlitz River, Kalama River, Satsop River, Bogachiel River, Sol Duc River, Hoh River, Wenatchee River
Rates: Half day: $80(1), Full day: $125(1), $250(2), 5 days: $1000 + gratuities
Call between: 7am-10pm
Provides: Light tackle, fly rod/reel, lures, bait, lunch
Handicapped equipped: Yes
Certifications: CPR, First aid

Woodie's Charter & Guide Service
Clallam Bay 360-963-2421
Species & Seasons: Steelhead June-Oct/Nov-April, Chinook Salmon June-Aug/Aug-Oct, Salmon, Bottom Fish June-Sept, Halibut June-July
Bodies of water: River Float Trips: Bogachiel River, Sol Duc River, Hoh River, Saltwater Charters: Strait of Juan de Fuca from Sekiu, WA
Rates: River trips (8 hrs.): $150(1), $250(2), Saltwater Charters (6 hrs.): Salmon: $70(1), Halibut, Bottom Fish: $80(1)
Call between: After 6pm or leave message
Provides: Light tackle, heavy tackle, lures, bait
Handicapped equipped: Yes
Certifications: USCG, Quantum, Cannon, Gamakatsu

LEWIS RIVER

FLY SHOPS...

Angler's Workshop
Woodland 360-225-9445
Hours: 9am-5pm, closed Sun.
Carries: Flies, maps, rods, reels
Bodies of water: Columbia River, Lewis River (north fork, east fork)
Services & Products: Rod building, fly tying
Guides: Yes
OK to call for current conditions: No

GUIDES...

C.C. Anderson Guide Service
Federal Way 206-839-3584
Species & Seasons: Steelhead June-Oct/Nov-Mar, Chinook Salmon April-May/Sept-Oct, Coho Salmon Sept-Nov
Bodies of water: Southwest Washington State Rivers: Cowlitz River, Lewis River, Columbia River
Rates: Full day: $175(1), $250(2), day trips only up to 10 hrs.
Call between: 6am-8pm
Provides: Light tackle, lures, bait, rain gear
Handicapped equipped: No
Certifications: USCG, CPR, First aid, fully licensed and insured

Clancy's Guided Sportfishing
Chehallis 360-262-9549
.... 800-871-9549
Species & Seasons: Steelhead June-Nov/Nov-April, Chinook Salmon Mar-June/Aug-Nov, Sturgeon Feb-Sept
Bodies of water: Lewis River, Chehalis River, Cowlitz river, Wynoochee River, Willapa Bay, Snake River, Satsop River, Columbia River
Rates: Full day: $150(1) + tax, $250(2) + tax
Call between: Anytime
Provides: Light tackle, lures, bait
Handicapped equipped: Yes
Certifications: USCG, CPR

NISQUALLY RIVER

BAIT & TACKLE...

Duffle Bag
Tacoma 206-588-4433
Hours: 9am-9pm Mon.-Fri., 9am-6pm Sat., 11am-5pm Sun.
Carries: Live bait, lures, flies, maps, rods, reels, licenses
Bodies of water: Puget Sound, American Lake, Nisqually River, Puyallup River
Guides: Yes
OK to call for current conditions: No

McKenna Bait & Tackle
McKenna 360-458-5720
Hours: 7:30am-6pm
Carries: Live bait, lures, flies, maps, rods, reels, licenses
Bodies of water: Nisqually River, Harts Lake, many other lakes
Services & Products: Food, beverages, fishing instruction
Guides: Yes
OK to call for current conditions: Yes

PACIFIC OCEAN

CHARTERS...

Bran Lee Charters
Westport 360-268-9177
Species & Seasons: Ling Cod, Sea Bass April-Sept, Halibut May-Sept, Tuna July-Sept
Bodies of water: Pacific Ocean
Rates: $55-$150 per day depending on fish
Call between: 9am-8pm
Provides: Light tackle, heavy tackle, bait, coffee
Handicapped equipped: Yes
Certifications: USCG

PACIFIC OCEAN - PUGET SOUND — WASHINGTON

Eagle Enterprises Charters
Bothell 206-481-4325
Species & Seasons: Salmon all year, Halibut May-June
Bodies of water: Puget Sound for Salmon, Pacific Ocean, Neah Bay, Washington for Halibut
Rates: Full day: $55(1)
Call between: 7am-9pm
Provides: Light tackle, bait
Handicapped equipped: Yes
Certifications: USCG

Pacific Salmon Charters
PO Box 519
Ilwaco 98624
Species & Seasons: Salmon July-Aug, Sturgeon all year, Bottom Fish May-Sept
Bodies of water: Columbia River, Pacific Ocean
Rates: Full day: $58-$85(1)
Call between: 8am-9pm
Provides: Light tackle, heavy tackle, lures, bait
Handicapped equipped: Yes

Westport Charters
Westport 360-268-9120
Species & Seasons: Salmon, Albacore July-Sept, Rockfish April-Sept, Ling Cod Mar-Sept
Bodies of water: Pacific Ocean
Rates: Full day: $60-$72(1)
Call between: 6am-6pm
Provides: Light tackle, heavy tackle, bait
Handicapped equipped: Yes
Certifications: USCG

LODGES...

Tahsis Lodge
Seattle 800-845-3476
Guest Capacity: 80
Handicapped equipped: Yes
Seasons: All year
Rates: $120/day Cdn.
Contact: Gilles or Barbara
Guides: Yes
Species & Seasons: Salmon, Halibut all year, Steelhead Jan-Mar/July-Aug, Rainbow Trout, Cutthroat Trout May-Oct
Bodies of Water: Nootka Sound, Vancouver Island, Pacific Ocean
Types of fishing: Fly fishing, light tackle, heavy tackle, salt water
Available: Licenses, bait, tackle, boat rentals, family activities, baby sitting

PUGET SOUND

BAIT & TACKLE...

Duffle Bag
Tacoma 206-588-4433
Hours: 9am-9pm Mon.-Fri., 9am-6pm Sat., 11am-5pm Sun.
Carries: Live bait, lures, flies, maps, rods, reels, licenses
Bodies of water: Puget Sound, American Lake, Nisqually River, Puyallup River
Guides: Yes
OK to call for current conditions: No

Jerry's Surplus
Everett 206-252-1176
Hours: 9am-9pm Mon.-Fri., 9am-6pm Sat., 11am-5pm Sun.
Carries: Live bait, lures, flies, maps, rods, reels, licenses
Bodies of water: Puget Sound, Strait of Juan de Fuca, Stillaquamish River, Snohomish River
Guides: Yes
OK to call for current conditions: Yes
Contact: Dave or Fabian

Northern Sales
Mount Vernon 360-424-8522
Hours: 9:30am-6pm Mon-Sat., 11am-5pm Sun.
Carries: Live bait, lures, flies, maps, rods, reels, licenses
Bodies of water: Puget Sound, Strait of Juan de Fuca, Stillaguamish River, Snohomish River
Services & Products:
Guides: Yes
OK to call for current conditions: Yes
Contact: Len Osborne

CHARTERS...

Admiralty Charters
Sequim 360-683-1097
Species & Seasons: Salmon May-Oct, Halibut May-Aug, Rockfish April-Nov
Bodies of water: Strait of Juan de Fuca, Puget Sound
Rates: Full day: $75(1), Bird, Whale trips: $40
Call between: 6am-6pm
Provides: Light tackle, heavy tackle, lures, bait
Handicapped equipped: Yes
Certifications: USCG

Eagle Enterprises Charters
Bothell 206-481-4325
Species & Seasons: Salmon all year, Halibut May-June
Bodies of water: Puget Sound for Salmon, Pacific Ocean, Neah Bay, Washington for Halibut
Rates: Full day: $55(1)
Call between: 7am-9pm
Provides: Light tackle, bait
Handicapped equipped: Yes
Certifications: USCG

GUIDES...

A Spot Tail Salmon Guide
Seattle 206-283-6680
Species & Seasons: Chinook Salmon May-Sept, Sockeye Salmon June-Aug, Coho Salmon, Aug-Sept, Chum Salmon Sept-Oct, Blackmouth Salmon Oct-April
Bodies of water: Puget Sound
Rates: 6 hrs: $325(1-2)
Call between: 9am-9pm
Provides: Light tackle, fly rod/reel, lures, bait, rain gear, beverages, lunch
Handicapped equipped: No
Certifications: USCG

MARINAS...

Lakebay Marina
Lakebay 206-884-3350
Hours: 8am-6pm
Carries: Live bait, lures, flies, rods, reels, licenses
Bodies of water: Puget Sound
Services & Products: Boat ramp, food, beverages, gas/oil
Guides: Yes
OK to call for current conditions: Yes
Contact: D.H. Hostetler

Point Defiance Boathouse Marina
Tacoma 206-591-5325
Hours: Sunrise-Sunset
Carries: Live bait, lures, flies, maps, rods, reels, licenses
Bodies of water: Puget Sound
Services & Products: Boat rentals, boat ramp, food, beverages, gas/oil
Guides: Yes
OK to call for current conditions: Yes
Contact: Skip Larsen or Tim Hartman

WASHINGTON

REGIONAL AREAS — SNOHOMISH RIVER

REGIONAL AREAS

BAIT & TACKLE...

Water Hole Sports Shop
Spokane 509-484-1041
Hours: 9am-7pm
Carries: Live bait, lures, flies, maps, rods, reels, licenses
Bodies of water: Spokane area
Services & Products: Fishing instruction, repair services
Guides: Yes
OK to call for current conditions: Yes
Contact: Larry Bryant

FLY SHOPS...

The Fly Fisher
Lacey 360-491-0181
Hours: 10am-6pm, closed Sun., Mon.
Carries: Flies, rods, reels
Bodies of water: Western Washington
Services & Products: Guide services, fishing instruction
OK to call for current conditions: Yes
Contact: George Beech

SATSOP RIVER

GUIDES...

Clancy's Guided Sportfishing
Chehalis 360-262-9549
.... 800-871-9549
Species & Seasons: Steelhead June-Nov/Nov-April, Chinook Salmon Mar-June/Aug-Nov, Sturgeon Feb-Sept
Bodies of water: Lewis River, Chehalis River, Cowlitz river, Wynoochee River, Willapa Bay, Snake River, Satsop River, Columbia River
Rates: Full day: $150(1) + tax, $250(2) + tax
Call between: Anytime
Provides: Light tackle, lures, bait
Handicapped equipped: Yes
Certifications: USCG, CPR

Mr. Steelhead Guide Service
Silvana 360-652-6850
Species & Seasons: Steelhead Jan-Jan, Salmon June-Jan, Trout June-April

Bodies of water: Sauk River Skykomish River, Skagit River, Stillaguamish River, Snohomish River, Cowlitz River, Kalama River, Satsop River, Bogachiel River, Sol Duc River, Hoh River, Wenatchee River
Rates: Half day: $80(1), Full day: $125(1), $250(2), 5 days: $1000 + gratuities
Call between: 7am-10pm
Provides: Light tackle, fly rod/reel, lures, bait, lunch
Handicapped equipped: Yes
Certifications: CPR, First aid

SILVER LAKE

LODGES...

Silver Lake Resort
Silver Lake 360-274-6141
Guest Capacity: Cabins/Motel: 11 rooms, RV: 23 sites, Tents: 14 sites
Handicapped equipped: No
Seasons: All year
Rates: Cabins/Motel: $45-$75/day, Tent/RV: $11-$16/day
Contact: Pat Hill
Guides: Yes
Species & Seasons: LM Bass, Crappie Mar-Nov, Bluegill, Perch April-Oct, Catfish May-Nov, Trout Feb-Oct
Bodies of Water: Silver Lake, Toutle River, Cowlitz River, Columbia River
Types of fishing: Fly fishing, light tackle, heavy tackle, wading
Available: Fishing instruction, licenses, bait, tackle, boat rentals, playground, boat launch, moorage, convenience store

SNAKE RIVER

GUIDES...

Clancy's Guided Sportfishing
Chehalis 360-262-9549
.... 800-871-9549
Species & Seasons: Steelhead June-Nov/Nov-April, Chinook Salmon Mar-June/Aug-Nov, Sturgeon Feb-Sept
Bodies of water: Lewis River, Chehalis River, Cowlitz river, Wynoochee River, Willapa Bay, Snake River, Satsop River, Columbia River
Rates: Full day: $150(1) + tax, $250(2) + tax
Call between: Anytime

Provides: Light tackle, lures, bait
Handicapped equipped: Yes
Certifications: USCG, CPR

Silver Bow Fly Fishing Adventures
Spokane 509-325-1960
Species & Seasons: Trout Mar-Nov, Steelhead Sept-Nov
Bodies of water: Spokane River, Wenatchee River, Grande Ronde River, Snake River & regional lakes
Rates: Half day: $150(1-2), Full day: $250(1-2)
Call between: 9am-6pm
Provides: Fly rod/reel
Handicapped equipped: No

MARINAS...

Columbia Park Marina
Richland 509-736-1493
Hours: 10am-7pm
Bodies of water: Columbia River, Snake River
Services & Products: Boat rentals, boat ramp, food, beverages, gas/oil
OK to call for current conditions: No

SNOHOMISH RIVER

BAIT & TACKLE...

Jerry's Surplus
Everett 206-252-1176
Hours: 9am-9pm Mon.-Fri., 9am-6pm Sat., 11am-5pm Sun.
Carries: Live bait, lures, flies, maps, rods, reels, licenses
Bodies of water: Puget Sound, Strait of Juan de Fuca, Stillaquamish River, Snohomish River
Guides: Yes
OK to call for current conditions: Yes
Contact: Dave or Fabian

Northern Sales
Mount Vernon 360-424-8522
Hours: 9:30am-6pm Mon-Sat., 11am-5pm Sun.
Carries: Live bait, lures, flies, maps, rods, reels, licenses
Bodies of water: Puget Sound, Strait of Juan de Fuca, Stillaquamish River, Snohomish River
Guides: Yes

SNOHOMISH RIVER - STRAIT OF JUAN DE FUCA

WASHINGTON

OK to call for current conditions: Yes
Contact: Len Osborne

GUIDES...

Mr. Steelhead Guide Service
Silvana 360-652-6850
Species & Seasons: Steelhead Jan-Jan, Salmon June-Jan, Trout June-April
Bodies of water: Sauk River Skykomish River, Skagit River, Stillaguamish River, Snohomish River, Cowlitz River, Kalama River, Satsop River, Bogachiel River, Sol Duc River, Hoh River, Wenatchee River
Rates: Half day: $80(1), Full day: $125(1), $250(2), 5 days: $1000 + gratuities
Call between: 7am-10pm
Provides: Light tackle, fly rod/reel, lures, bait, lunch
Handicapped equipped: Yes
Certifications: CPR, First aid

SOL DUC RIVER

GUIDES...

Bob Pigott Guide Service
Port Angeles 360-327-3554
Species & Seasons: Steelhead all year, Chinook Salmon May-Nov, Coho Salmon Aug-Nov, Sockeye Salmon June-Nov, Cutthroat Trout April-Nov, Rainbow Trout June-July
Bodies of water: Sol Duc River, Bogachiel River, Hoh River, Calawha River, Queets River, Elwah River, Olympic National Park
Rates: Full day: $190(1), $270(2)
Call between: 7pm-9pm
Provides: Fly rod/reel
Certifications: Olympic National Park Concession, WA State Dept. of Wildlife

Jeff Sahar Guide Service
Kent 206-631-4611
Species & Seasons: Steelhead Dec-Aug, Salmon Mar-Nov
Bodies of water: Sol Duc River, Bogachiel River, Quillayute River, Hoh River
Rates: Call for rates
Call between: 7am-9pm
Provides: All bait and tackle, heated boat
Handicapped equipped: No

Mr. Steelhead Guide Service
Silvana 360-652-6850
Species & Seasons: Steelhead Jan-Jan, Salmon June-Jan, Trout June-April
Bodies of water: Sauk River Skykomish River, Skagit River, Stillaguamish River, Snohomish River, Cowlitz River, Kalama River, Satsop River, Bogachiel River, Sol Duc River, Hoh River, Wenatchee River
Rates: Half day: $80(1), Full day: $125(1), $250(2), 5 days: $1000 + gratuities
Call between: 7am-10pm
Provides: Light tackle, fly rod/reel, lures, bait, lunch
Handicapped equipped: Yes
Certifications: CPR, First aid

Woodie's Charter & Guide Service
Clallam Bay 360-963-2421
Species & Seasons: Steelhead June-Oct/Nov-April, Chinook Salmon June-Aug/Aug-Oct, Salmon, Bottom Fish June-Sept, Halibut June-July
Bodies of water: River Float Trips: Bogachiel River, Sol Duc River, Hoh River, Saltwater Charters: Strait of Juan de Fuca from Sekiu, WA
Rates: River trips (8 hrs.): $150(1), $250(2), Saltwater Charters (6 hrs.): Salmon: $70(1), Halibut, Bottom Fish: $80(1)
Call between: after 6pm or leave message
Provides: Light tackle, heavy tackle, lures, bait
Handicapped equipped: Yes
Certifications: USCG, Quantum, Cannon, Gamakatsu

STILLAGUAMISH RIVER

BAIT & TACKLE...

Jerry's Surplus
Everett 206-252-1176
Hours: 9am-9pm Mon.-Fri., 9am-6pm Sat., 11am-5pm Sun.
Carries: Live bait, lures, flies, maps, rods, reels, licenses
Bodies of water: Puget Sound, Strait of Juan de Fuca, Stillaquamish River, Snohomish River
Guides: Yes
OK to call for current conditions: Yes
Contact: Dave or Fabian

Northern Sales
Mount Vernon 360-424-8522
Hours: 9:30am-6pm Mon-Sat., 11am-5pm Sun.
Carries: Live bait, lures, flies, maps, rods, reels, licenses
Bodies of water: Puget Sound, Strait of Juan de Fuca, Stillaguamish River, Snohomish River
Services & Products:
Guides: Yes
OK to call for current conditions: Yes
Contact: Len Osborne

GUIDES...

Mr. Steelhead Guide Service
Silvana 360-652-6850
Species & Seasons: Steelhead Jan-Jan, Salmon June-Jan, Trout June-April
Bodies of water: Sauk River, Skykomish River, Skagit River, Stillaguamish River, Snohomish River, Cowlitz River, Kalama River, Satsop River, Bogachiel River, Sol Duc River, Hoh River, Wenatchee River
Rates: Half day: $80(1), Full day: $125(1), $250(2), 5 days: $1000 + gratuities
Call between: 7am-10pm
Provides: Light tackle, fly rod/reel, lures, bait, lunch
Handicapped equipped: Yes
Certifications: CPR, First aid

STRAIT OF JUAN DE FUCA

BAIT & TACKLE...

Jerry's Surplus
Everett 206-252-1176
Hours: 9am-9pm Mon.-Fri., 9am-6pm Sat., 11am-5pm Sun.
Carries: Live bait, lures, flies, maps, rods, reels, licenses
Bodies of water: Puget Sound, Strait of Juan de Fuca, Stillaquamish River, Snohomish River
Guides: Yes
OK to call for current conditions: Yes
Contact: Dave or Fabian

WASHINGTON
STRAIT OF JUAN DE FUCA - WENATCHEE RIVER

Northern Sales
Mount Vernon 360-424-8522
Hours: 9:30am-6pm Mon-Sat.,
11am-5pm Sun.
Carries: Live bait, lures, flies, maps, rods, reels, licenses
Bodies of water: Puget Sound, Strait of Juan de Fuca, Stillaguamish River, Snohomish River
Services & Products:
Guides: Yes
OK to call for current conditions: Yes
Contact: Len Osborne

CHARTERS...

Admiralty Charters
Sequim 360-683-1097
Species & Seasons: Salmon May-Oct, Halibut May-Aug, Rockfish April-Nov
Bodies of water: Strait of Juan de Fuca, Puget Sound
Rates: Full day: $75(1),
Bird, whale trips: $40
Call between: 6am-6pm
Provides: Light tackle, heavy tackle, lures, bait
Handicapped equipped: Yes
Certifications: USCG

Woodie's Charter & Guide Service
Clallam Bay 360-963-2421
Species & Seasons: Steelhead June-Oct/Nov-April, Chinook Salmon June-Aug/Aug-Oct, Salmon, Bottom Fish June-Sept, Halibut June-July
Bodies of water: River Float Trips: Bogachiel River, Sol Duc River, Hoh River, Saltwater Charters: Strait of Juan de Fuca from Sekiu, WA
Rates: River trips (8 hrs.): $150(1), $250(2), Saltwater Charters (6 hrs.): Salmon: $70(1),
Halibut, Bottom Fish: $80(1)
Call between: after 6pm or leave message
Provides: Light tackle, heavy tackle, lures, bait
Handicapped equipped: Yes
Certifications: USCG, Quantum, Cannon, Gamakatsu

WENATCHEE RIVER

GUIDES...

Mr. Steelhead Guide Service
Silvana 360-652-6850
Species & Seasons: Steelhead Jan-Jan, Salmon June-Jan, Trout June-April
Bodies of water: Sauk River, Skykomish River, Skagit River, Stillaguamish River, Snohomish River, Cowlitz River, Kalama River, Satsop River, Bogachiel River, Sol Duc River, Hoh River, Wenatchee River
Rates: Half day: $80(1), Full day: $125(1), $250(2), 5 days: $1000 + gratuities
Call between: 7am-10pm
Provides: Light tackle, fly rod/reel, lures, bait, lunch
Handicapped equipped: Yes
Certifications: CPR, First aid

Silver Bow Fly Fishing Adventures
Spokane 509-325-1960
Species & Seasons: Trout Mar-Nov, Steelhead Sept-Nov
Bodies of water: Spokane River, Wenatchee River, Grande Ronde River, Snake River & regional lakes
Rates: Half day: $150(1-2), Full day: $250(1-2)
Call between: 9am-6pm
Provides: Fly rod/reel
Handicapped equipped: No

WEST VIRGINIA

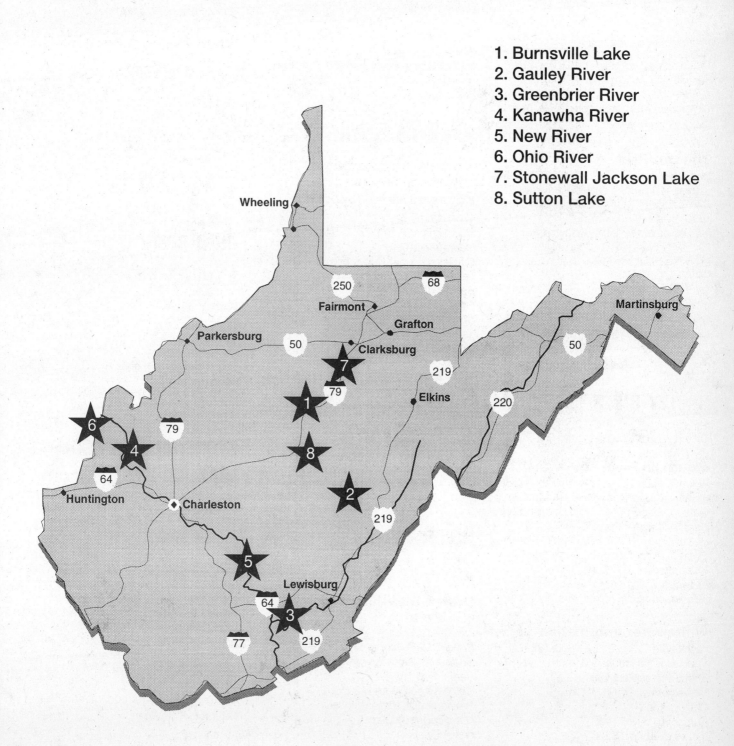

1. Burnsville Lake
2. Gauley River
3. Greenbrier River
4. Kanawha River
5. New River
6. Ohio River
7. Stonewall Jackson Lake
8. Sutton Lake

WEST VIRGINIA
BURNSVILLE LAKE - STONEWALL JACKSON LAKE

BURNSVILLE LAKE

BAIT & TACKLE...

Fishin Hole
Weston 304-269-4444
Hours: 6am-7pm
Carries: Live bait, lures, flies, maps, rods, reels, licenses
Bodies of water: Stonewall Jackson Lake, Stonecoal Lake, Burnsville Lake, West Fork River, Buckhannon River
Services & Products: Food, beverages, gas/oil, fishing instruction
Guides: Yes
OK to call for current conditions: Yes
Contact: Rick Wright

The Out Post
Burnsville 304-853-2909
Hours: 10am-8pm, closed Mon.
Carries: Live bait, lures, flies, maps, rods, reels
Bodies of water: Little Kanawha River, Burnsville Lake, Stone Coal Lake, Stonewall Jackson Lake, Sutton Lake, (Elk River)
Services & Products: Guide services, fishing instruction, repair services
Guides: Yes
OK to call for current conditions: Yes
Contact: Darrell D. Brown

GAULEY RIVER

GUIDES...

Mountain River Tours
Hico 800-822-1386
Species & Seasons: SM Bass, Catfish, Walleye, Striped Bass, Panfish June-Sept
Bodies of water: New River, Gauley River
Rates: Call for rates
Call between: 8am-7pm
Provides: Rain gear, beverages, lunch
Handicapped equipped: Yes

Whitewater Information
Fayetteville 800-782-RAFT
Species & Seasons: SM Bass, Spotted Bass April-Oct
Bodies of water: New River, Gauley River
Rates: Full day: $149(1), 2 days overnight: $260
Call between: 8am-8pm
Provides: Bait, rain gear, beverages
Handicapped equipped: Yes

GREENBRIAR RIVER

GUIDES...

Greenbrier River Company
Ronceverte 800-775-2203
Species & Seasons: SM Bass April-Oct
Bodies of water: Greenbrier River
Rates: Full day: $40(1-2), 2nd day: $30
Call between: 8am-8pm
Provides: Light tackle, lures, bait, rain gear, beverages
Handicapped equipped: No
Certifications: USCA, NACLO, ACA

KANAWHA RIVER

BAIT & TACKLE...

Kanawha Valley Sporting Goods
St. Albans 304-722-7247
Hours: 8am-9pm
Carries: Live bait, lures, flies, maps, rods, reels, licenses
Bodies of water: Kanawha River, Coal River
Services & Products: Food, beverages, gas/oil
Guides: No
OK to call for current conditions: No

Killer Bait
Davisville 304-485-7840
Carries: Lures, flies
Bodies of water: Ohio River, Kanawha River, Hughes River
Guides: Yes
OK to call for current conditions: Yes

NEW RIVER

GUIDES...

Drift-A-Bit White Water
PO Box 885
Fayetteville 25840
Species & Seasons: SM Bass April-Nov
Bodies of water: New River
Rates: Full day: $135(1)
Call between: 9am-5:30pm
Provides: Beverages, lunch
Handicapped equipped: Yes, depends on handicap
Certifications: WV DNR

Mountain River Tours
Hico 800-822-1386
Species & Seasons: SM Bass, Catfish, Walleye, Striped Bass, Panfish June-Sept
Bodies of water: New River, Gauley River
Rates: Call for rates
Call between: 8am-7pm
Provides: Rain gear, beverages, lunch
Handicapped equipped: Yes

Whitewater Information
Fayetteville 800-782-RAFT
Species & Seasons: SM Bass, Spotted Bass April-Oct
Bodies of water: New River, Gauley River
Rates: Full day: $149(1), 2 days overnight: $260
Call between: 8am-8pm
Provides: Bait, rain gear, beverages
Handicapped equipped: Yes

OHIO RIVER

BAIT & TACKLE...

Killer Bait
Davisville 304-485-7840
Carries: Lures, flies
Bodies of water: Ohio River, Kanawha River, Hughes River
Guides: Yes
OK to call for current conditions: Yes

STONEWALL JACKSON LAKE

BAIT & TACKLE...

Fishin Hole
Weston 304-269-4444
Hours: 6am-7pm
Carries: Live bait, lures, flies, maps, rods, reels, licenses
Bodies of water: Stonewall Jackson Lake, Stonecoal Lake, Burnsville Lake, West Fork River, Buckhannon River
Services & Products: Food, beverages, gas/oil, fishing instruction
Guides: Yes
OK to call for current conditions: Yes
Contact: Rick Wright

STONEWALL JACKSON LAKE - SUTTON LAKE

WEST VIRGINIA

The Out Post
Burnsville 304-853-2909
Hours: 10am-8pm, closed Mon.
Carries: Live bait, lures, flies, maps, rods, reels
Bodies of water: Little Kanawha River, Burnsville Lake, Stone Coal Lake, Stonewall Jackson Lake, Sutton Lake, (Elk River)
Services & Products: Guide services, fishing instruction, repair services
Guides: Yes
OK to call for current conditions: Yes
Contact: Darrell D. Brown

SUTTON LAKE

BAIT & TACKLE...

The Out Post
Burnsville 304-853-2909
Hours: 10am-8pm, closed Mon.
Carries: Live bait, lures, flies, maps, rods, reels
Bodies of water: Little Kanawha River, Burnsville Lake, Stone Coal Lake, Stonewall Jackson Lake, Sutton Lake, (Elk River)
Services & Products: Guide services, fishing instruction, repair services
Guides: Yes
OK to call for current conditions: Yes
Contact: Darrell D. Brown

Know before you go...

Look in the Angler's Yellow Pages

TRY THE NATIONAL DIRECTORY OF RECREATIONAL FISHING RESOURCES ORDER NOW & EXPLORE!

ANGLER'S YELLOW PAGES '96-97

KNOW BEFORE YOU GO!

- How & where the fish are biting
- Locate supplies & boat ramps
- Rates, species & seasons for guides, charter boats, fishing lodges, resorts, ranches & camps

---

Order Information
Mail this postage free card or call 1 800 242-9722
Major credit cards accepted for 800 number orders
❏ Yes! Send Angler's Yellow Pages & bill me $19.95 + $3.95 S & H
Name _____
Address _____
City _____ State _____ Zip _____
SATISFACTION GUARANTEED!

TRY THE NATIONAL DIRECTORY OF RECREATIONAL FISHING RESOURCES ORDER NOW & EXPLORE!

ANGLER'S YELLOW PAGES '96-97

KNOW BEFORE YOU GO!

- How & where the fish are biting
- Locate supplies & boat ramps
- Rates, species & seasons for guides, charter boats, fishing lodges, resorts, ranches & camps

---

Order Information
Mail this postage free card or call 1 800 242-9722
Major credit cards accepted for 800 number orders
❏ Yes! Send Angler's Yellow Pages & bill me $19.95 + $3.95 S & H
Name _____
Address _____
City _____ State _____ Zip _____
SATISFACTION GUARANTEED!

TRY THE NATIONAL DIRECTORY OF RECREATIONAL FISHING RESOURCES ORDER NOW & EXPLORE!

ANGLER'S YELLOW PAGES '96-97

KNOW BEFORE YOU GO!

- How & where the fish are biting
- Locate supplies & boat ramps
- Rates, species & seasons for guides, charter boats, fishing lodges, resorts, ranches & camps

---

Order Information
Mail this postage free card or call 1 800 242-9722
Major credit cards accepted for 800 number orders
❏ Yes! Send Angler's Yellow Pages & bill me $19.95 + $3.95 S & H
Name _____
Address _____
City _____ State _____ Zip _____
SATISFACTION GUARANTEED!

BUSINESS REPLY MAIL
FIRST-CLASS MAIL PERMIT NO. 88 DALLAS PA

POSTAGE WILL BE PAID BY ADDRESSEE

15 ELM DR
PO BOX 448
DALLAS PA 18612-9957

NO POSTAGE
NECESSARY
IF MAILED
IN THE
UNITED STATES

BUSINESS REPLY MAIL
FIRST-CLASS MAIL PERMIT NO. 88 DALLAS PA

POSTAGE WILL BE PAID BY ADDRESSEE

15 ELM DR
PO BOX 448
DALLAS PA 18612-9957

NO POSTAGE
NECESSARY
IF MAILED
IN THE
UNITED STATES

BUSINESS REPLY MAIL
FIRST-CLASS MAIL PERMIT NO. 88 DALLAS PA

POSTAGE WILL BE PAID BY ADDRESSEE

15 ELM DR
PO BOX 448
DALLAS PA 18612-9957

NO POSTAGE
NECESSARY
IF MAILED
IN THE
UNITED STATES

INTRODUCE A FEW FRIENDS TO...

YOUR SILENT FISHING PARTNER

ANGLER'S YELLOW PAGES

1 800 242-9722

WISCONSIN

1. Balsam Lake
2. Big Cedar Lake
3. Brule River
4. Clam Lake
5. Flambeau River
6. Fox River
7. Gile Flowage
8. Green Bay
9. Kangaroo Lake
10. Lac La Belle Lake
11. Lake Chippewa Flowage
12. Lake Geneva
13. Lake Mendota
14. Lake Michigan
15. Lake Poygan
16. Lake Superior
17. Lake Winnegago
18. Manitowoc River
19. Miller Dam Flowage
20. Mississippi River
21. Mohawksin Lake
22. Namekagon Lake
23. Oneida County
24. Petenwell Lake
25. Pewaukee Lake
26. Presque Isle Lake
27. Regional Areas
    Burnett County
    Forest County
    Hayward area
    Iron County
    Northern Wisconsin
    Price County
28. Shell Lake
29. Trout Lake
30. Turtle-Flambeau Flowage
31. Vilas County
32. Wind Lake
33. Wisconsin River
34. Wolf River

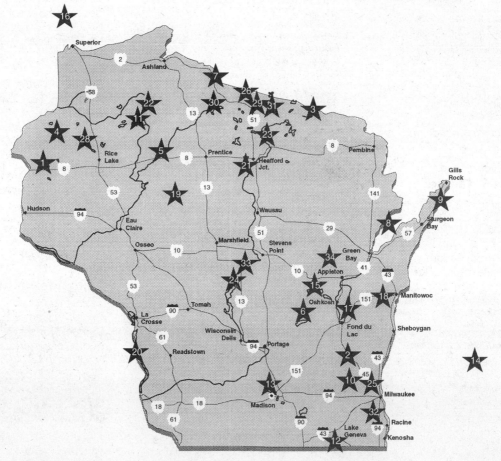

YOUR SILENT FISHING PARTNER

WISCONSIN

BALSAM LAKE

BAIT & TACKLE...

B & K Sports & Liquor
Milltown 715-825-3326
Hours: 8am-6or9pm
Carries: Live bait, lures, flies, maps, rods, reels, licenses
Bodies of water: Balsam Lake, Big Round Lake, Long Lake
Services & Products: Beverages
Guides: Yes
OK to call for current conditions: Yes
Contact: Gene

BIG CEDAR LAKE

BAIT & TACKLE...

Anglers Inn
Milwaukee........................ 414-527-2111
Hours: 6am-6pm Mon.-Thurs., 5am-8pm Fri., 4am-4pm Sat., 4am-Noon Sun.
Carries: Live bait, lures, flies, maps, rods, reels, licenses
Bodies of water: Pewaukee Lake, Okauchee Lake, Big Cedar Lake, Lac La Belle Lake, Keesus Lake, North Lake, Pine Lake, Silver Lake, Pike Lake, Little Cedar Lake, Friess Lake
Services & Products: Guide services, beverages, fishing instruction
Guides: Yes
OK to call for current conditions: Yes
Contact: Charlie Sapp

Barton Bait & Tackle
West Bend 414-338-9455
Hours: 6am-5pm
Carries: Live bait, lures, flies, maps, rods, reels
Bodies of water: Big Cedar Lake, Wallace Lake, Little Cedar Lake, Green Lake
Services & Products: Bulk bait by the pound
Guides: Yes
OK to call for current conditions: Yes
Contact: Jay Stone

BRULE RIVER

GUIDES...

Freestone Fly Fishers
Eagle River 715-545-2127
Species & Seasons: Trout May-Sept, SM Bass May-Oct, Walleye May-Feb, Muskellunge June-Nov
Bodies of water: Flyfishing for Trout on Brule River, Pine River, and area Spring Creeks, Three Lakes Chain, Butternut Lake, Eagle River Chain, North Twin Lake, South Twin and Kentuck Lake
Rates: Half day: $150(1-2), Full day: $200(1-2)
Call between: 7pm-9pm
Provides: Light tackle, heavy tackle, fly rod/reel, lures
Handicapped equipped: Yes

CLAM LAKE

BAIT & TACKLE...

Big Mike's Outdoor Sports Shop
Siren 715-349-2400
Hours: 6am-9pm
Carries: Live bait, lures, flies, maps, rods, reels, licenses
Bodies of water: Clam Lake, Big Sound
Services & Products: Boat rentals, charter boat service, food, beverages, fishing instruction, pontoon rentals
Guides: Yes
OK to call for current conditions: Yes
Contact: Mike

FLAMBEAU RIVER

GUIDES...

Northwoods Guide Service
W7820 Pine Avenue
Medford 54451
Species & Seasons: Muskellunge, Walleye June-Aug, LM Bass June-Oct, SM Bass May-Oct
Bodies of water: Jump River, Flambeau River, Rib Lake, Black River, Spirit Lake, Miller Dam Flowage
Rates: Half day: $95(1-2), Full day: $125(1-2), $30 additional pp over 2
Call between: 5pm-11pm
Provides: Light tackle, heavy tackle, lures, bait, rain gear, lunch
Handicapped equipped: No

FOX RIVER

GUIDES...

East Wisconsin Guide Service
Appleton 414-731-3287
Species & Seasons: Walleye all year, Panfish, Catfish June-Sept, Salmon, Trout April-Nov
Bodies of water: Lake Winnebago, Green Bay, Fox River, Wolf River, Lake Poygan, Lake Butte des Morts
Rates: Half day: $55(1), $100(2), Full day: $90(1), $175(2)
Call between: 6am-10pm
Provides: Light tackle, lures, bait, beverages
Handicapped equipped: No

J E Fishing Enterprises
Sturgeon Bay 414-743-7877
Species & Seasons: Walleye Mar-Nov, Brown Trout April-June, SM Bass May-Oct, Northern Pike Spring-Fall, Chinook Salmon, Rainbow Trout June-Oct
Bodies of water: Sturgeon Bay, Green Bay, Fox River, Lake Michigan
Rates: 18' boat: $150(1), $50 additional pp, 33' boat: 6 hrs. $360(6)
Call between: Evenings
Provides: Light tackle, heavy tackle, lures
Handicapped equipped: Yes
Certifications: USCG, State of WI

MARINAS...

Lakeside Marina
Green Bay 414-432-2400
Hours: 8:30am-5:30pm
Carries: Maps
Bodies of water: Lake Michigan, Fox River
Services & Products: Gas/oil, repair services, boat slips
Guides: Yes
OK to call for current conditions: No

FOX RIVER - GREEN BAY   WISCONSIN

Waterford Sport & Marine
Waterford 414-534-5530
Hours: 8am-7pm
Carries: Live bait, lures, flies, maps, rods, reels, licenses
Bodies of water: Fox River, Lake Michigan
Services & Products: Boat rentals, boat ramp, food, beverages, gas/oil, repair services, slip rental
Guides: No
OK to call for current conditions: Yes
Contact: Lauren

GILE FLOWAGE

GUIDES...

Don Pemble
Mercer 715-476-2718
Species & Seasons: Walleye, Muskellunge May-Nov, SM Bass, LM Bass June-Nov
Bodies of water: Turtle-Flambeau Flowage, Gile Flowage, Mercer Lake, Trude Lake, Long Lake, Moose Lake
Rates: Half day: $100(1-2), $125(3), Full day: $150(1-2), $175(3)
Call between: 6pm-9pm
Provides: Light tackle, heavy tackle
Handicapped equipped: Yes
Certifications: WI Licensed Guide

GREEN BAY

BAIT & TACKLE...

Highway 57 Bait & Tackle
Green Bay 414-866-3028
Hours: 24 hours
Carries: Live bait
Bodies of water: Green Bay
Services & Products: Fishing info, we tell it like it is
Guides: No
OK to call for current conditions: Yes
Contact: Brandy or Keith

Mac's Sport Shop
Sister Bay 414-854-5625
Hours: 9am-5pm
Carries: Live bait, lures, flies, maps, rods, reels, licenses
Bodies of water: Lake Michigan, Green Bay, Clark Lake, Kangaroo Lake, Europe Lake

Services & Products: Fishing instruction, repair services
Guides: Yes
OK to call for current conditions: Yes
Contact: Anyone

CHARTERS...

Ask Mee Charter Service
Sturgeon Bay 414-743-8595
Species & Seasons: Walleye, Lake Trout, Salmon, Rainbow Trout, Brown Trout June-Oct, Brown Trout, Walleye, Perch Dec-Mar, Northern Pike Dec-Mar
Bodies of water: Lake Michigan, Green Bay
Rates: Half day: $300(6), Full day: $600(6)
Call between: Anytime
Provides: Light tackle, heavy tackle, lures
Handicapped equipped: Yes
Certifications: USCG

Blue Fin Charters
Niagara 715-923-0007
.... 251-4452
Species & Seasons: Brown Trout, Rainbow Trout, April-Sept, Salmon July-Sept
Bodies of water: Lake Michigan, Green Bay at Port-Marinette Wisconsin
Rates: Half day: $250(2), $300(4), Full day: $325(2), $375(4), Pleasure cruise: $75 hr.
Call between: 7am-7pm
Provides: Light tackle, lures, bait
Handicapped equipped: Yes
Certifications: USCG, WI St. Lic.

East Wisconsin Guide Service
Appleton 414-731-3287
Species & Seasons: Walleye all year, Panfish, Catfish June-Sept, Salmon, Trout April-Nov
Bodies of water: Lake Winnebago, Green Bay, Fox River, Wolf River, Lake Poygan, Lake Butte des Morts
Rates: Half day: $55(1), $100(2), Full day: $90(1), $175(2)
Call between: 6am-10pm
Provides: Light tackle, lures, bait, beverages
Handicapped equipped: No

Ebben's Great Lakes Guide Service
Green Bay 800-752-7115
Species & Seasons: Steelhead June-Oct, Coho Salmon, Chinook Salmon July-Oct, Brown Trout Mar-Oct, Lake Trout April-Oct
Bodies of water: Lake Michigan, Green Bay
Rates: $50 an hour (6)
Call between: 8am-8pm
Provides: Light tackle, heavy tackle, lures, bait
Handicapped equipped: Yes
Certifications: USCG

J E Fishing Enterprises
Sturgeon Bay 414-743-7877
Species & Seasons: Walleye Mar-Nov, Brown Trout April-June, SM Bass May-Oct, Northern Pike Spring-Fall, Chinook Salmon, Rainbow Trout June-Oct
Bodies of water: Sturgeon Bay, Green Bay, Fox River, Lake Michigan
Rates: 18 ' boat: $150(1), $50 additional pp, 33 ' boat: 6 hrs. $360(6)
Call between: Evenings
Provides: Light tackle, heavy tackle, lures
Handicapped equipped: Yes
Certifications: USCG, State of WI

Lucky Lyle's Charter Fishing
Ellison Bay 414-854-4063
Species & Seasons: Rainbow Trout, Brown Trout May-June, Chinook Salmon July-Sept
Bodies of water: Green Bay, Lake Michigan
Rates: Half day: $45 + tax (minimum 4)
Call between: 7am-8pm
Provides: Downriggers and poles for deep water trolling
Handicapped equipped: Yes
Certifications: USCG

WISCONSIN

KANGAROO LAKE - LAKE GENEVA

KANGAROO LAKE

BAIT & TACKLE...

Mac's Sport Shop
Sister Bay 414-854-5625
Hours: 9am-5pm
Carries: Live bait, lures, flies, maps, rods, reels, licenses
Bodies of water: Lake Michigan, Green Bay, Clark Lake, Kangaroo Lake, Europe Lake
Services & Products: Fishing instruction, repair services
Guides: Yes
OK to call for current conditions: Yes
Contact: Anyone

LAC LA BELLE LAKE

BAIT & TACKLE...

Anglers Inn
Milwaukee 414-527-2111
Hours: 6am-6pm Mon.-Thurs., 5am-8pm Fri., 4am-4pm Sat., 4am-Noon Sun.
Carries: Live bait, lures, flies, maps, rods, reels, licenses
Bodies of water: Pewaukee Lake, Okauchee Lake, Big Cedar Lake, Lac La Belle Lake, Keesus Lake, North Lake, Pine Lake, Silver Lake, Pike Lake, Little Cedar Lake, Friess Lake
Services & Products: Guide services, beverages, fishing instruction
Guides: Yes
OK to call for current conditions: Yes
Contact: Charlie Sapp

Jim's Sports Heaven
Oconomowoc 414-567-6013
Hours: 9am-6pm Mon.-Thurs., 9am-5pm Fri., 9am-3pm Sat., 8am-2pm Sun.
Carries: Live bait, lures, flies, maps, rods, reels
Bodies of water: Lac La Belle Lake, Fowler Lake
Services & Products: Repair services
Guides: Yes
OK to call for current conditions: Yes

LAKE CHIPPEWA FLOWAGE

BAIT & TACKLE...

Eddie Bait Company
Hayward 715-462-3231
Hours: 9am-4pm, closed Sat., Sun.
Carries: Lures
Bodies of water: Lake Chippewa Flowage, Round Lake, Namekagon Lake, Lac Court Oreilles Lake, Grindstone Lake, Lost Land Lake, Teal Lake, Spider Lake
Services & Products: Guide services, fishing instruction
Guides: Yes
OK to call for current conditions: Yes
Contact: Dave Dorzaio

GUIDES...

Darwin Berry
Couderay 715-945-2321
Species & Seasons: Muskellunge, Walleye, Crappie, Northern Pike May-Oct, SM Bass, LM Bass June-Oct
Bodies of water: Lake Chippewa Flowage
Rates: Half day: $125(1-2), Full day: $175(1-2)
Call between: 6pm-9pm
Provides: Light tackle, heavy tackle, lures, bait
Handicapped equipped: No

Dave Dorazio
Hayward 715-462-3885
Species & Seasons: Muskellunge June-Nov
Bodies of water: Lake Chippewa Flowage
Rates: Full day: $190(1-2)
Call between: 7pm-10pm
Provides: Light tackle, heavy tackle, lures, rain gear
Handicapped equipped: No

Bill Gryzik
Hayward 715-462-3939
Species & Seasons: Muskellunge June-Nov, Crappie, Walleye May-Nov, SM Bass June-Sept
Bodies of water: Teal Lake, Lost Land Lake, Ghost Lake, Lake Chippewa Flowage
Rates: Half day: $100(1-2), Full day: $150(1-2), $50 additional pp over 2
Call between: 9am-9pm

Provides: Light tackle, heavy tackle, lures, bait, lunch, accomodations available
Handicapped equipped: No

Randy Gutsch
Hayward 715-462-9057
Species & Seasons: Muskellunge May-Nov
Bodies of water: Lake Chippewa Flowage and other Hayward area lakes
Rates: Full day: $175(1-2)
Call between: 6pm-10pm
Provides: Heavy tackle, lures

LODGES...

Indian Trail Resort
Couderay 715-945-3127
Guest Capacity: 50
Handicapped equipped: No
Seasons: May to Oct
Rates: $350/week
Contact: Pat
Guides: Yes
Species & Seasons: Muskellunge June-Nov, Bass June-Sept, Crappie, Bluegill May-Sept, Walleye May-Nov
Bodies of Water: Lake Chippewa Flowage
Types of fishing: Fly fishing, light tackle, heavy tackle
Available: Fishing instruction, licenses, bait, tackle, boat rentals, family activities

LAKE GENEVA

BAIT & TACKLE...

Diy Rod & Tackle
Racine 414-633-8292
Hours: 5am-6pm (Summer)
Carries: Live bait, flies, maps, rods, reels, licenses
Bodies of water: Lake Michigan, Lake Geneva, Powers Lake, Eagle Lake
Services & Products: Repair services
Guides: Yes
OK to call for current conditions: Yes
Contact: Anyone

Lake Geneva Rod & Reel
Lake Geneva 414-248-6610
Hours: 5am-5pm, closed Sun. afternoon
Carries: Live bait, lures, maps, rods, reels, licenses

LAKE GENEVA - LAKE MICHIGAN — WISCONSIN

Bodies of water: Lake Geneva, Deleuah Lake, Pell Lake, Powers Lake, Como Lake, Marie Lake, Elizabeth Lake
Services & Products: Near two launches
Guides: Yes
OK to call for current conditions: Yes
Contact: Jerry Asmus

Tri-Lakes Depth-Finder Repair
Fontana 414-275-5788
Hours: 6am-6pm
Carries: Live bait, lures, flies, maps, rods, reels, licenses
Bodies of water: Lake Geneva, Lake Delavan, Lake Como, Lake Comus
Services & Products: Guide services, boat ramp, food, fishing instruction, repair services
Guides: Yes
OK to call for current conditions: Yes
Contact: C. J. Bish or Hugh

LAKE MENDOTA

BAIT & TACKLE...

The Sportsman's Choice
Janesville 608-752-6743
Hours: 8am-5pm, closed Sun. except Mar.-June
Carries: Live bait, lures, flies, maps, rods, reels, licenses
Bodies of water: Rock River, Lake Koshkonong, Lake Mendota, Lake Menona, Lake Wabasa, Lake Kegonsa
Services & Products: Food, beverages, repair services
Guides: Yes
OK to call for current conditions: Yes
Contact: Dave Kessler

LAKE MICHIGAN

BAIT & TACKLE...

Art's Live Bait & Taxidermy
Sheboygan 414-452-2192
Hours: 5:30am-9pm
Carries: Live bait, lures, maps, rods, reels
Bodies of water: Lake Michigan
Services & Products: Fishing instruction, repair services
Guides: Yes
OK to call for current conditions: Yes
Contact: Art

Diy Rod & Tackle
Racine 414-633-8292
Hours: 5am-6pm (Summer)
Carries: Live bait, flies, maps, rods, reels, licenses
Bodies of water: Lake Michigan, Lake Geneva, Powers Lake, Eagle Lake
Services & Products: Repair services
Guides: Yes
OK to call for current conditions: Yes
Contact: Anyone

Mac's Sport Shop
Sister Bay 414-854-5625
Hours: 9am-5pm
Carries: Live bait, lures, flies, maps, rods, reels, licenses
Bodies of water: Lake Michigan, Green Bay, Clark Lake, Kangaroo Lake, Europe Lake
Services & Products: Fishing instruction, repair services
Guides: Yes
OK to call for current conditions: Yes
Contact: Anyone

Pigeon River Bait & Tackle
Sheboygan 414-457-2092
Hours: 5am-6pm May-Aug., 8am-6pm Sept.-April
Carries: Live bait, lures, flies, maps, rods, reels, licenses
Bodies of water: Lake Michigan and tributaries
Services & Products: Fishing instruction, repair services
Guides: Yes
OK to call for current conditions: Yes
Contact: Allan or Ed

Reef Runner Tackle
Racine 414-635-0651
Hours: 6am-3pm, closed Mon.
Carries: Live bait, lures, flies, maps, rods, reels, licenses
Bodies of water: Root River, Lake Michigan
Services & Products: Beverages
Guides: Yes
OK to call for current conditions: Yes
Contact: Rick or Clarence Coleman

Unco Industries Inc.
Racine 414-886-2665
Hours: 9am-5pm, closed Sat., Sun.
Carries: Live bait
Bodies of water: Lake Michigan
Guides: No
OK to call for current conditions: No

CHARTERS...

A-1 Mauer's Charter Service
Sturtevant 414-886-4050
Species & Seasons: Coho Salmon May-June, Chinook Salmon, Lake Trout, Rainbow Trout, Brown Trout May-Oct
Bodies of water: Lake Michigan
Rates: $300(6) + tax
Call between: 6am-10pm
Provides: Light tackle, heavy tackle, lures, bait
Handicapped equipped: Yes
Certifications: USCG

AAA-Unpredictable Charter Service
Manitowoc 414-684-0316
Species & Seasons: Rainbow Trout, Steelhead, Chinook Salmon, Coho Salmon, Brown Trout, Lake Trout June-Aug
Bodies of water: Lake Michigan
Rates: Full day: $400-$420(4), $420-$440(5), $440-$460(6), many other options available from $180
Call between: Anytime
Provides: Medium tackle, lures, bait, rain gear, beverages (limit to soda)
Handicapped equipped: Yes
Certifications: USCG, State of WI Trolling Lic.

Ask Mee Charter Service
Sturgeon Bay 414-743-8595
Species & Seasons: Walleye, Lake Trout, Salmon, Rainbow Trout, Brown Trout June-Oct, Brown Trout, Walleye, Perch Dec-Mar, Northern Pike Dec-Mar
Bodies of water: Lake Michigan, Green Bay
Rates: Half day: $300(6), Full day: $600(6)
Call between: Anytime
Provides: Light tackle, heavy tackle, lures
Handicapped equipped: Yes
Certifications: USCG

Belanger Charter Service
Westbend 414-338-8334
Species & Seasons: Chinook Salmon, Coho Salmon, Lake Trout, Rainbow Trout, Brown Trout April-Sept
Bodies of water: Lake Michigan
Rates: 5 hrs: $190
Call between: 7am-8pm
Provides: Rod/reel, lures
Handicapped equipped: No
Certifications: USCG

WISCONSIN — LAKE MICHIGAN

Black-Jac Fishing Charters
Kenosha 414-694-5878
Species & Seasons: Coho Salmon, Chinook Salmon, Rainbow Trout, Brown Trout, Lake Trout, Perch April-Oct
Bodies of water: Lake Michigan
Rates: Half day: $150(2), Full day: $225(2), other rates on request
Provides: Light tackle, bait
Handicapped equipped: Yes
Certifications: USCG, WI D.N.R.

Blue Fin Charters
Niagara 715-923-0007
.... 251-4452
Species & Seasons: Brown Trout, Rainbow Trout, April-Sept, Salmon July-Sept
Bodies of water: Lake Michigan, Green Bay at Port-Marinette Wisconsin
Rates: Half day: $250(2), $300(4), Full day: $325(2), $375(4), Pleasure cruise: $75 hr.
Call between: 7am-7pm
Provides: Light tackle, lures, bait
Handicapped equipped: Yes
Certifications: USCG, WI St. Lic.

Blue Max Charters
Elkhorn 414-246-6464
Species & Seasons: Coho Salmon May-Aug, Brown Trout May-Sept, Chinook Salmon June-Oct, Lake Trout, Rainbow Trout June-Sept
Bodies of water: Lake Michigan at Port of Milwaukee
Rates: Half day: $60(1), $120(2), $225(6)
Call between: 8am-10pm
Provides: Light tackle, lures, fish cleaning
Handicapped equipped: Yes
Certifications: State of WI, CPR, USCG

Clays Joy III Charter Service
Racine 414-633-7460
Species & Seasons: Coho Salmon April-Aug, Chinook Salmon June-Sept, Brown Trout, Rainbow Trout April-Sept, Lake Trout April-Oct
Bodies of water: Lake Michigan
Rates: Half day: $300(6), Full day: $600(6), 36' Sport fisherman: $60 hr.
Call between: 8am-8pm
Provides: Light tackle, heavy tackle, lures
Handicapped equipped: Yes
Certifications: USCG

Dale Schroeder Charter Fishing
Manitowoc 414-682-7477
Species & Seasons: Lake Trout, Brown Trout, Rainbow Trout May-Sept, Coho Salmon, Chinook Salmon July-Oct
Bodies of water: Lake Michigan
Rates: Half day: $300(1-6), Full day: $600(1-6)
Call between: 4pm-10pm
Provides: Light tackle, heavy tackle, lures, bait
Handicapped equipped: Yes
Certifications: USCG

Dead Reckon Lake Michigan
Sheboygan 414-467-1111
Species & Seasons: Lake Trout April-Sept, Rainbow Trout, Brown Trout, Coho Salmon, Chinook Salmon, Brook Trout, Skamania Trout April-Oct
Bodies of water: Lake Michigan
Rates: Half day: $200(1-2), Full day: $330(1-2), Rates as low as $50 for group of 6
Call between: 7am-9pm
Provides: Light tackle, heavy tackle, lures, bait
Handicapped equipped: Yes
Certifications: USCG

Dumper Dan Sportfishing Charters
Sheboygan 414-457-2940
Species & Seasons: Brown Trout, Coho Salmon April-Sept, Rainbow Trout, Chinook Salmon June-Sept, Lake Trout May-Sept
Bodies of water: Lake Michigan at Sheboygan Wisconsin
Rates: 3 hrs: $120(1-2), $140(4), $180(6), 6 hrs: $180(1-2), $220(4), $280(6), 9 hrs: $270(1-2), $330(4), $420(6) + tax
Call between: Anytime
Provides: Medium tackle, lures
Handicapped equipped: Yes
Certifications: USCG, D.N.R.

Ebben's Great Lakes Guide Service
Green Bay 800-752-7115
Species & Seasons: Steelhead June-Oct, Coho Salmon, Chinook Salmon July-Oct, Brown Trout Mar-Oct, Lake Trout April-Oct
Bodies of water: Lake Michigan, Green Bay
Rates: $50 an hour (6)
Call between: 8am-8pm
Provides: Light tackle, heavy tackle, lures, bait
Handicapped equipped: Yes
Certifications: USCG

Fiery Fox Charters
Greenfield 414-282-8919
Species & Seasons: Coho Salmon May-June, Chinook Salmon, Brown Trout, Rainbow Trout May-Oct, Lake Trout June-Sept
Bodies of water: Lake Michigan
Rates: Half day: $225(1-2), $290 (6 or less), Full day: $300(1), $350(2)
Call between: 9am-9pm
Provides: Medium tackle, lures
Handicapped equipped: Yes
Certifications: USCG

Fishing Bug Charters
Racine 414-633-8558
Species & Seasons: Coho Salmon May-July, Lake Trout May-Nov, Brown Trout, Rainbow Trout, Chinook Salmon May-Oct
Bodies of water: Lake Michigan at Racine, Wisconsin
Rates: Half day: $300(6), Full day: $600(6)
Call between: 5pm-10pm
Provides: Heavy tackle, lures, rain gear, licenses, fish cleaning
Handicapped equipped: Yes
Certifications: USCG, WI sport trollers license

Fishing Charters of Racine
Racine 800-475-6113
Species & Seasons: Coho Salmon May-June, Chinook Salmon, Brown Trout May-Oct, Steelhead May-Nov, Lake Trout June-Nov
Bodies of water: Lake Michigan at Port of Racine
Rates: Half day: $220(4) + tax, $300(6) + tax
Call between: 8am-9pm
Provides: Light tackle, heavy tackle, lures
Handicapped equipped: Yes
Certifications: USCG, Insured

Haasch Guide Service
Algoma 414-487-2705
Species & Seasons: Lake Trout, Brown Trout April-June, Steelhead June-Aug, Chinook Salmon July-Oct
Bodies of water: Lake Michigan
Rates: Half day: $250(1-6), Full day: $400(1-6), packages with lodging available

LAKE MICHIGAN — WISCONSIN

Call between: Anytime
Provides: Light tackle, heavy tackle, lures, bait
Handicapped equipped: Yes
Certifications: USCG, WDNR Licensed Guide

J E Fishing Enterprises
Sturgeon Bay 414-743-7877
Species & Seasons: Walleye Mar-Nov, Brown Trout April-June, SM Bass May-Oct, Northern Pike Spring-Fall, Chinook Salmon, Rainbow Trout June-Oct
Bodies of water: Sturgeon Bay, Green Bay, Fox River, Lake Michigan
Rates: 18 ' boat: $150(1), $50 additional pp, 33 ' boat: 6 hrs. $360(6)
Call between: Evenings
Provides: Light tackle, heavy tackle, lures
Handicapped equipped: Yes
Certifications: USCG, State of WI

Knudson Charter Fishing
Kewaunee 414-388-4805
Species & Seasons: Rainbow Trout June-Oct, Brown Trout, Lake Trout April-Nov, Salmon July-Oct
Bodies of water: Lake Michigan at Kewaunee
Rates: Half day: $150(2), $200(4), Full day: $300(2), $400(4)
Call between: 5am-10pm
Provides: Light tackle, heavy tackle, lures, bait
Handicapped equipped: Yes
Certifications: USCG

Leisure Time Charters
Waukesha 414-781-1704
Species & Seasons: Chinook Salmon June-Oct, Coho Salmon April-Sept, Lake Trout, Rainbow Trout May-Sept, Brown Trout April-Oct, Muskellunge June-Aug
Bodies of water: Lake Michigan, Pewaukee Lake, Okauchee Lake
Rates: Musky: Half day: $150(2), Full day: $325(2), Lake Michigan: Half day: $315
Call between: 8am-8pm
Provides: Light tackle, heavy tackle, lures, bait, beverages, lunch
Handicapped equipped: Yes
Certifications: USCG, State of WI

Lucky 7 Charter
Grafton 414-375-0308
Species & Seasons: Brown Trout, Rainbow Trout, Lake Trout, Coho Salmon, Chinook Salmon May-Sept
Bodies of water: Lake Michigan out of Port Washington
Rates: Half day: $110(1-2), $140(3), Full day: $200(1-2), $250(3)
Call between: 4pm-9pm
Provides: Light tackle, heavy tackle, lures, bait
Handicapped equipped: No
Certifications: USCG

Lucky Lyle's Charter Fishing
Ellison Bay 414-854-4063
Species & Seasons: Rainbow Trout, Brown Trout May-June, Chinook Salmon July-Sept
Bodies of water: Green Bay, Lake Michigan
Rates: Half day: $45 + tax (minimum 4)
Call between: 7am-8pm
Provides: Downriggers and poles for deep water trolling
Handicapped equipped: Yes
Certifications: USCG

Marlin
Oak Creek 414-764-7642
Species & Seasons: Salmon, Brown Trout, Rainbow Trout May-Oct, Lake Trout April-Sept
Bodies of water: Lake Michigan at Port of Milwaukee
Rates: Half day: $275(6)
Call between: 7am-9pm
Provides: Heavy tackle, lures, bait
Handicapped equipped: Yes
Certifications: USCG

Mauer's A-1 Adventure Charter Service
Racine 414-634-3911
Species & Seasons: Coho Salmon May-July, Chinook Salmon July-Oct, Lake Trout June-Oct, Brown Trout, Rainbow Trout May-Oct
Bodies of water: Lake Michigan
Rates: Half day: $300(6), Full day: $600(6)
Call between: 8am-9:30pm
Provides: Light tackle, heavy tackle, lures, bait
Handicapped equipped: Yes
Certifications: USCG, Sport Trolling Licenses

Darrell Mittlesteadt
Woodruff 715-356-1760
Species & Seasons: Walleye (in Vilas, Oneida Co, WI) May-Oct, Walleye (at Little Bay De Noc, Lake Michigan) Oct-Dec
Bodies of water: Inland lakes of Vilas County and Oneida County from May-Oct. 15th, Bay De Noc, Lake Michigan for Trophy Walleye Oct. 15-Dec. 15
Rates: Wisconsin: Full day: $185, Lake Michigan: Full day: $350
Call between: 4pm-10pm
Provides: Light tackle, lures, bait, rain gear
Certifications: USCG

Moody Blue Charters
2034 Mason Street
New Holstein 53061
Species & Seasons: Chinook Salmon, Coho Salmon, Rainbow Trout, Lake Trout, Brown Trout May-Sept
Bodies of water: Lake Michigan
Rates: Half day: $250(4), $275(5), $300(6), Full day: $500(4), $550(5), $600(6)
Call between: Anytime
Provides: Heavy tackle, lures, bait
Handicapped equipped: No

Night Flight Charters
Thiensville 414-242-4540
Species & Seasons: Salmon, Trout May-Oct
Bodies of water: Lake Michigan
Rates: 5 hrs: $265(6)
Call between: 7am-7pm
Provides: Light tackle, heavy tackle, lures
Certifications: USCG

Ozzie Charter Service
Oshkosh 414-233-1932
Species & Seasons: Lake Trout, Rainbow Trout, Salmon, Brown Trout June-Sept
Bodies of water: Lake Michigan at Two Rivers, Wisconsin
Rates: Half day: $175(1-2), $220(4), Full day: $300(1-2), $400(4)
Call between: 7am-7pm
Provides: Heavy tackle, lures, rain gear, lodging available
Handicapped equipped: No
Certifications: USCG, WI licensed

WISCONSIN
LAKE MICHIGAN - LAKE SUPERIOR

Prompt Delivery Charter Service
Sheboygan 608-849-6310
Species & Seasons: Lake Trout June-Aug, Chinook Salmon, Coho Salmon June-Oct, Rainbow Trout, Brown Trout May-Oct
Bodies of water: Lake Michigan
Rates: Half day: $250(6), Full day: $500(6)
Call between: 5pm-10pm
Provides: Light tackle, lures
Handicapped equipped: Yes
Certifications: USCG, WI Guide

Renegade Sportfishing Charters
Cedarburg 414-377-4560
Species & Seasons: Chinook Salmon, Coho Salmon, Rainbow Trout, Brown Trout, Lake Trout May-Sept
Bodies of water: Lake Michigan
Rates: Half day: $210(1-2)
Call between: 8am-10pm
Provides: Light tackle, lures, bait
Handicapped equipped: Yes
Certifications: USCG

Sea Dog Sportfishing Charters
Sheboygan 800-582-9694
Species & Seasons: Chinook Salmon, Coho Salmon, Rainbow Trout, Brown Trout, Lake Trout May-Oct
Bodies of water: Lake Michigan
Rates: Half day: $200(1-2), $220(4), Full day: $400(1-2), $420(4) + tax, evening rates available
Call between: 6pm-8pm
Provides: Light tackle, heavy tackle, lures, bait
Handicapped equipped: Yes
Certifications: USCG

Seahawk Charter
Port Washington 414-284-4693
Species & Seasons: Coho Salmon, Chinook Salmon, Rainbow Trout, Lake Trout, Brown Trout May-Oct
Bodies of water: Lake Michigan
Rates: Half day: $230(6), Full day: $460(6)
Call between: 8pm-10pm
Provides: Heavy tackle, lures
Certifications: USCG

Skinny Dipper Charters
Sheboygan 414-458-6657
Species & Seasons: Lake Trout May-Sept, Steelhead, Brown Trout, Coho Salmon, Chinook Salmon, Atlantic Salmon May-Oct
Bodies of water: Lake Michigan
Call between: 9am-3am
Provides: Light tackle, lures, bait
Handicapped equipped: Yes
Certifications: USCG, WI Guide

Stan Kupec Charter Service
Kewaunee 414-388-3732
Species & Seasons: Lake Trout, Rainbow Trout, Salmon, Coho Salmon, Brown Trout May-Oct
Bodies of water: Lake Michigan at Kewaunee, Wisconsin
Rates: Half day: $263(4-6), Full day: $525(4-6), more for 5 or 6
Call between: Anytime
Provides: Light tackle, lures
Handicapped equipped: Yes
Certifications: USCG

MARINAS...

Lakeside Marina
Green Bay 414-432-2400
Hours: 8:30am-5:30pm
Carries: Maps
Bodies of water: Lake Michigan, Fox River
Services & Products: Gas/oil, repair services, boat slips
Guides: Yes
OK to call for current conditions: No

Waterford Sport & Marine
Waterford 414-534-5530
Hours: 8am-7pm
Carries: Live bait, lures, flies, maps, rods, reels, licenses
Bodies of water: Fox River, Lake Michigan
Services & Products: Boat rentals, boat ramp, food, beverages, gas/oil, repair services, slip rental
Guides: No
OK to call for current conditions: Yes
Contact: Lauren

LAKE POYGAN
GUIDES...

East Wisconsin Guide Service
Appleton 414-731-3287
Species & Seasons: Walleye all year, Panfish, Catfish June-Sept, Salmon, Trout April-Nov
Bodies of water: Lake Winnebago, Green Bay, Fox River, Wolf River, Lake Poygan, Lake Butte des Morts
Rates: Half day: $55(1), $100(2), Full day: $90(1), $175(2)
Call between: 6am-10pm
Provides: Light tackle, lures, bait, beverages
Handicapped equipped: No

LAKE SUPERIOR
CHARTERS...

Anglers All
Ashland 715-682-5754
Species & Seasons: SM Bass, Walleye, Muskellunge May-Oct, Trout, Salmon April-June/Sept-Nov
Bodies of water: Lake Superior, Namekagon Lake
Rates: Half day: $150(1-2), Full day: $200(1-2)
Call between: 6am-6pm
Provides: Light tackle, heavy tackle, fly rod/reel
Handicapped equipped: Yes

Apostle Island Charter Services
Bayfield 715-779-5555
Species & Seasons: Coho Salmon May-June, Lake Trout June-Sept, Chinook Salmon, Brown Trout Sept-Oct
Bodies of water: Lake Superior (Apostle Islands)
Rates: Half day: $290(1-6), Full day: $400(1-6)
Call between: 8am-9pm
Provides: Heavy tackle, lures
Handicapped equipped: Yes
Certifications: USCG, WI Licensed Guide

LAKE SUPERIOR - MISSISSIPPI RIVER — WISCONSIN

Bayfield Fishing Charters Service
Bayfield 715-779-7010
.... 800-888-2378
Species & Seasons: Coho Salmon, Brook Trout, Rainbow Trout, Splake May-June, Chinook Salmon, Steelhead Sept-Oct, Lake Trout, Brown Trout June-Sept
Bodies of water: Lake Superior (Southern Shore/Apostle Islands)
Rates: Varies, Extended sportfishing and camping packages
Call between: Anytime
Provides: Heavy tackle, lures (downriggers)
Handicapped equipped: Yes, only on some yachts
Certifications: USCG, State of WI Certified/Lic. Guides (some are also Scuba Dive Masters)

Dave's Charter Service
Ashland 715-682-3379
Species & Seasons: Coho Salmon May-June, Lake Trout, Rainbow Trout June-Sept
Bodies of water: Lake Superior, Apostle Islands
Rates: Half day: $290, Full day: $390
Call between: 5pm-9pm
Provides: Light tackle, heavy tackle, fly rod/reel, lures, bait, rain gear
Handicapped equipped: Yes
Certifications: USCG

Northern Lite Charters
Port Wing 715-774-3673
Species & Seasons: Northern Pike April-Oct, Walleye May-Aug, Lake Trout, Brown Trout, Steelhead, Chinook Salmon, Coho Salmon May-Oct
Bodies of water: Lake Superior, rivers and tributaries
Rates: Half day: $200(4), Full day: $300(4), $30 additional pp over 4, maximum 6
Call between: 8am-10pm
Provides: Light tackle, heavy tackle, fly rod/reel, lures, bait, rain gear, beverages, lunch
Handicapped equipped: Yes
Certifications: USCG

Tracy Lee Charters
Saxon 715-893-2285
Species & Seasons: Lake Trout May-Oct, Coho Salmon May-July/Sept-Oct, Rainbow Trout, Brown Trout May-June, Chinook Salmon Sept-Oct

Bodies of water: Lake Superior
Rates: Half day: $150(4), $175(5), $200(6), Full day: $250(4), $275(5), $300(6)
Call between: 6pm-10pm
Provides: Heavy tackle, lures, bait
Handicapped equipped: Yes
Certifications: USCG WI and MI

LAKE WINNEBAGO

GUIDES...

East Wisconsin Guide Service
Appleton 414-731-3287
Species & Seasons: Walleye all year, Panfish, Catfish June-Sept, Salmon, Trout April-Nov
Bodies of water: Lake Winnebago, Green Bay, Fox River, Wolf River, Lake Poygan, Lake Butte des Morts
Rates: Half day: $55(1), $100(2), Full day: $90(1), $175(2)
Call between: 6am-10pm
Provides: Light tackle, lures, bait, beverages
Handicapped equipped: No

MANITOWOC RIVER

GUIDES...

Neshoto Guide Service
Two Rivers 414-793-2332
Species & Seasons: Steelhead Oct-May, Salmon Sept-Dec, SM Bass May-Aug, Crappie July-Aug, Channel Catfish June-Sept
Bodies of water: East Twin River, West Twin River, Kewaunee River, Manitowoc River, Branch River, Sheboygan River
Rates: Half day: $50(1), $80(2), Full day: $100(1), $160(2)
Call between: 4:30pm-10pm
Provides: Light tackle, heavy tackle, fly rod/reel, lures, bait

MILLER DAM FLOWAGE

GUIDES...

Northwoods Guide Service
W7820 Pine Avenue
Medford 54451
Species & Seasons: Muskellunge, Walleye June-Aug, LM Bass June-Oct, SM Bass May-Oct
Bodies of water: Jump River, Flambeau River, Rib Lake, Black River, Spirit Lake, Miller Dam Flowage
Rates: Half day: $95(1-2), Full day: $125(1-2), $30 additional pp over 2
Call between: 5pm-11pm
Provides: Light tackle, heavy tackle, lures, bait, rain gear, lunch
Handicapped equipped: No

MISSISSIPPI RIVER

BAIT & TACKLE...

Scott's Mobil & Sports Shop
Ferryville 608-734-3996
Hours: 6am-6pm
Carries: Live bait, lures, flies, maps, rods, reels, licenses
Bodies of water: Mississippi River
Services & Products: Food, beverages, gas/oil, fishing instruction, repair services
Guides: Yes
OK to call for current conditions: Yes
Contact: Scott

Williams Bait & Tackle
Necedah 608-565-7212
Hours: 5am-9pm
Carries: Live bait, lures, maps, rods, reels, licenses
Bodies of water: Mississippi River, Wisconsin River
Services & Products: Boat rentals, guide services, boat ramp, food, beverages
Guides: Yes
OK to call for current conditions: Yes
Contact: Paul or Charly

WISCONSIN — MISSISSIPPI RIVER - ONEIDA COUNTY

GUIDES...

God's Country Guide Service
LaCrosse 608-783-5160
Species & Seasons: Walleye Mar-April/Oct-Nov, LM Bass, SM Bass May-Oct, Crappie Aug-Oct, other species June-Oct
Bodies of water: Mississippi River pools 7 and 8
Rates: 6 hrs: $110(1), $130(2)
Call between: 6pm-9pm
Provides: Light tackle, heavy tackle, lures, bait, beverages

MOHAWKSIN LAKE

GUIDES...

Scott's Guide Service
Rhinelander 715-369-5929
Species & Seasons: Muskellunge May-Nov, SM Bass June-Aug, Northern Pike May-Sept
Bodies of water: Moen's Lake, Boom Lake, Wisconsin River, Mohawksin Lake, Lake George, Pelican Lake
Rates: Half day: $80(1-2), Full day: $175(1-2)
Call between: Anytime
Provides: Heavy tackle, lures, bait
Handicapped equipped: Yes

NAMEKAGON LAKE

BAIT & TACKLE...

Eddie Bait Company
Hayward 715-462-3231
Hours: 9am-4pm, closed Sat., Sun.
Carries: Lures
Bodies of water: Lake Chippewa Flowage, Round Lake, Namekagon Lake, Lac Court Oreilles Lake, Grindstone Lake, Lost Land Lake, Teal Lake, Spider Lake
Services & Products: Guide services, fishing instruction
Guides: Yes
OK to call for current conditions: Yes
Contact: Dave Dorzaio

GUIDES...

Anglers All
Ashland 715-682-5754
Species & Seasons: SM Bass, Walleye, Muskellunge May-Oct, Trout, Salmon April-June/Sept-Nov
Bodies of water: Lake Superior, Namekagon Lake
Rates: Half day: $150(1-2), Full day: $200(1-2)
Call between: 6am-6pm
Provides: Light tackle, heavy tackle, fly rod/reel
Handicapped equipped: Yes

ONEIDA COUNTY

BAIT & TACKLE...

R & R Live Bait Shop
Antigo 715-623-3051
Hours: 5am-10pm
Carries: Live bait, lures, flies, maps
Bodies of water: Wolf River, Pelican Lake, Summet Lake, Post Lake, Enterprise Lake
Services & Products: Repair services, rods
Guides: No
OK to call for current conditions: Yes
Contact: Dave M. Rusch

GUIDES...

C & R Guiding Service
Rhinelander 715-369-2283
Species & Seasons: Muskellunge June-Oct, Walleye May-June, Northern Pike May-Aug
Bodies of water: All lakes and rivers in Vilas County and Oneida County
Rates: Half day: $100(1-2), Full day: $180(1-2)
Call between: 5pm-10pm
Provides: Light tackle, heavy tackle, lures, bait
Handicapped equipped: Yes
Certifications: WI Licensed Guide

Gene Curtis
Phelps 715-545-4001
Species & Seasons: Muskellunge, Walleye, Northern Pike, Panfish May-Dec, SM Bass, LM Bass May-June
Bodies of water: Lakes in Vilas County, Oneida County, Forest County. Specialize in Muskellunge on North Twin Lake, Lac Vieux Desert Lake, Big Sand Lake, Eagle River Chain
Rates: Half day: $150(1-2), Full day: $200(1), $220(2), $240(3)
Call between: 7pm-10pm
Provides: Light tackle, heavy tackle, lures
Handicapped equipped: No

Jim Franson
Rhinelander 715-362-2176
Species & Seasons: Walleye, Muskellunge, Northern Pike, SM Bass, LM Bass May-Nov
Bodies of water: Inland lakes in Oneida County, Vilas County, Forest County
Rates: Half day: $125(2), Full day: $185(2)
Call between: 5pm-10pm
Provides: Light tackle, heavy tackle, lures, bait
Handicapped equipped: No
Certifications: WI Boating Safety, CPR, First aid

Freestone Fly Fishers
Eagle River 715-545-2127
Species & Seasons: Trout May-Sept, SM Bass May-Oct, Walleye May-Feb, Muskellunge June-Nov
Bodies of water: Flyfishing for Trout on Brule River, Pine River, and area Spring Creeks, Three Lakes Chain, Butternut Lake, Eagle River Chain, North Twin Lake, South Twin and Kentuck Lake
Rates: Half day: $150(1-2), Full day: $200(1-2)
Call between: 7pm-9pm
Provides: Light tackle, heavy tackle, fly rod/reel, lures
Handicapped equipped: Yes

Graser Guide Service
Mercer 715-476-3570
Species & Seasons: Muskellunge, Northern Pike May-Nov, LM Bass, SM Bass June-Sept, Walleye Sept-Oct, Crappie, Perch Sept-Nov
Bodies of water: Turtle-Flambeau Flowage, natural lakes and river systems in Oneida County, Vilas County, Iron County
Rates: Half day: $100(1-2), Full day: $160(1-2)

ONEIDA COUNTY — WISCONSIN

Call between: 5pm-9pm
Provides: Light tackle, heavy tackle, lures
Handicapped equipped: Yes

Elmer Jensen, Jr.
Eagle River 715-479-9228
Species & Seasons: Muskellunge, Northern Pike, Walleye, Crappie, Perch, Bluegill, SM Bass, LM Bass May-Nov
Bodies of water: Vilas County, Oneida County
Rates: Half day: $140(1-2), Full day: $190(1-2)
Call between: 5pm-10pm
Provides: Light tackle, heavy tackle, lures
Handicapped equipped: Yes
Certifications: USCG

Don Keister
Boulder Junction 715-385-2308
Species & Seasons: Muskellunge, Walleye, Northern Pike, SM Bass, LM Bass May-Oct
Bodies of water: Vilas County, Iron County, Price County, Oneida County
Rates: Full day: $170(1-2)
Call between: 6pm-10pm
Provides: Light tackle, heavy tackle, lures, bait, rain gear, beverages, lunch
Handicapped equipped: Yes

"Ranger" Rick Krueger
Eagle River 715-479-2250
Species & Seasons: Muskellunge June-Sept, Walleye May
Bodies of water: Vilas County most waters, Oneida County many waters, Forest County some waters
Rates: Full day: $225(2)
Call between: 5pm-10pm
Provides: Light tackle, heavy tackle, lures
Handicapped equipped: Yes

Darrell Mittlesteadt
Woodruff 715-356-1760
Species & Seasons: Walleye (in Vilas, Oneida Co, WI) May-Oct, Walleye (at Little Bay De Noc, Lake Michigan) Oct-Dec
Bodies of water: Inland lakes of Vilas County and Oneida County from May-Oct. 15th, Bay De Noc, Lake Michigan for Trophy Walleye Oct. 15-Dec. 15
Rates: Wisconsin: Full day: $185, Lake Michigan: Full day: $350
Call between: 4pm-10pm
Provides: Light tackle, lures, bait, rain gear
Certifications: USCG

Todd Powell
Eagle River 715-479-2422
Species & Seasons: Muskellunge June-Oct, SM Bass May-July, Trout May-Aug, Walleye May-Oct, Lake Trout April-Sept, Crappie May-Feb
Bodies of water: Vilas County, Oneida County lakes
Rates: Half day: $150(1-2), Full day: $200(1-2)
Call between: Anytime
Provides: Light tackle, heavy tackle, lures, bait, rain gear, beverages, lunch
Handicapped equipped: Yes
Certifications: WI Licensed Guide

Dave "Hawk" Pucci
Minocqua 800-688-7471
Species & Seasons: Muskellunge May-Nov, LM Bass, SM Bass, Northern Pike, Walleye May-Oct, Panfish May-Aug
Bodies of water: Trout Lake, Big St. Germain Lake, Little St. Germain Lake, Pike Lake Chain, Palmer Lake, lakes of Vilas County, Oneida County
Rates: Half day: $125(1-2), Full day: $185(1-2), $70 additional pp over 2
Call between: 6am-10pm
Provides: Light tackle, heavy tackle, fly rod/reel, lures
Handicapped equipped: No

Scott's Guide Service
Rhinelander 715-369-5929
Species & Seasons: Muskellunge May-Nov, SM Bass June-Aug, Northern Pike May-Sept
Bodies of water: Moen's Lake, Boom Lake, Wisconsin River, Mohawksin Lake, Lake George, Pelican Lake
Rates: Half day: $80(1-2), Full day: $175(1-2)
Call between: Anytime
Provides: Heavy tackle, lures, bait
Handicapped equipped: Yes

Terry J Strutz
Woodruff 715-356-7489
Species & Seasons: Muskellunge May-Dec
Bodies of water: Vilas County, Oneida County, Waters in Northern WI
Rates: Half day: $150(1-2), Full day: $200(1-2)
Call between:
Provides: Light tackle, heavy tackle, lures
Handicapped equipped: No

Thomas Urban
Rhinelander 715-362-3618
Species & Seasons: Walleye, Muskellunge, SM Bass, LM Bass Northern Pike May-Oct, Trout May-Sept, Panfish all year, (specialize in Muskellunge)
Bodies of water: Tomahawk Lake, Lake Minocqua, Pelican Lake, Wisconsin River, Wolf River, most lakes in Rhinelander area
Rates: Half day: $125(1-2), Full day: $185(1-2)
Call between: 6pm-10pm
Provides: Light tackle, heavy tackle, lures, bait, rain gear, beverages
Handicapped equipped: Yes
Certifications: Mepps, St. Croix, Mercury, Tuffy Boats

Nick "Fish Hawk" Van Der Puy
5013 Sundstein Road
Eagle River 54521
Species & Seasons: Walleye May-Nov, SM Bass, LM Bass May-Oct, Muskellunge May
Bodies of water: Vilas County, Oneida County
Rates: Half day: $150(1-2), Full day: $200(1-2)
Call between: Anytime
Provides: Light tackle, heavy tackle, lures, bait, rain gear, beverages, lunch
Handicapped equipped: No

Jim Voborsky
Rhinelander 715-282-5709
Species & Seasons: Muskellunge May-Oct
Bodies of water: Oneida County, Vilas County lakes
Rates: Full day: $200(1-2), Instructor (groups): $200/day
Call between: 6pm-10pm
Provides: Light tackle, heavy tackle, fly rod/reel, lures, bait, rain gear, beverages, lunch
Handicapped equipped: No

YOUR SILENT FISHING PARTNER

WISCONSIN
ONEIDA COUNTY - REGIONAL AREAS

The Walleye Man
Three Lakes 715-546-2576
Species & Seasons: Walleye, Northern Pike, Panfish May-Nov
Bodies of water: Lakes in Vilas County, Forest County, Oneida County, also ice fishing
Rates: Half day: $100(1-2), Full day: $160(1-2)
Call between: 7am-6pm
Provides: Light tackle, bait, rain gear, lunch
Handicapped equipped: Yes

PETENWELL LAKE

BAIT & TACKLE...

Pritzl's Corner Mart
Nekoosa 715-325-2281
Hours: 6:30am-7pm
Carries: Live bait, lures, flies, maps, rods, reels, licenses
Bodies of water: Wisconsin River, Petenwell Lake, Lake Arrowhead, Lake Sherwood, Lake Camelot
Services & Products: Food, beverages, gas/oil
Guides: No
OK to call for current conditions: Yes
Contact: John

PEWAUKEE LAKE

BAIT & TACKLE...

Anglers Inn
Milwaukee 414-527-2111
Hours: 6am-6pm Mon.-Thurs., 5am-8pm Fri., 4am-4pm Sat., 4am-Noon Sun.
Carries: Live bait, lures, flies, maps, rods, reels, licenses
Bodies of water: Pewaukee Lake, Okauchee Lake, Big Cedar Lake, Lac La Belle Lake, Keesus Lake, North Lake, Pine Lake, Silver Lake, Pike Lake, Little Cedar Lake, Friess Lake
Services & Products: Guide services, beverages, fishing instruction
Guides: Yes
OK to call for current conditions: Yes
Contact: Charlie Sapp

GUIDES...

Leisure Time Charters
Waukesha 414-781-1704
Species & Seasons: Chinook Salmon June-Oct, Coho Salmon April-Sept, Lake Trout, Rainbow Trout May-Sept, Brown Trout April-Oct, Muskellunge June-Aug
Bodies of water: Lake Michigan, Pewaukee Lake, Okauchee Lake
Rates: Musky: Half day: $150(2), Full day: $325(2),
Lake Michigan: Half day: $315
Call between: 8am-8pm
Provides: Light tackle, heavy tackle, lures, bait, beverages, lunch
Handicapped equipped: Yes
Certifications: USCG, State of WI

PRESQUE ISLE LAKE

BAIT & TACKLE...

Presque Isle Bait & Sweat Shop
Presque Isle 715-686-2636
Hours: 9am-5pm
Carries: Live bait, lures, flies, maps, rods, reels, licenses
Bodies of water: Presque Isle Lake Chain, Crab Lake, Oxbow Lake, Horsehead Lake, Armour Lake
Services & Products: Guide services, food, beverages
Guides: Yes
OK to call for current conditions: Yes
Contact: John

GUIDES...

Rodney Olsson
Presque Isle 715-686-2236
Species & Seasons: Muskellunge, Walleye May-Nov, SM Bass, LM Bass June-Oct
Bodies of water: Presque Isle Lake, Van Vliet Lake, Crab Lake, Papoose Lake, Harris Lake, Armour Lake
Rates: Half day: $95(1), $105(2), Full day: $150(1), $165(2), 5 days: $700(1), $800(2)
Call between: 7am-9am
Provides: Light tackle, heavy tackle, lures, bait
Handicapped equipped: No
Certifications: PADI (Scuba Diver)

REGIONAL AREAS

GUIDES...

Lorn Bown
Webster 715-635-7989
Species & Seasons: Walleye, Northern Pike, SM Bass, LM Bass in season
Bodies of water: All lakes and rivers in Burnett County, Washburn County
Rates: Full day: $40(1-2)
Call between: 6-9am/6-10pm
Handicapped equipped: Yes
Certifications: 50 years + experience

Gene Curtis
Phelps 715-545-4001
Species & Seasons: Muskellunge, Walleye, Northern Pike, Panfish May-Dec, SM Bass, LM Bass May-June
Bodies of water: Lakes in Vilas County, Oneida County, Forest County. Specialize in Muskellunge on North Twin Lake, Lac Vieux Desert Lake, Big Sand Lake, Eagle River Chain
Rates: Half day: $150(1-2), Full day: $200(1), $220(2), $240(3)
Call between: 7pm-10pm
Provides: Light tackle, heavy tackle, lures
Handicapped equipped: No

Dan Detko Fishing Guide Service
Park Falls 715-762-2884
Species & Seasons: Walleye May-Feb, Muskellunge May-Nov, Trout Oct-ice
Bodies of water: Northern Wisconsin lakes and rivers
Rates: Half day: $60(1-2), Full day: $120(1-2), Winter Walleye $30
Call between: Anytime
Provides: Light tackle, heavy tackle, lures, bait, beverages
Handicapped equipped: No
Certifications: WI Licensed Guide

Mary "Bwana" Elliott
Eagle River 715-479-4908
Species & Seasons: Walleye May-Oct, SM Bass June-Sept, Muskellunge May-Oct, Crappie, Bluegill June-July
Bodies of water: Northern Wisconsin
Rates: Half day: $140(1-2), Full day: $200(1-2)
Call between: 6pm-8pm
Provides: Light tackle, heavy tackle, lures, bait, rain gear
Handicapped equipped: Yes

REGIONAL AREAS - SHELL LAKE WISCONSIN

Jim Franson
Rhinelander 715-362-2176
Species & Seasons: Walleye, Muskellunge, Northern Pike, SM Bass, LM Bass May-Nov
Bodies of water: Inland lakes in Oneida County, Vilas County, Forest County
Rates: Half day: $125(2), Full day: $185(2)
Call between: 5pm-10pm
Provides: Light tackle, heavy tackle, lures, bait
Handicapped equipped: No
Certifications: WI Boating Safety, CPR, First aid

Graser Guide Service
Mercer 715-476-3570
Species & Seasons: Muskellunge, Northern Pike May-Nov, LM Bass, SM Bass June-Sept, Walleye Sept-Oct, Crappie, Perch Sept-Nov
Bodies of water: Turtle-Flambeau Flowage, natural lakes and river systems in Oneida County, Vilas County, Iron County
Rates: Half day: $100(1-2), Full day: $160(1-2)
Call between: 5pm-9pm
Provides: Light tackle, heavy tackle, lures
Handicapped equipped: Yes

Don Keister
Boulder Junction 715-385-2308
Species & Seasons: Muskellunge, Walleye, Northern Pike, SM Bass, LM Bass May-Oct
Bodies of water: Vilas County, Iron County, Price County, Oneida County
Rates: Full day: $170(1-2)
Call between: 6pm-10pm
Provides: Light tackle, heavy tackle, lures, bait, rain gear, beverages, lunch
Handicapped equipped: Yes

"Ranger" Rick Krueger
Eagle River 715-479-2250
Species & Seasons: Muskellunge June-Sept, Walleye May
Bodies of water: Vilas County most waters, Oneida County many waters, Forest County some waters
Rates: Full day: $225(2)
Call between: 5pm-10pm
Provides: Light tackle, heavy tackle, lures
Handicapped equipped: Yes

Last Wilderness Guide Service
Presque Isle 715-686-2813
Species & Seasons: LM Bass, SM Bass May-Sept, Muskellunge May-Nov
Bodies of water: Vilas County, Iron County, Chequamegon Bay
Rates: Half day: $90(1-2), Full day: $175(1-2)
Call between: 5pm-9pm
Provides: Light tackle, lures, bait
Handicapped equipped: Yes
Certifications: WI Licensed Guide, Author

Jodi Maina
Hayward 715-462-3952
Species & Seasons: Muskellunge May-Nov
Bodies of water: Hayward area (over 60 lakes)
Rates: Half day: $150(1-2), Full day: $250(1-2)
Call between: 7am
Provides: Heavy tackle, lures
Handicapped equipped: Some, inquire

Norb Wallock
Conover 715-479-6127
Species & Seasons: Walleye May-Mar, Muskellunge, Crappie May-Nov, SM Bass June-Nov
Bodies of water: Northern Wisconsin, UP of Michigan
Rates: Half day: $175(1-2), Full day: $250(1-2)
Call between: 6pm-10pm
Provides: Light tackle, heavy tackle, lures
Handicapped equipped: Yes
Certifications: WI Licensed Guide, Member of Eagle River Guides Assoc.

The Walleye Man
Three Lakes 715-546-2576
Species & Seasons: Walleye, Northern Pike, Panfish May-Nov
Bodies of water: Lakes in Vilas County, Forest County, Oneida County, also ice fishing
Rates: Half day: $100(1-2), Full day: $160(1-2)
Call between: 7am-6pm
Provides: Light tackle, bait, rain gear, lunch
Handicapped equipped: Yes

LODGES...

Candian Fishing Camps & Wisconsin Vacation Service
Milwaukee 414-466-6670
Guest Capacity: 100 facilities
Handicapped equipped: Yes, some
Seasons: All year
Rates: $285-$800/week
Guides: Yes
Species & Seasons: Muskellunge, Walleye May-Nov, Bass June-Nov, Northern Pike May-Mar, Panfish all year, Trout Spring/Fall
Bodies of Water: We represent facilities on over 100 bodies of water
Types of fishing: Fly fishing, light tackle, heavy tackle, wading, fly-out trips
Available: Fishing instruction, licenses, bait, tackle, boat rentals, family activities, children's program, baby sitting

SHELL LAKE
GUIDES...

Muskie Fever Guide Service
Rice Lake 715-234-6401
Species & Seasons: Muskellunge June-Nov
Bodies of water: Shell Lake, McKenzie Lake, Middle McKenzie Lake, Couderay Lake, Sissabagama Lake
Rates: Half day: $75(2), Full day: $150(2), "Prime Time" special w/video $65 pp
Call between: 6-8am/10-11pm
Provides: Heavy tackle, lures, bait
Handicapped equipped: No
Certifications: WI Licesed Guide

WISCONSIN

TROUT LAKE

GUIDES...

Dave "Hawk" Pucci
Minocqua.................. 800-688-7471
Species & Seasons: Muskellunge May-Nov, LM Bass, SM Bass, Northern Pike, Walleye May-Oct, Panfish May-Aug
Bodies of water: Trout Lake, Big St. Germain Lake, Little St. Germain Lake, Pike Lake Chain, Palmer Lake, lakes of Vilas County, Oneida County
Rates: Half day: $125(1-2), Full day: $185(1-2), $70 additional pp over 2
Call between: 6am-10pm
Provides: Light tackle, heavy tackle, fly rod/reel, lures
Handicapped equipped: No

Jim Stark
Boulder Junction............. 715-385-2480
.....................385-0133
Species & Seasons: Walleye Sept-Nov/May-July, LM Bass, SM Bass June-Sept, Muskellunge May-Nov, Brook Trout, Brown Trout May-Sept, Northern Pike May-Nov, Panfish May-Oct
Bodies of water: Big Muskellunge Lake, Cisco Chain, Trout Lake, Fishtrap Lake, Alequash Lake, Palmer Lake, White Sand Lake, Lost Canne, Diamond Lake, Boulder Lake, Jule Lake, Partridge Lake
Rates: Half day: $80(1-2), Full day: $160(1-2)
Call between: 9am-9pm
Provides: Light tackle, heavy tackle, lures

TURTLE-FLAMBEAU FLOWAGE

GUIDES...

Graser Guide Service
Mercer 715-476-3570
Species & Seasons: Muskellunge, Northern Pike May-Nov, LM Bass, SM Bass June-Sept, Walleye Sept-Oct, Crappie, Perch Sept-Nov
Bodies of water: Turtle-Flambeau Flowage, natural lakes and river systems in Oneida County, Vilas County, Iron County
Rates: Half day: $100(1-2), Full day: $160(1-2)

Call between: 5pm-9pm
Provides: Light tackle, heavy tackle, lures
Handicapped equipped: Yes

Don Gray
Mercer 715-476-3445
Species & Seasons: Walleye May-Oct, Muskellunge June-Oct
Bodies of water: Turtle-Flambeau Flowage
Rates: Half day: $90(2), Full day: $140(2)
Call between: 6pm-9pm
Provides: Bait
Handicapped equipped: No
Certifications: WI Licensed Guide

Jim Hemmy
Park Falls 715-762-2925
Species & Seasons: Walleye, Panfish May-Oct, Muskellunge June-Oct, SM Bass June-Sept
Bodies of water: Turtle-Flambeau Flowage
Rates: Half day: $90(2), Full day: $160(2)
Call between: 11am-6pm
Handicapped equipped: No

Killer's Professional Guide Service
Lac du Flambeau 715-588-7594
Species & Seasons: Walleye May-Nov, Muskellunge June-Nov, SM Bass, LM Bass May-Sept
Bodies of water: Turtle-Flambeau Flowage and Minocqua area (Walleye specialist)
Rates: Half day: $80(1-2), Full day: $150(1-2) + bait
Call between: Anytime
Provides: Light tackle, heavy tackle, rain gear, beverages
Handicapped equipped: Yes

Don Pemble
Mercer 715-476-2718
Species & Seasons: Walleye, Muskellunge May-Nov, SM Bass, LM Bass June-Nov
Bodies of water: Turtle-Flambeau Flowage, Gile Flowage, Mercer Lake, Trude Lake, Long Lake, Moose Lake
Rates: Half day: $100(1-2), $125(3), Full day: $150(1-2), $175(3)
Call between: 6pm-9pm
Provides: Light tackle, heavy tackle
Handicapped equipped: Yes
Certifications: WI Licensed Guide

VILAS COUNTY

BAIT & TACKLE...

Grizzly Bill's
Lac du Flambeau 715-588-3266
Hours: Winter: 7:30am-6pm Mon.-Sat., 8am-5pm Sun., Summer: 6am-8pm Mon.-Sat., 7am-7pm Sun.
Carries: Live bait, lures, maps, rods, reels, licenses
Bodies of water: Lac du Flambeau Indian Res.
Services & Products: Food, beverages, gas/oil, repair services, sweatshirts
Guides: Yes
OK to call for current conditions: Yes
Contact: Mark, Rich or Al

Presque Isle Bait & Sweat Shop
Presque Isle 715-686-2636
Hours: 9am-5pm
Carries: Live bait, lures, flies, maps, rods, reels, licenses
Bodies of water: Presque Isle Lake Chain, Crab Lake, Oxbow Lake, Horsehead Lake, Armour Lake
Services & Products: Guide services, food, beverages
Guides: Yes
OK to call for current conditions: Yes
Contact: John

GUIDES...

Boulder Junction Motor Lodge
Boulder Junction.............. 715-385-2825
Species & Seasons: Muskellunge, Walleye, LM Bass, SM Bass May-Dec, Panfish all year
Bodies of water: Vilas County
Rates: Half day: $120(1-2), $200(1-2)
Call between: 6am-10pm
Provides: Light tackle, bait, rain gear, beverages, lunch
Handicapped equipped: Yes
Certifications: WI Licensed Guide

C & R Guiding Service
Rhinelander....................... 715-369-2283
Species & Seasons: Muskellunge June-Oct, Walleye May-June, Northern Pike May-Aug
Bodies of water: All lakes and rivers in Vilas County and Oneida County
Rates: Half day: $100(1-2), Full day: $180(1-2)

VILAS COUNTY — WISCONSIN

Call between: 5pm-10pm
Provides: Light tackle, heavy tackle, lures, bait
Handicapped equipped: Yes
Certifications: WI Licensed Guide

Gene Curtis
Phelps 715-545-4001
Species & Seasons: Muskellunge, Walleye, Northern Pike, Panfish May-Dec, SM Bass, LM Bass May-June
Bodies of water: Lakes in Vilas County, Oneida County, Forest County. Specialize in Muskellunge on North Twin Lake, Lac Vieux Desert Lake, Big Sand Lake, Eagle River Chain
Rates: Half day: $150(1-2),
Full day: $200(1), $220(2), $240(3)
Call between: 7pm-10pm
Provides: Light tackle, heavy tackle, lures
Handicapped equipped: No

Jim Franson
Rhinelander 715-362-2176
Species & Seasons: Walleye, Muskellunge, Northern Pike, SM Bass, LM Bass May-Nov
Bodies of water: Inland lakes in Oneida County, Vilas County, Forest County
Rates: Half day: $125(2),
Full day: $185(2)
Call between: 5pm-10pm
Provides: Light tackle, heavy tackle, lures, bait
Handicapped equipped: No
Certifications: WI Boating Safety, CPR, First aid

Freestone Fly Fishers
Eagle River 715-545-2127
Species & Seasons: Trout May-Sept, SM Bass May-Oct, Walleye May-Feb, Muskellunge June-Nov
Bodies of water: Flyfishing for Trout on Brule River, Pine River, and area Spring Creeks, Three Lakes Chain, Butternut Lake, Eagle River Chain, North Twin Lake, South Twin and Kentuck Lake
Rates: Half day: $150(1-2),
Full day: $200(1-2)
Call between: 7pm-9pm
Provides: Light tackle, heavy tackle, fly rod/reel, lures
Handicapped equipped: Yes

Graser Guide Service
Mercer 715-476-3570
Species & Seasons: Muskellunge, Northern Pike May-Nov, LM Bass, SM Bass June-Sept, Walleye Sept-Oct, Crappie, Perch Sept-Nov

Bodies of water: Turtle-Flambeau Flowage, natural lakes and river systems in Oneida County, Vilas County, Iron County
Rates: Half day: $100(1-2),
Full day: $160(1-2)
Call between: 5pm-9pm
Provides: Light tackle, heavy tackle, lures
Handicapped equipped: Yes

Dick Gries
Arbor Vitae 715-356-2503
Species & Seasons: Muskellunge June-Nov, Walleye May-Oct
Bodies of water: Vilas County, premier Muskellunge/Walleye waters in Mid-west
Rates: Half day: $125(1-2),
Full day: $200(1-2)
Call between: 8am-9pm
Provides: Light tackle, heavy tackle, lures
Handicapped equipped: No

Harry's Guide Service
Boulder Junction 715-385-2404
Species & Seasons: Muskellunge, Walleye, Northern Pike May-Nov, SM Bass, LM Bass June-Sept, Panfish May-Sept
Bodies of water: Boulder Junction area (over 40 lakes)
Rates: Half day: $135(1-2), $155(3),
Full day: $200(1-2), $225(3)
Call between: 7pm-10pm
Provides: Light tackle, heavy tackle, lures
Handicapped equipped: Yes
Certifications: WI Licensed Guide

Elmer Jensen, Jr.
Eagle River 715-479-9228
Species & Seasons: Muskellunge, Northern Pike, Walleye, Crappie, Perch, Bluegill, SM Bass, LM Bass May-Nov
Bodies of water: Vilas County, Oneida County
Rates: Half day: $140(1-2),
Full day: $190(1-2)
Call between: 5pm-10pm
Provides: Light tackle, heavy tackle, lures
Handicapped equipped: Yes
Certifications: USCG

Don Keister
Boulder Junction 715-385-2308
Species & Seasons: Muskellunge, Walleye, Northern Pike, SM Bass, LM Bass May-Oct
Bodies of water: Vilas County, Iron County, Price County, Oneida County
Rates: Full day: $170(1-2)
Call between: 6pm-10pm

Provides: Light tackle, heavy tackle, lures, bait, rain gear, beverages, lunch
Handicapped equipped: Yes

"Ranger" Rick Krueger
Eagle River 715-479-2250
Species & Seasons: Muskellunge June-Sept, Walleye May
Bodies of water: Vilas County most waters, Oneida County many waters, Forest County some waters
Rates: Full day: $225(2)
Call between: 5pm-10pm
Provides: Light tackle, heavy tackle, lures
Handicapped equipped: Yes

Last Wilderness Guide Service
Presque Isle 715-686-2813
Species & Seasons: LM Bass, SM Bass May-Sept, Muskellunge May-Nov
Bodies of water: Vilas County, Iron County, Chequamegon Bay
Rates: Half day: $90(1-2),
Full day: $175(1-2)
Call between: 5pm-9pm
Provides: Light tackle, lures, bait
Handicapped equipped: Yes
Certifications: WI Licensed Guide, Author

Darrell Mittlestaedt
Woodruff 715-356-1760
Species & Seasons: Walleye (in Vilas, Oneida Co, WI) May-Oct, Walleye (at Little Bay De Noc, Lake Michigan) Oct-Dec
Bodies of water: Inland lakes of Vilas County and Oneida County from May-Oct. 15, Bay De Noc, Lake Michigan for Trophy Walleye Oct. 15-Dec. 15
Rates: Wisconsin: Full day: $185, Lake Michigan: Full day: $350
Call between: 4pm-10pm
Provides: Light tackle, lures, bait, rain gear
Certifications: USCG

WISCONSIN

VILAS COUNTY

Rodney Olsson
Presque Isle 715-686-2236
Species & Seasons: Muskellunge,
Walleye May-Nov, SM Bass, LM Bass
June-Oct
Bodies of water: Presque Isle Lake,
Van Vliet Lake, Crab Lake,
Papoose Lake, Harris Lake, Armour Lake
Rates: Half day: $95(1), $105(2),
Full day: $150(1), $165(2),
5 day: $700(1), $800(2)
Call between: 7am-9am
Provides: Light tackle, heavy tackle,
lures, bait
Handicapped equipped: No
Certifications: PADI (Scuba Diver)

Todd Powell
Eagle River 715-479-2422
Species & Seasons: Muskellunge
June-Oct, SM Bass May-July, Trout
May-Aug, Walleye May-Oct, Lake Trout
April-Sept, Crappie May-Feb
Bodies of water: Vilas County,
Oneida County lakes
Rates: Half day: $150(1-2),
Full day: $200(1-2)
Call between: Anytime
Provides: Light tackle, heavy tackle,
lures, bait, rain gear, beverages, lunch
Handicapped equipped: Yes
Certifications: WI Licensed Guide

Dave "Hawk" Pucci
Minocqua 800-688-7471
Species & Seasons: Muskellunge
May-Nov, LM Bass, SM Bass, Northern
Pike, Walleye May-Oct, Panfish May-Aug
Bodies of water: Trout Lake,
Big St. Germain Lake, Little St. Germain
Lake, Pike Lake Chain, Palmer Lake,
lakes of Vilas County, Oneida County
Rates: Half day: $125(1-2),
Full day: $185(1-2), $70 additional pp
over 2
Call between: 6am-10pm
Provides: Light tackle, heavy tackle,
fly rod/reel, lures
Handicapped equipped: No

Jerry Sobiek
Phelps 715-545-2515
Species & Seasons: Muskellunge
June-Oct, Walleye Dec-Feb
Bodies of water: North Twin Lake
Rates: Half day: $100(1-2),
Full day: $200(1-2)
Call between: 8am-4pm
Provides: Heavy tackle, lures
Handicapped equipped: No

Jim Stark
Boulder Junction 715-385-2480
.... 385-0133
Species & Seasons: Walleye
Sept-Nov/May-July, LM Bass, SM Bass
June-Sept, Muskellunge May-Nov, Brook
Trout, Brown Trout May-Sept, Northern
Pike May-Nov, Panfish May-Oct
Bodies of water: Big Muskellunge Lake,
Cisco Chain, Trout Lake, Fishtrap Lake,
Alequash Lake, Palmer Lake,
White Sand Lake, Lost Canne,
Diamond Lake, Boulder Lake, Jule Lake,
Partridge Lake
Rates: Half day: $80(1-2),
Full day: $160(1-2)
Call between: 9am-9pm
Provides: Light tackle, heavy tackle, lures

Terry J. Strutz
Woodruff 715-356-7489
Species & Seasons: Muskellunge
May-Dec
Bodies of water: Vilas County, Oneida
County, Waters in Northern Wisconsin
Rates: Half day: $150(1-2),
Full day: $200(1-2)
Call between:
Provides: Light tackle, heavy tackle,
lures
Handicapped equipped: No

Tom Swanson
Boulder Junction 715-385-2168
Species & Seasons: Walleye,
Muskellunge May-Nov
Bodies of water: Boulder Junction and
Vilas County area
Rates: Half day: $125(1-2),
Full day: $200(1-2), Night fishing: $150
Call between: 6pm-9pm
Provides: Light tackle, heavy tackle,
lures
Handicapped equipped: No

Nick "Fish Hawk" Van Der Puy
5013 Sundstein Road
Eagle River 54521
Species & Seasons: Walleye May-Nov,
SM Bass, LM Bass May-Oct,
Muskellunge May
Bodies of water: Vilas County,
Oneida County
Rates: Half day: $150(1-2),
Full day: $200(1-2)
Call between: Anytime
Provides: Light tackle, heavy tackle,
lures, bait, rain gear, beverages, lunch
Handicapped equipped: No

Jim Voborsky
Rhinelander 715-282-5709
Species & Seasons: Muskellunge
May-Oct
Bodies of water: Oneida County,
Vilas County Lakes
Rates: Full day: $200(1-2),
Instructor (groups): $200(day)
Call between: 6pm-10pm
Provides: Light tackle, heavy tackle,
fly rod/reel, lures, bait, rain gear,
beverages, lunch
Handicapped equipped: No

The Walleye Man
Three Lakes 715-546-2576
Species & Seasons: Walleye,
Northern Pike, Panfish May-Nov
Bodies of water: Lakes in Vilas County,
Forest County, Oneida County,
also ice fishing
Rates: Half day: $100(1-2),
Full day: $160(1-2)
Call between: 7am-6pm
Provides: Light tackle, bait,
rain gear, lunch
Handicapped equipped: Yes

Yutch's Deluxe Guide Service
Eagle River 715-479-8093
Species & Seasons: Muskellunge,
Walleye, Panfish May-Nov, SM Bass
June-Nov
Bodies of water: Eagle River Chain,
Kentuck Lake, Forest Lake,
Portage Lake and more
Rates: Half day: $95(1-2),
Full day: $175(1-2)
Call between: 6pm-10pm
Provides: Light tackle, heavy tackle
Handicapped equipped: Yes

LODGES...

Boulder Junction Motor Lodge
Boulder Junction 715-385-2825
Guest Capacity: 20 rooms
Handicapped equipped: Yes
Seasons: All year
Rates: $55-$85/day double occupancy
Contact: Sharon
Guides: Yes, recommend
Species & Seasons: Muskellunge,
Walleye, LM Bass, SM Bass May-Dec,
Panfish all year
Bodies of Water: Boulder Junction area
(197 lakes)
Types of fishing: Fly fishing, light tackle
Available: Hot tub, fish house,
fish freezing, comp. cont'l. breakfast

WIND LAKE - WOLF RIVER

WISCONSIN

WIND LAKE

BAIT & TACKLE...

Sportsman's Lounge
Wind Lake......................... 414-895-2216
Hours: 6am-7pm, closed in winter
Carries: Live bait, lures, licenses
Bodies of water: Wind Lake
Services & Products: Boat rentals, boat ramp, food, beverages, motor rentals
Guides: No
OK to call for current conditions: Yes
Contact: Ron

WISCONSIN RIVER

BAIT & TACKLE...

La-Va-Q's Live Bait & Tackle
Wisconsin Rapids 715-424-1723
Hours: 6am-9pm
Carries: Live bait, lures, flies, maps, rods, reels, licenses
Bodies of water: Nepco Lake, Lake Camelot, Lake Sherwood, Wisconsin River, 5 Mile Creek, Big Eau Pleine Res., 10 Mile Creek
Services & Products: Fishing instruction, repair services
Guides: No
OK to call for current conditions: No
Contact: Mike Lavaque

Pritzl's Corner Mart
Nekoosa 715-325-2281
Hours: 6:30am-7pm
Carries: Live bait, lures, flies, maps, rods, reels, licenses
Bodies of water: Wisconsin River, Peterwell Lake, Lake Arrowhead, Lake Sherwood, Lake Camelot
Services & Products: Food, beverages, gas/oil
Guides: No
OK to call for current conditions: Yes
Contact: John

Schleef's Bait Shop
Wisconsin Dells 608-254-2034
Hours: 6am-8pm
Carries: Live bait, lures, flies, maps, rods, reels, licenses
Bodies of water: Wisconsin Rver, Lake Delton, Mirror Lake, Lake Redstone, Jordan Lake
Services & Products: Boat rentals, guide services, food, beverages

Guides: Yes
OK to call for current conditions: Yes
Contact: Bob Haire

Williams Bait & Tackle
Necedah 608-565-7212
Hours: 5am-9pm
Carries: Live bait, lures, maps, rods, reels, licenses
Bodies of water: Mississippi River, Wisconsin River
Services & Products: Boat rentals, guide services, boat ramp, food, beverages
Guides: Yes
OK to call for current conditions: Yes
Contact: Paul or Charly

GUIDES...

Scott's Guide Service
Rhinelander 715-369-5929
Species & Seasons: Muskellunge May-Nov, SM Bass June-Aug, Northern Pike May-Sept
Bodies of water: Moen's Lake, Boom Lake, Wisconsin River, Mohawksin Lake, Lake George, Pelican Lake
Rates: Half day: $80(1-2), Full day: $175(1-2)
Call between: Anytime
Provides: Heavy tackle, lures, bait
Handicapped equipped: Yes

Thomas Urban
Rhinelander 715-362-3618
Species & Seasons: Walleye, Muskellunge, SM Bass, LM Bass Northern Pike May-Oct, Trout May-Sept, Panfish all year, (specialize in Muskellunge)
Bodies of water: Tomahawk Lake, Lake Minocqua, Pelican Lake, Wisconsin River, Wolf River, most lakes in Rhinelander area
Rates: Half day: $125(1-2), Full day: $185(1-2)
Call between: 6pm-10pm
Provides: Light tackle, heavy tackle, lures, bait, rain gear, beverages
Handicapped equipped: Yes
Certifications: Mepps, St. Croix, Mercury, Tuffy Boats

WOLF RIVER

BAIT & TACKLE...

R & R Live Bait Shop
Antigo 715-623-3051
Hours: 5am-10pm
Carries: Live bait, lures, flies, maps
Bodies of water: Wolf River, Pelican Lake, Summet Lake, Post Lake, Enterprise Lake
Services & Products: Repair services, rods
Guides: No
OK to call for current conditions: Yes
Contact: Dave M. Rusch

GUIDES...

East Wisconsin Guide Service
Appleton 414-731-3287
Species & Seasons: Walleye all year, Panfish, Catfish June-Sept, Salmon, Trout April-Nov
Bodies of water: Lake Winnebago, Green Bay, Fox River, Wolf River, Lake Poygan, Lake Butte des Morts
Rates: Half day: $55(1), $100(2), Full day: $90(1), $175(2)
Call between: 6am-10pm
Provides: Light tackle, lures, bait, beverages
Handicapped equipped: No

Thomas Urban
Rhinelander 715-362-3618
Species & Seasons: Walleye, Muskellunge, SM Bass, LM Bass Northern Pike May-Oct, Trout May-Sept, Panfish all year, (specialize in Muskellunge)
Bodies of water: Tomahawk Lake, Lake Minocqua, Pelican Lake, Wisconsin River, Wolf River, most lakes in Rhinelander area
Rates: Half day: $125(1-2), Full day: $185(1-2)
Call between: 6pm-10pm
Provides: Light tackle, heavy tackle, lures, bait, rain gear, beverages
Handicapped equipped: Yes
Certifications: Mepps, St. Croix, Mercury, Tuffy Boats

YOUR SILENT FISHING PARTNER

Look in the Species Index
to find service providers by species of fish

WYOMING

1. Fremont Lake
2. Green River
3. Medicine Lodge Creek
4. New Fork River
5. North Platte River
6. Platte River
7. Shoshone River
8. Snake River
9. Yellowstone Lake
10. Yellowstone National Park
11. Yellowstone River

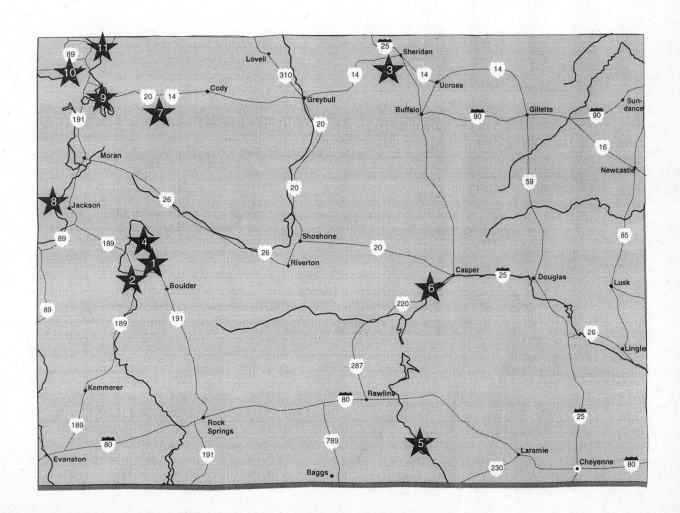

YOUR SILENT FISHING PARTNER

WYOMING
FREMONT LAKE – NEW FORK RIVER

FREMONT LAKE

LODGES...

Half Moon Lake Guest Ranch
Pinedale 307-367-6373
Guest Capacity: 12-24
Handicapped equipped: No
Seasons: May to Nov
Rates: Cabin: $53-$93/per cabin,
Pack trips: $185/day
Contact: Frank Deede
Guides: Yes
Species & Seasons: Rainbow Trout,
Brown Trout, Brook Trout, Mackinaw
June-Oct
Bodies of Water: Half Moon Lake,
Fremont Lake, Pole Creek, Fayette Lake
Types of fishing: Fly fishing, light tackle,
heavy tackle, horse/back pack, wading
Available: Fishing instruction,
boat rentals, baby sitting, waterskiing,
horseback trips

GREEN RIVER

GUIDES...

Arrowhead Outfitters
Jackson 307-733-4845
Species & Seasons: Cutthroat Trout
April-May/July-Sept, Rainbow Trout,
Brown Trout June-Aug
Bodies of water: Snake River,
Green River, horsepack fishing trips to
Bridger Wilderness Area
Rates: Full day: $200(1), $250-$300(2),
Horse trips: $175/day pp
Call between: 7pm-11pm
Provides: Light tackle, fly rod/reel,
rain gear, beverages, lunch
Handicapped equipped: Yes

Darby Mountain Outfitters
Big Piney 307-386-9220
Species & Seasons: Cutthroat Trout,
July-Sept, Brook Trout, Lake Trout,
Rainbow Trout June-Sept, Brown Trout
April-Sept
Bodies of water: Lake Alice,
South Piney Creek, North Piney Creek,
North Piney Lake, Middle Piney Lake,
Green River
Rates: Full day: $150(1)
Call between: 4:30pm-10pm
Provides: Lunch, rubber rafts, float tubes
Handicapped equipped: No

Green River Outfitters
Pinedale 307-367-2416
Species & Seasons: Trout May-Sept
Bodies of water: Green River,
New Fork River, Gros Ventre Wilderness
area, Bridger-Teton National Forest
Rates: Float trip: $250 per boat,
Horse pack trip: $200/day pp
Provides: Fly rod/reel, beverages, lunch
Handicapped equipped: Yes

John Henry Lee Outfitters
Jackson 307-733-9441
Species & Seasons: Trout (Snake River)
April-Nov, Trout (Yellowstone River)
June-Aug
Bodies of water: Snake River,
Green River, New Fork River,
Yellowstone River, Thorofare River
Rates: Half day: $185(1-2),
Full day: $260(1-2)
Call between: 6am-9pm
Provides: Light tackle, fly rod/reel,
rain gear, beverages, lunch
Handicapped equipped: Yes, on float
trips only

Snake River Anglers
Jackson 307-733-5223
Species & Seasons: Cutthroat Trout
April-Sept, Brown Trout, Rainbow Trout
June-July
Bodies of water: Snake River,
Green River, New Fork River, Flat Creek
Rates: Full day: $250-$300(2)
Call between: 7pm-11pm
Provides: Light tackle, fly rod/reel,
rain gear, beverages, lunch
Handicapped equipped: Yes

MEDICINE LODGE CREEK

GUIDES...

Outfitters Unlimited
Hyattville 307-469-2274
Species & Seasons: Rainbow Trout,
Brown Trout all year, Brook Trout
June-Sept, Golden Trout, Mackinaw
July-Sept
Bodies of water: Paintrock Creek
drainage, Medicine Lodge Creek
Rates: Half day: $150(1), $300(2),
Full day: $225(1), $450(2)
Call between: 7pm-10pm
Provides: Beverages, lunch
Handicapped equipped: Yes

LODGES...

Outfitters Unlimited
Hyattville 307-469-2269
Contact: Todd Jones
Guides: Yes
Bodies of Water: Paintrock Creek,
Medicine Lodge Creek, wilderness areas
Available: Guide services, Lodging, food,
fishing instruction

NEW FORK RIVER

GUIDES...

John Henry Lee Outfitters
Jackson 307-733-9441
Species & Seasons: Trout (Snake River)
April-Nov, Trout (Yellowstone River)
June-Aug
Bodies of water: Snake River,
Green River, New Fork River,
Yellowstone River, Thorofare River
Rates: Half day: $185(1-2),
Full day: $260(1-2)
Call between: 6am-9pm
Provides: Light tackle, fly rod/reel,
rain gear, beverages, lunch
Handicapped equipped: Yes, on float
trips only

Green River Outfitters
Pinedale 307-367-2416
Species & Seasons: Trout May-Sept
Bodies of water: Green River,
New Fork River, Gros Ventre Wilderness
area, Bridger-Teton National Forest
Rates: Float trip: $250 per boat,
Horse pack trip: $200/day pp
Provides: Fly rod/reel, beverages, lunch
Handicapped equipped: Yes

Snake River Anglers
Jackson 307-733-5223
Species & Seasons: Cutthroat Trout
April-Sept, Brown Trout, Rainbow Trout
June-July
Bodies of water: Snake River,
Green River, New Fork River, Flat Creek
Rates: Full day: $250-$300(2)
Call between: 7pm-11pm
Provides: Light tackle, fly rod/reel,
rain gear, beverages, lunch
Handicapped equipped: Yes

NORTH PLATTE RIVER - YELLOWSTONE LAKE   WYOMING

NORTH PLATTE RIVER

GUIDES...

Platt's Guides & Outfitters
Encampment 307-327-5539
Species & Seasons: Rainbow Trout, Brown Trout May-Oct, Cutthroat Trout July-Sept, Brook Trout June-Oct
Bodies of water: North Platte River, Encampment River, Big Creek, Mt. Zirkel Wilderness lakes and streams, private water
Rates: Full day: $200(1), $250(2), $300(3), $340(4), Customized pack trips 5 days: $875 pp
Call between: 6pm-8am
Provides: Beverages, lunch
Handicapped equipped: No

PLATTE RIVER

BAIT & TACKLE...

Now Catch Fishing Tackle
Casper 307-266-2627
Hours: 9am-4pm, closed Sat., Sun.
Carries: Lures
Bodies of water: Alcova Res., Glendo Res., Platte River
Guides: No
OK to call for current conditions: No

SHOSHONE RIVER

GUIDES...

Jiggs Pack & Guide Service
Riverton 307-856-3047
Species & Seasons: Cutthroat Trout, Rainbow Trout, Brook Trout June-Sept, Golden Trout July-Aug
Bodies of water: Yellowstone River, Buffalo River, South Fork Shoshone River, other wilderness areas
Rates: Horse back trips:
Full day: $150(1-2)
Call between: 7pm-9:30pm
Provides: Lunch

Schmalz Outfitting
Wapiti 307-587-5929
Species & Seasons: Cutthroat Trout, Rainbow Trout, Grayling June-Sept, Golden Trout July-Aug
Bodies of water: Yellowstone Lake, Shoshone River, Eagle Creek, Red Creek, Yellowstone Nat'l. Park and surrounding areas
Rates: 5 days: $800, 8 days: $1250, 9 days: $1350
Provides: Beverages, lunch
Handicapped equipped: Yes

SNAKE RIVER

GUIDES...

Arrowhead Outfitters
Jackson 307-733-4845
Species & Seasons: Cutthroat Trout April-May/July-Sept, Rainbow Trout, Brown Trout June-Aug
Bodies of water: Snake River, Green River, horsepack fishing trips to Bridger Wilderness Area
Rates: Full day: $200(1), $250-$300(2), Horse trips: $175/day pp
Call between: 7pm-11pm
Provides: Light tackle, fly rod/reel, rain gear, beverages, lunch
Handicapped equipped: Yes

John Henry Lee Outfitters
Jackson 307-733-9441
Species & Seasons: Trout (Snake River) April-Nov, Trout (Yellowstone River) June-Aug
Bodies of water: Snake River, Green River, New Fork River, Yellowstone River, Thorofare River
Rates: Half day: $185(1-2), Full day: $260(1-2)
Call between: 6am-9pm
Provides: Light tackle, fly rod/reel, rain gear, beverages, lunch
Handicapped equipped: Yes, on float trips only

Snake River Anglers
Jackson 307-733-5223
Species & Seasons: Cutthroat Trout April-Sept, Brown Trout, Rainbow Trout June-July
Bodies of water: Snake River, Green River, New Fork River, Flat Creek
Rates: Full day: $250-$300(2)
Call between: 7pm-11pm

Provides: Light tackle, fly rod/reel, rain gear, beverages, lunch
Handicapped equipped: Yes

LODGES...

Diamons D Ranch - Outfitters
Moran 307-543-2479
Guest Capacity: 30-36
Handicapped equipped: Yes
Seasons: All year
Rates: $1000/week
Contact: Rod Doty
Guides: Yes
Species & Seasons: Cutthroat Trout May-Oct, Brook Trout Aug-Oct
Bodies of Water: Snake River, Buffalo Fork River, lakes and streams in Teton Wilderness area
Types of fishing: Fly fishing, light tackle, horse/back pack
Available: Fishing instruction, children's program, lodging, food, guides

YELLOWSTONE LAKE

GUIDES...

Schmalz Outfitting
Wapiti 307-587-5929
Species & Seasons: Cutthroat Trout, Rainbow Trout, Grayling June-Sept, Golden Trout July-Aug
Bodies of water: Yellowstone Lake, Shoshone River, Eagle Creek, Red Creek, Yellowstone Nat'l. Park and surrounding areas
Rates: 5 days: $800, 8 days: $1250, 9 days: $1350
Provides: Beverages, lunch
Handicapped equipped: Yes

WYOMING — YELLOWSTONE NATIONAL PARK - YELLOWSTONE RIVER

YELLOWSTONE NATIONAL PARK
(also see Montana listings)

GUIDES...

Schmalz Outfitting
Wapiti 307-587-5929
Species & Seasons: Cutthroat Trout, Rainbow Trout, Grayling June-Sept, Golden Trout July-Aug
Bodies of water: Yellowstone Lake, Shoshone River, Eagle Creek, Red Creek, Yellowstone Nat'l. Park and surrounding areas
Rates: 5 days: $800, 8 days: $1250, 9 days: $1350
Provides: Beverages, lunch
Handicapped equipped: Yes

Rates: Half day: $185(1-2), Full day: $260(1-2)
Call between: 6am-9pm
Provides: Light tackle, fly rod/reel, rain gear, beverages, lunch
Handicapped equipped: Yes, on float trips only

Yellowstone Outfitters & Wagons West
Afton 800-447-4711
Species & Seasons: Cutthroat Trout, June-Aug
Bodies of Water: Yellowstone River, Thorofare River in Teton Wilderness
Rates: Varies
Types of fishing: Fly fishing, light tackle, horse/back pack, wading, 10 wilderness horse packtrips, 50 covered wagon trips

YELLOWSTONE RIVER

GUIDES...

Ron Dube Outfitter
Cody 307-527-7815
Species & Seasons: Cutthroat Trout June-Aug
Bodies of water: Thorofare River, Yellowstone River
Rates: 7 days: $1250 pp
Call between: Anytime
Provides: Beverages, lunch
Handicapped equipped: No

Jiggs Pack & Guide Service
Riverton 307-856-3047
Species & Seasons: Cutthroat Trout, Rainbow Trout, Brook Trout June-Sept, Golden Trout July-Aug
Bodies of water: Yellowstone River, Buffalo River, South Fork Shoshone River, other wilderness areas
Rates: Horse back trips: Full day: $150(1-2)
Call between: 7pm-9:30pm
Provides: Lunch

John Henry Lee Outfitters
Jackson 307-733-9441
Species & Seasons: Trout (Snake River) April-Nov, Trout (Yellowstone River) June-Aug
Bodies of water: Snake River, Green River, New Fork River, Yellowstone River, Thorofare River

CANADA

1. Albany River
2. Alberni Inlet
3. Arctic Ocean
4. Bay of Fundy
5. Berthelot Lake
6. Bras d'or Lake
7. Cedar Lake
8. Cecebe Lake
9. Chedabucto Bay
10. Dixon Entrance
11. French River Delta
12. Great Slave Lake
13. Kasba Lake
14. Lake of the Woods
15. Magaguadavic Lake
16. Margaree River
17. Miramichi River
18. Nagagami River
19. Ottawa River
20. Private Lakes
21. Queen Charlotte Strait
22. Rainy Lake
23. Remote Lakes
24. Sand Lake
25. Skeena River
26. St. Croix River
27. St. Lawrence River
28. Tyaughton Lake

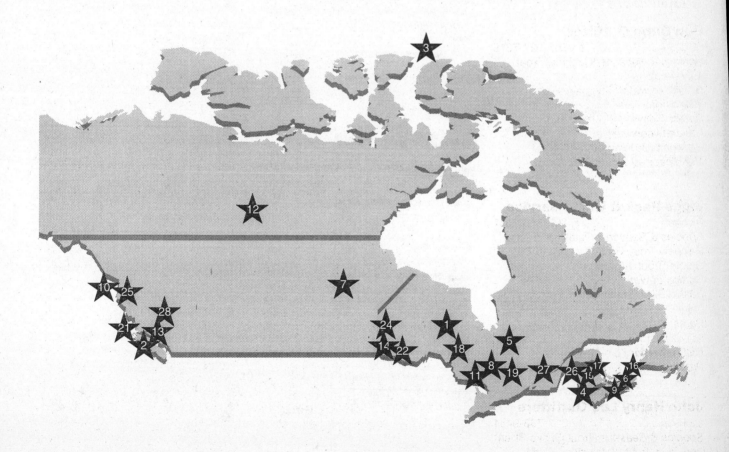

CANADA

ALBANY RIVER - CEDAR LAKE

ALBANY RIVER
LODGING...

Twin Lake Outfitters and Wilderness Camps Inc.
Nakina Ontario 807-329-5771
Handicapped equipped: No
Seasons: May to Oct
Contact: W. Pocock
Guides: No
Species & Seasons: Northern Pike, Walleye, Speckled Trout, Lake Trout, Yellow Perch, Whitefish
Bodies of water: Albany River Basin
Types of fishing: Fly-out trips
Available: Fishing licenses, bait, tackle, boat rentals

ALBERNI INLET
LODGING...

Haggard Cove Resort
Port Alberni B.C. 604-723-8457
Guest Capacity: 10
Handicapped equipped: No
Seasons: June to Oct
Rates: $250/day
Contact: Ron Clark
Guides: Yes/Included
Species & Seasons: Salmon, Halibut, Bottom Fish June-Oct
Bodies of water: Alberni Inlet, Barkley Sound, Pacific Ocean
Types of fishing: Light tackle, heavy tackle, fly-out trips
Available: Fishing instruction, fishing licenses, bait, tackle, boat rentals

ARCTIC OCEAN
LODGING...

High Arctic Lodge
Penticton B.C. 800-661-3880
.... 604-493-3300
Guest Capacity: 20
Handicapped equipped: No
Seasons: July 12 to Aug 25
Rates: $2995/week
Contact: Don Hamilton
Guides: Yes/Included
Species & Seasons: Arctic Char, Lake Trout July-Aug
Bodies of water: Arctic Ocean

Types of fishing: Fly fishing, light tackle, heavy tackle, wading, fly-out trips
Available: Fishing instruction, fishing licenses, bait, tackle

BAY OF FUNDY
LODGING...

Northern Outdoor Lodge
St. George N.B. 506-755-2373
Guest Capacity: 9
Handicapped equipped: No
Seasons: April to Oct
Rates: $59.95/day
Contact: Bruce Hanley
Guides: Yes, Half day: $125, Full day: $200
Species & Seasons: Brook Trout, Salmon April-Sept, SM Bass April-Oct, Striped Bass June-Aug, Mackerel, Flounder June-Sept
Bodies of water: Bay of Fundy, Digdeguash Lake, Harvey Lake, Lake Utopia, Magaguadavic Lake, Magaguadavic River, McDougall Lake
Types of fishing: Fly fishing, light tackle, wading
Available: Fishing licenses, bait, tackle, boat rentals

BERTHELOT LAKE
LODGING...

Berthelot Lake Lodge
Senneterre Quebec ....802-524-9486(W)
.... 819-737-4684(S)
Guest Capacity: 120
Handicapped equipped: No
Seasons: May to Oct
Rates: $210/week
Contact: Gary Koch
Guides: Yes/$100
Species & Seasons: Walleye, Northern Pike May-Oct
Bodies of water: Berthelot Lake
Types of fishing: Fly-out trips, main lodge and outpost
Available: Fishing licenses, bait, tackle, boat rentals, air service, bar

BRAS D'OR LAKE
GUIDES...

Donald Tutty
Baddeck NS 902-295-1900
Species: Atlantic Cod June-Oct, Trout June-Sept, Mackerel July-Oct, Tuna Sept-Oct, Shark Aug-Oct
Bodies of water: Bras d'Or Lake, Cape Breton Island, eastern Nova Scotia waters
Rates: $20 pp per hour
Call between: 6am-10pm
Provides: Heavy tackle, fly rod/reel, lures, bait, rain gear
Handicapped equipped: Yes
Certifications: YMCCG

Earl Rudderhan
Cape Breton NS 902-871-2549
Species: Atlantic Salmon June-Oct, Steelhead, Speckled Trout April-Sept, Cod, Halibut June-Dec, Mackerel July-Sept
Bodies of water: Bras d'or Lake, North River, Margaree River, other river systems
Rates: Full day: $125(1), $175(2) Packages available
Provides: Light tackle, heavy tackle, fly rod/reel, lures, bait, rain gear, beverages, lunch
Handicapped equipped: Yes

CEDAR LAKE
LODGING...

Moak Lodge
Eriksdale Manitoba 204-739-5398
Guest Capacity: 20
Handicapped equipped: No
Seasons: May to Oct
Contact: Glen Heroux
Guides: Yes/$100
Species & Seasons: Northern Pike May-Oct., Walleye June-Aug
Bodies of water: Cedar Lake, Cross Bay
Types of fishing: Light tackle, heavy tackle
Available: Fishing licenses, bait, tackle, boat rentals

CECEBE LAKE - MAGAGUADAVIC LAKE

CANADA

CECEBE LAKE

LODGING...

Woodland Echoes Resort
Magnetawan Ontario 705-387-3866
Guest Capacity: 65
Handicapped equipped: No
Seasons: May to Nov
Rates: $35/day, packages available
Guides: Yes/$20 hr
Species & Seasons: Northern Pike, Walleye May-Mar, SM Bass, LM Bass June-Nov, Panfish all year
Bodies of water: Cecebe Lake, Magnetawan River
Types of fishing: Fly fishing, light tackle, heavy tackle
Available: Fishing licenses, bait, tackle, boat rentals, family activities, baby sitting, hot tub, sauna, tennis, golf

CHEDABUCTO BAY

CHARTER...

Cape Breaker Outfitting
Canso NS 902-366-2949
Species: Blue Shark, Mako Shark July-Sept, Bluefin Tuna July-Nov
Bodies of water: Chedabucto Bay, other waters near Port of Canso
Rates: Packages available
Call between: Anytime
Provides: Light tackle, heavy tackle, lures, bait, beverages, lunch
Handicapped equipped: Yes

DIXON ENTRANCE

LODGING...

Eagle Pointe Lodge
PO Box 24184
Seattle, WA 98134
Guest Capacity: 12
Handicapped equipped: No
Seasons: May 20 to Sept 20
Rates: $1575/4 days, 3 nights
$1895/5 days, 4 nights
Guides: Yes
Species & Seasons: Halibut May-Oct, Salmon May-July, Coho Salmon June-Oct, Pink Salmon July-Oct, Sockeye Salmon June-Aug
Bodies of water: Dixon Entrance
Endorsements: BC Sports Fishing Mag.

Types of fishing: Fly fishing, light tackle, fly-out trips
main lodge and outpost
Available: Fishing instruction, licenses, bait, tackle

FRENCH RIVER DELTA

LODGING...

French River Lodge
Alban Ontario 705-383-2801
Guest Capacity: 55
Handicapped equipped: No
Seasons: May to Oct
Rates: $600/week Cdn.
Contact: Ann Ott
Guides: Yes/$150
Species & Seasons: Walleye, Northern Pike May-Oct, Muskellunge June-Oct, SM Bass July-Sept
Bodies of water: French River Delta
Types of fishing: Light tackle, heavy tackle
Available: Fishing instruction, fishing licenses, bait, tackle, boat rentals

GREAT SLAVE LAKE

LODGING...

True North Safaris Ltd.
Yellowknife N.W.T. 403-873-8533
Guest Capacity: 24
Handicapped equipped: Yes
Seasons: June to Oct
Rates: $300/day
Contact: Gary Jaeb
Guides: Yes/included
Species & Seasons: Northern Pike June-Sept, Lake Trout, Arctic Grayling July-Sept
Bodies of water: Great Slave Lake, Mackay Lake
Types of fishing: Fly fishing, light tackle, heavy tackle
Available: Fishing licenses, bait, tackle, boat rentals, family activities

KASBA LAKE

LODGING...

Kasba Lake Lodge
Parksville B.C. 604-248-3572
Guest Capacity: 46
Handicapped equipped: Yes
Seasons: June to Sept
Rates: $2095/5 days
Contact: Robert Hill
Guides: Yes
Species & Seasons: Lake Trout, Northern Pike, Arctic Grayling June-Aug
Bodies of water: Kasba Lake
Types of fishing: Fly fishing, light tackle, fly-out trips
Available: Fishing instruction, fishing licenses, bait, tackle

LAKE OF THE WOODS

LODGING...

Tomahawk Resort
Sioux Narrows Ontario 807-226-5622
Handicapped equipped: No
Seasons: May to Nov
Rates: $300-$500/week pp
Contact: Albert Kast
Guides: Yes/$100 (2)
Species & Seasons: Walleye, Northern Pike, SM Bass, LM Bass, Muskellunge, Lake Trout May-Nov
Bodies of water: Lake of the Woods
Types of fishing: Light tackle
Available: Fishing Instruction, fishing licenses, bait, tackle, boat rentals

MAGAGUADAVIC LAKE

GUIDES...

Malarkey Cabin Guiding Service
Zealand NB 506-363-2839
Species: Atlantic Salmon July-Aug, Trout, SM Bass June-Aug
Bodies of water: Magaguadavic Lake, Keswick River, Macta Quack Lake
Rates: Full day: $200(1), $180(2) each, 5 days: $850-$1,000
Call between: 8pm-10pm
Provides: Light tackle, fly rod/reel, bait, beverages, lunch
Certifications: NAHC

CANADA
MAGAGUADAVIC LAKE - MIRAMICHI RIVER

LODGING...

Chickadee Lodge
York Co. N.B.................. 506-363-2759
.... 363-2288
Guest Capacity: 8
Handicapped equipped: Yes
Seasons: May to Nov
Rates: $350/5days
Contact: Vaughan Schriver
Guides: Yes/$165
Species & Seasons: SM Bass May-Sept
Bodies of water: Magaguadavic Lake, Harvey Lake, Lake George, St. John River, Macta Quack Lake
Types of fishing: Fly fishing, light tackle
Available: Fishing licenses

Loon Bay Lodge
St. Stephen N.B............. 506-466-1240
Guest Capacity: 18
Handicapped equipped: No
Seasons: May to Nov
Rates: $144.90/day pp Cdn/$111.40/day pp US +3 meals, double occupancy
Contact: David Whittingham
Guides: Yes/$214(2) Cdn/$165(2) US
Species & Seasons: SM Bass May-Oct, Salmon, White Perch, Yellow Perch, Chain Pickerel, Brook Trout May-Sept
Bodies of water: Magaguadavic Lake, St. Croix River
Types of fishing: Fly fishing, light tackle, medium tackle, float trips
Available: Fishing instruction, fishing licenses, bait, tackle, canoes

Northern Outdoor Lodge
St. George N.B. 506-755-2373
Guest Capacity: 9
Handicapped equipped: No
Seasons: April to Oct
Rates: $59.95/day
Contact: Bruce Hanley
Guides: Yes, Half day: $125, Full day: $200
Species & Seasons: Brook Trout, Salmon April-Sept, SM Bass April-Oct, Striped Bass June-Aug, Mackerel, Flounder June-Sept
Bodies of water: Digdeguash Lake, Harvey Lake, Lake Utopia, Magaguadavic Lake, Magaguadavic River, McDougall Lake, Bay of Fundy
Types of fishing: Fly fishing, light tackle, wading
Available: Fishing licenses, bait, tackle, boat rentals

MARGAREE RIVER

GUIDES...

Bill Bryson
Stewiacke NS 902-673-2007
Species: Atlantic Salmon June-Oct, Brown Trout May-Aug, Brook Trout, Shad May-June
Bodies of water: Margaree River, other rivers and lakes throughout eastern Novia Scotia
Rates: 5 days 6 nights: $1200 pp, 2 days 3 nights: $600 pp
Call between: 8am-12midnight
Provides: Light tackle, fly rod/reel, lures, bait, rain gear, beverages, lunch
Handicapped equipped: Yes

Earl Rudderhan
Cape Breton NS 902-871-2549
Species: Atlantic Salmon June-Oct, Steelhead, Speckled Trout April-Sept, Cod, Halibut June-Dec, Mackerel July-Sept
Bodies of water: Bras d'or Lake, North River, Margaree River, other river systems
Rates: Full day: $125(1), $175(2) Packages available
Provides: Light tackle, heavy tackle, fly rod/reel, lures, bait, rain gear, beverages, lunch
Handicapped equipped: Yes

West Lake Ainslie Outfitters
Cape Breton NS 902-258-2654
Species: Trout May-Sept, Salmon June-Oct
Bodies of water: Margaree River, Lake Ainslie, Margaree River, Cape Breton rivers
Rates: Full day: $130(1-2) Cdn.
Call between: 10am-10pm
Provides: Light tackle, fly rod/reel, bait, beverages, lunch

MIRAMICHI RIVER

GUIDES...

Cail's Private Salmon Pools
Fredericton NB 506-450-3029
.... 365-1901(S)
Species: Atlantic Salmon June-Oct
Bodies of water: Miramichi River
Rates: Full day: $307 (1) includes lodging, guide, meals and private waters
Call between: 8am-10pm
Provides: Fly rod/reel, licenses
Handicapped equipped: No
Certifications: Canada Select Rating Program (2 star), Licensed NB Outfitter

Northway Outfitters
Hartland NB 506-375-6632
Species: Atlantic Salmon July-Sept
Bodies of water: Miramichi River
Rates: Half day: $95 (1-3), Full day: $150 (1-3)
Call between: 7pm-10pm
Provides: Fly rod/reel, rain gear
Handicapped equipped: No

The Bishop's View
Stanley NB. 506-367-2582
Species: Salmon July-Sept, Trout, LM Bass, SM Bass June-Sept
Bodies of water: Miramichi River, Nashwaak River, Macta Quac Lake
Rates: Half day: $50 (1), $100 (2), Full day: $100 (1), $200 (2) +expenses
Call between: 8am-8pm
Provides: Fly rod/reel, bait, rain gear, beverages, lunch, lodging available
Handicapped equipped: No

LODGING...

Burntland Brook Lodge
Boiestown N.B. 506-369-7405
Guest Capacity: 4
Handicapped equipped: No
Seasons: April to Nov
Rates: $150/day pp, $850/week pp
Contact: Joan or Barrie Duffield
Guides: Yes, 30 yrs. experience
Species & Seasons: Sea run Brook Trout May-June, Spring Salmon April-May, Atlantic Salmon June-Oct.
Bodies of water: Miramichi River, Cains River, Dungarvon River, Nahswaak River, Renous River, St. John River
Types of fishing: Fly fishing, wading, float trips, wilderness canoes and tenting
Available: Fishing instruction, boat rentals, family activities, great area to film moose, deer, bear, eagles

Flo's Fishing and Hunting Lodge
Doaktown N.B. 506-365-7920
Guest Capacity: 12-16
Handicapped equipped: No
Seasons: All year
Rates: $210/day pp + tax
Guides: Yes

MIRAMICHI RIVER - OTTAWA RIVER — CANADA

Species & Seasons: Spring Salmon April-May, Trout May-Sept, Bright Salmon June-Oct
Types of fishing: Fly fishing, wading
Available: Fishing licenses, bait, tackle

Miramichi Gray Rapids Lodge
Oromocto N.B. 800-261-2330
Guest Capacity: 14
Handicapped equipped: Somewhat
Seasons: All year
Rates: Fishing: $250/day, Hunting: $225/day
Contact: Guy A. Smith
Guides: Yes/Included
Species & Seasons: Atlantic Salmon April-Oct, Trout May-Sept
Bodies of water: Miramichi River, Cains River, Renous River, Dungarvon River
Types of fishing: Fly fishing, wading, float trips
Available: Fishing instruction, fishing licenses, boat rentals, family activities, dog sledding, snowmobile rentals, cross country ski, winter expeditions

O'Donnell's Cottage's on the Miramichi
Doaktown N.B. 506-365-7924
Guest Capacity: 6
Handicapped equipped: No
Seasons: April to Oct
Rates: $40/day
Contact: Valerie O'Donnell
Guides: Yes/$80
Species & Seasons: Atlantic Salmon April-May/June-Oct, Trout May-Sept
Bodies of water: Miramichi River
Types of fishing: Fly fishing, wading, float trips
Available: Fishing instruction, fishing licenses, boat rentals

Pettingill Lake Lodge
Arthurette N.B. 506-356-8375
Guest Capacity: 6
Handicapped equipped: No
Seasons: May to Nov
Rates: $600/week
Contact: Fred or Phyllis
Guides: Yes
Species & Seasons: Speckeld Trout, LM Bass, SM Bass May-Sept., Salmon June-Sept
Bodies of water: Miramichi River, Tobique Headpond, Tobique River, other area lakes and streams
Types of fishing: Fly fishing, light tackle, wading
Available: Fishing licenses, bait, tackle, boat rentals

South Ridge Sporting Camp
Juniper N.B. 506-246-5334
Guest Capacity: 8
Handicapped equipped: No
Seasons: All year
Rates: $750/week
Contact: William Prosser
Guides: Yes/Included
Species & Seasons: Brook Trout, Sea Trout May-Sept, Atlantic Salmon June-Sept, LM Bass, SM Bass July-Sept
Bodies of water: Miramichi River, St. John River
Types of fishing: Fly fishing, wading, float trips
Available: Fishing instruction, fishing licenses

Wilson's Sporting Camps Ltd.
McNamee N.B. 506-365-7962
Guest Capacity: 22
Handicapped equipped: No
Seasons: April to Oct
Rates: $390/day Cdn.
Contact: Keith Wilson
Guides: Yes/Provide
Species & Seasons: Atlantic Salmon April-Oct
Bodies of water: Miramichi River
Types of fishing: Fly fishing, wading, float trips
Available: Fishing instruction, fishing licenses, bait, tackle, boat rentals, family activities

NAGAGAMI RIVER

LODGING...

Tom Henry's Black Bear Fishing Lodge
Hornpayne Ontario 807-868-2802
Guest Capacity: 20
Handicapped equipped: Yes (partly)
Seasons: June to Aug
Rates: $250/week-children half price, under age of 10/free with paying adult
Contact: Tom Henry
Guides: No, give advice, maps
Species & Seasons: Brook Trout June-Sept, Northern Pike, Whitefish all year, Lake Trout June-?, Walleye May-Mar
Bodies of water: Nagagami River, Kabi River, Shekak River, Nagagamisis Creek, many others
Types of fishing: Fly fishing, light tackle, heavy tackle, wading, fly-out trips
Available: Fishing instruction, fishing licenses, bait, tackle, boat rentals, family activities, nature trails, ice fishing, snow mobile trails

OTTAWA RIVER

LODGING...

K/O Lodge
Deep River Ontario 613-584-2411
Guest Capacity: 107 (2 lodges)
Handicapped equipped: Yes
Seasons: May to Nov
Rates: Varies
Contact: Diane Carlin
Guides: Yes/$150 Cdn.
Species & Seasons: SM Bass, LM Bass, Muskellunge June-Dec, Northern Pike, Walleye May-Dec, Sturgeon all year
Bodies of water: Barron River, Corey Lake, Holden Lake, McConnell Lake, Ottawa River, Pettawawa River, Sullivan Lake
Types of fishing: Fly fishing, light tackle, heavy tackle, wading, bass boat trips
Available: Fishing instruction, fishing licenses, bait, tackle, boat rentals, family activities, children's program, baby sitting, hot tub, heated pool

Lakeside Cottages & Trailer Park
Cobden Ontario 613-646-7446
Guest Capacity: 30
Handicapped equipped: No
Seasons: May to Oct
Contact: Pamela McEwan
Guides: No
Species & Seasons: Northern Pike, Walleye May-Oct, SM Bass, LM Bass June-Oct, Panfish all year
Bodies of water: Bonnechere River, Muskrat Lake, Ottawa River
Types of fishing: Light tackle, heavy tackle
Available: Bait, boat rentals

CANADA

OTTAWA RIVER - ST. CROIX RIVER

Laurentian View Resort
Westmeath Ontario 613-587-4829
Guest Capacity: 50
Handicapped equipped: No
Seasons: May to Oct
Rates: Varies
Contact: Lorne Spotswood
Guides: No
Species & Seasons: Walleye, Northern Pike May-Oct, LM Bass, SM Bass June-Oct
Bodies of water: Ottawa River
Types of fishing: Fly fishing, light tackle, wading
Available: Fishing instruction, bait, tackle, boat rentals

PRIVATE LAKES

Picture Province Pond
Norton NB 506-485-2989
Species: Rainbow Trout, Speckled Trout all year
Bodies of water: Private Lake, ice fishing too
Available: Tackle, canteen

QUEEN CHARLOTTE STRAIT

LODGING...

Duval Point Lodge Ltd.
Port Hardy B.C. 604-949-6667
Guest Capacity: 16
Handicapped equipped: No
Seasons: June to Sept
Rates: $150/day
Contact: Tom Makinson
Guides: Yes/$100
Species & Seasons: Chinook Salmon June-Sept, Coho Salmon July-Oct, Pink Salmon July-Aug, Halibut April-Oct, Cod all year
Bodies of water: Queen Charlotte Strait
Types of fishing: Light tackle
Available: Fishing instruction, bait, tackle, boat rentals, package includes accommodations, boats, bait, tackle

God's Pocket Resort
Port Hardy B.C. 604-949-9221
Guest Capacity: 16
Handicapped equipped: No
Seasons: June to Aug
Rates: $849/4days
Guides: No
Species & Seasons: Chinook Salmon, Coho Salmon June-Aug, Sockeye Salmon, Chum Salmon Aug, Pink Salmon July-Aug
Bodies of water: Queen Charlotte Strait, Christie Pass, Goletas Channel, Gordon Channel
Types of fishing: Heavy tackle
Available: Fishing instruction, fishing licenses, bait, tackle

RAINY LAKE

LODGING...

Coppen's Resort
Ft. Frances Ontario 807-481-2564
Guest Capacity: 40
Handicapped equipped: Yes
Seasons: May to Oct
Rates: $25/day pp Cdn.
Contact: Kelly
Guides: Yes/$125 Cdn.
Species & Seasons: SM Bass May-July, Northern Pike, Crappie May-Sept, Walleye July-Sept
Bodies of water: Rainy Lake
Types of fishing: Fly fishing, light tackle, heavy tackle
Available: Fishing instruction, fishing licenses, bait, tackle, boat rentals, family activities, gas, store, ramp

REMOTE LAKES

LODGING...

Lukinto Lake Lodge
Longlac Ontario 807-876-2381
Guest Capacity: 40
Handicapped equipped: No
Seasons: May to Oct
Rates: $260/week
Contact: Bob Harkness
Guides: Yes/$75
Species & Seasons: Walleye, Northern Pike, Perch May-Oct, Brook Trout, Lake Trout May-Aug
Bodies of water: 12 remote lakes
Types of fishing: Light tackle
Available: Fishing licenses, bait, tackle, boat rentals

SAND LAKE

LODGING...

Birch Island Resort
Minaki Ontario 807-224-3471
Guest Capacity: 24
Handicapped equipped: Yes
Seasons: May to Oct
Rates: $102/day
Contact: Wendy Reid
Guides: Yes/$100
Species & Seasons: Walleye, Northern Pike, SM Bass, Muskellunge
Bodies of water: Sand Lake, Gunn Lake, Pistol Lake, Winnipeg River
Types of fishing: Light tackle, heavy tackle
Available: Fishing instruction, fishing licenses, bait, tackle, boat rentals

SKEENA RIVER

GUIDES...

Northwest Fishing Guides
Terrace BC 604-635-5295
Species: Steelhead Mar-May/Aug-Dec, Chinook Salmon May/June-July/Sept-Oct., Coho Salmon Aug-Nov, Trout, Arctic Char, Dolly Varden all year
Bodies of water: Skeena River, Kitimat River, Kalum River, Kasiks River, west coast ocean
Rates: Full day: $250(1), includes accomodations, guide, boat, food
Call between: 8pm-9pm
Provides: Light tackle, fly rod/reel, lures, bait, beverages, lunch
Handicapped equipped: Yes

ST. CROIX RIVER

LODGING...

Loon Bay Lodge
St. Stephen N.B. 506-466-1240
Guest Capacity: 18
Handicapped equipped: No
Seasons: May to Nov
Rates: $144.90/day pp Cdn/$111.40/day pp US +3 meals, double occupancy
Contact: David Whittingham
Guides: Yes/$214(2) Cdn/$165(2) US
Species & Seasons: SM Bass May-Oct, Salmon, White Perch, Yellow Perch, Chain Pickerel, Brook Trout May-Sept
Bodies of water: Magaguadavic Lake, St. Croix River

ST. CROIX RIVER - TYAUGHTON LAKE

Types of fishing: Fly fishing, light tackle, medium tackle, float trips
Available: Fishing instruction, fishing licenses, bait, tackle, canoes

Mohannes Camp
St. Stephen N.B. 506-466-3932
Guest Capacity: 12
Handicapped equipped: No
Seasons: May to Sept
Rates: $700/week
Contact: Wilfred Davidson
Guides: Yes
Species & Seasons: SM Bass, Trout, Pickerel, Salmon May-Sept
Bodies of water: St. Croix River, Canoose Flowage, Chamcook Lake, Magaguadavic River
Types of fishing: Fly fishing, light tackle, heavy tackle, wading
Available: Fishing licenses

Types of fishing: Fly fishing, light tackle, horse/back pack, wading, fly-out trips, float trips
Available: Fishing instruction, fishing licenses, bait, tackle, boat rentals, family activities, children's program, baby sitting

ST. LAWRENCE RIVER

MARINAS...

Peck's Marina
Landsdowne, Ont. 613-659-3185
Hours: 7am-11pm every day
Carries: Live Bait, lures, maps, rods, reels, licenses
Bodies of water: St. Lawrence River, Lake Ontario, Charelston Lake, Beverly Lake
Other services: Boat rentals, lodging, boat ramp, food, beverages, gas/oil, repairs, houseboats, dockage, propane, ice
Guides: Yes
Okay to call: Yes
Contact: Don Hunter

TYAUGHTON LAKE

LODGING...

Tyax Mountain Lake Resort
British Columbia B.C. 604-238-2221
Guest Capacity: 120
Handicapped equipped: Yes
Seasons: All year
Rates: $190/day
Contact: 604-238-2221
Guides: Yes
Species & Seasons: Rainbow Trout, Dolly Varden May-Nov
Bodies of water: Gun Lake, Spruce Lake, Tyaughton Lake

The business listings in the Angler's Yellow Pages are
full of valuable information.
"Know before you go…"

INTERNATIONAL DESTINATIONS

1. Alaska
2. Australia
3. Bahamas
4. Canada
5. Central America
6. Mexico
7. New Guinea
8. New Zealand
9. Russia
10. South America

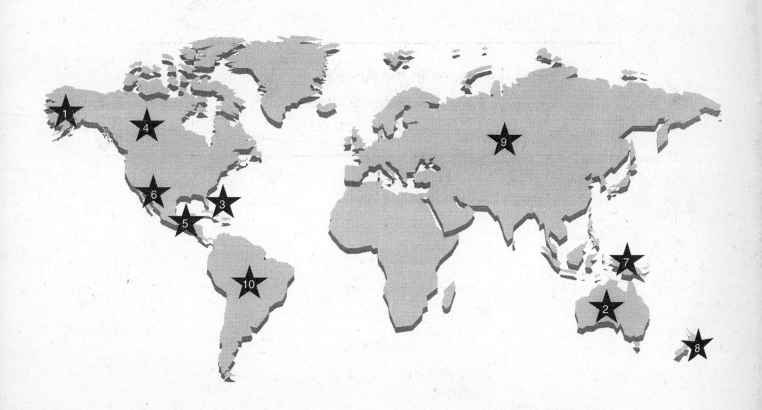

YOUR SILENT FISHING PARTNER

INTERNATIONAL DESTINATIONS

ALASKA - CENTRAL AMERICA

ALASKA

Alaskan Fishing Adventures
Soldotna, AK .... 907-262-9683(S)
.... 503-862-2021(W)
Destinations: Alaska: King Salmon, Halibut, Silver, Sockeye Salmon, Trout, Steelhead
Arranges: Trans from point of depart to fishing location, trans from point of arrival to fishing location, lodging, guides/charters
Evaluation: Yes
Free Consultation: Yes
Contact: Carol, Tim, Paul or Sharon

Cutting Loose Expeditions
Winter Park, FL 407-629-4700
Destinations: Florida: Salt/Fresh water, Alaska: Salmon, Rainbow Trout, Arctic Char
Central America: Halibut, Tarpon, Snook, general consulting on all areas
Price: $300 day to $6000 week
Arranges: Trans from point of depart to fishing location, trans from point of arrival to fishing location, lodging, guides/charters
Evaluation: Yes
Free Consultation: Yes
Contact: Neville Cutting

Ouzel Expeditions
Girdwood, AK 800-825-8196
.... 907-783-2216
Destinations: Alaska: Salmon, Rainbow Trout, Arctic Char
Kamchatka, Russia: Kunja Char, Arctic Grayling
Price: $2400 to $3500
Arranges: Trans from point of arrival to fishing location
Evaluation: Yes
Free Consultation: Yes
Contact: Paul Allred

Sporting Charters
Austin, TX 800-448-8994
.... 512-458-8900
Destinations: Bahamas, Belize, Costa Rica, Texas, Florida, Alaska, Canada, The Rockies, Brazil, Venezuela, Yucatan, Baja
Price: Varies

AUSTRALIA

Capt. Chris Jones
Kirwan, Qld., Australia
.... 011-61-18-778542
Destinations: Cairns, Australia: Black Marlin
Cape Bowling Green, Australia: Black Marlin, Sailfish
Price: $1000 to $1500 a day
Arranges: Trans from point of arrival to fishing location, charters
Evaluation: Yes
Free Consultation: Yes
Contact: Capt. Chris Jones

Dean Butler's Sportfishing Adventures
Cairns, Australia 011-61-70-531009
Destinations: Northern Australia: Barramundi, Queenfish, Threadfin Salmon, Giant Trevally
Saratoga/Cairns Townsville: Black Marlin, Sailfish
Papua New Guinea: LM Bass, Spot-tail Bass, Barramundi, All major game fish
Price: $1500 to $3500
Arranges: Trans from point of arrival to fishing location, lodging guides and charters. Specializes in salt water fly fishing for all species
Contact: Dean Butler

BAHAMAS

Bonefish Bay Camp
Tampa, FL 800-450-9908
Destinations: Andros Island: Bonefish
Price: $1200 to $3000
Arranges: Trans from point of depart to fishing location, trans from point of arrival to fishing location, lodging, guides/charters, meals
Evaluation: Yes
Free Consultation: Yes
Contact: Martha Fields

Sporting Charters
Austin, TX 800-448-8994
.... 512-458-8900
Destinations: Bahamas, Belize, Costa Rica, Texas, Florida, Alaska, Canada, The Rockies, Brazil, Venezuela, Yucatan, Baja
Price: Varies

CANADA

Sporting Charters
Austin, TX 800-448-8994
.... 512-458-8900
Destinations: Bahamas, Belize, Costa Rica, Texas, Florida, Alaska, Canada, The Rockies, Brazil, Venezuela, Yucatan, Baja
Price: Varies

CENTRAL AMERICA

Anglers Travel
Reno, NV 702-324-0580
Destinations: Costa Rica: Sailfish, Marlin, Dolphin, Wahoo, Tuna
South America: Black Marlin, Blue Marlin, Striped Marlin, Sailfish, Snapper, Tuna, Roosterfish
Arranges: Trans from point of depart to fishing location, trans from point of arrival to fishing location, lodging, guides/charters
Evaluation: Yes
Free Consultation: Yes
Contact: Chet Young

Cutting Loose Expeditions
Winter Park, FL 407-629-4700
Destinations: Florida: Salt/Fresh water, Alaska: Salmon, Rainbow Trout, Arctic Char
Central America: Halibut, Tarpon, Snook, general consulting on all areas
Price: $300 day to $6000 week
Arranges: Trans from point of depart to fishing location, trans from point of arrival to fishing location, lodging, guides/charters
Evaluation: Yes
Free Consultation: Yes
Contact: Neville Cutting

Hannibal Banic Lodge
Tampa, FL 800-450-9908
Destinations: Pacific Coast: Marlin, Sailfish, Shark
Panama: Roosterfish, Snook, Snapper, Wahoo
Price: $1800 to $3000
Arranges: Trans from point of depart to fishing location, trans from point of arrival to fishing location, lodging, guides/charters, meals
Evaluation: Yes
Free Consultation: Yes
Contact: Martha Fields

CENTRAL AMERICA - NEW GUINEA
INTERNATIONAL DESTINATIONS

Mike Kannapel
Mesa, AZ 800-658-5740
.... 602-929-0434
Rates: From: Half day: $35(1), $70(2)
From: Full day: $80(1), $150(2)
Call between: 11am-8pm
Provides: Beverages, lunch
Handicapped equipped: Yes

Roy's Zancudo Lodge
Tampa, FL 800-515-7697
Destinations: Gulfito: Marlin, Sailfish
Costa Rica: Roosterfish, Snook, Snapper,
Price: $1300 to $3000
Arranges: Trans from point of depart
to fishing location, trans from point of
arrival to fishing location, lodging,
guides/charters, food
Evaluation: Yes
Free Consultation: Yes
Contact: Martha Fields

Silver King Lodge
Tampa, FL 800-847-3474
Destinations: Rio Colorado River:
Tarpon, Snook
Costa Rica: Atlantic Sailfish
Price: $1400 to $3000
Arranges: Trans from point of depart
to fishing location, trans from point of
arrival to fishing location, lodging,
guides/charters, food
Evaluation: Yes
Free Consultation: Yes
Contact: Martha Fields

Sporting Charters
Austin, TX 800-448-8994
.... 512-458-8900
Destinations: Bahamas, Belize,
Costa Rica, Texas, Florida, Alaska,
Canada, The Rockies, Brazil, Venezuela,
Yucatan, Baja
Price: Varies

MEXICO

Fiesta Sportfishing & Diving Co.
Gilbert, AZ 602-814-0414
Destinations: Cabo San Lucas,
Baja-Mexico
Price: $595/pp, 5 days 4 nights, 2 days
fishing. Includes air and hotel

Mike Kannapel
Mesa, AZ 800-658-5740
.... 602-929-0434
Rates: From: Half day: $35(1), $70(2)
From: Full day: $80(1), $150(2)
Call between: 11am-8pm
Provides: Beverages, lunch
Handicapped equipped: Yes

Mexico Sportsman
San Antonio, TX 210-212-4566
Destinations: Acapulco,
Cabo San Lucas,
Cancun, Cozumel, Mazatlan,
Puerto Vallarta, Ixtapa
Contact: 210-212-4566

S & W Inc.
Malakoff, TX 903-489-1656
Destinations: Mexico: LM Bass
Brazil: Peacock Bass
Venezuela: Peacock Bass
Price: $1000 to $4000
Arranges: Trans from point of depart
to fishing location, trans from point of
arrival to fishing location, lodging,
guides/charters
Evaluation: Yes
Free Consultation: Yes
Contact: Ron Speed

Sporting Charters
Austin, TX 800-448-8994
.... 512-458-8900
Destinations: Bahamas, Belize,
Costa Rica, Texas, Florida, Alaska,
Canada, The Rockies, Brazil,
Venezuela, Yucatan, Baja
Price: Varies

Tony Reyes Fishing Tours
Orange, CA 714-538-5221
Species & Seasons: Yellowtail, Cabrilla
Mar-Nov, Grouper April-Nov, Dolphin,
Yellowfin Tuna July-Nov, Black Sea Bass
Mar-July, White Sea Bass Mar-June
Bodies of Water: Sea of Cortez
Rates: 6 day trips: $675
Call between: 10am-7pm
Provides: Bait, lunch
Handicapped equipped: No

Trophy Fishing Etc., Inc.
Lake Charles, LA 800-284-5210
Species & Seasons: Bass all year
Bodies of Water: Lake Guerrero
(Old Mexico)

Rates: Half day: $100(1),
Full day: $175(1)
Call between: 8:30am-5pm
Provides: Beverages, lunch
Handicapped equipped: Yes

Tropical Fishing Adventures
Montauk, NY 516-668-2019
Destinations: Costa Rica: Sailfish, Marlin,
Tuna
Panama: Tarpon, Dolphin, Bonefish,
Belize: Permit, Snapper, Roosterfish
Price: $900 to $15,000
Arranges: Trans from point of depart
to fishing location, trans from point of
arrival to fishing location, lodging,
guides/charters
Evaluation: Yes
Free Consultation: Yes
Contact: Capt. Gene Kelly

Dan Westfall
Glendale, AZ 602-843-4107
Species & Seasons: LM Bass Oct-May
Bodies of Water: Baccarac Lake
Rates: 4 days: $5500
Call between: 6pm-8pm
Provides: Light tackle, heavy tackle, lures
Handicapped equipped: No

NEW GUINEA

Dean Butler's Sportfishing Adventures
Cairns, Australia 011-61-70-531009
Destinations: Northern Australia:
Barramundi, Queenfish, Threadfin
Salmon, Giant Trevally
Saratoga/Cairns Townsville: Black Marlin,
Sailfish
Papua New Guinea: LM Bass, Spot-tail
Bass, Barramundi, All major game fish
Price: $1500 to $3500
Arranges: Trans from point of arrival to
fishing location, lodging guides and
charters. Specializes in salt water fly
fishing for all species
Contact: Dean Butler

INTERNATIONAL DESTINATIONS

NEW ZEALAND

The Best of New Zealand Fly Fishing
Santa Monica, CA 800-528-6129
Destinations: New Zealand: Brown Trout, Rainbow Trout
Arranges: Trans from point of depart to fishing location, trans from point of arrival to fishing location, lodging, guides/charters, other travel arragements
Evaluation: Yes
Free Consultation: Yes
Contact: Mike McClelland

Hanalei Sport Fishing & Tours
Hanalei Kauai, HI 808-826-6114
Species & Seasons: Rainbow Trout
Bodies of Water: North and South Islands, New Zealand (Jan 15 to April 15)
Call between: 7am-5pm
Provides: Light tackle, heavy tackle, fly rod/reel, lures, bait, rain gear, beverages, lunch
Handicapped equipped: No

Highland Fly Fishing
Bryson City, NC 800-258-9840
.... 704-488-8975
Call between: Anytime
Provides: Fly rod/reel, beverages, lunch
Handicapped equipped: Yes
Certifications: 26 years experience

RUSSIA

Ouzel Expeditions
Girdwood, AK 800-825-8196
.... 907-783-2216
Destinations: Alaska: Salmon, Rainbow Trout, Arctic Char
Kamchatka, Russia: Kunja Char, Arctic Grayling
Price: $2400 to $3500
Arranges: Trans from point of arrival to fishing location
Evaluation: Yes
Free Consultation: Yes
Contact: Paul Allred

SOUTH AMERICA

Anglers Travel
Reno, NV 702-324-0580
Destinations: Costa Rica: Sailfish, Marlin, Dolphin, Wahoo, Tuna
South America: Black Marlin, Blue Marlin, Striped Marlin, Sailfish, Snapper, Tuna, Roosterfish
Arranges: Trans from point of depart to fishing location, trans from point of arrival to fishing location, lodging, guides/charters
Evaluation: Yes
Free Consultation: Yes
Contact: Chet Young

Dick Ballard's Fishing Adventures
Republic, MO ...., 800-336-9735
Destinations: South America: Peacock Bass, Catfish
Brazil: Peacock Bass, Catfish
Venezuela: Bonefish, Billfish
Peru: Peacock Bass, Tarpon, Snook
Argentina/Chile: Rainbow Trout, Brown Trout
Paraguay: Saribin Catfish
Price: $2000 to $4000
Arranges: Trans from point of depart to fishing location, trans from point of arrival to fishing location, lodging, guides/charters, pre-trip packets
Evaluation: Yes
Free Consultation: Yes
Contact: Dick Ballard

Fishin' World
Dallas, TX 214-358-4941
Bodies of Water: Amazon River, Brazil
Call between: 9am-6pm Mon-Sat
Contact: Rob Cooper

Lost World Adventures
Marietta, GA 800-999-0558
Destinations: Amazonas, Venezuela: Peacock Bass
Cambean, Venezuela: Billfish, Bonefish
Chile: Trout
Price: $1595 to $4300
Arranges: Trans from point of depart to fishing location, trans from point of arrival to fishing location, lodging, guides/charters
Evaluation: Yes
Free Consultation: No
Contact: Robbie Cox

S & W Inc.
Malakoff, TX 903-489-1656
Destinations: Mexico: LM Bass
Brazil: Peacock Bass
Venezuela: Peacock Bass
Price: $1000 to $4000
Arranges: Trans from point of depart to fishing location, trans from point of arrival to fishing location, lodging, guides/charters
Evaluation: Yes
Free Consultation: Yes
Contact: Ron Speed

Sporting Charters
Austin, TX 800-448-8994
.... 512-458-8900
Destinations: Bahamas, Belize, Costa Rica, Texas, Florida, Alaska, Canada, The Rockies, Brazil, Venezuela, Yucatan, Baja
Price: Varies

WORLDWIDE

Blue Water Operations Inc.
Houston, TX 713-893-6791
Destinations: Worldwide: Blue Marlin
Price: Depends on location

Jim McCarthy Adventures
Harrisburg, PA 717-652-4374
Destinations: Worldwide: Sailfish, Tarpon, Marlin, Roosterfish, Salmon, Trout, Pike
Price: $150 to $800 a day
Arranges: Trans from point of depart to fishing location, trans from point of arrival to fishing location, lodging, guides/charters
Evaluation: Yes
Free Consultation: Yes
Contact: Jim McCarthy

Loon-A-Sea Charter Service
Trumansburg, NY 607-387-5474
Destinations: North America, Central America, South America, Africa
Contact: Paul Tatar

PRODUCTS

Electric Fishing Reel Systems
1700 Sullivan Street
PO Box 20411
Greensboro, NC 27420
.... 910-273-9101
Catalog: Yes/Free
Product Line: Electric fishing reel drives

Gamakatsu USA, Inc.
PO Box 1797
Tacoma, WA 98401 206-922-8373
Catalog: Yes/Free
Product Line: High carbon fish hooks

Humminbird
#3 Humminbird Lane
Eufaula, AL 36027 800-622-1468
Catalog: Yes/Free
Product Line: Humminbird fish finders, VHF waterproof radios, GPS navigational equipment

Hurst-Young Wholesale Bait, Inc.
PO Box 212
Savannah, TN 38372 901-925-4019
Catalog: Yes/Free
Product Line: Producer and wholesaler of live baits (crickets). Mail order shipped priority mail, or UPS Nationwide. Guaranteed live delivery.

Interphase Technologies Inc.
1201 Shaffer Road
Santa Cruz, CA 95060 408-426-2007
Catalog: Yes/Free
Product Line: Electronics: Scanning sonar depth sounder, fishfinders. Products: Probe, Sea Scout, Echo Scan, Advantage

Kingfisher Maps, Inc.
110 Liberty Drive Suite 100
Clemson, SC 29631 803-654-2207
Catalog: Yes/Free
Product Line: Topo lake maps - waterproof - tear proof

Lake Systems Division
315 E South Street
Mt. Vernon, MO 65712
.... 417-466-7136
Catalog: Yes/Free
Product Line: Accessories: Combo-C-Lector (measures water temp, pH, and tells best lure color), Power-Arm (lowers and raises trolling motor electrically)

Leatherman Tool Group, Inc.
PO Box 20595
Portland, OR 97294 503-253-7826
Catalog: Yes/Free
Product Line: Knives, tools

Max Systems Lures
PO Box 5094
Palatine, IL 60078 708-934-0515
Catalog: Yes/Free
Product Line: Max Craw, the cadillac of crayfish lures. Weights 1/50 oz-1/4 oz, 5 hook sizes, unique lifelife action. Very snag resistant, use on everything from fly rod thru casting.

FISHING IS GREAT WITH LIVE BAIT!

CRICKETS   WAXWORMS
REDWORMS   MEALWORMS

DIRECT FROM THE PRODUCER TO YOU

HURST-YOUNG WHOLESALE BAIT, INC.

P.O. BOX 212 - SAVANNAH, TN 38372
(901) 925-4019 • Fax (901) 926-2556

WE SHIP NATIONWIDE

PRIORITY MAIL - NEXT DAY OR 2ND DAY UPS

PRODUCTS

Niantic Bay Tackle Company
59 Pennsylvania Avenue
Niantic, CT 06357 860-691-4581
Product Line: Artificial Lures, spinners, rigs

North American Fiberglass Corp.
PO Drawer C, Dept. 2-B
Greenville, NC 27835 919-758-9901
Catalog: Yes/Free
Product Line: Sea Cat - powered catamarans

Northstar Technologies
30 Sudbury Road
Acton, MA 01720 508-897-0770
Catalog: Yes/Free
Product Line: Electronics

Orvis Company
1711 Blue Hills Drive NE
Roanoke, VA 24012 800-815-5900
Catalog: Yes/Free
Product Line: Fly fishing rods, tackle and clothing

Piranha Propellers
3681 Sacramento Street, Suite D
San Luis Obispo, CA 93401
.... 800-235-7767
Catalog: Yes/Free
Product Line: Composite, modular propellers 20hp to 260hp

Resolution Mapping
35 Hartwell Avenue
Lexington, MA 02173 617-860-0430
Catalog: Yes/Free
Product Line: Maptech electronic chart & navigation software

Shakespeare
Electronica & Fiberglass Division
PO Box 733
Newberry, SC 29108 803-276-5504
Catalog: Yes/Free
Product Line: Marine equipment

Simrad Inc.
19210 33rd Avenue W
Lynnwood, WA 98036 206-778-8821
Catalog: Yes/Free
Product Line: Radars, GPS, auto pilots, sonar

SI-TEX
11001 Roosevelt Boulevard
St. Petersburg, FL 33716
.... 813-576-5734
Catalog: Yes
Product Line: Electronics

Spot'em
10042 Mesita Drive
Dallas, TX 75217 214-285-1570
Catalog: Yes
Product Line: Transducer to trolling motor

The Most Effective Spinner for 50 Years!

All Stainless Steel

Works On All Fresh & Saltwater Game Fish

New Prizm Colors

Comes in 4 Sizes
1 1/4", 2 1/2", 3 1/2" & Double Blade

The Niantic Bay™ Spinner

Made in the U.S.A.

If you want to know how good it works just ask the guy next to you!

For more information call (860) 691-2516 or write to:

Niantic Bay Tackle™
P. O. Box 296
Niantic, CT 06357

CUSTOM BUILT FISHING RODS
All Types / All Brands
Any Size / Any Style

Custom Designed For Your Specific Needs.

Trust the company who makes one of the best spinners in the world...to make

the best fishing rods in the world!

Niantic Bay Tackle™
CALL US TODAY!
(860) 691-2516

Everything in the Angler's Yellow Pages is
alphabetically arranged for ease of reference

Look in the Species Index
to find service providers by species of fish

SPECIES INDEX

AFRICAN POMPA - CHINOOK SALMON

A

African Pompa 92

Aku 130

Albacore 64, 65, 66, 67, 84, 188, 190, 195, 198, 301, 303, 304, 308, 380, 457

Aligator 109, 117,

Aligator Gar 425

Amberjack 20, 21, 88, 90, 91, 92, 99, 101, 103, 104, 106, 107, 108, 124, 130, 348, 422, 427, 428, 435, 448, 449

Arctic Char 28, 29, 31, 34, 35, 488, 496, 498

Arctic Grayling 28, 29, 31, 34, 35, 41, 268, 269, 270, 272, 273, 274, 275, 278, 279, 280, 281, 282, 283, 485, 486, 489, 496, 498

Atlantic Cod 488

Atlantic Salmon 314, 318, 320, 323, 325, 326, 328, 329, 330, 332, 333, 334, 336, 337, 338, 339, 340, 342, 364, 444, 472, 488, 489, 490, 491

B

Barracuda 66, 88, 90, 91, 92, 99, 100, 101, 106, 107, 108, 109, 111, 428

Barramundi 496, 497

Bass 22, 45, 46, 47, 48, 50, 51, 94, 112, 113, 115, 117, 119, 136, 172, 173, 202, 205, 209, 211, 212, 226, 238, 242, 247, 348, 381, 416, 418, 424, 468, 477, 489, 491, 492, 497

Billfish 498

Black Bass 422, 433, 436

Black Drum 94, 97, 103, 121, 181, 182, 422, 423, 425, 426, 428, 435, 437, 448, 449

Black Grouper 91, 101, 104, 108

Black Marlin 130, 496, 497, 498

Black Sea Bass 124, 195, 497

Blackfin Tuna 91, 92, 101, 104, 106, 108, 427

Blackfish 78, 80, 301

Blackmouth Salmon 457

Blue Catfish 404, 405

Blue Marlin 21, 84, 85, 104, 130, 131, 301, 348, 349, 404, 422, 428, 430, 435, 496, 498

Blue Shark 176, 189, 191, 192, 195, 198, 489

Bluefin Tuna 67, 84, 85, 176, 189, 190, 191, 192, 193, 194, 196, 198, 301, 303, 304, 308, 316, 348, 349, 448, 489

Bluefish 78, 80, 84, 85, 97, 103, 104, 109, 176, 181, 182, 184, 185, 188, 189, 190, 191, 192, 193, 194, 195, 196, 197, 198, 251, 296, 301, 302, 303, 304, 305, 306, 307, 308, 316, 318, 321, 334, 349, 400, 401, 448, 449

Bluegill 24, 54, 58, 93, 94, 97, 98, 99, 110, 112, 113, 114, 115, 116, 117, 120, 121, 140, 141, 142, 143, 145, 158, 159, 166, 167, 168, 169, 170, 216, 217, 218, 219, 222, 223, 224, 225, 226, 227, 228, 229, 230, 232, 233, 234, 235, 236, 237, 239, 240, 241, 242, 243, 244, 245, 246, 247, 250, 251, 256, 257, 258, 259, 260, 263, 264, 265, 287, 289, 350, 353, 370, 384, 405, 406, 416, 417, 419, 424, 431, 434, 455, 458, 468, 475, 476, 479

Bonefish 91, 92, 93, 100, 101, 102, 108, 109, 110, 496, 497, 498

Bonito 66, 80, 84, 88, 91, 92, 101, 104, 106, 108, 188, 190, 191, 195, 198, 301, 302, 303, 304, 306, 308, 400, 401, 428, 448

Bottom Fish 62, 65, 380, 385, 454, 456, 457, 459, 460, 488

Bream 23, 24, 46, 50, 51, 98, 104, 112, 114, 116, 117, 118, 174, 405, 406, 407, 408, 419, 449, 450

Broadbill Swordfish 104

Brook Trout 57, 62, 72, 74, 75, 126, 134, 135, 136, 176, 177, 193, 197, 221, 268, 269, 270, 271, 272, 273, 275, 276, 277, 278, 279, 280, 281, 282, 283, 292, 293, 311, 314, 315, 319, 322, 323, 324, 325, 328, 331, 338, 340, 341, 345, 353, 374, 379, 381, 386, 396, 416, 419, 440, 441, 442, 444, 445, 470, 473, 478, 480, 484, 485, 486, 488, 490, 491, 492

Brown Trout 41, 44, 45, 46, 47, 48, 49, 51, 52, 57, 60, 62, 63, 72, 74, 75, 126, 134, 135, 136, 144, 145, 151, 176, 192, 196, 198, 202, 206, 207, 208, 209, 210, 211, 212, 213, 214, 256, 260, 263, 268, 269, 270, 271, 272, 273, 274, 275, 276, 277, 278, 279, 280, 281, 282, 283, 292, 293, 310, 311, 312, 314, 315, 318, 319, 320, 321, 322, 323, 324, 326, 327, 328, 329, 330, 331, 332, 333, 334, 335, 336, 337, 338, 339, 340, 341, 342, 345, 353, 364, 365, 377, 395, 396, 416, 419, 440, 441, 442, 444, 445, 466, 467, 469, 470, 471, 472, 473, 476, 478, 480, 484, 485, 490, 498

Bull Trout 134, 271, 272, 381

Bullhead 158, 159, 193, 197, 216, 223, 225, 240, 241, 319, 338, 345

C

Cabrilla 497

Calico Bass 66

Catfish 23, 24, 38, 39, 40, 44, 45, 46, 48, 49, 50, 51, 52, 54, 55, 58, 62, 69, 98, 99, 104, 110, 112, 114, 116, 126, 140, 141, 142, 143, 145, 157, 158, 159, 166, 167, 168, 169, 170, 181, 182, 208, 214, 225, 256, 257, 258, 259, 260, 261, 262, 263, 264, 265, 287, 289, 310, 311, 312, 320, 350, 351, 353, 362, 365, 367, 370, 371, 381, 384, 405, 406, 412, 416, 417, 419, 422, 424, 425, 432, 433, 434, 436, 437, 442, 455, 458, 462, 466, 467, 472, 473, 481, 498

Cero Mackerel 108

Channel Bass 448, 449

Channel Catfish 256, 260, 263, 264, 394, 397, 441, 442, 449, 450

Chinook Salmon 28, 29, 30, 31, 32, 33, 34, 35, 62, 64, 69, 134, 135, 144, 145, 151, 192, 196, 198, 202, 204, 206, 207, 208, 209, 210, 211, 214, 314, 318, 320, 321, 322, 323, 326, 327, 328, 329, 330, 331, 332,

SPECIES INDEX

CHINOOK SALMON - LING COD

335, 336, 337, 338, 340, 341, 342, 356, 357, 358, 364, 365, 374, 375, 376, 377, 378, 379, 380, 381, 382, 383, 384, 385, 386, 387, 388, 412, 413, 444, 454, 455, 456, 457, 458, 459, 460, 466, 467, 469, 470, 471, 472, 473, 476, 492, 496

Chum Salmon 28, 31, 34, 457, 492

Cobia 21, 88, 90, 91, 92, 97, 99, 100, 101, 102, 103, 104, 106, 107, 108, 109, 111, 117, 118, 119, 120, 172, 173, 182, 251, 348, 349, 428, 448, 449

Cod 176, 188, 189, 190, 191, 192, 193, 194, 195, 197, 198, 301, 303, 307, 316, 318, 334, 400, 401, 488, 490, 492

Coho Salmon 28, 29, 30, 31, 32, 33, 34, 35, 62, 144, 145, 151, 192, 196, 198, 206, 207, 208, 209, 210, 211, 214, 318, 320, 322, 326, 327, 328, 329, 330, 331, 332, 335, 336, 337, 340, 341, 342, 364, 365, 375, 380, 382, 383, 384, 385, 386, 387, 454, 455, 456, 457, 459, 467, 469, 470, 471, 472, 473, 476, 489, 492

Coosa Bass 124, 126, 127

Corvina 68

Crab 64

Crappie 22, 23, 24, 38, 39, 40, 44, 45, 46, 47, 48, 49, 50, 51, 52, 54, 58, 69, 93, 94, 97, 98, 99, 112, 113, 114, 115, 116, 117, 118, 119, 120, 121, 124, 125, 126, 127, 140, 141, 142, 143, 145, 146, 157, 158, 159, 166, 167, 168, 169, 170, 216, 217, 218, 219, 220, 221, 222, 223, 224, 225, 226, 227, 228, 229, 230, 231, 232, 233, 234, 235, 236, 237, 238, 239, 240, 241, 242, 243, 244, 245, 246, 247, 250, 251, 256, 257, 258, 259, 260, 261, 262, 263, 264, 265, 287, 289, 317, 344, 350, 351, 353, 370, 371, 374, 379, 381, 384, 386, 392, 398, 405, 406, 416, 417, 418, 419, 424, 425, 431, 432, 433, 436, 437, 449, 450, 455, 458, 468, 473, 474, 475, 476, 477, 478, 479, 480

Croaker 84, 85, 181, 182, 184, 185, 448

Cutthroat Trout 34, 44, 45, 46, 47, 48, 51, 52, 57, 72, 74, 75, 134, 135, 136, 137, 268, 269, 270, 271, 272, 273, 274, 275, 276, 277, 278, 279, 280, 281, 282, 283, 292, 310, 311, 312, 379, 381, 383, 440, 441, 442, 454, 456, 457, 459, 484, 485, 486

D

Dolly Varden 28, 30, 31, 32, 33, 35

Dolphin 67, 84, 85, 88, 90, 91, 92, 93, 100, 101, 102, 103, 104, 106, 107, 108, 110, 124, 130, 131, 173, 251, 301, 302, 303, 305, 348, 349, 400, 404, 427, 428, 430, 448, 496, 497, 498

Drum 88, 111, 302, 305, 306, 424, 448

F

False Albacore 448

Flathead Catfish 256, 260, 263, 404, 405

Flounder 20, 78, 80, 84, 85, 88, 97, 103, 111, 172, 173, 174, 181, 182, 184, 185, 189, 190, 191, 192, 194, 195, 197, 198, 250, 251, 300, 301, 302, 303, 305, 306, 307, 316, 318, 321, 334, 349, 352, 400, 422, 423, 425, 426, 428, 435, 437, 448, 449, 488, 490

Fluke 78, 80, 190, 191, 195, 196, 198, 300, 301, 302, 303, 304, 305, 306, 307, 316, 318, 321, 334, 400, 401

G

Golden Trout 268, 269, 272, 276, 277, 279, 280, 281, 283, 440, 484, 485, 486

Ground Fish 189, 192, 194, 196

Grouper 88, 90, 91, 92, 93, 94, 95, 99, 100, 101, 102, 103, 104, 106, 107, 108, 110, 111, 120, 121, 124, 172, 303, 305, 348, 349, 404, 428, 497

Grunts 348

H

Haddock 191, 193, 194

Hake 400

Halibut 29, 30, 31, 32, 33, 34, 35, 64, 66, 67, 191, 193, 380, 385, 454, 456, 457, 459, 460, 488, 490, 492, 496

Hybrids 6, 50, 124, 125, 126, 127, 350, 353, 370, 371, 407, 418, 424, 431

J

Jack Crevelle 88, 97, 110, 118, 119, 120, 251, 428

K

Kokanee Salmon 62, 292, 440

Kamloop 134, 135

Kelp Bass 66, 67

King Mackerel 20, 21, 88, 91, 92, 93, 99, 101, 102, 103, 104, 108, 109, 117, 124, 172, 251, 301, 348, 349, 404, 427, 428, 430, 448

Kingfish 88, 90, 91, 92, 93, 101, 102, 103, 106, 107, 108, 109, 110, 111, 427, 428, 430

Kunja Char 496, 498

L

Ladyfish 88, 97, 104, 110, 118, 119, 120

Lake Trout 28, 29, 31, 34, 50, 52, 60, 134, 135, 144, 145, 151, 177, 178, 193, 197, 202, 206, 207, 208, 209, 210, 211, 214, 218, 219, 220, 221, 231, 247, 269, 270, 272, 273, 274, 276, 277, 278, 280, 281, 282, 283, 310, 312, 314, 315, 316, 318, 320, 322, 323, 324, 325, 326, 327, 328, 329, 330, 331, 332, 333, 334, 335, 336, 337, 338, 339, 340, 341, 342, 344, 364, 440, 444, 445, 467, 469, 470, 471, 472, 473, 475, 476, 480, 488, 489, 491, 492

Landlocked Salmon 177, 192, 196, 198, 337, 340, 488, 490, 492

Ling 300, 302, 304, 307, 426, 427, 428

Ling Cod 31, 32, 35, 64, 66, 67, 456, 457

SPECIES INDEX

LM BASS - REDFISH

LM Bass 20, 21, 22, 23, 24, 25, 38, 39, 40, 44, 45, 46, 47, 48, 49, 50, 51, 52, 54, 55, 56, 57, 58, 59, 60, 62, 63, 69, 88, 93, 94, 95, 97, 98, 99, 103, 104, 109, 110, 111, 112, 113, 114, 115, 116, 117, 118, 119, 120, 121, 124, 125, 126, 127, 140, 141, 142, 143, 145, 146, 157, 158, 159, 166, 167, 168, 169, 170, 173, 174, 177, 178, 181, 184, 185, 186, 193, 197, 216, 217, 218, 219, 220, 221, 222, 223, 224, 225, 226, 227, 228, 229, 230, 231, 232, 233, 234, 235, 236, 237, 238, 239, 240, 241, 242, 243, 244, 245, 246, 247, 250, 251, 252, 256, 257, 258, 259, 260, 261, 262, 263, 264, 265, 287, 289, 292, 293, 310, 311, 312, 314, 315, 317, 319, 320, 321, 322, 323, 324, 325, 328, 330, 331, 332, 333, 334, 336, 337, 338, 339, 341, 342, 343, 344, 345, 350, 351, 352, 353, 363, 370, 371, 374, 379, 381, 386, 394, 397, 405, 406, 407, 408, 412, 413, 416, 417, 418, 419, 422, 424, 425, 431, 432, 433, 434, 436, 437, 441, 442, 444, 449, 450, 455, 458, 466, 467, 468, 473, 474, 475, 476, 477, 478, 479, 480, 481, 489, 491, 496, 497, 498

M

Mackerel 20, 66, 84, 91, 101, 103, 104, 108, 109, 176, 189, 191, 192, 193, 194, 195, 296, 301, 302, 303, 304, 306, 488, 490

Mackinaw 60, 134, 135, 292, 484

Mako Shark 84, 85, 189, 191, 192, 195, 198, 316, 489

Mangrove Snapper 91, 94, 101

Marlin 66, 67, 84, 88, 90, 91, 92, 93, 100, 101, 103, 104, 107, 108, 110, 121, 124, 130, 173, 188, 190, 195, 198, 302, 303, 305, 307, 316, 318, 334, 348, 400, 401, 427, 428, 430, 448, 496, 497, 498

Monkfish 191, 193

Muskellunge 141, 143, 144, 157, 158, 159, 204, 205, 206, 210, 216, 218, 219, 220, 221, 222, 223, 224, 225, 226, 228, 229, 230, 232, 233, 234, 235, 236, 237, 239, 240, 241, 242, 243, 244, 245, 246, 247, 257, 259, 262, 287, 289, 314, 315, 317, 318, 320, 321, 322, 323, 324, 325, 328, 330, 332, 334, 335, 336, 342, 343, 344, 365, 392, 398, 416, 466, 467, 468, 471, 472, 473, 474, 475, 476, 477, 478, 479, 480, 481, 489, 491, 492

Mutton Snapper 91, 101, 108

N

Northern Pike 28, 29, 31, 34, 35, 45, 75, 157, 158, 159, 193, 197, 216, 217, 218, 219, 220, 221, 222, 223, 224, 225, 226, 227, 228, 229, 230, 231, 232, 233, 234, 235, 236, 237, 238, 239, 240, 241, 242, 243, 244, 245, 246, 247, 270, 272, 278, 279, 280, 283, 314, 315, 317, 319, 320, 321, 322, 323, 324, 325, 326, 327, 328, 329, 330, 331, 332, 333, 334, 335, 336, 337, 338, 339, 340, 341, 342, 343, 344, 345, 356, 357, 358, 392, 398, 412, 413, 444, 445, 466, 467, 468, 469, 471, 473, 474, 475, 476, 477, 478, 479, 480, 481, 488, 489, 491, 492, 498

O

Oscar 116

P

Pacific Salmon 330, 340

Paddlefish 269, 272, 273, 276, 277, 279, 282

Pampano 103

Panfish 88, 94, 97, 98, 110, 111, 116, 118, 119, 126, 216, 218, 220, 221, 222, 223, 224, 226, 228, 230, 231, 232, 233, 234, 235, 236, 240, 242, 243, 244, 245, 246, 247, 259, 263, 264, 314, 315, 320, 321, 322, 330, 334, 336, 340, 343, 345, 407, 408, 417, 462, 466, 467, 472, 473, 474, 475, 476, 477, 478, 479, 480, 481, 489, 491

Peacock Bass 116, 497, 498

Perch 69, 157, 158, 159, 176, 178, 181, 204, 205, 206, 207, 208, 209, 210, 213, 214, 216, 218, 219, 220, 221, 222, 223, 224, 225, 228, 229, 230, 232, 233, 234, 235, 236, 237, 238, 241, 242, 243, 244, 247, 256, 260, 264, 287, 289, 316, 320, 327, 329, 331, 333, 336, 338, 344, 356, 362, 363, 364, 365, 367, 370, 371, 384, 392, 395, 396, 398, 419, 444, 445, 455, 458, 467, 469, 470, 474, 475, 477, 478, 479

Permit 91, 92, 100, 101, 102, 106, 107, 108, 109, 117, 497

Pickerel 114, 178, 319, 320, 338, 345, 493

Pink Salmon 28, 30, 31, 32, 33, 34, 206, 208, 489, 492

Pollock 191, 193, 194, 400

Pompano 20

Porgy 91, 101, 108, 188, 190, 192, 195, 196, 198, 300, 307

Q

Queenfish 496, 497

R

Rainbow Trout 28, 30, 31, 32, 33, 34, 35, 39, 41, 44, 45, 46, 47, 48, 49, 51, 52, 54, 57, 60, 61, 62, 63, 69, 72, 74, 75, 126, 134, 135, 136, 137, 145, 211, 212, 214, 219, 231, 256, 260, 263, 268, 269, 270, 271, 272, 273, 274, 275, 276, 277, 278, 279, 280, 281, 282, 283, 292, 293, 310, 311, 312, 314, 315, 319, 320, 321, 322, 323, 324, 326, 327, 328, 329, 330, 334, 335, 338, 340, 345, 353, 364, 374, 376, 377, 378, 379, 381, 383, 386, 395, 396, 416, 419, 440, 441, 442, 444, 445, 454, 455, 456, 457, 459, 466, 467, 469, 470, 471, 472, 473, 476, 484, 485, 486, 492, 493, 496, 498

Red Bass 88, 111

Red Drum 103, 251, 422, 423, 425, 426, 435, 437

Red Grouper 91, 101, 108

Red Snapper 20, 21, 35, 91, 103, 104, 124, 172, 251, 348, 422, 426, 427, 428, 430, 434, 435

Redfish 20, 88, 91, 93, 94, 95, 97, 99, 100, 101, 102, 103, 104, 106, 107, 108, 109, 110, 115, 117, 118, 119, 120, 121, 124, 172, 173, 174, 250, 251, 422, 423, 424, 425, 426, 428, 430, 435, 437

SPECIES INDEX — ROCK BASS - STRIPED BASS

Rock Bass 44, 45, 51, 223, 261

Rock Cod 64, 65, 66, 67

Rockfish 30, 31, 32, 34, 64, 66, 166, 167, 168, 169, 170, 380, 457, 460

Roosterfish 496, 497, 498

S

Sailfish 21, 88, 90, 91, 92, 93, 100, 101, 102, 103, 104, 106, 107, 108, 109, 110, 111, 348, 349, 404, 422, 428, 430, 435, 496, 497, 498

Salmon 34, 61, 62, 64, 65, 67, 69, 75, 135, 136, 141, 143, 144, 176, 177, 178, 193, 197, 202, 204, 205, 206, 207, 208, 209, 210, 211, 212, 213, 214, 314, 315, 316, 318, 320, 321, 322, 323, 324, 325, 326, 327, 328, 329, 330, 331, 332, 333, 335, 336, 337, 338, 339, 340, 341, 342, 343, 344, 345, 356, 357, 358, 374, 375, 376, 377, 378, 379, 380, 381, 382, 383, 384, 385, 386, 387, 388, 395, 396, 412, 413, 441, 442, 444, 445, 454, 455, 456, 457, 458, 459, 460, 466, 467, 469, 470, 471, 472, 473, 474, 481, 488, 489, 490, 491, 493, 496, 498

Sand Bass 66, 371

Sand Trout 426, 428

Saribin Catfish 498

Sauger 166, 167, 168, 169, 170, 229, 230, 231, 239, 243, 279, 356, 357, 358, 412, 416, 417, 419

Saugeye 357, 358

Scallops 104

Sea Bass 66, 84, 85, 88, 91, 92, 93, 97, 111, 115, 120, 190, 196, 198, 300, 301, 302, 303, 304, 305, 306, 307, 316, 318, 348, 400, 448, 449, 456

Sea Trout 84, 85, 88, 93, 95, 97, 99, 100, 101, 102, 103, 106, 107, 108, 109, 110, 111, 115, 118, 119, 120, 121, 124, 182, 185, 302, 305, 306

Shad 61, 62, 69, 88, 97, 98, 110, 112, 118, 119, 320, 321, 322, 323, 334, 336, 342, 375, 376, 377, 378, 379, 380, 382, 383, 384, 385, 386, 387, 388, 394, 397, 490

Shark 34, 66, 84, 85, 90, 91, 92, 97, 99, 100, 101, 103, 104, 106, 107, 108, 109, 110, 121, 124, 130, 176, 189, 190, 191, 193, 194, 196, 197, 198, 250, 251, 301, 302, 303, 304, 305, 306, 307, 316, 318, 319, 334, 400, 401, 422, 426, 427, 428, 435, 448, 488, 496

Sheafish 31, 33, 35

Sheepshead 20, 97, 103, 104, 124, 422, 425, 426, 435, 437

Shell Cracker 93, 94, 98, 99, 104, 112, 113, 114, 115, 116, 117

Shellfish 62, 65

Silver Snapper 348

Silver Trout 455

Skamania Trout 470

Skip Jack Tuna 130, 448

SM Bass 20, 21, 22, 23, 24, 25, 38, 40, 44, 45, 46, 47, 48, 49, 50, 51, 52, 59, 62, 69, 134, 135, 136, 137, 157, 159, 166, 167, 168, 169, 170, 176, 177, 178, 181, 184, 185, 186, 193, 197, 204, 205, 206, 210, 216, 217, 218, 219, 220, 221, 222, 223, 224, 225, 226, 227, 228, 229, 230, 231, 232, 233, 234, 235, 236, 237, 239, 240, 241, 242, 243, 244, 245, 246, 247, 256, 260, 261, 263, 264, 265, 292, 293, 310, 311, 312, 314, 315, 316, 317, 318, 319, 320, 322, 323, 324, 325, 326, 327, 328, 329, 330, 331, 332, 333, 334, 335, 336, 337, 338, 339, 340, 341, 342, 343, 344, 345, 362, 363, 364, 365, 367, 374, 375, 376, 377, 378, 379, 380, 381, 382, 383, 384, 385, 386, 387, 388, 392, 394, 395, 396, 397, 398, 412, 413, 416, 417, 418, 419, 422, 424, 433, 437, 440, 441, 442, 444, 445, 450, 455, 462, 466, 467, 468, 471, 472, 473, 474, 475, 476, 477, 478, 479, 480, 481, 488, 489, 490, 491, 492, 493

Smelt 62, 65

Snapper 88, 90, 91, 92, 93, 97, 99, 100, 101, 102, 103, 104, 106, 107, 108, 110, 111, 115, 120, 130, 172, 173, 251, 303, 305, 348, 349, 404, 428, 430, 496, 497, 498

Snook 88, 93, 94, 95, 97, 99, 100, 101, 102, 103, 106, 107, 108, 109, 110, 113, 115, 116, 117, 118, 119, 120, 121, 496, 497, 498

Sockeye Salmon 28, 29, 30, 31, 32, 33, 34, 35, 454, 456, 457, 459, 489, 492, 496

Spanish Mackerel 20, 84, 88, 97, 99, 103, 104, 108, 109, 111, 118, 120, 124, 172, 181, 182, 185, 188, 190, 195, 198, 251, 301, 348, 448, 449

Spearfish 130, 349

Speckled Trout 20, 104, 109, 117, 172, 173, 174, 250, 251, 422, 423, 424, 425, 426, 428, 430, 435, 437, 488, 490, 492

Splake 219, 221, 231, 473

Spoonbill 258, 263

Spot 181, 182, 184, 185, 448

Spot-tail Bass 496, 497

Spotted Bass 20, 21, 22, 23, 24, 25, 45, 46, 48, 49, 50, 51, 124, 125, 256, 260, 263, 264, 265, 424, 433, 436, 437, 462

Spotted Sea Trout 99, 107, 422, 423, 435

Steelhead 30, 31, 32, 33, 34, 61, 62, 65, 69, 134, 135, 136, 137, 144, 145, 151, 192, 196, 198, 202, 203, 206, 207, 208, 209, 210, 211, 212, 213, 214, 219, 231, 318, 320, 321, 322, 324, 326, 327, 328, 329, 330, 331, 332, 333, 335, 336, 337, 338, 339, 340, 341, 342, 363, 364, 365, 374, 375, 376, 377, 378, 379, 380, 381, 382, 383, 384, 385, 386, 387, 388, 389, 392, 398, 440, 444, 445, 454, 455, 456, 457, 458, 459, 460, 467, 469, 470, 472, 473, 488, 490, 492, 496

Striped Bass 22, 24, 38, 39, 40, 47, 48, 49, 54, 56, 57, 60, 61, 62, 78, 80, 84, 85, 88, 94, 97, 98, 110, 111, 112, 117, 118, 119, 124, 125, 126, 127, 166, 167, 168, 169, 170, 174, 176, 181, 182, 184, 185, 186, 188, 189, 190, 191, 192, 193, 194, 195, 196, 197, 198, 231, 239, 257, 258, 259, 261, 287, 296, 301, 302, 303, 304, 305, 306, 307, 308, 310, 311, 312, 316, 318, 321, 322, 323, 329, 334, 336, 337, 340, 342, 350, 351, 353, 371, 376, 377, 378, 379, 380, 382, 383, 385, 387, 388, 394,

395, 396, 397, 400, 401, 404, 405, 406, 407, 408, 416, 417, 418, 419, 422, 424, 430, 431, 432, 433, 434, 436, 437, 448, 449, 450, 451, 462, 488, 490

Striped Marlin 130, 131, 496, 498

Sturgeon 61, 64, 69, 134, 135, 136, 137, 218, 227, 228, 229, 230, 234, 236, 239, 242, 243, 244, 374, 375, 376, 377, 378, 379, 380, 381, 382, 383, 384, 385, 386, 387, 388, 454, 455, 456, 457, 458

Sunfish 226, 228, 229, 230, 234, 236, 238, 242, 247

Sunshine Bass 93, 114

Swordfish 302, 303

T

Tarpon 88, 90, 91, 92, 93, 95, 97, 99, 100, 101, 102, 103, 104, 106, 107, 108, 109, 110, 113, 115, 117, 118, 119, 120, 121, 124, 173, 426, 428, 430, 496, 497, 498

Tautog 84, 85, 188, 190, 191, 192, 194, 195, 196, 197, 198, 300, 301, 302, 303, 304, 307, 316, 318, 400, 401, 448, 449

Threadfin Salmon 496, 497

Tiger Trout 440

Tilapia 68

Trevally 496, 497

Triggerfish 20, 21, 103, 104, 172, 348

Triple Tail 95, 97, 99, 107, 109, 118, 120

Trout 31, 32, 33, 34, 35, 38, 39, 41, 44, 45, 46, 47, 48, 50, 51, 52, 58, 62, 69, 88, 94, 103, 104, 108, 110, 111, 121, 134, 136, 166, 168, 173, 206, 209, 211, 217, 218, 219, 220, 225, 226, 228, 232, 233, 236, 242, 245, 246, 256, 260, 261, 263, 265, 268, 269, 270, 271, 272, 273, 274, 275, 276, 277, 278, 279, 281, 282, 283, 284, 287, 310, 312, 315, 317, 319, 320, 321, 326, 327, 328, 329, 330, 332, 333, 334, 335, 336, 338, 342, 343, 345, 349, 352, 356, 357, 358, 374, 375, 376, 377, 378, 379, 380, 381, 382, 383, 384, 385,

386, 387, 388, 389, 392, 394, 395, 396, 398, 407, 416, 418, 441, 442, 444, 448, 449, 454, 455, 456, 458, 459, 460, 466, 467, 471, 472, 473, 474, 475, 476, 477, 479, 480, 481, 484, 485, 486, 488, 489, 490, 491, 492, 493, 496, 498

Tuna 66, 67, 84, 85, 88, 90, 91, 92, 93, 100, 101, 102, 104, 107, 108, 110, 111, 124, 130, 172, 173, 188, 190, 191, 194, 195, 198, 301, 302, 303, 304, 305, 306, 307, 316, 318, 334, 348, 380, 400, 401, 427, 428, 430, 448, 456, 488, 496, 497, 498

V

Vermillion Snapper 21

W

Wahoo 67, 84, 85, 88, 90, 91, 92, 93, 100, 101, 102, 103, 104, 107, 108, 124, 130, 131, 172, 173, 348, 349, 404, 428, 430, 448, 496, 498

Walleye 38, 40, 45, 46, 51, 52, 141, 143, 144, 157, 158, 159, 166, 168, 169, 203, 204, 205, 206, 208, 209, 210, 212, 213, 214, 216, 217, 218, 219, 220, 221, 222, 223, 224, 225, 226, 227, 228, 229, 230, 231, 232, 233, 234, 235, 236, 237, 238, 239, 240, 241, 242, 243, 244, 245, 246, 247, 256, 257, 258, 259, 260, 262, 263, 264, 265, 269, 272, 273, 276, 277, 279, 282, 287, 289, 310, 311, 312, 314, 315, 317, 318, 319, 320, 321, 322, 323, 324, 325, 326, 327, 328, 329, 330, 331, 332, 333, 334, 335, 336, 337, 338, 339, 340, 341, 342, 343, 344, 345, 356, 357, 358, 362, 363, 364, 365, 367, 375, 376, 377, 378, 383, 384, 385, 388, 392, 395, 396, 398, 412, 413, 416, 419, 422, 441, 442, 444, 462, 466, 467, 468, 469, 471, 472, 473, 474, 475, 476, 477, 478, 479, 480, 481, 488, 489, 491, 492

Warmouth 98, 99

Weakfish 84, 85, 181, 182, 184, 301, 302, 303, 304, 305, 306, 307, 308

White Bass 38, 40, 98, 112, 116, 117, 125, 140, 141, 142, 143, 145, 166, 167, 168, 169, 170, 256, 257, 258, 259, 261, 262, 263, 264, 265,

310, 311, 312, 356, 370, 371, 392, 398, 412, 416, 417, 419, 422, 424, 431, 432, 441, 442

White Marlin 84, 85, 104, 188, 195, 301, 348, 349, 400, 404, 422, 428, 435

White Perch 174, 181, 182, 184, 490, 492

White Sea Bass 66, 67, 497

Whitefish 177, 227, 235, 240, 243, 244, 270, 272, 278, 280, 283, 488, 491

Wolffish 191, 193, 194

Y

Yellow Bass 166, 167, 168, 169, 170

Yellow Perch 204, 205, 206, 208, 210, 230, 319, 338, 345, 362, 363, 364, 365, 392, 398, 488, 490, 492

Yellowfin Tuna 66, 67, 92, 84, 85, 101, 104, 108, 130, 131, 190, 191, 192, 195, 196, 198, 301, 348, 349, 404, 448, 497

Yellowtail 66, 67, 303, 305, 497

Yellowtail Snapper 91, 101, 108

LOCATION INDEX

ALABAMA - ARKANSAS

ALABAMA

Alabama River 20, 21, 22, 23
Black Warrior River 20
Bon Secour Bay 21
Cahaba River 20
Chatahoochee River 20, 21, 22, 23, 24, 25
Coosa River 20, 21, 22, 23, 24, 25
Dannelly Res. 20
Gulf of Mexico 20, 21
Guntersville Lake 20, 21, 22, 23, 24, 25
Harris Res. 20, 21, 22, 23, 24, 25
Joe Wheeler Dam 22
Jones Bluff Dam 20
Lake Eufaula 20, 21, 22, 23, 24, 25
Lake Jordan 20, 21, 22, 23
Lake Land Farms 20
Lake Martin 20, 21, 22, 23, 24, 25
Lake Nichol 20
Lake Purdy 20
Lake Tuscaloosa 20
Lay Lake 22, 23
Lewis Smith Lake 21, 22, 23, 24, 25
Logan Martin Lake 20, 21, 22, 23, 24, 25
Mitchell Lake 22, 23
Mobile Bay 21
Mobile River Delta 23
Neely Henry Lake 20, 21, 22, 23, 24, 25
Pickwick Lake 23, 24, 25
Tallapoosa River 20, 21, 22, 23, 24, 25
Tennessee River 20, 21, 22, 23, 24, 25
Walter F. George Res. 21
Warrior River 20, 21, 22, 23, 24, 25
Weiss Lake 20, 21, 22, 23, 24, 25
Wheeler Lake 20, 21, 22, 23, 24, 25
Wilson Lake 20, 21, 22, 23, 24, 25

ALASKA

8 Mile Creek 28
Aleutian Range 28
American River 33
Becharof NWR 28, 29
Bristol Bay 28, 29
Chena River 31, 35
Cook Inlet 29, 30, 31, 32, 33, 34
Cross Sound 31, 35
Donkey Creek 28
Fish Creek 28
Gulf of Alaska 31, 32, 35
Gulkana River 33
Hewitt Creek 28
Icy Straits 31, 35
Indian Creek 28
Innoko River 31, 35
Kachemak Bay 29, 30, 31, 32, 33, 34
Kasilof River 29, 30, 31, 32, 33
Katchamak Bay 31
Kenai Fjords 31, 32
Kenai River 29, 30, 31, 32, 33
Kodiac Island 29, 31, 34
Kvichak River 31, 34, 35
Lake Clark 31, 34, 35
Lake Creek 28
Lisianski Inlet 31, 35
Malone Creek 28
Mulchatna River 31, 34, 35
Nowitna River 31, 35
Nushagak River 31, 34, 35
Pacific Ocean 35
Resurrection Bay 31, 32
Salcha River 31, 35
Susitna River 28
Talachulitna River 28
Talkeetna River 28
Tanana River 31, 35
Ugaksik Lake 28, 29
Yukon River 31, 35

ARIZONA

Alamo Lake 38, 39, 40
Apache Lake 38, 40
Bartlett Res. 38, 40
Beaver Creek 39, 40
Big Lake 41
Black River 41
Canyon Lake 38, 40
Clear Creek 39, 40
Colorado River 38, 39
Crescent Lake 41
Eastern Region 39
Lake Havasu 38, 39
Lake Mary 39, 40
Lake Mead 38, 39
Lake Mohave 38, 39
Lake Pleasant 38, 40
Lake Powell 40
Lee Valley Res. 41
Lee's Ferry 39
Little Colorado River 41
Nelson Res. 41
Oak Creek 39, 40
Saguaro Lake 38, 40
Theodore Roosevelt Lake 38, 40
Topock Marsh 38, 39
Verde River 39, 40
Willow Beach 38, 39

ARKANSAS

96-Shoot 49
Arkansas River 44, 47, 49, 51
Bear Creek Lake 50
Beaver Lake 44, 50
Big Creek 44, 49, 51
Black River, 47
Blue Lake 49
Buffalo River 44, 45, 46, 47, 50, 51, 52
Bull Shoals Lake 44, 45, 46, 48, 49, 50, 51, 52
Caddo River 46, 48, 50
Cossatot River 46, 49, 50
Crooked Creek 44, 45, 46, 50, 51, 52
Crystal Lake 46
Dacus Lake 49
DeGray Lake 46, 48, 49, 50
Deirks Lake 46, 49, 50
DeQueen Lake 46, 49, 50
Eleven Point River 47
Greers Ferry Lake 46, 47, 48, 51
Hill Slough 47
Horshoe Lake 49
Illinois Bayou 44, 47
Lake Aptell Village Creek 50
Lake Charles 47
Lake Dardanelle 44, 45, 47, 48, 49, 50, 51
Lake Dunn Village Creek 50
Lake Hamilton 47, 48
Lake Merrisack 44, 49, 51
Lake Ouachita 45, 46, 47, 48, 50, 51
Lake Poinsett 50
Lake Wright Patmen 46, 49, 50
L'Anguille River 50
Little Red River 46, 47, 48, 49, 50, 51
Mid-Way 49
Millwood Lake 46, 49, 50
Mississippi River 44, 49, 51
Nimrod Lake 44, 47, 49
Norfork Lake 45, 46, 49, 50, 51, 52
North Fork River 46, 48, 49, 51
Ouachita River 46, 48, 50
Piney River 44, 47
Portia Bay 47
Red River 45, 46, 48, 49, 50, 51
Sardis 49
Spring River 47
St. Francis River 50
Swepco 46
Table Rock Lake 44, 50
White River 44, 45, 46, 48, 49, 50, 51, 52
White River National Wildlife Refuge Lakes 44, 49, 51

CALIFORNIA - CANADA
LOCATION INDEX

CALIFORNIA

Pt. Reyes 64
American River 56, 57, 61
Avacado Lake 69
Barrett Lake 57, 59, 63, 66, 68
Big Bear Lake 54, 59, 66, 68, 70
Black Butte Lake 54
Bridgeport Reservoir 54
Cachuma Lake 54, 55, 58, 59, 65, 68
Camanche Res.
    54, 55, 56, 57, 59, 60, 61, 67, 69
Carquinez Strait 70
Carson River 57
Castaic Lake 54, 55, 58, 59, 65, 68
Catalina Island 66
Channel Islands 67
Cibola Lake 55
Clair Engle Lake 55, 69
Clear Lake
    54, 55, 56, 57, 58, 59, 61, 64, 68, 69
Clementime Lake 57
Coffee Creek 62
Colorado River 55
Coronado Islands 67
Coronados Islands 66
Cortez Bank 66
Courtright Res 69
Delta
    54, 55, 56, 57, 59, 60, 61, 62, 63, 64, 67, 69
Don Pedro Res 54, 56, 57, 59, 69
Don Pedro Res. 54, 55, 56, 57, 59, 60, 69
East Park Res. 54
Edison Lake 69
Eel River 60, 61, 62, 65, 69
El Capitan Res
    57, 58, 59, 60, 63, 65, 66, 68
Fall River 60, 61, 63, 69
Farallon Islands 64
Feather River 61
Florence Lake 69
Folsom Lake
    54, 55, 56, 57, 59, 61, 69
Frank G. Bonelli Park 65
Gualala River 60, 61
Half Moon Bay 64
Harvey's Fishing Hole 55
Hat Creek 60, 61, 69
Hellhole Res. 57
Humboldt Bay 64
Huntington Flats 66
Huntington Harbor 67
Huntington Lake 69
Indian Creek Res. 57
Irvine Lake 58, 65
Kaweah River 59
Kings River 69
Klamath River 62, 65, 69
Laguna Niguel Lake 58, 65
Lake Amador 54, 55, 60, 61, 67
Lake Berryessa 55, 58, 61, 64, 68

Lake Casitas 54, 55, 58, 59, 65, 68
Lake Chabot 55, 61, 64
Lake Cuyamaca 58, 59, 66
Lake Dixon 57, 58, 59, 60, 63, 65, 68
Lake Hennessy 58, 61
Lake Henshaw 58
Lake Hodges
    57, 58, 59, 60, 63, 65, 66, 68
Lake Kaweah 59
Lake McClure 54, 56, 57, 60
Lake Merced 55, 61, 64
Lake Miramar 57, 58, 60, 65, 68
Lake Morena 57, 58, 59, 60, 63, 65, 66, 68, 69
Lake Oroville 54, 55, 56, 57, 59, 69
Lake Perris 54, 59, 66, 68, 70
Lake Piru 54, 55, 58, 59, 65, 68
Lake Poway 57, 58, 60, 65, 68
Lake Skinner 60
Lake Sonoma 60, 61
Lake Tahoe 60
Lake Wohlford
    57, 58, 59, 60, 63, 65, 68
Lewiston Lake 55, 63, 69
Lopez Lake 66, 69
Lost Lakes 57
Mad River 62
McCloud River 61, 62, 69
Mission Bay 67
Mokelumne River 56, 63
Monterey Bay 64, 65
Napa River 55, 58, 61, 64, 68
Natomas Lake 57
New Melones Lake
    54, 55, 56, 57, 60, 61, 67
Newport Beach 66
Otay Res. 57, 58, 59, 60, 63, 65, 66, 68
Outer Tuna Banks 66
Oxboe Lake 55
Pacific Ocean
    54, 55, 57, 58, 59, 60, 61, 62, 63, 64, 65, 66, 67, 68, 69, 70
Pardee Res. 54, 55, 60, 61, 67
Pine Flat Lake 69
Pit River 61, 69
Pleasant Valley Creek 57
Point Arena 64
Point Conception 66
Point St. George 64
Port San Luis 66, 69
Prado Regional Park 65
Pt. Reyes 64
Putah Creek 55, 58, 61, 64, 68
Pyramid Lake 54, 55, 58, 59, 65, 68
Redwood Creek 62, 65
Revilla Gegidos Islands 67
Russian River 60, 61
Sacramento River
    54, 55, 56, 57, 60, 61, 62, 63, 64, 67, 69
Salton Sea 54, 59, 66, 68, 70
San Clemente Island 66

San Diego Bay 67
San Francisco Bay 55, 61, 64, 65, 68
San Joaquin River
    54, 55, 56, 60, 61, 62, 63, 67
San Martin Island 66
San Miguel Island 66
San Nicholas Island 66
San Pablo Bay 55, 58, 61, 64, 65, 68
San Pablo Dam Resevoir 64
San Vicente Lake
    57, 58, 59, 60, 63, 65, 66, 68
Santa Ana River Lakes 58, 65
Santa Margarita Res. 66, 69
Santa Monica Bay 66
Santa Rosa Island 66
Sespe River 54, 55, 58, 59, 65, 68
Shasta Lake
    54, 55, 56, 57, 59, 61, 62, 69, 70
Shaver Lake 69
Siltcoos Lake 69
Silver Creek 57
Silverwood Lake 54, 59, 66, 68, 70
Smith River 62, 69
Stony Gorge Res 54
Suison Bay 70
Summit Lake 57
Tamarock 57
Trinity Lake 62, 69, 70
Trinity River 55, 60, 61, 62, 63, 65, 69
Van Duzen River 62, 65
Ventura River 54, 55, 58, 59, 65, 68
Wishon Lake 69
Whiskeytown Lake 69, 70

CANADA

Albany River Basin 488
Alberni Inlet 488
Arctic Ocean 488
Barkley Sound 488
Barron River 491
Bay of Fundy 488, 490
Berthelot Lake 488
Beverly Lake 493
Bonnechere River 491
Bras d'Or Lake 488, 490
Cains River 490, 491
Canoose Flowage 493
Cape Breton rivers 490
Cecebe Lake 489
Cedar Lake 488
Chamcook Lake 493
Charelston Lake 493
Chedabucto Bay 489
Christie Pass 492
Corey Lake 491
Cross Bay 488
Digdeguash Lake 488, 490
Dixon Entrance 489
Dungarvon River 490, 491
French River Delta 489
Goletas Channel 492

LOCATION INDEX

CANADA - FLORIDA

Gordon Channel 492
Great Slave Lake 489
Gunn Lake 492, 493
Harvey Lake 488, 490
Holden Lake 491
Kabi River 491
Kalum River 492
Kasba Lake 489
Kasiks River 492
Keswick River 489
Kitimat River 492
Lake Ainslie 490
Lake George 490
Lake of the Woods 489
Lake Ontario 493
Lake Utopia 488, 490
Mackay Lake 489
Macta Quac Lake 489, 490
Magaguadavic Lake 488, 489, 490, 492
Magaguadavic River 488, 490, 493
Magnetawan River 489
Margaree River 490
McConnell Lake 491
McDougall Lake 488, 490
Miramichi River 490, 491
Muskrat Lake 491
Nagagami River 491
Nagagamisis Creek 491
Nashwaak River 490
North River 490
Ottawa River 491, 492
Pacific Ocean 488
Pettawawa River 491
Pistol Lake 492
Port of Canso 489
Queen Charlotte Strait 492
Rainy Lake 492
Remote lakes 492
Renous River 490, 491
Sand Lake 492
Shekak River 491
Skeena River 492
Spruce Lake 493
St. Croix River 490, 492, 493
St. John River 490, 491
St. Lawrence River 493
Sullivan Lake 491
Tobique Headpond 491
Tobique River 491
Tyaughton Lake 493
Winnipeg River 492

COLORADO

Arkansas River 72, 73, 74, 75
Barbour Ponds 72, 75
Barr Lake 72, 75
Big Thompson River 72, 73
Blue River 72, 73, 74
Boyd Lake 72, 73
Castle Creek 73, 74
Chatfield Res. 72, 73, 74, 75
Cheeseman Canyon 74
Cherry Creek Lake 72, 73, 74, 75
Colorado River 72, 73, 74
Crystal River 73, 74
Del Norte area 75
Dolores River 74
Eagle River 72, 74
Elevenmile Canyon Res. 72, 73, 74, 75
Pueblo Res., 73
Fryingpan River 73, 74
Horseshoe Res. 72, 73, 74, 75
Horsetooth Res. 72, 73
La Garita 75
Lon Hagler Res. 72, 73
Maroon Creek 73, 74
McPhee Res. 74
Navajo Res. 75
Pueblo Res. 72, 73, 74, 75
Rio Grande Nat'l. Forest 75
Rio Grande Res. 75
Rio Grande River 75
Roaring Fork River 72, 73, 74
Ruby Lake 75
San Juan Mountains 75
Simpson Ponds 72, 73
South Platte River 72, 73, 74, 75
Spinney Mountain Res. 72, 73, 74, 75
Standley Lake 72, 75
Weminuche Wilderness Areas 75

CONNECTICUT

Amos Lake 79, 80, 81
Atlantic Ocean 78, 80, 81
Connecticut River 78, 79, 80, 81, 82
Dog Pond 78, 79, 81
Fisher's Island Sound 79, 80, 81
Hammonasset River 79, 80, 81
Highland Lake 78, 79, 81, 82
Housatonic River 78, 79, 80
Lake Candlewood 79, 80, 81, 82
Lake Lillinonan 79
Lake Quassapaug 79
Lake Zour 79
Long Island Sound 78, 79, 80, 81
Long Pond 79, 80
Naugatuck River 78, 79, 81
New Haven Harbor 81
Niantic Bay 78, 80, 81
Norwalk Islands 80
Norwalk River 79, 80, 81
Salmon River 79, 80, 81
Saugatuck Res 79
Saugatuck River 80, 81
Thames River 78, 79, 80, 81
Twin Lakes 78, 79, 82
Tyler Lake 78, 79, 81
West River 81
Westhill Pond 78, 79, 81
Wononskopomuc Lake 78, 82

DELAWARE

Assawoman Bay 84, 86
Atlantic Ocean 84, 85, 86
Broadkill River 84, 85, 86
Burton's Pond 85
Cape Henlopen 85
Chesapeake Bay 84, 85
Delaware Bay 84, 85, 86
Diamond Pond 84, 85
Indian River 85
Isle of Wight Bay 84, 86
Marshihope River 84, 85, 86
Nanticoke River 84, 85, 86
Pocomoke River 84, 85, 86
Red Mill Pond 84, 85
Rehoboth Bay 84, 85
Sinepuxent Bay 84, 86
Trappe Pond 85
Wagmon Pond 84, 85
Wicomico River 84, 85, 86

FLORIDA

Alligator Alley 94, 114, 115
Alligator Creek 106
Tampa Bay 105
Anclote River 97, 103
Anna Maria Island 99, 105
Apalachee Bay 96, 102, 112, 116
Apalachicola River
   94, 96, 97, 103, 111, 116
Atlantic Ocean 88, 89, 90, 91, 92,
   93, 94, 95, 96, 97, 100,
   101, 102, 105, 106, 107,
   108, 109, 110, 111, 113,
   114, 115, 116, 118
Atlantic Ocean Flats 91, 100, 109
Aucilla River 96, 102, 112, 116
Banana River 88, 96, 97, 118, 120
Banana River Lagoon
   88, 97, 110, 118, 119
Bear Lake 96
Biscayne Bay 89, 90, 94, 95
Black Creek 97
Blackwater River 96, 103
Blue Cypress Lake
   93, 97, 113, 114, 115, 119, 120
Boca Ciega Bay 105, 108
Boca Grande 95, 99, 103, 105, 106,
   107, 108, 109, 113, 115, 120
Boca Grande Pass 107, 108
Braden River 99, 110
Butler Chain 97
Caloosahatehee River 99, 107
Canal Systems 94, 116
Carribean Sea 90, 100, 105
Central Florida 119
Charlotte Harbor 95, 99, 105, 106,
   107, 108, 109, 120
Chipola River 96
Choctawhatchee Bay 96, 103, 105
Choctawhatchee River 96, 103

FLORIDA - GEORGIA LOCATION INDEX

Clear Lake 94, 116
Clearmont Chain 97
Clearwater 103, 108
Clearwater Bay 108
Clermont Chain 109, 113, 115, 120
Conway Chain 97
Crescent Lake 94, 97, 98, 111, 116, 119
Crystal River 104
Cypress Lake 94, 113, 117
Dead Lake 96
Doctors Lake 97
Dry Tortugas 92, 101, 108
East Bay 96, 102
East River 96, 102, 103
Econfina River 96, 102, 112, 116
Econolochattchee River 98, 112
Edison Reef 99, 107
Egmont Key 99, 105
Escambia River 96, 102
Everglades 90, 94, 95, 111, 114
Everglades Nat'l. Park 95, 107, 109, 120, 121
Faka Union Canal System 94, 121
Floral City Pool 121
Florida Bay 89, 93, 100, 101, 110
Florida Keys 90, 91, 92, 100, 101, 102, 106, 107, 108, 109
Ft. Pierce 92
Garcia Block 93, 114
Garcia Res. 93, 113, 119
Gasparilla Sound 107, 109
Gulf of Mexico 89, 90, 91, 92, 93, 95, 96, 97, 99, 100, 101, 102, 103, 104, 105, 106, 107, 108, 109, 110, 114, 115, 117, 120, 121
Gulf of Mexico Coastal Flats 109, 117
Gulf Stream 92
Halifax River 88
Hernando Pool 121
Holiday Park 94, 114
Holley Lake 104
Hollyland 94, 114
Homosassa River 104
Hurricane Lake 96
Indian River 88, 90, 93, 96, 97, 115, 118, 120
Indian River Lagoon 88, 89, 97, 110, 111, 118, 119
Intracoastal Waterways 88, 89, 90, 93, 95, 96, 105, 110, 111, 115
Inverness Pool 121
Jackson Lake 96, 102, 112, 116
Juniper Lake 96, 103
Karrick Lake 96
Key West 92, 101, 108
Key West Flats 100
King Lake 104
Kissimmee Chain 93, 110, 113, 114, 115, 117, 119

Kissimmee River 99, 112, 114
Lake Agnes 112
Lake Clarke 94, 116
Lake Delaney 95, 111, 113
Lake Dexter 98, 112, 118
Lake George 94, 95, 97, 98, 111, 112, 113, 116, 118, 119
Lake Harney 98, 112
Lake Hatchineha 94, 113, 117
Lake Ida 89, 94, 114, 116
Lake Istokpoga 99, 112
Lake Jackson 112, 117
Lake Juliana 112
Lake Kerr 95, 98, 111, 113, 119
Lake Kissimmee 88, 93, 94, 113, 114, 117, 119
Lake Kissimmee Chain 109, 113, 120
Lake Lamonia 112, 116, 117
Lake Marion 93, 114
Lake Mattee 112
Lake Miccosukee 114
Lake Mud 112
Lake Ocheesee 96, 116
Lake Okeechobee 89, 90, 93, 94, 97, 99, 105, 109, 111, 113, 114, 115, 116, 117, 119, 120
Lake Osborne 89, 94, 116
Lake Parker 93, 110, 114
Lake Rousseau 98, 116
Lake Seminole 96, 102, 112, 116, 117
Lake Talquin 94, 96, 97, 98, 102, 111, 112, 116, 117
Lake Tarpon 103, 109, 117
Lake Tohopekaliga 94, 113, 115, 117, 119
Lake Trafford 105, 114, 117, 120
Lake Wimico 96
Lake Woodruff 98, 112, 118
Lake Worth 115
Lochlossa Lake 99, 106, 118
Loxahatchee River 90, 111, 115
Makia River 106
Manatee River 99, 105, 110
Marco Island 95, 107, 109, 110, 120
Marquesas Keys 92, 101, 108
Matlacha Pass 99, 107
Miami Airport Lake 89, 105, 115
Mosquito Lagoon 88, 96, 97, 110, 118, 119, 120
Myakka River 99, 105
New River 99
Newman's Lake 99, 106, 118
Ochlockonee River 96, 98, 102, 112, 116, 117
Oklawaha River 95, 98, 111, 113, 119
Orange Lake 99, 106, 118
Palm Beach County Canal System 94, 116

Peace River 99, 108
Pensacola Bay 96, 102
Perdido Bay 96, 102
Perdido River 96
Perico Bay 99, 105
Pine Island Sound 99, 106, 107
Ponce Inlet 88, 96, 118
Port Canaveral 97, 118, 120
Port Everglades Inlet 90, 95, 111
Port of Miami 90
Private Pits 113, 119
Red Fish Pass 99, 107
Rodman Res. 94, 98, 111, 113, 119
Salt Run 89, 111
San Carlos Bay 99, 107
Sanibel Point 95, 99, 107, 120
Santa Rosa Sound 96, 102
Sarasota Bay 99, 105, 106, 109
Sawgrass 94, 114, 115
Sebastian Inlet 91
Sebastian River 93, 113, 119
Siesta Key 105
Singer Island 115
Snake Creek 94, 114
St. Andrews Bay 97, 103, 104
St. John's River 88, 94, 95, 97, 98, 110, 111, 112, 113, 116, 118, 119, 120
St. Marks River 96, 102, 112, 116
Steinhatchee River 96, 102, 112, 104, 116
Stick Marsh 88, 93, 97, 109, 110, 113, 115, 117, 118, 119, 120
Stone Lake 96
Straits of Florida 90, 92, 100, 101, 102, 105, 108
Suwannee River 94, 97, 111, 116
Tamiami Trail Canal System 89, 94, 95
Tampa Bay 99, 103, 105, 106, 108, 109, 117
Tarpon Springs 103, 106, 108
Ten Thousand Islands 94, 95, 105, 107, 109, 110, 114, 117, 120, 121
Terra Ceia Bay 99, 105
Tsala Apopka Chain of Lakes 121
Tsala Apopka Lake 98, 121
Wakulla River 96, 102, 112, 116
Weeki Wachee River 102, 105
West Lake Tohopekaliga 94
Winter Haven Chain of Lakes 93, 110, 114
Withlacoochee River 94, 97, 98, 99, 111, 116, 121
Yellow River 96, 102

GEORGIA

Alapaha River 125, 126
Atlantic Ocean 124
Brushy Branch 127

LOCATION INDEX

GEORGIA - INDIANA

Chattahoochee River 124, 125
Chattooga River 126
Chatuge Lake 126
Chestatee River 124, 125
Cooper Creek 126
Coosa River 124, 127
Etowah River 127
Hartwell Lake 124, 126, 127
Hiawassee River 126
Jackson Lake 124, 125, 126
Lake Allatoona 124
Lake Blackshear 125, 126
Lake Joy 125
Lake Juliette 125
Lake Oconee 124, 125, 126
Lake Olmested 126, 127
Lake Sidney Lanier 124, 125
Lake Sinclair 124, 125, 126
Lake Tobesofkee 125
Little River 125, 126
Noontootla Creek 126
Ocmulgee River 125
Oconee River 125
Paradise Fishing Park 125, 126
Rock Creek 126
Russell Lake 124, 125, 126, 127
Savannah River 126, 127
St. Simons Island 124
Strom Thurmond Lake (Clarks Hill)
    124, 126, 127
Toccoa River 126
Weiss Lake 124, 127
West Point Lake 127
Willacoochee River 125, 126

HAWAII

Hawaii 130
Kauai 130
Maui 130
Molokai 131

IDAHO

Big Wood River 134, 135, 136
Challis Nat'l. Forest 134, 136
Clark Fork River 134, 137
Clearwater River 134, 135, 137
Coeur d' Alene Lake 134, 135, 137
Coeur d' Alene River 134, 137
Lake Pend Oreille 134, 135
Lemhi River 134, 135
Little Wood River 134, 135, 136
Lost River 134, 135, 136
Priest Lake 134, 135
River of No Return 135
Salmon River 134, 135, 136, 137
Sawtooth Nat'l. Recreation Areas
    134, 136
Sawtooth Wilderness 136
Selway-Bitterroot Wilderness 136
Silver Creek 134, 135, 136

Snake River 134, 135, 136, 137
Spokane River 134, 137
St. Joe River 134, 137
Trail Creek 134, 135, 136
Warm Springs 134, 135, 136
Weitas Creek 136

ILLINOIS

Bangs Lake 140, 142
Banner Marsh 143, 145, 146
Big Muddy River 146
Braidwood Lake
    140, 141, 142, 143, 144
Carlyle Lake 140, 146
Cedar Lake 140, 141, 142, 143, 145
Chain O'Lakes 140, 141, 142, 143, 144
Clinton Lake 141, 147
Crab Orchard Lake 140, 141, 145
Crab Orchard Wildlife Refuge
    141, 142, 143, 145
Crystal Lake 140, 142
Des Plaines River 140, 141, 143
Devil's Kitchen Lake
    140, 141, 142, 143, 145
Du Page River
    140, 141, 142, 143, 144
Farm Ponds 146
Forth Lake 140, 144
Fox River 140, 141, 142, 143, 144
Frank Holten Lake 146
Gordon F. More Park Lake 146
Gran Creek 141, 143
Grays Lake 140, 144
Greenville Lake 140
Heideike Lake
    140, 141, 142, 143, 144
Hickory Creek
    140, 141, 142, 143, 144
Highland Old City Lake 146
Horseshoe Lake 146
Illinois River
    140, 141, 142, 143, 144,
    145, 146, 147
Jackson Creek 140, 142, 143, 144
Kankakee River
    140, 141, 142, 143, 144
Kinkaid Lake
    140, 141, 142, 143, 145
Kishwaukee River 146, 147
Lake Egypt 141, 142, 143, 145
Lake George 145, 146
Lake Michigan 140, 141, 142, 143, 144, 145
Lake Murphysboro 141, 140, 143, 145
Lake Springfield 143, 145, 147
Lake Storey 145, 146
LaSalle Lake 140, 142, 143, 144
Lincoln Trail Lake 146, 147
Little Grassy Lake
    140, 141, 142, 143, 145
Long Lake 140, 144
Mill Creek 145, 146, 147

Mississippi River
    140, 143, 145, 146, 147
Newton Lake 146, 147
Pierce Lake 146, 147
Red Hills (State Park) 146, 147
Rend Lake 146
Rice Lake 143, 145, 146
Rock River 145, 146, 147
Round Lake 140, 144
Salt Creek 141, 147
Sam Parr Lake 146, 147
Sangamon River 141, 143, 145, 147
Sangchris Lake 143, 145, 147
Spring Creek 140, 142, 143, 144
Strip Mine Lakes 143
Turtle Creek 146, 147
Wabash River 146, 147

INDIANA

Adams Lake 151
Atwood Lake 151
Barbee Chain of Lakes 150, 151
Bischoff Reservoir 150
Brookville Lake 150, 151, 152
Cecil M. Harden Lake 150
Clear Lake 151
Crooked Lake 151
Dallas Lake 151
Geist Res 151, 152
Greene-Sullivan State Forest 151, 152
Huntington Lake 150, 152
James Lake Chain 151
Jones Lake 151
Kankakee River 150, 152
Kokomo Res. 151, 152
Koontz Lake 150
Lake George 151
Lake Michigan 150, 151, 152
Lake Sullivan 151, 152
Lake Tippecanoe 150, 151
Lake Wawasee 151
Le-An-Wa Lake 153
Mississinewa Res 151, 152
Monroe Lake 150, 151, 152
Morse Res. 151, 153
Ohio River 150, 151, 152
Oliver Lake 151
Pine Lake 150, 152
Raccoon Lake 152
Rockville Lake 152
Salamonie Lake 150, 151, 152
Shakamak Lake 151, 152
St. Joseph River 150, 152
Steinbarger Lake 151
Stone Lake 150, 152
Sugar Creek 152
Summit Lake 150, 151, 152
Surgar Creek 152
Sylvan Lake 151
Turtle Creek 151, 152
Wabash River 151, 152
Waldron Lake 151

INDIANA - MAINE — LOCATION INDEX

Waveland Lake 152
Webster Lake 151
White River 151, 153
Whitmer Lake 151
Wildcat Creek 151, 152

INTERNATIONAL DESTINATIONS

Acapulco 497
Africa 498
Alaska 496
Amazon River 498
Amazonas 498
Andros Island 496
Argentina 498
Australia 496, 497
Baccarac Lake 497
Bahamas 496, 497, 498
Baja 496, 497, 498
Belize 496, 497, 498
Brazil 496, 497, 498
Cabo San Lucas 497
Cambean 498
Canada 496, 497, 498
Cancun 497
Central America 496
Chile 498
Costa Rica 496, 497, 498
Cozumel 497
Ixtapa 497
Lake Guerrero 497
Mazatlan 497
Mexico 497, 498
New Guinea 496, 497
New Zealand 498
Panama 496
Paraguay 498
Peru 498
Puerto Vallarta 497
Rio Colorado River 497
Russia 496, 498
Sea of Cortez 497
South America 498
Venezuela 496, 497, 498
Yucatan 496, 497, 498

IOWA

Big Creek 157, 159
Big Spirit Lake 157, 158, 159
Bobwhite State Park Lake 158
Cedar River 156, 157, 158
Center Lake 157, 158, 159
Clear Lake 156
Coralville Res 156, 157, 158
Corning Res. 157, 158
Des Moines River 156, 157, 158, 159
Iowa River 156, 157
Lake Ahquabi 157, 159
Lake Binder 157, 158
Lake Easter 157, 158, 159
Lake Icaria 157, 158
Lake Macbride 156, 157
Lake Okoboji 157, 158, 159
Lake Wapello 156, 158
Little River 158
Little Sioux River 157, 159
Little Spirit Lake 157, 159
Mississippi River 156, 157, 158
Nodaway River 157, 158
Pleasant Creek Lake 156, 157, 158
Raccoon River 157, 158, 159
Rathbun Lake 156, 158
Red Rock Res 157, 158, 159
Saylorville Res. 157, 158, 159
Silver Lake 157, 158, 159
Spirit Lake 159
Storm Lake 157, 159
Wapsipinicon River 156, 157
West Okoboji 157

KANSAS

Arkansas River 162
Big Hill Lake 162, 163
Cabondale City Lake 162, 163
Cedar Bluff Reservoir 162
Cheney Res. 162
Clinton Lake 162, 163
Cour Creek 162
Hills Lake 163
John Redmond Res. 162, 163
Kanopolis Lake 162
Kansas River 162, 163
Lake Parsons 162, 163
Lake Shawnee 162, 163
Little Arkansas River 162
Marais des Cygnes River 163
Melvern Lake 162, 163
Neosho County State Fishing Lake 162, 163
Neosho River 162, 163
Osage State Lake 162, 163
Perry Lake 162, 163
Pomona Lake 162, 163
Spring Creek 162
Wakarusa River 162, 163
Wolf Creek Nuclear Plant Lake 162, 163

KENTUCKY

Barren River 166
Beech Fork River 170
Cumberland River 166, 167, 168, 169, 170
Cumberland River Tailwaters 166, 168
Dale Hollow Lake 166, 169
Green River 168, 169, 170
Green River Lake 166, 169
Kentucky Lake 166, 167, 168, 169, 170
Kentucky River 167, 168
Kentucky State Game Farm Lakes 167, 168, 170
Lake Barkley 166, 167, 168, 169, 170
Lake Cumberland 166, 168, 169
Laurel Lake 169, 170
Nolin River Lake 169, 170
Ohio River 166, 167, 168, 169, 170
Rough River 169, 170
Rough River Lake 166, 168, 169, 170
Salt River 170
Taylorsville Lake 167, 168, 169, 170
Tennessee River 166, 167, 168, 170

LOUISIANA

Atchafalaya Basin 174
Barataria Bay 172, 173
Black Bay 172
Breton Sound 172
Caddo Lake 172, 173, 174
Calcasieu Lake 172, 173
Caney Lake 172, 173, 174
Delacroix Island 172
False River 174
Grand Isle 172, 173
Gulf of Mexico 172, 173, 174
Lake Bistineau 172, 173, 174
Lake Borgne 173
Lake Mechant 172
Lake Merchant 173
Little Lake 172, 173
Lost Lake 172, 173
Louisiana Coast 174
Louisiana Marsh 172
Mississippi Delta 173, 174
Mississippi River 174
Mississippi River Delta 173
Rigolets 173
Sister Lake 172, 173
Toledo Bend Res. 172, 173, 174
Vermilion Bay 172, 174

MAINE

Atlantic Ocean 176, 177
Bartlett Lake 177
Big Lake 176, 178
Casco Bay 176
Flat Iron Pond 176
Grand Falls Lake 176, 178
Grand Lake 177
Gulf of Maine 176
Kennebago Lake 176
Kennebago River 176
Kennebec River 176, 177
Kezar Lake 177, 178
King Lake 177
Little Kennebago Lake 176
Long Lake 176, 178
Moose Pond 177, 178
Moosehead Lake 176, 177
Penobscot River 176, 177, 178

LOCATION INDEX — MAINE - MICHIGAN

Piscataquis River 177, 178
Sebago Lake 177, 178
Sheepscot River 176
South Branch Lake 177, 178
Thomson Lake 177, 178
West Grand Lake 176, 178

MARYLAND

Atlantic Ocean 180, 181, 183
Back River 181
Bilhunting Creek 182, 184
Catoctin Mtn. Trout Streams 182, 184
Chesapeake Bay
 180, 181, 182, 183, 184, 185
Choptank River 181, 182
Conowingo Lake 180, 183, 185
Cunningham Falls 184
Cunningham Lake 182, 184
Deep Creek Lake 182, 183, 185
Elk River 180, 182, 185
Frank Bentz Pond 182, 184
Gunpowder River 180, 181, 183
Herring Bay 182
Jennings Randolph Lake 182, 183, 185
Liberty Lake 180, 183
Liberty Res. 180, 181, 183, 185
Loch Raven Res. 180, 181, 183, 185
Magothy River 180
Monocacy River 182, 184
North East River 180, 182, 185
North Point Creek 180
Patapsco River 180
Patuxent River 180, 184
Potomac River
 180, 182, 184, 185, 186
Prettyboy Res. 180, 183, 185
Rappahanock River 184
Rocky Gorge Res 180, 184, 185
Savage River Res. 182, 183, 185
Seneca Creek 184
Shenandoah River 182, 184
Susquehanna River
 180, 182, 183, 184, 185, 186
Tred Avon River 181
Tridelphia Res. 180, 184, 185, 186

MASSACHUSETTS

Assabet River 192
Atlantic Ocean 188, 189, 190,
 191, 192, 193, 194, 195,
 196, 197, 198
Block Island Sound 188, 190, 195, 197
Boston Harbor 189, 190, 191,
 192, 193, 194, 197, 199
Browns Pond 188, 195, 197
Buzzards Bay 188, 189, 190,
 191, 192, 195, 196, 197, 198
Cape Cod 188
Cape Cod Bay 188, 189, 190,
 191, 192, 193, 194, 195, 196,
 197, 198
Cape Cod Canal
 188, 190, 192, 196, 199
Cashes Ledge 191
Charles River 189, 199
Concord River 192, 199
Cuttyhunk Island 190, 195, 198
Fales Pond 199
Fore River 197, 199
Golden Hills Ponds 188, 195, 197
Goose Pond 193, 196
Great South Channel 198
Green River 193
Gulf of Maine 191, 194, 196
Hingham Bay 197, 199
Horn Pond 188, 195, 197
Houghton's Pond 189, 199
Ipswich River 188, 195, 197
Jamaica Pond 189
Lake Buell 193, 196
Lake Lashaway 193, 197
Lake Mirimichi 199
Laurel Lake 193, 196
Massachusetts Bay 188, 189, 191,
 192, 193, 194, 195
Merrimack River
 188, 189, 191, 194, 196
Monomoy Island 195, 198
Mossy Pond 198
Mystic River 188, 194, 195, 197
Nantucket Sound 188, 189, 190,
 191, 192, 194, 195, 196,
 197, 198
North Pond 193
Onota Lake 193, 196
Parker River 188, 194, 196
Peters Pond 188, 192
Plum Island River 188, 194, 196
Plymouth Harbor 191
Point of Pines River 188
Pontoosuc Lake 193, 196
Porkapaog Pond 189, 199
Prankers Pond 188
Quabbin Res. 188, 192, 193,
 196, 197, 198, 199
Quaboag Pond 193, 197
Quaboag River 193, 197
Quincy Bay 190, 191, 197, 199
Race Point 192, 197, 199
Rhode Island Sound 190, 197, 198
Saugus River 188, 195, 197
Sluice Pond 188
South Pond 193, 197
Spectacle Pond 188, 192
Stellwagen Bank 189, 190, 191,
 192, 193, 194, 196,
 197, 198
Stillwater River 198
Stockbridge Bowl 193
Sudbury River 192
Town River Bay 197, 199
Turnpike Lake 199
Vineyard Sound 188, 189, 190,
 191, 192, 195, 196,
 197, 198
Wachusett Res.
 188, 192, 196, 198, 199
Wakeby Pond 188, 192
Walden Pond 192, 199
Waushaccum East 198
Westport River 190, 197, 198
Weymouth Back River 197, 199
White Pond 192, 199
Whitings Pond 199
Whitmans Pond 189, 197, 199
Wickaboag Pond 193, 197

MICHIGAN

AuSable River
 202, 205, 206, 209, 211, 212, 214

Belleville Lake 203
Betsie River 202, 209, 211, 212
Black Lake 202, 205, 207, 211, 214
Black River 202
Boardman River 202
Bud Lake 203
Burt Lake 202, 205, 207, 211
Cass Lake 209, 213
Cedar Lake 202
Celar Lake 207, 214
Cheboygan River 202, 205, 211
Chippewa Lake 211
Chippewa River 211
Clam River 203, 210
Corey Lake 214
Crooked Lake 202, 203, 207, 210
Crystal Lake 202, 209
Detroit River
 202, 203, 204, 210, 212, 213
Escanaba River 203, 207
Ford Lake 203, 204, 210
Grand River 203, 212, 213
Greens Lake 213
Gull Lake 203, 204
Gun Lake 203, 204
Higgins Lake 203
Holloway Res. 203
Houghton Lake 203, 210, 213
Hubbard Lake 204
Huntoon Lake 213
Indian Lake 207, 214
Indian River 202, 205, 211
Jewel Lake 204
Kalamazoo River 203, 204
Kent Lake 209, 213
Klinger Lake 214
Lake Allegan 203, 204
Lake Erie 202, 203, 204, 205,
 206, 207, 209, 210
Lake Fenton 203
Lake Huron 202, 204, 205, 206,
 207, 208, 209, 210, 211,
 213, 214

MICHIGAN - MINNESOTA — LOCATION INDEX

Lake Isabella 211
Lake Mecosta 211
Lake Michigan 202, 203, 204, 206, 207, 208, 209, 210, 211, 212, 213, 214
Lake Missaukee 203, 210
Lake Nepessing 203
Lake Oakland 209, 212, 213
Lake Sapphire 203, 210
Lake St. Clair 203, 204, 205, 206, 209, 210, 212, 213
Lake Templene 214
Lake White 203, 212, 213
Little Manistee River 209, 210, 211, 212, 214
Long Lake 203
Loon Lake 202, 207, 209, 212, 213
Manistee Lake 209, 211
Manistee River 202, 203, 207, 209, 210, 211, 212, 214
Mantiny Lake 211
Menominee River 211
Michigamme Flowage 211
Mott Lake 203
Mullet Lake 202, 205, 211
Muskegon Lake 203, 212, 213
Muskegon River 202, 203, 209, 210, 211, 212, 213, 214
Peavy Falls Flowage 211
Pere Marquette River 202, 209, 210, 211, 212, 213, 214
Pickeral Lake 202, 207
Pigeon River 213
Pine River 210, 211, 212, 214
Platte River 202, 209, 211, 212
Pontiac Lake 209, 212, 213
Popple River 211
Rifle River 202, 205
Round Lake 202, 207
Sage Lake 202, 205
Saginaw Bay 203, 205, 206, 212, 213
Saginaw River 203, 205, 209, 212, 213
Sand Lake 202, 205, 214
Shiawassee River 205, 213
Spring Lake 203, 208, 212, 213
St. Clair River 209, 213
St. Joseph River 207, 208, 213, 214
Tippy Dam Pond 211
Tittabawassee River 205, 209, 212, 213
Tawas Lake 202
Van Etten Lake 202, 205
Walloon Lake 202, 207
White River 210, 211, 212, 214
Williams Lake 213
Woodhull Lake 209, 212, 213

MINNESOTA

4 Point Lake 235, 247
Alexandria Chain of Lakes 228, 229, 230, 234, 239, 242
Antler Lake 222
Bald Eagle Lake 246
Ball Club Lake 217, 231
Balm Lake 227
Baptism River 233
Bass Lake 224, 239
Basswood Lake 217, 219, 220
Battle Lake 216, 223, 224, 225, 240, 241, 244
Bay Lake 225, 236, 238
Bear Island River 217, 221, 246
Bearskin Lake 219, 231
Beaver River 233
Belle Taine Lake 216, 224
Benedict Lake 223
Big Boy Lake 235
Big Lake 223
Big Pine Lake 217
Big Sand Lake 222, 223, 232, 234
Big Sandy Lake 217
Bigfork River 217, 231, 238, 242
Birch Lake 217, 220, 221, 235, 246
Black Island Lake 224
Borden Lake 225, 236, 238
Boundary Waters Canoe Area 217, 218, 219, 220, 221, 245, 246
Bowstring Lake 217, 218, 231, 232, 233, 238, 242
Boy Lake 234
Boy River 234, 235
Burnside Lake 219
Burnt Shanty Lake 224
Caribow Lake 217, 220, 221
Cass Lake 221, 222, 223, 228, 232, 233, 234, 235, 236, 239, 244
Cedar Lake 225, 237, 238
Chain Lakes 222, 228, 233, 235, 239
Chippewa River 222
Chisago Lake 226
Clear Lake 226, 238
Clearwater Lake 227
Clitherall Lake 216, 224, 240
Crane Creek 244
Crane Lake 218, 219, 220, 227, 229, 239, 242, 243, 244
Crow River 226, 228, 240
Crow Wing Chain of Lakes 216, 224, 226, 235
Crow Wing River 227
Cut Foot Sioux Lake 218
Cuyuna Range Mine Pits 238
Deer Lake 216, 223, 224, 225, 239, 241
Eagle Lake 222, 236
Farm Island Lake 225, 236, 237, 238
Fish Hook Lake 225, 233
Fish Trap Lake 227
Floyd Lake 225
Forest Lake 226, 238
Fox Lake 245
Gilbert Lake 226, 237, 247
Green Lake 226, 228, 240
Greer Lake 226
Gull Lake 226, 227, 232, 233, 236, 237, 238, 241, 242, 246, 247
Gunflint Lake 221
Hay Lake 247
Horseshoe Chain 243
Hungry Jack Lake 219, 231
Island Lake 223, 224, 225, 236, 237, 238
Jack the Horse Lake 223
Jasper Lake 220
Jessie Lake 218, 232, 233
Johnson Lake 220
Kabetogama Lake 18, 219, 227, 229, 239, 240, 243, 244
Kawishiwi River 217, 220
Kid Lake 223
Lac La Croix 218, 227, 239, 244
Lake Alexander 227
Lake Andrusia 221, 223, 244
Lake Bemidji 222, 227, 228, 233, 235, 239
Lake Benton 231
Lake Calhoun 238
Lake Carlos 228, 230
Lake Elysian 236
Lake Emily 229
Lake Florida 226, 228, 240
Lake Frances 236
Lake George 223, 236
Lake Harriet 238
Lake Hendricks 231
Lake Hubert 226, 238, 241, 246
Lake Ida 228, 229, 230, 234, 236, 242
Lake Jefferson 236
Lake Koronis 243
Lake Lida 228
Lake Madison 231
Lake Mary 228, 230
Lake Miltona 228, 229, 230, 234, 236, 242
Lake Minnetonka 228, 229, 233, 236, 237, 238
Lake Minnewaska 228, 229, 230, 234, 236, 242
Lake of the Isles 238
Lake of the Woods 18, 227, 229, 230, 239, 242, 243, 244
Lake Osakis 228, 229, 230, 234, 236, 242
Lake Pepin 231, 238, 239
Lake Reno 228, 229, 230
Lake Sarah 231, 245
Lake Shetek 231
Lake Superior 219, 231, 245
Lake Thompson 231
Lake Washington 236
Lake Winnibigoshish 217, 218, 221, 222, 226, 231, 232, 233, 234, 236, 237, 238, 242, 247
Lake Zumbro 231, 238

LOCATION INDEX
MINNESOTA - MISSOURI

Lax Lake 233
Leech Lake
    216, 217, 221, 222, 224, 225,
    226, 228, 229, 230, 231,
    232, 233, 234, 235, 236,
    237, 238, 239, 242, 243, 247
Little Boy Lake 222, 223, 232,
    234, 247
Little Chippewa River 222
Little Floyd Lake 225
Little Fork River 218
Little Johnson Lake 220
Little Long 219
Little Moose Lake 225
Little Pine Lake 225
Little Rice Lake 221, 223, 244
Little Sand Lake 243
Little Trout Lake 222
Little Wolf Lake 222, 236
Little Thunder Lake 222, 233, 243
Long Lake 222, 226, 232, 233,
    236, 238, 241, 242, 246, 247
Lost Lake 216, 223, 225, 241
Madison Lake 236
Mantrap Lake 216, 224, 225, 233
Mille Lacs 225, 226, 228, 229,
    230, 232, 233, 234, 236,
    237, 238, 239, 242, 247
Minnesota River 228, 237
Mississippi River 217, 221, 222,
    223, 224, 225, 226, 228, 229,
    231, 232, 233, 235, 236, 237,
    238, 239, 241, 242, 243, 244,
    245, 246, 247
Mitchell Lake 220
Moose Lake 219, 220, 221,
    224, 225, 239
Movil Lake 245
Namakan Lake 218, 219, 227,
    229, 239, 240, 242, 243, 244
Nest Lake 226, 228, 240
North Star Lake 240
Ojibway Lake 220
Ossawinnamakee Chain of Lakes 242
Otter Tail Lake 216, 223, 224, 225,
    240, 241, 244, 245
Park Lake 231
Pelican Lake 218, 226, 229, 232,
    233, 236, 238, 241, 242,
    246, 247
Pine Lake 217, 225, 236
Pine Mountain Lake 226, 238, 241, 246
Pokegama Lake 217, 231, 238, 242
Poplar Lake 217, 220, 221
Quetico Provincial Park 218
Rabbit Lake 238
Rainy Lake 218, 227, 229, 239,
    240, 242, 243, 244
Rainy River 218, 227, 228, 229,
    230, 234, 236, 239, 242,
    243, 244
Red Lake 222, 228, 233, 235, 239

Rice Lake 221, 222, 223, 233,
    239, 243, 244
Root River 231, 238
Round Lake 236
Ruby Lake 224
Rush Lake 216, 241, 244, 245
Saganaga Lake 218, 221
Sand Lake 218, 232, 233, 243
Sand Point Lake 218, 219, 227,
    229, 239, 240, 242, 243, 244
Sauk Lake 230
Sea Gull Lake 221
Serpent Lake 238
Shagawa Lake 219, 220
Shamineau Lake 227
Side Lake 238, 245
Silver Lake 246
Sioux River 231
Snowbank Lake 219, 220
Spider Lake 224
Spring Lake 220, 243
Squaw Lake 217, 231
St. Croix River 226, 238, 246
Star Lake 216, 241, 244
Straight Lake 245
Straight River 244
Swamp Lakes 221
Swan Lake 238, 241, 244, 245
Tenmile Lake 217, 232, 235
Tetonka Lake 236
Tettegouche Lake 233
Thunder Lake 222, 233, 243
Tofte Lake 220
Triangle Lake 220
Trout Lake 219, 222, 232, 238, 245
Turtle Lake 245
Twin Lakes 231
Union Lake 245
Vermilion Lake 217, 219, 220,
    221, 231, 245, 246
Vermilion River 246
Victoria Lake 246
Voyageurs National Park
    218, 227, 229, 239, 242, 243, 244
Wabana Lake 222
Wabedo Lake 222, 223, 232, 234, 247
White Bear Lake 246
Whiteface Res. 231, 245
Whitefish Lake Chain 226, 232, 233,
    236, 237, 238, 241, 242,
    246, 247
Widow Lake 223
Wirth Lake 238
Wolf Lake 221, 222, 223, 236, 244
Woman Lake 222, 232, 234, 235, 247
Wood Lake 220
Zumbro River 231, 238

MISSISSIPPI

Arkabutla Lake 250, 252
Bee Lake 250, 251
Belzoni River 250, 251

Cat Island 251, 252
Chandeleur Sound 250, 251
Coldwater River 250, 252
Desoto Lake 252
Eagle Lake 250, 251
Enid Lake 250, 252
Flower Lake 250, 251, 252
Grenada Lake 250, 252
Gulf of Mexico 250, 251, 252
Jackson Lake 250, 251
Jordan River 250, 251, 252
Lake Pontchartrain 250, 251
Lake Washington 250, 251
Little Eagle 250, 252
Louisiana Marsh 251, 252
Mississippi River 250, 251
Mississippi Sound 251
Moon Lake 250, 251, 252
Pearl River 250, 251
Ross Barnett Reservoir 251
Sardis Lake 250, 252
Ship Island 251, 252
St. Louis Bay 251, 252
Tallahatchie River 250, 252
Tunica Cuttoff 250, 251, 252
Wasp Lake 250, 251
Wolf Lake 250, 251
Wolf River 251, 252
Yalobusha River 250, 252
Yazoo River 250, 252

MISSOURI

Bennett Spring 257, 262
Big Platte River 261
Bull Shoals Lake
    256, 260, 263, 264, 265
Grand River 256
Harry S. Truman Res. 256, 257, 258,
    261, 262
Indian Creek Conservation Lake 256
James River 259, 260, 265
Lake Jacomo 257, 261
Lake of the Ozarks
    256, 257, 258, 259, 261, 262
Lake Taneycomo
    256, 259, 260, 263, 264, 265
Little Blue River 257, 261
Little Platte River 261
Longview Res. 257, 261
Mark Twain Lake 261
Meramec River 261
Mississippi River 261
Missourii River 257, 259, 261
Niangua River 257, 262
Osage River 257, 259, 261
Platte River 262
Pomme de Terre Lake
    256, 257, 259, 261, 262
Salt River 261
Smithville Res. 261, 262
Stockton Lake
    256, 257, 259, 261, 262

Table Rock Lake
    256, 259, 260, 263, 264, 265
Thompson River 256
White River 256, 259, 260, 265

MONTANA

Absaroka Beartooth Wilderness
    268, 280, 281
Alpine Lakes 268, 274, 275, 276,
    277, 279, 280, 281, 283
Bear Creek 270
Beaverhead River 268, 269, 270,
    271, 273, 275, 276, 277,
    279, 284
Big Hole River 268, 269, 270, 271,
    273, 274, 275, 276, 277,
    278, 279, 282, 283, 284
Big Salmon Lake 271, 274
Bighorn River 269, 270, 272, 273,
    274, 276, 277, 278, 280,
    281, 282, 283
Bitterroot River 268, 269, 270,
    271, 273, 277, 278, 284
Blackfeet Indian Reservation 270, 271,
    272, 278, 279, 280, 283
Blackfoot River 268, 270, 271,
    272, 273, 274, 278,
    279, 280, 283
Bob Marshall Wilderness
    270, 271, 272, 274, 279
Boulder River 269, 270, 272, 273,
    275, 276, 277, 278,
    279, 280, 282, 283, 284
Canyon Ferry Lake 269, 272, 273,
    276, 277, 282
Clark Canyon Res 268, 269, 273, 279
Clark Fork River 268, 269, 270,
    271, 273, 274, 275, 276, 277,
    278, 279, 280, 283, 284
Clearwater River 271, 272
Cooney Res 269, 274, 280, 281
Cooper Lake 271, 272
Dearborn River 273, 274
Earthquake Lake 275, 277, 278, 282
Elbow Lake 280, 281
Elk River 268, 269, 276, 277
Ennis Lake
    269, 275, 276, 277, 278, 283
Flathead Lake 274
Flathead River
    271, 273, 274, 278, 280, 283
Fort Peck Lake
    269, 274, 280, 281, 282
Gallatin River 268, 272, 273, 274,
    275, 276, 277, 278, 279,
    280, 281, 282, 283, 284
Hauser Lake
    269, 272, 273, 276, 277, 282
Hebgen Lake
    269, 275, 276, 277, 278, 282, 283
High Mountain Lakes
    268, 269, 273, 279

Holter Lake
    269, 272, 273, 276, 277, 282
Jefferson River 268, 269, 273, 274,
    275, 276, 277, 278, 280,
    281, 282, 283, 284
Kootenai River 276, 281
Lake Koocanusa 276, 281
Lee Metcalf Wilderness
    274, 279, 281
Madison Mtn. Ranges 274, 279, 281
Madison River 268, 269, 270,
    272, 273, 274, 275, 276,
    277, 278, 280, 281, 282,
    283, 284
McGregor Lake 276, 281
Missouri River 269, 270, 271, 272,
    273, 274, 275, 276, 277,
    278, 279, 280, 281, 282,
    283, 284
Nevada Lake 271, 272
Paradise Valley 272, 275, 276,
    277, 281, 282, 283
Red Rock River 268, 269, 276, 277
Rock Creek 268, 269, 270,
    271, 273, 274, 277, 278,
    280, 281, 282, 283
Ruby River 268, 269, 276, 277
Seeley Lake 271, 272
Siah Lake 270
Smith River 270, 271, 272,
    273, 274, 275, 276, 277,
    278, 279, 280, 283
Stillwater River 268, 269, 270,
    272, 274, 275, 277, 278, 279,
    280, 281, 282, 283, 284
Storm Creek 270
Sun River 273, 274
Thompson Lakes 276, 280, 281
Thompson River 273, 279
Tongue River Res 274, 282
White River 271, 274
White Sand Creek 270
White Sand Lake 270
Whitefish Lake 281
Yellowstone Nat'l Park
    269, 274, 276, 280, 281, 282
Yellowstone River 268, 269, 270,
    271, 272, 273, 274, 275,
    276, 277, 278, 279, 280, 281,
    282, 283, 284
Yellowtail Res 269, 272, 274, 280, 282
Youngs Creek 271, 274

NEBRASKA

Blue River 288
Conestoga Lake 286, 288
Cunningham Lake 286, 288
DeSoto Bend NWR 288
Diamond Bar Lake 287, 288, 289
Elkhorn River 286
Elwood Res 286, 287
Harlan County Lake 286, 287, 288, 289

Jeffery Res 286, 287, 289
Johnson Res 286, 287, 289
Lake McConaughy 286, 287, 288, 289
Lake Ogallala 287, 289
Loup Canal 287, 288
Loup River 286, 287, 288, 289
Maloney Res 286, 287, 289
Merritt Reservoir 287, 289
Midway Lake 286
Missouri River 286, 288
Oak Lake 286, 288
Pawnee Lake 288
Platte River 286, 287, 288, 289
Plum Creek 286, 287
Republican River 288
Sherman Res 286, 287, 288, 289
Snake River 287, 289
Stagecoach Lake 286, 288
Standing Bear Lake 286, 288
Summit Lake 288
Sutherland Res 286, 287, 288, 289
Twin Lakes 286, 288
Valentine NWR 287, 289
Wagon Trail Lake 286, 288

NEVADA

Carson River 292
Crittenden Res. 292, 293
Lake Mead 292
Lake Mojave 292
Lake Tahoe 292
Pyramid Lake 292
Ruby Marsh 292, 293
Ruby Mountain High Lakes 292, 293
South Fork Res 292
Southfork Res. 292, 293
Walker Lake 292
Walker River 292
Wild Horse Res 292, 293
Wildhorse Res 293
Wilson Res 292, 293

NEW HAMPSHIRE

Atlantic Ocean 296
Contoocook River 296
Gilmore Pond 296
Gulf of Maine 296
Lake Contoocook 296
Lake Winnipesaukee 296, 297
Lake Winnisquam 296, 297
Newfound Lake 296, 297
Squam Lake 296, 297

NEW JERSEY

Absecon Bar 300, 303, 306
Absecon Inlet 300, 303, 306
Atlantic Ocean
    300, 301, 302, 303, 304,
    305, 306, 307, 308

LOCATION INDEX

NEW JERSEY - NEW YORK

Barnegat Bay
    300, 301, 304, 307, 308
Barnegat Inlet 301, 303, 304, 308
Bear Pond 306
Cape May 300, 301, 302, 303,
    304, 305, 306
Cranberry Lake 306
Delaware Bay
    300, 301, 302, 303,
    304, 305, 306, 308
Delaware River
    303, 305, 306, 307, 308
Essex Lakes 300
Great Bay
    300, 301, 302, 303, 305, 306
Greenwood Lake 305, 306
Hudson River 305, 306
Jersey Coast 303, 305
Lake Hopatcong 305, 306
Lake Musconetcong 306
Little Egg Harbor Bay 302
Little Egg Inlet 300, 304
Mansaquan Inlet 301
Mansaquan River 301, 304, 307
Maurice River 302, 303, 305, 306, 308
Musconetcong River 307, 308
Raritan Bay
    300, 301, 302, 303, 304, 306, 307
Raritan River 307, 308
Round Valley Res. 307, 308
Sandy Hook Bay
    300, 301, 303, 304, 307
Shark River 308
Shrewsbury River 300, 307
Spruce Run Res. 307, 308
Toms River 300, 304, 308
Union Lake 303, 305, 306, 308

NEW MEXICO

Avalon Res 310, 311
Brantley Res 310, 311
Caballo Res 310, 311, 312
Cimarron River 310, 311, 312
Cochiti Lake 310, 311, 312
Conchas Lake 310, 311, 312
Coyote Creek 310
Eagle Nest Lake 310
El Vado Lake 310, 312
Elephant Butte Res 310, 311, 312
Heron Lake 310, 312
Navajo Res 310, 311, 312
Pecos River 310, 311, 312
Red River 310
Rio Chama River 310, 311, 312
Rio Grande River 312
San Juan River 310, 311, 312
Ute Res 310, 311, 312

NEW YORK

Adirondack Lakes 314, 323, 328
Adirondack Mtns. 314
Adirondack Ponds 315
Adirondacks 314, 322, 323, 327
Alexandria Bay
    317, 326, 330, 333, 344, 345
Ashokan Res 315, 317, 319, 322, 339
Atlantic Ocean
    315, 316, 317, 318, 321, 329, 333, 334
Ausable River
    314, 315, 317, 319, 323, 324
Barge Canal 314, 323, 334
Batten Kill 315, 317, 319
Beaverkill River 315, 317, 319, 339
Big Bay Creek 330, 340
Big Pond 315, 317, 319
Black Lake 317, 332, 344
Black River 317, 318, 319, 325, 330,
    333, 337, 339, 340
Black River Bay 318, 333
Block Island Sound 316, 318, 334
Boquet River
    314, 315, 317, 319, 323, 324
Braddock Bay 333
Brandt Lake 314, 322, 325
Canadarago Lake 318, 338
Cape Vincent 316, 326, 329, 343
Cayuga Lake 320, 328
Chanango River 319, 338, 345
Chateauguay Lake 314, 322
Chaumont Bay 333
Chautauqua Lake 319, 324
Chenango River 319
Chazy Lake 314, 322
Conesus Lake 321
Connetquot River 315, 321, 333, 334
Crystal Lake 319, 345
Delaware River
    315, 317, 319, 320, 325, 339, 345
Eagle Lake 315, 324, 325
Erie Canal 324, 326, 335
Esodus Creek 315, 322, 339
Esopas Creek 315, 317, 319
Fall Creek 339
Finger Lakes 320, 321, 322, 323,
    330, 334, 336, 340, 343, 345
French Creek 330, 340, 344
Fulton Chain Lakes
    314, 322, 323, 325, 340
Genesee River 333
Glen Lake 314, 322, 325
Great Sacandaga Lake 314, 323, 334
Great South Bay
    315, 317, 321, 333, 334
Greenwood Lake 321, 322, 334
Grindstone 326, 336, 339
Hemlock Lake 321
Highland Lake 321, 334
Hudson River 314, 315, 321, 322,
    323, 325, 329, 334, 336, 339,
    340, 342, 343

Irondequoit Creek 321, 330, 340
Keuka Outlet 339
Kinderhook Creek 315, 317, 319
Lake Champlain 314, 315, 321,
    322, 323, 324, 325, 327, 328,
    334, 336, 340, 343
Lake Durant 315, 324, 325
Lake Erie
    319, 324, 325, 326, 329, 330, 334, 335
Lake George
    314, 315, 322, 323, 324, 325, 340
Lake Huntington 319, 345
Lake Luzern 314, 322, 325
Lake Ontario
    314, 316, 317, 318, 319, 320, 321,
    322, 323, 324, 325, 326, 327, 328,
    329, 330, 331, 332, 333, 334, 335,
    336, 337, 338, 339, 340, 341, 342,
    343, 344, 345
Lake Placid 314, 315, 323, 324, 328
Lake Ronkonkoma 333
Little Pond 315, 317, 319
Little Salmon River
    318, 326, 330, 332, 337, 338, 340, 342
Little Sandy Creek 331, 341
Little Sodus Bay 333
Long Island Sound
    315, 316, 318, 321, 333, 334
Loon Lake 314, 322, 325
Maxwell Creek 321, 330, 339, 340
Mexico Bay 326, 329
Mohawk River
    314, 321, 322, 323, 334, 336, 343
Naples Creek 321, 330, 340
Neversink River 317, 319
New Jersey Bay 316
New York Harbor 316
Niagara River
    324, 325, 326, 327, 329, 330,
    333, 334, 335
Oak Orchard Creek 321, 330, 340
Oak Orchard River 327
Oneida Lake
    321, 325, 326, 330, 331,
    332, 333, 335, 336, 337, 338,
    339, 341, 342, 345
Onondaga Lake 335, 337, 339
Oriskany Creek 317, 319, 325, 339
Oswego River
    318, 325, 326, 328, 330, 332,
    333, 335, 336, 337, 338, 339, 340,
    341, 342
Otsego lake 318, 338
Otselic River 319, 338, 345
Owosco Inlet 339
Paradox Lake 315, 324, 325
Pepacton Res 315, 317, 319, 322, 339
Perch Creek 333
Pharroah Lake
    314, 322, 323, 325, 340
Raritan Bay 316
Round Lake 321, 322
Salmon Creek 321, 330, 340

NEW YORK - OKLAHOMA — LOCATION INDEX

Salmon Res.
 332, 333, 336, 337, 338, 342
Salmon River 314, 317, 318, 319, 321, 322, 323, 325, 326, 328, 329, 330, 331, 332, 333, 335, 336, 337, 338, 339, 340, 341, 342
Salmon River Res 333, 342
Sandy Creek 326, 331, 336, 339, 341
Sandy Pond
 326, 331, 332, 336, 338, 341, 342
Saranac Lake 314, 315, 323, 324, 334
Saranac River 314, 315, 322, 323
Saratoga Lake
 321, 322, 323, 334, 336, 342, 343
Schoharie River 319
Schroon Lake
 314, 315, 322, 323, 324, 325
Schroon River 314, 315, 322, 324, 325
Seneca Lake 320, 321, 327, 328, 329
Siamese Ponds 322
Sodus Bay 325, 326, 333, 335
St. Lawrence River
 317, 326, 329, 330, 331, 343, 344
St. Regis Chain of Lakes 314, 323
Sunrise Lake 320
Swinging Bridge Res 319, 345
Taylor Pond 315
Thousand Islands 326, 343, 344
Tioughnioga River 319, 338, 345
Trout Lake 314, 322, 325
Union Falls Pond 315
Walton Lake 321, 322
West Canada Creek
 317, 319, 325, 330, 339, 340
White Lake 321, 334
Whitney Point Lake 321, 330, 336, 345
Willowemac River 317, 319, 339

NORTH CAROLINA

Albemarle Sound 348, 349, 352, 353
Atlantic Ocean
 348, 349, 350, 352, 353
Badin Lake 349, 351
Belews Lake 351
Big Creek 353
Bogue Inlet 349, 350, 353
Bogue Sound 348, 349, 350, 352, 353
Cape Fear River 348, 350
Catalochee Creek 353
Chowan River 348, 353
Core Sound 349, 352
Croatan Sound 348, 349, 352
Davidson River 353
Deep Creek 353
Drum Inlet 349, 352
Falls Lake 350, 351, 353
Fontana Lake 353
High Point City Lake 352
Jordan Lake 350, 353

Kerr Res 350, 351, 353
Lake Brandt 351
Lake Gaston 351
Lake Higgins 351
Lake Jeanette 351
Lake Norman 349, 351
Lake Tillery 349, 351
Lake Tom-A-Lex 352
Lake Townsend 351
Lake Upchurch 351
Lake Wylie 349, 351, 352
Neuse River 352
Oak Hollow Lake 352
Oconaluttee River 353
Oregon Inlet 348, 349, 352
Pamlico Sound 348, 349, 352
Pasquotank River 348, 353
Roanoke River 348, 353
Roanoke Sound 348, 349, 352
Sharon Harris Lake 350, 353
Sutton Lake 348, 350
Tar River 350, 351
Trent River 352
White Oak River 349, 350, 353

NORTH DAKOTA

Coal Mine Lake 356
Devils Lake 356, 357
Harvey Res 356
Indian Creek 356, 357
Jim Lake 356, 357
Lake Oahe 356, 357, 358
Lake Sakakawea 356, 357, 358
Lake Tschida 356, 357
Missouri River 356, 357, 358
Pipestem Res 356, 357
Powers Lake 358
Sheyenne River 356
Smishek Lake 358
Yellowstone River 357, 358

OHIO

Alum Creek Lake 360, 361
Beaver Creek 366
Brookville Lake 360, 361, 366, 367
Caesar Creek Lake 360, 361, 366, 367
Captina Creek 366
Chagrin River 361, 362
Cold Creek 361, 362, 365, 368
Conneaut Creek 361
Cowan Lake 360, 361, 367
Darby Creek 360, 368
Deer Creek Lake 360, 368
Delaware Lake 360, 361
Dillon Lake 360
East Fork Lake 360, 361, 366, 367
Fremont River 365, 366, 367, 368
Grand River 361, 362, 363
Great Miami River 360, 361, 366
Hargus Lake 360, 368

Highlandtown Lake 366
Hoover Res 360, 361
Huron River 362, 365
Lake Erie
 361, 362, 363, 364, 365, 366, 367, 368
Lake Gloria 361, 366
Lake Ontario 364
Leesville Lake 365, 366, 367, 368
Licking River 360, 361, 366
Little Miami River 360, 361, 366
Marseilles Reservoir 368
Maumee Bay 365, 367
Maumee River 365, 366, 367, 368
Monroe Lake 366
Mosquito Creek Lake 363
Muskingum River 360
Ohio River
 360, 361, 365, 366, 367, 368
Olentangy River 360, 361
Opossum Creek 366
Paint Creek Lake
 360, 361, 366, 367, 368
Pee Pee Creek 366, 368
Portage River 361, 365, 366, 367, 368
Pymatuning Res 367
Rocky Fork Lake 360, 361, 366, 367
Ross Lake 360, 368
Sandusky Bay 361, 362, 365, 367, 368
Sandusky River
 361, 365, 366, 367, 368
Scioto River 360, 366, 368
Sunfish Creek 366, 368
Tappan Lake 365, 366, 367, 368
Toussiant River 365, 367

OKLAHOMA

Arcadia Lake 370
Arkansas River 370, 371
Broken Bow Lake 370
Eufaula Lake 370, 371
Foss Lake 370
Ft. Cobb Lake 370
Grand Lake O' The Cherokees 370, 371
Kaw Lake 370, 371
Lake Eucha 370, 371
Lake Stanley 371
Lake Texoma 371
Lake Thunderbird 371
Lugert Lake 370
Robert S. Kerr Lake 370, 371
Shawnee Res 371
Skiatook Lake 371
Tenkiller Lake 371
Webber Falls Res 370, 371

LOCATION INDEX

OREGON — PENNSYLVANIA

OREGON

Alsea Bay
    374, 376, 378, 384, 387, 388
Alsea River 374, 376, 377, 378,
    379, 380, 382, 383, 384, 385,
    387, 388, 389
Applegate Lake 374, 379, 381, 386
Ben Irving Res. 386
Cascade Lakes 376, 377, 378
Chetco River 374, 375, 376, 378,
    379, 381, 382, 385, 386, 387
Clackamas River
    375, 377, 380, 383, 385, 386, 388
Columbia River 374, 375, 376, 377,
    378, 380, 383, 384, 385,
    386, 387, 388
Cooper Creek Res. 386
Coquille River 374, 376, 377, 378,
    379, 381, 382, 384, 385,
    386, 387, 388
Crane Prairie Res. 376, 377
Crooked River 376, 378, 379, 381, 386
Dairy Creek 386
Depoe Bay 380
Deschutes River 374, 375, 376, 377,
    378, 379, 380, 381, 382, 383,
    384, 385, 386, 387, 388
Diamond Lake 386
East Lake 376, 377
Elk River 374, 375, 376, 377,
    378, 379, 382, 383, 384,
    385, 387, 388
Emigrant Lake 374, 379, 381, 386
Fish Lake 374, 379, 381, 386
Gales Creek 386
Grande Ronde River
    376, 378, 379, 381, 386
Hagg Lake 386
Hells Canyon Res. 381
Howard Prairie Lake
    374, 379, 381, 386
Hyatt Res. 374, 379, 381, 386
John Day River 374, 375, 376, 377,
    378, 379, 381, 382, 383, 384,
    386, 387, 388
Klamath Lake 374, 379, 381, 386
Lake of the Woods 374, 379, 381, 386
Lemolo Lake 386
Lost Creek Res. 374, 379, 381, 386
McKenzie River 374, 376, 377, 378,
    379, 380, 381, 382, 383, 384,
    385, 386, 387, 388, 389
Nehalem Bay 375, 380, 385, 386
Nehalem River
    375, 377, 380, 383, 385, 386, 388
Nestucca River 374, 375, 376, 377,
    378, 379, 380, 382, 383, 384,
    385, 386, 387, 388
Owyhee River 376, 378, 379, 381, 386
Pacific Ocean 380, 385, 386, 388
Prineville Reservoir 381
Rogue River 374, 375, 376, 377,
    378, 379, 381, 382, 383, 384,
    385, 386, 387, 388
Salmon River
    379, 380, 381, 382, 383, 387, 388
Sandy River
    375, 377, 380, 383, 385, 386, 388
Santiam River 374, 375, 376, 377,
    378, 379, 380, 382, 383,
    384, 385, 386, 387, 388
Siletz River 374, 375, 376, 377,
    378, 380, 382, 383, 384,
    385, 386, 387, 388, 389
Siltcoos Lake 384
Siuslaw River 374, 376, 377, 378,
    379, 380, 382, 384, 385,
    387, 388, 389
Sixes River 374, 376, 377, 378,
    379, 382, 383, 384, 385,
    387, 388
Smith River 374, 376, 377, 378,
    379, 380, 381, 382, 384,
    385, 386, 387, 388, 389
Snake River 381
Tillamook Bay
    375, 377, 380, 383, 384, 385, 386, 388
Tillamook River 375, 380, 385, 386
Tokette Lake 386
Trask River
    375, 377, 380, 383, 385, 386, 388
Tualatin River 386
Umpqua River 374, 376, 377, 378,
    379, 380, 381, 382, 383,
    384, 385, 386, 387, 388
Willamette River 374, 375, 376, 377,
    378, 379, 380, 382, 383, 384,
    385, 386, 387, 388, 389
Wilson River
    375, 377, 380, 383, 385, 386, 388

PENNSYLVANIA

Allegheny Res 392, 395, 397, 398
Allegheny River
    392, 393, 395, 397, 398
Atlantic Ocean 392
Beltzville Lake 392, 393, 396
Blue Marsh Lake 392, 393, 394, 396
Brush Creek 397
Bushkill Creek 393, 398
Cedar Run 394
Chataqua Lake 392, 395, 397
Conestoga River 394
Conneaut Lake 392, 395, 397
Cononcocheague Creek 394, 398
Crooked Creek 392, 395, 397
Crooked Creek Res 392, 395, 397
Delaware Bay 392
Delaware River
    392, 393, 394, 395, 396, 397
Elk Creek 394
Elmhurst Res 393, 396
Falling Spring Branch 394, 398
Fishing Creek 394
French Creek 393, 394, 395, 397
Gouldsboro Lake 394, 397
Green Lane Res 392, 393, 396
Harveys Lake 395, 396
Juniata River 393, 394, 397
Keystone Lake 395, 398
Lackawanna River 393, 396
Lake Arthur 395, 396, 398
Lake Erie
    392, 393, 395, 396, 397, 398
Lake Marburg 396
Lake Nockamixon 392, 393, 396
Lake Redman 394, 396
Lake Wallenpaupack 393, 395, 396
Lake Wilheim 395, 396, 398
Lake Williams 396
Laurel Hill Creek 395, 396, 398
Lehigh River 392, 393, 396, 398
Letort Spring Run 394, 398
Little Buffalo River 393, 397
Little Lehigh Creek
    392, 393, 394, 396, 398
Loyalhanna Creek 395, 396, 398
Loyalsock Creek 393, 394
Lycoming Creek 393, 394
Mahoning Creek Lake 392, 395, 397
Mauch Chunk Lake 392
Middle Creek 394
Monocacy Creek 393, 398
Moraine State Park 392, 395, 397
Muddy Run Res 394, 396
Neshaminy Creek 393, 396
Neshannock Creek 398
North Park Lake 393, 398
Octoraro Res 394, 396
Ohio River 393, 398
Ontelaunee Lake 392, 394
Penns Creek 393, 394, 397
Pinchot Lake 393
Pine Creek 393, 394, 398
Pymatuning Res 392, 393, 395, 397
Raystown Lake 393, 394, 397
Roaring Brook 393, 396
Roaring Creek 393
Rose Valley Lake 393, 397
Schuylkill River 392, 393, 394, 396
Shawnee Lake 397
Slate Run 394
Slippery Rock 395, 396, 398
Stillwater Lake 394, 397
Stoney Creek 397
Susquehanna River 393, 394, 396, 397
Tohickon Creek 393, 396
Tulpehocken Creek 392, 394
Valley Creek 394
Walker Lake 393, 397
Whipples Dam 393, 397
Wills Creek 397
Yellow Breeches Creek 394
Youghiogheny River 398

RHODE ISLAND - UTAH

LOCATION INDEX

RHODE ISLAND

Atlantic Ocean 400, 401, 402
Block Island Sound 400, 401
Echo Lake 401, 402
Greenwich Bay 401
Narragansett Bay 400, 401
Pascoag Res 401, 402
Pawcatuck River 400, 402
Point Judith Pond 400, 401
Round Top 401, 402
Slatersville Res 401, 402
Watchaug Pond 400, 402
Wilson Res 401, 402
Wood River 400, 402
Worden Pond 400, 402

SOUTH CAROLINA

Atlantic Ocean 404
Calbogue Sound 404
Clarks Hill Lake
    404, 405, 406, 407, 408
Cooper River 405, 406
Hartwell Lake 404, 407, 408
Lake Cherokee 404
Lake Greenwood 404, 408
Lake Jocassee 404
Lake Keowee 404
Lake Marion 404, 405, 406, 407, 408
Lake Moultrie 405
Lake Murray 404, 405, 406, 407, 408
Lake Strom Thurmond 407
Lake Wylie 407, 408
Murrells Inlet 404
Port Royal Sound 404
Reedy River 404, 408
Russell Lake 404, 407, 408
Saluda River 404, 407, 408
Santee River 405, 406
Savannah River
    404, 405, 406, 407, 408
Stevens Creek 406, 407, 408
Wateree Lake 407, 408
White Water Lake 404

SOUTH DAKOTA

Elm Lake 413
Elm River 413
James River 413
Lake Francis Case 412, 413
Lake Louise 412, 413
Lake Oahe 412, 413
Lake Sharpe 412, 413
Mina Lake 413
Missouri River 412, 413
Richmond Lake 413

TENNESSEE

Cumberland River 416, 417, 419
Dale Hollow Lake 416
Douglas Lake 416
Finger Lakes of Smokies 416
Ft. Loudon Lake 417, 418, 419
Kentucky Lake 416, 417, 419
Lake Barkley 416, 417, 419
Lake Graham 417
Melton Hill Lake 417, 418, 419
Norris Lake 417, 418, 419
Obey River 416
Old Hickory Lake 418
Percy Priest Lake 418
Smoky Mountains 418
Tennessee River 416, 417, 418, 419
Tims Ford 419
Watts Bar Lake 417, 418, 419

TEXAS

Abilene Lake 429, 431
Amistad Res 422
Angelina River 436, 437
Aransas Bay 422, 423, 425, 426,
    427, 428, 429, 435, 437
B. A. Steinhagen Lake
    423, 431, 436, 437
Baffin Bay 423, 424, 425, 430
Baker Lake 432, 434
Bastrop Bay 427, 429
Belton Lake 424, 437
Bosque River 424, 433
Brazos River 424, 433, 437
Caddo Lake 424, 431
Calaveras Lake 424, 427
Canyon Lake 424, 425, 427
Carlos Bay 422, 425, 426, 435, 437
Cedar Creek 424, 435
Cedar Res 424
Choke Canyon Lake 425
Christmas Bay 427, 429
Clear Lake 426, 428
Coastal Bend 422, 435
Coleto Creek Res 425, 427
Colorado River 429, 434, 437
Concho River 429, 434, 437
Copano Bay
    422, 423, 425, 426, 428, 435, 437
Corpus Christi Bay
    422, 423, 425, 426, 427, 429, 430,
    435, 437
Cox Lake 427, 429
Drum Bay 427
East Bay 426
Estes Flats 422, 425, 435
Falcon Res 426, 436
Galveston Bay 426, 427, 428, 429
Guadalupe River 424, 425, 427
Gulf of Mexico
    422, 423, 425, 426, 427, 428,
    429, 430, 435
Hubbard Creek Res 429, 431
Inland Bay 422, 425, 427, 429, 435
Intracoastal Waterway
    422, 427, 429, 435
Ivie Res 429, 431, 434, 437
Laguna Madre
    422, 423, 424, 425, 427, 428,
    429, 430, 435
Lake Athens 435
Lake Buchanan 430, 431
Lake Fork 430, 431, 432, 434, 436
Lake Ft. Phantom Hill 429, 431
Lake Livingston 423, 431, 436, 437
Lake Lyndon B. Johnson 430, 431
Lake Madisonville 434
Lake Nasworthy 429, 434, 437
Lake O' The Pines 424, 431, 432
Lake Palestine 432
Lake Ray Roberts 430, 432, 434, 435
Lake Tawakoni 431, 432
Lake Texoma 430, 432, 433, 434, 435
Lake Travis 433
Lake Waco 424, 433
Lake Whitney 424, 433, 437
Lake Worth 433
Lost Lake 427, 429
Matagorda Bay 426
Mesquite Bay 422, 425, 426, 435, 437
Moss Lake 432
Navasota River 434
Nicks Lake 427
Nueces Bay 422, 425, 426, 427,
    428, 429, 435, 437
O. C. Fisher Lake 429, 434, 437
Pat Mayse Lake 434
Possum Kingdom Lake 430, 432, 434
Randall Lake 432, 434
Red River 434
Redfish Bay
    422, 423, 425, 426, 427, 428, 429,
    435, 437
Richland Cr. Res 431, 432, 435, 436
Rio Grande River 436
Salt Lake 427
Sam Rayburn Res 423, 431, 436, 437
San Antonio Bay
    422, 425, 426, 435, 437
San Antonio River 425, 427
Somerville Lake 424, 437
Stillhouse Hollow Lake 424, 433, 437
Swan Lake 427
Toledo Bend Res 423, 431, 436, 437
Tri-Lakes 430, 432, 434
Trinity Bay 426
Trinity River 434
Twin Buttes Res 429, 434, 437
West Bay 426

UTAH

Boulder Mountains 440
Boulder Mtns 440
Currant Creek 441, 442
Deer Creek Res 441, 442
East Canyon Res. 441, 442
Fishlake National Forest 440
Flaming Gorge Res. 440, 441

LOCATION INDEX

UTAH - WISCONSIN

Flaming Gorge Tailwater 440
Fremont River 440
Green River 440, 441
Jordanelle Res 441, 442
Mammoth Creek 441
Panguitch Creek 441
Panguitch Lake 441
Private Trophy Ponds 442
Provo River 440, 441, 442
Puffer Lake 440
Sevier River 441
Strawberry Res. 440, 441, 442
Uintas Mountains 442
Utah Lake 441, 442
Weber River 441, 442

VERMONT

Black River 444, 445
Caspian Lake 444, 445
Connecticut River 445
Crystal Lake 444, 445
Dog River 445
Echo Lake 444, 445
Hosmer Pond 444, 445
Lake Champlain 444
Lake Memphremagog 444, 445
Lake Willoughby 444, 445
Lamoille River 444, 445
Little River 445
Seymour Lake 444, 445
Shadow Lake 444, 445
White River 445
Winooski River 445

VIRGINIA

Atlantic Ocean 448, 449
Buggs Island 449, 450
Chesapeake Bay 448, 449
Chickahominy River 449, 450
Chincoteague Bay 448
James River 449, 450, 451
Kerr Res 449, 450
Lake Anna 449, 450
Lake Frederick 451
Lake Gaston 449, 450
Leesville Lake 449, 450, 451
Passage Creek 451
Potomac River 449, 450, 451
Rappahanock River 449, 450
Roanoke/Staunton River 450, 451
Rudee Inlet 448
Shenandoah River 449, 450, 451
Smith Mountain Lake 449, 450, 451

WASHINGTON

American Lake 456, 457
Bogachiel River
   454, 455, 456, 458, 459, 460
Calawha River 454, 456, 459

Chehalis River 454, 455, 456, 458
Columbia River
   454, 455, 456, 457, 458
Cowlitz River
   454, 455, 456, 458, 459, 460
Curlew Lake 455
Elwah River 454, 456, 459
Franklin D. Roosevelt Lake 455
Grande Ronde River 458, 460
Harts Lake 456
Hoh River
   454, 455, 456, 458, 459, 460
Kalama River
   454, 455, 456, 458, 459, 460
Lewis River 454, 455, 456, 458
Neah Bay 457
Nisqually River 456, 457
Nootka Sound 457
Olympic National Park 454, 456, 459
Pacific Ocean 454, 456, 457
Puget Sound 456, 457, 458, 459, 460
Puyallup River 456, 457
Queets River 454, 456, 459
Quillayute River 454, 456, 459
Satsop River
   454, 455, 456, 458, 459, 460
Sauk River
   454, 455, 456, 458, 459, 460
Silver Lake 454, 455, 458
Skagit River
   454, 455, 456, 458, 459, 460
Skykomish River
   454, 455, 456, 458, 459, 460
Snake River 454, 455, 456, 458, 460
Snohomish River
   454, 455, 456, 457, 458, 459, 460
Sol Duc River
   454, 455, 456, 458, 459, 460
Spokane River 458, 460
Stilliaguamish River
   454, 455, 456, 457, 458, 459, 460
Strait of Juan de Fuca
   456, 457, 458, 459, 460
Toutle River 455, 458
Vancouver Island 457
Wenatchee River
   454, 455, 456, 458, 459, 460
Willapa Bay 454, 455, 456, 458
Wynoochee River 454, 455, 456, 458

WEST VIRGINIA

Buckhannon River 462
Burnsville Lake 462, 463
Coal River 462
Elk River 462, 463
Gauley River 462
Greenbriar River 462
Hughes River 462
Kanawha River 462, 463
Little Kanawha River 462, 463
New River 462
Ohio River 462

Stone Coal Lake 462, 463
Stonewall Jackson Lake 462, 463
Sutton Lake 462, 463
West Fork River 462

WISCONSIN

Alequash Lake 478, 480
Apostle Islands 472, 473
Armour Lake 476, 478, 480
Balsam Lake 466
Bay De Noc 471, 475, 479
Big Cedar Lake 466, 468, 476
Big Eau Pleine Res 481
Big Muskellunge Lake 478, 480
Big Round Lake 466
Big Sand Lake 474, 476, 479
Big Sound 466
Big St. Germain Lake 475, 478, 480
Boom Lake 474, 475, 481
Boulder Lake 478, 480
Branch River 473
Brule River 466, 474, 479
Burnett County 476
Butternut Lake 466, 474, 479
Chequamegon Bay 477, 479
Cisco Chain 478, 480
Clam Lake 466
Clark Lake 467, 468, 469
Como Lake 469
Couderay Lake 477
Crab Lake 476, 478, 480
Deleuah Lake 469
Diamond Lake 478, 480
Eagle Lake 468, 469
Eagle River Chain
   466, 474, 476, 479, 480
East Twin River 473
Elizabeth Lake 469
Enterprise Lake 474, 481
Europe Lake 467, 468, 469
Fishtrap Lake 478, 480
Flambeau River 466, 473
Forest County
   474, 475, 476, 477, 479, 480
Forest Lake 480
Fowler Lake 468
Fox River
   466, 467, 471, 472, 473, 481
Friess Lake 466, 468, 476
Ghost Lake 468
Gile Flowage 467, 478
Green Bay 466, 467, 468, 469, 470, 471, 472, 473, 481
Green Lake 466
Grindstone Lake 468, 474
Harris Lake 476, 480
Horsehead Lake 476, 478
Iron County 474, 475, 477, 478, 479
Jordan Lake 481
Jule Lake 478, 480
Jump River 466, 473
Kangaroo Lake 467, 468, 469

WISCONSIN - WYOMING

Keesus Lake 466, 468, 476
Kentuck Lake 466, 474, 479, 480
Kewaunee River 473
Lac Court Oreilles 468, 474
Lac du Flambeau Indian Res 478
Lac La Belle Lake 466, 468, 476
Lac Vieux Desert Lake 474, 476, 479
Lake Arrowhead 476, 481
Lake Butte des Morts
    466, 467, 472, 473, 481
Lake Camelot 476, 481
Lake Chippewa Flowage 468, 474
Lake Como 469
Lake Comus 469
Lake Delavan 469
Lake Delton 481
Lake Geneva 468, 469
Lake George 474, 475, 481
Lake Kegonsa 469
Lake Koshkonong 469
Lake Mendota 469
Lake Menona 469
Lake Michigan 466, 467, 468, 469,
    470, 471, 472, 475,
    476, 479
Lake Minocqua 475, 481
Lake Poygan 466, 467, 472, 473, 481
Lake Redstone 481
Lake Sherwood 476, 481
Lake Superior 472, 473, 474
Lake Wabasa 469
Lake Winnebago
    466, 467, 472, 473, 481
Little Cedar Lake 466, 468, 476
Little St. Germain Lake 475, 478, 480
Long Lake 466, 467, 478
Lost Land Lake 468, 474
Manitowoc River 473
Marie Lake 469
McKenzie lake 477
Mercer Lake 467, 478
Middle McKenzie Lake 477
Miller Dam Flowage 466, 473
Mirror Lake 481
Mississippi River 473, 474, 481
Mohawksin Lake 474, 475, 481
Moose Lake 467, 478
Namekagon Lake 468, 472, 474
Nepco Lake 481
North Lake 466, 468, 476
North Twin Lake
    466, 474, 476, 479, 480
Okauchee Lake 466, 468, 471, 476
Oneida County
    471, 474, 475, 476, 477, 478, 479, 480
Oxbow Lake 476, 478
Palmer Lake 475, 478, 480
Papoose Lake 476, 480
Partridge Lake 478, 480
Pelican Lake 474, 475, 481
Pell Lake 469
Petenwell Lake 476

Pewaukee Lake 466, 468, 471, 476
Pike Lake
    466, 468, 475, 476, 478, 480
Pine Lake 466, 468, 476
Pine River 466, 474, 479
Portage Lake 480
Post Lake 474, 481
Powers Lake 468, 469
Presque Isle Lake 476, 478, 480
Price County 475, 477, 479
Rib Lake 466, 473
Rock River 469
Root River 469
Round Lake 466, 468, 474
Sheboygan River 473
Shell Lake 477
Silver Lake 466, 468, 476
Sissabagama Lake 477
Spirit Lake 466, 473
Sturgeon Bay 466, 467, 469, 471
Summet Lake 474, 481
Teal Lake 468, 474
Three Lakes Chain 466, 474, 479
Tomahawk Lake 475, 481
Trout Lake 475, 478, 480
Trude Lake 467, 478
Turtle-Flambeau Flowage
    467, 474, 477, 478, 479
Van Vliet Lake 476, 480
Vilas County
    471, 474, 475, 476, 477, 478, 479, 480
Wallace Lake 466
Washburn County 476
West Twin River 473
White Sand Lake 478, 480
Wind Lake 481
Wisconsin River
    473, 474, 475, 476, 481
Wolf River
    466, 467, 472, 473, 474, 475, 481

WYOMING

Alcova Res 485
Big Creek 485
Bridger Wilderness 484, 485
Bridger-Teton National Forest 484
Buffalo Fork River 485
Buffalo River 485, 486
Eagle Creek 485, 486
Encampment River 485
Fayette Lake 484
Flat Creek 484, 485
Fremont Lake 484
Glendo Res 485
Green River 484, 485, 486
Gros Ventre Wilderness Area 484
Half Moon Lake 484
Lake Alice 484
Medicine Lodge Creek 484
Mt. Zirkel Wilderness 485
New Fork River 484, 485, 486
North Piney Creek 484

North Platte River 485
Paintrock Creek 484
Piney Lake 484
Platte River 485
Pole Creek 484
Red Creek 485, 486
Shoshone River 485, 486
Snake River 484, 485, 486
South Piney Creek 484
Teton Wilderness 485
Thorofare River 484, 485, 486
Yellowstone Lake 485, 486
Yellowstone Nat'l. Park 486
Yellowstone River 484, 485, 486

	Number of Primary Locations					
State	Rivers*	Lakes	Bays	Oceans	Gulfs	TOTAL
Alabama	9	22	2		1	34
Alaska	22	6	7	1	1	37
Arizona	5	18				23
Arkansas	22	22				44
California	31	72	11	1		115
Colorado	16	17				33
Connecticut	9	13	5	1		28
Delaware	3		1	1		5
Florida	33	73	33	1	1	141
Georgia	17	18		1		36
Hawaii				1		1
Idaho	17	6				23
Illinois	18	41				59
Indiana	8	39				47
Iowa	10	22				32
Kansas	8	17				25
Kentucky	9	12				21
Louisiana	2	12	5		1	20
Maine	5	17	2	1		25
Maryland	7	9	1	1		18
Massachusetts	18	28	15	1		62
Michigan	30	63	1			94
Minnesota	19	185				204
Mississippi	9	21	3		1	34
Missouri	15	15				30
Montana	43	32				75
Nebraska	9	26				35
Nevada	2	11				13
New Hampshire	1	7	1	1	1	11
New Jersey	9	9	12	1		31
New Mexico	7	11				18
New York	47	60	14	1		122
North Carolina	13	22	6	1		42
North Dakota	2	9				11
Ohio	23	23	1			47
Oklahoma	2	17				19
Oregon	30	21	2	1		54
Pennsylvania	43	37				80
Rhode Island	2	7	3	1		13
South Carolina	7	13	3	1		24
South Dakota	3	6				9
Tennessee	2	14				16
Texas	11	52	21		1	85
Utah	11	11				22
Vermont	6	10				16
Virginia	6	5	2	1		14
Washington	27	5	7	1		40
West Virginia	11	5				16
Wisconsin	22	124	6			152
Wyoming	25	11				36

* Includes rivers, streams, and creeks

To order additional copies of the Angler's Yellow Pages
call 1-800-242-9722

THE ANGLERS EXCHANGE

FISHERMAN'S SWAP MEET MAGAZINE

Every month we print your classified ads for Ranger, Stratos, BassCat, Cajun bass boats. J Loomis, All Star, Shimano rods, Diawa, Lews, ABU reels, you name it, all at swap meet prices. A fishing gear "want ad" magazine by a fisherman.

Electronics, Lures, Tackle, Offshore Fishing Boats, Antique, Classic and Collectible Equipment and Outboards. Prop Swap Trolling Motors, Videos, Maps, Books and Magazines, Fly Fishing, Ice Fishing, Marine Engines and Outboards, Guides, Art...

Hundreds and hundreds of classified ads from Florida to California! If you have a product to sell, a service to offer, or marine or fishing equipment to buy, sell or trade....advertise it where the pros get results.

Sell some old stuff or buy some new gear. FREE classifieds!!

THE ANGLERS EXCHANGE SWAP MEET MAGAZINE
and
THE ANGLERS EXCHANGE "ON-LINE"
Computer BBS and World Wide Web Site.
You don't need a computer to get your ads on the Internet, We'll do it for you!

Get "World Wide Web exposure"
for the cost of a magazine subscription.

SUBSCRIBE TODAY, $20 (US)/12 MONTHLY ISSUES.
Visit our World Wide Web site:
http://sover.net:80/~anglerex

To become a member, send $20 US to: The Anglers Exchange Subscriptions, RR 1 Box 1323 Manchester Ctr., VT. 05255 or call: 802-362-4296. and get the power of the "internet" working for you.